DOCUMENTS ON BRITISH FOREIGN POLICY 1919–1939

EDITED BY

W. N. MEDLICOTT, M.A., D.Lit., D.Litt., Litt.D.
Emeritus Professor of International History, University of London

AND

DOUGLAS DAKIN, M.A., Ph.D.
Emeritus Professor of History, University of London

ASSISTED BY

GILLIAN BENNETT, M.A.

SECOND SERIES

Volume XXI

LONDON

HER MAJESTY'S STATIONERY OFFICE

© *Crown copyright 1984*
First published 1984
HER MAJESTY'S STATIONERY OFFICE
Government Bookshops
49 High Holborn, London, WC1V 6HB
13a Castle Street, Edinburgh EH2 3AR
Brazennose Street, Manchester M60 8AS
Southey House, Wine Street, Bristol BS1 2BQ
258 Broad Street, Birmingham B1 2HE
80 Chichester Street, Belfast BT1 4JY
*Government publications are also available
through booksellers*

Printed in the UK for HMSO
Dd 736097 c10 10/84
ISBN 0 11 591561 3*

DOCUMENTS ON BRITISH FOREIGN POLICY

1919–1939

Second Series, Volume XXI

Far Eastern Affairs

November 6, 1936–July 27, 1938

PREFACE

WE ARE mainly concerned in this volume with the British Government's reactions to the earlier stages of the Sino-Japanese war, which began with an apparently unrehearsed skirmish at Lukouchiao in North China on July 7, 1937. Once engaged, neither side could pull back or achieve victory in a struggle which merged into the world war in December 1941 and was ended only with the collapse of Japan in 1945. For the British Government, increasingly preoccupied with the lowering situation in Europe, there was an enduring threat to vast interests in the Far East which was difficult to meet, but which a revised Anglo-Japanese understanding might obviate. The present volume takes the story down to August 1938, after which it can be followed in Volumes VIII and IX, already published, of the Third Series of this Collection.

Chapter I deals with the period of uneasy expectancy which preceded the war, following the failure of the Leith-Ross mission of 1935–6 (Volume XX). Sir Frederick Leith-Ross's plan for Anglo-Japanese cooperation in financial aid to China had been given short shrift by the Japanese Government in 1935, and with it faded some of the Cabinet's hopes of strengthening British control of events and of halting the Japanese on their collision course with the China of General Chiang Kai-shek. In the circumstances the sanguine search for Anglo-Japanese agreement of Shigeru Yoshida, a new Japanese Ambassador in London, was puzzling rather than encouraging. Responsive no doubt to the Treasury interest revealed by the Leith-Ross mission, Mr. Yoshida had put his proposals into a memorandum which he handed to the Chancellor of the Exchequer, Mr. Neville Chamberlain, in November 1936. It proposed the maintaining of the spirit of the 'open door' in China by the elimination of trade boycotts and the upholding of the sovereignty of China 'south of the Great Wall'. Japan as the country most vitally interested in the restoration of political order in China should provide long-term credits for the obtaining of the arms and ammunition needed by the central Chinese Government, together with Japanese military officers as advisers. If China and Japan failed to come to agreement in this matter by direct negotiation, the British Government's sympathetic assistance would be welcomed (document No. 1).

The Foreign Office had had similar approaches from time to time in recent years, and was well aware that they might imply nothing more than a desire on the part of Mr. Hirota, the Foreign Minister, that Great Britain should divert and share the odium of Japan's unpopular policies in China (cf. Volume XX, No. 241). Nevertheless the Foreign Office saw possibilities as well as difficulties in the Yoshida programme, while doubting from the start his personal ability to carry it through. A detailed reply was prepared in the Foreign Office, and ran the gauntlet of comment by the Board of Trade, Dominions Office, and Treasury. Its presentation to the Japanese Ambassador on January 18, 1937 produced, however, a notable anti-climax: he had to confess three days later that all he could send his government was a document expressing the British Government's desire to negotiate a general agreement, 'in reply to which his Government might make definite proposals'. By this stage the Foreign Office had come to the conclusion that Mr. Yoshida was an 'accomplished blunderer' and that it might be better to 'try to do the job at the other end' (No. 52, note 6). The document asked for by Mr. Yoshida was, however, duly supplied and was well enough received in Tokyo, but what with cabinet changes there and the evident indifference or hostility of the military party to any development of Anglo-Japanese talks, these continued to be postponed. The Foreign Office in London did not at any time abandon hope, however tenuous, of agreement.

Whatever the relationship with Japan, the British Government hoped for joint action with the United States in defending Western interests in China: but the State Department seemed more than usually concerned at this period not to be drawn into any activity in the Far East. A British proposal in September 1936 for a re-affirmation of Article XIX of the Washington treaty (against refortification) had been rejected by the Americans with less than their usual urbanity (Volume XX, No. 562). When Mr. Chamberlain in March 1937 contemplated suggesting to Mr. Morgenthau a joint guarantee by Britain, China, Japan, U.S.S.R., and the U.S.A. of 'the territorial status quo' in the Far East, Mr. Eden, the Secretary of State for Foreign Affairs, commented that this might 'administer a shock that would be too much for American nerves' and Mr. Chamberlain had to be satisfied with a general reference to the desirability of trying to put relations between U.S.A., Japan, and Great Britain on a 'footing of harmonious cooperation' (cf. Volume XVIII, Nos. 268, 285). With regard to the Yoshida proposals the State Department seemed anxious only to be reassured that the British Government did not intend to change their policy with regard to China in order to secure Japan's friendship (No. 69). In April Mr. Norman Davis, President Roosevelt's 'Ambassador at large', broached with Mr. Eden a favourite project of the President's for the neutralization of the Pacific, a plan which even included the dismantling of the fortifications of Hong Kong. It appeared to be due to the President's desire to disembarrass his country of responsibility for the defence of the Philippines, and it was believed that he seriously contemplated advancing the date of complete Philippine independence to 1938 or 1939. The British reply was not encouraging, and the Americans seem to have had no answer to the British query as to how far Japan could ever be expected to join in and honour such a plan (Nos. 70, 76, 87). When the British Ambassador to China, Sir Hughe Knatchbull-Hugessen, pointed to the advantages of a Sino-Japanese-

Soviet *détente* the Foreign Office asked itself somewhat wryly whether such a development, even if practicable, was altogether desirable: there were certain advantages to Great Britain in mutual distrust between Russians and Japanese (No. 63, note 6).

The Lukouchiao incident of July 7/8 was at once interpreted in the Foreign Office as a Japanese offensive, probably aimed however at securing only local advantages. British relations with both the German and the Italian Governments were strained (see Volume XIX generally) and the last thing that Mr. Eden wanted at this moment was a major crisis in the Far East with possible British involvement.

In the intimate Anglo-American discussions over the Far Eastern crisis during the next five months the United States Government moved from a position of complete non-involvement to an acceptance at the highest level that in world affairs Britain and the United States must stand, if they did not wish to fall, together. In this sense, America's fate was involved in European as well as in Far Eastern developments, but it was in connexion with the latter that the President began to show his concern. Mr. Eden was perhaps more impressed by these indications than Mr. Chamberlain, who continued to grumble that nothing could be expected from the Americans but words. In a sense this was true, but the words were acquiring weightier promise as time went on.

The documents in Chapter II show that Mr. Eden's first moves in July and August were aimed at keeping the United Kingdom in close touch with the United States over the issues. He warned Mr. Yoshida on July 12 and other occasions that the projected Anglo-Japanese conversations 'would hardly be possible if existing conditions near Peking persisted or grew worse' (No. 105). Lukouchiao and the neighbouring city of Wanping were, it appeared, railway junctions commanding routes to Peiping: the Japanese forces, maintained in the Peiping-Tientsin area under the Boxer agreements, now numbered about 7,000, and were engaged on the 7th in manoeuvres including mock attacks on Wanping. Later there was shooting in which Chinese soldiers of the 29th Army were said to have fired on the Japanese troops. There were reports in Tokyo that the Japanese forces were to be reinforced, and that the Chinese Government planned to send four divisions north. Following a formal request on July 13 from the Chinese Ambassador for British good offices to preserve the peace, Mr. Eden proposed to Washington that the British and United States Governments should jointly express to the Japanese Government their apprehension at the report of large troop movements (No. 107). The reply was that Mr. Hull had already urged restraint on the Chinese and Japanese Ambassadors, and that the State Department feared that, in the existing temper of the Japanese Government, concerted action might defeat its own object (No. 110). The Foreign Office thought this reply 'characteristic', but was inclined to agree that concerted action in Tokyo was dangerous.

This might be so, but it was equally evident that the individual representations of foreign powers were quite ineffectual. At the opening of the crisis Sir H. Knatchbull-Hugessen was on holiday at Peitaiho. On July 12, following a request from the Chinese Foreign Minister he hurried to Nanking, and was able to follow up Mr. Eden's message to Washington of the 13th by extracting from the Foreign Minister a 'most categorical statement' that all Chinese troop movements in the crisis were solely self-defensive. The first form of the Chinese statement was in fact drafted on General Chiang Kai-shek's instructions in such emphatic language, with reference to the 'aggressive and provocative intentions of the Japanese troops' as to remind the ambassador of the Ems telegram. He secured a more innocuous version. The Foreign Minister then urged that as a preliminary measure troop movements on both sides should stop on July 17, after which arrangements could be made to restore the previous position. He hoped that Mr. Dodds, the British Chargé at Tokyo, could be instructed to pass this proposal on to the Japanese Government (No. 118). Mr. Eden, while agreeing that the statement had much to commend it, replied that His Majesty's Government could not act as a channel for communications of this sort: nor could it allow itself to be drawn in as a mediator 'unless both sides expressly desire it'.

This cautious approach, which was evidently reinforced by the State Department's isolationism, was almost immediately reversed by an early example of the Prime Minister's propensity for gingering up the Foreign Office (familiar enough in the field of European diplomacy). On the evening of June 20 he insisted that a 'last effort' should be made to avert war, and accordingly a telegram was despatched at 9 p.m. to Washington instructing the Ambassador to arrange to see Mr. Hull at once. He was to say that the British Government would be prepared to make a joint approach to the Chinese and Japanese Governments, who would be asked to agree to suspend all further troop movements and to agree to Anglo-American 'proposals to attempt to end existing deadlock' (No. 135). Mr. Hull was again unable to agree to anything more than 'parallel' as distinct from 'joint' representations (Nos. 135, 137, 139). Mr. Eden told the Cabinet on July 21 that it was not expedient to go further alone, and to create the impression in Tokyo that only the British Government were closely interested in the crisis (No. 140).

This, however, did not preclude continued efforts to devise effective means of Anglo-American pressure on Japan. News of a decisive victory on 27–28 July which gave the Japanese mastery of the Peking-Tientsin area caused Mr. Eden yet again, on the 28th, to urge joint representations, leading to Anglo-American mediation. Mr. Bingham, the United States Ambassador in London, said he regretted his government's previous refusal and would recommend Mr. Eden's renewed proposals to the State Department (No. 152). The State Department was evidently worried by the situation and anxious to know the British view, while still determined to avoid commitment. The Foreign Office now thought that it was no longer practicable to suggest the withdrawal of Japanese troops from

North China, and Sir R. Vansittart told Mr. Johnson, the U.S. Counsellor, on August 3 that the only practicable proposal seemed to be that both sides should offer to appoint plenipotentiaries and that the British and American Governments should offer their good offices in providing neutral ground for discussion and smoothing difficulties. When the State Department asked Mr. Grew, the U.S. Ambassador at Tokyo, what he thought of this plan he replied recommending that the proposal should be addressed to Japan alone, because of the importance of secrecy. Mr. Dodds thought that the proposal would do no harm, but like Mr. Grew he stressed the need to avoid any appearance of intervention by third parties, which the Japanese Foreign Minister had already told the Diet would be rejected. Mr. Grew saw Hirota on August 10. Mr. Dodds on the 11th presented pro memoria embodying Sir R. Vansittart's two proposals of August 3. Mr. Hirota read the pro memoria very slowly and said after a long pause that 'it might be possible to consider later taking advantage of it', a reply which seemed evidence to Dodds that he had no interest in the plan (No. 171).

It seems, however, that at the beginning of August some elements in the Japanese Government including Mr. Hirota still had hopes of a settlement, based on cessation of fighting and reciprocal withdrawals in North China; and General Chiang Kai-shek sent Mr. Kao Tsung-wu, head of the Asiatic Department of the Chinese Foreign Ministry, to talk to Mr. Kawagoe, the Japanese Ambassador, who took over the negotiations in Shanghai on August 7. Kao returned to Chiang Kai-shek on August 10, but with the outbreak of fighting there which followed the discussions were not continued (No. 179). Meanwhile Sir H. Knatchbull-Hugessen, who was viewing developments with increasing concern in Nanking, was rightly convinced by the beginning of August that Chiang Kai-shek intended to embark on large scale hostilities, although many people still doubted this.

The long and the short of it was that the largely uncoordinated eleventh-hour attempts of the British and other representatives of the powers to help in maintaining peace and in particular to keep the battle away from Shanghai had all proved futile, and serious fighting began there on August 13. The Chinese had moved up two divisions and other troops, and the Japanese were probably outnumbered by ten to one for a short time. The subsequent fighting went on at or around Shanghai until the heavily reinforced Japanese forces secured a general Chinese retreat at the end of October. After this a phase of more open warfare followed as the Japanese forces pressed on to Nanking, the walls of which were breached on December 13. There followed an appalling massacre of some 40,000 of the civilian population.

In an effort to limit the range of the fighting at Shanghai, the British Ambassador was instructed on August 17 to propose that both Chinese and Japanese should withdraw their battleships from the area and agree to entrust the protection of Japanese nationals to the foreign authorities, on the understanding that other powers should join in and that the action should be welcomed by the two belligerents (Nos. 189, 191). Tokyo however on the 19th declared the proposal to be 'unacceptable' at present, because of doubts as to whether the foreign authorities had sufficient troops for the purpose and also (no doubt the real reason) because it was 'the duty of the Japanese Government to protect Japanese nationals and interests' (No. 193). Later Japanese statements reiterated the view that it was the Japanese Government's policy to settle everything directly between China and Japan. In spite of using every argument, reinforced by a final intervention on the 25th, Mr. Eden could not budge the Japanese on this point (Nos. 198, 203). He had to listen to mild complaints from the State Department that it had not been adequately consulted in this case (No. 202).

The wounding of Sir H. Knatchbull-Hugessen by Japanese aeroplanes when he was travelling by car from Nanking to Shanghai on August 26 was not a surprising occurrence in the circumstances, but it was considered important that an apology should be offered and that the Japanese Government should accept full responsibility in suitable terms. There were immediate expressions of regret, but for some days it appeared that the Japanese might refuse to apologize on the ground that the facts had not been proved. Sir Robert Craigie, the new Ambassador to Japan, arrived in Tokyo at just this point, and was greeted with a telegram from London warning him that he might be withdrawn if the very modest degree of redress required by the Foreign Office were not granted. When the matter came before the Cabinet in London on September 8 the Japanese were still claiming not to be satisfied as to the facts; but it was realized that if the Ambassador were withdrawn and the Japanese still refused to give in it might be very hard to get him back again! Mr. Chamberlain proposed instead to the Cabinet a dignified reply to the effect that 'we did not consider it consonant with our dignity to press them any further in this matter, as apparently in matters of this kind Japan was unable to attain to the normal standards observed among civilized peoples' (No. 238). Fortunately the Japanese decided to admit responsibility, although coupling the admission with an expression of 'deep regret' rather than an 'apology' (No. 250): but this was judged by Mr. Eden and Mr. Chamberlain to be acceptable. Underlying this and similar incidents was a growing fear of escalating crises in which Britain might face the risk of a major confrontation or war alone.

For in the summer and autumn of 1937 the prolonged debate in the United States on the limits of intervention was still unresolved, although the all-sufficiency of American isolationism was no longer unchallenged. While its defenders redoubled their activities there were voices which insisted that integral neutrality was a programme of inactivity which might harm only the weak and the victims of aggression. The Neutrality Act of May 1, 1937, replacing two temporary earlier acts, provided that if a state of war existed the President should proclaim the fact and that it would then become unlawful to sell and transport arms and ammunition and grant loans to any of the belligerents, who could, however, under the 'cash and carry' system, purchase certain goods in the United States and transport them in foreign ships. When only a few weeks later there was undeclared war in China, opinion was divided; influential Senators and some newspapers called on the President to invoke the neutrality law, others were as strongly opposed to his doing so. In the absence of a clear lead the President was content to leave matters on a day-to-day basis, and in fact this continued indefinitely. Cordell Hull's statement of principles of foreign policy of July 16, 1937, was in the circumstances quite unhelpful: America, he said, advocated peace, peaceful change, respect for the rights of others, equality of commercial opportunity, armed forces maintained only up to the limit of national security, and so on; she eschewed 'alliances or entangling commitments' but favoured peaceful cooperative effort in favour of all the principles stated. On August 23, in a further press release, he reviewed his statement of principles and said that his government was 'endeavouring to see kept alive, strengthened, and revitalized, in reference to the Pacific and to all the world, these fundamental principles'. But this support of principles did not imply a willingness to support any form of specific joint representations over the China question in Tokyo, and it was generally assumed in London that American cooperation with a League sanctions policy could not be expected. This automatically ruled out British and French action, and Chinese pressure was a corresponding embarrassment.

However, the Chinese case had already been communicated on August 30 to the Secretary General of the League, and the Chinese Government was loath to abandon the hope of some League endorsement, and of at least using Geneva as a good platform to expound the Chinese case. On September 12 Dr. Wellington Koo formally requested the League to take cognizance of the fact that China had been invaded. Mr. Eden had arrived in Geneva on September 9 for the Nyon Conference but had time on the 15th to join with M. Delbos and M. Avenol in urging the Chinese representatives not to give the impression of aiming at the immediate application of sanctions under Article XVI. This it appears was not their intention and they readily agreed to suggest to the Assembly that the matter should be referred to the Advisory Committee appointed by the Assembly in 1933 (No. 242; cf. No. 246). The collection of Foreign Office telegrams at this point has suffered from the apparently erratic hands of the weeder, but we know that the Advisory Committee held its first meeting on September 22, and during the next twelve days prepared the way for a conference of the nine Pacific powers of the Washington treaty, a basis which would allow the United States to take part (No. 253, note 2).

Meanwhile there was no agreement in London as to the possibility of launching a successful sanctions programme even with American support. When on September 29 Mr. Eden told the Cabinet that he proposed to make another attempt to secure joint Anglo-American cooperation in the

Far East, Mr. Chamberlain made it clear that he hoped this would stop short of an economic boycott of Japan. On the following day in a draft telegram to Washington Mr. Eden remarked that a strong feeling seemed to be growing in Britain and elsewhere in favour of some form of economic boycott of Japan; the Prime Minister added to the draft, to Mr. Eden's annoyance, the comment that 'we are not convinced that the sort of action suggested here would be effective' (No. 272). Departmental opinion was indecisive, but not on balance hostile. Mr. Jebb however argued boldly that a thorough-going economic blockade applied by both the USA and Great Britain would have a devastating effect on Japan and necessarily involve American cooperation in European affairs (No. 274). He could quote J.M. Keynes, who wrote to the Foreign Office on September 29 strongly recommending economic sanctions against Japan, 'which would be without risk, certain to be successful' – always providing of course that America would play (No. 271). On the other hand a letter from the Admiralty of October 4 was full of reservations as to the ultimate chance of success (No. 283), and these doubts were shared by Mr. Jebb's colleagues and certainly by Mr. Chamberlain, who again spoke strongly to the Cabinet on the subject on October 13 (No. 304). It was evident that a decisive lead from Washington might overcome the hesitations of some, but not all, English opponents of coercion. In reply to Mr. Eden's enquiry of September 30 the Assistant Secretary of State, on October 5, simply referred to Mr. Hull's statements of July 16 and August 23 as a summary of the 'controlling factors of American policy' and promised 'careful consideration' of any British plan of peaceful settlement based on them (No. 286). However, he indicated that action under the Nine Power treaty was likely to appeal to his government (No. 287).

This coyly circumscribed approach to acceptance of the conference project was not greatly illuminated by President Roosevelt's speech, also of October 5, in which he said that 'an epidemic of world lawlessness is spreading' and that when 'an epidemic of physical disease starts to spread the community approves and joins in a quarantine of the patients'. It is well known that the President's mind at this time was ranging over many plans for the severance of economic links with an aggressor without using the traditional machinery of sanctions and blockade and still less of naval or military intervention, and there was sufficient alarm at the quarantine speech for him to emphasize only its peaceful setting: 'America hopes for peace . . . Therefore America actively engages in the search for peace.' Ultimately after Pearl Harbour the United States was to evolve a system of economic blockade based on 'control at source' which did to a large extent eliminate traditional blockade practices, and something on these lines seems to have been in his mind and that of his naval advisers as early as 1937. The position was evidently not very clear, however, to Mr. Norman Davis, who before setting off for Brussels as the United States' chief delegate was aware of a difference of opinion between his State Department advisers as to whether in the last resort it was necessary to contemplate ultimate armed resistance to Japanese aggression. In London there was disappointment in the Foreign Office at the non-committal character of the State Department's reply of October 5.

October went by with preparations for the conference, which did not hold its first meeting until November 3. The delay was of little significance, for Japan declined to have anything to do with it throughout, and Britain and the United States were not yet ready to act together, although each had excellent reasons for not acting alone. The State Department's anxiety to avoid any suggestion of being 'dragged along by the British' was seen in its proposal that a small power, Holland or Belgium, should issue the invitation (No. 294) and in a general avoidance of joint pronouncements or representations by the two governments. There was some apprehension in London lest the quarantine speech meant a belief that effective economic sanctions were possible without the risk of war, and might result in the Japanese seizure of some Far Eastern territory by way of reprisal. These apprehensions were put to the State Department by Mr. Eden on October 12 (No. 300) and caused some resentment. On the 28th Mr. Bingham told Mr. Eden that the President was 'a little disappointed' at being asked so promptly to explain his Chicago speech. (According to his own account he described the request for definition in somewhat undiplomatic language as 'objectionable and damaging', but Mr. Eden's version merely reports the Ambassador as saying that it was 'rather a pity' (No. 323, note 3)). The State Department was unresponsive to several urgent invitations to the American delegates to the conference to come to London for preliminary discussions (Nos. 295, 300, 301, 305), as was Mr. Davis himself to a similar invitation after the conference. It was understood that the President valued the conference mainly as a means of educating American public opinion, and it was kept going for three weeks with singularly little to show for its deliberations. Mr. Eden was encouraged by these signs that America was moving away from isolationism, albeit with much uncertainty and ambiguity. He did not wish to be accused either of trying to hurry her on before she was ready, or of failing in support if and when she decided to act; but neither did he wish to move into a clear confrontation with Japan without a binding commitment of military support from Washington, the mere suggestion of which might be treated by Mr. Bingham and others as objectionable. And his attempts to strike exactly the right note with the State Department did not always convince the Prime Minister.

Faced with the flat refusal of Japan to make even a pretence of collaboration the representatives of the powers at Brussels could not but speculate on the wider implications of their rebuff and the possible reactions of their governments. Much the most interesting part of our documentation for the next three months concerns the process of high level thinking and perhaps alarm in Washington, and the varying British reactions to it. Norman Davis said on November 2, if we can believe Mr. Eden's account: 'All liberty depends in the President's view upon the course of the conference and state of American opinion at the end of it.' The President, deeply concerned at the world outlook, was 'sincerely anxious to co-operate in an attempt to stop the rot' and the failure of the conference would confront the world with a situation in which further action by the United States 'could not be excluded'. This might happen if Great Britain was compelled to withdraw from her position in the Far East leaving the United States some day to deal, maybe alone, with a greatly strengthened Japanese power (No. 328). Commenting on the European situation Mr. Hull told Sir R. Lindsday on November 16 that the 'British Empire might go down and if that happened the United States would go down soon afterwards'; the one gleam of hope, he said, was Anglo-American co-operation, which had been very close at Brussels (Nos. 364, 365, 369).

Mr. Eden was no doubt glad to hear this, for it had not been altogether easy to discover the real American objectives, and in spite of his anxiety to encourage American participation, he was not at all anxious to find himself advancing alone. The possibility of this arose from the tendency of members of the American delegation—possibly merely in an attempt to keep the conversation going—to speculate about means of coercing Japan and to hint at the possible unwillingness of the European powers to follow an American lead. Thus on November 2, at a meeting with the United Kingdom delegation, Mr. Davis said that 'he supposed we had had enough of sanctions' which led Mr. Eden to insist on Britain's willingness to take part in any international action, although in view of the European situation she could not act except in full co-operation with the United States (No. 328). On the following day when Mr. Davis suggested that if Japan continued recalcitrant, public opinion in his country might be prepared to consider the possibility of action, Mr. Eden warned him against ineffective sanctions, 'which achieved nothing beyond embitterment of the country against which sanctions were directed'. Mr. Eden gave this warning as he had 'gathered from a previous conversation that he might have had the idea of enlisting our co-operation in some comparatively mild (and therefore useless) action which he might maintain called for no guarantee of assistance but which might in fact provoke Japan whose retaliation would be directed in the first instance against ourselves' (No. 330). At another meeting on November 3 Mr. Norman Davis was told bluntly by M. Delbos and Mr. MacDonald that France and Britain could not undertake to act alone in the Far East in view of the European situation, but were prepared to consider action taken jointly with other governments, in particular that of the United States. Mr. Davis replied that as a democracy America was unable to undertake any precise commitments in advance (No. 332).

However, the American delegates at Brussels continued somewhat confusingly to talk about modes of pressure on the Japanese for which there seemed to be little interest in the State Department or in public opinion: as Sir R. Lindsay pointed out, the education of American public opinion which the President so earnestly desired had hardly begun (No. 337). Mr. Eden was clearly anxious not to pour too much cold water on Mr. Davis's fairly precise plans, which included a refusal to buy Japanese goods, and at which Mr. Chamberlain in turn showed alarm in a conversation with Mr. Eden in London on November 8 (No. 339, and note 2). Back in Brussels, Mr. Eden listened on the same day to further details of Mr. Davis's programme. How would it be if Britain and the United States were both to sell arms to China? Or they might declare that they would not recognize any Japanese aggression or lend money to Japan for development of those territories taken by force. A third procedure which 'he thought quite possible' would be for both governments to refuse to take Japanese products. He also hoped that the President would suspend, as far as this conflict was concerned, the operation of the Neutrality Act. Mr. Eden had doubts about all these proposals, which he promised however to examine carefully.

In the Foreign Office there was some uneasiness at the possibility of a press campaign of accusations of failure to follow an American initiative (No. 344). But Mr. Eden was evidently aware of this possibility, and determined to do nothing to weaken the President's confidence in the British in spite of Mr. Chamberlain's opposition to sanctions against Japan (which had been endorsed by the Cabinet on October 13, see No. 304). He accordingly sent off on November 10 from Brussels a long telegram to Sir R. Lindsay in which, after stressing all the dangers of ineffectual sanctions, he asked whether they would not be well advised 'to agree for the sake of the education which it would bring to the American people and the fostering of the habit of Anglo-American co-operation. Such joint action might be the foundation for later co-operation in Europe and it might be a capital error to discourage it.' Lindsay might discuss this with the President (No. 346). This telegram was sent to the Foreign Office, with instructions not to show it to the Cabinet. Mr. Chamberlain apparently never saw it. But the need to do so did not arise, for Sir Robert replied reassuringly. He thought it best to speak to Sumner Welles rather than the President in order to avoid publicity, and the Assistant Secretary of State, in conversation on November 13, said that Mr. Davis's suggestions were strictly exploratory, there was no intention to introduce the legislation needed for the 'so-called sanctions', and in his view Anglo-American co-operation had been perfectly satisfactory throughout. Formal instructions had now been given to Mr. Davis indicating that what the United States Government now desired was the appointment of a standing committee to follow up future possibilities (Nos. 355, 356). On November 24 the conference adjourned *sine die* after affirming that 'a prompt suspension of hostilities in the Far East would be in the best interests not only of China and Japan, but of all nations' (No. 391).

In the meantime the British delegation had to point out that the effect of Japanese intransigence during the conference on American opinion seemed to have been nil, and that there was as yet no prospect of popular support for the indictment of Japan and hint of possible pressure that Mr. Norman Davis proposed. Telegram No. 81 of November 22 gives a graphic account of plain speaking by the British spokesman, Mr. MacDonald, whose remarks on this point reduced Mr. Davis to 'a painful silence' (No. 381). On the following day Mr. Davis declined a pressing invitation to visit London because otherwise isolationists might say that the United States had entered into commitments to the United Kingdom (No. 384). However, American pressmen seemed more inclined to blame the United States Government for the conference's lack of success and Mr. Eden earned some credit for discouraging such attacks (No. 399). He at least took seriously the willingness of the United States Government to act in certain circumstances, and instructed Lindsay on November 27 to offer staff conversations with a view to naval demonstrations if the U.S. Government considered the time for this had come (No. 392). In a further telegram on December 6 after conversations with Lord Chatfield he made it clear that the despatch of a British force of capital ships with auxiliary craft not inferior to the Japanese would seriously denude other stations and could only be contemplated if vital British interests were threatened: but if the U.S. Government were disposed to take similar action he would be prepared to recommend the sending of a proportionate British force, and he had good reason to think that the Cabinet would consider it (No. 402). This was sent only for the ambassador's information, but on December 12 came the Wuhu incident with a Japanese bombardment of H.M.S. *Ladybird* and other British ships on the Yangtse, and the sinking of a U.S. ship, the *Panay*. Mr. Eden at once promised to support any U.S. protest and to consider joining in any more menacing action that was contemplated (No. 411).

It is clear that for over a week after the *Panay* crisis President Roosevelt did consider seriously both economic and naval action against Japan, and the British were enlivened and perhaps alarmed by frank and widely ranging projects given in what Lindsay called the President's 'worst "inspirational" mood'. He proposed to send a suitable naval expert to London to arrange in the first instance for a blockade of Japan but also to establish a more permanent exchange of secret information similar to that which had taken place between 1915 and 1917 (No. 433). The naval blockade in the Pacific might be accompanied by the freezing of Japanese assets, which it was thought would be possible under the existing U.S. Trading with the Enemy Act, although it would be wise to secure the co-operation of the British Treasury in order to prevent the Japanese conversion of dollars to pounds sterling. For this purpose Mr. Morgenthau on December 17 telephoned Sir John Simon, the Chancellor of the Exchequer, who passed the information on to Mr. Chamberlain and the Foreign Office. A thoroughgoing apology and promise of inde-mnification by the Japanese Foreign Office on December 14 was however followed by a more elaborate apology on December 24, by which date the President had evidently decided that further American reaction to this particular incident was unnecessary. But the President's naval expert, Captain R. E. Ingersoll, duly arrived in England at the end of December to investigate what to do 'if the United States and England would find themselves at war with Japan', and this included the economic aspects which Morgenthau had raised with Sir J. Simon. Discussions proceeded frankly with great secrecy during the first half of January. We print the joint Anglo-American record of the conversations as document No. 486 below.

It is evident that Mr. Chamberlain hoped for more than this. He privately told his sister on December 17 that he thought the Americans were nearer to 'doing something' than he had ever known them, 'and you can bet your bottom dollar I am making the most of it' (No. 431). By mid-December Eden was able to inform Lindsay that the British Government was contemplating the possibility of sending to Far Eastern waters 'a fleet of eight or nine capital ships with the necessary accompaniment of other units if the United States would make at least an equivalent effort': the Foreign Office prepared a memorandum on the objects which His Majesty's Government would hope to achieve by this action, and Sir A. Cadogan commented that he did not see why the U.S. Government should find much difficulty in declaring their intention to take corresponding action, especially as their delegation at the Brussels Conference had been very keen on reserving all rights under the Nine Power Treaty (No. 438).

However, the President's talk with Lindsay on December 17 made it clear that he did not contemplate a blockade or any other coercive action against Japan until some further outrage occurred, although he was ready for some more peaceful demonstration. The Foreign Office stated the case for some preparatory action by the two navies at once; this might be sufficient to deter the Japanese, and in any case would put the two navies in a position to act quickly if the need arose (No. 441) but this did not make any impression, although following an invitation from the Australian Government of December 23 it was agreed that four American cruisers should go to Australia for the Sydney celebrations of January 26 and that a visit to Singapore should follow. Then on January 7 came press reports of a Japanese assault on two British police officers in Shanghai, and a telegram from the Foreign Office (where Mr. Chamberlain was temporarily in charge) sounded the State Department as to whether, if the British Government announced that it was completing 'certain naval preparations' the United States would take any parallel action (No. 471). The President agreed on January 10, although not with any alacrity, that if the British did make the suggested announcement, it would be announced that vessels of the United States fleet in the Pacific were being sent to dry-dock to have their bottoms scraped. Weighing up the position in an interesting minute, Mr. Chamberlain was confirmed in his customary view that the United States could offer 'nothing helpful' and that if a threat to send the British fleet to the Far East were ineffective it would be necessary actually to send it, and this would be a most unfortunate moment to do so. He preferred a strongly worded note, but without any announcement about the fleet's movement (No. 480).

It is interesting to note that Mr. Chamberlain's minute was written, and the limited nature of American support over the Shanghai incident recognized, on January 11, that is, the day before the receipt in the Foreign Office of the telegrams concerning Mr. Roosevelt's peace conference proposal (see Volume XIX, Nos. 421–8). There seems to be no indication in the Foreign Office papers as to whether Mr. Chamberlain's unenthusiastic reaction to this proposal was coloured by disappointment at the President's preference for talk rather than action over China; in the circumstances, however, no one in London seems to have been greatly impressed by Sumner Welles's suggestion to Lindsay on the 12th that if 'German and Italian Governments enter on serious negotiations they will by force of circumstances have to withdraw support to such an extent that Japanese Government will have to make peace within the terms of the Nine-Power Treaty' (*ibid.*, No. 427). In fact the increasing gravity during the following months of the European situation imposed a corresponding caution on British Far Eastern diplomacy, of which the Japanese Government were quite aware. The 'strongly worded note' about the Shanghai assaults which Sir R. Craigie was instructed to deliver to the Japanese Government on January 12 (No. 482) was, as the Foreign Office noted later, intended 'to impress on the Japanese Government that the issue was really grave and, failing a satisfactory solution, would tend to serious impairment of our relations' (No. 530, note 3). But the Japanese were not much impressed, the hint of stronger action could not be followed up, and the ambassador was left to settle the incident with as much dignity as possible (Nos. 522, 525, 530, 533 etc.). It was, however, announced on May 21, long after the Wuhu incident for which he had been responsible on December 12, that Colonel Hashimoto had been placed on the retired list (No. 579).

The unsatisfactory exchanges between the British and American Governments concerning possible naval action also gave rise to a protracted and inconclusive correspondence between Sir A. Cadogan and Dr. Hornbeck of the State Department regarding suggestions for peace terms to be offered to the belligerents in the Far East if mediation were called for (No. 450, note 3). The possibility of mediation by one or more Powers was a red herring exploited by both the Japanese and Chinese Governments on a number of occasions in the next few months, but the Cadogan-Hornbeck correspondence also raised the question of possible economic retaliation against Japanese threats to Western interests in China. Although in November 1937 the A.T.B. Committee had effectively ruled out economic sanctions against Japan (No. 334), Dr. Hornbeck's statement that the U.S. Government were considering commercial reprisals (No. 592, note 1) prompted a reconsideration of the issue in the Foreign Office in the early months of 1938, and despite Treasury objections the matter came before an Interdepartmental Committee on July 12 (No. 598).

Although the Committee's findings were inconclusive, they were linked with the more significant issue of possible financial assistance to China, which came under renewed consideration at the beginning of 1938 although it had been a vexed question between Treasury, Foreign Office, and Chinese Government since 1934 (cf. Volume XX). Dr. Kung had been authorized to make a formal request for a loan on his visit to London in May 1937, and the request had been renewed on several occasions, always receiving the reply that no loan or credit for China would be possible without special legislation, and that such legislation was not contemplated. An approach in March 1938 from the Chinese Ambassador, however, for a loan of £20m (No. 534) led to more serious consideration, partly because of the British Government's interest in the Chinese antimony and wolfram monopolies, offered as security (Nos. 535, 541). Sir J. Simon favoured this idea for a while, on the grounds that these metals were 'of the first order of importance on defence grounds'. Lord Halifax, meanwhile, was also inclining to the view that the Chinese deserved the support and stimulus of a loan, and that 'the necessity and possibility of doing something to protect British interests and prestige in China and in Asia should on balance outweigh the risk and consequences of Japanese resentment' (cf. Nos. 567, 570, 595).

The Treasury, however, had second thoughts, and by the time the issue came before the Cabinet Committee on Foreign Policy on June 1 opposing viewpoints were clearly defined (No. 584). Mr. Chamberlain felt that the matter was sufficiently serious to call for Foreign Office and Treasury memoranda (Nos. 595 and 596), and the Cabinet agreed on July 6 that the arguments for and against a loan were 'very nicely balanced' (No. 597). By the next Cabinet meeting, however, Lord Halifax had also developed doubts and had been discouraged by the U.S. Ambassador's reply to a suggestion of collaboration in a loan to China. The final verdict, that 'in view of the serious international situation and the reactions that might be caused in Japan and subsequently in Europe' the loan proposals should not be adopted, would have come as no surprise to Sir F. Leith-Ross, in view of his own experiences (No. 599). It should be mentioned that it has been necessary to obtain many of the documents on this question from the Cabinet Office and from the Confidential Print, as the relevant Foreign Office file (25/10) has been completely destroyed.

Anglo-French preoccupation with European developments during the first half of 1938 precluded anything approaching a major confrontation with Japan, who for her part did not propose at this stage to fall out with Britain, France, the Soviet Union, or the United States—four possible and untried rivals for influence in Asia. Germany's friendship too remained in some respects equivocal. But she pressed on with her plans to dominate mainland China, and undoubtedly considered the British the major obstacle in her path. The British were able to make one contribution to

Chinese resistance with the Burma Road. In October 1937, when it became clear that persistent Japanese air attacks on Chinese railways were seriously threatening the transport of munitions from the coast, the Chinese Government had asked whether the Burmese Government would agree to the importation of munitions by means of a motor road through Burma. The plan, which had actually been foreshadowed by Sir F. Leith-Ross in the summer of 1936 (Volume XX, No. 569), was warmly supported by the British mission in Nanking and the acting consul-general in Yunnanfu, Mr. R. A. Hall, reported favourably on the technical possibilities (No. 316). The Government of Burma made no objection; the British Government's approval in principle was given on November 3, 1937. The Foreign Office saw no reason to be deterred by objections which could be anticipated in due course from Tokyo, and there already existed roads within Burma up to the frontier which could be made serviceable without great effort. There was a possibility of future commercial advantage (No. 518). On the Chinese side hundreds of miles of new road building would be needed, but by the end of the year a route from Lungling to Yungch'ang (Paoshan) had been selected (No. 444); in March 1938 it was reported that 170,000 labourers were at work on it. In the New Year Mr. Gage, Second Secretary in H.M. Embassy at Peking, after being relieved by Mr. MacKillop, elected to return to England by the proposed new highway and gave the Foreign Office a full and interesting report on the project (No. 549). In the summer of 1938 it began to appear that anticipations of the completion of the road had been somewhat optimistic, but it remained potentially one of the more hopeful assets of the Chiang Kai-shek regime.

For the rest, however, the British Government could do no more than hold on as far as possible to its existing positions in mainland China and Shanghai, and in prolonged negotiations about the customs administration had in fact to yield considerable ground. The documentation about this major problem will be found mainly in Chapter VI. For some unexplained reason the relevant file in the Foreign Office archives has been destroyed, but fortunately the essential documents survive in the Confidential Print, although without of course the minutes and possible inter-departmental correspondence about the problem which might be illuminating at certain points. The Japanese military authorities in Northern China had secured a success at Tientsin in October 1937 when after a great deal of pressure Mr. Myers, the local Customs Commissioner, agreed to deposit the customs revenue that he collected in the Japanese controlled Yokohama Specie Bank, on the understanding that the normal functioning of the customs service and the payment of interest on foreign loans would continue (Nos. 302, 303, 329). In November Japan made similar demands in Shanghai, but here the Inspector General, Sir Frederick Maze, resisted their pressure during December and January. It seemed all too evident that the Japanese intended to use the revenues for their own purposes as soon as they had obtained control of them. Sir R.

Craigie was instructed to take up the matter directly with the Japanese Government, and the help of the French and United States Governments was sought for alternative arrangements (No. 514). These the United States Government was not prepared to support, although it did not wish to interfere with the British effort; but by the end of February the Foreign Office decided that in view of the American attitude it must abandon its basic demand that the revenues should be deposited in a neutral bank, and as favourable a settlement as possible be worked out on the basis of that concession. Lengthy negotiations followed in which the Japanese Government certainly made some concessions, but with no guarantee that it would carry out its side of the bargain. The agreement was announced on May 3: General Chiang Kai-shek refused to agree to it, and it never came into force (Nos. 565, 580). But Sir Frederick Maze decided later in the year to deposit current revenues in the Yokohama Specie Bank, which postponed crises for the time being.

The customs issue was one of many, closely affecting British interests in the Far East, which required delicate and often difficult negotiations on the part of British representatives with the Chinese and Japanese authorities. Limitations of space have made it impossible to cover all such issues in this Volume, but a number of them find mention in the documentation, as do some local issues of interest, such as the enthusiastic if misguided attempts by the colourful British Military Attaché at Tokyo, Major General F. S. G. Piggott, to improve relations with the Japanese military authorities (Nos. 577, 586, 587, 590). No attempt has been made to remove or call attention to inconsistencies in the spelling of Chinese and Japanese personal and place names in the texts of documents, and documents have been printed in chronological order irrespective of differences between Far Eastern and Greenwich Mean times.

With this Volume we complete the publication of the Second Series of this Collection of documents on British foreign policy, 1919–1939. The origin of the Collection is described in the preface to Volume I of this Second Series, the first to be published in 1947. It was originally intended to have only two series (1919–1929: 1929–1939), but in the summer of 1947 it was decided to cater for the widespread interest in the immediate origins of the war in Europe by starting a third series dealing with the period March 1938 to September 1939. Accordingly the now completed Second Series runs from 1929 to the spring of 1938. Although the predominant interest of readers was in the story of Anglo-German relations it was recognized that Far Eastern developments had an interest and importance of their own, and they have accordingly been dealt with in separate volumes of the Collection. Thus of the 21 volumes which make up the Second Series, six deal with the Far East, one with Anglo-Soviet relations, and one with the origins of the Italo-Ethiopian crisis, while in the remaining thirteen the predominant interest is in Anglo-German relations. Within each volume the classification of documents is normally chronological. The Editors can say again, of this Volume as of the others in the Collection, that the conditions under which they accepted the task of producing these volumes for publication, namely access to all Papers in the Foreign Office archives and freedom in the selection and arrangement of documents, continue to be fulfilled.

Use has been made of the private papers of Mr. Neville Chamberlain with the kind permission of the Librarian of the University of Birmingham, and the papers of Sir F. Leith-Ross, Sir R. V. Hopkins, and successive Chancellors of the Exchequer have been consulted at the Public Record Office. I have to thank Miss E. Blayney, the Head of the Library and Records Department of the Foreign and Commonwealth Office, and her staff for all necessary facilities. We have relied as ever on the efficient services provided by the Public Record Office, and would also like to thank the Records Branch of the Cabinet Office for much willing help given in connection with this and previous Volumes. Mrs. I. Ennis too has given much valuable assistance over the years in the preparation of material for the Series. Finally I must say a special word of thanks to Mrs. Gillian Bennett, M.A., the Assistant Editor: we have had a long editorial collaboration since 1974 in the production of nine volumes of this Series, and her enthusiasm, good judgment, and assistance have been invaluable to me at every stage.

September 1983   W. N. MEDLICOTT

CONTENTS

LIST OF ABBREVIATIONS

A.T.B.	Advisory (Committee) on Trade and Blockade Questions in Time of War.
B.F.S.P.	*British and Foreign State Papers* (London).
Cmd.	Command Paper (London).
D.D.F.	*Documents Diplomatiques Français 1932–1939* (Paris).
D.G.F.P.	*Documents on German Foreign Policy 1918–1945* (London).
D.V.P.S.	*Dokumenty Vneshney Politiki SSSR* (Moscow).
F.R.U.S.	*Papers relating to the Foreign Relations of the United States* (Washington).
H.C.Deb. 5 s.	*Parliamentary Debates (Hansard), Official Report, 5th Series,* House of Commons (London).
H.L.Deb. 5 s.	*Parliamentary Debates (Hansard), Official Report, 5th Series,* House of Lords (London).
L/N.O.J.	*League of Nations Official Journal* (Geneva).

An asterisk following the file number of a document indicates that the text has been taken from Confidential Print.

CHAPTER SUMMARIES

CHAPTER I

The Anti-Comintern Pact: the Sian incident: discussions with Mr.
Yoshida on Anglo-Japanese relations
November 6, 1936–June 29, 1937

CHAPTER II

The Lukouchiao Incident and after
July 8–August 25, 1937

XXXV

CHAPTER III

The wounding of Sir H. Knatchbull-Hugessen: Chinese appeal to
the League of Nations
August 26–October 6, 1937

xli

CHAPTER IV

The Brussels Conference
October 7–November 25, 1937

l

CHAPTER V

Japanese attacks on British and American shipping: Anglo-American naval conversations
November 27, 1937–January 14, 1938

CHAPTER VI

Discussions on financial assistance to China and possibilities for mediation: Anglo-Japanese agreement on Chinese Customs administration
January 17–July 27, 1938

CHAPTER I

The Anti-Comintern Pact: the Sian incident: discussions with Mr. Yoshida on Anglo-Japanese relations

November 6, 1936—June 29, 1937

No. 1

Mr. Eden[1] to Sir R. Clive[2] (Tokyo)

No. 531 [F 6826/89/23]

Confidential   FOREIGN OFFICE, *November 6, 1936*

Sir,

I asked the Japanese Ambassador[3] to come and see me to-day, when I told him that the Chancellor of the Exchequer[4] had given me the memorandum on Anglo-Japanese relations which his Excellency had handed to him.[5] I was glad to have this document, since at our earlier interview[6] the Ambassador had said in general terms that he wished to improve Anglo-Japanese relations, and that he might at some later date be able to speak more specifically on the subject. Since our objective was also an improvement in such relations, we were naturally glad to have some concrete proposals.

2. The Ambassador replied that since he had last spoken to me at length on Anglo-Japanese relations at the end of July he had received

[1] Mr. Anthony Eden was Secretary of State for Foreign Affairs.
[2] H.M. Ambassador at Tokyo.
[3] H.E. Shigeru Yoshida, K.C.V.O. Born 1878, he married the daughter of Count Makino, and was to become Prime Minister of Japan 1946–7 and 1948–54. He had served as First Secretary at the Japanese Embassy in London 1920–22, Consul General at Tientsin and then Mukden (1922–8), Vice Minister for Foreign Affairs 1928–30, and Ambassador at Rome 1930–2 when he was delegate to the League of Nations during the later stages of the Manchurian crisis. He was known for his pro-Anglo-Saxon outlook and sympathies, and events were to show that his plans for Anglo-Japanese cooperation in China were largely his own.
[4] Mr. Neville Chamberlain.
[5] See Annex to this document: for further details of the presentation of the memorandum see Volume XX, Nos. 590 and 594.
[6] See Volume XX, No. 543.

from his Government definite instructions to endeavour to bring about an improvement in the relations of our two countries. His instructions were not detailed. Indeed, he described himself as having been given virtually *carte blanche*.

3. We then entered upon a discussion of the Ambassador's memorandum, which he explained to me had not been prepared by himself, but on the basis of certain ideas which he had suggested. I told Mr. Yoshida that I understood that the memorandum represented his personal suggestions and that I would respond in the same way. We then went through the points one by one. With reference to point (*a*), I remarked that the respect for the territorial integrity of China was, of course, an obligation to which we had each of us subscribed. I did not include in my reference the words 'south of the wall'. The assurance contained in (*b*) was, I told his Excellency, very welcome to us. As regards (*c*), this paragraph seemed to contemplate joint representations in China on behalf of Anglo-Japanese interests. I was myself a little doubtful whether this was a wise method by which to proceed. We had certain interests in China which we should certainly seek to uphold. So had Japan, and we fully understood that Japan would wish to uphold her interests also. But to combine for the purpose seemed to us of doubtful wisdom. Such a course might result in misunderstanding in other quarters. It might, therefore, be wiser for us each to look after our own interests while maintaining friendly understanding. The Ambassador did not take exception to these remarks, and explained that what had been in his mind was that we should each undertake to respect each other's interests in China. He had noted since he had been in this country a considerable tendency to believe that Japan wished to injure British interests in the centre of China. This was not the truth, and his object in this paragraph had been to give us some reassurance on this point. I replied that, if this was his Excellency's purpose, then it seemed to me that it could be attained without the suggestion of joint representations.

4. As regards the proposals in (*d*) and (*e*), some of which I told the Ambassador were very interesting, I should probably be making the most helpful contribution if I were to explain what were our views on the subject of assistance to China generally. We felt that we could not impose control upon China, and that any attempt to do so would defeat its own ends and arouse hostility among the Chinese. On the other hand, if China wished for financial aid or for technical advice we should be glad to join with others in giving it.

5. I then asked his Excellency the meaning of the reference in this paragraph to 'political assistance'. Mr. Yoshida, somewhat to my surprise, explained that this referred to Japanese relations with Chinese generals. In the past he confessed that Japan had, from time to time, used Chinese generals against the Central Government in order to put pressure on the latter. If these proposals went through it would be Japan's object to have a strong Central Government in China. Therefore they would not wish to

continue this policy of supporting individual generals. The Ambassador added cheerfully that our own people in China would understand what he meant. I told him that so far as I understood his explanation he seemed to have in mind some form of doctrine of non-intervention in China in respect at least of Chinese generals. The Ambassador said that this was his thought. I then asked Mr. Yoshida whether he really believed it likely that China would agree to buy her arms exclusively from Japan. It seemed to me that this proposal could hardly be a practical one unless relations between the two countries were very different from what they were to-day. The Ambassador replied that it was essentially on the basis of better relations that this suggestion was made. It was intended, he explained, to give a certain satisfaction to the military and naval authorities in Japan. China now received her arms from a number of sources, and if relations with Japan were once established on a friendly basis it would be of great assistance to the political element in Japan if this concession could be granted. The Ambassador added that all he was asking from us was that we would raise no objection if China and Japan came to an agreement on this subject of their own accord.

6. We then discussed points (f), (g) and (h). These, I told the Ambassador, we should be glad to have examined by the departments concerned with the desire to do our utmost to find a basis of discussion between us. Mr. Yoshida then gave me some explanation of the financial difficulties with which Japan was faced. Her credit in this country was unhappily low. The Ambassador considered it undeservedly so, for Japan had never defaulted on her obligations, whereas China, who had defaulted, had now better credit in London than Japan. It seemed, remarked the Ambassador somewhat sadly, as though it would therefore pay Japan to default. She might then get better terms. Mr. Yoshida also maintained that the heavy financial charges which Japan had to bear, not only in paying interest on her foreign loans, but also owing to the high cost to her of trade bills, in its turn due to the low value of the yen, resulted in Japan having to export more in order to meet her obligations. It was therefore, he argued, in the interests of this country that Japan's credit should stand high.

7. Finally, we spoke of points (i) and (j). I told the Ambassador that it was a little difficult for us to accept the conception that if there were to be an Anglo-Japanese agreement on other points Japan might subsequently come into a naval agreement. After all the latter agreement concerned many countries, and was not by any means an Anglo-Japanese issue alone. The Ambassador did not contest this, but explained that in his view naval matters would be much easier to handle after we had settled some of our other problems.

8. I took the opportunity of speaking to the Ambassador again on the matter of the 14-inch gun. We had already asked the Japanese Government what their intentions were in this connexion, and I should be grateful for anything the Ambassador could do to assist us. His

Excellency's reply was not hopeful. He stated that Japan's naval plans were not yet determined, and indicated that there was a certain confusion in the situation.[7] I understood that whereas the naval authorities wanted the largest possible ships there was also the financial consideration, which presented certain difficulties. The Ambassador was not therefore hopeful that we should receive an early reply.

9. Earlier in the conversation he had intimated that if our talks made sufficient progress he wished himself to return to Tokyo in order to speak to his Government of the whole situation and endeavour further to facilitate matters. On the occasion of that visit it might be possible for him to obtain information about the 14-inch gun. I showed my disappointment at such delay, but his Excellency was unable to give me any further comfort.

10. In a further reference to point (*i*) I pointed out that we could not of course accept any obligations which were contrary to the Covenant of the League of Nations which we had signed. It was interesting to note what his Excellency had to say about a return to the League. If Japan were able to reconsider her attitude towards that institution and resume collaboration with it, His Majesty's Government would of course be pleased to welcome her back. The Ambassador replied that the difficulty in connexion with the League was that whereas Japan had been ready to collaborate in the early stage, they had soon felt themselves diplomatically at a disadvantage there. Mr. Yoshida feared that the Japanese were not good diplomatists, and did not state their points of view effectively. The Chinese, on the other hand, excelled in these methods.

11. On parting I thanked his Excellency for letting us have his personal views in so much detail and undertook to communicate with him again as soon as the necessary interdepartmental exchanges had taken place.[8]

I am, &c.,

ANTHONY EDEN

ANNEX TO No. 1

Draft memorandum communicated by the Japanese Ambassador to the Chancellor of the Exchequer

[*F 6511/89/23*]

Strictly Confidential

The Ambassador for Japan has received instructions from Tokyo to

[7] The Japanese Government had not signed the naval treaty of March 25, 1936, which had provided for the limitation of capital ships to 35,000 tons and 14″ guns. See Volume XIII, No. 718.

[8] A record of Mr. Eden's conversation with Mr. Yoshida was sent to the Board of Trade, Colonial Office, Dominions Office, and Treasury: a draft reply based on their comments had been agreed by the first three of these departments by mid-January 1937, but was criticized on some points by the Treasury; see No. 46, note 3 below.

approach the British Government with a view to establishing a definite understanding between Japan and Great Britain concerning all matters in which their joint interests are affected.

No specific instructions as to the form of this understanding have been laid down, so that the Ambassador judges that he has full authority to use his own initiative in the matter, and he accordingly puts forward the following suggestions for the consideration of the British Government, the result of which he will communicate to the Japanese Government.

The Ambassador considers the present situation in China not only constitutes the principal source of mutual misunderstanding, but also represents the most vital issue to Japan. He is of the opinion that any agreement between Great Britain and Japan for stabilising this situation will have far-reaching results on other issues outstanding between the two Governments, in addition to securing a stabilising force for peace in the Far East.

The Ambassador is fully aware that there are many difficulties before a satisfactory solution can be arrived at, but he believes that a genuine desire to overcome these difficulties in a spirit of mutual understanding can bring about the desired result, and to this end he submits the following proposals for consideration:

(*a*) Both countries will undertake to respect in full the territorial rights and sovereignty of China, south of the Great Wall.

(*b*) Both countries will support in its entirety the principle of the 'open door' in China, as established by existing treaties, and will respect the integrity of the Chinese Maritime Customs in all treaty ports in China.

(*c*) Both countries will recognise and respect foreign rights and interests in China. It must, however, be pointed out that in recent years foreign rights in China have not been respected in their entirety by the Chinese Government. Specific examples of this are to be found in the trade boycotts, which the Chinese Government have taken no measures to oppose, and in the student agitations, which no effective measures have been taken to check. The Japanese Government feels that this state of affairs is partly due to lack of co-operation between the interested Powers, and it is therefore suggested that when instances occur of failure on the part of the Chinese Government to respect such rights, or in the event of unacceptable attempts being made by the Chinese Government to undermine those rights, or in the event of boycotts against the trade of any country, the British and Japanese Governments should consult together with a view to joint representation on the matter at issue. Similarly, it is suggested that before any action is taken by either Great Britain or Japan to alter or modify the existing treaties concerning China, the matter should be frankly and fully discussed between the two countries.

(*d*) The principle of a stabilised and commercially prosperous China is fully admitted to be a vital necessity to Japan, seeing that a prosperous China affords the natural market for the output of Japanese industry. It

5

cannot be gainsaid, however, that existing conditions in China militate to a dangerous extent against China's recovery to a normal state, and it is therefore suggested that a scheme of active co-operation should be evolved with a view to terminating the recurrent disorders now prevalent in China.

It is felt that the Chinese Government is seriously attempting to restore order and to develop China's resources, but success in this attempt must be dependent upon financial and political assistance from other Powers, which alone can enable China to effect the maintenance of order, steps for flood prevention, and the extension of communications, which are necessary to real reconstruction. It is therefore proposed that there should be frank discussion on the possibility of giving the requisite financial and political aid to the Chinese Government.

In connexion with this financial aid, it is considered that a more rapid and satisfactory conclusion can be arrived at by initial discussion between Great Britain and Japan, and it is therefore suggested that a plan should be evolved before being jointly submitted to China, the United States of America and other interested Powers. It is understood that the possibility of rendering financial aid to China has been explored by Sir Frederick Leith-Ross[9] and his recommendations on this point could form the basis of such discussion.[10]

(e) The Japanese Government feels that one of the prevalent dangers which obstruct the Nanking Government in its attempt to secure order in China is the steady spread of Communist influence by the Soviet Government. It is feared that the British Government fails to realise the danger to all foreign interests in China which will result if the steady extension of this influence is not checked by the Chinese Government. The attention of the British Government is especially drawn to the danger existing in Western China from the Soviet advance in Sinkiang. It is suggested, therefore, that discussions with the Chinese Government should include the question of assistance in checking the spread of communism.

It is recognised, however, that the problem of restoring political order in China must depend upon the military force of the Central Government. Seeing that Japan is the country most vitally interested in the restoration of that order, it is suggested that an arrangement should be come to between the Nanking Government and Japan for the provision by Japan of long-term credits for the arms and ammunition that may be required for the forces of the Central Government. It is also suggested that an adequate number of Japanese military officers should be employed by the Central Government in an advisory capacity.

The Ambassador thinks it right to make it quite clear that this

[9] Chief Economic Adviser to His Majesty's Government, who went to the Far East in September 1935 to explore the possibilities of financial aid to China: see Volume XX, Chapters V and VI.

[10] Cf. *ibid.*, No. 569.

suggestion does not imply any intention to obtain military domination of China. The objects aimed at are twofold; firstly, to ensure that the channel for the importation of arms and ammunition into China should be limited to one country only, so as to obstruct as far as possible the opportunities of independent generals obtaining supplies elsewhere; and, secondly, to strengthen the unification of Japanese Government policy in China. At the present moment the non-uniformity of Japanese policy in China is due to the fact that the Foreign Office deals direct with the Central Government at Nanking and army policy is chiefly directed towards North China, while naval policy is directed more towards the South. By the appointment of naval and military officers in an advisory capacity to the Nanking Government the present lack of unification can be avoided.

The Ambassador is of the opinion that the two questions raised in this suggestion should be dealt with by direct negotiations between Japan and China, but if the two countries should fail to come to agreement in the matter, the British Government's sympathetic assistance would be welcomed.

(f) One of the principal results of the slow disintegration of China as a world market has been the inability of Japan to find her natural market for her increased industrialisation. A direct consequence of this loss of the Chinese market has been the increased export of Japanese goods to Great Britain and her Colonies in quantities which have caused unfortunate trade controversies. The Japanese Government feels with justice that a fair market should be accorded to the products of Japanese industry, and that trade barriers, such as high tariffs and arbitrary quotas, represent a cause of ill-feeling between the two countries which it is desirable to remove by a mutual understanding of each other's difficulties.

On the premises that the two countries will jointly assist in bringing about the restoration of China's prosperity, it is suggested that Great Britain and Japan should give evidence of their mutual goodwill by discussion of a reasonable quota for Japanese exports. Such a proposal might include the acceptance by the British Government, on their side, of the quantities of textiles and rayon exported by Japan during 1935 as a basis, less a reduction on the Japanese side of 20 per cent. Such an arrangement might be accepted for a period of five years, at the termination of which further negotiations could be reopened as circumstances dictate.

(g) It is suggested that if an agreement on these lines can be arrived at, the British Government should use its good offices to obtain similar agreements between the British Dominions and Japan.

(h) It is suggested that there should be closer financial relations between the two countries. An exchange of views on the Treasury policies might be considered.

(i) It is clear that any agreement on the above lines arrived at between the two countries would result in a similarity of the view of both countries on the naval question, so that in the event of such agreement being arrived at, it might be considered feasible to revive the Naval Conference on the basis of this similarity of view.

It is also suggested that any understanding arrived at might be extended on the lines of a defensive agreement, embodying an understanding of benevolent neutrality on the part of Great Britain in the event of war between Japan and the Soviet, in return for an undertaking by the Japanese Government to protect British possessions and trade routes in the East in the event of Great Britain being involved in a war elsewhere.

(j) Similarly, if an agreement on the above lines is arrived at, it is suggested that the Japanese Government might consider co-operation with Great Britain in any plan accepted by the latter for the reconstruction of the League of Nations.

No. 2

Sir R. Clive (Tokyo) to Mr. Eden (Received December 1)

No. 577 [F 7400/89/23]

Confidential   TOKYO, *November 6, 1936*

Sir,

The Military Attaché to this Embassy[1] has addressed to me a report, of which I have the honour to enclose a copy,[2] on the subject of Anglo-Japanese relations.

2. The gist of General Piggott's remarks is that at the present moment the Japanese Army are favourably disposed towards an Anglo-Japanese understanding, or at least more cordial relations, that this friendly feeling towards Great Britain is widespread amongst all classes of Japanese, and that if the opportunity is missed to grasp the outstretched hand of friendship it may not recur.[3]

3. It is only two years since the famous Army pamphlet of October 1st, 1934 (enclosed in my despatch No. 564, Confidential, of October 25th, 1934)[4] was published. I quote the following extract: 'The British and Dutch peoples for the benefit of a small number of the governing classes are trying to supply a large number of the coloured races in their territories or colonies with their manufactures at high prices . . . If either the British or the Dutch should obstinately carry on their unjust competition to the last, the (Japanese) Empire may be forced to resort to war for the rectification of such an attitude'. The publication of this

[1] Major General F.S.G. Piggott took up his post at Tokyo in May, 1936: see Volume XX, No. 486, note 5. He described his experiences in Japan in his autobiography, *Broken Thread* (1950).

[2] Not printed.

[3] General Piggott concluded his eleven page report with the remark that it was 'just possible, as suggested to me earlier in the year by several good judges among our countrymen at home, that the Last Bus is coming round the corner'.

[4] See Volume XX, No. 188, note 6.

pamphlet coincided with the visit of an industrial 'goodwill' mission to Japan headed by Lord Barnby.[5] During that visit and at various times subsequently allusion has been made in the press and by high officials, including the present Prime Minister, to the desire felt in Japan for collaboration and even some sort of political understanding with Great Britain. Excepting therefore as regards the Army, the desire for a friendly understanding recorded by General Piggott presents no new phenomenon. On the other hand, apart from the action of the military authorities in Tokyo in restraining the press in Japan from writing up the Sasaki and Onishi cases this summer,[6] I cannot call to mind one single instance in which the Japanese Government or the military or naval authorities have done anything to meet us since I returned to Japan in June 1934. Beyond fair words we are still waiting for any practical sign of this change of heart, this desire for friendship. At the same time I readily admit that sentiment plays a larger part in Japan than in any other country in which I have served, and I can well believe that with any encouragement from our side the Japanese nation could in a short time be brought to endorse a national policy based on friendship with Great Britain.

4. The feeling of isolation which first seriously came to be recognised five years ago still haunts the Japanese, who would gladly know that they had a friend in need. One of their first reactions to the brutal murders of February 26th[7] was 'What will the world, what will England think of us?'

5. It is from that date, I believe, that the attitude of the Army towards Great Britain began to change. The improving relations between Great Britain and the U.S.S.R. have been watched with concern, and doubt has entered the military mind as to how far British sympathy could be counted on in the event of war. From one point of view especially—namely the continued supply of raw materials under British control—this is vital to Japan. The most essential of these are oil, iron ore, and cotton from India. There can be only two alternatives, friendship with Great Britain or sufficient force to seize in the last resort the sources of these commodities. The risks inherent in the latter alternative are at present too great to be contemplated.

6. The Japanese desire various things from the British Empire:
(1) Recognition that they are the predominant Power in China.
(2) What they are pleased to call free trade, i.e. the right to export their goods freely to all parts of the British Empire.
(3) Our benevolent neutrality in case of war with Russia.
(4) Sympathy of the London money market in order to assure British financial support and assistance in certain eventualities.

[5] See *ibid.*, Nos. 170, 171, and 174.
[6] In July 1936 two British soldiers appeared before a Consular Court in Peking, accused of assaulting two Japanese, Sasaki and Onishi, the former of whom died of his wounds. The trial was reported in *The Times* of July 1, 2, 4, and 7.
[7] See Volume XX, No. 467.

In return they might be prepared to come to a naval understanding with us in the Pacific, to guarantee the security of our vested interests in China generally, and even to recognise a certain predominance of British interests in South China.

7. Now if such an understanding involved
(a) an economic agreement covering world markets,
(b) a satisfactory naval agreement in the Pacific in which the United States of America also participated,
(c) real security for our interests in China,
(d) a guarantee that Hong Kong, Singapore and British territory and interests generally in the Pacific were secure from attack,
the advantages seem obvious.

8. On the other hand to what extent would our relations with other countries, notably the United States of America and the U.S.S.R., be affected by such an agreement? We cannot afford to antagonise either of these countries, and any political agreement with Japan to which His Majesty's Government would consent would have to take into the fullest consideration the reactions in these two countries. Again, the effect in China could not be ignored. If an understanding with Japan were to be interpreted in China as a *désintéressement* on our part in their political fate, there might, in fact there almost certainly would, be a violent reaction leading perhaps to another boycott.

9. As Sir George Sansom says in a minute, which I enclose,[2] on General Piggott's despatch, 'a comprehensive arrangement in my opinion is likely to be extremely difficult, because our interests are fundamentally opposed at almost every point'.

10. That the Japanese Government are cautiously sounding the ground is clear from your despatch No. 453[8] of October 1st and your telegram No. 232[9] of November 1st, but as indicated in my telegram No. 318[10] of November 3rd the general view of this Embassy is that, time being in our favour, it would appear to be the best policy to be as little precise as possible in responding to the Japanese advances, but to 'keep the ball in play'.

11. In conclusion I would add that I am not unmindful of our obligations to the League in case the consideration of an eventual understanding with Japan becomes a matter of practical politics.[11]

I have, etc.,

R.H. CLIVE

---

[8] See *ibid*., No. 561, note 2. [9] *Ibid*., No. 590. [10] *Ibid*., No. 594.

[11] Minutes on this despatch expressed general agreement with the views of Sir R. Clive and of Sir G. Sansom (Commercial Counsellor to H.M. Embassy at Tokyo), and tended to dismiss General Piggott's views as 'sentimental'. Mr. C.W. Orde, Head of the Far Eastern Department of the Foreign Office, drew particular attention to a postscript to Sir G. Sansom's minute (see para. 9 above) which concluded: 'I don't suggest that the Japanese are given to breaking their promises . . . but they have peculiar readings of the spirit of an undertaking, and I am sure that we should find their interpretation of words cooperation

and reciprocity very shocking'. Sir A. Cadogan, Deputy Under Secretary of State for Foreign Affairs, commented on December 14: 'I am quite ready to believe that there exists in Japan a body of opinion sentimentally inclined to friendship with us (just as there still exists in England a reminiscent—and also rather sentimental—feeling for Japan). But unfortunately it is difficult to find bases on which a real understanding leading to cooperation can be built.'

No. 3

Sir H. Knatchbull-Hugessen[1] (Nanking) to Mr. Eden
(Received November 13, 6.15 p.m.)

No. 189 Tour Telegraphic: by wireless [F 7011/96/10]

NANKING, *November 13, 1936*

My telegram 186 Tour.[2]

I asked the Japanese Consul General on November 9th about the result of his visit to Tokyo. He stated that he had received instructions from Hirota[3] and Japanese Minister for Foreign Affairs[4] who were anxious to secure a settlement, and in general he gave me the impression that the Japanese were modifying their attitude and their methods—if not their actual demands. He told me that since his return he had been in negotiation with the head of the Asiatic department and claimed that he had succeeded in reaching some measure of agreement which was to be registered in a forthcoming conversation between the Minister for Foreign Affairs[5] and Japanese Ambassador.[6]

2. Last night after dinner at Waichiaopu[7] I asked the Minister for Foreign Affairs if he could give me any information.

3. The Minister for Foreign Affairs said that he had had an interview with the Japanese Ambassador on the previous afternoon. After earlier conferences *communiqués* had been issued announcing in general terms that no progress had been made. This time at the suggestion of the Japanese Ambassador who said that Japanese public opinion had been disappointed . . .[8] by which the *communiqué* announced that there had been a slight rapprochement of views. This was not true: both Chinese and Japanese adhered to their own point of view and no progress

[1] H.M. Ambassador at Peking.

[2] Of November 10, not printed: cf., however, Volume XX, Nos. 582 and 592. These telegrams referred to the Sino-Japanese negotiations which had been proceeding intermittently since September 1936 regarding the series of demands presented to China by Japan which appeared to encompass the creation of an autonomous buffer state in North China and an anti-Communist agreement, as well as Japanese economic and administrative penetration in wider areas of China: cf. *ibid.*, No. 565. The progress of the negotiations so far is described *ibid.*, Nos. 583, 586, 588, and 589.

[3] Japanese Prime Minister.   [4] Mr. Arita.   [5] Chang Chun.   [6] Mr. Kawagoe.

[7] i.e. the Chinese Foreign Office.

[8] The text was here uncertain: a note on the filed copy suggested that the missing words should read 'there had been a compromise'.

whatever had been made. It was impossible for the Chinese to make any concessions regarding the anti-red bloc to which the Japanese attached much importance.

4. I asked the Minister for Foreign Affairs what was the position taken up by the Soviets in this matter. He replied that the press had indicated that if the Chinese Government did come to any arrangement with the Japanese for an anti-communist front Soviet Government would regard it as an unfriendly act.

5. The Minister for Foreign Affairs emphasised that the Chinese Government were following a definite policy of not entering into any engagement damaging to the other's foreign interests and stated in general that they were guided by two main considerations (a) to rid themselves of present position in which they were deprived of freedom of action in almost every sphere owing to possibility of encountering Japanese pressure and (b) to preserve territorial integrity and independence.

6. His Excellency agreed with me that though the problems remained as before the atmosphere was slightly better.

7. The Minister for Foreign Affairs next referred to your speech in the House of Commons on November 5th[8] and asked whether your statement that the situation had eased was based on any communication or assurance from the Japanese Government. I replied in the negative: I thought it must have been based only on reports received from myself and Sir R. Clive recording our impressions.

Repeated to Peking, Tokyo, Commander-in-Chief, Rear Admiral Yangtse, General Officer Commanding Saving and Financial Adviser.

[8] In the course of the debate on the Address in the House of Commons on November 5 Mr. Eden referred to the Sino-Japanese negotiations and remarked: 'I am happy to say that there have been definite indications lately of a distinct easing of the tension'; see 317 *H.C. Deb. 5 s.*, col. 283.

No. 4

Sir R. Clive (Tokyo) to Mr. Eden (Received November 14, 9.30 a.m.)

No. 329 Telegraphic [F 7005/303/23]

Confidential   TOKYO, *November 14, 1936, 11 a.m.*

German Ambassador[1] returned from leave November 9th and great publicity has been given to visit paid to the Prime Minister. There are widespread rumours that some sort of German-Japanese Treaty is on tap. My German colleague called on me yesterday and in the course of a long conversation assured me that no treaty had been arranged and in case one was made it would be published. I said he might not wish to answer if, very undiplomatically, I asked him a direct question. Were there any

[1] Dr. Herbert von Dirksen.

12

German-Japanese negotiations going on for a common front against Communism? He said that he preferred not to answer but as I knew German-Japanese views about Communism were very similar. I said that I had the impression that there was a pro-German wave in Japan today. He said that this was true. I asked how Japanese liked the presence of 80 German instructors with Chinese army and recent barter agreement between Germany and China.[2] He said that the Japanese did not like either but they had not referred to them in conversation since his return.[3]

[2] Cf. *D.G.F.P.*, Series C, vol. v, pp. 886–7.

[3] In his immediately following telegram No. 330 of November 14 Sir R. Clive added that there seemed 'to be little doubt that some Japanese-German understanding is imminent'. In fact Japanese-German agreements including the so-called 'Anti-Comintern Pact' had already been initialled in Berlin on October 23: see No. 9, note 3 below.

No. 5

Mr. Eden to Sir R. Clive (Tokyo)

No. 545 [F 7043/303/23]

FOREIGN OFFICE, *November 16, 1936*

Sir,

During the course of a conversation with the Japanese Ambassador today I remarked to M. Yoshida that I had seen in the press a number of reports of an impending agreement between Germany and Japan.[1] Was His Excellency in a position to give me any information on this subject?

2. The Ambassador replied that some little time ago, he thought in March or April, the Japanese Military Attaché in Berlin had been strongly advocating some joint German-Japanese declaration about communism.[2] Both Germany and Japan were opposed to communism: hence the advocacy of this joint statement. M. Yoshida added that a few weeks ago he had received a telegram from Tokio instructing him to deny any reports of an agreement between Germany and Japan. He had no information later than this, and was therefore unable to tell me whether there had been any subsequent development. The Ambassador was clear, however, that in any event it could only have to do with communism, which His Majesty's Government themselves did not favour.

3. I replied that it was quite true that we did not like communism as a form of government, but as the Ambassador would be aware the basis of our foreign policy was to seek to promote friendly relations between nations, whatever their forms of government. We would never join in a crusade in favour of any ideology. While, therefore, I had of course no comment to make about any attempts which might be made to improve relations between Germany and Japan, the Ambassador would appreciate

[1] Cf. No. 4. [2] Cf. *D.G.F.P.*, Series C, vol. iv, Editor's Note on p. 948.

that if an agreement between those two countries were aimed at a third country, then its completion might be expected to complicate the progress of our conversations for the betterment of Anglo-Japanese relations.

4. M. Yoshida replied that he perfectly understood the point. He would report what I had said to his Government and would let me know at once whether there was any information he could give me.

I am, etc.,

ANTHONY EDEN

No. 6

Extract from Cabinet Conclusions No. 66(36) of November 18, 1936

[F 7118/303/23]

6. The Secretary of State for Foreign Affairs recalled that for some time there had been rumours that Germany was seeking closer relations with Japan. Recently he had received a telegram from His Majesty's Ambassador at Tokio that Germany and Japan were on the verge of reaching an understanding.[1] Consequently he had seen the Japanese Ambassador[2] and warned him, *à propos* of tentative suggestions that the Ambassador had made for improving relations with this country,[3] that we could not enter into a combination against any other country, and that if there was a combination between Japan and any other country against some third party it would make the Anglo-Japanese conversations more difficult. Relations with Japan would not be improved by a regrettable leading article in *The Times*,[4] which had not consulted the Foreign Office before writing it. A further complication was that he could not postpone beyond that very day making a statement on the recent Keelung incident, in the course of which he was bound to show that the Fleet could not visit Japanese ports until the matter had been cleared up.[5] He added that the German-Japanese understanding was not thought to be directed against this country. It did indicate, however, that Japan might act contrary to our interests if Germany was at war with us. There was, however, no new

---

[1] See No. 4.   [2] See No. 5.   [3] Cf. No. 1.

[4] A copy of this article, published in *The Times* of November 18, p. 15 and entitled 'Three's Company?', is filed at F 7085/303/23. Referring to a report in the same issue of the paper about Italy's attitude to the German-Japanese agreement, the article was critical of all three powers, using the phrase 'mutual admiration among thieves': see Volume XVII, No. 393, note 3. Japan's choice of friends was described as 'not only ill-timed but ill-made'.

[5] See Volume XX, No. 593, note 2. Deadlock had been reached in Anglo-Japanese discussions on the incident: the Japanese authorities maintained that their police had behaved with propriety and refused to apologise. After long efforts to find a form of words by which Japan could express regret without apologising, the episode was finally closed in April 1937 by an exchange of notes, the texts of which were read to the House of Commons by Mr. Eden on April 13: see 322 *H.C. Deb. 5 s.*, cols. 797–8. The tortuous negotiations leading to this conclusion can be followed on file 147/23 of 1937.

factor there, as it had long been thought a possibility. One result of the understanding was that Russo-Japanese relations were likely to become more tense.

The First Lord of the Admiralty[6] added some information that had reached him as to the nature of the pact. He apprehended that in addition to an anti-Communist part of the understanding there might be a second part containing a military agreement.[7] There were indications that moderate opinion in Japan was by no means pleased with this arrangement, and one of the most regrettable aspects of the understanding was the probability that the moderates in Japan had once more been overborne.

[6] Sir S. Hoare.   [7] See No. 9, note 3 below.

No. 7

Sir H. Knatchbull-Hugessen (Nanking) to Mr. Eden
(Received November 20, 9.30 a.m.)

No. *198 Tour Telegraphic: by wireless* [F 7125/399/10]

Important   NANKING, *November 19, 1936*

My telegram No. 189 Tour.[1]

Vice Minister for Foreign Affairs[2] informed me in the course of conversation before the last conversation between Chinese Minister for Foreign Affairs and Japanese Ambassador that Minister for Foreign Affairs intended to intimate to Japanese Ambassador that if existing situation in Suiyuan[3] developed it would be impossible for him to continue negotiations. Minister for Foreign Affairs today informed Chancellor of Reuters that he now intends to suspend conversations as long as existing situation continues. Meanwhile Head of Asiatic Department has been sent to Suiyuan. He will first get in touch with Futsoi [*sic*] at Kweihua and subsequently proceed to the scene of operations, returning after about two weeks to report to the Minister for Foreign Affairs.

2. Chancellor has (? however) been informed in strict confidence by Head of Publicity Department of Waichiaopu that Chiang Kai-shek[4] now intends to take firm measures to oppose attacking forces in Suiyuan and to clear them out. It was also indicated that operations might if necessary be

[1] No. 3.   [2] Hsu Mo.

[3] Suiyuan, a province of Inner Mongolia, was invaded on November 15 by a force of Mongolian troops and bandits, who, according to War Office reports, were armed with Japanese weapons and aircraft; there were also reports that Manchukuoan troops were involved. The attackers were meeting with fierce resistance from the Governor, Fu Tso-yi, and his troops.

[4] General Chiang Kai-Shek was President of the Executive Yuan, head of the National Military Affairs Commission, and Chief of the General Staff, as well as holding a number of other posts.

extended to Chahar.[5] All resources of the Central Government would be used for this purpose.

3. I saw Vice Minister for Foreign Affairs this morning who told me there were Central Government forces in the district but not at present in the front line.

4. Both Vice Minister for Foreign Affairs in conversation with me and Minister for Foreign Affairs in conversation with Chancellor expressed considerable anxiety regarding reported German-Japanese understanding.[6] Both feared that this understanding would . . .[7] Japan to take a stronger line in China.

5. Chiang Kai-shek has gone to Taiyuan.

Repeated to Tokyo, Peking, Commander-in-Chief, Rear Admiral Yangtse, General Officer Commanding, Commander-in-Chief, Financial Adviser.

[5] The province of Chahar, which had already been infiltrated by Japanese troops and Manchukuo forces in 1935 (see Volume XX, Chapter V, *passim*), was the next province to Suiyuan. Mr. Orde commented on November 23: 'I should doubt C.K.S. deciding to clear the Manchukuo troops out of Chahar. If he tries the situation may well become serious.'
[6] See Nos. 4–6, and No. 9, note 3 below.
[7] The text was here uncertain.

No. 8

Minute by Mr. Orde for Sir R. Vansittart[1] on Japanese foreign policy

[F 7146/553/23]

FOREIGN OFFICE, *November 19, 1936*

Mr. Collier[2] tells me that you wish to have a note on the prospect of Japan being so far satisfied with the position vis à vis Russia as to be encouraged to strike forcibly in a southern direction. I believe the Japanese army to have their eyes more or less permanently fixed on Russia in view of her strategic position. The Japanese mind is slow to abandon a more or less fixed idea and I think that it will take a great deal of evidence of a pacific attitude on Russia's part, including probably a definite understanding to change this state of mind. If by *any* means Russia were neutralised the position would become more alarming.

In 1932 there were strong indications of a desire on the part of the Japanese army for a trial of strength with Russia. The latter took urgent steps to strengthen her Far Eastern forces and to double-track the Trans-Siberian railway and the Japanese ardour diminished. Then came the sale of the Chinese Eastern Railway by Russia,[3] influenced by the way

[1] Permanent Under Secretary of State for Foreign Affairs.
[2] Mr. Lawrence Collier, Counsellor in the Foreign Office and Head of the Northern Department.
[3] See Volume XX, Nos. 22, 34, 36, and 166.

in which Japanese control of Manchukuo, new railway construction and deliberate starvation of the Chinese Eastern Railway were tending to make it a useless asset. The sale seemed to indicate that Russia might decide in her growing fear of Germany to settle with Japan by liquidating her position in the Far East to the extent of abolishing all occasion of friction with Japan.[4] Subsequently indeed she offered a non-aggression pact, which Japan, under army influence, refused.[5] But the prospect of Russia throwing in her hand in the Far East receded and relations have remained uneasy. Japan cannot forget the possibility of Russian air and submarine activities from Vladivostok, only 450 miles from Japan and much less from the quickest Japanese communications with Manchukuo, or Russia's position half encircling Manchukuo.[6] An additional factor in preventing Japan from coming to terms with Russia is her obsession with the danger of communism. The army, in pursuit of a Mongolian policy which would weaken Russia's strategic position, attempted to penetrate into Outer Mongolia and there were a number of minor armed clashes on the Outer Mongolian frontier. On their side the Russians, relying on their increased strength, met these pin-pricks with firmness and made it plain that any attack on Russian territory would meet with determined resistance. These tactics have been successful. The frontier incidents have ceased and the Japanese have come to a clearer realisation of Russia's strength and have lost any inclination to an armed adventure against her. At the same time there are contradictory currents; the Japanese have not yet reached the point of being ready for a non-aggression pact to which the Russians for their part have become indifferent. A recent despatch from Sir R. Clive[7] concludes 'The impression left on me by all this is that the Japanese for very obvious reasons of their own do not wish to have serious trouble with the Soviet Government at present, that the Soviet Government feel sufficiently strong to hit back at the Japanese on the slightest provocation and that the two countries are still far from a state of genuinely normal and friendly relations'. Now the Japanese flirtation with Germany appears to have just come to a head,[8] not it would seem in the form of a military alliance but in that of cooperation in measures against communist propaganda. We do not yet know the contents of the agreement, but it seems unlikely to be of a character to dispose of any chance of a rapprochement between Russia and Japan. Japan may still come to the conclusion that the facilitating of her aims in China and elsewhere will be worth the price of an understanding with Russia. But if an understanding is reached it is likely to be precarious. Russia is not likely to be so

---

[4] Cf. *ibid.*, Nos. 160 and 166.   [5] Cf. *ibid.*, No. 258.

[6] Sir A. Cadogan commented in a minute of November 19: 'The Japanese, whose towns are still largely built of wood and paper, are obsessed with the fear of air bombardment, and their military adventures on the mainland have been designed as much to outflank Vladivostok as to gain elbow-room for their enterprises in N. China.'

[7] No. 543 of October 9, not printed: cf., however, Volume XX, No. 558.

[8] See Nos. 4–6.

complaisant as to remove the permanent sources of Japanese apprehension unless she is completely dominated by fear of Germany; and the circumstances which would justify a fear of that intensity might well induce Japan to reverse any policy of understanding.

Assuming that a real understanding, in fact if not explicit, were reached the effect on British interests in the Far East might be far-reaching. Japan would be strengthened as against China and if she found that force could be more profitably exercised elsewhere the temptation to an adventure towards the South would be greatly increased. Her interest in the South Seas is strong, and while at present it is taking an economic form, the danger of military action must be taken seriously. Financial weakness, which at present seems to be inclining Japan towards moderation, is a factor which works both ways. If financial and economic embarrassment reaches a certain point it may produce a reckless spirit in external affairs. We must unquestionably reckon with this possibility and southward aggression will have at least a strong rival attraction compared with an attack on Russia. The latter would bring greater strategic security, the former great economic advantages. If the United Kingdom and Russia were simultaneously engaged in war with Germany Japan's choice would be doubtful. If only one were engaged there could be little doubt that Japan would attack that one. The only safeguard to us will come from the completion of the Singapore Base and the possession of a really strong fleet based upon it.

No. 9

Sir R. Clive (Tokyo) to Mr. Eden (Received November 23, 11.15 a.m.)

No. 347 Telegraphic [F 7169/303/23]

Confidential   TOKYO, *November 23, 1936, 6.5 p.m.*

Your telegram No. 245[1] and my telegram No. 340.[2]

Minister for Foreign Affairs asked me to call today and said he wished to tell me something about German-Japanese agreement in reply to enquiry you made of Japanese Ambassador. Protocol and supplementary protocol would be signed this week.[3] They were directed against no third State but only against Comintern, with a view to exchange of information and adoption of common measures against communism. Japan was not

[1] This was a telegraphic version of No. 5.
[2] Of November 19, not printed (F 7092/303/23).
[3] Details of the German-Japanese Anti-Comintern pact and supplementary secret agreements, initialled on October 23 and signed on November 25, 1936 in Berlin, are given in *D.G.F.P.*, Series C, vol. v, pp. 1138–40: the text of a secret agreement regarding measures to be taken in the event of a Soviet attack against Germany, and stating that neither party should conclude any treaty with the Soviet Union 'without mutual consent', is printed *ibid.*, Series D, vol. i, p. 734. Cf. also Volume XVII of this Series, No. 421, note 3.

concerned with communism in Europe but would like to see formed an anti-communist bloc. Japan had no interest in fascism, only in fighting communism.

In reply to my question His Excellency assured me that there was no secret treaty at all. Supplementary protocol was in regard to measures to give effect to protocol. Both would be published and he would send me copy before publication. He was gratified by my letter to Vice Minister for Foreign Affairs (see my telegram No. 338)[4] and expressed interest in probable reactions in British press.

[4]. This telegram of November 19 referred to a personal letter from Sir R. Clive to the Vice Minister for Foreign Affairs, Mr. Horinouchi, regarding the article in *The Times* of November 18 which had been critical of both the Rome-Berlin Axis (see Volume XVII, No. 345, note 9) and the Anti-Comintern Pact: see No. 6, note 4; cf. also Volume XVII, No. 393, note 3, and *D.G.F.P.*, Series C, vol. v, pp. 1136–8. Sir R. Clive quoted the concluding sentence of his letter: 'I wish to let you know that this article in no sense represents the views of my Government who regard such premature criticism as unfortunate and have an open mind on this subject until they are in a position to know the terms of the agreement.'

No. 10

Letter from Sir E. Drummond[1] (Rome) to Sir A. Cadogan

[F 7427/553/23]

Confidential   ROME, *November 23, 1936*

My dear Alec,

I am sending you a record of a conversation which I had on Saturday last with Sugimura.[2] You know the very friendly relations which have always existed between him and me and you too know him; I therefore need make no comment on this aspect of our talk. In view of Yoshida's very important move in London,[3] an account of which I read in the print, I thought it might be of some interest if I could find out what Yoshida really represented in Japan and, as you see, I got some response to the fly that I threw. Will you make such use of the information as you think fit, but if you do use it, please do not reveal the source.

For your own information only, I may add that Sugimura told me very confidentially that Prince and Princess Chichibu would come to London for the coronation.[4] They would first spend a considerable time in Paris and it was probable that he (Sugimura) and his wife would be attached to them; indeed there was some likelihood that he might be nominated as Japan's Ambassador in Paris at a not very distant date. He emphasised that I must keep the last matter entirely secret.

Yours ever,
ERIC DRUMMOND

[1] H.M. Ambassador at Rome.   [2] Japanese Ambassador at Rome.   [3] See No. 1.
  [4] i.e. in May 1937: the date of the coronation was not changed when H.M. King George VI succeeded H.M. Edward VIII on December 14, 1936.

Record by Sir E. Drummond of a conversation with Mr. Sugimura

November 21, 1936

M. Sugimura and I had a long discussion to-day on various questions relating to Japanese policy. It turned first on Japan's relations with Germany. He said that I must remember that the military party in Japan based their policy on the assumption that war with the Soviets was inevitable. The Soviet forces in the Far East were more numerous than those of Japan; therefore the Japanese soldiers felt it essential that they should have a definite military alliance with some strong country hostile to the Soviets, and clearly to-day this would be with Germany. The Emperor and the Government were not, however, prepared to go to these lengths, though M. Sugimura, who was not very explicit on the point, indicated that the policies of the two Governments were proceeding on more or less convergent lines. He explained that when there was unrest in Europe the Soviet attitude towards Japan was more or less conciliatory; if things were quiet in Europe they became almost provocative. There was, therefore, a large party in Japan who thought it desirable that Europe should not settle down. He said that while he did not in any way defend certain provocative acts by the Japanese military in Manchuria, the Soviets were also provocative. For instance, when the Japanese Minister of War went to inspect Japanese troops in Manchuria the Soviets chose this opportunity to make a great aerial demonstration over Manchukuo territory. This had infuriated the General in question.

I asked him what the position of M. Yoshida was in Japan and whether he enjoyed any considerable authority. M. Sugimura replied that he had a certain position as the son-in-law of Count Makino and therefore connected with the immediate advisers of the Emperor. He had been Vice-Minister for Foreign Affairs but was not popular with the army and when he had been proposed as a Cabinet Minister the army had refused to accept him.[5] It was then suggested to him that he should go to London. M Yoshida refused at first but was persuaded to do so by M. Matsudaira[6] and the Government; he had, however, only consented provided he was to be given a more or less free hand. M. Sugimura said that this free hand could only be exercised within certain limits and he feared that M. Yoshida might perhaps over-estimate his position, since he could not in effect make any far reaching political arrangements (he implied that the Government was in the same position) unless the military party approved, and, as he had already said, the military party were not favourable to M. Yoshida. At the same time, he said, the Emperor was anxious for an

[5] See Volume XX, No. 470, note 5.
[6] Former Japanese Ambassador at London, appointed Minister of the Imperial Household in March 1936.

Anglo-Japanese rapprochement and this of course was a highly important factor.[7]

He then expressed himself as greatly depressed by the recent article in the *Times*[8] and said that he feared that the effect would be the same on many Japanese since the *Times* was highly respected in Japan and looked upon as a Government organ. I told him that I had definite knowledge that that article did not meet with the approval of the Secretary of State,[9] but M. Sugimura continued that unhappily Japanese who had been in London had reported that feelings there were very anti-Japanese and that there was nothing to be done in the way of restoring Anglo-Japanese friendship. The military party in Japan were opposed to England. They respected Germany because of her force and because many of the officers had been trained there. The Navy, on the other hand, was still in favour of friendship with England.[10]

[7] In a minute of December 8 Mr. Orde suggested that Mr. Chamberlain 'should see the passage about M. Yoshida's standing, in case he sees more of him'. Sir A. Cadogan, however, wrote on December 9: 'I rather prefer to assume that the Chancellor will *not* have to conduct further conversations with Mr. Yoshida and I don't think it necessary to give the Treasury this inf[ormatio]n . . .' Cf. Volume XX, No. 590, note 1.

[8] See No. 6, note 4.   [9] Cf. No. 9, note 4.

[10] In his reply to Sir E. Drummond, dated November 30, Sir A. Cadogan expressed himself 'extremely sceptical about [Yoshida's] approach to us leading to anything tangible; his suggestions at the present stage are extremely vague and only serve, I fear, to veil a fundamental difference of outlook between the two countries. But we will, of course, follow them up as far as we possibly can, as an Anglo-Japanese rapprochement is naturally highly desirable, or at least the reverse is greatly to be apprehended'.

No. 11

Sir R. Clive (Tokyo) to Mr. Eden (Received November 25, 9.30 a.m.)

No. 348 Telegraphic [F 7223/303/23]

TOKYO, *November 25, 1936, 12.25 p.m.*

My telegram No. 347.[1]
Soviet Ambassador[2] called yesterday evening.

He said that his Government had definite knowledge that there was additional secret agreement to Japanese-German protocol one of the terms of which was that neither party would conclude non-aggression pact with the U.S.S.R.[3] I told him that the Minister for Foreign Affairs had formally denied to me existence of any secret agreement. In that case he said the Minister for Foreign Affairs had lied. Secret agreement had been arranged between German and Japanese military authorities in Berlin last summer. I asked how his Government knew this. Had they seen copy? He said they had copy.

I told him that the Minister for Foreign Affairs had replied to my

[1] No. 9.   [2] M. Yurenev.   [3] Cf. No. 9, note 3.

enquiry November 23rd, that he had no knowledge that Soviet Government in view of Japanese-German agreement had refused to sign fishery convention. He said that this was untrue as Japanese Chargé d'Affaires in Moscow had been told that Soviet Government did not consider moment opportune to sign convention. If later they agreed to sign it would only be after modification of present text. He added that other probable reactions of his Government would be to increase their forces in the Far East and to have closer relations with China. At the same time his Government believed agreement was directed as much against Pacific Powers especially Great Britain as against the U.S.S.R. Germany and Japan both wanted Colonies. Best rejoinder would be pact between Great Britain, the United States, the U.S.S.R. and China which Japan should be invited to join. I said this hardly seemed practical ideal. In any case Japan never wished to antagonise Great Britain and the United States at the same time.

He returned to the question of reaction in England. He asked if I had told the Minister for Foreign Affairs that His Majesty's Government had an open mind as there was rumour to this effect. I asked where he had heard this. After some hesitation he said that a member of his staff had learnt this. I told him I had privately written to inform Vice Minister for Foreign Affairs that His Majesty's Government had had nothing to do with recent article in *The Times* and had an open mind until they knew all the facts.[4]

Finally he said that his Government did not take this affair tragically. They now knew where they stood and would take measures accordingly.[5]

Repeated Saving, to Peking, Nanking and Commander-in-Chief.

[4] See No. 9, note 4.

[5] There was some discussion in Foreign Office minutes on the probability of a secret German-Japanese agreement, but Mr. Collier maintained in a minute of November 26: '. . . I don't think it matters much . . . whether there are any secret arrangements or not. If the object of the Agreement were merely to exchange information and coordinate police arrangements, no Agreement would be necessary at all . . . Our information shows that the Japanese military authorities pressed for this Agreement in the hope that it would put them in a stronger position to carry out their designs in China and generally, and it also shows that on the German side, the object has been to draw Japan as much as possible, and as publicly as possible, into the German-Italian political bloc, whose aim, as is well-known, is to upset the present status quo in Europe and to blackmail France and this country in the colonial question.' Mr. Collier thought that the British press were right in regarding the German-Japanese agreement as 'inimical to British interests', and regretted that the disavowal at Tokyo and Rome (see No. 9, note 4, and Volume XVII, No. 393) of the *Times* article might have given the impression 'that we were deceived by the transparent pretence of an anti-Communist front whereas I should have thought that if we wanted our often-repeated objection to the formation of political or idealogical [*sic*] blocs in the world to be taken seriously, we should have made it plain that we disapproved of the formation of this new bloc both for that reason and because the activities of its members are known to be incompatible with British interests, in Europe and in the Far East.'

Sir A. Cadogan, however, maintained on November 27 that 'we were quite right to lose no time in dissociating ourselves' from the article: 'The whole tone was wrong—it gave an impression of baffled fright, which was the last effect we wished to create . . . the article was offensive incidentally also to Italy, with whom we are engaged upon trying to improve our relations [cf. Volume XVII, Nos. 410 and 415].' Mr. Eden commented on November 29: 'I am not prepared to take this matter tragically, still less to believe that if we play our cards well the agreement need lead to any closer cooperation between Germany and Japan. Some such contact existed before. The publication of the agreement appears to have been ill received in Japan, while it has irritated, to put it mildly, Washington. It is important that we should show the Japanese that we think they have done a bad day's work for themselves and generally been "had for mugs" . . . we must be active and not lament.' He asked what was the 'next step', and it was suggested that the matter might be discussed with the Americans, but Mr. Orde, Sir A. Cadogan, and Sir R. Vansittart agreed that no further action should be taken until a memorandum had been prepared: see No. 27 below.

No. 12

Record by Sir R. Craigie[1] of a conversation with Mr. Millard[2]

[F 7661/89/23]

FOREIGN OFFICE, *November 26, 1936*

After discussing one or two points relating to the naval question, Mr. Millard suddenly presented me with a copy of the *Morning Post* leading article of November 19th, headed: 'Horizons in the Far East'. He drew attention to the last paragraph which states that it is an open secret in diplomatic circles that within the last two or three months Japan has approached Great Britain with proposals for an agreement which offered the prospect of a mutual accommodation in the Far East.[3] Mr. Millard enquired if I could tell him whether such proposals had in fact been made.

I said that, as I understood it, the position was as follows. Mr. Yoshida had received general instructions to put forward proposals for improving Anglo-Japanese relations, though the Japanese Government appeared to have no very definite idea as to how this was to be done. Mr. Yoshida had had one or two talks of a general nature with the authorities here but it would, in my opinion, be incorrect to call them 'negotiations' at the present stage. It was rather a question of ascertaining whether any basis existed for setting our relations on a more satisfactory footing. It seemed to me that, so far as China was concerned, the idea running through Mr. Yoshida's mind was that satisfactory relations between our two countries—and presumably also with the United States Government—could best be established by the strengthening of the Central Government in China and the restriction of negotiations between China and Japan to the proper diplomatic channels, i.e. the Central Government in Nanking and the Government in Tokyo. This was obviously an objective with which both we and the United States would sympathise, but we were at the moment

[1] An Assistant Under Secretary in the Foreign Office, superintending the American Department, and official Foreign Office representative in the naval negotiations 1934–36: see Volume XIII.
[2] A First Secretary in the U.S. Embassy at London.
[3] Cf. Volume XX, Nos. 590 and 594, and No. 1 above.

doubtful whether anything along these lines could be achieved. Another point with which Mr. Yoshida was concerned was the improvement of the economic relations between the two countries. I said that I knew it was the intention of the Secretary of State to keep the United States Government informed, should anything develop out of the rather vague ideas which were now current, but that it could only be misleading if we were at this stage to notify the American Government that anything more than a mere survey of the ground—and a very unofficial survey—had taken place up to the present.

Mr. Millard thanked me for this information and said he knew his Government would be glad to learn that it was the intention of the Secretary of State to keep the United States Government informed should anything of interest emerge from the present exchange of views.[4]

[4] Mr. Millard's report of this conversation to the State Department is printed in *F.R.U.S.*, 1936, vol. iv, p. 389. In a minute of November 26 Sir R. Craigie deplored the leakage concerning Mr. Yoshida's proposals, but explained that he had felt it would be 'a great mistake to appear to be entirely uncommunicative' and that he had hesitated to refer Mr. Millard to Mr. Orde or Sir A. Cadogan 'seeing that it might have been a little difficult for them to be as studiously vague as I was'. He suggested, however, that it might be desirable to 'take the Americans rather more into our confidence', and also that the Japanese should be told of his conversation with Mr. Millard. Sir R. Vansittart did not see the necessity for this (November 27): 'The Japanese leaked. The Americans enquired. Such things happen constantly alas. But I don't think that is a reason to go to the Japanese about the American enquiry. It seems an unnecessary complication.' After further discussion with Sir R. Craigie, however, he agreed that the latter might inform the Japanese Embassy of what had happened 'in the course of an interview on some other matter', and this was done on December 3: according to Sir R. Craigie, Mr. Terasaki (Third Secretary in the Japanese Embassy at London) was shocked by the *Morning Post* article and denied Japanese responsibility for the leakage; see No. 14 below.

No. 13

Sir H. Knatchbull-Hugessen (Nanking) to Mr. Eden
(Received November 27, 4 p.m.)

No. 202 Tour Telegraphic: by wireless [*F 7327/399/10*]

NANKING, *November 27, 1936*

Vice Minister for Foreign Affairs told me this morning[1] that although military operations at Suiyuan[2] were very successful a serious situation had arisen. Irregulars and bandits had their headquarters in Chahar, it was impossible to deal with them effectively without following them into that province. Central Government had determined to take such measures as might be necessary even to the extent of entering Chahar, and Suiyuan troops have already been crossing the provincial border on one or two occasions during fighting. Kwantung army had however

[1] This telegram was drafted on November 25.　　　　[2] See No. 7, note 3.

immediately protested to Fu Tso-yi on basis of an agreement alleged to have been made betwen Doihara[3] and Sung Che-yuan[4] when latter's troops were expelled last year.[5] Central Government had no official knowledge of any such agreement and were considering ignoring it.

2. Some leading members of Government were advocating making an announcement that Central Government refused recognition of any pacts or agreements alleged to have been made with Chinese authorities not authorised for the purpose. This would cover Tatan agreement of February 1935[6] as well as alleged Sung-Doihara agreement but not Tangku truce[7] or Ho Ying-chin-Umetsu agreement[8] since these were concluded by authorised representative of Central Government. Matter was under consideration and no announcement would be made for some days. Government realised that if Kwantung army's warning was ignored there was serious danger of direct conflict with Japanese. He asked me what I thought would be reaction abroad to such action. Bearing in mind your telegram No. 332[9] I said that apart from rights and wrongs of the case I knew you were anxious as to possible results of anything savouring of over-assertiveness. From this point of view you hoped that Chinese Government would not adopt too uncompromising an attitude and would count well the cost before taking a step which might produce very serious developments.

3. He said that although it was common knowledge that Japanese were supporting bandits, Central Government were not as yet in possession of such conclusive evidence as would justify official representations to Japanese Government. They were awaiting report from their investigator who would return to Nanking in a few days.

4. Vice Minister for Foreign Affairs added that negotiations here were at standstill though not officially broken off. (? Japanese Ambassador) was still here but Vice Minister for Foreign Affairs thought he might shortly return to Shanghai 'or even Tokyo'.

Repeated to Peking, Commander-in-Chief, General Officer Commanding, Tokyo and Saving to Rear Admiral Yangtse and Financial Adviser.

[3] General Doihara was head of the Mukden Mission of the Kwantung Army.
[4] Chairman of the Hopei-Chahar Political Council.
[5] See Volume XX, No. 447, para. 11.   [6] See *ibid.*, No. 268, para. 10.
[7] See Volume XI, Nos. 590–2.
[8] See Volume XX, No. 306, note 4, and No. 39 below.   [9] Volume XX, No. 591.

No. 14

Record by Sir R. Craigie of a conversation with Mr. Yoshida

[*F 7660/89/23*]

Very confidential   FOREIGN OFFICE, *December 4, 1936*

The Japanese Ambassador called today and said he had received through Mr. Terasaki my message in regard to what I had said to Mr. Millard on the subject of Mr. Yoshida's proposals for improving Anglo-Japanese relations.[1] He agreed that I had had no alternative but to say what I had and he appeared to concur in the line I had taken. He was, however, most concerned and puzzled at the leakage that had occurred. So important had he considered secrecy to be that he kept all the papers in his own possession and not even one of his secretaries had seen the text of the proposals he had made. The Ambassador emphasised that, in his opinion, the only hope of success lay in the preservation of complete secrecy until such time as he was able to return to Japan, as unobtrusively as possible, in order to discuss the whole matter with his Government. Whether he would return must, of course, depend on the nature of His Majesty's Government's reply. He therefore expressed the earnest hope that we on our side would take similar measures to preserve complete secrecy in this matter.

I said I would pass on His Excellency's message to the Far Eastern Department. From the wording of the *Morning Post* article, we had certainly gained the impression that the leakage must have come from the Japanese side and I did not believe it could have come from here. We fully understood the need for complete secrecy at this stage.

As regards the United States, the Ambassador fully agreed that, at the proper moment, the United States Government must be taken fully into our confidence and he had, in fact, already informed Mr. Bingham[2] that one of the main purposes of his mission was to improve Anglo-Japanese relations. But he considered that it would only be misleading to enter into anything in the nature of conversations with the United States Government until it was certain that there was a basis for an agreement as between Japan and the United Kingdom. To attempt to exclude the United States would, of course, be absurd, since it would always be possible for the United States Government to wreck any plan which Japan and the United Kingdom might work out in disregard of that country's interests. I remarked that, when this subject had cropped up at an earlier date in connexion with the naval negotiations, the United States Government had taken the line that it would not be possible for them to come into any Far Eastern agreement which did not include China and other Powers interested in the Far East. Mr. Yoshida answered that he saw no reason why China should not also be included in any agreement, seeing that the main purpose of his proposals was to secure a genuine rehabilitation and strengthening of the Central Government of China.

The Ambassador then said he would like to give me a general review of the relations of Japan and the United Kingdom in regard to the Far Eastern question during recent years. I pointed out to His Excellency that this was somewhat outside my beat. But he said that for this very reason it might be easier for both of us to discuss these matters more frankly and

---

[1] See No. 12.　　　　　　　　　　　　　　　　[2] U.S. Ambassador at London.

26

less officially.[3] He then proceeded to give a survey of the principal events in Sino-Japanese and Anglo-Japanese relations since the termination of the Anglo-Japanese alliance. The main conclusion he appeared to draw from this survey was that, with the disappearance of the Anglo-Japanese alliance, Japan's foreign policy had lost its former orientation and, not to put too fine a point on it, had been devoid of any orientation at all. The military element had steadily taken more and more control of policy on the ground that, since Japan no longer had any friends, it was necessary to increase armaments to the limit. As a further justification of this policy it was necessary to have an enemy. For this rôle Soviet Russia was cast, at a time when Russian power in the Far East was relatively weak. The only result of this policy had been the strenghening of Russia's Far Eastern defences to such an extent that her position was now completely impregnable. Another serious result was that Japanese trade had found itself cut off progressively from China as a result of political boycotts, and had sought compensation for this by increasing Japanese exports to the British Dominions and Colonies. This in turn had led to a commercial controversy with the British Empire. In Japanese eyes our policy also had not been blameless in bringing about the progressive decline in Anglo-Japanese relations, for we had appeared to be only too ready to benefit by any deterioration in Sino-Japanese relations. In other words, it was felt by some in Japan that we had endeavoured to exploit the situation to our own advantage. (At this I, of course, protested and tried to put the matter in its proper perspective.)

This being the course of events, it seemed to the Ambassador and to many who shared his views in Japan to be essential to reverse the process; to secure a really friendly relationship between China and Japan and to re-establish confidence in the former country. He would not hide from me that, of the increase in trade which might be expected to result from a marked improvement in China's economic and political situation, Japan would expect to get the lion's share; but this in turn would automatically reduce the Japanese pressure on British markets and would make a commercial agreement between the two countries far easier.

I said that I felt quite sure that, if the Japanese Government were sincerely to adopt and follow such a policy, they would have the full support not only of this country but also of the United States. The difficulty was that we saw no signs at present of such a change of policy, which meant, so far as I could see, that the military element in Japan should once more be put in its proper place and that diplomacy should be conducted by the diplomatists. I was frankly rather sceptical as to whether the moment had come for this most desirable change in the situation. What did the Ambassador think?

[3] Sir A. Cadogan commented in a minute of December 9: 'The Ambassador has an irresistible desire to discuss policy with everyone except those who are primarily and directly concerned with it [cf. No. 10, note 7]. (Perhaps he feels that he is thus less exposed to some of the more obvious retorts).'

Mr. Yoshida replied that, with the recent increase in taxation, there was every evidence that the people of Japan were beginning to tire a little of the constant demands of the military and were beginning to wonder whether there was not an alternative policy which would be less exacting. It was surely in our interest to encourage and facilitate the adoption of that alternative policy. He did not deny, however, that if our reply to Japan's present advances were unfavourable or inadequate, this would be a great discouragement for those in high place in Japan who held the same views as he had expressed to me. Among these, he hinted, was the Emperor himself. If there was no hope of an alternative policy, which could only be worked in close cooperation with this country, then the liberal elements in Japan would suffer discouragement and he feared that Japanese foreign policy would evolve in a much less desirable direction.[4] What I gathered he feared was that, unless a sound alternative policy could be found, those who favoured an even closer relationship between Japan and Germany would have their way. It was, Mr. Yoshida said, as easy for us to read the signs as for him, but he regarded these tendencies, which fortunately had not gone far at present, as highly dangerous for his own country.

Finally, the Ambassador said that he had wished to put these very frank observations to me in the hope that I would do what I could, within my own sphere, to assist in promoting friendship between our two countries. I assured His Excellency that this had always been my ideal and that, if the Japanese Government were ready to adopt a liberal and broadminded policy such as he had outlined, they could fully count on British cooperation, without the need of any recommendation from me.[5]

[1] Sir A. Cadogan commented on December 9: 'We must remember that Mr. Yoshida was banned from office by the military [cf. No. 10] and therefore of course has no love for them. But I am afraid the wish is father to the thought when he speaks of the possibility of strengthening the liberal elements in Japan at the expense of the military.'

[5] A copy of this record was sent to Sir R. Clive under cover of a letter from Sir A. Cadogan of December 14 marked 'private and secret'.

No. 15

Sir H. Knatchbull-Hugessen (Nanking) to Mr. Eden
(Received December 7, 7 p.m.)

No. 209 Tour Telegraphic: by wireless [F 7566/303/23]

NANKING, *December 7, 1936*

German and Italian understandings with Japan[1] are viewed here with great disfavour and some suspicion.

It is feared that German-Japanese Agreement will render possible a

[1] See No. 9, note 3.

return to a more forward policy on the part of Japan and that Japanese Army in the North will assume agreement places a check on Russia and therefore gives them a freer hand. Vice Minister for Foreign Affairs expressed to Chinese Counsellor[2] the conviction that secret clauses existed.[3] He stated German Ambassador[4] had been unable to answer his enquiry as to the meaning of provision in published document for joint invitation 'to other States whose internal peace is menaced by Commintern [sic]' and for stringent measures by competent authorities 'against persons at home *and abroad* who assist in activities of the Commintern' [sic]. He had asked whether the first passage alluded to China and as regards the second passage whether the German Government was considering measures against Chinese or other nationals in China. The Ambassador had undertaken to refer this question to his Government.

The Italian Ambassador[5] came to Nanking on instructions from his Government to explain their agreement with Japan. He denied that the Italian Government were recognising Manchukuo and said the Japanese Government were merely informing the Italian Government that the Manchukuo authorities were willing to accept an Italian Consul at Mukden. When pressed on the subject of exequatur,[6] Ambassador became extremely embarrassed and undertook to refer to his Government. He emphasized that Italian attitude to China remained one of cordial friendship.

Vice Minister for Foreign Affairs expressed the view that the two agreements were inter-connected and that if Chinese Government had not strenuously resisted Japanese pressure to form anti-communist bloc they would have been jockeyed into fascist combination. In general there is considerable soreness with Germany although Chinese Government do not credit her with intention to interfere in their affairs. They are inclined to suspect German inspiration behind Japanese pressure to join anti-communist bloc.

Attitude to Italy is one of complete distrust coupled with certainty that recognition of Manchukuo has been bartered against recognition of Ethiopian conquest.

Repeated to Peking, Tokyo, Commander-in-Chief, Rear Admiral Yangtse, General Officer Commanding and Saving to Financial Adviser.

[2] Mr. A.D. Blackburn.
[3] Cf. No. 11.
[4] Dr. Oskar Trautmann.
[5] Signor Lojacono.
[6] i.e. the authorization given to a Consul by a government to pursue his functions.

No. 16

Sir H. Knatchbull-Hugessen (Nanking) to Mr. Eden
(Received December 7, 7 p.m.)

No. 210 Tour Telegraphic: by wireless [F 7567/166/10]

Confidential   NANKING, *December 7, 1936*

My immediately preceding telegram.[1]

One result has been to make Chinese Government consider seriously the advisability of dismissing German Military and Air Advisers. This would actually have been done in the case of Italian Advisers had not Italian Government succeeded in hedging here as regards recognition of Manchukuo sufficiently to deprive Chinese Government of a good excuse for action. But in any case question of dismissal of both Italians and Germans is still under very serious consideration.

Dr. Kung[2] informed me yesterday that it was the wish of Chinese Government to have British Advisers both as regards air and military affairs and also as regards finance and it is not unlikely if present Air and Military Advisers are dismissed we shall be approached with a direct request. Similar request as regards Financial Advisers is also possible.[3]

Donald[4] informed me that the whole trend of thought was in favour of increased confidence in and reliance on ourselves. He also stated that establishment of income tax organisation on British model is in contemplation. He had expected Dr. Kung to speak to me about this but Dr. Kung did not do so.

Repeated as before.

---

[1] No. 15.

[2] Chinese Minister of Finance.

[3] It was generally agreed in the Foreign Office that a Chinese request for advisers should be treated sympathetically, despite the fact that, as pointed out by Mr. N.B. Ronald, a First Secretary in the Far Eastern Department, the War Office and Air Ministry were 'deplorably short of suitable officers at the moment'. Mr. Orde and Sir R. Vansittart were especially concerned that an air advisership should be taken up, but there was some concern that the appointment of a military adviser would be badly received by the Japanese. Sir A. Cadogan pointed out on December 10 that as far as the supply of war material was concerned 'China must come very low on the priority list . . . much as we should desire to secure China's goodwill I fear we can't buy it with war material . . . That is all the more reason why we should make every effort to try to find suitable advisers, if they are wanted'. Mr. Eden agreed (December 15), but thought that 'we could wait for the request': meanwhile telegram No. 145 Tour to Nanking of December 17 cautioned Sir H. Knatchbull-Hugessen that he 'should not of course encourage [the Chinese] in any way to dismiss the German advisers but leave the matter to their initiative'.

[4] Mr. W.H. Donald, Personal Adviser to Chiang Kai-shek.

No. 17

Sir H. Knatchbull-Hugessen (Nanking) to Mr. Eden
(Received December 9, 5.40 p.m.)

No. 217 Tour Telegraphic: by wireless [F 7589/96/10]

NANKING, *December 8, 1936*

My telegram No. 214 Tour.[1]

After Japanese Ambassador's interview on December 3rd, Japanese Embassy issued through Domei News Agency a statement that partial agreement had been reached in five out of eight major ...[2] in Sino-Japanese negotiations viz: (1) direct China-Japan air service (2) tariff revision (3) control of all Korean nationals (4) employment of advisers (5) restraint of anti-Japanese activities.

2. Ministry of Foreign Affairs have now issued counter-statement in which the foregoing points are dealt with seriatim as follows: (1) question of direct air service between Fukuoka and Shanghai had reached stage of draft agreement when Japanese aeroplanes began to fly illegally in North China and Chinese Government have refused to discuss question further until illegal flying has ceased. (2) Tariffs are an internal matter and can be adjusted to ...[2] requirements of national trade and finance; but first essential to a consideration of tariff adjustment is suppression of smuggling and restoration of customs right of search. (3) Chinese Government strongly discountenance illegal activities of any sort by any foreigners in China; but at the same time Japanese authorities must curb illegal activities of Koreans, Formosans and other Japanese whose activities are carried on under the aegis of Japan. (4) Chinese Government of its own motion employs foreign advisers according to its requirements and would be prepared to employ Japanese as technical advisers if a favourable turn took place in Sino-Japanese relations. (5) Chinese Government is doing all possible to produce harmonious relations but a change of policy on Japan's part is only real solution for anti-Japanese feeling.

3. Vice Minister for Foreign Affairs told me today that five points mentioned above were continued[3] in memorandum read by Japanese Ambassador at his interview with the Minister for Foreign Affairs on December 3rd. Memorandum was he said grossly misleading: it not only

---

[1] Sir H. Knatchbull-Hugessen's telegrams Nos. 212 and 214 Tour of December 7 referred to an interview on December 3 between the Chinese Foreign Minister and the Japanese Ambassador, when despite the former's refusal to continue negotiations in view of the situation in Suiyuan (see Nos. 7 and 13) Mr. Kawagoe insisted on leaving with him a document summarizing the discussions which Chang Chun 'declined to accept on the grounds that it was inaccurate'. According to Mr. Hsu Mo, however, discussions were 'not broken off but only put into cold storage'.

[2] The text was here uncertain.

[3] A note on the filed copy suggested that this should read 'contained'.

ignored entirely Chinese side of the case but it alleged agreement in principle when there had been no agreement and continually introduced matters which had never been mentioned. It was clear that Japanese were playing their old trick of presenting Chinese with a document containing their own requirements and thereafter treating it as an agreement. That was why the Minister for Foreign Affairs had so vigorously rejected it. Document after being returned to Japanese Embassy had been returned again to Ministry who rather than keep up this undignified game had eventually retained it but had informed Japanese Embassy in writing that the contents were inaccurate.[4]

Repeated as before.

[4] Mr. J. Thyne Henderson, a First Secretary in the Far Eastern Department, commented on December 10: 'A childish performance but the Domei report is useful as showing Japan's immediate objectives. Of course the Japanese people will not see the Chinese Govt.'s *démenti* and will think, when the "agreement" is not immediately implemented, that the Chinese are being insincere again, but both sides seem to be heading for war anyway, so it probably doesn't make much difference'. Sir R. Vansittart noted on December 10: 'The S. of S. shd. see this paper and Mr. Henderson's minute. The Japanese are behaving with deliberate provocativeness.' Mr. Eden initialled the minutes on December 14.

No. 18

Sir H. Knatchbull-Hugessen (Nanking) to Mr. Eden
(Received December 9, 6.15 p.m.)

No. 221 Tour Telegraphic: by wireless [F 7619/96/10]

NANKING, *December 8, 1936*

Sino-Japanese relations.

My recent telegrams[1] show situation as seen from here to be as follows:

(a) General negotiations are . . .[2] in unfavourable atmosphere Japanese Government having completely failed to carry any of their points.

(b) Japanese designs in Suiyuan[3] have up to now been checked but there is some possibility of complications owing to threat of Kwantung army if Chinese forces advance against irregular activity in Chahar.

(c) New incident which appears to have been provoked by Japanese has arisen at Tsingtao and as stated in my telegram No. 218 tour Japanese Government have made threat regarding similar action elsewhere if occasion arises.[4]

[1] Cf. Nos. 15 and 17.   [2] The text was here uncertain.   [3] See Nos. 7 and 13.

[4] A party of Japanese marines had landed at Tsingtao on December 2 following an outbreak of strikes in Japanese cotton mills which the Japanese said were part of an organised anti-Japanese campaign. The marines made a number of arrests, harassed Kuomintang officials and searched their offices. The Chinese Foreign Minister protested to the Japanese Ambassador at their interview on December 3: see No. 17, note 1. In his telegram No. 218 Tour drafted on December 7 (received December 9) Sir H. Knatchbull-Hugessen reported that according to Hsu Mo the Mayor of Tsingtao had been presented

2. Until announcement of German-Japanese agreement[5] I had thought it probable that Japanese Government would refrain from pressing things beyond a certain point. Indeed trend of events up to Tsingtao incident confirmed this theory. But future developments seem to depend on two factors (1) How far Japanese Government may be emboldened as a result of German-Japanese agreement and (2) How far Government in Tokyo can restrain their extremists. Japanese movements in China appear to be mainly prompted by considerations of party politics at home. Kuantung army are having a new fling in Suiyuan and navy are now following suit at Tsingtao. Danger of serious complications must continue unless moderating control of government in Tokyo can be established.

3. As reported in my Telegram No. 208 Tour[6] Donald spoke of possible representations at Tokyo and Vice Minister for Foreign Affairs yesterday produced idea of some declaration of much wider scope—see my telegram No. 219 Tour[7]. I refrained from pursuing Donald's suggestion and tried to be as non-committal as possible to Vice Minister for Foreign Affairs.

4. But in view of present situation and in particular German-Japanese agreement and Tsingtao affair I would venture to put before you question whether the moment has not arrived for some further representations at Tokyo, if possible in conjunction with United States and French Governments both of whom appeared ready to make some *démarche* at the time of the crisis last September. (See Sir R. Lindsay's telegram No. 244,[8] last paragraph and your telegram No. 312[9] of October 7th to Foreign Office from Geneva.)[10]

Repeated as before.

---

with twelve demands 'of a far-reaching character. . . Japanese were in fact using labour trouble as a pretext for putting forward political demands under naval pressure with a view to establishment of another puppet régime'. Strong support from the Central Government for the local authorities, however, led to a moderation of the Japanese attitude and the affair was settled locally. Sir H. Knatchbull-Hugessen reported in telegram No. 225 Tour of December 11 that the Chinese authorities considered the landing of the marines 'a political move to set off non-success of Nanking negotiations and the rebuff suffered by Manchukuo forces in Suiyuan'.

[5] See No. 9, note 3.

[6] Of December 5, not printed (F 7506/399/10).

[7] In this telegram of December 9 Sir H. Knatchbull-Hugessen reported that Hsu Mo had asked his opinion 'as to feasibility of some joint statement based on the Covenant of the League, Kellogg Pact, and Nine Power Treaty reaffirming principles of non-aggression etc. embodied in those documents'. He proposed as signatories China, France, Russia, Great Britain, and the United States: Germany, Italy, and Japan would also be welcome. Sir H. Knatchbull-Hugessen replied that His Majesty's Government had made it clear that they could undertake no further commitments in any circumstances, and referred to Mr. Eden's recent speech at Leamington in which he deplored the tendency to divide the world into opposing camps: see Volume XVII, No. 400, note 1.

[8] Volume XX, No. 570.

[9] This was a repeat of Geneva telegram No. 75 Saving: see Volume XX, No. 582, note 1.

[10] A note on the filed copy of this telegram by Mr. O.C. Harvey, Private Secretary to Mr.

Eden, read: 'S. of S. wd. like to see minutes in due course.' Mr. Orde (December 10) did not think the moment right for representations in Tokyo, although 'something might be said to show the Japanese that we are concerned'. Sir A. Cadogan, however, thought it better to say nothing (December 12): 'Our relations with the Japanese are not at the moment good, and we don't want to make them worse unless it is necessary and unless we can do any good thereby.' Sir R. Vansittart agreed (December 12): 'I wouldn't move yet. We are *en froid* with Japan anyhow just at present. I hope she will rectify this by burning her fingers a little.' Mr. Eden noted: 'I agree.'

No. 19

Mr. Eden to Sir R. Clive (Tokyo)

No. 601 [F 7569/89/23]

FOREIGN OFFICE, *December 8, 1936*

Sir,

I asked the Japanese Ambassador to come and see me this morning when I told His Excellency that the various Government departments concerned were still actively engaged in the study of the memorandum which he had left with us.[1] We were anxious that the Ambassador should not think that because of the time that we were taking in this study we were not interested. The reverse was the truth, but the variety and importance of the subjects raised inevitably entailed much work.

2. In the meanwhile however, there was one matter in connexion with this memorandum about which I would like to speak to him. In para. (d) of his draft memorandum the Ambassador referred to conditions in China and stated that in connexion with the projected financial aid to China it was considered 'that a more rapid and satisfactory conclusion can be arrived at by initial discussion between Great Britain and Japan, and it is therefore suggested that a plan should be evolved before being jointly submitted to China, the United States of America and other interested Powers. It is understood that the possibility of rendering financial aid to China has been explored by Sir Frederick Leith-Ross, and his recommendations on this point could form the basis of such discussion'. Personally I entirely shared the view expressed in those sentences. In this connexion I understood that Sir Charles Addis[2] had recently approached Viscount Kano[3] in order that conversations might be initiated with reference to the possibility of a joint loan for railway construction in China, but that Viscount Kano had felt unable to agree to this. He had, I understood, consulted His Excellency and the reason given had been the political negotiations at present in progress between Tokio and Nanking.

[1] See No. 1.

[2] Head of the British group of the China Consortium. The Consortium was formed by an agreement signed in 1920 between British, French, Japanese, and American banking groups for international cooperation in financial aid to China.

[3] Representative of the Japanese group of the China Consortium in London.

This reply was so much at variance with the suggestion in the memorandum that I was drawing His Excellency's attention to it in the hope that it might be possible to reconsider the attitude at present taken up by Viscount Kano. We were ourselves anxious to begin conversations with the Japanese representatives on this subject.[4]

3. After some further conversation M. Yoshida stated that he did not think there could be any serious objection to private and informal conversations being begun between Viscount Kano and Sir Charles Addis.

4. We then spoke of general Anglo-Japanese relations. The Ambassador explained that he was most anxious to return to Tokio in order to arrive there about the 10th January. The Japanese Diet opened on the 20th of the same month and if he was to obtain the ear of Cabinet Ministers it was desirable that he should be in Tokio before that date. M. Yoshida explained that he quite understood that it would not be possible for him to be given an answer to his memorandum before he left. All that he asked, however, was for an indication that H.M. Government were sincerely desirous of improving Anglo-Japanese relations. What many Ministers in Tokio felt was that Anglo-Japanese Commercial rivalry was now so intense that it had become virtually impossible to improve political relations. Personally he thought the German-Japanese Agreement[5] unfortunate, but he was sure that it would never have come about but for this fear that the improvement of Anglo-Japanese relations presented difficulties so serious, especially in trade matters, as to be well-nigh insuperable. The Ambassador himself wished to counter this point of view. He fully admitted the intensity of our trade rivalry. At the same time he felt that this was in a large measure due to the situation in China. Japan had lost a large part of her Chinese market owing to the boycott of Japanese goods in that country and to other causes. If the position in China could be improved and Japanese trade with that country increased, the pressure of her competition in the Dominions and in the Colonies would be correspondingly relaxed. In any event the Ambassador repeated

[4] The suggestion that Mr. Eden should speak to Mr. Yoshida on this point was made in a letter of November 27 from the Treasury to the Foreign Office commenting generally on Mr. Yoshida's memorandum (Annex to No. 1). The letter referred to Sir C. Addis's conversation on November 3 with Viscount Kano, who said that after consultation with Mr. Yoshida on the question of a meeting to discuss an international railway loan he felt it 'might be better to approach the other groups first and "apply for Japanese assent at a later stage"'. Sir C. Addis disagreed, maintaining that 'an assurance in advance of the cordial cooperation of Japan was . . . an indispensable step to approaching the other groups in the Consortium'. The Treasury strongly supported this view, and felt that the discrepancy between Mr. Yoshida's memorandum and what he told Viscount Kano should be pointed out. Foreign Office officials agreed. Sir A. Cadogan (December 4) thought that the issue was a 'test of Japanese sincerity: there is no good reason for their refusal to cooperate on these lines, if they are in earnest when they profess their desire to assist in the consolidation and development of China'. Sir R. Vansittart agreed (December 4), but thought there was little hope that they would 'survive the test, for their attempts to delay in this very category smell strong of insincerity'. Mr. Eden noted on December 5: 'Very well: let us try.'

[5] See No. 9, note 3.

that he was anxious to assure his Government of this country's real desire for improved relations, for he feared that without it further steps such as had recently been taken might be contemplated.

5. After some further conversation we agreed that further exchanges of view should take place between the Ambassador and the Foreign Office during the next few days, and that I should see His Excellency again before his departure.

I am, etc.,
ANTHONY EDEN

No. 20

Sir R. Clive (Tokyo) to Mr. Eden (Received December 11, 9.30 a.m.)

No. 365 Telegraphic [F 7635/96/10]

TOKYO, *December 11, 1936, 12.55 p.m.*

In an official statement issued to the press yesterday after outlining the course of negotiations it is alleged that agreement in principle had been reached on five points indicated in Nanking telegram No. 217 Tour[1] to Foreign Office but that Chinese Government had subsequently informed Japanese representative that it would be difficult to bring negotiations to successful conclusion so long as East Suiyuan question was not settled[2]. Japanese Ambassador considering Suiyuan question irrelevant to negotiations had replied requesting Chinese Government to translate into action as soon as possible the point on which the agreement had been reached.

'Japanese Government now await reply of Chinese Government. Should Chinese Government fail to take effective steps for control of anti-Japanese movement, and lives and property of Japanese be jeopardized and their rights and interests violated, Japanese Government is prepared in view of conditions in China to take adequate measures to cope with the situation.'

[1] No. 17.　　　　　　　　　　　　　　　　　　[2] Cf. Nos. 7 and 13.

No. 21

Sir R. Clive (Tokyo) to Mr. Eden (Received December 12, 11 a.m.)

No. 366 Telegraphic [F 7649/96/10]

TOKYO, *December 11, 1936, 3.38 p.m.*

My immediately preceding telegram.[1]

I told Vice Minister for Foreign Affairs yesterday that last paragraph sounded ominous. Minister of War had recently said the same thing in an

[1] No. 20.

interview. I trusted that Japanese Government were not contemplating forcible action. He assured me that they were not. He added that the trouble at Tsingtao[2] was on the road to settlement. Kuomintang and Communist agitators had caused strike and the landing of marines was reasonable precaution and should protect Japanese.

Press reports today that Chinese are going to expostulate on the solution agreed to on . . .[3] for settlement of Chengtu and Pakhoi incidents and are objecting to the opening of Japanese Consulate at Chengtu[4].

I am convinced that any joint representation whatever suggested by Sir H. Knatchbull-Hugessen in his telegram No. 221 Tour series to Foreign Office[5] would be inadvisable at present. Japanese Government have been much criticised for German-Japanese Agreement[6] and for failure of Sino-Japanese negotiations but the press appear to support determination of Japanese Government not to tolerate indefinitely postponement of settlement with China.[7]

Repeated to Peking Saving and Nanking.

[2] See No. 18, note 4.   [3] The text was here uncertain.
[4] See Volume XX, No. 549, note 3, and No. 555, note 3. These two incidents were settled by an exchange of notes on December 30, 1936 between the Chinese and Japanese authorities. The Chinese note expressed regret and gave details of measures to punish the offenders: compensation was also paid. The question of the Chengtu Consulate was not mentioned, but Sir H. Knatchbull-Hugessen reported in his telegram No. 8 of January 4, 1937 that the Japanese Foreign Office spokesman had announced that 'reopening will take place shortly': the Ambassador thought this 'would seem somewhat dangerous proceeding'.
[5] No. 18.   [6] See No. 9, note 3: cf. No. 15.
[7] Minutes on this telegram agreed that the time was not right for joint representations. Sir A. Cadogan commented on December 14 that the Japanese were 'a little bit frightened at what they have done, and they can be left in that mood for the moment. A move on our part now might stir them into a fresh aggressive mood'. He agreed with Mr. Orde, however, that it would be a good idea to discuss the matter with Mr. R. Atherton, Counsellor of the U.S. Embassy at London: see No. 27 below. Meanwhile with the approval of Sir R. Vansittart and Mr. Eden telegram No. 142 Tour of December 16 was despatched to Sir H. Knatchbull-Hugessen as follows: 'Your telegram 221 Tour [No. 18]. I agree with Sir R. Clive that joint representations would be inadvisable at present.'

No. 22

Sir H. Knatchbull-Hugessen (Nanking) to Mr. Eden
(Received December 13, 10 a.m.)

No. 230 Tour Telegraphic [F 7652/166/10]

Important   NANKING, *December 13, 1936, 3.50 p.m.*

You will no doubt have seen Reuters report of Chang Hsueh-liang rebellion, his arrest of Chiang Kai-shek at Sian and issue of circular telegram advocating overthrow of the government and alliance with

Soviet Russia against the Japanese.[1] This information is confirmed by Waichiaopu.

2. At emergency meeting of the central executive committee and central political council last night Dr. Kung was put in charge of Executive Yuan and Ho Ying-chin[2] was put in command of military operations.

3. Vice Minister for Foreign Affairs states that Chang Hsueh-liang has for some time been under suspicion, that he had withdrawn some of his troops from fighting the communists and had been suspected of arranging to combine with the communists against the Japanese. Government have been making different dispositions and think they have the situation in hand.

4. See my immediately following telegram.[3]

[1] A copy of the Reuter's report as published in the *Morning Post* on December 14 is filed with this telegram. General Chiang Kai-shek had been captured on December 12 at Sian, capital of Shensi province, by troops under the command of the 'Young Marshal', Chang Hsueh-liang, who was appointed in February 1934 to suppress Communist bands in that area.

[2] Minister of War.   [3] No. 23 below.

No. 23

Sir H. Knatchbull-Hugessen (Nanking) to Mr. Eden
(Received December 13, 6.40 p.m.)

No. 231 Tour Telegraphic: by wireless [F 7653/166/10]

Important   NANKING, *December 13, 1936, 5.15 p.m.*

My immediately preceding telegram.[1]

Report seems to show that Japanese doubts about Chang Hsueh-liang were well-founded while we were misled by Donald's assurances of his absolute loyalty to Chiang Kai-shek.

2. We knew of course that some of Chang Hsueh-liang's forces were fraternising with communists, that Chiang Kai-shek's visit to Sian in October[2] was partly for the purpose of clearing up this situation and we had heard report that he would try to arrange for transfer of these troops to another garrison area and their substitution by forces under his own control. It is reported that the immediate cause of present revolt is an order issued by Chiang Kai-shek for the suspected portion of Chang Hsueh-liang's troops to be transferred to Fukien. I am inclined to think this is the key to the situation.

3. Crisis bears strong . . .[3] that in the south-west last summer:[4] one militarist angling for support of others against Central Government on anti-Japanese war cry; but as Chang Hsueh-liang refused to support south-west leaders then, it seems unlikely they will support him now and I

[1] No. 22.   [2] Cf. Volume XX, No. 589, note 2.   [3] The text was here uncertain.
[4] See Volume XX, Nos. 522, 525, 538, 540, and 544.

think Han Fu-Chu,[5] Yen Hsi-shan[6] etc. can be relied on to support Central Government.

4. Chang Hsueh-liang may have obtained agreement with the Soviet but I consider this most unlikely. Chiang Kai-shek and Central Government have throughout been at great pains to maintain friendly relations with the Soviet. They are bound together by common bond of hostility to Japan and I cannot believe Soviet would be so foolish as to support Chang Hsueh-liang in his adventure, thereby weakening Chinese front against Japan.

5. Failing support from the Soviet or other Chinese militarist it should be only question of time before revolt dies out as Chang Hsueh-liang alone or in combination with Chinese communists unsupported from Russia could hardly withstand Central Government's troops which now need not be prevented by considerations of Chang Hsueh-liang's prestige from taking over control of north-west.

6. Question of Japanese attitude arises. In my opinion they will wait and see how Central Government deals with the emergency and will not intervene unless situation turns against the government.[7]

7. I am inclined to think Chiang Kai-shek is not in personal danger and that he may succeed in turning this serious situation to the advantage of the Central Government as he has done others in the past.[8]

[5] Chairman of Shantung province.

[6] Pacification Commissioner for Shensi province.

[7] In telegram No. 372 of December 14 Sir R. Clive described the Japanese attitude as 'wait and see, combined with scarcely disguised feeling of satisfaction that the world must now realise that Chinese are hopeless, as Japanese always knew. Japanese have the utmost contempt for Chang Hsueh-liang and the inevitable chaos which must ensue if Chiang Kai-shek disappears is not to their interest'.

[8] Sir A. Cadogan expressed agreement with this view in a minute of December 16 on file F 7688/166/10: 'It is all very obscure, and may be calamitous, but Chiang Kai-shek has the skill of a Houdini in extricating himself from tight places, and I still have hopes.' He also doubted that there was any foreign involvement in the incident, commenting that Chang Hsueh-liang had probably been prompted to the kidnapping by his own 'vanity and jealousy'.

No. 24

Sir H. Knatchbull-Hugessen (Nanking) to Mr. Eden
(Received December 17, 9.30 a.m.)

No. 236 Tour Telegraphic [F 7757/166/10]

Important   NANKING, *December 17, 1936, 1.4 p.m.*

Following received from His Majesty's Ambassador [*sic*].
My telegram No. 235 Tour Series.[1]

[1] Owing to a delay in repetition this telegram concerning the situation in Sian did not reach the Foreign Office until December 23, by which time it was out of date.

Suggestion has been made to me that something might be effected if representatives of the Powers here or as many of them as possible were to address strong representations to Chang Hsueh-liang on behalf of Chiang Kai-shek and on the grounds of serious danger to political position of China if the present situation is allowed to continue. These representations could be made personally by Ambassadors here without implicating their governments.

2. I mentioned this suggestion very privately to Vice Minister for Foreign Affairs this afternoon making it clear that I had as yet reached no decision on it myself and had spoken to none of my colleagues.

3. Vice Minister for Foreign Affairs expressed the view that good might possibly be done in this way and that Chang Hsueh-liang with his knowledge of the outer world might perhaps be influenced.

4. I should be grateful for your views and instructions as to whether I should proceed further.

5. Alternative methods of expressing our own disapproval occur to me such as statement in the House of Commons. Possibly other governments could find similar methods. Procedure here would inevitably take time as my colleagues would have to consult their governments.[2]

Repeated to Peking.

[2] In his telegram No. 238 Tour, received at 10.15 a.m. on December 17, Sir H. Knatchbull-Hugessen reported that he had now received through a third party 'a fairly direct request from Chinese Government that I should make some statement indicating adverse opinion of action of Chang Hsueh-liang and anxiety for speedy settlement': the Ambassador, however, felt that a statement in the House of Commons would have more effect. Sir R. Vansittart agreed with Mr. Orde and Sir A. Cadogan on December 17 that there would be 'no harm in this', and Mr. Eden made a statement in the House on these lines in answer to a question on December 18; See 318 *H.C. Deb. 5 s.*, col. 2804.

Following a suggestion made by the economist Sir A. Salter to Sir A. Cadogan on December 17, Sir H. Knatchbull-Hugessen was also consulted on the possibility of a guarantee to Chang Hsueh-liang of his safety if he were to release Chiang Kai-shek: see No. 26 below.

No. 25

Sir H. Knatchbull-Hugessen (Nanking) to Mr. Eden
(Received December 17, 4.20 p.m.)

No. 237 Tour Telegraphic: by wireless [F 7797/166/10]

NANKING, *December 17, 1936*

My telegram No. 235.[1]

Donald returned to Loyang yesterday whence he telephoned to Madame Chiang Kai-shek that he had seen Chiang Kai-shek who was well and in good spirits; that Chang Hsueh-liang had urged Chiang Kai-shek to accept his demands but Chiang Kai-shek had refused to discuss a

[1] See No. 24, note 1.

matter which he said was in the province of the Central Government.

2. Vice Minister for Foreign Affairs told me today that government had decided to send punitive expedition under the command of Ho Ying-chin and that there is to be no parley and no concessions. He also said that Soviet Government had expressly disassociated themselves from the coup. In these circumstances Chinese Government are confident of localising military activity.

3. It is now clear that Chiang Kai-shek had determined to remove effective control of bandit suppression in the north west from Chang Hsueh-liang and put it in charge of one of his trusted henchmen General Chiang Ting-wen director of Fukien pacification headquarters. Announcement of latter's appointment 'as Commander-in-Chief of north west bandit suppression forces at the front' was published in Sian on the morning of December 12th and I think affords sufficient explanation of Chang Hsueh-liang's subsequent actions. Chiang Ting-wen is amongst those held captive by Chang Hsueh-liang.[2]

Repeated to Peking.

[2] In a minute of December 19 Mr. G. W. Aldington, a member of the China Consular Service serving in the Far Eastern Department since January 1936, noted that according to press reports General Chiang Ting-wen had been released to carry a letter from Chiang Kai-shek to Nanking, and commented that this move to open negotiations was 'a hopeful sign'.

No. 26

Mr. Eden to Sir H. Knatchbull-Hugessen (Nanking)

No. 147 Tour Telegraphic [F 7761/166/10]

Immediate   FOREIGN OFFICE, *December 17, 1936, 7 p.m.*

Your telegrams Nos. 236 and 238.[1]

I am considering possibility of making a statement in Parliament.

Meanwhile, I am not aware of the exact situation in Sian nor of the course of any negotiations that may have taken place, but it occurs to me that it may be that Chang Hsueh-liang might be persuaded to release General Chiang Kai-shek if he could be assured of his own personal safety. If that is so, would it help matters if we were to express our willingness to do our best to assure his safety? It might be possible for him to be removed by air to Tientsin or Shanghai where we could probably guarantee him, and whence he could leave the country. You might be able to make arrangements locally.

Can you ascertain from Donald if this would be of any assistance? If so, I would ask United States, Japanese, Italian and French Governments to join in action proposed.

[1] No. 24, and *ibid.*, note 2.

If you cannot communicate with Donald, you may sound whichever Chinese authorities you think most suitable.

Repeated to Peking, Washington, Tokyo, Paris, and Rome.

No. 27

Record by Sir A. Cadogan of a conversation with Mr. Atherton

[F 7926/303/23]

FOREIGN OFFICE, December 17, 1936

Mr. Ray Atherton of the American Embassy called yesterday and I asked him if he could give me any idea of the reactions of his Government to the German-Japanese Agreement.[1]

Mr. Atherton, who returned to England about ten days ago, said that he had had some conversation on the subject with Dr. Hornbeck.[2] The latter did not appear to regard the agreement with undue concern. His view appeared to be that it did not of itself effect any essential change in the situation, and was rather in the nature of a registration of a situation which already existed. Mr. Atherton added that his Government had information to show that beside the public agreement there were subsidiary agreements which went considerably further.[3] These, however, were not of a positive but rather of a negative character, i.e. the signatories bound themselves in certain circumstances to refrain from certain action rather than to take positive action. From information in our possession we know this to be the case, and the United States Government are evidently well informed.

As regards the immediate future effect of the agreement, Mr. Atherton said that he thought it would rather produce a stalemate in Russo-Japanese relations; the provocation given to Russia by the signature of the agreement would render it necessary for Japan to watch her northern neighbour very closely, and this might set a limit to Japanese adventures on the mainland further south.

I told Mr. Atherton that we, for our part, did not take the agreement too tragically, and that our views coincided generally with those which he had outlined to me.

Mr. Atherton mentioned incidentally Anglo-Japanese relations, but did

[1] The question of whether to discuss the German-Japanese agreement with the Americans had been deferred pending the preparation of a memorandum: see No. 11, note 5. A memorandum dated December 4, drawn up by Mr. Ronald in consultation with the Northern and Central Departments, is filed at F 7504/303/23. In a minute of December 7 on this file Sir A. Cadogan concluded that it might be useful to have a talk with Mr. Atherton, and Sir R. Vansittart and Mr. Eden minuted their agreement on December 7 and 13 respectively. Cf. also No. 21, note 7.

[2] Head of the Far Eastern Division of the State Department.

[3] Cf. No. 9, note 3.

not put any direct question as to the conversations with the Japanese Ambassador.[4] He observed that Mr. Yoshida on his way through America to take up his post in London had given it out that his mission was to improve Anglo-Japanese relations, but he (Mr. Atherton) doubted whether Mr. Yoshida had sufficient authority from his Government to be able to carry the matter very far. I told him that Mr. Yoshida had approached us with what amounted to little more than pious aspirations; that we had received these sympathetically, and were perfectly ready to examine any suggestions that he might be able to put forward, but that at present nothing very concrete had emerged. I mentioned that Mr. Yoshida had been planning to return shortly to Japan if he could take back with him sufficient material to enable him to further the matter, but that quite recently he had told me that he was now doubtful whether he would return or not. Mr. Atherton said that he thought this was quite likely; when in the last few weeks the position of the Tokyo Government appeared to be shaken he thought Mr. Yoshida possibly had hopes of returning and obtaining some post in a new administration. Now that events in China had possibly come to the rescue of the Tokyo Cabinet Mr. Yoshida might see less chance of his employment at home.

I told Mr. Atherton that if anything concrete should emerge from the conversations with the Japanese Ambassador we should, of course, like to take the American Embassy into our confidence.[5]

[4] Cf. No. 14.
[5] Mr. Eden wrote on this record on December 20: 'This is satisfactory. If M. Yoshida *is* going back I must see him before I leave on Tuesday.' Mr. Eden saw Mr. Yoshida on the morning of December 22 (see No. 35 below), and left London the same day to spend Christmas in Yorkshire.

A copy of this record was sent to Tokyo in despatch No. 635, and to Washington in despatch No. 1080, on December 23.

No. 28

Sir H. Knatchbull-Hugessen (Nanking) to Mr. Eden
(Received December 18, 10.30 a.m.)

No. 245 Tour Telegraphic [F 7798/166/10]

Immediate   NANKING, *December 18, 1936, 1.40 p.m.*

Your telegram No. 147 (Tour).[1]
Donald is in Sian. I saw Kung who welcomes your proposal and would be most grateful if you would proceed with it. I explained that consultation with other Powers would be necessary.

2. Chang Hsueh-liang's wife and family are in England (Hove).
3. Latest information is (a) that Chiang Ting-wen has arrived here (see

[1] No. 26.

my telegram No. 243 tour series[2]) (b) an aeroplane belonging to Chang Hsueh-liang has flown to Taiyuan with representatives of Chang Hsueh-liang (c) Government troops are being moved into position but order to attack has been suspended.

4. Rear Admiral (? told me) Yen Hsi-shan is We Pei-fu's mediat(or?).
Please repeat to Paris and Rome as my telegram No. 1 tour series.
Repeated to Peking, Washington, Tokyo, Paris and Rome.

[2] Of December 17, not printed: cf. however No. 25, note 2. In telegram No. 243 Sir H. Knatchbull-Hugessen reported that Dr. Kung was in touch with both Chiang Kai-shek and Chang Hsueh-liang and had proposed that they should both go to Taiyuan for negotiations, with a full guarantee of safety for Chang Hsueh-liang.

No. 29

Mr. Eden to Sir R. Lindsay[1] (Washington)

No. 431[2] Telegraphic [F 7798/166/10]

Immediate   FOREIGN OFFICE, December 18, 1936, 6.10 p.m.

Nanking telegram No. 245.[3]
Please now ascertain whether Government to which you are accredited would cooperate in carrying out suggestion contained in my telegram No. 147 Tour[4] to Nanking, and would instruct their representative in China to concert details with his colleagues.

It must be quite understood that we do not propose any intervention in negotiations but would only offer our good offices in the hope that they might assist in the carrying out of any arrangement that may be reached by the parties.
Repeated to Peking.

[1] H.M. Ambassador at Washington.
[2] No. 304 to Paris, No. 278 to Tokyo, No. 480 to Rome.   [3] No. 28.   [4] No. 26.

No. 30

Sir H. Knatchbull-Hugessen (Nanking) to Mr. Eden
(Received December 19, 6.25 p.m.)

No. 251 Tour Telegraphic [F 7842/166/10]

NANKING, December 19, 1936, 1 p.m.

My telegram No. 245 Tour[1] and Washington telegram No. 342[2] and Tokyo telegram No. 383.[2]
My United States colleague and I have discussed the matter. We feel

[1] No. 28.   [2] Not kept in F.O. archives.

there are no other measures which could be adopted. Question therefore is only one of guarantee already proposed.

2. We think that if Chinese Government are able to find a solution themselves without bringing in foreign Powers it would be better. On the other hand the fact that certain foreign Powers are willing in certain circumstances to guarantee safety of Chang Hsueh-liang and if necessary of Yang Hu-cheng[3] might be of value.

3. We suggest that Doctor Kung be informed that United States Government and His Majesty's Government are willing if necessary to take all possible steps to ensure the safety of Chang Hsueh-liang and if necessary of Yang Hu-cheng in leaving the country. This undertaking would be given also by such of the other three Powers as may be willing.

4. As to the exact method of carrying out this undertaking we feel that the only feasible plan would be for Central Government to be responsible for passage of either or both generals to some post where the Powers can undertake their safe conveyance out of China. Obvious plan would be Tientsin where they could be put on board a warship until safe passage from China could be arranged.

5. I am uncertain whether you are willing to proceed in concert with one or more of the Powers consulted or whether you intend only to act if all agree.

6. My United States colleague is telegraphing in the same sense.[4]

Please repeat to Paris and Rome as my telegram No. 2 Tour.

Repeated to Peking, Washington, Tokyo, Commander-in-Chief, Paris and Rome.

[3] Pacification Commissioner for Shensi province, and an accomplice of Chang Hsueh-liang in the kidnapping of Chiang Kai-shek.
[4] See *F.R.U.S.*, 1936, vol. iv, pp. 438–9.

No. 31

Sir E. Drummond (Rome) to Mr. Eden (Received December 20, 10 a.m.)

No. 756 Telegraphic [F 7838/166/10]

ROME, *December 19, 1936, 11.30 p.m.*

Your telegram No. 480.[1]

I spoke to Minister for Foreign Affairs[2] this morning in the sense of your instructions. His Excellency after reading the aide-mémoire I left with him promised to send instructions to Italian representative in China accordingly. He then told me that at the instance of the Chinese Ambassador[3] here he had already two or three days ago sent a personal telegram to Chang Hsueh-liang who had been an intimate friend of his.

[1] No. 29: see *ibid.*, note 2.   [2] Count Ciano.   [3] Liu Wen-tao.

This telegram which he showed to me was to the effect that he sincerely trusted that Chang would take no irrevocable step but would reach an agreement with Chiang Kai-shek for the maintenance of peace and order in China; and he appealed to Chang's chivalrous sentiments and to the gratitude which such a generous action would arouse throughout China.

No. 32

Sir R. Clive (Tokyo) to Mr. Eden (Received December 21, 2.40 p.m.)

No. 384 Telegraphic [*F 7909/166/10*]

TOKYO, *December 21, 1936, 9.45 p.m.*

My telegram No. 383.[1]

Vice Minister for Foreign Affairs told me this evening that Japanese authorities had been instructed to report on proposal[2] and to enquire of Nanking Government. In reply to his questions I explained again that there was no question of pressing this solution on Chinese, all that was suggested was guarantee of safety of Chang Hsueh-liang presumably from arrival at port until embarkation if this was likely to help the release of Chiang Kai-shek. United States Government approved your proposal[3] but I did not know the reactions of French[4] and Italians.[5]

Repeated to Peking and Saving to Nanking.

[1] See No. 30, note 2.   [2] Cf. No. 29.   [3] See No. 30.

[4] The French reply was given in Paris telegram No. 567 Saving of December 19, not kept in F.O. archives. The French Government expressed their willingness to cooperate if necessary.

[5] See No. 31. Now that all the Powers had replied to the enquiry in No. 29 instructions were drawn up to implement the proposal to offer safe conduct to Chang Hsueh-liang: see No. 36 below.

No. 33

Mr. Eden to Sir R. Clive (Tokyo)

No. 281 Telegraphic [*F 7922/89/23*]

FOREIGN OFFICE, *December 21, 1936, 10 p.m.*

I informed Japanese Ambassador on December 8[1] that we were actively studying the memorandum which he had communicated to us as reported in my telegram No. 232.[2] Meanwhile I understood that Sir C. Addis in his approach to Viscount Kano with a view to conversations regarding the possibility of a joint loan for railway construction in China, had been put off on the Ambassador's advice on the ground of the political negotiations

[1] See No. 19.   [2] Volume XX, No. 590.

proceeding between the Japanese and Chinese Governments.[3] This seemed at variance with the suggestion contained in his memorandum, and as we were anxious for conversations I asked whether they could not take place. The Ambassador replied, after some further conversation, that he did not think that there would be any serious objections to private and informal conversations being begun, and Sir C. Addis has now had talks with Viscount Kano and the Ambassador, but finds them very unresponsive.[4]

The Ambassador said that he wished to return to Japan very shortly, and in order to influence those members of the Japanese Government who thought it impossible, in view of the commercial rivalry between our two countries, to improve their political relations, he would like to take back with him some indication of our real desire to improve these relations. On December 14 Sir A. Cadogan, on my instructions, asked Mr. Yoshida to call and reminded him of the desire which he had expressed to me. We were of course sincerely desirous of improving Anglo-Japanese relations, but a general declaration to that effect would not seem to carry us very far. Could His Excellency give us any clearer idea of what was in his mind? The Ambassador (who said it was no longer certain that he would be returning to Japan soon) had no definite suggestion to make and finally said that declarations alone were of little value. In answer to a further enquiry he appeared to think that it would be useful if we were to give him a preliminary and general reply to his memorandum, full study of which would take some time.

I see little utility in a vague declaration of desire for friendly relations and am considering advisability of sending the Ambassador a preliminary

[3] See No. 19, note 4.
[4] On December 10 Sir C. Addis sent Sir F. Leith-Ross a memorandum of a conversation on December 9 with Viscount Kano, who referred to the fact that Mr. Yoshida had agreed that discussions could go ahead on a railway loan. Sir C. Addis, however, now replied that he was 'not convinced that the Addis-Kano conversations could be continued as an integral part of the negotiations between the two Governments', and that there was no point in pursuing hypothetical talks on loans if Sino-Japanese relations were not settled: cf. No. 19, note 4. In his reply to Sir C. Addis on December 10 Sir F. Leith-Ross agreed that it was desirable to move slowly and allow Sino-Japanese negotiations to progress.

Copies of this correspondence were sent to the Foreign Office, where they caused some alarm. Sir A. Cadogan pointed out in a minute of December 11 that Sir C. Addis' attitude was in direct contradiction to that put forward by the Treasury in their letter of November 27 (No. 19, note 4): 'The Japanese will think we are dodging.' He did not now know what to say to Mr. Yoshida: 'I can't help saying . . . that I believe our policies aims and methods in the Far East are at present so fundamentally different that it is almost impossible to get an agreement. This question of cooperation in the rehabilitation of China is the test of Japanese sincerity, and if we pressed it hard enough, I think we should burst the bubble. We don't want to do that: we rather want to keep the Japanese in play, in the hope that Japanese policy *may* undergo a change. Therefore I agree with Sir F. Leith-Ross to the extent that I think we ought to move slowly, but I think we ought to move.' He suggested that the situation should be explained to Sir C. Addis, and Mr. Eden agreed. Sir A. Cadogan spoke on December 14 to Sir C. Addis, who said he 'quite understood and was certainly ready to do his best to keep the discussion going for as long as might be possible'.

reply on the lines shown in my immediately following telegram.[5] I shall be glad of your views as soon as possible as to the manner in which it would be likely to be received and the effect which it might have, e.g. would the Japanese Government take it as an indication that we were frightened by the conclusion of their agreement with Germany?[6] The repercussion on the naval question must also be considered since it has now become a matter of the highest importance for us to secure Japan's acceptance of the 14″ gun maximum for capital ships.[7] Do you think it might be better to leave the matter alone for the moment? Or would some such advance on our part help the moderate elements in the Japanese Government and contribute anything towards improving Anglo-Japanese relations or towards saving Japan from a worse régime than the present one?

[5] Not printed. At the end of a long minute of December 15 recording his conversation with Mr. Yoshida Sir A. Cadogan suggested that the moment might be not 'altogether unpropitious' for an approach to Japan and that Sir R. Clive should be consulted with a view to giving a preliminary reply on the lines of minutes in F 6511/89/23 (see Volume XX, No. 590). Mr. Eden agreed (December 16): 'On balance I believe we should gain by giving an interim reply. It might help the moderates in Tokyo.' Telegram No. 282 to Sir R. Clive, despatched at 6.30 p.m. on December 22, closely followed the lines of telegram No. 232 of October 31: Volume XX, No. 590.

[6] Cf. No. 9, note 3.   [7] Cf. No. 1, note 7.

No. 34

Sir H. Knatchbull-Hugessen (Nanking) to Mr. Eden
(Received December 23, 9.30 a.m.)

No. 225 Tour Telegraphic [F 7953/166/110]

NANKING, *December 22, 1936, 12.47 p.m.*

My telegram No. 251 Tour.[1]

My United States colleague has instructions in the following sense:[2]

United States Government consider caution is necessary and that no guarantee should be undertaken which would leave us with the responsibility in the event of Chinese interfering in attempt to save lives of the two Generals or failures to guarantee their security. United States Ambassador is authorised to collaborate with me in informing Kung of willingness of United States Government to co-operate with His Majesty's Government and other governments mainly . . .[3] to effect safe conduct of the two Generals, say from Tientsin to some . . .[3] outside China, it being understood that when this has been effected our responsibility for lives of the two Generals ceases.

2. Japanese Consul-General and French Ambassador have both called on my United States colleague and myself with instructions to enquire as to exact scope of proposal. Their governments had evidently misinter-

[1] No. 30.   [2] See *F.R.U.S.*, *op. cit.*, pp. 439–40.   [3] The text was here uncertain.

preted it as one for . . .[3] involving some form of mediation. The matter has been explained to them by both of us.

3. Italian Embassy have shown no signs of life.

4. I am hoping for answer to my telegram under reference.[4]

Repeated to Peking and Washington, Tokyo, Commander-in-Chief, Paris and Rome.

[4] Cf. No. 32, note 5, and No. 36 below.

No. 35

Mr. Eden to Sir R. Clive (Tokyo)

No. 633 [F 7928/89/23]

FOREIGN OFFICE, *December 22, 1936*

Sir,

I asked the Japanese Ambassador to come and see me this morning when I told him that Sir A. Cadogan had given me an account of his last conversation with His Excellency[1] when it had been suggested that it would be of considerable assistance to the Ambassador if some form of interim reply to his memorandum could be submitted. We were now considering the possibility of doing this.[2] In the meanwhile it would assist us if the Ambassador could be good enough to state what decision, if any, he had come to as to his plans for returning to Tokio. M. Yoshida replied that he had no plans. He was very content to wait for our answer. It was quite true that he did wish, were it possible, to be back in Tokio before the meeting of the Diet, but this was not as important as that he should have some indication, however general, of the views of His Majesty's Government on his memorandum. After some further conversation we agreed that I would endeavour to let His Excellency have some form of interim reply during the next ten days. I explained to the Ambassador that I could give no binding undertaking, since until I had further examined this possibility I could not be certain whether it was a practical proposition to give such an interim reply. We would, however, do our best.

2. I then told His Excellency that there were two other matters about which I wished to speak to him. The first was the Keelung incident.[3] It would be of the greatest assistance to our conversations if we could get this unhappy incident cleared up. I felt sure that the Japanese Government must wish to do so as we did in the interests of good Anglo-Japanese relations, and I hoped therefore that if His Excellency were telegraphing to Tokio he would urge the importance of an early liquidation of this affair. The Ambassador undertook to do this.

[1] See No. 33.

[2] See *ibid.*, note 5.

[3] See Volume XX, No. 593, note 2, and No. 6, note 5 above.

49

3. Finally I said that I wished to speak to him about the position of British oil interests in Japan. I understood that last year after prolonged negotiation some arrangement had been come to between the Asiatic Petroleum Company and the Japanese Government, but that the latter had never yet declared their attitude to this arrangement.[4] The result was that British companies found themselves in a position of the greatest difficulty and embarrassment, being unable to look with any certainty towards the future. His Majesty's Government would therefore be most grateful to M. Yoshida if he could inform the Japanese Government of our preoccupations on this score. This also His Excellency said that he would be glad to do, adding that he would ask Sir A. Cadogan to supply him with further details.

I am, etc.,

ANTHONY EDEN

[4] See Volume XX, Nos. 273 and 274. Throughout 1935 and 1936 protracted negotiations were carried on between the oil companies and the Japanese authorities concerning arrangements for the companies to fulfil their obligations under the Petroleum Industry Law. By the end of 1936 the position was still unclear, and the announcement of new Japanese import tariffs and kerosene quotas seemed to contradict the terms of the original agreement. Sir R. Clive presented an aide-mémoire on December 24 protesting that the Japanese Government's petroleum policy involved 'discrimination against British oil interests and will result in driving them out of Japan'.

No. 36

Foreign Office[1] *to Sir H. Knatchbull-Hugessen* (*Nanking*)

No. 156 Tour Telegraphic [*F 7909/166/10*]

Immediate   FOREIGN OFFICE, *December 23, 1936, 4.50 p.m.*

Your telegram No. 251 Tour.[2]

Present position is that the Italians have promised to send instructions to their representative in China;[3] the French are 'prepared if necessary to cooperate' as suggested[4]; the Japanese have asked for the observations of their Embassy in China[5]; and the U.S. Government have instructed their Ambassador to cooperate with you on the lines suggested in paragraph 4 of your telegram under reference but they say that it must be clearly understood that their 'responsibility would cease as soon as Chang is out of China'[6].

You are therefore now authorized to proceed as you propose in concert with your U.S. colleague and such of the others as have received instructions and whose collaboration you think desirable in the circumstances. You should anyhow keep your French, Italian and Japanese

[1] After his conversation with Mr. Yoshida on December 22 (see No. 35) Mr. Eden left to spend Christmas in Yorkshire. He returned on January 4, 1937.
[2] No. 30.   [3] See No. 31.   [4] See No. 32, note 4.   [5] See No. 32.   [6] See No. 34.

colleagues informed of any action you take.

Repeated to Peking, Washington, Tokyo, Rome, Paris.

No. 37

Sir R. Clive (Tokyo) to Foreign Office
(Received December 24, 11.50 a.m.)

No. 391 Telegraphic [F 7963/89/23]

TOKYO, *December 24, 1936, 6.55 p.m.*

Your telegram No. 281.[1]

I am inclined to leave the matter alone for the present. While giving Japanese Ambassador to understand that he will receive in due course reply to his memorandum His Excellency might be perhaps told that, failing some satisfaction about Keelung incident (see my telegram No. 388[2]), not to mention oil question[3] . . .[4] which Japanese Government have in my opinion and that of my United States colleague shown deliberate bad faith, the atmosphere is not very favourable for serious negotiations.

On January 22 after opening the Diet Minister for Foreign Affairs makes a speech on foreign relations. He would no doubt like to indicate that 'traditional friendship' is being maintained with Great Britain. I consider that on Japanese side they have given no proof of this during the past year beyond vague expressions of goodwill on the part of the military. Moreover many Japanese are upset at unfortunate effect on Anglo-Japanese relations which may result from German agreement.[5]

---

[1] No. 33.   [2] Not printed: cf. No. 6, note 5.   [3] See No. 35, note 4.
[4] The text was here uncertain.
[5] Sir R. Craigie expressed strong disagreement with Sir R. Clive's views in a minute of December 31. He said that 'the administration of a rebuff to Mr. Yoshida such as Sir R. Clive suggests would be quite fatal at this moment, when the question of Japan's attitude on the 14-inch gun question is under active consideration [cf. No. 1, note 7] . . . The line proposed . . . would play straight into the hands of Admiral Nagano and other naval extremists who largely for considerations of "face" would like to make difficulties for us . . . My belief is that if we now return a reply . . . on the lines proposed, this will just tip the balance in favour of a more reasonable Jap attitude towards the naval question'. He also felt that 'we have as much interest as Japan in improving our mutual relations and the mere fact that the recent proposals have come from the Japanese side should not lead us to look upon the grant of our friendship as something so desirable in itself that we can afford to hold ourselves disdainfully aloof and leave the field to the Germans. Evidently Sir R. Clive has a greater belief than I have in the efficacy of the policy of the "cold douche" '.

Mr. Orde and Sir A. Cadogan also expressed surprise at Sir R. Clive's views, and did not think his objections to a reply were strongly held. Sir A. Cadogan commented on January 1, 1937 that 'hitherto in our dealings with Japan no-one could complain that our attitude has not been fair and conciliatory, and the fact that (as I believe) we have not met with much response is no reason for changing it'. He proposed that the idea of a preliminary reply to Mr. Yoshida's proposals should be proceeded with, and Sir R. Vansittart agreed (January 1): see No. 42 below.

No. 38

Mr. D. J. Cowan[1] *(Peking) to Foreign Office*
(Received December 26, 12.5 p.m.)

No. 936 Telegraphic [F 7972/166/10]

PEKING, *December 26, 1936, 6.15 p.m.*

Following from Nanking telegram 138 of December 26th, begins:

Waichiaopu confirm release of Chiang Kai-shek who is expected to arrive at Nanking midday today from Loyang. Waichiaopu have no information regarding the course of events leading up to Chiang Kai-shek's release beyond what is contained in Reuter's message last night.[2]

[1] First Secretary in H.M. Embassy at Peking, acting as Chargé d'Affaires.

[2] According to the account given in Sir H. Knatchbull-Hugessen's despatch No. 15 of March 2, 1937, many explanations were put forward for the sudden release of Chiang Kai-shek on Christmas Day. Madame Chiang Kai-shek, her brother T.V. Soong, and Mr. Donald had all visited Sian and were widely thought to have entered negotiations with Chang Hsueh-liang: there were rumours of 'the payment of a huge ransom, coupled with the acceptance of some of the Young Marshal's terms and a promise of immunity'. Sir H. Knatchbull-Hugessen himself, however, took the view that Chang Hsueh-liang, 'conscious of the rectitude of his own purpose', hoped to 'impress the Government and the people, capture their attention and attract their sympathy, by a gesture theatrical perhaps, but none the less in the best Confucian tradition. This is probably as near the real explanation as we shall ever get'. For Mr. Donald's views on the episode see No. 40 below: cf. also No. 56 below. The release of Chiang Kai-shek also naturally put an end to plans for a joint guarantee of Chang Hsueh-liang's safety: cf. Nos. 29, 31, 32, 34, and 36.

No. 39

Mr. Cowan (Peking) to Foreign Office (Received February 9, 1937)

No. 1320 [F 824/35/10]

PEKING, *December 28, 1936*

Sir,

With reference to Peking telegram No. 933 of 24th December 1936,[1] I have the honour to transmit herewith a translation into English of a Chinese translation and the Chinese text[2] respectively of the letter alleged

[1] In this telegram Mr. Cowan reported that broadsheets were being distributed in Peking attacking the Minister of War, Ho Ying-ch'in, for his part in the Ho-Umetsu agreement of June 1935, and calling for opposition to civil war in China and the immediate declaration of war with Japan. For the background to the Ho-Umetsu agreement, the existence of which was denied by the Chinese authorities at the time, see Volume XX, No. 306, note 4. The present despatch, transmitted the alleged texts of the agreement to the Foreign Office for the first time.

[2] The Chinese texts of the letters are not filed with this despatch.

to have been sent by General Umetsu to General Ho Ying-ch'in of 9th June 1935 and the latter's reply of 6th July 1935.[3]

2. A similar version of the former was published in the *China Weekly Review* of 14th March 1936, and the Chinese text of the latter also appeared in an article contributed by Dr. Hu Shih to the Tientsin *Ta Kung Pao* of 2nd February 1936.

I have, etc.,
D. J. COWAN
(For H.M. Ambassador)

ENCLOSURE I IN NO. 39

Translation of a letter from General Umetsu to General Ho Ying-Ch'in of June 9, 1935

Clause I

The matters which the Chinese authorities have already agreed with the Japanese military authorities to accept are as follows:

1. Dismissal of General Yu Hsüeh-chung and Chang T'ing-ô from their respective posts in Hopei Province.

2. Dismissal of Chiang Shou-hsien (Chiang Kai-shek's nephew), Ting Chang, Tseng Kwang-ch'ing, and Ho I-fei.

3. Removal of the 3rd Regiment of Gendarmes (Hsien Ping).

4. Withdrawal of the Peking Branch of the National Government's Military Affairs Commission, the Political Training Corps, and further issues of the Peking Military Magazine.

5. Control of all secret organizations said by the Japanese to be inimical to Sino-Japanese international relations, and prohibition of their further existence.

6. Withdrawal of all Kuomintang party offices in Hopei Province and withdrawal of the Peking Moral Endeavour Association.

7. Removal of the 51st Army from Hopei Province.

8. Withdrawal of the 2nd and 25th Divisions and dissolution of the Students Training Corps attached to the latter.

9. Prohibition of all anti-Japanese activities by Chinese.

Clause II

The above mentioned terms must be at once carried out by China and at the same time, China must agree to the following additional terms:

1. All conditions which China has orally promised to carry out, must be carried out *in toto* within the stipulated period. Any person or organ tending to cause Sino-Japanese relations to be bad must not again be employed or established as the case may be.

2. In the appointment of provincial and municipal officials it is absolutely necessary to take into account the expectations of the Japanese

[3] General Umetsu was Commander of the North China Garrison of the Japanese Army, and General Ho was at that time also head of the Peiping Military Council.

authorities and no person likely to injure Sino-Japanese relations may be appointed.

3. Japan is entitled to carry out supervisory and inspection activities during the period of execution of the above mentioned demands.

The above has been specially reduced to writing to serve to you as an aide-mémoire.[4]

ENCLOSURE II IN No. 39

Translation of a letter from General Ho Ying-ch'in to General Umetsu of July 6, 1935

'The various matters proposed by Chief of Staff Sakai on 9th June are all agreed to, and (the Chinese authorities) of their own accord are taking steps to carry them into effect. A special notification, addressed to General Umetsu (signed) Ho Ying-ch'in. 6th July, 1935.'

[1] Mr. Thyne Henderson commented on February 13: 'If China had been defeated in war with Japan these demands might have appeared reasonable, but the feeling of humiliation experienced by the students and all who have the good of China as an entity at heart is easily understandable.'

No. 40

Sir H. Knatchbull-Hugessen[1] (Peking) to Foreign Office (Received December 30, 6 p.m.)

No. 946[2] Telegraphic [F 8078/166/10]

Secret   PEKING, *December 30, 1936*

Following received from Nanking telegram No. 140 December 28th.

Donald called today. Following is gist of what he told me: Chiang Kai-shek has a very difficult temper which makes it almost impossible for him to discuss questions or take advice. He had adopted policy of conciliation to Japanese and had brought into the government 'pro-Japanese' such as Ho Ying-chin, Chang Chia-ao, and Chang Chun under whose influence he was blinded to the real temper of the country which was against conciliation and demanded firm, positive policy. Madame Chiang Kai-shek and Donald had for a long time been urging him to take a stronger bolder line but without success. Chang Hsueh-liang was firmly convinced policy of using the people's forces against Chinese so-called

[1] The Ambassador had evidently returned to Peking: this telegram and No. 41 below, however, referred to events which took place while he was still in Nanking.

[2] This telegram was actually received in the Foreign Office one hour later than telegram No. 948 (No. 41 below), but they have been kept in numerical order.

communists instead of against Japanese invaders and of suppressing patriotic 'national salvation' movement at the behest of Japanese was disastrous but he could not get Chiang Kai-shek even to discuss the matter. Anti-Japanese feeling in the North West was very strong. Arrest on orders of Central Government of seven prominent Chinese in Shanghai for participation in national salvation movement provoked student demonstration in Sian which was dispersed by armed force resulting in death of one student. Turmoil followed and Chang Hsueh-liang exasperated by Chiang Kai-shek's refusal to open his eyes to the realities of the situation determined to follow well-established Chinese precedent and detain him till he did.

3 (*sic*). In holding Chiang Kai-shek Chang Hsueh-liang played into the hands of the former's enemies in Nanking the chief of whom are according to Donald the (pro-Japanese) clique who would be glad to see him out of the way. Had expeditionary force attacked Sian or planes bombed the town nothing could have saved Chiang Kai-shek and both Donald and Madame Chiang Kai-shek were convinced that expeditionary force was deliberately launched as a means of getting Chiang Kai-shek out of the way in a . . .[3] appearing manner.

4. It was only gradually that Chiang Kai-shek came to appreciate the seriousness of the situation and in the result Chang Hsueh-liang's coup drove home the lesson that Donald and Madame Chiang Kai-shek had been trying to impress to him for a long time that the country would not follow him indefinitely unless he led in the right direction and at last he began to discuss the question more freely. Original eight demands were whittled down to the following: (1) Enunciation of a definite anti-Japanese national policy, (2) release of political prisoners, (3) re-organisation of the Cabinet, (4) discontinuance of civil war. Although (if I understood Donald correctly) Chiang Kai-shek was released unconditionally he was already half-converted. He was satisfied that Chang Hsueh-liang was actuated by honest patriotic motives. Chang Hsueh-liang voluntarily accompanied him to Nanking to prove his good faith and his loyalty to Central Government in spite of appearances.

5. Donald denies that any question of money was involved or at any time discussed. He denies even press report that there was misunderstanding owing to misappropriation of funds destined for payment to Chang Hsueh-liang's troops.

6. He says that communists in the North West will not be further molested and he anticipates that there will be a domestic purge of Central Government and adoption of more positive policy. Chiang Kai-shek will, he thinks, tender his resignation for the sake of form but will be re-called with acclamation and will not only be a stronger but a better leader for his lesson.[4]

[3] The text was here uncertain.
[4] In his telegram No. 947 of December 30 (Nanking telegram No. 141) Sir H. Knatchbull-Hugessen commented that Mr. Donald's views in the last paragraph of telegram

No. 946 were 'clearly in line with his own wishes' and that he took 'too partial a view' of Chang Hsueh-liang's conduct: 'I cannot believe his motives were entirely patriotic (though misguided) and were uninfluenced by personal consideration.' Mr. Orde agreed in a minute of January 1 that the Young Marshal 'took too narrow and hasty a view', and Sir A. Cadogan (January 1) was convinced that Chiang Kai-shek was *not* pro-Japanese . . . but he has a much more realist grasp of possibilities than some of his erratic subordinates'.

No. 41

Sir H. Knatchbull-Hugessen (Peking) to Foreign Office
(Received December 30, 5 p.m.)

No. 948 Telegraphic: by wireless [F 8072/166/10]

PEKING, December 30, 1936

Following received from Nanking telegram No. 142 of December 28th. Begins.

My immediately preceding telegram.[1]

I called on the Minister for Foreign Affairs this morning and offered congratulations on behalf of His Majesty's Government and yourself on the release of Chiang Kai-shek. He thanked me and added that Chiang Kai-shek had asked him to express his gratitude for support accorded to him by His Majesty's Government.

2. I asked the Minister for Foreign Affairs if he could give me any indication of the political consequences of the coup and its settlement. He said that disciplinary question was in the hands of the military commission and he had no idea how they would deal with the situation. He volunteered the statement that the coup would not involve any change in either the policy or personnel of the Government.[2]

[1] See No. 40, note 5.
[2] Chang Hsueh-liang was sentenced to ten years' imprisonment by a military tribunal, but the sentence was immediately remitted by the State Council. He was, however, kept under close surveillance and debarred from resuming command of his troops or holding any official post. For the political repercussions of the incident see Nos. 56, 60, and 61 below.

No. 42

Foreign Office to Sir R. Clive (Tokyo)

No. 1 Telegraphic [F 7963/89/23]

FOREIGN OFFICE, January 4, 1937, 1.15 p.m.

Your telegram No. 391.[1]

In conversation with Japanese Ambassador on December 22nd[2] I found

[1] No. 37.
[2] See No. 35.

him anxious to have some indication of our views and I promised to see whether it would not be possible to let him have an interim reply. I should therefore prefer to send one unless you have any positive objection, which I do not so far gather to be the case.[3] I am anxious not to seem to be rebuffing a friendly advance, even though it may not lead to much. I have already in conversation mentioned above laid stress on importance of Keelung case[4] and referred to the oil matter[5], and can bring them in again later. Meanwhile interim reply would not give anything away. To the outline contained in my telegram No. 281[6] we are now contemplating adding on point (f) that we should be disposed to welcome in principle an agreement as to amounts of textile exports from our respective countries in substitution for British colonial import quotas, which we gather is what is proposed, but would like certain elucidations of the Japanese attitude.

Please telegraph whether you have any further observations.

[3] Cf. No. 37, note 5.　　　[4] See No. 6, note 5.　　　[5] See No. 35, note 4.　　　[6] No. 33.

No. 43

Mr. Eden to Sir R. Clive (Tokyo)

No. 7 Telegraphic [A 397/6/45]

Important　　　　　　　　　FOREIGN OFFICE, *January 15, 1937, 10.30 p.m.*

As you are aware, all the naval Powers with whom we have been in negotiation (which include the United States, France, Italy, Germany and Soviet Russia, in addition to a number of other countries with smaller navies) are willing to adopt the 14-inch gun as the maximum size of gun for capital ships, but quite naturally feel that this self-denying ordinance must be universal, and therefore must include Japan.[1] Despite the representations of the Japanese Ambassador here, his Government have

[1] Cf. No. 1, note 7. The draft of this telegram was prepared by Sir R. Craigie, who sent it to Sir A. Cadogan on January 14 with the following minute: 'Despite the efforts of Mr. Yoshida it has been quite impossible to elicit a reply from the Japanese Government in regard to the 14-inch gun. There is reason to think that the Japanese Ministry of Marine are taking up an uncompromising attitude and the time has therefore come when we should bring the full weight of our pressure to bear on the Japanese Government in regard to this question . . . it is important that it should be brought home to the Japanese Government as a whole in no uncertain terms that considerable disadvantages are likely to accrue to Japan from a failure to oppose the Navy Department in this matter.' Sir R. Craigie suggested that the telegram should be sent off *'after* we have handed to Mr. Yoshida our preliminary answer to his proposals for improving Anglo-Japanese relations' (see No. 37, note 5, and No. 42). Sir A. Cadogan, however, thought that there was no need to wait, and Mr. Eden agreed (January 15): 'If Sir A. Cadogan does not think that our memorandum for Mr. Yoshida will produce any material improvement in Anglo-Jap relations, then perhaps there is no need to wait for its delivery which must take place at latest on Tuesday [see No. 46 below]'. Sir A. Cadogan replied on January 15: 'I don't think our memo. can be expected to have any immediate effect.'

so far been silent on this subject, which is now becoming very urgent owing to the necessity on the part of the various countries to proceed with the construction of new capital ships and to put the London Naval Treaty into force without further delay.

There is no need to recount at length the history of recent negotiations, full details of the position having been given to the Japanese Ambassador from time to time. It is sufficient to lay down the general proposition that all the other naval Powers consulted have accepted the 14-inch gun contingently on a similar acceptance by Japan. The issue, therefore, now is whether this measure of naval limitation can be made generally acceptable or whether the world is to be faced with the problems inherent in a steadily upward trend in the sizes of capital ships and guns.

The Japanese Government will, I think, admit that, since their departure from the London Naval Conference,[2] everything possible has been done by His Majesty's Government to allow for their susceptibilities and to smooth their path. While other Powers are preparing to enter into definite agreements on the lines of the London Naval Treaty, 1936,[3] Japan is asked to do no more than (a) give the assurance necessary to permit of the London Naval Treaty entering into force with the 14-inch gun as a maximum calibre (Article 4); and (b) take no action which in practice would entail the invocation of the escalator clauses by other Powers and so bring the whole treaty system to the ground.

From such information as reaches us it would appear that the Japanese Government are disposed to consider this question almost exclusively from a technical point of view. We trust, however, that, before a final decision is reached, the serious political implications of the problem will also be given full weight. It has been with great pleasure that His Majesty's Government have received from time to time the assurance of Japan's desire to maintain the most friendly relations with His Majesty's Government—a desire which they fully reciprocate. If, however, Japan, by adopting an uncompromising attitude, were to negative the treaty system, which elsewhere has been accepted, for the qualitative limitation of armaments, with the consequential diminution of international tension, the favourable effect produced in this country by such professions of friendship would be inevitably undermined. Indeed the only interpretation of such an attitude would be that Japan had determined to impose upon the world the evils of unrestricted competition in naval armaments, except on her own terms that the numerical strength of all fleets was to be identical irrespective of self-evident variations in national conditions, and was quite indifferent to the consensus of opinion among all other naval Powers in favour of a certain measure of qualitative restriction. It is because of our real desire for better relations with Japan that we feel that these issues should be frankly placed before the Japanese Government while they are considering their decision.

[2] See Volume XIII, No. 622. [3] See *ibid.*, No. 718.

This is, of course, not merely a British interest; it is one of world-wide importance and the Japanese Government will appreciate that, in playing the leading rôle in the recent series of naval negotiations, His Majesty's Government have been acting in pursuance of the wishes of the other Powers concerned. The object is to prevent an absolutely unrestricted race in naval armaments being superimposed on the existing rivalry in land and air armaments, and it is only if these efforts fail that His Majesty's Government must reluctantly conclude that there will be no alternative for this country but to use to the full the technical and financial resources which it commands.

Your Excellency should speak clearly to the Minister for Foreign Affairs in the above sense, leaving a carefully worded aide-mémoire in accordance with the present telegram as a record of your conversation. You should add that we have now been waiting for three months for an answer from the Japanese Government to a question which was, for their own convenience, put to them as late as possible, and that we should greatly appreciate a definite reply, in one sense or the other, at the earliest possible moment.

No. 44

Sir R. Clive (Tokyo) to Mr. Eden (Received January 16, 9.30 a.m.)

No. 17 Telegraphic [F 324/28/23]

TOKYO, *January 16, 1937, 1 a.m.*

There are definite signs with the New Year of a tendency towards better Anglo-Japanese relations. Reply on oil question is better than companies anticipated and is fairly satisfactory.[1]

The Japanese Government are most anxious to keep the door open about Keelung.[2]

Japanese Foreign Office are very gratified at our note about perpetual leases and will urge acceptance of our offer.[3]

Prince Chichibu proposes in the late summer after his continental engagements to return to England in the hope, as high Court official told Sir G. Sansom, of re-establishing more friendly feeling between our two countries.

[1] See No. 35, note 4. The Japanese reply to Sir R. Clive's aide-mémoire was received on January 15, and stated that there was no intention to discriminate against British oil interests or drive them out, and that if the companies obeyed Japanese laws they would receive favourable consideration. The Foreign Office thought that this was 'generally satisfactory', although the oil companies continued to complain about the treatment they received.

[2] See No. 6, note 5.

[3] Perpetual landleases held by foreigners, mainly British and American, were regarded as an 'unnatural institution' resulting from the 'unequal' treaties of Japan's earlier develop-

ment. Sir R. Clive took the initiative in proposing their abolition. Notes were to be signed on March 25 at the Japanese Foreign Office between the Foreign Minister, Mr. Naotake Sato (see No. 54, note 3 below) and Sir R. Clive, and between Mr. Sato and Mr. Joseph Grew, the American Ambassador at Tokyo, providing for the entire abolition within five years of the perpetual leases held by British and American subjects. In the Tokyo press the agreement was attributed to 'Sir Robert's consistent endeavours made in drawing closer traditional bonds of friendship between England and Japan'.

No. 45

Sir R. Clive (Tokyo) to Mr. Eden (Received January 18, 9.30 a.m.)

No. 20 Telegraphic [A 415/6/45]

TOKYO, *January 18, 1937, 4.20 p.m.*

Your telegram No. 7.[1]

I left with the Minister for Foreign Affairs today aide-mémoire based on your telegram. I endeavoured to make it clear to His Excellency that Japanese refusal to accept the 14 inch gun would not only throw on Japan the odium of unlimited and unending race in naval armament but must inevitably have very unfavourable reaction on Anglo-Japanese relations at a moment when there were signs of improvement; he seemed more impressed by the second argument than by the first.

He spoke of the common upper limit and our refusal to accept Japanese proposal.[2] I said that no country had accepted it. I said that I understood that the United States had with great difficulty been induced to accept the 14 inch gun but only on the understanding that every other country did so. I emphasised the high political importance of the present question. He admitted this. Successful solution I said might lead the way to arms limitation in other directions. He said that the Japanese Government objected to qualitative without quantitative limitations. I said that the Japanese Government were only being asked at present for qualitative limitation on one vital point. Finally he promised to reply as soon as possible—a week or a little more.

[1] No. 43.   [2] Cf. Volume XIII, Chapter VIII.

No. 46

Mr. Eden to Sir R. Clive (Tokyo)

No. 40 [F 357/28/23]

FOREIGN OFFICE, *January 18, 1937*

Sir,

I asked the Japanese Ambassador to come and see me this afternoon, when I handed him a copy of our aide-mémoire[1] in response to the memorandum which His Excellency communicated to us towards the end of October.[2] I explained to His Excellency that the preparation of this reply had involved a good deal of consultation between the departments concerned, and that it represented a genuine attempt to promote progress in our conversations[3]. The Ambassador read the memorandum through and then stated that he would study it carefully and when he had done so would like to discuss any points that occurred to him with Sir Alexander Cadogan or myself. I told Mr. Yoshida that we should be glad to fall in with this arrangement.

2. The Ambassador went on to say that it was now in his mind that the best way to promote progress in the Far East might be for Japan to attempt to negotiate two separate agreements, one with China and one with ourselves. His idea was that the agreement with China might be negotiated with our knowledge and good-will and that we should be kept informed of the course of the negotiations. It was not the intention of the Japanese Government in this connexion to press a settlement on China, but to attempt to negotiate one. In such circumstances the Japanese Government might perhaps be permitted to look for some help from His Majesty's Ambassador in Peking. Mr. Yoshida continued that if his Government allowed him to go home he thought that he might take the opportunity of going on to China, so as to study the position on the spot and see what were the chances of concluding two parallel agreements such as he had suggested.

3. I then told His Excellency that I had been glad to receive a telegram from you from which it appeared that progress was being made on the

---

[1] See Enclosure below.   [2] See Annex to No. 1.

[3] In telegram No. 12 to Tokyo of January 19 Sir R. Clive was informed that the aide-mémoire 'generally followed lines indicated in my telegram No. 282': see No. 33, note 5. However, the British reply has been printed here in full as a useful indication in many respects of official thinking on Far Eastern problems on the eve of the Sino-Japanese war. The Foreign Office draft reply to Mr. Yoshida's memorandum had been circulated to four interested departments in November 1936: see No. 1, note 8. At the Treasury Mr. Chamberlain, Sir Warren Fisher (Permanent Secretary to the Treasury and head of the Civil Service) and Sir F. Leith-Ross made changes which Sir R. Vansittart thought 'altered our draft more than necessary', but which were recommended to Mr. Eden by Mr. Chamberlain in a letter of January 13. The Foreign Office objected to several of the Treasury amendments, in particular Mr. Chamberlain's wish to retain the wording of paragraph (a) of Mr. Yoshida's memorandum which limited respect for Chinese territorial rights and sovereignty to 'south of the Great Wall'. Mr. Eden explained in a letter to Mr. Chamberlain of January 15 that 'it was not from inadvertence that in our reply we omitted the words "south of the Great Wall" '. To accept this limitation would be to recognize by implication that Japan 'had some right to interfere in the northern provinces, such as Chahar and Suiyuan'. The Treasury accepted this, and after further discussion on the afternoon of January 15 between Sir F. Leith-Ross and Sir A. Cadogan agreement was reached on the rest of the text. Papers relating to these discussions are filed at F 290 and F 345/28/23.

vexed subject of oil interests.[4] We were grateful to the Ambassador's help in this matter.

4. Mr. Yoshida replied that he was glad to hear what I had reported to him, for it seemed to him also that the negotiations on this subject were proceeding satisfactorily.

5. I then said that there was another subject on which I wished to speak to him and which appeared to be likely to present difficulties. You had informed us that the Japanese Government were proposing to increase the import duty on woollen tops, yarns and tissues. It appeared that in respect of some duties the rates were being increased by over 200%. This was clearly prohibitive, since Japanese woollen imports I understood, amounted to some half-million a year and were almost exclusively made up of exports from this country. The Ambassador would understand that if action were taken which would gravely injure, if not destroy, this United Kingdom trade, then pressure from interests in this country for maintaining and increasing restrictions on imports from Japan would become very difficult to resist. This would be all the more unfortunate at the present time. I therefore asked the Ambassador whether he would be good enough to communicate with his Government on the subject without delay and to tell them of the concern which we had felt on learning of these proposals. At my suggestion Mr. Yoshida took a note of what I had told him and said that he would speak to his Government in the matter.

6. We then spoke of the Keelung incident,[5] when the Ambassador told me that he had recently been informed of a new proposal made by the Minister for Foreign Affairs. I replied that you too had given me particulars of this. I added that I felt sure the Ambassador would appreciate the importance of settling the incident as soon as possible. Parliament was now reassembling and questions would inevitably be asked that could only prove embar[r]assing to Anglo-Japanese relations. Therefore if His Excellency could say a word in Tokio to hurry matters up that would be all to the good. The Ambassador replied that he appreciated the importance of this and would do what he could.

I am, etc.,
ANTHONY EDEN

ENCLOSURE IN NO. 46

Aide-mémoire presented to the Japanese Ambassador on January 18, 1937

[F 345/28/23]

Towards the end of October[6] the Japanese Ambassador was good enough to communicate a memorandum in which he announced the receipt of instructions from his Government to approach His Majesty's Government in the United Kingdom with a view to establishing a definite

---

[4] Cf. No. 44, note 1.   [5] See No. 6, note 5.   [6] October 1936: see Volume XX, No. 590.

understanding between Japan and Great Britain concerning all matters in which their joint interests are affected.

In that memorandum his Excellency put forward certain proposals for the consideration of His Majesty's Government. These proposals, his Excellency explained, were tentative and constituted his personal suggestions as to the general lines on which such an understanding might be reached.

His Majesty's Government, needless to say, are as anxious as the Japanese Government to do everything that may be possible to ensure close, friendly and harmonious relations, and they are therefore examining the Ambassador's proposals with the most sympathetic attention. The suggestions being of very wide scope, however, some time may elapse before it is possible to return a definite reply on all the points raised. This being so, it may be that it would be useful to the Ambassador to set out for his information the results of the preliminary examination which is now complete, taking his Excellency's suggestions *seriatim*.

(*a*) His Majesty's Government regard themselves as already bound by existing treaties to respect the territorial integrity of China. But they would welcome the reaffirmation of this principle by the Japanese Government. This principle implies, in their view, abstention, not only from actual territorial encroachment but also from interference with the Chinese administration.

(*b*) His Majesty's Government welcome the idea of a declaration by both countries to the effect that they will support in its entirety the principle of the 'open door' in China as established by existing treaties, and will respect the integrity of the Chinese maritime customs in all treaty ports in China. They would expect that such a declaration would be implemented both in the spirit and the letter and that a stop would be put to the importation of goods into China otherwise than through the treaty ports in contravention of the Chinese customs tariff.

(*c*) His Majesty's Government, like the Japanese Government, are naturally concerned to protect the rights and interests of their own nationals in China. They would always be happy to consult with the Japanese Government on all occasions when their respective rights were in any way threatened. Such a procedure would naturally not exclude consultation with other Governments on matters in which they were also interested. His Majesty's Government hesitate, however, to agree without reservation to the procedure of joint representation to the Chinese Government. While Governments whose interests are similarly affected should consult together and, if possible, agree upon a similar line of policy, joint action may not always be the most helpful procedure and may, in some cases, lend itself to misrepresentation.

His Majesty's Government gladly agree that there should be frank and full discussion between them and the Japanese Government before action is taken by either Government to alter or modify the existing treaties concerning China.

(*d*) His Majesty's Government welcome the recognition that a stable and prosperous China is a Japanese interest. They for their part are convinced that it would be in the best interests of all countries. They fully agree with the views expressed that the Chinese Government is seriously attempting to restore order and to develop China's resources, but that success in this attempt must be dependent upon financial and political assistance from other Powers. His Majesty's Government are prepared to consider with the utmost sympathy proposals for active co-operation with a view to helping China to consolidate herself and to develop her resources. They would, however, observe that such co-operation to be effective must be directed to objects desired by China herself, and must be in a form acceptable to her. Any attempt to impose any form of control on an unwilling China would only arouse hostility and defeat its own ends. His Majesty's Government fully agree with the suggestion that practical proposals might be first discussed between Great Britain and Japan, and that Sir F. Leith-Ross's recommendations might be the basis of such discussions. In accordance with the Ambassador's suggestion His Majesty's Government have already begun to consider what financial assistance can be given in the most promising field, that is to say the development of Chinese railways, and they have been somewhat disappointed to find that the Japanese representatives on the consortium have not been able as yet to respond to the approaches made to them by the British representatives.[7] They trust that the Japanese representatives will soon be in a position to co-operate fully in the examination of concrete proposals in this field.

As regards political aid to China, to which his Excellency refers, it is difficult to express an opinion without knowing more precisely what is intended. Presumably his Excellency has in mind the supply of technical guidance and advice. His Majesty's Government would certainly agree that the Chinese Government might be expected to profit greatly by the appointment of foreign experts and advisers. But here, again, they consider, and they trust the Japanese Government will agree, that foreign advisers, to be effective, must have the goodwill of the Chinese Government, who must be free to recruit them where they may choose.

In general, it is clear to His Majesty's Government that there can hardly fail to be vicissitudes in the course of the comprehensive experiment in political and social reorganisation which is being undertaken on such a vast scale in China, and that stability in China can only be attained if all the Powers exercise the greatest patience and restraint in the face of the occasional disappointments with which they are bound to be confronted.

(*e*) His Majesty's Government would not wish to set up their view against that of the Japanese Government as to the degree of danger presented by communism in China. The efforts of the Chinese Government to deal with this danger seem to be limited by their present lack of

---

[7] See No. 19, note 4, and No. 33, note 4.

internal strength and general political cohesion. It may well be that some foreign military advice may be of assistance to them, but always on the condition referred to in the preceding paragraph, that it is desired and expressly requested by the Chinese Government; the imposition of advisers would be likely to weaken rather than strengthen the political system in China at its present stage of evolution. The Chinese Government must, in the opinion of His Majesty's Government, be allowed the fullest liberty to draw for their requirements in arms on any sources that may be available to them. If all countries limit the supply of arms to China to consignments approved by the Central Government, they can be sure that by so doing they are helping to diminish the danger of internal disturbance. The majority of countries already follow this practice, and His Majesty's Government would welcome the assistance of the Japanese Government in securing its universal adoption. His Majesty's Government would add, however, that they are disposed to think that, in this field, too, economic help to China may well be the best means of promoting the political stability which both Governments desire.

(f) His Majesty's Government are fully alive to the importance of ensuring a fair market for Japanese exports, and the desirability, if it is feasible, of reaching an agreement mutually satisfactory to both countries. His Majesty's Government for their part have never desired to impose any unfair restrictions on Japanese exports, and they regret that any ill-feeling should have been caused by the imposition of import quotas on certain textiles in the Colonial Empire. His Majesty's Government were forced to adopt this method in order to prevent the disastrous effects on their industries of the excessive and unregulated competition then taking place, and they only took action after negotiations between the industries of the two countries had failed to achieve results.[8] These negotiations broke down because the Japanese industrial representatives were only prepared to discuss a limitation of exports to the United Kingdom and British Colonies, whereas the British representatives did not consider that such a limited agreement would be of any substantial value, and their desire was to obtain an agreed allocation of markets generally between the industries of the two countries. His Majesty's Government fear that, if the Ambassador's suggestion is to limit Japanese exports only to the United Kingdom and Colonies, it would not appear any more attractive to the British manufacturing industries now than in 1934; and before expressing any definite view on the precise proposal as to the amount of Japanese exports which would be permitted (viz., the 1935 level of exports less 20 per cent.) they would be glad to learn

(1) Which are the classes of textile goods which would be covered by the proposal; and
(2) Whether the Japanese Government would undertake to give effect to any agreement by an effective control of their export trade.

[8] See Volume XX, Chapter II.

On receipt of further information on these points, His Majesty's Government would be ready to sound the United Kingdom industries as to the possibility of a negotiation on this basis; but His Majesty's Government would again urge the Japanese Government to consider whether it would not be in the best interests of the producers in both countries to negotiate an agreed allocation of their respective exports to all markets.

(g) His Majesty's Government will be glad to communicate to His Majesty's Governments in the Dominions the results of their study of the whole question. The Japanese Government will understand that it will be for those Governments to reach their own conclusions in the light of their own conditions and of the general situation as they view it.

(h) It has always been the desire of His Majesty's Government to maintain close touch with the Japanese Financial Commissioner in London, and they will be glad to arrange for exchanges of views at any time and on any question which the Japanese Government may desire to raise.

(i) A naval agreement being a matter of concern to several other countries, His Majesty's Government doubt the wisdom of linking it to any general political or economic agreement with Japan alone. This does not, of course, mean that His Majesty's Government would not be prepared to conclude a separate bilateral naval agreement with Japan at any time in the same way that they are concluding bilateral agreements with other Powers. In any event, the Japanese Government will be the first to recognise that any action by Japan which would have the effect of destroying the system of qualitative limitation now laboriously being built up between all the other naval Powers, and which would thus bring about a resumption of unrestricted naval competition in new types of vessels, would be a retrograde step which is not in the interests of either country, and must hamper that improvement in Anglo-Japanese relations to which His Majesty's Government attach so much importance.

(j) The reform of the Covenant being a matter for the world in general, it is similarly difficult for His Majesty's Government to deal with it in connexion with a special agreement with Japan, but they welcome the suggestion that in suitable conditions Japan might be looked to for co-operation in this direction.

The Ambassador will appreciate that the observations set out above represent only the first reaction of His Majesty's Government to the very comprehensive proposals contained in his Excellency's draft memorandum, and are liable to modification as the detailed examination of his proposals progresses. His Majesty's Government hope, however, that these preliminary observations will assist the Ambassador in formulating those definite proposals which his Excellency had in mind when he drew up his draft. In the meantime they wish to repeat that they fully share the desire of the Ambassador to establish co-operation between the two countries on a basis which will consolidate the good relations between them and promote the peace and stability both of the Far East and of the world generally, and they will be ready to collaborate with him in seeking to overcome the difficulties that exist in a spirit of mutual understanding.

No. 47

Mr. Eden to Sir R. Clive (Tokyo)

No. 14 Telegraphic [A 415/6/45]

FOREIGN OFFICE, *January 19, 1937, 10.30 p.m.*

Your telegram No. 20[1].

Your language approved.

Calculation of Japanese Ministry of Marine is probably twofold. They may perhaps believe that by adopting a stiff attitude on qualitative limitation they may yet be able to oblige the other naval Powers to accept some form of Japanese common upper limit proposal. As you rightly stated, this proposal is acceptable to no country. It is indeed abundantly clear from course of naval negotiations during the last year that, at the present moment, there is no chance whatever of putting into operation any system of quantitative limitation. This does not mean that His Majesty's Government would not still favour some form of quantitative limitation should there at some future date be a better prospect than there is at present of securing international agreement on this point.

In the second place, Japanese Ministry of Marine probably calculate that by secretly building types of ship superior to those in existing categories they may be able to obtain a sufficient start in the naval race which would ensue. This calculation leaves out of account the fact that the United States Government have made it clear that, if Japan seeks to initiate a qualitative race, the United States will build two ships for every one to be built by Japan. Japanese Government will, we hope, realise before it is too late financial strain which such a competition would impose on their country. They will also, we hope, realise that this country will similarly be obliged to take up any such challenge and that we are admirably equipped for meeting it.

The above observations may be useful in case the Japanese Minister for Foreign Affairs should revert to the matter in conversation with you.

---

[1] No. 45.

Record by Sir A. Cadogan of a conversation with Mr. Yoshida

[F 417/28/23]

FOREIGN OFFICE, *January 21, 1937*

The Japanese Ambassador called this morning to discuss the memorandum which was handed to him by the Secretary of State on January 18th.[1]

His Excellency was rather more unintelligible than usual. He said that he found our memorandum 'embarrassing', though he did not clearly explain why.

He said that originally he had meant to put certain ideas to Sir Warren Fisher, and he seemed to wish me to understand that his memorandum did not represent exactly those ideas. For instance, as I understood him, he never meant to suggest that we should make joint representations to the Chinese: only that Japan should reach agreement with us before tackling Nanking. But if so, his memorandum was distinctly misleading. I said that we quite understood that his document was informal, and our reply was meant to be of the same nature. We knew, of course, that he had approached the Treasury in the first instance, but they had naturally referred the matter to us, as it was here that such questions should be discussed.[2] His Excellency had been good enough to give us these suggestions, and we had thought it best to reply to them frankly.

However, he now reverted to his former idea that we should simply give him a document expressing our desire to negotiate a general agreement, in reply to which his Government might make definite proposals.

I said I didn't think there would be much difficulty about that, but that it seemed to me this would be rather a step backward. I reminded him of our former conversation on this point,[3] which had resulted in our agreeing that this would be rather too vague and general, and that it would be more practical and useful if we were to give His Excellency a reply to his memorandum. Nevertheless, he urged that we should now confine ourselves to a vague statement on the lines which he had indicated. He has asked for permission to go to Tokyo, and he would like to start almost at once, taking such a document with him.

What his real motives are, I don't know. Either he went ahead of his Government in presenting his memorandum and now does not dare produce our reply, or he led them to believe that the latter would be more favourable than it is.

I tried to elicit from him whether he had reported any of our reply to his Government, and I gathered he had only told them that His Majesty's Government would be ready to discuss relations between the two countries, and in particular their respective Far Eastern policies on the basis of existing Treaties, that His Majesty's Government would also be

---

[1] See No. 46.　　　[2] Cf. Volume XX, No. 590, note 1.　　　[3] See No. 33.

prepared to examine trade questions, and that they would be ready to discuss financial matters 'from time to time'.

He again pressed very strongly for some general assurance, to 'encourage his people'. I pointed out that this really only meant delay: inevitably, as a second stage, we should come up against the questions dealt with in our exchange of memoranda. But he was quite insistent, and obviously we can't ram our memorandum down his throat, so I said I would see what could be done.

I said that I supposed the kind of draft he wanted would be on the lines that we should refer to his approach to us and say that we welcome the idea of a general understanding, and sincerely desire it. He agreed and suggested that we should add that we are ready to discuss our respective policies in the Far East *on the basis of existing Treaties* (he emphasized this), and trade questions. We might also repeat what he had said about arranging exchanges of views at any time on financial matters. I said I would see what we could do to meet his wishes in this matter.

I told the Ambassador that so far as I knew the Secretary of State would not be back before Feb[ruary] 2nd or 3rd, and asked him whether the matter could wait until then.[4] He said, however, that he would be very glad if he could receive the memorandum before that date, as he would wish if possible to start for Japan via Siberia before the end of this month. His idea was to go first to Tokyo and then to Shanghai to see the Japanese Ambassador in China, and also if possible Sir Hughe Knatchbull-Hugessen. He would have to be back here in April in time for Prince Chichibu's visit.

As he was going he suggested that he might perhaps give us a short memorandum to which ours could be a reply, and I agreed that this might perhaps simplify the procedure. He promised to let me have a short memorandum as soon as possible.

I am at a loss to know what all this means, and the Ambassador is being extremely tiresome: he has put us to a good deal of trouble in drafting our memorandum. He now, without expressing any appreciation of the effort we have made, asks that we should revert to his original suggestion and give him a piece of paper which will mean nothing and will not advance matters at all. However, he maintains that during the coming session of the Diet the position of the Japanese Cabinet will be rather precarious and he professes to hope that out of the crisis there may emerge a Government which will be more liberal and more independent of the military party, and he always hints that some vague friendly declaration on our part might help to bring this about and strengthen the more moderate elements in Japan. He must be assumed to be a better judge of this than we are, and consequently I suppose there is nothing for it but to comply with his suggestion.

[4] Mr. Eden travelled to Paris on January 20 en route for Geneva to attend a meeting of the League of Nations Council. He was back in the Foreign Office on January 31: see Volume XVIII, No. 128, note 3.

At the same time I think we should inform Sir Robert Clive fairly fully of what has happened and ask him what his views are and whether he is able to suggest any explanation of the Ambassador's rather extraordinary manoeuvres.[5]

[5] A brief account of this interview was sent to Sir R. Clive in telegram No. 24 of January 26, which concluded: 'It may well be that our "interim reply" brought the Ambassador nearer to certain realities than he found altogether comfortable. Have you any other explanation to suggest of his rather peculiar manoeuvres or comment on his expectations?' Meanwhile Sir A. Cadogan produced 'a first draft of the sort of memorandum we might give H. E.': see No. 51 below. Sir R. Vansittart commented on the interview on January 21: 'All this is very crooked and a definite step backward. The Japanese always recede when it comes to practical issues . . . but if they wish to resort to this crab-like procedure, we must humour them and keep them in play . . .'

No. 49

Sir H. Knatchbull-Hugessen (Nanking) to Foreign Office (Received March 15)

No. 4 [F 1551/5/10]

NANKING, *January 21, 1937*

Sir,

Mr. Suma, the Japanese Consul-General in Nanking who is leaving China in the next few days after eleven years residence in this country, called upon me on January 20th to say Goodbye. I have the honour to enclose a minute of our conversation on that occasion.

2. Mr. Suma, as you know, has played the most active part in the recent negotiations between the Japanese and Chinese Governments.

3. Mr. Suma confirmed that in future the Japanese Ambassador would make his headquarters at Nanking. For this reason, he explained, no successor to himself in the capacity which he had actually filled, would be appointed. I presume therefore that Mr. Kawagoe will be furnished with a Counsellor and the usual diplomatic staff and that the Japanese Consulate-General will exist at Shanghai.

I have, etc.,

H. M. KNATCHBULL-HUGESSEN

ENCLOSURE IN NO. 49

Record by Sir H. Knatchbull-Hugessen of a conversation with M. Suma

January 20, 1937

Mr. Suma called this morning to say good-bye before leaving for Japan. He was not quite definite as to his final departure and said it was possible that in course of time he might return, but it was evident from further conversation that he is leaving for good and expects another post. I should hazard a guess that his departure may involve a change of method on the part of the Japanese Government and that if the new method fails Mr. Suma may return in due course. He is going to Japan for one or two months in any case, and I suspect that he is to take part in discussions on future Japanese policy with regard to China.

After a few preliminary remarks, Mr. Suma mentioned that he had met Mr. Kirkpatrick[1] and that there had been some conversation between them on the subject of Great Britain and Japan working together in China. I agreed that this was a very desirable solution, but reminded him that it was of course necessary that any such cooperation should admit China on an equal basis. This led to a more general conversation on the subject of Sino-Japanese relations. As Mr. Suma drifted into this more general talk, I said that I had been here for four months and had watched with regret the failure to reach a solution of Sino-Japanese problems. Giving it as my purely personal opinion, I said that I thought the mistake the Japanese had made had been to begin at the wrong end. There were certain questions which were concrete and definite and probably capable of solution: there were others which had been raised by the more extreme parties in Japan, which could hardly be described as capable of solution with the consent of the Chinese. This last category of questions had been made the main topic of negotiation, while the others had been left to look after themselves. In my opinion it was quite hopeless ever to expect the Chinese to be persuaded to enter, for instance, into an anti-Red combination with Japan. On the other hand, there were questions, such as smuggling and tariff, which should be capable of solution. Mr. Suma immediately expressed agreement and of his own accord added to my list of questions capable of solution that of the East Hopei Autonomous Government. He said, however, that the feeling in China was so strong that it really seemed hopeless to get anything done. The Japanese had tried for a considerable time to come to an agreement, but without success. I replied that this lack of success was really for the most part due to the Japanese themselves and, as I had already said, to their method of approach. In my opinion the Chinese were only too anxious to reach a settlement with Japan on a fair basis, and I was strongly inclined to think that if the Japanese once showed any understanding of what was reasonable on the Chinese side of the case the atmosphere would improve. Still more could they improve the atmosphere by seriously trying to clear away those outstanding points which were capable of solution. I emphasized that these were only my personal opinions and that I had not discussed this aspect of the matter with anyone on the Chinese side. It was impossible to build a house by putting the roof on first, and if the Japanese

[1] Mr. William Kirkpatrick had been appointed representative in China of the Export Credits Guarantee Department of the Board of Trade in October, 1936. Although reporting to the Department, he was officially attached to the British Embassy and under the direction of the Ambassador.

really wanted good feeling with China they must begin at the beginning. I instanced previous cases of how understandings between nations had been brought about and mentioned the Anglo-French Entente, which was founded upon the settlement of outstanding concrete difficulties. Mr. Suma listened and expressed agreement. He then said he would be very frank. The Japanese had no serious intentions of absorbing or annexing any more of China. The underlying consideration in everything they did was Russia. It was essential to them to protect Manchukuo strategically. I said I quite understood that Japan had serious political considerations to bear in mind, but did he think that they were really improving their position by maintaining in North China institutions like the East Hopei Autonomous Government, which was a thorn in the side of the National Government and a perpetual source of irritation against Japan? I admitted that the situation was very difficult, but it seemed to me that the most politic line of approach would be to do everything that was possible to ensure good feeling between China and Japan, without necessarily expecting this good feeling to be directed against a third country. I said that if Japan were to attempt to draw China into a combination against Russia, the immediate result would be a counter-move by Russia, who would attempt to draw China on to her side against Japan. It was utterly unreasonable to expect China to lean either to one side or the other.[2]

On the same question, later in the conversation, Mr. Suma remarked that he saw considerable danger in the present pressure being brought to bear upon the Chinese Government by the disaffected elements in Sian to adopt an anti-Japanese policy. He affected to believe that this was a real danger existing throughout the country, to which the National Government might be forced to give way. I said I did not believe this. He knew as well as I did what Chiang Kai-shek's own policy was and he must have realised from recent events that if China as a whole supported any one individual or form of government, that individual was Chiang Kai-shek. He would also remember that the apostle of a militant anti-Japanese policy was Chang Hsueh-liang, and he had only to read the newspapers of the last few days to see that protests against Chang Hsueh-liang's policy and his light sentence were coming in from all quarters.[3] I thought it probable that the present trouble would be localised. He must also have seen Wang Ching-wei's[4] recent declarations, which were definitely anti-communist.

[2] In a minute of March 22 Sir A. Cadogan commented that he did not know what Sir H. Knatchbull-Hugessen meant by this sentence: 'I shd. have thought that in any difference or conflict between Japan & Russia it wd. be very difficult to restrain the Chinese from thinking they could fish in troubled waters & get some benefit by espousing one side or the other. And they have a natural instinct almost, for playing off one country against another.'

[3] See No. 41, note 2.

[4] Wang Ching-wei, who had been recuperating in Europe since the attempt on his life in November 1935 (see Volume XX, No. 379), returned to China when he heard of the kidnapping of Chiang Kai-shek, arriving in Shanghai on January 18. Although he had

We then turned back to the subject of Anglo-Japanese relations, especially as regards China. I repeated that I agreed that Anglo-Japanese cooperation was very desirable, but it must be Anglo-*Sino*-Japanese cooperation, nor should it necessarily exclude any other country from the economic field. Mr. Suma agreed and we spent a few minutes considering how this end could be pursued. I pointed out that it was hopeless to expect any progress until relations between China and Japan were on a better footing. At present the feeling against Japan was too great to make progress possible. After some conversation on these lines, Mr. Suma expressed himself as entirely in agreement that the first thing to be done was to clear up the Sino-Japanese difficulties.

We went on to talk about Anglo-Japanese relations in the wider field. Mr. Suma said he would ask me a very indiscreet question. This question turned out to be: What did H.M. Government think of the German-Japanese agreement?[5] He added that it had clearly had an unfortunate effect in China, because, since the date of its announcement, the Chinese had been far more difficult to deal with. I said as regards our own views, firstly that it had always seemed to me difficult to understand the making of an agreement between two governments against what was in effect purely a political theory. It was only natural to suppose that there must be something more concrete behind this. It was obvious that Russia lay between Germany and Japan geographically, Russia was the apostle of communism: the agreement was directed against communism, therefore it was directed against Russia. It was only natural that people who thought logically should conclude that the agreement was directed against Russia. With regard to the effect in China, I thought that this was what had happened. The Chinese were afraid that Japan, having succeeded in relieving the danger of Russian pressure, would be freer to exercise pressure on China.

Turning to another subject, Mr. Suma then said that in certain quarters the recent increased interest in British commercial expansion in China had created suspicions. I assured him that we had no intention of impinging upon legitimate Japanese interests, that we felt that China was big enough for all, and that any suspicions that we were trying to drive Japan out were quite unjustified. (I mentioned this last point because the Japanese 1st Secretary in Peking had asked me outright the other day whether it was the object of Great Britain to drive out Japanese trade from China.)

I said I was certain that there was nothing my Government desired so strongly as to pursue friendly relations and understanding with Japan in general. Mr. Suma agreed and went on to mention the various other difficulties which existed, such as Japanese trade in the Dominions and

resigned his government posts in 1935 he was still a member of the Standing Committee of the Central Political Council.
  [5] Cf. Nos. 5, 6, and 9.

Colonies, the recent trouble with Australia, trade difficulties with India, etc. He suggested that it would be an excellent thing if the whole question of Anglo-Japanese outstanding difficulties could be examined and that there should be a general talk over the whole subject. I said it was not for me to deal with these wider matters but that I was convinced that His Majesty's Government, in their desire for friendly relations with Japan, would be ready to examine all points and that in any case ventilation could do no harm. I said that he had mentioned matters which presented great difficulties and that a satisfactory solution might be impossible on all of them but that seemed to me personally to be no reason why the whole position should not be examined.

Mr. Suma returned once more to Mr. Kirkpatrick's appointment. I explained as closely as I could what Mr. Kirkpatrick's functions were, as defined in his letter of appointment. I dwelt on this point rather particularly because Mr. Suma mentioned the possibility that Mr. Kirkpatrick should visit Japan—a suggestion which he himself warmly advocated. I said I thought such a visit would be quite a good thing provided it did not arouse any distrust or suspicion in China. I added that it would, however, be rather outside the main object of Mr. Kirkpatrick's presence here, which was to examine and report to the Export Credit Guarantee Department upon proposals for contracts in China which were taken up by British firms who might require the assistance of that Department.[6]

H.M.K-H.

[6] Sir A. Cadogan commented on March 22: 'Mr. Suma's departure from China is not to be lamented. In speaking frankly to him of the mistakes of Japanese policy the Ambr. was speaking to the right man as Mr. Suma probably bears a fair share of responsibility for Japan's recent policy in regard to China.'

No. 50

Sir R. Clive (Tokyo) to Foreign Office (Received January 25, 10 a.m.)

No. 33 Telegraphic [A 621/6/45]

TOKYO, January 25, 1937, 4.58 p.m.

My telegram No. 20.[1]

Minister for Foreign Affairs asked me to call today. Japanese Government having resigned, he said, were only awaiting the formation of the new Government to go[2]. In these circumstances they had decided to leave

[1] No. 45.

[2] Criticism of their financial policies and pressure from the Army faction had caused the Japanese Cabinet to resign on January 23, although the Emperor ordered them to remain at their posts until a new government was formed. Prince Saionji first recommended General Ugaki as the new premier, but the Army would not accept him and on January 29 General Hayashi, Minister of War 1934–35, was ordered to form a government: see Nos. 54 and 55 below.

decision about 14″ guns to their successors. He regretted the inevitable delay but the question was so important that they were unwilling to take a decision. I asked what were the views of the present Government. He said that the Cabinet had only been able to discuss the question once.

I propose to invite the immediate attention of the new Minister for Foreign Affairs to the question as soon as I see him after he is appointed.

No. 51

Record by Sir A. Cadogan of a conversation with Mr. Yoshida

[*F 546/28/23*]

FOREIGN OFFICE, *January 25, 1937*

The Japanese Ambassador called, at my request, this afternoon and I pointed out to him the difficulty in which we found ourselves in regard to his aide-mémoire[1]; namely, that the reply which we proposed to send him[2] and which was on the lines that he had approved would not balance his own document. The latter made a number of suggestions, more or less in detail, as His Excellency had done in his first memorandum[3], and to give a reply in merely general terms would appear to be inadequate. For instance, I pointed out that in his paragraph (A) he mentions again the 'integrity of the Chinese Maritime Customs in all Treaty Ports in China'. His Excellency would remember that in reference to a similar passage in his original memorandum we had felt bound to make allusion to the importation of goods into China otherwise than through the Treaty Ports in contravention of the Chinese Customs tariff. If he repeated this passage in his present memorandum we could not pass it over in silence but would have to insert in our reply something to the effect of what we had said in our original aide-mémoire[4].

The Ambassador seemed to see the point and did not demur to redrafting his aide-mémoire. I went through it with him and suggested that the first three paragraphs might stand and that his paragraph (A) might be covered by the insertion in the third paragraph of some reference to existing treaties. For instance, in the last sentence of that paragraph he might refer to an 'agreement between Great Britain and Japan for stabilising this situation on the basis of the existing treaties'.

[1] On January 23 Mr. Yoshida sent Sir A. Cadogan the following letter:
'Dear Sir Cadogan [*sic*],
Referring to our conversation of Thursday last, I enclose herewith a memorandum, which is written in simple form and taking out misunderstandable points. Judging from the actual situation in Tokio I firmly believe that encouraging words from your side will go a long way towards reestablishing friendly relations between two countries. I need not to say that your reply will not never [*sic*] be publicly quoted. I only wish to have liberty to use it to show your friendly feeling to a very limited person in the responsible quarter.' Cf. No. 48. Mr. Yoshida's memorandum has not been printed as it was superseded by No. 53 below.
[2] See No. 48, note 5.   [3] Annex to No. 1.   [4] See Enclosure in No. 46.

As for the rest of his memorandum, it might be confined to indicating that the Japanese Government were anxious to discuss trade and financial matters (covering paragraphs (D) and (F)). I would see no objection to his adding his paragraph (G) at the end of his new draft.

I think the Ambassador understood, and promised to let me have an aide-mémoire on these lines as soon as he could[5].

Meanwhile Mr. Harvey rang up this morning from Geneva to say that the Secretary of State, while approving our re-draft of our aide-mémoire in F 417[6], was inclined to think that the first two paragraphs were a little bit sweeping and committal. I understand that he did not lay very much emphasis on this point, and I confess I do not quite see how we can water them down. The first paragraph is simply a reference to the Japanese Ambassador's memorandum and reproduces his wording, and the second paragraph really only expresses our good intentions and our readiness to discuss. I suggest, therefore, that they might be allowed to stand as they are.

The Ambassador said that he had just received a telegram from Tokyo, from the outgoing Minister for Foreign Affairs[7], of course saying that he was unable to give him permission to leave his post. He will therefore be unable to obtain such permission until the new Government is formed and until the new Minister for Foreign Affairs can decide whether Mr. Yoshida should return to Tokyo or not.

[5] See No. 53 below.
[6] See No. 48, note 5: the aide-mémoire in its final form is printed in No. 55 below.
[7] Mr. Arita: cf. No. 50, note 2.

No. 52

Sir R. Clive (Tokyo) to Foreign Office (Received January 27, 10.45 a.m.)

No. 42 Telegraphic [F 570/28/23]

Confidential   TOKYO, *January 27, 1937, 4.48 p.m.*

Your telegram No. 24.[1]

In my recent conversations with Minister for Foreign Affairs and Vice Minister for Foreign Affairs I have made it abundantly clear that while His Majesty's Government sympathetically view Mr. Yoshida's efforts to promote an agreement between us, with a view to improving Anglo-Japanese relations, settlement of Keelung incident[2] must precede any agreement while refusal to accept 14 inch gun[3] will have the worst possible effect in England.

With all respect to Japanese Ambassador, his statement that document he hopes to obtain would strengthen the chance of a more liberal

[1] See No. 48, note 5.   [2] See No. 6, note 5.   [3] Cf. Nos. 43, 45, and 50.

Government in Japan, is nonsense. Relations with Great Britain do not enter into the present political crisis.

I am afraid that Mr. Yoshida is not taken very seriously in Japan and I do not understand his persistent desire to return here nor do I see what he hopes to accomplish. He was sent to London to save his face when the military refused to have him as Minister for Foreign Affairs in the Government which has now resigned.[4] He has made two blunders which have much annoyed the Court.

(1) He told journalists before leaving that he had a letter to the King besides his credentials. Questions were to have been asked in the Diet about this letter.

(2) He had no personal message to communicate from the Emperor (see your despatch No. 602 of December 8th[5]). He had misread his instructions which were merely that the Emperor wished to be kept fully informed about British constitutional crisis as His Majesty deeply sympathized with unprecedented difficulties of the situation.

Mr. Matsudaira told me this himself.[6]

---

[4] See No. 50, note 2.   [5] Not printed.

[6] Foreign Office comment by Mr. Orde, Sir A. Cadogan, Sir R. Vansittart, and Mr. Eden was now critical of Mr. Yoshida. Mr. Orde wrote on January 28 that Mr. Yoshida 'seems to be an accomplished blunderer. This throws no further light on his recent wriggling'. Sir A. Cadogan agreed (January 28): 'It would be quite impossible to negotiate anything serious with M. Yoshida. But as he makes advances, we cannot rebuff him and must . . . keep him in play without committing ourselves to anything in particular.' Sir R. Vansittart wrote (January 28): 'Mr. Yoshida is just plainly no good. We can leave it at that: play him, but don't take him seriously. If the moment comes for that—it hasn't yet come but may possibly be coming soon—we must try to do the job at the other end. S. of S. on return.' Mr. Eden added on February 1: 'I agree. I am sorry for Sir A. Cadogan but it cannot be helped!'

No. 53

Letter from Mr. Yoshida to Sir A. Cadogan

[F 586/28/23]

JAPANESE EMBASSY, *January 28, 1937*

Dear Sir Alexander,

With reference to my conversation with you the other day,[1] I have pleasure in enclosing herewith an Aide-Mémoire for your perusal.

Believe me,

Yours very sincerely,

SHIGERU YOSHIDA

[1] See No. 51.

Aide-Mémoire communicated by the Japanese Ambassador

LONDON, *January 27, 1937*

The Japanese Ambassador has received instructions from Tokyo to approach the British Government with a view to establishing a definite understanding between Japan and Great Britain concerning all matters in which their joint interests are affected.

As a means of establishing a common ground for such an understanding, the Ambassador puts forward on his own initiative the following suggestions for the consideration of the British Government.

The Ambassador considers the present situation in China not only constitutes the principal source of mutual misunderstanding but also represents the most vital issue to Japan. He is of the opinion that any agreement between Great Britain and Japan for stabilizing this situation will have far-reaching results on other issues outstanding between the two Governments, in addition to securing a stabilizing force for peace in the Far East.

The Ambassador suggests that mutual re-affirmation by the two countries to respect in full the territorial rights and sovereignty of China and all the principles of the 'Open Door' in China as established by existing Treaties might form a fundamental basis of any agreement.

It is also suggested that frank discussions might be opened as to the possibilities of giving the requisite aid to China in her present programme of reconstruction.

The Ambassador proposes that the differences existing between the two countries concerning trade matters should be settled on a basis of goodwill and mutual understanding of each other's difficulties.

It is proposed that the principle of closer financial relations between the two countries might be adopted.

The Ambassador believes that agreements arrived at between the two countries might later be extended in other directions which may be considered desirable in the interests of both countries.

No. 54

Sir R. Clive (Tokyo) to Mr. Eden (Received February 2, 2.10 p.m.)

No. 50 Telegraphic [F 683/233/23]

TOKYO, *February 2, 1937, 8.43 p.m.*

My telegram No. 48[1].
Prime Minister[2] with skeleton Cabinet was appointed today by the

---

[1] Of February 1, not printed.　　　　[2] General Hayashi: see No. 50, note 2.

Emperor. Prime Minister will temporarily act as Foreign Minister and Education Minister while several other Cabinet posts are duplicated. No member of political parties is included. It is not yet settled who will be offered the post of Minister for Foreign Affairs[3] nor whether the Diet will be dissolved.

Position is really *chaotic*. General view is that Premier is a child in politics. Minister of War[4] is a nonentity and will merely take orders from military hierarchy. The latter feared to be put in (? office) in view of unanimity of press against Military Government and issued statement January 31st that they did not hold Fascist ideas[5]. Minister of Finance[6] alone inspires any confidence.

Repeated Saving to Nanking.

[3] The appointment of Mr. Naotake Sato, formerly Japanese Ambassador at Paris, as Minister for Foreign Affairs was announced on March 3.

[4] Lt.-General Nakamura, who resigned on February 9 and was succeeded by General Sugiyama.

[5] This statement was quoted in a postscript to Sir R. Clive's despatch No. 61 of January 31, not printed (F 1258/233/23).

[6] Mr. Toyataro Yuki.

No. 55

Mr. Eden to Sir R. Clive (Tokyo)

No. 75 [F 754/28/23]

FOREIGN OFFICE, *February 5, 1937*

Sir,

I asked the Japanese Ambassador to come and see me to-day when I told him that Sir Alexander Cadogan had informed me of the conversations which he had had with the Ambassador on the subject of the memorandum which we had handed to him on January 18th[1]. I understood that the Ambassador had not wished to accept this memorandum as a contribution to the conversations which His Excellency had been seeking to initiate. I was sorry for this myself, since it seemed to me that there was much useful material in the document. Perhaps the objection in the Ambassador's judgment to it was that it was too detailed for so early a stage. The Ambassador replied that this was just it: too detailed and too truthful about difficulties.

2. I replied that I hoped His Excellency would not consider the present memorandum,[2] which I was handing to him, any less truthful as regards the realities of the situation even though more general in terms. The last thing we should wish to do was to start conversations on a false basis. The Ambassador said that he fully understood and shared my preoccupation; at the same time it was necessary to look at the matter to some extent from

[1] See Nos. 46, 48, and 51.   [2] See Enclosure below.

the Japanese end. There were many people in Japan who believed that the trade rivalry between our two nations all over the world was now so acute that no return to the previous good relations between us was possible. Mr. Yoshida did not share that view, but if the Japanese Government was to be persuaded of this it was wiser not to set out all the difficulties in the way of negotiation at the outset. The Ambassador then read the attached memorandum and described it as 'very better'.

3. I then asked Mr. Yoshida about his plans. Did he still hope to return to Tokio? The Ambassador replied that we would be aware of the recent Government crisis in his country.[3] He had at present no chief at the Foreign Office, but he understood that his request to be allowed to return to Tokio on a visit was under consideration. In reply to further questions the Ambassador explained that in his view the present Government in Japan could not be expected to enjoy a long life. Recent developments were encouraging for the Moderates and he himself was convinced that it would not be possible for any government to survive without the support of the Diet. Japan was passing through a difficult transition period and in the meanwhile he much hoped that this country would show all possible sympathy and understanding with her in her difficulties.

I am, etc.,
ANTHONY EDEN

ENCLOSURE IN No. 55

Aide Mémoire for Japanese Ambassador
[*F586/28/23*]

FOREIGN OFFICE, *January 28, 1937*

The Japanese Ambassador has been good enough to communicate a memorandum intimating that he is instructed to approach His Majesty's Government with a view to establishing 'a definite understanding between Japan and Great Britain concerning all matters affecting their joint interests'[4].

His Majesty's Government warmly welcomes this intimation, and are ready to join in any effort to achieve a progressive betterment of relations between the two countries. To that end they will be ready to discuss with all frankness and sympathy all questions affecting the relations between the two countries, including their respective policies in regard to China, on the basis of the existing treaties.

His Majesty's Government would be willing to include in this discussion a consideration of questions relating to trade.

As regards financial questions, it has always been the desire of His Majesty's Government to maintain close touch with the Japanese Financial Commissioner in London, and they will be glad to arrange for exchanges

[3] See No. 54.   [4] See Enclosure in No. 53.

of views at any time and on any question which the Japanese Government may desire to raise.

His Majesty's Government would repeat that they fully share the desire of the Japanese Ambassador to establish cooperation between the two countries on a basis which will consolidate the good relations between them and promote the peace and stability both of the Far East and of the world generally, and they will be ready to collaborate with him in seeking to overcome the difficulties that exist, in a spirit of mutual understanding.

They hope that the Japanese Government may be able and willing to make definite proposals which, they can assure the Ambassador, would receive their fullest and most sympathetic consideration.

No. 56

Sir H. Knatchbull-Hugessen (Nanking) to Foreign Office[1]
(Received March 24)

No. 7 [F 1767/223/10]

NANKING, *February 12, 1937*

Sir,

I have the honour to refer to your despatch No. 586 (F 6262/42/10) of November 6th, 1936[2], enclosing a copy of a document which the Japanese Ambassador had communicated to the Foreign Office on the subject of Communist activities in China, and calling for my observations.

2. The burden of the Japanese Ambassador's memorandum is the decision of the Communist Party to intensify its anti-Japanese activities and to work for a united front against Japan. We have been inclined to make somewhat light of Japanese fears, sincere though I believe them to be, of the communist menace in China, but this view clearly needs examination and possibly revision in the light of recent events in North West China. At first sight these events would seem to afford ample justification for the Japanese point of view, but a closer survey puts a somewhat different complexion on them.

3. It is always difficult to ascertain the precise extent to which the Communists are responsible for incidents and disturbances and how far they are merely opportunist and take advantage of conditions which they find ready made and apt for their purpose. This is exactly the difficulty in the present instance. Between the time when the Communist armies were ejected from Kiangsi in 1934 and the end of 1935 Communist stock in

[1] Mr. Eden left London on February 6 for a holiday in the South of France. Lord Halifax, Lord Privy Seal, took charge in his absence, and he returned to the Foreign Office on February 23.
[2] Not printed.

China stood very low and communism as a political force seemed to have ceased to exist in this country. Then it began to take a new lease of life. The communist armies which, after having been harried all round western China, had collected in Kansu and Shensi were, we were told, the most patriotic of the patriots and were only asking to be allowed to join in saving China from the Japanese. It was then that we first heard of the 'common front' – the union of all parties and cliques (including of course the Communists) against Japan, and the folly of internecine strife while there was an external enemy battering in the gates. This idea was enthusiastically taken up by two separate groups who reacted mutually on each other: (1) the Young Marshal's North-Eastern armies, and (2) the students and intellectuals who for all their scholarship would seem never to have heard of the Trojan horse.

4. When the Young Marshal and his Manchurian armies were evicted from Manchuria at the time of the Japanese occupation in 1931 they first took up their quarters in Hopei but when the Japanese objected that they were still uncomfortably close to Manchuria they were transferred to Shensi and Kansu, where they were given the title of 'North-West Bandit Suppression Forces' and the task of dispersing the Communist armies which were congregating there. They were from the first unhappy and discontented. They disliked the country, the climate and the conditions of their service; they felt that those in power were taking rather too lightly the loss of the Manchurian provinces and that their own prospects of returning to their homes and families were becoming more and more remote; added to this the subsidies from the Central Government were not arriving as regularly as had been promised, and in comparison with the new-model armies of the Central Government the North-Easterners were ill-clad, ill-fed and ill-armed. They were in fact exactly in that state of mind which is most suitable for the reception of communist propaganda. The anti-communist campaign became a farce since the disaffected troops, so far from fighting, began to fraternise with the enemy.

5. Among the students and intellectuals the movement for a popular front was launched at the time of, and in reply to, the intensive Japanese campaign for North China autonomy in November and December 1935. The objects of the movement as they then began to take shape were to put an end to the nine-years civil war between the Kuomintang and the Communists, to unite all 'parties, cliques, classes and armed forces' for a nation-wide war of defence against Japan, and to demand a truer form of democratic government, and freedom of expression and organisation in order to awaken the people to the need of real political unity as the essential condition of successful resistance to Japan. In spite of opposition from the Government based largely on their fear of Japanese reactions, the movement, which had by now become known as the 'National Salvation Movement', gained considerable momentum, receiving support both from the right and from the left.

6. Whether the communists deliberately inspired the united front

movement in the first instance or whether they adopted it for their own purposes is, as I have suggested above, difficult to say. According to the Japanese Ambassador in London the intensification of anti-Japanese activities was the outcome of a resolution passed at the 7th Conference of the Comintern held at Moscow last summer and the common-front policy was adopted by the Chinese Communist Party in a declaration dated August 1st. I have not seen any report of the proceedings referred to and so can neither confirm nor deny the correctness of these statements. They are, however, in line with the well-known tactics of the Third International, and are supported by a mass of other information.[3] At all events it is certain that by the summer of 1936 the tactics of the Chinese Communist Party had changed. There was no longer any word of the class warfare, the dictatorship of the proletariat or anti-imperialism, attention being directed solely to the new policy of the united front of all parties against Japan. The move was a clever one, for thus the extreme anti-Japanese elements became identified with the Communists and whenever the Government attempted to strike at the latter they found themselves in the false position of appearing to attack the most patriotic party in the country.

7. The national salvation movement was given further impetus by the Suiyuan invasion[4] and the Tsingtao incident[5] of November 1936, when it took a more pronounced anti-Governmental turn. Throughout most of the country the Government were able to keep the movement within bounds. The arrest of seven well-known Chinese at Shanghai for implication in the movement formed the subject of your telegram to me No. 133 Tour series of December 9th[2] and of Shanghai telegram to Nanking No. 49 of December 11th[2]. But in Shensi the situation was complicated by the disaffected Manchurian troops, by the presence of thousands of students who had formerly been in Manchurian schools and universities and who were among the most ardent supporters of the national salvation movement and the anti-Japanese front, and by the enthusiastic prompting of the propaganda agents from the nearby Communist armies.

8. It is not my intention in this report to deal with the Sian incident and it is sufficient for my present purpose to point out that the immediate cause of the coup was the forcible dispersion on the Generalissimo's orders of a 'national salvation' demonstration and that the eight demands which the Young Marshal presented to the Generalissimo were the slogans of the national salvationists, namely:

(1) Reorganise the Nanking Government and admit all parties to share the responsibility for saving the nation;

[3] Sir J. Pratt noted on March 31 that 'we know that the political line of the Common Front was laid down by the Executive Committee of the Comintern early in 1935 & that its effects have been felt not only in China, but in France, Spain, England & possibly other countries as well'.

[4] See Nos. 7 and 13.　　　　　　　　　　　　　　　[5] See No. 18, note 4.

(2) Put an end to all civil wars;

(3) Release the patriotic leaders arrested in Shanghai;

(4) Release all political prisoners throughout the country;

(5) Give freedom to the people for patriotic purposes;

(6) Safeguard the right of the people to organise and enjoy all political liberties;

(7) Comply strictly with the terms of Sun Yat-sen's will (i.e. co-operate with the U.S.S.R. and the Communist Party);

(8) Summon forthwith a National Salvation Conference.

9. From the time of the Generalissimo's arrest there was no further attempt to conceal the close association of the communists with the movement which had led to his arrest: though the Communist armies did not enter Sian their agents were there, open and avowed; indeed the Military Attaché and Captain Scott were able to converse freely with some of them.

10. Given the close association of the Communists with the national salvation movement and the disaffected North-Eastern armies, it is reasonable to enquire what exactly the Communists are after. This is a question which in my opinion hardly admits of two answers. The change is a change of tactics and not a change of purpose. The Chinese Communist Party must obtain recognition and get back a place in the government or perish. The only way it can do so is by playing on popular feeling and identifying itself with the popular indignation against Japan, and that is what I believe to be happening. At present the cry is 'a common front against Japan', and the rest of the communist ideology has been put into cold storage until the 'common front' shall have enabled the Communists to resume the position in the Chinese Government which they held before 1927, and when they have done that the Kuomintang would be quietly assassinated and a Soviet system introduced.

11. It is astonishing that the North-Eastern troops and the student patriots do not see what the Communists are working for. They appear to envisage the 'common front' as a sinking of ideological differences and a merging of material forces for the common purpose. Yet the communists are frank enough in avowing that that is not their intention. In an article by a Chinese contributor in the *International Press Correspondence* of September 26th, 1936, the writer is at pains to emphasise with the assistance of italics that for the Chinese Communists the establishment of a united front does not mean any weakening of the Party or its organs: on the contrary, a 'determined struggle must be carried on against the tendencies which may lead to the dissolution of the Communist Party in some sort of general political alliance of anti-Japanese forces ... The united national front presupposes the establishment of a united all-China anti-Japanese army, which must be established on the basis of a political agreement between the Red Army, the Kuomintang and other troops ... While each body participating in this Army will be responsible for a definite sector of the common front it will wholly and completely

maintain its political and organisational system, its commanding and political officers'.

12. What chance, it will be asked, is there of the Kuomintang Government accepting such a partnership of compromise with the Communist Party. Here one is in the realm of pure speculation, and I give my own opinion with diffidence. I consider such a solution unlikely. Sympathy with Communist ideas is practically non-existent in China at present. Communism is generally hated and detested for the havoc which has been wrought in its name during the past decade and for the trick which it played on Dr. Sun Yat-sen and the Kuomintang in the years culminating in 1927. Though there is a great deal of sympathy with the common front idea while it remains merely a theory I am inclined to think that this sympathy would evaporate as soon as any discussion of terms and conditions revealed the exact nature of the communist aims.

13. There remains one point, regarding which further information would be interesting if it were procurable, and that is the actual extent to which the Chinese Communist Party and the Communist Armies receive practical help as well as verbal encouragement from the Third International and the Soviet Government. The Soviet Government, it will be remembered, hastened to dissociate itself from the coup of December 12th and I am inclined to think that the disclaimer was genuine; nor has there ever been any indication in recent years that the Soviet Government is giving material assistance to the Communists in China. As regards the Third International – in so far as one can dissociate the Comintern from the Soviet Government – it is impossible for me to speak with any assurance since I am without any information on the subject. The United States Assistant Military Attaché, who visited Sian during the rebel occupation, was assured emphatically by a representative of the Communist forces that they had had no relations whatever with Russia since they left Kiangsi in 1934.

14. To sum up, my conclusions are that communism in China was moribund until it was galvanised into an appearance of revival by association with the anti-Japanese movement, that even now there is little Communist sentiment in China and that though the Communists may continue to be a nuisance there is small danger of their being able to regain a footing in the government or seriously to affect national policy. But so long as Japanese pressure on China continues, so long will the Communists be able to make a specious appeal to the patriotic sentiments of the population, especially among its younger elements.

I have, etc.,

H. M. KNATCHBULL-HUGESSEN

No. 57

Sir H. Knatchbull-Hugessen (Nanking) to Foreign Office[1]
(Received February 16, 3.30 p.m.)

No. 37 Telegraphic: by wireless [F 951/35/10]

NANKING, *February 16, 1937*

My telegram No. 31.[1]

Preliminary meeting of plenary session of Central Executive Committee was held yesterday. In opening speech Wang Ching-wei stressed recovery of lost territory as well as defence of remaining territory as being objects of Chinese efforts. This is something more positive than earlier declarations have been and may prelude bolder front to Japan on Manchuria and North China issues[2].

2. Japanese Ambassador called on Wang Ching-wei yesterday afternoon and spent an hour with him. That he should have chosen this occasion which must have been most inconvenient for Wang might be taken to indicate that he wished to warn plenary session against yielding to anti-Japanese feeling.

3. General and Madame Chiang Kai-shek returned to Nanking February 14th. He is taking things quietly and did not attend yesterday's ceremonies.[3]

Repeated to Peking, Commander-in-Chief, General Officer Commanding, Rear Admiral Yangtse, Saving Tokyo and Financial Adviser.

[1] In this telegram of February 9 Sir H. Knatchbull-Hugessen reported that the rebel troops in Sian had been persuaded to withdraw, although opposition from Communist and Radical elements led to the murder of General Wang I Che and three other officers of the North Eastern Army on February 2.

[2] Sir A. Cadogan commented on February 18: 'This from the "pro-Japanese" Wang Ching-wei!'

[3] Sir J. Pratt commented on February 18: 'Public opinion influences Government policy in China no less than in England. It failed to support the anti-Japanese cry when raised by the leaders of the S.W. because it had been raised for purely private and selfish reasons [see Volume XX, Chapter VII]. But when raised by the N.E. Army and the Communists of Shensi it seemed to be the expression of an opinion that had been silently gathering force for some time past. The politicians of the Kuomintang and Nanking Government have therefore had to trim their sails to the breeze.'

No. 58

Foreign Office to Sir R. Lindsay (Washington)

No. 145 [F 957/5/10]

Secret   FOREIGN OFFICE, *February 18, 1937*

Sir,

The Counsellor of the American Embassy called on Sir A. Cadogan on the 10th February[1]. Sir Alexander took the opportunity to refer to his previous conversation with him, which was recorded in my secret despatch No. 635 to Tokyo, a copy of which was forwarded to Your Excellency in despatch No. 1080 of the 23rd December[2].

2. Sir Alexander Cadogan reminded Mr. Atherton that the Japanese Ambassador had professed a desire to improve generally the relations between Japan and this country and had communicated to His Majesty's Government a preliminary, personal and very vague aide-mémoire[3]. His Majesty's Government would have been ready to discuss this document in some detail[4], had not His Excellency said that he hoped that they would be able to return a reply of as indefinite a nature as his own document, although cordial in the expression of their desire to 'get together'[5]. His Majesty's Government had seen no difficulty in acting on this suggestion, and an informal aide-mémoire had accordingly been given to Mr. Yoshida reciprocating his sentiments and declaring His Majesty's Government's readiness to discuss all questions, including the respective policies of Japan and this country in China, on the basis of the existing Treaties[6]. Mr. Yoshida hoped to return to Japan with this reply and thereby encourage his government to put forward proposals of a more definite nature.

3. It was explained to Mr. Atherton that the above was a comprehensive statement of the position and that it remained to be seen whether any more concrete proposals would, or could, develop out of the Japanese Ambassador's *démarche*.

4. Mr. Atherton expressed gratitude for the information, and volunteered his opinion that Mr. Yoshida was trying to play politics on his own account (a view in which Mr. Atherton is very probably correct).

6. A copy of this despatch is being sent to His Majesty's Ambassador at Tokyo.[7]

I am, etc.,

[HALIFAX]

---

[1] Sir A. Cadogan had minuted to Mr. Ronald on January 15: 'After the reply has been given to Mr. Yoshida [cf. No. 46], please remind me to take up the question of taking the Americans into our confidence.' Cf. No. 12, note 4, and No. 27.

[2] See No. 27, note 5.   [3] See Annex to No. 1.   [4] Cf. Enclosure in No. 46.
[5] See No. 48.   [6] See Enclosure in No. 55.
[7] Minutes on this file also discussed the question of what to say if the Chinese Ambassador should make enquiries regarding Mr. Yoshida's approaches. Sir A. Cadogan noted on February 10 that he had discussed the matter with Mr. Eden who agreed that the Chinese

should be told that they 'may rest assured that we should agree to nothing with the Japanese that would be aimed against China or detrimental to Chinese interests'. Sir A. Cadogan added: 'Fortunately the Chinese Ambr. has not yet embarrassed me with an enquiry on the point.'

No. 59

Mr. Eden to Sir H. Knatchbull-Hugessen (Peking)

No. 75 [F 881/320/10]

FOREIGN OFFICE, *February 23, 1937*

Sir,

In my telegram No. 113 Tour of the 13th November, 1936[1], I outlined to Your Excellency the lines on which His Majesty's Government in the United Kingdom would have wished that the Chinese Government might have been able to obtain financial assistance from abroad for the purpose of railway construction; these were, briefly, that an international loan, on as wide a basis as possible, might be negotiated and that each national group should apply the tranche for which they were responsible to the railway or railways in which they were more particularly interested. International co-operation in a loan of this character, while in harmony with the obligations assumed in the Consortium Agreement[2], would, it was hoped, avoid many of the difficulties that had hitherto been encountered in attempting to apply the cumbrous machinery of the Consortium to all the undertakings in China. A project of this nature, however, could only be realised after negotiations not only between banking groups both within and without the Consortium, but also between the Governments concerned, including the Chinese Government. The most important prerequisite conditions would be the readiness of the Japanese Government to sanction the participation of the Japanese group and the willingness of the Chinese Government to acquiesce in such participation; and it was to this end that Sir Charles Addis was requested, in October, 1936, to initiate preliminary discussions with Viscount Kano, the representative in London of the Japanese group[3].

2. A further question which Sir C. Addis was requested to take up with the other national groups members of the Consortium was that of the open-tender resolution adopted by the Consortium Council on the 15th May, 1922. The principle that Consortium contracts should be put up to tender open to all the world is now in conflict with the policy both of His Majesty's Government and, it is believed, of the other Governments concerned in regard to foreign lending. Sir C. Addis, accordingly, on

[1] Not printed (F 7003/38/10): cf., however, Volume XX, No. 557, note 4, and Nos. 569 and 595.
[2] See No. 19, note 2.   [3] Cf. No. 19, note 4: cf. also No. 33, note 4.

October 1st last, addressed a letter to the other members of the Consortium, proposing the rescission of the resolution in question.

3. Very little progress had been made with either of these questions when, as reported in your telegram No. 27 of the 12th January last[4], the Chinese Government put the whole question of the Consortium in issue by inviting British financial assistance with a view to the immediate construction of the Canton-Meihsien Railway. As it was considered desirable that full advantage should be taken of the desire of the Chinese Government to enlist the co-operation of British capital and enterprise in railway construction and economic development generally in South China, it was decided in principle, as Your Excellency will be aware from my recent telegrams on the subject[5], that the investment of British capital in this project should be facilitated. Had it been possible to get the open tender principle out of the way and to secure general assent to international co-operation on the lines laid down in my telegram No. 113, referred to in paragraph 1 above, it might have been possible to overcome the difficulties arising from the extreme reluctance of the Chinese Government to deal with the Consortium in any shape or form. The possible failure of the attempts of the Consortium to get round these difficulties (see my telegram to British Embassy Offices Shanghai No. 3 of January 28)[5] has led His Majesty's Government to the conclusion that the time has now arrived when British finance and enterprise in China must be freed from the disabilities imposed upon them by the Consortium Agreement in its present form.

4. You will recall that the Consortium policy of His Majesty's Government came under review in 1929. In his despatch No. 879 of the 6th September[6] of that year Mr. Henderson transmitted to Sir M. Lampson a copy of a memorandum by Sir John Pratt, in which British withdrawal from the Consortium was recommended. As this recommendation was opposed by Sir M. Lampson and was not supported by all the Departments of His Majesty's Government concerned, no action was taken on it at that time. There seems, however, no reason to reject the conclusions reached by Sir John Pratt in 1929, the validity of which appears in no way to have been impaired by subsequent events.

5. The only ponderable difficulty inherent in a dissolution or radical reform of the Consortium, once it is admitted that this action is in itself desirable, is the attitude of the United States Government. It has always been realised that that Government attached far greater weight to the maintenance of the Consortium Agreement than any of the other governments concerned. When, therefore, it became clear that the policy of His Majesty's Government in regard to railway financing in China must involve substantial modification of the Agreement, or, if the consent of the other governments to such modification were not forthcoming, the withdrawal of the British group, it was considered advisable that a full and

[4] Not printed (F 210/79/10).   [5] Not printed.   [6] Volume VIII, No. 95.

frank discussion of the issue should be initiated with the United States Government.

6. Sir Alexander Cadogan accordingly saw the U.S. Chargé d'Affairs on the 10th February[7] and, on my instructions, handed him the memorandum of which a copy is enclosed. Mr. Atherton offered no comment, but enquired whether the matter was regarded as urgent. When he was informed that Sir C. Addis had already been in correspondence with the other Groups and that the State Department would hence be likely shortly to be seized of the matter, he promised to telegraph to his Government and to communicate to me without delay any reply that might be received.

7. You will observe that His Majesty's Government have invited the views of the United States Government on the whole question of the Consortium. I shall at the same time be glad to receive at an early date any recommendations which you may have to make.

8. I am sending copies of this despatch to H.M. Ambassadors at Washington, Paris and Tokyo and to your Financial Adviser at Shanghai.

I am, etc.,
ANTHONY EDEN

ENCLOSURE IN No. 59

Foreign Office Memorandum respecting the China Consortium handed to the United States Embassy on February 10, 1937

The Consortium in its present form, applying both to Administrative and to Industrial loans to China, was formed in 1920 mainly on American initiative with strong British support after prolonged negotiations lasting some eighteen months. Its purpose was the same as that which animated the signatories of the Nine Power Treaty, namely to provide the fairest possible conditions for the political and economic development of China by substituting co-operation for competition in the field of international action.

During the War and post-War period the economic development of China had been brought to a standstill by prolonged political confusion. But China has now reached a degree of political stability which makes further foreign borrowing both justifiable and expedient. During the past few years the National Government of China has been carrying through a large programme of internal development including not only many improvements and extensions of her existing railway lines, bridges and road communications. Upon the achievement of this programme will largely depend the political and economic progress of the country. The cost is being met, in the main, by the issue of domestic loans. But it appears that the capacity of the internal market has been strained by the

[7] Cf. No. 58. Mr. Atherton's report of this interview is printed in *F.R.U.S.*, 1937, vol. iv, pp. 568–9.

loans so raised and the financial structure in China would be greatly strengthened if a part, at any rate, of the capital required could be raised abroad. With this in view, the Chinese Government have recently negotiated settlements of existing defaults. Thus for the first time there is a reasonable basis for new development loans which would both strengthen the position of the Nanking Government and promote the prosperity of the country.

But under existing conditions the Consortium in its present form, instead of promoting the economic progress of China, as its authors intended, is an obstacle which stands in the way of such action.

The Chinese have always regarded the Consortium with dislike and suspicion. The terms of any loan made by the Consortium would, it was well known, include provisions for adequate security and proper conditions as regards the purposes to which the funds were to be applied and the methods of applying them. Each of the countries, members of the Consortium, including Japan, though it is not a lending country, would have a voice in the settling of these conditions. The Chinese Government apparently feared that this power might be used to impose political conditions and in any case, they objected to such 'group treatment' which, like the unequal treaties, seemed to them to touch the independence of China as a sovereign State. They have therefore consistently refused to have any dealings with the Consortium or to recognise its existence in any way. Moreover, the Consortium itself, with its arrangements for joint negotiations, rotation of engineers, participation in the supply of materials etc., was an exceedingly cumbrous machine either for negotiating with the Chinese or for the practical execution of industrial undertakings. This had been found to be the case with the Consortium as it existed, say, in 1912, before Chinese national feeling had risen to its present height; and in the post war period the same obstacle prevented even the beginning of negotiations for the rehabilitation of railways in which British interests were deeply interested.

This explains the situation which during the last twelve months has actually arisen in China. A number of agreements for financing the import of materials for the construction of new railways have been signed with German, French and Belgian groups; but China has consistently refused to borrow from the Consortium.

As the United States Government are aware, some special loans have been negotiated with the Trustees for the British Indemnity Funds (in particular, for the completion of the Canton-Hankow Railway). But as regards any ordinary market loan towards the rehabilitation of China, His Majesty's Government felt that it was incumbent upon them to ensure that a genuine effort should be made to use the machinery of the Consortium, cumbrous though it was. With this end in view Sir C. Addis, the British representative of the Consortium group, after consultation with His Majesty's Government addressed to the other members of the Consortium on October 1 last a letter proposing the rescission of the open tender resolution adopted by the Consortium Council on 15th May 1922. The principle that all orders for goods supplied in execution of Consortium contracts should be put up to tender open to all the world formed no part of the Consortium Agreement itself of 1920 the terms of which had been so fully discussed between the Foreign Office and the State Department. The principle of open tender now conflicted with the existing restrictions on foreign lending in the United Kingdom. These restrictions were adopted by His Majesty's Government in order to prevent foreign loans being issued in London which would cause heavy transfers over the exchange and thereby prejudice their monetary policy of seeking inter alia to avoid undue fluctuations in the value of sterling.

Their policy in this matter was endorsed in the Three Power Declaration of last September and they would therefore expect that these restrictions would meet with the understanding and support of the United States Administration. The principle of open tender is believed also to conflict with the policy which other Consortium governments have adopted, for similar reasons, as regards foreign lending in their markets. Therefore it seemed to His Majesty's Government that if the Consortium were to be free to negotiate loans with China an essential preliminary must be the rescission of the Resolution relating to open tender. The other groups have either not yet replied to Sir C. Addis' proposal or have refused to accept it.

While this point yet remained unsettled the Chinese Government put the whole question of the Consortium in issue by making an offer to British interests of a contract for the construction of a railway line from Canton to Meihsien, a town near the Fukien border not far from Swatow. On being informed that the British group would have to offer a share of this contract to its Consortium partners the Chinese authorities expressed strong objection to any dealings whatever with the Consortium and, after hearing from Japanese sources that the Japanese wished to participate, refused to continue discussions on these lines. They have indicated that if the British interests approached are not willing to negotiate a purely British loan to China, they will open negotiations with German or French groups.

It would seem therefore that the continued existence of the Consortium in its present form is, in fact, defeating its own object. It is preventing the members of the Consortium from participating in the economic rehabilitation of China, and it is impeding instead of assisting such rehabilitation. In these circumstances His Majesty's Government desire to consult frankly with the United States Government in order to ascertain their views on the whole subject and discover whether there is any method by which, while restoring to its individual members the required liberty of action as regards industrial enterprises, the major objects of the Consortium could be attained by keeping in being co-operation between the governments concerned (including the Chinese Government).

An additional reason for entering upon a full consideration of, and frank consultation as regards, the policy which the United States Government and His Majesty's Government should now pursue in regard to the Consortium is to be found in the fact that, as His Majesty's Government understand, the American group, at any rate as at present constituted, could not in fact take any active share in a Consortium operation.

His Majesty's Government, for their part, would have been willing to co-operate in attempting to revise the existing Consortium agreement, to take account of the actual conditions that prevail to-day, if there were any prospect of obtaining the goodwill of the Chinese Government for such a revised arrangement. Having regard however to the attitude of the Chinese Government it appears to them that no good purpose would be served by attempting to proceed on these lines and in their opinion the agreement should now be dissolved by mutual consent. They understand that in the view of the banking groups the initiative in this matter should come from the Governments concerned and His Majesty's Government hope that they may be able to obtain the agreement of the Government of the United States.

His Majesty's Government have thought it desirable to submit the whole position to the United States Government before approaching the other Governments concerned and they hope to be favoured with an early expression of the views of the United States Government.

No. 60

Sir H. Knatchbull-Hugessen (Nanking) to Mr. Eden
(Received February 24, 9 p.m.)

No. 49 Telegraphic: by wireless [F 1125/35/10]

NANKING, *February 24, 1937*

My telegram No. 37 of February 16th[1].

Plenary session has closed yesterday. It took a very firm line with regard to Sian and communists. It refused to consider the eight demands of the National Salvation Association and declared that reconciliation was possible with the communists only on the following terms.

1. Abolition of the Chinese Red army and unification of command of all armed forces of the state.

2. Unification of governing power in hands of Central Government and dissolution of 'Chinese Soviet Republic' and other organisations detrimental to national unity.

3. Absolute cessation of communist propaganda.

[1] No. 57.

4. Cessation of class struggle.[2]

2. It was also decided that national assembly postponed from last November should be convoked on November 12th this year.

3. I have not yet seen final manifesto.[3]

Repeated to Tokyo, Commander-in-Chief, Rear Admiral Yangtse, General Officer Commanding and Financial Adviser.

[2] Mr. Thyne Henderson commented on February 25: 'There is nothing in this to which the Japanese could take objection.'
[3] See No. 61 below.

No. 61

Sir H. Knatchbull-Hugessen (Nanking) to Mr. Eden
(Received February 24, 9 p.m.)

No. 51 Telegraphic: by wireless [F 1136/35/10]

NANKING, *February 24, 1937*

My immediately preceding telegram[1].

It is clear from published proceedings of session that there is to be no compromise with Communist armies, Communist doctrines, or common front and that government propose to pursue exactly the same policy as in the past. So far as I can learn meetings were harmonious and no serious difference of opinion appeared.

2. Chiang Kai-shek, I am told, now intends to use Central Government forces to break up Communist armies (if latter still resist) and since he has apparently succeeded in breaking their alliance with north eastern troops he should not have much difficulty. North west problem is however not yet solved.

3. A disquieting note was introduced by failure of Kuangsi and Szechuen militarists to attend session and their reactions are awaited with some uneasiness. I am inclined to think they will accept situation since feeling in the country seems overwhelmingly to support government policy.

4. Only important change in government yet announced is resignation of Chang, [?Ch'eng] Chien becoming Minister of the Interior vice Chiang Tso-pin who will get governorship. Wang Chung-hui has been offered post of Minister for Foreign Affairs but I am told will not accept unless he

[1] Telegram No. 50, also received at 9 p.m. on February 24, transmitted the principal points of the manifesto issued by the Plenary Session, which included 'forbearance in domestic issue and non-toleration of aggression and non-conclusion of any agreement detrimental to China's territorial sovereignty', and the readjustment of Sino-Japanese relations on a basis of 'equality, reciprocity, and mutual respect of each other's territorial integrity'.

is also appointed concurrently Vice-President of Executive Yuan, about which there are difficulties[2]. From our point of view it would be good appointment. Chang is pleasant but futile.

5. Line taken by session on Communist question should allay Japanese fears and coupled with conciliatory tone of recent Japanese offer allows one to hope that new atmosphere is about to enter Sino-Japanese relationships.

6. Great emphasis has been laid on economic, particularly agricultural, reconstruction. Breakdown of peasant economy is one of the most serious problems now facing the Government and one of the most fertile sources of Communism.

7. You will note reference in manifesto to currency (and financial stability).

Repeated Saving to Peking, Tokyo, Commander-in-Chief, General Officer Commanding, Rear Admiral Yangtse, Financial Adviser.

[2] Sir H. Knatchbull-Hugessen reported in telegram No. 60 of March 4 that Wang Chung-hui had accepted the post of Foreign Minister.

No. 62

Mr. Eden to Sir R. Clive (Tokyo)

No. 101 [F 1001/28/23]

FOREIGN OFFICE, *February 24, 1937*

Sir,

The Japanese Ambassador called on Sir Alexander Cadogan on the 17th February. He informed Sir Alexander that he had now received a telegram from his Government instructing him to remain at his post. He said that Prince Chichibu would arrive in this country in the middle of April[1] and that he would therefore, in any case, hardly have had time usefully to return to Japan and to get back to this country in time to make arrangements for His Royal Highness's reception.

2. In these circumstances His Excellency had telegraphed to Tokyo informing his Government of the suggestions which he had made in his original memorandum on Anglo-Japanese relations[2], and inviting them to make definite proposals on which the negotiation might be continued.

3. M. Yoshida added that in the present uncertain political state in Japan, and particularly in the absence of a Minister for Foreign Affairs[3], he could not expect any rapid progress in the negotiations. In reply to Sir Alexander Cadogan's enquiry he said that on the whole he thought it

[1] Cf. No. 10.   [2] See Annex to No. 1.   [3] See No. 54, note 3.

likely that M. Sato, the Japanese Ambassador in Paris, would be appointed Minister for Foreign Affairs.[4]

I am, etc.,
ANTHONY EDEN

[1] Sir R. Vansittart commented on February 18: 'I do not think that it matters much where the Japanese Ambassador in London is.'

No. 63

Sir H. Knatchbull-Hugessen (Nanking) to Mr. Eden
(Received March 2, 7 p.m.)

No. 59 Telegraphic: by wireless [F 1325/597/61]

NANKING, *March 2, 1937*

Following for Sir A. Cadogan.
My telegram No. 17, second paragraph.[1]

I should like to put before you certain considerations regarding general situation in the Far East which appear to me to deserve examination, even if in present circumstances they may not indicate a practical line of action. I send this by telegraph owing to delay in correspondence by bag, but would ask you to regard it as a private letter.

2. It is clear that all progress towards general improvement in the Far East and towards realisation of our own political and commercial objects in China is blocked by Sino-Japanese politics. Hitherto it has been impossible to do anything in promotion of *détente* but if any progress is to be made here it will be necessary for this obstacle to be removed.

3. I have always felt that favourable opening for British policy should arrive when recent Japanese methods of dealing with China became discredited and when a period of uncertainty and even domestic difficulty opened in Japan. Unless Military Party in Japan throw prudence to the winds it seems possible that this situation may now develop. It is difficult to believe that Japan can embark on a really vigorous foreign policy with present conflict of creeds and interests at home. This theory is supported by fact that Japanese pressure on Chinese has not been maintained recently. Further point likely to lead to greater moderation in Japan is our own rearmament programme not to mention that of U.S.A., while China's increased powers of sticking up for herself should contribute an additional detriment to policy of bullying. In fact that policy may be proved to be unworkable, unprofitable, and even dangerous.

4. It is I suppose still possible that Military Party in Japan may run amok: it is not for me to assess these possibilities. But if that is still on the cards it remains worth while to consider whether any moderating influence could be exercised before it is too late.

[1] Of January 23, not printed (F 567/166/10).

5. On this basis a Sino-Japanese *détente* is seen to be necessary. But it seems clear that no Sino-Japanese understanding is possible without Russian participation. It would not be possible for China to side with either neighbour against the other[2] and Japan would agree to nothing which did not provide some solution of her strategical problems vis-à-vis Russia.

6. Is there any basis on which such a tripartite understanding would be possible?

7. On broadest lines it would seem reasonable to calculate that (a) China would consider it worth something to be relieved of Japanese pressure; (b) Japan would welcome measures tending to diminish anxiety vis-à-vis Russia; (c) Russia might regard settlement of the more acute Far-Eastern problems as a desirable set off to recent German-Japanese agreement.

8. Crux of the matter is North China and it would be necessary to examine the extent to which settlement of North China questions would be feasible in the event of the situation in Japan admitting of any attempt to deal with this problem.

9. If question is examined in its widest aspects following considerations suggest themselves: it seems improbable that China would agree to anything short of restoration of complete sovereignty over North China and Inner Mongolia including abolition of demilitarized zone and all other servitudes. Japan would have to agree to withdraw all claims to a special position in North China together with withdrawal of all troops including perhaps those maintained by virtue of Boxer Agreement. (This raises position of other Boxer Powers and may even develop into a question of withdrawal of all foreign troops). It would be a big price for Japan to pay but she might consider it in return for guarantee of security from Russia and China in regard to Manchukuo and for certain tariff and economic advantages.

10. It is difficult to see how Manchukuo could be left out of general settlement since much of the trouble arises from undefined Manchukuo-Soviet and Manchukuo-Mongolian frontiers and non-recognition of Manchukuo by China. Weng Wen-hao[3] remarked to me . . .[4] sort [?short] while ago that China and Japan were both agreeable to leaving Manchukuo out of a settlement and added that if it was left out it was in practice left to Japan. But Chinese public opinion is very strong on this point as appeared during Sian affair[5] and anything like a surrender would be extremely difficult. But if China would admit status quo in Manchuria, maintenance of a demilitarized zone in North China would become unnecessary and an agreed frontier between U.S.S.R. and Manchukuo and between Outer Mongolia and Manchukuo would put an end to all these frontier incidents.

[2] Cf. No. 49, note 2.

[3] Secretary General of the Executive Yuan, and an eminent geologist.

[4] The text was here uncertain.   [5] See No. 56, para. 7.

11. Japan would no doubt require from Russia not only frontier delimitation but reduction or withdrawal of troops and settlement of fisheries and other pending questions.

12. It is less easy to forecast Russian desiderata though they would presumably include withdrawal of Japanese troops from North China. She might make conditions about Japanese troops in Manchukuo and possibly as to recognition of independence of Outer Mongolia. Russia possibly has least to gain though it might be worth her while to sacrifice something to ease her relations with Japan to get rid of Japanese threat to Inner Mongolia and to secure restoration of general tranquil[l]ity.[6]

13. It will be seen that problems may range very far. A wholehearted settlement might even raise questions such as Shanghai situation arising out of 1932 (Demilitarized zone and Japanese garrison) and we might find ourselves up against some general discussion on Washington Conference lines involving even extra-territoriality. I think it would clearly be essential to set a definite limit to prevent such subjects being raised. In fact in present circumstances if anything should prove possible at all I should suggest desirability of a limited objective aiming at laying foundations of wider understanding in the future by clearing away most pressing problem of North China.

14. I do not suggest that these views are worth more than examination at present. Question seems to be not whether any definite action is called for, but whether a situation may not be imminent in which a discreet exchange of views with other interested Powers (especially U.S.A.) might not be undertaken with a view to deciding whether anything could be said tentatively to any of the three Powers most closely concerned.[7]

[6] In a letter of April 1 Mr. Orde asked Lord Chilston for his views on the probable attitude of the Soviet Government towards an understanding on the lines suggested by Sir H. Knatchbull-Hugessen. In his reply of April 19 Lord Chilston said he considered such a development 'entirely out of the range of practical politics, for I cannot conceive that the Soviet Government, after building up, with the utmost intensity, their military strength in the Far East during those years when their position undoubtedly was dangerously liable to a Japanese attack, should now be prepared to reduce that strength which they believe now to be so overwhelming that their anxiety as to a Japanese menace has fallen to a minimum'.

[7] Sir H. Knatchbull-Hugessen's proposals were subjected to an elaborate and rigorous scrutiny in the Foreign Office: 19 pages of minutes by Sir J. Pratt, Mr. Orde, Mr. Collier, Mr. C.W. Baxter (a First Secretary in the Central Department), Mr. W. Strang (Head of the Central Department), Sir O. G. Sargent (Assistant Under Secretary of State), Sir A. Cadogan, and Mr. Eden are preserved with this telegram. An analysis of the advantages and disadvantages to China, Japan, and Russia respectively of a *détente* on the lines suggested was made by Mr. Orde, who thought, however, that the 'most important question is whether the suggested *détente* would really be advantageous to ourselves'. All the writers had doubts on this point. Mr. Strang said that he was 'heretical enough' to think that 'we fare best . . . when our potential enemies are in a state of mild friction with other Powers; when relations between them are bad enough for them to keep an eye on each other, but not bad enough to threaten a disturbance of the peace'. In a final note of March 21, quoted in his memoirs (*Facing the Dictators*, (London, 1962), pp. 529–30), Mr. Eden, after praising the minutes, agreed with Sir A. Cadogan, who had written on March 17: 'I see (cynically) certain advantages in mutual distrust on the part of the Russians & Japanese (which is likely in any

15. I am sending copy of this privately to Sir R. Clive. If you think it necessary you will no doubt send it to Moscow from London.[8]

case to continue).' Mr. Eden added the comment that 'a Sino-Japanese *détente* could presumably be accompanied by better relations between Japan and this country, and this is what we should work for.' A memorandum replying to this telegram was sent to Sir H. Knatchbull-Hugessen by Mr. Orde on April 1 (F 1325/597/61).

[8] It may be noted that on March 11, in the draft of his reply to the U.S. Secretary to the Treasury, Mr. Henry Morgenthau, as to the possibilities of Anglo-American cooperation for peace, Mr. Chamberlain showed interest in a regional pact in the Far East in which Great Britain and the United States would join with China, Japan, and the U.S.S.R. in guaranteeing the status quo. On Mr. Eden's request, however, he agreed to substitute a more anodyne statement welcoming the advent of a new government in Japan as an opportunity to put relations between the U.S.A., Japan, and Great Britain on a footing of harmonious cooperation: see Volume XVIII, Nos. 250, 268, and 285.

No. 64

Sir R. Clive (Tokyo) to Mr. Eden (Received March 6, 9.30 a.m.)

No. 93 Telegraphic [F 1366/28/23]

TOKYO, *March 6, 1937, 1.10 p.m.*

My telegrams Nos. 17[1] and 86[2].

Deliberate campaign appears to have been started to show how strong is our desire for friendship for Japan. Leader from *Daily Telegraph* about perpetual lease settlement is cited as a British gesture towards Japan. Recent articles in *Daily Mail* and *Daily Express* are quoted. *Times* is commended for having modified its criticism of policy. At the same time my German colleague tells me of immense relief felt by Japanese Government at being invited unconditionally to send a ship to the Coronation Review. Naval Attaché tells me of impression made on naval officers by our building programme. As I have repeatedly said, might will always command indefinitely more respect than right in Japan. From Osaka Commercial Counsellor learns that feeling is growing in favour of Anglo-Japanese understanding. Yesterday at reception of Heads of Missions I had twenty minutes conversation with the new Minister for Foreign Affairs[3] who after most flattering remarks about yourself and Sir A. Cadogan expressed determination of Japan for closer relations with Great Britain. While reciprocating their friendly sentiments I said that Japan had opportunity to give effect to them at once by accepting our very reasonable proposal for settlement of Keelung incident.[4] He promised to study the question and agreed that it was essential to settle it.[5]

Repeated Saving to Peking and Commander-in-Chief.

[1] No. 44. [2] Not kept in F.O. archives. [3] Mr. Sato: see No. 54, note 3. [4] See No. 6, note 5.
[5] Foreign Office comment was cautiously hopeful about Mr. Sato. Sir A. Cadogan wrote on March 8: 'I am sure that the Japanese wish to be friendly with us. The question is

whether their policy and methods will admit of it. M. Sato should be an excellent M.F.A.: we know that he is sane, reasonable and moderate, and that he has disapproved a number of the worst manifestations of Japanese policy. Whether, in the atmosphere of Tokyo he will, during his term of office, be able to retain his outlook—and to impose it to any degree on others—remains to be seen. We have responded with the utmost cordiality to Mr. Yoshida's rather fumbling approach to us: we cannot be accused of failing to respond to Japanese advances, and for the moment I don't think we can do more. We cannot ourselves make advances to them.'

No. 65

Sir R. Clive (Tokyo) to Mr. Eden (Received March 9, 1.5 p.m.)

No. 95 Telegraphic [*F 1428/28/23*]

TOKYO, *March 9, 1937, 7.18 p.m.*

At interview today with Minister for Foreign Affairs I referred to his speech in the Diet on March 7th in which after expressing warmest desire of Japanese Government and people for co-operation and friendship with Great Britain he said 'Unfortunate misunderstandings and difficulties have arisen between the two countries in recent years. One lies in China question. Another is economic question and a third is that of disarmament'.

I asked His Excellency to tell me what he had in mind. He said he favoured economic co-operation in China between us but there were many elements in Japan who would have to be persuaded. He was agreeably surprised at finding military as represented by the present Minister and Vice Minister of War far more reasonable than he had expected. I mentioned the urgent necessity of stopping smuggling scandal in which we were doubly interested both commercially and as parent and strongest supporter of the integrity of maritime customs. With regard to economic question he referred to this in the widest sense. He had no knowledge of Japanese Ambassador's negotiations in London but felt effort must be made to reach an understanding.

As to disarmament he was referring to the past and told me he had refused to be second delegate last year to Admiral Nagano[1] because he knew Admiral's mind was made up before he started. I pressed for a reply about the 14 inch guns.[2] He said he had spoken to Minister of Marine but found him still quite undecided. I urged that the matter should be decided by Japanese Government and not left to the Admirals. Favourable reply would make excellent impression in England. In any case we hoped for reply as soon as possible[3].

[1] i.e. at the London Naval Conference: see Volume XIII, Chapters VI–VIII.
[2] Cf. No. 50.
[3] Telegram No. 63 of March 16 to Tokyo (A 1861/6/45) instructed Sir R. Clive to 'continue to use all your influence to secure favourable Japanese reply' on the 14 inch gun question: 'Failure to reply at all would, of course, be tantamount to a refusal of our proposals.'

Finally I pressed for reply to my letter of March 1st to Vice Minister for Foreign Affairs about Keelung[4]. He said he was dining alone with Vice Minister for Foreign Affairs tonight and promised reply as soon as possible. 'Owing to Prince Chichibu's departure[5] and your departure[6] I shall find a settlement' he said.[7]

Repeated Saving to Peking and Nanking.

[1] Cf. No. 6, note 5. [5] Cf. No. 62.

[6] It was announced in *The Times* on March 13 that Sir R. Clive was to succeed Sir E. Ovey as H.M. Ambassador at Brussels: Sir E. Ovey was appointed Ambassador at Buenos Aires. Sir R. Craigie was to replace Sir R. Clive at Tokyo, and took up his post on August 4, 1937.

[7] Minutes of March 10 by Mr. Orde, Sir A. Cadogan, and Mr. Eden were as follows. 'I wonder whether he has discovered yet all the obstacles to overcome before he can give us satisfaction.' 'We mustn't expect him to work miracles.' 'But the general Japanese attitude does appear to show improvement.'

No. 66

Letter[1] from Mr. S. M. Bruce[2] to Mr. M. MacDonald[3]

[F 1772/28/23]

AUSTRALIA HOUSE, *March 9, 1937*

My dear Secretary of State,

The Commonwealth Government have been watching with great interest the private discussions which have recently taken place with the Japanese Ambassador, which are summarised in your secret circular despatch B.No.26 of the 23rd February[4]. This question is one which vitally concerns Australia and I have now been instructed to convey the following communication to the United Kingdom Government.

'The Commonwealth Government has followed with the closest attention and interest the question of Anglo-Japanese relations as indicated in various Foreign Office memoranda and especially those conversations on the Japanese Ambassador's memorandum of last November.

The Commonwealth Government feels that the promotion of better relations and a closer understanding between Great Britain and Japan would be h[i]ghly desirable from the point of view of Australia. The recent agreement against communism between Germany and Japan, the attitude of Japan towards naval disarmament, and other international agreements and the campaign for a southward advance policy have created a feeling of perturbation in Australia which a definite understanding with Japan, in general terms on the lines of the recent Anglo-Italian exchange, would go a long way to dispel.

[1] A copy of this letter was sent to the Foreign Office by the Dominions Office on March 17.
[2] Australian High Commissioner in London. [3] Secretary of State for the Dominions.
[4] Not traced in F.O. Archives.

The fact that the overtures were initiated by Japan and the conversations continued after the German agreement was concluded seems to be an indication that the Japanese Government is anxious to arrive at some definite understanding.

The Commonwealth Government hopes that, should the present political situation in Japan not jeopardise this favourable atmosphere, His Majesty's Government in the United Kingdom will lose no opportunity of pursuing the matter to a mutually satisfactory conclusion'.[5]

Yours sincerely,
S. M. BRUCE

[5] Sir R. Vansittart commented: 'The answer is that we would if we could, & we could if they would.' Mr. Bruce's letter was circulated to the Cabinet Committee on Foreign Policy as F.P. 36(25).

No. 67

Sir R. Clive (Tokyo) to Mr. Eden (Received April 26)

No. 165 [F 2368/597/61]

TOKYO, March 25, 1937

Sir,

In his telegram No. 59[1] of March 2nd His Majesty's Ambassador at Nanking expresses the view to Sir A. Cadogan that a favourable opportunity for a Sino-Japanese *détente*, and for the realisation, in consequence, of British aims in China, should arise now that the recent Japanese policy towards China has become discredited. Sir H. Knatchbull-Hugessen suggests that the time may be approaching when a moderating influence to this end might be exercised by His Majesty's Government on the Japanese, Soviet and Chinese Governments. As her part in bringing about such a *détente* Japan would be required to withdraw her claims to a special position in North China and to withdraw her troops including those maintained under the Boxer Agreement.

2. In my view the time is not yet ripe, so far as Japan is concerned, for action by His Majesty's Government on the lines suggested by Sir H. Knatchbull-Hugessen. It is natural that, as he observes, the Chinese would demand 'the restoration of complete sovereignty over North China and Inner Mongolia'; but it is certain that the new Japanese Foreign Minister (whatever he may think) would never be allowed even to discuss this. Mr. Sato's policy, as I understand it, is to limit himself to endeavouring, at the opportune moment, to settle individual questions, e.g. smuggling against tariff decrease, etc., very gradually.

3. Nor do I see any chance in the near future of Japan agreeing 'to withdraw all claims to a special position in North China'.

[1] No. 63.

4. There is, perhaps, something to be said for considering whether the Boxer Powers should not exchange views on the subject of withdrawing their troops from North China. Japan would no doubt stoutly resist this and accuse us and the United States of America of 'insincerity'. Any such suggestion would therefore have to be made with great tact and without publicity in order to avoid defeating the object in view by giving offence to the Japanese. In any case it would be premature to make it just yet. If Mr. Sato is to have any success he must not be put in an impossible position vis-à-vis his own countrymen. Moreover I am convinced that any change in Japanese policy must come from within. If there are moderating influences at work in this country—and it is not certain that they amount to anything—any move that savours of external pressure or even advice would, in my opinion, be fatal. In the present phase of Japan's development the sentiment of self-sufficiency is paramount.

5. I feel hardly competent to consider Russian desiderata for a *détente* of this kind, but I find it difficult to believe that the Soviet Government would ever request Japan to withdraw its troops from North China. Moreover, the Japan-German Anti-Comintern Pact[2] must surely postpone any understanding between Japan and the Soviet Union. The Soviet Ambassador, however, is shortly returning from leave and it is quite possible that he may have new instructions to try to come to terms with Japan.

6. The abolition of the demilitarized zone is, of course, eminently desirable, but it is difficult to see how it can be achieved without a Sino-Japanese understanding about Manchuria, and that for the present seems out of the question.

7. Finally, I venture to express the opinion that it must never be forgotten that the Chinese have their own Oriental way of settling difficulties (e.g. the treatment of Chang Hsueh Liang after the kidnapping of General Chiang Kai-shek), a way that the European mind does not understand and would never have thought of. I am therefore in principle opposed to too much talk and conferences among the Powers as to how the Chinese and the Japanese should settle their affairs.[3]

I have, etc.,

R. H. CLIVE

[2] See No. 9, note 3.
[3] Sir J. Pratt, Mr. Orde, Sir A. Cadogan, and Sir R. Vansittart all agreed with Sir R. Clive's conclusions. Sir A. Cadogan wrote on May 1: 'If, as we hope, a change of policy is being initiated in Japan, I am sure . . . that anything savouring of external pressure would be fatal to it. If that new policy really develops and is maintained, it may be possible for us to take advantage of it and to put matters in the Far East on a better footing.' Sir R. Vansittart added (May 3): 'I agree. I think Sir R. Clive is probably right.'

No. 68

Sir R. Clive (Tokyo) to Mr. Eden (Received March 27, 9.30 a.m.)

No. 111 Telegraphic [A 2333/6/45]

TOKYO, *March 27, 1937, 3.40 p.m.*

Minister for Foreign Affairs handed me this morning the reply of the Japanese Government declining to accept the 14″ gun limitation as foreshadowed in paragraph 1 of my telegram No. 106.[1] It is stated 'Japanese Government trust that the British Government will understand that Japan is not at this juncture in a position to accept apart from quantitative restriction only limitation of gun calibre for capital ships as this constitutes in fact the most important part of qualitative restriction'. And again 'policy that guides Japan in her armament policy is based on consistent regard for principle of non-menace and non-aggression', and finally 'British Government have stressed political implications of the question from the point of view of promoting cordial relations with this country. Japanese Government are of course no less anxious for further advance of trading between the two countries. It is, however, a pre-requisite to its realisation that both countries should adequately understand and appreciate the position of the other, and the Japanese Government hope that this position will be fully appreciated by the British Government.[']

Full text by Siberia.[2]

[1] In this telegram of March 19 Sir R. Clive reported that Mr. Sato had warned him the previous day that he would shortly receive a note refusing to accept the 14″ gun limitation: 'He had been unable to move naval authorities. He realised that this decision would be very badly received in England.' Cf. Nos. 43, 45, 47, 50, and 65.

[2] Not printed. Sir R. Vansittart wrote across a copy of this telegram filed at A 2457/6/45: 'I shd. like to see an attempt to appreciate Japan's *real* motives (and her ulterior ones) in this refusal.' In a minute of March 31 addressed to Sir R. Vansittart Mr. Holman, a First Secretary in the American Department, assessed the importance of the naval authorities in Japan, and said he thought it 'not unlikely that the Japanese Government are secretly experimenting with specially large guns and ships which, in the absence of any contractual obligations, they may hope to spring on the world at a moment's notice'. He concluded, however: 'I cannot help feeling that the main consideration which has prompted the Japanese Government to refuse their cooperation in the size of capital ship guns is represented by their intense desire for prestige, secrecy and liberty of action.'

No. 69

Mr. Eden to Sir R. Lindsay (Washington)

No. 299 [F 1633/28/23]

FOREIGN OFFICE, *April 5, 1937*

Sir,

With reference to my despatch No. 1080 of December 23[1] I have to inform you that the Counsellor of the American Embassy, Mr. Atherton, came to see Sir A. Cadogan on March 12, the principal object of his visit being to communicate the substance of a letter which he had received from Mr. Hornbeck on the subject of what had been told him about the exchange of views with the Japanese Ambassador regarding Anglo-Japanese relations.

2. Mr. Hornbeck expressed great satisfaction that His Majesty's Government had kept the United States Government informed of what was proceeding. His letter referred to an account which Mr. Atherton had given him of Sir A. Cadogan's conversation with the latter on December 16th. This conversation, of course, related to an early stage of the discussions with Mr. Yoshida. Mr. Hornbeck expressed the hope that His Majesty's Government would make an encouraging reply to a friendly advance on the part of the Japanese Government. At the same time he observed that the Japanese Government were inclined to elicit or extract messages of friendship and goodwill from other Governments and then to brandish these if ever they should get into difficulties with the Government concerned. This appears to be guarded against in the present case because the aide-mémoire[2] which was handed to Mr. Yoshida referred very specifically and clearly to his approach to His Majesty's Government, and it was clear from the text of the British document that it arose purely out of a Japanese initiative. Mr. Atherton added that he had since received a short note from Mr. Hornbeck referring to a further report which he had sent him after he had been told of the final result of the exchange of views with Mr. Yoshida.[3] For some unexplained reason Mr. Hornbeck in this note said that he gathered that His Majesty's Government were unfavourable to the Japanese proposals. Sir A. Cadogan said that this represented the British attitude incorrectly: the Japanese advance was welcomed and His Majesty's Government were anxious to give it a friendly reception and to pursue the discussions if possible in a friendly spirit. The Japanese had not submitted anything very definite to His Majesty's Government in the way of proposals, and that consequently it remained to be seen whether any basis existed for improving relations between the two countries. Sir A. Cadogan told Mr. Atherton that the Japanese Ambassador had informed him that he had telegraphed to Tokyo the terms of the British reply[4] and had suggested to his Government that the next step

[1] See No. 27, note 5.   [2] See Enclosure in No. 55.   [3] See No. 58.   [4] See No. 62.

would be for them to make concrete proposals, and these were awaited.

3. In general Mr. Atherton said that, while he would not attach too much importance to the possibility of a real change of attitude on the part of Japan, he nevertheless thought that the present moment might be a favourable one for examining the possibility of reaching an agreement in the Far East, and he was glad to think that His Majesty's Government were not discouraging it.

4. Mr. Atherton then proceeded to put a number of questions, evidently on instructions from Mr. Hornbeck. He asked in the first place whether His Majesty's Government expected to obtain any definite advantage from better relations with Japan: what, in fact, was the British objective? Sir A. Cadogan replied that it was obviously a British interest to keep on good terms with Japan. If the latter pursued an aggressive policy in China, she would necessarily constitute a threat to the very considerable British interests there and, if His Majesty's Government had to reckon with Japanese hostility, that would evidently increase their embarrassment were they to become involved in complications in Europe. Thus one of their aims was strategic, but they had the further objective of trying to induce the Japanese instead of following aggressive tactics against China to co-operate with them in helping China to develop herself. The development of the China market would be in the interests of everyone. Mr. Atherton asked which of these objectives had priority, to which Sir A. Cadogan replied that they were parallel aims. Obviously the strategic aim was of more direct and more vital importance. He then enquired whether it was intended to sacrifice the one to the other, that is to say whether, in order to secure Japan's friendship His Majesty's Government would be prepared to change their policy in regard to China. He was told that the reply to this question was definitely in the negative: His Majesty's Government could have no idea of following Japan along the road she had recently followed as regards China: if they were to associate themselves with Japanese aims and methods, they would retard the unification and progress of China and would share with Japan the odium which at present attaches to her alone. Consequently such a policy would benefit no one and they should not contemplate it.

5. Mr. Atherton then said that it seemed that Japan was dissatisfied with her treaty position in China and might wish to modify it in such a way as to emphasise her special position in that region. Sir A. Cadogan said that there was no idea at present of tackling the treaty question. Really the whole aim was to try and influence Japan to drop her present tactics and to join with His Majesty's Government and the United States Government and other Governments interested in helping to develop China rather than in hindering the unification of the country by the enforcement of selfish and exclusive claims.

6. Mr. Atherton expressed himself as very satisfied with these explanations, which he thought would be of great interest to his Government, and Sir A. Cadogan assured him that the Foreign Office should of course in

future, if the discussions developed, keep in the closest contact with him, as they attached the greatest value to co-operation with the United States.[5]

I am, etc.,

ANTHONY EDEN

[5] Mr. Eden commented on Sir A. Cadogan's record of this conversation: 'This is satisfactory; Sir A. Cadogan has well disabused some baseless U.S. apprehensions. We must continue to keep U.S. Govt. informed of any subsequent developments. A.E. March 29.'

No. 70

Mr. Eden to Sir R. Lindsay (Washington)

No. 329 [F 2214/597/61]

Confidential   FOREIGN OFFICE, April 16, 1937

Sir,

During the course of a conversation with Mr. Norman Davis[1] on April 9th he stated that he had a message to deliver which President Roosevelt had instructed him only to deliver to myself and to the Chancellor of the Exchequer should he see the latter. This concerned relations in the Pacific. I might be aware, Mr. Norman Davis explained, that a favourite project of President Roosevelt's was the neutralisation of the Pacific. The President felt that if this objective could be secured we should perhaps be able to remove the danger of war in an important part of the world. I asked Mr. Davis what areas exactly it was intended to neutralise. He replied that the United States were willing to neutralise the Philippines and I understood Guam also. He thought it might be possible to extend this treatment to the Dutch East Indies and maybe if we wished to do so to Hong Kong also, since he imagined that Hong Kong would in any circumstances be very vulnerable in the event of a war between this country and Japan.

2. I asked whether it was intended that Japan should also neutralise some area, and did neutralisation include the removal of fortifications? Mr. Davis replied that it was certainly contemplated that Japan should make some contribution, and the President did mean that neutralisation should include the abolition of fortifications. I replied that if this was the proposal we should certainly have to know more about it, and more of what was to be asked of Japan for it to be possible for us to express any opinion.[2]

I am, etc.,

ANTHONY EDEN

[1] Mr. Davis, U.S. 'Ambassador at large', had been head of the U.S. delegation to the London naval conference, 1935–6: see Volume XIII, Chapters VII and VIII. He was in London as head of the American delegation to the International Sugar Conference.

[2] Mr. Davis reverted to the subject of a possible neutralization of the Pacific in conversation with Sir A. Cadogan on April 22: see No. 76 below.

No. 71

Sir H. Knatchbull-Hugessen (Nanking) to Mr. Eden
(Received April 21, 9 p.m.)

No. 108 Telegraphic: by wireless [F 2303/14/10]

NANKING, April 21, 1937

Following are extracts (slightly abridged) from a report by Financial Adviser on Japanese economic mission.[1]

2. The impression I gathered was that the main possibility to be exploited by mission was whether Chinese would be prepared to agree to a reduction in Customs tariff in return for Japanese collaboration in the suppression of smuggling in North China.

3. I had an interview with Soong[2] before he saw Kodama. He informed me that the agreed policy of all Chinese in contact with members of Kodama mission was that before any economic understanding was possible between Japan and China three preliminary conditions had to be fulfilled.

(a) Suppression of East Hopei Chinese administration.

(b) Suppression of smuggling in North China (including smuggling of narcotics).

(c) Suppression in North China of espionage agencies masked as Japanese military bureaux.

4. I subsequently had an interview with Kodama. The main points emerged that:

(1) He was taking a keen interest in the financial developments here and that he fully shared British point of view as to the necessity of establishing a reformed central bank and of securing unification of note issue.

(2) He desired to secure co-operation between Great Britain-Japan in railway developments in China but he realized that before this was possible an amelioration of Sino-Japanese relations was necessary. He also held the view that much of the present financing of railway projects in China was on too short terms.

(3) He was anxious on general grounds to secure a better understanding between Great Britain and Japan and regretted opportunity to secure

---

[1] An economic mission composed of Japanese bankers and industrialists, headed by Mr. Kenji Kodama, former president of the Yokohama Specie Bank, visited Shanghai and Nanking in March 1937, and attended the first general meeting of the Sino-Japanese trade association in Shanghai. In his despatch No. 173E of April 5 commenting on the mission Sir R. Clive expressed the opinion that 'Much was expected in Japan of this Mission, representing as it did the first outward expression of the conciliatory China policy of the new Government who openly sponsored it, and its cool reception has come both as a disappointment and a surprise . . . the Mission found China united in her hostility towards Japan while Japan is by no means united in her policy of friendship towards China'.

[2] T. V. Soong, former Minister of Finance, was head of the National Economic Council.

this better understanding afforded by visit of Sir F. Leith-Ross[3] had been missed.

(4) He saw necessity of some settlement of question of East Hopei even in face of opposition from Japanese military.

(5) He was of opinion that Japanese military were gradually modifying their unreasonable attitude.

(6) He thought there were definite possibilities of reaching a settlement of Sino-Japanese difficulties if patience were exercised and that thereafter co-operation might be possible.

(7) He proposed to press for a Japanese export credit scheme for China immediately Japanese banks had arranged to surrender their silver holdings to Chinese authorities. (These have since been surrendered.)

(8) He felt as long as Mr. Ikeda and Mr. Tsushima remained as Governor and Vice-Governor of Bank of Japan respectively that finances of Japan would be managed relatively with prudence.

5. According to a prominent Chinese who was present at many discussions between the Mission and Chinese much time had been taken up by Chinese airing their grievances. The Chinese while friendly had been quite uncompromising on certain essential points and Japanese had been on the defensive and considerably embarrassed. Towards the end of second meeting it had been felt by both sides that only harm would result if discussions were continued on these lines and it was agreed that each side having stated its case no further progress could be made for the present. My informant was of opinion that Japanese representatives had now a much clearer idea of possibilities of an economic understanding with China and he thought they would genuinely endeavour to take steps in Japan to bring about such an understanding. In conversation with Mr. Kodama my informant had gathered that present Japanese Cabinet were going to be left a free hand by the military for a limited period in which to try their new policy in China. Mr. Kodama felt that every effort would be made by Hayashi Cabinet to obtain some concrete result in this limited period and my informant thought Mr. Kodama would recommend first of all a settlement of vexed question of East Hopei so as to pave the way for an opening of tariff discussions.[4]

Repeated Saving to Peking telegram No. 87 Tokyo, Financial Adviser and Commercial Counsellor.

[3] See Volume XX, Chapters V and VI.
[1] Sir J. Pratt commented on April 23: 'Though the Mission appeared to have been a failure this exchange of views between reasonable men on both sides can hardly fail to have done good.' Sir A. Cadogan agreed (April 23), but worried about the Chinese attitude: 'If the "new policy" of Japan is really on trial for only a short time, it might be important that there shd. be something to show for it. I am always afraid of the Chinese, when things are going better with them, overplaying their hand.' He suggested that it might be useful 'to try and save the Chinese from their own folly by advising them to be reasonable', and Mr. Ronald noted on April 24 that he had discussed the suggestion with Sir J. Pratt: 'It is some five months since we last urged moderation on the Chinese [see Volume XX, No. 591] and . . . a word now might be very opportune.' Telegram No. 70 of April 27 to Sir H.

Knatchbull-Hugessen instructed him to impress on the Chinese that His Majesty's Government 'earnestly trust that in their own interests they will go as far as they can to meet the Japanese while the latter remain in this comparatively reasonable mood'.

No. 72

Sir H. Knatchbull-Hugessen (Nanking) to Mr. Eden
(Received April 22, 6 p.m.)

No. 109 Telegraphic: by wireless [F 2305/14/10]

NANKING, *April 22, 1937*

My telegram 108.[1] In interview with press on April 15th Japanese Ambassador while admitting there was some ground for Chinese view that removal of political obstacles must precede talk of Sino-Japanese economic rapprochement expressed opinion that economic co-operation might also lead to settlement political differences. He denied that Japan was trying to use Sino-Japanese economic rapprochement to obtain necessary raw materials from China for military purposes. He maintained that smuggling in North China was due to special conditions and not to be regarded in same light as ordinary smuggling. Regarding bogus régime East Hopei he said that theoretically it was Chinese domestic issue but he hoped that by the time general relations between China and Japan had been amicably adjusted Japan would be able to enter into negotiations on the matter with China and assist in settlement.

2. Chinese press reactions to this interview are unanimously unfavourable. Criticisms take the following lines.

(a) There is nothing special about North China which is an integral part of the Republic and only the underhand activities of the Japanese military complicate the situation.

(b) Japan's idea is to keep the general political issues open while extending a colonial form of economic penetration in North China and only after this will she be ready to discuss the abolition of the puppet régime in East Hopei and the settlement of other Sino-Japanese issues. From (*sic*) point of view economic co-operation without the removal of political handicaps will reduce her to the Status of a Colony.[2]

Repeated Saving Peking, Tokyo, Financial Adviser, Commercial Counsellor.

[1] No. 71.

[2] Mr. Thyne Henderson commented on April 23: 'The Japanese still seem to think that constant reference to "special" conditions or position will make the Chinese accept the idea, whereas just the opposite is the case—they lose their temper when they hear the word.' Sir A. Cadogan noted on April 23 that this telegram was 'rather in contrast with F 2303' (No. 71).

No. 73

Mr. Eden to Sir H. Knatchbull-Hugessen (Peking)

No. 208 [F 2288/320/10]

Confidential   FOREIGN OFFICE, *April 26, 1937*

Sir,

With reference to my despatch No. 75[1] of the 23rd February last on the subject of the China consortium, and in confirmation of my telegram No. 100[2] of the 19th March, I have to inform Your Excellency that a reply, favourable in term as you will see from the enclosed reply[3], was received from the United States Embassy to the memorandum enclosed in that despatch.

2. Memoranda, differing only slightly from that communicated to the Counsellor to the Embassy, on the 10th February last, were accordingly prepared for communication to the French and Japanese Ambassadors, and were handed to Their Excellencies on the 20th and 21st April respectively; copies of these documents are also enclosed for your information[4]. An oral intimation of the fact that an approach had already been made to the United States Government and a favourable reply received was conveyed to them at the same time. It was emphasised that His Majesty's Government would welcome an early reply, and the necessity was impressed upon the Japanese Ambassador of getting in touch with his Government by telegraph[5]. Mr. Yoshida, after studying the memorandum said that he might require to be enlightened on certain

---

[1] No. 59.

[2] This telegram to Peking, also sent to Washington, Tokyo, and Paris, read: 'United States Government have now replied that they do not desire to raise any objection to negotiations between the groups with a view to the dissolution of the Consortium.'

[3] Not printed: the U.S. memorandum is published in *F.R.U.S.*, 1937, vol. iv, pp. 576–7. Dated March 13, the reply stated that in view of difficulties mentioned by the Foreign Office the American Government would 'although with sincere regret, inform the American banking group party to the consortium agreement of the British Government's proposal that the agreement be dissolved and will state that this Government will interpose no objection to participation by the American group in negotiations, if and when proposed, among the banking groups, looking toward dissolution of the consortium'. Comment in the Foreign Office was that this reply was 'unexpectedly satisfactory'.

[4] Not printed.

[5] Mr. Yoshida had not yet telegraphed to Tokyo when he called on Sir A. Cadogan on April 24 to express the fear that to put the consortium memorandum to his Government now 'might prejudice the chances of reaching an Anglo-Japanese agreement on the lines which he had suggested'. Sir A. Cadogan pointed out that 'we were only too anxious for cooperation with the Japanese in China but we could not cooperate if there was no business to be done, and the continuance of the Consortium ... prevented the doing of any business'. Sir A. Cadogan commented in a minute of April 29 that Mr. Yoshida's attitude was 'simply that of the dog in the manger ... [the Japanese] probably couldn't finance much at the moment ... so it is convenient for them that the Consortium should bar us *all* from doing anything'.

points in order that 'misunderstandings' might be avoided; he was informed that any further explanations which might be required would readily be furnished.[6]

I am, etc.,
ANTHONY EDEN

[6] A meeting of the China Consortium was held in London on May 6: the delegates, while 'averse to a general release of the Groups from their obligations', agreed that while discussions were proceeding concerning the future of the Consortium, no objection would be raised to the British group conducting separate negotiations for the Canton-Meihsien railway loan; see No. 59. Sir C. Addis sent a copy of the minutes of the meeting to Mr. Orde on May 10 with a covering letter stating that if he had 'moved a general resolution in favour of dissolution by mutual consent it would have been lost. The most I could do was to secure for the British Group a breathing space before the Governments proceed to pronounce the doom of the Consortium'.

No. 74

Mr. Eden to Sir R. Clive (Tokyo)

No. 230 [F 2494/28/23]

FOREIGN OFFICE, April 30, 1937

Sir,
The Japanese Ambassador told me in the course of conversation at the Japanese Embassy last night that he had heard from Tokio that the Japanese Government would shortly be sending to us proposals designed they hoped to bring about an improvement in Anglo-Japanese relations. The Ambassador regretted that owing to pressure of work on M. Sato since he had taken over the Foreign Office there had been delay in the preparation of these proposals. But he himself clearly attached considerable importance to them.

I am, etc.,
ANTHONY EDEN

No. 75

Sir H. Knatchbull-Hugessen (Nanking) to Mr. Eden
(Received May 1, 8 p.m.)

No. 128 Telegraphic: by wireless [F 2491/14/10]

NANKING, May 1, 1937

Your telegram No. 70.[1]
I spoke accordingly last night to the Minister for Foreign Affairs[2] who

[1] See No. 71, note 4.   [2] Wang Chung-hui: see No. 61, note 2.

saw the force of the argument. He was unable offhand to think of any particular point but remarked that it might be a good thing to make some gesture without giving away anything important. He said that he would think it over and may speak to me again.[3]

Repeated to Tokyo, Saving to Peking No. 103.

[3] Sir A. Cadogan noted on May 6 that he had spoken in a similar sense to the Chinese Finance Minister, H. H. Kung, who was in England as a member of the delegation to the Coronation. Dr. Kung was 'sceptical as to the possibility of any real change of attitude on the part of the Japanese, but agreed as to the danger of discouraging it'.

No. 76

Mr. Eden to Sir R. Lindsay (Washington)

No. 375 [F 2214/597/61]

FOREIGN OFFICE, *May 3, 1937*

Sir,

In my despatch No. 329 of the 16th April[1] I recorded a conversation which I had had with Mr. Norman Davis on the subject of a possible neutralisation of the Pacific. A few days later[2] Mr. Davis called on Sir A. Cadogan and reverted to this subject.

2. He began by referring to the British proposal for maintaining in force Article 19 of the Washington Treaty of 1922.[3] He explained that when this proposal had reached Washington he had been sent for and had discussed it with the President. He said that he could not understand what His Majesty's Government had hoped to gain from their proposal and he personally considered that, in view of the violation by Japan of almost every international instrument to which she had set her name, there would not be much value in continuing an agreement with them in regard to non-fortification.

3. Mr. Davis then went on, rather inconsequently, to speak of the neutralisation of the Pacific, an idea which he said he had put before the President.[4] He had in mind an agreement between His Majesty's Government, the United States and Japan whereby the area covered by Article 19 should be completely neutralised, by which Sir Alexander

[1] No. 70.
[2] On April 22: a record of this conversation is filed at F 2348/597/61. Mr. Davis's account of the interview is printed in *F.R.U.S.*, 1937, vol. iii, pp. 975–8.
[3] See Volume XX, Nos. 550–2, 562–3, and 575–6.
[4] According to the documents printed in *F.R.U.S.*, discussion of this subject began with the presentation of a memorandum dated February 16, 1937 prepared for the President by the Far Eastern division of the State Department: see *F.R.U.S.*, *ibid.*, pp. 954–71; cf. also pp. 974–5. There is nothing to suggest that Mr. Davis originated the proposal: according to his account of his interview with Sir A. Cadogan he himself was 'not at all confident of the feasibility of such a plan' and was merely asking Sir A. Cadogan 'if he thought it was a matter which might be worth considering'.

understood him to mean that no fortifications or naval bases should be allowed. This would, of course, mean the dismantling of Hongkong. Mr. Davis explained that the United States did not require the Philippines as a naval base, but would be content with Hawaii: they would even be prepared to forego the right to establish any bases in the Aleutian Islands. He suggested that if the U.S.A. could be satisfied with Hawaii, Great Britain might equally be satisfied with Singapore.

4. It was difficult to comment on any such vague proposals and Mr. Davis, as usual, showed some skill in evading being pinned down to any particular points. Sir Alexander, however, did refer him to his remark made earlier in the conversation about the worthlessness of a Japanese signature, and suggested that everyone would be taking a considerable risk in abandoning fortified points on the strength of a Japanese undertaking that they would do the same in regard to such places as Formosa. Mr. Davis agreed that there was some force in this and went on to speak of other things, but at the end of the conversation when he asked Sir Alexander to think over what he had said, Sir Alexander replied that he presumed this did not apply to their discussion of the proposal for the neutralisation of the Pacific, as it seemed to him that they were agreed that for the moment this was impracticable. Mr. Davis agreed.

5. It may be that in the light of what Sir Alexander said to Mr. Davis no more will be heard of the project to neutralise the Pacific, but the fact of the idea having been broached may indicate that the United States Government, when they eventually formulate their proposals for the neutralisation of the Philippines, as contemplated under Section 11 of the Tydings-MacDuffie Act,[5] intend to broaden the neutralisation area in the Pacific in the hope of spreading the responsibility involved. As you are aware, any proposals emanating from the United States Government for the neutralisation of the Philippines will be welcomed and favourably examined by His Majesty's Government, but it is clearly for the United States authorities to take the initiative and clarify their views.

6. The rather vague scheme now propounded by Mr. Davis, however, which would presumably cover the question of Philippine neutralisation, appears to be of a much wider scope, and in the absence of elucidation can hardly be given serious consideration by His Majesty's Government. Moreover, as it is not certain that the State Department have ever been consulted in the elaboration of Mr. Davis's proposals,[6] it would be undesirable that you should make any enquiries about the scheme or make any approach in the matter to the United States authorities. At first sight it appears that, under Mr. Davis's plan, neutralisation would take the form of undertakings by certain governments to dismantle fortifications in a given area and to refrain from constructing others in their place,

[5] This act, Public Law 127, passed both houses of the U.S. Congress and received Presidential approval on March 24, 1934: it was ratified by the Philippines legislature on May 1, 1934. It provided for the independence of a Philippine Commonwealth in 1946.
[6] Cf. note 4 above.

rather than that the parties to the agreement should guarantee to maintain neutrality of the areas involved by force. Mr. Davis gave no hint that the United States Government would be prepared to give any explicit guarantees, nor is it likely, in view for example of the United States attitude towards the Kellogg Pact, that any such guarantees would be forthcoming. Without guarantees on the part of the United States of America, it is scarcely likely that any of the other Powers concerned in the Pacific would be prepared to undertake any fresh commitments. If that be the case, Mr. Davis's proposals really amount to the destruction of certain existing fortifications in the hope that such action may be conducive to a more peaceful atmosphere of security in the Pacific and result in a state of non-menace and non-aggression in that hemisphere. How far the United States Government would be ready to implement Mr. Davis's proposals for dismantling fortifications, and to what extent Japan would be prepared to co-operate, it is difficult to judge, and I should accordingly be grateful for any observations which you or Sir Robert Clive, to whom I am sending a copy of this despatch, may desire to furnish.[7]

I am, etc.,
ANTHONY EDEN

[7] The comments in paragraph 6 follow copious minutes. Sir A. Cadogan remarked: 'It might be thought that if America negotiated the perpetual neutralisation of the islands they would logically have to attach some explicit guarantee. But they didn't in the case of the Kellogg Pact, where it would have been just as natural and logical. A. C. April 27, 1937.'

No. 77

Sir H. Knatchbull-Hugessen (Nanking) to Mr. Eden
(Received May 5, 8.20 p.m.)

No. 133 Telegraphic: by wireless [F 2634/2595/10]

NANKING, *May 4, 1937*

My telegram No. 132.[1]
Chiang Kai-shek sent Donald from Shanghai today with a message to me to the following effect. Begins.
He was somewhat disturbed at reports from London regarding attempts of Japanese to effect a rapprochement with Great Britain.
He supposed that Great Britain was not ready to cooperate with Japan unless China's interests were safeguarded but he could not help feeling

[1] In this telegram of May 4 Sir H. Knatchbull-Hugessen reported a conversation with the Chinese Foreign Minister who said that Chiang Kai-shek had instructed him to make enquiries about reports of Anglo-Japanese conversations on cooperation in China, and whether these reports 'were being circulated from Japanese sources to damage Sino-British relations which were now so good'.

that there was a danger of our being hoodwinked by Japan whose promises and talk of cooperation might not be entirely reliable.

2. He was anxious to know whether in the view of His Majesty's Government this was not the right time to discuss question of Anglo-*Chinese* cooperation and he wished me to put this question to you. If in your opinion the moment was favourable for such discussions he would telegraph to Doctor Kung[2] who had full powers to act both for government and for General Chiang Kai-shek personally. The cooperation which he envisaged would be (a) military and (b) economic. As to the former Chiang Kai-shek realised that His Majesty's Government would not favour a military pact but there could be an understanding as to exchanges of military intelligence and staff officers. He spoke also of engaging British military adviser and inviting British officers to strategic points along the Yangtse. (I am aware that this is all rather vague but Donald himself was vague). As regards economic cooperation Doctor Kung had authority to make with British any arrangement he thought advisable and if we on our side had any ideas we should put them to Doctor Kung.

3. I told Donald for information of Chiang Kai-shek about my conversations with Minister for Foreign Affairs and said that while I had no official information regarding Anglo-Japanese conversations it was perfectly certain that they were directed to a general appeasement of Far Eastern situation and that there was no question of our making any bargain with Japan at the expense of China.[3]

4. Donald says Chiang Kai-shek is continually the victim of mischief-makers who are pointing to these reports from London as evidence that general attitude of His Majesty's Government towards China is changing and that all he really wants is an assurance from an authoritative quarter that this is not the case.[4] I said I thought it probable that any misconception on this point had already been cleared up in London but that I would report to you General Chiang Kai-shek's *démarche* and inform Minister for Foreign Affairs of any reply which I might receive.

5. The Chinese are extremely suspicious of references (such as that in yesterday's *Times*[5]) to recognition of Japan's 'special position' in China and may be excused for readiness to . . .[6] in this political inferences which are no doubt not intended. Japanese too make the most of such references. I suggest therefore that it might be advisable to make clear both to Chinese and to Japanese that we still stand on principle of the open door and equal

[2] Cf. No. 75, note 2.

[3] Telegram No. 77 of May 7 to Nanking, sent in reply to Sir H. Knatchbull-Hugessen's telegram No. 132 (see note 1 above) referred to a conversation between Sir A. Cadogan and the Chinese Ambassador concerning Mr. Yoshida's proposals, and stated that 'the Chinese Government could rest assured that His Majesty's Government would do nothing to the detriment of Chinese interests'.

[4] A marginal note by Mr. Eden here read: 'We can do this.'

[5] See *The Times*, May 3, 1937, p. 15.   [6] The text was here uncertain.

opportunity throughout China and do not admit that Japan has rights in . . .[6] any part of China which we have not.[7]

Repeated to Tokyo and Saving to Peking No. 107, and Commercial Counsellor.

[7] A note by Mr. Eden on the filed copy of this telegram read: 'My statement at Chinese dinner and answers in Parliament should meet this.' In an after-dinner speech of welcome to Dr. Kung on May 4 Mr. Eden said that 'British policy has but one objective in China, to assist the Chinese people . . .': see *The Times*, May 6, 1937, p. 18. Cf. also No. 79 below.

No. 78

Sir H. Knatchbull-Hugessen (Nanking) to Mr. Eden
(Received May 10, 8.15 p.m.)

No. 143 Telegraphic: by wireless [F 2722/5/10]

NANKING, *May 10, 1937*

General Chiang Kai-shek in conversation on [May] 8th on the subject of Sino-Japanese relations remarked that if Japan would be prepared to settle East Hopei, Northern Chahar, and the smuggling question, a new basis would be created on which he would be perfectly ready to engage in amicable conversations with Japan. In such an atmosphere China would be willing to discuss (? such) matters as economic co-operation in the north and could be relied on to abide strictly by what was legal and reasonable.

He was anxious for some representation in above sense to be conveyed to Japanese Government and asked how this could be done. When I hesitated he asked me directly to telegraph to you in above sense.

This conversation arose out of my speaking to him in the sense of your telegram No. 70.[1] I felt bound in view of his insistence to undertake to telegraph as he asked. I realise that you feel (? difficulty) in complying with such a request especially as Chiang Kai-shek's proposal contains nothing new or particularly hopeful. Possibly you might allow me to speak here to newly arrived Japanese Chargé d'Affairs, Hikada, who appears friendly and most moderate and states that he is a strong follower of Sato, or an opportunity might occur with Japanese delegation.[2]

Repeated to Tokyo Saving.

[1] See No. 71, note 4.
[2] Commenting on this telegram in his telegram No. 154 of May 11, Sir R. Clive reported that he knew the Japanese Chargé well and that he had a 'very good position here . . . I agree with Sir H. Knatchbull-Hugessen that if it is a question of passing on to Japanese any proposals of Chiang Kai-shek it had much better be done in Nanking in informal conversation . . .' Sir A. Cadogan wrote on May 13 that he was 'a little doubtful myself about our acting as intermediaries in a negotiation of this kind', but was willing to agree in view of Sir R. Clive's comments. Telegram No. 144 to Peking of May 18 instructed Sir H. Knatchbull-Hugessen to speak informally to the Japanese Chargé, but told him to 'indicate

Chinese conditions in the form of an estimate that you personally had formed . . . of what they would be likely to demand': he should 'try to avoid acting as an intermediary'.

No. 79

Mr. Eden to Sir H. Knatchbull-Hugessen (Peking)

No. 143 Telegraphic [F 2634/2595/10]

FOREIGN OFFICE, *May 11, 1937, 6.45 p.m.*

Your telegram No. 133.[1]

My telegram No. 77[2] should reassure Chiang Kai-shek that the general attitude of His Majesty's Government towards China is not changing.

Meanwhile you will probably have seen the remarks reported in the Press to have been made yesterday by the Japanese Foreign Minister for Foreign Affairs to foreign journalists[3]. Present Japanese Government would not appear to lay claim to any exclusive or monopolising interest in North China. His Majesty's Government would certainly not admit such a claim if made. We have made it clear and will continue to do so in our conversations with the Japanese that His Majesty's Government still stand for respect for Chinese territorial integrity and for the principle of the 'open door' and 'equal opportunity' throughout China.

You may so inform Donald for communication to the Generalissimo. As regards Anglo-Chinese cooperation it is not clear what answer is expected. Our general readiness to assist China in well-considered economic enterprises should be evident since Sir F. Leith-Ross's mission[4] if not earlier, while as regards military advice we are prepared (see my telegram No. 145 Tour[5] of last year) to consider carefully any request that Chinese Government may make for British advisers. You may reply in this sense if you think it desirable.

[1] No. 77. [2] See *ibid.*, note 3.
[3] According to a report in *The Times* of May 7, 1937, Mr. Sato, addressing foreign journalists on May 6, said that Japan did have a 'special interest' in North China but that it was not exclusive or monopolising.
[4] See Volume XX, Chapters V and VI. [5] See No. 16, note 3.

No. 80

Sir R. Clive (Tokyo) to Mr. Eden (Received June 18)

No. 269 [F 3537/28/23]

TOKYO, *May 13, 1937*

Sir,

I have the honour to report that Lady Clive and I were entertained to luncheon at the Palace by Their Majesties The Emperor and Empress on May 11th. Their Majesties were extremely gracious both to Lady Clive and to myself. Prince and Princess Takamatsu were also present at the luncheon. After luncheon I was accorded a farewell audience[1] by The Emperor.

2. His Majesty began by expressing his great appreciation of the very friendly welcome to Their Imperial Highnesses Prince and Princess Chichibu in England. It was His Majesty's wish that the friendliest relations should exist between our two countries. His Majesty then said 'I am very glad that the Keelung affair has been satisfactorily settled'. I was much surprised at His Majesty's referring to this unfortunate incident, as such conversations are usually confined to generalities[2]. I replied that the settlement of this affair was a matter of satisfaction to my Government and I begged His Majesty to believe that, in spite of occasional troubles and differences of view, I felt sure that fundamentally Great Britain and Japan were destined to be friends and that the traditional friendship would remain. His Majesty also expressed his pleasure at the presence at Portsmouth of the Japanese cruiser which had been invited to attend the Coronation review.

3. The Emperor spoke of the Coronation and requested me to convey to Their Majesties an expression of his good wishes and of his enduring regard. I promised to convey this message.

4. Finally His Majesty was kind enough to express his regret at my departure and added that though my official connection with Japan would shortly cease he hoped that my interest in this country would remain and that I would continue to work for the strengthening of Anglo-Japanese friendship. I replied expressing my respectful thanks and adding that a very happy connection with Japan lasting over 32 years could not lightly be forgotten and that His Majesty could count on my permanent interest in Japan and on my doing what lay in my power to help the cause of Anglo-Japanese friendship and understanding.

I have, etc.,

R. H. CLIVE

[1] See No. 65, note 6.
[2] See No. 6, note 5. The Emperor's reference to the Keelung incident was considered surprising in the Foreign Office, since he was 'usually kept sedulously apart from matters of policy'. Mr. Ronald commented on June 21: 'The reference to Keelung makes it look as though M. Matsudaira informs the Emperor on matters on which His Ministers prefer to say little or nothing.'

No. 81

Sir H. Knatchbull-Hugessen (Nanking) to Mr. Eden (Received July 12)

No. 44E [F 3975/14/10]

NANKING, *May 14, 1937*

General Review of Japanese Economic Activities in China

Sir,

I have the honour to enclose a copy of a most interesting and important despatch[1] by Sir Louis Beale[2] in which he presents a general review of Japanese economic activities in China, and of their effect on British interests. Copies of this despatch have been communicated direct to the Department of Overseas Trade.

2. I have found particularly illuminating Sir Louis' analysis of the manner in which China and Japan, so far from following divergent lines of development, are in reality travelling the same road, with Japan only one stage ahead of China. 'If', he says, 'Japan is dreaming of industrial development for herself, with China supplying agricultural and mineral raw products she will have a rude awakening to an industrial China treading on her heels'. He points out that the difference in price between British goods and those of the Japanese and Chinese is fundamentally one of labour costs and that as soon as countries, such as China and Japan, with comparatively low standards of living and cheap but skilful labour, turn their attention to modern methods of manufacturing, we can no longer expect to sell our goods, with a content of high-priced labour, in competition against goods with a content of low-priced labour. It is, he maintains, a delusion to imagine that high-priced labour, necessarily produces goods of a superiority commensurate with the difference in the two costs.

3. The picture drawn by Sir Louis, of China rapidly progressing towards the point where she can supply herself with the cheaper grade of products which she has in the past obtained from Japan, thus compelling Japan to turn more and more to the production of the higher grade articles which we have hitherto regarded as our own preserve, is not a pleasant one for the British manufacturer to contemplate and it presents a problem to which no satisfactory solution is apparent. By more efficient organisation and a freer grant of credit we may delay the decline but we can hardly stop it. Sir Louis suggests that it is only by reorganising our own machinery and by partnership between our own interests and Chinese interests that we can assure for ourselves a permanent and secure place in the economy of China. Though this may cheer the investor, I fear it will be cold comfort to the manufacturer in the United Kingdom who is interested not in investing but in marketing his goods.

4. Sir Louis has of course based his survey on consideration of

---

[1] No. 134 of April 6, not printed.   [2] Commercial Counsellor at Shanghai.

economic factors alone. The political factors are almost imponderable, and might alter the picture within wide limits, but it would still probably retain its essential form. Internal unrest in China may delay the process of industrialisation, internal unrest in Japan may relieve for a time the economic pressure of Japan on China, war between the two countries or in which they were involved would have the same temporary results, but it seems to me inevitable that in the long run the economic factors must prevail. I would, however, venture the opinion that we need not now consider the more remote future. There is no doubt that we ought to do well in the first of the three periods or phases which Sir Louis describes (namely that during which equipment for industrialisation is supplied). The second period may be a lean one, but the third is so remote that what it may hold for us is impossible of calculation. Nevertheless I cannot but feel that the more development takes place in China the greater will be the share in it for all—including ourselves.

5. I have not attempted in this despatch to do more than indicate the merest outline of the scope of Sir Louis Beale's survey and of my own reactions to it. It is a compilation of the highest value and will no doubt receive the closest study from all those concerned in the development of British commercial policy in China.[3]

I have, etc.,
H. M. KNATCHBULL-HUGESSEN

[3] Foreign Office officials were agreed that Sir L. Beale's views were too pessimistic. Sir J. Pratt (July 28) found it 'difficult to believe that the industrialisation of China can do us any harm . . . A wealthy China would mean more wealth for all the world'. Mr. Orde agreed (August 8) but thought that Sir L. Beale had been deliberately pessimistic 'for we shall not escape serious trouble unless we show great adaptability and greater sense and organising power than Lancashire has shown in recent years'.

No. 82

Sir R. Clive (Tokyo) to Mr. Eden (Received May 17, 10 a.m.)

No. 155 Telegraphic [F 2801/414/23]

Very Confidential   TOKYO, *May 17, 1937, 12.5 p.m.*

In the course of long conversation after dinner yesterday Count Makino[1] assured me that the Emperor's desire was to see close relations established with Great Britain and the United States and that this should in fact be the objective of Japan's foreign policy.

He did not allude to Mr. Lyons reported proposals in London[2] but

[1] Count Makino resigned from the office of Lord Keeper of the Privy Seal in December 1935, but was still closely connected with the Imperial Household.
[2] In his opening statement at the first meeting of the Imperial Conference, held at St. James's Palace on May 14, Mr. J. A. Lyons, Prime Minister of Australia, said that Australia 'would greatly welcome a regional understanding and pact of non-aggression by the countries of the Pacific, conceived in the spirit of the principles of the League'. Mr. Lyons

insisted that things must go very slowly. When I said that friendly attitude of army leaders had been noticeable recently in contrast to very reserved attitude of the navy, he replied that time must be allowed to bring about the change. He emphasised extremely friendly attitude of the whole Japanese press and people towards the Coronation and asked if I did not consider atmosphere much clearer than three years ago. I said I had no doubt of it but equally agreed that it would be a mistake to attempt to force the pace.[3]

He said he felt optimistic for the future but repeated that great caution and much patience were essential if any understanding in the Pacific was to be achieved.[4]

He doubted whether a government could survive the growing opposition of political parties and the press. This was unfortunate as it would disturb everyone's atmosphere this summer. Government was not bad and opposition was solely due to action of Prime Minister in dissolving Diet. Sudden decision of Prime Minister might be justified in a general but was less so appropriate to a statesman.[5]

Repeated Saving to Peking, Nanking and Commander in Chief.

elaborated his proposal at the fourth meeting of principal delegates on May 22: see No. 86 below. Cf. also Volume XVIII, No. 510.

[3] Marginal comment by Mr. Eden, who marked this sentence: 'I agree. A. E.'

[4] The preceding sentence was marked by Mr. Eden, who wrote on the filed copy of this telegram: 'This seems to me sound sense and the marked passages without quoting source of course, might be useful as guidance for news dept.'

[5] General Hayashi had secured Imperial agreement to the dissolution of the Diet on March 31, saying that the obstructionist attitude of the political parties prevented all progress. His decision was criticized as 'unconstitutional and unprecedented', and in the general elections held on April 30 the government received little support, the majority of votes going to the traditional Seiyukai and Minseito parties. General Hayashi still had the support of the Army, but was unable to come to terms with any of the political parties and resigned on May 31: see No. 89 below.

No. 83

Letter from Sir A. Cadogan to Sir M. Hankey[1]

[F 2930/597/61]

Secret   FOREIGN OFFICE, *May 21, 1937*

Van[2] passed to me your letter of the 7th May[3], enclosing a paper on defence matters prepared by the Australian Delegation, which we have

[1] Secretary to the Cabinet, and also to the Committee of Imperial Defence (C.I.D.).

[2] i.e. Sir R. Vansittart. Opening salutation omitted from the filed copy of this letter.

[3] In this letter Sir M. Hankey explained that Sir Archdale Parkhill, Australian Minister of Defence, who was in London for the Imperial Conference, had attended a meeting of the Chiefs of Staff Sub-Committee of the C.I.D. on May 6 to discuss a number of papers prepared by the Australian delegation on defence matters.

read with much interest.[4]

The only points which appear specifically to concern the Foreign Office are the questions raised in Section 11 of the paper.[5] I enclose a note, together with a few spare copies in case they may be of use to you, containing our observations on these points which you may wish to pass on to those interested.

Yours ever,

A. CADOGAN

ENCLOSURE IN NO. 83

Reply to Australian questionnaire

FOREIGN OFFICE, *May 20, 1937*

Section 11. (i) and (ii). His Majesty's Government in the United Kingdom naturally aim at the establishment of the friendliest possible relations with Japan and the adjustment of differences that exist between the two countries, *but not* at the expense of China or at the expense of their good relations with China, on the maintenance of which British interests depend.

They cannot be openly associated with a Japan that adheres to the policy which Japan has in recent years followed in regard to China. Happily there are signs that Japanese policy has taken a new direction, and His Majesty's Government may therefore now work in a more hopeful spirit for an improvement of the general situation in the Far East.

(iii) (*a*) His Majesty's Government's hope is for permanent friendship and a harder attitude in the future is not in contemplation.

(*b*) His Majesty's Government in the United Kingdom are certainly

[4] A copy of this paper of March 8, signed by Sir Archdale Parkhill, is filed at F 2930/597/61.

[5] The questions were as follows. '(i) What are the guiding considerations in British policy for the realization of the aim of permanent friendship with Japan? (ii) What is their relation to the maintenance of British interests in China in view of Japan's penetration in Asia and her claim to a special position in the Far East, which amounts to the dictation of the conditions under which she will co-operate in Chinese or Pacific questions? (iii)(a) Is the present policy of accommodation to Japan a temporary one pending the strengthening of British defences, and does the United Kingdom Government propose to stiffen its attitude when its rearmament is complete? (b) Is the United Kingdom Government prepared to go to war in defence of its interests in China and Hong Kong? (iv) In the opinion of the United Kingdom Government, is the maintenance of the integrity of the Netherlands East Indies vital to the security of Singapore and the scheme of defence of Empire interests that hinges on this base? (v)(a) To what degree is British Policy in harmony with that of the United States on matters relating to Asia and the Pacific Region generally? (b) If a firm stand is taken, to what extent can the United States be relied on for co-operation in view of: The general American attitude of isolation from the League, even where they may have special interests as in the Sino-Japanese dispute in 1932/33; The desire to maintain neutrality as indicated by the recent legislation by Congress; The independent attitude revealed by their unwillingness to renew Article 19 of the Washington Treaty?'

resolved to defend to the utmost of their ability British interests in China and Hong Kong. It is of course impossible to say beforehand what circumstances or what degree of menace might lead His Majesty's Government to consider that a resort to arms was necessary for their defence.

(iv) The answer to this question may be in the affirmative, but it is rather for the Service Departments to advise in the first instance.

(v) (*a*) General harmony appears to exist, but there is nothing in the shape of a definite agreement apart from the Nine-Power-Treaty.

(*b*) Nothing specific can be relied upon from the United States of America.[6]

[6] The Chiefs of Staff's Appreciation of the Situation in the Far East in 1937 (C.O.S. 596 of June 14, 1937, not printed) gave full details of Service views on the defence of British interests in the Far East, and was communicated to the Dominions representatives at the Imperial Conference. Substantial quotations from this report are printed in N.H. Gibbs, *Grand Strategy*, Vol. I (London, *1976*), pp. *415–20.*

No. 84

Sir H. Knatchbull-Hugessen (*Nanking*) to Mr. Eden
(*Received May 22, 7.20 p.m.*)

No. 171 Telegraphic: by wireless [F 2989/5/10]

Immediate Confidential   NANKING, *May 22, 1937*

I called on Minister for Foreign Affairs on May 22nd to say good-bye before leaving for Peking.

His Excellency spoke about Sino-Japanese relations saying that during the last three weeks there had been a noticeable stiffening in Japanese attitude here. This only had relation to small incidents and nothing had appeared in the press. Nevertheless it seemed to him that Japanese were once again casting about to find cases which they could press against Chinese Government and out of which they could make grievances if required. For instance despatch of a few troops to the north to assist in counter smuggling operations had been represented as an insult to Japanese army and action of some aviation students who had flown a military machine low over a Japanese cruiser in Yangtze at Nanking had equally been represented as an insult.

I asked whether he felt any apprehension with regard to reported resumption of military preparations in Suiyuan.[1] He replied not yet but in

[1] Cf. Nos. 7 and 13. Sir J. Pratt commented on May 25: '. . . I believe the Kwantung army always intended to return some day and finish the job with Japanese troops in order to make the Manchurian frontier secure against the Soviet menace from outer Mongolia. If the moves here reported are preparatory to resumption of Japanese aggression at Suiyuan in the summer a serious situation may develop.'

July and August situation there might become serious. It depended on internal developments in Japan and on position between Japanese Government and the Diet. In his view there were four solutions open to Japanese Government.

(1) Another dissolution.
(2) Compromise.
(3) Resignation.
(4) Distraction abroad.

Of these (2) was practically impossible. He feared that in certain circumstances recourse might be had to (4).

With reference to consideration put to him on lines of your telegram 70[2] he said that he thought that some progress might possibly be made on lines of inducing Japanese to give . . .[3] some of their illegal proceedings on Chinese territory. In action Chinese Government might make some concession and the whole business could be represented as a friendly agreement implying no censure on past Japanese doings. He recognized that it was important to give Mr. Sato some success. But he was unable to be more specific.[4]

Repeated to Tokyo, Saving to Peking No. 140.

[2] See No. 71, note 4. [3] The text was here uncertain.
[4] Mr. Ronald commented on May 25: 'I am inclined to think that the Kwantung Army, although outwardly pretending to comply with orders from Tokyo to behave themselves, are surreptitiously preparing the ground for further adventures in case (–perhaps in the hope that) M. Sato's policy of conciliation and accommodation will not produce results within the time allotted to it for trial.'

No. 85

Sir H. Knatchbull-Hugessen (Nanking) to Mr. Eden
(Received May 22, 7.20 p.m.)

No. 172 Telegraphic: by wireless [F 2990/597/61]

Immediate   NANKING, *May 22, 1937*

My telegram No. 164.[1]

Minister for Foreign Affairs seemed reassured as to possible effect of Anglo-Japanese conversations on Chinese interests when I saw him today. He realized that these conversations could not have proceeded very far. He asked me if I would keep him informed on their progress. I said that I would do so in so far as I was able.

With regard to proposal for a Pacific pact[2] he doubted whether the material though plentiful was of a kind which would admit of embodiment in anything formal.

Repeated to Tokyo, Saving to Peking No. 141.

[1] In this telegram of May 19 Sir H. Knatchbull-Hugessen reported that he had spoken to the Chinese Foreign Minister in the sense of paragraph 2 of F.O. telegram No. 143 (No. 79).
[2] See No. 82, note 2.

No. 86

Extract from the minutes of the fourth meeting of principal delegates to the Imperial Conference 1937, held at 10, Downing Street, S.W.1, on Saturday, May 22, 1937, at 11 a.m.[1]

[*T 9200/226/384*]

Secret   2, WHITEHALL GARDENS, S.W.1, *May 22, 1937*

The Far East[2]

MR. EDEN said that the last two years had seen attempts by Japan to carry further her aggressive policy on the mainland, and, recently, a decided check to her activities outside Manchuria. These ambitions had two sides, the one strategic against Russia and the other economic. The strategic side had been shown not only in the active building of railways in Manchuria, but also in attempts to penetrate eastwards into both Outer and Inner Mongolia. After a series of Frontier incidents an unsuccessful attempt was made to open up some kind of official relations between Manchuria and Outer Mongolia, but the Mongolians, with the backing of the Soviet Union, had resisted the attempt and an alliance was concluded between Outer Mongolia and the Soviet Union which had given Japan clear warning that her interference would not be tolerated. To the South, the Japanese had attempted to penetrate westwards so as to bring Inner Mongolia into their orbit, but here again they had met with a check.

These and other difficulties had recently induced what appeared to be a more moderate policy on the part of Japan. At the same time China had made decided progress politically and economically of late. The authority and prestige of the Central Government had notably increased, and signs were not lacking that China's limit of patience had been reached and that there was a genuine risk of armed resistance to further Japanese encroachments.

In November last an agreement was concluded between Japan and Germany for co-operation against Communism.[3] In its published form the agreement had no other object than close collaboration in combating the subversive activities of the Comintern, but secret provisions are understood to be directed against the Soviet Union. These did not amount to a military alliance but to ensure that there should be no divergence of political attitude towards the Union. The whole Agreement had not

---

[1] For details of the work of the Imperial Conference see Volume XVIII, No. 510, note 1. At the meeting on May 22 Mr. Neville Chamberlain was in the Chair and the United Kingdom delegation included Mr. Eden, Lord Halifax, and the Home Secretary, Sir John Simon, with Sir R. Vansittart and Sir A. Cadogan as advisers. The Canadian, Australian, New Zealand, and South African delegations were headed by their Prime Ministers, and India was represented by the Secretary of State for India, Lord Zetland.

[2] The meeting opened with a discussion on matters raised at previous sessions, and on Central European and Abyssinian affairs, which has here been omitted.

[3] See No. 9, note 3.

unnaturally irritated the Soviet Government whose reply had been to refuse to sign a new Fisheries Agreement with Japan, and it seemed to have removed for the time being any likelihood of an improvement in Russo-Japanese relations. The Agreement, which was the outcome of military diplomacy on the part of the Japanese, had had a bad reception in Japan.

In China the Japanese had made some progress in an economic direction in the North, but their general aims had met with effective resistance from the Chinese Government, and a deadlock had been reached which they did not feel inclined to resolve by force. It was recognised in many quarters in Japan that her China policy had failed, and the Minister for Foreign Affairs in the new Japanese Government had announced that a fresh start must be made on the basis of the recognition of China as an equal. It remained to be seen whether this would really be the case but there was ground for the hope that a gentler policy would be followed. China appeared to be ready to respond to genuine advances, and recently a Chinese Minister (Dr. Kung) had stated that China would be ready to go half way in order to secure a really satisfactory arrangement with Japan.

As regards the possibility of Japanese expansion in the South Seas, there had been no very recent development. In 1934, the Dutch authorities had made a firm and successful stand against exorbitant Japanese demands in certain trade negotiations. These negotiations had been broken off, and had not been resumed, with the result that the import trade had been regulated; the Japanese imports being confined to a reasonable percentage.

The general situation confronting Japan at home, and her difficulties with Russia and China, undoubtedly had had their influence in restricting her power of expansion in other directions. While her ambitions had to be continually watched, the situation in this respect did not appear at the moment to warrant undue apprehension.

Non-Aggression Pact in the Pacific

At the opening Session of the Conference[4] Mr. Lyons had alluded to the possibility of concluding a 'regional understanding and Pact of Non-Aggression by the countries of the Pacific conceived in the spirit of the principles of the League'. No doubt in due time Mr. Lyons would elaborate this idea which must be of the greatest interest to all present. Though he (Mr. Eden) was not yet quite clear in his own mind as to what Mr. Lyons had in view, it might perhaps assist clarification if he were to submit one or two observations. Great Britain was not opposed to Pacts of Non-Aggression if there was a general desire for them and if they represented a real intention for peace and collaboration. They might play a part in producing a *détente* and he would do nothing to discourage any

---

[4] See No. 82, note 2.

attempt to consolidate the situation in any part of the world. He did think, however, that we must be sure that a Pact of Non-Aggression would contribute to that end before we embarked upon it, because after all a simple Pact of Non-Aggression only repeated what was already contained in the Kellogg Pact, and to reaffirm Treaties might only have the effect of casting doubt on their validity—a doubt which in a few years' time might attach to the reaffirmation. Constant reaffirmation of obligations risked undermining the validity of international engagements. In the past we had attempted to supplement the Covenant by regional agreements of which the Treaty of Locarno was the prototype, but these agreements were in the form of a Treaty of Mutual Guarantee. If what Mr. Lyons had in mind was anything of this nature, Mr. Eden was sure that he would not be unconscious of the difficulties:

(1) we should be assuming a new, definite and very grave commitment in joining in any guarantee of the status quo;

(2) our experience taught us that it would almost certainly be impossible for the United States to join in such an arrangement, and without their participation the scheme would lose much of its value.

Since China in 1931 failed to find protection in the League, the Chinese Government had on various occasions approached us tentatively with the idea of such a regional Pact. We had always indicated to them the necessity of sounding the United States Government on the subject, but if they had done so we certainly had not heard that they had obtained any result.

Reverting to the idea of a simple Non-Aggression Pact he (Mr. Eden) fully realised that there might be, so to speak, a great moral value in securing a United States signature to such a document if that could be done as a specific indication of the particular interest which the United States took in that region, an interest very similar to our own in that she was concerned for the maintenance of the status quo and for the peace and well-being of all countries in the Far East, but whether it would have more than a moral value was doubtful. If Russia could be included in such a Pact it might be very useful, but this of course might well raise difficulties with Japan. It would be very helpful to hear at a later stage exactly what was in the minds of the Australian Delegation and other Delegations interested in the matter, but if any action was taken it would be necessary to move with extreme caution, and in particular to ensure that Japan was favourable to what was proposed from the outset.

MR. EDEN said that he had nothing to add to the admirable, lucid and complete summary of the situation in the United States which Mr. Mackenzie King[5] had laid before the Conference.[6] There were certain difficulties, such as war debts and the conclusions of a Trade Agreement, but, as he had already mentioned, our relations with the United States were excellent, and indeed had never been closer or more cordial.

[5] Canadian Prime Minister.
[6] At the third meeting of the principal delegates on May 21.

MR. MACKENZIE KING said that he did not wish to make any further observations at the present stage.

MR. LYONS said that the Australian Delegation had in mind the making of a Non-Aggression Pact on the lines of the old Quadruple Treaty.[7] If such a pact covering the Pacific could be made this would be a very important first step towards the bringing together of the countries concerned with a view to the improvement of their relations and the growth of closer and more intimate collaboration between them. He (Mr. Lyons) had mentioned the suggestion to the President of the United States, who might perhaps have been expected to react somewhat unfavourably. In point of fact, however, Mr. Roosevelt had stated that the preservation of peace was the first and most important consideration, and that he would be quite ready to enter into an agreement with Japan or with any other country to secure this end. If it was found possible to bring about some understanding of the kind in contemplation, it might be found possible to relieve Great Britain to some extent of the heavy burden of her defensive preparations in the Pacific and the same would apply to Australia and the other Dominions concerned.

Mr. Lyons suggested that the proposed pact should in general be based on the old Quadruple Treaty which contained provisions to the following effect:

'With a view to the preservation of the general peace and the maintenance of their rights in relation to their insular possessions and insular dominions in the region of the Pacific Ocean

1. The High Contracting Parties agree as between themselves to respect their rights in relation to their insular possessions and insular dominions in the region of the Pacific Ocean.

If there should develop between any of the High Contracting Parties a controversy arising out of any Pacific question and involving their said rights which is not satisfactorily settled by diplomacy and is likely to affect the harmonious accord now happily subsisting between them, they shall invite the other High Contracting Parties to a joint conference to which the whole subject will be referred for consideration and adjustment:

2. If the said rights are threatened by the aggressive action of any other Power, the High Contracting Parties shall communicate with one another fully and frankly in order to arrive at an understanding as to the most efficient measures to be taken, jointly or separately, to meet the exigencies of the particular situation.'

Australia's objective in this matter was the preservation of peace and the maintenance of ever-increasing friendly relations with Japan. It was true that Japan had objected to the measures which Australia had taken to protect British exports to Australia against Japanese competition. These

[7] i.e. the Kellogg Pact of 1928: see *B.F.S.P.*, vol. 128, pp. 447–9.

objections had now been overcome. It would no doubt take a long time to achieve the proposed Pact, but it would be helpful if the Conference could give the proposal encouragement and support.

MR. MACKENZIE KING enquired whether the signatories to the proposed pact would be the same as the signatories to the Kellogg Pact. It should be remembered that the United States had been responsible for the Kellogg Pact. There was some danger that in any new Pact it might eventually be found that responsibilities had been incurred by the Commonwealth Governments, which were not shared by the United States.

MR. LYONS said that he fully appreciated difficulties of this kind. At the same time Mr. Roosevelt had told him that if serious trouble arose in the Pacific the United States would be prepared to make common cause with the members of the Commonwealth concerned.

MR. MACKENZIE KING added that Mr. Roosevelt had spoken to him of his desire to see the fortification of the islands of the Pacific dismantled as a measure of furthering peace in the Pacific.

MR. EDEN said that there was of course a considerable difference between an expression of opinion by Mr. Roosevelt in private conversations and the entering into by him, as President of the United States, of undertakings and commitments in a formal document.

MR. CASEY[8] enquired whether Mr. Eden was ready to say anything about the Philippines. The grant of independence to the Islands would raise certain problems as regards the Pacific generally.

MR. EDEN said that he did not know whether the attitude of the United States would undergo modification before that time. His impression was that Mr. Roosevelt was thinking of the neutralisation of the Pacific as a means of safeguarding the Philippines during the transition period.

MR. CASEY enquired whether anything would be done as regards a guarantee of the independence of the Philippine Republic.

MR. EDEN said that he had no definite information, but he understood that the United States would like the other Pacific powers to have the same commitment towards the Islands as the United States had now. In any case, the grant of complete independence was still eight years off.

MR. CHAMBERLAIN asked whether Mr. Savage[9] wished to make any observations.

MR. SAVAGE said that he would like to thank Mr. Eden for his simple and frank exposition of the problems.

As regards a Pacific Pact, he did not yet know enough to express an opinion and he would like to have more information before doing so. He rather imagined that any such arrangement would necessarily have an economic foundation. He was prepared to go a very long way for peace, but he would not much like a Pact which necessitated New Zealand shifting her trade from the United Kingdom to Japan.

LORD ZETLAND said that India and Burma were vitally concerned in

[8] Mr. R. G. Casey, Australian Treasurer.   [9] New Zealand Prime Minister.

relations between the British Commonwealth and Japan. His chief apprehension in this connection at the present time was the penetration in Eastern waters of Japanese shipping and more particularly Japanese fishing fleets. The latter were scattered over all the coasts from the Persian Gulf to New Zealand, and comprised very efficient boats fitted with wireless which were undoubtedly carrying on intelligence work for the Japanese Admiralty.

The matter was under consideration in consultation with the Admiralty here, with a view to plans being devised for dealing with the situation.

MR. CHAMBERLAIN said that the suggestion made by Mr. Lyons appeared to be the most important matter arising out of the discussion. It seemed desirable, however, to work it out in greater detail before it was in a form on which the Conference could express an opinion. He felt that the best course would be for those present to turn the matter over in their minds during the forthcoming week and for the matter to be discussed between individuals.

Further discussion could take place at the meetings which would be held on Mr. Eden's return from Geneva[10] and a decision could then be reached whether there should be a resolution by the Conference on the subject.[11]

[10] Mr. Eden left London on May 23 to attend League of Nations meetings in Geneva. He returned on May 29.
[11] The rest of the discussion dealt with the Franco-Soviet Pact and German affairs, and has here been omitted.

No. 87

Sir R. Lindsay (Washington) to Foreign Office[1] (Received June 9)

No. 476 [F 3372/597/61]

Confidential   WASHINGTON, *May 28, 1937*

Sir,

With reference to your despatch No. 375[2] of the 3rd May relative to Mr. Norman Davis' suggestions for a possible neutralisation of the Pacific, I have the honour to submit the following observations on your question how far the United States Government would be ready to implement Mr. Davis' proposals for dismantling fortifications.

2. My information goes to show that the American military authorities consider the Philippine Islands a dangerous outpost to hold and, if political considerations could be eliminated, would on strategic grounds be glad to be rid of such a commitment. American naval opinion, on the other hand, is less likely to be enthusiastic about the demilitarisation of the naval base at Cavite, but realises that this base is not strong enough on its

[1] See No. 86, note 10.   [2] No. 76.

own and cannot be safely retained without the assistance of a military force provided by the United States Army. It is doubtful whether the naval authorities would be satisfied with the protection of General MacArthur's native militia.

3. From certain confidential information enclosed in a private letter[3] from Mr. Mallet[4] to Mr. Troutbeck[5] of March 12th last I understand that President Roosevelt is seriously considering advancing the date of complete Philippine independence to 1938 or 1939, but that he would like to retain a small naval base in the Philippines after independence has been granted and that President Quezon would be delighted if the United States would do this. Such a base in any case would probably be practically unfortified and mainly useful for submarines and aircraft. The above is probably Mr. Roosevelt's own personal view; he has always been particularly interested in naval matters since the time when he was Assistant Secretary of the Navy and he is in advance of public opinion and of the opinion of his advisers, which he surely realises. In order therefore to attain the wider objectives envisaged by Mr. Norman Davis I fancy that Mr. Roosevelt would readily abandon the idea of retaining such a base in the Islands.

4. When under the instructions contained in your telegram No. 283[6] of the 9th September, 1936 Mr. Mallet took up with the State Department the question of the renewal of Article 19 of the Washington Treaty with modifications which would have enabled His Majesty's Government to place their defences at Hong Kong on a proper footing, Mr. Mallet tells me that he had a feeling that the Department was being less sympathetic than usual in turning down the proposals made. It occurs to me that the real reason for the attitude of the United States Government at that time may well have been that they were pondering this very idea of neutralisation which Mr. Norman Davis has now propounded. Such an idea would involve the demilitarisation of Hong Kong and thus run absolutely counter to our proposals. It looks to me therefore as if the United States Government, realising that there is no interest here in the Philippines, have more or less decided to give President Quezon his independence as soon as he likes to have it and would welcome the chance of a clear cut to get right away from a potentially awkward commitment. Although they would not want any other nation to take their place in the Islands, they will, according to their present ideas, make the best of a bad job if such a thing were to happen. The triangle Formosa—Philippine Islands—Hong Kong represents three close and therefore dangerous points of contact between the three great Pacific Powers. Assuming that the United States will anyhow be clearing out of the Philippines, it would save the American face towards their former protégés in the Islands if this

[3] Not printed (A 2369/20/45).
[4] Mr. V. A. Mallet, Counsellor in H.M. Embassy at Washington.
[5] Mr. J. M. Troutbeck, Acting Head of the American Department of the Foreign Office.
[6] Volume XX, No. 551.

country could point to an agreement which had demilitarised the two neighbouring angles of the triangle. I am therefore inclined to answer your question by saying that I believe that the United States Government would go the whole way to dismantling their fortifications. They would then concentrate upon fortifying the main defence line of the Aleutian Islands—Hawaii—Panama Canal Zone, which should be quite sufficient to ward off any risk of attack upon the coasts of America.

5. If I may trespass a little beyond the immediate question, I would add that a neutralisation, or rather disarmament policy in the Pacific could not possibly hurt the United States strategically once they are rid of the Philippines commitment, even if the Japanese were to fail to keep their part of the bargain. Their influence for the protection of their commercial interests in China would of course diminish, but the average American voter would not worry about that. On the other hand, we might well be taking an unnecessary risk unless the United States were to join with us and the other Powers concerned not merely in a pact of non-aggression but in an actual pact of mutual guarantee. Now, as I have said above, public interest here in the Philippines is practically nil and beyond a feeling that Japan is a vague menace there are few people who think about or study the problems of the Pacific Ocean. It would therefore be extremely difficult for President Roosevelt to arouse Congress to a sufficient interest in the subject to approve of any commitment involving guarantees against an aggressor, at any rate until the European situation is less threatening and there is less appearance of Japan becoming involved in a world war as a satellite of Germany.[7]

I have, etc.,

R. C. LINDSAY

[7] Mr. Troutbeck commented on June 14: 'The U.S. Govt. seem to be playing—or at any rate contemplating—rather a low game. That they shd abandon the Philippines to their fate is of course their own affair—and in a way one feels some sympathy for them in that after all the Filipino cries for independence. But it is a very different thing when they ask us to dismantle Hong Kong in order to make their desertion easier.' Sir A. Cadogan wrote on June 16: 'The "Pacific Pact" idea will have something in its favour if it pushes the "neutralization" idea into the background.' Sir R. Vansittart agreed (June 16): 'If this is the American game we obviously cannot play it.'

On June 11 the Foreign Office received another definition of American Far Eastern policy in Mr. Cordell Hull's memorandum of June 1 (Volume XVIII, No. 560) replying to Mr. Chamberlain's message to Mr. Morgenthau of the previous March (*ibid.*, No. 297: see also No. 63, note 8 above). In his memorandum Mr. Hull recognized that in various matters in and with regard to the Far East the rights and obligations of the two countries were alike; he was not able to state in advance what measures of protection his country would employ in the event of a resort of any country to measures of aggression there. It was 'the traditional policy of this country not to enter into those types of agreement which constitute or which suggest alliance'. The Foreign Office described this reply as a 'masterpiece of negation' (*ibid.*, No. 560, note 6).

No. 88

Record by Sir R. Craigie of a conversation with Mr. Yoshida

[*F 3416/28/23*]

Confidential   FOREIGN OFFICE, *June 2, 1937*

The Japanese Ambassador called this morning to inform me unofficially of the present position of his discussions between himself and his Government on the subject of the proposed Anglo-Japanese negotiations. I enquired whether it would not be better for the Ambassador to see Sir Alexander Cadogan, but he said that at the moment he had no proposals to make and that there was a danger, should he call on Sir Alexander, of the press asserting prematurely that the discussions had been resumed. He therefore thought it best to defer his visit to Sir Alexander Cadogan until he had received his final instructions from Tokyo.

Mr. Yoshida then said that he had telegraphed to Tokyo his final draft of the proposed answer to His Majesty's Government on the day before he received the news of the fall of the Hayashi Cabinet.[1] He knew that his draft was in accordance with the views of Mr. Sato, and he believed that Mr. Sato would probably continue in the new Cabinet; but for the moment there was no Minister for Foreign Affairs and there might, therefore, be a delay in the Japanese reply. The Ambassador then handed to me his draft of the Japanese answer[2] and asked me to hand it to Sir Alexander Cadogan, who would, he hoped, give it his personal consideration, pending the receipt of the official document. By this means he hoped we might reduce the delay consequent upon the fall of the Hayashi Cabinet.

In reply to my enquiry as to whether the Japanese Government were likely to have any concrete suggestions to make for the settlement of our commercial difficulties, Mr. Yoshida said that he personally was in favour of pushing ahead with that part of the problem which related to Sino-Japanese relations, as he believed that this would prove easier of solution than the more complicated trade question, and that progress with the former question would ultimately facilitate the solution of the latter. As regards the Japanese Trade Mission, due next July, the Ambassador knew little in regard to its personnel and believed that it should be regarded primarily as a good-will mission.[3] There was, of course, every

---

[1] See No. 82, note 5. On June 1 Prince Konoye, President of the House of Peers, agreed to try to form a government. In telegram No. 178 of June 3 Mr. J. L. Dodds, Acting Counsellor in H.M. Embassy at Tokyo, reported that the former Premier and Foreign Minister, Mr. Koki Hirota, had been appointed Vice Premier and Minister for Foreign Affairs in Prince Konoye's cabinet. General Sugiyama retained his post as War Minister, and Admiral Yonai became Minister of Marine.

[2] See Annex to this document.

[3] A Japanese Economic Mission, headed by Mr. Chokyuro Kadono, Senior Director of the Japan Economic Federation, was to visit the United Kingdom in July, following visits to Germany and the United States. In telegram No. 141 of April 23 Sir R. Clive had reported

advantage in the industralists of the two sides 'getting together', but he would consider it unwise to take the mission too much into his confidence (meaning, I think, that he did not propose to inform the mission of the proposals for a settlement of the trade difficulty contained in the accompanying document). The Ambassador also mentioned that a Japanese-American Joint Trade Committee had recently been set up in Washington, with excellent results, and that it was for this reason that his Government were proposing the establishment of a similar committee in London to deal with the detailed application of any trade agreement that might be reached.

I promised to hand the draft memorandum to Sir Alexander Cadogan and to inform him of the Ambassador's observations.

R. L. C.

ANNEX TO No. 88

Memorandum by Mr. Yoshida

June 2, 1937

Recollecting the cordial relations which existed in the past between Japan and Great Britain, and considering the complicated situation which has arisen in China since the Washington Conference 1921–22, and realizing the inseparable connection between peace in the Far East and the general prosperity of the world, it is deemed of vital importance that the relations between Japan and Great Britain should be adjusted and placed on a more satisfactory footing.

The principal source of discord between Japan and Great Britain is commercial conflict, and though the commercial conflict between the two countries has developed all over the world, its main cause is to be found in China, where the anti-Japanese movement drove Japanese industry out of its natural market and forced it to find an outlet in other parts of the world. The boycott of Japanese goods in China was followed by the general trade depression all over the world, and these two factors working together have brought about the present world-wide conflict between Japanese and British commercial interests. It is, therefore, felt that, if co-operation between Japan and Great Britain can bring about the maintenance of order and increase of prosperity in China, not only will trade competition between Japan and Great Britain be everywhere alleviated, but also the prospect of a general trade recovery will appear from the direction of the Far East.

The chief questions which require frank discussion between the British and Japanese Governments may be summarized under three heads as follows:

that according to Mr. Kadono the Mission would not take any initiatives, but hoped to 'clear the ground' for future discussions on trade and the textile industry.

(1) Co-operation between Japan and Great Britain with a view to China's reconstruction as a solid factor in world trade.

With regard to this, it is deemed essential:

(a) That Japan and Great Britain should mutually reiterate their policy of respecting the sovereignty of China and should co-operate for the maintenance of order and the promotion of prosperity in China;

(b) That the Japanese and British Governments should continue as occasion may demand to exchange their frank views on any development, political or economic, which may arise in connection with China.

(2) The question of Anglo-Japanese trade competition.

Recent negotiations with various Dominions have resulted in the conclusion of trade agreements, but the Japanese Government feel that the ground might be explored for a more lasting solution. To this end, it is deemed necessary that the present position of Japanese and British commercial requirements in world trade should be studied jointly, and measures to arrive at a satisfactory solution might be discussed on the following lines:

(a) The British Government might give their consideration to the existing barriers or discrimination against Japanese goods in the British Dominions and Colonies and render any assistance possible in obtaining a basic equality of treatment as each opportunity arises.

(b) With regard to the importation of Japanese goods into the United Kingdom, the Japanese Government propose the establishment of an Anglo-Japanese Joint Trade Committee in London.

(c) With regard to Anglo-Japanese trade conflict in other world markets, the Japanese Government are most anxious to find a mutually satisfactory solution and would welcome a proposal from the British Government.

(3) Closer financial contact between Japan and Great Britain.

With a view to cementing the friendly relations between the two countries and to promoting the long established connection between the Japanese and British financial markets, it is considered desirable that views should be exchanged between the Japanese Financial Commissioner in London and the British Treasury on the financial policies of the two countries and on any other financial questions that may arise.

The Japanese Government take this opportunity to enquire whether financial assistance could be rendered by the British Government in either of the following methods:

(a) Provided that the market prices of Japanese loans permit, the possibility of securing another loan to Japan could be considered, or

(b) Arrangements could be made, through the machinery of the Exports Credits Guarantee Department for the purchase of British goods on long term credits.

Explanatory remarks on questions relating to China

1. The Japanese Government categorically affirm that they have no intention either to sever North China from the Nanking Government or to exclude foreign interests from that region.

The Japanese Government, however, feel fully justified in pointing out that, owing to the territorial contiguity of North China to Manchoukuo, they cannot remain indifferent to any disorder in North China or to any action on the part of the local authorities which is inimical to Japan and Manchoukuo. The Japanese Government realize that the present situation in North China is the direct outcome of the fact that the status of Manchoukuo has not yet been agreed upon by China. It is felt, however, that the existing situation in North China might be relieved if the British Government could advise the Nanking Government to refrain from any action inimical to Japanese interests in North China and the peaceful development of Manchoukuo.

2. The Japanese Government are anxious to negotiate with China upon all outstanding questions and to establish the relations of the two countries upon an assured foundation.

The Japanese Government are fully prepared to lay before the British Government a frank exposé of their aspirations with regard to the relations between Japan and China. The Japanese Government expect to return the assistance and support of the British Government by friendly counsel to the Chinese Government should occasion arise.

3. With a view to eliminating individual competition in investment in China, it is suggested that the Japanese and British Governments should consult with each other whenever financial aid to China in any form is contemplated by either party.

4. The Japanese Government will support in its entirety the existing organization of the Chinese Maritime Customs.

The Japanese Government realize that as any reconstruction of China must involve financial assistance, it is important that the Chinese customs organization should be strengthened. The Japanese Government expect that the British Government will co-operate with the Japanese Government in ensuring that Japanese representation in the Chinese Customs Service will be maintained in accordance with the fundamental principles governing foreign representation in that Service.

5. The Japanese Government also suggest that the British Government should co-operate with the Japanese Government to secure a modification of the existing Customs tariff, which is regarded as an impediment to trade.

6. The Japanese Government affirm their desire for the establishment of a peaceful and prosperous China and welcome the opportunity to discuss any proposals which the British Government may have already considered desirable to effect this purpose.

With a view to promoting the mutual interests of both countries, the

Japanese Government undertake to respect in toto all British rights and interests in China and affirm that they have no intention whatever of obstructing British economic development. It is hoped that Great Britain on her part will assist Japan in obtaining the complete cessation of the anti-Japanese boycott or of any other movement which interferes with Japanese interests.[4]

4. Preliminary examination of Mr. Yoshida's memorandum in the Foreign Office resulted in a number of objections being noted. In a minute of June 4 Sir A. Cadogan commented with regard to paragraph 3 that there 'must be nothing in any agreement about cooperation for the *maintenance of order* in China'; similarly '(1)(b) might look like combined interference in Chinese affairs'. He also noted that 'if the situation as regards Manchukuo remains unchanged, we could, of course, say nothing in any agreement about "Manchukuo"'. On the other hand we, like the Japanese, think the Chinese tariff too high'. On June 8 Mr. Orde made some further points, and remarked that 'we can probably do extremely little to influence Dominion policy towards Japanese imports'.

Sir A. Cadogan discussed the memorandum with Mr. Yoshida on June 11 and drew his attention to these points, stressing also that 'we should have to be very careful that nothing emerged from our negotiations which could be construed as in any way being directed against third parties'. Mr. Yoshida said that his memorandum was only a rough draft, and that he was awaiting further instructions from Tokyo.

No. 89

Mr. Dodds (Tokyo) to Mr. Eden (Received June 7, 2 p.m.)

No. 181 Telegraphic [F 3308/28/23]

TOKYO, *June 7, 1937, 7.10 p.m.*

At a reception for Heads of Missions this afternoon Minister of Foreign Affairs[1] informed me that an understanding with United Kingdom was the most important work which new Japanese Government had to perform. This had been his ambition when he was Minister for Foreign Affairs in 1935 but when he became Prime Minister he had not enough time to devote to it. He believed it was possible and hoped to put it through within the next two or three months and before Prince Chichibu left England to return to Japan. He had accordingly told officials of the Ministry of Foreign Affairs to speed up final instructions to Japanese Ambassador in London. Such an understanding was essential to the peace of the world or at all events the Far East. He did not know why Anglo-Japanese alliance had been abrogated but 'look at the result ever since'.[2]

Repeated to Peking Saving and Nanking.

[1] Mr. Hirota: see No. 88, note 1.
[2] Mr. Eden read out this telegram at the fifteenth meeting of principal delegates to the Imperial Conference on June 8. He also read out his record of a conversation with Mr. Yoshida on Mr. Lyons' proposal for a Pacific pact: see No. 91 below. He commented that the two documents 'confirmed our previous information that Japan was anxious for some relaxation of the present tension in the Pacific', but noted that 'the two messages did not

entirely coincide': Mr. Hirota's statement, however, 'must of course be taken as the more authoritative'.

No. 90

Sir H. Knatchbull-Hugessen (Peking) to Mr. Eden
(Received June 7, 10 p.m.)

No. 218 Telegraphic: by wireless [F 3330/2595/10]

Very Secret   PEKING, June 7, 1937

Following from Nanking No. 205 of June 4th.

1. Following for His Majesty's Ambassador from Military Attaché:
Reference telegram No. 133[1] to the Foreign Office. Paragraph 2; exchange of military intelligence *and* staff officers. Suggest this should read '*between* staff officers'.[2]

2. This has evidently been passed on to Chinese General Staff. Head of intelligence section has asked me unofficially whether it would be possible to exchange military intelligence. He added *in strict confidence* that Chinese military were considering despatching specially selected officer to Singapore with the intention of watching Japanese activities. He emphasised that this action was not directed against us. He asked whether I could give letters of introduction to selected officers and suggested exchange of information at Singapore.

3. In my case I see no objection to a liaison with military authorities at Nanking but I see difficulties in the way of Chinese starting a private enquiry agency at Singapore with our official knowledge.[3] Should the Home Government agree to the plan for exchange of military intelligence between staff officers in China *and Singapore* that would be a different matter but up to the present the Government have not replied to Chiang Kai-shek's proposal to this effect. There is also possibility that suggestion has a political motive[4] and is another line of approach for an entente aimed at the Japanese. Suggest that Foreign Office be informed of above and asked for a ruling.[5]

---

[1] No. 77.   [2] It was later established that 'and' was in fact correct.
[3] Mr. Eden wrote in the margin at this point: 'Yes indeed.'
[4] The preceding ten words were underlined by Mr. Eden with the marginal comment: 'Yes, we must be careful.'
[5] In a further telegram No. 219, also received at 10 p.m. on June 7, Sir H. Knatchbull-Hugessen commented that he agreed with the Military Attaché's views in para. 3 of telegram No. 218 but wished for a ruling. On June 12 copies of the two telegrams were sent to the War Office, Admiralty, Air Ministry, and Colonial Office, with a covering letter asking their views on the exchange of information and on the suggestion that a Chinese officer should be stationed at Singapore.

No. 91

Mr. Eden to Mr. Dodds (Tokyo)

No. 285 [F 3346/597/61]

FOREIGN OFFICE, *June 7, 1937*

Sir,

The Japanese Ambassador asked to see me today when he said that he wished to put certain questions to me which might seem somewhat indiscreet at this stage, on the subject of the projected Pacific Pact to which Mr. Lyons had referred in his opening speech at the Imperial Conference.[1] Had we as yet any definite proposals in mind?

2. I replied that we had not. So far matters had not proceeded further than an informal exchange of views on the proposal.[2] If and when we were in a position to put forward anything more definite we would of course make preliminary soundings among other Governments, when I would ask His Excellency to speak to me again on the subject. In response to a question the Ambassador then gave me what he described as his own personal impressions of his Government's attitude to a non-aggression pact for the Pacific. He said that he thought that they would have no objection in principle to such a pact, but that they might regard its negotiation as a little premature at this time. The first necessity in his judgment was to seek to improve relations with other Powers in the Pacific and more especially with His Majesty's Government in the United Kingdom. From such improvement a Pacific Pact would flow naturally. The Ambassador also showed a certain apprehension lest the new Pact should be similar in form to the Nine-Power Treaty, and I had the impression that this would not be welcome to Japan.

3. M. Yoshida also asked me whether I had any information as to the attitude of the United States to a Non-Aggression Pact in the Pacific. Mr. Davis when he had been here had spoken to M. Yoshida on the subject[3] and had appeared to consider that the correct way to proceed was through bilateral arrangements which could gradually be extended to include an ever larger number of Powers. He wondered therefore whether it was our intention to widen the basis of an Anglo-American trade agreement which might be reached in order that that might include Japan. I replied that we were acutely conscious of the significance of economic matters and their relation to any political agreement, but that we had as yet much work to do before anything in the nature of an Anglo-American trade agreement was in sight. In the circumstances any question of extending it must inevitably be remote. There was no reason, however, why trade and economic matters which affected Japan and ourselves should not be discussed *pari passu* with any discussion of political problems. I had the impression that the Ambassador's main object in raising this question at the present time

[1] See No. 82, note 2.   [2] Cf. No. 86.   [3] Cf. *F.R.U.S.*, 1937, vol. iii, pp. 74–6.

was to ensure that the Japanese Government might not suddenly be presented with a fully drafted Pacific pact and asked to sign it. I therefore gave His Excellency the assurance that no such procedure was in contemplation.

4. Finally the Ambassador remarked that he had some little time ago received from the Japanese Government certain proposals for the betterment of Anglo-Japanese relations. He had wished to make certain changes in the texts and had submitted his amendments to Tokio. These were now being considered by the new Government and he hoped to receive a reply in the near future.[4]

I am, etc.,
ANTHONY EDEN

[4] Mr. Yoshida continued during the next few weeks to refer hopefully to arrangements for the improvement of Anglo-Japanese relations. No progress had been made however before July 8, when the Lukouchiao incident brought talk of an Anglo-Japanese agreement to a standstill (see No. 105 below).

No. 92

Mr. Eden to Mr. Dodds (Tokyo)

No. 138 Telegraphic [F 3488/4/10]

Very Confidential   FOREIGN OFFICE, *June 19, 1937, 6.30 p.m.*

Following is text referred to in my immediately preceding telegram.[1] Begins.

1. The Chinese Minister of Finance, Dr. Kung, during his recent visit to England, raised the question of the issue in London of a Currency Loan for China.[2] Discussions in regard to this proposal are still in an early stage, but His Majesty's Government of the United Kingdom desire to inform the French Government confidentially of their course as they are anxious

[1] In telegram No. 137, also despatched at 6.30 p.m. on June 19, Mr. Dodds was informed that telegram No. 138 contained the text of a memorandum handed to the French Ambassador that morning. Similar memoranda were handed to the American and Japanese Ambassadors on June 21.

[2] Sir L. Beale had reported in his telegram No. 24 to the Department of Overseas Trade on April 2 that Dr. Kung proposed to seek a large loan during his visit to England as a member of the delegation to the Coronation, and this information was confirmed in subsequent reports from Sir H. Knatchbull-Hugessen, who also said that Chiang Kai-shek had given personal instructions to Dr Kung: cf. No. 77. A currency loan scheme was discussed on May 5 and 11 by Dr. Kung and Sir F. Leith-Ross, who approved the idea in principle. As Mr. J. Chaplin, a Third Secretary in the Far Eastern Department, pointed out in a memorandum of July 8 reviewing the whole question of a loan, the idea had 'been in Sir Leith-Ross' mind for two years': cf. Volume XX, Chapters V and VI; the present scheme 'was not entirely woven in Dr. Kung's brain'. The Foreign Office were more critical of the scheme, and the present telegram represents the culmination of copious minuting on the subject.

that in matters of this kind there should be close consultation between the Governments principally concerned.

2. His Majesty's Government are disposed to view Dr. Kung's proposal with favour, provided that it forms part of a well-considered programme for maintaining the stability of the Chinese currency and for the execution of a sound financial policy on the part of the Chinese Government. They feel that the carrying out of such a programme is essential in the interests of China and is to the advantage of all countries which trade with China and intend to co-operate in her economic development.

3. In particular, His Majesty's Government attach importance to the establishment in China of an independent and non-political Central Reserve Bank. The principles for the setting up of a Central Reserve Bank have already been adopted by the Chinese Government and it is satisfactory to note that Dr. Kung has stated his intention of putting these principles into practical effect without delay. In discussing the question of a Currency Loan, it was made clear to Dr. Kung that His Majesty's Government regard it as very important that satisfactory legislation for a Central Reserve Bank should be put into force as soon as possible and that it would be essential that this step should have been taken before the issue of any Currency Loan.

4. The programme envisaged would, of course, include provisions as to the disposal of the proceeds of a Currency Loan. The sterling proceeds would be sold by the Chinese Government to the Central Reserve Bank and would be used by the Bank solely for foreign exchange transactions in order to maintain the stability of the Chinese currency. It would clearly not be desirable that the Chinese dollars thus received by the Chinese Government from the Central Reserve Bank should be available for current budget expenditure, and the programme would provide that these dollars should be used by the Chinese Government gradually over a period for the redemption of existing domestic bonds, which would have the effect of improving the credit of the Chinese Government in their own internal market. It would also be part of the programme that the Chinese Government should pursue a policy of balanced budgets.

5. Provided that a Currency Loan formed part of a well considered programme on these lines, His Majesty's Government felt that they could themselves view it with favour and could hope that the proposal would be viewed sympathetically by the French Government and the other Governments concerned. But it was made clear to Dr. Kung that His Majesty's Government could not express any opinion as to whether, and on what terms, a Loan could be successfully issued in the London market and that this must depend on negotiations with the financial institutions concerned.

6. Dr. Kung proposed that the Loan should be secured on the Maritime Customs Revenue, in which connexion His Majesty's Government stated that they would expect an assurance that the existing system of the Maritime Customs would be continued. They here emphasised the

importance of the resumption of the recruitment of foreign personnel.

7. The discussions with the financial institutions concerned are still at an early stage, and it is not yet clear whether the Chinese Government will be in a position to offer security which the market would regard as adequate, even for a comparatively small Currency Loan of say not more than £10 millions to £20 millions. (If the total were more than £10 millions, only £10 millions would be issued in the first instance). Discussions on this point are understood to be continuing.

8. Should these discussions be successfully concluded, it is understood to be the desire of Dr. Kung to issue a Currency Loan in the Autumn. In this connexion the question of the Consortium has, of course, to be taken into account.[3] His Majesty's Government trust that they will shortly receive from the French and Japanese Governments, as they have already received from the United States Government,[4] an intimation that they agree to negotiations between the Groups for the dissolution of the existing Consortium by mutual consent. In that event, it may be expected that the Consortium will have been dissolved before the Autumn and no question of a formal decision by the Groups will be involved; but it would, of course, continue to be the policy of His Majesty's Government to keep in close touch on the matter with the other three interested Governments. In the alternative event of the Consortium not having been dissolved by the Autumn, His Majesty's Government trust that the French Government would find no difficulty in using their influence with the French group to secure the consent to the issue in London of a Currency Loan as part of a well considered programme on the lines described above.

Repeated to Peking No. 197, to Nanking No. 108, to Embassy Offices, Shanghai No. 93, to Washington No. 15 (Saving), and to Paris No. 100 (Saving).

[3] Cf. No. 59.   [4] See No. 73.

No. 93

Letter from Mr. A. E. Widdows[1] (War Office) to Foreign Office (Received June 21)

[F 3567/2595/10]

Confidential   WAR OFFICE, *June 21, 1937*

Sir,

I am commanded by the Army Council to acknowledge the receipt of your letter No. F.3330/2595/10 dated 12th June, 1937, transmitting copies of two telegrams from His Majesty's Ambassador in China on the subject of certain proposals for Sino-British military co-operation.[2]

[1] An Assistant Under Secretary of State in the War Office.   [2] See No. 90.

2. In reply I am to say that no such interchange of military intelligence as has been suggested is in force with any foreign Power and there is, in the Council's opinion, no sufficient military advantage to be gained by establishing a precedent in favour of the Chinese Government.

3. The Council further considers that the political object which has prompted the present proposals could only be attained by the publication of any agreement which might be concluded between His Majesty's Government and the Chinese Government. Such an announcement, in the Council's opinion, could not fail to produce the most unfavourable reactions in the Japanese Army and, consequently, in the Japanese Government.

4. In view of these considerations, the Council cannot agree to the proposal for an official interchange of military intelligence. For similar reasons, the proposal that a Chinese officer should be officially stationed at Singapore cannot be entertained.

5. I am further to say that, in the opinion of the Council, the mere existence of such proposals constitutes a potential danger to the establishment of friendly relations between Great Britain and Japan; it therefore seems desirable that an early opportunity should be taken to define the extent of possible British military assistance to China, and inform the Chinese Government accordingly.

6. The Council suggest, for the consideration of Mr. Secretary Eden, that this assistance should be limited to such purely military facilities as are available to any other nation which may request them of His Majesty's Government. As applied to China these facilities might include the training of Chinese military students in England, the provision of instructors and/or advisers to the Chinese Army, and the supply on normal terms of such material as may be available to meet China's legitimate defensive requirements.[3]

7. A copy of this letter is being sent to the Admiralty, Air Ministry and Colonial Office.

I am, etc.,

A. E. WIDDOWS

[3] Mr. Thyne Henderson noted on June 22: 'This is what we expected.' Similar replies were received from the Colonial Office, Admiralty, and Air Ministry. For the reply to Sir H. Knatchbull-Hugessen see No. 115 below.

No. 94

Mr. Dodds (Tokyo) to Mr. Eden (Received June 23, 9.30 a.m.)

No. 191 Telegraphic [F 3602/4/10]

TOKYO, *June 23, 1937, 12.38 p.m.*

Your telegrams Nos. 137 and 138.[1]
Following for Treasury from Financial Adviser. Begins:
Explanations given to Vice Minister of Finance June 21st. He expressed appreciation as real situation could be explained at meeting of the Cabinet on June 22nd and erroroneous [*sic*] impression created by press reports from Shanghai removed.

2. In agreement with Vice Minister I saw Tsushima[2] June 22nd to give similar explanations. He asked if British Adviser to Central Reserve Bank would be a condition of loan. As no mention was made of this in telegram No. 138 I replied that I had no instructions on this point but to ensure success of Central Reserve Bank it seemed desirable to have expert advice and that Chinese Government appreciated this. Tsushima asked if none of the present American advisers had Central Banking experience and I replied in the negative.

3. Tsushima suggested that I remain here till the Cabinet had had time to consider forms of formal notification. He would keep me advised of developments as far as possible. He added that he felt that Japanese Government would wish to know if Bank Adviser was to be a condition of loan and if so his nationality.

4. He asked if there was to be any American participation. I replied that I thought this improbable.

Repeated to Peking for repetition to Nanking, Shanghai (Shanghai please paraphrase to Rogers).

[1] See No. 92, and *ibid.*, note 1. [2] Vice President of the Bank of Japan.

No. 95

Mr. Dodds (Tokyo) to Mr. Eden (Received June 26, 4.15 p.m.)

No. 194 Telegraphic [F 3664/233/23]

TOKYO, *June 26, 1937, 4.28 p.m.*

I read present situation here as follows.
Prince Konoye is proceeding with great caution and certainly with more political astuteness than either of the two previous Prime Ministers. He is (? pupil of) Prince Saionji who has nursed him politically and is said to have advised him to refuse the premiership at the time of the February

revolt last year[1] on the ground that the situation then demanded a rough and ready politician of the type of Hirota and that Konoye should not take the helm until the situation had eased, namely until the military had had time to calm down. The fact that he has now done so suggests therefore that the military are now beginning to see reason and this proposition is borne out by his enunciation of three principles on which his policy is to be based, viz: expansion of production, equilibrium of international payments, and Government control of imports and exports. So far as these are reconcilable with policy of. . .[2] normal commercial imports will be severely restricted in favour of imports for armaments and allied industries. To this extent the realities of the situation are being brought home to the military. A sign of common sense (? is) appointment of two parliamentary secretaries both from Lower House to each Government department. They will not count much in practice but the fact of their appointment is an indication of Prime Minister's ability to smoothe over friction between the military and political parties. He is by birth of a family which has been anti-militarist for centuries and whose tradition it has been to defend Imperial privileges against feudal, i.e. military aspirations. He is therefore regarded in certain, e.g. financial, circles as a kind of white hope who may guide the country into safer waters.

On the other hand he is I understand quite capable of throwing in his hand if bored or disgusted: in fact a Japanese Rosebery.

Japanese Ambassador to China has returned there after two months' leave here and is apparently to be. . .[2] This is also not a bad sign and supports the belief which is growing here that Japanese policy in China is to be one of no demands and no concessions. This again suggests that military are putting some water in their wine.

If the above diagnosis is correct and I do not pretend that it is more than a possible one (and moreover one made before Government can be said to have got into its stride), deductions are that both China and ourselves would be well advised for the present to go very slowly in any negotiations with Japan.

Time is on our side, for the longer we can wait the more must reason and economic facts prevail here. But reason will not prevail if military are not allowed to calm down but are agitated by Chinese pretensions or European unrest.[3]

Repeated to Peking and Nanking Saving.

[1] See Volume XX, No. 467.   [2] The text was here uncertain.
[3] Foreign Office officials were not optimistic about the new Japanese Government. Mr. Orde commented on June 29: 'I am afraid that the policy of "standing pat" in China is a backward step from the position of the late Govt. of which we knew, as it happens, more than Mr. Dodds, and can only mean deadlock.' Sir A. Cadogan agreed (June 29): 'I'm afraid I don't see much prospect of any very positive improvement in Sino-Japanese relations.'

No. 96

Sir H. Knatchbull-Hugessen (Peking) to Mr. Eden
(Received June 29, 8.40 p.m.)

No. 258 Telegraphic: by wireless [F 3700/5/10]

PEKING, *June 29, 1937*

You will have seen reports of statements made by Kawagoe to press in Tokyo on June 24th on the eve of his return to China.[1] He is reported to have dwelt on importance (presumably for China) of recognising the inevitability of the relations between Manchukuo and North China, to have emphasized the impossibility of cancelling the Tangku truce[2] and Ho-Umetsu agreement,[3] and to have said that he would continue to negotiate with local administrations on local issues.

2. Chinese press is bitterly disappointed at this indication that Japanese policy towards China remains unchanged and that hoped for liberalisation is not to take place.

3. Your statement in the House on June 25th[4] has been well received and has had a reassuring effect.[5]

Repeated Saving to Tokyo, Embassy Nanking, Commander-in-Chief, General Officer Commanding.

---

[1] Cf. No. 95.
[2] Of May 1933: see Volume XI, Nos. 590–2.
[3] See No. 39.
[4] See 325 *H.C. Deb. 5 s.*, cols. 1601–2.
[5] Mr. Thyne Henderson commented on June 30: 'It would not be surprising if Mr. Kawagoe roared loudly in Tokyo for the benefit of the Army and that his real intentions are less intransigent than his words. . .' Sir J. Pratt, however, (June 30) was inclined 'to think that the liberal policy has in fact received a check', and Mr. Orde agreed (July 1).

CHAPTER II

The Lukouchiao Incident and after

July 8—August 25, 1937

No. 97

*Sir H. Knatchbull-Hugessen (Peking) to Mr. Eden
(Received July 8, 8 p.m.)*

No. 280 Telegraphic: by wireless [F 3888/9/10]

PEKING, *July 8, 1937*

Japanese troops who were holding manoeuvres near Lukouchiao west of Peking, came into conflict with a battalion of the 29th Army garrisoning that town, early this morning. There was considerable firing audible in Peking. Each side charges the other with provocation. Reliable details not yet available.

2. Japanese have indicated the desire to treat matter as a 'local incident' but Hsiang Hsiao-hao (Secretary of Hopei Chahar Council) has expressed the view that Japanese deliberately staged the incident as an excuse to evict the Chinese troops from Lukouchiao in view of its strategic importance in the same way that they evicted them from Fengtai last year.[1]

Repeated to Peitaiho, Nanking, Commander-in-Chief, General Officer Commanding and Tientsin.

[1] See Volume XX, No. 559, note 6.

No. 98

Mr. Cowan (Peking) to Mr. Eden (Received July 8, 8 p.m.)

No. 281 Telegraphic: by wireless [F 3898/9/10]

PEKING, *July 8, 1937*

My telegram No. 280.[1]
Shima, secretary in charge of Japanese Embassy here, called this

[1] No. 97.

evening to explain the position. He said that Japanese were insisting that Chinese troops (who number only about 100) in Luko[u]chiao should evacuate the city and had proposed that Chinese should cross the river which flows past the town while the Japanese should remain on the opposite bank pending negotiations. Chinese had refused. Japanese reinforcements were coming from Tientsin. If the Chinese did not evacuate peaceably forcible measures would have to be used and if Chinese brought up reinforcements (of which there was no sign at present) a very serious situation would arise. He said that there had been a number of casualties but could give me no idea as to numbers.

2. He added that part of the Embassy guard which was at Tungchow when the incident began had been called in but on arrival at Peking had been refused entrance. It had, he thought, gone on to Luko[u]chiao. City gates are closed and railway communication is interrupted. Shima enquired our attitude to this interruption in view of Boxer protocol.[2] I replied that I did not consider a temporary interruption would call for diplomatic action.

3. Chinese troops involved include those of 37th division, commanded by Feng Chih-an, chairman of Hopei Provincial Government. Shima told me that Feng has refused to deal with Japanese who are referred to the Chairman of Foreign Affairs Commission of Hopei Chahar Council.

4. Hsiung Hsiao-hao has just telephoned to me to say that Chinese had not submitted and did not intend to submit to Japanese demands. So the situation is full of dangerous possibilities.[3]

Repeated to Nanking, Commander-in-Chief, General Officer Commanding, Tientsin, His Majesty's Ambassador at Peitaiho.

[2] Concluded in September 1901 after the Boxer uprising.
[3] Minutes on this telegram showed that the Foreign Office shared this view. Mr. Ronald wrote on July 9: 'It looks very much as though the Japanese, desiring to control an important bridgehead, had had recourse to their own peculiar methods to achieve their purpose.'

No. 99

Note[1] by Sir J. Pratt on the Lukouchiao incident

[F 4078/9/10]

FOREIGN OFFICE, *July 10, 1937*

The following points should be noted. (1) This clash has nothing to do with the demilitarised zone which was set up by the Tangku truce[2] early in 1933 after the fighting consequent on the Japanese seizure of Jehol and in

[1] This note was drafted in preparation for a reply to parliamentary questions on July 12: see 326 *H.C. Deb.* 5 s., cols. 848–50.
[2] See Volume XI, Nos. 590–2.

which the East Hopei autonomous government is now established. Lukouchiao is outside this area.

(2) In July 1935 a mysterious agreement was made between a Chinese general and a Japanese general, the terms of which have never been officially acknowledged[3] on either side. It is believed however that under this agreement, known as the Ho-Umetsu Agreement, the Japanese military claim that *no* Chinese troops but only militia may be stationed in the Province of Hopei. This may be at the bottom of the present clash, but it seems best not to say anything about it until we have more definite information.

(3) Numbers of troops: the number of Japanese troops in North China is estimated to amount to about 7,000. The total of all other foreign troops stationed in North China under the terms of the Boxer Protocol is 4,489 made up as follows:

	G.B.	U.S.A.	France	Italy
Tientsin	390	528	232	99
Peking	278	743	1350	279
Shanhaikwan	340		218	32
	1008	1271	1800	410

(4) The papers this morning (Saturday) report that, in accordance with an agreement reached with the Japanese military authorities, the Chinese troops have withdrawn and their places have been taken by militia. Japanese troops except those garrisoning the railway station have also withdrawn.

[3] A marginal note by Mr. Orde here read: 'I am not sure. I have seen it stated that the Chinese recognise this as well as the Tangku truce agreement. But its terms are not known to us.' See, however, No. 39.

No. 100

Mr. Eden to Sir R. Lindsay (Washington)

No. 224 Telegraphic [*F 4084/9/10*]

Important   FOREIGN OFFICE, *July 12, 1937, 4.30 p.m.*

I have informed U.S. Ambassador that I am anxious that our two Governments should keep in close touch on the situation in North China.

Our present information is insufficient to enable us to form a judgment on the responsibilities for the outbreak or an estimate of probable developments. I told His Excellency however in confidence that I had decided to give the Japanese Ambassador this afternoon[1] a friendly warning to the effect that so long as the present situation lasted it might

[1] See No. 105 below.

not be opportune to open the Anglo-Japanese conversations to which we have been looking forward.[2]

I said I should be very glad to be informed of the views of the U.S. Government and in particular to know whether they contemplated any move or would like to suggest any joint *démarche*. His Excellency promised to communicate at once with his Government.[3]

Repeated to Tokyo No. 156 and Nanking No. 120.

[2] Cf. No. 88.
[3] On the afternoon of July 13 Mr. Bingham called on Sir A. Cadogan to deliver his government's message that the State Department had issued a statement to the effect that both the Japanese Ambassador and the Counsellor to the Chinese Embassy in Washington had been warned that 'an armed conflict between Japan and China would be a great blow to the cause of peace and world progress'. The U.S. Government did not have any further action in mind at the moment, but would welcome 'continuous and frank exchange of information' with the British Government. See *F.R.U.S.*, 1937, vol. iii, pp. 147–8 and 154–5.

No. 101

Sir H. Knatchbull-Hugessen (Peking) to Mr. Eden
(Received July 12, 1 p.m.)

No. 297 Telegraphic [F 4016/9/10]

PEKING, *July 12, 1937, 7.15 p.m.*

My telegram No. 296.[1]

Japanese Embassy informed me that document was signed yesterday evening by the Mayor of Tientsin and Staff Officer of 29th Army to the following effect:

(1) 29th Army agree not to re-occupy Wanping.

(2) They apologise for the incident and undertake to punish those responsible for it.

(3) They promise to take all steps to control anti-Japanese activities.

2. Document was not signed by Japanese side and press report regarding *mutual* apologies incorrect.

3. Fuller report will be sent by wireless tonight.[2]

Repeated to His Majesty's Ambassador etc.

[1] Not kept in F.O. archives. It evidently referred to the Lukouchiao incident (see Nos. 97 and 98).
[2] See No. 103 below.

No. 102

Mr. Dodds (Tokyo) to Mr. Eden (Received July 12, 4.30 p.m.)

No. 213 Telegraphic [F 4034/9/10]

TOKYO, *July 12, 1937, 8.40 p.m.*

My immediately preceding telegram.[1]

Soviet Chargé d'Affaires tells me that he has little doubt that Japanese military authorities are gambling on preoccupation of Europe with its own affairs on . . .[2] and they undoubtedly believe Soviet régime has suffered by the execution of Soviet Generals[3] and on the successful manipulation of the Diet by the Prime Minister to stage an adventure in North China which shall deliver it finally into their hands. He appears to be convinced that Japanese deliberately started this latest incident and that the situation depends entirely on whether Chiang Kai-shek calls their bluff. He agreed however that a military adventure on the scale necessary would completely upset the present delicately balanced Japanese financial structure. I told him I believed Japanese Government were genuinely seeking an understanding with ourselves and that an adventure of the kind he described would postpone it indefinitely. He was not convinced by this argument.

Repeated to Nanking for repetition to Peking.

[1] Not kept in F.O. archives.   [2] The text was here uncertain.
[3] See Volume XVIII, Nos. 599 and 602.

No. 103

Sir H. Knatchbull-Hugessen (Peking) to Mr. Eden (Received July 12, 9.10 p.m.)

No. 298 Telegraphic: by wireless [F 4038/9/10]

PEKING, *July 12, 1937*

My telegram No. 297.[1]

Chinese Counsellor[2] called on Shima this morning to enquire which of the conflicting reports regarding the fighting, conclusion of agreement and present demands was correct. Following is substance of Shima's replies:

A. Agreement in principle had been reached between Chinese and Japanese Military Authorities yesterday afternoon and a document was signed by Chang Tzu-chung (Mayor of Tientsin) and Chief of Staff of 29th Army at 7 p.m. For the terms of this document see my telegram under reference. Document was not signed by Japanese side. There was no question of *mutual* apologies as mentioned in the press since Japanese

[1] No. 101.   [2] Mr. A. D. Blackburn.

152

did not admit they had anything to apologise for. Document did not mention that the Chinese were to take anti-communist measures but this was really implied in the undertaking contained in the third clause.

B. Japanese regarded the obligation of the 29th Army not to re-occupy Wanping as 'semi-permanent'.

C. All Japanese troops had now been withdrawn except 200 still posted North-East of Wanping to 'watch' Chinese movements. He could not say how long they would remain there. Embassy guard returned to Peking this morning.

D. With regard to firing which took place at 11 p.m. last night and again between 2 a.m. and 3 a.m. today he said no Japanese were involved. Chinese troops on the West of the river had mistaken gendarmerie moving on East of river for Japanese.

2. Situation is still quiet. Railway line is open but trains are running spasmodically being stopped or diverted apparently at the whim of Japanese at Fengtai.

Repeated to Peitaiho, Tokyo, Nanking, Commander-in-Chief, General-Officer-Commanding, Tientsin.

No. 104

Mr. Cowan (Peking) to Mr. Eden (Received July 12, 9.10 p.m.)

No. 300 Telegraphic: by wireless [F 4059/9/10]

PEKING, *July 12, 1937*

My telegram No. 298.[1]

Reuter reports from Tokyo that . . .[2] 'is taking all necessary steps to despatch military forces to North China though there is still hope of amicable solution of Lukouchiao affair'.

It is possible that Japanese may regard the affair as having been amicably settled by 'agreement' reported in my telegram No. 297[3] but Chinese Government may take different view. Essential fact which Central Government cannot ignore is that Chinese forces are excluded from Wanping by Japanese pressure. Japanese allege that several divisions of Central Government forces are on the move creeping northward along Peking-Hankow line. This is partly confirmed by statement by Donald to Mr. Gage[4] in Kuling yesterday that Central Government had sent two divisions to the north. If these movements continue Japanese are certain to take counter measures, so all elements of serious trouble on a large scale are present. It looks as if Japanese may have decided that the moment has come to teach Chinese another lesson and Chinese encouraged by good opinion of German advisers may accept the challenge.

[1] No. 103.   [2] The text was here uncertain.
[3] No. 101.   [4] Mr. B. E. F. Gage was Second Secretary in H.M. Embassy at Peking.

2. In view of Chinese assertions that Lukouchiao incident was deliberately staged by Japanese I should perhaps state my conviction that this was not the case. Evidence that they were taken by surprise is overwhelming: General Tashiro was ill in Tientsin and bulk of Japanese Embassy guard was at Tungchow and most of the battalion engaged in manoeuvres had already returned to Fengtai. It is impossible to say who fired the first shot but Japanese know very well that these manoeuvres around Peking are keenly resented by many Chinese and holding of night exercises at a time of political tension like this can only be regarded as an act of grossest stupidity.

3. As frequently happens on such occasions all Chinese in authority have gone to ground and I have been unable to confirm from Chinese side signature of 'agreement' about which some [? same] doubts had already arisen as arose in connexion with Ho Umetsu agreement[5] but I think that anyone with local experience must recognise authentic Japanese touch. Authority of two signatories to commit anyone but themselves may be open to doubt but that is unlikely to deter Japanese.

[5] See No. 39.

No. 105

Mr. Eden to Mr. Dodds (Tokyo)

No. 157 Telegraphic [F 4071/9/10]

Immediate   FOREIGN OFFICE, *July 12, 1937, 9.15 p.m.*

I saw the Japanese Ambassador this evening when I spoke to him of my preoccupation at reports of fighting near Peking. It was the earnest hope of His Majesty's Government that what appeared to be a serious situation would not be allowed to develop further with unhappy consequences for all concerned. The Ambassador replied that he had on two occasions received reports from his Government stating that the differences were settled, but that each of these telegrams had been followed by another saying that fighting had started again. He had just received a third telegram once again reporting a settlement which he hoped this time would have no unhappy sequel. The Ambassador begged me to believe that his Government desired a settlement. I replied I was glad to hear this, since the Ambassador was aware of the importance we attached to conversations with Japanese which we had hoped would shortly begin. His Excellency would appreciate, however, that such conversations would hardly be possible if existing conditions near Peking persisted or grew worse.

The Ambassador replied that he fully appreciated the situation and hoped that we would make some communication to the Chinese Government so that if Japanese military became more reasonable they would not seek to profit by the fact. He emphasised that he was absolutely convinced that his Government did not desire this fighting to spread and have serious consequences. I asked His Excellency whether I might inform His Majesty's Ambassador to China of this statement. He replied that I might because he was absolutely convinced it represented his Government's point of view.

Repeated to Peking No. 231, Nanking No. 121, and Washington No. 225.

No. 106

Mr. Dodds (Tokyo) to Mr. Eden (Received July 12, 4.30 p.m.)

No. 214 Telegraphic [F 4035/9/10]

TOKYO, July 12, 1937, 9.45 p.m.

My telegram No. 213.[1]

It is too soon for me to express opinion on the acuteness of this latest Sino-Japanese clash but I think it might be as well if I were to be authorised to say to the Minister for Foreign Affairs in certain eventualities that you know from his message conveyed in my telegram No. 181[2] how genuinely anxious he is for an understanding with Great Britain and that nothing could defer such an understanding so effectually as an attempt at the present moment by the Japanese to turn North China into a second Manchukuo.[3]

Repeated to Nanking for repetition to Peking.

[1] No. 102. [2] No. 89.
[3] Mr. Eden wrote on the filed copy of this telegram: 'I agree. Mr. Dodds could be authorised to speak in this sense.' Telegram No. 158 to Tokyo of July 13 read: 'I approve your suggestion and you should take earliest opportunity of making communication you propose.'

No. 107

Mr. Eden to Sir R. Lindsay (Washington)

No. 228 Telegraphic [F 4086/9/10]

Immediate   FOREIGN OFFICE, July 13, 1937, 7.30 p.m.

My telegram No. 225.[1]

Chinese Ambassador[2] called on me this morning and made formal request that His Majesty's Government should offer their good offices in attempt to preserve peace between China and Japan. He added that similar request was being made to U.S., French and Soviet Governments.

[1] i.e. No. 105. [2] Dr. Quo Tai-chi.

French Ambassador has subsequently informed me that his Government were agreed in principle to urge moderation, on *both* sides, and had instructed their representatives in Nanking and Tokyo to be ready to cooperate with their British colleagues if the latter should receive instructions to make representations.[3]

As the U.S. Ambassador here knows, I have already warned Japanese Ambassador that it would be inopportune to open expected Anglo-Japanese conversations so long as present situation is allowed to continue, and I hope His Excellency has conveyed this warning to his Government.

I am somewhat disturbed at reports of large Japanese reinforcements, and further I feel we should be foolish to ignore altogether reiterated Chinese declarations that they would have to resist further Japanese encroachment on Chinese territory. While still prepared to believe that the Government in Tokyo have not deliberately planned an aggression, I fear there is a risk that the situation may get out of hand, and result in a clash on a considerable scale. In these circumstances I have been considering whether it might not be desirable to express to the Japanese Government our apprehension at the reports of the despatch of large reinforcements. It is of course for them to judge what measures are necessary for their security: to us it seems that their existing forces must be amply sufficient to ensure and maintain their position until the recent unfortunate incidents can be cleared up and a satisfactory settlement reached. I should be inclined to tell the Japanese Government that I was at the same time using such influence as His Majesty's Government may possess at Nanking to persuade the Chinese Government to take no action which might make situation more difficult. If, in the course of any negotiations that might take place for a settlement of the whole dispute, His Majesty's Government could be of any assistance, they would gladly listen to any suggestions that the Japanese Government would care to make.

I should at the same time instruct His Majesty's Ambassador in Nanking to inform the Chinese Government that we were preaching restraint at Tokyo and to beg them to do nothing that will make our task more difficult. I should say that mediation cannot usefully be attempted unless both sides desire it, and that we cannot say, without a further exchange of views with Japan, whether there is any way in which we can assist towards a settlement of the whole question.

Please at once try to obtain Secretary of State's reaction to these ideas and, if he approves, ask whether he would be disposed to instruct U.S. representatives in Nanking and Tokyo to cooperate with their British colleagues along these lines.

It would appear that, if any move is to be made, it must be made without delay. Chinese Ambassador expressed the fear that the Japanese would make a forward move on July 15.

[3] Cf. *D.D.F.*, Series 2, vol. vi, Nos. 220 and 235.

No. 108

Mr. Dodds (Tokyo) to Mr. Eden (Received July 13, 4.30 p.m.)

No. 216 Telegraphic [F 4070/9/10]

TOKYO, *July 13, 1937, 8.50 p.m.*

Your telegram No. 156.[1]

I venture to suggest that His Majesty's Ambassador at Peking and I should be instructed to approach Governments to which we are accredited *simultaneously*, asking if there is anything His Majesty's Government can do to ease the situation.

Anything more than this from us would in my opinion be almost certain to be misinterpreted by the Japanese military authorities who are not yet in the mood for advice of any kind from abroad. We should inform the Governments to which we are accredited that our *démarches* are simultaneous.

I believe that civil authorities here might welcome this. There is the bare chance that we might be able to help to discover some face-saving solutions.

United States Ambassador agrees that an enquiry of this kind could do no harm. He has heard nothing yet from United States Government as a result of your conversation with Bingham.[2] Similar action by United States representatives would of course be helpful.

In my opinion the principal factor which might make for peace would be realization by the Japanese military:

(1) that Soviet régime is not weakened (as they were led to suppose over Amur incident[3] and by recent executions[4]) and

(2) that an understanding with Great Britain will be indefinitely postponed if they attempt to establish a hegemony in North China. We have done what we can about (1); as regards (2) I doubt, however, if they care about it enough. Civilian authority cares of course very much but military have not been allowed to calm down (last sentence of my telegram No. 194[5]) and now appear in full control.[6]

Repeated to Washington and Nanking for repetition to Peking.

[1] i.e. No. 100. [2] Cf. *ibid.*, note 3.
[3] A dispute was in progress between the Japanese and Soviet Governments regarding rival claims to islands in the Amur river which formed the border between the Soviet Union and Manchukuo. Japanese, Manchukuo, and Russian forces clashed at the end of June 1937 and a Russian gunboat was sunk on June 30.
[4] See No. 102, note 3. [5] No. 95.
[6] Mr. Orde commented on this telegram: 'This is in line with our suggestions to Washington, which go a little further but not much.' See No. 107.

No. 109

Mr. Eden to Mr. Dodds (Tokyo)

No. 160 Telegraphic [F 4070/9/10]

Most Immediate   FOREIGN OFFICE, July 14, 1937, 1.20 a.m.

Your telegram No. 216.[1]

You will have seen, from my telegram to Washington No. 228,[2] that I have suggested to the U.S. Government joint representations to Japanese Government. You are authorised, the moment you hear from your U.S. colleague that he is authorised to join you, to act as indicated in that telegram, and you need not await instructions from here. In the meanwhile I am not at present prepared to authorise you to take action alone on these lines without U.S. cooperation, though you should of course act at the earliest possible moment on my telegram No. 158.[3]

Repeated to Washington No. 229.

[1] No. 108.   [2] No. 107.   [3] See No. 106, note 3.

No. 110

Sir R. Lindsay (Washington) to Mr. Eden (Received July 14, 10.10 a.m.)

No. 181 Telegraphic [F 4087/9/10]

Immediate   WASHINGTON, July 14, 1937, 1.55 a.m.

Your telegram No. 228[1] and my telegram No. 180.[2]

Head of Far Eastern Department has tonight brought me answer to the following effect:

You have already been informed[3] by American Ambassador of conversations held yesterday by Secretary of State with Japanese and Chinese Ambassadors and he had further conversations with them to-day.

In all four of these conversations he urged at length the importance of maintaining peace and he covered most of points mentioned in your telegram except that no reference was made to possibility of mediation.

State Department is heartily in accord with idea of representations at Tokyo and Nanking by His Majesty's representatives as outlined by you. Such action would be parallel though not identical with that already taken here and which it is intended to repeat here. American representatives in Japan and China are being kept informed of action taken.

State Department consider it important that His Majesty's Government and United States Government co-operate closely in exchanging information and in working on parallel lines.

[1] No. 107.   [2] Not kept in F.O. archives.   [3] See No. 100, note 3.

Head of Department added orally that in the present temper of Japanese Government it was feared that concerted action might defeat its own object.[4]

[1] Mr. Orde commented on July 14: 'This is characteristic but I think there is force in the argument that concerted action in Tokyo is dangerous. Independent but similar action will, I suggest, do all that is necessary. Words spoken in Washington may not be reported very faithfully in Tokyo, but they will be vague anyhow, and will almost certainly be reported in the press. I suggest that Mr. Dodds and Sir H. Hugessen should act now on the lines indicated in our tel. No. 228 to Washington.' Sir A. Cadogan agreed, but pointed to 'one slight difficulty in that the French are ready to act with us'. He was 'rather afraid that if we and the French act together *without* the U.S. that may give an impression of lack of solidarity', and thought 'we had better act alone' (July 14). Mr. Eden agreed (July 14). Mr. Orde noted that he had so informed the French Embassy by telephone. Foreign Office telegram No. 230 of July 14 to Washington instructed Sir R. Lindsay to thank Mr. Hull for his message and inform him of the instructions which were being sent to H.M. Ambassadors at Tokyo and Nanking: see No. 111 below.

No. 111

Mr. Eden to Mr. Dodds (Tokyo)

No. 162 Telegraphic [F 4087/9/10]

Immediate   FOREIGN OFFICE, *July 14, 1937, 5.20 p.m.*

My telegram No. 160[1] and Washington telegram No. 181.[2]

You should communicate with the Japanese Government independently and as soon as possible on the lines indicated in my telegram No. 228[3] to Washington, informing them of action taken in Nanking.[4]

I understand your French colleague may have authority to take joint or similar action, but as U.S. Government do not favour that course, I should not desire a purely Anglo-French representation. You should therefore go ahead on your own, telling your French colleague afterwards that you have done so. If his Government wish to follow suit, there can be no objection.

Repeated to Nanking, Peking, Washington, Moscow and Paris Saving.

[1] No. 109.   [2] No. 110.   [3] No. 107.
[4] Sir H. Knatchbull-Hugessen was given almost identical instructions in telegram No. 125 to Nanking, despatched at 4.58 p.m. on July 14.

No. 112

Mr. Dodds (Tokyo) to Mr. Eden (Received July 14, 2 p.m.)

Nos. 220 & 221 Telegraphic [F 4108/9/10]

Important   TOKYO, *July 14, 1937, 7.22 p.m.*

Your telegram No. 158.[1]

Minister for Foreign Affairs received me this afternoon. I reminded him that he had told me that the principal work his Government had to perform was the conclusion of an understanding with the United Kingdom.[2] It was very unfortunate that the North China affair had broken out just as Anglo-Japanese conversations were about to begin as in your opinion it might not be opportune moment to carry them on. I concluded by expressing the purely personal hope that His Excellency would let me know if I could be of any service in present difficult situation.

Minister for Foreign Affairs did not seem to have been informed of your warning the Japanese Ambassador in London on these lines.[3] He said situation would not develop if China were 'sensible'. Had I noticed Japanese Government had issued no propaganda since the incident began, whereas Chinese were inviting people up and down the country to resist Japan? I said I had informed you that no efforts were being made in Japan to rouse the people. He appeared to appreciate this. Interview then ended.

I did not use language contained in my telegram No. 214[4] because I am beginning to believe, and United States Ambassador takes same view, that Japan did not want this incident, does not want to have to push it through, and is not being provocative, and that peaceful solution depends on ability of Chinese Government to restrain their nationals. United States Military Attaché was categorically informed by Ministry of War this morning that no troops had yet been despatched for North China from Japan or Korea, and this was confirmed to the Naval Attaché this afternoon at Ministry of Marine as regards Japan, and by G.S.O. to Military Attaché as regards Korea. There is as Minister for Foreign Affairs says no attempt being made here to rouse emotions of the people. United States Ambassador has therefore recommended his Government that inaction is the best course for United States Government at present,[5] and telegram which he has received from the latter containing substance of your telegram No. 228[6] to Washington is accordingly 'for information only'.[7]

I thought therefore that threat suggested in my telegram No. 214 would at present stage be ill-timed and trust you will approve. I had originally intended that it should be used only 'in certain eventualities', i.e., if it became clear that Japan had premeditated this business. I venture to

[1] See No. 106, note 3.   [2] See No. 89.   [3] See No. 105.   [4] No. 106.
[5] See *F.R.U.S.*, 1937, vol. iii, p. 157: cf. also *ibid.*, pp. 164–6.
[6] No. 107.   [7] Cf. *F.R.U.S.*, *ibid.*, pp. 159–61.

suggest the time to use it may be if Japan obtains a settlement and presumes on it (see last paragraph of my immediately following telegram).[8]

Repeated to Washington and Nanking for repetition to Peking.

[8] Telegram No. 222 of July 14 summarized a conversation between General Piggott and General Homma. The last paragraph stated that according to the Japanese General 'certain elements in Japan would press for "final" settlement of North China problem now this unexpected "golden opportunity" had occurred', but that he thought that the government would resist this pressure if the present incident were peacefully settled.

No. 113

Mr. Eden to Mr. Dodds (Tokyo)

No. 164 Telegraphic [F 4108/9/10]

Immediate   FOREIGN OFFICE, *July 15, 1937, 11 a.m.*

In the light of your telegrams Nos. 220 and 221[1] the instructions contained in my telegram No. 162,[2] based as they were on your telegram No. 212,[3] may not seem to be entirely appropriate. As however the Chinese Government are being approached on similar lines it will be necessary for you to take action roughly analogous to that contemplated. You should therefore make your communication in the friendliest possible way, explaining that much the same thing is being said to the Chinese Government and that the sole object of His Majesty's Government in making these representations is to do all they can to ensure the maintenance of peace between two powers with whom Great Britain is always anxious to remain on the best of terms.

Repeated to Nanking No. 127, Peking No. 238, Washington No. 234, Moscow No. 73 and Paris Saving No. 119.

[1] No. 112.   [2] No. 111.   [3] See No. 102, note 1.

No. 114

Mr. Eden to Sir N. Henderson[1] (Berlin)

No. 136[2] Telegraphic [F 4168/9/10]

FOREIGN OFFICE, *July 15, 1937, 3.35 p.m.*

Please inform Government to which you are accredited that His Majesty's Government have thought it desirable to show their concern at the situation in North China. It is impossible on the information at their disposal to form any final opinion as to the rights and wrongs of the recent incident but the reports of reinforcements being sent to the scene by

[1] H.M. Ambassador at Berlin.   [2] No. 238 to Rome.

Japanese and possibly also Chinese Government suggest that there is danger of a clash on a major scale which would appear to be contrary to the interests of everyone. His Majesty's representatives in Tokyo and Nanking have therefore been instructed to urge moderate and calm handling of the situation on both governments, and we are also informing Japanese Government that if there is any way in which we could contribute to a peaceful settlement we would gladly consider any suggestions they may have to make. We understand that U.S. Government is giving similar moderating advice in Washington and that French Government are disposed to act in the same sense.

The above is being sent to you because we desire as an act of courtesy to keep German/Italian Governments informed of what we are doing. We should appreciate any information or comments they may wish to give us.[3]

[3] This paragraph was added to the draft in Mr. Eden's handwriting.

No. 115

Mr. Eden to Sir H. Knatchbull-Hugessen (Peking)

No. 240[1] Telegraphic [F 3913/2595/10]

FOREIGN OFFICE, July 15, 1937, 4 p.m.

Your telegrams Nos. 218[2] and 289.[3]

No such interchange of military intelligence as suggested in former telegram is in force with any foreign Power, and His Majesty's Government are not prepared to establish a precedent in favour of the Chinese Government. The publication of such an agreement could not fail to produce the most unfavourable reactions in Japan, and the mere existence of such proposals constitutes a potential danger to the maintenance of friendly relations between Great Britain and Japan.

You should therefore inform Donald that British military assistance to China must be limited to such purely military facilities as are available to any other nation. They might in the case of China include the training of Chinese military students in England, the provision of instructors and/or advisers to the Chinese Army, and the supply on normal terms of such material as may be available to meet China's legitimate defensive requirements.

As regards the proposed stationing of a Chinese officer in Singapore, it is considered most undesirable that His Majesty's Government should be

[1] In a minute of July 13 Mr. Orde noted that this telegram was 'based on the W[ar] O[ffice] and C[olonial] O[ffice] views, in which the Adm[iral]ty and Air Ministry have concurred'. Cf. No. 90, note 5, and No. 93.

[2] No. 90.

[3] In this telegram of July 10 Sir H. Knatchbull-Hugessen reported that Chiang Kai-shek had again enquired 'when it will be possible "to exchange staff officers"'.

placed in the position of recognising in Singapore the secret agent of one friendly Power or of assisting him in discharging his Government's instructions to watch and report upon the activities of the nationals of another friendly Power.

Subject to the foregoing considerations I approve of the suggestion that the Chinese Government be invited to send someone in Nanking to discuss their requirements with the Military Attaché.

No. 116

Sir R. Lindsay (Washington) to Mr. Eden (Received July 16, 9.30 a.m.)

No. 184 Telegraphic [F 4160/9/10]

WASHINGTON, *July 15, 1937, 5 p.m.*

1. I had some conversation last night about China with Under Secretary of State[1] and Mr. Norman Davis. The latter had been brought into the discussion[2] of your proposal of the day before for concerted representation at Tokyo and Nanking.[3] Both expressed satisfaction that you seemed not to be seriously disconcerted at the failure of the United States Government to agree on suggested action.[4] This they attributed to adverse effect which in their judgment it would have on the Japanese at this moment.

2. Mr. Norman Davis also said that United States Government was rather reluctant to 'get mixed up with all Europe' in the Far East. On this point Under Secretary of State said nothing. In my opinion this may have been a subsidiary element in their decision but not one of the first importance.

3. Both evinced curiosity as to how we were now proceeding with regard to French-Soviet cooperation and I told them of instructions in your telegram No. 162[5] to Tokyo.

4. On general situation they were pessimistic. They said that neither His Majesty's Government nor United States Government were prepared to push their opposition to extremes and Japanese Government knew this perfectly well. United States Ambassador in Tokyo reported that Japanese opinion was now more solidly behind the Japanese Government than ever before in his experience and they therefore expected that the Japanese would go right ahead. The one thing which might stop them would be the imponderable element, in fact well known at Tokyo, that both our two Governments strongly disapproved of such a course.

---

[1] Mr. Sumner Welles. [2] See *F.R.U.S.*, 1937, vol. iii, pp. 160–1. [3] See No. 107.
[4] See No. 110. [5] No. 111.

No. 117

Mr. Dodds (Tokyo) to Mr. Eden (Received July 15, 3.45 p.m.)

No. 224 Telegraphic [F 4151/9/10]

TOKYO, *July 15, 1937, 6.55 p.m.*

Your telegram No. 162.[1]

I told Vice Minister for Foreign Affairs this afternoon that His Majesty's Government were using such influence as they might possess etc. (down to 'Japanese Government would care to make' in your telegram No. 228[2] to Washington).

He thanked me profusely and said he was certain that Japanese Cabinet would much appreciate this act of friendship on the part of His Majesty's Government.

He then discussed situation which he said was definitely improving though still critical. Without any prompting from me he said that no re-inforcements had yet been sent from Japan or Korea nor had any troops been mobilized. I said you would be very glad to hear this as wild rumours of large re-inforcements being rushed across had reached England.

Previous to this interview French Ambassador had told me that he had been told by his Government that he might collaborate in a *démarche* with United States Ambassador and myself. He had not answered the telegram but said he would do so this afternoon stating that he would not collaborate unless explicitly instructed as he believed Japanese Government were doing their best to stop this affair developing and that counsels of moderation from outside would only do harm.[3] I shall inform him of my action in due course.

Repeated to Paris, Washington, Moscow and Nanking for repetition to Peking, and C. in C.

[1] No. 111.   [2] No. 107.   [3] See *D.D.F., op. cit.*, No. 231.

No. 118

Sir H. Knatchbull-Hugessen (Nanking) to Mr. Eden (Received July 15, 6 p.m.)

No. 192 Telegraphic [F 4142/9/10]

Important   NANKING, *July 16, 1937, 1.30 a.m.*

My telegram No. 190.[1]

Minister for Foreign Affairs has now communicated with Chiang Kai-shek who has made a most categorical statement to the effect that all

[1] No. 120 below.

Chinese troop movements have been solely for self-defence in view of troop movements by Japan and that he entertains no intentions whatever of starting hostilities.

2. Chinese Government are ready to put an end to all troop movements in the area affected and to withdraw troops to their positions prior to the incident if Japanese Government will do likewise. Minister for Foreign Affairs attaches the utmost importance to avoidance of aggravation of the situation and suggests that as a preliminary measure troop movements on both sides stop on July 17th after which arrangements could be made for restoration of previous position. The above on the understanding that neither side in the meantime will attempt to occupy any position of strategical importance or in other words a gentleman's agreement under which no attempt will be made to take advantage of this intervening period.

3. Minister for Foreign Affairs agrees to statement on the above lines being made to Japanese Government if you are willing to instruct His Majesty's Chargé d'Affaires to make it.

Repeated to Peking, Commander-in-Chief, Tokyo, Rear-Admiral Yangtse, General Officer Commanding, Washington and Moscow.

No. 119

Sir H. Knatchbull-Hugessen (Nanking) to Mr. Eden
(Received July 16, 9.30 a.m.)

No. 193 Telegraphic [*F 4159/9/10*]

Important   Very secret   NANKING, *July 16, 1937, 4.20 a.m.*

My immediately preceding telegram.[1]

Minister for Foreign Affairs read to me and handed to me a statement of which following is actual text, begins:

'I am directed by General Chiang Kai-shek to . . .[2] the following statements: in view of the fact that large numbers of Japanese troops have been despatched from Manchuria, Corea and Japan proper to Tientsin, Fengtai and elsewhere in preparation for a war on a large scale Chinese Government is compelled to move troops as a precautionary measure solely for self-defence and not for starting hostilities. In a word, the mobilization of Chinese troops has no other purpose than that of preparing for resistance. This is entirely different from aggressive and provocative intentions of the Japanese troops'.

I said at once that it was impossible for me to make use of this statement in its existing form, that if it became known it would have the effect of

[1] No. 118.   [2] The text was here uncertain.

another Ems telegram.[3] I must be allowed to omit certain portions and I said he should ensure the utmost secrecy for the document itself. The Minister for Foreign Affairs fully realized implications of Chiang Kai-shek's statement and said that he would only . . .[2] it to a few chosen colleagues, but he felt bound to give it to me as it showed Chiang Kai-shek's state of mind. I said I would pass it on to you but to no-one else.

My immediately preceding telegram which is based on innocuous passages in Chiang Kai-shek's statement was drafted in collaboration with Minister for Foreign Affairs and Vice Minister for Foreign Affairs and has their full approval. I am communicating copy to them.

Repeated to Peking No. 272.

[3] Of July 13, 1870, from Abeken to Bismarck: the traditional cause of the Franco-Prussian war.

No. 120

Sir H. Knatchbull-Hugessen (Nanking) to Mr. Eden
(Received July 16, 9.30 a.m.)

No. 190[1] Telegraphic [F 4157/9/10]

Important   NANKING, *July 16, 1937, 11.5 a.m.*

Your telegram No. 125.[2]

I have seen Minister for Foreign Affairs and spoke to him in sense of paragraph 5 of your telegram No. 228[3] to Washington.

Minister for Foreign Affairs expressed serious apprehension at Japanese designs and said that military party were in complete control in Tokyo. I expressed some doubt of this and said that it seemed to me inconsistent with recent trend of Japanese policy that an incident should be created at present and force a serious issue. It was quite reasonable to argue that present Japanese troop movements were purely precautionary as it was necessary for them to guard against a situation in which their troops in north China would be seriously outnumbered by Chinese. Chinese themselves were moving troops and I had received a message from General Chiang Kai-shek that Central Government troops had been sent to Paotingfu. (Minister for Foreign Affairs confirmed this but added that these troops were not to go beyond Paotingfu).

I said that it seemed to me that neither Government desired to force a serious crisis and that both were moving troops merely for defensive measures with no ambitious motive. It was essential to stop troop movements on both sides and if it could be shown that movements on each side were purely defensive and precautionary a standstill might be possible after which a settlement would be easier. Could I assure you that

[1] This telegram was despatched after telegrams Nos. 192 and 193 (Nos. 118 and 119).
[2] See No. 111, note 4.   [3] No. 107.

Chinese Government had no aggressive intention whatever and that their measures were purely precautionary? Minister for Foreign Affairs gave me most categorical assurance that this was the case but said he would telephone to Chiang Kai-shek at Kuling and give me a more official answer later. I am to see him again shortly and will telegraph again.

Repeated to Peking, Tokyo, Washington, Moscow, Rear Admiral Yangtze, Commander-in-Chief and General Officer Commanding.

No. 121

Mr. Eden to Sir H. Knatchbull-Hugessen (Nanking)

No. 129 Telegraphic [F 4159/9/10]

Immediate   FOREIGN OFFICE, *July 16, 1937, 5 p.m.*

Your telegrams Nos. 192,[1] 193[2] and 194.[3]

In my telegram No. 228[4] to Washington I made it clear that we cannot allow ourselves to be drawn in as mediators unless both sides expressly desire it. So far there has been no sort of hint that the Japanese would accept our, or indeed any, mediation.

The suggestion for a standstill agreement contained in para. 2 of your telegram No. 192 appears to us to have much to commend it, but it seems to me that it is one for the Chinese Government themselves to put direct to the Japanese Government through the ordinary diplomatic channel, and that it should be put without delay. It is not as though diplomatic relations had been broken off between China and Japan and until they are His Majesty's Government could certainly not accept the responsibility of acting as a channel for communications of this sort.

I cannot go further than to inform the Japanese Government that, in reply to representations which you made, Chinese Government have indicated that their attitude is as discussed in your telegram No. 192 (see my telegram to Tokyo No. 168[5]). You should not, however, inform Chinese Government that I have given this information to Japanese Government, for I consider that it is for them to do so.

Repeated to Tokyo No. 167.

[1] No. 118.   [2] No. 119.   [3] Not traced in F.O. archives.
[4] No. 107.   [5] No. 122 below.

No. 122

Mr. Eden to Mr. Dodds (Tokyo)

No. 168 Telegraphic [F 4159/9/10]

Immediate   FOREIGN OFFICE, *July 16, 1937, 5.30 p.m.*

Your telegram No. 224.[1]

I appreciate the spirit in which Vice Minister for Foreign Affairs received your communication.

You may tell him in confidence that, in reply to representations which, as he knows, His Majesty's Ambassador in Nanking was instructed to make, Chinese Government have declared that they are ready to put an end to all troop movements in the area affected and to withdraw troops to their positions prior to the incident if Japanese Government will do likewise. Chinese Minister for Foreign Affairs attaches utmost importance to avoidance of aggravation of the situation and declares Chinese Government would for their part stop all troop movements, if Japanese will do likewise, so that arrangements can be made for restoration of previous position. This would be on understanding that neither side in the meantime would attempt to occupy any position of strategical importance.[2]

This attitude seems reasonable and I am encouraging Chinese Government to make proposals on these lines to Japanese Government.[3]

Repeated to Nanking No. 130.

[1] No. 117.   [2] See No. 118.   [3] Cf. No. 121.

No. 123

Mr. Dodds (Tokyo) to Mr. Eden (Received July 17, 9.30 a.m.)

No. 227 Telegraphic [F 4192/9/10]

TOKYO, *July 16, 1937, 8 p.m.*

Your telegram No. 164.[1]

It was announced late last night that 'a contingent' would be sent from Japan. I saw Vice Minister for Foreign Affairs accordingly at 11.45 this morning and said that Japanese Government must of course be judge of what measures were necessary for security of their troops in North China. It was hoped tht representations being made at Nanking by His Majesty's Ambassador would succeed in persuading Chinese Government to take no action which might make the situation more difficult. Chinese might, however, be unwilling to listen to his representations if they were able to show that large reinforcements were being sent to Japanese garrison in North China.

[1] No. 113.

2. Sole object of His Majesty's Government was to do all they could to ensure maintenance of peace between the two Powers with whom Great Britain was always anxious to remain on the best of terms.

3. Reception accorded to communication I made yesterday and reported in my telegram No. 224[2] was so good that I thought that the Japanese Government could now hear more easily communication reported in first paragraph of this telegram. Vice Minister for Foreign Affairs took it quite well.

4. I reinforced it by informing him that His Majesty's Ambassador at Nanking had impressed on Chinese Minister for Foreign Affairs that it was absolutely essential that troop movements should be stopped on both sides at the earliest possible moment and that he thought both were moving troops merely for defensive purposes, etc., quoting suitable extracts from Nanking telegram No. 190[3] to you. Finally I said that I had no instructions[4] but had reason to believe that the Chinese Government were ready to put an end to all troop movements, etc., as in second paragraph of Nanking telegram No. 192[5] to you.

5. He refused to make any comment but said he would let me know reactions of his Government as soon as possible.

6. Nanking telegram No. 192 reached me just as I was leaving the Embassy for this interview. As every moment is vital I trust that you will approve of my acting without instructions.

7. Vice Minister for Foreign Affairs said that no reinforcements had yet left Japan or Korea and that those under orders to leave were mainly transport and supplies. It is absolutely essential that he should not be quoted as giving me this information.

8. I have kept United States Ambassador informed.[6]

Repeated to Washington, Commander-in-Chief, Nanking for repetition to Peking.

[2] No. 117.　　　　　　　　　　　　　　　　　　[3] No. 120.
[4] Mr. Orde wrote in the margin at this point: 'They were on their way.' See No. 122.
[5] No. 118.
[6] Mr. Orde minuted on July 19: 'Mr. Dodds anticipated in a more disguised form the instructions in our tel. No. 168 [No. 122] and will have been reassured by its receipt. He has spoken well throughout and I suggest sending him a tel. to say so.' This was done in telegram No. 171 to Tokyo of July 19.

No. 124

Mr. Eden to Sir H. Knatchbull-Hugessen (Peking)

No. 387 [F 4177/9/10]

FOREIGN OFFICE, *July 16, 1937*

Sir,

The Chinese Ambassador asked to see me this morning when he stated that he feared there was no improvement in the situation in the Far East which in certain respects seemed to him to be even more ominous. His Excellency then handed me the attached memorandum[1] which he informed me had been communicated to all the countries signatories of the Nine-Power Treaty except Japan. It was also being communicated to Germany and Russia.

2. The Ambassador continued that he feared that the objective of the Japanese Government was to separate the Northern Provinces from China. As he had explained to me before, this would be quite unacceptable to the Chinese Government—much as they desired peace. He thought it indicative of Japanese intentions that they were seeking to insist that the provinces of Hopei and Chahar should not be allowed to take part in the elections of the new Government of China. Japan was, in short, attempting to revive her separatist plans of a year ago which had then failed of fruition.[2] Nevertheless the Ambassador did not despair: he was hoping against hope for better things. It was something gained that the Japanese offensive which it had been reported must be on the 15th July had not in fact taken place.

I am, etc.,
ANTHONY EDEN

ENCLOSURE IN NO. 124

Memorandum by the Chinese Government

CHINESE EMBASSY, *July 16, 1937*

Since the outbreak of the Loukouchiao incident in the night of July 7 when Japanese troops in the course of their manoeuvres, which were not permissible even under the terms of the Protocol of 1901 (as the points where foreign troops may be are specifically enumerated in Article Nine of the final Boxer Protocol and neither Loukouchiao nor Wanping nor Fengtai are included), suddenly opened attack on the city of Wanping and met with resistance from the local garrison, Chinese authorities, anxious to reach a peaceful settlement, have used their best efforts to arrange for cessation of hostilities by mutual withdrawal of troops. But almost immediately after each successive arrangement was made it was nullified by resumption of attack by Japanese forces. In the meantime fighting has been extended to the immediate environs of Peiping, while large numbers of Japanese reinforcements are being rapidly sent into the province of Hopei from Manchuria, Korea and Japan proper. It is estimated that over 100 aeroplanes and 20,000 troops have already been concentrated n the Peiping and Tientsin area ready to precipitate a major clash at any moment.

It need scarcely be pointed out that the sudden attack on Loukouchiao

---

[1] See Enclosure in this document.
[2] Cf. Volume XX, Nos. 511, 512, 518, 524, and Chapters VI and VII, *passim.*

and the invasion of North China by large Japanese military forces constitute a clear violation of China's sovereignty contrary to the letter and spirit of the Nine Power Treaty, the Paris Peace Pact and the Covenant of the League of Nations. The crisis thus precipitated by Japan's aggressive action in China if permitted to take its own course will not only immediately disturb the peace in-East Asia but may entail unfor[e]seen consequences to the rest of the world. While China is obliged to employ all the means at her disposal to defend her territory and national honour to the end of her existence, she nevertheless holds herself in readiness to settle her differences with Japan by any of the pacific means known in international law and treaties.

No. 125

Sir H. Knatchbull-Hugessen (Nanking) to Mr. Eden
(Received July 18, 9.30 a.m.)

No. 211 Telegraphic [F 4201/9/10]

Immediate   NANKING, *July 18, 1937, 12.45 p.m.*

Donald has informed Gage at Kuling confidentially that General Chiang Kai-shek is preparing a statement to the Chinese Nation main points of which are:
(1) Chinese patience has resulted in loss and suffering;
(2) Present situation is in the fullest sense premeditated by the Japanese;
(3) When talking of localization he cannot forget Manchukuo;
(4) If there is no hope of peace China will fight to the last Province and man. See however my immediately following telegram.[1]
Repeated to Peking, Tokyo, Commander-in-Chief, Rear Admiral Yangtse and General Officer Commanding.

[1] No. 126 below.

No. 126

Sir H. Knatchbull-Hugessen (Nanking) to Mr. Eden
(Received July 18, 9.30 a.m.)

No. 212 Telegraphic [F 4202/9/10]

Immediate   NANKING, *July 18, 1937, 12.55 p.m.*

My telegram No. 211.[1]
Mr. Gage has just telephoned from Kuling that the Japanese Govern-

[1] No. 125.

171

ment have telegraphed suggesting they should send representatives to Kuling to negotiate.

He states that Chiang Kai-shek is inclined to regard this as a move to gain time.

I asked him to express to Donald my view that suggestion should receive serious consideration and that in view of it it would be the height of folly to issue statement referred to in my telegram referred to.

Repeated Tokyo, Peking, Rear-Admiral Yangtse, Commander-in-Chief, and General Officer Commanding.

No. 127

Sir H. Knatchbull-Hugessen (Nanking) to Mr. Eden
(Received July 18, 3 p.m.)

No. 216 Telegraphic [F 4203/9/10]

Immediate   NANKING, July 18, 1937, 5.50 p.m.

Counsellor of the Japanese Embassy has just called to inform me that at 11.30 p.m. on July 17th he called on Chinese Minister for Foreign Affairs and on instructions from his Government made a verbal communication calling upon the Chinese Government.

A. To cease immediately all provocative acts and

B. To refrain from obstructing execution of agreement of July 11th[1] between the local authorities.

Communication went on to say that if this action of the Chinese Government continues a very grave situation will arise whose consequences cannot be foreseen.

Counsellor left with Minister for Foreign Affairs a written note of this communication pro-memoria. He did not ask for immediate reply but expects the Chinese Government to answer [? by] July 19th.

He stated similar pressure being exerted at Tientsin to expedite local negotiations now proceeding there.

Yesterday also representations were made by Japanese Assistant Military Attaché to Chief of General Staff to the effect that movement of Central troops to Paotingfu constituted a breach of the Ho-Umetsu agreement.[2]

Repeated to Tokyo, Peking, Commander-in-Chief, Rear Admiral Yangtse and General Officer Commanding.

[1] See No. 101.
[2] Mr. Orde minuted on this telegram on July 19: 'No definition of "provocative acts"; it may well cover troop movements. But there is some reassurance in the second condition . . . this warning seems not to conflict with the assurances given to us in Tokyo and Peking that the Japanese are not aiming at further political advantages.' Sir A. Cadogan wrote on July 19: 'But of course trespassers should not be the sole judges of the "provocativeness" of the attitude of the landlord or his agent. It is impossible to say how the clash originated, but it is

really otiose to say that Japanese troops ought not to have been in the neighbourhood of Lukouchiao. It might be difficult to prove they had no *right* to be there, but I should have no difficulty in asserting that they had no *reason* to be. It is all part of the deliberate process of encroachment. Today we are reassured if we learn that Japanese troops are returning from Lukouchiao to "their positions at Fengtai". And we are inclined to forget that Fengtai was last year's Lukouchiao.' He also remarked that the Chinese had 'always assured us that the "Ho-Umetsu agreement" doesn't exist': cf. No. 39.

Mr. Eden commented on July 20: 'While I agree that we should not rush ahead alone, it is surely important that the Japanese should not be able to pretend that our silence was encouragement. Are we going to hold any further communication with Washington? Should we for instance ask them to join in speaking about bombing. . .' See No. 135 below.

No. 128

Sir H. Knatchbull-Hugessen (Nanking) to Mr. Eden (Received July 18, 8.35 p.m.)

No. 210[1] Telegraphic: by wireless [*F 4234/9/10*]

NANKING, *July 18, 1937*

Vice Minister for Foreign Affairs urged upon me this evening that good might be done if His Majesty's Government were to make some statement and indicate importance attached by them to pacific settlement of present dispute owing to damage to British interests and subjects in the event of hostilities. He had seen recent answer in the House of Commons[2] and suggested some more widely issued statement might produce similar declarations from other Powers.

I avoided all commitments but said I would pass this on.

He also stated that Chinese Government were considering possible appeal to League of Nations either under article 17 or article 11 of Covenant. This idea at present was only remote in their minds but it existed.[3]

Repeated to Peking, Tokyo, Commander-in-Chief, Rear Admiral Yangtse and General Officer Commanding.

[1] This telegram was received after telegrams Nos. 211, 212, and 216 (Nos. 125–7).
[2] See No. 99, note 1.
[3] Mr. Orde minuted on July 20: 'It seems to me that we have now said all that is desirable for the moment.' This was a reference to Mr. Eden's speech of July 19 opening the House of Commons debate on foreign policy. It included the statement: 'We ourselves enjoy very good relations with both the Governments concerned, and we do not believe that the interests of those two Far Eastern nations need conflict.' See 326 *H.C. Deb. 5s.*, cols. 1799–1802.

No. 129

Mr. Dodds (Tokyo) to Mr. Eden (Received July 18, 7.30 p.m.)

Nos. *229 & 230 Telegraphic [F 4208/9/10]*

Immediate   TOKYO, *July 18, 1937, 11.50 p.m.*

I saw Vice Minister for Foreign Affairs at 4 this afternoon. He said that no reinforcements had yet left Japan. Some had gone from Korea and Manchukuo. The hopes of local settlement were brighter and Japanese Government were doing their best to expedite it in order to prevent further movements of troops by China or Japan. As they wished to conclude settlement locally they were not prepared to act on 'standstill' proposal made by Nanking Government (paragraph 4 of my telegram No. 227[1]) which they had heard of only from me and not from the Japanese Counsellor at Nanking. (This conflicts with information in Nanking telegram No. 207[2]).

2. I said I thought Nanking Government would not object to local settlement if terms were reasonable[,] (I had in mind Nanking telegram No. 208[3]) and suggested they should be informed of them as soon as possible if they were not aware of them already. I added that His Majesty's Ambassador at Nanking feared that there was grave risk that if Chiang Kai-shek did not resist Japanese, he would disappear. I said Vice Minister for Foreign Affairs would realise that this would mean the end of the chance of local settlement.

3. Vice Minister for Foreign Affairs said that Japanese terms included no political demands. They appear to be those mentioned in Peking telegram No. 297.[4]

4. I said that Nanking Government feared Japanese military would demand more than Japanese Government authorised them to. He said this would not be so and repeated it when I referred to our own experience of difficulty of dealing with local Japanese officials, outside Japan.

5. My purpose in drawing his attention to apprehension of Nanking Government referred to in preceding paragraph was in order to quote him, if military do in fact exceed their instructions. If he had shown any hesitation in giving me assurance asked for I should have observed that excess by military would have unfortunate effect on Anglo-Japanese conversations about to begin, but he did not, and I refrained.

---

[1] No. 123.   [2] Not kept in F.O. archives.
[3] In this telegram of July 18 Sir H. Knatchbull-Hugessen reported that according to the Chinese Foreign Minister the Japanese interpretation of 'localisation' was 'to settle present dispute direct with 29th army and northern leaders to the complete exclusion of Central Government. . . In his view Japan would demand complete separation at least of Hopei province on lines similar to East Hopei'.
[4] No. 101.

6. He then asked me what His Majesty's Government had asked the United States and French Governments to do, and what replies had been received. I said it had been suggested to United States Government that their representatives at Nanking and Tokyo should co-operate with their British colleagues on lines with which he was familiar from my conversations with him and that they had not seen fit to do so. His Majesty's Government had not asked French Government nor, in reply to his further question, Soviet Government or any other Government.

I will report further on situation tomorrow morning.

Repeated to Washington, Nanking for repetition to Peking.

No. 130

Mr. J. B. Affleck[1] (Tientsin) to Mr. Eden (Received July 19, 5 p.m.)

No. 3 Telegraphic [F 4274/9/10]

Important   Most Secret   TIENTSIN, *July 19, 1937, 5.48 p.m.*

Addressed to Peking telegram No. 31 July 19th.

Following is a secret and confidential report received through Kailan Mining Administration of a meeting between Sunk [Sung] Cheh-yuan and Katsuki at Japanese garrison at 1 p.m. on July 18th. This information was obtained from an officer in the Japanese garrison and from Cheng Chung-fu, Cheng Chueh-sung and others who were assisting Sung Cheh-yuan. Begins.

The terms formally agreed to by Sung Cheh-yuan[2] at meeting were as follows:

1. Apology by the 29th Army for Lukouchiao incident.
2. Punishment of those responsible for the incident. Removal of Feng Chuh-an from his command of 37th Division.
3. Compensation to be made by Chinese.
4. Ho-Umetsu agreement[3] to be fully carried out. It is understood that according to that agreement no Chinese troops will be allowed in the area concerned, in present case Chahar and Hopei. (No distinction was made at the time between Nanking troops and local troops in province. Su[ng] said that 29th Army would be allowed to remain although it is believed that this permission on the part of Japanese would only be given for a limited time).

[1] H.M. Consul-General at Tientsin.
[2] According to a personal message of July 16 from T.V. Soong to Sir F. Leith-Ross (F 4268/9/10), Sung Che-yuan had already 'been coerced into signing agreement whereby Hopei-Charhar [sic] reduced to status of Eastern Hopei becomes Japanese protectorate'. Dr. Soong concluded: 'Personally I believe that serious conflict is inevitable unless chance of outside mediation by the Foreign Powers.'
[3] See No. 39.

The above was agreed to in a formal way although no document was signed. Besides above terms, Sung Cheh-yuan also agreed that Hopei and Chahar would be made an 'independent and autonomous area'.

Sung Cheh-yuan left the garrison at about 3 p.m. and General Chang Tsu-chung remained further to discuss with Katsuki the method of carrying out an 'independent and autonomous' Government in this area. No-one else who went with Sung was allowed to be present during the latter part of the meeting when Chang Tsu-chung and Katsuki were closeted together.

Japanese troops are now moving from Fengtai to Peking-Hankow line and will advance south to meet Nanking troops that are at present in Paotingfu. It is expected that fighting will occur on Peking-Hankow line and Tientsin-Pukow railway between Nanking troops and Japanese Army. The 29th Army will withdraw to convenient areas so that they themselves should not be involved. Ends.

It is estimated that at least 5,000 more Japanese troops with equipment, guns, etc., have entered through Shanhaikuan during the twenty-four hours. Definite and extensive preparations are being made for a large landing at Tangku. Number given is 35,000 and date July 22nd. At the same time (? reliable) reports reach us of large movements of Chinese troops towards Paotingfu and of movements from Paotingfu towards Peking.

There are indications therefore that operations on a large scale may materialize.[4]

Repeated to Nanking, Commander-in-Chief, General Officer Commanding.

[4] Mr. Ronald commented on July 20: 'I think that this version of the projected agreement must be correct, having regard to the terms of the Chinese reply' (Nos. 131–2 below). Mr. Orde agreed (July 20) that it 'must be pretty near the truth'.

No. 131

Sir H. Knatchbull-Hugessen (Nanking) to Mr. Eden
(Received July 20, 9.30 a.m.)

No. 226 Telegraphic [F 4261/9/10]

Immediate   NANKING, *July 20, 1937, 2.10 a.m.*

Part One

Following is position as it appears at 10 p.m. July 19th.

Chinese Government have replied to Japanese representations reported in my telegram No. 216[1] see my immediately following telegram.[2] I understand through a third party that Japanese Counsellor does not take favourable view of this reply.

[1] No. 127.   [2] No. 133 below.

2. Sung C[he] Y[uan] has returned to Peking. Minister for Foreign Affairs interprets this as a sign that some agreement has been reached locally at Tientsin.[3]

3. It is reported from Chinwangtao that eleven Japanese troop trains containing infantry, cavalry, artillery, mechanical transport etc. passed Chinwangtao during 24 hours up to 6 p.m. July 18th. These are understood to be units from Korean army. It is also stated that seven Chinese divisions have been sent to Shantung.

Repeated to Tokyo, Peking, Commander-in-Chief, Rear Admiral Yangtse and General Officer Commanding.

[3] See No. 130.

No. 132

Sir H. Knatchbull-Hugessen (Nanking) to Mr. Eden
(Received July 20, 9.30 a.m.)

No. 226 Telegraphic [F 4273/9/10]

Immediate   NANKING, *July 20, 1937, 3.13 p.m.*

Part Two[1]

4. General Chiang Kai-shek is issuing a declaration to the Chinese nation on lines of my telegram 211.[2] Main points of this document are as follows. Begins:

1. Any kind of settlement must not infringe upon the territorial integrity and sovereign rights of our nation.

2. The status of Hopei-Chahar political council is fixed by the Central Government; we should not allow any illegal interference.

3. We will not agree to removal by outside pressure of those local officials appointed by Central Government such as Chairman of Hopei-Chahar political council.

4. We will not allow any restriction being placed upon positions now held by the 29th army.

These four points constitute minimum conditions possible as a basis for negotiation no matter how weak we may be. Ends.

5. I learn that it is not true that Shihchiachuang was bombed (see my telegram 219[3]). Chinese general staff inform Military Attaché that on July 18th three separate attacks with machine guns were made by Japanese aeroplanes on trains on Peking-Hankow railway. About 20 Chinese were killed or wounded. You will notice that this account speaks of machine guns and not bombs.

[1] See No. 131.   [2] No. 125.   [3] Not kept in F.O. archives.

No. 133

Sir H. Knatchbull-Hugessen (Nanking) to Mr. Eden
(Received July 20, 10 p.m.)

No. 227 Telegraphic: by wireless [F 4299/9/10]

NANKING, *July 20, 1937*

My immediately preceding telegram.[1]

Following English translation of aide-mémoire presented by the Waichiaopu to the Japanese Embassy here at 2.30 o'clock this afternoon is being issued as a *communiqué*. 'Since the outbreak of the Lukouchiao incident China having not the least desire to aggravate the situation or provoke a conflict with Japan has repeatedly declared her readiness to seek a settlement by pacific means. The Japanese Government while professing anxiety not to see the situation aggravated has at the same time despatched large numbers of troops to the province of Hopei. The movements of Japanese troops which have not yet ceased indicate a clear intention on the part of Japan to resort to force. In the circumstances the Chinese Government has been compelled to take adequate precautionary measures for self-defence but the Chinese Government has not relaxed its consistent efforts for peace. On July 12th the Minister for Foreign Affairs in discussing the situation with Mr. S. Hi[d]aka Counsellor of the Japanese Embassy proposed mutual cessation of military movements and withdrawal of troops on both sides to their original positions. It is to be regretted that no reply to this proposal has yet been received from Japan. The Chinese Government now wishes to reiterate its desire for a peaceful settlement of the incident as well as its intention not to aggravate the situation. It is therefore proposed that the two parties jointly fix a definite date on which both sides shall simultaneously cease all military movements and withdraw their respective armed forces to the positions occupied prior to the incident. In view of the peaceful aspirations voiced by the Japanese Government the Chinese Government trusts that the proposal will be acceptable to Japan as regards the procedure to be followed for a settlement of the Lukouchiao incident. The Chinese Government is prepared immediately to enter into negotiations with the Japanese Government through regular diplomatic channels, the settlement of questions of a local nature susceptible of adjustment on the spot shall be subject to the sanction of the Chinese National Government. In short the Chinese Government is ready to exhaust all pacific means for the maintenance of peace in Eastern Asia. Therefore all methods provided by international law and international treaties for the pacific settlement of international disputes such as direct negotiations good offices mediation arbitration etc. are equally acceptable to the Chinese Government.

Repeated to Peking No. 300 and Tokyo.

[1] Nos. 131 and 132.

178

No. 134

Sir H. Knatchbull-Hugessen (Nanking) to Mr. Eden
(Received July 20, 3.40 p.m.)

No. 229 Telegraphic [F 4290/9/10]

Immediate   NANKING, July 20, 1937, 4.45 p.m.

My telegram No. 226.[1]

Situation is now extremely grave.

Counsellor of Japanese Embassy saw Minister for Foreign Affairs this morning and discussed Chinese reply.[2] Hidaka informs me that Minister for Foreign Affairs was most conciliatory in general but stated

(a) that Chinese Government would not undertake to cease provocative acts because this would be to admit that they had committed acts. (Hidaka explained to me that act which the Japanese Government have particularly in mind is despatch of Central Government troops to Paotingfu);

(b) that while Chinese Government had not wished to prevent conclusion of local agreement (? they could not) sanction it themselves until it had been submitted to and approved by them.

Beyond this Minister for Foreign Affairs was most conciliatory and anxious to explore every possibility through diplomatic channel. Counsellor had forwarded Chinese reply to Tokyo yesterday evening and expressed to his Government view that it was unsatisfactory on two specific points.

He informed me that late last night Japanese Government issued *communiqué* expressing dissatisfaction with Chinese reply.

Counsellor also said that Chiang Kai-shek's declaration reported in my above-mentioned telegram would have bad effect.

Counsellor tells me Japanese Ambassador has no plan for returning here. Counsellor intends to remain as long as possible.

Repeated to Peking, Tokyo, Commander-in-Chief, Rear-Admireal Yangtse, General Officer Commanding

[1] Nos. 131 and 132.   [2] See No. 133.

No. 135

Mr. Eden to Sir R. Lindsay (Washington)

No. 239 Telegraphic [F 4302/9/10]

Most Immediate   FOREIGN OFFICE, July 20, 1937, 9 p.m.

His Majesty's Government are gravely preoccupied by recent developments in Far East and have been considering whether one more effort cannot be made to avert hostilities which may have far-reaching consequences.[1] In the circumstances we should be willing to make with the United States Government joint approach to Japanese and Chinese Governments and ask them to agree:

(1) to issue instructions that all further movement of troops be suspended;

(2) to agree that the United States Government and ourselves should put forward proposals in attempt to end existing deadlock.

Please arrange to see Mr. Hull at once and ask him whether he agrees with such a course of action and whether he would join with us in it. We appreciate that the chances of success may be slender, but in view of serious consequences to prosperity of Far East and to peace in those regions which must result from a clash between armed forces of Japan and China, we consider attempt should be made. It will be clear that if approach is to be made it should be done with least possible delay.[2]

Repeated to Nanking No. 137, Tokyo No. 174 and Paris (Saving) No. 121.

[1] Cf. No. 127, note 2.
[2] This telegram was despatched after Mr. Eden's conversation with Mr. Bingham recorded in despatch No. 694 to Washington (No. 136 below). According to a telegram from the U.S. Ambassador to the State Department despatched at 12 noon on July 21 (*F.R.U.S.*, 1937, vol. iii, p. 229) Mr. Eden telephoned Mr. Bingham at 8.45 p.m. on July 20 to say that since their meeting in the late afternoon 'the Far Eastern situation had taken a still graver turn for the worse'. He had had discussions with Mr. Neville Chamberlain (who had succeeded Mr. Baldwin as Prime Minister on May 28) and they had agreed on a suggestion to be made to the U.S. Government: 'while he did not wish to read this to me over the telephone he wanted me to know that such a message was going forward.'

No. 136

Mr. Eden to Sir R. Lindsay (Washington)

No. 684 [F 4301/9/10]

FOREIGN OFFICE, *July 20, 1937*

Sir,

I asked the United States Ambassador to come and see me this afternoon when, after expressing satisfaction at His Excellency's recovery in health, I said I wished to speak to him about the situation in the Far East. So far as I had been able to gather from telegrams and from the conversations which had taken place here with the United States Counsellor, the views of our two Governments on the present situation were very similar,[1] and I was glad to have an opportunity of expressing to

[1] Cf. Nos. 100, 107, 110, and 116.

the Ambassador our appreciation of Mr. Cordell Hull's recent public statement.[2]

2. At the same time the situation seemed to us to be growing ever graver. As the Ambassador would be aware we were willing to co-operate with the United States Government in any step which they might think fit to take. That was still the position, and if the United States Government had anything further to suggest we should be only too glad to consider it. At the same time I thought I ought to tell the Ambassador frankly that we were not anxious to take any further action alone. Mr. Bingham would perhaps be aware that some days ago we had been approached by the Chinese Government and asked to take joint action with the French, United States and perhaps the Soviet Government also in Tokio, counselling restraint and offering our good offices towards negotiations for a settlement.[3] We had ourselves consulted with the United States Government on the subject of this approach and Mr. Cordell Hull had taken the view that action should be parallel rather than complementary.[4] We had in consequence on our own used language in Tokio, advising restraint and offering good offices, while I understood that Mr. Hull had spoken in Washington to the Japanese Ambassador. From telegrams which reached us from Tokio last night we understood that the Japanese had the impression in consequence that we were rather more interested than the United States Government. I felt sure that the Ambassador would agree that it was undesirable that this impression should be created. This was why I attached great importance to joint action in any further step we might agree to take. By this I did not mean necessarily that our two Ambassadors should actually proceed in unison, but that there should be no doubt at Tokio that we thought alike.

3. The Ambassador replied that he fully understood our point of view on this subject which he felt sure should be shared in Washington. He wished me to bear in mind that the collaboration of the U.S. Government would be easier to obtain in respect of Far Eastern issues than it was in respect of Europe. The Western States of the United States were always apprehensive of Japanese intentions and the U.S. Government therefore received a considerable measure of support from that quarter in any action they took vis-à-vis Japan. At the same time though the Ambassador shared my view as to the gravity of the outlook it was difficult to see what further action could be taken. We could not go to war in the matter. Neither of us was in a position to do that. And short of such action it was

[2] On July 16 Mr. Cordell Hull issued what he called 'a statement of this Government's position in regard to international problems and situations with respect to which this country feels deep concern'. The United States, he said, advocated 'constantly and consistently' the maintenance of peace, 'national and international self-restraint', economic stability and the lowering of trade barriers, and the limitation of armaments. The statement is printed in *F.R.U.S.*, 1937, vol. i, pp. 699–700: see also *ibid.*, pp. 697–9 for Mr. Hull's remarks at a press conference relating his statement to the Far Eastern situation.
[3] See No. 107.   [4] See No. 110.

very difficult to think of anything which would have an effect. I fully agreed as to the difficulty and as to the opinion that we could neither of us go to war. Nonetheless in view of the gravity of the situation I had thought it desirable to have this conversation with the Ambassador and to express once again through him to the U.S. Government our willingness to co-operate in any way that seemed practicable in Washington. I also gave Mr. Bingham an account of the varying degrees of contact which we have maintained with the French, German and Italian Governments in this same connexion. Mr. Bingham thanked me and undertook to transmit what I had said to his Government. In conclusion I told His Excellency that I was at his disposal at any time should he wish to communicate with me tomorrow.[5]

I am, etc.,
ANTHONY EDEN

[5] See No. 137 below. Mr. Bingham's account of his conversation with Mr. Eden is printed in *F.R.U.S.*, 1937, vol. iii, pp. 224–5.

No. 137

Sir R. Lindsay (Washington) to Mr. Eden (Received July 21, 9.30 a.m.)

No. 194 Telegraphic [F 4317/9/10]

Immediate   WASHINGTON, *July 21, 1937, 1.16 a.m.*

Your telegram No. 239.[1]

I made representations to Secretary of State late this afternoon.[2] This evening at 11 p.m. he sent Head of Far Eastern Department to me at Embassy who told me Secretary of State expects to speak again tomorrow to the two Ambassadors in Washington and reiterate views which he has already expressed to both that it is of the utmost importance that hostilities be avoided. Head of Department said that it had not been possible this evening to reach any further decision than this but that further consideration would be given tomorrow to the question of joint action. Language he used however gives me very little expectation that Secretary of State will agree to joint action. Head of Department believes that military element have taken charge of government in Japan and that nothing will stop them, and he seems convinced that joint action will merely exacerbate an already desperate situation.[3]

State Department had already received report of your conversation of today with United States Ambassador (your telegram No. 238).[4]

[1] No. 135.   [2] i.e. on July 20: see *F.R.U.S.* 1937, vol. iii, pp. 226–7.
[3] Cf. *F.R.U.S.*, *ibid.*, pp. 227–8.
[4] This was a telegraphic version of No. 136: cf. *ibid.*, note 5.

No. 138

Sir H. Knatchbull-Hugessen (Nanking) to Mr. Eden
(Received July 21, 9.30 a.m.)

No. 230 Telegraphic [F 4320/9/10]

Immediate   NANKING, *July 21, 1937, 2.17 a.m.*

My telegram No. 229.[1]

I feel I must emphasise extreme seriousness of present situation. I see no possibility of hostilities being avoided unless Japanese Government and military party modify their attitude either voluntarily or in response to representations from other Powers.

I have just seen Donald who returned on July 20 to Nanking with Chiang Kai-shek. It is quite clear that Chiang Kai-shek still desires peaceful solution but that anything amounting to complete surrender to present Japanese demands would bring about his fall. As member of Chinese general staff (Major General Chu) informed Military Attaché today it is no longer a question of settling Luk[o]uchiao incident but of loss or retention of two Chinese provinces (Hopei and Chahar).

Position of Central Government is that they are entirely willing to negotiate with Japan through diplomatic channels on present dispute in all its aspects and have even offered arbitration and other methods of settlement but that they cannot allow themselves to be jockeyed with blind acceptance of some local settlement which will destroy their position in the north once and for all. If Japanese Government imagine that there is any element of bluff in Chinese attitude they are making a great mistake. As regards Chinese Government the weakness of their military position is fully realised but they feel there is a point beyond which public opinion will not allow them to go in the direction of compliance with Japanese demands.

If Japanese Government insist on settlement with local authorities in north China to the exclusion of Central Government they must realise that war will be inevitable.

Repeated to Tokyo, Peking, Commander-in-Chief, Rear Admiral Yangtse and General Officer Commanding.

[1] No. 134.

183

No. 139

Sir R. Lindsay (Washington) to Mr. Eden (Received July 22, 9.30 a.m.)

No. 196 Telegraphic [F 4352/9/10]

Immediate   WASHINGTON, *July 21, 1937, 7.35 p.m.*

My telegram No. 195.[1]

Following is text of aide-mémoire received from State Department this evening.[2]

Government of United States share[s] grave preoccupation of British Government as a result of developments in the Far East. It fully concurs in feelings expressed by British Government that every practicable effort should be made to avert hostilities which undoubtedly might have far-reaching consequences. It desires to co-operate with British Government in urging upon both parties that hostilities are not warranted and should be avoided. It further believes that co-operation between the two Governments in urging a peaceful solution of the controversy which has arisen is eminently desirable.

In the light of all information which has come to us—and we assume British Government has received much the same information—we feel that courses of action thus far pursued by our two Governments on parallel lines have been truly co-operative and that, in continuation of a common effort to avert hostilities, both Governments should again, each in its own way, urge upon the Japanese and Chinese Governments the importance of maintaining peace.

It is understanding of this Government that Chinese Government has already suggested to Japanese Government, and that British Government has already called to attention of the Japanese Government, the Chinese Government's suggestion, that troops' movements be suspended. This Government also understands that Japanese Government has indicated that it is not receptively disposed towards any such suggestion.

Secretary of State has this morning once more expressed to Japanese and Chinese Ambassadors at Washington solicitude of this Government that their countries respectively exercise effective self-restraint, has emphasised view of this Government that hostilities between their countries would be a calamity both to them and to the world, and has again invited any suggestions that either of their Governments may feel inclined to make for assistance which this Government might appropriately render towards a solution of issues over which they are contending. American Ambassadors to Japan and to China are being informed by telegram[3] of representations made by Secretary of State and have been

[1] Not kept in F.O. archives: it apparently reported that Mr. Hull had spoken to the Japanese and Chinese Ambassadors, but that no decision had yet been reached by the U.S. Government on the question of joint action with His Majesty's Government.

[2] The aide-mémoire is also printed in *F.R.U.S.*, 1937, vol. iii, pp. 235–6.

[3] See *F.R.U.S.*, *ibid.*, pp. 236–9.

instructed carefully to inform the Governments to which they are accredited of these representations. Might not British Government feel that similar action by it at this moment would be helpful?

No. 140

Extract from Cabinet Conclusions No. 31(37) of July 21, 1937

[*F 4399/9/10*]

3. The Secretary of State for Foreign Affairs said that he had no encouraging information from the Far East. He had done his best to keep in close touch with the Government of the United States of America. He had seen the American Ambassador on the previous evening[1] and had informed him of communications he had made to Tokyo and Peking, adding that we were not prepared to go further alone, for the reason that the fact that we had taken action in Tokyo and the American Government only in Washington, had given rise in Tokyo to the impression that we only were closely interested. On the previous evening the Prime Minister had suggested that a last effort might be made to avert war, and he had accordingly sent telegram No. 239[2] to Washington, which he read to the Cabinet. This, at any rate, would place on record our offer of joint action with the United States Government.

[1] No. 136.   [2] No. 135.

No. 141

Letter from Sir A. Cadogan to the French Ambassador[1]

[*F 4103/9/10*]

FOREIGN OFFICE, *July 21, 1937*

My dear Ambassador,

M. de Margerie[2] enquired by telephone a few days ago whether the Chinese Ambassador here had asked our views as to the desirability of the North China situation being laid before either the League of Nations or the signatories of the Washington Nine Power Treaty.[3]

The Chinese Ambassador called on me on the 14th July and told me he had received a telegram from his Government saying that they were considering the possibility of an appeal to the League. I replied that in my opinion this would neither be very useful nor effective. The Chinese Government could only invoke Article 17 and this Article was very

[1] M. André Corbin.   [2] First Secretary in the French Embassy at London.
[3] Cf. *D.D.F., op. cit.,* Nos. 220, 228, and 246.

difficult to work and action under it could be obstructed by the Japanese Government. Dr. Quo said that he was inclined to share my opinion and had advised his Government against an appeal to the League. He gathered, however, that they felt that Geneva was a good platform from which to put their case to the world. I told him that at the present moment I was rather inclined to dissent from that view as anything emanating from Geneva was bound to meet with an unfavourable reaction in Rome and Berlin. I did not know whether the Chinese Government expected any sympathy from those two capitals, but I did not think their chances of obtaining it would be increased by attempting to make use of the League at this juncture.

The Chinese Ambassador did not invite our views on the advisability of referring the present dispute to the signatories of the 9 Power Treaty. If he were to make such an enquiry, our present inclination would be to deprecate the idea of such an appeal, but, if the French Government have other views, we shall of course be only too happy to consider them.[4]

ALEXANDER CADOGAN

[4] M. Corbin transmitted a French translation of this letter to Paris in a telegram of July 22: see *D.D.F., ibid.*, No. 263.

No. 142

Mr. Eden to Sir R. Lindsay (Washington)

Unnumbered Telegraphic [F 4301/9/10]

Most Secret and Personal   FOREIGN OFFICE, *July 22, 1937, 5.30 p.m.*

The United States Ambassador asked to see me this morning,[1] when he said that he had been considering the position in the Far East. As he had told me the day before[2] this was an issue on which he thought that the United States Government could give a greater measure of co-operation than would be possible in Europe. The Ambassador had received no instructions of any kind from his Government, but at the same time he wished to put to me a suggestion which had occurred to him. He was making it, he several times emphasised, on his own responsibility only.

Could we not consider the possibility of approaching the United States Government to ask them to join with us in an embargo on Japanese trade? I asked the Ambassador whether he meant an embargo on Japanese imports into our respective countries, or an embargo on our exports to

[1] i.e July 21. It is clear that the interview between Mr. Eden and Mr. Bingham recorded in this telegram took place early on the morning of July 21, before Mr. Eden had seen Sir R. Lindsay's telegram No. 194 (No. 137). Mr. Bingham's account of the interview was telegraphed to the State Department at noon on July 21: see No. 135, note 2. The delay in the despatch of the present telegram until 5.30 p.m. on July 22 is not explained, but it may have been held up for Mr. Chamberlain's perusal.

[2] See No. 136.

Japan. The Ambassador replied that he meant both. There should be a cessation of all trade. In his view the present situation was extremely serious, and if some attempt were not made to call a halt to Japanese aggression there would soon be an end not only to the trade of both our countries with China, but also a total loss of the large investments both our countries possessed in the Far East.

I asked the Ambassador whether the United States Neutrality Legislation would allow the United States Government to put into force the policy to which the Ambassador referred. Mr. Bingham replied that he thought so, but on my expressing my doubt undertook to look into the matter further.

I then told His Excellency that while I was grateful to him for putting to me his personal view which I fully understood was exclusively his own, I wished to inform him of the telegram which I had sent Your Excellency the evening before (my telegram No. 239).[3] It seemed to me that before considering the Ambassador's proposal it was desirable to see what the response of the United States Government would be to the line of action we had already proposed. The Ambassador agreed and added that if the United States Government were not prepared to co-operate to the extent we had already suggested it was hardly possible to expect them to agree to the more drastic action which the Ambassador himself had in mind. Meanwhile Mr. Bingham begged that I would keep his suggestion to myself. He would never have dreamt of making it, but for the very intimate friendship that subsisted between us. I replied that [I] would certainly not make known what he had said to me to my colleagues in general, but that I must tell the Prime Minister. To this Mr. Bingham at once agreed.

Finally we agreed to meet later in the day, by which time I hoped to be in possession of Your Excellency's reply to my telegram No. 239.[4]

[3] No. 135. In his telegram to the State Department of July 21 (see *ibid.*, note 2) Mr. Bingham noted that Mr. Eden had read him the text of No. 135 but made no mention of his own suggestions for a trade embargo.

[4] In a further unnumbered telegram dated July 21 marked 'most secret and personal' Sir R. Lindsay was informed that at an interview later that day Mr. Eden and Mr. Bingham had agreed that they would wait for 'the further response which had been promised in your telegram No. 194 [No. 137] . . . before even considering the line of policy which the Ambassador himself put forward. . .' Cf. No. 139.

No. 143

Sir R. Lindsay (Washington) to Mr. Eden (Received July 23, 9.30 a.m.)

Unnumbered Telegraphic [*F 4463/9/10*]

Immediate   Secret   WASHINGTON, *July 23, 1937, 1.31 a.m.*

Your two unnumbered telegrams of today.[1]

I am sure you will have nothing to do with United States Ambassador's fantastic scheme. I am shocked to learn that he can talk such nonsense. Of course as you surmise such an embargo as he mentioned is impossible without legislation and idea of Congress, just emereging from a bitter five months' battle over Supreme Court, should now take up such a thorny topic as neutrality is not worth a moment's consideration. Exactly how many miles he is out of touch with the State Department you will see from my conversation of today with Under Secretary of State (my telegram No. 197)[2] which took place before I had received your telegram under reference. Mr. Welles may be 'a somewhat rigid individual' but he has a very level head on his shoulders and a pretty firm grasp of foreign policy of United States Government.[3]

[1] i.e. July 22: see No. 142, and *ibid.*, note 4.

[2] In this telegram of July 22 Sir R. Lindsay reported a conversation with Mr. Sumner Welles who denied that there was any failure of Anglo-American cooperation: the U.S. Government refused to take part in joint representations 'solely and entirely' because 'the two governments take different views of effect which such representations would have in that United States Government are convinced that effect would be bad in Japan'.

[3] In an unnumbered telegram to Washington of July 28 Sir R. Lindsay was informed that in conversation with Mr. Eden that day (see No. 152 below) Mr. Bingham remarked that 'the United States Government's reply reported in your telegram No. 196 [No. 139] clearly ruled out the possibility of giving further consideration to the suggestion which he had personally made on July 21st'.

No. 144

Sir G. Ogilvie-Forbes[1] (Berlin) to Mr. Eden (Received July 25, 10 a.m.)

No. 188 Telegraphic [*F 4483/9/10*]

BERLIN, *July 24, 1937, 10.58 p.m.*

Your telegram No. 140.[2]

I spoke as instructed to Acting Minister for Foreign Affairs who informs me that since conversation reported in Sir N. Henderson's

[1] H.M. Minister at Berlin.

[2] In this telegram of July 22 (No. 135 to Paris, No. 251 to Rome) Sir N. Henderson was instructed to inform the German Government of recent representations made by the British Government at Tokyo and Nanking.

telegram No. 446 Saving[3] July 17th, German Ambassadors in Japan and China had been instructed to express in a friendly manner to the Governments to which they were accredited the earnest hope and desire of the German Government for a peaceful solution.

In expressing the opinion that the situation had improved he repeated the assurance that Germany had no political aims in the Far East but only economic interests on both sides. He repudiated reports appearing in French press that Germany was committed to the support of Japan in view of anti-Communist agreement. This he said applied only to German-Japanese police matters and was not intended to be an interference in the internal affairs of China.

[3] Not kept in F.O. archives.

No. 145

Mr. Cowan (Peking) to Mr. Eden (Received July 26, 8.30 p.m.)

No. 347 Telegraphic: by wireless [F 4558/9/10]

PEKING, *July 26, 1937*

Following from Financial Adviser:[1]

Addressed to Nanking telegram No. 14 of 24th July. Repeated to Peking, copied to Tokyo.

Saionji, grandson of Genro,[2] arrived from Japan yesterday and dined with me.

I gathered he was acting as an unofficial emissary from Konoye and *inter alia* was to ascertain whether chances of a settlement of existing difficulties would be improved if Japan made a proposal to send an important statesman to China to explore possibilities of such a settlement. He emphasised the time-factor and, as Soong is the only important Chinese figure in Shanghai, has already expressed a wish to meet him as soon as possible. I have arranged a meeting this afternoon.

2. When I saw Soong in this connexion he told me that Yoshida[3] (the Mitsubishi manager here who is a recognised Japanese intermediary) had just been to see him to convey unofficially that Japan did not want a major war and was prepared to settle present dispute on following terms:

(a) Recognition by Nanking of local settlement reached by Sung Che-yuan,

(b) Withdrawal of troops on both sides but Japanese withdrawal to be slower than Chinese as the latter can send troops into Hopei faster than Japanese reinforcements can reach China.

[1] Mr. E. Hall-Patch.
[2] i.e. Prince Kimmochi Saionji, the last surviving Japanese elder statesman.
[3] Mr. Masaji Yoshida of the Mitsubishi Bank.

(c) Immediate discussion of general settlement of all Sino-Japanese differences and for this discussion Japan would be prepared to send Hirota (and perhaps Sujiyama also) to China.

(d) No further territorial encroachment was intended by Japan and if a general settlement of other questions can be reached China would receive suitable assurances that there was no intention to annex Hopei.

3. I have since gathered from Saionji that condition (b) above is Yoshida's own suggestion and did not come from Konoye. I have been unable to ascertain from him on whose authority Yoshida made these proposals to Soong but my impression is that Saionji and Yoshida are acting in concert to some extent but Saionji represents Konoye personally and Yoshida is acting as unofficial emissary of Japanese Foreign Office.[4] Yoshida expected to meet Soong early this morning and there are indications he wished to forestall Saionji. It is quite clear that the latter is acting independently of Japanese diplomatic machine.

4. If I obtain information from either Soong or Saionji as to what transpires this afternoon, I will telegraph further.[5]

[1] In a minute of July 28 Mr. Ronald commented: 'That a man of M. Yoshida's views should be acting as unofficial emissary of the Japanese foreign office, if he really is, seems worth noting: his employment under the late M.F.A., M. Sato, would have seemed perfectly natural; possibly M. Hirota after all has not abandoned all the "illusions" of his predecessor. . .'

[5] In telegram No. 271 of July 30 Sir H. Knatchbull-Hugessen reported that according to Mr. Hall-Patch, T.V. Soong and Chiang Kai-shek had given careful consideration to Mr. Saionji's proposals, but thought 'they offered no real solution of Chinese difficulties unless China was again to yield to Japanese pressure . . . it had been decided to make no response to feeler thrown out by Konoye as it was felt that if negotiations were opened they would only break down and Chinese would then be accused of having rejected reasonable proposals'.

No. 146

Sir E. Drummond (Rome) to Mr. Eden (Received July 28)

No. 150 Saving: Telegraphic [F 4596/9/10]

ROME, *July 26, 1937*

Your telegram No. 251.[1]

I spoke to the Minister for Foreign Affairs this evening in the sense of your instructions. Count Ciano told me that after my last conversation with him on this subject he had got into touch with Berlin and the two Governments had made a *démarche* with the Chinese and Japanese Governments saying that they trusted that both would maintain an attitude of moderation and offering to co-operate in any way they could

[1] See No. 144, note 2.

with a view to a settlement of the dispute. They had done nothing more as yet.

After this His Excellency discussed with me at considerable length the present position in the Far East. In his view China would never declare war upon or take action which must bring about war with Japan unless she had considerable hopes that some outside Power would intervene. Japan, particularly at this time of year, could send her fleet up the Yangtse; could set fire to and bombard the more important Chinese towns; could act militarily from the north and equally attack China from the south from the important air base established at Formosa; the Chinese really had no chance whatever of putting up any prolonged opposition. Her air force was efficient but small.

I replied that, however this might be, the time might come when Chiang Kai-shek would be faced with the risk not only of his own disappearance but also of that of the Nankin Government if he agreed or permitted the extension of Japanese authority over the five provinces in the north. It might be true that China could put up a small military resistance, but it was one thing to conquer a country and another to hold it down and the results must ultimately be very serious for Japan from an economic point of view.

Count Ciano admitted all this but nevertheless held that unless Russia was prepared to intervene, and he himself did not think this likely at the present time, the Chinese statesmen while talking very loudly would not run the risk of war. However, as he remarked at the end of our conversation which went on for a long time, no one ever knows what is going to happen in the Far East and we can only watch developments. Meanwhile Italy would do what she could again to counsel moderation should the necessity arise.[2]

[2] In a minute on this telegram Mr. Ronald commented (July 29): 'it is interesting that the Italians deemed it necessary to concert with the Germans before saying anything at all to either disputant and that, the line decided, the representations were apparently made jointly. Possibly the Berlin Rome axis is an object of veneration and respect in Tokyo, but Nanking regards it in quite another light.' Sir R. Vansittart wrote: 'An interesting illustration of the closeness of the Rome-Berlin axis. And so long as it continues to be quite as close as this . . . I shall continue to be sceptical of Italian professions, unless they are accompanied by concrete and satisfactory actions. Of that there is at present little or no trace. R.V. July 29.'

No. 147

Mr. Eden to Sir H. Knatchbull-Hugessen (Peking)

No. 412 [F 4535/9/10]

FOREIGN OFFICE, July 26, 1937

Sir,
    The Chinese Ambassador asked to see me this morning when he stated

that General Chiang Kai-shek had seen you on Saturday,[1] when he had told you of the progress of peace negotiations. The terms demanded by Japan were: (1) an apology, together with punishment of those guilty of the incident, and a guarantee that such an incident would not recur. (2) The demilitarisation of L[o]ukouchiao and Lung Wang Miao. These places should in future be occupied by militia and not by troops. (3) The suppression of blue-shirts and all other Communist and other anti-Japanese activities.

2. General Chiang Kai-shek had informed you that bad as these terms were if they had been agreed by General Sung they would be accepted by the Chinese Government. If they had not been agreed then the Chinese Government would like certain modification. The Ambassador added that this meant that the Nanking Government had accepted the terms, for it was known that General Sung had done so.

3. General Chiang Kai-shek further informed you that he was much preoccupied by the fact that Japanese troop movements had been intensified since July 22nd when these terms had been agreed. He wished it to be realised that the Chinese Government had made the maximum concession in their power and that if the Japanese Government were to bring fresh demands, then China would have to resist. General Chiang Kai-shek was all the more preoccupied because he had information tending to show that the Japanese Government proposed to submit fresh demands in about a week's time. These would include [1] a request that the Central Government should not interfere in the conduct of foreign affairs by the Hopei-Chahar Political Council. (2) That there should be a common front against Communism, by which, the Chinese Ambassador explained, Soviet Russia was meant. (3) There might also be a request for the recognition of Manchuria.

4. It was in these conditions that General Chiang Kai-shek asked once again for our good offices. He argued that we should jointly with the United States and with France make it clear to the Japanese that China had gone to the limit of concession and that if anything more was demanded she would be compelled to resist. He also hoped that we should suggest that the troops on both sides should now be withdrawn. General Chiang Kai-shek was of the opinion that Tokio did regard the incident as closed, but the Army was 'greedy' and unless a word of warning were uttered would formulate fresh demands with disastrous consequences.

5. The Ambassador explained that a similar communication had been made to the United States and French Ambassadors[2] by General Chiang

---

[1] i.e. July 24. Sir H. Knatchbull-Hugessen reported this conversation in his telegram No. 246, drafted on July 24, but it was delayed in transmission and did not reach the Foreign Office until 7 p.m. on July 29. According to this telegram Chiang Kai-shek told Sir H. Knatchbull-Hugessen that Sung Che-yuan 'had reported to the Central Government the conclusion of agreement with the Japanese. . .': cf. No. 130.

[2] See *F.R.U.S.*, 1937, vol. iii, pp. 256–8, and cf. *D.D.F.*, *op cit.*, No. 278. See also No. 148 below.

Kai-shek, and it was hoped that after consultation we should be able to take joint action in the matter.

I am, etc.,
ANTHONY EDEN

No. 148

Sir. H. Knatchbull-Hugessen (Nanking) to Mr. Eden
(Received July 27, 9.30 a.m.)

No. 252 Telegraphic: by wireless [F 4562/9/10]

NANKING, *July 27, 1937*

United States Ambassador saw Chiang Kai-shek on July 25th. Latter spoke on the same lines as those reported in my telegram No. 246.[1] But he was more explicit as regards further details of demands which he expected Japanese Government will make. He outlined these as follows:

(a) Settlement of all questions connected with Manchuria.

(b) Withdrawal of all troops from Hopei (for which Ho-Umetsu agreement[2] would be invoked).

(c) Suppression of anti-Japanese activities and communism on a *national* scale (the July 11th agreement[3] only providing for these measures *locally*). Chiang Kai-shek repeated in this connexion his expectations that some measures against Russia would be included.

2. Chiang Kai-shek expressed hope that United States Government and His Majesty's Government would not cease to display active interest about North China and said that some more positive declaration of our position was necessary if Japan was to be discouraged from presenting further demands.

3. United States Ambassador formed impression with which I agree that if any joint action were found possible by our two Governments an element in it to which Chinese Government would attach importance would be that we should endeavour to assume position of guarantor for any Sino-Japanese agreement so as to prevent the concealment and distortion which have taken place e.g. with Ho-Umetsu agreement (see last sentence of paragraph 3 of my telegram No. 235[4]). United States Ambassador seemed however, to think it undesirable that we should go too far as we . . .[5] such risk of serious embarrassment. He thought Japan had a fixed policy of domination in (?North) China which would be pursued by successive stages of which this is one. In his view China must decide for herself when the moment for serious resistance has come.

4. There is much in my United States colleague's view and it may not be thought desirable to become involved too deeply, for instance as in

[1] See No. 147, note 1.   [2] See No. 39.   [3] See Nos. 101 and 103.
[4] Of July 22, not printed (F 4388/9/10).   [5] The text was here uncertain.

Shanghai in 1932.[6] In this connexion unless we can place complete faith in Japanese declarations of moderation contained in Tokyo telegram No. 246[7] and unless development reported in F[inancial] A[dviser]'s telegram No. 14 to Nanking[8] has any real meaning I still see no possibility of concerting policy other than action by United States Government and His Majesty's Government.[9] Chinese General Staff consider situation still very grave, and there are reports of fighting today at Lanfang on Peking-Tientsin line.[10]

Repeated to Peking, Tokyo, Commander-in-Chief, General Officer Commanding, Rear Admiral Yangtse.

[6] See Volume IX, Chapters III-V.

[7] In this telegram of July 23 Mr. Dodds reported that the Japanese Vice Minister for Foreign Affairs had assured him that the terms of the proposed local settlement (see No. 130) were 'not political' and that 'military would not exceed their instructions'.

[8] No. 145.

[9] Foreign Office minutes generally agreed with Mr. Ronald's comment of July 28 that 'Our position as mediators would be sufficiently difficult—as guarantors I feel it would be unthinkable'. Mr. Orde wrote on July 29: 'I trust that we shall not get involved in negotiations between the two parties. The Chinese are such inveterate wrigglers and self-deceivers that they are really best helped by leaving them to face hard facts by themselves. . .' Sir R. Vansittart concluded (July 29): 'We can be mediators, but we cannot possibly be guarantors', and authorized the despatch of telegram No. 268 to Washington on July 29, instructing Sir R. Lindsay to inform the U.S. Government that 'we could certainly not agree to act as guarantors of any settlement that might be reached between China and Japan': presumably the U.S. Government 'would equally find it impossible to assume such a role'.

[10] On July 25 a Japanese force of 100 men, which had been sent to Langfang on the Tientsin-Peiping railway, fought with the Chinese troops stationed there; on the same day Japanese forces seeking to reinforce the Japanese Legation guard in Peking came into conflict with Chinese troops at the south-west gate of the city. There was renewed fighting at Wanping. On July 26 General Katsuki, newly appointed commander of Japanese forces in the area, demanded the withdrawal of Chinese troops from Lukouchiao and Wanping on the 27th, and of the whole of the 37th Division from the Peking area on the 28th. On that day the Japanese forces attached the Chinese who were speedily defeated, leaving the Japanese in control of the whole Peking-Tientsin area. General Katsuki's ultimatum had been authorized by the Japanese General Staff in Tokyo, but as a limited operation which was not to extend beyond the Yungting river.

No. 149

Mr. Dodds (Tokyo) to Mr. Eden (Received July 27, 6 p.m.)

No. 251 Telegraphic [F 4585/9/10]

TOKYO, *July 27, 1937, 9.45 p.m.*

Your telegram No. 185.[1]

My first reaction when I read paragraphs 2 and 3 of Nanking telegram No. 246[2] was that Chiang Kai-shek was attempting to save face by

[1] This was a telegraphic version of No. 147.   [2] See *ibid.*, note 1.

exaggerating Japanese menace. I still think there is some truth in my view. Military activity in Japanese ports is consistent with declaration of Japanese Government that though they wish to avoid war they are ready for it if necessary. I do not agree that war fever is being worked up by the Japanese Government. Japanese people are naturally apathetic and a great deal of effort would be required to stir them to war fever heat. Little of such effort is evident.

2. In short, approaches made by Chiang Kai-shek to His Majesty's Ambassador and United States and French Ambassadors as seen from here suggest:

A. That he wishes to impress on these representatives that Japanese threat is so great that his concession in recognising local settlement was inevitable in order to stave off something much worse.

B. That he wants naturally to throw on them odium of making representations to Japanese in case there is substance in his fears.

3. I do not question the danger of Japanese Army exceeding their instructions (see paragraph 4 of my telegram No. 229[3], paragraph 5, of my telegram No. 230[3], and paragraph 2 of my telegram No.246[4]) and if the Chinese do not act on the settlement they signed the danger may recur. But assurance given me twice over by Vice Minister for Foreign Affairs was so categorical that I am not yet prepared to believe in the Japanese putting forward fresh demands if the Chinese carry out their part of the bargain. Unfortunately the latest news [5] and present Japanese ultimatum are not encouraging.

4. I agree with view of United States Ambassador at Nanking (paragraph 3 of Nanking telegram No. 252[6]) that Japan has a fixed policy of domination in North China which would be pursued by successive stages of which this is one and that China must decide for herself when to resist seriously. But I do not think Japanese Government intended this stage to take place at present.

5. Without further evidence therefore, I should not be prepared to recommend agreeing to Chiang Kai-shek's request which appears to be that we should ask Japanese Government not to present further demands. In my view this would only provoke the retort that they had no intention of doing this and had already told me so.[7] But the Chinese must carry out local settlement or my argument is invalid.

6. I have shown this telegram to United States Ambassador who tells me that he agrees with it one hundred per cent.[8]

Repeated to Nanking and Washington.

[3] No. 129.   [4] See No. 148, note 7.   [5] Cf. No. 148, note 10.   [6] No. 148.
[7] Mr. Orde (July 28) did not agree that there was no point in trying to prevent further Japanese demands: 'I don't think we can do anything to stop them, but I don't think there can be any particular harm in making an attempt so long as it is not of such a kind as to encourage the Chinese to think that we can really do something effective'. Sir R. Vansittart commented on July 29: 'I hope the U.S. G[ovt]. will let us hear from them soon. Every day is of value now'; cf. No. 152 below.
[8] See F.R.U.S., 1937, vol. iii, pp. 277–8.

No. 150

Sir E. Phipps[1] (Paris) to Mr. Eden (Received July 29)

No. 447 Saving: Telegraphic [F 4610/9/10]

PARIS, *July 28, 1937*

Minister for Foreign Affairs[2] tells me that Chinese Ambassador in Paris[3] informed him today confidentially that German Government intimated to Chinese Government a few days ago that if the latter invoked Russian assistance against Japan the German Government would be obliged to go to Japan's assistance.

Two days later a similar communication was made to the Chinese Government by the Italian Government.[4]

Repeated to Berlin and Rome by telegraph in cypher.

[1] H.M. Ambassador at Paris.   [2] Mr. Yvon Delbos.   [3] Dr. Wellington Koo.
[4] This telegram led to considerable minuting in the Foreign Office. Sir R. Vansittart wrote on July 29: 'This, if true, is very sinister and far-reaching. What might *we* expect if we got into trouble with Japan. But I think we must verify this rather more before we can accept it. And I wd ask the Chinese Government if it is true. *If* they say yes, then I wd ask the Germans and Italians if they really did hold the language alleged. We ought to know where we stand.' According to documents printed in *D.G.F.P.*, however, the German Government were anxious to maintain strict neutrality in the Far Eastern conflict: see Series C, vol. vi, Nos. 479, 480, and 493, and Series D, vol. i, No. 463.

No. 151

Extract from Cabinet Conclusions No. 32(37) of July 28, 1937

[F 4676/9/10]

5. The Secretary of State for Foreign Affairs recalled that at the Meeting referred to in the margin[1] he had reported that he had sent a telegram to washington suggesting joint action with the Government of the United States of America with a view to averting war in the Far East.[2] After some delay the American Secretary of State had made clear that he was not prepared for joint representations to China and Japan as he thought they would be liable to exacerbate the situation.[3] He himself, however, had made his own representations to Peking and Tokio. On the previous day, on receipt of grave reports from Peking, he had telegraphed to Tokio to try and restrain the Japanese Government,[4] and had

[1] i.e. on July 21: see No. 140.   [2] No. 135.   [3] See No. 139.
[4] The 'grave reports from Peking' were contained in two telegrams from Mr. Cowan on July 27 reporting information that the Japanese military intended to launch a general attack on Chinese forces either on July 27 or 28: see No. 148, note 10. Telegram No. 186 to Tokyo, despatched at 1.30 p.m. on July 27 and marked 'Most Immediate', stated that 'Any form of attack is certainly bound to endanger lives of foreigners and on this ground alone

asked the United States of America and some other Powers to take similar action. He gathered from the Press that the American Secretary of State had made representations to China as well as to Japan.[5] He regretted to report that the outlook was now bad and for the moment he could suggest no further action that could usefully be taken.

The Prime Minister recalled that the American Secretary of State's refusal to co-operate had not been owing to an objection in principle to joint representations, but on the ground that it was not likely to prove useful on the present occasion. It was only fair that the Cabinet should note the distinction.

The Chancellor of the Exchequer[6] recalled that at the time of the Shanghai affair the position had been reversed.[7] The United States Government had made proposals to us for joint representations that did not commend themselves, and we had preferred to proceed independently.

The Lord President of the Council[8] expressed the hope that if the crisis in the Far East developed unfavourably and it was suggested to bring the matter before the League of Nations, we should lose no time in making clear that we did not regard a reference to the League as useful.

The Foreign Secretary said that hints to this effect had already been given in reply to Questions in Parliament, and he did not think that a reference to the League of Nations would be pressed. He proposed, however, to see the United States Ambassador and to discuss with him as to whether any further useful action could be taken.[9]

The Prime Minister expressed the view that joint representations by the British and United States Governments were likely to produce more results than simultaneous and parallel representations. It would be deplorable if any major war were to develop.

The Foreign Secretary reported that some of his experts considered it possible that there would be no major war, but a long period of skirmishes interspersed with parleys.

apart from other considerations the strongest representations to the Japanese Government would be justified'. Mr. Dodds was instructed to make immediate representations to Mr. Hirota, 'adding anything which in your opinion is calculated to have a restraining effect on Japanese'.

[5] See *F.R.U.S.*, 1937, vol. iii, pp. 263–7, and 275–6.

[6] Sir J. Simon.

[7] Sir J. Simon was presumably referring here to his discussions as Secretary of State for Foreign Affairs with the U.S. Secretary of State, Mr. Henry Stimson, in February–March 1932. The two governments did act together over Shanghai, but it was in the British view bad tactics to make representations simultaneously to Japan over both the Manchurian and Shanghai questions. See Volume IX, Nos. 455 and 469, and Appendix II to Volume XX.

[8] Lord Halifax.   [9] See No. 152 below.

No. 152

Mr. Eden to Sir R. Lindsay (Washington)

No. 717 [F 4620/9/10]

FOREIGN OFFICE, *July 28, 1937*

Sir,

I asked the United States Ambassador to come and see me this afternoon when I read to him the recent telegrams which we had received from the Far East and also discussed the communications which we had each had from Washington. I pointed out that the sum total of this information went to show that the situation was rapidly deteriorating. In the circumstances I was anxious to examine with him whether there was any step that might yet be taken to attempt to avert the serious consequences which seemed imminent. I fully understood that the United States Government had been of the opinion that up to the present parallel representation rather than joint representation had been desirable, and I much appreciated the co-operation which had existed between us. At the same time I wondered whether the time had not now come for some joint representation and whether the U.S. Government might not now be willing to consider some such action as I had suggested in my telegram 239[1] to you. I appreciated that the chances of success might be slight, but it did seem that in any event such an attempt could do no harm, whereas it might conceivably have a steadying effect in Tokio.

2. The Ambassador who indicated that he shared my point of view in the matter and remarked that he regretted the reply contained in your telegram No. 196,[2] undertook to speak to his Government in this sense and to support the suggestion which I had made. His Excellency expressed special gratification at my action in keeping him fully informed of all the news which we received from the Far East—a procedure which he knew would be much appreciated in Washington.[3]

I am, etc.,

ANTHONY EDEN

---

[1] No. 135.   [2] No. 139.

[3] Mr. Bingham's account of this interview is printed in *F.R.U.S.*, 1937, vol. iii, pp. 286–8.

No. 153

Mr. Dodds (Tokyo) to Mr. Eden (Received July 29, 10.30 a.m.)

No. 258 Telegraphic [F 4631/9/10]

TOKYO, *July 29, 1937, 1.20 p.m.*

My telegram No. 257.[1]

I received strong impression from my conversation with Soviet Chargé d'Affaires which took place after my interview with Minister for Foreign Affairs that he believes Soviet Government might be prepared to threaten Japanese Government if His Majesty's Government would do so also but that *in any case* they would use the methods in China if Nanking Government were involved which they have used in Spain during the past year.[2]

2. I had contemplated saying to Vice Minister for Foreign Affairs with reference to conversation reported in last paragraph of my telegram No. 212[3] that in my personal opinion Japanese Government are running an additional most serious risk if they are counting on Soviet Government standing aside and that in the event of Nanking Government intervening they ought not to exclude possibility of Soviet Government taking similar line in China to that which they have taken in Spain. But I fear this warning would at present stage do no good and might arouse suspicions.

3. Minister for Foreign Affairs yesterday gave me the impression of being impervious to argument but I find it difficult to believe the arguments I have during the crisis presented to him or Vice Minister for Foreign Affairs (and which they cannot pretend to have misunderstood as I usually left documents *pro memoria* though conversations were of course oral) are not in fact carefully weighed. United States Ambassador seems to take the view that representations from him or me or any foreigner are useless or harmful but I am unwilling to accept what seems to me a defeatist view.

Repeated to Nanking and Moscow.

---

[1] In this telegram of July 28 Mr. Dodds reported the Soviet Chargé d'Affaires as saying that 'the only argument that Japanese recognised was force and the only way to stop them therefore was active cooperation by non-aggressive powers'. He added that if 'Soviet Government and His Majesty's Government were together firm with Japanese Government the latter would stop their aggressive policy at once', but admitted that he had 'heard nothing on the subject from Soviet Government since this trouble started'.

[2] For documents on the Spanish civil war see Volumes XVII and XVIII.

[3] Not kept in F.O. archives.

No. 154

Mr. Dodds (Tokyo) to Mr. Eden (Received July 31, 11 a.m.)

No. 267 Telegraphic [F 4732/9/10]

TOKYO, *July 31, 1937, 3.40 p.m.*

Shanghai telegram No. 14 to Nanking.[1]

I hear on fairly good authority that the Prime Minister[2] has with difficulty been prevented from resigning during the past week. It had been his wish a fortnight ago to try to settle Sino-Japanese difficulties by sending Minister for Foreign Affairs to China with wide powers but this is now of course out of the question as military have forced the . . .[3] He is said to be remaining in office as last hope of retaining some brake on the army. Please see my telegram No. 194.[4]

Navy are said to be very deprecating about the North China campaign. Repeated to Nanking.

[1] No. 145. [2] Prince Konoye. [3] The text was here uncertain.
[4] No. 95.

No. 155

Sir H. Knatchbull-Hugessen (Nanking) to Mr. Eden (Received July 31, 8.10 p.m.)

No. 275 Telegraphic: by wireless [F 4724/9/10]

Very confidential   NANKING, *July 31, 1937*

Your telegram No. 159.[1]

I questioned Vice Minister for Foreign Affairs who was present at my interview with Chiang Kai-shek [? when] the subject of Russia had been mentioned (see my telegram No. 239[2]) and he told me confidentially that nothing had been said either by German or Italian Governments in Nanking. What had happened was that German representative in Moscow had spoken as reported to the Chinese Ambassador and Italian representative had done the same later. He was even vague as to whether representatives had spoken to Chinese Ambassador or to a member of his staff but in any case the Ambassador had reported it.

I asked Vice Minister for Foreign Affairs if he could tell me whether Chinese Government had in fact approached the Russian Government. He replied that the Chinese Government had made no 'concrete suggestions' to Soviet Government and had found them disappointingly

[1] This telegram of July 29 asked Sir H. Knatchbull-Hugessen for his comments on No. 150.
[2] Of July 23, not printed (F 4469/9/10).

unforthcoming (see my telegram No. 260[3]). In reply to direct question he added that any suggestions which had been made were for diplomatic support only.

Vice Minister for Foreign Affairs expressed the view that in the present circumstances any repetition of frontier incident round Manchuria might have immeasurable consequences. Judging from the recent Amur affair[4] the Soviet Government were anxious to avoid trouble but it would be easy for Japanese to create an incident which would force them to resist.

He thought that Stalin seemed to have strengthened (*sic*) himself by recent purges, if he were forced into a war there might be a revolution in Russia. He evidently meant to suggest that Japan and others might be counting on this.

Vice Minister for Foreign Affairs' views are at least logical if his information is correct. I have no outside information beyond that given in my telegram No. 239 and 249.[5] Soviet Ambassador was here for a few days laying very low and has returned to Shanghai.[6]

---

[3] In this telegram of July 29 Sir H. Knatchbull-Hugessen reported that according to the French Ambassador Chiang Kai-shek had spoken 'very bitterly regarding complete detachment and disinterestedness of Soviet Government in the present crisis': cf. No. 153, note 1.

[4] Cf. No. 108, note 3.   [5] Not kept in F.O. archives.

[6] Telegram No. 170 to Nanking of August 3 asked Sir H. Knatchbull-Hugessen to 'ascertain whether Chinese Government attach importance to language said to have been used in Moscow', and warned him that it might eventually be desired to enquire in Berlin and Rome 'what real attitude of German and Italian Governments is'. In telegram No. 297 of August 6, however, Sir H. Knatchbull-Hugessen replied that according to the Vice Minister for Foreign Affairs the 'whole matter had been exaggerated' and no importance should be attached to it. On August 10 Sir R. Vansittart agreed to let the matter drop: 'We have not enough to go on.'

No. 156

Sir H. Knatchbull-Hugessen (Nanking) to Mr. Eden
(Received July 31, 9 p.m.)

No. 277 Telegraphic: by wireless [F 4726/9/10]

NANKING, *July 31, 1937*

Addressed to Commander in Chief telegram No. 67 July 31st.

My telegram No. 276[1] to Foreign Office.

However unlikely these dangers might appear at present I feel that it would be imprudent not to be prepared for them. In particular I think that we should make every effort to prevent 1932 situation from recurring

---

[1] In this telegram of July 31 Sir H. Knatchbull-Hugessen reported a warning by the Chinese Vice Minister for Foreign Affairs that serious consequences might follow if the Japanese again used the international settlement at Shanghai as a base for hostilities.

in Shanghai[2] and it is perhaps not too soon to concert with other interested Powers in joint representations on the subject to be made at the appropriate moment to Japanese Government. The minimum required is an undertaking from the Japanese Government that neither the settlement itself nor the river fronting the settlement will be used in any way in connexion with hostilities. I do not however think this in itself would be sufficient to avert trouble of which there is always a danger so long as Japanese landing party is allowed to remain. The only certain safeguard would be the complete withdrawal of the latter possibility [sic] in return for an undertaking from other Powers to make themselves responsible for external security of the settlement. This would involve an obligation on their part to bring in an adequate number of troops for the purpose. However unlikely it may be that Japanese would accept such a proposal I presume . . .[3] would more squarely place on them the responsibility for any untoward consequences.

Representations might include a request for an undertaking that international settlement at Kulangsu also would not be used in any way in connexion with hostilities but we should not undertake any obligations for defence here since the situation is quite different from that at Shanghai.

I should be grateful for Your Excellency's observations in the first place and would then refer to the Foreign Office.

Repeated to Peking, General-Officer Commanding, Tokyo, Foreign Office and Shanghai.

[2] See Volume IX, Chapters III–V.   [3] The text here was uncertain.

No. 157

Mr. Cowan (Peking) to Foreign Office[1] (Received August 2, 8.20 p.m.)

Nos. 381 & 382 Telegraphic: by wireless [F 4792/9/10]

PEKING, *August 2, 1937*

Addressed to Nanking No. 318 of August 2nd.

Please consider following as a series of notes for pencil [sic] letter which I should send you if ordinary means of communication were not cut and please remember that three weeks ago my personal bias was:

    (A) An intense dislike of Japanese as a result of my experience during Sasaki case[2] last year.

    (B) Genuine affection for Peking Chinese—especially coolie and peasant class.

[1] Mr. Eden had left London for a three week holiday at Fawley on Southampton Water: see Volume XIX, No. 79, note 1. Lord Halifax took charge of the Foreign Office during his absence.
[2] See No. 2, note 6.

(C) Mild contempt (*increasing daily* as a result of Embassy site scandal)[3] for 'Soong dynasty' and for Nanking officials.

2. During the past few weeks interesting factor has been behaviour of Japanese Embassy as regards their attitude towards foreigners and as regards way in which they have imparted information. The attitude to foreigners has been extremely correct—I might almost say forthcoming— and their soldiery within the quarter have behaved no worse than they do in normal times. As regards information they have been most accessible and handed out to foreign representatives and to the press most precise and accurate details of their military operations and of their next day's plan of campaign. They have made no effort to conceal their nervousness regarding certain points where they were weak and their frank admittance of the one bad mistake that they have made to date namely their misjudgment of character of 132nd division. They seem on the whole to have been considerate in their dealing with the Chinese but I have impression since Tungchow massacre[4] the gloves are off.

3. Attitude of local Chinese officials vis-à-vis this Embassy has been hopeless and helpless—Blackburn will have told you about that and I can assure you that there has been no change since he left. At the moment local Chinese officials are trying to involve the United States Embassy by asking them to make arrangements to evacuate 132nd division units. But the story is going round in Chinese circles that I am 'third party' referred to in Chang Tzu-chung's declaration as having helped to arrange for Sung's departure. Chinese police authorities both inside the City and in Western hills have been most helpful.

4. Attitude of Chiang Kai-shek during the whole time that hostilities were in progress disgusted foreign opinion here. But his broadcast denunciation of Sung[5] has really turned our stomachs. I find foreigners who three weeks ago would have gone out of their way to avoid sitting at same table with Japanese now expressing view that Hopei would be better off under Japanese than under Nanking. Sung as we know during past two years has out Chinesed the Chinese in devising obstructive methods of irritating resistance to Japanese penetration. His army were a decent lot and made no trouble in any of the towns which they garrisoned.

5. A few days ago I had hoped that Japanese would halt short of Paotingfu and with a view to maintaining fiction that whole affair is a local

[3] A reference to attempts to find a suitable site for a new British Embassy building at Nanking.

[4] It was reported in *The Times* on July 28 that 800 men of the Chinese 29th Army quartered in a compound outside the walls of Tungchow (capital of East Hopei) had been virtually annihilated by aerial bombing after refusing to surrender their arms to the Japanese. On August 3 it was reported that some 200 Japanese and Koreans at Tungchow had been massacred.

[5] According to a report in *The Times* of July 30, p. 14, Chiang Kai-shek in a press statement of July 28 had blamed Sung Che-yuan for the military débâcle and the loss of Peking: cf., however, No. 160 below.

incident would have delivered ultimatums rather on lines of those delivered in (?1918). But now it seems more probable that Japanese would attack without further warning. Perhaps in the long run this will be as well for I feel the more the Central Government people come into contact with General Sazuki's mechanised column the sooner they will come to their senses. That column was in action around Peking clearing up Tungchow salient and has made a great impression.

    6. My efforts have been directed chiefly on the following points:

A. Insisting on Japanese not taking action in advance of times fixed in their ultimatums regarding military action within and without Peking.

B. Insisting vis-à-vis Japanese Embassy on their military protecting our nationals and property: and that we have exactly the same rights that they have in North China.

C. Discouraging them from attempting any military action within the City.

As regards A & C I can only hope that my efforts were of some use. As regards B. I seem to have been not unsuccessful as I understand Paomachang has been made into a special area which is being guarded and patrolled by Japanese troops. Outside that area I understand there has been looting.

    7. I am repeating this to Foreign Office.[6]

[6] Minutes on this telegram revealed concern in the Foreign Office as to whether 'armed resistance by the Chinese at the present time would be foolhardy', and it was decided to consult the War Office 'in case we are later led to consider putting in a serious, though of course perfectly friendly, word of warning at Nanking'. The War Office replied in a 'Note on the Sino-Japanese military situation in North China' dated August 8 (F 4990/9/10), which the Foreign Office found on the whole reassuring. Mr. Orde commented on August 12: 'This is a very interesting appreciation. It bears out on military grounds of the right Chinese tactics our guess of what Chiang Kai-shek would be likely to do—viz. avoidance of massacre of his best troops while threatening the Japanese & forcing them to keep large forces at great expense in N. China. But he may be unable to pursue this course owing to faulty discipline & national cohesion. . .'

No. 158

Sir H. Knatchbull-Hugessen (Nanking) to Foreign Office
(Received August 3, 10 p.m.)

No. 284 Telegraphic: by wireless [F 4828/9/10]

NANKING, *August 3, 1937*

My telegram No. 275.[1]

Situation is quiet on the surface so much so that many people are inclined to believe even now that Chiang Kai-shek does not seriously

[1] No. 155.

intend to embark on large scale hostilities though I hold the opposite view. Apart from continuous movement of Central Government troops northwards along Peking-Hankow line there are numerous other indications that extreme measures are intended e.g. government have ordered from Asiatic Petroleum Company five million gallons of petrol to be distributed to 62 points in central provinces mostly north of the Yangtse; notice has been given to commercial and taxi companies here of intention to requisition; Waichiaopu are moving six cases of valuable archives to Hongkong for storage.

2. There is a very deep current of anti-Japanese feeling which is only restrained because people feel that the Generalissimo is at last about to lead them forward; but my impression is that if he failed them now there would be serious danger of an outburst of national feeling which would destroy him.

3. Military preparations are however far from complete nor are preparations being made of such a kind as to inspire confidence. There is in particular a lack of co-ordination due to personal jealousies amongst the military leaders which will bring disaster unless it can be corrected. Chiang Kai-shek is I understand at this moment dealing with this problem. His purpose is to eliminate the old militarist gang entirely from control in the field or at least let them destroy themselves and to conduct the serious operations himself through his own generals. Han Fu-shu and Yen Hsi-shan are both in Nanking and Li Tsung-jen is expected.

4. The Chinese while realising that their best policy is to lengthen Japanese line are most anxious to keep hostilities north of the Yangtse since their lines of communication and chances of obtaining munitions would be gravely prejudiced by hostilities on the Yangtse and a blockade of southern ports.

Repeated to Peking, Tokyo, Commander-in-Chief, General Officer Commanding and Rear Admiral Yangtse.

No. 159

Foreign Office to Sir R. Lindsay (Washington)

No. 277 Telegraphic [F 4890/9/10]

FOREIGN OFFICE, *August 4, 1937, 7.15 p.m.*

My telegram No. 239.[1]

1. U.S. Ambassador called on July 30th and enquired what sort of proposals we had in mind and whether we had considered possibility of suggesting suspension of hostilities for the purpose of and based on a proposal for the evacuation of Peking by *all* foreign personnel, both

---

[1] No. 135.

civilian and military, including the Japanese, and by all Chinese military forces, exclusive of the Peking gendarmerie, or any variant of such a proposal.[2]

2. In reply, Sir R. Vansittart informed U.S. Counsellor on August 3rd[3] that, in our view, the only practical proposals which could be put forward, at this date would seem to be that both sides should appoint plenipotentiaries to discuss terms for a settlement; His Majesty's Government and the U.S. Government might offer their good offices (a) in providing neutral ground where the plenipotentiaries might meet and (b) during the negotiations in smoothing any difficulties which might arise. If both sides agreed in principle to negotiations, then it might be urged that no more Chinese Central Government troops should be sent northward and no more Japanese troops should enter Hopei either from Manchuria or from Japan. Further arrangements with regard to troops would be a matter for the plenipotentiaries to discuss. It would be made clear that proposals were no more than an offer of good offices and in no sense constituted intervention. Any appearance of intervention might inflame public opinion in Japan and strengthen military party; it might also encourage the Chinese Government to believe that the U.S. Government and His Majesty's Government intended to take active measures to restrain Japan.

3. Recent developments made it clear that it would be impracticable to propose that the evacuation of Peking should be made the basis for suggesting the suspension of hostilities. In fact, hostilities seemed likely to continue until the Chinese and Japanese had agreed on some new form of administration for North China.

4. Repeated to Nanking No. 172, Peking No. 275, Tokyo No. 200, Paris Saving No. 139.

[2] Cf. *F.R.U.S.*, 1937, vol. iii, pp. 289–90. Mr. Eden had noted on July 30 on Sir R. Vansittart's record of this conversation: 'If this means that U.S. Govt. considers joint action discussable we should follow it up and explain a little more fully what we have in mind. We must no [sic] lose no opportunity of cooperating with U.S. Govt.'

[3] See *F.R.U.S.*, *ibid.*, pp. 319–20.

No. 160

Sir H. Knatchbull-Hugessen (Nanking) to Foreign Office
(Received August 4, 10 p.m.)

No. 289 Telegraphic: by wireless [F 4885/9/10]

NANKING, *August 4, 1937*

Addressed to Peking No. 404 of August 4th.
Your telegrams Nos. 318 and 319.[1]
Following for Mr. Cowan:

I have been meaning for some days to express my appreciation of the measures taken by you and military authorities for the safety of British subjects during the recent very trying time. Policy adopted by you as stated in paragraph 6 of your telegram No. 319 has been most successful and I congratulate you.

I do not wish to go into main subject of your telegrams in detail but in my opinion there is an appearance of being . . .[2] policy by obliging attitude of Japanese towards foreigners. It is clearly in their interest to avoid anything likely to annoy foreign Powers and I think this consideration should explain their whole attitude. Presence of Japanese soldiers must be viewed with background described in my telegram No. 263[3] to Foreign Office. It would be difficult to controvert contention that they are the aggressors and naturally they will do all they can to present themselves in the most favourable light.

I think you misjudge Chiang Kai-shek.[4] His position is exceedingly difficult. If the development to which you refer is the interview he gave to Central News Agency on July 29th we do not read it here as a denunciation of Sung but rather as a[n] exculpation.

Repeated to Foreign Office No. 289 for Sir R. Vansittart.[5]

---

[1] i.e. No. 157.   [2] The text was here uncertain.
[3] In this telegram of July 30 Sir H. Knatchbull-Hugessen referred to No. 149 and pointed out that the Sino-Japanese conflict must be viewed against the background of 'the immense exasperation of the Chinese in seeing Japan carrying out step by step a policy for domination of North China . . . the Japanese soldier regards himself as a demigod; the army adopt a haughty and truculent attitude on these occasions which would make the settlement of the simplest incident a difficult matter even if there were no element of chronic tension'.
[4] Cf. No. 157, note 5.
[5] In a note on the filed copy of this telegram Sir R. Vansittart indicated his agreement with Sir H. Knatchbull-Hugessen's comments.

No. 161

Sir H. Knatchbull-Hugessen (Nanking) to Foreign Office
(Received August 6, 9.30 a.m.)

No. 294 Telegraphic [*F 4919/9/10*]

NANKING, *August 5, 1937, 1.45 a.m.*

My telegram No. 278.[1]

I conclude from the silence which has followed your telegram No. 261[2] to Washington that all possibility of further action by ourselves and United States Government, whether joint or otherwise, has disappeared. In existing circumstances this seems inevitable. Nevertheless I would venture to put before you following considerations in the hope that some last-moment action may be thought possible.

Chinese decision to fight to a finish has been frequently declared and military preparations are sufficiently indicative that this decision will in the last resort be carried out. I understand tonight indirectly from Madame Chiang Kai-shek that Chinese army is preparing successive lines of defence southward from Machang (Tsinpu railway) to Paotingfu (Kinhan railway) and she states that when these preparations are complete the army will take the offensive against Japanese in Tientsin and Peking area. Military Attaché's opinion as to complete inadequacy of material etc. and as to inevitable result will have been clear from my recent telegrams. Indeed there are indications now that Chinese Government view the immediate future with increasing anxiety and are still anxious to keep an opening for negotiations.

On Japanese side even though military party must now have complete control there must be elements who view a prolonged war with serious misgiving. Civilian authorities have always appeared moderate and reassuring—see for instance last paragraph of your telegram No. 187[3] to Tokyo.

It seems to me almost unprecedented that a war on such a scale should be begun when there have been no direct negotiations between the governments of the potential belligerents. Only communications that have passed hitherto have been Japanese *démarche* reported in my telegram No. 216[4] and Chinese reply (my telegram No. 227[5]) followed by conversation reported in my telegram No. 229.[6] These exchanges seem purely ad hoc in relation to the immediate situation. There has been no attempt to deal with fundamentals.

[1] In this telegram of July 31 Sir H. Knatchbull-Hugessen explained why he did not think it was practical to suggest a simultaneous suspension of hostilities by China and Japan.

[2] This telegram of July 29 transmitted to Sir R. Lindsay the substance of No. 152.

[3] The last paragraph of this telegram of July 28 quoted the Japanese Foreign Minister as saying in the House of Peers on July 27: 'We have only friendly feelings for the Chinese people. We do not want war.'

[4] No. 127.   [5] No. 133.   [6] No. 134.

Japanese Ambassador is now returning to Nanking.

Would it be possible as a last effort for peace to suggest that before outbreak of hostilities a serious attempt at direct negotiations between the two governments should be made? If it is thought undesirable to make this suggestion officially to the two governments it could presumably be put forward without involving us in the responsibilities implied in point two of your telegram No. 239[7] to Washington, though if anything were to come of it the resulting negotiations would have to cover all outstanding questions.[8]

Repeated as usual.

[7] No. 135.
[8] On Sir R. Vansittart's instructions Mr. Orde asked Mr. Herschel V. Johnson, who had succeeded Mr. Atherton as Counsellor at the U.S. Embassy in London, to call on August 6 and read to him the greater part of this telegram, pointing out that it seemed to strengthen the argument for action on the lines proposed in No. 156. Mr. Johnson said he would telegraph to Washington, and that the U.S. Ambassador in Japan was being consulted: see F.R.U.S., 1937, vol. iii, pp. 339–40. An account of the interview was sent on August 7 to Tokyo and Nanking in telegrams Nos. 204 and 175 respectively, repeated to Washington as No. 284.

No. 162

Mr. Cowan (Peking) to Foreign Office (Received August 5, 8.20 p.m.)

No. 402 Telegraphic: by wireless [F 4937/9/10]

PEKING, *August 5, 1937*

Addressed to Nanking No. 341 August 5th.

I am very grateful for message contained in your telegram 404.[1]

I can assure you I am not hoodwinked by the apparent 'gentlemanly' attitude of Japanese. In fact at no moment since their local military success would I have been surprised to have received rude and abrupt notification that presence of Embassy guard and use of Embassy wireless was distasteful to them. But apparently it still suits their book to pretend that this is China and that they cannot even send their troops through the city without permission of local people. So long as they continue to play that game it suits our book for I am able to maintain that we together with American, French and Italians have absolutely equal rights with the Japanese in this part of China and the Japanese cannot do otherwise than acquiesce.

I regret that I misinterpreted Chiang Kai-shek's announcement which in the absence of comprehensive Chinese text was taken from Reuter report dated Nanking July 29th which states that on that date Chiang Kai-shek affirmed immediately after outbreak of Lukouchiao incident he gave Sung orders which he disobeyed.

Repeated to the Foreign Office for Sir R. Vansittart.

[1] i.e. No. 160.

No. 163

Foreign Office to Sir H. Knatchbull-Hugessen (Nanking)

No. 173 Telegraphic [F 4828/9/10]

Important   FOREIGN OFFICE, August 5, 1937, 10.35 p.m.

Your telegram No. 284.[1]

It is difficult to see what suggestions could be put forward by His Majesty's Government which might (a) be justifiable and (b) possibly have the effect of averting more serious hostilities, other than those contained in my telegram No. 277 to Washington,[2] but I shall naturally welcome any which you may be able to make.

The following points suggest themselves on which it would be useful to crystallise our views, and I shall be glad to have your comments upon them after such consultation as you may find possible and useful with your Service Attachés and with Financial Adviser before latter leaves for Japan.

(1) What are the chances of the Chinese army being able to offer effective resistance and how long could they keep it up;

(2) What are the chances of feeling in Japan hostile to the Army's continental adventures manifesting itself before the Army has completely crushed Chinese resistance;

(3) Does the expenditure probably involved (a) in consolidation of recent Japanese gains in North China, (b) in dealing with continued Chinese resistance (if any) seem likely to be so heavy as seriously to discredit Japanese military party and enhance influence of more moderate party, and if so, can any estimate be given of the time this process would take?

(4) What would be the effect of an early and complete Chinese military débâcle on

    (a) Chiang Kai-shek personally:

    (b) Chinese Central Government and process of unification:

    (c) Chinese finances:

    (d) British interests in China, existing and potential:

(5) Are these risks greater for Chiang Kai-shek and Central Government than those involved in immediate acquiescence in extension of Japanese hold on North China, assuming for the sake of argument that this would take the form of alternative 2 in Peking telegram to Nanking No. 322.[3]

(6) And if so, does it seem desirable that His Majesty's Government and U.S. Government, jointly or separately, should offer advice to Chiang

---

[1] No. 158.   [2] No. 159.

[3] In this telegram of August 2, transmitted to the Foreign Office as Peking telegram No. 385 of August 3, Mr. Cowan reported information that negotiations were proceeding on three alternative proposals for local administration: the second of these was the formation of a Hopei-Chahar anti-Communist autonomous government on the same lines as that in East Hopei.

Kai-shek that he should in the best interests of his Government and his country temporarily bow to the storm. Could such action (a) in any way damage our interests, (b) appear in the eyes of the Chinese people as providing Chiang Kai-shek with a valid excuse for not maintaining a hopeless struggle.

(7) Are risks to British interests greater if Chinese resist or acquiesce.

Have you any reason to suppose that communications contained in your telegrams Nos. 265[4] and 266[5] were addressed to any other Power besides ourselves? if so, to whom?, if not, why were we singled out?

Repeated to Peking No. 275 and Tokyo No. 202.

[4] In this telegram of July 30 Sir H. Knatchbull-Hugessen reported that Chiang Kai-shek had sent Mr. Donald to him with a message stating that China was going to fight to the bitter end, and was preparing to sever diplomatic relations with Japan. Chiang Kai-shek was 'prepared for a long struggle lasting perhaps two years and is determined to make the adventure so expensive for the Japanese that they will never attempt it again'.

[5] Not kept in F.O. archives.

No. 164

Sir H. Knatchbull-Hugessen (Nanking) to Foreign Office
(Received September 4)

No. 65 [F 6115/9/10]*

NANKING, *August 5, 1937*

Sir,

I have the honour to submit the following report and observations on the so-called Lukouchiao incident and its aftermath.

2. Lukouchiao, known to foreigners as the 'Marco Polo Bridge,' is an old stone bridge which crosses the Hun (or Yungting) River, 3½ miles north-west of Fengtai, which is itself 8 miles south-west of Peking. The name Lukouchiao is also loosely applied to the small walled city of Wanping, which stands at the east, or Peking, end of the bridge. Whatever importance Lukouchiao may have derives, not from the old road bridge, but from the neighbouring railway bridge carrying the tracks of the Peking-Hankow line across the river. A glance at the attached sketch map[1] will show that on the east side of the bridge the main line runs directly to Peking, while it is connected on the south by a branch with the Peking-Mukden line at Fengtai, and on the north by a branch with the Peking-Suiyuan line. Control of the bridge at Lukouchiao has accordingly a considerable strategic importance. Control of both Lukouchiao and Fengtai by the Japanese gives them effective command of all rail communication between Peking and the south; control of Tungchow and the Nankou Pass gives them a complete stranglehold on Peking and points northwards.

[1] Not printed.

3. The district between the western suburbs of Peking and the Hun River is flat, open and sparsely populated. It has been a favourite manœuvre ground of the Japanese troops. Whether the choice of this terrain was dictated by considerations other than its convenience I cannot say; it seems probable. The *right* of Japanese or any other foreign troops to hold manœuvres and field exercises in this district is denied by the Chinese, and has, I believe, been the subject of repeated protest. I deal with this point more fully in an appendix.[1]

4. At the time of the incident the Japanese forces in and near Peking consisted of one battalion, about 550 officers and men, at Fengtai, and the Embassy guard, about 460 officers and men, the majority of whom were actually at Tungchow on the evening in question.

5. The Chinese forces consisted of units of the 37th and 38th Divisions of the XXIXth Army under the command of General Feng Chih-an, Chairman of Hopei Province, and General Chang Tzu-chung, Mayor of Tientsin, respectively together with cavalry and other miscellaneous troops and gendarmerie. At the time of the incident there were at least 15,000 Chinese troops in and around Peking. The majority of them were stationed at the Nanyuan barracks south of Peking, the Peiyuan barracks to the north of Peking, and the Hsiyuan barracks near the Summer Palace. There was a post of about 100 men in Wanping and other parties guarding the bridges and other points in the neighbourhood. So far as I am aware, there was nothing abnormal in these dispositions. The Japanese, who see in every Chinese defensive measure an act of offence against themselves, have since put forward that the Chinese troops were engaged in building 'pill boxes' in the neighbourhood of the bridge, and that this was provocatory.

6. As to the incident itself, it is difficult to determine the facts from the many versions which have been published, but up to a point the story seems fairly clear. The Japanese battalion stationed at Fengtai, about 550 strong, was carrying out night manœuvres in the neighbourhood of the Marco Polo Bridge on the evening of the 7th July. Shortly before midnight, when two of the three companies in this battalion had already returned to Fengtai, the third company was engaged in a sham fight. Suddenly rifle shots rang out. The Japanese commanding officer immediately stopped the fight, assembled his men and put a telephone call through to the battalion headquarters at Fengtai, who in turn communicated with the Embassy in Peking. On receipt of the first message the two companies, which had just returned to barracks, were rushed back to Lukouchiao, and Colonal Matsui, 'Special Military Commissioner of the Japanese Army in Tientsin, stationed at Peking,' got into touch with the Hopei-Chahar Political Council. To the latter Colonel Matsui asserted that according to the information received from the field the man who had fired the shots had entered the walled city of Wanping, and he insisted that the Japanese must be allowed to enter the city and search for him. When the request was refused Colonel Matsui replied that the Japanese

would, if necessary, use force. (According to the Chinese version of the story the Japanese commander, on assembling his men, found that one was missing, and that it was to search for this man that he wished to enter Wanping City. This, however, seems unlikely. The Japanese version says nothing of a missing man, and the difference between the two versions is probably due to language difficulties.)

7. The Hopei-Chahar Council had, in the meantime, received reports from the Chinese side that the Japanese were closing in on the city in a threatening manner. So they hurriedly came to an arrangement with Colonel Matsui that a joint commission of investigation should proceed immediately to Lukouchiao. The party, consisting of Captain Teradaira (Colonel Matsui's assistant), Colonel Sakurai (Japanese adviser to the XXIXth Army), Mr. Wang Lei-chai (Magistrate of Wanping), Mr. Lin Keng-yu (of the Foreign Relations Commission of the Hopei-Chahar Council) and Colonel Chang Yung-nien (of the Hopei-Chahar Pacification Commissioner's headquarters) arrived at Wanping at 4 a.m. on the 8th July.

8. But in the meantime the alarm caused by these midnight commotions was leading to panic measures. Chinese troops from Nanyuan were rushed to the assistance of Wanping. The portion of the Japanese Embassy guard which was out at Tungchow was hastily recalled, to find the city gates closed, sandbagged and heavily guarded. Being unable to gain admittance it trudged round the outskirts of the city of Fengtai. Further Japanese reinforcements from Tientsin were rushed up to Fengtai by road.

9. The investigation party on reaching Wanping found the situation tense, with the two sides glaring at each other at close quarters, but not actually at blows. They entered the city and discussions were in progress (the Japanese still insisting that their troops be allowed to enter and search the city) when firing broke out again, and there was a heavy fusillade which lasted for an hour or more. The discussions, nevertheless, continued uneasily, interrupted from time to time by bursts of gun and rifle fire for nearly twenty-four hours, and at length on the early morning of the following day (9th July) a truce was arranged on the terms that the Chinese troops in the area of hostilities (including the garrison of Wanping) should withdraw to the west bank of the Hun River, and that the Japanese should also withdraw.

10. The terms of the truce were apparently not embodied in writing, and at once that difficulty arose which anyone familiar with Japan's relations with China from 1931 onwards could have foretold. It seems to be regarded as an insult to the Japanese army that they should be expected ever to deal with the Chinese army on a footing of exact equality. An arrangement for mutual withdrawal, by which the Chinese mean a simultaneous withdrawal, means for the Japanese that the Chinese must be humiliated by being compelled to withdraw first, whereupon the Japanese withdraw at leisure with all the prestige of victory. So it was at

Lukouchiao. The Chinese would half withdraw, but finding that no corresponding movement was taking place on the other side, they would rush forward again and reoccupy their original positions, with an inevitable aftermath of charges of insincerity and broken faith. There was further 'misunderstanding' regarding the point to which the Japanese were to withdraw. The Chinese asserted that, according to the terms of the truce, the Japanese were to withdraw to their original garrison quarters; the Japanese maintained that they need only withdraw a short distance from Wanping, provided they remained east of the river.

11. Meanwhile, the incident was having other and more far-reaching repercussions. General Chiang Kai-shek, Dr. Wang Chung-hui (Minister for Foreign Affairs) and the principal members of the Chinese Government were in Kuling, where also were beginning to assemble a large number of the leading educationalists and scholars from all parts of China whom it was the generalissimo's intention to put through a sort of summer school course in civics.

12. On the 9th July the Waichiaopu, acting on instructions from Kuling, lodged an oral protest with the Japanese Embassy in Nanking. On the following day a counter-protest was received from the Japanese Embassy. At the same time, alarming reports were reaching both Tokyo and Nanking regarding the extent and implications of the conflict, and of the military measures which each side was alleged by the other to be taking. By the 11th July all available men from the Tientsin Japanese garrison had been sent to Fengtai and reinforcements were beginning to arrive from Manchukuo. On the Chinese side, units of the XXXIInd, XLth and LIIIrd Armies already stationed in Hopei began to concentrate towards Shihchiachuang and Paoting (Peking-Hankow Railway), whilst three divisions of the XXVIth Route Army were ordered to move from Hupeh to Paoting. On the 11th July the Japanese Cabinet met in extraordinary session to consider 'fundamental decisions' said to have been reached with regard to the Government's North China policy and a Cabinet *communiqué* announced that the Government was taking all the necessary measures for the despatch of military forces to North China, though it was still hopeful that an amicable solution might be reached and the affair localised.

13. The Chinese authorities were also anxious to localise the incident, and there can be no doubt that their anxiety was increased by the extent of the Japanese military preparations which were now becoming evident. Late in the evening of the 11th it was announced that an agreement had been reached for the settlement of the incident and that—once more—both sides were to withdraw. The terms of this agreement have never been officially published, but were to the following effect:

(1) Withdrawal of Chinese troops from the Wanping area and their replacement by gendarmerie.

(2) An apology to be tendered on behalf of the XXIXth Army, and those persons responsible for the incident to be punished.

(3) Appropriate measures to be taken for the suppression of 'Blueshirt,' Communist and anti-Japanese activities.[2]

14. According to the Japanese Embassy these terms were embodied in a document which was signed by General Chang Tzu-chung (Vice-Commander of the XXIXth Army and concurrently Mayor of Tientsin) and Chang Yun-jung (Chief of Staff of the XXIXth Army) on behalf of the Hopei-Chahar Political Council and the XXIXth Army. This, it was said, was only an agreement on principles and discussions were then begun in Tientsin between military representatives of the two sides with regard to the enforcement of the terms. Wanping had already been evacuated by the Chinese troops, and was now garrisoned by gendarmerie; and the first half of the second term of the 11th July pact was executed on the 18th July, when General Sung Che-yuan expressed his regrets in person to General Katsuki, the Commander-in-chief of the Japanese forces in North China.[3] But there remain the questions of punishment and of suppression of anti-Japanese activities, &c. These two were difficult of settlement, particularly the latter, which was a sort of omnibus clause under the terms of which the Japanese could demand the removal of any person and the suppression of any form of activity which they might dislike throughout the jurisdiction of the Hopei-Chahar Political Council. As a first step they demanded the removal from the Peking area of the 37th Division, which they regarded as especially anti-Japanese and responsible for the Lukouchiao incident. This demand caused great indignation among the Chinese, and not least among the troops of that division, but General Sung Che-yuan decided that discretion was the better part of valour and eventually the evacuation of the 37th Division to points further south along the Peiping-Hankow Railway was begun, and units of the 132nd Division from Hokien, which the Japanese purported to regard as less unfriendly, brought in to take its place. All this was performed to the accompaniment of 'incidents' and 'misunderstandings' of more or less gravity which threatened at any moment to develop into large-scale hostilities.

15. General Sung Che-yuan had since the beginning of May been 'sweeping the tombs of his ancestors' at his home in Loling, in other words he was using a time-honoured device to evade the constant pressure of the Japanese military authorities who were endeavouring to wring from him concessions in connexion with the Langyen Iron Mines and the Tsanghsien-Shihchiachuang Railway. These were two of the schemes to which the Japanese attached great importance as part of their economic co-operation plans for North China, but which the Central Government had forbidden him to sanction. General Sung had accordingly gone into hiding, and it required the urgency of the present serious crisis to bring him out again. He had arrived in Tientsin on the 12th July to find the port had already been sold by his subordinate Chang Tzu-chung. All he could

[2] See Nos. 101 and 103.　　　　　　　　　　　　　[3] See No. 130.

do then was to make the best of a bad business. On the 18th July he met General Katsuki and tendered an expression of regret as mentioned above. On the 19th July he went to Peking to supervise the withdrawal of the 37th Division, and the further negotiations for the implementation of the 11th July agreement were left in the hands of General Chang Tzu-chung and General Hashimoto (Chief of Staff of the Japanese forces in North China).

16. On this same day (the 19th July) these two officers appear to have reached an understanding regarding the implementation, in part at least, of the 11th July agreement. According to Japanese official sources it was embodied in a note addressed by the Chinese to the Japanese military representative, undertaking to carry out the following terms:

(1) The elimination of 'those Chinese who are impeding good relations between China and Japan.'
(2) The suppression of Communists generally.
(3) The control of anti-Japanese organisations and their activities, including education of an anti-Japanese character.

The exact nature of this agreement (which came to be called the Chang-Hashimoto Agreement) are enveloped in the same mystery as shrouds most of the other Sino-Japanese pacts. As late as the 24th July General Sung Che-yuan denied that he knew its exact contents, and on the 25th July the Minister for Foreign Affairs informed me, personally, that the Central Government knew nothing about it.

17. Meanwhile, the Central Government were much disturbed at the turn which events in the north were taking. While anxious that the Lukouchiao incident should be localised if possible, they were even more anxious to prevent the conclusion of any more local pacts such as the Tangku Truce and the 'Ho-Umetsu Agreement,'[4] which could be used by the Japanese as pretexts for further tightening their grip on North China. On the 12th July the Waichiaopu informed the Japanese Embassy that no agreement for the settlement of the Lukouchiao incident would be regarded as valid unless it was sanctioned by the Central Government. On the 13th July all the members of the Chinese Government who were summering at Kuling returned to Nanking with the exception of General Chiang Kai-shek. On the 17th July the counsellor of the Japanese Embassy in Nanking called on the Minister for Foreign Affairs and, on instructions from his Government, made an oral communication (also embodied in an aide-mémoire) requiring the Chinese Government (a) to cease immediately all provocative activities, and (b) to refrain from obstructing the execution of the 11th July agreement.[5] The communication went on to say that, if the action of the Central Government continued, a very grave situation would arise whose consequences could not be foreseen. On the following day the Japanese military attaché made representations to the Chief of the General Staff to the effect that the

[1] See No. 39.   [5] See No. 127.

216

movement of Central Government troops into Hopei constituted a breach of the Ho-Umetsu agreement.

18. The Waichiaopu's reply to these representations was in the form of an aide-mémoire which was presented to the Japanese Embassy on the 19th July.[6] This aide-mémoire was to the following effect: China had not the least desire to aggravate the situation or provoke a conflict with Japan; she had, on the contrary, repeatedly declared her readiness to seek a settlement by pacific means; the Japanese Government, however, while professing anxiety not to see the situation aggravated, had despatched large numbers of troops to North Hopei, these movements—which had not yet ceased—indicating a clear intention on the part of Japan to resort to force; in the circumstances, the Chinese Government had been compelled to take adequate precautionary measures for self-defence; it had not, however, relaxed its efforts for peace; on the 12th July the Minister for Foreign Affairs, in discussing the situation with Mr. Hidaka, the counsellor of the Japanese Embassy, had proposed the mutual cessation of military movements and the withdrawal of troops on both sides to their original positions, but it was to be regretted that no reply had been received from Japan; the Chinese Government now wished to reiterate its desire for a peaceful settlement of the incident as well as its intention not to aggravate the situation; it therefore proposed that the two parties jointly fix a definite date for the simultaneous cessation of all military movements and the withdrawal of their respective armed forces to the positions occupied prior to the incident; as regards the procedure to be followed for the settlement of the Lukouchiao incident, the Chinese Government was prepared to enter into immediate negotiations with the Japanese Government through the regular diplomatic channels, the settlement of questions of a local nature susceptible of adjustment on the spot to be subject to the sanction of the National Government. In short, the aide-mémoire concluded, the Chinese Government was ready to exhaust all pacific means for the maintenance of peace in East Asia, and therefore all methods provided by international law and treaties for the pacific settlement of international disputes—such as direct negotiations, good offices, mediation or arbitration—would be equally acceptable to the Chinese Government.

19. On the same day (the 19th July) General Chiang Kai-shek took advantage of a speech to his conference of educational and other leaders in Kuling to make an important announcement to the people as a whole. After recalling the declaration of policy which he had made at the fifth plenary session of the Kuomintang Central Executive Committee in November 1935 ('while there is the slightest hope for peace we will not abandon it; so long as we have not reached the limit of endurance we will not talk lightly of sacrifice'), he asked his audience to consider well the meaning of the phrase 'the limit of endurance' and to realise its

[6] See No. 133.

217

importance, since once the decision to resist was taken, there could be no half-way measures and no turning back; the war must be waged to the bitter end with all its inevitable sacrifices. He then went on to consider the Lukouchiao incident. It was not, he said, a sudden and unpremeditated step. For a month past there had been indications that something was going to happen: there had been statements made in the Japanese press and through diplomatic channels, and news had been received from various sources that the Japanese were aiming to expand the scope of the Tangku Truce, to enlarge the bogus 'East Hopei Government,' to drive out the XXIXth Army, to force out General Sung Che-yuan, &c.; it was clear that the Japanese had a very definite policy towards China and that the Lukouchiao incident was only one step in its execution; the only way apparently in which the incident could have been avoided was by allowing foreign troops to go and come freely within Chinese territory while the Chinese army must be shackled; the four north-eastern provinces had gone, then there was the Tangku Truce, and now the point of conflict was at the very gates of Peiping; if Peiping became a second Mukden, what was to prevent Nanking from becoming a second Peiping? Finally, he enunciated the minimum conditions for a settlement beyond which the Chinese Government could not retreat. These were as follows:–

(1) Any settlement must be such that it did not impair the territorial integrity and sovereign rights of the Chinese nation.

(2) The status of the Hopei-Chahar Political Council being fixed by the Central Government, no illegal alteration of it could be permitted.

(3) There must be no removal by outside pressure of those local officials appointed by the Central Government, such as the chairman of the Hopei-Chahar Political Council.

(4) No restriction must be placed on the positions now held by the XXIXth Army.[7]

20. This speech was very well received in the country as much as for the fact that it showed that the generalissimo was resuming his grip on public affairs as for its reasonably clear definition of what was his last ditch.

21. The Japanese Government did not directly reply to the Waichiaopu's aide-mémoire, but early on the morning of the 20th July the Gaimusho issued a statement in Tokyo to the following effect: The Chinese reply to the Japanese communication evaded the two points raised by Japan, namely, that the Nanking Government should refrain from interfering with the 11th July local settlement and should cease all action hostile to Japan. The three following points were made: (1) Local agreements for mutual withdrawal had been broken by the Chinese, and it was therefore impossible to entertain seriously the Chinese proposal for the suspension of military movements on both sides and withdrawal to original positions; (2) China could hardly claim that the despatch of troops northwards in such huge numbers was self-defence; in view of these

[7] See No. 132.

218

Chinese actions, the Japanese Government had taken the decision to send reinforcements, it was true, but actually, except for a small contingent, these had not been sent; (3) Nanking had hitherto recognised the Hopei-Chahar Council, and had not interfered with agreements into which it had entered; a change of policy now was unjustified, particularly as it could only be an obstacle to peace. The assumption underlying the second of these points, that the movement of Chinese troops in Chinese territory is offensive while the movement of Japanese troops in China is defensive, could hardly be expected to appeal to the Chinese, while the third point is simply grotesque when the history of the formation of the Hopei-Chahar Council and the efforts of the Central Government to retain control of foreign relations is considered.

22. While these diplomatic exchanges were taking place the situation in North China was deteriorating rapidly. On the 18th July a Japanese military aeroplane, scouting along the Peking-Hankow Railway, had machine-gunned a train near the Hopei-Honan border. The pilot alleged that the train was carrying troops, and that as he flew low to investigate he was fired on. (It is yet to be explained by what right he was flying where he was, or what other action the Chinese troops could reasonably have been expected to take.) On the 19th and 20th July there was considerable firing around Peking, and the Japanese bombarded Wanping as a reprisal for the wounding of a Japanese officer. All seemed to turn at this moment on whether or not the 37th Division would evacuate Peking and neighbourhood peacefully. The Japanese anticipated that there might be some resistance, and the situation became so threatening that arrangements were made to bring all British subjects into the city, even, if necessary, into the Legation quarter. On the 22nd July, however, the Japanese Embassy expressed themselves satisfied with the progress of the withdrawal of the 37th Division, and for a brief space there was ground for thinking that, if no hitch occurred, some modus vivendi might be arranged on the basis of the 11th July terms, and a major conflict avoided. It was reported from Tientsin that powerful influences were working for peace, and that a special emissary had flown from Tokyo with orders to General Katsuki to avoid further hostilities. As to the Central Government's attitude, the generalissimo, on the 21st July, told me that he was most earnestly desirous of reaching a peaceful solution. His only proviso was that it should be consistent with the four points of his declaration.

23. When I saw him again on the 24th[8] he told me that General Sung Che-yuan had reported the terms of the 11th July settlement to the Central Government for approval, and that the Central Government had replied that they did not wholly approve of the agreement, but if it had already been signed they were prepared to ratify it. I gained the impression that at this time the generalissimo did not realise how far surrender to the Japanese demands had already gone. Not only did he

[8] See No. 147, note 1.

seem to be unaware that the 37th Division was even then withdrawing, but he also denied all knowledge of the further agreement which was said to have been reached in Tientsin on the 19th July; indeed, in reply to a question from myself, based on the third clause of this alleged agreement, he stated most emphatically that there could be no question of conceding to the Japanese any right to interfere in educational matters. He expressed himself, however, as most apprehensive that the Japanese would not rest content with the terms of the 11th July settlement, but would make further demands; if they did so, he said, it would be a serious matter, since the 11th July terms, which the Central Government had now ratified, represented the absolute limit of the concessions they were prepared to make.

24. On the 24th July, the very day on which I had the foregoing interview with the generalissimo, the Japanese Embassy in Peking informed Mr. Cowan that they were no longer satisfied with the manner in which the withdrawal of the 37th Division was being carried out; not only was it going too slowly, but certain units were stating openly that they had no intention of withdrawing. The Japanese military authorities were also uneasy about the arrangements for the replacement of the Peking garrison by units of the 132nd Division, since it seemed that advantage was being taken of the change-over to increase the garrison by 1,000 men. Unless matters could be settled by negotiation, the Japanese Embassy indicated that a definite time-limit would be given for the withdrawal of the 37th Division, accompanied by a threat of force.

25. At 11 p.m. on the 25th July Japanese troops came into collision with the small Chinese garrison, consisting of troops of the 38th Division, at Langfang, a station on the Peking-Mukden Railway about half-way between Peking and Tientsin. The Japanese troops were alleged by the Japanese to have gone there for the purpose of repairing telephone wires which had been cut, but it seems reasonable to suppose that they were determined to evict the Chinese troops, whose presence was a menace to the Japanese lines of communication. Whatever the purpose, the Chinese were driven out with very severe casualties, chiefly the result of aerial bombing. The fact that this allegedly treacherous attack by Chinese troops on the Japanese resulted in eleven Japanese casualties and at least forty times that number of Chinese casualties tells its own story.

26. The following afternoon (the 25th July), at 4.45 o'clock, an ultimatum in the name of the Imperial Japanese Army was presented to General Sung Che-yuan in Peking by Colonel Matsui, acting on behalf of General Katsuki. This ultimatum demanded:

(1) The withdrawal of the units of the 37th Division at Lukouchiao, Papaoshan and Wanping to Changsintien before noon on the 27th; and

(2) The withdrawal of the units of the same division inside the city and at Hsiyuan and other places west of Peking, to points west of the Yungting River before noon on the 28th.

In the event of failure to comply with these demands, it was indicated that the Japanese troops would take all necessary steps to enforce them. It was further indicated that the 37th Division would be required to withdraw eventually south of Paoting.

27. As the Japanese, later that evening, were bringing back into Peking part of the Embassy guard which had been out at Fengtai, another serious incident occurred. It seems that permission for the guard to pass through the Changyimen Gate had been obtained from some Chinese authority, but there was some dispute as to the numbers who were to be allowed in, and when one-third of the party had entered, the Chinese closed the gate, whereon a pitched battle ensued, with a number of casualties on both sides.

28. For the Japanese military authorities this was the last straw. At 9.30 a.m. on the following day (27th July) the Senior (American) Commandant of the Embassy guards was informed by the Japanese liaison officer that at noon a general attack would be launched on all Chinese forces, both inside and outside the city, irrespective of whether the withdrawal of the 37th Division was proceeding satisfactorily or not. Mr. Cowan at once instructed His Majesty's consul-general at Tientsin to lodge a strongly-worded protest with the Japanese Ambassador, imploring him to exercise his authority to prevent any unnecessary violence, and pointing out that, if at noon the 37th Division was in fact withdrawing, an attack by the Japanese forces could only be regarded by the entire civilised world as an act for which there was no possible justification. Brigadier Hopwood made similar representations to the Japanese military authorities in Tientsin; and I asked the counsellor of the Japanese Embassy here to inform his Ambassador that I strongly endorsed Mr. Cowan's remarks. These representations proved successful, and the Japanese military authorities were persuaded not to anticipate the programme laid down in their ultimatum.

29. General Sung Che-yuan had, however, in the meantime issued a proclamation that it was impossible for him to accept the Japanese demands. Consequently, the Japanese troops, in the afternoon of the 27th July, began to carry out their threat to evict the 37th Division by force. At the last moment the 132nd Division was also included in the interdict, since men of that division had been involved in the Changyimen Gate clash on the previous evening. Thus the Japanese demands now amounted to the virtual demilitarisation of the Peking area. Heavy fighting ensued all round Peking. Extraordinary and—to anyone with any knowledge of the comparative fighting value of the forces engaged—quite incredible reports of Chinese victories were broadcast all over China, but the fact is that the immense superiority of the Japanese armament, aided by treachery in the Chinese camp, made short work of the Chinese resistance, and by the evening of the 28th all units of the XXIXth Army in the area (excluding the two or three regiments of the 132nd Division which were inside the city and neither attacked nor were molested by the Japanese) were in full retreat. The Chinese casualties were enormous;

estimates vary from 5,000 to 15,000; the Japanese casualties negligible. Late that evening General Sung Che-yuan, commanding the 29th Army and chairman of the Hopei-Chahar Political Council, accompanied by the mayor of Peking (General Chin Te-ch'un) left by motor car for Paoting, after hastily appointing General Chang Tau-chung (mayor of Tientsin and commander of the 38th Division) to act in the dual capacity of acting chairman of the Hopei-Chahar Council and acting mayor of Peking.

30. During these operations around Peking on the 27th July a Japanese unit, assisted by aircraft, almost annihilated the Chinese force (XXIXth Army) which by a strange anomaly had still garrisoned the western or Peking gate of Tungchow City, the headquarters of the East Hopei Government. There were 400–500 Chinese casualties; ten Japanese casualties were reported. Two days later the East Hopei gendarmerie (Paoantui) which had been concentrated at Tungchow, turned on their Japanese masters. The small Japanese garrison was beleaguered and about 250 Japanese and Korean civilian refugees in the city were massacred. The Japanese took a swift revenge; the garrison was relieved by a mechanised unit and bombing planes; the gendarmerie were routed and almost exterminated in a chase which continued nearly to the gate of the Summer Palace.

31. An even more serious affair had broken out almost simultaneously at Tientsin. At about 3 a.m. on that day (29th July) units of the 38th Division and gendarmerie made a surprise attack on the East Station, the aerodrome on which a considerable number of Japanese military machines were standing, and the barracks in the Japanese concession. The Japanese were taken off their guard, but reacted with characteristic vigour and ruthlessness and at the end of twenty-four hours had the situation under control; though 'mopping up,' which necessitated the use of aircraft and artillery, continued for several days more; by that time the Nankai University and other important buildings were in flames and enormous loss of Chinese life and damage to property had occurred. The foreign concessions were for a time in great danger, and there were a few casualties caused apparently by stray bullets. As always happens on these occasions, the foreign communities were faced with special problems arising from the hundreds of thousands of Chinese refugees who crowded into the concessions or clustered round the confines, most of them foodless, homeless and completely destitute.

32. On the same day, the 29th July, Japanese destroyers lying off Tangku bombarded the village of Taku, from which a number of rifle shots had been fired, whereafter a landing party drove off the Chinese troops, which appear to have been units of the 38th Division.

33. On the 27th July the Minister for Foreign Affairs, Dr. Wang Chung-hui, sent for my American colleague and myself and made a statement for confidential communication to our respective Governments. The Japanese, he said, had now expanded the terms of the original agreement far beyond its intended limits, and it was clear that they did not

intend to rest content with a local solution on the basis of the 11th July agreement, but would engage in a gradual crescendo of demands. In face of this continual and increasing pressure and of the growing threat from the Japanese side, the Chinese Government had now reached the 'limit of endurance' (phrase made familiar by Chiang Kai-shek) and would be forced to make a stand. In reply to a question, he implied that the Chinese Government were considering the severance of diplomatic relations with Japan. Similar communications were subsequently made to my French, German and Italian colleagues. Both Mr. Johnson and I were struck by the vagueness of the phraseology employed by Dr. Wang, which seemed to us to indicate that perhaps the situation was not so desperate as it seemed, and that the generalissimo was still hopeful of a solution other than by an appeal to arms.

34. As, however, reports came in of clash after clash—Peking, Tungchow, Tientsin, Taku—and the complete rout and enormous casualties of the XXIXth Army, all hope of a peaceful solution seemed to vanish. On the afternoon of the 29th the generalissimo sent me a message by his Australian adviser, Mr. [W. H.] Donald, to the effect that the loss of Peking and Tientsin was not of any military consequence at the moment; it had always been allowed for in the Chinese plans and the most that had been expected of General Sung Che-yuan was that he would fight a delaying action while the Central Government made its preparations; but now the Government was going to fight to the bitter end. Mr. Donald added that the Chinese plans, which had been drawn up with the help of the German advisers, were designed with a view to pushing the Japanese back beyond the Great Wall and involved an advance along four columns, one of which would proceed via Suiyuan and Chahar.

35. There is good ground for believing that the decision to embark on war with Japan on a national scale was only accepted with the greatest reluctance by the generalissimo, who realises, probably better than any other Chinese, how totally inadequate the Chinese organisation is to meet the Japanese military machine which has been constructed and maintained in readiness for just such a crisis. But, the decision having been taken, such dispositions as the imperfect organisation permits are being put into effect. Troop movements indicate that a line from Paoting (on the Peking-Hankow Railway) to Tsangchow (or Tsanghsien, on the Tientsin-Pukow Railway) will form the first Chinese front, and two divisions are reported to have reached Kalgan from Suiyuan; so the initial movements at any rate are taking place according to plan.

36. Behind the front strenuous preparations are being made to meet the national emergency, but they are not of a kind to inspire confidence; the material appliances of war are hopelessly inadequate, the supply and medical services are of the sketchiest, there is hasty improvisation on the most vital matters, and a lack of co-ordination due to personal jealousies among the provincial militarists which alone will bring disaster unless it can be speedily corrected. The generalissimo is, I understand, working on

this last problem, his purpose being to eliminate the old militarist gang entirely from control in the field, or at any rate give them and their provincial armies subordinate rôles and to conduct serious operations himself with his own forces through the generals and subordinate officers from his own military academies.

37. This seems a suitable point at which to close this account of the origin and development of the present conflict. Major hostilities have for the moment ceased, and the stage is now being set for the next scene in the drama. What it will be it is impossible to forecast with accuracy. By ordinary standards war would seem to be inevitable, but in China, rather more than in most countries, ordinary standards do not apply. At all events the Japanese, as a result of their activities up to date, find themselves in complete military command of the whole of North Hopei as far south as the line of the Hun Ho and Hai Ho Rivers, and within the area of their occupation there is not now a single organised body of Chinese troops. With regard to the civil government of this area, I have as yet no information except in respect of Tientsin and Peking. General Sung Che-yuan, before leaving Peking, appointed General Chang Tzu-chung to be Acting Mayor of Peking (as mentioned in paragraph 29 above). At the same time he made a number of other appointments, including that of General Lo Wen-tien (Deputy Commander of the 38th Division) to be Acting Mayor of Tientsin. The one characteristic that all the appointments had in common was that the appointees had all recently been in close contact with the Japanese régime in North China. The anomaly whereby the Commander and Deputy Commander of the 38th Division were assuming posts in Peking and Tientsin by favour of the Japanese, while the forces under their nominal command were waging war against the Japanese will already have been noticed. The Chinese press has no hesitation in calling them roundly traitors, and putting them in the same category of Japanese puppets as Yin Ju-keng. The truth of the accusation remains to be seen.

38. What future the Japanese intend for North China—whether it is to be another Manchuria or merely an extended East Hopei— is not yet clear, though the indications point rather to the latter. It only needs to be said that they can find tools in any number to give a Chinese or 'independent' complexion to any organisation they like to establish. It is said that the ex-Emperor Pu Yi, now Kang Teh of Manchukuo, would not be averse to remounting the Dragon Throne.

39. One point remains to be mentioned. The question whether the incident which precipitated this crisis was or was not deliberately arranged by the Japanese has been hotly argued. The view held by probably all Chinese and certainly by many foreigners is that it was deliberately engineered; it so much resembled the Mukden *coup*; there had been rumours among the Chinese that something was afoot for days before; the holding of night manœuvres at such a time and in such a place was in itself suspicious; such are the arguments used. Mr. Cowan, in his telegram No.

300 of the 12th July,[9] expressed his conviction that the incident was not deliberately staged, and after reviewing the evidence I have reached the same conclusion, at least so far as the Japanese command is concerned (I have to make this reservation because I cannot overlook the possibility that the first shots were fired by some ultra-patriotic Japanese soldier who wanted to force a situation in which the Japanese Government would be driven into taking vigorous action in North China; but there is no evidence to support this hypothesis nor do the facts require it). We are assured from Tokyo that the Japanese Government were taken aback and seriously embarrassed at the occurrence of the incident just then. Locally, the evidence that the Japanese were caught unawares was overwhelming; of the battalion which was carrying out night manœuvres two companies had already returned to Fengtai and had to be hurriedly brought back when the incident occurred; the bulk of the Embassy guard was at Tungchow and also had to be hastily summoned in the middle of the night, and when it was not allowed to enter the city gates of Peking, instead of using force, tramped quietly round to Fengtai; the Commander-in-chief of the Japanese North China Command was so ill that a successor had to be rushed over from Japan by aeroplane. These are only a few of the indications of unpreparedness which occur to me. In fact, the Lukouchiao incident could hardly have been more different than it was from the Mukden incident, which was an example of what the Japanese can do in stage management.

40. Did the Japanese then not realise the danger of starting an incident if they held night exercises at a time of nervousness and near a strategic point known to be guarded by Chinese troops? To this I can only reply that the Japanese have repeatedly held manœuvres in the same place; and, as to the danger of precipitating an incident, do they not time after time hold night exercises in the streets of Shanghai without paying the slightest attention to the protests of the authorities or the exasperation of the inhabitants? Yet no one can suppose they wish to have an incident there. Then, if the incident was fortuitous, why was it allowed to develop in this fantastic manner? In my view the answer is: firstly, because the Japanese army is always and at every moment ready to 'teach the Chinese a lesson' and to react extravagantly to the least supposed insult (there have been incidents enough in other parts of China to illustrate this); and, secondly, because, the incident having occurred, the army thought the opportunity was too good to lose and deliberately exploited it for the purpose of obtaining a settlement of the North China situation once and for all. There was absolutely nothing in the incident to justify the despatch of reinforcements from Manchuria or Japan and it is obvious that the army misled the Japanese Government as to the seriousness of the situation and deliberately worked up feeling. They had, of course, plenty of background material to work on: the Swatow and other incidents,

[9] No. 104.

which undoubtedly were used to show that all Japanese were going in fear of their lives, the irritation caused by the refusal of the Central Government to discuss a general settlement of Sino-Japanese relations, and a feeling that if the Chinese army was not well beaten now it might get too big to beat.

41. To get the Chinese point of view the incident must be looked at (as I explained in my telegram No. 263 of the 29th July)[10] against the background of the history of Sino-Japanese relations since 1931 and of the immense exasperation of the Chinese at seeing Japan carrying out, step by step, a plan for the domination of North China about which there has never been any secret. The feeling of the Chinese when they see Japanese troops overrunning provinces to which their own troops are denied access must be appreciated. However true it may be that Japan did not *intend* the incident as an excuse for another step forward at the present time, the Chinese can hardly be blamed for thinking otherwise, in view of the manner in which it was immediately exploited by the Japanese; within forty-eight hours of the incident political demands had been introduced (suppression of anti-Japanese agitation, communism &c.), which were quite irrelevant to the incident.

42. In my opinion the Japanese have no one to blame but their army for their present predicament. Whatever the military outcome—and no unbiased observer can anticipate other than an overwhelming victory for Japan—China will have had the satisfaction of compelling Japan to spend millions she can ill afford, use up military supplies accumulated for another purpose, and destroy for a term, possibly of years, her trade with her best customer.[11]

I have, &c.,
H. M. KNATCHBULL-HUGESSEN

[10] Not printed.
[11] Mr. Randall commented on September 12 that he found this despatch 'most useful': 'The dispassionate and impartial manner in which the story is told seems somehow to make the underlying indictment of the Japanese all the more telling.' Sir A. Cadogan agreed (September 13): 'The Japanese haven't got a leg to stand upon.'

No. 165

Viscount Chilston (Moscow) to Foreign Office
(Received August 7, 2.30 p.m.)

No. 129 Telegraphic [F 4977/9/10]

MOSCOW, *August 7, 1937, 1.39 p.m.*

My telegram No. 124.[1]
Yesterday after lunch with Monsieur Litvinov[2] in the country he

[1] In this telegram of July 30 Mr. D. MacKillop, H.M. Chargé d'Affaires at Moscow, gave his opinion that the principal aim of Soviet policy in the Far East at the present time was 'to

volunteered to me interesting information that Chiang Kai-shek had several times conveyed to him an enquiry whether Russia would give any help against Japanese attacks. But Soviet Government would not embark on such a venture (which would mean being at war with Japan) nor did he (Monsieur Litvinov) think that Nanking Government would really be able to organize a serious resistance to Japan especially as generals in North China were so corruptible.

Speaking about Germany he said that he did not think she was at all bound to assist Japan if the latter was at war with China:[3] secret German-Japanese agreement – although it existed – was not a military alliance. In this connexion (and with reference to your telegram No. 81[4]) I may mention that the French Ambassador tells me that he had heard that Germans had given the Chinese Embassy here some sort of warning in the event of any Soviet aid to China.

Incidentally I was rather surprised when Monsieur Litvinov observed that he was thinking of going on a few weeks' leave soon to do a short cure, unless Spanish non-intervention crisis detained him and as to Far East he did not think that need necessarily prevent his doing so.

Repeated to Berlin, Nanking and Tokyo.

avoid war with Japan at almost any cost'. He thought that 'in spite of advantage afforded by absence of any effective frontier between U.S.S.R., Outer Mongolia and China proper it appears to me that idea of intervention on as large a scale as that practised in Spain would be considered too dangerous to be worth while'

[2] Soviet Commissar for Foreign Affairs.   [3] Cf. No. 150.

[4] A repeat of No. 155.

No. 166

Mr. Dodds (Tokyo) to Foreign Office (Received August 7, 11.55 a.m.)

No. 277 Telegraphic [F 4961/9/10]

TOKYO, *August 7, 1937, 4.58 p.m.*

Your telegram No. 173[1] to Nanking.

Point two. There are no chances of feeling in Japan manifesting itself against the army before latter has crushed Chinese resistance if this is done soon say within a year, attitude of Diet is to urge Government forward rather than the reverse.

Point three. No doubt financial circles dislike idea of a war but feel that it is useless or dangerous to say so at present and are gambling on prospects of gain if military bring it off. They cannot be expected to make their influence felt unless or until prospect of speedy finish to a war is eliminated. It would be premature to try now to estimate when this may

[1] No. 163.

be; but Commercial Counsellor does not think it likely that financial difficulties will develop soon enough to affect situation for about a year and in any case we doubt whether military party would be discredited by anything but obvious military reverses.

Repeated to Nanking and Commander-in-Chief.

No. 167

Mr. Dodds (Tokyo) to Foreign Office (Received August 7, 2.30 p.m.)

No. 278 Telegraphic [F 4962/9/10]

TOKYO, *August 7, 1937, 6.37 p.m.*

Your telegram No. 204.[1]

We have already offered our good offices and they have not been accepted and the Minister for Foreign Affairs has moreover made it clear in the Diet that intervention by third parties would be rejected (my telegram No. 266[2]). I agree that any appearance of intervention might inflame public opinion in Japan so far as it exists at present. Military party is paramount and nothing we do or have done can weaken it. But it might become even more obstinate if it suspected our offer was intended to help China.

2. Massacre of Japanese at Tungchow[3] makes pacification even more difficult.

3. There are no signs of a basis for compromise. Japanese are confident of victory. Minister for Foreign Affairs has just reiterated his intention of going on with one at least of his three China principles viz cooperation of Japan and China versus communism. Military regard the present as one of the stages towards the achievement of their destiny to control East Asia. They have as you are aware little perception of statesmanship and nothing but fear that they may lose is likely to have much influence with them. Financial difficulties for example are not yet likely to weigh much with them (my immediately preceding telegram[4]) and on the other side C[h]iang Kai-shek will apparently disappear unless he yields to popular demand to try conclusions with Japan. Moreover even if peace is achieved now on perhaps the basis of the demands of July 11, though Japanese are sure to ask for more, what hope is there of it lasting? Japan started defalcating in 1931 and has no option but to go on or pay the penalty and China has to submit to loss of sovereignty in North China or fight.

4. However, I do not think harm can be done by one more effort on lines suggested in second paragraph of your telegram No. 277[5] to Washington. Bases for hope appear to be (1) that neither side wished for war at this moment (2) that it is probably true that the more that intelligent

---

[1] See No. 161, note 8.   [2] Not kept in F.O. archives.   [3] See No. 157, note 4.
[4] No. 166.   [5] No. 159.

Japanese contemplate the idea of war with China the more they dislike it (3) Japanese appreciate impartial and helpful attitude we have adopted so far in London, Nanking and Tokyo, and will not be disposed therefore to resent a further attempt for peace.

5. United States Ambassador agrees and is recommending his government to act on suggestion contained in second paragraph of your telegram No. 277 to Washington but only as an informal, confidential and exploratory step.[6]

Repeated to Nanking, Washington and C.-in.-C.

[6] See *F.R.U.S.*, 1937, vol. iii, pp. 350–1: cf. also pp. 340–1 and 349–50. Mr. Orde noted on August 9 that Mr. Johnson of the U.S. Embassy had called and confirmed 'that Mr. Grew considered that we should approach the Japanese Govt. only, owing to the importance of secrecy. The State Dept. emphasised this. They had authorised Mr. Grew to act accordingly if Mr. Dodds were instructed likewise [see *F.R.U.S.*, *ibid.*, p. 353]. It is a forlorn hope anyhow, but I think our best chance of achieving something is on these lines...' With Sir R. Vansittart's agreement telegram No. 206 was despatched to Tokyo on August 9 instructing Mr. Dodds to approach the Japanese Government as proposed.

No. 168

Sir H. Knatchbull-Hugessen (Nanking) to Foreign Office (Received August 9, 9.30 a.m.)

No. 307 Telegraphic [F 5020/9/10]

NANKING, *August 8, 1937, 10.25 p.m.*

My telegram No. 306.[1]

American, French, German and Italian Ambassadors and I are meeting tomorrow August 9th when question of representations to the Japanese will be discussed. I had preliminary conversations today with my United States colleague to decide on the best course of action. It seemed to both of us that the matter was so urgent that interested Ambassadors should make immediate joint representations to our Japanese colleague on our own responsibility without further delay. My United States colleague was insistent that these representations should be of most general character and we drafted a formula for discussion at tomorrow's meeting after which I will report by telegraph action decided on.

[1] This telegram of August 8 forwarded the text of an oral communication made to the British, American and French Ambassadors that morning by a representative of the Waichiaopu to the effect that the Chinese military authorities had no intention of launching an attack on Japanese forces already at Shanghai. The situation would, however, be entirely altered if the Japanese should open an attack, which would be immediately resisted, or should unjustifiably send more forces to Shanghai. If the Japanese forces used any part of the settlement as a base of operations the Chinese forces would be compelled to take necessary action, and in such a case 'it would be clear that the responsibility for all consequences does not rest with China'.

My United States colleague and I both felt strongly that our action . . .[2] that it should be brought home to Japanese Government in most urgent and unmistakable manner that the Powers concerned view possibility of trouble in Shanghai with the utmost anxiety. We propose at tomorrow's meeting to urge that all Ambassadors present should request their governments to speak seriously at Tokyo and in addition to general representations in favour of maintaining neutrality of Shanghai to press in particular that Japanese Government should refrain from using Shanghai as a base of operations and from increasing numbers of their troops there.

My United States colleague and I consider this so important that we propose to urge our governments to take this action whether others agree or not. I do not however anticipate objections from other colleagues.

In the meanwhile in view of the urgency of the matter I propose to take early opportunity of speaking personally to Japanese Ambassador or in his absence Counsellor quite frankly in the same sense. It will be necessary for the present to avoid mentioning suggestion at the end of paragraph 1 of my telegram No. 67[3] that landing party should be withdrawn altogether as we are without information as to whether British or other troops could be employed in the Settlement.

Repeated as usual.

[2] The text was here uncertain.   [3] i.e. No. 156.

No. 169

Sir H. Knatchbull-Hugessen (Nanking) to Foreign Office
(Received August 9, 9.30 p.m.)

No. 313 Telegraphic: by wireless [F 5044/9/10]

Important   NANKING, *August 9, 1937*

Following received from Financial Adviser No. 19 of August 8th begins:
Addressed to Nanking, repeated Saving to Peking and Tokyo.
Foreign Office telegram No. 173 to Nanking.[1]

A. In accordance with your request I give below my comments on paragraphs 2 and 3 of telegram under reference but my knowledge of Japan is limited.

B. Second paragraph of telegram under reference. Chances are small before Japanese army has crushed organised forces of present Chinese government.

C. Third paragraph of telegram under reference. While warlike conditions exist nothing short of an internal débâcle will discredit Japanese military and such a débâcle is unlikely until sacrifices demanded of civilian population become intolerable.

[1] No. 163.

D. My comments on sub-paragraphs (c) and (d) of paragraph 4 are as follows:

E. Sub-paragraph (c). If hostilities on a major scale are prolonged beyond a month or six weeks the budget deficit will become out of hand and inflation and its effects abroad inevitable. Possibilities of domestic loan issues are remote. If conflict is short and sharp it may be possible to avoid complete disorganisation of financial machinery but only if neutrality of Shanghai is respected: otherwise complete and immediate disorganisation is certain. In either case currency would most probably fail.

F. Sub-paragraph (d). This depends on length of hostilities and again on maintenance of neutrality in the Settlement and Concessions. Early and complete Chinese military débâcle would injure British business interests mainly through financial repercussions though naturally the answer depends on what Japan would demand as the fruits of victory. We may be sure that our status in any territory effectively controlled by Japan would in the long run approximate to our present unsatisfactory status in Manchuria. I am inclined to think that elsewhere in China British interests would show their usual recuperative powers in course of time and from some points of view might even profit inasmuch as weak cover obtainable would postpone extension of Chinese large-scale enterprise.

G. On the other hand a long drawn out struggle would be much more disastrous to British interests all over China including Hongkong as it would result not only in currency crisis but in suspension of ordinary trading, shipping and other British business activities, and possibly their partial extinction.

H. Third possibility is Chinese acceding to Japanese demands without major military engagement. Effects of this would be similar to effects of military débâcle but on minor scale. Immediate financial repercussions would not be so grave but there would be a tendency gradually to eliminate British interests from areas gained by Japan—whether by force or agreement is immaterial. I . . .[2] comments in paragraphs F. to H. are drafted in consultation with Acting Commercial Counsellor.

[2] The text was here uncertain.

No. 170

Sir H. Knatchbull-Hugessen (Nanking) to Foreign Office (Received August 9, 10 p.m.)

No. 310[1] Telegraphic: by wireless [F 5045/9/10]

NANKING, *August 9, 1937*

My telegram No. 307.[2]
At the meeting this morning August 9th it was agreed that joint note

[1] This telegram was received after telegram No. 313 (No. 169). [2] No. 168.

should be addressed to Japanese Ambassador and Chinese Minister for Foreign Affairs. Agreed texts are contained in my immediately following telegram.[3] Action however awaits receipt by United States Ambassador of authority from Washington.[4]

2. I saw the Japanese Counsellor yesterday and impressed on him strong necessity of avoiding hostilities at Shanghai and particularly that the Japanese should not use Shanghai as a base for increase . . .[5] number of troops. I added that we would shortly be approaching his Ambassador officially. He replied that the Japanese were equally anxious to avoid involving Shanghai and had no intention of using it as a base. He added that the present Commander-in-Chief of Japanese third fleet, commanding Japanese forces at Shanghai was a man of much tact and discretion who could be counted upon not to take any action likely to provoke hostilities at Shanghai.

Repeated as usual.

[3] Not printed. The agreed texts are printed in *F.R.U.S.*, 1937, vol. iii, pp. 356–8 and 360–1.
[4] Sir H. Knatchbull-Hugessen reported in telegram No. 321 of August 12 that the U.S. Ambassador had been authorised to send the notes subject to changes in the text to indicate that prior to the Chinese communication of August 8 (see No. 168, note 1) the interested Powers were already preparing an approach to the Chinese and Japanese governments regarding Shanghai. See *F.R.U.S., ibid.*, pp. 363–4. The notes were signed as amended and delivered to the Chinese Foreign Minister and Japanese Ambassador on August 11: see *ibid.*, p. 376.
[5] The text was here uncertain.

No. 171

Mr. Dodds (Tokyo) to Foreign Office (Received August 11, 11.30 a.m.)

No. 283 Telegraphic [F 5070/9/10]

TOKYO, *August 11, 1937, 3.55 p.m.*

My telegram No. 281.[1]
I gave Minister for Foreign Affairs this morning brief pro memoria containing suggestion in paragraph 2 of your telegram No. 277[2] to Washington explaining that this was of course purely verbal informal communication.

2. He read it very slowly and with great care and said after a long pause that it might be possible later to consider taking advantage of it.

[1] In this telegram of August 10 Mr. Dodds reported that the U.S. Ambassador had called on Mr. Hirota that afternoon to offer his good offices as instructed: see No. 167, note 6. Mr. Dodds added that Mr. Grew regarded it as 'essential that Chiang Kai-shek should keep the door open and suggests that United States and British Ambassadors at Nanking should urge him to do so'. See *F.R.U.S.*, 1937, vol. iii, pp. 368–9.
[2] No. 159.

3. He then said that Kao[3] had been sent by Chiang Kai-shek to see Kawagoe[4] at Shanghai on August 9 to discuss (a) settlement of Sino-Japanese relations and (b) how to stop fighting in North China. He had returned to Chiang Kai-shek on August 10 and if Chiang Kai-shek gave him without delay a reasonable reply to deliver to Kawagoe negotiations might be begun and war averted.

4. Minister for Foreign Affairs said he was optimistic. For the first time however he seemed to be less certain that Chiang Kai-shek would not fight and admitted that latter was 'in a difficult position'. By this however he explained that he meant that Chiang Kai-shek was surrounded by generals who did not want to fight. But he said later that the younger generation in China were 'pro-war'.

5. He added that situation was 'critical': much if not everything depended on Chiang Kai-shek's reply to Kawagoe.

6. I said His Majesty's Ambassador at Nanking was doing everything in his power to keep the way open for a peaceful solution.[5]

7. No reference was made either by Minister for Foreign Affairs or myself to the fact that practically identical conversation took place yesterday between him and United States Ambassador.

8. He impressed on me that what he had told me should be treated as most confidential.

9. I venture to think action taken by Unites States Ambassador and myself was well worth while and His Excellency agrees.

Repeated to Nanking.

[3] Chief of the Asiatic Bureau of the Chinese Ministry for Foreign Affairs.
[4] Japanese Ambassador to China.
[5] Telegram No. 186 to Nanking of August 12 referred to Tokyo telegrams Nos. 281 and 283 (see note 1 above) and read: 'It seems desirable that you should express to Chinese Government the hope that they are keeping the way open for negotiations and you have my authority to do so.'

No. 172

Sir H. Knatchbull-Hugessen (Nanking) to Foreign Office
(Received August 13, 9.30 a.m.)

No. 323 Telegraphic [F 5116/9/10]

Immediate   NANKING, *August 12, 1937, 1.50 p.m.*

Japanese first battle fleet minus battleships reached Shanghai yesterday, and I learn from Acting Consul General that additional marines are being landed.[1] The situation against which we were warned by Minister for

[1] It was reported in *The Times* on August 12, 1937, p. 10, that 4,000 Japanese marines were in the process of landing at Shanghai, bringing the total Japanese landing force up to 9,000. Fighting between Chinese and Japanese forces at Shanghai began on August 13. For the next few days the Japanese were heavily outnumbered, and on the 15th the Japanese

Foreign affairs on August 8th (see my telegram No. 306[2]) has arisen.

Acting Consul General also reports that Japanese Consul General yesterday notified the Mayor that Paoantui[3] must be withdrawn. No limit of time or distance was mentioned and notification was not in the form of an ultimatum. Nevertheless the situation is I consider most serious since the Chinese are in no mood to make further concessions and show an inclination to 'damn the consequences'. Any suggestion from us that Paoantui should be withdrawn would be very badly received unless at the same time we suggested to the Japanese that their landing forces should be withdrawn. It is a question whether in view of the extreme seriousness of the situation the Japanese would be prepared to consider this solution.

I am meeting my colleagues this afternoon to consider if we can usefully take any further action. Meanwhile I would urge that representations in Tokyo be strengthened in view of the challenge to the Chinese, afforded by arrival in Shanghai of fresh naval forces.[4]

Repeated as usual.

Government decided to send army reinforcements to Shanghai under the command of a retired General, Iwane Matsui. The Chinese 87th and 88th Divisions nevertheless held out against the Japanese forces for some weeks, and were not finally evicted from their last stronghold at Chapei until October 27.

[2] See No. 168, note 1.　　　　　　　　　　　　[3] The Peace Preservation Militia.

[4] Telegram No. 194 of August 13 to Nanking read: 'You will see that my telegram No. 193 [No. 173 below] which had already been decided upon meets the suggestion contained in your telegram No. 323 last paragraph.'

No. 173

Foreign Office to Sir H. Knatchbull-Hugessen (Nanking)

No. 193[1] Telegraphic [F 5164/9/10]

Most Immediate　　　　　　　　　　　　　　　FOREIGN OFFICE, *August 13, 1937*

Reports today of fighting having broken out in Hongkew district of Shanghai[2] make it urgently necessary to impress on Japanese and Chinese Governments once more in the strongest terms the importance of avoiding hostilities in that city. Each side is under the strongest moral obligation to refrain from any action likely to lead, whether through their own immediate fault or that of the other party, to such hostilities and to incalculable danger which will ensue to many thousands of foreigners in no way concerned. Not only contact between troops of opposing parties but their presence in that area must be recognised as constituting a naked flame in a powder magazine and responsibility cannot be avoided by petty

[1] No. 218 to Tokyo. No time of despatch is given on the filed copy of this telegram, but it was apparently sent off during the afternoon of August 13.

[2] See No. 172, note 1.

arguments as to who started firing or what technical right exists to have troops on the spot. Both sides will be responsible for the disastrous results which cannot humanly speaking be avoided if their present attitude is maintained. To the impartial onlooker that attitude is the one most certain to lead to the very trouble which each side professes to wish to avoid. No words can alter this fact and His Majesty's Government must appeal to both Japanese and Chinese Governments with the utmost insistence to make their deeds conform to their assurances. To the Japanese we must point out that it is preposterous and a glaring contradiction of their assurances to imperil Shanghai as they have done by the measures recently taken simply, as would seem, because two members of their landing party have been killed far outside the city boundary. It is their duty to their own good name and to the rest of the world to avoid not only recurrence of such incidents, but exaggerated measures if and when they do occur and in general such disposition and use of their forces as will lead to Chinese counter measures. Under this heading certainly comes use of the International Settlement as a base in any form. They ought rather to take every possible measure to prove to the Chinese that serious action is not intended at Shanghai.

To the Chinese we must point out the folly and inconsistency of bringing their troops into contest with the Japanese at Shanghai. They cannot ultimately do themselves any good by such action but will in fact only increase the danger of Japanese ultimately controlling the destiny of Shanghai and the main source of Chinese customs revenue, while endangering the city itself and the countless foreign lives in it.

Please urge these considerations so far as applicable to the Government to which you are accredited. You should in any case act at once, but you should try to enlist the support of your foreign colleagues.

Repeated Immediate to Washington No. 298,[3] Paris No. 143, Rome No. 270, Berlin No. 157 and Shanghai No. 126.

[3] Telegram No. 299 to Washington, despatched at 5.30 p.m. on August 13 and also marked 'Most Immediate', instructed Sir R. Lindsay to 'do your best to persuade [U.S. Government] to send similar instructions to U.S. representatives' at Nanking and Tokyo.

No. 174

Mr. Dodds (Tokyo) to Foreign Office (Received August 13, 10 a.m.)

No. 288 Telegraphic [F 5138/9/10]

Immediate   TOKYO, *August 13, 1937, 3.37 p.m.*

It goes without saying that Japanese Government will make what use they can of ourselves and the Americans in their dealings with Chinese during the present crisis. I am thinking e.g. of blatant suggestion to

235

Military Attaché reported in paragraph 3 of my telegram No. 263[1] (see Nanking telegram No. 278[2]) and of Minister for Foreign Affairs' remarks to United States Ambassador and myself that war would be averted if Chiang Kai-shek returned a reasonable answer to Japanese proposals (my telegrams Nos. 281[3] and 283[4]) while Director of Military Intelligence was simultaneously informing Military Attaché that the Japanese would drive the Chinese to war unless diplomacy stopped it (my telegram No. 184[1]). The object of these three communications can be interpreted as an attempt by force and diplomacy to obtain the surrender of North China without fighting. Japanese know that we are trying to keep the peace and would no doubt like to use us to press Chiang Kai-shek to accept it at any price.

2. Financial circles here as you are aware have so far been completely silent in public but I do not doubt they are making themselves felt in private. They know better than the military the risks involved in war with China and in particular the damage to Japan's market in China which would be caused for many years by wholesale butchery in battle by Japan of Chinese armies.

3. In such circles it is I understand said that the present crisis involves continued existence of Japan as a class [sic] Power.

4. I therefore conclude though it it perhaps sound for Chiang Kai-shek to keep the door open it would be highly dangerous for him to yield.[5]
Repeated to Nanking.

[1] Not kept in F.O. archives.   [2] See No. 161, note 1.   [3] See No. 171, note 1.   [4] No. 171.
[5] Sir R. Vansittart wrote across the filed copy of this telegram: 'This is a telegram to be remembered.' Mr. Orde commented on August 14: 'We have avoided the trap which this tel. exposes and I trust will continue to do so.'

No. 175

Mr. Dodds (Tokyo) to Foreign Office (Received August 13, 2.45 p.m.)

No. 289 Telegraphic [F 5167/9/10]

TOKYO, *August 13, 1937, 7.35 p.m.*

Your telegrams Nos. 213[1] and 216.[2]
I carried out your instructions in interview with Vice Minister for Foreign Affairs this afternoon. He said that Counsellor of Japanese Embassy Nanking had today informed representatives of Powers interested that if the Chinese would withdraw forces near the Settlement and destroy defences there, Japanese would withdraw to their original positions and would also reduce the number of Japanese troops now

[1] This telegram of August 12 instructed Mr. Dodds to communicate immediately with the Japanese Government in the sense indicated in Nanking telegram No. 307 (No. 168).
[2] Of August 12, not printed (F 5164/9/10).

there. It was for foreign representatives at Nanking and Shanghai to act accordingly. He assured me that the Japanese Government were as averse as ourselves to hostilities taking place at Shanghai and referred to the unprofitable nature of 1932 operations there.

2. United States Ambassador is only authorised, not instructed, to take similar action to mine only if Germans, Italians, French and British representatives also do so. Germans and Italians have no instructions and French will only act if America does. So I have acted alone but I think Japanese are genuinely anxious to avoid hostilities in Shanghai if possible and that concerted representations could not do much good and might be misrepresented in the press. I think, however, Vice Minister for Foreign Affairs welcomed the opportunity of repeating to me what the Japanese Counsellor is saying in Shanghai or Nanking.[3]

Repeated to Nanking and Shanghai.

[3] See No. 176 below.

No. 176

Sir H. Knatchbull-Hugessen (Nanking) to Foreign Office (Received August 19,[1] 1.15 p.m.)

No. 328 Telegraphic [F 5427/9/10]

Immediate   NANKING, *August 13, 1937, 7.37 p.m.*

My telegram No. 325.[2]

Counsellor of Japanese Embassy called upon me this morning and informed me that he was instructed by his government and in particular by his Ambassador to state that Japanese Government considered the situation in Shanghai very serious. He was to express the hope that I would concur as to the necessity of inducing the Chinese to withdraw their troops.

Similar message was given to my United States colleague last night.

From subsequent conversation it became clear that Japanese Counsellor was not asking me to take any action. In my reply I made it clear that I understood that no request was addressed to me to approach the Chinese Government and that I was only being informed of the views and action of the Japanese. I said that in my opinion it was quite useless to suggest to the Chinese that they should withdraw unless the Japanese Government were

[1] Mr. Ronald noted on August 20 that this telegram had 'suffered long delays in transmission'.

[2] This telegram of August 12 was also delayed in transmission and did not reach the Foreign Office until August 17. It referred to No. 172 and stated that the French, German, and Italian Ambassadors had agreed on August 12 to make representations at Tokyo on the lines recommended by the British and U.S. Ambassadors. By the time the telegram was received, instructions had already been sent to Sir H. Knatchbull-Hugessen and acted on: see No. 172, note 4, and No. 173.

prepared to give them a hard and fast guarantee that they would withdraw their troops simultaneously and proportionately. I urged him in view of extreme seriousness of the position to put this to his government immediately and I expressed the hope that they would realise the importance of this.

Finally Mr. Hiidia [sic][3] made the following statement to me of possible attitude of his government explaining that it was personal, non-committal, and confidential.

1. Japanese Government required withdrawal of Paoantui and regular troops and destruction of all defence works erected in the last few days.

2. In return Mr. Hiidia [sic] presumed that Japanese forces would 'resume their original positions'. He added that he inferred that this expression did not include re-embarkation of additional troops recently landed.

I said that this might afford a slight hope but that it would be necessary to expand it to include a Japanese guarantee of simultaneous and proportionate withdrawal with Chinese. I added that even then it was essential that troops which had recently been landed should be re-embarked and I said that the best final arrangement would be that Japanese landing force embark when they should be reduced to the numbers before 1932 incident and that Chinese forces should be reduced to their numbers just after the incident.

Mr. Hiidia [sic] agreed to my informing my colleagues of the above at the next meeting.[4]

Repeated to Peking, Tokyo, General Officer Commanding, Commander-in-Chief and Rear Admiral Yangtse.

[3] This should presumably read: 'Mr. Hidaka'.

[4] In telegram No. 332 of August 13 Sir H. Knatchbull-Hugessen transmitted the text of a memorandum communicated that day to the British, American, French, Italian, and German Ambassadors by the Japanese Counsellor. The memorandum began: 'It goes without saying that safety of lives and property of foreigners as well as Japanese in Shanghai falls under solicitous care of Japanese Government', and went on to repeat the offer to withdraw the Japanese landing party 'to their original positions' if the Chinese withdrew all their troops and demolished military constructions. The text of the memorandum as transmitted to the State Department by the U.S. Ambassador is printed in *F.R.U.S., op. cit.*, p. 400: cf. also note 94 on p. 399.

No. 177

Sir H. Knatchbull-Hugessen (Nanking) to Foreign Office
(Received August 14, 9.30 a.m.)

No. 330 Telegraphic [*F 5166/9/10*]

Important   NANKING, *August 13, 1937, 7.27 p.m.*

My telegram No. 329.[1]

I informed my four colleagues of what the Japanese Counsellor had said.[2] They all agreed with the line which I took and we remain convinced that it would be useless to make representations to the Chinese alone regarding withdrawal.

2. It was agreed that our best and most helpful attitude would be in the event of a direct understanding being reached between Chinese and Japanese Governments regarding withdrawal to offer the services of joint commission as umpire or in any helpful capacity in connexion with the execution of the withdrawal agreement. It would be made clear that this function was performed not in virtue of 1932 agreement[3] which set up commission but independently.

3. We regard it as essential to dissociate any present arrangement from 1932 agreement since that agreement would place an obligation on the Chinese with no corresponding obligation on the Japanese. This would in the present case be quite unacceptable nor would it be fair because despatch of Chinese military forces is due to the arrival of Japanese naval reinforcements.

4. We all agreed that any mediation or intervention with either side would be out of the question and that the Japanese and Chinese should be left to make this agreement direct but that once made we could offer the services of this international body in manner proposed above.

5. My four colleagues and I agreed to telegraph identically to our governments proposing the appointment of representatives to serve on a board of observers to watch simultaneous withdrawal of Chinese and Japanese armed forces in Shanghai area in the event of Chinese and Japanese authorities agreeing to such withdrawal. This would in effect be joint commission minus Chinese and Japanese. The feeling amongst the majority of my colleagues was that owing to the extreme urgency of the crisis we should proceed on these lines without awaiting replies from our governments in the event of Sino-Japanese agreement as to withdrawal making this offer advisable.[4]

Repeated to Peking, Tokyo, General Officer Commanding, Commander-in-Chief and Rear Admiral Yangtse.

---

[1] Not kept in F.O. archives.   [2] See No. 176.
[3] i.e. the Sino-Japanese agreement of May 5, 1932: see Volume X, No. 324.
[4] In Foreign Office telegram No. 197 of August 14, Sir H. Knatchbull-Hugessen was authorized to 'join in offer proposed in para. 5'.

No. 178

Sir R. Lindsay (Washington) to Foreign Office
(Received August 14, 9.30 a.m.)

No. 232 Telegraphic [F 5165/9/10]

WASHINGTON, *August 13, 1937, 10.38 p.m.*

Your telegram No. 299.[1]
I handed memorandum of these instructions this afternoon to Under Secretary of State who informed me that according to a telegram just received United States Ambassador Tokyo had made almost identical representations to Japanese authorities and had received an answer very similar to that returned to His Majesty's Chargé d'Affaires.[2] I was also informed that only this morning Secretary of State had sent for Japanese Ambassador and had spoken to him precisely in the sense of first part of your instruction to Nanking and Tokyo about neither side being able to avoid responsibility for a collision if one takes place at Shanghai.[3] Moreover it has been suggested to United States Ambassador at Nanking that he might consult his foreign colleagues with a view to confidential representations being made to the effect that Chinese forces serve no useful purpose in their present positions and merely give to the Japanese pretext for further action. No special form of action was recommended but some withdrawal might remove a provocation.

[1] See No. 173, note 3.   [2] Cf. *F.R.U.S.*, 1937, vol iii, pp. 399–400.   [3] See *ibid.*, pp. 400–1.

No. 179

Sir H. Knatchbull-Hugessen (Nanking) to Foreign Office
(Received August 24, 9.30 a.m.)

No. 333 Telegraphic [F 5638/9/10]

NANKING, *August [13][1], 1937*

My telegram No. 331.[2]
General Chiang Kai-shek sent for United States, French, German and Italian Ambassadors and myself this afternoon August 13th.
2. He enquired what news we had from Japan. This brought up the subject of Japanese attitude regarding Shanghai and in the course of discussion Japanese memorandum reported in my telegram No. 332[3] was read to General Chiang Kai-shek. He then asked each of us for our views regarding the memorandum. We all said that it appeared to afford some

[1] This telegram was drafted on August 13 but was not despatched until August 23. For the sake of continuity, however, it has been printed under the date to which its contents refer.
[2] Not kept in F.O. archives.   [3] See No. 176, note 4.

opening and we urged him to approach the Japanese Embassy and follow it up. He avoided expressing any definite opinion regarding Japanese memorandum, but stated that the Waichiaopu would examine it. He said that Chinese Government were in continual touch with Japanese Embassy as diplomatic relations were still in existence.

3. General Chiang Kai-shek thanked us for the interest taken by our Governments in the position and asked whether we would be prepared to vouch for any Japanese undertaking regarding withdrawal of Japanese troops and the avoidance of hostilities. We said quite emphatically that this would be impossible. I pointed out that it was out of the question for us either to act as mediators or guarantors and my United States colleague said the same.[4]

4. We then said that if an agreement in principle were reached between the two parties we should be prepared to suggest in order to facilitate technical execution and to smooth away differences of opinion the neutral members of West Commission should act as umpires as indicated in my telegram No. 330.[5] Chiang Kai-shek thanked us for this proposal.

5. After the meeting my colleagues and I discussed things and came to the conclusion that progress would be held up unless Japanese Counsellor were informed in some desirable manner of what had passed regarding Shanghai question. We therefore arranged for my French colleague who was expecting to see Japanese Counsellor this evening to inform him that we had apprised General Chiang Kai-shek unofficially of the contents of the Japanese memorandum, that General Chiang Kai-shek had not rejected the suggestions although he had referred [sic] to commit himself but that he had instructed the Waichiaopu to examine them. My French colleague will also inform Japanese Counsellor of statement made by General Chiang Kai-shek as reported in paragraph 6 below.

6. Chiang Kai-shek informed us that he had asked us to come in order to make a categorical statement that China had no wish to start hostilities or to take aggressive action either in Shanghai or in any other part of China: the Chinese Government wished for peace. He went on to say that the Chinese Government had been compelled to send troops into Woosung area as a defensive measure because they had positive information that it was the Japanese intention to occupy Sungkiang and Soochow and establish a special régime covering the whole area of which Shanghai is the centre.

7. We laid stress upon our anxiety regarding the safety of our nationals in Shanghai. When asked my views on Japanese memorandum as reported in paragraph 1 above, I took the opportunity of speaking in the sense of your telegram No. 186.[6] I repeated this after the meeting to the Vice Minister for Foreign Affairs and said that it was a matter to which you attached great importance.

Repeated as usual and Shanghai.

[4] Mr. Nelson Johnson's report of this meeting is printed in *F.R.U.S.*, *op. cit.*, pp. 397–9.
[5] No. 177.   [6] See No. 171, note 5.

No. 180

Mr. Dodds (Tokyo) to Foreign Office (Received August 14, 9.30 a.m.)

No. 291 Telegraphic [F 5186/9/10]

TOKYO, *August 14, 1937, 3.52 p.m.*

Your telegram No. 218.[1]

I carried out your instructions this morning in a letter which I handed to Minister for Foreign Affairs.

2. He said that he had just seen Chinese Ambassador and had impressed on His Excellency that he earnestly desired that peace should ensue at Shanghai. I said that essential thing was that troops on both sides should be removed as far away as possible from contact with each other. He said that he most emphatically agreed. If the Chinese troops would withdraw to some two miles outside the city Japanese troops would also 'withdraw'. He could not undertake to bring them back to Japan as he did not wish to risk another Tungchow.[2]

3. United States Ambassador is telegraphing text of my letter to his Government in case they instruct him to support my representations.[3] I am trying to obtain support of the other representatives concerned but do not think much can be expected from them. German Ambassador has informed United States Ambassador that he has instructions not to concert.

4. United States Ambassador was sent for last night[4] by Vice Minister for Foreign Affairs and had similar conversation to that recorded in paragraph 1 of my telegram No. 289.[5]

Repeated to Nanking.

[1] No. 173.   [2] See No. 157, note 4.   [3] See *F.R.U.S.*, 1937, vol. iii, pp. 409–10.
[4] Cf. No. 178, note 2.   [5] No. 175.

No. 181

Foreign Office to Sir H. Knatchbull-Hugessen (Nanking)

No. 200 Telegraphic [F 5185/9/10]

FOREIGN OFFICE, *August 14, 1937, 9 p.m.*

Chinese bombing at Shanghai.[1] No doubt you are already making representations against this senseless action. You may say you are doing so on my instructions.

Repeated Peking, Shanghai.

[1] It had been reported that 1047 people were killed and 100 injured in Chinese bombing attacks on the Central District of the Shanghai settlement. On the evening of August 14 the Chinese Foreign Minister expressed regret to Sir H. Knatchbull-Hugessen on behalf of Chiang Kai-shek for the bombing, and 'explained that this was due to the wounding of

pilots and intensive attack from Japanese anti-aircraft guns and consequent loss of control'. It was understood that one of the main Chinese objectives was the Japanese Coast Defence Vessel *Idzumo*, stationed alongside the N.Y.K. Wharf in the International Settlement. H.M.S. *Cumberland* had suffered a hit, and Sir H. Knatchbull-Hugessen was instructed in telegram No. 207 of August 15 to protest against the attack: 'Inadvertent as it no doubt was, it is an added illustration of the terrible dangers of this air activity.'

No. 182

Foreign Office to Mr. Dodds (Tokyo)

No. 222 Telegraphic [F 5229/9/10]

Immediate   FOREIGN OFFICE, *August 15, 1937, 3 p.m.*

Nanking telegram No. 332.[1]

Please make urgent representations to Government to which you are accredited that greatest and most immediate danger to lives and property from combatants in International Settlement arises from presence of *Idzumo* adjacent to Settlement wharves[2] and that, without prejudice to other aspects of the situation, best practical demonstration that Japanese could give of their expressed desire to avert danger to foreign life and property would be removal of *Idzumo* to a more distant station.

Please urge Japanese Government to order this removal without delay and explain that we are at the same time urging upon Chinese Government in most insistent manner possible that they should refrain from any repetition of their bombing raids.[3]

Repeated to Nanking No. 203 and Shanghai No. 36.

[1] See No. 176, note 4.   [2] Cf. No. 181, note 1.
[3] A note on this file stated that Sir R. Vansittart, Rear Admiral Cunningham (Assistant Chief of Naval Staff), and Major General Haining (Director of Military Operations and Intelligence) met on the morning of Sunday, August 15, to decide what action was necessary in the Shanghai crisis. The decisions taken are shown in a number of telegrams sent off that afternoon, based on a pencilled note by Sir R. Vansittart preserved in this file. These include the present telegram and Nos. 183 and 184 below. Telegram No. 41 to H.M. Consul General at Shanghai authorized him to take such steps as he might judge necessary for carrying out any arrangements made for evacuating British nationals from Shanghai. He was also asked whether he had any apprehensions in regard to the food situation. See also No. 191 below.

No. 183

Foreign Office to Sir E. Phipps (Paris)

No. 146[1] Telegraphic [F 5229/9/10]

Immediate   FOREIGN OFFICE, *August 15, 1937, 3.20 p.m.*

Please inform Government to which you are accredited that Comman-

[1] No. 300 to Washington.

der in Chief has represented need for reinforcement of foreign troops at Shanghai. His Majesty's Government have despatched one battalion from Hong Kong and at least one other will follow immediately. His Majesty's Government will be glad to know as soon as possible what Government to which you are accredited contemplate doing in this direction.[2]

[2] Telegram No. 234 of August 17 from Washington reported that a regiment of 1200 marines was to leave San Diego for Shanghai in a few days time, and another company was on its way from Manila. Paris telegram No. 150 of August 18 reported that the French Government had already despatched one battalion from Hanoi and hoped to send another immediately.

No. 184

Foreign Office to Mr. Dodds (Tokyo)

No. 223 Telegraphic [F 5229/9/10]

Immediate   FOREIGN OFFICE, August 15, 1937, 3.55 p.m.

Please represent to Japanese Government that the situation that has arisen at Shanghai must be considered as ultimately due to the presence of Japanese landing party there. The best practical contribution which they can make to a solution of it would be to withdraw their landing party. His Majesty's Government are urging Chinese Government on their part to guarantee that there will be no attack on Japanese quarter, and to dispose of their forces so as to remove apprehension of any attack.[1]

Repeated to Nanking No. 204, Shanghai No. 38, and Washington No. 301.

[1] Telegram No. 205 to Nanking, despatched at 4 p.m. on August 15, instructed Sir H. Knatchbull-Hugessen to take corresponding action with the Chinese Government.

No. 185

Sir H. Knatchbull-Hugessen (Nanking) to Foreign Office (Received August 15, 8.15 p.m.)

No. 336 Telegraphic: by wireless [F 5201/9/10]

NANKING, August 15, 1937

Your telegram No. 193.[1]

I saw the Minister for Foreign Affairs immediately on receipt and gave him substance on paper omitting passage dealing with the Japanese. I spoke most seriously and in particular urged on him the vital importance of effective measures to prevent . . .[2] flying over Settlement. I also asked Donald to pass similar requests to Madame Chiang Kai-shek.

[1] No. 173.   [2] The text was here uncertain.

244

In reply to the Minister for Foreign Affairs' question I said that equally strong representations are being made in Tokyo.

Minister for Foreign Affairs put forward arguments to show that the fault lay with the Japanese. I said that this was not the immediate point. Things had been so serious that essential point was at once to stop fighting in Shanghai. Question of right and wrong could be decided later.

My United States and French colleagues have already associated themselves with me. I hope to hear later from German and Italian Ambassadors.

Minister for Foreign Affairs will see Chiang Kai-shek tonight and report our conversation.

Minister for Foreign Affairs then raised the question of proposals contained in Shanghai telegram No. 27.[3] I informed him of what passed at interview with Chiang Kai-shek (my telegram No. 333)[4] and urged him to discuss proposals in Shanghai telegram with Chiang Kai-shek and if the latter agreed to speak at once to the Japanese Counsellor.

Repeated as usual and Shanghai.

[3] Not traced in F.O. archives.   [4] No. 179.

No. 186

Mr. Dodds (Tokyo) to Foreign Office (Received August 16, 3.15 p.m.)

No. 296 Telegraphic [F 5276/9/10]

TOKYO, *August 16, 1937, 6 p.m.*

Your telegrams Nos. 222[1] and 223[2] and 225[3]. I led the conversation accordingly with Vice Minister for Foreign Affairs. I pointed out to him efforts now being made by His Majesty's Ambassador at Nanking to urge Chinese Government to guarantee not to attack Japanese quarters and to dispose their forces etc., and said that this was giving both sides another chance. I would undertake to emphasise to His Majesty's Government and His Majesty's Ambassador at Nanking extreme importance of obtaining such a guarantee if I could say at the same time that Japanese Government would on this understanding withdraw the whole of their landing party from China. I trusted that his government would very earnestly consider this in order to avoid all sorts of complications which might arise if fighting continued.

As regards *Idzumo* prospects of Japanese agreement are dubious.

Vice Minister for Foreign Affairs will let me know decision of Japanese Government on these two points as soon as possible.

Repeated to Nanking, Commander-in-Chief.

[1] No. 182.   [2] No. 184.
[3] This telegram of August 15 (No. 206 to Nanking) read: 'Please inform Government to which you are accredited that arrangements are being made to evacuate a large number of

British nationals from Shanghai and that His Majesty's Government count upon them to enable this to be done.'

No. 187

Mr. Dodds (Tokyo) to Foreign Office (Received August 16, 3.15 p.m.)

No. 297 Telegraphic [*F 5252/9/10*]

TOKYO, *August 16, 1937, 8.15 p.m.*

Your telegram No. 291[1] paragraph 3.

United States Ambassador has been authorised to support my representations if he thinks fit and to use such language as he thinks suitable.[2] He is accordingly seeing Minister for Foreign Affairs this afternoon and giving him letter of which he has given me copy which is similar in substance to mine. It includes the following sentence 'important issue at present moment is not a question of determining initial responsibility for outbreak but there can be no doubt that if Shanghai region continues to be made the theatre of battle neither side can divest itself of responsibility.'[3]

When giving me copy of this letter United States Ambassador referred to statement in paragraph 6 of my telegram No. 230[4] which I showed him at the time that United States Government 'had not seen fit' to co-operate with us at Tokyo and suggested that it was no longer valid. I reassured him with emphasis. He has been extremely helpful (a welcome contrast to my other interested colleagues) and perhaps an expression at Washington of your appreciation of this if you thought it desirable to make it might be useful for the future.[5]

Repeated Nanking.

---

[1] No. 180.　　　　　　　　　　　　　　　[2] See *F.R.U.S.*, 1937, vol. iii, p. 412.
[3] See *F.R.U.S. Japan 1931–1941*, vol. i, pp. 347–9.　　　　　　　　　[4] No. 129.
[5] In a minute of August 17 referring to this sentence Mr. Ronald wrote: 'I take it that the contrast in brackets must be principally with the attitude of the German who according to Mr. Dodds's tel. No. 291 was instructed *not* to concert.' In telegram No. 308 of August 19 to Washington Sir R. Lindsay was informed that Sir R. Vansittart had expressed appreciation of Mr. Grew's help to Mr. Bingham. It was left to Sir R. Lindsay's discretion whether he said anything to the State Department.

Sir H. Knatchbull-Hugessen (Nanking) to Foreign Office
(Received August 16, 7 p.m.)

No. 345 *Telegraphic: by wireless* [F 5292/9/10]

Immediate   NANKING, *August 16, 1937*

Addressed to Shanghai telegram No. 66 of August 16th.

Commander-in-Chief's telegram No. 119[1] to Admiralty.

I am firmly convinced that it is a complete waste of time to discuss any solution based on a 'withdrawal to original positions'.

The Japanese maintain that presence of forces of landing party is necessary for the protection of their nationals the danger envisaged being:

1.   Organised attack by the Chinese armed forces from outside the Settlement.

2.   Sporadic attacks on individuals by anti-Japanese fanatic[?s] inside Settlement; in which connexion they complain that they receive insufficient protection from Shanghai Municipal Police.

It is clear that it is the presence of Japanese armed forces in Shanghai which is attracting danger to life and property of Japanese nationals. The Japanese authorities . . .[2] make up their minds whether they are more interested in the prestige of their armed forces or in the safety of their nationals. If the former there is nothing for it and the issue must be fought out; if the latter then they can assure most positively best way of securing safety of their nationals in Shanghai is to withdraw their armed forces subject to arrangements on following lines: (a) Simultaneous withdrawal of all Chinese armed forces from Shanghai zone, (b) Temporary protection to be afforded by other foreign forces *pari passu* with Japanese withdrawal to Japanese nationals until Chinese evacuation is completed and until (c) a considerable increase has been effected in number of Japanese officers of Shanghai Municipal Police so as to afford confidence to Japanese community. The figure I have in mind is about one hundred.

In my opinion if these terms could be accepted they would afford complete security to the Japanese.

It may be pointed out to them that once Chinese armed forces withdraw all that Japanese nationals in Shanghai need fear is an outcrop of incidents with which augmented police force should be quite capable of dealing. I am well aware it will be increasing Japanese personnel of police but

[1] This telegram of August 14 argued that the case for sending two further battalions to Shanghai should be seriously considered, and that it was important that foreign reinforcements should also be sent. The Commander in Chief felt that the crisis at Shanghai could only be alleviated in two ways: (a) by the withdrawal of the Japanese landing party and nationals from Shanghai and the withdrawal of Chinese to outside the demilitarized zone; or (b) by the complete evacuation of foreign nationals other than Japanese, the defence force remaining to protect property.

[2] The text were here uncertain.

situation is so serious that that consideration takes second place.

Please discuss urgently with Commander-in-Chief ...² authorities Mayor and your Japanese colleague and any others you think desirable and see whether there is any possibility of a solution on these lines.

In order to show our own disinterestedness His Majesty's Government might perhaps be willing to give an undertaking to withdraw our own forces from Shanghai as soon as situation calms down but you should say nothing of this at present since I have not consulted Foreign Office.³

Repeated to Peking, Tokyo, Commander-in-Chief and General Officer Commanding.

³ This telegram was discussed at the meeting of Ministers held on August 17 at 4 p.m. (see No. 191 below), but Sir R. Vansittart had already despatched a private telegram, No. 213, to Sir H. Knatchbull-Hugessen at 2.30 p.m. on August 17, stating that the suggestion that British troops might eventually be withdrawn from Shanghai 'does not appeal to me and I much doubt whether His Majesty's Government would consider it'.

No. 189

Foreign Office to Sir H. Knatchbull-Hugessen (Nanking)

No. 217¹ Telegraphic [F 5292/9/10]

Immediate   FOREIGN OFFICE, August 17, 1937, 8.55 p.m.

Nanking telegram No. 66 to Shanghai.²

If both Chinese and Japanese will agree to withdraw their forces including warships from the Shanghai area and will both agree that protection of Japanese nationals in the International Settlement and on extra settlement roads should be entrusted to foreign authorities, His Majesty's Government will be prepared to undertake this responsibility if other powers will join them in doing so. You may so inform Government to which you are accredited adding that in putting forward this proposal His Majesty's Government are actuated solely by the desire to keep the International Settlement free from hostilities and the commitment contemplated would be of a temporary nature to hold good during the continuance of the crisis.

Repeated to Peking No. 303, G.O.C., C. in C. C. in C. please pass to Consulate General Shanghai en clair.

¹ No. 226 to Tokyo. This telegram and No. 190 below were despatched after discussion at the Ministers' meeting on the afternoon of August 17: see No. 191 below.
² No. 188.

No. 190

Foreign Office to Sir H. Knatchbull-Hugessen (Nanking)

No. 218 Telegraphic [F 5292/9/10]

Immediate   FOREIGN OFFICE, *August 17, 1937, 9.20 p.m.*

My telegram No. 217.[1]

In making your communication you should point out to the Chinese Government that the proposal covers and more than covers their point about Japanese use of the International Settlement as a military base.

I am not prepared at this moment to put forward the suggestion for an increase in Japanese police strength; if you have any further observations on this point I shall be glad to have them in due course.

His Majesty's Government are unable to give any undertaking to withdraw British forces.[2] I have just been informed that French Government are not prepared to withdraw French troops, feeling, I understand that if they were once withdrawn it would be impossible ever to send them back.

Definition of Shanghai area for purpose of withdrawal proposed will require to be reached. Apart from this a necessary condition of the scheme will be certainty that the Chinese will carry out and maintain any undertaking that they give.

Repeated to Tokyo No. 227, Peking, G.O.C. C. in C. C. in C. please pass to Consulate General Shanghai en clair.

[1] No. 189.   [2] Cf. No. 188, note 3.

No. 191

Extract from notes of a meeting of Ministers[1] held at the Foreign Office on August 17, 1937, at 4 p.m.

[F 5384/9/10]

Most Secret   2, WHITEHALL GARDENS, S.W.1, *August 17, 1937*

PRESENT: Lord Halifax (*in the Chair*); Mr. Eden, Mr. Ormsby-Gore[2], Mr. Duff Cooper[3], Mr. Hore-Belisha[4], Sir R. Vansittart, Rear Admiral Cunningham, Field Marshal Sir C. J. Deverell[5], Major General Haining, Sir L. Oliphant[6], Mr. Orde, Sir J. Pratt, Sir L. Wakely[7], Colonel Ismay (Deputy Secretary, C.I.D.).

[1] For the background to this meeting see Volume XIX, No. 94, note 1. Mr. Eden came up to London to attend the meeting, and returned to Southampton to resume his holiday.
[2] Secretary of State for the Colonies.   [3] First Lord of the Admiralty.
[4] Secretary of State for War.   [5] Chief of the Imperial General Staff.
[6] Deputy Under Secretary of State for Foreign Affairs.
[7] Deputy Under Secretary of State for India.

1. *The Situation in Shanghai*

THE LORD PRESIDENT said that his object in summoning a Meeting of those Ministers who happened to be in London was first to run over what had been done in regard to the crisis in Shanghai, and secondly to see whether there was anything further that could be done.

SIR ROBERT VANSITTART said that he had had a Meeting last Sunday[8] with representatives of the Admiralty and War Office, as a result of which a number of decisions had been taken, and telegrams despatched.[9] There was one point, however, on which they had not thought it right to take the responsibility of a decision without reference to Ministerial authority—namely the possibility of persuading the Japanese to withdraw their landing party, the Chinese to withdraw all their armed forces from the Shan[g]hai zone, and of our undertaking the responsibility together with other foreign forces, of affording protection to Japanese nationals in Shanghai.

He proceeded to read out a telegram (see Appendix I to these Minutes[10]) which showed that Sir Hughe Knatchbull-Hugessen had the same sort of idea in mind. Attention was drawn to the fact that it might be difficult to afford protection to those Japanese nationals who lived outside the international settlement. It was also observed that the precise definition of the Shanghai area for the purposes of the proposed withdrawals would have to be a matter for subsequent consideration.

THE SECRETARY OF STATE FOR WAR pointed out that the Chinese had about eight divisions, including two German-trained divisions, in the vicinity of Shanghai, and that the Japanese had only something like 34,000 men. In these circumstances it seemed likely that the Chinese would decline to abandon the initiative which their numerical superiority at present gave them, and with it the chance of scoring a spectacular success, which would have such a tremendous moral value in the early stages of the conflict. Consequently there was the danger that we should find ourselves trying to protect the Japanese withdrawal against an overwhelming Chinese attack.

THE FIRST LORD OF THE ADMIRALTY agreed, and added that the Japanese position was at present somewhat precarious. If they were compelled to retire, we should have the extraordinary position of British soldiers losing their lives in fighting for the Japanese cause.

THE SECRETARY OF STATE FOR FOREIGN AFFAIRS thought it extremely unlikely that the Chinese would give up their chance of an outstanding success, but nevertheless the proposal was worth giving a trial.

THE LORD PRESIDENT said that there could be no question of our undertaking any commitment to protect Japanese nationals unless three conditions were satisfied. First, that both Chinese and Japanese should agree to withdraw their forces, including, in the case of the Japanese, their warships, from the Shanghai area. Secondly, that both parties to the

---

[8] See No. 182, note 2.   [9] See Nos. 182–184.   [10] No. 188.

conflict would welcome this undertaking on our part, and thirdly that other Powers were prepared to co-operate with us in implementing the commitment. This third condition was, in his view, essential, in order to emphasise the international character of the enterprise, and it was immaterial if only meagre numbers could be supplied by some of the co-operating Powers. He felt that if these three conditions were satisfied, there would be no question of our troops becoming engaged with the Chinese forces, and that their work would be primarily that of the maintenance of law and order. He assumed that the numbers that we should have available in Shanghai would be sufficient for this latter purpose.

THE CHIEF OF THE IMPERIAL GENERAL STAFF expressed some doubts as to whether the British forces at Shanghai were adequate to implement the proposal. He said that he would like the opportunity of consulting the local Commander on this point.

Conclusion 1

After some further discussion, it was agreed:
that the Secretary of State for Foreign Affairs should inform Nanking and Tokyo by telegram that, if both the Chinese and Japanese would agree to withdraw their forces (including warships) from the Shanghai area, and if they would both agree that the protection of Japanese nationals in the Shanghai area should be entrusted to the forces of foreign Powers, His Majesty's Government would be prepared to undertake this responsibility, provided that the other Powers were willing to co-operate in doing so. It should be emphasised in putting forward this proposal that His Majesty's Government were actuated solely by the desire to keep the International Settlement free from hostilities, and that the commitment contemplated would be of a temporary character, and would hold good only during the continuance of the crisis.[11]

The discussion then turned to the proposal put forward by Sir Hughe Knatchbull-Hugessen (see telegram attached as Appendix I) that there should be 'a considerable increase in the number of Japanese Officers of the Shanghai Municipal Police so as to afford confidence in the Japanese community'.

Conclusion 2
It was agreed:
that the Secretary of State for Foreign Affairs should inform His Majesty's Ambassador at Nanking that His Majesty's Government were disinclined at present to adopt his suggestion that the number of

[11] The telegrams despatched in accordance with this conclusion are printed as Nos. 189 and 190 above.

Japanese Officers of the Shanghai Municipal Police should be increased, but that they would welcome any further observations on this point that he might care to make.

As regards the suggestion contained in Appendix I that His Majesty's Government 'might perhaps be willing to give an undertaking to withdraw our own forces from Shanghai as soon as the situation calms down', it was generally agreed that such a suggestion could not be entertained since once troops were withdrawn it would be very difficult ever to send them back.

Conclusion 3

It was agreed:

that the Secretary of State for Foreign Affairs should inform His Majesty's Ambassador at Nanking that His Majesty's Government were not prepared to contemplate the idea of giving an undertaking to withdraw British forces.[12]

The discussion then turned to the question of the evacuation of women and children from Shanghai.

THE SECRETARY OF STATE FOR FOREIGN AFFAIRS asked whether it would be possible to expedite the evacuation by using warships for the purpose.

REAR ADMIRAL CUNNINGHAM said that the Commander in Chief was evacuating 700 women and children to-day and that he hoped to evacuate about 2,000 more on the 19th August. It was true that a figure of 4,500 had been mentioned as the number of women and children to be evacuated, but it would almost certainly be found that a very large number of these would refuse to leave. The evacuation of men as well as women and children was out of the question. As regards the question of using warships for evacuation purposes, the only two cruisers in China Seas were being kept out of the way, and destroyers were entirely unsuitable for the purpose.

SIR ROBERT VANSITTART raised the question of the evacuation of foreigners. He said that the Portuguese Ambassador had recently told him that there were some 4,000 Portuguese Nationals in the Shanghai Area, and that, without making any specific request that we should assist in their evacuation, he was obviously toying with the idea. All that he had in fact asked was that our Consul-General should be instructed to keep in close touch with the Portuguese Consul-General.

REAR ADMIRAL CUNNINGHAM suggested that the Commander in Chief might be asked to give favourable consideration to assisting the evacuation of the Esthonians in Shanghai to the number of about 120.

THE LORD PRESIDENT thought that any assistance that we might give to the Nationals of other Powers should be confined to the smaller nations, which were unable to help themselves.

[12] See No. 190.

THE SECRETARY OF STATE FOR THE COLONIES observed that accommodation in Hong Kong was very tight and that we would soon be reaching saturation point there. Would it not be possible to approach the United States of America with a request to permit evacuation to Manila?

Conclusion 4
It was agreed:
   (a) that the Secretary of State for the Colonies should ascertain the position as regards the accommodation of refugees at Hong Hong.
   (b) that the Secretary of State for Foreign Affairs should take up the question of whether the United States Government would be prepared to receive a number of refugees from Shanghai at Manila.
   (c) that the Naval Commander in Chief should be requested to give favourable consideration to the possibility of assisting the evacuation of Nationals of those small Powers who were unable to help themselves, provided that this did not interfere with the evacuation of British Nationals.

The discussion then turned to the question of the reinforcements required from India.

THE CHIEF OF THE IMPERIAL GENERAL STAFF said that it was necessary to get two battalions from India in order to replace the battalions that had been, or were to be, sent from Hong Kong to Shanghai. He would agree to both the battalions being Indian Battalions. If this were done, the position would be briefly as follows. At Shanghai there would be 4 British battalions; at Hong Kong there would be 1 British battalion and 3 Indian battalions; and at Singapore there would be two British battalions.

SIR LEONARD WAKELY said that Lord Zetland agreed to ask the Government of India for these reinforcements. He observed, however, that there had been considerable arguments about the financial adjustments for the reinforcements sent to China on the last occasion. It would, therefore, be of definite assistance if some indication of the financial arrangements proposed by His Majesty's Government could be included in the telegram to the Government of India asking for two battalions.

THE LORD PRESIDENT thought it was impossible for this question to be settled at the meeting. He asked whether these reinforcements were required to enable the British garrison at Shanghai to cope with the extra work occasioned by the crisis or whether they were for increased moral effect. He added that the larger our garrison, the greater the target for air attack.

THE CHIEF OF THE IMPERIAL GENERAL STAFF pointed out that there was a large perimeter to be held, and that the authorities on the spot had strongly urged the necessity for these reinforcements.

Conclusion 5
It was agreed:
   that the Secretary of State in India should request the Government of

253

India to send two battalions (which might both be Indian Battalions) to Hong Kong as soon as possible.

There was some discussion as to whether a *communiqué* should be issued to the Press on the subject of the meeting.

Conclusion 6

It was agreed:

that there should be no formal Press *communiqué*, but that the News Department of the Foreign Office should inform the Press that there had been a meeting of those Ministers who happened to be in London, in order to consider what further representations might be made to the Japanese and Chinese Governments with a view to keeping the International Settlement free from hostilities, and what further arrangements could be devised for the protection of British Nationals and British Interests.

No. 192

Mr. Dodds (Tokyo) to Foreign Office (Received August 18, 10 a.m.)

No. 299 Telegraphic [F 5331/9/10]

TOKYO, *August 18, 1937, 3.40 p.m.*

Your telegram No. 226.[1]

I so informed Vice Minister for Foreign Affairs this morning. He observed this was a very important communication. He added personally he doubted whether troops at disposal of foreign authorities were sufficient to protect Japanese nationals and interests and that it might be difficult for Japanese Government to accept in face of Chinese aggressive tactics at Shanghai. He will inform me of decision of Japanese Government as soon as possible.

2. In reply to my enquiry he said that reinforcements for Shanghai referred to in my telegram No. 294[2] had not yet left Japan. I said they need not leave at all if Japanese accepted proposal I had just made to him and pointed out that this was at least the 4th or 5th proposal for peace which we were offering.

3. He said *Idzumo* had been moved down stream from the Settlement wharves.

4. United States Ambassador is informing United States Government of my communication to Vice Minister for Foreign Affairs.[3]

Repeated to Nanking and Commander in Chief.

---

[1] No. 189.   [2] Not kept in F.O. archives.   [3] See *F.R.U.S.*, 1937, vol. iii, pp. 440–1.

No. 193

Mr. Dodds (Tokyo) to Foreign Office (Received August 19, 2.30 p.m.)

No. 301 Telegraphic [F 5428/9/10]

TOKYO, *August 19, 1937, 7.6 p.m.*

Your telegrams Nos. 228[1] and 229[2].

I left pro memoria and note with Vice Minister for Foreign Affairs on these two subjects today. At the same interview he told me that Japanese Government would not *at present* accept proposals reported in my telegrams Nos. 296[3] and 299[4] because they were not convinced that foreign authorities had sufficient troops at their disposal for the purpose and also because it was the duty of the Japanese Government to protect Japanese nationals and interests. Also Sino-Japanese hostilities in Shanghai had been caused by Chinese violation of 1932 Agreement. Hostilities would cease when the Chinese regular troops and Peace Preservation Corps were withdrawn to district outside agreed area and it was to be hoped that the Powers would persuade Chinese Government to do this. Similar language was used to Military Attaché by Military Affairs Bureau who added that if the Chinese did this all Japanese troop movement to Shanghai and preparations for attack there would cease.

I am inclined to let Japanese Government think about our proposal for a day or two before approaching them again on the subject. It seems just possible that they may discover it to be to their interest to accept it though I fear I cannot hold out much hope on this score.[5]

Repeated to Nanking and Commander-in-Chief.

---

[1] This telegram of August 18 (No. 220 to Nanking) instructed Mr. Dodds to represent urgently to the Japanese Government that the extension of hostilities into the area of the Whangpoo river between Garrison Bend and Junk Boom would greatly increase the danger to all foreign interests.

[2] This telegram of August 18 referred to the reported occupation of the property of Messrs. Jardine, Matheson & Co. by the Japanese.

[3] No. 186. [4] No. 192.

[5] Foreign Office telegram No. 237 to Tokyo of August 20 agreed that for the moment it might 'be better to say nothing further to the Japanese Government though you might consider whether it would not be useful to point out that if the scheme is accepted by both sides a small number of foreign troops should suffice for protection of Japanese nationals'.

No. 194

Sir R. Lindsay (Washington) to Foreign Office
(Received August 20, 9.30 a.m.)

No. 237 Telegraphic [F 5452/9/10]

Immediate   WASHINGTON, *August 19, 1937, 8.10 p.m.*

Your telegram No. 305.[1]

United States Government have returned the following reply to enquiry made in accordance with your instructions:

'Careful and close attention has been given to His Majesty's Government's enquiry whether United States Government would be prepared to accept with His Majesty's Government joint responsibility in carrying out action proposed by the latter at Shanghai and whether they would be prepared to instruct United States Ambassadors at Nanking and Tokyo accordingly.

2. Shortly after receipt of this enquiry, United States Government received in a telegram from United States Ambassador Tokyo information to the effect that His Majesty's Chargé d'Affaires Tokyo had presented to Japanese Vice Minister for Foreign Affairs His Majesty's Government's proposal and that reaction of Vice Minister was of a character which could only be construed as unfavourable.[2] There has subsequently appeared no indication of an affirmative interest on the part of Japanese Government in this proposal. In the light of this evidence, it appears to United States Government that the question of a possible assumption of a joint responsibility such as is envisaged in His Majesty's Government's proposal has already been disposed of adversely by the attitude of Japanese Government. However, towards avoiding any possible misunderstanding, it should not be expected that United States Government would be favourably inclined towards any project envisaging military or police responsibilities over and above those which relate to already existing Missions of their armed forces now present in China'.[3]

---

[1] This telegram of August 18 referred to No. 217 to Nanking (No. 189) and instructed Sir R. Lindsay to enquire immediately whether the U.S. Government would accept the joint responsibility indicated therein and instruct their representatives at Nanking and Tokyo accordingly. The same instructions were sent to Paris in telegram No. 150 for communication to the French Government, who agreed late on August 18 to support the British plan: see *D.D.F., op cit.*, p. 616, note 2.

[2] Cf. No. 192, note 3.

[3] In a minute of August 23 Mr. Orde commented on the American eagerness 'to assume that there was no chance of our proposal succeeding and that no action was therefore proper. The fact is that there *was* a faint chance: the proposal probably was too late but that only made the utmost promptitude essential. The real reason for this attitude is that Roosevelt is being pressed not to protect American lives and property but to evacuate nationals and let property go west & that he prefers to hedge instead of acting'.

No. 195

Foreign Office to Sir R. Lindsay (Washington)

No. 313 Telegraphic [F 5452/9/10]

Immediate   FOREIGN OFFICE, *August 20, 1937, 2.15 p.m.*

Your telegram No. 237.[1]
Please inform U.S. Government that Japanese Government while indicating preliminary doubts have not given their final answer to our proposal. You should point out that if Chinese and Japanese Governments genuinely accept the scheme quite small numbers of foreign troops should suffice for protection of Japanese nationals. Since the scheme appears to be the only chance of averting further and even more terrible dangers to International Settlement His Majesty's Government earnestly trust that U.S. Government will be able to declare their readiness to cooperate. French Government, though mainly concerned with French concession, are understood to be ready to contribute something to indicate their solidarity outside their concession.

Repeated to Nanking, Peking, Tokyo, G.O.C. Hong Kong, C. in C., C. in C. please pass to Consulate General Shanghai en clair.

[1] No. 194.

No. 196

Foreign Office to Mr. Dodds (Tokyo)

No. 239 Telegraphic [F 5428/9/10]

FOREIGN OFFICE, *August 20, 1937, 7 p.m.*

Your telegram No. 301.[1]
I understand that the Japanese Government have not yet formally rejected our proposal. With all allowance for hesitation, precious time is passing. It is therefore in my view necessary that it should be represented urgently to them that damage to British property and danger to British lives is continuing and that they should realise the extent to which they are endangering our interests by their operations at Shanghai. The magnitude of these operations has been out of all proportion to the comparatively trivial incident, namely the killing of two members of the Japanese landing party, which gave rise to them. According to our information the Chinese reinforcements of which the Japanese complain were only brought up after the Japanese had as a result of that incident more than doubled their naval strength at Shanghai and landed a large additional number of men there. The Japanese Government must realise

[1] No. 193.

that public opinion in this country and in the world in general necessarily attributes the course of events at Shanghai mainly to Japanese action there. His Majesty's Government consider it therefore particularly incumbent on the Japanese Government to assist in measures to end a state of affairs potentially disastrous to others. The acceptance of our proposal for withdrawal would at least be a helpful contribution.

Please communicate accordingly with the Japanese Government.

No. 197

Sir R. Lindsay (Washington) to Foreign Office
(Received August 22, 11 a.m.)

No. 240 Telegraphic [F 5540/9/10]

Confidential   WASHINGTON, *August 21, 1937, 10.7 p.m.*

My immediately preceding telegram.[1]

I have had an unofficial message from Secretary of State of which following is substance though actual language is not necessarily his.[2] Begins:

State Department is somewhat embarrassed at being pressed more than once to co-operate in this scheme of neutralization of a zone in Shanghai or for assumption of a joint responsibility for Japanese lives. It is not that they are not very anxious to have Anglo-American co-operation which in general and certainly in suitable cases they regard as of utmost value but in present instance, and perhaps in another, during the currency of the present crisis they feel that a scheme has been launched from London and simultaneously acted upon in the Far East and that then their co-operation has been sought when for one reason or another scheme lacks or has ceased to have any utility. Of course they realise that in moments of pressure this sort of thing may well happen. As regards scheme of neutralisation etc., it was present in their minds well before you invited them to join in its support and they have already decided on ample evidence that it was impracticable because with military influence paramount at Tokyo Japanese Government would never be able to allow other nations to protect their nationals or to admit foreign forces would be adequate for the task or to agree that necessary good faith on part of Chinese would be forthcoming. They were aware that Vice Minister for Foreign Affairs' refusal had been pro tempore and subject to reconsideration but had never regarded this as anything more than common Japanese

[1] Not kept in F.O. archives.
[2] Cf. No. 195. A formal note of acknowledgement from the State Department to the British Embassy dated August 21, which reiterated the U.S. Government's view that the Japanese attitude made any idea of 'joint responsibility' impracticable, is printed in *F.R.U.S.*, 1937, vol. iii, p. 456.

form and virtually meaningless. They felt they were being offered a dead horse and invited to join in flogging it into a canter and this has made them a little restive.

The immediately practical point, however, is that this scheme has been launched and widely publicised and they are being questioned as to what they are doing about it all the more keenly because of French acceptance of it in principle and on a purely pro forma basis with nature of which they were familiar from the first. With all this they can deal and they have not complained of what has come forward so far but should messages come from London to the effect that scheme has failed because United States Government refused to participate that would not only be unfair to them in their view but would also cause recriminations to arise and would give a check to Anglo-American co-operation. Present message is sent just to avoid such a check and because recrimination is the last thing they desire. Ends.

No. 198

Foreign Office to Mr. Dodds (Tokyo)

No. 242 Telegraphic [F 5552/9/10]

FOREIGN OFFICE, *August 21, 1937, 11 p.m.*

Your telegram No. 304.[1]

Prime Minister's statement to the press cannot be accepted as a final answer to us, and his interpretation of our proposal as intervention should be rebutted. You should renew your efforts and add to the communication you were instructed to make in my telegram No. 239[2] an explanation that it is incorrect to look on our proposal as intervention. It was not made for that purpose but as the only possible means apparent to us by which the immense British interest at stake in Shanghai might be saved. The Japanese have professed to wish not to endanger our interests but it will be impossible to believe them if they persist in their present attitude. Since Chinese Government (as shown by Nanking telegram No. 370[3]) are considering our proposal we earnestly trust that the Japanese Government will not close the door. Every day that passes means further great

[1] In this telegram of August 21 Mr. Dodds reported that the Japanese Prime Minister had told the press on August 20 that 'there was no alternative to answer given by Ministry of Foreign Affairs to British proposal for establishment of a neutral zone at Shanghai as intervention by a third party had to be considered in the light of its possible after effects. Government policy was not to allow third party to intervene but to settle everything direct between China and Japan'.

[2] No. 196.

[3] In this telegram of August 20 Sir H. Knatchbull-Hugessen reported a conversation with Chiang Kai-shek as a result of which he was convinced that the General 'would in fact give the undertaking [in No. 189] if Japanese did likewise'.

damage to life and property in Shanghai and a very early and favourable decision is of the greatest importance.[4]

Repeated to Nanking No. 235, Peking, G.O.C. Hong Kong, C. in C. C. in C. please pass to Shanghai Consulate General en clair.

[4] In telegram No. 308 of August 23 Mr. Dodds reported that he had been told on August 21 by the Vice Minister for Foreign Affairs that 'as the situation at Shanghai had not changed he saw no possibility of attitude of Japanese Government towards British proposal changing'; Mr. Dodds had 'used every possible argument but could not budge him'.

No. 199

Mr. Eden[1] to Sir R. Lindsay (Washington)

No. 317 Telegraphic [F 5540/9/10]

Confidential   FOREIGN OFFICE, August 23, 1937, 3.30 p.m.

Your telegram No. 240.[2]

Please thank the Secretary of State for his message and inform him in such terms as you think suitable that the information at our disposal did not lead us to take quite so pessimistic a view regarding acceptability of our suggestions for a truce. We also have not been hopeful of the result of our proposal, but did not consider that a reason for abstaining from at least an attempt to alleviate a situation which had grown so urgent and so profoundly serious. On the contrary having regard to the large international interests at stake we felt bound in default of any alternative constructive proposals to put forward the suggestions submitted to us by the Ambassadors at Nanking. The State Department is in error in describing this as 'a scheme launched in London': it originated in Nanking where it was discussed by all the responsible foreign representatives, including that of the United States. Moreover the moment for making an effort towards a peaceful solution seemed specially opportune as Japanese Military Attaché in China was reported to be then on his way to Tokyo to urge on Japanese military party necessity of a speedy cessation of hostilities in Shanghai area on account of great damage being done to Japanese interests there. In all these circumstances inaction would have seemed to us impossible, and indeed unpardonable. Mr. Hull may however of course rest fully assured that everything possible has been and will be done here to ensure that failure of scheme will not in any way be attributed here to U.S. refusal to participate. Principal blame in the nature of things will probably be laid at Japan's door if she turns proposal down.

[1] Mr. Eden resumed charge of the Foreign Office on August 23.   [2] No. 197.

No. 200

Sir H. Knatchbull-Hugessen (Nanking) to Mr. Eden
(Received August 24, 8.30 p.m.)

No. 382 Telegraphic [F 5690/1098/10]

Very Secret   NANKING, *August 23, 1937*

Chiang Kai-shek sent for me August 23rd and after a preliminary enquiry as to nature of relations between His Majesty's Government and U.S.S.R. told me in strict confidence that the Chinese Government was considering entering into a Pact of mutual non-aggression with the U.S.S.R.[1] It would he said be strictly in accordance with League Covenant and would be registered with the League and published and would contain no secret clauses. Effect would be that Russia would not support China against any third party or vice versa.

2. From subsequent conversation I gathered that advantage[s] which China expects to obtain from this are (a) moral effect (b) it will avert danger of Russia giving in to Japanese pressure to side against China . . .[2] (c) in particular it will prevent Russia withdrawing troops from Manchu-kuo frontier and thereby releasing Japanese troops for action against China.[3]

3. Chiang Kai-shek stated that discussions with Soviet Government had already been opened in Moscow.

4. I gathered that Chiang Kai-shek's desire in imparting this information was to ascertain reaction of His Majesty's Government. He did not however put this question to me and I merely said I would report the conversation confidentially to you. I also said that in my opinion the matter was very delicate[,] it was vital to avoid giving Japan any pretext for accusing China or Russia of plotting against her and it was essential that every word of the Pact should be published officially. I was rather struck by an evident fear on Chiang Kai-shek's part that unless precautions were taken Russia might not be able to withstand Japanese pressure aimed through Russia at China. He said he was not mentioning the matter to any of my colleagues and wished it to be kept secret.

5. I have not repeated to Tokyo.

Repeated to Peking No. 534.

---

[1] In fact a Sino-Soviet non-aggression pact had been signed on August 21: see No. 217 below.

[2] The text was here uncertain.

[3] Mr. Ronald commented in a minute of August 25: '. . . I cannot understand why Chiang Kai-shek fears that Russia will give in to Japanese pressure to side against China. One would have thought this inconceivable. . . It may be that the Chinese have heard the rumour that the Russians are once more toying with the idea of a Soviet Japan Non-Aggression Treaty and hope in some obscure way to head them off. . . Alternatively I suppose it is just possible that the Chinese are banking on the Japanese suspecting the existence of secret sinister additional clauses if an innocuous Sino-Russian agreement is published and retaining

valuable manpower in Manchukuo against a possible move by Russia in conformity with one of these secret clauses. . .'

No. 201

Memorandum by Sir J. Pratt on the possible effects on British interests of hostilities at Shanghai

[F 5642/9/10]

FOREIGN OFFICE, *August 23, 1937*

If the efforts which we are now making to stop the hostilities in Shanghai should fail (and the American attitude leaves little doubt that they will fail) there are three possible ways in which they can end:

(1) A stale-mate,
(2) A Japanese victory,
(3) A Chinese victory.

It seems worth enquiring which of these three alternatives would be most favourable (or least favourable) to British interests.

A stale-mate would mean most of Hongkew and Yangtzepoo in ruins, the Japanese forces in possession of the ground, no political settlement and, therefore, a prospect of fighting breaking out again, and continued paralysis of all trade. Such a situation would be only slightly less disastrous than a complete Japanese victory. If the Japanese defeat and drive away the Chinese armies they would establish a wide demilitarised zone all round Shanghai, their own forces would remain in sole possession of Hongkew and Yangtzepoo, and any Chinese authority exercising jurisdiction in the demilitarised zone would be completely under Japanese control. Most of Hongkew and Yangtzepoo and possibly other districts, such as Pootung, might be destroyed. Hongkew and Yangtzepoo constitute the shipping and industrial centre of Shanghai where all the docks, public utilities and many factories and commercial enterprises are situated. The value of the British investment in this district is said to amount to £180 million. Nowhere else in the world can there be found a parallel of this vast concentration of British capital invested within an area of a few square miles. Nevertheless, the total destruction of the whole of this property would be less disastrous to British interests in China than the occupation of the area itself by Japanese troops or the control by the Japanese of the local Chinese administration, for in this latter event British enterprise would be driven out of the Yangtze valley as surely as it has been driven out of Manchukuo and Korea. It would mean the final extinction of British interests in this region.

A Chinese victory, on the other hand, apart from the actual physical damage to British property, would be favourable to British interests, and the sooner it is won the less the amount of damage done. Chinese municipal administration would almost certainly replace the present foreign administration in at least Hongkew and Yangtzepoo. The process of adjustment would involve political problems of great delicacy and complexity, but there is no reason to doubt that British enterprise would prosper under Chinese administration just as it has prospered in Pootung, Hankow and in other areas where no foreign municipalities exist.

The conclusions reached are that a stale-mate or a Japanese victory would, from our point of view, be a complete disaster from which British interests in China from the Yangtze valley northwards might never recover, and that a Chinese victory, the speedier the better, would save British interests from extinction and offer a fair prospect of renewed prosperity in the future. Unfortunately it does not seem likely that the Chinese will win without foreign help. Unless, therefore, we are prepared to issue an ultimatum to Japan and back it with sufficient force, (the only argument that Japan appreciates) there is nothing we can do to protect British interests. Whether that is a practicable policy is another matter. The question whether we should go to war with Japan—or stand ready to go to war with her—in order to save British interests in China from extinction is not within the scope of this note.[1]

[1] Mr. Orde commented on August 23: 'I agree with the general conclusions in Sir J. Pratt's memo. . . There is nothing that we can do to influence the outcome of the present struggle, and we can but look forward with gloom to the future.'

No. 202

Sir R. Lindsay (Washington) to Mr. Eden
(Received August 25, 11 a.m.)

No. 247 Telegraphic [F 5683/9/10]

WASHINGTON, August 24,[1] 1937, 6.50 p.m.

Your telegram No. 317.[2]

I have given your message to Hornbeck who confidently assures me that it would be warmly appreciated by Secretary of State. I emphasised that perfect frankness between the two governments was the best basis for co-operation and he agreed. I suggest[ed] that as regards China at present, whereas here the main pressure from the banks is in the direction of inaction, in London there is considerable pressure to do something towards minimising the disasters of the situation and the knowledge that neither side had fully appreciated the different outlook of the other. He rather agreed with this but made two points, firstly that insistence of Washington on parallel rather than on joint action had been due only to the belief that joint action would defeat its own purpose and secondly that if His Majesty's Government desired to propose any joint action they

[1] The date of despatch is given on the filed copy as August 25, apparently in error.
[2] No. 199.

would be generally well advised to consult United States Government first and not first to issue instructions to their representative in the Far East and then ask United States Government to join in support of *démarche*. In case of such consultation State Department would always do its best to attend to matter with utmost celerity.

Tone of our conversation as indeed of Secretary of State's message was entirely friendly.[3]

[3] A memorandum of this conversation by Mr. Hornbeck is printed in *F.R.U.S.*, 1937, vol. iii, pp. 464–7. Mr. Ronald commented in a minute of August 25 on this telegram: 'Mr. Hornbeck is no doubt right when he says that, if we want U.S. cooperation, we must consult the State Dept. before taking action: I would go further and say that we must always frame our approach to the State Dept. in such a way that any action which may ultimately be taken may be represented as an American idea acted on through American initiative. And we must never complain if the State Dept. act without consulting us. . . In other words we must be prepared to take all the knocks and get none of the credit. But Anglo-American cooperation being so important, I venture to think that we should be wise to submit to this, humiliating though it may be.' Mr. Orde agreed (August 25): 'Up to a point where it isn't actually harmful. Urgent action is sometimes necessary. This seems quite a good close to the conversation for the moment.' Sir R. Vansittart added on August 26: 'I wouldn't go as far as Mr. Ronald suggests! But we can now let *this* suggestion rest.'

No. 203

Mr. Eden to Mr. Dodds (Tokyo)

No. 248 Telegraphic [F 5589/9/10]

Important   FOREIGN OFFICE, *August 25, 1937, 4.35 p.m.*

Your telegram No. 308.[1]

I should like to make a final effort to persuade the Japanese Government to accept these proposals. Even though you may already have used these arguments, you might say that objections mentioned in your telegram No. 301[2] have largely disappeared: there are now more foreign troops available to work the scheme than there were; and the Chinese Government have stated that they are 'prepared to accept the British proposal in principle, provided it is accepted by the Japanese Government'.[3] Of their expressed objections there remains only their reluctance to delegate protection of Japanese lives and interests to foreigners. This would be understandable in normal circumstances, but should not be allowed to prevail when so much is at stake. Japanese Government surely would not wish on this point alone to incur the responsibility of rejecting a scheme which admittedly offers a practicable way out of a situation of peculiar difficulty and enormous danger. You should act on the above lines unless you see strong objection, and feel that

[1] See No. 198, note 4.   [2] No. 193.
[3] Sir H. Knatchbull-Hugessen had reported the receipt of a message to this effect from the Chinese Foreign Minister in telegram No. 377 of August 23.

it may do more harm than good. In such case you should refer to me at once.

Repeated to Nanking No. 242, Peking, G.O.C. Hong Kong, C. in C. C. in C. please pass to Shanghai Consulate General en clair.

CHAPTER III

The wounding of Sir H. Knatchbull-Hugessen: Chinese appeal to the League of Nations

August 26—October 6, 1937

No. 204

Mr. J. W. O. Davidson[1] (Shanghai) to Mr. Eden (Received August 26)

No. 28 Telegraphic: by wireless [F 5728/5727/10]

Immediate   SHANGHAI, *August 26, 1937*

Ambassador's car flying Union Jack was fired on with machine gun and bombed about 14.30 to-day by two Japanese planes. Ambassador[2] seriously wounded in stomach now in country hospital. Doctors preliminary examination spinal region affected but not paralysis. Military Attaché and Financial Adviser unhurt.

Repeated British Legation Peking No. 68, British Embassy at Nanking No. 48.

[1] Acting Consul General at Shanghai.   [2] i.e. Sir H. Knatchbull-Hugessen.

No. 205

Mr. Eden to Mr. Davidson (Shanghai)

No. 52 Telegraphic [F 5727/5727/10]

Most Immediate   FOREIGN OFFICE, *August 26, 1937, 12.15 p.m.*

Please telegraph urgently particulars of Sir H. Knatchbull-Hugessen's condition[1] and circumstances in which he was wounded. Convey to him also if he is in a fit condition warmest sympathy and good wishes from myself and all in the Foreign Office.[2]

[1] See No. 204.
[2] This telegram was followed by two others to Mr. Davidson on August 26 urgently requesting more detailed information. No. 53 (despatched at 4.45 p.m.) wanted to know, in

order to decide what reparation should be demanded, 'whether car was open or closed, whether any one in it wore uniform, and whether Union Jack should have been visible to attacking aeroplanes'. Telegram No. 54 was despatched at 7.30 p.m. and asked for information as to the height of the aeroplane and other details. In telegram No. 331 to Peking, despatched at 8 p.m., Mr. Eden also sent a message of sympathy and good wishes to Lady Hugessen.

No. 206

Mr. Dodds (Tokyo) to Mr. Eden (Received August 26, 11 a.m.)

No. 318 Telegraphic [F 5716/9/10]

Immediate   TOKYO, August 26, 1937, 4.45 p.m.

Your telegram No. 248.[1]

I regret that I must express my opinion that it would be useless and would probably merely irritate Japanese Government if I attempted again to persuade them to accept our proposal. Situation has now much changed (see Commander-in-Chief's telegram No. 155 to the Admiralty[2] and my telegram No. 314[3]) and it is no longer a question of Japanese withdrawing merely a landing party reinforced by two or three thousand marines.[4]

Repeated to Nanking and Commander in Chief.

[1] No. 203.   [2] Not traced in F.O. archives.   [3] Of August 25, not printed (F 5692/9/10).
[4] It was agreed in the Foreign Office that the matter could not be pressed further. Mr. Orde noted on August 26: 'I feel myself that Mr. Dodds is right. The Japanese still however owe us a final reply as a matter of form. I should be inclined not to ask for one since it might irritate and the reply being final and certainly negative would close any remaining chink in the door. . .' Sir R. Vansittart agreed (August 27): 'I would certainly not override Mr. Dodds. And in any case we now have other fish to fry with the Japanese. These may sizzle quite a lot.' Mr. Eden wrote on August 27: 'My only remaining anxiety in this connexion is that we shall have to tell the world in due course that we have had no answer, as in the case of Germany [cf. Volume XIX, pp. 612–3, 'Five-Power Treaty']. This makes us appear rather snubbable? But perhaps we need not put it that way?' A note of August 28 by Mr. Ronald read: 'Sir R. Vansittart says this paper can now go by.'

No. 207

Mr. Dodds (Tokyo) to Mr. Eden (Received August 26, 12.45 p.m.)

No. 317[1] Telegraphic [F 5735/9/10]

TOKYO, August 26, 1937, 5.58 p.m.

Secretary at the Ministry of Foreign Affairs left statement here in English this morning which has been issued to the press that Japanese naval authorities have closed Chinese coast to Chinese vessels from 32

[1] Telegram No. 317 was despatched after No. 318 (No. 206).

degrees 4 minutes north latitude and 121 degrees 44 minutes east longitude to 23 degrees 14 minutes north latitude and 116 degrees 48 minutes east longitude beginning with 6 p.m. August 25th, 1937.

Statement adds that this measure applies only to Chinese vessels and that peaceful commerce carried out by other Powers will be fully respected.[2]

Do you wish me to ask what is meant by term 'peaceful'.

In United States Ambassador's opinion Japanese are anxious to avoid establishment of proper blockade for fear of complications with third parties but he does not know whether it would mean application of American neutrality act. Press is showing more signs of nervousness than usual about Anglo-American cooperation regarding the present situation in China.[3]

Repeated to Nanking and the Commander-in-Chief.

[2] In telegram No. 321 of August 27 Mr. Dodds added that the U.S. Naval Attaché had been told that the Japanese would remove only troops and armament stores but not normal cargoes from Chinese ships, and would not interfere in any way with neutral ships even if known to be carrying munitions.

[3] In a minute of August 28 on Tokyo telegram No. 321 Sir J. Pratt suggested that it was 'on the face of it reassuring', but that it was 'just possible that it may be deliberately intended to keep us quiet while the blockade step by step is tightened and extended'. He thought that '[w]e cannot resist, or protect our shipping, because we are not prepared to use force against Japan'. He concluded: 'There is only one thing that might conceivably prevent or at least delay developments along the above lines, namely, the fear that we and the Americans were acting together as regards interference with shipping. It may, therefore, be worth while trying to get the U.S.A. to join us in asking the Japanese Government to clarify their attitude.' Mr. Orde and Sir R. Vansittart agreed, and in telegram No. 338 to Washington of August 30 Sir R. Lindsay was instructed to ask whether the U.S. Government would be prepared to authorize their representative at Tokyo to concert with Mr. Dodds with a view to eliciting precise statement of measures which the Japanese Government intended to take. See *F.R.U.S.*, 1937, vol. iv, pp. 440–43. The enquiry was also addressed to the French Government.

No. 208

Mr. Cowan (Peking) to Mr. Eden (Received August 26, 8 p.m.)

No. 475 Telegraphic: by wireless [*F 5767/5727/10*]

PEKING, *August 26, 1937*

We received the sad news of the wounding of His Majesty's Ambassador this evening. We at once informed Japanese Embassy and Counsellor in charge of Embassy called to express regret. It was explained to him that so far as we knew it was impossible to attach any blame to any particular person for the incident.

Ambassador's wife is still at Peitaiho and will receive news (which has already been broadcast from London) at the latest tomorrow morning and I have accordingly asked Japanese Embassy to provide aeroplane to take my wife to Peitaiho in case she may be of immediate use. Japanese Embassy have arranged for an aeroplane to be here at 9 tomorrow morning and Shima, Japanese secretary, has undertaken to accompany my wife.[1]

Repeated to His Majesty's Ambassador, Tokyo, Commander-in-Chief, General Officer Commanding, Nanking and Rear Admiral Yangtse.

---

[1] But in his telegram No. 477 of August 27 to the Foreign Office Mr. Cowan had to report that his plan to send his wife to Peitaiho had not been entirely successful. As the Japanese pilot did not know the situation of the airfield at Peitaiho and as the plane could carry only two passengers it was arranged that Mr. Cowan's eldest son who knew the local geography should accompany Mr. Shima, who had been instructed to express condolences to Lady Knatchbull-Hugessen in person (F 5793/5727/10).

No. 209

Letter from Mr. Dodds (Tokyo) to Mr. Orde (Received September 25)

[F 6926/9/10]

Confidential   TOKYO, *August 26, 1937*

My dear Orde,

It may be of some interest if I send you a few impressions which have forced themselves upon me since the crisis here began but which are hardly suitable for a despatch.

2. In the first place my relations with the United States Embassy. Mr. Grew appears to enjoy the complete confidence of the State Department. It was therefore of the first importance to have him on our side. He has an open mind and has on at least one important occasion viz. when it was a question of recommending his Government to act on our proposal to provide neutral ground where peace plenipotentiairies [*sic*] might meet and to help during negotiations (paragraph 5 of my telegram No. 278[1]), accepted my opinion and rejected that of his Counsellor, Dooman. He had drafted a telegram to his Government recommending them not to accept our proposal. I discovered that the argument which seems to have been the principal reason why he turned the other way was a reference by myself to the record which history would show of the respective parts played by our two Governments in this crisis. (This seems a good argument to use on Americans for some reason, I suppose because they are young!) He came round at once on the ground that the United States could not allow it to be said that they had not done all they could for peace.

3. I have the impression that Grew was relieved that the Sino-Japanese trouble has put an end for the time being at all events to the Anglo-Japanese conversations.

[1] No. 167.

4. My other Colleagues have so far behaved more or less true to form. The French Ambassador partly I suppose on instructions but certainly partly owing to temperament has been completely passive, except when it came to undertaking to collaborate with us in the plan to protect Japanese nationals at Shanghai, when he had to do as he was told. The Germans have been sitting on the fence though superficially friendly to ourselves. The same may be said of the Italians.

5. As regards the Japanese I reject for good the suggestion that it is dangerous and useless even to say 'Boo' to them shared by most of my Colleagues including to a certain extent even Grew. He was fond of saying that it is useless or dangerous to make representations to them as they loathe occidental interference in Asia more than anything (my telegram No. 239 of 21st July[2]); but on my pointing out that on the British mind, at least, this argument has about as much effect as water on a duck's back, and that we are a much greater Asiatic power than Japan, he has not referred to it again.

6. Just as the Japanese respect force more than anything else so they despise anyone who does not stand up for his rights. But I am convinced that there are ways and ways of doing this. One can say almost anything to the Japanese: but the manner in which it is said is infinitely important. A formal note such as seemed necessary on the receipt of Foreign Office telegram No. 239[3] annoys them considerably. A verbal communication, with a *pro memoria*, saying the same thing, or a semi-official letter such as the one I handed to the Minister for Foreign Affairs on receipt of Foreign Office telegram No. 218[4] has for some curious reason some effect without apparent irritation. A verbal communication, without the support of a *pro memoria*, often, I am sure, does not penetrate at all.

7. The Japanese are bad propagandists. To us the justification they produce for their activities in China is puerile and won't bear investigation for a moment. I am not convinced that they have justification of any kind: but they could make a better case than they do. This point is not badly put in a leading article in the *Japan Advertiser* of August 24th. I enclose an extract from it.[5]

8. I am naturally the target of panic-mongers and alarmists. I now do not, for example, question the truth of our belief (Sir R. Clive's letter to you of the 22nd March 1937[5]) that Günther Stein is unduly pessimistic and gloomy. He also looks at any problem through the financier's eyes. Byas is always sound and reliable.

9. The Soviet Embassy were without an Ambassador or Counsellor when the trouble started and up to date have been run by a first secretary called Deitchman. He is an unattractive specimen who speaks with the voice that breathes over the *Pravda* and *Izvestia*. Comparatively friendly at first when he thought there was a chance that Britain might take up the cudgels hand in hand with his Government he has lately referred to our

[2] Not printed (F 4325/9/10)   [3] No. 196.   [4] No. 173.   [5] Not printed.

expecting other Governments to pull our chestnuts out of the fire and has effectively extinguished the faint flickers of benevolence towards him and his country which I cherished on arriving here.

10. The Japanese enjoy the advantage in the conduct of their foreign policy, due partly no doubt to their recent arrival in the world and singular ignorance of other countries, of being quite exceptionally blind to any other point of view but their own. It is therefore in my opinion all the more necessary that we, especially since others won't, should open their eyes as often as possible. For this kind act they ought of course to be grateful but, such is human nature, they probably aren't!

This letter has gone on longer than I intended. I apologise.[6]

Yours ever,

J. L. DODDS

[6] Mr. Orde's reply to Mr. Dodds, dated October 1, is printed as No. 279 below.

No. 210

Mr. Davidson (Shanghai) to Mr. Eden (Received August 27, 9.30 a.m.)

Unnumbered Telegraphic: by Admiralty wireless [F 5755/5727/10]

SHANGHAI, *August 27, 1937*

Your telegram No. 53.[1]

Two obviously private black saloon cars each flying Union Jack approximately 18 inches by 12 inches on the near side of the cars projecting above the roofs. Aeroplane which fired machine gun dived from the off side at a right angle to the cars. Military Attaché is of opinion that flags should have been visible but Air Attaché considers they might not have been seen by a pilot diving towards the cars.

Military Attaché states that without any doubt that planes were Japanese. On arrival at Shanghai Military Attaché had a conversation with Mr. Matsumoto Head of Domei news agency and a Japanese Vice Consul who made no attempt to deny the nationality of the planes.

No Chinese troops were encountered until about an hour's drive from the scene of the incident.[2]

[1] See No. 205, note 2.
[2] In his telegram No. 31 of August 27 Mr. Davidson said that the above unnumbered telegram had been sent off early that morning before he had seen it. He wished the following to be added to it as the last sentence. 'No previous notice was given to any Japanese authority of His Majesty's Ambassador's intention to visit Shanghai. No Japanese officials remain in Nanking and telegram to Shanghai stating that His Majesty's Ambassador had left was handed in at Nanking 14.55 and received here at 16.40 when His Majesty's Ambassador was already in hospital.'

No. 211

Mr. Dodds (Tokyo) to Mr. Eden (Received August 27, 9.30 a.m.)

No. 320 Telegraphic [F 5760/5727/10]

Immediate   TOKYO, *August 27, 1937, 12.6 p.m.*

Your telegram No. 250.[1]
Minister for Foreign Affairs sent Vice Minister for Foreign Affairs to see me this morning to express his regrets and concern. Vice Minister for Foreign Affairs said it was unimaginable that any Japanese airman would intentionally fire at a British motor car and I said that of course no one believed that. Japanese Government are evidently extremely upset. Vice Minister for Foreign Affairs said they were calling for an immediate report from their authorities at Shanghai and had provided Mrs. Cowan with a military aeroplane to go from Peking to visit Lady Knatchbull-Hugessen at Peitaiho.[2] Ministry of War and Ministry of Marine have also sent representatives.
Repeated to Nanking.

[1] A repeat of No. 204.   [2] Cf. No. 208.

No. 212

Mr. Davidson (Shanghai) to Mr. Eden (Received August 27, 9.30 p.m.)

No. 35 Telegraphic: by wireless [F 5804/5727/10]

SHANGHAI, *August 27, 1937*

My telegram unnumbered of August 27th.[1]
Following from Sir H. Knatchbull-Hugessen:
Japanese Ambassador called this morning August 27th to enquire and express regret. He told me he had at once telegraphed to Tokyo and had received instructions from Mr. Hirota to express sincere regret and to inform me that a thorough investigation is being made.

[1] No. 210.

No. 213

Mr. Eden to Mr. Dodds (Tokyo)

No. 427 [F 5806/5727/10]

FOREIGN OFFICE, *August 27, 1937*

Sir,

The Japanese Ambassador asked to see me this afternoon when he stated that he had been instructed by his Government to express their very deep regret at the incident which had befallen His Majesty's Ambassador in China.[1] The Prime Minister and the Foreign Secretary had specially asked to be associated with this expression of regret. The Japanese Ambassador asked also to be allowed to add his own expression of very sincere regret. He said that the Japanese Government were very much upset at what had happened.

2. In reply I thanked the Ambassador for his message and stated that we were, as he could imagine, deeply concerned at what had happened. This was a deplorable event. In acknowledging the Japanese Government's expression of regret I must, however, point out that this was different from an official apology. The Ambassador at once rejoined that such an official apology might follow. He felt sure moreover that those responsible must certainly be dealt with and repeated that the tone of the telegram he had received showed clearly how much upset the Japanese Government were. I told His Excellency that I would not on this occasion make any further comment on what had happened. As he would have seen from the *communiqué* issued last night,[2] we were making certain further enquiries after which we proposed to take the appropriate action with the Japanese Government. This we would do through His Majesty's Embassy at Tokio in the course of the next few days.

I am, etc.,
ANTHONY EDEN

[1] See No. 204.   [2] See *The Times*, August 27, 1937, p. 12.

No. 214

Mr. Dodds (Tokyo) to Mr. Eden (Received August 28, 9.30 a.m.)

No. 325 [F 5836/9/10]

TOKYO, *August 28, 1937, 3.50 p.m.*

I have now lengthy confidential note from Japanese Government in reply to my note based on your telegram No. 239.[1] Following is summary. Begins.

[1] No. 196.

It is not the Japanese army which is endangering British interests in Shanghai but illegal Chinese attack on Settlement. Recent Japanese military operations were not in retaliation for killing of two members of landing party but were merely measures of self-defence by small Japanese squadron and landing party to protect 30,000 Japanese residents from attack by Chinese forces which disregarded armistice agreement of May 1932 who had invaded the neighbourhood of Japanese residential district.

Referring to statement that Chinese reinforcements were only brought up after Japanese had doubled naval strength and landed men, note points out that Peace Preservation Corps (as well equipped as regular troops if not better) had been considerably increased, had constructed strong points in army's area, and were in a position to attack force. In view of Oyama incident Japanese Government were responsible both as a Government and for humanitarian reasons for the protection of Japanese residents with the minimum military force which moreover had to cross several hundred miles of sea. In the event Japanese reinforcements were . . .[2] inferior to the Chinese.

Security of British lives and property at Shanghai is always a matter of concern to the Japanese Government and their forces constantly devote themselves to this end.

Vice Minister for Foreign Affairs informed me in detail of Shanghai situation on August 18th (see my telegram No. 299[3]) and that Japanese Government were directing all their efforts towards peace and it is regretted that 'public opinion in Great Britain is without reliable information on these points'. Regardless however of British public opinion Japanese Government desire a speedy end to the state of affairs and continues [sic] to use the best efforts to attain this object.

Ends.

Note is throughout courteous in tone.

Translation follows.[4]

Repeated to Nanking Saving and Commander-in-Chief.

---

[2] The text was here uncertain.　　　　　[3] No. 192.　　　　　[4] Not printed.

No. 215

Mr. Eden to Mr. Dodds (Tokyo)

No. 256 Telegraphic [F 5838/5727/10]

Immediate　　　　　　　　　　　FOREIGN OFFICE, August 28, 1937, 6 p.m.

Following is text of note[1] which you should hand at once to Japanese Government.

---

[1] This note was based on a draft by Mr. G. G. Fitzmaurice, Third Legal Adviser in the Foreign Office. It was finalised after consultation between Mr. Eden and Mr. Chamberlain.

The Japanese Government will be aware of the injuries sustained by Sir H. Knatchbull-Hugessen, His Majesty's Ambassador in China, as a result of shooting from Japanese military aeroplanes when motoring with members of his staff from Nanking to Shanghai on August 26th last.

The facts were as follows:

His Majesty's Ambassador was proceeding from Nanking to Shanghai on August 26th accompanied by the Military Attaché and the Financial Adviser to His Majesty's Embassy, and a Chinese chauffeur. The party occupied two black saloon cars of obviously private character, each flying the Union Jack, approximately 18" by 12" in size on the near side of the car projecting above the roof. At about 2.30 p.m. and about 8 miles north-west of Taitsang,[2] i.e. some 40 miles from Shanghai, the cars were attacked by machine-gun fire from a Japanese aeroplane. The aeroplane which fired the machine gun dived from the off-side of the car at a right angle to it. This was followed by a bomb attack from a second Japanese aeroplane from a height of about 200 feet. The Ambassador was hit by a nickel steel bullet (subsequently found embedded in the car) which penetrated the side of the abdomen and grazed the spine.

His Majesty's Government in the United Kingdom have received with deep distress and concern the news of this deplorable event, in respect of which they must record their emphatic protest and request the fullest measure of redress.

Although non-combatants, including foreigners resident in the country concerned, must accept the inevitable risk of injury resulting indirectly from the normal conduct of hostilities, it is one of the oldest and best established rules of international law that direct or deliberate attacks on non-combatants are absolutely prohibited; whether inside or outside the area in which hostilities are taking place.

Aircraft are in no way exempt from this rule, which applies as much to attack from the air as to any other form of attack.

Nor can the plea of accident be accepted where the facts are such as to show, at the best negligence and a complete disregard for the sanctity of civilian life. In the present case the facts which have been recorded above make it clear that this was no accident resulting from any normal hostile operation and it should have been obvious to the aircraft that they were dealing with non-combatants.

The plea, should it be advanced, that the flags carried on the cars were too small to be visible is irrelevant. There would have been no justification for the attack even had the cars carried no flags at all. The foreign, even the diplomatic, status of the occupants is also irrelevant. The real issue is that they were non-combatants. The aircraft no doubt did not intend to

[2] In an unnumbered telegram of August 29 the Air Attaché at Shanghai reported that the Military Attaché had now 'established definitely position of attack which took place six miles south of Taitsang'. The Military Attaché had apparently been 'misled by Chinese driver of car who at the scene of attack stated Shanghai was 50 miles distant and by local map which did not show newly constructed road'.

attack His Majesty's Ambassador as such. They apparently did intend to attack non-combatants, and that suffices in itself to constitute an illegality.

It is, moreover, pertinent to observe that in this particular case the Ambassador was travelling in a locality where there were no Chinese troops nor any actual hostilities in progress. No Chinese troops were in fact encountered by the Ambassador's party until about an hour's drive from the scene of the attack.

His Majesty's Government feel that they must take this opportunity to emphasise the wider significance of this event. It is an outstanding example of the results to be expected from indiscriminate attack from the air. Such events are inseparable from the practice, as illegal as it is inhuman, of failing to draw that clear distinction between combatants and non-combatants in the conduct of hostilities which international law, no less than the conscience of mankind has always enjoined.

The fact that in the present case no actual state of war has been declared or expressly recognised by either party to exist emphasizes the inexcusable nature of what occurred.

His Majesty's Government must therefore request:
(1) A formal apology to be conveyed by the Japanese Government to His Majesty's Government;
(2) Suitable punishment of those responsible for the attack;
(3) An assurance by the Japanese authorities that the necessary measures will be taken to prevent the recurrence of incidents of such a character.[3]
Repeated to Nanking, Peking, Shanghai.

[3] In telegram No. 327 of August 29 Mr. Dodds reported that he had delivered the note to Mr. Hirota at 2 p.m. that day. In telegram No. 328, also of August 29, he reported that the Vice Minister for Foreign Affairs had telephoned suggesting that the 'text of note should not be published for the present on the ground that it would make a settlement easier'. Mr. Grew, the U.S. Ambassador, thought that the note was 'couched in reasonably moderate terms': see *F.R.U.S.*, 1937, vol. iii, p. 494.

No. 216

Mr. Eden to Mr. Dodds (Tokyo)

No. 259 Telegraphic [F 5839/5727/10]

Immediate   FOREIGN OFFICE, *August 29, 1937, 2.15 p.m.*

Your telegram No. 328.[1]

Publication cannot be postponed. It is essential in view of imaginative versions of our protest which have already appeared and which will inevitably continue in enhanced degree and form if facts are not made known.[2]

[1] See No. 215, note 3.
[2] The Japanese Embassy in London, on instructions from Tokyo, also asked the Foreign

Office on the afternoon of August 29 that publication of the note should be withheld as it was undesirable that Japanese public opinion should be further excited. The Foreign Office reply, given at 6.45 p.m., was that publication could not be deferred, and that the note had been given to the press at 5 p.m. See *The Times*, August 30, 1937, p. 10.

No. 217

Mr. Gage (Nanking) to Mr. Eden (Received August 29, 8.15 p.m.)

No. 400 Telegraphic: by wireless [F 5832/1098/10]

Immediate NANKING, *August 29, 1937*

My telegram No. 395.[1]

Only the American and French Ambassadors and I (representing His Majesty's Ambassador) were present at the meeting.

2. Minister for Foreign Affairs announced that a pact of mutual non-aggression with Soviet Russia had been signed on August 21st[2] and that public announcement had been deferred for . . .[3] days by mutual agreement. He stated that pact consisted of 3 clauses:

(1) Neither party to commit any act of aggression on the other.

(2) Neither party to assist any third party which might commit an act of aggression on either of signatories and

(3) All existing agreements whether bilateral or multi-lateral to which signatories are parties to remain in force.

3. Minister for Foreign Affairs said that this pact was outcome of negotiations which had commenced some considerable time ago. It had been originally intended that there should be a commercial treaty as well as a pact of non aggression but commercial treaty had been abandoned as no agreement could be reached. He added that pact was purely negative in nature, that it partly fulfilled China's fixed purpose of living in peace with her neighbours, and that she was quite ready to make a similar pact with Japan. He particularly wished to emphasise he said that it did not signify any abandonment on the part of China of her fixed policy of anti-communism. In this connexion he pointed out that the third clause kept alive Article 6 of Sino-Soviet Agreement, signed in Peking on May 31st, 1924.[4]

---

[1] This telegram of August 28 ran: 'Minister for Foreign Affairs has asked the four Ambassadors and myself to call on him at 9 a.m. Sunday August 29th. It is reasonable to suppose he has some important announcement to make.'
[2] Cf. No. 200. [3] The text was here uncertain.
[4] Mr. Orde noted on August 30 that 'Article 6 of the Sino-Russian treaty of May 31st 1924 forbad [sic] propaganda against the political and social systems of the two countries or toleration in either of organisations or groups whose aim is to struggle by acts of violence against the Govt. of either'. The text of the agreement is printed in *B.F.S.P.*, vol. 122, pp. 263–70.

4. Peking texts of pact and accompanying declaration are being released in various capitals and in Shanghai today.[5] I therefore propose not to telegraph them in full unless you so instruct me.

5. I understand that German and Italian Ambassadors have been informed separately.

Repeated to Peking, Shanghai, C. in C., Tokyo, G.O.C. and R.A.Y.

[5] The text of the Sino-Soviet Pact is printed in *B.F.S.P.*, vol. 141, pp. 882–3, and also in *D.V.P.S.*, Volume XX, No. 300: cf. also No. 315.

No. 218

Mr. Dodds (Tokyo) to Mr. Eden (Received August 31, 1.30 p.m.)

No. 331 Telegraphic [F 5926/5727/10]

Immediate   TOKYO, *August 31, 1937, 5.55 p.m.*

My telegram 327.[1]

I have some reason to believe that Japanese Government are contemplating refusing to agree to our request on the grounds that Chiang Kai-shek was expected on the road on which His Majesty's Ambassador was travelling, that Chinese aeroplanes used Japanese markings and aeroplane in question was to blame for taking this journey without notifying Japanese authorities.

2. I am doing what is possible through third parties in a position to bring some influence to bear on the Japanese Government to persuade the latter that to turn down our request would be a colossal blunder. Chinese have alienated foreign opinion to a certain extent by their bombings at Shanghai and Japanese have an excellent opportunity of improving their own position vis-à-vis world opinion by a handsome apology. If they reject our request world will turn unanimously against them and opinion in England will be affected for who knows how long?

3. Japanese navy are I understand principally responsible for the line which is apparently being taken and no one is big enough to overrule them.

4. His Majesty's Ambassador[2] is due September 3rd and must shortly be received by the Emperor. It is just possible that this may be held to turn the scales in favour of accepting our request. But I am not optimistic.

5. Press is restrained.

Repeated to Nanking, Commander-in-Chief.

[1] See No. 215, note 3.   [2] i.e. Sir R. Craigie.

No. 219

Mr. Eden to Mr. Dodds (Tokyo)

No. 267 Telegraphic [F 5926/5727/10]

Immediate   FOREIGN OFFICE, *August 31, 1937, 8.50 p.m.*

Your telegram No. 331.[1]

I am in entire agreement with your views. Public opinion in this country and throughout the Empire will not permit of any weakening in the attitude of His Majesty's Government in a matter of this importance. You should let the Japanese Government know by any means you consider suitable that we could not abate the very moderate measure of redress for which we ask.

2. For your own information, if we do not receive satisfaction, His Majesty's Government will probably decide to withdraw Sir R. Craigie.

3. As to the line which you anticipate Japanese Government may take, you should as occasion offers point out that

(a) An attack on the effective head of a State with which they are still in diplomatic relations would be a manifest illegality, and

(b) from the evidence of eye-witnesses and from the admissions by Japanese local authorities at the time it is clear beyond all possibility of doubt that attacking machines were Japanese; what object could Chinese planes have in attacking traffic on that road?

(c) His Majesty's Government have yet to learn that a British Ambassador proceeding on his lawful occasions in the country to which he is accredited and where no professed state of war exists is obliged to give notice of his intentions to the authorities of a foreign Power or else run the risk of a lawless outrage.

4. In addition you should make such use as you see fit of the supplementary information contained in the three unnumbered telegrams from Shanghai repeated to you from here on August 29th and August 30th[2] and of the fact that Military Attaché and Financial Adviser had made use of the road two days previously without taking any special precautions.

---

[1] No. 218. Mr. Orde minuted on August 31 for Sir R. Vansittart: 'Some immediate instructions to Mr. Dodds on his tel. 331 ... seem desirable', and submitted a draft prepared by Mr. Ronald and Mr. Fitzmaurice, remarking that Sir R. Vansittart might 'think it goes rather far'. Sir R. Vansittart commented: 'This telegram is strong, but not unduly strong, and it is not threatening. I think it is justifiable to send it for, if we don't take a very firm line now, we are clearly likely to be in far worse troubles still.' Mr. Eden made a number of amendments to the draft.

[2] Not printed.

No. 220

Mr. Mallet (Washington) to Mr. Eden (Received September 1, 9.30 a.m.)

No. 259 Telegraphic [F 6013/9/10]

WASHINGTON, *August 31, 1937, 9.55 p.m.*

Your telegram No. 338.[1]

In reply to my representations United States Government explain that they do not believe it would be advisable to make an enquiry of Japanese Government on lines suggested. In their opinion statement made by Japanese Government of their intention to blockade a portion of the China coast against Chinese shipping seems sufficiently precise within its own limits.[2] In amplification of this, however, State Department add that on August 27th an officer of the Ministry of the Navy of Japanese Government gave to an officer of the United States Embassy in Tokyo statements in reference to Japan's intentions, one of which was to the general effect that interference with merchant vessels other than Chinese was not intended.[3] Further they say that on August 30th, the Japanese Vice Minister for Foreign Affairs gave to French Ambassador at Tokyo what was apparently a pro memoria in which it was stated in effect that intensive blockade applies only to Chinese vessels and not to vessels of third Powers.[4] Neither Japanese Government nor Chinese Government has made a declaration of war or assumed for itself status of a belligerent. Both of these governments are aware of the principles and rules of International Law which apply. State Department add that whatever may be the intentions of the Japanese Government or their agents, those intentions would not, in the opinion of the United States Government, be altered by there being addressed to the Japanese Government a request for a more precise statement of their intentions, whether that request were made by one Power or by several Powers. In fact, such approach or approaches if made now, in the light of statements which Japanese Government have already made, would, in the opinion of the United States Government, have only effect of disclosing to the Japanese Government uneasiness on the part of governments which might make them.

[1] See No. 207, note 3. [2] See *F.R.U.S.*, 1937, vol. iv, pp. 440–1. [3] See *ibid.*, pp. 435–6.
[4] See *ibid.* pp. 437–8.

No. 221

Mr. Mallet (Washington) to Mr. Eden (Received September 1, 8.15 p.m.)

No. 260 Telegraphic [*F 6030/9/10*]

WASHINGTON, *September 1, 1937, 1.10 p.m.*

My telegram No. 259.[1]

I gathered privately that State Department were a little disturbed at this fresh request for joint action. They are all for close consultation locally but in general prefer parallel though not necessarily simultaneous representations. This procedure has the advantage of minimizing delays inevitable if joint action has to be concerted through London and Washington.

Present proposal was not however rejected for this reason but on its merits.

---

[1] No. 220.

[2] Sir J. Pratt commented on September 3: 'It will evidently be best to take the hint and in future act independently merely giving U.S. the opportunity to take similar action if they feel disposed. This procedure will be applied to the telegram now under consideration re. air attack on merchant ships.' See No. 239 below.

No. 222

Mr. Affleck (Tientsin) to Mr. Eden (Received September 1, 10.30 p.m.)

No. 11[1] Telegraphic: by wireless [*F 6032/220/10*]

TIENTSIN, *September 1, 1937*

Following is repetition of my telegram No. 33 to Nanking, repeated to Peking telegram No. 83, Commander-in-Chief, General Officer Commanding, Financial Adviser telegram No. 9.

My telegram No. 32,[2] last paragraph.

Commissioner[3] has at last[4] been tentatively approached by Japanese

---

[1] This telegram was received one hour later than telegram No. 12 (No. 223 below), but they have been printed in the order obviously intended.

[2] This telegram of August 26 from Mr. Affleck to Nanking stated that so far no move had been made by the Japanese to interfere with the Chinese customs administration.

[3] Mr. W. R. Myers was Commissioner of Customs at Tientsin.

[4] On August 16 the China Association had drawn the attention of the Foreign Office and Treasury to a cable from its representative in Tientsin suggesting the likelihood that if Japan in effect added North China to Manchuria the Japanese would withdraw control of the Maritime Customs at the Northern ports from the present Inspectorate General, whether or not they withdrew that portion of the customs revenue collected at Tientsin. The China Association suggested the negotiation of an agreement with China and Japan to anticipate and prevent Japanese interference with the existing administration. In a minute of September 1, however, Sir J. Pratt suggested that 'any initiative on our part would only provoke the danger that is feared', and Mr. Orde agreed.

Consulate-General on the subject of customs administration. It is expected from a verbal statement made to him that proposals for taking over . . .[5] Japanese occupied areas will be on lines of following:

(1) Customs revenue will be deposited and remitted for loan service account only: none of surplus will be used either by Tientsin or by Chinese administrations in Japanese occupied areas.

(2) A certain proportion of these customs funds will be required to be deposited in Yokohama Specie Bank.

(3) Customs in Japanese occupied areas will not permit any arms to be imported by Chinese: arms for foreigners will be permitted only under license (obtainable from Japanese military).

Question for the present only concerns Tientsin and Chinwangtao but may shortly be extended to Chefoo Tsingtao and possibly Shanghai. Unless therefore Chinese Government is prepared to agree to some compromise on lines indicated Commissioner of Customs anticipates that maintenance of Customs Administration and China credit will be in danger. In order to arrive at permanent adjustment of this question it may in his opinion be necessary that the various Powers interested should prevail on Chinese Government to declare customs as responsible for loan service consistently with revenues to be utilised for payment of existing internal and external loans and surplus to be retained in a controlled fund for credit of China and any further commercial loans.

[5] The text was here uncertain.

No. 223

Mr. Affleck (Tientsin) to Mr. Eden (Received September 1, 9.30 p.m.)

No. 12 Telegraphic: by wireless [F 6041/220/10]

TIENTSIN, *September 1, 1937*

Following is repetition of Saving telegram No. 34 to Nanking, repeated to Peking No. 85, C. in C. G.O.C. and Financial Adviser No. 10.

My telegram No. 33.[1]

Following is gist of telegram sent today by Commissioner of Customs to Inspector General of Customs begins:

At interview today Japanese Consul made following verbal communication to me;

Subject to faithful observance of following conditions there was no desire on the part of Japanese authorities to interfere with or disrupt Customs service in Japanese occupied or controlled areas. (a) Regular quotas of foreign loans may be remitted but surplus must be retained on deposit in an acceptable bank pending general settlement of situation (b)

[1] No. 222.

Customs to pass no arms or ammunition for Chinese within these areas even if covered by *huchao*[2] (c) Yokohama Specie Bank to be utilised as bank for deposit above all, or other acceptable means to be devised to guarantee that surplus will not be improperly administered. Against this Japanese agree to give full protection and assistance to Customs officers and offices, to suppress all attempts at smuggling in these areas by Japanese, and not to require any alteration of existing . . .[3] until this matter shall be dealt with by negotiation. Refusal to accept these conditions would entail taking over of Customs administration in these areas and a purely Japanese controlled service. Internal loans quotas will not be considered except in so far as they concern foreign nationals or groups or until some international agreement may be reached. Figure at present covers only Tientsin and Chinwangtao but extension down to Tsingtao and even Shanghai and further is visualised by Japanese.

As regards (a) and (b) I can see no alternative but to suggest acceptance and, as regards surplus, to negotiate for its retention in Hongkong and Shanghai Bank under some general international guarantee. I doubt whether it will be possible to suggest any modification of terms outlined above which have been drawn up by Japanese military commander and Consul-General. Ends.[4]

[2] A type of import licence: see Volume XX, Nos. 95, 131, and 132.
[3] The text was here uncertain.
[4] In telegram No. 90 of September 3 Mr. Hall-Patch reported that he had discussed the situation arising from telegrams Nos. 33 and 34 with Sir F. Maze, Inspector General of the Chinese Maritime Customs, who afterwards sent him the following note: 'I have informed [Chinese] Government that in the circumstances terms are not unreasonable and that it would be impolitic for Government to reject them; but if they do not feel that direct action is possible I have suggested that I be authorised to instruct Tientsin Commission to make informal arrangement on lines indicated by Japanese authorities. Furthermore in the interest of Chinese Bondholders and bankers, I have urged that internal loans be included within the scheme.' In a further telegram, No. 97 of September 10, Mr. Hall-Patch reported that the Japanese demands had been referred to General Chiang Kai-shek, who however wished to leave the matter in abeyance to the end of the month. Sir F. Maze was accordingly asked by the Chinese to hold up the question as long as possible.

No. 224

Mr. Eden to Mr. Mallet (Washington)

No. 344 Telegraphic [F 6047/9/10]

FOREIGN OFFICE, *September 2, 1937, 3.45 p.m.*

Chinese Ambassador stated to Sir R. Vansittart on August 31 that Mr. Hull a few days ago informed Chinese Ambassador in Washington that America 'Believed in and stood for sanctity of treaties' and had added that 'if His Majesty's Government contemplated taking any action, either alone or with other Powers, with a view to the maintenance of the sanctity of treaties, the U.S. Government would be glad to associate itself with them'.

2. Ambassador was not sure of exact words and Chinese optimism has probably led them into considerable overstatement, but Mr. Hull may have said something not too discouraging of which it would be well for us to know.

3. Please do your best to ascertain exactly what was said and report by telegraph.[1]

[1] On September 3 Mr. H. R. Wilson, Assistant Secretary of State, told Mr. Mallet that Mr. Hull had not intended to offer more than sympathetic consideration for any defence of the sanctity of treaties: see *F.R.U.S.*, 1937, vol. iii, pp. 509–10.

No. 225

Mr. Eden to Mr. Dodds (Tokyo)

No. 272[1] Telegraphic [F 5926/5727/10]

Immediate   FOREIGN OFFICE, *September 2, 1937, 9 p.m.*

1. Time is running on and we have as yet no reply from the Japanese Government to our communication of last Sunday.[2] From your telegram No. 331[3] it would also appear that you think us unlikely to receive a satisfactory one.

2. In these circumstances I think it advisable to give you an outline of what we have in view, with particular respect to the timetable.

3. If we have received no reply from the Japanese Government by Saturday next, September 4th, we shall send you official instructions to ask that the reply may be expedited, and you will be informed that it is in particular necessary for us to have this reply before the next meeting of the Cabinet which is due on Wednesday, September 8th.[4] If either no reply at all has been received by that date or if the reply is wholly unsatisfactory, it is probable that His Majesty's Government will decide to withdraw Sir R. Craigie.

4. I am giving you this probable outline in advance for it seems certain that some further and immediate pressure on the Japanese Government is likely to be required, and you will no doubt consider with Sir R. Craigie on his arrival on September 3rd how far he will be able advantageously to take part in exercising that pressure himself. In other words, you and he

[1] This telegram was despatched following a meeting of Ministers held at the Foreign Office on September 2 at 11 a.m.: cf. Volume XIX, No. 114. The meeting considered the question of the action to be taken if no satisfactory reply was received from Japan to the British note protesting against the wounding of Sir H. Knatchbull-Hugessen. After discussion it was agreed that the question of whether to withdraw Sir R. Craigie from Tokyo should be reserved for the decision of the Cabinet on September 8, but that meanwhile Mr. Dodds should be informed of the importance of pressing for a reply before that date.
[2] See No. 215.   [3] No. 218.   [4] See No. 238 below.

284

might judge it opportune to expedite his reception by the Minister for Foreign Affairs and possibly the presentation of his credentials. I do not of course know what dates have as yet been fixed for these ceremonies but there may be advantage in seeing that they take place at once.

If Sir R. Craigie has to be withdrawn we hope that the Canadian Government would also wish to withdraw the Canadian Minister, for indeed the adoption of any other course might render the position difficult and anomalous, but we have not yet consulted the Canadian Government about this, though we are now taking steps to sound them informally. In view of this it is desirable that you should take your Canadian colleague into your confidence and on receipt of this telegram let him know the contents of the paragraphs 1–4 above. You can no doubt ensure that the utmost secrecy should be observed.

It has furthermore appeared to us that the attack on His Majesty's Ambassador in Peking is a matter which really concerns the Diplomatic Body of all countries having representation in the Far East. It would of course hardly have been possible to invoke their support for our communication to the Japanese Government, but it would be obviously less difficult and quite appropriate for them to take some step to show their corporate interest in the matter, and this in itself might tend to induce the Japanese Government to give an early and favourable reply. Unless therefore you see any objection or consider that such a suggestion would inevitably be refused, you should sound your United States, French, German and Italian colleagues on this possibility.

I should be grateful if you would take action in this sense at once or alternatively if you would report to me immediately any misgivings that you may have.[5]

[5] A further telegram to Mr. Dodds, No. 274 of September 3, instructed him to see the Foreign Minister on Sunday (September 5) at the latest and, if a reply had not been received before then, to press for one 'as soon as possible emphasising that His Majesty's Government desire to have one in any case before the meeting of the Cabinet to be held on September 8th'.

No. 226

Mr. Eden to Mr. Mallet (Washington)

No. 849 [F 6055/9/10]

FOREIGN OFFICE, *September 2, 1937*

Sir,

The United States Chargé d'Affaires came to see me to-day when he gave me a memorandum to read (copy attached)[1] setting forth the views of the United States Government in response to my query as to the

[1] Not printed: cf. note 2 below.

attitude to be adopted by ourselves, the French and the United States Governments in the Far East to the Japanese demand to stop non-Chinese ships on the high seas for the purposes of verification only.[2] Having read the memorandum I remarked that I thought perhaps I had not quite made myself plain at our last interview. I had not contemplated any form of negotiation with the Japanese Government, still less any form of bargaining. As I understood it Mr. Hull now suggested that we should in fact acquiesce in the Japanese demand without making any communication to them. We should confine ourselves to giving advice to our shipping to submit to this procedure.

2. The Chargé d'Affaires said that he also understood that to be the meaning of the communication. I replied that there seemed to me to be much force in the United States arguments on this point and that we would be glad to conform our procedure to theirs. It would however be inevitable that the Japanese should come to know what instructions had been issued, since we should have to tell our merchant ships. The Chargé d'Affaires admitted this. After some further discussion I undertook to let the Chargé d'Affaires know what actual advice we were going to give our merchant ships.[3]

I am, etc.,

Anthony Eden

[2] Mr. Eden's enquiry was prompted by the French Government's note of August 30, communicated to him by the French Chargé d'Affaires, M. Cambon, which contained a passage asking whether His Majesty's Government had issued instructions in case British vessels were stopped by Japanese ships in Far Eastern waters in order to ascertain their nationality: see Volume XIX, No. 108, para. 3. Mr. Eden told M. Cambon on August 31 that His Majesty's Government were prepared to agree that their ships would stop, if challenged by Japanese ships, 'solely for the purpose of verification of nationality', and were also prepared to consider issuing a statement on these lines jointly with the French and American Governments. Mr. Eden discussed this later on August 31 with Mr. Herschel V. Johnson; see *F.R.U.S.*, 1937, vol. iv, pp. 439–40. In his memorandum replying to Mr. Eden's enquiry Mr. Cordell Hull rejected the idea of a statement, taking the view that it would 'be better for the powers concerned merely to understand *inter se* that none of them expects to resist with force the overhauling of its merchant vessels for purposes of identification': see *ibid.*, pp. 441–3.

[3] This question had been discussed at the meeting of Ministers held earlier on September 2: see No. 225, note 1, and cf. Volume XIX, p. 217. The meeting decided that British shipping should be advised to comply with a demand from a Japanese warship to stop for purposes of verification of nationality. A formula on these lines was agreed upon, with the added provision that the right was reserved to claim compensation for 'damage sustained by the owners of British ships delayed or stopped under this procedure'. It was agreed, however, that this decision should not be notified to the Japanese Government or to British shipping companies until the Dominion Governments had been consulted. A memorandum was prepared on the subject, C.P. 212(37) of September 7, which was circulated to the Cabinet on September 7: see No. 239 below.

Sir R. Craigie (Tokyo) to Mr. Eden (Received September 3, 4.30 p.m.)

No. 345 Telegraphic [F 6099/5727/10]

Immediate   TOKYO, *September 3, 1937, 10.35 p.m.*

Your telegram No. 272.[1]

I hope to arrange interview with the Minister for Foreign Affairs tomorrow afternoon at which I shall make every endeavour to obtain an immediate answer.

I am afraid that it is no use approaching the Ambassadors as suggested in the penultimate paragraph of your telegram as there is no question but that they will all reply that they must consult their own Governments first. If anything is to be done on these lines, therefore, I submit that it should be from London[,] particularly as an exchange through that channel is less likely to become prematurely known here.[2]

[1] No. 225.
[2] The Foreign Office acquiesced, apparently with some reluctance, in this view. Sir R. Vansittart wrote: 'I see no reason why this shd. not have been tried locally. We never expected the prospects to be favourable, but it might have been worth trying out. The one thing that has been clear from the start is that this is not a manoeuvre which shd. be tried from here. R.V. Sept. 6.'

No. 228

Sir R. Craigie (Tokyo) to Mr. Eden (Received September 4, 1.20 p.m.)

No. 347 Telegraphic [F 6143/5727/10]

TOKYO, *September 4, 1937, 6.45 p.m.*

Your telegram No. 274.[1]

I made my first call on the Minister for Foreign Affairs today to present copies of my credentials and was told that September 10th would probably be the date on which I would be received by the Emperor, no earlier date being convenient owing to the meeting of the Diet.

I impressed on His Excellency the vital necessity of a satisfactory answer to our Note[2] in regard to the wounding of Sir H. Knatchbull-Hugessen being received by next Wednesday's Cabinet meeting and spoke of the growing and very legitimate indignation of His Majesty's Government at continued absence of any direct apology from Government to Government. He replied that no report had yet been received from the Ministry of Marine who were conducting a careful investigation but that as soon as it had been received Japanese Government would be glad to reply to our

[1] See No. 225, note 5.   [2] See No. 215.

Note. On my pointing out that this would probably be too late and that even if technical report were not available in time there should at least be a full apology by next Tuesday possibly reserving other points for later settlement, Minister for Foreign Affairs promised to consider this course.[3] I said that our evidence that a Japanese plane was involved was overwhelming and that I was quite ready to discuss this evidence informally with the proper authorities should this seem likely to facilitate an early reply.

Other topics were touched on lightly and His Excellency evidently desires to discuss with me situation in China and Sino-Japanese relations at an early opportunity.

I note from your telegram No. 272[4] that if either no reply or an unsatisfactory one is received by September 8th, His Majesty's Government may decide to withdraw me. This is not a matter on which I can properly give an opinion beyond expressing the hope that as I only arrived yesterday I may be given a little more time to see what I can do before a final decision is taken.

[3] The Foreign Office disliked this proposal. On Mr. Eden's instructions, Sir R. Craigie was told in telegram No. 281 of September 6 'to make it clear that this was your own personal suggestion and that you have not obtained my approval for it'.
[4] No. 225.

No. 229

Mr. Eden to Mr. Dodds (Tokyo)

No. 279 Telegraphic [*F 6032/220/10*]

FOREIGN OFFICE, *September 4, 1937, 7.30 p.m.*

Tientsin telegrams Nos. 33 and 34 to Nanking.[1]

You should inform Japanese Government that His Majesty's Government have been made aware of certain measures which the Japanese authorities in Tientsin have taken or contemplate taking with a view to preventing revenues collected in areas under the *de facto* control of the Japanese Military authorities being remitted for the benefit of the Chinese Government at Nanking. His Majesty's Government desire to remind the Japanese Government of the substantial British interest in both the Customs and the Salt administrations and in the revenues which they collect. His Majesty's Government do not doubt that the Japanese Government intend scrupulously to respect the interests in question but would be glad to receive an assurance that this is in fact their intention.

For your own information. It is feared that total customs collections may at best barely cover foreign loan obligations and proposals have been made to us and to His Majesty's Embassy in China (whose views are

[1] Nos. 222 and 223.

awaited) for appointment of Hongkong and Shanghai Bank or Inspector General of Customs as trustee for bondholders and custodian of revenues. It would be disastrous if with a view to sterilising surplus (probably in any case non-existent) measures were adopted in any port which might lead to disruption of the administration.[2]

Repeated to Nanking No. 266, Peking No. 351, Tientsin No. 9, Shanghai No. 75, Washington No. 351, Paris (Saving) No. 158.

[2] Instructions were sent at the same time to H.M. representatives at Washington and Paris (telegrams Nos. 352 and 159) to inform the American and French Governments of the action to be taken at Tokyo and to ask whether they proposed to take similar action.

No. 230

Sir R. Craigie (Tokyo) to Mr. Eden (Received September 5, 3.45 p.m.)

No. 351 Telegraphic [F 6147/5727/10]

TOKYO, *September 5, 1937, 6.40 p.m.*

My telegram No. 347.[1] (not repeated elsewhere).

At unofficial meeting yesterday with Vice Minister for Foreign Affairs and Vice Minister of Marine I went over carefully all the circumstances connected with the wounding of Sir H. Knatchbull-Hugessen. The Vice Minister for Foreign Affairs stated that my . . .[2] seeming indictment of Japanese Government could hardly lie seeing that sincere regrets of Japanese Government had already been expressed through four different channels, namely, Japanese Ambassador to yourself, Vice Minister for Foreign Affairs to Chargé d'Affaires here, Japanese Admiral at Shanghai to Commander-in-Chief, and Japanese Ambassador to Sir H. Knatchbull-Hugessen himself. Vice Minister for Foreign Affairs admitted that these communications had been unofficial but said that they should at least be regarded by us as an indication of the deep concern of the Japanese Government. Vice Minister of Marine after indicating reasons for delay in original investigation stated that first report received from Admiral at Shanghai stated that only three naval planes had been operating at the moment of attack and that all personnel concerned had denied any knowledge of it. Ministry of Marine had considered this report inadequate and had ordered thorough-going investigation, report of which had not yet been received.

While unable for obvious reasons to give final reply to our note until result of second investigation is known they recognise that further delay in answering would be undesirable and result in misinterpretation of Japanese Government's attitude. They therefore undertook that an interim answer would be sent to me on Monday or at latest Tuesday morning. This I understand will probably contain an admission of

[1] No. 228.　　　　　　　　　　　　　　　　　　[2] The text was here uncertain.

strength of circumstantial evidence that a Japanese plane was involved while reserving final opinion until result of investigation is known and will state that in the circumstances Japanese Government desire to express their deep regret at this deplorable incident. As regards the other demands in our note namely punishment of officers responsible and guarantees for the future, Japanese Government will probably ask that answer on these points should be deferred until report from Shanghai which is expected shortly has been received.

My impression of Japanese official attitude is as follows: They deeply regret the incident and admit appearances point to a Japanese aeroplane being involved but they are perplexed at absence of corroborative evidence from their side and cannot altogether eliminate possibility of foul play by another party. (They state for instance that shortly before incident Chinese planes bearing Japanese markings and displaying Japanese flags had bombed Japanese warships).

I cannot of course guarantee that interim reply will be in terms which His Majesty's Government will consider acceptable but I am at present disposed to believe that given the necessary time it should be possible for us ultimately to obtain full satisfaction from Japanese Government in this matter.[3]

Repeated to Nanking and Commander-in-Chief.

[3] Mr. Orde commented on September 6: 'Sir R. Craigie is optimistic; I wish I were.'

No. 231

Sir R. Craigie (Tokyo) to Mr. Eden (Received September 6, 9.30 a.m.)

No. 354 Telegraphic [F 6169/9/10]

TOKYO, *September 6, 1937, 1.35 a.m.*

During my journey and since my arrival here I have been struck by the flow of press telegrams originating allegedly in Washington the general burden of which is that while Great Britain is constantly trying to arrange for joint Anglo-American cooperation at Japan's expense, the United States Government are firmly rejecting all such overtures. Impression conveyed is that Japan's real enemy is Great Britain with whom United States is refusing to cooperate except in joint action with which other interested Powers are also associated.

While making every allowance for tendentious activities of Domei Agency I cannot help feeling that this turn of affairs is not altogether unwelcome to United States Government. This impression is confirmed by a Domei report from Washington dated September 3rd that Mr. Hull has just re-emphasised the United States stand in avoiding joint action with any foreign Power in current Far Eastern situation.[1] Mr. Hull is

[1] Cf. *F.R.U.S.*, 1937, vol. iii, pp. 505–8.

reported to have added that United States Government intend 'to pursue an independent and separate policy regarding threatened developments under any circumstances'. There may, he adds, be occasions on which cooperation with *all* foreign Powers concerned may be desirable but this is taken by Japanese agency as affording additional evidence that first part of Mr. Hull's remarks were intended to refer to British efforts to secure Anglo-American cooperation.

While not underestimating enormous value of cooperation with United States whenever this can be made a reality I venture to think that any further initiative on our part to secure such cooperation will in present circumstances tend to diminish influence which we can exercise here on our own without any corresponding advantage to our relations with United States.[2]

Above observations are not of course intended to refer to admirable arrangements for cooperation between the five principal Powers which have been made at Nanking and Shanghai.

[2] Mr. Ronald remarked on September 7 that the 'somewhat sombre and dispiriting story of our efforts to collaborate closely with the Americans' had been set out in a recent paper (F 5868/9/10, not printed).

No. 232

Sir R. Craigie (Tokyo) to Mr. Eden (Received September 6, 2.45 p.m.)

No. 356 Telegraphic [F 6182/5727/10]

Immediate   TOKYO, *September 6, 1937, 8.30 p.m.*

My telegram No. 351.[1]

Following is text of interim reply received from the Japanese Government this evening. Begins:

I have the honour to acknowledge receipt of Note No. 125 under date August 29th addressed to me by Mr. Dodds, the Chargé d'Affaires at the British Embassy concerning the incident in which Sir H. Knatchbull-Hugessen was wounded.[2]

The Japanese Government on receiving news of the event in question took a grave view of the incident and hastened to convey expressions of profound sympathy to His Britannic Majesty's Government and to Sir H. Knatchbull-Hugessen through myself and the Ambassadors to the Court of St. James's and to China respectively and at the same time they sent urgent instructions to the authorities on the spot to investigate the case thoroughly. Although results of these investigations have so far failed to produce any evidence to establish that the shooting was done by a Japanese aeroplane the Japanese Government are taking measures for

[1] No. 230.   [2] See No. 215, note 3.

further investigations by the authorities on the spot in order to spare no efforts to ascertain the facts of the case.

In these circumstances it is still impossible to determine whether or not responsibility for incident rests with Japan. Nevertheless in view of traditional ties of friendship which binds [sic] Japan and Great Britain Japanese Government express their profound regret that Sir H. Knatchbull-Hugessen should have met with such a misfortune incident to . . .[3] hostilities that were actually in progress in the region of Taitsang on that particular day.

2. In this connexion I wish to assure Your Excellency that Japanese forces always take fullest precaution against causing injuries to non-combatants and it is certainly very far from the desire of the Japanese Government that such an unfortunate event should ever occur in the future through any fault of their own. Fresh instructions have consequently been sent to their authorities on the spot to exercise the strictest caution in this regard. I earnestly hope therefore that British authorities will on their part kindly co-operate with the Japanese authorities with a view to forestalling the recurrence of a similar event by taking such necessary measures as giving notice in advance to Japanese authorities on the spot when entering a zone of danger.

In making the above *ad interim* reply I avail myself, etc.,

(Signed) Minister for Foreign Affairs.[4]

Repeated to Nanking.

[3] The text was here uncertain.

[4] Telegram No. 283 to Tokyo, despatched at 7 p.m. on September 6, read: 'You should bear in mind essential difference between apology and mere expression of regret at incident, such as interim reply contains. I have already observed to Japanese Ambassador that expression of regret which he conveyed was not the same thing as an apology.' Cf. No. 233 below.

No. 233

Sir R. Craigie (Tokyo) to Mr. Eden (Received September 6, 4.30 p.m.)

No. 358 Telegraphic [F 6193/5727/10]

Immediate   TOKYO, *September 6, 1937, 10.3 p.m.*

My telegram No. 356.[1]

I feel this note represents a genuine effort to meet our demands as far as it is possible to do so in advance of final report on investigation now in progress. Pending the receipt of that report we cannot logically press either for the punishment of the offenders or for a more definite admission of responsibility than is implicit in the terms of the note. If you share this view I hope the British press may be guided accordingly because

[1] No. 232.

a report of the reception at this stage will increase our chance of securing full satisfaction later.[2] Request in last sentence relating to prior notification of such journeys in future, Vice Minister for Foreign Affairs informs me that during Shanghai troubles in 1932 Sir M. Lampson invariably notified Japanese authorities of frequent journeys he made by air between Nanking and Shanghai. Whatever may be the legal position, such notification would seem to be a wise precaution if we are to deal with realities of the situation and request for future notification is a tacit admission that a Japanese plane may have been involved.

You may perhaps consider it unnecessary to return any official reply to this note pending receipt of the next Japanese communication.

Repeated to Nanking.

[2] The Foreign Office did not consider the Japanese reply satisfactory: see No. 236 below. In the course of a long minute of September 7 Mr. Ronald commented: 'It seems to me that if we give the impression of being pleased with this sort of stuff, there is no knowing to what lengths of impudence the Japanese will go in their final reply. I suggest that News Dept. if they give the press any guidance at all should ask them to adopt an attitude of extremely distant reserve, tempered possibly with an occasional acid comment.'

No. 234

Sir R. Craigie (Tokyo) to Mr. Eden (Received September 7, 10 a.m.)

No. 361 Telegraphic [F 6229/5727/10]

Important   TOKYO, *September 7, 1937, 3.33 p.m.*

My telegram No. 360.[1]

I should perhaps make it clear that my original suggestion was that only point (two) of our note (punishment of those responsible) should be reserved until completion of investigation. In subsequent conversation (see my telegram No. 351[2]) I gathered that Japanese authorities might also wish to reserve point (3) (prevention of recurrence) but they eventually decided to deal with it in interim reply. I have made it clear throughout that final reply will be expected to follow very shortly.

I greatly regret if this procedure is not approved but I am quite sure that nothing more could have been obtained at the moment and I acted on the assumption that His Majesty's Government would not wish a complete break on this question (as forecast in your telegram No. 272[3]) with serious consequences that may be entailed as long as a reasonable chance remained of securing our desiderata in a few days' time.

In the opening paragraph of your telegram No. 272 emphasis is laid on

[1] In this telegram of September 7 Sir R. Craigie referred to Foreign Office telegram No. 283 (see No. 232, note 4) and asked whether the use of the word 'apology' was essential 'or would expression of deep regret *coupled with* admission of responsibility meet the case?'.
[2] No. 230.   [3] No. 225.

fact that 'no reply' had as yet been received from the Japanese Government and it would presumably have created the worst impression if no answer at all had been forthcoming before tomorrow's Cabinet.

No. 235

Mr. Mallet (Washington) to Mr. Eden (Received September 8, 9.30 a.m.)

No. 266 Telegraphic [F 6284/9/10]

WASHINGTON, *September 7, 1937, 7.2 p.m.*

My telegram No. 262.[1]
Assistant Secretary of State told me today that Secretary of State was slightly disturbed at rumours through London press that United States Government were embarrassed by our efforts for co-operation in Far Eastern crisis.[2] Mr. Hull particularly wished me to know that we had done nothing to embarrass him and that he saw every advantage in our working together in matters where our interests coincide so closely.

While I was with Mr. Wilson Secretary of State asked him to take me in to see him. Mr. Hull then repeated to me emphatically what Mr. Wilson had said. I assured him that as far as I knew you were not under this misapprehension. I had informed you of his press statement of September 3rd (see my telegram No. 262) and had also conveyed to you my impression that United States Government preferred parallel to joint action. Mr. Hull, while not entirely ruling out joint action if its utility could be proved, said that he decidedly preferred parallel action as more expeditious and less liable to involve him in criticism here, but once again asked me to tell you that he was *not* embarrassed.

Mr. Hull was most cordial. I think his object in sending for me was to reciprocate my confidence in discussing privately with Mr. Wilson your telegram No. 344.[3] He seemed to want us to know that he valued collaboration even if he could not speak in the sense Chinese Ambassador had misreported.

---

[1] Not kept in F.O. archives. This telegram apparently referred to a press statement issued by Mr. Cordell Hull on September 3. No such statement was reported in *The Times*: cf. however No. 231. See also *The Memoirs of Cordell Hull*, vol. i (London, 1948), pp. 541–2.
[2] Cf. Nos. 197 and 221.   [3] No. 224.

No. 236

Mr. Eden to Sir R. Craigie (Tokyo)

No. 284 Telegraphic [F 6193/5727/10]

Important   FOREIGN OFFICE, *September 7, 1937, 11 p.m.*

Your telegram No. 358.[1]

I cannot but regard Japanese interim reply as unsatisfactory. In particular I regret that they should have included their request that British authorities should 'co-operate'. (What Sir M. Lampson may or may not have done is not to the point and cannot be appealed to as any excuse. After all, we have no official cognizance of a 'danger zone' which, if it exists, might be found to have arisen from a violation of the Kellogg Pact and the Nine-Power Treaty. The Japanese therefore should be rather chary of referring to it).

Expressions of regret accompanied by disclaimers of responsibility do not approximate to an apology, though I agree that regret coupled with admission of responsibility (your telegram No. 360[2]) would meet the case.

I trust Japanese final reply will not be delayed for more than a week or so. In the meanwhile you should at once let Japanese Government know unofficially that we realise that this is an interim reply but that if the final reply were to be of this nature we should find it unacceptable.

[1] No. 233.   [2] See No. 234, note 1.

No. 237

Viscount Chilston (Moscow) to Mr. Eden (Received September 10)

No. 439 [F 6347/1098/10]

Confidential   MOSCOW, *September 7, 1937*

Sir,

Since sending my telegram No. 133[1] of the 30th August regarding the Pact of Non-aggression between China and the Soviet Union[2] I have had the opportunity of discussing the significance of the Pact with certain of my colleagues. What I have heard tends to confirm the impression recorded in my telegram, that the Pact in no way represents a new forward tendency in Soviet foreign policy.

2. I asked the Chinese Ambassador, who was lunching with me to-day, whether there was any truth in the rumours emanating chiefly from Japanese sources that the Pact implied military assistance from the Soviet Union in the present war with Japan, and that Soviet aeroplanes and

[1] Not printed.   [2] See No. 217.

perhaps other military supplies were already being sent to China. The Ambassador said he could tell me quite frankly that he only wished these rumours could be correct, for he had been trying for some time to obtain some Soviet assistance, but he had met with no success at all. As for the Pact, it was purely one of non-aggression. The idea, as I knew, had been started long ago, but at that time the Soviet support of the Chinese communists had been an obstacle. For some time past however the Soviets had no longer been active in that respect and were now giving no help at all to the Chinese communists. Therefore it was not true that Soviet desistence from the support of the communists constituted a bargain in concluding the present Pact. I asked whether the question about Outer Mongolia had played any part, and he said that on that matter there was a tacit understanding that it should be 'put into cold storage' (where I imagine that in fact it has already been for some time). I referred to certain press reports that Japan had been trying some time ago to induce the Chinese Government to come into a position of guaranteed neutrality in the event of a war with the Soviet Union. The Ambassador said this was so, but China could have none of this, because the proposed guarantee amounted to a Japanese control of the five Northern provinces.

3. According to the German Embassy the German Ambassador in China has reported that in a recent interview Marshal Chiang Kai-shek assured him that the Pact would not involve communist participation in the Nanking Government. He explained that he could not fight against Japan and his own communists at the same time. A tacit understanding had accordingly been reached to the effect that in future the Chinese communists would, under orders from Moscow, refrain from giving the Nanking Government any more trouble. In return for this the Nanking Government would say no more about Sinkiang and Outer Mongolia.[3]

4. According to this version, it will be seen, the use of Soviet influence as a means of bringing the Chinese communists into line with the Nanking Government was one of the elements of the bargain, and although, as I pointed out in my telegram No. 38 (Saving)[1] of 31st July, there have for some time past been indications of a change of heart in the Chinese communists, such an assurance would no doubt have been welcome to the Nanking Government. It is at the present moment clearly to the interest of the Soviet Government to bolster up the Nanking Government against Japan and it would be characteristic that the Comintern should be made to serve this aim of Soviet national policy. It is undoubtedly a cause of great satisfaction to the Soviet Government that Japan should be wearing out her strength against China. Indeed the longer the hostilities in China last the better pleased they will be. Their interest clearly lies in preventing the

[3] Mr. Ronald commented on September 14 that 'it would be interesting to know whether the Germans, usually well informed, had reason to believe that there was more behind the Pact. . .' Mr. Collier remarked (September 15): 'If the Germans had any evidence that the Pact was more than this, I am sure they would have said so.' Cf. *D.G.F.P.*, Series D, vol. i, pp. 756–7.

Japanese from coming to an understanding with the Chinese and then turning their whole strength against the Soviet Union. This danger they no doubt hope to have averted by means of the Non-aggression Pact.

5. As to the possibility of Soviet 'intervention' in China on a large scale, I still do not consider it likely. As I explained in my telegram No. 124[1] of 30th July, the Soviet Government are anxious to make as much trouble for the Japanese as they can, but in my opinion are not prepared to risk war themselves. (In this connexion I may mention that on enquiring at the People's Commissariat for Foreign Affairs as to the nature of the Pact the French Chargé d'Affaires was assured that there was no question of mutual assistance, the surprisingly frank comment of the competent official at the People's Commissariat for Foreign Affairs being 'Ce serait trop dangereux!')

6. So long as a state of war between China and Japan has not been declared there is of course in theory no reason why the Soviet Government should not supply the Chinese forces with any amount of war material, and one hears it said that Outer Mongolia is being made into a regular base for that purpose. With the Japanese at Kalgan, however, and Prince Teh in Inner Mongolia, communication by land with the Nanking Government forces must be becoming daily more difficult. Nor would transport by sea from Vladivostok be an easy matter. On the other hand there is no reason why numbers of Soviet aeroplanes should not be flown to China if desired, and indeed most of the rumours of Soviet aid to China current here concern the departure of flights of aeroplanes.

7. I am sending a copy of this despatch to His Majesty's Ambassadors at Tokyo and Nanking.

I have, etc.,
CHILSTON

No. 238

Extract from Cabinet Conclusions No. 34(37) of September 8, 1937

[F 6353/5727/10]

1. The Cabinet had before them a Note by the Deputy Secretary (Paper C.P.208(37))[1] covering the draft Notes of a Meeting of Ministers held at the Foreign Office on Thursday, 2nd September, 1937, for the examination of certain urgent questions which had arisen in connection with recent developments in the situation in the Far East and in the Mediterranean. At this Meeting four questions had been specifically reserved for consideration by the Cabinet.

The Cabinet were reminded by the Secretary of State for Foreign Affairs that when the Meeting of Ministers had discussed the question of

[1]Not printed: see No. 225, note 1.

the attack on His Majesty's Ambassador in China it had been agreed *inter alia* that the question of the withdrawal of our Ambassador in Tokyo should be reserved for the decision of the Cabinet at their Meeting on September 8th, when the Cabinet could reach a decision in the light of further developments and information (see Conclusion 2 on page 11 of Notes of Meeting, Paper C.P.208(37)).

Since the Meeting of Ministers an interim reply had been received from the Japanese Government (for the text of which see Appendix I[2]). This interim reply could not in the view of the Secretary of State be regarded as satisfactory, and if the final reply of the Japanese Government was similar in character to their interim reply the final reply would have to be regarded as unsatisfactory. Sir Robert Craigie had been so informed,[3] and we had also expressed to him the hope that the Japanese final reply would not be unduly delayed. The Secretary of State suggested that the Cabinet might wish to consider what action should be taken in the not improbable event of the Japanese final reply proving unsatisfactory.

The Prime Minister thought that examination by the Cabinet of the procedure to be followed in the event of the Japanese final reply proving unsatisfactory would be valuable. At the Meeting of Ministers on the 2nd September it had been assumed that the final reply of the Japanese Government would by now have been received. In the events which had happened all that we had got at present was an interim reply which, while friendly and conciliatory in tone, was undoubtedly unsatisfactory. The reply intimated that the Japanese investigations had so far failed to produce any evidence to establish that a Japanese aeroplane had been guilty of the outrage, and that in these circumstances it was still impossible to determine whether or not any responsibility for the incident rested with the Japanese Government. The interim reply added insult to injury by suggesting that in order to prevent the recurrence of such an incident we should co-operate with the Japanese authorities on the spot by giving them notice in advance when British subjects proposed to enter a danger zone. It looked very much as if the Japanese were adopting the same dilatory and unsatisfactory attitude which they had taken up in the Keelung affair.[4]

He (the Prime Minister) did not believe that the Japanese Government dared to go further in the direction of giving us satisfaction in view of the violent manner in which the Japanese military and naval elements would react. It should be observed in particular that the Japanese had so far failed to tender any apology, and to undertake suitably to punish those responsible for the attack, two of the requirements contained in our Note to the Japanese Government of the 28th August, 1937.[5]

He (the Prime Minister) had been considering the suggestion that our Ambassador in Tokyo should be withdrawn in the absence of any satisfactory reply, and he wished to suggest to the Cabinet an alternative

[2] See No. 232.   [3] See No. 236.   [4] See No. 6, note 5.   [5] No. 215.

proposal which he had had no opportunity as yet of discussing with any of his colleagues. He assumed that the Cabinet would agree that we could not simply acquiesce and do nothing, but the difficulty that he foresaw about withdrawing our Ambassador from Tokyo was that such action would not seriously injure Japan, and would moreover leave the situation entirely unliquidated. Should we withdraw our Ambassador the time would come in the future when it would be necessary that he should return to Tokyo. It was most improbable that in the interval the Japanese Government would give us the satisfaction we were demanding, and we should then be placed in a humiliating and embarrassing position. In order to avoid difficulties of this kind he proposed that the action to be taken should consist of two parts. In the first place we should answer the final reply of the Japanese Government (assuming that reply to be unsatisfactory) in stinging terms, to the following effect:

We had received their final reply with disappointment and regret. Having regard to the undoubted fact, as proved beyond question by evidence in our possession, that this outrage had been committed by a Japanese airman, we could not understand the failure at once to comply with our reasonable and moderate demands. As the Japanese Government did not feel able to take this course, in this second case where a British subject had been subjected to gross outrage by persons in the service of the Japanese Government, we did not consider that it was consonant with our own dignity to press them further in the matter, as apparently in matters of this kind Japan was unable to attain to the normal standards observed among civilised peoples. In this way the incident could be closed by us with dignity and without loss of prestige.

Secondly, he (the Prime Minister) thought that an announcement should be made very soon after the despatch of our reply to Japan to the effect that in view of the grievous injuries sustained by His Majesty's Ambassador and the possible prejudice to his future health resulting from the outrage, the Government had decided to make a compensatory grant to him of £5,000. Such action would relieve the mind of the Ambassador from undue anxiety.

If we proceeded on these lines, the incident would be liquidated in a way which he thought public opinion would approve, and it would be unnecessary to consider further the question of withdrawing Sir R. Craigie from Tokyo.

The Secretary of State for India was of the opinion that the Japanese would only pay attention to force, or to the display of force. Rebukes, however strongly worded, would have no effect upon them and would certainly not deter them from committing further outrages.

The Minister of Health[6] favoured the line suggested by the Prime Minister and doubted whether the Japanese would be much impressed by the withdrawal of our Ambassador from Tokyo. Moreover, the difficulty

[6] Sir Kingsley Wood.

regarding the Canadian Minister in Tokyo would remain.

The Secretary of State for Dominion Affairs said that the position in regard to the Canadian Minister presented no immediate difficulty. The Canadian Minister had been spending his leave in Victoria, British Columbia, and had been due to return to Japan on 4th September. He had been instructed by the Canadian Government to postpone his return indefinitely. Should it be decided to withdraw Sir Robert Craigie it would be very quickly realised in Japan that the Canadian Government, by postponing the return of their Minister to Tokyo, were keeping in step with us. But he thought that the difficulty of getting the Ambassador back once he had been withdrawn was a very grave one, and it would be every bit as embarrassing and difficult for the Canadian Government to allow their Minister to return if he was withdrawn as it would be for us in the case of H.M. Ambassador. He therefore was inclined to favour the alternative proposal made by the Prime Minister.

The Secretary of State for the Colonies thought that a profound sensation would be caused in Japan if we were to brand the Japanese as not coming up to ordinary civilised standards.

The Secretary of State for Foreign Affairs agreed and warned the Cabinet that the Japanese might, on receipt of a Note of the kind contemplated by the Prime Minister, decide to sever diplomatic relations with us. It was very difficult indeed correctly to assess Japanese mentality but there was no doubt that they would attach great importance to our withdrawing our Ambassador. There were, of course, precedents for withdrawing Ambassadors, and no insuperable difficulties had been found in other cases in resuming normal diplomatic relations. In a year's time the whole situation in the Far East might have been profoundly altered, possibly to the detriment of the Japanese, who might then be much more anxious for our friendship than they were at present. He was in full agreement with the Prime Minister's suggestion that a pecuniary grant should be made to Sir Hughe Knatchbull-Hugessen. He did not think that any decision on the question of withdrawing our Ambassador need, as yet, be taken by the Cabinet.

The Prime Minister agreed that no decision need be taken that day.

Some discussion then took place as to whether we could regard as satisfactory anything short of full compliance with the three requirements in our Note of August 28th. In this connection the Secretary of State for Foreign Affairs drew attention to the following passage in his telegram No. 284[7] of the 7th September to Sir R. Craigie:

'Expressions of regret accompanied by disclaimers of responsibility do not approximate to an apology, though I agree that regret coupled with admission of responsibility (Your telegram No. 360[8]) would meet the case.'

[7] No. 236. [8] See No. 234, note 1.

The view was expressed that it would be unwise for us to insist on the punishment of the actual perpetrators of the outrage, and that in any case it would be very difficult to insist on our second requirement, namely, suitable punishment for those responsible for the attack, as it might well be argued that the ultimate responsibility lay with those who had decided on warlike operations in China.

The Prime Minister suggested that if the Japanese Government admitted responsibility and tendered their apologies and regrets but added that after further exhaustive investigations they had failed to identify the airmen who had committed the outrage, that we should accept as satisfactory a reply on these lines.

The Secretary of State for Foreign Affairs agreed but was emphatically opposed to Sir Robert Craigie being informed at present that we were prepared to make any concession on our original demands. If we appeared to be weakening it would be impossible for Sir Robert Craigie to negotiate any satisfactory settlement.

The Lord President of the Council agreed that it was unnecessary at this stage for the Cabinet to decide whether our Ambassador to Tokyo should be withdrawn or not. He hoped that a communication could be sent to Sir Robert Craigie emphasising the strong feelings of the Cabinet on the subject. If we then received a final reply from the Japanese containing expressions of regret it would be possible for Sir Robert Craigie to start negotiations with a view to getting the best possible settlement.

The Prime Minister feared that if we embarked on negotiations the matter would drag on interminably and he thought that we should endeavour to reach some decision at the earliest possible moment.

The Minister for Co-ordination of Defence[9] agreed but hoped that it would be possible to avoid anything of the nature of an ultimatum. He would not therefore ask for a final reply by any fixed date, but would give the Japanese two or three weeks.

The Secretary of State for Foreign Affairs pointed out that in his telegram No. 358[10] of 7th September to Sir R. Craigie he had asked that the Japanese final reply should not be delayed for more than a week or so.

The Prime Minister thought that the position might be summed up as follows. The Government were in no way seeking a quarrel with Japan. On the contrary they would like to reach an amicable settlement of this incident on the basis of the moderate and reasonable request already made to Japan. It was impossible to reach any decision until the final reply from Japan was received, and in any case the Cabinet were not prepared to decide that our Ambassador at Tokyo should be recalled if that reply was unsatisfactory without further consideration. In the meantime the Secretary of State for Foreign Affairs would examine the alternative procedure which he (the Prime Minister) had suggested earlier in the

[9] Sir T. Inskip.
[10] The reference should presumably be to Foreign Office telegram No. 284 (No. 236).

discussion. The Prime Minister added that the Cabinet agreed in principle with his suggestion that some £5,000 should be awarded to Sir Hughe Knatchbull-Hugessen and that Sir Hughe should be informed privately of this decision.

The Secretary of State for War said that he was entirely in favour of making this grant to Sir Hughe Knatchbull-Hugessen, but suggested that it might be desirable for the precedents to be examined as it was possible that the award to Sir Hughe might give rise to other claims.

The Cabinet approved the course to be taken in regard to this question as set out in the Prime Minister's summing up of the position given above.

No. 239

Extract from Cabinet Conclusions No. 34(37) of September 8, 1937

[*F 6354/130/10*]

2. With reference to the Conclusions on pages 1 to 11 of the Draft Notes of the Meeting of Ministers held on the 2nd September, 1937 (C.P.208(37)),[1] the Cabinet had before them a Memorandum by the Secretary of State for Foreign Affairs (C.P.212(37)),[2] copies of which were handed round at the Meeting.

The Secretary of State for Foreign Affairs pointed out that his Memorandum raised two main points. The first point, which was discussed in paragraphs 1 to 7 of the Memorandum, related to the action which had already been taken in regard to the verification by Japanese warships of the right of a British ship to fly the British flag. The second point, which was discussed in paragraphs 8 and 9 of the Memorandum, concerned the question of what action should be taken in the event of the Japanese taking further steps against British shipping other than the mere verification of their right to fly the British flag. With regard to the first question, we had not as yet informed the Japanese Government of our decision, for the reasons set out in the Memorandum.

The view was expressed that it would be impracticable to carry out the agreed formula in paragraph 2 of C.P.212(37) without telling the Japanese what was proposed, and that the best line to take might be to tell the Japanese that we will tolerate verification of British registry, notwithstanding that this meant granting them a right which they could not properly claim in the circumstances now existing.

In this connection the Chancellor of the Exchequer pointed out that at the Meeting of Ministers on the 2nd September it had been clearly understood that we were making these concessions to the Japanese in return for undertakings on their part that their interference with British shipping would be strictly limited in the manner proposed.

[1] See No. 226, note 3. [2] Not printed: see *ibid.* A copy of this paper is filed at F 6354/130/10.

The Secretary of State for Foreign Affairs pointed out that since the Meeting on September 2nd we had learnt that the United States Government was strongly opposed to the Japanese being informed of the agreed formula.[3]

The Prime Minister thought that if nothing was said to the Japanese, and interference with British shipping continued, the tendency would be for the Japanese to proceed from one improper kind of interference to other and more improper kinds. He preferred, therefore, notwithstanding the American objections, to inform the Japanese Government that, while we did not admit that they had any rights in the matter, we would agree to verification of British registry on the terms and conditions set out in the formula. At the same time it should be borne in mind that whatever decision was reached in the matter in regard to British shipping in Chinese Waters would have to be applied to British shipping in similar circumstances in the Mediterranean.

In the course of discussion the Cabinet were informed that while certain of the Government's advisers were opposed to the Japanese being informed of the formula, the First Sea Lord strongly favoured the information being given to the Japanese. In this connection it was pointed out that the addendum to the formula, relating to our reservation of the right to claim compensation for damage sustained by the owners of British ships delayed or stopped under the procedure, would have little or no meaning if the Japanese were not informed of it.

Some discussion then took place in regard to the question of ships recently transferred to the British Register. It was pointed out that in the absence of any definition in the formula it would be very difficult, if not impossible, for the Japanese to know where the line could be drawn between a British and a non-British ship. The best course might be to inform the Japanese that, while we were entirely opposed to abuse of the British flag, we intended to extend the fullest protection in our power to genuine British ships; that a British ship was a ship on the British Register; and that the formula must be interpreted accordingly.

The Secretary of State for Foreign Affairs said that he was advised that grave difficulties might be anticipated in the case of ships owned by British subjects of Chinese race having dual nationality. In the case of such ships the Japanese would allege that it was impossible without exhaustive examination to decide whether such ships were British or not and that this could not be done by mere verification of the flag on the spot.

The President of the Board of Trade doubted whether there was any substance in this suggestion. A ship was either on the British Register or it was not, and this must be the criterion.

The Prime Minister thought that the general view of the Cabinet favoured the communication of the formula to the Japanese Government.[4]

[3] See No. 226.
[4] On September 9 Mr. Herschel Johnson had a conversation with Sir A. Cadogan, who

The Secretary of State for Dominion Affairs agreed, and stated that the Dominions concerned had all agreed to the procedure proposed, and that those most interested had expressed their readiness to adopt the same procedure.

The Minister of Agriculture and Fisheries referred to the second paragraph on page 2 of C.P.212(37), and suggested that difficulties might be avoided if the matter could be treated on general lines in a statement of Government policy regarding misuse of the flag which would be applicable both to the China Seas and the Mediterranean.

The Minister for Co-ordination of Defence observed that our system had throughout been based on the principle of getting as many ships as possible onto the British Register. The paragraph to which the Minister of Agriculture and Fisheries had referred needed clarification, in that it made no reference to the important fact that a ship could only be placed on the British Register if the principal place of business of the owner was in British territory.

The Prime Minister pointed out that the paragraph in question was concerned simply with the question of fact whether the ship was a British ship or not. It was not concerned with the question of possible fraudulent registration.

The President of the Board of Trade informed the Cabinet that he would be most strongly opposed to any suggestion that the existing rules and regulations regarding the registration of British ships should be materially altered.

The Secretary of State for War pointed out that both the Japanese and General Franco objected to the very easy procedure under which ships which were in no real sense British ships could get onto the British Register. Morally there was much to be said for their complaints, and if the matter was not fully investigated and remedied it must give rise to many embarrassing incidents.

The Prime Minister thought that this aspect of the question could more conveniently be discussed when the Cabinet considered the situation in the Mediterranean.[5]

The Secretary of State for Foreign Affairs warned the Cabinet that the second point discussed in paragraphs 8 and 9 of his Memorandum raised further difficult questions. He had learnt that morning that the Chinese

informed him of the Cabinet decision to communicate the formula to the Japanese Government: see *F.R.U.S.*, 1937, vol. iv, pp. 454–5. According to Mr. Johnson, Sir A. Cadogan told him that although Mr. Eden had for several days agreed with the American view that the shipping formula should not be notified to the Japanese, other government departments, especially the Admiralty had held different views. Mr. Johnson commented: 'Although Cadogan stated that the American view had been held by the Foreign Secretary for several days, he gave no indication that the policy finally agreed upon by the Departments and approved by the Cabinet yesterday did not have the full concurrence of the Foreign Office'.

[5] See Volume XIX, No. 142.

Government were likely to appeal to the League of Nations under Article 17 of the Covenant.[6] This was the Article which dealt with cases of disputes between a Member of the League and a State which is not a Member of the League. It was most unlikely that Japan would accept an invitation of the League to accept the obligations of Membership, and in that event the provisions of Article 16 of the Covenant would come automatically into operation. It had been ascertained that France and other Powers were most anxious to avoid the difficult situation which might thus arise. The questions discussed in the concluding paragraphs of his Memorandum were technical and difficult, and the best way to handle them might be to refer them to a Cabinet Committee for consideration.

The Prime Minister expressed the view that it would be a great mistake to tell the Japanese in advance what action we proposed to take in the event of their taking measures against British shipping of a more drastic character than was contemplated in the formula. As regards possible action on our part, he enquired whether consideration had been given to the possibility of reinforcing our naval strength in the Far East.

The Secretary of State for Foreign Affairs thought that this matter might be examined by the proposed Cabinet Committee.

The Chancellor of the Exchequer suggested, and the Cabinet agreed, that words such as 'suspected of not being entitled to fly the flag' should be substituted for the words 'suspected of being an impostor' in lines 2 and 3 of the formula in paragraph 2 of C.P.212(37).

After further discussion, the Cabinet agreed:

(1) That the formula amended as suggested by the Chancellor of the Exchequer should be communicated to the Japanese Government.[7]

(2) That a Cabinet Committee composed as follows:

> The Home Secretary (*In the Chair*),
> The Secretary of State for Foreign Affairs,
> The Secretary of State for Dominion Affairs (or Representative),
> The President of the Board of Trade,
> The First Lord of the Admiralty,
> The Minister for Co-ordination of Defence,
> The Attorney-General,

should meet to examine the question of the Japanese taking further steps against British shipping than the mere verification of the right

---

[6] See No. 241 below.

[7] Cf. note 4 above. In telegram No. 297 to Tokyo, despatched at 9.40 p.m. on September 9, Sir R. Craigie was instructed to inform the Japanese Government of the formula agreed upon for British shipping: see No. 226, note 3. However, in a note on the file of September 11 Mr. Ronald stated that on his way through Paris on September 9 (see No. 241, note 1 below) Mr. Eden was asked by the French Government to defer taking action on the Cabinet decision, and Sir R. Craigie was told in telegram No. 299, despatched at 11.50 p.m. on September 9, to suspend action on telegram No. 297. On September 10, however, Mr. Eden telephoned from Geneva to say that Sir R. Craigie should be told to delay no longer, and this was done in telegram No. 303 to Tokyo, despatched at 5.35 p.m.

of British shipping to fly the British flag and of the measures to be adopted in such an event.

The Committee should also consider the possible reinforcement of British naval forces in the Far East, and, should it be thought necessary or desirable to send such reinforcements, to advise as to the kind of reinforcements which could be contemplated.

The Committee to hold their first Meeting at 2, Whitehall Gardens, immediately after the conclusion of the adjourned Meeting of the Cabinet that afternoon, and Ministers to be at liberty to bring to that Meeting such officials or advisers as they might think fit.[8]

(3) That, in the event of the Chinese Government appealing to the League of Nations under Article 17 of the Covenant, the Secretary of State for Foreign Affairs and his colleagues at Geneva should be at liberty to deal with the matter as they thought best.

[8] The Cabinet Committee on British shipping in the Far East held a somewhat discursive meeting at 3.30 p.m. on September 8, with Sir S. Hoare in the chair. The meeting decided that 'from the point of view of British Trade, the system of verification of British shipping in the Far East by the Japanese was preferable to the exercise of belligerent rights by Japan', and agreed that the Admiralty should be asked their views on the possibility of reinforcing British naval forces in the area. They also agreed, however, that the Committee should only meet again 'when considered necessary by any of the members'. A copy of the draft conclusions of the meeting is filed at F 6355/130/10.

No. 240

Mr. Gage (Nanking) to Mr. Eden (Received October 4)

No. 85 [F 7355/35/10]

NANKING, *September 8, 1937*

Sir,

With reference to His Majesty's Ambassador's despatch No. 65 of August 5th, 1937,[1] I now have the honour to report on developments in the political situation and in Sino-Japanese relations since that date.

2. As stated in paragraph 35 of the despatch under reference, the Chinese Government, having taken the decision to embark on war with Japan on a national scale, set about making such dispositions as its imperfect organisation permitted to put the decision into effect. The first problem with which the Government had to deal was that of producing a united front. There were two groups of people to be won over, firstly the provincial leaders, and secondly the Communist-National Salvationists. In order to secure the whole-hearted co-operation of the provincial militarists, the Generalissimo had to satisfy them that this time he was really

[1] No. 164.

going to take up the Japanese challenge. In this he appeared to be singularly successful. Han Fu-chu, Yen Hsi-sham, Liu Hsiang, Yu Hanmou all came to Nanking to discuss arrangements and troop dispositions; more important, they placed their forces at the disposal of the Central Government for the common purpose, and one saw—a strange phenomenon in China—Szechuen troops in Hupei, and Kwangsi troops in Shantung, not as invaders, but as partners in a common enterprise. Most important of all, perhaps, General Pai Chung-hsi, the inveterate enemy of General Chiang Kai-shek, at last buried the hatchet and came to Nanking. After the Generalissimo, General Pai is perhaps the most trusted figure in China. He is in popular estimation the best strategist in the country, and the news that he was not only going to remain in Nanking, but was to take up the post of Vice-Chief of the General Staff under General Cheng Chien was hailed with a sigh of relief.

3. As an earnest to the Communist-Salvation Association group the Government ordered the release of the seven Shanghai intellectuals (see Nanking Embassy despatch No. 7 of February 12th, 1937,[2] paragraph 7) and even of Mr. Chen Tu-hsiu, the veteran Communist professor, who had already served three years of an eight years' sentence.

4. During the first days of August there were no major hostilities, but both sides were feverishly moving troops into position, and the tactics which they proposed to follow gradually became clear. The Japanese plan was evidently to make a drive for Kalgan and to secure control of the whole Peking-Suiyuan line, while holding the Chinese forces along the rest of the front; the Chinese plan to stand on the defensive on all fronts, and to play for time in the belief that long-drawn-out hostilities would impose a greater strain on the Japanese financial and economic structure than on their own. At the outset, therefore, the Chinese began to dig themselves in on a line roughly from Nankow Pass to Changsintien, and thence south-east to Chinghai on the Tientsin-Pukow Railway, while the Japanese assembled troops north of Peking for the drive on Chahar, leaving only sufficient forces south of Peking and Tientsin to meet any possible Chinese attack. The Chinese were also very apprehensive lest the Japanese should turn their flank by a landing in the Tsingtao area, and the considerable forces were massed in Shantung province to meet any such movement. Other Chinese forces were massed in the Hankow, Amoy and Shanghai areas, and, indeed, at any point where either there were considerable numbers of Japanese residents or there was reason to apprehend a Japanese landing.

5. The Japanese, whose fundamental policy was to concentrate on the north and to avoid being drawn into expensive and strategically useless sideshows in other parts of China, had at first intended to withdraw their communities from all except a few of the more important centres, such as Hankow and Tsingtao, but as they felt the strength of the hostility against

[2] No. 56.

307

them and realised the danger of massacres, they reluctantly withdrew even from these centres until the whole of China south of the Tientsin-Peking zone had been completely evacuated by Japanese nationals and officials, with the single exception of Shanghai. The situation at some of the ports was for a time exceedingly tense. At Hankow the small Japanese concession was to all intents and purposes invested by a large Chinese army. It was impossible for the Japanese to defend it, and I am convinced that it was only the tardily reached and hastily executed resolve to evacuate it completely that averted a shocking tragedy. A graphic account of these events is contained in Mr. Consul-General Moss's despatch to Peking, No. 58 of August 10th[3] and No. 60 of August 13th.[3]

6. At Tsingtao a crisis was precipitated by the shooting of two Japanese sailors by an unidentified assailant on August 15th. The situation was the more serious from the point of view of ourselves and other neutrals in that Tsingtao was crowded not only with the normal quota of summer visitors, but also with refugees from other places. Urgent representations were made by the representatives of the principal Powers both in Nanking and Tokyo to prevent this seaside resort from becoming involved in hostilities and eventually the Japanese Government, to their general relief, decided to evacuate the port completely. Japanese mill and other property, estimated by the Japanese to be worth yen 300,000,000, was handed over to the custody of the Chinese authorities.

7. All this took time. The evacuation of Hankow was completed on August 11th, that of Amoy on August 28th, and that of Tsingtao only on September 4th.

8. Meanwhile, most serious developments had taken place at Shanghai. It will be remembered that, as the result of the 1932 Truce Agreement, the Japanese forces were withdrawn inside the International Settlement and Chapei 'salient,' while the Chinese undertook to remain outside the line to which they had been driven by the Japanese 'pending further arrangements,' the intervening area to be policed meanwhile by a force of gendarmerie to be established by the Chinese for the purpose. Inevitably, the two sides, and the foreign friendly Powers who had participated in the truce conference, could not agree on the scope of the 'further arrangements'. The Japanese had envisaged a round-table conference at which all the international problems of Shanghai would be discussed; the Chinese maintained that the 'further arrangements' dealt only with the restoration of peaceful conditions in the Shanghai area, whereafter the Truce Agreement lapsed, and they would have nothing to do with any round-table conference unless it dealt with Manchuria as well as Shanghai; and the foreign Powers, who had half agreed to the idea of a round-table conference, hastily drew back when it became evident that they were to be used for the purpose of extracting further concessions

[3] Not printed.

from China in the Japanese interest.

9. Thus Japan has always regarded herself as having been betrayed by the Powers, and, failing a fundamental solution by international agreement securing her position to her own satisfaction, has taken her own measures to assure the safety of her nationals. The Marine Landing Force permanently stationed in Shanghai was greatly increased, fortress-like headquarters to accommodate 2,000 men, as well as equipment and stores for several times that number, were built, and night exercises covering the whole of the Hongkew and 'salient' areas became a regular institution. Naturally, even this force could not protect the Japanese residents, or even the landing force itself, from the activities of gunmen and anti-Japanese fanatics, so that incidents were constantly occurring. Helpless to *prevent* such incidents, all the landing force could do—and did—when they occurred was to demonstrate in force, thrash around and make the situation as uncomfortable as possible for the wretched Chinese in the neighbourhood.

10. The Chinese argued that the military preparations being made by the Japanese went far beyond what was necessary for the defence of Japanese interests in the settlement, and could only be interpreted as evidence of an intention once again at the appropriate moment to use the settlement as a base for operations outside. China's national spirit was growing, and there was a general determination that if there was another 1932 affair it should have a different result. Accordingly, and as an answer to the Japanese military preparations, the Chinese began unostentatiously to increase the numbers of the gendarmerie, provide them with machine guns and modern equipment and generally assimilate them more and more to a military unit. 'Pill boxes' and other defensive positions were constructed in the truce zone, and even, so the Japanese alleged, the refortification of Woosung was begun. The Japanese became very uneasy at these preparations, which they alleged were a breach of the spirit, if not of the words, of the 1932 Truce Agreement, and in June 1937 they appealed to the Joint Commission (comprising representatives of the friendly participating Powers, as well as of China and Japan) for a ruling. The Powers, however, who regarded the Truce Agreement as an *ad hoc* arrangement for the settlement of a long-past emergency, and who had allowed the Joint Commission to be kept alive merely because it provided a useful buffer between the Chinese and the Japanese, were not prepared to support the Japanese thesis. The neutral members of the Joint Commission refused to express any opinion on the fundamentals of the Japanese complaint, and confined themselves to an enquiry to the Chinese side whether, as a gesture of conciliation and goodwill, they would be prepared to make any voluntary declaration as regards the composition and members of the gendarmerie in the Shanghai area and/or on the question of any fortifications within the truce zone. This the Chinese refused to do, and the matter was dropped (see Peking despatch No. 696 of July 5th, 1937).[3]

11. A few days later the Lukouchiao incident occurred. Although at first the situation at Shanghai remained calm on the surface, the tension below the surface began to increase. As hostilities in the north developed and the Japanese communities evacuated from the Yangtze ports began to arrive in Shanghai these tensions became more and more acute. China and Japan were now virtually at war and the Chinese forces in the Shanghai zone took up dispositions obviously arranged beforehand for such a contingency. The gendarmerie, which had grown into a well-armed force of at least 6,000, began to draw in towards the International Settlement, to build barricades on the outlying roads and challenge passers-by. Two, and possibly more, of the Central Government's best divisions were concentrated within easy distance of Shanghai. The Japanese became increasingly uneasy. They were undoubtedly anxious to avoid trouble at Shanghai, since their whole policy was, as mentioned in paragraph 5 above, to shorten their line and concentrate their effort in the north, instead of dissipating it in costly expeditions in other parts of the country. It was partly for this reason (partly also that effective protection was out of the question) that they were evacuating the Yangtze Valley. They were not, however, prepared to follow this policy to its logical conclusion by evacuating Shanghai as well; such an evacuation would, they felt, be too great a blow to their prestige.

12. The position of the Chinese was different; while it was greatly in their interest, too, to avoid trouble in Shanghai, the industrial and financial centre of the country, they were desperate and quite determined not to yield another inch to the Japanese, whatever the cost might be; and, of course, the more the Japanese effort was dissipated, the better for China.

13. The seriousness of the situation was impressed on me when the Vice-Minister for Foreign Affairs told me on July 31st that there might be disastrous consequences if the Japanese again used the International Settlement in Shanghai as a base for hostilities, since in such an event the Chinese might not exercise the same restraint as in 1932.[4] I immediately consulted the Commander-in-chief regarding the possibility of obtaining an undertaking from the Japanese Government that neither the setlement itself nor the river fronting the settlement would be used in any way in connexion with hostilities. I was convinced, however, even then that it was the Japanese landing force which was attracting the danger to Shanghai, and I suggested that the only certain safe-guard would be the complete withdrawal of the latter, in return perhaps for an undertaking from the other Powers to make themselves responsible vis-à-vis the Japanese for the security of the settlement.

14. But it was already too late to avert the ensuing tragedy. And I may say here, in parenthesis, that, in my opinion, nothing that the Powers could have done, short of direct military action, would at any time have

---

[4] See No. 156, note 1.

changed the course of events. The train was laid and only the spark was needed. There was a false alarm when, on August 1st, a Japanese sailor disappeared from Shanghai in mysterious circumstances which suggested that he might have been murdered. After a preliminary flurry, however, the Japanese got their feelings under control and the incident was turned off with an apology and a laugh when the sailor was found a few days later swimming in the Yangtze near Chinkiang, having apparently committed some offence against discipline and then run away to avoid punishment.

15. But the final conflagration was not long delayed. On August 9th a Japanese sub-lieutenant of the landing force and a Japanese seaman acting as his chauffeur, both in uniform, were shot and killed on the Monument Road (the most outlying of the so-called extra-settlement roads in the western district of Shanghai) in the vicinity of Hungjao Aerodrome. According to the Japanese version, the officer was unarmed and was taking a motor drive in the ordinary way along a road where he had a right to be, when the car was surrounded by gendarmerie, who opened fire with machine guns and rifles. According to the Chinese version the officer was trying to force his way into the airfield, and when he was stopped by the guards he opened fire, killing some of the guards, whereupon the rest of the party returned the fire in self-defence. The Chinese version is certainly incorrect, since it does not tally with the facts as subsequently ascertained; the Japanese version is incorrect, because it is only half the truth. It can hardly be doubted that the officer was driving round by the airfield to see what information he could pick up; as much was subsequently admitted by the Japanese consul-general. Even for a British officer in uniform such a drive at such a time would have seemed hazardous; for a Japanese officer it was suicidal. Indeed, it is not an unreasonable supposition that the officer deliberately sought death as a form of *hara-kiri* to force the hands of his Government. In saying this, I must not be thought to condone the killing, still less the brutality with which it was accomplished (the officer was not only killed; he was riddled with bullets and bayonet stabs and his brains battered out); but it is a well-known characteristic of the normally placid Chinese that under the stress of excitement and passion they quickly lose their self-control and then are capable of the most horrible outrages.

16. The Mayor of Shanghai and the Japanese consul-general immediately met and agreed to settle the incident through diplomatic means. But the conditions of the problem were rapidly altering. On August 8th, that is, on the day preceding the murder, the Chinese Government, through the Waichiaopu, had informed His Majesty's Ambassador and the other diplomatic representatives in Nanking that, while the military authorities were anxious to maintain peace in and around Shanghai and entertained no intention of attacking the Japanese forces already there, they could not allow the Japanese to consolidate a position from which they could launch attacks on the Chinese forces, and that, accordingly, if the Japanese armed forces in Shanghai were

augmented, the Chinese forces would 'take the first opportunity to prevent them from disturbing peace and order in Shanghai' (see Nanking telegram No. 306 of August 8th[5]). His Majesty's Ambassador and his American, French, German and Italian colleagues, who were by now meeting in almost daily conferences, after consulting their respective Governments, addressed a joint note to the Japanese Ambassador on August 11th informing him of the above-mentioned communication and urging him to give an assurance that the Japanese authorities would do all in their power to exclude the Shanghai area from the scope of any possible hostilities. At the same time they addressed a note to the Minister for Foreign Affairs, referring to the communication which he had made to some of their number, informing him of the note which they were addressing to the Japanese Ambassador, and saying that they should welcome any additional assurances that the Chinese Government would do all in its power to exclude the Shanghai area from the scope of any possible hostilities.[6]

17. Simultaneously, however, with the despatch of these representations, the Japanese First Battle Fleet (minus battleships) appeared at Shanghai, and additional marines were landed. The situation against which the Minister for Foreign Affairs had warned us on August 8th had accordingly arisen.[7] The Japanese Consul-General at Shanghai at the same time notified the mayor that the gendarmerie forces, which were pressing the Japanese landing force at uncomfortably close quarters, must be withdrawn. He also appealed to the Joint Commission to find means to compel the Chinese to withdraw. The Japanese Counsellor of Embassy in Nanking likewise called on His Majesty's Ambassador and his colleagues to invoke their assistance in the same cause. But the Chinese were by this time in no mood to make any further concessions, and any suggestion from the Ambassadors that the gendarmerie should be withdrawn would have been very badly received, unless at the same time the suggestion was made to the Japanese that their landing forces should be withdrawn, a solution which the Japanese, in the extremely serious situation which had now arisen, were not in the least likely to consider.[8]

[5] See No. 168, note 1. [6] See No. 170.

[7] In the printed version of this despatch the Foreign Office added the following note at this point: The normal strength of the Japanese landing party was 2,000, and that was the number at the beginning of August. 300 marines at Hankow formed part of the landing party, and when Hankow was evacuated they were sent to Shanghai, arriving on the critical day of the 9th August. 1,000 men were landed from the First Battle Fleet on the 11th August (within forty-eight hours of the incident), making a total of 3,300. With reservists, the total number of Japanese under arms on land at the beginning of hostilities was probably about 5,000. On the 11th August four cruisers and about twenty destroyers of the First Battle Fleet arrived off Woosung and subsequently steamed up to Shanghai. There were also, either in Whangpoo or near Woosung, two aircraft carriers, two aircraft tenders and all the Japanese Yangtze river gunboats. Approximately 150 naval aircraft had arrived in carriers, tenders and cruisers.

[8] The Foreign Office added the following note at this point: The Commander, Shanghai Area, was reliably informed that the Japanese consul-general at Shanghai requested an

18. The Japanese had undoubtedly been caught in a dilemma. They had evacuated the whole of the Yangtze valley, and many thousands of Japanese civilians had been concentrated in Shanghai as in a city of refuge. Anxious as they might be to keep hostilities away from Shanghai, their whole China policy and recent activities in North China had aroused passions which the sight of a Japanese uniform drove to the edge of madness. Though many solutions were discussed during the ensuing weeks, in fact, the only alternatives before the Japanese were either to withdraw their armed forces from Shanghai completely or else to strengthen them sufficiently to afford adequate protection to their nationals. Unwisely, I think, they chose the latter course, and from the moment when the First Battle Fleet appeared on the scene all hope of keeping Shanghai out of the arena vanished.

19. It quickly became evident that the Chinese threat to take action in the event of reinforcements being landed was not a bluff. They immediately threw a barrage of sunken ships across the Yangtze at Kiangvin to prevent the Japanese fleet from entering the river, and another across the Whangpoo at the upper limit of the French concession to prevent access to the Chinese city of Shanghai and the Lunghwa arsenal and aerodrome; and the 87th and 88th Divisions—considered to be among the best in the Chinese army—closed in and occupied the North Railway Station and Kiangwan. Hostilities commenced with sniping and desultory firing, appropriately enough on Friday, August 13th. On the following day the Chinese launched a furious air attack on the Japanese flagship *Idzumo* and the other Japanese craft in the river. The *coup*, if skilfully executed, might well have had a paralyisng effect on the Japanese. Unfortunately, however, the inexperienced Chinese pilots caused almost no injury to their naval objectives, while, on the other hand, they dropped bombs at two of the most crowded street corners in the International Settlement, inflicting casualties which ran into four figures. These air attacks and the anti-aircraft action of the Japanese caused complete chaos. The whole of the water-front became practically untenantable; the banks closed their doors, and the British Consulate-General, situated in a particularly dangerous spot, was hastily evacuated.

20. All British subjects and other foreign nationals had been called in from the Hongkew and Yangtzepoo districts at the first sign of serious danger and the Volunteer Corps mobilised. In order, however, not to be caught in the same trap as in 1932, the council did not declare a 'state of emergency' which would have brought the joint defence scheme into operation, and once more given the Japanese the chance to say that they were merely carrying out their part in the international defence of the settlement. Indeed, the possibility was even discussed of withdrawing volunteers completely from Hongkew (the predominantly Japanese area)

assurance from the mayor of Greater Shanghai that the Japanese landing party would not be attacked. The assurance was not given. (Telegram to the War Office No. 4726 of the 7th August last).

313

so as to dissociate them as much as possible from the Japanese, and defending only that part of the settlement south the Soochow Creek. Though the proposal was dismissed as impracticable, the officers commanding the foreign defence forces announced that the area south of the creek was to be considered as a place of refuge from which the Japanese armed forces, equally with Chinese, would be excluded.

21. The avowed intention of the Chinese was to drive the Japanese forces out of Shanghai altogether before further reinforcements could be brought up, and, simultaneously with the air action, a heavy attack in overwhelming numbers was commenced on the Japanese positions all the way from the North Railway Station to the tip of the International Settlement in Yangtzepoo. The attack failed, and though it was renewed time after time in the ensuing days, the Japanese continued to hold intact, except for brief intervals, the whole of their original front. Though an offensive carried on through the streets of a city is, I believe, one of the most expensive and difficult forms of warfare, nevertheless, the Chinese, with the overwhelming forces at their command, should have been able to press it home, and their failure to do so seems to me a fair indication of the immense disparity between the Chinese and Japanese military machines.

22. The hostilities spread round to the Pootung shore of the Whangpoo, and Nantao, on the further side of the French Concession, became a target for naval and air bombardment. As the scope of the hostilities spread, the position of the foreign communities became more precarious. There was already one British battalion in Shanghai. Immediately the gravity of the situation was realised Brigadier Telfer-Smollett asked for two more battalions. The first of these arrived from Hong Kong on August 17th and the second on August 18th. The French also brought up reinforcements from Indo-China, the Italians landed a company of marines, and the Americans as a first instalment increased their landing force by about the same number, the 4th Regiment of Marines, 1,200 strong, being at the same time ordered over from San Diego.

23. Meanwhile the evacuation of women and children of all nationalities had commenced. So far as the British nationals were concerned, evacuation, while strongly recommended, was kept on a voluntary basis; the appalling effect of the reckless use of aircraft, and in particular of the bombs which fell in Nanking Road and the French Concession on August 14th, were so demoralising, however, that little other inducement was required, and in the event 3,391 British women and children, representing 85 per cent. of all British women and children in Shanghai, were evacuated.

24. As in 1932, the Japanese navy found that it had taken on more than it could manage and the army had to come to the rescue. On August 23rd the first portion of the Japanese Expeditionary Force reached Woosung and covering forces supported by warships managed to establish themselves ashore both at Woosung and further up the Yangtze at Liuho. The

Chinese appear to have put up a stubborn resistance and there were large casualties on both sides. The Japanese at this time voiced the somewhat optimistic estimate that they would have cleared the Shanghai area of Chinese troops in three to four weeks' time. They possibly counted on the Chinese forces cracking. If so, they were mistaken, for up to the present the Chinese show no sign whatever of weakening, and are making the Japanese pay dearly for every yard they gain. The Chinese were, however, compelled to abandon the attempt to force the Japanese out of the International Settlement. As the Japanese Expeditionary Force landed at Woosung and Liuho, the Chinese forces opposite the settlement withdrew to defensive positions a few hundred yards in the rear. This change in tactics brought great relief to the much tried foreign community, and the machinery of trade began slowly to turn again.

25. Though the Shanghai hostilities received all the limelight, and gradually absorbed more and more of Japan's effort, this was merely casual and accidental. For the Japanese, as I have already mentioned, the first strategic objective after their occupation of the Peking and Tientsin area was the control of the Peking-Suiyuan Railway. They began their drive along this line on the 2nd August by an attack on the Chinese positions in the Nankow Pass. The Chinese forces (which included Central Government divisions) resisted strongly, but were out-manœuvred, and by the end of the month the Japanese were in control of Nankow, Kalgan and the whole of South Chahar, with the Chinese in full retreat towards Tatung. It seems that the regular Japanese forces received considerable assistance from Mongolian irregulars, whose co-operation was given in return for a promise of Japanese support for Inner Mongolian independence. Since the occupation of Kalgan, reports from this area have been very meagre and, being entirely from Japanese sources, have to be accepted with caution, but it seems fairly well established that the formation of a new puppet State embracing the whole of Chahar south of the Great Wall is under way. The Japanese penetration into the heart of Inner Mongolia can hardly fail to be disturbing to the Soviet Government, whose reactions will be awaited with interest.

26. The Chinese air attack on the Japanese naval unit in the Whangpoo on August 14th was the signal for a comprehensive and searching bombing by Japanese aircraft of Chinese aerodromes as far west as Hankow and Nanchang and as far south as Canton. At first the attacks were carried out by large machines from Formosa, flying without any protection. The results were disastrous for the Japanese, since the Chinese met the machines in the air and brought down a large proportion of them. Subsequent raids were made by carrier-borne planes flying at a great height, which, though more successful in avoiding disaster, seemed to produce little damage to military targets. Nanking was subjected to a number of raids which appeared to be directed principally against military objectives, although considerable damage was done to the Central University, and some bombs were dropped in a night raid on a poor

315

residential quarter inflicting a large number of casualties. It may, however, be said that contrary to general expectation no raid has yet been made on Nanking with the primary purpose of demoralising the Government and destroying the nerve centres of the Administration. I hesitate to say what the effect of systematic and ruthless attack for that purpose might be. The Government have let it be known that they will remain in Nanking so long as it is physically possible to carry on the administration from here, and from present appearances have every intention of doing so. All valuable archives have been moved elsewhere and Government offices, such as the Ministries for Foreign Affairs and Communications, which form excellent targets from the air, are occupied only by skeleton staffs, the work of the departments being carried on in private houses scattered in different parts of the town. Three-quarters of the Chinese population has migrated elsewhere; the rest seem disposed to face what may come. A liberal number of dugouts has been prepared by the municipality and the system of air-raid alarms and 'blacking-out' works with the greatest effectiveness.

27. As soon as the Japanese realised that hostilities were likely to be prolonged, they began casting about for some means of cutting off China's supply of arms, for which she is almost entirely dependent on imports from abroad. The Chinese Government, who were only too well aware of their vulnerability in this respect, had, almost immediately after the trouble began, diverted all shipments to Hong Kong whence they could carry them by water, or, if the Japanese blockaded the river, by rail, to Canton and thence northward by the Canton-Hankow Railway. For this the co-operation of the Hong Kong authorities was vital; indeed, it may be said that it was for the Chinese a matter of life or death that this route should be kept open and that they should be able to continue to use Hong Kong as an entrepôt.

28. The Japanese made their first move in the matter of cutting off China's supplies of war materials on August 25th when the admiral commanding the Third Fleet announced that navigation on the lower Yangtse and along the Central China coast from (and including) Shanghai to a point south of Swatow was closed to Chinese shipping as from 6 p.m. on that date.[9] In a statement to the press Dr. Jimpei Shinobu, a professor of international law acting as legal adviser to the Japanese Third Fleet, described this as a 'pacific' or 'peace-time' blockade for which he said there was precedent in the Greek war of 1827, a precedent which had been recognised by international jurists in 1887, and followed by the Allies when they had banned native shipping along the coast of Montenegro in 1917. Chinese vessels operating in the forbidden zone would, he explained, be detained regardless of whether or not they were carrying munitions.[10] Since, however, this was not a war-time blockade foreign

[9] See No. 207.
[10] The Foreign Office added the following note at this point: The Ministry of Marine nevertheless informed the United States naval attaché in Tokyo on the 27th August, *inter*

vessels could not be seized, or compelled to change their course, even if they were carrying arms to China, but they were liable to be boarded by Japanese naval officers for the purpose of verifying their nationality [in] case of doubt. 'However,' he added, 'we can take such effective measures as exercising the privilege of pre-emption towards foreign bottoms found to be carrying cargo which in war-time would constitute contraband.'

29. Further light was thrown on this statement by a communication made by the Vice-Minister for Foreign Affairs in Tokyo to the Counsellor of the French Embassy on August 31st (and issued to the press in Shanghai on September 1st) to the following effect:

'Although the measures which had been announced by Admiral Yoshisawa on the 25th August did not apply to arms and ammunition carried by vessels of third Powers, Chinese ships had been flying foreign flags, and so the Japanese navy were forced to inspect suspects in order to identify their nationality. To avoid misunderstandings the Japanese would find it convenient to have advance notice of ships of third Powers entering the prescribed area, viz., their names, captains and 'matters concerning capital invested in them.' The measures were designed to prompt China's reconsideration and bring about a speedy settlement. If China received large supplies of arms and ammunition from abroad her antagonism to Japan would be strengthened and the conflict prolonged and intensified. The Japanese Government hoped, therefore, that the Governments of third Powers would refrain as far as possible from doing anything likely to encourage China in this direction. And finally, the Japanese Government did not contemplate for the time being any action to prevent the importation of arms and ammunition into China by foreign vessels, but future developments might compel them to devise more effective and suitable measures to stop all importation of arms and ammunition into China' (see telegram from Tokyo to the Foreign Office No. 333 of the 31st August[11]).

30. On September 5th the embargo zone was extended to cover the whole Chinese coastline from Chinwangtao in the north to the Indo-China frontier in the south, with the exception of Tsingtao and 'leased territories of third Powers.' In making this announcement the Japanese Government again declared that they would respect the 'peaceful commerce of third Powers,' with which they had no intention of interfering. The only points on the Chinese coast to which the embargo does not extend are, accordingly, Tsingtao, Hong Kong, Macao and Kwangchowan. The exclusion of Tsingtao is at first sight somewhat surprising; the Japanese explain that it is due to their desire at any cost to

alia, that only troops and armament stores, but not normal cargoes, would be removed from Chinese ships and that Chinese-registered ships would not be confiscated (Tokyo telegram No. 321 of the 27th August last).

[11] Not printed: cf. No. 220.

avoid any cause of friction which might lead to hostilities in that area; in any case it is of no practical importance.

31. On September 1st the Aide-de-Camp to the Minister of Marine informed the naval attaché to His Majesty's Embassy in Tokyo that Japan was concerned over the fact that Hong Kong was being used as an entrepôt for the import of munitions for the Chinese, and he indicated that the object of the air raid which had taken place at Canton on the preceding day was to interrupt the transportation northwards of the munitions which were known to have already arrived in Hong Kong. The extension of the embargo zone cut off one line of entry of such arms into China, namely, carriage in Chinese vessels from Hong Kong to Canton; it remains now for Japan to devise means of cutting off the other lines, namely, carriage in foreign steamers or by rail.

32. There this matter rests for the moment. Chinese shipping in the prohibited area has been brought to a complete standstill. In regard to foreign shipping, all that has yet happened as a result of the embargo is that a number of vessels have been stopped by signal from Japanese warships, but allowed to proceed after signalling their name, ports of origin and destination and that they were not on charter. In reply to enquiries from British shipping companies as to the position of British merchant vessels, the Commander-in-chief has informed them that the question is under consideration and that meanwhile British ships should obey all orders received from Japanese warships, reporting on the circumstances afterwards.

33. The Chinese Government and educated classes are, as was pointed out in my telegram No. 417 of September 4th,[3] awaiting with the keenest anxiety the reaction of His Majesty's Government to the Japanese manœuvres to prevent arms reaching China via Hong Kong. They feel that, as co-signatories with them of the Kellogg Pact and other agreements which Japan is trampling underfoot, we owe them something more than benevolent neutrality in what is for them a life or death struggle against a powerful aggressor. Japan's suggestion that the neutral Powers should help her to shorten the hostilities by cutting off China's supply of arms has called forth particularly cynical comment.

34. On August 21st a Treaty of Non-Aggression was concluded at Nanking between the Chinese and Soviet Governments.[12] The treaty follows the usual formula for such pacts. The high contracting parties, after expressing their desire to strengthen the friendly relations existing between them and to confirm and define the obligations mutually undertaken under the Paris Pact of 1928, undertake to refrain from any aggression against each other (article 1), or, in the event of one party being attacked by one or more third Powers, from affording assistance, direct or indirect, to such attacking Powers (article 2), and it is stated that the present treaty is not to be interpreted in such a way as to affect or

[12] See Nos. 200, 217, and 237.

modify existing international obligations of the parties (article 3). The treaty is valid for five years and then for periods of two years, subject to six months' notice of denunciation (article 4).

35. In informing the American and French Ambassadors and myself (in the absence of His Majesty's Ambassador) officially of the conclusion of the pact, the Minister for Foreign Affairs outlined briefly the history of the negotiations. The Sino-Soviet Agreement of May 31st, 1924, had envisaged both a commercial treaty and a pact of non-aggression, but for one reason and another, though numerous attempts had been made, the discussions had always broken down until the present, and even now it had been found impossible to conclude a commercial treaty. He added that the pact was purely negative in character, that it partly fulfilled China's fixed purpose of living in peace with her neighbours and that she was quite ready to make a similar pact with Japan. He particularly emphasised that the conclusion of the pact did not signify any abandonment on the part of China of her fixed policy of anti-communism. In this connexion he pointed out that the third clause of the pact kept alive article 6 of the Sino-Soviet Agreement of 1924. The Minister for Foreign Affairs asserted in the most positive manner that there were no secret clauses attached to the pact. General Chiang Kai-shek had given a similar assurance to His Majesty's Ambassador a few days earlier. The advantages which the Chinese Government expected to obtain from the conclusion of the pact at this time were, it seemed, twofold: moral, in that it would act as a tonic for the Chinese and a warning to the Japanese; and practical, in that it would prevent Russia from withdrawing troops from the Manchurian frontier and thereby releasing Japanese troops for action against China.

36. No clear indication has yet appeared as to the nature of the final Japanese plans for North China, and it seemed likely that the Japanese have as yet no very clear ideas on the object themselves. They have been content to leave the actual details of local administration for the time being in the hands of the Chinese subject to the over-riding demands of their own military control. At the beginning of August 'Peace Preservation Associations' were set up in Peking and Tientsin, consisting of members of the local gentry and commercial and cultural organisations. These associations were theoretically in charge of civic affairs in conjunction with the mayor, but they also acted as buffers between the Chinese population and the Japanese invaders. In Peking the chairman of the Peace Preservation Association was a venerable ex-official of Yuan Shih-kai's régime, General Chiang Chao-tsung, who seems to have accepted the position out of a sense of public duty rather than out of any goodwill towards the Japanese.

37. On August 6th General Chang Tzu-chung (who had been nominated acting Mayor of Peking and acting Chairman of the Hopei-Chahar Council by General Sung Che-yuan, before the latter's hasty departure— see paragraph 29 of the despatch under reference) resigned both these

posts, much to the indignation of the Japanese military authorities, who seemed to anticipate some difficulty in finding a successor. However, after a lapse of a fortnight, General Chiang Chao-tsung assumed the post of mayor, the appointment being made by the Peace Preservation Association, but no new appointment was made to the Hopei-Chahar Council, which in consequence quietly died. Though it was pretended that the council was in temporary abeyance rather than abolished, the transfer of its functions to the mayor and the local Peace Preservation Association seemed a necessary preliminary to the formation of an 'autonomous' Government, in support of which popular demonstrations of a now familiar type were already being staged. By the dual fiction that the council dissolved of its own accord and that the Peace Preservation Association is the spontaneous creation of the people, the Japanese will be able to disclaim any hand in the establishment of the 'autonomous' Government when the time comes to bring it into existence.

38. Though it is not strictly germane to the subject matter of this despatch, I may perhaps be excused for making a passing reference to the wounding of His Majesty's Ambassador. Mr. Hall-Patch, the financial adviser to this Embassy, who had been in Shanghai during the first difficult days of the fighting in and around the International Settlement, came to Nanking by road on the 24th August in company with Colonel Lovat-Fraser, the military attaché. Colonel Lovat-Fraser had done the same journey in the reverse direction a few days earlier. Mr. Hall-Patch informed His Majesty's Ambassador that the British community in Shanghai were much discouraged, and that a visit from the Ambassador would be welcome, as giving them moral support. He also expressed the view that the Japanese Ambassador, who was then in Shanghai, was very uneasy at the way in which the situation was developing, and that some good might come of an informal meeting and discussion between the two Ambassadors. It was under the influence of these considerations that His Majesty's Ambassador decided to take what seemed at that time to be the very slight risk involved in making the journey to Shanghai by road— which was, indeed, then the sole practical line of communication, since the river had already been closed, and the railway was subject to constant attacks from the air, trains running only intermittently, and making a detour via Soochow and Kashing. It happened, however, that on that day the Japanese had received intelligence that General Chiang Kai-shek was on the road (as, indeed, he was) and the attack on the Ambassador's car was one of many attacks which were made along the roads between Nanking and Shanghai on that day with the intention of killing the Generalissimo.

I have, &c.,
(In the absence of the Ambassador),
B. E. F. Gage

No. 241

Foreign Office[1] to Mr. Mallet (Washington)

No. 363 Telegraphic [F 6357/9/10]

FOREIGN OFFICE, *September 10, 1937, 6 p.m.*

Your telegram No. 261.[2]

Chinese Ambassador informed Sir A. Cadogan on the 7th September that, as Chinese delegate to the League of Nations, he had received instructions from his Government to invoke Article 17 of the Covenant. He gave the impression that he did not himself entirely approve of these instructions and was fully aware that nothing effective could be done at Geneva. He supposed that pressure was being brought to bear on the Government in Nanking to leave nothing untried in an attempt to obtain intervention or at least an amelioration of the Chinese position. In any case, public discussion at Geneva would afford the Chinese delegates a good platform from which to expound Chinese case.[3]

2. U.S. Chargé d'Affaires was informed of this yesterday.[4] He agreed that consequence of this might be application of American Neutrality Act.[5] He had not heard of Chinese Government's intention, but promised to inform U.S. delegate to Geneva, advising him to keep in close touch with British delegation.[6]

Repeated to Tokyo, Nanking and Peking.

[1] Mr. Eden flew to Paris on the afternoon of September 9, en route for Geneva: see Volume XIX, No. 147, note 1.

[2] Not kept in F.O. archives. It apparently said that Mr. Leland Harrison, U.S. Minister at Berne, would be available for contact with the U.K. delegation at Geneva regarding discussion of the Far Eastern situation. See *F.R.U.S.*, 1937, vol. iv, pp. 9–10.

[3] The Chinese case had already been stated by Mr. Hoo Chi-tsai, Director of the Permanent Bureau of the Chinese delegation at Geneva, in a communication of August 30 to the Secretary General of the League of Nations, M. Avenol. It gave the Chinese Government's account of the development of the Sino-Japanese dispute since the Lukouchiao incident: see *L/N.O.J., July-December 1937*, pp. 653–7.

[4] See *F.R.U.S., op. cit.*, pp. 454–5.   [5] See Volume XVIII, Nos. 88, 332, and 333.

[6] In a letter of September 12 from Dr. Wellington Koo to M. Avenol, the Chinese Government formally requested the League of Nations 'to take cognisance of the fact that Japan has invaded China'. The letter concluded: 'In the name of my Government, I hereby invoke the application of Articles 10, 11, and 17 of the Covenant and appeal to the Council to advise upon such means and take such actions as may be appropriate and necessary for the situation under the said articles.' See *L/N.O.J., ibid.*, p. 1100. The Council agreed on September 14 to include the Chinese Government's appeal on the agenda for the current session (*ibid.*, p. 887).

No. 242

Mr. C. A. Edmond[1] (Geneva) to Foreign Office
(Received September 15, 9.30 a.m.)

No. 40 Telegraphic [F 6505/9/10]

GENEVA, *September 15, 1937, 12.25 a.m.*

Following from the Secretary of State:

I had a long conversation with Chinese Ambassador this morning. In view of its outcome and of Chinese appeal to the League in which article 10, article 11 and article 17 are mentioned[2] I thought it desirable to arrange a meeting this evening with French Foreign Minister, Chinese representatives and Secretary General.

Monsieur Delbos, Monsieur Avenol and I were unanimous in suggesting to Chinese representatives that they should not insist on Council proceeding under article 17 as this would give the impression that they aimed at immediate application of article 16 which they admitted was not their intention but that they should agree to Council referring matter to Advisory Committee set up by the Assembly in 1933.[3] Chinese representatives seemed to appreciate the force of arguments used and said that while they could not pledge their government they thought the latter would concur. I suggested further to Mr. Koo, Chinese first delegate, that in his speech before the Assembly he should mention the possibility of the matter being referred to Advisory Committee in order to obviate any future criticism that such a procedure had been forced on the Chinese Government. This also Mr. Koo promised to consider.

We pointed out that the United States was already member of Advisory Committee. There was therefore greater likelihood of the United States Government co-operating with that body than with the Council. We all attached the greatest importance to co-operation of that government.

I am convinced that this meeting during which we frankly surveyed the problems confronting us and League's manifest limitations for dealing with them has been most useful. There is good reason to hope that Chinese who emphasised their earnest desire to co-operate with His Majesty's Government and French Government will now take no action to precipitate declaration of state of war by Japan which would be against their own interest.

---

[1] H.M. Consul at Geneva. [2] See No. 241, note 6.

[3] The Advisory Committee on the Sino-Japanese dispute was set up under the League Assembly resolution of February 24, 1933, and held its first meeting on March 15, 1933. Its membership was basically the same as that of the Committee of Nineteen appointed by the Assembly in March 1932: see Volume XI, No. 462.

No. 243

Sir R. Craigie (Tokyo) to Foreign Office (Received September 15, 3 p.m.)

No. 392 Telegraphic [F 6540/9/10]

Confidential   TOKYO, *September 15, 1937, 7.50 p.m.*

In the course of an interview today Minister for Foreign Affairs enquired whether I had any news as to the attitude of the Chinese Government. I replied that I had no direct news but understood from journalistic sources that any genuine offer of reasonable peace terms would be likely to be well received. His Excellency then stated that Japanese Government had no intention of putting forward terms which were unreasonable and in particular would make no territorial demands; they were still anxious to find some way of putting Sino-Japanese relations on a permanent friendly footing. Asked if Japan's terms would be likely to remain reasonable even if conflict continued for some months His Excellency said he feared not though he personally considered it would be a mistake to seek to impose harsh terms on China. He added that according to his information Russian arms and munitions were being supplied to Chinese forces but as the bulk of these supplies were going to Communist armies the Nanking Government felt some resentment.

Minister for Foreign Affairs asked that our conversation should be regarded as entirely confidential. If however Chinese Government make any enquiries as to attitude of Japanese Government, they might I suggest be informed that we learn from a good source that Japanese Government are still in the mood to make peace on reasonable terms.[1]

I was careful not to probe any further at this stage because any premature effort to 'put our oar in' is likely to do more harm than good. When the proper time comes however I believe Japanese Government are likely to be more responsive to suggestions from His Majesty's Government than from any other quarter. His Excellency was very insistent on his desire to resume the Anglo-Japanese discussions as soon as possible after liquidation of present incident.[2]

Repeated to Nanking.

[1] The Foreign Office was inclined to dismiss Mr. Hirota's message as mostly 'just propaganda to prove the essential reasonableness of Japan'. Sir A. Cadogan wrote on September 17: 'I am afraid that what the M.F.A. says at the present juncture means nothing. This—to me—is borne out by his assurance that Japan will "make no territorial demands".'

[2] Mr. Ronald commented on this sentence on September 16: 'I hope that the "incident" referred to . . . is the "China incident" not the "Knatchbull-Hugessen incident", for there can be no question of resuming the Yoshida conversations before peace is made with China.'

No. 244

Foreign Office to Sir R. Craigie (Tokyo)

No. 321 Telegraphic [F 6609/5727/10]

Immediate   FOREIGN OFFICE, *September 17, 1937, 2.40 p.m.*

Your telegrams Nos. 383, 384, 385 and 386.[1]

Sir A. Cadogan, at the request of the Japanese Embassy here, received Mr. Sugimura, Japanese Ambassador at Paris, yesterday afternoon. In a letter received from H.M. Chargé d'Affaires in Paris,[2] it was explained that Mr. Sugimura had come to London at the urgent request of Mr. Yoshida for consultation as to the best means of producing some early improvement in Anglo-Japanese relations, which have so markedly deteriorated during the last three months.

2. Mr. Sugimura said he thought the first essential for an ultimate peaceful settlement was that Tokyo should remain on good terms with and retain the confidence of London, Washington and Paris. It was therefore absolutely necessary to obtain a settlement of the affair of the shooting of Sir H. Knatchbull-Hugessen. He had given this much thought, but he feared that he, even in conjunction with Mr. Yoshida, could exercise very little influence in Tokyo. It occurred to him that something might be done through Prince Chichibu,[3] who was inclined to adopt the proposal he had made to him that H[is] I[mperial] H[ighness] should telegraph to the Emperor suggesting that to the usual telegram of thanks to be sent when H[is] I[mperial] H[ighness] leaves the country an expression of regret should be added at the accident to Sir H. Knatchbull-Hugessen. Mr. Sugimura admitted at once that this would not be a 'solution juridique', but he felt that it would have a great *moral* effect and might facilitate a solution.

3. Sir A. Cadogan expressed appreciation of Mr. Sugimura's efforts and goodwill, and said he hoped that this might make a solution easier. He

---

[1] In these telegrams of September 14 Sir R. Craigie reported details of the investigations carried out by the Japanese authorities into the wounding of Sir H. Knatchbull-Hugessen. It was admitted that Japanese planes had been bombing cars on the road some ten miles from the spot where the attack on the Ambassador was supposed to have occurred, but the Japanese insisted that they could not comply with the request for an apology unless agreement was reached as to the exact location of the incident. In telegram No. 386 Sir R. Craigie commented that he was 'satisfied that Japanese representatives have put all their cards on the table'.

[2] A copy of this letter from Mr. H. Lloyd Thomas to Sir A. Cadogan is also filed at F 6609/5727/10. Mr. Lloyd Thomas reported that according to Mr. Sugimura, Mr. Yoshida had begged him to come to London to help him, and Mr. Sugimura felt that he 'would like to go if he thought that he could be of any assistance in arriving at a settlement as he had many friends like you [i.e. Sir A. Cadogan] in London and he felt frankly that Yoshida was completely at sea and without personal contacts or real understanding of British mentality'.

[3] According to Mr. Lloyd Thomas's letter Prince Chichibu was due to arrive in London on September 15 or 16 for a three day visit.

pointed out the difference between 'regret', even coming from the highest quarter, and an admission of responsibility. He took the opportunity to give Mr. Sugimura the gist of your recent conversations with the Vice-Ministers, pointing out that the Japanese now admitted that their machines *were* machine-gunning and bombing the road, that two of them in fact did so attack two cars on that day and that this attack was delivered only a few minutes and a few miles from the time and place indicated by the Military Attaché. His Majesty's Government had never sought to suggest that the attack was deliberately made on the Ambassador: it was plain that it was an accident. Seeing what the Japanese now admitted as regards their aeroplanes' activities, was it so difficult, he asked, for them to admit that they were responsible for the accident? Mr. Sugimura clearly thought the Japanese ought to accept responsibility and do it at once. I have no idea whether he will telegraph any representations to his Government.

Repeated to Geneva No. 34 L.N., to Nanking No. 303, Commander in Chief unnumbered.

No. 245

Sir R. Craigie (Tokyo) to Foreign Office
(Received September 17, 3.30 p.m.)

No. 398 Telegraphic [F 6619/9/10]

Secret   TOKYO, *September 17, 1937, 7.30 p.m.*

1. I learn from an absolutely reliable source that Japanese terms for a settlement now are as follows:[1]

(a) Northern provinces of China: (1) establishment of a neutral zone (from which both Japanese troops and troops of Central Chinese Government would be excluded) to be policed by Peace Preservation Corps, zone to extend to south of Peking-Tientsin; (2) undertaking by Nanking that régime in North China which would be subject to Nanking would not be unfriendly to Japan and that in particular 'war lords' unfriendly to Japan would be eliminated; (3) Japan to receive certain economic concessions but to ask for no exclusive rights and to respect in full the interests of third parties without whose co-operation it is recognised that full economic development of China is impossible.

(b) Settlement of outstanding Sino-Japanese questions. By this is meant in particular settlement of Manchurian question. Chinese recognition of Manchukuo would not be insisted upon but Chinese Government would be expected to undertake in most definite terms to abstain from making further difficulties for Japan in Manchukuo.

[1] Cf. No. 243.

325

(c) Future of Sino-Japanese relations. Japanese Government would wish the most express undertakings to be forthcoming that in future China would meet halfway any genuine Japanese attempt to put Sino-Japanese relations on a new and friendly footing. In particular Japanese Government would wish for undertaking that Nanking Government would resist spread of communism in China. They would like to see China join anti-communist pact but realise that this may not be possible in present circumstances.

(It will be noted that no demands are being made in regard to Shanghai though for future protection of Settlement Japanese Government think there would be advantage in establishing a neutral zone there also.)

2. While the above outline[2] may be taken as representing majority view in Cabinet, position is extremely delicate because army are opposed to any premature opening of negotiations and wish first to secure a decisive success in the field. More moderate statesmen on the other hand realize folly of prolonging present conflict, of which they have never been in favour. But they have to proceed with utmost caution.

3. What I think would be appreciated here is any assistance which His Majesty's Government may feel disposed to give in ascertaining probable attitude of Chinese Government towards settlement on lines indicated without disclosing source of information. In view of position here vis-à-vis the military it will be appreciated that peace party can make little progress until they receive reliable information as to dispositions of Chinese Government. It is of course true that direct diplomatic relations still exist with China but it appears that this channel is not proving satisfactory for such soundings and I doubt whether anything short of direct approach to Chiang Kai-shek would serve a useful purpose.

4. I presume that if His Majesty's Government desired to take any action at all they would merely authorise Mr. Howe to say he has heard from a very reliable source that paragraphs 1(a), (b) and (c) above represent basis on which Japanese Government would be prepared to negotiate and that he thinks it well to let Chinese Government know, without expressing any opinion on merits of these terms. He would no doubt be able to gather Chinese reaction without actually asking for any expression of opinion.

5. Even this action you will no doubt wish to reserve until His Majesty's Government have received full satisfaction in regard to wounding of Sir H. Knatchbull-Hugessen.[3]

[2] Further comments on the Japanese terms from the 'reliable source' were transmitted in Tokyo telegram No. 440 of September 25, not printed.
[3] In a minute of September 20 Sir A. Cadogan expressed agreement with the last paragraph of this telegram, and added: 'Ultimately, when the moment comes, I shouldn't mind mediating to this extent. If we are careful, we ought to be able to avoid being inconveniently involved, and there is this advantage, that if terms or proposals are passed through us we can bear witness to what they *are*, whereas if China and Japan negotiate direct there is no knowing how much shuffling and dodging takes place. But of course that

is where we might become inconveniently involved, and if ever the time comes for passing on actual proposals the Japanese—or Chinese—would have to trust us sufficiently to give us their point of view in writing. Which they would hate doing!'

No. 246

Mr. Edmond (Geneva) to Foreign Office
(Received September 17, 9.30 p.m.)

No. 51 Telegraphic [F 6634/9/10]

Immediate   GENEVA, *September 17, 1937, 8 p.m.*

Following from Secretary of State:
My telegram No. 40.[1]
I understand from Mr. Koo that Chinese delegation have instructions to try to obtain something on the following lines from the Advisory Committee.

1. A declaration of Japanese aggression and a condemnation of inhuman methods of warfare adopted by the Japanese.

2. A refusal to supply war material and credit to Japan. Further if possible a refusal to supply certain raw materials such as wool, cotton, oil, iron and other minerals and a refusal to accept Japanese exports.

3. Facilities for purchase and delivery of arms to China together with credit arrangements and general financial assistance.

As regards (1) Mr. Koo made it clear that what was required was a moral if not actually a legal basis for co-ordinated action on lines of points (2) and (3). It was pointed out to Mr. Koo that a declaration of aggression would probably be a matter of considerable difficulty and might not be to the advantage of China as it would almost certainly entail application of neutrality legislation by the President of the United States of America. To this Mr. Koo replied that the United States Government had already gone a considerable distance towards application of neutrality legislation in forbidding government owned ships to carry war material to the Far East and warning to privately owned ships that they did so at their own risk. It was also represented to Mr. Koo that Advisory Committee could hardly declare Japan to be an aggressor without an enquiry. This might well take a considerable time. Mr. Koo said that he appreciated this but public opinion in China and he thought throughout the greater part of the world would demand a clear expression of opinion on the subject by the Advisory Committee basing itself on the Covenant of the League, Kellogg Pact and Nine Power Treaty. The Chinese Government were bound to press for a declaration of aggression in order to justify the attitude which they had maintained from the beginning in the face of Japanese action.

As regards (2) a refusal of arms and credits to Japan was really a

[1] No. 242.

327

minimum and the Chinese Government hoped they would be able to obtain its extension to raw materials mentioned and that a boycott of Japanese exports could be arranged.

As regards (3) Mr. Koo made it clear that facilities for delivery of arms to China should include transit through Hongkong.

No. 247

Mr. Affleck (Tientsin) to Foreign Office (Received September 17, 11 p.m.)

No. 23 Telegraphic: by wireless [F 6655/220/10]

TIENTSIN, *September 17, 1937*

Addressed to Nanking No. 49 of September 17th.

My telegram No. 37 to Nanking repeated to Foreign Office telegram No. 14, Peking telegram No. 95, Tokyo Financial Adviser telegram No. 12.[1]

Following is text of telegram sent by Myers to Inspector General of Customs September 16th begins:

Confidential.

Your telegram No. 613.[2]

Japanese authorities will come to definite terms but only on one condition namely that our revenue is deposited with Yokohama Specie Bank. Their requirement is that such deposits shall remain untouched except for what is required to meet foreign loan quota and local current expenses until present situation is liquidated. They are prepared through Consul General to give a written guarantee that these moneys quartered with Yokohama Specie Bank will not be seized and ultimate disposal will be arranged together with settlement of present incident. They require an undertaking that revenue moneys in Hongkong & Shanghai Bank and secured . . .[3] revenue in Central Bank of China will not be remitted except as part of foregoing loan quota. In all other respects with common sense give and take on both sides I and Japanese authorities find it possible to work harmoniously. Our general regulations are respected and I have every reason to believe that from now on we may expect support without interference and the complete check of the smuggling which has arisen through existing abnormal conditions provided I am put in a position to agree to one outstanding condition. Strongly recommend you give me your *personal* authority to . . .[3] currency question to a final settlement on lines indicated also suggest for time being you do not insist upon any quota remittance and leave outstanding moneys here in suspense. Apart from service integrity, our banking with Yokohama Specie Bank will help to solve local currency problem. Large quantities of Japanese imported

[1] Not kept in F.O. archives.   [2] Not traced in F.O. archives: cf. Nos. 222, 223, and 229.
[3] The text was here uncertain.

credits not necessarily of Japanese origin are frozen as Japanese merchant accounts are all in yen and insufficient standard dollars are available to meet our demands. Under proposed arrangement merchants can come to a settlement with Yokohama Specie Bank and probably there will be a gradual general movement of cargo and legal tender. Yokohama Specie Bank will invariably credit us with standard dollars. Sincerely hope you will agree to this suggestion as no other is acceptable to Japanese who are now impatient for a settlement. Post Office and Salt Gabelle have already come to settlement on comparatively similar lines. Ends. I agree to suggestions made by Mr. Myers.

No. 248

Foreign Office to Sir R. Craigie (Tokyo)

No. 324 Telegraphic [F 6637/5727/10]

Immediate   FOREIGN OFFICE, September 18, 1937, 5.20 p.m.

Nanking telegram to the Foreign Office No. 453.[1]

It appears to me[2] that it will never be possible to reconcile the two accounts in all details. As I pointed out to Mr. Sugimura,[3] however, the Japanese have now admitted that their machines *were* machine-gunning and bombing the road along which the Ambassador must have travelled, that two of them in fact did so attack two cars on that day, and this attack was delivered only a few minutes and a few miles from the time and place indicated by the Military Attaché. Can you not persuade Japanese Government to admit that by accident these machines must have attacked car in which Ambassador was travelling? His Majesty's Government have never suggested that the attack was deliberately made on the Ambassador, and naturally will take no exception if the Japanese reply brings out the accidental character of the occurrence so far as the wounding of the Ambassador is concerned, though they must admit responsibility for having made a deliberate attack on a motor-car. Time is getting on and His Majesty's Government, like the Japanese Government, feel that it is essential to reach a settlement at the earliest possible moment. You should therefore, in the interests of Anglo-Japanese relations press for a very early reply.[4]

[1] This telegram of September 17 forwarded the comments of the Military Attaché on Tokyo telegrams Nos. 383–6: see No. 244, note 1. Major Lovat-Fraser stated that the account given by the Japanese of the 'activities of two Japanese planes in vicinity of Taitsang and Kiating in no way agrees with what happened when the Ambassador's car was attacked', and went on to refute the Japanese account on other points of detail.

[2] This telegram was initialled by Sir A. Cadogan.   [3] See No. 244.

[4] In a letter to his sister Ida of September 19, preserved in his private papers, Mr. Chamberlain wrote: 'I feel rather more hopeful about the Japanese reply to our note about the Ambassador. Their enquiry clearly shows that 2 Japanese planes machine gunned and

bombed two cars "camouflaged with grass" at a place about 10 miles away from the scene of the attack on the Ambassador at about the same time [cf. No. 244, note 1], and the discrepancy is thus reduced so much as to amount practically to admission. Whether they dare to admit responsibility publicly remains to be seen, but I hope they may at least be prepared to reply in such a way that we may close the incident. I am most reluctant to withdraw our Ambassador which would leave us with the problem of how to get him back again.'

No. 249

Mr. Edmond (Geneva) to Foreign Office
(Received September 18, 10.15 p.m.)

No. 57 Telegraphic [F 6640/9/10]

GENEVA, *September 18, 1937, 8.15 p.m.*

Following from Secretary of State:

My telegram No. 51.[1]

I discussed last night with M. Delbos desires of Chinese Delegation as set forth in my telegram under reference. M. Delbos' first reaction was that the Chinese were asking Advisory Committee to do exactly what they would have proposed to the Council under articles 17 and 16 of the Covenant. Such proposals were far outside purview of Advisory Committee. It was however in deference to representations of United Kingdom and the French Delegations that the Chinese Delegation had agreed to reference to the Advisory Committee. It would not be possible therefore to interpret the powers of that Committee too narrowly but M. Delbos thought that the Chinese would probably be satisfied with about 20% of what they demanded.

We discussed possibility of refusing credits to Japan and considered that some tacit arrangement might be made to this end.

We discussed export of arms to China and agreed that this should be continued until the war should actually be declared when a meeting of the Council would presumably be called.

We agreed that in general our countries should be prepared to go as far as United States but not further.

First meeting of the Advisory Committee will probably be on Tuesday next.[2]

[1] No. 246. [2] i.e. September 21: see No. 253, note 2 below.

No. 250

Sir R. Craigie (Tokyo) to Foreign Office
(Received September 20, 11.10 a.m.)

No. 410 Telegraphic [F 6685/5727/10]

Immediate   TOKYO, September 20, 1937, 3 p.m.

Your telegram No. 324[1] crossed my telegram No. 405[2] from which it will be seen that I have already urged immediate action in the sense you desire.

I have had further private discussion today with two Vice-Ministers on draft of proposed note, which, subject to one or two modifications I have proposed, will, I think, be quite satisfactory:

Paragraph 1 contains admission that two Japanese planes attacked two cars, believed to be military.

Paragraph 2 explains delay due to difficulty of determining the exact spot where the Ambassador was wounded, but states that the position is now established as being to the southward of Kating.

Paragraph 3 states that incident may accordingly have been caused by Japanese aircraft. 'As therefore wounding of the Ambassador may have been due to action however involuntary of Japanese aircraft, Japanese Government desire to convey to His Majesty's Government a formal expression of their deep regret'.

Paragraph 4 on the question of punishment draft states: 'It is needless to say that Japanese Government would take suitable steps whenever it was established that Japanese aviators had killed or wounded, intentionally or through negligence, Nationals belonging to a third country.'

Paragraph 5 repeats statement in note of September 6th[3] in regard to sending of further instructions to Japanese forces in China 'it being the desire and policy of Japanese Government to limit, so far as this can possibly be done, the dangers to non-combatants resulting from existing hostilities in China'.

We had some difficulty over last point. Japanese representatives were disposed to have this out altogether unless they could revive their request for cooperation.

I strongly objected to latter proposal, but as it seemed to me important to obtain this formal statement of Japanese policy in regard to non-combatants, pressed for retention of sentence reported in preceding paragraph.

Japanese representatives finally agreed, on the understanding that Vice Minister for Foreign Affairs could address to me confidential and unofficial letter[4] stating that while the Japanese Government understood the necessity for avoiding legal issues involved in any formal request for

---

[1] No. 248.   [2] Of September 18, not printed (F 6652/5727/10).
[3] See No. 232.   [4] See No. 252 below.

331

cooperation they were nevertheless most anxious to avoid occurrence of further incidents and hoped that without prejudice to legal position, local authorities on the spot may exchange information unofficially in regard to movements of non-combatants.

I earnestly hope that it will not be necessary to take exception to the despatch of this unofficial letter. It seems really important to avoid further incidents of the kind at this critical time and seeing that we have asked for 'safety zone' in Nanking and have in a number of other ways invoked Japanese help for protection of non-combatants, it hardly seems likely that our legal position can be prejudiced through the giving of unofficial notification as proposed.

Draft note has still to be approved by higher authority here, but will be despatched tomorrow. The fact that I have seen the draft is to remain entirely confidential.[5]

[5] The full text of the note was transmitted to the Foreign Office in Tokyo telegram No. 419 of September 21, not printed (F 6769/5727/10). A note of September 22 by Sir A. Cadogan stated that both Mr. Eden and Mr. Chamberlain judged the texts of the note and the letter to be acceptable: cf. No. 254 below.

No. 251

Mr. Howe (Nanking) to Foreign Office (Received September 20, 9 p.m.)

No. 464 Telegraphic by wireless [F 6763/9/10]

Confidential   NANKING, *September 20, 1937*

Tokyo telegram No. 392.[1]

I doubt very much whether any terms which Japanese would consider reasonable would have any chance of acceptance by the Chinese Government in its present temper. The Chinese want Japanese armies to clear out of China and leave them to run their country in their own way. My impression after talking to Chinese leaders here and in Shanghai is that they are prepared for all eventualities and to retire further and further into the interior. They will not consider any question of local settlements e.g. Shanghai. They envisage the possibility of a year's resistance believing the strain of a year's war will be at least as disastrous to Japan as to China. German adviser considers that China can resist for this length of time. The so-called pro-Japanese party through whom any approach would probably have to be made have gone completely to ground and it would be as much as their lives were worth to be suspected of any such dealings with Japanese.

I will of course watch carefully for appearance of any signs on the part of Chinese Government of a desire to come to terms with Japanese but I

[1] No. 243.

do not expect to see any yet.[1]

Repeated to Tokyo, Peking, Commander-in-Chief, General-Officer Commanding and Rear Admiral Yangtse.

[2] Mr. Orde commented on September 22: 'This is not hopeful for the success of a Conference of Pacific Powers as suggested by M. Delbos. . .' See No. 253 below.

No. 252

Sir R. Craigie (Tokyo) to Foreign Office (Received September 21, 5 p.m.)

No. 420 Telegraphic [F 6770/5727/10]

TOKYO, *September 21, 1937, 8 p.m.*

My immediately preceding telegram.[1]

Following is text of confidential and unofficial letter from Minister for Foreign Affairs referred to in eighth paragraph of my telegram No. 410.[2]

Confidential.

My dear Ambassador,

With reference to misfortune that befell Sir H. Knatchbull-Hugessen I wish to assure Your Excellency that Japanese forces always take fullest precautions against causing injuries to non-combatants and it is certainly very far from desire of Japanese Government that an unfortunate event should ever occur in future through any fault of their own. Consequently fresh instructions have, as stated in my note No. 172 . . .[3] of September 21st, 1937, been sent to their authorities on spot to exercise strictest caution in this regard.

I earnestly hope therefore that British authorities will, on their part, kindly co-operate with Japanese authorities with a view to forestalling recurrence of a similar event by taking, without prejudice to the legal position of either Government, such necessary measures as giving notice in advance to local Japanese authorities when entering a zone of danger.

Believe me etc.

(Signed) Vice Minister for Foreign Affairs.[4]

Repeated to Nanking, Shanghai (for Commander-in-Chief No. 100).

[1] See No. 250, note 5.   [2] No. 250.   [3] The text was here uncertain.
[4] In an unnumbered telegram of September 22 Sir R. Craigie asked that this should be corrected to read 'Minister for Foreign Affairs'.

No. 253

Mr. Edmond (Geneva) to Mr. Eden[1] *(Received September 22, 4.5 a.m.)*

No. 68 L.N. Telegraphic [F 6774/9/10]

Most Immediate   GENEVA, September 22, 1937, 2.20 a.m.

Following (? for) Mr. Eden.

My telegram No. 67.[2]

Lord Cranborne[3] received a message this evening[4] shortly after meeting of Sino-Japanese Advisory Committee from M. Delbos to the effect that he was giving notice in an informal manner to the United States observer on Committee (Mr. Harrison) that he proposes, at the meeting of the Committee on Monday next, that Sino-Japanese dispute should be referred to the Powers interested in the Pacific. In view of the fact that at their last discussion such a procedure had seemed most favourable to Mr. Eden and himself he asked Lord Cranborne to associate himself with this notice to United States Government. He was making it clear to Harrison that no reply was expected from United States Government pending adoption of proposals by Advisory Committee and consequent official notification to Washington. On the receipt of this message Lord Cranborne informed United States observer while he was aware that Secretary of State was most anxious to work in closest collaboration with United States Government and was, he knew, in principle, in favour of procedure proposed by M. Delbos he could not associate himself with the communication made by the latter without referring to Mr. Eden who would certainly have views as to the exact method of making so very important and delicate a *démarche*. Lord Cranborne therefore begged Mr. Harrison not to communicate with his Government until at any rate tomorrow Wednesday. Mr. Harrison agreed.

Lord Cranborne also explained matter to M. Delbos who entirely appreciated his reason for delay. He said he had spoken to Mr. Harrison exactly in the sense of his message to Lord Cranborne and when asked by Mr. Harrison what Powers would be considered as being interested in the Pacific had given off-hand the following list: Great Britain, France, United States, Soviet Russia, Netherlands, Australia, New Zealand; (he did not mention Canada).

---

[1] Mr. Eden flew to London on the evening of September 21 and returned to the Foreign Office on September 22.

[2] For some reason this rather important telegram has not been preserved in the Foreign Office archives. It apparently described the first meeting of the League of Nations Sino-Japanese Advisory Committee on September 21. M. Munters, the Latvian representative, was elected chairman. It was decided to invite China, Japan, Germany, and Australia to participate in the committee's deliberations, and to hold these deliberations in private. The committee met on September 21, 27, and 29, and October 1 and 5. A set of the provisional minutes, prepared by the League Secretariat, is filed at F 7133/6799/10.

[3] Parliamentary Under Secretary of State for Foreign Affairs.   [4] i.e. September 21.

United States observer had asked whether Italy and Germany would be invited and M. Delbos stated he had been evasive on this point. M. Delbos asked that if matter was being referred to Mr. Eden it might be pointed out that there were two methods of procedure: either Committee could proceed on analogy to Nyon Conference[5] and convoke a meeting of the Pacific Powers somewhere away from Geneva though under the auspices of the League of Nations; or alternatively Advisory Committee could establish sub-committee if necessary of these same Powers. He was inclined to favour the latter method because as sub-committee would be an integral part of the Advisory Committee itself it would obviate the awkwardness of the question of the participation of Germany and Italy who would certainly be absent from the Committee. If you approve of initiative taken by M. Delbos, Lord Cranborne will associate himself with it. If you feel matter is being rushed he would explain this to M. Delbos. But in any case it is M. Delbos' view that United States Government should be informed before Monday next. In any event Lord Cranborne would be most grateful if you could, after considering the matter, telephone him at midday tomorrow Wednesday.[6]

[5] See Volume XIX, Nos. 154–6.
[6] A note of September 23 by Mr. Orde read: 'This was answered by the Sec. of State by telephone. See now Geneva tel. No. 71 (F 6830/6799/10) [No. 255 below].'

No. 254

Mr. Eden to Sir R. Craigie (Tokyo)

No. 334 Telegraphic [F 6758/5727/10]

FOREIGN OFFICE, *September 22, 1937, 2.10 p.m.*

Your telegrams Nos. 419[1] and 420.[2]

Note is acceptable to His Majesty's Government and you should address a Note to the Japanese Government in the following terms.

'I have the honour to inform Your Excellency that I duly communicated to His Majesty's Government in the United Kingdom the terms of the Note which Your Excellency addressed to me on the 21st instant in regard to the attack on His Majesty's Ambassador in China by two aeroplanes in the neighbourhood of Shanghai on the 26th August last. I have now received instructions from His Majesty's Government to state that they have received this communication with satisfaction and regard the incident as closed.'

In reply to the Vice Minister's letter, you should say that the British authorities will be ready to assist the Japanese authorities by giving notice where possible of any intention to enter a zone of danger. If any case arises where it may not have been possible to give such warning, His

[1] See No. 250, note 5.   [2] No. 252.

Majesty's Government could not consider that the Japanese authorities were thereby absolved from responsibility.

The reply to the Japanese Note will be published, together with the Japanese Note, tomorrow morning.[3]

Repeated to Nanking, Shanghai (for C. in C.).

[3] See *The Times*, September 23, 1937, p. 12. Foreign Office telegram No. 339 to Tokyo of September 23 conveyed Mr. Eden's congratulations to Sir R. Craigie on the success of his efforts to obtain 'an acceptable settlement of the incident in which Sir H. Hugessen was involved. I feel that they have been invaluable'.

No. 255

Mr. Edmond (Geneva) to Mr. Eden (Received September 23, 12.5 p.m.)

No. 71 Telegraphic [F 6830/6799/10]

Immediate   GENEVA, *September 23, 1937, 11.5 a.m.*

Following from Mr. Elliot.[1]

My telegram No. 68.[2]

Lord Cranborne saw Monsieur Delbos this evening[3] and informed him of your preference for establishment of a sub-advisory committee as a first step in dealing with the Far Eastern problem. He informed Monsieur Delbos of importance which you attached to close cooperation of United States and of your proposal that Mr. Harrison should be asked to obtain the views of his government before next meeting of Advisory Committee on September 27. Monsieur Delbos agreed that this should be done but pointed out that United States Government in agreeing to send an observer had said that 'it would not be prepared to state it's [*sic*] position in regard to policies or plans submitted to it in terms of hypothetical enquiry'. Monsieur Delbos would therefore prefer that Mr. Harrison should be consulted as to the best way of handling the matter.

Lord Cranborne then saw Mr. Harrison[4] and explained to him that His Majesty's Government and French Government were most anxious not to do anything to embarrass United States Government. He therefore suggested that Mr. Harrison should make unofficial soundings of his government whether they would be prepared to participate if asked in a sub-committee. Mr. Harrison did not seem perturbed and said that he would enquire of his government and would let Lord Cranborne know the result.

[1] Mr. Walter Elliot, Secretary of State for Scotland, was a member of the U.K. delegation at the League of Nations.

[2] No. 253.   [3] i.e. September 22.   [4] See *F.R.U.S.*, 1937, vol. iv, p. 29.

No. 256

Major G. A. Herbert[1] *(Tientsin) to Mr. Eden*
(Received September 23, 8.30 p.m.)

No. 28 Telegraphic: by wireless [F 6982/220/10]

TIENTSIN, September 23, 1937

Addressed to Nanking telegram No. 56 of September 23rd.

My telegram No. 49 to Nanking, repeated to Foreign Office telegram No. 23, Peking telegram No. 111, Financial Adviser telegram No. 14 and Tokyo.[2]

Inspector General of Customs' reply to Myers' telegram of September 16th was merely to the effect that he was to carry on negotiations. Following is text of further telegram dated September 22nd sent by Myers to Inspector General of Customs, begins:

My telegram No. 450.[3] Japanese authorities demand date . . .[4] bonds. They will not listen to suggestion of neutral bank as opposed to Yokohama Specie bank. I must give an immediate answer otherwise the terms will be withdrawn and we must face the consequences. I recommend that you give me your permission to arrange the best terms possible and remove permanent danger of break up of service here. I am convinced the only means of maintaining the service here intact is to agree immediately to terms as already outlined. If we do not agree I am afraid there will be no service here when the time for final settlement arrives, ends. The best and only solution would appear to be for Inspector General of Customs to get Myers to come to arrangement locally on lines indicated in his telegram of September 16th and I must stress the urgency for an early decision.

Repeated to Peking No. 118 and Financial Adviser telegram No. 17.

[1] Acting Consul at Tientsin.   [2] No. 247.   [3] Not traced in F.O. archives.
[4] The text was here uncertain.

No. 257

Mr. Hall-Patch (Shanghai) to Mr. Eden
(Received September 29, 9.30 a.m.[1]*)*

No. 115 Telegraphic [F 7124/220/10]

SHANGHAI, September 25, 1937, 12.25 a.m.

Customs

No instructions yet received in Shanghai as a result of action reported in Nanking telegrams 461[2] and 62,[2] 63.[2]

2. On September 22 I saw Soong and emphasized once more that

[1] A corrupt text of this telegram was received in the Foreign Office at 9.30 a.m. on September 25, but the amended repetition was not received until September 29.
[2] Not printed.

Chinese tactics might result in total loss of Tientsin customs. I urged him without further delay to authorize Maze (who refused to act without covering authority) to instruct Myers to negotiate best terms possible with Japanese. He summoned Vice Minister of Finance (Hsu Kan) and Chinese head of customs (Loy Chang) and finally agreed to instruct Maze to send a telegram to Myers the terms of which are given in my immediately following telegram.[3] I pointed out the impossibility of expecting Myers to obtain all these concessions and that he should give Myers latitude to reach the best settlement possible. This Soong would not do without instructions from Nanking and he stated that he was already exceeding his powers in instructing Maze to open negotiations with Japanese on any terms. He would be prepared to take up the question again with Nanking if Myers was unsuccessful in obtaining agreement to the settlement he suggested. I again emphasized danger of not giving Myers free hand but could not move him. It is however step forward to have secured Myers has instructions to open negotiations on any basis.

3. I have seen trade counsellor and financial adviser of the Japanese Embassy and Kishimoto.[4] In each case I have emphasized that disruption of customs will destroy the main support of China's credit and jeopardize currency stability without which trade after cessation of hostilities will be hazardous for all countries including Japan. Also that if present customs administration is destroyed it is hopeless to expect China will accept any measure of foreign guidance and setting up of new administration. Future trade will then be handicapped by purely Chinese administration probably hostile [to] all foreign interests.

4. They admit these dangers but say that military are exercising severe pressure owing to refusal of Myers to discuss relatively satisfactory settlement put forward at the end of August and reported in Tientsin telegrams 33[5] and 34[6] to Nanking. Kishimoto informed me privately on September 23 that if Myers is given authority to act speedily he may still be able to obtain settlement on these lines but otherwise it is only a question of time before Japanese will take over Tientsin customs.

5. I have just received Tientsin telegram 56[7] to Nanking and will see Maze and Soong again but I am not sanguine that they will act. The latter's hesitation is understandable in view of his difficulties with Nanking. Attitude of the former is inexplicable. Had he acted vigorously in first...[8] present situation might have been avoided.

6. Meanwhile will you consider if any further representations can be made in Tokyo to supplement those mentioned in Foreign Office telegram No. 279 to Tokyo.[9]

Repeated to Nanking, Peking, Tientsin and Tokyo.

[3] No. 260 below.
[4] Mr. Hirokichi Kishimoto was Chief Secretary to the Inspector General of the Chinese Maritime Customs.
[5] No. 222.   [6] No. 223.   [7] No. 256.   [8] The text was here uncertain.
[9] No. 229. Mr. chaplin commented on September 29: 'It is deplorable that neither Mr.

Soong nor Sir F. Maze will take a decision. We can hardly make representations in Tokyo if we do not know how far the Chinese are prepared to go.'

No. 258

Sir R. Craigie (Tokyo) to Mr. Eden (Received September 25, 9.30 a.m.)

No. 439 Telegraphic [F 6972/9/10]

Confidential   TOKYO, *September 25, 1937, 12.55 p.m.*

I believe next few weeks may prove decisive in determining the length and outcome of the struggle in China and it is for this reason that I venture to make the following observations after so short residence here.

So far as Japanese Government are concerned it would still I think be possible to-day to secure peace on terms which would leave Nanking with an authority in Northern Provinces not less and possibly even somewhat greater than that exercised before the present incident occurred. There would it is true be a demand for economic concessions but apparently the intention is that latent economic resources should be developed by means of Japanese organisation and capital.

It is obvious however that Japan's terms will harden in proportion to the magnitude of her effort and what may be possible to-day will be impossible to-morrow. Furthermore any solid military success, by raising prestige of the army in Japan, must necessarily increase its control of domestic affairs and lead automatically to a stiffening of terms. Question to my mind is not so much whether Japan will crush Chinese armies but how long it will take to do so.

Judging from Mr. Howe's telegram No. 464[1] Chinese Government's objective remains 'to clear Japanese armies out of China'. They believe the strain of a year's war will be at least as disastrous to Japan as to China.

If China really expects to achieve this end by force of arms and if this is Nanking's last word the outlook is indeed unpromising. Nanking's calculations are presumably based on possibility of

1. Japan's financial collapse and (2) foreign intervention by (a) Soviet Russia or (b) the League or (c) Great Britain and/or United States (in the latter case through steady exasperation of public opinion in those countries).

As regards (1) with the example of Italy's conquest of Abyssinia before her, China would appear most unwise to trust in those economists who predict early financial collapse here. Price in economic disequilibrium to be paid by Japan *after* the war may be a high one but that will not help a defeated China.

2(a). Direct Russian intervention is on the whole unlikely and if it were to happen, might have fatal results for peace of Europe. Russia has only to

[1] No. 251.

339

sit back and enjoy the fruits of Japan's folly in China while encouraging Nanking to resist *à l'outrance*.

2(b). League intervention by raising false hopes would do China more harm than good unless backed by overwhelming force and the same consideration applies to British and United States intervention.

But what China is never likely to regain by force of arms she might, with our help, recover by diplomatic means. While making all allowances for present state of feeling in China and for considerations which may not be present to my mind, it should not be impossible to bring Chinese leaders to look the above facts squarely in the face before there sets in the process of inevitable disintegration which I am told by neutral observers must be expected sooner or later.

Collective mediation internationally by the League or by parties to the nine power treaty or even by Great Britain and United States in collaboration is in my opinion most unlikely *in initial stages* to achieve desired results here because of element of intimidation inherent in it. On the other hand good offices of a single power, carried out with the utmost secrecy in so far as concerns Japan is the only possible medium at the moment and Great Britain is the only power which could undertake so delicate, if ungrateful, a task with any hope of success. That hope lessens with every week that passes. Risks to us of such an undertaking are obvious, but are not the risks inherent in indefinite prolongation of the conflict far greater? Between impact of Japanese imperialism in the North and steady infiltration of Russian influence in the South (with its memories of 1926–1927) the prospects for future of British interests in China would be grim indeed. In addition there would be the ever present danger of serious complications with a Japan steadily more dominated by extreme militarists prone to proceed in China from one outrage to another.

I recognise that . . .[2] pressure in certain circles in Europe for 'collective' action of some kind. But I can only say in the particular case before us and viewed from this post, I can conceive of no form of collective action which is not likely to leave things rather worse than it found them.[3]

Not repeated to Nanking pending instructions to do so.

[2] The text was here uncertain.
[3] Mr. Eden wrote across the filed copy of this telegram that he was 'always ready to assist any effort towards restoration of peace ... for this purpose our good offices always available', and authorized a reply to Sir R. Clive (No. 263 below), noting, however, 'Don't hope much from it'.

No. 259

Mr. Edmond (Geneva) to Mr. Eden (Received September 25, 3.15 p.m.)

No. 75 Telegraphic: by telephone [F 6960/6799/10]

Most Immediate   GENEVA, *September 25, 1937*

My immediately preceding telegram.[1]

Following from Mr. Elliot:

I learn confidentially that Monsieur Avenol's views on Far Eastern question are briefly as follows:

Meeting of Advisory Committee means in fact that League has taken up a position in regard to Japan. If powers interested in Far East are now ready to abandon all hope of achieving anything it would be better to make no attempt in Committee to take any definite action. In the same way however as Governments make diplomatic protests without any real intention of following them up by physical force, Committee can assume an attitude in regard to present situation which while expressing the world public opinion of today, may prepare for possible future action. If Japan succeeded in conquering China and in holding her gains against world, obviously nothing could be done. But question is what will be Japan's position in six months or a year if she has not succeeded in making this conquest? In Monsieur Avenol's view Committee should therefore

(a) without perhaps going so far as giving verdict of aggression set forth main facts in a manner which while being objective would contain its own conclusion.

(b) say that China is not exclusively the affair of Japan and though the latter can forcibly impose measures affecting the life and property of Chinese and foreigners this cannot be regarded as a right or as the basis of a future right.

(c) deal with air bombardments and other military measures against civilian populations.

(d) assume an attitude for the future and reserve possibility of any later action for conciliation.

(e) organise medical assistance in China.

We think something might be done by Committee on lines suggested by Monsieur Avenol.[2]

Repeated to Washington, Tokyo and Nanking by Foreign Office.

[1] Of September 25, not printed (F 6959/6799/10).
[2] Mr. Orde noted on September 28: 'The Sec. of State gave general approval to this programme in a telephone conversation with Lord Cranborne yesterday.' Cf. No. 261 below.

No. 260

Mr. Hall-Patch (Shanghai) to Mr. Eden
(Received September 25, 6.45 p.m.)

No. 116 Telegraphic: by wireless [F 6981/220/10]

SHANGHAI, September 25, 1937

Following from Financial Adviser:

Text of telegram from Inspector General of Customs to Commissioner at Tientsin dated September 23rd,[1] begins:

Confidential

You are authorised to negotiate with Japanese authorities on the following lines, viz.

1. All revenue of collection of funds to be banked in neutral non-Japanese bank.

2. Deduct and remit cost of collection.

3. Deduct and remit Tientsin and Chinwangtao quotas for service which will be foreign and domestic loans.

4. After new deduction the surplus remaining is to be held on deposit in new neutral non-Japanese bank until present crisis is liquidated.

For your guidance very important you cite argument in favour of including domestic loans, that these loans form one of the main bases of currency structure in China which it should be the interest of all foreign Powers to maintain. I trust that you will exercise every endeavour to secure acceptance of new terms. Ends.

Repeated to Nanking, Peking, Tientsin and Tokyo.

[1] See No. 257.

No. 261

Sir R. Craigie (Tokyo) to Mr. Eden (Received September 27, 9.30 a.m.)

No. 446 Telegraphic [F 7020/6799/10]

TOKYO, September 27, 1937, 10.15 a.m.

Geneva telegram No. 75 to Foreign Office.[1]

I fear, with memories of League action during Manchurian crisis still fresh in public memory, issue of any denunciatory statement by the League at this juncture can only have effect of strengthening influence of extreme militarists here. At the same time it may be difficult for the League to avoid 'assuming an attitude' and if any pronouncement must be made it might follow the lines proposed by M. Avenol, subject to following

[1] No. 259.

suggested amendments.

(A) Statement of main facts should be as objective as possible and no effort should be made to gloss over such responsibility as can fairly be attributed to China particularly for development at Shanghai.

(B) Should be omitted altogether as being unnecessary in law and dangerous in practice. I suggest substitution of appeal to both sides to endeavour to put early end to costly struggle by seeking basis of peace honourable to both sides.

C D and E seem unobjectionable.[2]

Repeated to Geneva telegram No. 1.

[2] The Foreign Office did not entirely agree with Sir R. Craigie's comments. Sir A. Cadogan remarked on September 28: 'As regards (A), even if the Chinese were proved to have started the Shanghai campaign ... I'm not sure that that necessarily involves them in any "responsibility" if in fact Japan (as we are inclined to believe) started the *war*. Once hostilities are engaged, subsequent offensives and changes in the theatre of war do not affect the question of original guilt.' Sir R. Vansittart wrote: 'I entirely agree, and there is surely no question but that Japan started the war. . .' Sir A. Cadogan also remarked that he did not 'see much harm in (B). We and other nations *have* large interests in China and I should have thought we were quite entitled to give notice that we denied the right of Japan to interfere with them by violence.' Sir R. Vansittart wrote: 'I agree again. Sir R. Craigie's objection to B. seems rather feeble.' A telegram on these lines was despatched to Geneva: see No. 266 below; cf. also No. 259, note 2.

No. 262

Mr. Hall-Patch (Shanghai) to Mr. Eden
(Received September 27, 10.15 p.m.)

No. 120 Telegraphic: by wireless [F 7070/220/10]

SHANGHAI, *September 27, 1937*

Copy of telegram received from Tientsin[1] September 25th by Inspector General of Customs.

Confidential

Your telegram No. 632.[2]

The situation as stated in my telegram No. 456[3] which has crossed yours remains unchanged. I had used all arguments cited by you over and over again but to no avail. The Japanese military have laid down terms and the Japanese Consulate refuse again to approach them for any alteration in these terms. I cannot see any possible likelihood that the Japanese military will change their present attitude unless perhaps you find it possible to bring pressure to bear from some outside source. If this pressure can be brought it should be immediate and effective if the situation is to be saved.

Repeated to Nanking, Peking, Tientsin and Tokyo.

[1] i.e. from Mr. Myers.   [2] Presumably No. 260.   [3] Not traced in F.O. archives.

No. 263

Mr. Eden to Sir R. Craigie (Tokyo)

No. 355 Telegraphic [F 6972/9/10]

Confidential   FOREIGN OFFICE, September 27, 1937, 10.30 p.m.

Your telegram No. 439.[1]

I concur generally in the views which you express. I only wonder whether it would be possible to get in touch with the forces that in fact direct Japanese policy. It is conceivable that statesmen in Tokyo may have moderate and long-sighted views, but have they any influence over events, and with the passage of time are they more likely or less likely to regain ascendancy?

However that may be, His Majesty's Government would always be ready to further any effort towards restoration of peace, and for that purpose their good offices would always be available. You may make that intimation in whatever manner and to whatever quarter you think most suitable. It occurs to me that you could if you wished base any such intimation on statement, reported in yesterday's press, by Japanese military spokesman in Peking to the effect that Japanese army would welcome a change in the atmosphere enabling them to halt hostilities, and you might endeavour to ascertain what is at the back of this statement.

Repeated to Nanking.

To Tokyo only.[2]

Can you give me indication of 'reliable source' referred to in your telegram No. 398.[3]

---

[1] No. 258.

[2] The rest of this telegram was added to the draft in Mr. Eden's handwriting.

[3] No. 245. According to a note of September 27 by Mr. Chamberlain (PREM 1/314) he had discussed Tokyo telegram No. 398 with Mr. Eden: 'The Foreign Secretary agreed with me that this was an important communication, and that we ought not to neglect any opportunity of bringing about a cessation of the present horrors if we could do so without undue risks to British interests.' They had agreed that the Chinese should be told that 'we had informed the Japanese that we held ourselves available for our good offices if they cared to make any proposals to us; that we had reason to believe that we could obtain from them (the Japanese) particulars of the terms which they would be prepared to accept, and that we would inform the Chinese accordingly . . . I suggested to the Foreign Secretary that if things went favourably we might suggest to the Chinese that they should ask that joint proposals should be made by the United States and ourselves. I thought it was possible that the United States would be willing to come in with us if we could convince them that our joint proposals were likely to be accepted by both sides, and the fact that we were associated would, I thought, help to make our proposals acceptable, not only to the Chinese but to the world in general which otherwise might get some idea that we had sold the Chinese pass. The Foreign Secretary, though doubtful whether things would work out like this—since such a result would seem almost too good to be true—nevertheless agreed that it was worth trying for.' The telegram sent to Mr. Howe on September 29, however, was in rather more cautious terms than those suggested by Mr. Chamberlain: see No. 267 below.

Mr. Edmond (Geneva) to Mr. Eden (Received September 28, 10.30 a.m.)

No. 79 Telegraphic [F 7068/6799/10]

Immediate   GENEVA, *September 28, 1937, 8.15 a.m.*

Following from Mr. Elliot [*sic*].

Advisory Committee met in private today[1] and welcomed representatives of China and Australia. On proposal of Chairman meeting then . . .[2] public. Mr. Wellington Koo in a speech that was much applauded denounced Japan's policy towards China. He gave details of air bombardments and urged that Committee should condemn this violation of public law. He concluded by requesting that Committee should study without delay feasibility of measures of assistance that might be rendered to China but refrained, in view of representations made by us and French representative this morning, from making any concrete suggestions as to sanctions as he had intended. Lord Cranborne proposed that Committee should postpone general discussion and should confine itself today to question of air bombardments. This was supported by representatives of France, Sweden and Russia and Committee proceeded to resolution condemning bombardment of open towns. For texts of Lord Cranborne's speech and resolution see my two Saving telegrams Nos. 52[3] and 53.[4]

[5]Lord Cranborne deprecated suggestion made by Chinese delegate to insert words 'by Japan' in first paragraph of resolution which originally read 'taking into urgent consideration question of aerial bombardment of open towns in China'.

Lord Cranborne pointed out that it was important to condemn general practice of bombing from the air, that resolution was already a very strong one, and that the words were in any case superfluous. Chinese delegate however with support of a number of other delegations, notably New Zealand, pressed their insertion. After some discussion it became apparent that vast majority of Committee were in favour of naming Japan and it was eventually decided to add the words 'by Japanese aircraft' to the end of first paragraph of resolution.[6]

---

[1] i.e. September 27. This was the committee's second meeting: see No. 253, note 2. The attitude of the member governments had been largely defined at the important private meeting in M. Avenol's room at 12 noon that day: see No. 270 below. There was a short private meeting of the full committee from 5.30 to 5.45 p.m., followed by a public session, which was mainly taken up with a long speech by Dr. Wellington Koo.

[2] The text was here uncertain.   [3] Not printed.   [4] Not kept in F.O. archives.

[5] The committee resumed in private session at 7.30 p.m., when the discussion summarized in the next two paragraphs took place.

[6] The text of the resolution was as follows. 'The Advisory Committee, Taking into urgent consideration the question of the aerial bombardment of open towns in China, by Japanese aircraft, Expresses its profound distress at the loss of life caused to innocent civilians, including great numbers of women and children, as a result of such bombardments, Declares that no excuse can be made for such acts which have aroused horror and

indignation throughout the world, And solemnly condemns them.' The resolution was unanimously adopted by the League Assembly on September 28 (*L/.N.O.J.*, *Records of the 18th Assembly*, *1937*, pp. 89–90).

No. 265

Sir R. Craigie (Tokyo) to Mr. Eden (Received September 29, 9.30 a.m.)

No. 459 Telegraphic [F 7121/9/10]

Immediate   Secret   TOKYO, *September 29, 1937, 11.10 a.m.*

Your telegram No. 355.[1]

I have had to preserve secrecy as to the source owing to special conditions here but informant definitely assures me Japanese High Command favour an early peace and may confidently be expected to acquiesce in peace terms as things stand. Some junior officers at the front may display desire to push things to a finish, but no trouble is anticipated on this score.

Difficulty is of course that the Japanese Government are as reluctant as Chinese Government to take the first step.

Only action which it is desired that we should take at the moment is to authorise Mr. Howe to make an oral and private approach in the proper quarter in the sense suggested in my telegrams Nos. 398[2] and 440[3]. He might state that this information having reached His Majesty's Government from a reliable source, they have considered it sufficiently interesting to pass it on to Chinese Government, without however accepting any responsibility in the matter. He would do well to add, according to our information, these terms would only be available for an *early peace*. If Chinese Government desire, without necessarily disclosing their identification, to express an opinion on these terms, means could no doubt be found to ensure reply reaching proper quarter.

I am also authorised to say, for the information of His Majesty's Government only, that if Chinese reply were sufficiently favourable Japanese Government would consider sending special representative on secret mission to China to undertake direct negotiations.

Position may however change radically in the next ten days as I learn from the same source that heavy reinforcements are on their way to both Shanghai and northern front. It seems therefore important to act before next offensive starts, particularly in view of Mr. Howe's telegram No. 475[4] to the Foreign Office.[5]

Repeated to Nanking.

---

[1] No. 263.   [2] No. 245.   [3] See *ibid.*, note 2.

[4] In this telegram of September 23 Mr. Howe reported that according to the Chinese Foreign Minister the Chinese Government would be receptive to suggestions leading to a cessation of the conflict with Japan, but that as China was the injured party Japan must make the first move.

[5] In minutes of September 29 Sir A. Cadogan and Sir R. Vansittart declared that they

were still suspicious of the sincerity of the Japanese peace terms, but agreed with Mr. Orde that 'we might pass them on and see how the Chinese take them': see No. 267 below, and cf. No. 263, note 3.

No. 266

Mr. Eden to Mr. Edmond (Geneva)

No. 4 Saving: Telegraphic [F 7020/6799/10]

FOREIGN OFFICE, *September 29, 1937, 7.30 p.m.*

Tokyo telegram No. 446.[1]

A. We shall shortly receive a report on the sequence of events which led to hostilities at Shanghai, but our belief is that Japan began the hostilities in North China and that the Chinese could incur no 'responsibility' by thereafter enlarging the theatre of war.

B. We consider that we may justifiably and without danger warn Japan not to offer violence to our great interests in China, though this action may of course be ineffective.

Repeated to Tokyo No. 360.

[1] No. 261.

No. 267

Mr. Eden to Mr. Howe (Nanking)

No. 337 Telegraphic [F 7121/9/10]

Secret   FOREIGN OFFICE, *September 29, 1937, 10 p.m.*

Tokyo telegram No. 459.[1]

You should inform Chinese Government, preferably Chiang Kai-shek himself, orally that definite indications have reached us that Japanese would be willing to make peace now on terms indicated in Tokyo telegrams Nos. 398[2] and 440[3]. If asked on what authority they rest you should say that while we cannot guarantee their genuineness we believe them to represent authoritative opinion and pass the information on as being in our opinion of interest (for your own information we are satisfied that authority behind them is fully sufficient to justify their communication to Chinese Government). You will of course express no opinion of them, still less of course in any way advocate their acceptance,[4] but will explain that we thought it our friendly duty to communicate the information.

[1] No. 265.   [2] No. 245.   [3] See *ibid.*, note 2.
[4] The preceding ten words were added to the draft in Mr. Eden's handwriting: cf. No. 263, note 3.

You should not offer to act as a channel for any reply but can agree to report to me any request to do so. If only for our own information I shall be glad if you can elicit the impression which the suggested terms make on the Chinese.

Repeated to Tokyo.

No. 268

Mr. Edmond (Geneva) to Mr. Eden (Received September 30, 9.30 a.m.)

No. 83 Telegraphic [F 7213/6799/10]

GENEVA, *September 29, 1937, 11 p.m.*

Following from Mr. Elliot.

Advisory Committee met this evening.[1] American representative on instructions of his government had [? read] a statement made public yesterday by American Secretary of State relating to committee resolution on bombing.[2] Representative of Ecuador demanded that committee should pronounce moral condemnation of violation of covenant. French representative proposed reference of problem to sub-committee. Lord Cranborne in a speech, text of which will be sent to you by airmail[3] supported this proposal. Chinese representative urged that there should be a condemnation of aggression to serve as a basis for sub-committee's labours.

Committee agreed to setting up of a Sub-committee constitution of which was to be settled at next meeting of committee. After considerable discussion of term of reference this question was also referred to next meeting of committee tomorrow.

[1] The committee held its third meeting at 5.30 p.m. on September 29.
[2] See *F.R.U.S.*, 1937, vol. iv, pp. 40–1. [3] Not printed.

No. 269

Extract from Cabinet Conclusions No. 35(37) of September 29, 1937

[F 7339/9/10]

4. The Secretary of State for Foreign Affairs said that already the Chinese Government was suffering from a shortage of aeroplanes as well as of anti-aircraft ammunition. The possibility of a Chinese collapse could not be ruled out. He had kept in touch with the American State Department, but there was no more sign of any anxiety on their part for joint action than there had been when last the Cabinet met. He was advised that any approach on our part would embarrass the American

Government and perhaps interfere with the existing good relations. The American Chargé d'Affaires had spoken to him of the strong isolationist feeling in the United States. He had instructed our Chargé d'Affaires at Washington to watch the situation carefully and report if any change took place. He thought our policy should be to take no step without the support of the United States of America. So far as the League of Nations was concerned, the Secretary-General had made a proposal for a resolution which appeared reasonable.[1] In Germany opinion was reported to be divided. Dr. Schacht[2] was anxious to keep the German markets in China, which were important to their exchange position, but Nazi sympathy was with Japan. He thought that we ought to do anything we could towards helping to clear up the situation if an opportunity offered. He had intimated to the Japanese Government that we were prepared to do our best.[3] At the moment there was no other step open to us.

In reply to a question he said he was conscious of the dangers run by a go-between, but the longer the present situation endured the worse it would be for everyone, including China. If the moment came for some action of the kind, he would have to consider whether to approach the United States, but he would not do so at this stage.

The question was asked as to what should be the attitude of the Government towards the proposals in the press for an economic boycott of Japan.

The Prime Minister expressed the hope that no-one would give any support to any such proposal. He was most anxious to avoid the position which had been reached with Italy over Abyssinia. As regards the prospects of peace, there seemed some ground for the belief that both sides would welcome it. His Majesty's Ambassador in Japan had suggested that Japan might now be willing to make peace on terms that were not too bad,[4] and he thought that General Chiang Kai-shek would probably be glad to escape from the present position.

A suggestion was made that if peace came about as the result of our acting as a go-between, the Chinese Government would say that we had forced it on them.

The Prime Minister thought it might be necessary to risk that.

The Secretary of State for Foreign Affairs said that, in view of possible developments in public opinion here, he did not want absolutely to exclude the possibility of an approach to the United States in the last resort, though he wanted to avoid it if he could. No-one here knew that we had approached the American Government at the beginning to co-operate with us in stopping the threatened developments.

At the conclusion of this discussion the Secretary of State for Foreign Affairs informed the Cabinet that the Foreign Office and the Treasury had agreed in the matter of the grant that Parliament was to be asked to

[1] See No. 259.   [2] Reich Minister of Economics and President of the Reichsbank.
[3] See No. 263.   [4] See Nos. 243 and 245, and cf. No. 263, note 3.

vote for His Majesty's Ambassador in China, and an announcement would be made in the near future.[5]

The Secretary of State for Foreign Affairs also referred to the attitude taken at Geneva by the High Commissioner for New Zealand, who had expressed strong views as to the policy that ought to be adopted and had reproached the Government in the United Kingdom.[6] He paid a tribute to the restraining influence of the Secretary of State for Dominion Affairs.

The Secretary of State for Dominion Affairs said he had done his best, but one difficulty was that the present Government in New Zealand adopted the policy of the Labour Opposition here on this subject.

The Prime Minister recalled that the Secretary of State for Dominion Affairs had impressed on the New Zealand representative that if His Majesty's Government were to adopt the policy they proposed, they would very soon have to extricate both themselves and New Zealand from the dangerous situation that would be created.

[5] It was reported in *The Times*, September 30, p. 12 that Parliament was to be asked to vote £5000 for Sir H. Knatchbull-Hugessen.
[6] Cf. No. 264.

No. 270

Mr. Edmond (Geneva) to Mr. Eden (Received October 1)

No. 110 [F 7228/6799/10]

GENEVA, *September 29, 1937*

The United Kingdom Delegate to the League of Nations presents his compliments, and has the honour to transmit copies of the under-mentioned paper:

No. and Date	*Subject*
Record of Meeting, September 27th.	Sino-Japanese dispute.

ENCLOSURE IN No. 270

At the request of the Chinese First Delegate, a small meeting was held in M. Avenol's room today at mid-day.[1] There were present:

M. Delbos
Mr. Walter Elliot
Lord Cranborne
Mr. Wellington Koo
Mr. Quo Tai Chi
M. Avenol

[1] See No. 264, note 1.

Mr. Wellington Koo said that he proposed, at the meeting of the Sino-Japanese Advisory Committee, to make a statement of what the Chinese Government hoped that the Advisory Committee would be able to do, and would present a resolution to the Committee. First of all the Chinese Government desired that the Committee should make a declaration of Japanese aggression, basing themselves on Articles 10 and 11 of the Covenant. This should be combined with a condemnation of the methods of warfare used by the Japanese. Further, the Chinese Government desired that the Committee should organise the following practical measures:

(1) That Members of the League should abstain from supplying Japan with credits, munitions of war, and certain raw materials such as coal, iron, wool, and cotton.

(2) That the Committee should organise medical assistance for China.

(3) That the Committee should recommend to League Members an embargo on exports of oil to Japan. This should be linked with a condemnation of aerial bombardment.

M. Delbos said that he appreciated the force of the arguments used by the Chinese First Delegate, and shared his sentiments regarding the methods of warfare used. It was, however, necessary to take account of practical possibilities. China was in fact asking for sanctions, without the invocation of Article 16. He thought, however, that the League could well organise humanitarian work in China under Articles 23 and 25 of the Covenant. He referred to the proposal that a sub-committee of Pacific Powers should be set up. He suggested that the Chinese First Delegate should confine himself to generalities at the forthcoming meeting of the Advisory Committee, and might put forward concrete proposals for action to the projected sub-committee.

Mr. Walter Elliot agreed that it would be a great mistake for Mr. Wellington Koo to put forward a concrete request for sanctions.

Lord Cranborne said that he thought the lesson which had been learned by the League in the Abyssinian affair had been that the imposition of sanctions without the determination to go to all lengths in support of them was useless. In the present political circumstances he doubted whether the League would be willing to go so far as the Chinese Government wished, and if Mr. Wellington Koo put forward concrete proposals, the Committee would have to modify them.

Mr. Wellington Koo said that world public opinion was much excited and shocked by Japanese action, and would expect the League to do something. It was not precisely sanctions that he asked for, but a recommendation that the Powers should take certain action to assist China. The oil embargo particularly might be put on humanitarian grounds, in that its successful imposition would restrict the bombing of open towns from the air.

Mr. Walter Elliot explained that constitutionally His Majesty's Government in the United Kingdom could not apply any restrictive measures without a definite decision by the League of Nations on the basis of the Covenant.

Lord Cranborne said that he very much sympathised with the position of the Chinese delegates, but he thought it to be his duty to emphasise his doubt whether the Committee would be able to accept any such proposals as those outlined by Mr. Wellington Koo.

M. Delbos then asked Mr. Wellington Koo whether he considered it absolutely essential to put forward precise demands. He referred in veiled terms to the possibility of action outside the League which might be arranged by the projected sub-committee.

Mr. Wellington Koo then asked whether that would lead to much delay.

M. Delbos said that the sub-committee could begin its sittings at once.

Mr. Walter Elliot agreed that there should be as little delay as possible. With regard to the sanctions asked for by the Chinese Government, he very much doubted whether China would in fact gain as much, by putting forward a claim which would inevitably be rejected, as by leaving it to the Powers particularly interested in the Pacific to do what they could to help her quietly. It would be constitutionally impossible for His Majesty's Government to place a prohibition on credits to Japan unless a definite League decision was reached on the subject. Such a decision would probably not be forthcoming, and if the Chinese request were thus publicly rejected, the effect might be to encourage financiers to assist Japan, whereas, if nothing were said about it, the City of London could probably arrange that in fact no credits would be forthcoming.

Lord Cranborne made it clear that His Majesty's Government wanted to keep the door open. The situation might evolve, and although China's demands could not be granted now, it was quite possible that in the future something definite might be done to help her, particularly if co-operation in the United States could be obtained.

Mr. Quo Tai Chi then asked what measures could be taken to stop air raids on open towns, now being carried out by the Japanese. If some definite action could be taken by the League, he thought that the latter would regain its influence and authority throughout the world. It was for this reason, as well as for his country's sake, that Mr. Wellington Koo wanted to put forward his proposal for an oil embargo.

Lord Cranborne pointed out that 60% of the oil used by Japan came from the United States, and was therefore outside the control of League Members. He thought that all that was possible for the moment was a firm declaration condemning the aerial bombardment of open towns. He did not under-estimate the value of such a declaration.

Mr. Walter Elliot said that it was necessary to rally public opinion throughout the world. If the League were in a position to organise medical assistance to China, this could be taken as a sign of sympathy with her. As to methods of putting a stop to aerial bombardments, the only thing that was likely to succeed would be a declaration of war.

Mr. WELLINGTON KOO then asked what line he should take at the next meeting of the Committee.

LORD CRANBORNE said that he thought the Committee would have to face the situation itself, and should do so without delay, but he strongly advised Mr. Wellington Koo not to put forward concrete demands for sanctions.

Mr. WELLINGTON KOO then suggested that the Committee might adopt a resolution condemning air bombardment, and that the discussion of definite action by League Members should be carried out in the sub-committee.

M. DELBOS and Mr. ELLIOT agreed with this.

M. AVENOL pointed out that one of the members of the sub-committee would be only an observer.

Mr. WELLINGTON KOO then said that they had excellent reason to believe that the United States Government would consider favourably any concrete proposals. He thought it essential to avoid the League trying to put responsibility for its inaction onto Washington.

LORD CRANBORNE said that the co-operation of the United States was absolutely essential. The truth was that the sub-committee could take no decision without knowing in advance that they would have United States co-operation.

He wished to emphasise his view that it would be a bitter disappointment for China if the impression were given by the establishment of a sub-committee, that the League was going to take action which in fact it could not take.

M. AVENOL then spoke of the possible mandate which might be given to the sub-committee. He suggested that no precise instructions should be given. It should in fact have the same task as the full Committee, but being a smaller body, it might find it more easy to decide on what could be done.

M. DELBOS then suggested that the sub-committee might meet very shortly.

Mr. WELLINGTON KOO reserved his right to present concrete proposals to the sub-committee, and asked whether he could take it for certain that China would be a member of the sub-committee.

M. DELBOS and Mr. WALTER ELLIOT agreed that China should be invited to participate in the sub-committee's work.

M. DELBOS then suggested that in the course of the Committee Meeting this afternoon, a drafting sub-committee might be set up to prepare and submit a resolution condemning air bombardment.[2] The meeting might be suspended for a short time for this purpose. This was agreed to.

LORD CRANBORNE once again emphasised his view that it was most important not to give the impression that the sub-committee would take any immediate action to assist China.

DR. QUO TAI CHI suggested that the Committee might be given the task

---

[2] See No. 264, note 6.

of studying measures of assistance for China.

M. AVENOL then said that the Committee would in fact be substituted for the full Committee, and should have the same terms of reference. This was agreed to.

No. 271

Letter from Mr. J. M. Keynes[1] to Mr. H. M. G. Jebb[2]

[*F 7822/6799/10*]

46, GORDON SQUARE, LONDON, W.C.1, *September 29, 1937*

My dear Jebb,

You will probably have seen my letter in to-day's *Times*[3] about economic sanctions against Japan. I do feel that this moment is one of the clear opportunities for decisive action, which would be without risk, certain to be successful and with the most fruitful consequences.

I felt the same at one moment about Abyssinia. I have never felt it in the case of Spain, for there has never been a really clear case. But the present case is surely the clearest of all.

If America will not play, then, of course, we cannot proceed. But it would be a splendid thing at least to put the proposition to her. It is high time that she was forced into the position of having to take clear responsibility one way or the other.

And who knows but she would not welcome the invitation. I shall never forget how, when I visited Washington about three years ago,[4] when Simon was Foreign Secretary, no-one would talk to me (who wanted to discuss nothing but New Deal) except on the question whether I could give an even plausible explanation of why our Foreign Office was refusing to play with them over Japan.[5] I got the same question from the President himself, from Morgenthau and from the State Department. They were begging me even to produce some barely plausible explanation of our attitude. I am sure that the world immensely underestimates the effect of economic sanctions. The case of Italy is, of course, no proof to the

---

[1] Mr. John Maynard Keynes, the economist, had been the principal Treasury representative at the Paris Peace Conference in 1919, and was editor of the *Economic Journal*, Fellow of King's College, Cambridge, and a member of the Economic Advisory Council.

[2] A First Secretary in the Economic Relations Section of the League of Nations and Western Department of the Foreign Office.

[3] In this letter (see *The Times*, September 29, 1937, p. 13) Mr. Keynes suggested that there were 'at least nine chances in 10' that a threat of economic sanctions against Japan by Great Britain, America, and 'the other 23 nations' would be effective.

[4] R. F. Harrod, *The Life of John Maynard Keyes* (London, 1951), pp. 448–50, refers to a visit by Keynes to the United States in the summer of 1934, but does not mention Japan.

[5] Cf. Volume XX, Appendix II.

contrary. Everyone knows that they were never applied to any adequate extent. If they had been, it would have been another story.[6]

Yours sincerely,

J. M. KEYNES

[6] Mr. Jebb's reply to this letter is printed as No. 274 below.

No. 272

Foreign Office[1] *to Mr. Mallet (Washington)*

No. 409 Telegraphic [F 7240/7240/10]

FOREIGN OFFICE, September 30, 1937, 9.15 p.m.

Please communicate with the United States Government in the following sense.

They will be aware that strong feeling is growing not only in this country but in other countries that some effective action should be taken to put a stop to the conflict in the Far East, if such action could be agreed upon internationally. At present this pressure, though not yet fully formulated, seems to be taking the shape that a lead should be given by the United Kingdom and the United States in some form of economic boycott on Japan. His Majesty's Government would be glad to know what is the attitude of the United States Government to such views. We recognise that it would not be reasonable to ask the United States Government about their attitude without informing them of our own. This is as follows: we should be ready to consider this or any other action likely to curtail the present conflict, but only if we were convinced of the effectiveness of whatever course might seem advisable. At present we are not convinced that the sort of action suggested here would be effective but we should be quite prepared to examine it further ourselves or with the United States Government if the latter consider it worth pursuing. It is recognised here that action by us alone would certainly not be effective, and for this reason we should be grateful for any expression of the views of the United States Government.[2]

[1] Mr. Eden left the Foreign Office on the evening of September 30 to spend a long weekend in Yorkshire: cf. note 2 below.

[2] With regard to the drafting of this telegram, Mr. Eden said in his memoirs (*Facing the Dictators, op. cit.*, p. 534) that by the end of September he had 'decided to make another attempt at joint Anglo-American intervention in the Far East'. On his instructions Mr. Orde submitted a draft after discussion with Mr. Chamberlain, which concluded with the following passage: 'This is indeed a capital consideration. What are the views of the United States Government? We are prepared to consider with the United States Government any course that may fulfil these requisites; but we can obviously say no more without knowing their views or alternatively without knowing the views that might emerge from such consideration.'

As Mr. Eden had to leave for Yorkshire (see note 1), he asked Sir R. Vansittart to take the draft to Mr. Chamberlain for his approval: the Prime Minister substituted the last two sentences of the above version for Mr. Eden's draft. According to Mr. O. C. Harvey (*The Diplomatic Diaries of Oliver Harvey 1937–1940* (London, 1970), pp. 48–9) Mr. Eden did not see the amended telegram until October 2, when he 'immediately rang me up in great annoyance at this ending which he regarded as an invitation to America to reject idea. . . He was in no way appeased when told that these were the *ipsissima verba* of the P.M.'. Cf. No. 281 below.

No. 273

Mr. Edmond (Geneva) to Foreign Office (Received October 1, 8 a.m.)

No. 88 L.N. Telegraphic [F 7235/6799/10]

Immediate   GENEVA, *September 30, 1937, 10.45 p.m.*

Following from Mr. Elliot.

My immediately following telegram[1] contains text of resolution to be put before Committee of Twenty-three by Chinese Delegation tonight. It will it is hoped, be referred to sub-committee which will be appointed according to present plan at this evening's meeting. I would however point out that this is not an isolated step on their part. It is likely to be the first instalment of a series of progressive demands.

This afternoon Lord Cranborne had talk with Mr. Wellington Koo in which His Excellency after mentioning resolution referred to above said he hoped that it would be within competence of sub-committee when it was set up to consider other aspects of general situation. On Lord Cranborne asking what aspects Mr. Wellington Koo had in mind the latter stated he thought that it might be useful if committee passed resolutions before assembly came to an end setting forth certain general principles, as for instance, that no members of League should give any assistance to aggressor and every member of League should give such assistance as was in their power to aggressee.

Lord Cranborne said that he must tell Mr. Koo quite frankly that he did not consider that it was desirable at present time to lay down such principles. It would be leading Chinese people and others to think League intended to take stronger action than was in fact possible—though Mr. Koo gave impression of acquiescing Lord Cranborne had strongest impression that he intended to proceed with his course of action. It is to be expected therefore that Chinese may during next two days put forward proposals of a general character and also individual proposals such as that

[1] Not printed. The draft resolution set out in blunt terms the acts of aggression against China by Japanese army, navy, and air forces, and proposed that the Advisory Committee should declare that these facts 'constitute a case of external aggression against a member of the League of Nations within the meaning of Article [10] of the Covenant'. In a minute of October 1 Mr. Orde wrote that he had 'telephoned to Geneva on Sir R. Vansittart's instructions that in our view the text was "overheated" and should be toned down as likely to lead to trouble which was to be avoided in view of all that H.M.G. had on their hands elsewhere. . .' See No. 277 below.

of oil sanctions. In view of attitude of smaller Powers here amounting to exciting of expectation of support for proposals especially as they involve no risk to themselves and of public opinion in England which appears almost equally excited, I should be glad to know what in your opinion should be attitude of British Delegation. I should in particular be glad to know what is your view with regard to resolution contained in my immediately following telegram. I would emphasize that if it is accepted it will probably prove jumping off place for a series of further demands.

No. 274

Letter from Mr. Jebb to Mr. J. M. Keynes

[F 7822/6799/10]

FOREIGN OFFICE, *September 30, 1937*

Dear Keynes,

Many thanks for your interesting letter of September 29.[1] The points you raise are of course very present in our minds just now, and I'm afraid I can't say anything more than that at the moment. I agree that sanctions against Italy failed because they were never applied to an adequate extent. After all, the U.S., Germany, Japan, Austria, and Hungary were definitely outside the scheme, the bulk of S. America only applied it very partially, and the French Government were nervous of the whole business and most reluctant to extend the scheme's operation. Moreover before sanctions had really begun to work Italy had conquered Ethiopia.[2] If therefore such a scheme is to be successfully applied to an 'aggressor' in the future it is obviously essential for it to be more widely adopted than were the ill-fated measures of 1935.

Incidentally I need hardly say that Colonel Stimson's version of the F.O.'s attitude in 1932 is in many respects directly contrary to the Dept.'s, and I think that if you heard the latter you would agree that it was at least plausible![3]

[1] No. 271. [2] Cf. Volume XVI, Nos. 235, 360, and 361. [3] See Volume XX, Appendix II.

No. 275

Sir. R. Craigie (Tokyo) to Foreign Office (Received October 1, 9.30 a.m.)

No. 470 Telegraphic [F 7313/6799/10]

TOKYO, *October 1, 1937, 10.35 a.m.*

Your telegram No. 4 Saving to Geneva.[1]

My reason for considering Monsieur Avenol's proposal (b) a little

[1] No. 266.

dangerous from our point of view is that Japanese Government have during present hostilities shown every desire to safeguard British interests whenever individual cases have been been brought to their attention. A resounding phrase of this description pronounced from platform of Geneva is not the best way of ensuring due regard for British interests in the future. This can best be done by energetic action here.

But Japanese Government have refused responsibility for damage done by Japanese forces to foreign property and I believe Chinese Government have done the same. A warning from an international body that responsible government must be held to account for damage to foreign lives and property might not be out of place.

No. 276

Mr. Edmond (Geneva) to Foreign Office (Received October 1, 8.25 p.m.)

No. 91 Telegraphic [F 7303/6799/10]

GENEVA, *October 1, 1937, 6.32 p.m.*

Following from Mr. Elliot.

Advisory Committee on Sino-Japanese dispute met this morning and agreed to revised terms of reference for sub-committee proposed by Lord Cranborne as follows:

To examine the situation arising out of Sino-Japanese conflict in the Far East, to discuss the questions involved and to submit to Advisory Committee such proposals as it might think fit.

Following were then appointed members of the sub-committee: Australia, Belgium, United Kingdom, China, Ecuador, France, Netherlands, Poland, Sweden, U.S.S.R., United States (as observer). Latvia was added as chairman on the proposal of Lord Cranborne and New Zealand was added to the sub-committee on the proposal of Monsieur Litvinov. Polish representative explained that he would have to seek instructions of his government before taking part in the work of the sub-committee.

Chinese resolution (see my telegram No. 89[1]) was referred to sub-committee.

Sub-committee met immediately after the meeting of the full committee and after beginning examination of the Chinese resolution agreed on the motion of Lord Cranborne to adjourn until tomorrow morning by which time an exposé of the facts setting forth publicly official statements of the parties would be prepared and circulated by Secretariat.

[1] See No. 273, note 1.

No. 277

Foreign Office to Mr. Edmond (Geneva)

No. 54 Telegraphic [F 7235/6799/10]

FOREIGN OFFICE, *October 1, 1937, 7.15 p.m.*

Your telegram No. 88 L.N.[1]

Following for Mr. Elliot.

Our views on resolution quoted in your telegram No. 89[2] will have reached you by telephone. As regards further Chinese proposals which you apprehend we can, I fear, at the present stage only offer general hope that it will be possible for the present at least to stave off anything leading towards imposition of sanctions. As regards any differential treatment as regards supply of arms this question is to be considered by the Cabinet shortly.

Public opinion here is undoubtedly strong and proposals are being put forward in some quarters for a trade boycott of Japan of a more or less extensive character. The idea does not appear practicable to His Majesty's Government but they have felt it wise and necessary to sound confidentially the U.S. Government and to define their attitude to extent shown in my telegram to Washington No. 409.[3] It seems to be realised by public here that participation of U.S. Government would be essential. Pending a reply to our sounding and further consideration of the whole question I fear it will be impossible to define exactly our attitude in any other quarter. In order to avoid isolation in such necessarily somewhat temporising attitude every effort should be made to keep the French delegation at least in line with us.

[1] No. 273.   [2] See *ibid.*, note 1.   [3] No. 272.

No. 278

Mr. Edmond (Geneva) to Foreign Office (Received October 5)

No. 113 [F 7415/6799/10]

GENEVA, *October 1, 1937*

The United Kingdom Delegate to the League of Nations presents his compliments and has the honour to transmit copies of the undermentioned paper.

No. and Date	Subject
Lord Cranborne. September 30th	Sino-Japanese dispute: conversation with Mr. Amau.[1]

[1] Mr. Eiji Amau, the former Japanese Foreign Office spokesman, had been Japanese Minister at Berne since August 11, 1937.

Record by Lord Cranborne of a conversation with Mr. Amau

GENEVA, *September 30, 1937*

Mr. Amau, the Japanese Minister at Berne, came to see me this morning. His Excellency explained that he had not had time at our last interview[2] a few days ago to finish all he had to say. Moreover, events had occurred since which made a further conversation desirable.

He then spoke of the League resolution with regard to bombing[3] and said that it had had a deplorable effect in Japan. The strong resolution had been based on very imperfect and one-sided information. The Japanese Government could not agree that Canton and Nanking were open towns. Moreover, the Japanese Air Force had taken particular precautions to limit their activities to buildings of military importance. He added that the Japanese were producing a document this afternoon giving, as I understand it, a true version of the facts, and said that he would send me a copy.

I told His Excellency that, whatever the intentions of the Japanese Air Force, there could be no doubt that in these raids very large numbers of women and children had been killed. Public opinion in Great Britain, as in other countries, had been profoundly shocked, and the resolution which had been passed expressed not merely the views of Governments but of the general opinion of the countries represented at Geneva.

Mr. Amau then turned to the question of the debate which is now going on in the Committee of Twenty-three. He hoped very much that this would not lead to a resolution declaring Japan guilty of aggression. This would still further inflame Japanese public feelings. I said that I could not tell him what would be decided by the Committee. It had not yet finished its deliberations. I could, however, tell him this. The feeling that had been shown there was not only very general but very strong. It would be a great mistake if he had the impression that the only nation to hold very strong views on this question was Great Britain. On the contrary, I myself had been surprised at the violence of the feeling shown, especially by the small nations. So far as His Majesty's Government were concerned, we had made our position known perfectly well again and again in the course of this dispute. We desired a peaceful settlement, satisfactory to both parties, to be reached at the earliest possible moment. We only hoped that this might be the view of the Japanese Government also. I reminded Mr. Amau of what I had said to him at our last meeting as to the danger of Japan by her policy completely isolating herself in the world. I said that there was real danger that this might come to pass, not merely through the attitude of other Governments but of the people whom they represented.

---

[2] A record of an interview of September 17 between Lord Cranborne and Mr. Amau is filed at F 6996/6799/10.

[3] See No. 264.

The strength of their feelings was not due merely to membership of the League of Nations but to the fear that, if war was allowed to take such horrible forms without protest, it would be repeated later in their own countries. I, therefore, urged His Excellency in any way he could to recommend counsels of moderation.

Mr. Amau was throughout perfectly friendly, indeed much more so than on his last visit. I also thought him, if not definitely nervous, at least certainly more anxious as to the situation than he had been. He showed no special animosity to His Majesty's Government, indeed he said that he had heard that in the Committee of Twenty-three they had tried to exercise a calming and moderating influence.[4]

[4] Cf. No. 273.

No. 279

Letter from Mr. Orde to Mr. Dodds (Tokyo)

[*F 6926/9/10*]

Confidential   FOREIGN OFFICE, *October 1, 1937*

Dear Dodds,

Thank you for your interesting letter of August 26th[1] giving some of your impressions during the earlier developments of the N. China crisis.

We are fully in agreement with your views on how to behave with the Japanese. It is unquestionably a fact that one can talk very bluntly to them so long as one is not rude; Butler[2] told me that in Mukden they seemed to like him all the better for his frequent outspokenness. Anyway it is becoming increasingly clear that this is the only method of obtaining the desired effect. In the past the western powers, ourselves included, have treated them gently and with marked forbearance, and it is perhaps not astonishing that as a result they have come to believe that a policy of swagger and bluster can sweep all before it. By all means let us try methods of firmness and standing up for our rights on every possible occasion. It is, of course, exhausting and exasperating to have to keep on hammering away at people who are blinded by an overweening national vanity; but when we know, as we do, how large an element of bluff there really is in their pretentions when one looks behind the surface we are, I think, justified in assuming that the dangers attending such a process are for the most part largely imaginary and it is well worth while to keep on hammering away in spite of the tedium and strain involved. Of course there is a point at which they may go off their heads, and sanctions may be that point.

Your point that we are a much greater Asiatic power than Japan is

[1] No. 209.   [2] Mr. P. D. Butler was H.M. Consul General at Mukden.

excellent. This they must be made to realise and accept. They are fond of talking of the 'realities of the case'. Let us also be realists and keep this fact well in the forefront of our mind in framing our attitude towards their claims to Asiatic supremacy.

When they have a case, and have learned to state it properly and reasonably, we will, I do not doubt, be prepared to listen to them with respect and magnanimity: but meanwhile we shall have to let them see we are not to be intimidated and we must endeavour, with or without their gratitude, to open their eyes as often as possible. In this I agree with you that if no-one else will do so, it is all the more necessary that we should, in our own interests as well as those of the world in general.

The poor things here would like to 'enlighten' us, 'correct' and 'rectify' our attitude; but they are hard put to it. We are getting shoals of letters and telegrams from people full of indigation at the bombings.

Yours ever,

C. W. ORDE

No. 280

Mr. Mallet (Washington) to Foreign Office
(Received October 2, 8.15 p.m.)

No. 317 Telegraphic [F 7310/7240/10]

Important   WASHINGTON, *October 2, 1937, 12.16 p.m.*

Your telegram No. 409[1] reached me when I was about to take Mr. Geoffrey Lloyd[2] to see the Secretary of State.

2. At the end of this interview I intimated to Mr. Hull that I had a message from him and Mr. Lloyd made a gesture to leave the room but Mr. Hull motioned him to stay.

3. I made oral communication in exact sense of your telegram and then gave Mr. Hull a written version of what I had said explaining that this should be treated as a mere record of conversation. I thought this method desirable because I felt that before replying he would probably want to consult the President who is in Seattle.

4. Mr. Hull gave no indication of what his answer would be but his amiability which had been marked during the talk with Mr. Lloyd was in no way diminished by my communications. He said that he would have to think this over.

[1] No. 272.
[2] Mr. Lloyd was Parliamentary Under Secretary of State at the Home Office, and had been Parliamentary Private Secretary to Mr. Baldwin, 1931–5.

No. 281

Foreign Office to Mr. Mallet (Washington)

No. 414 Telegraphic [F 7240/7240/10]

Most Immediate   FOREIGN OFFICE, October 2, 1937, 2.25 p.m.

My telegram No. 409.[1]

In view of the maintenance of keen public interest in the Far East, as well as for our own information, it would help me to learn as soon as convenient the reactions of the United States Government to the enquiry you have already made. You should therefore renew your enquiry as soon as possible and in doing so make it quite plain that the question of whether or not the kind of action suggested here would in fact prove effective clearly requires further examination. We should be very glad to undertake such an examination with United States Government if the latter felt able to join with us in doing so.[2]

---

[1] No. 272. In his diary for October 2 (The Diplomatic Diaries of Oliver Harvey, op. cit., p. 49) Mr. Harvey wrote that when Mr. Eden discovered the amendments which Mr. Chamberlain had made to telegram No. 409 (see No. 272, note 2) he attempted to cancel it, but action had already been taken. 'He therefore decided to send a second telegram [No. 414] instructing Mallet to go again to State Department under pretext of impressing them with urgency for an early reply . . . In other words to emphasise that the British attitude was an open and unprejudiced one on the subject, and that we really were anxious to examine possibilities with the U.S. The truth is that here again there is a divergence between A.E. and P.M. as latter is strongly opposed to any sort of economic boycott in the Far East even with U.S.A. A.E. on the other hand would welcome joint action with U.S.A.'

[2] In telegram No. 318, received at 10 p.m. on October 2, Mr. Mallet reported that he had given this message to Mr. Hornbeck who was seeing Mr. Hull immediately. Mr. Hornbeck 'privately expressed himself pleased at the keen public interest of the United Kingdom' but stressed the 'difficulty of Governmental action to encourage boycott' which would require legislation in the United States.

No. 282

Mr. Hall-Patch (Shanghai) to Foreign Office
(Received October 4, 4.15 p.m.)

No. 133 Telegraphic: by wireless [F 7416/220/10]

SHANGHAI, October 4, 1937

My telegram No. 130 to Foreign Office.[1]

Myers' reply just received to Inspector General of Customs telegram quoted in my telegram under reference begins:

---

[1] Not kept in F.O. archives. It apparently forwarded some suggestions from Sir F. Maze on October 2 as to lines on which Mr. Myers might continue to discuss the customs problem in Tientsin with the Japanese authorities.

No further negotiations are possible. The Japanese absolutely refuse to consider any other bank than Yokohama Special [*sic*] Bank.[2] If we accept now it is practically certain that we save everything. If we refuse it is equally certain that we lose everything. I urge for immediate authority to accept. If we delay much longer we can only accept the consequences. Ends.

Inspector General of Customs still declines to act without covering authority but is seeking it. I will see Dean immediately and press for Myers to be given the authority to settle.

Repeated to Peking, Nanking, Tientsin, Tokyo.

[2] In Tientsin telegram No. 33 of September 29 Mr. Affleck reported that according to Mr. Myers the Japanese military authorities insisted that customs monies should be deposited in the Yokohama Specie Bank, although 'when so deposited he as Commissioner of Customs will retain full control except that no remittances will be permissible to government until a final settlement has been reached'. Mr. Myers did not consider that a Foreign Office suggestion that the funds should be deposited in an account in the Hongkong and Shanghai Bank in the joint names of the Yokohama Specie Bank and the Central Bank of China would be acceptable either to the Japanese or the Chinese governments.

No. 283

Letter from Mr. S. H. Phillips[1] (Admiralty) to Foreign Office
(Received October 5)

[*F 7372/6799/10*]

Secret and Immediate   ADMIRALTY, *October 4, 1937*

Sir,

I am commanded by My Lords Commissioners of the Admiralty to state that they have had under consideration telegrams Nos. 88[2] and 89 L.N.[3] from the United Kingdom Delegation at Geneva and Foreign Office telegram No. 409[4] to Washington. They note that the Chinese delegate to the Committee of 23 has drafted a resolution which winds up by declaring that Japan has committed an act of external aggression against a member of the League of Nations within the meaning of the Covenant and that Mr. Elliot fears that he will shortly put forward proposals such as a suggestion for oil sanctions; also that it has been considered desirable to consult the United States Government with a view to ascertaining their views on possible economic action against Japan.

2. Their Lordships desire, in the first place, to associate themselves very fully with the views expressed in telegram No. 409 to Washington to the effect that no such action should be taken unless we are convinced of its effectiveness. They would point out that in this connection there are two

[1] A Principal Assistant Secretary in the Admiralty.

[2] No. 273.   [3] See *ibid.*, note 1.   [4] No. 272.

aspects of effectiveness which must be clearly distinguished and borne in mind. In the first place it might be interpreted as meaning that the measures taken are effective in preventing the boycotted articles from reaching (or from leaving) Japan, and in the second place that such measures would be effective in actually preventing Japan from further prosecution of the war.

3. My Lords suggest that it is very doubtful whether any measures, even if taken by all the League Powers in conjunction with the United States, would be effective in preventing such supplies as oil from reaching Japan, having regard to the probable attitude of Powers such as Italy and Germany, and to the difficulty which the less highly organised League Powers would be likely to have in enforcing restrictions upon their nationals. It must also be borne in mind that Japan is likely to have considerable stocks of such supplies, sufficient, at any rate, for the prosecution of a war such as the present where Naval operations on a large scale are not essential and where the Chinese are not highly equipped with modern war-like appliances.

4. As regards the effectiveness of economic measures in deterring Japan from further prosecution of the war, I am to observe that if Japan had been faced, from the beginning, with a comprehensive League system such as was originally envisaged before the defection of the U.S.A., and had known throughout that her action in China would almost certainly have subjected her to a virtually complete economic boycott, it is unlikely that she would have allowed herself to get in the position in which she now stands. The fact however remains that she has openly committed herself to the adventure, and it can hardly be thought that a threat which would have been sufficient to deter her in the earlier stages would be sufficient for that purpose now.

5. The extent to which a highly organised and resolute State can face economic difficulties resulting from sanctions, and the extent to which such action can exacerbate international relations and lead to a prolonged period of political instability and possibility of war, have been well illustrated in the case of Italy and the sanctions arising out of the Italo-Abyssinian war.

6. Their Lordships anticipate that the result of an appeal to the United States of America might well be that support will be secured for sanctions such as an oil embargo, which would be imposed by the United States through the agency of the recent Neutrality legislation (i.e. by way of an embargo on both belligerents). It would seem possible that in this way the President might be able to satisfy both the extreme non-interventionists, who sponsored the Neutrality Bill,[5] and the rising tide of feeling against Japan which, no doubt, exists in the United States of America as elsewhere.

7. Their Lordships' object in writing this letter is to make clear the risks

[5] Cf. Volume XVIII, No. 88.

to this country of any action of this character. Although the United States of America might be prepared to assist by an embargo directed against both belligerents, at the present time there seems to be little reason to hope that they would take part in sanctions directed against Japan only or that they would be prepared to afford us military support if, as is possible, the consequences of imposing sanctions were to exasperate Japan and to divert some of her aggressive intentions from China to provocative action against the chief League Powers. Although it might not be that the imposition of sanctions would lead Japan to take immediate aggressive action against ourselves or the Dutch, it cannot be doubted that her hostility would be mainly and most easily directed against us as the leading League Power with heavy Far Eastern commitments. The assuagement of feelings of hostility thus aroused might be a very lengthy process.

8. It must be borne in mind that we alone of the League Powers possess the necessary Naval power to deal with Japan and that League action against Japan, therefore, means British action.

9. My Lords would therefore suggest that the proper approach to this problem is to face the ultimate consequences before any action against Japan is taken. It is in fact necessary that we should ask ourselves the question whether or not we are prepared to go to war with Japan in order to deter her from her present adventure on the Chinese mainland. In so doing, it would be essential to bear in mind that, in the present unsettled political state of Europe, there would be a serious possibility that, once we became involved in hostilities in the Far East, the opportunity of our military unpreparedness might be seized by Germany or Italy to take advantage of our pre-occupation. Recent investigations have shown how great are the difficulties, in the present state of re-armament (or indeed at any time), of engaging in war with both Japan and Germany at the same time, while the intervention of Italy when we were so engaged would be a most serious matter; in fact, it may be said that unless we are assured of the armed support of the United States and France, the risks to the Empire involved in the situation contemplated above would be very great.

10. The proper approach to America would, therefore, seem to be to draw attention to the possible ultimate consequences of action of the type contemplated, and to state that H.M. Government would not be prepared to consider sanctions against Japan (even of a 'token' character in order formally to comply with Article 16 of the Covenant) unless we were firmly assured, in advance, that we could count on the fullest military support and collaboration of the U.S.A., not only if war ensued during the continuance of the present emergency, but also throughout the whole period of disturbed conditions in the Far East which might be expected to follow. In this manner the moral responsibility of America would be clearly brought home and it would be impossible for her to evade that responsibility by agreeing to collaborate in the imposition of sanctions without having any real intention of seeing the matter through. We are faced at the present time with a resolute, aggressive and warlike country,

which has openly committed itself to action in China and which sets great store on questions on 'face', and it would only be possible to deter her if we were prepared, if necessary, to go to the utmost limit.[6]

A copy of this letter has been sent to the Air Ministry, War Office and Treasury.[7]

I am, etc.,
S. H. PHILLIPS

[6] Mr. Chaplin (October 5) thought this letter 'clear-headed' and asked with regard to telegram No. 409 whether a negative decision by the British Government 'after receiving a favourable reply from the U.S. would be likely to have an unfortunate effect on our relations with that country'. Mr. Orde replied on October 5: 'I don't know. I shd. think the U.S. will *at most* agree to examine the question & will be glad if they do examine it with us to find economic measures unlikely to be effective.' He added: 'I confess that I should strongly deprecate for my part running any risk of war with Japan at the present time.' Sir R. Vansittart agreed (October 6): 'We shall presumably not embark on any action with the U.S.A. unless we receive assurances of their willingness to share the consequences.'

[7] A letter from the Air Ministry of October 13 indicated their wish to associate themselves fully with the views of the Admiralty.

No. 284

Mr. Edmond (Geneva) to Mr. Eden[1] (*Received October 5, 2.10 p.m.*)

No. 95 Telegraphic: by telephone [F 7444/6799/10]

Immediate   GENEVA, *October 5, 1937*

Following from Mr. Elliott [*sic*].

Advisory Sub-committee by 7 p.m. on Monday[2] completed draft of report. Last section contains conclusions which are in effect strong condemnation of action of Japan, avoiding however use of word 'aggression'. It was agreed that proposals for action should be put forward in separate document, and at night session which lasted till 1.15 a.m. Lord Cranborne circulated document proposing that Assembly should invite member-states parties to the 9 Power signatories in order to seek method of ending conflict by agreement and failing such a solution to make other proposals to the Assembly should they consider it desirable to do so. Other States having special interests in the Far East would be associated with the work.

Mr. Wellington Koo urged that there should be parallel action by the League, declaration of aggression and agreement (1) not to hinder China and (2) not to assist Japan. He was supported by M. Litvinov who argued that what states could do as parties to 9 Power treaty they could equally do as members of the League, that sanctions might be effective though not universal and that reference to 9 Power Conference might involve long delay, Lord Cranborne's proposal was supported by representatives of

[1] Mr. Eden returned to the Foreign Office on October 5.
[2] i.e. October 4.

367

France, Australia, Netherlands, Sweden and Belgium. Three latter countries declared that League in present circumstances being absolutely powerless the only Chinese proposal to which they could accede was proposal not to hinder China. Netherlands representative (M. de Graeff) was particularly frank and emphatic in this respect. Mr. Bruce pointed out that China could hope for nothing under articles 17 and 16, that only under Lord Cranborne's plan was there any hope of securing co-operation of the indispensable non-member States. Lord Cranborne replying to M. Litvinov denied that reference to 9 Powers need involve delay and referred to Nyon Conference[3] as example of successful application of special machinery to deal with the special cases.

Lord Cranborne's proposal was dealt with by small drafting committee this morning and it has been brought before sub-committee this afternoon. Report and recommendations must thereafter be considered by the Advisory Committee and subsequently by the Assembly. This procedure should be completed by tomorrow.

[3] See Volume XIX, Chapter II.

No. 285

Mr. Howe (Nanking) to Mr. Eden (Received October 5, 5.45 p.m.)

No. 525 Telegraphic: by wireless [F 7479/9/10]

Secret   NANKING, *October 5, 1937*

Your telegram No. 337.[1]

I had tea with Chiang Kai-shek and Madame and at an appropriate turn of the conversation I spoke to him as instructed. Madame's reaction to terms regarding North China was one of anger but Chiang Kai-shek listened quietly until I had finished reading them all. He then remarked that Japan . . .[2] evidently hoping to get all she wanted without further fighting but that China would go on until she had complete sovereignty and administrative rights in North China.

Chiang Kai-shek enquired from what source in Tokyo these conditions had emanated and whether I had received them direct. I replied that we believed them to represent authoritative opinion in Tokyo and that they had reached me from Tokyo through you. He asked whether we had been invited to put forward these terms in capacity of mediators. I replied in the negative. Then he asked me for a copy of terms and I gave him a rough note which I had previously prepared. You will realise that it is a difficult matter to gather definite impression from a Chinese of Chiang Kai-shek's stamp who is slow to make up his mind especially when conversation is conducted through an interpreter like Madame Chiang

[1] No. 267.   [2] The text was here uncertain.

Kai-shek who is of a more volatile temperament. But my feeling which I admit is purely intuitive is that while the conditions mentioned were not regarded as worth serious consideration (Madame remarked 'what cheek') or as affecting their determination to carry on the struggle, the view taken was that they might in any case have been worse.

Earlier in the interview I had mentioned that sooner or later a possibility of mediation might arise and I thought His Majesty's Government would like to keep their hands free to take advantage of any opportunity which might arise rather than become involved in a futile attempt to impose sanctions again Japan. To this Madame Chiang Kai-shek replied 'please make it plain to your Government that there is no possibility of any mediation between China and Japan'.[3]

Repeated to Peking and Tokyo.

[3] In a minute of October 7 Mr. Orde referred to Mr. Howe's telegram No. 511 of October 2, in which he reported Chiang Kai-shek as saying that no compromise was possible unless Japan withdrew her troops from China, and commented 'the two telegrams [Nos. 511 and 525] are conclusive for the moment'. Mr. Eden wrote across the filed copy of telegram No. 459 [No. 265]: 'I am inclined to think that we have done all we can, & that in view of Chiang Kai-shek's reception we should do no more.' Also filed with telegram No. 525 was a cutting from *The Times* of October 2, reporting a statement by a Japanese Foreign Office spokesman to the effect that 'we do not think mediation is called for at the present stage . . . we are determined to fight to the bitter end until China reconsiders her attitude . . .'

No. 286

Mr. Mallet (Washington) to Mr. Eden (Received October 6, 9.30 a.m.)

No. 324[1] Telegraphic [F 7477/7240/10]

Immediate   WASHINGTON, *October 5, 1937, 7.39 p.m.*

Your telegram 409.[2]

Assistant Secretary of State has just given me answer in an informal and confidential memorandum which states my enquiries of October 1st relate to a situation to which American Government has been giving earnest consideration.

'The people of the United States, as do the people of the United Kingdom, stand conspicuously in the forefront among the nations that desire peace, justice and order; and both countries deplore the conflict in the Far East and are desirous that it be brought to an end.

Naturally, in both countries thought runs towards the problem of the methods of preserving peace.

The American Government feels thus far since the present conflict

[1] Telegrams Nos. 324 and 325 (No. 287 below) were despatched in reverse order, but have been printed in numerical order as they were received in the Foreign Office at the same time.

[2] No. 272.

unfortunately began, there have been made available clear indications of attitude and policy of both of the United Kingdom and of United States. In a number of important respects the policy of the Government of the United States is reflected in enactment of neutrality legislation with which the British Government is familiar[3] and which indicates that this country intends not to be drawn into any armed conflict. The American Government has constantly in mind and is guided by this expression of the desire and determination of the American people.

The American Government, through Secretary of State, on July 16th[4] stated the principles which in its opinion should prevail in international relations, and on August 23rd[5] stated those principles applied in its opinion in regard to the Far East as well as to all other regions of the world and made expressed reference to the Nine Power Treaty and Kellogg-Briand Pact. The American Government has forbidden the carrying by government-owned ships of arms, ammunition and implements of war to countries parties to the conflict and discouraged such carrying by any other vessels under American flag. The American Government has in communication with Japanese and Chinese Governments strongly urged respect for law, for treaty pledges and for principles of humanity; and it has declined to give assent to any action by either of the parties to the conflict in the impairment or in violation of law or of treaties. The substance, the general direction, and purpose of American Government policy are clearly discernable by reference to this record.

If, with the foregoing summary of control[l]ing factors of American policy in mind, the British Government sees some plan whereby the Government of the United States might cooperate by pacific methods with the British and other Governments towards bringing to an end the present hostilities in the Far East, the American Government would be glad to give its careful consideration and to consult fully.'[6]

[3] Cf. Volume XVIII, Nos. 88, 332, and 333.

[4] See No. 136, note 2. [5] See *F.R.U.S., Japan 1931–41*, vol. i, pp. 355–7.

[6] This memorandum is printed in *F.R.U.S.*, 1937, vol. iii, pp. 582–3. It is evident that the Foreign Office were disappointed with it, although Mr. Eden's comment to this effect is missing from the relevant file. Mr. Orde wrote on October 7: 'We could I suppose reply by expressing disappointment at the lack of any indication that the U.S. Govt. will themselves, with or without our assistance, proceed to examine the possibilities of a boycott from the technical point of view. It seems useless to do more than that at the moment. And perhaps it would be better to wait till we have looked into the matter ourselves?' Mr. Jebb noted on October 7 that a technical examination of the effects of a boycott of Japan was under way: his preliminary observation was that an economic boycott if fully applied by both the U.S.A. and British Empire would be so devastating in its effects as to face Japan with the alternatives of having practically no stocks of vital raw materials at the end of six months, or 'going and getting the bulk of them by force from the Dutch East Indies and Malaya'.

No. 287

Mr. Mallet (Washington) to Mr. Eden (Received October 6, 9.30 a.m.)

No. 325 Telegraphic [F 7478/7240/10]

WASHINGTON, *October 5, 1937, 6.49 p.m.*

My immediately preceding telegram.[1]

Mr. Wilson went on to refer to the latest news from Geneva especially Lord Cranborne's statement to the sub-committee[2] and hinted that action under the Nine Power Treaty would be the course most likely to appeal to the United States Government.

It was clear from his friendly manner that the State Department do not want us to consider the door in any way closed to consultations. I think they are afraid of giving any countenance to boycott movements as contrary to the strict neutrality policy to which they are committed by the Congress. Even so they might be less nervous of doing so if they could represent their action as taken in agreement with other signatories of the Nine Power Treaty.

Mr. Wilson also remarked that the boycott movement in the United Kingdom appeared from today's press to be dying down.[3]

[1] No. 286.
[2] Cf. No. 284.
[3] According to a letter from Sir R. Vansittart to Mr. Chamberlain of October 8 [PREM 1/314), he and Mr. Eden had discussed Washington telegrams 324 and 325 and felt 'it would be unwise and unpractical to leave things as they are, seeing that we shall soon probably be in a Nine Power Conference'. Sir R. Vansittart enclosed a draft reply to these telegrams prepared in the Foreign Office, which described them as 'redolent of caution and an almost resolute avoidance of the explicit', and asked the Prime Minister to consider the draft over the weekend and discuss it with Lord Halifax with whom he was going to stay. According to a note by Sir H. Wilson of October 11 Mr. Chamberlain had discussed the draft with Lord Halifax, Sir J. Simon, and others, and incorporated his views in notes which he gave to Sir R. Vansittart: see No. 304, note 7 below. The original Foreign Office draft was superseded by No. 300 below: cf. also Nos. 311 and 312 below.

No. 288

Mr. Edmond (Geneva) to Mr. Eden (Received October 6, 8.10 a.m.)

No. 98 Telegraphic: by telephone[1] [F 7457/6799/10]

Immediate   GENEVA, *October 6, 1937*

My telegram No. 95.[2]

Following from Mr. Elliot.

1. Drafting Committee which met at 9.30 a.m.[3] completed the drafts of

[1] This telegram was telephoned to the Foreign Office before the despatch of telegram No. 97 (No. 289 below).
[2] No. 284.
[3] On October 5.

the recommendation by 2 p.m. and report on recommendations was submitted to the sub-committee at 4 p.m. Agreement had not been reached on two points raised by the Chinese delegate viz: re-affirmation of the non-recognition proposal contained in the Assembly resolution of March 11th 1932, and the pronouncement regarding assistance to China. After prolonged discussion in sub-committee the former point was dropped and Chinese delegate accepted phrase proposed by Lord Cranborne after consultation with Mr. Bruce that the Assembly should recommend that Member States 'should consider how far they should individually extend aid to China'.

2. Advisory Committee met at 7 p.m. and adopted practically without discussion report on recommendations of the sub-committee. Swiss and Canadian representatives abstained from voting on ground that there had been no time to obtain instructions. Advisory Committee also adopted short report on resolution prepared by the chairman submitting for the approval of the Assembly a resolution adopting the report on recommendations, requesting the president to take necessary action with regard to proposed meeting of parties to the 9 Power treaty, expressing moral support for China, and recommending that Member States 'should refrain from taking any action which might have the effect of weakening China's power of resistance and thus of increasing her difficulties in the present conflict and should also consider how far they can individually extend aid to China'.

3. These documents were submitted to the Assembly at 9 p.m. Several delegates indicated that they had had insufficient time to read the documents or consult their governments. The meeting was accordingly adjourned after a few speeches had been made till 5 p.m. on Wednesday.[4] Monsieur Litvinov explained that the active part he had played was due to loyalty to the Covenant and a desire to help victims of aggression. He would have preferred to give China substantial assistance but was prepared to try the procedure suggested. He thought, however, that it would be necessary for the League to do its full duty towards China. Mr. Willington [*sic*] Koo while grateful for what had been done explained that the proposals fell far short of the Chinese Delegation's demands which he preserved the right to present again on any future appropriate occasion. I briefly emphasised that the situation called for a review that was swift realistic and constructive and that conciliation should be on as wide a basis as possible.

4. Results achieved in Advisory Committee are in our view here satisfactory. Report is an objective statement of facts beginning with clash of July 7th and concluding with severe condemnation of Japan but in spite of constant pressure of Chinese delegate definition of aggression was avoided. Mr. Koo throughout aimed at securing (1) condemnation of

[4] At the Assembly meeting on Wednesday, October 6, the Advisory Committee's resolution was adopted: see *L/N.O.J., Records of the 18th Assembly*, pp. 124–5.

aggressor. (2) Refusal of assistance to Japan and (3) some formula which would enable any state that might in future come to China's assistance to claim that it was acting under League Mandate. Dangers of (1) and (2) are obvious and were we think successfully though with difficulty resisted; British delegate nevertheless securing the gratitude of Chinese delegate by according him satisfaction as regards (3) in formula quoted at the end of paragraph 2 above.

No. 289

Mr. Edmond (Geneva) to Mr. Eden (Received October 6, 9.50 a.m.)

No. 97 Telegraphic [F 7476/6799/10]

Immediate   GENEVA, *October 6, 1937, 8.25 a.m.*

Following from Mr. Elliot:

My telegram No. 95.[1]

Letter will be addressed to the President of the Assembly[2] tomorrow to member States, parties to Washington Nine Power Treaty, to initiate consultation at the earliest practicable moment.

Advisory Committee suggested in its recommendations that the Powers should meet forthwith to decide the best and quickest means of giving effect to the President of the Assembly's invitation and has expressed the hope that they will be able to associate with them in their work other States which have special interests in the Far East.

I suggest the best procedure would be for His Majesty's Government to propose to the above-mentioned Powers that they should authorize their representatives in London to meet there and concert next step, which would presumably be an invitation to non-member signatories of the Washington Treaty to participate in a Conference.

As such an invitation would include the United States it might be well that His Majesty's Ambassador at Washington should sound the United States Government privately regarding their views on the projected conference and in particular on the method of issue and form of invitation.[3]

---

[1] No. 284.   [2] See No. 292 below.   [3] See No. 290 below.

No. 290

Mr. Eden to Mr. Mallet (Washington)

No. 419 Telegraphic [F 7476/6799/10]

FOREIGN OFFICE, *October 6, 1937, 7.30 p.m.*

Your telegram No. 325.[1]

Please inform U.S. Government that, according to our information, President of the League Assembly, following on a recommendation by the Advisory Committee, will today address a letter to members of the League who are parties to the Nine-Power Treaty inviting them to initiate consultation as soon as possible.[2] The Advisory Committee have expressed the hope that other States having special interests in the Far East would be associated with member States in such consultation.

This seems to leave open decision as to how consultation should be organised. We should be glad to know as soon as possible any views U.S. Government may have as to how effect should be given to the invitation of the President of the Assembly, since we are naturally anxious to do everything possible to facilitate U.S. cooperation. Amongst points to be considered are: how further invitations should be issued, what form they should take and where a conference, which is in our view clearly necessary, should take place. If the U.S. Government felt able themselves to call the Conference or were willing that it should take place in Washington, His Majesty's Government would, for their part, warmly concur.

It seems clear that in accordance with the hope expressed by the Advisory Committee the Soviet Government should be invited to take part in the proposed consultation. It would, we presume, be for consideration whether Germany should be added.[3]

[1] No. 287.　　　　　　　　　　　　　　　　　　　　　[2] See No. 289.
[3] Mr. Orde noted that this telegram was drafted on Mr. Eden's instructions: the draft was extensively amended by Mr. Eden.

No. 291

Extract from Cabinet Conclusions No. 36(37) of October 6, 1937

[F 7593/9/10]

5. The Secretary of State for Foreign Affairs reported that Viscount Cranborne, at Geneva, had informed him that a resolution of a fairly satisfactory character was likely to be passed the same day. It would be in two parts. The first part, without naming Japan as an aggressor, would contain an indication that that country had in fact committed an aggression. The second part would contain a suggestion for summoning a

meeting of the signatories of the China Nine-Power Treaty of 1922.[1] He thought that this was the best step that could be taken, and it would give the fullest scope to the United States of America to give any co-operation they could. After President Roosevelt's speech[2] it was hardly possible for the American Government to reject the suggestion. The passing of this resolution might involve within the next few days a meeting of the six Powers signatories of the Nine Power Treaty who were also Members of the League of Nations, in order to make arrangements for carrying out the recommendation of the League.

Some discussion took place as to the probable effect of such a meeting on the three Powers who were not Members of the League of Nations. There was general agreement that it would be necessary to act in accordance with any provisions that might be contained in the Treaty for summoning a meeting of signatories.

Some discussion took place as to the significance to be attached to President Roosevelt's speech on the previous day.

The Prime Minister pointed out that the speech introduced a new factor into the situation, and, whatever its real significance, it was likely to be made use of for political purposes by the Opposition Parties in this country. It would be important for the Government not to be manoeuvred into a position in which it could be said that the United States had offered to co-operate in economic sanctions if the United Kingdom would join them and that we were standing in the way of such action. The speech, however, was so involved that it was very difficult to discover its meaning. Nevertheless, some reply ought to be made at once, without waiting for the occasion of a Parliamentary Debate, and as he himself would be making a public speech in two days' time he could hardly avoid some comment. His present inclination was to say that President Roosevelt's remarks voiced the feelings of people in this country and that he welcomed a statement on the sanctity of treaties coming from such a quarter and would await any proposals that might be made. This would bring out the point that the intentions of the President's speech were not very clear.[3]

[1] See Nos. 288 and 289.
[2] The reference is to the important 'Quarantine' speech made on October 5 in Chicago by President Roosevelt, in which he spoke of the necessity of a quarantine to protect the community from an 'epidemic of world lawlessness', and implied that while the United States wished to avoid war they could not insure themselves against the danger of involvement: see Volume XIX, No. 222. Sir R. Vansittart remarked that 'we must see how far we can develop this change of tone in the U.S.A., though we may well be disappointed' (see *ibid.*, note 2). For Mr. Chamberlain's views on the speech see note 3 below.
[3] In a letter to his sister Hilda of October 9 Mr. Chamberlain remarked that President Roosevelt's speech 'sounded very fierce but when one examined it carefully it was contradictory in parts and very vague in essentials. What does he mean by "putting them in quarantine"? And seeing that patients suffering from epidemic diseases do not usually go about fully armed is there not a difference here & something lacking in his analogy . . . my first impression [is] that the President's pronouncement was intended to sound out the

The Secretary of State for Foreign Affairs agreed with the Prime Minister, but added that in addition to a public reply it would be necessary to take some diplomatic action. He recalled that the British Chargé d'Affaires at Washington had been asked to make some enquiries as to the American attitude towards the idea of action to bring to an end the conflict in China. As yet he had received no reply.[4] It was not unlikely that the American Secretary of State would intimate that the President had given the answer in his speech. He proposed to instruct the Chargé d'Affaires in that event to ask for certain clarification as to the meaning of the speech.

The Secretary of State for War said that the General Staff were disturbed about the possible developments of events in the Far East. At Shanghai there were small British forces adjacent to relatively overwhelming Japanese forces. Hong-Kong also could not, in present circumstances, be held against a Japanese attack. The General Staff also held that the actions of the Japanese had not been unjustified. For example, the bombing of the Capital was a justifiable act of war which was likely to be undertaken by any country in the event of hostilities. The bombing attack on the British Ambassador[5] ought, they thought, to have been avoided, as the Military Attaché ought not to have allowed him to take this risk.

The Secretary of State for Air reminded the Cabinet that captured maps showed that the Japanese objectives were of a military character.

The Cabinet were also reminded that the Japanese aeroplanes in some cases had probably been getting rid of their bombs to avert a forced descent; that since the strong expressions of public opinion the Japanese had been more careful in their raiding attacks; and that if the nations were to proceed beyond remonstrances or threats the Japanese would have no further incentive to mitigate their action and the Chinese civilians would suffer.

The Prime Minister pointed out that the real ground for objection to the Japanese attitude was that they should have engaged in hostilities at all. He appreciated the preoccupations of the General Staff about the dangers of the situation, and with this in mind he had seen the Archbishop of Canterbury and had done his best to damp down the

ground & see how far his public opinion was prepared to go but that he himself had thought nothing out and in any case had no present intention of doing anything that wasn't perfectly safe. Now in the present state of European affairs with the two dictators in a thoroughly nasty temper we simply cannot afford to quarrel with Japan and I very much fear therefore that after a lot of ballyhoo the Americans will somehow fade out & leave us to carry all the blame & the odium. It is not a pleasant prospect, but I am setting my mind now to see how we can avoid it and I think some straight speaking to U.S.A. (in private) before they go any further will be necessary.' Mr. Chamberlain took a close interest in the drafting of a reply to Washington telegrams Nos. 324 and 325: see No. 300 below.

[4] Mr. Eden evidently did not see Washington telegrams Nos. 324 and 325 (Nos. 286 and 287) until after the Cabinet meeting on October 6.

[5] See Nos. 204, 205, and 210 above.

nature of the speeches made at the Albert Hall on the previous day.[6] He could not imagine anything more suicidal than to pick a quarrel with Japan at the present moment when the European situation had become so serious. If this country were to become involved in the Far East the temptation to the Dictator States to take action, whether in Eastern Europe or in Spain, might be irresistible.

In the course of the discussion the view was expressed that public opinion and the Press tended to isolate Far Eastern affairs too much from the general world situation.

The Secretary of State for Foreign Affairs said that the Foreign Office had done what they could to give the Press a right view of the situation. He thought it possible that events in Spain in the near future might draw attention away from the Far East.

The Prime Minister pointed out that the attitude of the Press had not been unhelpful in this matter, and drew attention to an article in the *Manchester Guardian* on the previous day at the end of which it had been pointed out that sanctions, if effective, involved the risk of war, and, if they were not effective, were of no value. That was a point which might have to be put to the United States of America, namely, as to whether, in the event of their favouring economic sanctions, they were prepared for the consequences, which might well include co-operating in the defence of our own possessions in the Far East. For the moment he felt that President Roosevelt had rather embarrassed the situation, but he did not under-rate the importance of his statement, especially as a warning to the Dictator Powers that there was a point beyond which the United States of America would not permit them to go. Consequently, if embarrassing today, the speech might prove useful later on.

The Cabinet agreed

(a) That the Prime Minister should consider the inclusion in his speech on Friday, October 8th, of some comments on President Roosevelt's speech:[7]

(b) That the Secretary of State for Foreign Affairs should consider appropriate diplomatic action at Washington.[8]

[6] The reference is to a national protest meeting against 'Japan's war on Civilians' held at the Royal Albert Hall on the night of October 5: see *The Times*, October 6, 1937, pp. 14 and 16.

[7] Mr. Chamberlain referred to the President's speech in his address to the National Union of Conservative and Unionist Associations at Scarborough on the evening of October 8: see *The Times*, October 9, 1937, p. 14.

[8] See Nos. 300 and 311–2 below.

No. 292

Letter from The Aga Khan[1] *(Geneva) to Mr. Eden*
(Received October 8)

[*F 7568/6799/10*]

GENEVA, *October 6, 1937*

Sir,

By a resolution of October 6th, 1937, the Assembly of the League of Nations adopted two reports submitted to it by its Advisory Committee regarding the dispute which is the subject of the appeal made to the League by the Chinese Government.[2]

The resolution and reports in question are reproduced in documents A.78.1937, A.79.1937, and A.80.1937, enclosed.[3]

As you will see, the second report A.80.1937 contains the following paragraph:-

'The Sub-Committee notes that under the Nine-Power Treaty signed at Washington, the contracting Powers, other than China, agreed *inter alia* to respect the sovereignty, the independence, and the territorial and administrative integrity of China, and that all contracting Powers, including China, agreed that whenever a situation should arise which involved the application of the stipulations of the Treaty and rendered desirable the discussion of such application, there should be full and frank communication between the Powers concerned. It appears, therefore, to the Sub-Committee that the first step which the Assembly should take, in the name of the League, would be to invite those Members of the League who are parties to the Nine-Power Treaty to initiate such consultation at the earliest practicable moment. The Sub-Committee would suggest that these Members should meet forthwith to decide upon the best and quickest means of giving effect to this invitation. The Sub-Committee would further express the hope that the States concerned will be able to associate with their work other States which have special interests in the Far East, to seek a method of putting an end to the conflict by agreement'.

In conformity with the aforementioned resolution, I have the honour, in the name of the League of Nations, to address to your Government the invitation contemplated in the paragraph quoted above.

I have, etc.,
AGA KHAN
Le Président de l'Assemblée

---

[1] President of the 18th Assembly of the League of Nations.   [2] See No. 288.
[3] Not printed. Copies of documents A.78 and A.79 are filed at F 7568/6799/10.

CHAPTER IV

The Brussels Conference

October 7–November 25, 1937

No. 293

Mr. Howe (Nanking) to Mr. Eden (Received October 7, 5.45 p.m.)

No. 539 Telegraphic: by wireless [F 7595/9/10]

NANKING, *October 7, 1937*

Tokyo telegram No. 457[1], last paragraph, and Tokyo telegram No. 439[2].

The immediate Japanese military objective in North China seems to be to clear the five provinces (Hopei, Chahar, Suiyuan, Shansi and Shantung) of Central Government troops so as to open the way for the special autonomous régime they envisage. They have made considerable progress having met with little resistance in Hopei and Shansi and are now only about sixty miles from the Yellow River on Tsinpu front. There is no doubt they have been hoping to win over Han Fu-chu and so get Shantung without fighting for it. This presumably seems doomed to failure since Han Fu-chu is no longer completely master of the province but is surrounded by troops from other provinces.

On reaching the Yellow River Japanese will have to decide whether (a) to remain on that line and consolidate their gains or (b) to go on as far as line of Lunghai railway and then consolidate or (c) push beyond railway towards Nanking.

(a) would leave them with only half the province of Shantung without Tsinanfu, Tsintao and Kiaochao railway. It is probable therefore that they will decide to force the Yellow River and continue down to Lunghai railway where they will come up against Chinese main defence line. In fact there are already indications that this is their intention.

A good deal however may depend on how situation develops in Shanghai. The Chinese put their best troops in the field here and efforts of Japanese to break through their line have hitherto failed. The Chinese are confident of their ability to hold Japanese in this area but they are

---

[1] The reference should apparently be to Tokyo telegram No. 459 (No. 265).
[2] No. 258.

doing so by denuding other fronts of essential equipment and Japanese may find it pays them better to press attack from the north than to attempt to force Shanghai line.

The Military Attaché takes the view that Japanese are likely to break Central Government forces and that they will smash away until they have done so. If pressure is kept up on all fronts it should not be long before Chinese stores are used up, and they cannot import enough in face of Japanese command of the sea to keep large scale hostilities going short of help from outside; therefore it is only a question of time before Chinese resistance is broken on all fronts and inevitable disintegration sets in.

I would like to make it clear however that there are at present no signs of disintegration and that Chinese morale is still high and is likely to continue as long as supplies of war material can be obtained. A danger point will come if it does not come earlier, when Chinese Government is forced by military or air action to vacate Nanking.

Present indications are however that Japanese are unwilling to proceed to extremes against Nanking as long as there is any hope of obtaining a political settlement with Chiang Kai-shek and I am inclined to think they may go on waiting before taking the gloves off to see latter's reaction to terms which I communicated to him.[3] At any rate it has been very obvious that they have been holding their hand here whatever the reason: even without indiscriminate bombing in cities they could by continued air action not only make it almost impossible for the Government to function at all (we have ourselves experienced extreme difficulty of working in the midst of air raid alarms) but they could it seems to me without much difficulty cut all communications between Nanking and Shanghai and between Nanking and the North. It is a matter of surprise to us that they have not already done so.

As regards assistance from abroad I think that Chinese have few delusions on the subject of the League and their request for application of sanctions was rather a forlorn hope. They still hope that something may occur to force Russia to take direct action against Japan. Russia however seems unlikely to do so except as a member of the League. To what extent she is a present or potential supplier of armaments it is impossible to say. There are however indications that she has been holding out hopes of indirect assistance in the form of supplies of aircraft and other military supplies in return for acceptance by China of certain political terms which would bind her more closely to Russia than recently signed Sino-Soviet Pact of Non-Aggression.[4] To what extent Russia is a present or potential supplier of armaments it is difficult to ascertain. I question whether, apart from aircraft, she is or ever will be on a large scale as question of transport between Russia and China is very difficult. In spite of reports regarding arrival of Soviet aeroplanes Donald still affirms not a single[5] (? machine)

[3] See No. 285.   [4] See Nos. 200, 217, and 237.
[5] A marginal note here drew attention to Nanking telegram No. 549 of October 10 (F 7705/130/10), which reported that 96 Russian aircraft had already arrived at Lanchow.

has been received from Russia. Nevertheless the sources of these reports, which are several, are usually quite reliable and I am inclined to believe that negotiations for supply of Russian aircraft on a large scale are on foot. At present there is no doubt that Germany is main foreign supporter of China from military point of view. Not only is she supplying arms and ammunition more abundantly than any other country but her military advisers are virtually running the war and are gradually pushing out other foreign advisers particularly the Italians. They are represented on every front and moreover are also in charge of ground anti-aircraft defence of Nanking and of the settlement of Kiangyin . . .[6] on the Yangtse the defence of which they have taken over permanently from Italians. As a result of their attitude there is no doubt that Germans have more than regained the confidence in them lost at the time of signature of German-Japanese anti-communist pact.[7] That German Government hope to reap a reward after termination of hostilities in the form of economic concessions goes I should think without saying.

How far their attitude will be modified by any active intervention of Russia on behalf of China is difficult to estimate from here.

From conversations with German advisers however I am under the impression that strong German military support at present being afforded is dictated partly by a desire to prevent China from falling back too much on Russia.[8]

Repeated to Tokyo, Commander-in-Chief, General Officer Commanding and Peking.

[6] The text was here uncertain.
[7] Cf. No. 15.
[8] Mr. Ronald commented on October 11: 'I wonder what the Japanese think of these transactions? Perhaps it would be too much to hope that they will be led to the reflexion "If this is what Germans do when we make a treaty with them, what ever would the slippery Italians do if we made one with them?" '

No. 294

Mr. Mallet (Washington) to Mr. Eden (Received October 8, 9.30 a.m.)

No. 332 Telegraphic [F 7574/6799/10]

Immediate   WASHINGTON, *October 7, 1937, 10.5 p.m.*

My immediately preceding telegram.[1]

Further conversation with Mr. Wilson somewhat elucidated above six points.

[1] Not kept in F.O. archives. This telegram transmitted Mr. Wilson's reply to the aide-mémoire presented to him by Mr. Mallet as instructed in Foreign Office telegram No. 419 (No. 290). The text of Mr. Mallet's communication is printed in *F.R.U.S.*, 1937, vol. iv, p. 64. The main points of Mr. Wilson's reply are those set out in the memorandum of his conversation with Mr. Mallet printed *ibid.*, pp. 65–6. The paragraph numbers in telegram No. 332 refer to the numbers of the points listed *ibid.*

1. United States Government would be reluctant to issue invitations themselves for internal political reasons. They would also prefer that if their suggestion of six convening powers is not found practicable convening government should not be His Majesty's Government alone but one of the smaller countries party to the treaty. The idea is to obviate criticism that the United States Government were dragged along by the British. I see that Senator Borah is already asserting this.

3. Mr. Wilson had in view either the Hague, Brussels or preferably for climatic reasons some Swiss town other than Geneva. He admitted, however, that the Hague seemed ruled out owing to the Netherlands Government not being in relations with Soviet Government. He felt that Japanese Government might find it easier to attend the meeting in such a place than if invited to Washington or London where feeling runs high against them.

4. I think nearly three weeks would be needed, one week for preparation here, one week for travel, and a few days in London on the United States delegation's way to the Conference. Mr. Wilson thought this might be valuable contact.

5. I do not think the United States Government will hold out for procedure outlined. Mr. Wilson seems to think it would not entail much extra delay if signatories met first and then decided who else to invite.

No. 295

Mr. Howe (Nanking) to Mr. Eden (Received October 8, 5 p.m.)

No. 546 Telegraphic: by wireless [F 7604/220/10]

Immediate   NANKING, October 8, 1937

Addressed to Embassy Offices for Financial Adviser No. 55.
Tokyo telegram No. 501[1] to Foreign Office.
I have just seen Minister for Foreign Affairs who asked me my opinion on the following suggestion for a solution of Customs question which he emphasized was a personal suggestion and had not yet been approved by the Government.

Central Bank to nominate Hongkong and Shanghai Bank 'neutral' Bank as custodian Bank for *all* customs revenue. Custodian Bank to open an account with Yokohama Specie Bank in which all customs revenues collected in Tsientsin [*sic*] and (? Chinwangtao) will be deposited, the Custodian Bank undertake vis-à-vis the Yokohama Specie Bank that this account will be drawn upon by Custodian Bank by cheque for foreign loan quota and current local expenses only and balance to remain in Yokohama Specie Bank pending settlement of present hostilities.

2. The proposal is intended to combine two proposals supported by us

[1] Not kept in F.O. archives.

both locally and generally. There are of course . . .[2] in it so far as it deals with general situation but as far as Tientsin is concerned it offers a possible solution and I am instructing Consul-General at Tientsin (to whom this telegram is being repeated) to inform his Japanese colleague that a proposal on these lines is being considered and to urge him to induce his military authorities to allow Government reasonable time to consider proposal before taking any action against customs. The Minister for Foreign Affairs is anxious that his own responsibility for proposal should not be disclosed and that we should use our influence in Tokyo in its support.

3. I asked Minister for Foreign Affairs whether in the event of Japanese refusing to entertain above proposal he thought Chinese Government would accept their ultimatum. Minister for Foreign Affairs replied that Chinese Government would be unlikely to give way.[3]

Repeated to Peking, Tientsin, Tokyo.

---

[2] The text was here uncertain.

[3] Both Foreign Office and Treasury officials considered this Chinese proposal to be 'satisfactory, indeed better in so far as Tientsin is concerned than that which we have been pressing on the Chinese'. Telegram No. 379 to Tokyo of October 9 instructed Sir R. Clive to urge the proposal strongly on the Japanese Government, subject to the conditions that the funds in the Hongkong and Shanghai Bank should be in the name of the Inspector General of Customs, and that the Japanese agreed not to touch the funds in the Yokohama Specie Bank.

No. 296

Mr. Eden to Mr. Mallet (Washington)

No. 423 Telegraphic [F 7574/6799/10]

FOREIGN OFFICE, October 8, 1937, 6.15 p.m.

Your telegrams Nos. 331 and 332.[1]

Please inform Mr. Wilson that we are in general agreement with views he conveyed to you, particularly as regards the choice of a place for the conference, a meeting as soon as possible and the character of the invitation. We ourselves would prefer The Hague to any alternative and are sounding the Dutch Government to-day as to whether this would meet with their approval. If they object, we propose to try for Brussels. Our idea is when we hear from the Dutch Government (or, if necessary, Belgian Government) to sound other Governments receiving the League invitation with a view to a joint invitation being issued to the U.S. Government. If this invitation is accepted, we would suggest that these Governments, together with the U.S. Government, should then consider

---

[1] No. 294, and ibid., note 1. Mr. Orde noted on October 10 that telegram No. 423 was drafted as a result of a discussion with Mr. Eden of these two telegrams on October 8.

the issue of invitations to the Soviet and German Governments, both of whom we think should be invited, together of course with any other Governments which the U.S. Government might think should also be invited.

The choice of representatives will to some extent depend on the place of meeting, but we feel that the conference should have a powerful personnel. I should very likely attend myself and would of course certainly do so if Mr. Hull were to represent U.S. Government.[2]

We cannot at present throw any light on the probable attitude of the Soviet or German Governments, but if any information reaches us we will be glad to let the State Department have it.

We should ourselves strongly desire preliminary contact in London with the U.S. delegation.

[2] This sentence was added to the draft in Mr. Eden's handwriting.

No. 297

Mr. Hall-Patch (Shanghai) to Mr. Eden
(Received October 9, 4.15 p.m.)

No. 142 Telegraphic: by wireless [F 7675/220/10]

Immediate   SHANGHAI, *October 9, 1937*

Following from Hall-Patch:
Addressed to Tientsin telegram No. 24 October 9th; repeated to Peking, Nanking, Foreign Office and Tokyo.
My telegram No. 23 to Tientsin.[1] Following from Financial Adviser:
Japanese Ambassador is ill but I have seen Counsellor. I first outlined proposal in Nanking telegram No. 55 to me[2] and then spoke in approximately the same terms as Nanking telegram No. 27 to Tokyo[1] just received. I asked Kishimoto to support my request for extension of the time limit[3] and he has done so. Counsellor saw Japanese Ambassador and subsequently told me Japanese Embassy will do everything possible to extend time limit.

2. Counsellor stated in confidence that the Japanese military wished to take over customs and were chafing at the delay. Japanese Embassy advised by Kishimoto opposed this course and would make this clear once more to Tokyo with whom the matter now rested. I urged the most immediate action with Tokyo which he agreed to take.

[1] Not traced in F.O. archives.   [2] No. 295.
[3] In Tientsin telegram No. 38 of October 7 Mr. Affleck reported that the Japanese Consul General had told Mr. Myers that 'no more negotiations are possible' and given him until the evening of October 9 to accept the Japanese terms for the customs administration.

3. I have asked Japanese Financial Attaché to put urgently direct to the Ministry of Finance considerations referred to in the third paragraph of my telegram No. 115 to the Foreign Office.[4]

[4] No. 257.

No. 298

Mr. Eden to Sir R. Clive (Brussels)

No. 52 Telegraphic: by telephone [F 7771/6799/10]

Immediate   FOREIGN OFFICE, *October 9, 1937, 5 p.m.*

1. League of Nations proposal for consideration of Far Eastern situation by parties to the Nine Power Washington Agreement of 1922.[1]

2. His Majesty's Government in the United Kingdom feel it will be best if proposed meeting is not held in London, Washington or Paris, but rather at the capital of some party which has not large political interests in the Far East. In their opinion there could be no more suitable or indeed agreeable meeting place than Brussels. They have reason to believe that the United States Government share this view.[2]

3. Please endeavour to get into immediate touch with Prime Minister or Minister for Foreign Affairs and represent to him, in terms you consider best calculated to secure favourable reply, how gratified His Majesty's Government would be if the Belgian Government could see their way to allow the Conference to be held in Brussels. If they agree to this, you should say that it has been suggested that the Prime Minister of Belgium might issue invitations on behalf of the group to those signatories of the Nine Power Agreement who are not members of the League, i.e. United States and Japan. His Majesty's Government would further suggest that the Conference should meet about October 25th and that the consideration of what other States should be invited should be completed not later than the first meeting of the Conference.

Repeated to Paris No. 204 Saving (by bag).

---

[1] On the morning of October 9 the Foreign Office had learned through the Counsellor of the Netherlands Legation at London that the Dutch Government were 'not at all keen to have the Conference in The Hague'. The main argument was that it would be preferable to hold the conference in the capital of a country which had practically no political interest in the Far East, and it was also felt that the Dutch Government's non-recognition of the Soviet Government might cause difficulties. The Counsellor was told that Mr. Eden 'very much appreciates the spirit of this reply' and was therefore approaching the Belgian Government.

[2] Mr. Herschel Johnson called on Sir R. Vansittart on the evening of October 8 to deliver a message giving President Roosevelt's views on the proposed conference: see *F.R.U.S.*, 1937, vol. iv, pp. 67–8. The President's suggestions were incorporated in the present telegram to Sir R. Clive.

No. 299

Sir R. Craigie (Tokyo) to Mr. Eden (Received October 11, 1.20 p.m.)

No. 515 Telegraphic [F 7723/9/10]

TOKYO, *October 11, 1937, 8.5 p.m.*

On October 9th Ministry of Foreign Affairs issued statement refuting charges made against Japan in the League of Nations resolution[1] and statement made by United States Government.[2]

Statement expresses regret that real circumstances and true intentions of Japan are not understood, places full blame for incident on China and asserts that Japan is acting in self-defence, that she is merely seeking for 'abandonment by China of its anti-Japanese policy and establishment of enduring peace in East Asia through sincere co-operation between Japan and China' and that she has no territorial designs. Japanese action in China 'contravenes none of the existing treaties which are in force'; it is the Chinese Government who have brought about the present hostilities by 'persistent and malicious anti-Japanese measures', and by attempting to do away with the rights and vital interests of Japan in China by force of arms and it is they who should be regarded as having violated the spirit of the Treaty for renunciation of war.[3]

Repeated to Nanking.

[1] See No. 288.

[2] The reference is to a statement on the Far Eastern situation issued by Mr. Hull on October 6: see *F.R.U.S.*, 1937, vol. iv, pp. 62–3.

[3] Mr. Ronald commented on October 11: 'The Japanese are past masters at the art of studied stupidity. Up to a point it certainly pays to be wholly unable to see any one else's point of view and in a way it is actually a source of strength, but one must also at the same time be impervious to what other people think of you and this the Japanese appear not to be.'

No. 300

Mr. Eden to Mr. Mallet (Washington)

No. 433[1] Telegraphic [F 7477/7240/10]

Most Immediate   FOREIGN OFFICE, *October 12, 1937, 2 p.m.*

In his recent speech I noted that the President made use of the expression 'quarantine'. I have no doubt that the President recognises the implications of this phrase but I am somewhat concerned lest public opinion here and in the United States should too hastily and too easily assume that quarantine means economic sanctions without the risk of war. This is in fact the interpretation openly put upon the phrase by Senator

[1] For the origins of this telegram see No. 291.

386

Pit[t]man, and it is in this sense that there is already a tendency to interpret the expression here. It is an interpretation that in fact needs qualification. It would surely be unjustifiable and therefore highly dangerous to assume that Japan would in her present mood submit to a boycott or to economic sanctions that were effective without seeking to rectify the consequences. She might for instance seize some territory in the Far East under the control of those applying the embargo with a view to counteracting its effect, or with a view to acquiring bases, or by way of retaliation. There are possibilities which must necessarily be faced in good time, that is at an early stage in the full consideration to which I have referred in my telegram 409.[2]

I will in any case send to you in due course a further appreciation of the situation before the American delegation to the Nine Power Conference starts,[3] but I think it important that you should in the first instance pass on this indication to the State Department in the course of today.

All this however seems to me to reinforce the need for discussion of the problem in all its bearings, and I would therefore attach particular importance to the suggestion contained in your telegram No. 332,[4] viz. that the American Delegation on its way to Brussels should spend a day or even possibly two days in London so that full opportunity may be afforded to attain complete understanding between us.

[2] No. 272.   [3] See Nos. 311 and 312 below.   [4] No. 294.

No. 301

Mr. Mallet (Washington) to Mr. Eden
(Received October 12, 8.15 p.m.)

No. 340[1] *Telegraphic* [F 7792/7240/10]

Immediate   WASHINGTON, *October 12, 1937, 1.55 p.m.*

Your telegram No. 433.[2]

I spoke to Under Secretary of State accordingly.[3] He interprets 'quarantine' as a remote and vague objective. President did not intend to suggest it as in any way an immediate policy. On the contrary emphasis should be placed on the last sentence of the speech 'America hates war. America hopes for peace. Therefore America actively engages in search for peace'. Pittman's remarks had no official authority. Press had also distorted State Department's statement (my telegram No. 329[4]) into 'America brands Japan as aggressor'. It did nothing of the kind. United

[1] This telegram and No. 300 have been printed in reverse order as telegram No. 340 was in reply to No. 433, although despatched five minutes beforehand because of the time difference between Washington and London.
[2] No. 300.   [3] See *F.R.U.S.*, 1937, vol. iii, pp. 600–2.
[4] Not kept in F.O. archives: see No. 299, note 2.

States Government intended at the Conference to promote a constructive policy for peace in the Far East. President's broadcast tonight[5] would help to elucidate.

I urged strongly that United States Delegation should visit London on the way to Brussels but Mr. Sumner Welles was non-committal. He expressed keen desire to see further appreciation of the situation promised in your telegram and said that after studying that it would be easier to judge of the utility of London visit. In any event time was getting short and if Conference was really to meet on October 25th he hoped that invitations would not be delayed.

He indicated that the Secretary of State would be unable to leave Washington but that Delegation would be headed by a person in whom the President reposes entire confidence. I suppose Mr. Norman Davis.

[5] See *The Times*, October 13, 1937, p. 14.

No. 302

Mr. Howe (Nanking) to Mr. Eden (Received October 13, 9.30 a.m.)

No. 565 Telegraphic [F 7798/220/10]

Immediate　　　　　　　　　　　　　　　NANKING, *October 13, 1937, 4 a.m.*

Addressed to Tientsin No. 65.

Your telegram No. 83.[1]

Please communicate following statement to Myers and inform him that instructions will be sent to him by Inspector General of Customs that if Japanese authorities at Tientsin agree to terms contained therein he is authorised to accept them.[2]

1. The procedure now in force is that all customs revenues are deposited with Central Bank of China. The Chinese Government is willing to instruct on its own initiative the Central Bank of China to authorise as a provisional measure a bank of a third country as custodian bank to receive such revenues, details of arrangement to be fixed by the two banks.

2. The revenues referred to above shall include those of Tientsin and Chinwangtao customs.

3. The period for which authorisation is given will only cover the duration of present hostilities.

4. The custodian bank shall be responsible for Central Bank of China

[1] In this telegram of October 12 (No. 46 to the Foreign Office) Mr. Affleck gave the text of a telegram from Mr. Myers to Sir F. Maze informing him that he had obtained three days' respite from the Japanese Consul General: cf. No. 297, note 3.

[2] Embassy Offices Shanghai telegram No. 147 of October 14 F7934/220/10 transmitted the text of the instructions sent to Mr. Myers by Sir F. Maze: the terms he was authorized to offer were essentially the same as those in the present telegram.

for safe custody of all customs revenues so deposited. With regard however to revenues collected by Tientsin and Chinwangtao customs the custodian bank is permitted to deposit them with another bank.

5. The custodian bank shall during the period of authorisation mentioned in No. 1 above make necessary monthly payments as heretofore. As regards however the revenues deposited temporarily with other bank mentioned in No. 4 it may draw by cheque on such other bank as they fall due the necessary amounts for payment of quota . . .[3] loans assigned to Tientsin and Chinwangto and for defraying if necessary current local expenses of those stations.

6. The custodian bank shall not concern itself with matters other than arrangements above mentioned.

Repeated to Financial Adviser, Tokyo and Peking.

[3] The text was here uncertain.

No. 303

Mr. Howe (Nanking) to Mr. Eden (Received October 13, 9.30 a.m.)

No. 566 Telegraphic [F 7799/220/10]

Immediate   NANKING, *October 13, 1937, 4 a.m.*

My telegram No. 65[1] to Tientsin confidential.

After constant persuasion and representations during the last few days, I was sent for by the Minister for Foreign Affairs at 11.30 p.m. tonight October 12th when his Excellency handed to me the terms set out in my above mentioned telegram. He hoped very much that the Japanese would accept them as he had had a hard struggle to induce the other members of the Government to agree to them and said that it would not be possible to get them to accept any modification.

It seems to me that the Japanese would be foolish to reject the arrangement which gives them all and even more than they ask, since it makes no mention of any balance left over in Yokohama Specie Bank after payment of loan quotas and expenses.

The Minister for Foreign Affairs was evidently anxious that the Japanese should not be given the impression that the Chinese Government were willingly agreeing to the arrangement. Rather should it be regarded as their limit of concession.[2]

Repeated to Peking, Financial Adviser, Tokyo, Tientsin.

[1] No. 302.
[2] The Foreign Office considered it 'very satisfactory that the Chinese should have given way'. Sir J. Pratt commented on October 14 that the special arrangement at Tientsin and Chinwangtao 'should be satisfactory to the Japanese military authorities in control at these places . . . The advantage of handling the matter in this way is that the special arrangement can be extended to any other Treaty ports that may fall under the control of the Japanese military'.

No. 304

Extract from Cabinet Conclusions No. 37(37) of October 13, 1937

[*F 8000/6799/10*]

5. The Secretary of State for Foreign Affairs said he hoped that Brussels would be accepted as the place for the proposed Conference to be summoned under the Nine-Power Treaty regarding China, of February, 1922, and that the date would be October 25th. A telegram setting out the views of His Majesty's Government was in course of preparation in the Foreign Office,[1] and it was hoped to send it to Washington before the departure of the United States Delegation. He drew attention to telegram No. 433,[2] which had been sent to Washington in order to give the American Government a preliminary indication of our views on economic sanctions. In reply to a question, he said that no invitations to the Conference were to be sent out until the place of meeting was definitely settled.

The Prime Minister thought it important that the Cabinet should consider our objectives at the coming Conference, as well as what we should avoid. He also thought it very desirable that an understanding should be reached with the United States representatives as to the line to be taken, as if a difference arose our position would be weakened. He recalled that President Roosevelt had used the expression 'quarantine',[3] which had been generally interpreted as a boycott. He himself had noticed, however, that the President's speech was so worded that he could escape from that interpretation. In the House of Commons the Opposition Parties might well interpret the phrase as an offer to impose economic sanctions, and would suggest that we were standing in the way of an effective restraint on Japan. If this occurred it might be necessary to come into the open. He himself had been thinking over the whole matter, and, after discussion with the Secretary of State for Foreign Affairs, had arrived at certain conclusions, in which he thought the Secretary of State agreed.

[1] An interdepartmental meeting was held at the Foreign Office on the afternoon of October 13 to consider the terms of a draft telegram to Washington giving an appreciation of the probable effects of taking economic measures against Japan: a record of the meeting is filed at F 8143/6799/10. There was considerable disagreement on the terms of the draft: Mr. Waley, for the Treasury, disagreed 'with almost every word', feeling that it 'did not sufficiently stress the difficulties of imposing sanctions'. Mr. Jebb for the Foreign Office thought Treasury objections 'far too categorical. Sanctions might or might not be desirable, but if generally adopted they might very well be successful'. Representatives of other Departments expressed equally strong views on both sides. The meeting finally agreed to leave the decision to Ministers, and the telegrams finally drafted (see Nos. 311 and 312 below) were based on the decisions of the present Cabinet meeting. Captain Phillips of the Admiralty also suggested that the whole question should be considered by the Advisory Committee on Trade and Blockade Questions in Time of War (A.T.B. Committee), a Sub-Committee of the C.I.D.: see No. 315 below.

[2] No. 300.

[3] Cf. No. 291, note 2.

These were as follows:

(1) It was impossible to put in force *effective* sanctions without a risk of war.

(2) We could put in force ineffective sanctions, but these would not accomplish their purpose and would result (as in the case of Italy) in prolonged bitterness and ill-will.

(3) He doubted whether, even if a sufficient number of countries could be induced to put economic sanctions in force effectively, they would operate in time to save China, whose collapse appeared possible and might even be imminent. The Japanese armies appeared to be rolling up the Chinese. They might in due course capture Nanking, Hankow and Canton, in which case the condition of the Chinese would be comparable to that of Abyssinia, Chiang Kai-shek taking the place of the Emperor.[4]

(4) If sanctions proved effective there was no guarantee that Japan, possibly egged on by Germany and Italy, would not make some retaliatory attack, e.g., on some oil supplies in the East Indies, or on Hong-Kong, or the Philippines. If they did so what could we do in present conditions? It would not be safe to send the Fleet to the Far East in the present position in Europe. We could not go into sanctions, therefore, without a guarantee from the United States of America that they would be prepared to face up to all the consequences which might fall on nations with large interests in the Far East. Even then it was impossible to foresee how long public opinion in America would be prepared to maintain the position. His conclusion, therefore, was that economic sanctions were of no use unless backed by overwhelming force.

He had considered the alternative that the Powers should render assistance to China in the form of war material and munitions. This, however, would have to be carried by sea, and supplies could not be ensured without command of the sea, which brought us back to the question of force.

He had then asked himself the question whether the Conference was to do nothing. He thought he discerned a possibility that Japan, if treated diplomatically, might consent to some possible terms. China at present was holding out against the negotiation of terms, being in a position when she was bound not to show weakness. It must not be assumed, however, that this was their last word. He would like to say, therefore, that we had come to the Conference in the interests of peace and were not going to think of compulsion until conciliation had been exhausted. That would not commit us on the ultimate issue, since we should only say that we 'would not think of' compulsion. In his belief that Japan might be induced to make terms he was encouraged by recent telegrams from His Majesty's

[4] Cf. Volume XVI, Chapter IV.

Ambassador in Tokyo. At his request the Secretary of State for Foreign Affairs had sent a telegram to the Ambassador asking him to keep his channels of communication open.[5] That was the most fruitful line of action, and if it succeeded it had the advantage of leaving no bitterness. He thought that the Foreign Secretary shared his view, except that he required some precautions as to our communications with the United States of America. He asked if that view commended itself to the Cabinet.

The Minister for Co-ordination of Defence said that on the previous evening he had seen Lord Runciman, who had told him that the Japanese had made great efforts to finance their purchases of Australian wool but had failed. This information, he thought, supported the view that the Japanese, whose financial position was very difficult, might be willing to discuss peace terms now, though if their financial position became worse their attitude might harden.

The Secretary of State for Air said that the Prime Minister's line must appeal to the Service Departments.

The Chancellor of the Exchequer also agreed with the Prime Minister. He suggested that the success of the Conference would depend upon Japan's willingness to attend. From this point of view it was rather unfortunate that the Conference was to be summoned in relation to the Nine-Power Treaty regarding China, the first Article of which stated that the Contracting Powers agreed 'to respect the sovereignty, the independence, and the territorial and administrative integrity of China.' It was rather difficult to reconcile this with the Prime Minister's suggested approach to the Conference.

The Secretary of State for Foreign Affairs feared that the prospect of Japan being represented at the Conference was remote. He endorsed the Prime Minister's description of the effect of sanctions. He himself would never agree to the imposition of sanctions without the agreement of the United States of America and the other signatories of the China Treaty to support those sanctions by the use of force, if need be. He thought that President Roosevelt's speech was a most important new factor in the situation, and that Anglo-American co-operation was vital. He thought that in the communication to the United States Government the question should be approached on the lines of the *Manchester Guardian* article mentioned by the Prime Minister at the Meeting of the Cabinet referred to in the margin,[6] namely, to make clear that we could not go into sanctions without a definite undertaking by all concerned to support them in all circumstances. He would, however, not like to indicate that, in the

[5] Cf. Nos. 245, 265, and 267. In telegram No. 508 of October 8 Sir R. Craigie had urged that the fact that the Japanese terms had been passed to him gave His Majesty's Government 'a means of influencing the Japanese Government . . . far more potent than that provided by joint action of a number of Powers'. Telegram No. 385 to Tokyo of October 12 instructed Sir R. Craigie to 'keep open any channel that holds any promise': in view of the proposed Nine Power Conference, however, 'we must not appear to be acting behind the backs of our associates'.

[6] See No. 291.

extremely unlikely event of the American Government being prepared to act on those lines, we should refuse. For his part, in spite of all the dangers, he thought we should take the risk in such an eventuality.

The Secretary of State for Scotland doubted whether the odds against such an offer were quite so great as had been suggested. President Roosevelt's speech had been made after his own Observer had reported what had happened at Geneva. He thought there were some not unhopeful features in the situation. The Chinese representatives at Geneva had expressed the view that the Japanese armies were not attempting to over-run China, but that their object was to push the Chinese across the Yellow River in order to get them out of the way with a view to an eventual attack on the U.S.S.R. in Eastern Siberia. He saw no difficulty, however, in laying emphasis on conciliation as the object of the Conference. Our Delegation at Geneva had put all the stress on this point. He agreed, however, that we should explore the possibility of close co-operation with the United States. Dictators had a habit of going on until they were stopped, and the example of one might be followed by others, with dangerous results in Europe.

The President of the Board of Education agreed in the Prime Minister's proposals. As to the military situation, he thought it possible that the Japanese might soon find themselves marching across a vast country in the grip of a hard winter, getting nowhere, like Napoleon in Russia. If the Chinese could hold out until the end of the year and then adopt guerilla warfare, the Japanese might be unable to bring the war to an end. This prospect might incline them to negotiations.

The Secretary of State for War read a Report from the Military Attaché indicating the probability of an early victory for Japan. He thought it important not to put Japan 'in the dock' at the Conference. If we made clear that our object was to bring about peace, the prospects were not unhopeful.

The Secretary of State for Dominion Affairs agreed with the Prime Minister. The situation in Europe was too critical to justify our taking any risks in the Far East. It was important, from the point of view of home politics, to make clear to the world that the United States of America were whole-heartedly with us in this matter. He thought it quite possible that the Japanese might be willing to make an effort to secure peace. Later he reminded the Cabinet that some of the Dominions were signatories of the Nine-Power Treaty. He thought we ought to get into line with them even before we approached the United States of America, and suggested that the Dominions Office and the Foreign Office should arrange for discussions. He agreed that care would have to be exercised owing to the indiscretions of the representative of one Dominion. He proposed to approach them by way of informal discussion.

The Lord Chancellor agreed with the Prime Minister's analysis. He thought it unnecessary for the Cabinet to make up their minds today what to do if the United States of America wanted to impose sanctions.

393

The Lord President of the Council agreed with the Lord Chancellor. He thought we should be content with stating the situation frankly to the United States of America. Even if America did take a more bellicose line than we, we should have to think carefully before committing to them the defence of our interests in the Far East.

The Secretary of State for Foreign Affairs said that it was important to avoid putting the American Government in a position to say that they could have cleared up the situation but for our unwillingness.

The Prime Minister thanked his colleagues for the expression of their views. It was very useful to the Foreign Secretary, other members of the Cabinet, and himself, to know the general lines on which both foreign policy and public statements should be based. He thought nothing should be done to suggest the imposition of sanctions.

The Cabinet agreed:

(a) That our policy towards the Conference should be framed on the lines of the Prime Minister's statement, summarised on the first three pages of this record and marked 'C',[7] for the subsequent discussion:

(b) That the Secretary of State for Dominion Affairs, in concert with the Secretary of State for Foreign Affairs, should take such action as he might deem appropriate for informing the Governments of the Dominions of our policy and, so far as possible, for securing their agreement.

[7] i.e. the second, third, and fourth paragraphs of this Extract. Mr. Chamberlain's views on the policy to be adopted towards the Brussels Conference had been more fully elaborated in notes which he gave to Sir R. Vansittart on October 11: a copy of these notes, and of the draft telegram to Washington which Sir R. Vansittart based on them, is preserved in PREM 1/314. Mr. Eden and Mr. Chamberlain discussed the draft further on October 12, and telegram No. 455 to Washington of October 18 (No. 312 below), although amended in the light of the Cabinet discussion, corresponds closely to Mr. Chamberlain's notes. Cf. No. 287, note 3.

No. 305

Record by Mr. Eden of a telephone conversation with Mr. Davis on October 13, 1937, at 6.45 p.m.

[F 7860/6799/10]

FOREIGN OFFICE, *October 13, 1937*

Mr. Norman Davis telephoned to explain that a cable had just been received from Tokyo[1] to say that the Belgian Ambassador in Tokyo was reported to have said to the Japanese Vice Minister for Foreign Affairs that the Belgian Government did not wish to have the Nine Power

[1] See *F.R.U.S.*, 1937, vol. iv, p. 74.

Conference at Brussels, but that they did wish to know whether the Japanese Government would come. The Japanese Vice Minister replied that the Japanese Government was not interested in these conditions. Mr. Davis hoped that we would do our best to hasten a decision from the Belgian Government as it was essential to get the invitations out without further delay.

Mr. Davis, who explained that he was speaking for Mr. Hull who had a bad cold and could not shout on a Trans-Atlantic telephone, added that the United States Government considered it desirable to make an approach to the Japanese Government before the actual invitation reached them and to say how much we both hoped that Japan would attend the Conference. It should be explained to the Japanese Government that the purpose of the Conference was to put an end to the conflict by agreement. It should also be explained to them that the present situation was causing the gravest anxiety and we therefore earnestly hoped for their co-operation to put an end to it.

We agreed that our two Ambassadors should speak in Tokyo in this sense previous to the receipt of the invitation by Japan and that they should concert together the expressions which they would use. The approach would not be a joint one, but the language used would be similar. Mr. Davis added: 'Don't think we are going to drop you a bomb over this'.[2] I replied that I had never had the least anxiety on that score. I understood him to mean that U.S. Government were not going to put potentially dangerous proposals to us.

I then asked Mr. Davis whether he was coming to London on his way to Brussels or Paris and he replied that he thought this difficult for a variety of reasons. He very much hoped, however, that I should be able to attend the Conference in person. I replied that I hoped to be able to do so at least for a period.

A.E.

[2] Mr. Eden referred to this phrase in telegram No. 444 to Washington, despatched at 11 p.m. on October 13. Mr. Mallet was instructed that if he should think 'that the U.S. Government entertain any suspicion that they cannot count upon our cooperation in any proposals which are designed to give effect to the President's policy', he should 'at once make plain that such suspicion is groundless'. The concluding paragraph, in Mr. Eden's handwriting, read: 'I do not want U.S. Government to pretend even to themselves that we are acting as a brake for which impression there is not of course the slightest foundation.'

No. 306

Mr. Mallet (Washington) to Mr. Eden (Received October 15, 9.30 a.m.)

No. 346 Telegraphic [F 7927/6799/10]

Important   WASHINGTON, *October 14, 1937, 4.52 p.m.*

Your telegram No. 444.[1]

I took the opportunity during interview this morning with Under Secretary of State[2] to make this clear.

He welcomed my statement and said most earnestly that United States Government were anxious to cooperate with us and to avoid any possible cause for misunderstanding. He had in fact been slightly uneasy after our conversation reported in my telegram No. 340.[3] I explained the object of that message had been to emphasise the importance of co-operation such as he desired. I did not think you had been inclined to place undue emphasis on word 'quarantine' but rather that it was the press in both countries which has distorted its meaning.

Mr. Sumner Welles again stressed importance of hastening invitations. Delay was having a bad effect on opinion here.

[1] See No. 305, note 2.   [2] See *F.R.U.S.*, 1937, vol. iii, pp. 608–9.   [3] No. 301.

No. 307

Record by Sir R. Vansittart of a conversation with Mr. Herschel Johnson

[F 7994/6799/10]

FOREIGN OFFICE, *October 14, 1937*

The Counsellor of the United States Embassy called this afternoon and communicated to me the instructions that were being sent to the United States Ambassador in Brussels.[1] These were to the effect that it was the American view that though the Nine Power Treaty arose out of a suggestion of the League Assembly, the meeting itself was not under the auspices of the League but autonomous. The United States Government wished on no account to cross wires with His Majesty's Government in preliminary conversations with the Belgian Government. The British Government had approached the United States Government in the matter and the United States had expressed their view that Brussels would be the best meeting-place. The United States Government had therefore only been attempting to support His Majesty's Government for this purpose.

The United States Chargé d'Affaires went on to say that his Government attached great importance to the Nine Power Conference and

[1] See *F.R.U.S.*, 1937, vol. iv, p. 73: cf. p. 72.

thought it was of the greatest importance that the delegations to be present there should be strong ones. Mr. Hull was happy to note that Mr. Eden would presumably be there himself. Mr. Hull for his part had found it impossible to undertake the journey at this moment, and Mr. Norman Davis would represent the United States in his place. The United States Government wished, however, that this information should be regarded as confidential until an official announcement was made.

The United States, Mr. Johnson added, were becoming considerably concerned at the delay in fixing the date and place of the meeting, and considered the general effect of this delay was bad. They earnestly hoped that the British Government might soon be able to remove the hesitations of the Belgian Government.[2]

[2] Mr. Eden wrote on the filed copy of this record: 'I agree emphatically as to harm of delay. Belgians really must decide yes or no *tomorrow*.' After further exchanges between Mr. Orde and the Belgian Embassy on October 15, the formal invitation of the Belgian Government reached the Foreign Office on October 16: see No. 309 below.

No. 308

Sir R. Craigie (Tokyo) to Mr. Eden (Received October 15, 7 p.m.)

No. 545 Telegraphic [F 8006/6799/10]

TOKYO, *October 15, 1937, 11.15 p.m.*

My telegram No. 534.[1]
United States Ambassador having received his instructions[2] saw the Minister for Foreign Affairs this afternoon. I saw him later and spoke as directed in your telegram No. 391[3] leaving a note of what I had said.

Minister for Foreign Affairs after remarking that Japanese Government had not so far received invitation to Conference, stated that while no definite decision had yet been taken in the matter the 'general tendency here was against acceptance'. He mentioned the fact that Japan had already been stigmatized as an aggressor by the Powers composing the Conference[4] adding that Japanese opinion was strongly in favour of direct settlement with China.

I emphasized the point about the Conference being called to promote settlement by agreement and said that I interpreted this to mean that its

[1] Not kept in F.O. archives.
[2] See *F.R.U.S.*, 1937, vol. iv, p. 77.
[3] This telegram of October 13 referred to No. 305 and instructed Sir R. Craigie, after consultation with his American colleague, to point out to the Japanese Government, in view of indications that they were thinking of refusing an invitation to the Nine Power Conference, that the Sino-Japanese conflict was 'causing grave and continuing anxiety': it was to be hoped that the Japanese Government would accept the invitation and cooperate in the aim of the Conference, which was to settle the conflict by peaceful agreement.
[4] Cf. Nos. 264, 288, and 292.

purpose would be conciliation rather than pressure. Speaking for myself I believed that Japanese Government were sincerely anxious to bring incident to a speedy termination and that it would be a great mistake to miss this opportunity of doing so, particularly if Japan's terms were to be reasonable and possibly even generous. Diplomatic possibilities of such a Conference from Japan's point of view should not be overlooked. Refusal of invitation on the other hand would lead the world to believe Japan's intentions were not sufficiently defensible to permit of them being explained at an International Conference.

Minister for Foreign Affairs listened attentively and did not deny that there was some force in this, but repeated that opinion here was in general strongly opposed to any idea of mediation by a number of Powers.

Assistance in securing settlement from a single Power such as Great Britain or United States of America would be another matter and might be welcomed at appropriate moment. I replied that as he knew our good offices were at his disposal but that amount of assistance we could offer must depend on character of terms and particularly on their freedom from any limitations on Chinese sovereignty.

Finally Minister for Foreign Affairs said that it would be extremely difficult for the Japanese Government to authorise their diplomatists to start discussing peace terms at an International Conference while their soldiers and sailors were still fighting for their country in China. However no final decision had, he repeated, been taken in the matter.[5]

[5] Mr. Eden wrote across the filed copy of this telegram: 'A. C[adogan]. We must be very careful not to let Japs refuse on ground that we are go-between already. Another telegram to Craigie is called for.' See No. 310 below.

No. 309

Aide-Mémoire communicated by the Belgian Ambassador[1]

[F 8008/6799/10]

LONDRES, le 16 octobre, 1937

Donnant suite à une demande du Gouvernement de Sa Majesté Britannique faite avec l'approbation du Gouvernement des États-Unis d'Amérique, le Gouvernement du Roi propose aux Etats signataires du Traité du 6 février 1922 de se réunir à Bruxelles le 30 de ce mois,[2] à l'effet d'examiner, conformément à l'article 7 de ce Traité, la situation en

[1] Baron de Cartier de Marchienne.

[2] On October 26 the Foreign Office agreed, on the urgent request of M. Spaak, the Belgian Foreign Minister, to postpone the opening of the conference until November 3, following the resignation of the Belgian Government on October 25 (cf. Volume XIX, No. 440, note 1).

Extrême Orient, et d'étudier les moyens amiables de hâter la fin du conflit regrettable qui y sévit.

L'Ambassade de Belgique serait très reconnaissante des instructions que M. le Secrétaire d'Etat Principal pour les Affaires Etrangères croirait pouvoir donner en vue de lui faire savoir aussitôt que possible si le Gouvernement de Sa Majesté Britannique serait disposé à assister à cette réunion.[3]

[3] The British Government's acceptance of the invitation was notified to the Belgian Embassy on the same day, October 16.

No. 310

Mr. Eden to Sir R. Craigie (Tokyo)

No. 400 Telegraphic [F 8006/6799/10]

FOREIGN OFFICE, October 18, 1937, 7 p.m.

Your telegram No. 545.[1] Penultimate paragraph.

It is important that Japanese Government should not be given any excuse for refusing to attend the Conference on the ground that His Majesty's Government are already acting or prepared to act as go-between for them with the Chinese Government. You should take steps to remove any misapprehension which may conceivably exist as to our attitude. Japanese attendance at the Conference represents the best chance of peace, indeed the only one so far as we can see at present, and a Japanese refusal to attend could only reduce the power of His Majesty's Government to help in the promotion of peace.

You should therefore again urge on the Japanese Government the importance, from every point of view, of their representation at the Conference. Their case went by default at Geneva and it would seem essential, in their own interests, that they should be present at Brussels to put their side of the case. The other Governments represented there will be ready and anxious to give careful consideration to anything that the Japanese Government may wish to put forward.

[1] No. 308: cf. ibid., note 5.

No. 311

Mr. Eden to Mr. Mallet (Washington)

No. 456 Telegraphic [F 8013/6799/10]

Immediate   FOREIGN OFFICE, *October 18, 1937, 9.10 p.m.*

My immediately preceding telegram.[1]

For your own information only it may be useful to you to have the following indications of our attitude.[2]

It seems to us unlikely that sanctions on any conceivable scale could take effect until after the military defeat of China. Although this is not necessarily a decisive objection to their imposition, we feel in any case that, if they were applied and seemed likely to succeed in their object, Japan might well resort to force either against the Powers applying them or against territories of vital interest to them such as the Dutch East Indies. Situation in Europe is such that we, for our part, should not be prepared to incur this risk of Japanese retaliation, unless we were assured in advance of full military support from the United States.

It is of vital importance to us not to discourage in any way the present tendency of the United States Government to emerge from their isolation. For this reason and to avoid subsequent misrepresentation of our attitude it is essential that we should not give an impression of lagging behind the United States Government in our desire to put an end to the present conflict by any practicable means, including sanctions if necessary.

On the other hand to offer directly, or even to appear eager to apply sanctions and at the same time to ask outright for a guarantee of military assistance would probably appear to the United States Government as an attempt to rush them into a system of collective security and might perhaps strengthen their isolationist tendencies. Moreover, any such offer, if disclosed later, would do irreparable harm to our subsequent relations with Japan.

It is accordingly desirable to steer a middle course between two dangers outlined in the two preceding paragraphs. In any conversation you may have on this subject with United States officials, you should therefore, if questioned on the point, adopt the general attitude that, while we have not yet completed our investigation into the efficacy of sanctions, we are fully prepared to discuss this or any other possible course of action with them. The necessity of a military guarantee has been made quite clear in my appreciation of the situation and should if possible not be further emphasised in conversation.

---

[1] No. 312 below: telegrams Nos. 455 and 456 were despatched in reverse order.

[2] In a minute of October 15 Mr. Jebb stated that this telegram and No. 312 below were drafted in the light of departmental criticism of the original draft telegram to Washington (see No. 304, note 1), and of the Cabinet discussion (No. 304). In a long minute of October 15 Mr. A. Holman, a First Secretary in the American Department of the Foreign Office,

expressed a strong preference for the new drafts, although he concluded: 'I think that we can expect to get little out of America in the way of concerted action in regard to economic or other measures against Japan . . . It is true that the President's Chicago speech [see No. 291, note 2] was delivered in rather strong terms, but it seems unlikely that it will have any immediate effect on the country and Congress . . . Personally I should have thought that America would never take any strong line unless the national emotions were aroused again, as in the last war. This takes time, and so far is certainly not the case.'

Mr. Orde and Sir A. Cadogan also preferred the new drafts, and Mr. Ronald noted on October 19 that Mr. Eden had approved the despatch of the telegrams on the previous evening after discussion with Mr. Chamberlain.

No. 312

Mr. Eden to Mr. Mallet (Washington)

No. 455 Telegraphic [F 8013/6799/10]

Immediate　　　　　　　　　　　　FOREIGN OFFICE, October 18, 1937, 11 p.m.

Following is further appreciation of situation referred to in my telegram No. 433, paragraph 2.[1]

2. First objective of Brussels Conference must be to reach peace by agreement. It is still uncertain whether Japan will attend, and in her absence it is doubtful whether we can attain this object unless or until some considerable change occurs in Japan's military or economic position. Conference may thus be faced with choice of

(a) deferring any action in the hope that such a change will supervene.
(b) expressing moral condemnation of Japan, without taking or promising any positive action.
(c) embarking on positive action in the form either of active assistance to China or of economic pressure on Japan.

3. Both (a) and (b) are open to the obvious objection that they are tantamount to acquiescence in aggression. Either course could only serve as encouragement to peace-breakers. Course (b) has the additional disadvantage that it would further exasperate opinion in Japan to no purpose.

4. In these circumstances His Majesty's Government feel that it is necessary for both the United States Government and themselves to go to Brussels in the full realization of the implications of course (c).

5. So far as assistance to China is concerned, (even if the United States Neutrality Law were not an insuperable objection to it) it must be remembered that there are material difficulties in the way of rendering assistance. If it is to be effective it must directly or indirectly involve supplying China with war material. The sea route is, or will shortly be, the only practicable one, and if such supplies were to reach China on a scale large enough to affect the issue of hostilities, it is hardly conceivable that

[1] No. 300: for the origins of this telegram, see No. 304, note 7.

Japan would not extend the blockade to neutral ships. We should then be faced with the alternatives of acquiescing in this extended blockade or of keeping the sea routes open by armed force.

6. So far as economic measures against Japan are concerned, a preliminary investigation suggests that they might be effective if they were applied by the United States of America, all the countries of the British Empire, and some six or eight other countries, provided that satisfactory measures could be evolved to prevent evasion through third parties and provided that the measures extended both to imports and to exports. His Majesty's Government are pursuing their study of this matter and would be happy to discuss it in all its aspects with the United States Delegation if they would agree to such a discussion. Whether economic measures would become effective in time to affect the issue of the war, unless China were simultaneously assisted, is perhaps doubtful. But, irrespective of this, it seems to His Majesty's Government that if sanctions appeared likely to succeed in their object, there would be a very real danger of Japan taking violent action to prevent their success, either by making war on one or more of the sanctionist countries or by seizing the territory of some other power from which essential raw materials could be derived. In view of this danger it appears to His Majesty's Government that no country could afford to impose effective sanctions unless it first received from the other participating countries an assurance of military support in the event of violent action by Japan. It would also be necessary to guarantee the territorial integrity of third parties. If such assurances were forthcoming it is possible, although of course not certain, that Japan would be deterred from taking any such action, and that the knowledge that sanctions would eventually prove successful might lead her to consider an early peace.

7. These are briefly the considerations which present themselves to His Majesty's Government in their preliminary examination of the problem. In conveying them to the United States Government you should emphasize that they are not a statement of policy, but an appreciation of the difficulties which must be faced and if possible discussed between our two governments before the Brussels Conference meets. It is for this reason that we hope the United States delegation will be able to call here on their way to Brussels.

8. You should accompany this statement with an informal intimation that foregoing represents views of His Majesty's Government in the United Kingdom. It has been impossible to obtain views of Dominion Governments, but they are being consulted urgently.

No. 313

Mr. Mallet (Washington) to Mr. Eden (Received October 20, 9.30 a.m.)

No. 357 Telegraphic [F 8191/6799/10]

Immediate   WASHINGTON, *October 19, 1937*

Your telegram No. 455.[1]

Mr. Wilson sent for me this evening and expressed thanks of United States Government for this interesting aide-mémoire.[2]

He states that United States Government was of the opinion that, for the moment, considerations such as those raised under point (c) did not arise in a conference which had for its objective the finding of a solution of conflict in the Far East by agreement.

United States Government had been giving much thought to question of possible procedure with two objectives, that of inducing the two parties to the conflict to enter upon an armistice, to be followed by peaceful negotiation and that of endeavouring to find a means of stabilizing conditions in the Far East. Mr. Norman Davis is fully conversant with such thoughts and it had occurred to the Secretary of State that it might be advisable to invite your attention to this phase of the problem, in anticipation of your talks with Mr. Norman Davis in Brussels.

Above was handed to me in the form of a record of conversation. I questioned Mr. Wilson on phrase 'stabilizing conditions' and it was evident that State Department's ideas are still very fluid and undefined. Mr. Wilson thought conversations between our delegations might elucidate better than cable messages but was ready, if you desired it, to attempt a fuller explanation in the next few days.

He admitted that point (c) might eventually have to come up and seemed personally glad that you had raised it now.

It seems clear to me however that United States delegation do not intend to be drawn into discussion of sanctions during preliminary stages.[3] The fact that they are not taking an economic expert with the delegation seems to confirm this.

---

[1] No. 312.   [2] See *F.R.U.S.*, 1937, vol. iv, p. 92.   [3] Cf. *F.R.U.S.*, *ibid.*, pp. 85–6.

Sir R. Craigie (Tokyo) to Mr. Eden (Received October 20, 3.50 p.m.)

No. 566 Telegraphic [*F 8218/6799/10*]

Important   TOKYO, *October 20, 1937, 10.10 p.m.*

My telegram No. 559.[1]

Although Japanese Government have not yet received invitation, I thought it better not to delay longer and spoke to Minister for Foreign Affairs this evening in sense of your telegram No. 400.[2]

His Excellency replied that since he had last discussed this question with me he had had numerous consultations and found opinion running very strongly against Japanese participation in conference. There were a few responsible people who favoured participation as a means of putting Japan's case before the world but they were small minority. Japanese public opinion had hitherto been so united in face of present emergency that government were not prepared to risk a serious rift in opinion on this issue.

I used every argument I could think of to persuade him of unwisdom of a refusal to participate. Japanese public opinion seemed to me clearly anxious to bring Chinese affair to a speedy termination and as conference probably represented the last opportunity of finding a peaceful solution for months to come it was difficult to understand how there could be such strong opposition to Japan's attendance. But I was unable to move His Excellency and I left with the impression that there is now very little hope of Japan's acceptance of invitation.

Minister for Foreign Affairs for the first time showed signs of fatigue and depression. I believe he has put up a fight for Japanese representation but has lost. He did not appear at all interested in the question of composition of the conference.

[1] Not kept in F.O. archives.   [2] No. 310.

No. 315

Extract from Cabinet Conclusions No. 38(37) of October 20, 1937

[*F 8306/6799/10*]

5. The Minister for Co-ordination of Defence said that a proposal had been received from the Foreign Office that the Advisory Committee on Trade Questions in Time of War should be asked to examine the effect on Japan of the imposition of economic sanctions.[1] As the matter had a political bearing he had thought it right to bring the proposal to the notice

[1] Cf. No. 304, note 1.

of the Cabinet. In that connection he drew attention to a Report on this very subject that had been prepared by the Sub-Committee in March, 1932 (C.I.D. Paper No. 1083B[2]) some parts of which were appropriate to the present situation, though they would require to be brought up to date.

The Cabinet agreed

> That the Advisory Committee on Trade questions in Time of War should be instructed
>
>> 'To consider and report to the Committee of Imperial Defence what results could be achieved by the imposition of economic sanctions against Japan by the British Empire and the United States of America in conjunction, alternatively with or without the co-operation of other countries.'[3]

[2] Not printed.

[3] A preparatory memorandum on economic measures against Japan was drawn up in the Foreign Office and circulated to the A.T.B. Committee on October 22 as A.T.B. 154: a copy of this paper is preserved in F.O. 837/528. The memorandum stated that 'Anglo-Japanese trade is on too small a scale to permit of any effective unilateral action by the United Kingdom' and even complete interruption of trade with the Empire would only involve Japan in serious, not overwhelming difficulties, although these would be intensified if the United States agreed to participate. A number of detailed criticisms of this paper (especially its tables of trade figures) were made by Major Desmond Morton of the Industrial Intelligence Centre: his comments are also preserved in F.O. 837/528.

Mr. Walter Elliot, Chairman of the A.T.B. Committee, directed that the question of economic measures against Japan should be considered by the Sub-Committee on Economic Pressure on Germany. This Sub-Committee met on October 26 to consider a draft report, and prepared a revised draft (A.T.B. 155) by October 28, a copy of which was taken to Brussels by the U.K. Delegation. This revised draft was approved by the full A.T.B. Committee at its 25th meeting on November 4 and was circulated as C.I.D. 1365B on November 5: see No. 334 below.

No. 316

Mr. Howe (Nanking) to Mr. Eden (Received October 23, 5 p.m.)

No. 603 Telegraphic: by wireless [F 8430/130/10]

NANKING, *October 22, 1937*

Chinese Government are seriously concerned at persistent air attacks on railways which are making transport of munitions very difficult and they are anxious to investigate the possibility of importing munitions by motor road via Burma. They enquire whether Burmese Government would agree to a connexion being established across the frontier if a road is made on Chinese side joining existing Yunnanfu-Hssakuan motor road with border.

I venture to suggest that proposal should receive most careful consideration and that in present circumstances strategical considerations referred to in India Office letter to the Foreign Office of June 12th last[1] may no longer constitute a ruling factor.

There seems to be at least two possible routes which would necessitate no new road construction just yet, (1) Hssakuan-Tengyueh-Lungling-Namhkam. (2) Mitu-Kunlong.

Acting Consul-General Yunnanfu[2] reports that Hssakuan-Tengyueh route has been surveyed and instructions issued for its completion with minimum delay. Latter has so far been surveyed for railway only but it is considered to be topographically much easier.

Repeated to Peking, Rangoon and Yunnanfu.

[1] Not printed. [2] Mr. R. A. Hall.

No. 317

Mr. Eden to Sir R. Craigie (Tokyo)

No. 426 Telegraphic [F 8499/6799/10]

Important FOREIGN OFFICE, *October 25, 1937, 8.20 p.m.*

If not already too late I hope that you may find opportunity once more to urge on Japanese Government importance, not least in their own interests, of being represented at Brussels.

Even if they cannot see their way to this, you should express the strong hope that they will not display an attitude of determined hostility to the Conference, that they will give careful consideration to any communication Conference may address to them and that they will not slam any doors. They are probably obsessed with idea that many members of Conference go to Brussels with their minds already prejudiced against Japanese case. If this is so, absence of Japanese representative makes it all the more difficult to remedy. Probably no amount of protestation would convince Japanese Government that it is not so. I can only give assurance that His Majesty's Government are determined to do their utmost to seek a way of ending hostilities and reaching an agreed solution. Though I cannot speak for them, I am confident that that is the attitude of the principal Powers to be represented at Brussels.

I leave to your discretion the manner and form in which you should convey contents of preceding para. to Japanese Government.[1]

[1] This telegram was drafted by Sir A. Cadogan and initialled by Mr. Eden. A memorandum of October 22 on the prospects for the Brussels Conference by Sir A. Cadogan (which began 'In the absence of any representative of Japan it is difficult to see exactly how the Brussels Conference can proceed') is filed at F 8467/6799/10.

No. 318

Sir R. Craigie (Tokyo) to Mr. Eden (Received October 26, 10.50 a.m.)

No. 587 Telegraphic [F 8498/6799/10]

Important   TOKYO, *October 26, 1937, 5.45 p.m.*

Your telegram No. 426.[1]

I saw Minister for Foreign Affairs for a few minutes this afternoon. He told me reply was being drafted and would be despatched in a day or two. While technically final decision has not yet been taken, in practice mind of Japanese Government has been made up and I soon realized that nothing I could now say would change it.

I therefore spoke in the sense of second paragraph of your telegram. Minister for Foreign Affairs replied emphatically that no doors were closed. Reply when it went would contain a full statement of grounds for Japanese refusal and, I gather, an indication of terms on which Japan would be prepared to make peace (though I do not think final decision has been reached on the latter point). Conference could best help to promote peace by persuading China to enter upon direct negotiations with Japan.

I said that everything must depend on Japanese terms and I did not see how conference could be expected to give advice to China if terms contained or implied any limitation on Chinese sovereignty. Minister for Foreign Affairs replied that as I knew, Japanese Government had no desire to set up autonomous régime in Northern China but that if present situation lasted much longer (he instanced one or two years) the Northern Chinese themselves might well refuse to accept again the overlordship of Nanking. He also referred to desire of Japanese military authorities to establish a cordon sanitaire from which regular troops would be excluded.

As soon as Japanese reply had been drafted and was ready to go off, he proposed to ask me to call again in order to explain Japanese position more fully.[2]

---

[1] No. 317.

[2] This telegram engendered a round of exasperated comment by the Foreign Office officials. 'The Japanese still regard China in the past tense, i.e. a collection of provinces ruled by "lords" of which Nanking is "overlord" ... J. Thyne Henderson 27/10.' 'The Japanese are the most extraordinary people: even the M.F.A. appears not to appreciate that a veto on the movements of Central Govt. troops would constitute a serious limitation on Chinese sovereignty. N. B. Ronald 27/x.' 'I fear nothing but defeat, exhaustion or Russian intervention will alter this attitude. C. W. Orde 27/10.' 'I am afraid not. Japanese apologists have a blatancy that compels admiration. Japan invades China in self-defence and then proceeds to crush her completely in order to win her from "anti-Japanism". That is one version. The other, which is used here, is that she is delivering the Chinese from Nanking. The fighting in the north and at Shanghai doesn't look as if the Chinese were acclaiming their salvation with any marked degree of enthusiasm. And the two-year-old (or more) experiment of the East Hopei autonomous area makes it look as if the Chinese do not take very kindly to "autonomy". A. C[adogan]. Oct. 27 1937.'

No. 319

Record by Sir A. Cadogan of a conversation with Baron Guillaume

[*F 8630/6799/10*]

FOREIGN OFFICE, *October 26, 1937*

Baron Guillaume, the Belgian Ambassador in China, called on me this morning in regard to the arrangements for the Brussels Conference.

He began by emphasizing the desire of the Belgian Government to postpone for a few days from October 30th, and I told him that we had just sent a message to his Government indicating that, although we should have preferred the Conference to meet on that date, we were prepared, if they wished it, to agree to postponing until November 3rd.[1] Baron Guillaume said that his instructions were that the Conference should meet on November 4th so as to give delegations one day beforehand for consultation. (The Chinese Ambassador, who has just been to see me on the same subject, tells me that his colleague in Brussels has reported to him that the Belgian Government have indicated November 3rd as the date of the meeting of the Conference.)[2]

Baron Guillaume went on to speak of various other points. In the first place his Government viewed with considerable distaste the idea of a Belgian presidency of the Conference. To this I replied that I very much hoped that they would nevertheless accept this task: they were the obvious people to fill the chair, and as the Conference was being held in Brussels it was only suitable that it should be presided by a Belgian. I gathered that however much they disliked it the Belgian Government were more or less resigned to the necessity, but Baron Guillaume later returned to the point and again emphasized his Government's reluctance to accept the duty.

He then went on to enquire whether we had any ideas regarding the line which the Conference should take. If the President were to be a Belgian he would require to know what sort of opening speech to make and in what sort of direction to lead the Conference. I said that I supposed in the opening speech he would refer to the circumstances which had brought about the meeting in Brussels and the letter from the President of the Assembly.[3] Baron Guillaume said that he thought it was rather important to minimise as far as possible the connexion with the League. With this I fully agreed, but on the other hand the connexion existed already and was a matter of public knowledge, and moreover the Aga Khan's letter contained at the end a suggestion which was of some value and constituted some sort of guidance to the Conference in that it emphasized that its primary duty would be to seek peace by agreement.

---

[1] Cf. No. 309, note 2.

[2] A marginal note by Sir A. Cadogan here read: 'We have since recd. a tel. from Brussels saying definitely that the date is Nov. 3rd.'

[3] No. 292.

As regards the further procedure of the Conference, I said that we had no hard and fast ideas and should not have until we had had an opportunity of discussing the matter with a number of other delegations. But we did feel strongly that in the first instance at least it must be our object to see whether there were any possibilities of arresting hostilities or setting in motion some form of mediation. This, of course, would be rendered all the more difficult by the absence of Japan, but I could imagine that the Conference might, through the diplomatic channel, approach the Japanese with a request to indicate their attitude in general in regard to the question of mediation.

Baron Guillaume asked if we should make any proposals for an armistice, to which I replied that we should certainly do so if there seemed any possibility of such a proposal meeting with acceptance; there remained the question of the moment at which a proposal of that kind could be made, i.e. whether it should be made in the first instance, or whether we should first ascertain whether there was any prospect at all of mediation.

Baron Guillaume then asked whether, seeing that this was primarily a meeting of the Nine Powers, we should take our stand on the principles of the Nine-Power Convention; to which I replied that our first object was to try and do something practical without proclaiming hard and fast principles which had, in point of fact, already been discredited. It could not be denied that since 1931 the principles of the Nine-Power Treaty had been violated and there was nothing practical to be gained by shutting one's eyes to that fact and making speeches in support of them, more particularly if such a course touched the conscience of the violator of those principles and made him more difficult to deal with in our attempt to restore peace and order.

I was sorry to be unable to give Baron Guillaume any further indication of what our attitude would be, but he must understand that we could not take any definite line until we had had an opportunity of exchanging views with others. He inevitably enquired what our attitude was to be in regard to sanctions; if the Conference found that all prospect of mediation was denied to them, what would be their attitude and would anyone propose that they should consider the possibility of bringing pressure to bear? I said that though we should insist on first exploring all the possibilities of mediation, it could not of course be excluded that if that failed other courses of action might have to be discussed. Quite evidently the question of economic pressure depended on common action and common determination to follow it through to the end, and until we had had some discussion with the other Governments most closely interested it was impossible for us to form an estimate of what might be possible or what might not. For our part we were perfectly ready to discuss the matter with other delegations, and in fact we had a certain amount of material ready to hand.

Baron Guillaume asked whether we should initiate a discussion on sanctions. I said that it was quite impossible to answer that question. The matter would almost inevitably crop up in private discussions which would precede the meeting, from which we should be able to ascertain what the prospects were. If they should be unfavourable for the reason that certain of the interested Governments were unable to see their way to embark on such a course, it would be unlikely that we should make any proposal, as it would in that event be ineffective and might prove embarrassing to those who were unable to join in it.[4]

[4] Mr. Eden wrote on the filed copy of this Record on October 27: 'Sir Alexander Cadogan spoke very well, but I am more and more in doubt as to what this conference can achieve.'

No. 320

Sir R. Craigie (Tokyo) to Mr. Eden (Received October 27, 5.30 p.m.)

No. 596[1] Telegraphic [F 8590/6799/10]

TOKYO, *October 27, 1937, 11.5 p.m.*

My telegram No. 587.[2]

Minister for Foreign Affairs asked me to call this evening and handed to me text of note in which Japanese Government decline Belgian Government's invitation. He wished to give me advance information of reply because [of] interest which he knew His Majesty's Government took in this conference and he wished to draw special attention to concluding paragraph of his note. Japanese Government were sincerely desirous of bringing conflict in China to an end at earliest possible moment and he felt that if His Majesty's Government desired to give practical help in restoring peace the best course would be to persuade Chinese Government to enter into direct negotiations with Japanese Government.[3]

Minister for Foreign Affairs has handed to me copy of statement in which Japanese Government define their attitude on Sino-Japanese relations in general and towards conflict in particular. Summaries of both these documents are contained in my immediately following telegrams.

My United States colleague was received immediately after me and handed same document: he was followed by Belgian Ambassador to whom Japanese reply was then handed.[4]

Repeated to Nanking No. 240.[5]

[1] Although according to the filed copies telegram No. 596 was despatched after No. 597 (No. 321 below) it was received earlier in the Foreign Office.

[2] No. 318.

[3] In a minute of October 29 Sir A. Cadogan commented on this advocacy of direct negotiations: 'The [Japanese] Ambassador said much the same to me this morning . . . But I had to express a doubt as to whether this was "mediation", as he described it. (I suppose that is their stupid game—to strike a successful blow at Shanghai and then get us to advise the Chinese to sue for peace.)' Sir R. Vansittart wrote (October 30): 'I hope we shall make it very clear to them that we will do nothing of the kind.'

[4] See No. 321 below. The substance of the Japanese statement was transmitted in Tokyo telegram No. 598 of October 27, not printed (F 8606/6799/10). The statement was printed in full in *The Times*, October 28, 1937, p. 15.

[5] On the same day, October 27, the Japanese forces after heavy fighting completed their mastery of the whole Shanghai area by throwing the Chinese from their last footing at Chapei. The Chinese forces made on the whole an orderly retreat to defensive positions on a line from Kiangyin on the Yangtse to Hangchow on the coast, defending Nanking. The Japanese breached this line on November 25, after capturing Soochow on November 20, and a direct assault on Nanking followed: the city fell on December 13.

No. 321

Sir R. Craigie (Tokyo) to Mr. Eden (Received October 27, 6.40 p.m.)

No. 597 Telegraphic [F 8622/6799/10]

TOKYO, *October 27, 1937, 2.55 p.m.* [sic]

Following is summary of reply of Japanese Government to invitation to attend Nine Power Conference:

Contrary to League of Nations declaration[1] based on statements that only one party to the action of Japan in China lies outside the purview of the Nine Power Treaty . . .[2] being self-defence in the face of China's anti-Japanese policy and provocative acts of force. League of Nations by assuring China of moral support recommending members to abstain from action that might weaken China etc., has taken sides with one of the parties, encouraged its hostile disposition and taken no account of Japanese intention to achieve Sino-Japanese cooperation and assuring peace in East Asia.

Although invitation makes no mention of the League Japanese Government cannot but conclude that the conference is linked thereto and as the League have imputed [?impugned] the honour of Japan and adopted unfriendly resolution Japanese Government believe that frank and full discussion, with a view to just, equitable and realistic solution of the conflict cannot be expected from the conference of the Powers.

The very existence of Japan and China is involved and attempt to seek solution by a gathering of Powers whose interests in East Asia vary in importance or who practically have none there will only complicate matters and hinder just solution.

For these reasons Japanese Government regret they cannot acccept invitation.

Present conflict was forced by Chinese Government which has for years entertained anti-Japanism as a matter of national policy and in collusion with Communist elements menaced East Asiatic peace by virulent agitation against Japan. Consequently what is most urgently needed is the realization by the Chinese Government of common responsibility with

[1] Cf. Nos. 288, 291, and 292.   [2] The text was here uncertain.

411

Japan for stability of East Asia and change of policy to one of cooperation with Japan. Only if this is comprehended can cooperation of Powers contribute effectively towards stabilization of East Asia.

Repeated to Nanking No. 241.

No. 322

Extract from Cabinet Conclusions No. 39(37) of October 27, 1937

[F 8801/6799/10]

4. The Secretary of State for Foreign Affairs said that he was exercising all possible pressure on the Japanese Government to accept the invitation to the Brussels Conference. He then called attention to a telegram he had received from His Majesty's Ambassador at Brussels reporting that, according to Baron von Neurath's son, who was a Secretary in the German Embassy in Brussels, Baron von Neurath was thinking of attending the Brussels Conference in person.[1] He himself had telegraphed to say that this would be a great advantage, and he had also telegraphed to the Italian Foreign Minister suggesting that he also should try and attend. Their presence, apart from the Far Eastern discussions, might afford an opportunity to discuss affairs in Spain.

He had discussed with the Prime Minister the composition of the United Kingdom Delegation at Brussels, and understood that the Prime Minister proposed to ask the Secretary of State for Dominion Affairs to be his colleague.

The Cabinet agreed:

(a) That the United Kingdom representatives at the Brussels Conference on the Far Eastern Situation should be
    The Secretary of State for Foreign Affairs,
    The Secretary of State for Dominion Affairs,
and should be announced in Parliament the following day:

(b) That the Secretary of State for Foreign Affairs should enquire as to the precedents for announcing the names of senior officials who would be attached to the Delegation, and should have discretion to announce them if he thought advisable:

(c) That the Secretary of State for Foreign Affairs should give consideration to the suggestion of the Secretary of State for Dominion Affairs that in the event of his having to return to London the Earl of Cranborne should join Mr. Malcolm MacDonald at Brussels during his absence:

(d) To take note that the Government of India had nominated Sir Ramaswami Mudaliar as their representative at the Brussels Conference and that his instructions will be to conform to the

[1] See Volume XIX, No. 272, note 4.

attitude of His Majesty's Government in the United Kingdom; but if the question of sanctions should arise, to refer to the Secretary of State for India for instructions;

(e) To take note that the Secretary of State for Scotland, as Chairman of the Advisory Committee on Trade Questions in Time of War, hoped to be able to communicate to the Secretary of State for Foreign Affairs, if he required it, a draft of his Report by the end of the present week, and probably a Final Report to follow early next week.[2]

[2] Cf. No. 315: see No. 334 below.

No. 323

Mr. Eden to Sir R. Lindsay (Washington)

No. 998 [A 7748/228/45]

FOREIGN OFFICE, *October 28, 1937*

Sir,

I saw the United States Ambassador this morning, when Mr. Bingham told me that he wished to deliver a message with which President Roosevelt had charged him.[1] In the first place the President wished to assure His Majesty's Government of his desire to collaborate fully with us. The President had been a little disappointed at the rapidity with which he had been asked to explain exactly what he intended by his Chicago speech[2]. He thought that rather a pity.[3] I interjected that we had not done this, to which the Ambassador at once rejoined that he knew we had not, but that the press had done so and this had proved embarrassing. The President's intention which he wished to make clear to me was to attempt to deal with the Conference at Brussels as he had dealt with the Pan-American Conference at Buenos Aires.[4] There a large number of American States had been present, jealous nearly all of them and some mutually hostile. The United States had not played any rôle publicly greater than that of the smallest State present, and yet by her presence and by the atmosphere of cooperation, something in the nature of a common front had been created, and the President truly believed that the risk of war on the American continent had now been wholly removed.

[1] Details of this message are given in Mr. Bingham's account of this interview in *F.R.U.S.*, 1937, vol. iv, pp. 114–6.

[2] See No. 300

[3] In his own account Mr. Bingham reported himself as using somewhat more abrasive language at this point: he described the attempt 'to pin the United States down to a specific statement as to how far it would go, and precisely what the President meant by this Chicago speech' as 'objectionable and damaging' (*F.R.U.S., ibid.*, p. 115).

[4] Cf. Volume XVII, Nos. 435, 451, and 458.

And so at the Brussels Conference he hoped that we should not 'rush ahead' for this would prove embarrassing for the United States, where the Administration was frequently accused of being dragged along at Britain's tail. At the same time the United States Government did not intend to take the lead. They hoped that some smaller Powers would begin discussions and that ultimately, as the result of Anglo-American cooperation, an important degree of unity would emerge. I remarked to the Ambassador that I thought there was more than a risk that if neither we nor the United States were willing to take the lead, then the smaller Powers might be shy of doing so in such a serious situation. The Ambassador thought that this situation also might be dealt with by careful management.

2. As the result of some further questioning, it emerged that President Roosevelt's main hope in this Conference was that it would familiarise the people of the United States with the idea of cooperating with His Majesty's Government in international affairs. This had never been possible for them at Geneva, since the League had many enemies in the United States. It would be easier for them at Brussels. I had the impression that President Roosevelt even thought it possible that out of the beginnings of this cooperation at Brussels might grow some larger organisation of world Powers.

3. I thanked Mr. Bingham for what he had told me and said that I wished to make it quite clear to him that His Majesty's Government were very ready and anxious to cooperate fully with the United States Government. At the same time it would be a help to me if I could glean a little more what was in the mind of the President. When he spoke of quarantine did President Roosevelt mean economic action against Japan? The Ambassador replied that he was fairly confident that quarantine did not mean sanctions at the present stage. It was too early for any conception of that kind. Nor could he speak with confidence at this time of future developments. He was, however, sure that the speech was intended to lay the foundation for future Anglo-American cooperation.

When I remarked that the President's speech seemed directed in part at least to the education of the American public, His Excellency agreed.

I am, etc.,
ANTHONY EDEN

No. 324

Sir R. Craigie (Tokyo) to Mr. Eden (Received October 29, 9.30 a.m.)

No. 605 Telegraphic [F 8754/414/23]

Confidential   TOKYO, *October 29, 1937, 12.55 p.m.*

In view of persistent reports that Italy is on the point of joining

Japanese-German anti-Communist Pact[1] I asked Minister for Foreign Affairs yesterday whether he could give me any information on the subject. His reply was that the question of Italian accession to the Pact had been under consideration ever since its conclusion and discussions were still proceeding.

As I gained the impression that conclusion of Japanese-Italian Agreement might be imminent,[2] I expressed personal opinion that the moment for such a step could scarcely be more inopportune. After emphasizing that I had no instructions I reminded him of the bad impression created in England on the announcement of German-Japanese Agreement[3] and said that conclusion of Japanese-Italian Agreement at a moment when there were so many difficulties between our two countries would be taken by many people as an indication that Japan has definitely decided to link her fortune with those two Powers in Europe whose policy was responsible for so much of the present unrest. This in turn would certainly not facilitate eventual re-establishment of personal, real friendly relations between our two countries which I knew to be His Excellency's aim.

Mr. Hirota scoffed at the idea that conclusion of an anti-Communist Pact with Italy could be held to imply any new orientation in Japan's foreign policy. Speaking with more emphasis than is usual with him he declared that cultivation of good relations with Great Britain was the fundamental objective of Japan's foreign policy.[4] Japanese Government had sincerely regretted, while they understood, decision to discontinue Anglo-Japanese negotiations for they believed that an agreement on the lines contemplated might be profitable for both countries. It was their hope that if the present Sino-Japanese controversy could be settled on satisfactory lines Anglo-Japanese negotiations could be taken up again without delay. This was the policy of Japanese Government as a whole and had been laid down in letter from the Emperor to the King[5] to which His Excellency attached great importance. Proposed agreement with Italy on the other hand was a mere incident to Japan's fear and dislike of Communism and he would not conceal from me that in a moment of crisis like the present large sections of Japanese opinion were deeply grateful

[1] See No. 9, note 3.

[2] Herr von Ribbentrop, German Ambassador at London, travelled to Rome on November 5 for the signature on November 6 of the protocol whereby Italy adhered to the Anti-Comintern Pact: see Volume XIX, No. 274, note 3, and No. 311. The protocol is printed in *D.G.F.P.*, Series D, vol. i, No. 17.

[3] Cf. Nos. 5, 6, and 19.

[4] Sir R. Vansittart commented on this sentence on November 1: '. . . the Japanese have strange notions of cultivation. I am afraid these professions are largely eyewash with some colouring matter of their favourite word "sincerity".'

[5] The reference is apparently to a letter from the Emperor of Japan to the late King Edward VIII dated May 15, 1936, written in reply to the King's letter of August 1935: see Volume XX, No. 346, note 3: cf. also No. 529. The Emperor's letter, of which a copy is filed at F 8754/414/23, was delivered by Mr. Yoshida when he took up his post as Ambassador at London: see *ibid.*, No. 541.

for the support which Japan had been receiving from Germany and Italy.

I asked His Excellency whether he thought that this support had been altogether disinterested and he laughingly admitted that it might not be so but that the effect on public opinion here was nevertheless considerable.

From what I have been able to learn initiative in these discussions has rested with Italy. I do not know whether my observations will have effect of slowing down negotiations but I fancy that they have proceeded too far to permit of delay. I am convinced of Mr. Hirota's sincerity when he speaks of a close understanding with us as being the fundamental objective of the Government and I believe this view to be shared by many of the most influential and best informed people here not excluding the army leaders (see my letter dated October 22nd to Sir A. Cadogan sent by the last bag[6]). But there is no doubt that both Germany and Italy are coming increasingly to be regarded as Japan's only friends by the public at large and I fear the strain imposed on Anglo-Japanese relations by the present conflict may, if continued much longer, so estrange opinion in the two countries as to render impossible a return to the old and most valuable terms of friendship. I dislike intensely seeing dictator States 'getting away with it' but for the moment there is little we can do here to arrest a tendency which may ultimately have very unfortunate results.[7]

[6] Not printed.
[7] Sir A. Cadogan commented on November 1: 'This only seems to show that those who affect to direct Japanese foreign policy are as irresponsible as they are foolish.'

No. 325

Sir G. Ogilvie-Forbes (Berlin) to Mr. Eden
(Received October 29, 11 a.m.)

No. 255 Telegraphic: by telephone [F 8669/6799/10]

Immediate   BERLIN, *October 29, 1937*

Minister for Foreign Affairs informed me last night that Germany had just received an invitation to the Brussels Conference and would decline.[1]

I understand Herr Hitler is shying at conferences associated with the League of Nations. Moreover since it is expected that atmosphere at Brussels will be pro-Chinese, alleged connexion of China with communism (see last sentence of my telegram No. 623 Saving[2]) makes him reluctant to associate himself with conclusions which may be reached.

[1] Cf. *D.G.F.P.*, Series D, vol. i, Nos. 14 and 505–7. Cf. also Volume XIX of this Series, No. 278.
[2] This telegram of October 20 referred to a cleavage of opinion in Germany over the Far Eastern question. The last sentence read: 'Herr Hitler himself is of course particularly susceptible where communism is concerned.'

No. 326

Sir R. Craigie (Tokyo) to Foreign Office[1]
(Received November 3, 10 p.m.)

No. 632 Telegraphic [F 8982/9/10]

TOKYO, *November 3, 1937, 12.5 p.m.*

My immediately preceding telegram.[2]

I am seriously perturbed by growth of anti-British sentiment here as evidenced by the tone of the press and public demonstrations. During the last few days feeling has assumed such proportions that I consider possibility of some incident in China, perhaps deliberately (?encouraged) by young officer group in the navy or army, cannot be precluded and that action rashly directed might immediately gain wide support here.

Between 40 and 50 persons instigated by Rash Behair Se[3] made a demonstration in front of the Embassy some days ago and very anti-British sentiments were expressed at a crowded public meeting held on October 31st under the auspices of pan Asiatic leaders. Violent anti-British articles are appearing in some of the *less* well known papers and there is evidence that the authorities themselves are nervous as police guard at the entrances to the Embassy has recently been considerably increased.

I do not believe that the agitation is due to official inspiration or that the government desires a quarrel with us. But I do not like the situation and there is . . .[4] of great public resentment at evidences of anti-Japanese feeling in England. As I have reported once or twice since I arrived reports coming from Europe and United States always give impressions that Great Britain is leader of all anti-Japanese activities and instigator of every international movement to checkmate Japan with United States as a somewhat reluctant second (temporary flurry caused by Roosevelt's speech[5] has almost been forgotten). It is obvious that with feeling inflamed as it is in Japan today the continuation of exacerbation of public opinion by this method is a dangerous process. We must I think make up our minds whether or no we are prepared for trouble with this country. If not then a concerted effort must be made promptly by both governments to put the brake on.[6]

---

[1] Mr. Eden left London on November 1 to attend the Brussels Conference. Sir A. Cadogan accompanied him.

[2] Of November 2, not printed (F 8942/9/10).

[3] According to a minute of November 4 by Mr. H. H. Thomas, a member of the Consular service in Japan who served in the Foreign Office from March to December 1937, the reference was to 'Rash Bihari Bose, the well-known Indian agitator in Tokyo, a leader of the Pan-Asiatic movement'.

[4] The text was here uncertain.   [5] See No. 291, note 2.

[6] Mr. Thomas protested on November 4: 'I do not like Sir R. Craigie's implied suggestion that we must adopt the humiliating and even immoral role of aiding and abetting Japan in

My concrete suggestions are (1) if I could be informed that His Majesty's Government will do whatever is in their power to exercise moderating influence on British press. I can, with this assurance, bring strong pressure to bear on Japanese government to do the same (our press seems to have lost all sense of proportion and in its efforts to champion the cause of China is doing irreparable harm to our own interests here).[7] (2) Serious consideration should be given to stop arms traffic via Hongkong (whether by general prohibition of export to both sides or otherwise).[8] (3) Every effort should be made to improve relations between British and Japanese military authorities in Shanghai. I realize that the role of our authorities in Shanghai is a very difficult one but there never was a moment when restraint and display of impartiality were more necessary than now. I do not of course suggest that any change in our policy of resolutely defending our own interests whenever these are threatened. In this sphere I have always found a readiness to meet us halfway and I should feel far more confident of being able to defend these in the future if our press could display more impartiality in the issue as between Japan and China.

Lest you should think that I am painting a picture in too vivid colours I may mention that at one time or another my Belgian, Netherlands, French and United States colleagues have all volunteered an expression of their concern at the growing antagonism here against Great Britain which transcends in strength similar to [sic] ebullitions of feeling in the past (my Belgian colleague has been here sixteen years and my Netherlands colleague fourteen years).

her aggression against China. It is both stupid and unnecessary to be afraid of Japan. She has sufficient preoccupations at present to prevent her from striking at us, and I feel sure that it is most unlikely that she will unless given a great deal more provocation than we have yet offered . . . If the present régime in Japan remains in the saddle and is successful in its policy, nothing is more certain than that Japan will eventually come into collision with the British Empire. Our policy must surely be to do everything we can, with reasonable safety anyhow, to hasten the downfall of that régime whose gospel is the sword and whose economics is spoliation.'

[7] In a minute of November 4 Mr. Orde agreed with Mr. Thomas that Japanese press agitation should not be taken too seriously, and pointed out that the British press had given a 'full hearing' to Japan's 'very bad case': 'to restrain criticism might meet with a very unpleasant reaction.'

[8] Mr. Orde disagreed strongly with Sir R. Craigie's suggestion, commenting that an embargo on the export of munitions from Hong Kong 'would be a very serious step in Japan's favour and totally illogical if we maintain the policy of allowing export of munitions from this country to Japan and China; it would be at variance with the League resolution against weakening China's power of resistance and increasing her difficulties'. Mr. Eden, who was in London between November 5 and 9, saw this telegram: cf. *Facing the Dictators, op. cit.*, p. 539. He wrote on November 7: 'I am in entire agreement with Mr. Orde . . . I found many at the Brussels Conference who thought that Japan was going to her "1812" in China. This may not be so but we should do what we cautiously can to make it possible.' It was agreed that a paper on the question of the export of arms from Hong Kong should be prepared for submission to the Cabinet Committee on Shipping in the Far East on November 9: see No. 345 below.

No. 327

Foreign Office to Mr. Howe (Nanking)

No. 438 Telegraphic [F 8797/130/10]

Immediate   FOREIGN OFFICE, November 3, 1937, 5 p.m.

Your telegram No. 603.[1]

1. My two immediately following telegrams[2] repeat telegrams on this subject between the Secretary of State for Burma and the Governor of Burma.

2. His Majesty's Government and the Government of Burma welcome in principle the establishment of direct road connection between Burma and China, and you may so inform the Chinese Government. Actual route must depend on latter's decision, but for the immediate purpose the route from railhead at Lashio via Muse and Lungling to connect with the motor road between Yunnanfu and Siakwan would seem most suitable. On a longer view route via Kunlong would perhaps be more advantageous; this would, however, raise question of territorial rights in Hopang salient.

3. Government of Burma could not incur any considerable outlay on improving existing roads or on new construction without being assured that trade in arms (and other goods) would produce enough in transit charges to make it a reasonable proposition and that these charges would be promptly paid.

Repeated to Peking No. 506, to Yunnanfu No. 5, and to Burma No. 177.

[1] No. 316.   [2] Not printed.

No. 328

Sir R. Clive (Brussels) to Foreign Office (Received November 3, 9 p.m.)

No. 76 Telegraphic [F 9046/6799/10]

BRUSSELS, November 3, 1937, 6.5 p.m.

Following from Secretary of State:

Mr. Malcolm MacDonald, Sir A. Cadogan and I had a conversation with Mr. Norman Davies [sic] and his advisers this morning.[1]

Mr. Davies began by saying that he supposed we had had enough of sanctions to which I replied that while the present business of conference was mediation Mr. Davies must not assume we were unwilling to take part in any international action. I begged him to understand that His Majesty's

[1] This telegram was drafted on November 2. Lord Avon referred to this conversation in *Facing the Dictators, op. cit.*, pp. 536–7. See also *F.R.U.S.*, 1937, vol. iv, pp. 145–7.

Government were ready for fullest co-operation with United States Government. They would not find us backward in working with them or in joining with them in any action which they desired to take. It was however useless to ignore European situation and we could take no action with Far East while the present conditions persisted in Europe except in full co-operation with United States. Mr. Davies then explained that sanctions were not in any event on our present agenda. Our first attempt must be to try to make peace. After further conversation it emerged that programme which United States delegation have in mind is that having elected our chairman who we hope will be Monsieur Spaak and having devoted one day to public speeches conference should then go into private session. During this private session a small committee will probably be set up to be charged with approaching the two parties. This committee will endeavour to obtain Japanese information as to their general attitude, as to their willingness to co-operate with conference and even as to possibility of a cessation of hostilities.

It is clear that United States delegation do not wish this conference merely to appoint two or three States, even for example His Majesty's Government and United States Government, and then to adjourn. They would much prefer that the conference, using all possible means of conciliation, should continue for as long as possible its endeavours to make peace and that, if it ultimately fails, it would then have to make plain to the world that it has failed and why. There is little doubt in our minds that this procedure is intended among other things to ensure that, if the conference does fail, world opinion in general, and American opinion in particular, will have been educated in the process.[2]

Mr. Davies in private conversation with me made it plain that the President is deeply concerned at world outlook and sincerely anxious to co-operate in an attempt to stop the rot. Mr. Davies explained that the President had put it to him that the conference would either succeed or, having failed, would confront the world with a futile situation in which further action by the United States could not be excluded. All liberty depends in the President's view upon the course of the conference and state of American public opinion at the end of it. Mr. Davies also intimated that the President was deeply perturbed at the prospects in the Far East. He thought that Great Britain might be compelled to withdraw from her position there and that as a consequence United States might some day have to deal, may be alone, with a greatly strengthened Japanese Power across the Pacific Ocean. It was this formidable prospect that was making the President wish, if he could, to do something to check the tendency now.

During the course of a luncheon which United States delegates had with us today, Mr. Hornbeck admitted to me that United States Government

[2] In a minute of November 5 on this passage Mr. Ronald remarked: 'It is a little hard to expect a number of people who have a great deal of work to do elsewhere to hang about in Brussels while American opinion is being educated . . .'

had certain ideas in mind as to means of pressure on Japan, should the conference fail. He added however that he did not even wish to mention them just now, since it was too early to do so. He added that he was sure that much propaganda, including an (?oil) sanction, was misguided.

According to United States information Japan possesses reserves of oil for nearly two years. He also said that he thought that we were over-estimating the power of Japan. He was convinced that she was not sufficiently formidable to attempt to attack either Great Britain or the United States in the Far East.

Our general impression from these first contacts is that United States representatives do attach a great importance to this conference as an important factor in the process of educating their own public. We do not believe that they themselves yet know what next step they may be able to take, but they are hopeful that the effect of the conference will enable them to visualise that next step with a greater measure of public support behind them.[3]

[3] The first plenary session of the conference took place in the Palais des Académies, Brussels, on the morning of November 3 at 11 a.m. M. Spaak, Belgian Minister for Foreign Affairs, took the chair. A second plenary session took place at 4.30 p.m. on the same day. Mr. Davis, Mr. Eden, Mr. Delbos, and Count Aldevrando-Marescotti (Italy) spoke at the first meeting. The second was notable for a long speech by Dr. Wellington Koo. The official minutes are filed at F 9132, 9133/6799/10.

No. 329

Memorandum by Sir J. Brenan[1] on the Customs administration in North China

[F 8951/220/10]

FOREIGN OFFICE, *November 3, 1937*

The recent developments are as follows.

On October 14 the Inspector-General, Sir F. Maze, instructed the Customs Commissioner at Tientsin, Mr. Myers, to offer the Japanese the following terms, referred to in the correspondence as the six point proposal.[2]

Customs revenues in all China to be deposited in a neutral custodian bank for the duration of the hostilities. Tientsin and Chinwangtao revenues, however, to be deposited by the Custodian Bank with another bank (meaning the Yokohama Specie Bank). The Custodian Bank to make necessary monthly payments as heretofore and to draw on the Yokohama Specie Bank for quota of *foreign* loans assigned to Tientsin and

[1] Sir J. Brenan, former Consul General at Shanghai, was employed in the Far Eastern Department of the Foreign Office from November 1, 1937. He was succeeded at Shanghai by Mr. Herbert Phillips, formerly Consul General at Canton.

[2] See No. 302.

Chinwangtao and for local expenses of those stations.

The above offer was confirmed by the Chinese Minister for Foreign Affairs to Mr. Howe on October 12 (Nanking telegram to Foreign Office 566 of October 12[3]).

On October 20th the Finance Minister, through the Inspector-General, further authorised the Tientsin Commissioner to agree, in the last resort, to deposit the Tientsin and Chinwangtao customs revenue locally in 'a reliable bank of good standing' (meaning the Yokohama Specie Bank)[4] 'but remittance of cost of collection destined for foreign and internal loans and indemnity and regular local obligations such as conservancy and quarantine are to be made therefrom as due and if considered necessary by you any balance remaining to be left to accumulate in the bank.'

Mr. Myers evidently took the phrase 'if considered necessary by you' as relating to the words preceding it and not to those following it and assumed that he was given discretion to refrain from making loan remittances if he thought such a course to be necessary.

At all events on October 27 he reported to the Inspector-General that acting on the above instructions he had offered to deposit all local customs revenues in the Yokohama Specie Bank, and as withdrawals from that bank for loans purposes had been left to his discretion he did not intend to make any such withdrawals for the time being.

He explained that this was the best arrangement he could make, and although in practice it meant that all revenues would be deposited in a Japanese bank without withdrawals for any loan service foreign or domestic, the right to make such withdrawals was maintained and was left over for subsequent negotiation. In the meantime the integrity of the Customs administration was preserved.

The Inspector-General did not feel happy about this arrangement and on October 29th asked the Commissioner for further information about remittances for the service of the foreign and domestic loans. The Commissioner replied that, as stated in his previous telegram, while the right to remit loan quotas was maintained it was not being exercised for the time being. He added that any attempt at remittance, agreement or no

---

[3] No. 303.

[4] The local Japanese authorities had taken strong objection to the fact that under the terms offered by the Chinese the Tientsin and Chinwangtao customs revenues would be handled by the custodian bank before being deposited in the Yokohama Specie Bank. Tientsin telegram No. 48 of October 15 reported that the military faction at Tokyo also felt themselves tricked 'first by the Chinese Government and secondly by the British Embassy from whom the terms were received in Tokyo'. Mr. Myers urged that the only way to save the customs service from disintegration was to agree at once to place the Tientsin and Chinwangtao revenues directly in the Yokohama and Specie Bank. Despite Sir R. Craigie's protests at Tokyo the Japanese attitude remained uncompromising, and following representations by Mr. Howe in Nanking it was reported in Shanghai telegram No. 152 of October 20 that Dr. Kung, while maintaining that no further concession was possible, had agreed that as a final alternative Mr. Myers could use his discretion to deposit the revenues in a local bank.

agreement, would entail immediate seizure of customs functions and the disappearance of all revenue.

In the meantime, while the Tientsin Commissioner was trying to conclude, or had concluded (it is not clear which), this agreement with the Japanese Consul-General there was a tendency on the part of the military authorities on both sides to wreck it.

On October 19 Chiang Kai-shek told Mr. Howe that in no circumstances whatsoever would he agree to hand over the customs revenues to the Yokohama Specie Bank. He would rather see the whole customs go by the board first. In spite of his uncompromising attitude, however, Mr. Howe thought that he would not repudiate the six point proposal if the Japanese accepted it.

On the other hand a section of the Japanese Military Authorities in Tientsin were of the opinion that there had been too much delay in coming to an agreement, and that it was better simply to take over the Customs administration in the North as had been done in Manchuria.

The next development was indicated in a message of October 30th[5] from the Inspector-General to the Tientsin Commissioner to the effect that as Chiang Kai-shek might repudiate the proposals which the Commissioner had been authorised by the Minister of Finance to make to the Japanese, the 'tentative arrangement' with the Yokohama Specie Bank should not be regarded as 'necessarily binding' and the door must be kept open for further negotiations.

Sir Frederick Maze's telegram is curiously worded and contains the unwarranted assumption that 'the present tentative arrangement of course allows for regular remittance to Shanghai of full Tientsin Chinwangtao share of foreign and internal loans and indemnity to conform with the conditions laid down by the Minister'.

As the unfortunate Commissioner had already twice clearly explained that he was precluded from making these remittances on pain of seeing the Customs administration disrupted altogether, the Inspector-General's message is somewhat disingenuous.

His latest instructions to Mr. Myers[6] are to the effect that unless he can arrange to make remittances periodically for internal as well as foreign loans and indemnity without differentiation he should endeavour to introduce again the six point proposal or in any case to keep the question open locally pending support from elsewhere.

Mr. Myers replies that, as already explained, he has done the best he can locally in very difficult circumstances and suggests that the matter be taken up in Tokyo.

Mr. Myers undoubtedly stretched the discretion given him to the utmost to meet the Japanese demands, but he evidently believed that it

[5] Transmitted to the Foreign Office in Shanghai telegram No. 165 of October 30 (F 8846/220/10).
[6] Transmitted to the Foreign Office in Tientsin telegram No. 57 of November 1 (F 8951/220/10).

was the only way to save the integrity of the Customs administration for China.

On the other hand if his arrangement is allowed to stand it means that the northern revenues will make no further contribution to the foreign loan services, a serious business for China's credit and for the interests of the bondholders.

The Chinese are holding out for both the foreign and internal loan service, but would probably be content with the foreign quota only (see their six point proposal). Presumably we shall presently receive comment on the Tientsin telegram from Nanking or Shanghai when the question of further representations at Tokyo should be considered.

No. 330

Sir R. Clive (Brussels) to Foreign Office (Received November 4, 6.5 p.m.)

No. 78 Telegraphic [F 9072/6799/10]

BRUSSELS, *November 4, 1937, 4.6 p.m.*

Following from Secretary of State.

(? Mr. Norman Davis) called on me this afternoon.[1] Mr. . . .[2] and Sir A. Cadogan were also present.

Mr. Norman Davis began by saying that he hoped I should not hurry away from Brussels after opening meetings of the Conference and be no more seen. He felt it would be disastrous to give the appearance at an early stage of helplessness and futile obstinacy. He wished very much— more particularly for education of public opinion in the United States—to keep Conference going and to keep up a pressure on Japan which he thought would not be entirely ineffective.

I assured Mr. Davis that for the sake of achieving co-operation of the United States Government and of making a real contribution to peace I should be willing to stay indefinitely in Brussels.

Mr. Davis expressed conviction that public opinion in his country would develop and he seemed to hint that if Japan continued to be recalcitrant to every suggestion made with a view to restoration of peace it might be prepared to consider possibility of action.

I at once said that if it came to action, or to put it more bluntly, sanctions, it seemed to me that these were of two kinds, ineffective and effective.

The former was merely an empty gesture which achieved nothing beyond embitterment of the country against which sanctions were

[1] This telegram was drafted on November 3. The conversation with Mr. Davis presumably took place in the afternoon of that day before the second plenary session of the Conference: see No. 328, note 3.

[2] The text was here uncertain.

directed. The latter on the other hand might drive the victim to desperate acts and we had to bear that in mind: before embarking on any course of effective sanctions we should have to consider risks to which we might be exposed—and to which in fact we might expose others—and be prepared to give (? each other) fully mutual guarantees of assistance in case of need. We ourselves had many anxieties in Europe: we could not be expected alone to bear the brunt of a conflict because of the Far East. Assured of assistance of United States we should be in a different position and I made it plain once more to Mr. Davis, as I had already done on a previous occasion, that we should be ready to enter into a discussion with him of co-operation in any action which United States Government might feel prepared to take. Mr. Davis professed to be interested in this statement and implied that he had expected that we should not have been able to encourage him to think that we could do anything.

As is his wont, he guarded himself from making any definite statement but he evidently wished me to understand that he contemplated the possibility, in the event of Japan's attitude causing further resentment in the United States, of United States Government considering action of some sort. I felt it well to give him the warning against ineffective sanctions as I had gathered from a previous conversation that he might have had the idea of enlisting our co-operation in some comparatively mild (and therefore useless) action which he might maintain called for no guarantee of assistance but which might in fact provoke Japan whose retaliation would be directed in the first instance against ourselves.

Turning to another point Mr. Davis expressed his conviction that it would be of the greatest value if we at this Conference could in any way enlist co-operation of Germany. Germany's reply declining invitation to the Conference[3] was carefully designed to leave the door open and gave a hint that at the proper moment she might be disposed to co-operate. Mr. Davis enquired whether it might be possible to approach Germany again: her co-operation might prove most important not only from point of view of present case but also in the interest of general appeasement.

I fully agreed though I thought approach would have to be made with greatest discretion. To provoke a second refusal from Germany would be only to commit her more firmly to abstention. It was finally agreed that M. Spaak (who yesterday evening had spoken to us in the same sense as Mr. Davis on the subject of value of German co-operation) might be asked to take purely private and unofficial soundings and Mr. Davis undertook to put this to M. Spaak.

Rest of our conversation was devoted mainly to question of procedure. We agreed that when present opening discussion was at an end, Conference might—perhaps tomorrow—go into private session at which it would discuss how to address itself to its immediate task of attempting mediation. Conference might appoint a small sub-committee consisting of

[3] Cf. No. 325.

two or three members with duty of drawing up a communication to be made to the Japanese Government. This might be to the effect that, Chinese Delegation having made known their point of view to the Conference, the latter were anxious to hear what the Japanese Government had to say, reminding the latter that under Nine Power Treaty they were committed to consultation, and enquiring whether they would be prepared to designate someone who would get into contact with the Conference, perhaps through its Committee.

It remains to be seen whether this idea will commend itself to other Delegations and various conversations have been arranged to take place before secret session tomorrow afternoon.

No. 331

Sir R. Clive (Brussels) to Foreign Office (Received November 5)

No. 52 Saving: Telegraphic [F 9071/6799/10]

BRUSSELS, *November 4, 1937*

Following from Secretary of State.

The Conference met in private this afternoon. M. Spaak suggested that it might be useful to examine the texts of the reply sent by the Japanese Government to the Belgian invitation[1] and of the Japanese Foreign Office statement regarding the dispute[2]. He had observed from these documents that Japan did not dispute the fact that the Treaty[3] was still in force, while her statements that she did not harbour any territorial designs and that she was prepared to continue cultural and economic collaboration with the Powers having interests in China, amounted to substantial acceptance of its provisions. The complaints made by Japan were such as should normally lead to an appeal to Article 7 of the Treaty, and consequently the Conference might be thought to be essential from the juridical point of view. The Japanese, however, had said that the Conference was too numerous and consisted of Powers having interests in the Far East of varying degree; it might therefore be best to have a smaller group and to invite the Japanese to enter into discussions with it.

2. Mr. Norman Davis expressed agreement and emphasised that we could not accept the theory that the dispute only concerned China and Japan.

3. I said that I thought that the points made by M. Spaak were very good and should certainly be used. It would be for the Conference to decide how to use them, and it might well be best to submit them for guidance to a small committee.

---

[1] See No. 321. [2] See No. 320, note 4.
[3] i.e. the Nine Power Treaty of February 6, 1922.

4. Count Aldrovandi had no objection to consideration being given to the Japanese communications if it was clear that any points needed elucidation, but it should be made clear that the Conference or its sub-committee were entirely without *parti pris*. A communication should also be addressed to both China and Japan asking them to come together and negotiate direct. In answer to Mr. Norman Davis, he said he did not mean that any agreement they might reach should be approved by the Conference in advance, but that it was essential that some agreement should be reached quickly, after which the Powers could make such comments as they pleased.

5. M. Delbos said he thought it would not be enough if the sub-committee had a mandate merely to reply to the Japanese notes; it should also offer its good offices, which were appropriate in view of all the interests involved, of the right possessed by signatories of the Washington Treaty to intervene in any agreement made, and of the interests of peace in general. He thought that the sub-committee, in order to be of use, should have a mandate to make practical suggestions, and that the conference should consider what these suggestions should be. Did the Italian Delegation accept the idea of such a mandate?

6. Mr. Bruce (Australia) said that it was important that the reply sent to Japan should be in sympathetic terms making it clear that the issue was not prejudged. He agreed with Count Aldrovandi that it was desirable that China and Japan should get together, but that was the last step, and the good offices of a sub-committee such as had been proposed would help to enable it to be taken. The smaller this committee was the better. It should make an appeal to the good will of either side, without emphasising the rights and interests of neutrals.

7. Mr. Jordan (New Zealand) supported the suggestion that a small sub-committee of Powers having material interests in the Far East should get in touch with Japan and he hoped it would be possible to arrange an armistice during negotiations.

8. Count Aldrovandi explained that his proposal was that a communication should be addressed to China and Japan, with a view to making possible direct contact between them. This might include an offer of good offices, and the proposed sub-committee could, after making its communication, go on to study other means of attaining its objective.

9. M. Spaak, summing up the discussion, said that it seemed to be agreed (1) that a small committee should be appointed, (2) that this committee should study the two Japanese documents and draw up replies; the conference could not of course at this stage suggest the nature of those replies (3) that it should establish contact with China and Japan with a view to seeing how its good offices might be of use.

10. This summing up was agreed to by the Conference.

No. 332

Memorandum[1] *of an interview between Mr. MacDonald, Mr. Davis, and M. Delbos at Brussels on November 3, 1937*

[*F 9291/6799/10*]

BRUSSELS, *November 4, 1937*

Mr. Norman Davis, having indicated that he would like a further interview[2] with the British and French delegations, Mr. MacDonald called upon him at 9.30 p.m. on November 3rd accompanied by Sir A. Cadogan. M. Delbos and M. de Tessan[3] were also present, together with Mr. Moffat of the American Delegation.

Mr. Norman Davis began by addressing himself to M. Delbos, inviting him to indicate the attitude of the French Government in regard to the possible outcome of this Conference. He referred to reports of French policy in regard to the transit of arms through Indo-China to China, and enquired whether, if this Conference failed to put an end to the present conflict, the French Government would be prepared to take any action, or whether they would, as he put it, hand over Indo-China to Japan.

M. Delbos jokingly replied that they would prefer to give Japan the Philippines, and this retort rather deflected Mr. Davis from his original line. M. Delbos pointed out that although it might be desirable to adopt a firm attitude we must avoid going too far in that direction, and we must be careful not to utter any threats which we might be unable to carry out. If we adopted a firm line with Japan, there were two things that might result. Firstly, Japan might tighten her blockade of China, an action which would cause us all considerable embarrassment and would almost inevitably lead to unpleasant incidents. Secondly, she might even go further and resort to reprisals against any Government possessing territory in the Far East that took action against her. He thought that in regard to the blockade, it might be possible for the Governments interested to consult together and devise some means of protection for their shipping. As regards direct reprisals, we could only be protected against these by a concerted mutual guarantee of security. Mr. MacDonald said that he might repeat what had already been explained to Mr. Davis, namely that while, owing to the anxieties of the European situation, His Majesty's Government could not undertake alone to embark on any action in the Far East, yet they were prepared to consider the possibility of any action that might be taken jointly with other Governments, in particular that of the United States.

Mr. Norman Davis observed that America was a democracy, and that one of the drawbacks of democracies, as compared with totalitarian States, was that it was impossible for the Government to undertake any precise

[1] Transmitted to the Foreign Office in despatch No. 12 of November 8 from the U.K. Delegation at Brussels.
[2] See No. 330.   [3] French Under Secretary of State for Foreign Affairs.

commitments in advance. The feeling in the United States was that America's direct interests in the Far East were not so great as those of certain other countries. If those countries who had territorial possessions appeared reluctant to assume any risk in defending them, the United States would lose interest. America's whole interest was in the maintenance of peace throughout the world, and in particular the re-establishment of respect for international treaties, which seemed lately to be vanishing. The American people would be prepared to play their part in any action to re-establish the rule of international law.

M. Delbos agreed that what we were dealing with now was not only a Japanese question. We had to consider it as part of a general tendency manifested in the policy of Germany and Italy. We had in the last few years gone back several centuries; treaties were ignored, war was embarked on without any proper declaration of war, open cities were bombarded from the air, and so on. And he therefore agreed with Mr. Davis that what was required was some concerted action to re-establish the rule of law. He thought that there was only one person who could properly take the initiative in this respect, and that was the President of the United States. If he would summon a conference it would be necessary to prepare carefully for that conference and to work out by prior agreement the principles which we desired to establish. There was one further thing that we must do, and that was that, pending a successful outcome of such a conference, we must take steps to ensure against further encroachment by the lawless Powers and to guarantee each other against further attack.

Mr. Norman Davis said that he was convinced that the President of the United States would have no appetite for such an enterprise in present circumstances, and that indeed it was too big an undertaking for any one man. He said that it was plain that the situation in Europe and the situation in the Far East interacted on each other: if one could be settled that would go far towards the settlement of the other. It was probably impossible to settle both together and it was necessary to begin either at one end or at the other. Did M. Delbos think that it was easier to settle first the European problem, or would it be easier to deal in the first instance with the Sino-Japanese situation, in the discussion of which he reminded M. Delbos that the United States happened to be involved by their obligation under the Nine-Power Treaty. He thought it important for M. Delbos to reflect upon that and to consider whether every effort should not be made with the co-operation of the United States to bring about a settlement of the dispute which was engaging the attention of the present Conference.

He went on to express regret that Germany had found herself unable to take part in the present Conference, and the conviction that it was necessary to take every possible step to get her to reverse that decision.

M. Delbos agreed, but urged that above all we must not expose ourselves to a further rebuff from Germany. He reminded Mr. Davis that a short while ago the French and British Governments invited Germany to take part in the Nyon Conference, but were rebuffed.[4] Again, Germany had been asked to Brussels, and again she had refused.[5]

Mr. Davis said that he was well aware of that fact, but again stressed the importance of trying to get into better contact with Germany: he was convinced that Germany, with her inferiority complex, would be greatly gratified to be treated by France and Great Britain on a footing of greater equality and with greater respect for her feelings.

M. Delbos retorted that the French and British Governments had indeed lately tried to adopt that attitude towards Germany; there had been no reason to invite Germany to the Nyon Conference, which was dealing entirely with Mediterranean affairs, whereas Germany was not a Mediterranean Power. Nevertheless, she had been invited on account of her being a great Power with direct and important interest in European affairs. Equally she had not been a signatory of the Nine-Power Treaty, and yet again we had invited her to Brussels on account of her importance and prestige.

M. Delbos however admitted that Franco-German relations had recently improved somewhat and agreed that we should consider every possible means of drawing Germany into our counsels, and he suggested that although it would be merely inviting a rebuff to repeat the invitation, which she had already received, yet it might be possible at some later stage to represent that a new situation had arisen, such as might meet the condition which Germany had indicated in her refusal, which might permit of her changing her mind. For instance, it had been suggested that the Conference might appoint a sub-committee to get into contact with Japan and he thought that if such a sub-committee were appointed, it might be possible to ask Germany whether she also would be prepared to enter into contact with it.

Mr. MacDonald said that he thought they should give very serious thought to the possibility of getting Germany's cooperation in their proceedings. He agreed that an invitation in the old circumstances would meet with the old refusal. But the last sentence of the German reply had left the door open, and informal soundings might show that Germany would be willing to co-operate with a sub-committee of a few Powers.

Mr. Norman Davis agreed, but thought that the matter might be made even easier if instead of the Conference appointing a sub-committee of its own it nominated the representatives of certain Governments to undertake soundings in different quarters. He thought that the speeches that had already been made at the Conference would have shown Germany the spirit in which the Conference was approaching its work and might reassure her as to its intentions and prospects.

M. Delbos entirely agreed with this suggestion, though he felt bound to add that he saw certain other difficulties in the way of Germany's

[4] See Volume XIX, No. 147, note 3.   [5] See No. 325.

participation. Neither Russia nor Italy would welcome it, Russia for obvious reasons (though he did not think that they would insist on their objection), and Italy because in the absence of Germany she found herself in rather an important position, representing herself, Japan and Germany, and that flattered her vanity.[6]

[6] In a minute of November 11 Mr.Ronald remarked: 'Mr. Davis is a woolly old man, but I think he deserves every credit for stamping on M. Delbos' idea of a world conference to be summoned by Mr. Roosevelt . . .' Mr. Orde wrote on November 15: '. . . the idea of a world conference was thrown out I suspect as a pointed form of the pertinent argument that the U.S.A. must not expect others to settle definitely what they are prepared to do while remaining completely non-committal themselves.' A note of November 6 by M. Delbos in which he recorded conversations at Brussels with Mr. Eden, Mr. Davis, M. Spaak and M. Litvinov, is printed in *D.D.F.*, Series 2, vol. vii, pp. 346–50.

No. 333

Sir R. Clive (Brussels) to Foreign Office (Received November 6)

No. 54 Saving: Telegraphic [F 9151/6799/10]

BRUSSELS, *November 5, 1937*

Following from Secretary of State:
The Conference met again in private this morning. The Chinese Delegation said that they had deliberately abstained from taking part in the previous day's discussion[1] on the question of procedure, and as they understood that the question was to be discussed further, they offered to withdraw from the Conference while this was done, if their presence were thought embarrassing. Count Aldrovandi (Italy) said that he for his part had no objection to the Chinese remaining and they were unanimously invited to do so.

2. The President then read out a draft reply to the Japanese communications which had been prepared by the Belgian Ministry of Foreign Affairs (for text see my immediately following telegram[2]), and the Conference proceeded to discuss this draft.

3. It was generally agreed that it would be premature to attempt to designate the Powers who were to serve on the proposed sub-committee, and that as a first step Japan should be asked whether she was prepared to discuss matters with a small group of Powers, in which case the Conference would gladly designate one. There was some divergence of opinion as to whether the Japanese case should be outlined, or, if it were, whether a statement of the Chinese counter-arguments should not also be included. Dr. Wellington Koo said that if Japan's case was stated he felt it his duty to ask that it should be balanced by the Chinese case. M. Litvinov (Russia) urged that the Conference should not imply that they were taking

[1] See No. 331.   [2] Not kept in F.O. archives: see however No. 338 below.

the Japanese case at its face value, since it was only a piece of propaganda and was to a great extent irrelevant, because even if the facts alleged were true it constituted no defence. It would therefore be best not to mention either the Japanese 'grievances' or the Chinese reply to them. M. de Castro (Portugal) and Senator Dandurand (Canada) agreed with M. Litvinov's conclusion: Mr. Bruce (Australia) thought that a recapitulation of Japan's grievances was important because they were the reasons advanced by Japan for departing from her policy of friendly co-operation with China: Mr. Norman Davis (United States) thought that it would be enough if emphasis were laid on the fact that China was present at the Conference and had shown thereby her desire to collaborate, and the question put, whether Japan would do as much on her side. Mr. Jordan (New Zealand) pointed out that if the points of detail which had been raised were to be dealt with at all they would have to be dealt with at great length.

4. M. Litvinov further observed that account must be taken of the fact that the Conference was not entirely composed of signatories of the Washington Treaty: moreover, it was not quite in accordance with what had been agreed on the previous day to say that the aim of the small group would be to 'facilitate a settlement between the two parties.'

5. It was agreed that Delegates should present their amendments in writing in the course of the afternoon, the President emphasising that it was necessary to avoid giving the impression that the Conference was unable to agree or was delaying matters unnecessarily.

6. Shortly before the Conference adjourned it was announced that there had been some leakage into the press, and a *communiqué* was agreed stating that any document purporting to emanate from the Conference was entirely without authority.

No. 334

Report[1] *of the Advisory Committee on Trade Questions in Time of War on Economic Sanctions against Japan*

Cab. 4/26

Secret   2, WHITEHALL GARDENS, S.W.1, *November 5, 1937*

I PRELIMINARY CONSIDERATIONS

1. Our terms of reference are as follows:

'To consider and report to the Committee of Imperial Defence what results could be achieved by the imposition of Economic Sanctions against Japan by the British Empire and the United States of America

[1] Circulated to the C.I.D. as C.I.D. 1365B (A.T.B. 155): see No. 315, note 3.

in conjunction, alternatively with or without the co-operation of other countries.'

2. This Committee considered a somewhat similar problem in March 1932,[2] and, although there have been important changes in the situation in the last five years, certain basic factors remain unaltered.

One of the changes in the basic situation which has taken place is the fact that Japan has ceased to be a member of the League of Nations. The legal position has consequently been affected in regard to the possibility of applying measures of economic pressure in respect (a) of the treaty obligations of the United Kingdom, and (b) the procedure by which the measures could be enforced under United Kingdom law.

As regards (a), most of the possible measures would conflict with the obligations of this country under the Anglo-Japanese Commercial Treaty of 1911. In the case of sanctions against Italy, the analogous difficulty was overcome owing to the fact that Italy, being a member of the League, could be held to have debarred herself from protesting against action taken under the Covenant, and from invoking her rights under pre-existing treaties. The same doctrine could not be applied in the case of Japan unless the procedure of Article XVII of the Covenant had first been followed, i.e., Japan had been invited to become a member of the League for the purposes of the dispute and had refused, with the result that Article XVI became applicable; and even in that case the question might arise whether, Japan not being a member of the League, the provisions of the Covenant would constitute an adequate defence to Japanese complaints based on the commercial treaty.

In the absence of League action under the Covenant, a legal justification for action over-riding this country's treaty obligations could only be sought in reprisals for a breach by Japan of her treaty obligations under the Briand-Kellogg Pact and the Nine-Power Treaty.

As regards (b), His Majesty's Government could not, unless action were being taken under the Covenant, proceed, as was done in the case of sanctions against Italy, by Order-in-Council under the Treaty of Peace Act. Special legislation would be necessary.

In view of our terms of reference, we have thought it unnecessary to deal with the political and constitutional aspect of this question so far as the countries of the British Empire are concerned, and have confined ourselves to the consideration of a hypothetical case in which all the Members of the British Commonwealth were prepared to co-operate in a policy of applying sanctions against Japan.

3. The imposition of economic sanctions against Japan carried with it, of course, the risk of grave counter-measures by that country. In the first place, there is the danger that the adoption of such a policy in time of peace might lead to war either through acts of retaliation on the part of Japan or through some other eventuality. The more effective sanctions

[2] *Note in original*: Paper No. A.T.B. 86; also C.I.D. Paper No. 1083B. [Not printed.]

are, the more likely this is to occur, and this danger of retaliation would inevitably lead to a demand by the more vulnerable States that they should be effectively guaranteed against Japanese attack in the event of their agreeing to apply sanctions. The States which might be expected to make such guarantees a condition of their participation would doubtless include France in respect of Indo-China, the Netherlands in respect of their East Indian colonies, Siam, the United States in respect of the Philippines, the U.S.S.R., Portugal in respect of Macao, ourselves, presumably, in respect of all our Far Eastern possessions, and (to a lesser degree, owing to their greater distance from the scene of conflict) Australia, New Zealand, India and Burma. In the second place, there is the possibility that, in the event of sanctions being applied, Japan, who is not at present exercising belligerent rights at sea against neutrals and is operating only against Chinese shipping, might be led to increase her economic pressure on China by admitting the existence of a state of war and exercising full belligerent rights against neutral trade with that country. Moreover, there is the risk that Japan, in her anxiety to force a speedy decision before sanctions could become effective, might resort to a greater degree than hitherto, to measures of unrestricted warfare against the Chinese civilian population, and even perhaps, against neutral shipping. We do not consider that our terms of reference require us to pursue these possibilities further.

4. There are two other general considerations of great importance, to which we refer again later, which must also be kept constantly in mind in considering any scheme for the application of economic sanctions to Japan:

(*a*) the extent to which any scheme can be vitiated by evasion, either by design or through inefficient administration, or by the existence of alternative sources of channels of supply.

(*b*) that, although the United Kingdom would not remain entirely unaffected commercially and financially by the consequences of an interruption in Japanese trade, the dislocation and loss would fall to a much greater extent on other countries of the British Empire, particularly India and Australia.

II EXTENT OF JAPANESE SELF-SUFFICIENCY

Foodstuffs and Raw Materials for industry generally

5. Rice is normally the only essential foodstuff import, but this year's crops in Japan, Formosa and Korea are so large that, taking existing stocks into account, no import of foodstuffs will be necessary for at least eighteen months.

Japan is, however, dependent in varying degrees on overseas supplies of a number of raw materials for her industrial activity of which, as seen from Annex I[3], the chief are iron (ore, scrap and pig), non-ferrous metals,

---

[3] Not printed.

petroleum, rubber, cotton, wool, wood pulp and jute. Annex II[3] shows that Japan was importing during the first six months[4] of 1937 supplies of many important materials at a rate of importation much above that of previous years. Together with stocks in hand at the beginning of the year, Japan probably had at the start of hostilities sufficient supplies to meet all demands for these raw materials without further addition for between six and nine months at the peace-time rate of expenditure. Moreover, whilst on the one hand, the mobilisation of industry to meet the needs of the military operations in China has raised the consumption of practically all industrial raw materials above the normal rate, any interference with her export trade would result in a slowing up of the rate of consumption of certain, though not all, of these raw materials.

Capacity to manufacture war stores
  6. If kept supplied with raw materials, Japanese industry is now able to manufacture an adequate quantity of all the war stores essential to the Forces she has put into the field against China with three possible exceptions—explosives, mechanised transport and aviation spirit.

As regards explosives, there is already evidence that the rate of expenditure has severely strained Japanese manufacturing capacity and that she is trying—not altogether successfully—to purchase explosives abroad in considerable quantitites. Even if there is no weakening of the Chinese defence which might lead to a decrease in the present rate of Japanese munitions expenditure, it would be unsafe to assume that a shortage will develop on the Japanese side so acute as to make her military operations ineffective.

As regards mechanised transport, we have information that the Japanese Armies in North China are already embarrassed by the inability of Japanese-made mechanised vehicles to stand up to local conditions. The domestic output, which is largely dependent on components imported from the United States (see Annex III[3]) is insufficient to make good the wastage. This embarrassment will increase with the extension of the Japanese lines of communication.

So far as aviation spirit is concerned, there is evidence that during the past two months Japan has been buying considerable quantities in the United States of America for urgent delivery. We have, however, no information regarding the size of stocks of aviation spirit available in Japan. Reserves of oil stocks for other purposes, however, are known to be exceptionally large, and it appears unlikely that the need for a proportionate reserve of aviation spirit has been overlooked. The current purchases may be prompted rather by fear of future eventualities than by an immediate or prospective shortage. The position of Japan in regard to oil is set out in Appendix VII[3].

[4] *Note in original*: Figures for July and August suggest that the abnormal imports have continued in these months except in the case of wool, rubber and cotton, of which the August imports were below the monthly average for 1936.

7. So far as war stores for the operations in China are concerned, we conclude, with some reservation in the case of explosives, mechanised transport (including component parts) and aviation spirit, that Japan is in a position, having regard to her present stocks of war stores, and principal raw materials, and to her industrial capacity, to continue fighting on the present scale for some months without further importation of these goods.

III METHODS OF ECONOMIC PRESSURE

8. There are four methods by which economic pressure can be exercised against Japan. Steps can be taken to interfere with her
(a) Imports.
(b) Exports.
(c) Finance.
(d) Shipping.

IIIA ACTION IN REGARD TO JAPANESE IMPORTS

9. In 1936 nearly 70 per cent. by value of Japanese imports, other than those from Manchuria and the Kwantung Leased Territory, were derived from the British Empire, the United States and its Dependencies (*vide* Annex IV[3]). Annex I[3] is even more impressive as showing by commodities the extent to which Japan is normally dependent upon the British Empire and the United States for her principal imports, all of which are of the first importance in war. It also indicates the most important alternative sources of supply of the principal Japanese imports. Certain of these are controlled by British or United States interests, but the possibility of using this control to prevent supplies being sold to Japan requires further examination.

10. It is, however, certain that in view of the great proportion of her imports derived directly from the British Empire and the United States, Japan would experience grave difficulties in rapidly acquiring alternative sources of supply. It would appear, therefore, that a refusal on the part of the British Empire and the United States to export certain essential commodities to Japan would cause extensive dislocation in Japanese economy and industry as soon as accumulated stocks had been used up.

On the other hand, Japan would undoubtedly endeavour to reorganise her import trade so as to obtain her supplies from new sources and by alternative channels, e.g., by the direct importation from producing countries not taking part in the policy of economic sanctions or by the indirect importation from participating countries by means of an entrepôt trade established in non-participating countries. Such a procedure would entail certain disadvantages for her, but no insuperable difficulties are seen in the way of its accomplishment during the period that existing stocks are being used up. As shown in paragraph 15 below, Japan would have no difficulty in financing such purchases for a considerable period of time.

11. No effective counter-measure against this sort of evasion would appear to be possible without some form of rationing scheme on a world-wide international basis.

In practice it was not found possible when sanctions were imposed on Italy in 1935 to attempt any rationing of supplies to non-participating States, whether members of the League or not, and in our Tenth Annual Report,[5] reviewing the results of applying economic sanctions to Italy, we stated *inter alia*:

> 'The general conclusion of our first Report was that, without a state of war, a prohibition of essential imports to Italy would be comparatively ineffective even over a long period. This is confirmed, as there was no apparent shortage of essential military requirements during the war, although the efficacy of including petroleum products, with the possible co-operation of the United States of America, was never tried.'

We think the organisation by the British Empire and the United States of America of a far-reaching scheme of effective international rationing would be out of the question. It seems to us out of the question to suppose that Germany and Italy, for example, would consent to the restrictions on their trade which such a scheme would involve.

Another deduction from the Italo-Abyssinian experience is that collective action against a country's imports by a large number of different countries can only be applied in a comparatively crude form, i.e., in respect of a limited number of easily specified raw materials, and that this has the effect of fostering an increased trade in semi-manufactured articles or processed materials in lieu of the normal trade in the prohibited raw materials. This form of evasion can only be countered by making the list of forbidden goods so extensive that administration is rendered too complicated to be practicable.

IIIB ACTION IN REGARD TO JAPANESE EXPORTS

12. Whilst in the case of Japanese imports it would be impracticable to apply sanctions save in respect of certain major commodities primarily required for war purposes, in the case of exports there would be no administrative necessity for any differentiation and an embargo could apply to all Japanese exports of any kind.

In 1936 the British Empire and the United States between them took 65 per cent. of the total Japanese exports by value (excluding those to Manchuria and the Kwantung Leased Territory). As can be seen from Annex V[3], the remainder of Japanese exports were distributed over a large number of countries. The complete loss of British Empire and United States markets would, therefore, restrict the external resources at

---

[5] *Note in original*: Paper No. A.T.B. 143; also C.I.D. Paper No. 1292B. [Not printed.]

the disposal of Japan for the acquisition of necessary imports to a marked degree, even if allowance is made for some diversion to alternative markets.

13. Japanese exports to the British Empire and the United States in 1936 were 1,420 million yen.[6] After allowing for diversion to other markets and other adjustments, the net reduction in export is unlikely to exceed 1,000 million. Whatever the amount is, it must be met out of Japan's available external resources.

14. The Japanese gold reserve is estimated at a market value of 1,220 million yen, and her production in 1937 has been estimated at 200 million yen. There are other resources in the form of Japanese balances in foreign centres and Japanese-held foreign securities. The nominal amount in September 1936 has been estimated[7] at £137 million. No estimate of present holdings and their market value is available, and Japanese Foreign Bonds would be difficult to sell in any volume; but, whatever the value of this asset is, there is something to set against it for Japanese external liabilities.

The Treasury have been furnished with a confidential estimate that the present figure of short-term facilities (advances, discounts, credits, &c.) granted to the Japanese in the London market lies between £15 million and £20 million. The total amount has not been increased during recent months, and it is now in process of gradual and general reduction. A considerable proportion of the indebtedness is secured.

But whereas most or all of the short-term indebtedness would have to be paid off, it may be assumed that the service of Japan's long-term indebtedness to British and American creditors would be suspended. It is estimated that nearly £59 million of British money is invested in Japan and Japanese territory, the annual charge being £3.4 million. The suspension of this (the equivalent of nearly 60 million yen) would be a further relief to the balance of payments.

15. On the basis of the estimates contained in the preceding paragraphs it appears that some two years might elapse before Japan's resources would be exhausted, assuming that, in the absence of any interruption, her exports would pay for her imports.[8] But it would not be safe to assume that the large additional imports required by war conditions could be compensated by equivalent further reduction of non-essential imports. Moreover, account must be taken of the decrease in Japan's production for export, which may be expected under war conditions, apart from any embargo, and also of the diminution of the Chinese markets which Japan has in any case to face. On the other hand, the possibility of obtaining supplies on credit from non-sanctionist

[6] *Note in original*: The present rate of exchange is 17 yen to £1 sterling.

[7] *Note in original*: Tokyo despatch No. 295E of March 5, 1937. (The estimate is in several points very obscure.)

[8] *Note in original*: Expressed in the form of a balance sheet over this period the calculation

countries must not be overlooked nor the stocks at present held by Japan (see paragraph 5 above) which are known to be large.

Again, we have made no attempt to estimate the effect of sanctions on the Japanese Budget position and on the standard of living in Japan. The position just before the outbreak of hostilities was summarised as follows by the Financial Adviser to the Tokyo Embassy:

> In 1937 the political conditions of the country have been more than usually unsettled and the financial position has become steadily worse. The rapid rise in world prices has upset all calculations, and the adverse trade balance reached 624.9 million yen for the first five months and twenty days of this year as compared with 323.5 million yen for the corresponding period last year. This represents the highest adverse trade balance since 1924, the year following the Kwanto earthquake, and, although exports usually exceed imports in the second half of the year, it seems probable that the adverse trade balance at the end of 1937 will be unusually large. Wholesale and retail price indices have shown a further sharp rise; sporadic strikes for higher wages indicate that domestic wage levels cannot be prevented from rising very much longer; there is an increasing demand on the banks for accommodation from their industrial clients and the banking system has become still more illiquid;[9] the Bank of Japan is finding it more and more difficult to dispose of deficit bonds;[10] interest rates are hardening and the underlying tendency of the yen is weaker in spite of gold shipments.

Since the outbreak of hostilities special credits to a total of 2,550 million yen (£149 millions) have been voted and the inflation must have developed at a greatly increased pace.

Sanctions would involve additional expenditure for purchases by indirect methods, and in particualr the interruption of silk exports would

on the assumption above, would appear as follows:

Resources	Million yen.	Liabilities	Million yen.
Gold reserve	1,220	Net loss of exports	2,000
Gold production	400	Withdrawal of short-term facilities in	
Sale of securities	? 500	U.K. and U.S.A.	? 250
Default to British and U.S.A. creditors	? 120		
	? 2,240		? 2,250

[9] *Note in original*: It should, however, be noted that for reasons peculiar to Japan (small investing public, prevalence of long-time deposits, low wage and salary structure) the liquidity of Japanese banks in normal times is very much less than in English banking practice.

[10] *Note in original*: The amount of Government bonds held by the Bank of Japan at the end of 1936 was 764.9 million yen. This figure fell to 571.2 million yen at the end of February, but by the end of May had risen to 782.7 million yen.

presumably be met by very large subsidies in some form or other to the silk farmers of Japan, who would be rendered destitute, and assistance to the cottage industries of Japan. Thus the distress of a population, a large part of which is never far from destitution, would be intensified. How far and for how long this would be countered by a determination to endure every sacrifice rather than give in to sanctions is a psychological question. Such considerations are always difficult to assess at their true value, and the difficulty is enhanced in dealing with an oriental nation, whose habits and character are alien to our own. In the case of Japan the difficulty is still further increased by the impossibility of estimating the probable effects, both material and psychological, upon the subject races of Manchukuo, Formosa and Korea.

Taking these and other factors into account it seems a reasonable estimate that the prohibition of imports from Japan to the British Empire and the United States—though ultimately a very potent weapon—*would not have a decisive effect for between* 1 *and* 2 *years*. But in view of the many unknown factors this estimate is given with every reserve[11]; on the one hand we may well have under-estimated the difficulties which economic sanctions on the part of the British Empire and the United States of America would cause to Japan, whilst, on the other hand, the very fact that sanctions are being imposed would make it possible for the people of Japan to endure a degree of sacrifice otherwise intolerable.

IIIC FINANCIAL PRESSURE

16. The calculation in the preceding paragraphs is based on the assumption that Japan will not be able to borrow abroad. Economic pressure would include a prohibition of lending or granting credit to anyone resident or carrying on business in Japan. In present circumstances, with existing credits in process of repayment, such a prohibition in this country would have no very great practical effect on Japan. Possibly it might have more effect if imposed in the United States[12] if it were effectively enforced. This is a matter on which we have no information.

It is possible that Japan may receive important facilities in other countries whether economic pressure is applied by the British Empire and the U.S.A. or not. Even those countries which are the most embarrassed in their finances can afford to supply goods on credit.

IIID ACTION AGAINST JAPANESE SHIPPING

17. Measures against Japan's foreign trade would automatically react

[11] *Note in original*: It is interesting to note from F.O. telegram from Tokyo 580 of 23rd October, 1937 [not printed], that the Japanese Minister of Commerce is believed to have stated recently in private conversation that Japan had all the foodstuffs she needed, and stocks of other essential commodities to enable her to hold out against a boycott for two years.

[12] *Note in original*: Japan does not come within the scope of the Johnson Act which places an embargo on countries in default to the United States Government.

upon Japanese shipping, but pressure could be increased by a refusal of bunker facilities or by prohibiting Japanese shipping from using the ports of participating countries and, conversely, by prohibiting the shipping of participating countries from carrying goods to and from Japan.

The adoption of such measures if combined with sanctions against trade would no doubt add to the economic pressure on Japan, who in 1935 obtained a net gain in foreign exchange of about £10 million from her shipping. An additional strain would, moreover, be placed on Japanese shipping by the necessity of trading with countries other than the British Empire and the United States.

18. Although the elimination of Japanese competition might be of some benefit to the shipping of participating countries, the carrying trade of non-participating countries would benefit generally at the expense of that of participating countries. It is doubtful, for instance, if Japanese trade were cut off, whether the trade remaining would allow certain British shipping lines normally plying in the Far East to continue to operate without running at a loss.

19. At the same time it seems likely that Japan would regard measures directed against her shipping as especially provocative, and might well retaliate against British shipping in the Far East. Moreover, such measures would not, like prohibitions on imports or exports, be confined to the character of a 'long range blockade' and the risk of incidents would be greatly increased.

It will be recalled that shipping sanctions were never imposed on Italy.

The adoption of such measures as are mentioned in paragraph 17 would not effectively prevent the conveyance of goods to or from Japan inasmuch as Japanese shipping could still be used for trade between Japan and the non-participating countries, and the ships of those countries could be chartered by Japan for use in the trade (which would in any case be greatly reduced by the export and import prohibitions) between Japan and participating countries. In addition, Japanese ships might, if necessary, be temporarily transferred to the flags of the non-participating countries for the purpose of taking part in the last-mentioned trade.

In these circumstances, we feel that the adoption of the measures under discussion would not by itself inflict sufficient injury on Japan to justify the risks and disadvantages involved.[13]

[13] Commenting on this paper in a note of November 1 which was circulated to the A.T.B. Committee as A.T.B. 156, Mr. Clauson of the Colonial Office expressed the opinion that the A.T.B. Report made an insufficient examination of the possibility of sanctions on shipping. He thought that the risk of Japanese retaliation had been exaggerated, and referred to the exploits of Italian and Spanish ships in the Mediterranean: cf. Volume XIX, Chapter I. At the A.T.B. Committee meeting on November 4, however (see No. 315, note 3), when Mr. Clauson aired his views, Sir J. Foley, Under Secretary at the Board of Trade, continued to maintain that an embargo on Japanese shipping was impossible.

IV COUNTER-EFFECT UPON THE BRITISH EMPIRE OF ECONOMIC PRESSURE ON JAPAN

20. Although, as already stated in paragraphs 10 and 12, so large a proportion of Japanese trade is normally carried on with the British Empire and the United States, the share of the United Kingdom is very small, representing only about 1 per cent., both of United Kingdom imports and exports. The cessation of trade between the United Kingdom and Japan would, therefore, have no very serious effect upon the former, but certain trades in this country would suffer: in particular our natural silk industry, which depends almost entirely on Japan for its raw material. (On the other hand, our cotton industry would receive a considerable but purely temporary stimulus through the removal of Japanese competition in various markets.)

The possible loss of interest on British capital employed in the Japanese Empire, Manchuria and the Kwantung Leased Territory has been estimated in paragraph 14 above at about £3.4 million per annum, whilst, in addition, there is a risk that some of the invested capital might be permanently lost.

British shipping might have to face a loss in the carrying trade, for reasons indicated in paragraph 18 above, but the information available does not allow us to estimate the extent of the possible loss entailed.

21. Annex VI[3] suggests that the most serious risk of loss would be incurred by certain British oversea countries. The closing of Japanese markets to Australian wool, Indian cotton and jute and Malayan rubber, for example, would be relatively a much more serious matter for those countries, if they should be unable to find alternative markets, than the loss of Japanese trade with the United Kingdom. It is not possible to estimate how far alternative markets could be found without a prolonged and detailed study of international trade. In so far as Japan substituted staple fibre, &c. for wool and cotton there would be a net and continuing loss to the producers of these raw materials.

22. As regards India, we are advised that the elimination of Japanese trade would involve a number of special problems. The cessation of Japanese exports to India would cause a serious loss to the customs revenue, though it would bring profits to some Indian manufacturers. It would also tend to benefit some branches of British trade, especially that of Lancashire, and, although Indian sympathies appear to be strongly with China, a policy of economic pressure against Japan might, nevertheless, be represented in certain quarters in India as an attempt by His Majesty's Government to force British products, and cotton goods in particular, upon India. As regards Japanese imports from India, the Japanese market for raw cotton is of very great importance to India, and its loss would be a most serious matter to the producers, especially at a time when there is a surplus of raw cotton in the world. It may be anticipated that India would not be ready to face this strain upon her

economic resources unless she were sure that the burden of economic pressure was being fairly shared among the States participating in it, and she would probably expect some relief from outside in respect of her cotton which fails to find a market.[14]

V THE EFFECT OF THE CO-OPERATION OF COUNTRIES OTHER THAN THE BRITISH EMPIRE AND THE U.S.A.

23. Our terms of reference do not specifically require us to consider which countries would in practice be willing to participate in sanctions, but the following observations may be of use as showing the countries whose participation would be necessary or desirable, and the effects which might be expected from their participation.

24. So far as sanctions directed against the supply of certain articles to Japan are concerned, the effect of the co-operation of other countries depends largely on two factors: first, whether those countries are likely to include all, or nearly all, the principal sources of supply of essential commodities, and, secondly, whether their co-operation would sufficiently reduce the risk of evasion. As regards the first of these considerations, Annex I[3] suggests that the participation of the undermentioned countries would be required to cut Japan off from direct access to the principal sources of the commodities shown, viz., Argentine, Belgium, Bolivia, Brazil, Chili, Colombia, Egypt, France, Mexico, Netherlands, Norway, Peru, Siam, Uruguay, Sweden, Venezuela, Roumania and the U.S.S.R.

Theoretically, of course, equally decisive results as far as direct supply is concerned could be attained if Japan were deprived of access to any one foreign product which was at once irreplaceable and essential to the prosecution of the war. In that case the co-operation of a much smaller number of States might prove effective.

25. But even the participation of these countries, or of some of them, would not, *eo facto*, prevent Japan from purchasing their products through non-participating countries of which there would inevitably be a certain number, among them, no doubt, Germany and Italy, where all material facilities for the speedy establishment of an entrepôt trade already exist.

We have considered the possibility that the sanctionist countries might agree so to control their exports of essential commodities to non-sanctionist countries that the latter would be unable to obtain a surplus for re-exports to Japan. We do not, however, regard such a measure as practicable, even if, as suggested above, control were to be limited to any one essential commodity.

26. We are therefore forced to the conclusion that the participation in sanctions of any number of countries conceivable in present circumstances would be incapable of preventing Japan from acquiring the necessary

[14] *Note in original*: This would have repercussions in the United States of America, whose record cotton crop is an important factor in the surplus referred to above.

supplies of raw materials. The only effect of their participation, so long as other countries, through which a transit trade could be organised, remained outside, would be to increase the temporary dislocation of Japan's trade and, ultimately, to force her to pay somewhat higher prices for her purchases.

27. As regards an embargo on Japanese exports, the co-operation of at least the following countries, which, after the British Empire and the United States of America, are Japan's chief markets, would be desirable: the Netherlands, France, Siam, Egypt, Germany, Belgium, the U.S.S.R. and Argentine. Of these, Germany and Siam are unlikely to participate. The remainder in 1936, took Japanese goods to the value of about 340 million yen, of which 151 million yen were accounted for by the Netherlands and her colonies. If all these countries participated it would be more difficult for Japan to find new markets for the goods normally exported to the British Empire and the United States of America, and we may therefore assume that Japan's net annual loss of exports would be in the order of 1,300 to 1,400 million yen. At this rate, and on the basis of the tentative calculations made in Section IIIB the period of time in which serious difficulties for Japan might be expected to occur would be reduced by some months. A further reduction in this period might be effected by the participation of other countries, which although not normally large importers of Japanese goods, might provide Japan with potential alternative methods.

VI CONCLUSIONS

28. Our Conclusions, which are summarised in the next paragraph, should be read in conjunction with the following considerations of a more general character:-

(a) In view of the Anglo-Japanese Treaty of 1911 and of the fact that Japan is not a member of the League of Nations, the application of sanctions by the United Kingdom might involve certain legal difficulties. Special legislation might be required (paragraph 2).

(b) The imposition of sanctions might involve Japanese retaliation and a demand from the more vulnerable of the participating States for military guarantees against it (paragraph 3).

(c) Sanctions might lead Japan to intensify her economic pressure on China as claiming belligerent rights and to resort to measures of unrestricted warfare against non-combatants and even against neutral shipping in order to force a quick decision (paragraph 3).

29. For the reasons set out in our report, we conclude that

(a) stocks of war stores and of many of the principal materials imported by Japan stand at present at abnormally high levels. It is considered that Japan would be able to continue military operations on the present scale for some months without further importation of these goods. The chief possible deficiencies are likely to be in explosives, mechanised transport and, perhaps, aviation spirit (paragraphs 5–7).

(b) an embargo by the British Empire and the United States of America on selected commodities required by Japan would cause her serious difficulty, but in the absence of a world-wide scheme of international rationing, which we regard as quite impracticable, she could not, without a state of war between her and the participating countries, be prevented from acquiring supplies from alternative sources in non-participating countries or by entrepôt trade through such countries (paragraphs 9–11).

(c) an embargo by the British Empire and the United States of America on all Japanese export trade would be highly embarrassing for her, and might ultimately prove decisive owing to her inability to pay for imports. Having regard, however, to Japan's gold reserve and other resources, no decisive effect could be expected for a considerable period which may be put at between one and two years (paragraphs 12–15).

(d) a refusal by the British Empire and the United States of America of bunker facilities and of the use of their ports to Japanese shipping would increase the economic pressure on Japan, although it would not prevent the conveyance of goods to and from Japan. Such action, which was not taken against Italy, would entail special risks (paragraphs 17–19).

(e) The co-operation of other countries with the British Empire and the United States of America would intensify to varying extents all the different forms of pressure.

   (i) As regards Japanese imports, the participation of any number of countries conceivable in present circumstances could not entirely prevent Japan from acquiring the necessary supplies of raw materials. Their participation would, however, increase the temporary dislocation of Japan's trade and force her to pay higher prices for her supplies.

   (ii) The effect on Japanese exports would be more pronounced. If the Netherlands, France, Egypt, Belgium, the U.S.S.R. and the Argentine co-operated, the period of 'between one and two years' referred to in (c) above might be reduced by some months.

(f) as regards the counter-effect on the British Empire, by far the largest part of the loss of trade will fall on certain oversea countries, notably India and Australia.[15]

Signed on behalf of the Committee,
WALTER E. ELLIOT, *Chairman*
C. N. RYAN, *Secretary*

[15] In his note of November 1 (see note 13 above) Mr. Clauson further criticized the

Report for ignoring the possible effects of the financial and social dislocation which sanctions might cause in Japan. He also pointed out that Japan's existing financial difficulties had been disregarded, and concluded: 'I find it impossible personally to believe that the Government would be able for long to face the economic and social dislocation which would be occasioned by sanctions in Japan proper, let alone the additional difficulties in Korea, Formosa and Manchukuo where there is an alien and potentially, if not actually, hostile population.'

Mr. Clauson's paper was discussed by the A.T.B. Committee on November 4, but the Report was adopted with only slight amendment and submitted to the 301st meeting of the C.I.D. on November 18. In presenting the Report Mr. Elliot drew attention to the fact that it was impossible to assess the psychological effects of sanctions on Japan, and also to the view of the Service Departments that sanctions would involve 'a grave risk of war'. Mr. Eden expressed gratitude for the Report, which was approved by the C.I.D. The A.T.B. Committee were subsequently instructed to work out plans to exert economic pressure on Japan in the event of war and in their 11th annual report of February 9, 1938 (A.T.B. 160) noted that in view of the 'change in circumstances towards the end of the year [1937]' Japan had been given priority in this respect over Germany. On February 23 the Economic Pressure Sub-Commitee of the A.T.B. circulated 'Preliminary notes on some aspects of the economic situation in the Far East in the event of war between the British Empire and Japan in 1938' (A.T.B.(E.P.G.)11). Another paper, (A.T.B.(E.P.G.)12 of March 5, 1938) set out naval measures for the interception of Japanese trade, and more detailed plans were to be formulated by July. Further details of these plans can be found in W. N. Medlicott, *The Economic Blockade* (revised edn., 1978), vol. i, pp. 383–8.

No. 335

Mr. Affleck (Tientsin) to Mr. Eden[1] *(Received November 6, 6 p.m.)*

No. 58 Telegraphic: by wireless [F 9207/220/10]

TIENTSIN, *November 6, 1937*

Addressed to Nanking No. 105 of November 6th.

Foreign Office telegram to Tokyo No. 441 of November 3rd.[2]

Following is my studied appreciation of local situation in regard to customs.

I am quite satisfied that Myers, the Commissioner of Customs, has dealt with a most difficult situation in the only way possible to save breakdown of Chinese customs administration in North China.

The Japanese military authorities have from the beginning adopted a most uncompromising attitude, making it difficult even for their own Consul-General through whom alone Myers was able to communicate with them, to have any dealing with them, except on basis of complete submission to their dictates. They throughout flatly refused even to discuss Six Point proposals and Myers was warned that unless revenues were without further parley deposited in Yokohama Specie Bank the Chinese customs would be ignored and other arrangements made. Myers

[1] Mr. Eden flew back to London on the afternoon of November 5, returning to Brussels on November 9.

[2] Not printed (F 8773/220/10).

held out as long as he could in face of this ultimatum but on October 22nd he decided, under continual and daily pressure from Japanese, and in order to save Chinese customs service in North China, that the time had now come when he must exercise discretion conveyed to him in Maze's confidential telegram No. 678, October 19th[3].

3. The wording of this telegram was somewhat equivocal and it subsequently appeared that there had been a rather important word omitted from it (see Financial Adviser's telegram to Tientsin No. 39[3] of October 19th and No. 48[4] of October 25th). In the circumstances Myers took the only line left open to him. He deposited revenues in Yokohama Specie Bank at the same time reserving all rights in regard to remittances for loan quotas etc. He had previously been repeatedly assured by the Japanese Consul-General that there was no intention on the part of the Japanese military to divert any part of these revenues to their own use and that as far as external loans were concerned remittances could be made as usual. But as regards other remittances Japanese military were adamant in determination to stop, while the present campaign lasted, any money reaching Nanking which might be used against them. In view of this statement Myers wisely decided to make no remittances at all for the time being so as not to differentiate between external loans and other obligations and thus leave an open field for future negotiations. As Myers put it to me, it was better to have revenues coming into and accumulating in Yokohama Specie Bank than to run the risk of losing them altogether by continued opposition to insistent demands of Japanese military.

4. Myers informed me yesterday that everything was now working towards a return to normal. He had just seen Japanese Consul-General and received his assurance that military will give the Customs full co-operation both here and at Chinwangtao and that integrity of customs will be fully maintained. A remittance of $200,000 is to be made today to Inspector General of Customs.

5. Much credit is in my opinion due to Myers for the level headed and able manner in which he has tided over an admittedly critical situation for Chinese customs.[5]

Repeated to Peking telegram No. 187, Shanghai, for Financial Adviser No. 40, Tokyo.

[3] Not printed: cf. No. 329.   [4] Not printed.
[5] Following the settlement reached by Mr. Myers the customs service ran fairly smoothly for some time, although difficulties were caused by the refusal of the Japanese authorities to allow any remittances to reach the Chinese Government other than collection costs and the service of foreign loans. On November 15 a new crisis arose over the customs at Shanghai: see No. 371 below.

No. 336

Sir R. Craigie (Tokyo) to Mr. Eden (Received November 6, 2 p.m.)

No. 653[1] Telegraphic [F 9147/6799/10]

Important   TOKYO, *November 6, 1937, 8.20 p.m.*

Sir R. Clive's telegram No. 84.[2]

I feel sure that Japanese Government would decline to join deliberations of such a committee if invited. But I believe its constitution (minus Soviet Russia) would be step in the right direction particularly if the door were left open to an offer of good offices by *one* of the Powers represented in it, see my telegram No. 616.[3] I have since had further reason to think such an outcome of conference would be welcome to Japanese Government.

What contact could be established between such a committee and Japanese Government (beyond exchange of written communications) it is difficult to determine at the moment. Japanese Government are still resolutely opposed to anything in the nature of collective mediation and all I can elicit is that they would appreciate action of any friendly Power which would advise China in her own interests to start direct negotiations with Japan. Naturally Japanese Government would be only too pleased if such advice were to be offered to China by the Committee as a whole but in the course of any ensuing Sino Japanese negotiations the Japanese Government would be more responsive to advice or good offices of a single Power than of a group of Powers.

I hope I have made it clear in earlier telegrams that these people are now determined to see this thing through to the end winter campaign or not and I am personally at a loss to understand what Chinese Government can hope to gain by prolonging the struggle unless Japanese terms prove to be quite impossible. Why not find out what the terms are?

Apart from Press reports I have no information as to the nature of message which is being drafted by the Committee.[4]

For immediate repetition to Brussels.

[1] Although this telegram was despatched after No. 337 below, it was received a day earlier in the Foreign Office.

[2] In this telegram of November 6 Mr. MacDonald referred to Conference discussions on the drafting of a message to the Japanese Government and said that Mr. N. Davis had told him that Count Aldovrandi had reason to believe that 'if a small committee for negotiating with the Japanese were set up, and provided Russians were not on the committee, Japanese would agree to make contact with it'.

[3] Of October 30, not printed (F 8783/6799/10).

[4] In a note on the filed copy of this telegram, Sir R. Vansittart asked for it to be minuted, and remarked: 'We have had one look at the terms already and they were impossible. That was some time ago, and they have probably risen since. Sir R. Craigie seems bent on urging the Chinese to surrender. But he is Ambassador at Tokyo and not to China. R. V.' Mr. Ronald, in a minute of November 9, said that in deciding to resist the Japanese by force the Chinese 'calculated that they must expect frequent reverses, but that, if only they could

draw Japanese forces further and further into China, the expense of a long campaign would be ruinous to Japan . . . They would not bless us therefore if we pressed them to ask Japan what terms of settlement she now proposed . . .' Mr Orde wrote: 'My fear is that the Chinese have fought only too stoutly & have suffered heavier losses then it was wise to incur. It was a difficult game that they had to play. Terms of peace which *some* Chinese are ready to contemplate are given in F 9052/9/10 [not printed].' He thought that Sir R. Craigie was 'unduly optimistic about them. What is really needed is something precise and neither side really like precision unless it gives them everything they want. Each side hopes to (and the Japanese intend to and will effectively) stretch anything vague in their own favour. The Chinese are constitutionally optimistic and face-saving and the Japanese are ruthless and exorbitant . . . I fear that one side or the other has to be nearer the breaking point than is apparent now before any terms with a proper chance of permanence can be agreed upon. The Powers can work towards clearing up the position but they cannot well advise China in the sense which Sir R. Craigie appears to advocate. C. W. Orde 9/11.'

No. 337

Sir R. Lindsay (Washington) to Mr. Eden
(Received November 7, 10 a.m.)

No. 385 Telegraphic [F 9185/6799/10]

WASHINGTON, *November 6, 1937, 7.35 p.m.*

Your telegram No. 489.[1]
My first impression on reading your telegrams Nos. 76[2] and 78[3] from Brussels was that while I would not quarrel with any statement of fact in them their general tone is too sanguine. For instance Hornbeck certainly has plans for putting further pressure on Japan just as American General Staff has plans for invasion of Canada but while the former are of more immediate importance neither has yet come out of the pigeon hole.

I agree with Mr. Norman Davis that opinion here will develop but important question is the pace at which this will take place. There is here perhaps a reluctance to recognise necessity of educating public opinion which President so earnestly desires but this recognition is only the first step and actual education has hardly begun. It will go on but it will be slow and might have setbacks. Brussels Conference is not exciting very wide interest here now. Japanese recalcitrance has been discounted in advance and more than that will be wanted to accelerate progress in any marked degree. I certainly do not think opinion will be ready to support United States Government in any positive action just because the Conference fails.

Present circumstances are not favourable for the country is unfortunately in a 'new depression' and the gradual emergence of labour into politics creates difficult situations for many politicians. While the

---

[1] Not kept in F.O. archives. It apparently asked for Sir R. Lindsay's views on the evolution of American public opinion as foreshadowed by Mr. N. Davis in Nos. 328 and 330.
[2] No. 328.   [3] No. 330.

President is making an open campaign of education others must surely be preparing one to counteract his efforts and old congressional technique for alleviating difficulty of domestic situations is to draw across the trail the red herring of isolationism etc., I rather expect this when Congress meets on November 15th and we shall then see. I should not much mind this for itself because it is not now so dreadful for us as it used to be but time element gives it grave importance and I fear it will set us back somewhat.[4]

[4] Minutes on this telegram showed some anxiety in the Foreign Office over possible American press coverage. Mr. Ronald wrote on November 9 that 'there are a large number of American journalists hanging about in Brussels with little to do and next to no opportunities for "educating" their readers as there is nothing for them to report. And in their anxiety to provide something of news value they may make all sorts of mischief.' Mr. Orde, however, commented on November 9: 'Every one I imagine will set a higher value on Sir R. Lindsay's opinion than on Mr. Norman Davis's.'

No. 338

Sir R. Clive (Brussels) to Mr. Eden (Received November 7)

No. 57 Saving: Telegraphic [F 9154/6799/10]

BRUSSELS, *November 6, 1937*

Following from Mr. MacDonald.
My immediately preceding telegram.[1]
Following is text of communication to Japanese Government adopted by Conference this morning:

1. The representatives of the States met in Brussels on November 3rd last have taken cognisance of the reply which the Japanese Government sent in on October 27th to the invitation of the Belgian Government, and the statement which accompanied this reply.

2. In these documents the Imperial Government states that it cherishes no territorial ambitions in respect of China and that on the contrary it sincerely desires 'to assist in the material and moral development of the Chinese nation', that it also desires 'to promote cultural and economic co-operation' with the foreign Powers in China and that it intends furthermore scrupulously 'to respect foreign rights and interests in that country'.

3. The points referred to in this declaration are among the fundamental principles of the Treaty of Washington of February 6th 1922 (the Nine Power Treaty). The representatives of the States parties to this Treaty have taken note of the declarations of the Imperial Government in

[1] Telegram No. 56 Saving reported that in a private meeting on the morning of November 6 the Conference had adopted a revised text for immediate communication to the Japanese Government. The Conference then decided to adjourn until the following Tuesday morning (November 9).

this respect.

4. The Imperial Government moreover denies that there can be any question of a violation of the Nine Power Treaty by Japan and it formulates a number of complaints against the Chinese Government. The Chinese Government for its part contends that there has been violation, denies the charges of the Japanese Government, and, in turn, makes complaint against Japan.

5. The Treaty has made provision for just such a situation. It should be understood that the exchange of views taking place in Brussels is based essentially on the terms of the Nine Power Treaty and constitutes 'full and frank communication' as envisaged in Article 7. This Conference is being held with a view to assisting in the resolving by peaceful means of a conflict between parties to the Treaty. One of the parties to the present conflict, China, is represented at the Conference and has affirmed its willingness fully to co-operate in its work. The Conference regrets the absence of the other party, Japan, whose co-operation is most desirable.

6. The Imperial Government states that it is 'firmly convinced that an attempt to seek a solution at a gathering of so many Powers whose interests in East Asia are of varying degree, or who have practically no interests there at all, will only serve to complicate the situation still further and to put serious obstacles in the path of a just and proper solution'.

It should be pointed out that all of these Powers which are parties to the Treaty are, under the terms of the Treaty, entitled to exercise the rights which the Treaty confers upon them; that all Powers which have interests in the Far East are concerned regarding the present hostilities; and that the whole world is solicitous with regard to the effect of these hostilities on the peace and security of the members of the family of nations.

However, the representatives of the States met at Brussels believe that it may be possible to allay Japan's misgivings referred to above; they would be glad to know whether the Imperial Government would be disposed to depute a representative or representatives to exchange views with representatives of a small number of Powers to be chosen for that purpose. Such an exchange of views would take place within the framework of the Nine Power Treaty and in conformity with the provisions of that Treaty. Its aims would be to throw further light on the various points referred to above and to facilitate a settlement of the conflict. Regretting the continuation of hostilities, being firmly convinced that a peaceful settlement is alone capable of ensuring a lasting and constructive solution of the present conflict, and having confidence in the efficacy of methods of conciliation, the representatives of the States met at Brussels earnestly desire that such a settlement may be achieved.

7. The States represented at the Conference would be very glad to know as soon as possible the attitude of the Imperial Government towards this proposal.[2]

[2] The text of this document was published in *The Times* of November 8, 1937, p. 11.

No. 339

Mr. Eden to Sir R. Lindsay (Washington)

No. 1024 [F 9234/7240/10]

FOREIGN OFFICE, *November 6, 1937*

Sir,

In the course of a conversation which I had with Mr. Norman Davis on our way back from a meeting of the Conference at Brussels yesterday, the United States Ambassador at Large began to express his anxiety lest Japan should, within the next few days, declare war on China. This would put President Roosevelt in a most embarrassing position. Mr. Davis himself was convinced that the Neutrality Act[1] was virtually dead. Nonetheless, if war were declared before Congress met in ten days' time, it would be very difficult for President Roosevelt to avoid applying that instrument.

2. At a later stage Mr. Davis discussed what action was to be taken if our policy towards Japan failed and, lowering his voice confidentially, he added: 'I'll tell you, we won't put on any of these sanctions, we will just refuse to buy Japanese goods, that's what we'll do. We won't refuse to allow our ships to take their goods, or our goods to go to them—we will just refuse to buy.'

3. I had to explain to Mr. Davis that this particular measure had formed the most serious of the sanctions imposed upon Italy and had not been conspicuously successful in that instance. Mr. Davis, however, maintained that since, he said, we and the United States took 75% of Japan's goods, sanctions must be effective. It entered my mind, though I did not mention it, that this was the same proportion of Italian export trade as was taken by the League in 1935.

4. During the course of a subsequent conversation Mr. Davis mentioned that he was most anxious that we should not create a situation such as was reputed to have occurred in 1932. In respect of that year he knew that we blamed them and they blamed us. I replied that I cordially shared his view and in order to make the position absolutely clear I wished to explain to him how the sanctions problem appeared to us. There were two kinds of sanctions—effective and ineffective. To apply the latter was provocative and useless. Mr. Davis agreed. If we were to apply the former, I continued, we ran the risk of war and it would be dangerous to shut our eyes to the fact. As we had previously explained to the United States Government we were perfectly willing to examine this question with them and examine what steps if any could be taken, but it must be with our eyes open and with a willingness to share the risks, whatever they might be, right through to the end.

5. Mr. Davis appeared fully to appreciate the force of this and did not demur to my analysis. He appeared to think, however, that it was easy to

[1] See Volume XVIII, Nos. 88, 332, and 333.

exaggerate the action which Japan could take in reply to sanctions that might be imposed upon her.[2]

I am, etc.,
ANTHONY EDEN

[2] This conversation with Mr. Davis is referred to in *Facing the Dictators, op. cit.*, p. 538, and *The Diplomatic Diaries of Oliver Harvey, op. cit.*, pp. 56–7. Both accounts went on to record a conversation of November 8 between Mr. Eden and Mr. Chamberlain which, according to Mr. Harvey, 'went very badly'. They discussed the Brussels Conference, and Mr. Chamberlain stated 'On no account will I impose a sanction'. Mr. Eden asked whether the Prime Minister wished him to say this to Mr. Davis, but Mr. Chamberlain agreed that he did not. Mr. Harvey noted on November 9 that in describing this conversation Mr. Eden had expressed doubts about Mr. Chamberlain's health: 'Sixty too old for a P.M. nowadays' (*ibid.*, p. 58).

No. 340

Sir R. Clive (Brussels) to Mr. Eden (Received November 10)

No. 58 Saving: Telegraphic [F 9271/6799/10]

BRUSSELS, *November 8, 1937*

Following from Mr. MacDonald.

Mr. Norman Davis came to have a talk with me this morning about the general work of the Conference. He said that he thought we had to contemplate three stages: first, the stage of making contact with the Japanese. That stage we were in the middle of now. Second, supposing that the Japanese reply to our message was favourable, there would be the stage of conciliation or negotiation. It would involve sitting down with the Japanese and Chinese and trying to work out a comprehensive settlement of the Far Eastern question. The third stage need only be faced if the Japanese refuse to make contact with us, or if the contact proved to be fruitless. This third stage was that in which we should consider what further action we might take by way of influencing the situation, and putting that action into execution. He asked whether we had done any work with regard to the third stage.

I replied that we had given the matter some purely preliminary consideration. Moreover, we had learned a few lessons at the time of the Abyssinian trouble. As a result of that we knew that the worst policy of all was a policy of ineffective pressure. That policy should be dismissed in any case. It was only worth considering taking action, if that action was going to be effective; and effective action meant putting on stiff sanctions and being prepared to support our action by military measures if necessary.

Mr. Davis said that he completely agreed. Later on he said that he thought we were making a mistake when we occasionally said that we would be ready to do anything that the Americans would do. That meant that if nothing were done the Americans would be likely to get the blame.

We must try to avoid what had happened in 1932, when each of us was inclined to blame the other for the failure.

I replied that the position surely was that we in the British Commonwealth could not take any really effective action by ourselves. If such action were contemplated we would depend on complete co-operation in that action from at least the United States. In the same way, the United States could not by themselves take really effective action, and they therefore were dependent on co-operation from at least us. We were both really in a similar position. I agreed with him that it would be most unfortunate if it were said by opinion in either country that the other country was solely responsible for what might or might not happen. We must conduct the whole business in such a way that if the policy in the third stage which he had mentioned was to be one of comparative inaction, then we were both responsible for that decision, and if the policy was on the other hand one of action, then we were both equally responsible for that. I asked Mr. Davis whether he had any indications as to the state of mind of his public opinion.

He replied that he was completely satisfied at the way American opinion was moving so far. He had had reports of what the newspapers, not only in the Eastern States but in the Middle West, were saying, and he thought there were encouraging indications that opinion was taking the Far Eastern dispute seriously and recognising United States interest in a proper settlement of it. He quoted one or two instances which, he said, showed that the Americans were beginning to contemplate the possibility of action.[1]

[1] Mr. Thomas commented on November 10 that there was 'an increasing atmosphere of unreality about the proceedings at Brussels', and that it 'remains to be seen whether Mr. Davis' optimistic view of the evolution of American public opinion towards "possibility of action" is justified'. Mr. Orde commented on November 10: 'I find difficulty in believing it.' Cf. No. 337.

No. 341

Sir R. Clive (Brussels) to Mr. Eden (Received November 10)

No. 59 Saving: Telegraphic [F 9273/6799/10]

BRUSSELS, *November 8, 1937*

Following from Mr. MacDonald.
My telegram (Saving) No. 58.[1]
In the course of my talk with Mr. Norman Davis this morning, we discussed the procedure at the Committee meeting to be held tomorrow. In quite a general way we explored the possibility of setting up a

[1] No. 336.

sub-committee which should not, however, be the committee for 'negotiation' with the Japanese. By creating such a sub-committee on which the French would sit, we might possibly be able as a second stage to appoint a smaller committee for 'negotiation' representing two or three Powers, excluding the French.

Mr. Norman Davis mentioned to me that he was having lunch with Monsieur Litvinov and would discuss the matter with him. Remembering the effect on Mr. Norman Davis of an earlier lunch with the Commissar for Foreign Affairs, I said that I hoped that he (Mr. Davis) agreed with me that it would be disastrous for Russia to be a member of either the larger or the smaller sub-committee. Mr. Davis agreed, but said that he felt somewhat uncertain as to the reason we could give for excluding the Russians.

I replied that I thought there was a perfectly sound reason in that the committees would be considering questions connected with a contact with the Japanese. Such contact was to take place strictly under the terms of Article 7 of the Nine Power Treaty. Russia was neither a signatory of nor an acceder to the Treaty and therefore it would really be inappropriate for her to be represented on these committees. If she were a member of either of them Japan could easily excuse herself from co-operating on the ground that we clearly were not proceeding in accordance with our mutual obligations under the Treaty.

Mr. Davis expressed agreement with this argument, and said that he would take that line with Monsieur Litvinov and do everything he could to get him to agree that Russia need not be on the sub-committee to be appointed tomorrow.

No. 342

Foreign Office to Sir R. Craigie (Tokyo)

No. 458 Telegraphic [F 9147/6799/10]

FOREIGN OFFICE, *November 9, 1937, 3.35 p.m.*

Your telegram No. 653.[1]

I quite understand that it would suit Japanese Government if Chinese Government were advised by third parties to open negotiations direct with Japan. But His Majesty's Government could not contemplate giving such advice to a weaker Power which has been attacked by a stronger one.[2]

---

[1] No. 336.
[2] A note on the file stated that this telegram was despatched on Sir R. Vansittart's instructions.

No. 343

Sir R. Clive (Brussels) to Foreign Office (Received November 11)

No. 63 Saving: Telegraphic [F 9384/6799/10]

BRUSSELS, *November 9, 1937*

Following from Secretary of State.[1]

M. Litvinov came to see me this afternoon when he told me that he was returning to Moscow tonight, leaving M. Potemkine in charge of the Soviet Delegation. He thought it desirable to re-establish contact with the Soviet Government, who might otherwise be puzzled by proceedings here. His Excellency added that he had not been altogether happy at the turn events had taken in relation to the formation of the Committee of the Conference. It would be quite impossible for him to be outside a Committee if the Italians were in it.[2] Soviet Russia had infinitely greater interests in the Far East than Italy. Moreover the Italian Government's signature of the Three Power Pact with Japan[3] made it fantastic to suggest regarding that Government as in any way impartial to the dispute. I said that I would like to mention that in a conversation which I had had with Mr. Norman Davis on my arrival I had suggested to him that it might be preferable to leave this matter of the Committee in abeyance. It had never seemed to me that any organisation other than the actual negotiating Committee, which must be a small one, was called for. There was clearly no need for, and indeed there might be some disadvantage in setting up a negotiating Committee at this stage. M. Litvinov agreed and said that he had been much relieved to hear from Mr. Norman Davis that he shared the point of view I had expressed. It would make M. Potemkine's task much easier.

M. Litvinov went on to explain that in his view we should have no very definite reply from Japan for some time. Germany and Italy would manoeuvre with hints and suggestions that Japan would on this condition or on that be ready to negotiate and so much time would be spent but nothing would result.

---

[1] Cf. No. 335, note 1.

[2] M. Litvinov had already discussed this point with Mr. Davis, whose account of the conversation was transmitted to the Foreign Office by Mr. MacDonald in Brussels telegram No. 60 Saving of November 8. According to Mr. Davis, M. Litvinov had been 'obstinate about Russia being a member of the sub-committee', complaining that he had only accepted the invitation to the Conference 'because he wished to make a last effort at co-operation in a great collective policy': now he 'wondered why he had been invited to the Conference at all'. In a minute of November 10 on file F 9273/6799/10 Mr. Thomas remarked that he found M. Litvinov's views 'readily comprehensible', and Mr. Collier agreed on November 13: 'I cannot understand why Italy was ever proposed for the sub-committee.' Mr. Ronald, however, commented on November 10: 'M. Litvinov may have made up his mind that Brussels is not likely to achieve anything and prefers that the U.S.S.R. should have got away on some pretext or other before failure becomes too obvious.'

[3] See No. 324, note 2.

When we spoke of the actual progress of the war M. Litvinov said that what reports he received showed that the Chinese were resisting with a truly wonderful courage. All the same there must be a limit to such resistance unless China could receive supplies of arms from abroad. In reply to a question M. Litvinov said that China was receiving certain supplies from Russia, but these must inevitably be small owing to the very great difficulty of transport.

With reference to the general world situation, M. Litvinov remarked that we must be aware that the anti-Communist Pact was not directed against Soviet Russia alone. In his own view there were two alternatives before the world; either the Powers who had territorial possessions and no territorial designs must draw closer together than they had done hitherto and combine their action, or Germany, Italy and Japan would one day virtually dominate the world and Britain and France would be reduced to playing the rôle of second-class Powers in Europe. This was his own sincere conviction. As regards the present Far Eastern situation, the Soviet Government were willing to cooperate in any international action that might be decided upon, provided that the necessary guarantees were given by all participants. I replied that I thought that M. Litvinov's attitude on the last question was an eminently reasonable one. With regard to the position of the 'haves' among the Great Powers, it was, I thought, true that our relations with France were at least as close as and probably more friendly than those between Germany and Italy. Even though our relations with Soviet Russia could not be comparable in cordiality, if only on account of the feelings about Communism held by many people in Great Britain, yet between us also relations surely could be regarded as very fairly satisfactory. M. Litvinov replied that the trouble was that the Rome-Berlin axis worked better than the cooperation between England and France. Germany and Italy appeared less questioning in their support of each other. So far as Soviet Russia and His Majesty's Government were concerned, M. Litvinov said that he could not understand how anybody in Great Britain today could have any reason to apprehend the intentions of the Soviet Government. At no point in the world did the Soviets in any way threaten a British interest, nor was there any reason why those interests should clash.[4]

---

[4] Mr. Collier commented on November 12 that 'a good deal of what M. Litvinov said seems very true to me'.

Sir R. Clive (Brussels) to Foreign Office (Received November 11)

No. 64 Saving: Telegraphic [F 9385/6799/10]

BRUSSELS, *November 9, 1937*

Following from Secretary of State:

In the course of a conversation which I had alone with Mr. Norman Davis this afternoon, the United States Ambassador at Large mentioned that it was now necessary to consider what steps we should take if the Japanese Government refused to co-operate at all. He would like to start with those suggestions which did not involve an element of risk. How would it be if we were both to sell arms to China? I agreed with Mr. Norman Davis as to the desirability of our jointly examining the situation which might be expected to confront us, for, as we had already explained in Washington before Mr. Davis left, we were very ready to do this with the United States Government on any hypothesis. At the same time I was very doubtful at first sight whether Mr. Davis' propositions could be regarded as free from risk. If we and the United States Government were to sell arms in considerable quantities to China, then it was to be anticipated that Japan would wish to stop this. I did not mean, of course, that we should refuse to examine any proposition which Mr. Norman Davis might like to make. No Government could be expected to join in collective action which would entail risks unless there were collective undertakings for mutual support.

Mr. Davis then mentioned another proposal that occurred to him and to his colleagues in the United States delegation, though this had not been as yet approved by the United States Government. It seemed to Mr. Davis to constitute a minimum of what we might do. We might declare that we would in no circumstances recognise Japan's aggression either in China proper or in Manchuria and that, moreover, we would neither of us lend money to Japan for the development of these territories which she had taken by force. Mr. Norman Davis felt that this was a gesture which would be approved the world over and which, if we could take it together, would show Anglo-American solidarity. It must also in due course prove most embarrassing to Japan who would be in desperate need of money once this war was over. I told Mr. Davis I agreed with him that it was almost impossible to exaggerate the significance of some common Anglo-American decision at this conference. It was indeed the one solid achievement which we all hoped to obtain from it. So far as his suggestion was concerned, I would certainly be glad to have it examined.

The United States Ambassador at Large went on to explain that there was a third procedure which he thought quite possible. We and the United States Government might both refuse to take Japanese products. If this course were pursued by the British Empire and the United States

Government, it would affect 75 per cent of Japan's foreign trade. This was a very formidable proportion. Mr. Davis explained that he preferred action of this kind to attempting to stop trade going to Japan, which would be infinitely more difficult to put into execution. I remarked that this was, of course, the action which the League had taken against Italy during the Abyssinian dispute, and it had not been successful. Indeed the conflict had been over before the time we had always visualised as necessary for this sanction to become effective had elapsed. The Ambassador at Large said that he appreciated the significance of what I had said and that, of course, these questions required careful examination. At the same time, he did feel convinced that President Roosevelt would be anxious to take some action in this conflict. In the first instance Mr. Norman Davis hoped that President Roosevelt would ask Congress to suspend, insofar as concerned this dispute, the operation of the Neutrality Act. He also had some hopes that the President would send a special message to Congress urging them to this course. In general Mr. Davis believed that it was the President's conviction that some attempt must be made to put a stop to the increasingly menacing challenge of the totalitarian States before it was too late for democracies to do so with any chance of success. If Japan were really to overrun China, it would only be a question of time before she swallowed India also. This, Mr. Davis knew, was the President's view and, therefore, he was anxious to do everything he could to meet this state of affairs. I told the Ambassador that I much appreciated the frankness with which he had spoken. I too, thought the one important contribution to peace that could emerge from the present conference was closer Anglo-American cooperation. Fortunately our two delegations were working together very well at present. (To this Mr. Davis at once assented.) We would carefully examine the proposals which Mr. Davis had made, or any other he might like to make. At the same time, I would ask the Ambassador to bear in mind the distinction which I had made to him a few nights ago between the effective and the ineffective sanction. I was confident that nobody who had experienced the Abyssinian dispute would wish to repeat the errors practised on that occasion. Yet the application of effective sanctions, if indeed such could be devised in the case of the present dispute, must provoke a risk of conflict. As I had already explained to the Ambassador at Large we were nonetheless ready to examine all these questions with the United States Government and they would not find us backward in full cooperation. In the present state of Europe, however, it was clearly not possible for us to act alone in Far Eastern matters. Mr. Davis said he fully understood this, but, at the same time, he was inclined to contend that the risk was not really very great as Japan would never dare to attack Hongkong while she had a dispute such as this on her hands. So far as the United States attitude was concerned, it was, of course, important to watch how public opinion developed. It would then be possible for the President to decide how far he could go. At the same time, he thought that the kind of action which he had mentioned to me would receive a full measure of support in the United States and that, therefore, any accompanying action that might be necessary would also be more palatable to American opinion.[1]

Substance repeated to Washington No. 3 of November 11th.

[1] A minute of November 12 by Mr. Ronald summarized the Foreign Office's uneasiness over this American initiative. It included the comment: 'Of course Mr. Davis' suggestions are all equally impracticable, but the mere fact of his having made them and meeting with only destructive criticism from us may be very damaging to us in America if the pestilential Mr. Pell one day chooses to preach to his press gang on this text. [Mr. R. T. Pell was Press Officer to the U.S. delegation at the Brussels Conference.] The danger of this will only be passed when we elicit from the Americans an admission that the suggestions for coercive action which they have proposed are not likely to produce the desired effect . . .' A minute by Mr. Jebb, favouring a more positive approach, is printed as No. 352 below. Mr. Orde decided that the first step should be to ascertain from Washington whether Mr. Davis's proposals were supported by the U.S. Government, and in Sir R. Vansittart's absence he telephoned a suggestion in this sense to Brussels on November 13. Cf., however, No. 346 below.

No. 345

Conclusions of the second meeting of the Cabinet Committee on British Shipping in the Far East, held in the Home Secretary's Room, Home Office, S.W.1, on Tuesday, November 9, 1937, at 11.30 a.m.

[*F 9709/130/10*]

Secret   2, WHITEHALL GARDENS, S.W.1, *November 9, 1937*

PRESENT: Sir S. Hoare, Home Secretary (*in the Chair*); Sir T. Inskip, Minister for Co-ordination of Defence; Mr. O. Stanley, President of the Board of Trade; Sir D. Somervell, Attorney-General; Mr. W. Ormsby-Gore, Secretary of State for the Colonies; The Marquess of Hartington, Parliamentary Under Secretary of State, Dominions Office; Mr. G. Shakespeare, Parliamentary and Financial Secretary, Admiralty; Lord Chatfield, First Sea Lord and Chief of the Naval Staff (for item 1 only); Sir R. Vansittart, Mr. Orde, and Mr. Fitzmaurice (Foreign Office); Sir R. B. Howorth and Mr. W. D. Wilkinson (Joint Secretaries).

1. The Committee had before them a Note by the First Lord of the Admiralty (F.E.S.(37)4) covering a Memorandum by the Chief of the Naval Staff on the possibility of reinforcing the British Naval Forces in the Far East by two capital ships, bearing in mind the state of preparedness of the Singapore base and the effect of such a reinforcement on the British Naval Forces in other parts of the world.[1]

The Naval Staff had considered this question on two alternative assumptions (1) that the situation in the Mediterranean remains as at

[1] Not printed: cf. No. 239, and *ibid.*, note 8.

present, and (2) that a new situation arises in the Mediterranean with the discontinuance of piracy as a result of the successful issue of the Nyon Conference.[2]

The conclusion reached by the Naval Staff was that a reinforcement of two capital ships only should not be despatched to the Far East on either assumption.

THE HOME SECRETARY recalled the fact that a Note had been circulated by his instructions on September 27th stating that he himself accepted the conclusions reached by the Chief of the Naval Staff and was prepared to recommend them to the Cabinet. No disagreement with his view had been recorded. Was the Committee now prepared to make a formal report to the Cabinet in this sense?

General agreement was expressed.

SIR ROBERT VANSITTART informed the Committee that the Secretary of State for Foreign Affairs (who could not be present at the Meeting) shared this view.

It was agreed to make a recommendation to the Cabinet on the lines noted above.

(The First Sea Lord withdrew at this point.)

2. The Committee took note of the following documents:

A Memorandum prepared in the Foreign Office containing a statement of the position of Hong Kong in relation to the Sino-Japanese dispute (F.E.S.(37)2).[3]

A Note by the Secretary covering exchange of telegrams between the Colonial Office and the Officer Administering the Government of Hong Kong (F.E.S.(37)3).[3]

3. The Committee had before them the following documents:

Memorandum prepared in the Colonial Office (F.E.S.(37)6).[3]
Telegrams received from H.M. Ambassador in Tokyo (F.E.S.(37)7).[4]
Memorandum by the Secretary of State for Foreign Affairs (F.E.S.(37)8).[5]

The Committee considered the request in Sir R. Craigie's telegram No. 632 of November 3rd that in view of the serious anti-British feeling now being displayed in Japan further consideration should be given to stopping the passage of arms through Hong Kong. Now that France had stopped such passage through Indo-China and Portugal had stopped such passage through Macao, Hong Kong was left as the one effective neutral channel through which munitions could reach China.

SIR ROBERT VANSITTART informed the Committee that there appeared to be a choice between three courses:

[2] Cf. Volume XIX, Nos. 156, 214, and 279.   [3] Not printed.
[4] These were Tokyo telegram No. 632 (No. 326), and telegram No. 628 of November 2, not printed (F 8989/130/10).
[5] Not printed (F10650/130/10).

(a) No new action by His Majesty's Government, i.e. the present thin 'trickle' of munitions into China through Hong Kong would be allowed to continue.

(b) Action by His Majesty's Government to stop the 'trickle' by an embargo on the export of munitions from Hong Kong.

(c) To explain the position to the Chinese Government and to ask them which they regard as the lesser of the two evils, an embargo on the passage of arms through Hong Kong or a Japanese blockade.

Sir Robert added that course (b) would appear to present insuperable difficulties. It could hardly be reconciled with the League of Nations Resolution,[6] and it was likely to provoke a storm of opposition at home.

THE HOME SECRETARY said that he felt much hesitation about course (c), viz. taking China into our confidence in this matter. If we did, the news of our action would be sure to leak out and the probability of the Japanese declaring a blockade would be vastly increased.

THE PRESIDENT OF THE BOARD OF TRADE said that the general position of his Department was that they were anxious for Anglo-Chinese trade to continue so far as possible. They were apprehensive of the consequences of a Japanese blockade. He was inclined to the view that the present 'trickle' of munitions through Hong Kong should be allowed to continue. If it did not increase in size the Japanese might not think it worth while to make a protest.

The President referred to the discussion in Cabinet on October 6th on the subject of the export of munitions to Japan. It had been decided on that occasion that he must refer to the Cabinet in the event of any applications for licences to export arms to Japan. He would have to do so very shortly, since three applications for the export of munitions to Japan were now before him. One of the firms concerned might be persuaded not to press its application, but the other two were unlikely to be amenable. The quantity of arms involved in these two applications was very small, e.g. it included only one tank.

THE ATTORNEY-GENERAL referred to the passage at the foot of page 2 and the beginning of page 3 of F.E.S.(37)8 to the effect that it could be pointed out to the Chinese Government 'that if the Colonial Government forbade the passage of arms through Hong Kong the Japanese would have little or no excuse for intensifying the blockade'. We should hardly be justified in going as far as this unless we were in possession of a firm undertaking from the Japanese—an undertaking of a kind which we were unlikely ever to receive.

THE MINISTER FOR CO-ORDINATION OF DEFENCE thought that the Government would be in a very weak position if it became known that, seeing no solution of this difficulty ourselves, we had taken counsel of the Chinese Government. It seemed to him to be out of the question that the Chinese should agree to the closing of Hong Kong to the traffic in arms.

[6] See Nos. 288, 291, and 292.

The 'trickle', he thought, must be allowed to go on. It might result in a declaration of war by Japan on China; it might equally well have no result at all, apart from the value of the actual consignments of arms.

THE HOME SECRETARY said that he had formed the view that the present very small traffic in arms from this country to both Japan and China should be allowed to continue. The trade with Japan was by far the smaller of the two.

The Committee accepted the Home Secretary's view as the basis of their Report to the Cabinet on this item.

The Committee were not prepared to recommend either of the other alternative courses, viz. the closing down of the arms trade through Hong Kong or consultation with the Chinese Government.

The Committee noted that the President of the Board of Trade was about to ask for a further Cabinet decision regarding the issue of licences for the export of munitions to Japan.

4. The Committee had before them a Memorandum by the Secretary of State for Foreign Affairs (F.E.S.(37)9).[5]

The Committee were informed that the Chinese Government were reported to have evolved a scheme for an aeroplane assembly depot in the Hong Kong New Territories; the proposal was that a company should be registered in Hong Kong, ostensibly for training air mechanics but in reality for receiving and erecting new aeroplanes destined for the Chinese air force. It was in practice to be controlled and operated by the Chinese Government. It was proposed that the company should have an assembly depot near the frontier with a runway in Chinese territory, from which the actual take-off would be made.

The question on which the Cabinet Committee's opinion was desired was whether, in informing the Hong Kong Government (as we had done) that this project was to be regarded as incompatible with the neutral position which the colony should maintain, we had acted inconsistently with the League Resolution, which recommended that Members 'should refrain from taking any action which might have the effect of weakening China's power of resistance . . . and should also consider how far they can individually extend aid to China'.

THE MINISTER FOR CO-ORDINATION OF DEFENCE thought this a very undesirable project. It was comparable in his view to our inviting one of the belligerents in a naval war to make use of special dockyard facilities at a British port.

SIR ROBERT VANSITTART pointed out that the balance of argument was in favour of continuing our present policy at Hong Kong. Nobody had yet argued that this contravened the League Resolution.

THE SECRETARY OF STATE FOR THE COLONIES believed that the scheme for the aeroplane assembly depot was so drawn up as not to infringe the terms of the Air Navigation Order in Council. It might be a dangerous scheme, nevertheless. If it were successful in practice, the depot might be bombed by the Japanese.

In the course of discussion the view was expressed that the scheme, if approved, might do China more harm than good.

The question was raised whether the scheme under examination had been put to us officially by the Chinese Government, and whether there was any necessity to return an answer. The Committee were reminded that telegram No. 602 of October 23rd from Nanking[7] asked for a definite ruling on this question for the information of the Chinese Government. This telegram put the matter in a general way without reference to the particular scheme.

> The Committee agreed to report to the Cabinet against the assembly in Hong Kong of aircraft for delivery to China, on account of the serious complications to which it might give rise.

If the Cabinet approved, the Chinese might be advised unofficially not to raise the matter formally, since the greatest difficulty would be found in giving a favourable reply.

5. The Home Secretary, as Chairman of the Committee, was invited to circulate a draft Report on the matters dealt with in the discussion.

If the draft was acceptable to Members of the Committee, the Chairman was authorised to submit it to the Cabinet, without calling a further Meeting of the Committee.[8]

[7] Not printed (F8440/31/10).
[8] The Committee's report was submitted to the Cabinet on November 17 as C.P.270(37). Its recommendations were substantially the same as those set out in the present Conclusions. The Cabinet approved the recommendations, and also agreed that applications by private firms for the export of war material to China and Japan should be dealt with by a policy of 'masterly inactivity', and that 'sales of surplus Government war material to China and Japan should not be permitted while the present hostilities lasted'.

No. 346

Sir R. Clive (Brussels) to Sir R. Lindsay (Washington)

No. 2 Telegraphic [F 9736/6799/10]

Immediate   Very Confidential   BRUSSELS, *November 10, 1937*

Following from Secretary of State.[1]

[1] Mr. Harvey, who had accompanied Mr. Eden to Brussels, sent a copy of this telegram to Mr. Hoyer Millar on November 10 with a covering letter. He wrote: 'This is the only copy which we are sending to you and the Secretary of State would like you to show it to Van. He does not wish it to be given any circulation outside the Office, but Van may think that it will be all right to give it "No Distribution" circulation in the Office. The Secretary of State does not want it to be seen by the Cabinet, at any rate at this stage. We will send you a copy of

Your telegram No. 385.[2]

You will have seen from my telegrams which have been repeated to you the course of my conversations with Mr. Norman Davis on the possible outcome of the Far Eastern Conference.[3]

Our position, as I have continually impressed on Mr. Norman Davis, is this. There are two kinds of sanctions, effective and ineffective. To apply the latter would be useless. In view of our Abyssinian experience we should be reluctant to embark again on ineffective sanctions which would only have the effect of further weakening the principle of international action. On the other hand, to apply effective sanctions would involve at least some risk of war. We are perfectly prepared to consider their application provided it is understood that we expect mutual guarantees for the protection of our Far Eastern territories.

It is clear that Mr. Norman Davis does not contemplate at present anything approaching what we would regard as effective sanctions. He has indicated that what the United States Government might be prepared to consider would be to impose an embargo on the purchase of Japanese goods in America, and he appears to hold the view that such a sanction would be effective and, furthermore, that the likelihood of Japan reacting violently is remote.

Mr. Norman Davis' whole case, moreover, rests on the assumption that American opinion will be so stirred by the refusal of Japan to come to reasonable terms as a result of the Brussels Conference that it will be prepared to approve at least the modest form of sanctions indicated above.

Having in mind the vital importance for the future of maintaining and developing the present trend of Anglo-American relations, I naturally wish to take all possible steps which may lead to closer Anglo-American co-operation, whether in Europe or in the Far East. Any suggestion that we are lukewarm in the matter of joint action might fatally impair the good will of President Roosevelt, and we should be made to appear once more as having rebuffed an American offer of co-operation as in the case of Manchukuo. From what you say in your telegram under reference as well as from my conversations with Mr. Norman Davis, it is clear that, unless some quite unforeseen development takes places, it is out of the question that the United States will ever embark on anything approaching full and effective economic sanctions, if indeed there are any such in this conflict. That being so, we are left with the probability that we shall be pressed to adopt ineffective sanctions, such as an embargo on purchases from Japan or a refusal of loans. If the United States Government are

Lindsay's reply, and, if he should telegraph it to the Foreign Office direct, perhaps you would take similar precautions to prevent its being given "Political Distribution".' Sir R. Vansittart wrote on November 11: 'I wd. keep this telegram quite quiet at present. We can consider no distribution when the reply is in, i.e. when the S. of S. is also back and may wish to consider whether the moment has not come to enlighten his colleagues.'

[2] No. 337.   [3] Cf. Nos. 339 and 344.

prepared and are able to take such action, even though modest and probably ineffective, it is for consideration whether we should be well advised to agree for the sake of the education which it would bring to the American people and the fostering of the habit of Anglo-American co-operation. Such joint action might be the foundation for later co-operation in Europe and it might be a capital error to discourage it.

On the other hand, I feel that, even though we regard such action as almost certain to be ineffective, we should have to be prepared for Japanese counter-action of a violent description. In view of the difficult situation in Europe today we should obviously be unable to concentrate overwhelming naval forces in the Far East; we should, therefore, be obliged to insist on making our concurrence in such a policy dependent on guarantees being forthcoming to the possessions of those applying sanctions, since otherwise the temptation to Japan might prove too great. Provided, however, that such guarantees were given, the arguments in favour of acceptance would be strong. M. Delbos, M. de Graeff and M. Litvinoff have all made it clear that they would be willing to join in international action if such guarantees were given by all including the United States. I also believe that the Dominions would similarly be prepared to do so in the major interests of co-operation between the United States and the British Commonwealth of Nations.

A further consideration, however, is whether United States opinion will react in the sense anticipated. Whilst it is important that we should do nothing to impair President Roosevelt's confidence in us, it is equally important that we should not be identified with a failure to bring the United States into collective action and should not expose ourselves to the risk of being misrepresented as having sought to inveigle America into the protection of British interests in the Far East.

I am not certain, moreover, that Mr. Norman Davis, who is a profuse rather than a clear thinker, has put to President Roosevelt the position as clearly as I have put it to him. I feel, therefore, that it might be useful for you yourself to talk to the President in order to go through with him the points which I have put to Mr. Norman Davis, so that we can be quite certain that he grasps our position clearly. Before, however, instructing you to do so, I shall be glad if you would telegraph your own views on the desirability of doing this, as well as on the general considerations as to the best line for us to follow in regard to Anglo-American relations as indicated above.

Since dictating the above, I have had a further conversation with Mr. Norman Davis who told me that he is sending a cable today to President Roosevelt, stating that the time is rapidly drawing near when some decision as to future international action will have to be taken and putting certain alternative courses.[4] I anticipate, though Mr. Norman Davis did not tell me so, that these courses will range between condemnation of

[4] Cf. *F.R.U.S.*, 1937, vol. iv, pp. 175–7.

Japan's action, coupled with an intimation that the fruits of conquest will not be recognised and that Japan will not receive from the United States financial help for their development, on the one hand, and a refusal to buy Japanese goods on the other. Mr. Norman Davis remarked that he hoped that the first act of President Roosevelt would be to induce Congress to suspend the operation of the Neutrality Act for the purposes of this dispute. He added that the movements of the American Fleet were, of course, entirely a matter for the President himself to decide, but he would have to take careful account of the state of public opinion. Mr. Davis summed up the situation to me in these terms. 'The President is sincerely desirous of putting a check to the present disintegration of international relations. On the other hand we are most anxious not to let you down and however much the President may want to do, it is difficult for him to know how much he can do at present. The next few days, together with the meeting of Congress, may bring developments in American opinion.'

No. 347

Sir R. Clive (Brussels) to Foreign Office (Received November 12)

No. 68 Saving: Telegraphic [F 9473/6799/10]

BRUSSELS, *November 10, 1937*

Following from Secretary of State.

I had a conversation to-day at luncheon with M. Delbos and Mr. Norman Davis.

The main subject of discussion at the luncheon was what was to be done by the Brussels Conference on receipt of Japan's reply to the communication made to her on November 6th.[1] M. Delbos put forward a suggestion that the representatives of the United Kingdom, the United States and France should, in the likely event of an unsatisfactory reply from Japan, make a declaration, each in his own words, but with the same general sense, to the effect that the basis of international relationships was the sanctity of treaties and not ideological conceptions. After some discussion it was decided that the declaration should cover the following points.

1. The three great Democracies regarded with disfavour any attempt to govern the relations between peoples on an ideological basis.

2. That the only basis for international relationships was the respect for treaties.

3. That each country is entitled to have the régime that suits it best, without interference from outside.

[1] See No. 338.

467

It was thought that such a declaration would be welcomed by all the smaller States and might eventually form part of a resolution by the Conference on the Japanese reply.

Some discussion then ensued regarding possible mediation between the parties to the conflict. M. Delbos said that the French Government had heard that the Japanese would prefer mediation by one Power and that that Power would be the United States. If that was so, France would be perfectly ready to accept such a procedure. Mr. Norman Davis objected that such a proposal might well be a Japanese manoeuvre. What, he asked, would be the position of a single Power, in such circumstances, without the whole weight of and authority of the Conference behind it? It would either have to 'sell out' China to Japan or would have to sit and watch Japan spinning out negotiations while she continued her spoliation of China. M. Delbos rejoined that France would give a complete mandate to any Power, represented at the Conference (he made an exception in the case of Italy) to act as mediator, and he pledged the whole-hearted support of France.

Some allusion was made to the possibility of collective action against Japan in the event of conciliation failing. In this connexion M. Delbos said categorically that France was ready to co-operate to the utmost limit of her available resources and that just as she would undertake to do her share in protecting and helping any nation which might be victimised by Japan on account of its part in any collective action, so she would expect that any help and protection which might be necessary should be accorded to her by the other Powers concerned. I said that the position taken up by France must be that of any country, taking part in collective action in this dispute, including my own, but that in fairness to the United States it should not be forgotten that in the event of collective action a great part of the burden of protective measures would fall on the United States. Mr. Norman Davis said that he appreciated M. Delbos's statement, but he let it be understood that the United States, owing to their neutrality legislation, were in an extremely difficult position when it came to considering questions of collective pressure on Japan.[2]

[2] Mr. Orde commented on November 15: 'It is interesting to find France taking up the same position as ourselves and Holland. The next move is surely with the U.S. Government.' Mr. Davis's account of this conversation is printed in *F.R.U.S.*, 1937, vol. iv, pp. 177–8.

No. 348

Sir R. Lindsay (Washington) to Sir R. Clive (Brussels)
(Received November 11, 10.15 p.m.)

No. 1[1] Telegraphic [F 9682/6799/10]

Immediate   Very Confidential   WASHINGTON, *November 11, 1937, 2.20 p.m.*

Your telegrams regarding your conversations with Mr. Norman Davis.[2]
Following for Secretary of State.

While the course of the Brussels Conference must give you anxiety I think you are unduly preoccupied over the effects of its outcome in this country. It resembles previous conferences so much that minor results or even barely disguised failure is discounted in advance. Sanctions, whether mild or severe, are hardly in the atmosphere at all and the only talk is about some form of purely private boycott of Japanese goods and I have no reason to think even this is seriously thought of in official circles. When I was speaking in th[is] sense incidentally yesterday to Dunn at the State Department they expected the Conference would end fairly soon with the appointment of a standing sub-committee of the Nine Powers minus Japan and China which would be available at short notice for any future action. This is not to be taken as a sure indication of what the President has in mind, but I should regard it as a faithful reflection of the State Department's atmosphere.

Japanese recalcitrance and collective impotence will be the two leading features in the final outcome of the present Conference and to some extent they cancel each other out, though on balance I think something in the way of education will have been achieved, but at present opinion is undecided and the public would prefer if possible to avert its eye from the disagreeable prospect.

As to what we can do I have little to say you do not already know. There are two axioms:

(a) United States, like other countries, will take important action only in its own interests, but differs from other countries in that for

---

[1] This telegram was addressed to Mr. Eden at Brussels.
[2] Cf. No. 346. It appears from a note of November 17 by Mr. H. A. Caccia, Assistant Private Secretary to Mr. Eden, that the copy of Sir R. Lindsay's telegram No. 1 which was received by Mr. Eden in Brussels began with a reference to Mr. Eden's telegram No. 2 to Washington: No. 346. However, when Mr. Eden wished to send a copy of the telegram, together with further telegrams from Sir R. Lindsay (see Nos. 354, 355, and 355, note 5 below) to the Prime Minister, he specified that Mr. Chamberlain should *not* receive a copy of No. 346. Mr. Caccia noted that 'the only alteration that need be made is the ommission [sic] of the telegram under reference in Sir R. Lindsay's telegram No. 1. Instead, the words "your telegrams regarding your conversations with Mr. Norman Davis" might be substituted.' The alteration was also made on the copy for distribution within the Foreign Office.

geographical and historical reasons it is slower both to recognise where its best interest lies and to take action in its defence.

(b) For psychological reasons there is always reaction against deference to British pressure. For His Majesty's Government it is therefore more important to avoid errors than to seek out positive action even of a wise nature. So far as is possible we must neither openly lag behind as in 1932 nor attempt or appear to attempt to inveigle them into situations for which they are not prepared. Your policy in the present situation is a perfectly honest effort to pursue this line, and the only danger at present is that President and State Department may not fully understand it. Unless therefore you telegraph urgently to the contrary, I propose to re-state your attitude tomorrow to Sumner Welles, who is perfectly competent and not to the President with whom an interview is too much a matter of sensational interest to the public. Incidentally more will be done in the way of education by apparent developments in Latin America than by any efforts of our diplomacy. See Lima telegram to you No. 46[3] received here this morning. Ideological struggles in South America will indeed bring difficulties of isolation home to the United States.

[3] Not printed.

No. 349

Mr. Howe (Shanghai) to Foreign Office (Received November 11, 1 p.m.)

No. 192 Telegraphic [F 9388/9/10]

Important   SHANGHAI, *November 11, 1937, 7.25 p.m.*

I had long conversation with Soong this morning on general situation and on prospects of move being made either in the direction of cessation of hostilities or on the question of peace. He confirmed as far as Nanking Government was concerned that there was no departure from policy of resistance even in the event, which now seems quite possible, of Japanese forces here penetrating as far as the capital.[1] In that case the Government would move to the interior and carry on. I replied and he agreed that if that were indeed the policy there appeared to be no immediate end to the struggle and I said that it seemed to me most desirable that some attempt should be made to start the ball rolling. The difficulty which I found in Nanking was that no one in authority appeared to be able or willing to formulate terms which would serve as a basis for approach to Japanese either for an armistice or for peace nor did any direct approach appear feasible. He replied that no one in Nanking except Chiang Kai-shek would dare to discuss such matters with any third parties. He did not know

[1] Cf. No. 320, note 5.

whether even Chinese delegates at Brussels Conference had any instructions in this sense.

2. After some further conversation he asked me whether I thought it would be possible for me to talk frankly to Chiang Kai-shek on the same lines and I replied that I should be only too glad to clear my own mind by such a discussion but I had no idea whether Chiang Kai-shek was in the mood. It would be purely personal talk on my part as I had no instructions from you.

3. He then said he would telegraph to Chiang Kai-shek today putting forward this suggestion which I said I would follow up on my return to Nanking.

4. Soong was nervous but this may have been due to the fact that our discussions took place with Japanese shells screaming overhead and exploding nearby in Nantao. Atmosphere in Nanking is calmer but it is a question whether politicians there realise the tremendous hammering Chinese army has been getting here in the last few days. Whether the latter can take much more punishment of this kind is a matter of conjecture but there is a possibility that army leaders may soon have to admit that they cannot hold the military situation and that this may induce another form of mind in the capital.[2]

Repeated to Tokyo, Peking, General Officer Commanding Hongkong, copies to Commander-in-Chief, Major General.

[2] Some anxiety was expressed in the Foreign Office that if Mr. Howe spoke as he proposed to Chiang Kai-shek it would be embarrassing in view of Tokyo telegram No. 653 (No. 336) and the Foreign Office reply to it (No. 342), neither of which had been repeated to Mr. Howe. In telegram No. 199 of November 12 from Sir R. Vansittart Mr. Howe was informed that his telegram would be discussed with Mr. Eden on his return from Brussels. Meanwhile, however, although 'early peace is of course eminently desirable', on the other hand 'Japan *may* be more tired of the war than appearances would seem to indicate and we must be careful to refrain from encouraging China to agree to terms which leave this possibility out of account'. Mr. Howe was told, as Sir R. Clive had been (No. 342) that His Majesty's Government could not encourage a weaker power (China) to open direct negotiations with Japan: nor must anything be said to cut across the work of the Brussels Conference. Mr. Howe's remarks, therefore, should 'be on a purely personal basis . . .'

No. 350

Mr. Gage (Nanking) to Foreign Office (Received November 11, 9 p.m.)

No. 646 Telegraphic: by wireless [F 9425/6799/10]

NANKING, *November 11, 1937*

Addressed to Embassy Offices, Shanghai, telegram No. 127.
Following for Mr. Howe. Begins:
My telegram No. 118.[1] Following is the text of telegram sent by Chiang

[1] Not printed (F 9270/9/10).

Kai-shek to Mr. Wellington Koo yesterday. Begins:

Withdrawal yesterday of our troops from the immediate vicinity of Shanghai foreign . . .² necessary for tactical reasons in order to continue long resistance. Our Government and the whole nation are determined to resist to the end. The enemy can never harden (*sic*) our spirit to resist. Please inform Brussels delegates that as long as enemy troops on our soil we shall continue to resist with all our strength.³ So long as our sovereignty is endangered, we will not consider peace for we will not sell our birthright for a mess of pottage. We will under all circumstances uphold Nine Power Treaty in spirit as well as in fact and expect all the signatories to this Treaty to do likewise. Also assure the Powers that with our firm determination to resist we are confident that their efforts for a just and equitable settlement of Far Eastern situation will not be exerted in vain.

Repeated to Peking.

² The text was here uncertain: the word 'settlement' was suggested on the filed copy.
³ Cf. No. 349.

No. 351

Sir R. Clive (Brussels) to Foreign Office
(Received November 12, 2.5 p.m.)

No. 88 Telegraphic: by telephone [F 9474/6799/10]

Important   BRUSSELS, *November 12, 1937*

From Secretary of State.

I have had some discussion this morning with Mr. Norman Davis on Japanese reply¹ and on further procedure.

Idea which emerged from our conversation was that conference should lose no time in sending reply to Japanese controverting their main contention that Sino-Japanese conflict is a matter that concerns only the two combatants. This communication while it might indicate that conference would always be ready to offer its good offices if required would not specifically call for a reply. It would indicate that conference without adjourning would suspend its sittings while delegates consulted

¹ The Japanese note, dated November 12, was transmitted to the Foreign Office in U.K. Delegation's despatch No. 21 of November 13, not printed (F 9547/6799/10). In it the Japanese Government expressed their regret that they were unable to modify the views set out in their note and statement of October 27 (see No. 320). They denied that their actions in China came within the scope of the Nine Power Treaty, and 'could not agree to take part in a meeting based on the provisions of the Treaty while it is accused of having violated the terms of that Treaty'. The Sino-Japanese conflict, they maintained, had its origin in conditions peculiar to the Far East. An endeavour to reach a solution by the only two parties having a direct interest therein constituted the means of securing the most equitable settlement.

their governments. It would meet again probably in about a week's time to draw up a resolution. This would be in the form of an indictment of Japan and Mr. Norman Davis hopes it might go further and announce some positive action on the part of the governments represented. He says he has suggested to United States Government that governments represented in conference should declare that they would not recognise any changes brought about by Japanese action and will not extend to her any credits enabling her to reap fruits of her invasion of China.[2] He has not yet received any reply but in view of line we have taken with United States Delegation here it seems to me that it would be very useful now that Mr. Norman Davis has given us some definite indication of what he hopes United States government might do, if we could tell him at once that His Majesty's Government would be prepared to take these steps with United States government. I do not know whether it is possible for me to receive immediate authorisation to give Mr. Norman Davis such an assurance but if it were, I do think it would be most useful in convincing United States Government of our readiness to co-operate.[3] We could not be suspected of trying to inveigle United States Government into action for which they are not prepared as suggestion emanates from United States Delegate.

Mr. Norman Davis says idea is that during contemplated week's recess governments could consider whether they would be prepared to go even further than above, and in any case next week's resolution might indicate that governments would remain in consultation as to any further steps that might progressively be taken.

[2] See *F.R.U.S.*, 1937, vol. iv, pp. 175–7.
[3] It became unnecessary however for Mr. Eden to press for this authorization in view of the evidence that soon reached him as to the absence of any support for Mr. Davis's proposals in Washington (see No. 355 below). There was no enthusiasm for the proposals in the Foreign Office, to judge from the minutes on this telegram, which included a lengthy discussion by Sir H. W. Malkin and Mr. Fitzmaurice on the interpretation of articles 1 and 2 of the Nine Power Treaty. Mr. Orde commented on November 15: 'In view of Sir W. Malkin's opinion we can argue if necessary that article 2 does not compel us not to "recognise" any changes brought about by the Japanese action. Except for the possibly over-riding factor of cooperation with the U.S. Govt. I should be opposed to any non-recognition declaration. It is hardly necessary to enlarge on the disadvantages of burying one's head in the sand, but I would mention a point made by Sir J. Pratt that we shall be greatly hampered in coping with Japanese pretentions in Shanghai if we tie ourselves up with a doctrinaire principle precluding any give and take.' Sir R. Vansittart wrote on November 15: 'I agree. And in general I shd. strongly deprecate—in view of the state of our armaments and the extent of our dangers—any joint minatory pronouncements as regards Japan unless we are assured of full American support, if need be. Otherwise we are risking something quite vital for the sake of an ineffective set of words, which we shd. not at this time of day be considering at all except for our desire to cooperate with the U.S.A. But such a pronouncement without a guarantee is not cooperation. It is a risk—for *us*.' Mr. Eden initialled these minutes on November 16.

No. 352

Minutes by Mr. Jebb on Anglo-American coercive action against Japan

[*F 9385/6799/10*]

FOREIGN OFFICE, *November 12, 1937*

I hope that I may be excused if in minuting this paper[1] I go rather outside my province, for, as I see it, the really essential question now is, not whether any form of sanctions would be 'effective' or 'ineffective', but how we can best take some action—no matter what—in conjunction with the United States.

So far as the efficacy of the first two measures suggested by Mr. Norman Davis is concerned I think there can be no two opinions. The suggestion that we and the United States should sell arms to China would undoubtedly be met by the institution of a Japanese blockade. There is, therefore, every reason to suppose that the arms would never get to China beyond some small amounts which might eventually be despatched by the road through Yunnanfu.[2] I do not, therefore, think that this suggestion need be seriously entertained. The proposed joint declaration of non-recognition and of refusal to lend money would act purely as an irritant.[3] Refusal to recognise in the long run merely makes the non-recogniser look silly; while as for not lending money, nobody in his senses is likely to lend Japan money so long as her finances are in their present state.[4]

We are therefore left with the third suggestion, namely, that the British Empire and the United States should refuse to take Japanese products. There is no doubt whatever that such a refusal, if it came about in practice, would be a very severe blow to Japan; but there is equally no doubt that she could in such circumstancces continue to finance her imports for a considerable time by drawing on her gold and foreign exchange reserve, by increased trade with third parties and possibly also by getting a certain amount of her products into the United States and the British Empire by round about means. The Advisory Committee on Trade and Blockade does not consider, however, that Japan would be able under these conditions to finance her imports for more than two years, while the period might not in practice exceed one year.[5] It is true that, owing to the large proportion of her exports which is taken by Anglo-Saxon countries, the strain on her economy might be considerably greater than the strain on Italy involved by the application of sanctions; but it is also true that this strain would be to a certain extent counteracted by the intense patriotic feeling that such an action would engender and by

---

[1] i.e. Brussels telegram No. 64 Saving (No. 344).

[2] Marginal comment at this point: 'That is true.' This and further marginal comments on this paper (see notes 3, 4, 6, 7, 8, 9 below) were by Sir R. Vansittart.

[3] 'I agree.'   [4] 'Of course not.'   [5] See Nos. 315 and 334.

the economic support which Japan might in present circumstances be expected to receive from her partners in the Anti-Communist Pact, limited though this would necessarily be. It is also quite obvious that Japan might in the circumstances be tempted to rectify the situation by seizing the Dutch East Indies and other territory in that part of the world.[6]

On the other hand, the advantages from our point of view of taking such action in concert with the United States, provided always that it were accompanied by some kind of guarantee of mutual support in the event of trouble, would be enormous.[7] Even if there were no war, the U.S. would become our associate and active partner in world policy and we should be committed to a path of strict co-operation in Far Eastern affairs. In such co-operation it would be most probable that we should be joined by the U.S.S.R. But should our action lead to war then it is evident that the U.S. would be our ally; and if she were our ally in the Far East she would necessarily be our ally in the event of trouble in Europe. The knowledge of this fact would be about the most effective deterrent to precipitate action on the part of the European Dictators that one can possibly imagine.[8] Indeed, it might solve most of our problems at a single blow.

I therefore think that, far from discouraging Mr. Norman Davis' third suggestion, we should actively encourage it, not indeed to the extent of appearing to wish to drag the United States into war, but certainly to the extent of not letting the Americans think we were lagging behind because of any risk involved.[9] Even the first two suggestions—useless though they might in practice turn out to be—would be worth considering, if only because their adoption would represent a first step towards co-operation with America.

Would it be possible for some or all of these considerations to be conveyed to Brussels?[10]

[6] 'We shd. be attacked too.'   [7] 'The guarantee is essential to any move.'   [8] 'Yes, indeed.'
[9] 'But always with the guarantee of course. (And I'm afraid the U.S.A. are not ready for it.)'
[10] Commenting on Mr. Jebb's minute on November 12, Mr. Holman referred to the British 'fear of complications in the Far East with a possibility of America at the last moment not being able to give us full support', and felt that he could not therefore 'be quite so optimistic as Mr. Jebb as regards the real value and effect of carrying close co-operation to its extreme limit'. Mr. Orde wrote on November 13: 'I agree with Mr. Holman and with paras. 1–4 of Mr. Jebb's minute, the rest of which I hesitate to endorse.'

No. 353

Sir R. Clive (Brussels) to Foreign Office (Received November 13)

No. 19 [F 9509/6799/10]

BRUSSELS, *November 12, 1937*

The United Kingdom Delegation to the Nine Power Conference presents its compliments to the Under Secretary of State for Foreign

Affairs, and has the honour to transmit herewith the under-mentioned document.

Paper	*Subject*
Conference memorandum, November 10	Meeting with Dominion Delegates, November 10

ENCLOSURE IN No. 353

Record of meeting with Dominion Delegates to the Brussels Conference held at 11.15 a.m. on November 10, 1937

BRUSSELS, *November 10, 1937*

Present: *United Kingdom*: Mr. Eden, Sir J. Pratt, Mr. J. P. L. Thomas, Mr. Harvey, Mr. Stevenson, Mr. Hankinson, Mr. Cockram, Mr. Heppel; *Canada*: Senator Dandurand, Mr. Wrong; *Commonwealth of Australia*: Mr. Bruce, Mr. Stirling; *New Zealand*: Mr. Jordan, Mr. Knowles; *Union of South Africa*: Dr. Gie, Mr. Stoker; *India*: Sir R. Mudaliar, Mr. Morley.

Mr. Eden began by referring to the procedure to be adopted at the meeting of the Conference that afternoon. As a result of his talks with Mr. Norman Davis he had gathered that the latter had dropped his idea of proposing that the Conference should appoint a 'Steering' Committee, and from M. Spaak he had learnt that the Japanese reply to the communication sent by the Conference on the preceding Saturday would not be available until the 12th November. It would therefore be possible simply to take note of this information at their meeting that afternoon and to decide to meet again on Friday afternoon.

As regards the question of what they should do after the Japanese reply had been received, it was necessary to discuss their future work on the basis that the Japanese reply would be unfavourable. He had gathered that Mr. Norman Davis' idea was that the Conference ought not to disperse before taking some action, and that he had in mind a refusal to recognise any results of Japanese aggression and possibly a refusal to assist Japan with any funds for the development of any territories which she might acquire in this way. This would be an extension of the action adopted in 1932 in connexion with Manchuria.

Mr. Bruce explained that he had gained the definite impression that Mr. Davis had also in mind a proposal that the countries represented at the Conference should, in the event of the Japanese reply being unfavourable, agree to a boycott of all imports from Japan. This would deprive Japan of the necessary funds for making purchases abroad, and would, in effect, be very similar to the imposition of sanctions on the lines previously attempted in the dispute between Italy and Abyssinia.

Doubts were expressed as to whether the United States Government would be able to give effect to any such policy (which would require the

476

passage of legislation by Congress as well as the approval of the Senate) and whether the Conference, which had been called to consider means of securing peace by agreement, was in any case the correct body to initiate any such proposals. It was, however, pointed out that they had met under Article 7 of the Washington Treaty which did not prescribe any particular means by which they should act.

There was general agreement however that before any such proposals were initiated it would be desirable for the Conference, in the event of a negative reply being received from Japan, to draw up an impartial resumé of the facts, which would amount to an indictment of Japan.

The discussion then concentrated upon the possibility of any further action. In the first place it was pointed out that what this raised in effect was the whole question of the effectiveness of sanctions, and that they had to face the fact that probably Japan had laid in sufficient stocks of necessary materials to prevent any action which they might take from being effective for, at the very least, the first six months, even if the United States and all other Governments participated. There was also the possibility of a Chinese collapse before any action which they might take could be effective. In these circumstances it was important to avoid the humiliation of another unsuccessful attempt at coercion.

There was also general agreement that while it was desirable that if any action were taken, the League should have an opportunity to participate, it was essential that the question should be decided at Brussels and not referred to Geneva primarily, because the United States was participating in the work of the Brussels Conference, and would only be present at Geneva in the quality of an observer, but also because it might be found that the members of the League had already gone as far as they were prepared to go. They had already condemned Japanese action, agreed to take no steps which might hinder China, and approved of members of the League giving China such assistance as they might individually be able to give.

The paramount necessity was to keep the United States co-operating in their work, not primarily because of the effects of any joint action which they might take, but because of the effect on the whole international position in the world if the United States ceased to co-operate, and Mr. Eden said that personally he would like to tell Mr. Davis that if the United States wished to consider certain possible courses of action on the lines they had indicated then the United Kingdom (he would not speak for the Dominions) was also ready to consider it. The representatives of some of the Dominions then indicated what they thought the attitude of their Government would be.

Dr. Gie said that his Government were opposed to sanctions after the failure of sanctions in the Abyssinian dispute, and that they were on the verge of a general election into which it would be dangerous for them to introduce this question. But if the United States were prepared to take action, and if it could be shown that there was a good prospect of their

477

action, and that of other countries in co-operation with them, proving effective, then the South African Government might be prepared nevertheless to review the situation in the light of these facts.

Mr. Bruce explained that the Australian Government, like the South African and Canadian Governments were strongly opposed to any further experiment in sanctions. In fact, he had instructions in his pocket to oppose any proposal for Sanctions. On the other hand, if the United States wished to take certain action and if the United States and the United Kingdom, on full consideration, were prepared to take it, then he felt that the Commonwealth Government would probably withdraw their objection.

Mr. Jordan said that the New Zealand Government offered their assistance, for what it was worth, and would be prepared to back the United Kingdom and the United States in any joint action which they might take.

Mr. Eden in conclusion emphasised that it was of vital importance that no word should get abroad at the present moment about their discussions, and Mr. Bruce added that he did not think that the moment had yet come to consult their Governments as to any proposal for action against Japan. Before they could do so it was necessary to have something which was much more definite than they had at present.

It was agreed that a meeting the following day might be desirable.[1]

[1] Further meetings between the British and Dominion delegates during the conference were recorded in Brussels despatches to the Foreign Office Nos. 20 (November 11), No. 26 (November 15), and No. 27 (November 15).

No. 354

Sir R. Lindsay (Washington) to Sir R. Clive (Brussels)
(Received November 14, 10 a.m.)

No. 2[1] *Telegraphic* [F 9683/6799/10]

Very Confidential   WASHINGTON, *November 13, 1937, 8.30 p.m.*

Following for Secretary of State.
My telegram No. 1.[2]
I saw Under Secretary of State this morning and said to him that it was clear that while Anglo-American conversations at Brussels so far had been exploratory, important decisions were now imminent and I thought it well to let him see the picture of the present state of affairs as it appeared to me from a close study of telegrams I had received.

2. Your own attitude had been governed by certain axioms. Firstly you would be very careful always to proceed closely in step with the United States Government. Anglo-American co-operation was of great general

[1] This telegram was addressed to Mr. Eden at Brussels.   [2] No. 348.

importance; it was now being subjected to a severe test; and the way in which it stood the test would be most important in the future. You were anxious to avoid such a situation as arose in 1932 when Mr. Stimson got ahead of all other Powers and you would be equally anxious yourself not to get unduly ahead of other Powers now. You also desired to avoid even the appearance of attempting to inveigle the United States into situations for which they were not prepared or into defence of interests which were not American. And you thought that any recriminations between Great Britain and America in the sense that either would have been ready to go ahead faster but for the other must be carefully avoided.

3. I said that there had been a certain amount of rather inconclusive talk between yourself and Mr. Norman Davis about sanctions of various kinds. Of greater or effective sanctions there had been comparatively little mention and they seemed hardly to come into the picture. Among minor sanctions there was every kind of gradation, from measures of considerable severity down to those which where [sic] comparatively insignificant, and several of them had arisen in conversations between you and Mr. Norman Davis.

4. Our own experience was that ineffective sanctions only had the effect of embittering Government against which they were directed without weakening it; and they also cast discredit on the system of collective action. But all sanctions, whether severe or mild, were liable to provoke a violent reaction from the party to whom they were applied and violence of the reaction would always be in direct proportion to the severity of the measures proposed. In this connexion I reminded him of this Embassy's memorandum of October 19th (your telegram No. 455[3]).

5. You yourself had looked on all these possibilities with an open mind and you had not refused to take into consideration any of the measures which had come up in my conversation and it was even possible that British opinion would be more advanced than American opinion. But all sanctions, whether greater or less, must involve some greater or less military danger. Owing to the situation in Europe we should not be able to concentrate overwhelming naval forces in the Far East and we should not be able to meet a military risk single-handed. The same consideration must inevitably apply to any third parties who might be involved in the same dangers.

6. I said we were thus this time . . .[4] with a situation which was familiar to every person in private life, namely that nothing desirable can be obtained without paying the price. If it was desired to bring Japan to desist from her present course of action we must pay in terms of military risk and in our view that risk should be shared fairly by all. If on the other hand we decided on comparative inaction, price must be paid in coin of a different kind, and it must be made clear that responsibility for decision reached was a joint one (see my immediately following telegram).[5]

[3] No. 312.   [4] The text was here uncertain.   [5] No. 355 below.

No. 355

Sir R. Lindsay (Washington) to Sir R. Clive (Brussels)
(Received November 14, 10 a.m.)

No. 3[1] *Telegraphic* [F 9684/6799/10]

Very Confidential   WASHINGTON, *November 13, 1937, 8.30 p.m.*

My immediately preceding telegram.[2]

Mr. Welles then took the points which I had made one by one. He said that Anglo-American co-operation had in his view been perfectly satisfactory and he only wished that there had been some sign of co-operation made by the others. He considered there was no danger either of the United States or of Great Britain being left out on the end of a branch by the other. He himself had no fear of inveiglement and he felt confident that there would be no recriminations.

2. As to sanctions he agreed to the view I had expressed that their effect was only to envenom the situation; and he further pointed out that to be of any use at all co-operation of even most of the small Powers must be necessary. Mr. Norman Davis' original instructions had been perfectly definite that he was to do no more than explore these fields and his discussion of them with you had been strictly exploratory. Mr. Norman Davis had now been told that in so far as any of these so-called sanctions involved legislation it was not contemplated here to introduce that legislation into Congress. He believed Congress generally approved of the attitude of the President in not applying the Neutrality Law to the present conflict and so long as this approval continued the question would not arise of suspending the Act. A movement of the Fleet had been mentioned and thought about but it had been decided not to issue any orders in this sense at present.

3. As to the immediate future, I gather formal instructions have now been sent to Mr. Norman Davis.[3] He indicated that the issue of the Conference now desired by the United States Government was the appointment of a standing committee to follow up the future possibilities. He spoke very bitterly about French insistence on their own inclusion whereby the committee had been unduly enlarged. He thought the conference should insist that the principles of the Nine Power Treaty were still valid and should appeal to all the Powers of the world for support of them. He held it as important we should both insist first that the conference had not been a failure and secondly that the Nine Power Treaty was not dead.

4. He made no reference to what I had said about military danger, but his tone throughout was friendly and his general satisfaction at the relations between the American and British Delegations was evident, and

---

[1] This telegram was addressed to Mr. Eden at Brussels.   [2] No. 354.
[3] See *F.R.U.S.*, 1937, vol. iv, pp. 180–1.

I should conclude his silence was due to the fact that in the present circumstances this particular point does not arise.[4]

See my immediately following telegram.[5]

[4] Mr. Welles's memorandum of this conversation is printed *ibid.*, pp. 152–5.

[5] Not kept in F.O. archives: it apparently referred to Anglo-American trade negotiations. Mr. Eden and Mr. Harvey returned from Brussels on November 14, presumably bringing with them copies of Sir R. Lindsay's telegrams. Copies of the four telegrams, but not of Mr. Eden's telegram No. 2 (No. 346) were sent to Mr. Chamberlain: see No. 348, note 2. A copy of telegram No. 4 was sent to the President of the Board of Trade. Mr. Caccia wrote on November 17 that 'Within the Foreign Office the Secretary of State wishes the four telegrams from Sir R. Lindsay to receive "No distribution" '. Mr. Orde noted on November 17: 'Action as above is being taken.'

No. 356

Mr. Eden to Sir R. Lindsay (Washington)

No. 510[1] *Telegraphic* [*F 9548/6799/10*]

FOREIGN OFFICE, *November 14, 1937, 9.30 p.m.*

Position reached at Brussels Conference may be briefly summed up as follows.

In spite of Japan's refusal to attend Conference itself, enquiry was addressed to her as to whether she would enter into discussion with limited number of Delegates. She has flatly turned down that proposal, reiterating her contentions that this is not a case to which the Nine Power Treaty applies and that the matter can only be settled direct between Japan and China.[2]

The Conference (with the practically certain exception of Italy) will approve, probably on Monday, a declaration refuting Japan's contentions and finding that the Governments represented at the Conference 'must consider what is to be their common attitude in a situation where one party to an international treaty' has unilaterally repudiated that Treaty. The results of that consideration should be announced at the next meeting of the Conference which must take place within about a week.

We are thus confronted with a problem that requires immediate consideration. At the outset of the Conference Mr. Davis gave it to be understood—though he was careful to make no definite commitment—that his Government might be ready, if necessary, to exert certain pressure in Japan. It was not until a few days ago that he made the definite suggestion that the U.S. Government might advocate doctrine of non-recognition and refusal of credits, which he said he had proposed to Washington.[3] We have always taken the line that His Majesty's Govern-

[1] This telegram was drafted in Brussels, but despatched from the Foreign Office. Mr. Eden returned to London late on Sunday, November 14.

[2] See No. 351, note 1. [3] See No. 351.

ment would go with the United States. Mr. Davis has now evidently received a discouraging reply from Washington and is distinctly uneasy.[4] The only hope he has is that the President may be contemplating some announcement in his message to Congress on Monday and does not want his thunder stolen.

When Conference reassembles after a week's recess it will have, so far as I can see, to choose between 3 alternatives—1. an indictment of Japan, with an implied confession of impotence, 2. the announcement of such doubtfully effective measures as non-recognition and refusal of credits, 3. the foregoing coupled with an intimation that there may be more rods in pickle.

Judging from Mr. Davis' present mood, 2. and 3. seem most improbable, and we may be driven to 1. which, from the broader aspect of maintaining sanctity of treaties and world peace, is discouraging, to say the least. It may be that President's message may give hope of more than we seem at present justified in expecting. But if it does not, I fear that nett result of this Conference will show nothing on the credit side.[5]

All this, I am sure, is present to the mind of the U.S. Government, and it might be useful if you could discuss the prospects with Mr. Hull or Mr. Sumner Welles, and report their reactions.

Even though he is in a baffled mood, Mr. Davis still affects to comfort himself with thoughts of what might yet be possible. For instance, he suggests that Congress might be brought to vote that the Neutrality Act shall not apply in this dispute, even though war may be formally declared. I do not know whether this is possible. It might have a great minatory effect in present circumstances, and any precedent for the setting aside of the Act might be valuable. Do you think there is any possibility of this?

Mr. Davis himself reluctantly admits that he sees no sign of American opinion being 'brought along' by the doings of the Conference.

The only bright spot is that I can confidently say that Anglo-American relations at this Conference have been excellent, and that the 2 Delegations have been working in perfect harmony.

In any conversation which you may have at the State Department you will of course emphasise how cordial Anglo-American cooperation at the Conference has been and how much we have appreciated this.[6]

[4] Cf. No. 355, note 3.

[5] This view of the Conference was shared by Mr. Chamberlain, who in his rather stormy interview with Mr. Eden on November 16 concerning Lord Halifax's forthcoming visit to Germany referred to the Brussels Conference as a 'complete waste of time': see Volume XIX, No. 319, note 11.

[6] The last paragraph of this telegram was added to the draft by Mr. Harvey who noted on it: 'Approved by S. of S. O.C.H. 14/xi.' The rest of the draft was in Sir A. Cadogan's handwriting.

No. 357

Sir R. Clive (Brussels) to Mr. Eden (Received November 15)

No. 73 Saving: Telegraphic [F 9568/6799/10]

BRUSSELS, November 14, 1937

Following from Mr. MacDonald.

My telegram No. 67 Saving.[1]

The Conference met in private on Saturday morning[2] and again in the afternoon to consider the text of reply of Japanese Government[3] to the communication addressed to them by the Conference on November 7th[4]. (See Brussels Conference despatch No. 21 of November 13th[3]).

Doctor Wellington Koo said that after ten days effort the Conference was back where it had started. Japan had taken the studied moderation of the communications addressed to her as a sign of weakness. There was nothing new in the present document, which merely repeated all the old flimsy excuses. Even supposing that she were acting in self-defence it did not follow that the Washington Treaty did not apply to the present situation. For years China had tried to settle her differences with Japan peaceably and she was now unhappily convinced of the futility of direct negotiation. The treaty breaker was now asking the Conference to recognise a *fait accompli*. He urged the conference to withhold war material and credits from Japan and to give China the supplies she needed.

Monsieur Delbos said that the policy of France was inspired by the principle of respect for international obligations and for the right of peoples to govern themselves as they pleased and to choose their institutions freely. Respect for international obligations did not mean that there could be no change, but changes must be brought about by agreement. The security and welfare of nations could not be established by ideological blocs, but depended on this principle. Japan's answer had set a problem which the Conference must face.

Mr. Eden said that the conflict, so far from interesting only China and Japan concerned all countries whose interests it had damaged, or who were signatories of the Nine Power Treaty, or who desired to see international obligations respected. His Majesty's Government believed that international law alone should govern the relations between States and that the dislike, however sincere, of the political institutions of another country conferred no right whatever to interfere in its affairs. There was no reason why treaties should not be modified, provided this was done by agreement. He regretted the refusal of Japan to co-operate with the Conference and he suggested that, while the Conference would no doubt wish at once to express its opinion of the situation created by that

---

[1] Not kept in F.O. archives.

[3] See No. 351, note 1.

[2] i.e. November 13.

[4] See No. 338.

483

refusal, the fundamental problem would require careful study by all the States represented at the Conference.

Mr. Norman Davis also emphasised the necessity of respect for treaties. Change was possible and even desirable but it must be brought about by mutual agreement. The Conference would have welcomed Japan's collaboration: every effort had been made to meet her susceptibilities and he believed that the Conference could have helped her as well as China. Her treaty obligations, her own interests and the interests of international peace and fair dealing should all have led her to co-operate and he hoped she would still see her way to do so.

Monsieur Potemkine (U.S.S.R.) said that conciliation had failed but there was still hope that the conflict might be settled on a basis of equity and of respect for treaties and national sovereignty. The U.S.S.R. would assist in any steps taken for this purpose, which would need for its achievement combined and effective action by the Powers interested.

Count Aldrovandi (Italy) said that he agreed with what had been said regarding respect for treaties and their possible modification, but he did not think it was for the Conference to discuss measures to be taken with regard to one of the parties to the dispute. He asked what in fact there remained for the Conference to do.

The President then announced that he was in possession of a draft statement of views prepared by the United States, United Kingdom and French Delegations. It was decided that this draft should be circulated and that the Conference should meet again to discuss it later in the day. The text of this draft as amended after the afternoon's discussion is contained in Brussels Conference despatch No. 24 of today[5].

A record of the latter meeting is contained in my telegram No. 74 Saving.[6]

[5] Not printed: the draft text was published in *The Times* of November 15, 1937, p. 13. The final text of the declaration, as amended after discussions on November 14 and 15 (see Nos. 358 and 360 below) was sent to the Foreign Office in Brussels Conference despatch No. 31 of November 15: No. 364 below.

[6] No. 358 below.

No. 358

Sir R. Clive (Brussels) to Mr. Eden (Received November 15)

No. 74 Saving: telegraphic [F 9569/6799/10]

BRUSSELS, *November 14, 1937*

Following from Mr. MacDonald.
My telegram No. 73 Saving.[1]
At this afternoon's session Count Aldrovandi said that he was unable to

[1] No. 357.

484

comment in detail on the draft without consulting various relevant documents, but he must declare himself unable to support it either as a whole or in detail. He thought that more attention should be paid to the Japanese request for a 'contribution' from the Conference 'in conformity with the real situation'. The Japanese Government might be asked what they meant by this phrase.

M. Michel (Mexico) supported the draft. The situation must be examined with equanimity, prudence and frankness, and the world had a right to know why wars were made and what was the price of peace. He concluded by saying that we must not be pessimistic but must use all our resources to bring about a just solution.

Mr. de Castro (Portugal) and M. Costa du Rels (Bolivia) also in principle supported the draft.

M. de Graeff (Netherlands) supported it in general, subject to certain amendments.

Mr. Bruce (Australia), in a speech which was received with applause, also supported it. The Conference had to consider whether its own approach to Japan had been a reasonable one and whether Japan's reply had been unreasonable. The answer to both questions was surely 'Yes'. Japan's complaints against China would have been investigated with complete impartiality and the Conference would have been ready to consider the desirability of making changes. The essence of the draft statement was to show that the line taken by Japan was one with which the Powers disagreed, and to refute her contention that the dispute concerned only herself and China and that the best way to settle it was by direct negotiation. It was also right to refer to the larger issue, which was really more important even than all the sufferings of China. The action of Japan brought the world face to face with the most momentous problem which it had ever had to solve.

As there was no support for Count Aldrovandi's suggestion that further explanations should be sought from Japan, it was decided that the draft should be considered paragraph by paragraph. Count Aldrovandi reserved his position. The delegates of Norway, Sweden and Denmark also made reservations, especially as regards the last paragraph which they thought might be taken as committing the Conference to action lying outside its scope.

Various amendments were then incorporated in the draft, and it was agreed to postpone further consideration of it until Monday afternoon, November 15th, in order that Delegates might have an opportunity of consulting their Governments.[2]

[2] See No. 360 below.

No. 359

Sir R. Craigie (Tokyo) to Mr. Eden (Received November 15, 3 p.m.)

No. 682 Telegraphic [F 9578/9/10]

Important   Very Confidential   TOKYO, *November 15, 1937, 9.40 p.m.*

Your telegram No. 474.[1]

I understand confidentially from Vice Minister for Foreign Affairs that position as regards the Germans and mediation is as follows:

Shortly after despatch of my telegram No. 649[2] German Ambassador called and sounded the Minister for Foreign Affairs on desirability of mediation by the German Government. About the same time the German Ambassador at Nanking was making similar soundings among certain Chinese leaders (including possibly Chiang Kai-shek). He discovered that Chinese terms—particularly stipulated [*sic*] for the withdrawal of all Japanese troops as condition for armistice—provided no basis for further negotiations. Thereafter my German colleague called on the Minister for Foreign Affairs again and stated that for the present there did not seem to be any opening for German mediation. This is all that has happened up to date. As regards Italian mediation no official steps appear to have been taken as yet though press is full of reports that it is impending.

2. As regards adjournment of Conference[3] I think effect can only be good in so far as Japanese public opinion is concerned providing no resolution is previously passed condemning Japan. Any resolution in this sense or in favour of lending some assistance to China could only have effect of debarring any participating Powers from acting as intermediary when the right moment arrives, as collective mediation of the Conference or of a group of Powers may be definite.

3. In so far as Japan is concerned effect of such a resolution could only

---

[1] In this telegram of November 14 Sir R. Craigie was asked for his views as to the value to be attributed to rumours which were reaching Europe 'regarding the possibility of a German or an Italian-German mediation in the Chino-Japanese [*sic*] dispute. Is such mediation at all likely to be asked for or offered?'

[2] Not kept in F.O. archives: it apparently reported on November 6 an official Japanese denial of press reports that Japan had received an offer of mediation from Herr Hitler. According to *D.G.F.P.*, Series D, vol. i, No. 506, Dr. Herbert von Dirksen, German Ambassador at Tokyo, was told on October 28 that Japan would welcome Germany's friendly influence on the Chinese Government 'with a view to the initiation of peace negotiations by China'. Dr. Oskar Trautmann, German Ambassador in China, was instructed on October 30 not to go beyond the role of letter carrier between the Chinese and Japanese Governments at this stage (*ibid.*, No. 510). In this role he passed on to Chiang Kai-shek on November 5 (*ibid.*, No. 516) Japanese peace terms which had been given to Dr. von Dirksen on November 3 (*ibid.*, No. 514). General Chiang Kai-shek said that he could not accept any Japanese demands as long as the Japanese were not prepared to restore the status quo ante.

[3] In telegram No. 474 Sir R. Craigie had also been asked his opinion as to the effect likely to be created by the adjournment of the Brussels Conference for a week.

be to open the door to ultimate German mediation (or German-Italian if Italy abstains from voting). It would moreover greatly exacerbate opinion here and combined with successive Japanese military successes tend further to stiffen Japan's terms.

From various indications that have reached me I am inclined to think offer of good offices by Great Britain and United States jointly might not be so unacceptable to the Japanese Government as I had at one time thought.

Repeated to Nanking No. 287.

No. 360

Sir R. Clive (Brussels) to Mr. Eden (Received November 16)

No. 76 Saving: Telegraphic [F 9620/6799/10]

BRUSSELS, *November 15, 1937*

Following from Mr. MacDonald.
My telegram No. 74 Saving.[1]
The Conference met again in private this afternoon to consider further the draft submitted by the United States, United Kingdom and French Delegations.

Monsieur de Dardel (Sweden) expressed regret that the efforts of the Conference were without result. While fully adhering to the principles embodied in the draft, he would abstain from voting the text because Sweden did not possess political interests in the Far East.

Monsieur Aubert (Norway) likewise declared himself in agreement with these principles and said that he still hoped that a settlement based on them might be attained by means of mediation. He referred to his statement of the 13th November and said that he would abstain from voting. (In this statement he made a reservation in so far as the declaration might be construed as suggesting any action which lay outside the scope of the Conference as defined by the terms of the invitation.)

Monsieur de Kauffmann (Denmark) said he would abstain from voting on the same grounds as his Scandinavian colleagues, though he agreed with the principles of the draft.

Count Aldrovandi (Italy) said that Italy considered that this draft left a door open not towards a settlement of the conflict but towards very serious complications. She dissented categorically from it and reserved her attitude as regards future phases of the conflict.

The other delegations signified their acceptance of the draft.

It was agreed that the Conference should issue the declaration in an amended form showing which delegations had associated themselves with

---

[1] No. 358.

it and setting forth the position adopted by the representatives of Norway, Sweden, Denmark and Italy.[2] It was decided not to bring this declaration officially to the notice of the Japanese Government.

Conference then adjourned until 3 p.m. on Monday November 22nd.

[2] See No. 364 below.

No. 361

Sir R. Clive (Brussels) to Mr. Eden (Received November 16)

No. 77 Saving: Telegraphic [F 9621/6799/10]

BRUSSELS, *November 15, 1937*

Following from Mr. MacDonald.

Mr. Quo Tai-chi[1] came to see me this evening. He said that the Chinese military situation in the Shanghai area was serious: Chinese forces no longer outnumbered to any great extent the Japanese forces (which he put at 180,000) and lack of material hampered them very considerably. He believed Germans and Italians were both offering their mediation[2], and I gathered from his conversation (though he did not actually say so) that he was afraid that, if Brussels Conference failed, the Nanking Government rendered helpless by divided counsels, might reluctantly throw itself upon the mercy of Germany and Italy.

It is difficult to believe that intervention of these Powers would produce a satisfactory or lasting settlement, but if it brought hostilities to an end and produced the semblance of a peace, that might be a great apparent diplomatic success for the Dictator Powers.

I wonder whether, if the Conference has to confess failure, we and the Americans, if we were agreed to do so, could spontaneously and at once offer our good offices to both sides. Our idea originally was that best chance of a settlement lay in Anglo-American mediation. Our difficulty here has been to get other members of the Conference to leave it to us. But if Conference fails there would seem to be no reason why we should not take initiative into our own hands, and forestall German and Italian initiative. Sir R. Craigie would have views on the likelihood of such initiative meeting with any success.

Dr. Wellington Koo was meanwhile talking to Mr. Davis, with whom I subsequently had exchange of views. Dr. Koo had said that French Government had been holding up for three weeks in Indo-China a consignment of arms destined for Chinese Government, which they would not allow to proceed unless British and Americans would guarantee

[1] The Chinese Ambassador at London was a member of his country's delegation to the Brussels Conference.

[2] Cf. No. 359.

safety of their railway. Dr. Koo said that if this became known in China it would have deplorable effect. He appears to have spoken more or less on same lines as Mr. Quo on subject of possible German-Italian mediation. As a purely personal suggestion I put to Mr. Davis possibility and desirability of His Majesty's Government and United States Government offering their good offices if and when Conference declared itself unable to take any positive action. He did not commit himself. Members of his Delegation who were present raised not very well founded objections, which he did not seem to accept, and my impression was that he thought there might be something in the suggestion.[3]

He reverted to an idea, which he has expressed before, that mediation might be offered by the 'Shanghai Powers', i.e. Great Britain, United States, France and Italy.

[3] A minute of November 17 by Sir A. Cadogan read: 'The S. of S. this evening author[ize]d tels. to Tokyo and Washington exploring possibility of offer of Anglo-U.S. good offices before reassembly of the Brussels Confce.' See No. 368 below.

No. 362

Sir R. Clive (Brussels) to Mr. Eden (Received November 16)

No. 28 [F 9628/6799/10]

BRUSSELS, *November 15, 1937*

The United Kingdom Delegation to the Nine Power Conference presents its compliments to the Under Secretary of State for Foreign Affairs and has the honour to transmit herewith the under-mentioned document.

Paper	*Subject*
Minute, Mr. Harcourt-Smith, November 15	Message from Japanese Ambassador in Brussels

Enclosure in No. 362

Record by Mr. Harcourt-Smith of a conversation with M. Kurusu

BRUSSELS, *November 15, 1937*

The Japanese Ambassador asked me, in the absence of Sir R. Clive, to call and see him urgently this afternoon. I did so at 2 p.m., when M. Kurusu told me that he had a message of great importance which he would like to see communicated to Mr. MacDonald. He wished, however, to make it perfectly clear that in what he was going to say he was not acting upon instructions from Tokyo, but entirely upon his own initiative. He had, however, consulted M. Yoshida in London by telephone 10 minutes before, and the latter was in entire agreement with what he was going to say.

He belonged, he said, (as did M. Yoshida) to the party in Japan who looked upon good relations between England and Japan as essential to the peace of the world. For some time past there had been, as I would know, efforts to bring about an improved understanding between our two countries. These efforts had been brought to nought by recent events and now, with the probable passing this afternoon of a resolution condemning Japan and providing for assistance of various kinds to China, we were at the parting of the ways. He still refused to believe that we should ever come to blows, but it was a case of the wish being father to the thought. The passing of the resolution would bring the possibility of an Anglo-Japanese war immeasurably closer than it had ever been and he trembled to think what the outcome would be.

When the Japanese Minister for Foreign Affairs declined the invitation to the Nine Power Conference, he had intimated in vague terms to Sir R. Craigie and Mr. Grew that Japan would welcome Anglo-American mediation with a view to stopping Sino-Japanese hostilities.[1] Neither London nor Washington had reacted in any way to this hint. The Japanese reply of November 12th,[2] M. Kurusu went on to say, had been most unfortunately worded, and had thus created in the Conference the impression that Japan slammed the door in our faces. This was the last impression she wished to create, and for the Japanese Government the kernel of the communication lay in the sentence which says 'the Japanese Government would be very glad if the Powers ... could make their contribution to stability in East Asia in conformity with the real situation.' This phrase, cryptic though it might seem, was really meant to repeat the hint given by M. Hirota to Sir R. Craigie and Mr. Grew that Japan would welcome Anglo-American, as opposed to Nine Power, mediation. What Mr. Hirota had in mind was some form of Anglo-American mediation on the lines of the part played by Sir Miles Lampson and Mr. Johnstone in the Shanghai Settlement in 1932.[3]

Mr. Kurusu felt that, if given a little time, he could induce the Japanese Government to make their meaning clearer and thus render their reply of November 12th less unpromising; but this would of course be impossible if the resolution were to be passed this afternoon. In fact, he imagined that they would even feel themselves obliged to retract their hints of welcoming Anglo-American mediation. Could not therefore the taking of a resolution be postponed for a few days, until, for instance next Saturday? During that time he and M. Yoshida from London would exert all their powers to induce their Government to make some gesture along the lines he had indicated. If they failed, then let the Conference pass the

---

[1] Marginal comment by Mr. Orde: 'What he said was that H.M.G. shd. advise the Chinese to *negotiate direct* with Japan.' See No. 320.   [2] See No. 351, note 1.
[3] Cf. Volume X, Chapters I–III.

resolution. At least he (and M. Yoshida) would feel that their consciences were clear and that they had done everything they could to prevent still further bad feeling and misunderstanding accumulating between our two countries.[4]

[4] In a minute of November 19 Mr. Orde commented: 'It is difficult to deal with people who express themselves with such caution and obscurity and leave it to unauthorized (and inaccurate) spokesmen to say what is meant. It all savours of manoeuvering rather than of policy . . .' Mr. R.C.S. Stevenson, Foreign Office Adviser on League of Nations Affairs, noted on November 19 that the American, French, Scandinavian, and Netherlands Delegations had received similar communications and that 'Mr. MacDonald discussed the matter with Mr. Norman Davis and M. de Tessan. It was decided that as M. Kurusu had no authority to speak for his Govt. there were no grounds for a postponement of the Conference's meeting.'

No. 363

Sir R. Clive (Brussels) to Mr. Eden (Received November 16)

No. 29 [F 9629/6799/10]

BRUSSELS, *November 15, 1937*

The United Kingdom Delegation to the Nine Power Conference presents its compliments to the Under Secretary of State for Foreign Affairs and has the honour to transmit herewith the under-mentioned document.

Paper	Subject
Minute, November 15, 1937	Conversation between Mr. MacDonald, Sir A. Cadogan and Mr. Norman Davis

ENCLOSURE IN No. 363

Record by Mr. MacDonald of a conversation with Sir A. Cadogan and Mr. Norman Davis

BRUSSELS, *November 15, 1937*

Sir Alexander Cadogan and I had a talk with Mr. Norman Davis this morning to consider future procedure. Mr. Davis said that he thought that there were three possible stages of action regarding the Japanese refusal to modify their attitude. First, we might try moral pressure on Japan. Second, we might put on some form of material pressure which would not involve any risk of hostilities between Japan and ourselves. Third, we might put on material pressure which would involve such a risk. He was inclined to think that at the present time we should not do more than try the first policy. He could not help feeling that if we could put Japan in moral isolation, that would have a great effect. We should declare that the Japanese were not playing the game according to civilised standards, and that until she mended her ways we would have nothing to do with her.

In the course of further discussion it appeared that all that Mr. Davis meant by this was that we should agree to withdraw our ambassadors from Tokio. In reply, whilst saying that the Government of the United Kingdom would be ready to consider any proposal, Sir Alexander Cadogan and I pointed out the numerous obvious objections to this course, and Mr. Davis agreed that they were weighty. However, he has apparently put up this proposal to his Government. He has also proposed to them a declaration of non-recognition of any alteration in the status quo in China, and a declaration that no financial assistance would be given to the Japanese in developing any conquest that they may make.[1]

I asked him whether he thought it would be possible at the present time for us to take any action of a more effective nature. He answered that he thought not; American public opinion would require to move some way further before that became possible. He is in rather a pessimistic mood, and is becoming increasingly afraid that the Conference will have to end in our taking no action at all, though I think that he still hopes that the President may consent to something more or less mild.

I indicated once more that we in the United Kingdom would be ready to consider really effective action, if the Americans would be prepared to co-operate. But I added that whatever we did or refrained from doing, the policy so far as we were concerned would be one for which the United States and ourselves shared responsibility equally. I thought it very important that the world should recognise our agreement and co-operation.

Mr. Davis heartily agreed with the importance of this.

[1] Cf. No. 351.

No. 364

Sir R. Clive (Brussels) to Mr. Eden (Received November 16)

No. 31 [F 9631/6799/10]

BRUSSELS, *November 15, 1937*

The United Kingdom Delegation to the Nine Power Conference presents its compliments to the Under Secretary of State for Foreign Affairs and has the honour to transmit herewith the under-mentioned document.

Paper	*Subject*
November 15, 1937	Declaration by the Brussels Conference

The Brussels Conference

Confidential   BRUSSELS, *November 15, 1937*

The Representatives of the Union of South Africa, The United States of America, Australia, Belgium, Bolivia, Canada, China, France, The United Kingdom, India, Mexico, Netherlands, New Zealand, Portugal and The Union of Socialist Soviet Republics have drawn up the following declaration:[1]

1. The representatives of the above-mentioned States met at Brussels having taken cognisance of the Japanese Government's reply of November 12, 1937[2], to the communication addressed to the latter on November 7, 1937[3], observe with regret that the Japanese Government still contends that the conflict between Japan and China lies outside the scope of the Nine Power Treaty and again declines to enter into an exchange of views for the purpose of endeavouring to achieve a peaceful settlement of that conflict.

2. It is clear that the Japanese concept of the issues and interests involved in the conflict under reference is utterly different from the concept of most of the other nations and governments of the world. The Japanese Government insist that, as the conflict is between Japan and China, it concerns those two countries only. Against this, the representatives of the above-mentioned States now met at Brussels consider this conflict of concern in law to all countries party to the Nine Power Treaty of Washington of 1922 and to all countries party to the Pact of Paris of 1928, and of concern in fact to all countries members of the family of Nations.

3. It cannot be denied that in the Nine Power Treaty the parties thereto affirmed it to be their desire to adopt a specified policy designed to stabilise conditions in the Far East and agreed to apply certain specified principles in their relations with China and, in China, with one another; and that in the Pact of Paris the parties agreed 'that the settlement or solution of all disputes or conflicts of whatever nature or of whatever origin they may be, which may arise among them, shall never be sought except by pacific means.'

4. It cannot be denied that the present hostilities between Japan and China adversely affect not only the rights of all nations but also the material interests of nearly all nations. These hostilities have brought to some nationals of third countries death, to many nationals of third countries great peril, to property of nationals of third countries widespread destruction, to international communications disruption, to international trade disturbance and loss, to the peoples of all nations a

---

[1] See Nos. 357, 358, and 360.   [2] See No. 351, note 1.   [3] See No. 338.

sense of horror and indignation, to all the world feelings of uncertainty and apprehension.

5. The representatives of the above-mentioned States met at Brussels therefore regard these hostilities and the situation which they have brought about as matters inevitably of concern to the countries which they represent and—more—to the whole world. To them the problem appears not in terms simply of relations between two countries in the Far East but in terms of law, orderly processes, world security and world peace.

6. The Japanese Government has affirmed in its note of October 27th[4], to which it refers in its note of November 12th, that in employing armed force against China it was anxious to 'make China renounce her present policy'. The representatives of the above-mentioned States met at Brussels are moved to point out that there exists no warrant in law for the use of armed force by any country for the purpose of intervening in the internal régime of another country and that general recognition of such a right would be a permanent cause of conflict.

7. The Japanese Government contends that it should be left to Japan and China to proceed to a settlement by and between themselves alone. But, that a just and lasting settlement could be achieved by such a method cannot be believed. Japanese armed forces are present in enormous numbers on Chinese soil and have occupied large and important areas thereof. Japanese authorities have declared in substance that it is Japan's objective to destroy the will and the ability of China to resist the will and the demands of Japan. The Japanese Government affirms that it is China whose actions and attitude are in contravention of the Nine Power Treaty; yet, whereas China is engaged in full and frank discussion of the matter with the other parties to that Treaty, Japan refuses to discuss it with any of them. Chinese authorities have repeatedly declared that they will not, in fact that they cannot, negotiate with Japan alone for a settlement by agreement. In these circumstances, there is no ground for any belief that, if left to themselves, Japan and China would arrive in the appreciably near future at any solution which would give promise of peace between those two countries, security for the rights and interests of other countries, and political and economic stability in the Far East. On the contrary, there is every reason to believe that if this matter were left entirely to Japan and China the armed conflict—with attendant destruction of life and property, disorder, uncertainty, instability, suffering, enmity, hatreds and disturbance to the whole world—would continue indefinitely.

8. The Japanese Government, in their latest communication, invite the Powers represented at Brussels to make a contribution to the stability of Eastern Asia in accordance with the realities of the situation.

9. In the view of the representatives of the above-mentioned States met at Brussels, the essential realities of the situation are those to which they draw attention above.

[4] See No. 320.

10. The representatives of the above-mentioned States met at Brussels are firmly of the belief that, for the reasons given above, a just and durable settlement is not to be expected of direct negotiations between the parties. That is why, in the communications addressed to the Japanese Government, they invited that Government to confer with them or with representatives of a small number of Powers to be chosen for that purpose, in the hope that such exchange of views might lead to acceptance of their good offices and thus help towards the negotiation of a satisfactory settlement.

11. They still believe that if the parties to the conflict would agree to a cessation of hostilities in order to give an opportunity for such a procedure to be tried, success might be achieved. The Chinese Delegation has intimated its readiness to fall in with this procedure. The representatives of the States met at Brussels find it difficult to understand Japan's persistent refusal to discuss such a method.

12. Though hoping that Japan will not adhere to her refusal the above-mentioned States represented at Brussels must consider what is to be their common attitude in a situation where one party to an international treaty maintains against the views of all the other parties that the action which it has taken does not come within the scope of that treaty and sets aside provisions of the treaty which the other parties hold to be operative in the circumstances.[5]

The representative of Sweden made the following statement:

No one can regret more deeply than does the Swedish Government the fact that the Conference's efforts at mediation have so far remained without result. Having to take note of this fact, my Government, which adheres to the principles of the declaration but which does not possess the same political interests in the Far East as certain other Powers, feels that it is its duty to abstain from voting for this text.

The representative of Norway made the following statement:

The Norwegian Government accepted the invitation to this Conference in the desire thereby to contribute if possible to a settlement of the conflict in the Far East by peaceful mediation.

Nobody deplores more than my Government that the efforts of the Conference towards such mediation have hitherto been fruitless.

I am quite in accord with the principles underlying the declaration before us and venture to express the hope that it may still prove possible to obtain through mediation a settlement on the basis of those principles.

Referring, however, to my previous declaration made on the 13th instant, I find it proper to abstain from voting.

The representative of Denmark made the following statement:

I should like to associate myself with the statements just made by my colleagues from Sweden and Norway. Also my country deplores that the

---

[5] This declaration is also printed in *F.R.U.S. Japan 1931–1941*, vol. i, pp. 410–3.

efforts for mediation have hitherto not met with success, and I fully share the hope that through means of mediation it may still be possible to obtain some results. For similar reasons as those given by my Scandinavian colleagues, also I think it proper to abstain from voting on the text of this declaration, while fully in accord with the principles laid down therein.

The representative of Italy made the following statement:

Italy considers the declaration before us as a door open not towards the settlement of the conflict, but rather towards the most serious complications.

Italy does not intend to assume the responsibilities that might devolve therefrom, and she therefore expresses her definitely contrary vote, whilst reserving her attitude as regards all that concerns the subsequent phases of the dispute.

No. 365

Sir R. Lindsay (Washington) to Mr. Eden
(Received November 17, 9.30 a.m.)

No. 399[1] Telegraphic [F 9655/26/23]

Immediate   Very Secret   WASHINGTON, November 16, 1937, 1.44 p.m.

Mr. Hull showed that he was fully alive to the great dangers of the present situation. Besides talking of 'the menace of the three desperadoes' which I have heard before he twice asked specifically what you know about the precise relations now existing between Germany, Italy and Japan.[2] His own impression was that anything said in one capital was instantly repeated to the other two. He thought it was ten to one that there was a definite alliance between them. If this was so the situation in his opinion was one of the utmost danger. 'The British Empire might go down and if that happened the United States would go down soon afterwards'. It would be well if you would send him your appreciation of the situation as regards alliance with any reliable secret information about it you may possess.[3]

---

[1] This telegram was despatched before telegrams Nos. 397 and 398 (Nos. 366 and 367 below): it evidently referred to Sir R. Lindsay's interview with Mr. Hull reported in those telegrams.

[2] Cf. No. 324: cf. also Volume XIX, No. 311.

[3] In a minute of November 18 Mr. Ronald recommended that Mr. Hull's enquiry should be answered 'as fully as the circumstances permit . . . to let Mr. Hull see that, while we are alive to the implications of the Pact, we do not take it quite so tragically as he seems to do'. A draft statement on the anti-comintern pact was prepared: see No. 385 below. This interview appears to have been the first of a series of requests by the State Department for confidential information: see Volume XIX, Nos. 356, 413, and 451.

No. 366

Sir R. Lindsay (Washington) to Mr. Eden
(Received November 17, 9.30 a.m.)

No. 397 Telegraphic [A 8259/228/45]

Immediate   WASHINGTON, *November 16, 1937, 5.12 p.m.*

My immediately preceding telegram[1] and your telegram No. 510.[2]

After expressing the utmost satisfaction at terms of this memorandum I referred to situation with which we are confronted as a result of Brussels Conference. That Conference was clearly ending in a very definite set-back to orderly conduct of international affairs and to system of collective action. It must constitute a severe diplomatic rebuff to all interested in the cause of right and I need not disguise that the rebuff would be more severe to those who are nearest to actual conflict. This must be a severe disappointment to the greater part of the world who have the cause of peace at heart. The one gleam of hope arising was Anglo-American co-operation. This had been very close at Brussels and as I understood it afforded great satisfaction to both our governments. The announcement that we were now contemplating an intention to embark on trade agreement negotiations would hold out prospect of further, stronger and more fruitful Anglo-American co-operation in the future. As international co-operation declined Anglo-American co-operation would arise. I was therefore anxious to join Brussels failure to trade agreement success (so far as it goes) and as I said frankly to lend political importance to the latter. This I suggested should be brought out in announcement to be made about trade negotiations.

My suggestion met with no disapproval from either Mr. Hull or Mr. Sayre.[3] Mr. Hull in concurring generally with my views did indeed launch into one of his usual lengthy disquisitions of a general and abstract character, but Mr. Sayre who is a practical man perfectly grasped the implications. They said that they were perfectly willing to contemplate some procedure such as I had foreshadowed and would anxiously await your views on it. They thought statement should be issued simultaneously in London and in Washington and that the hour and day for issue should be agreed on. They would be willing to have it on Monday if that was the day you preferred. They even seemed prepared to contemplate a joint statement. Above all they emphasized that your immediate attention to this question is urgently necessary.

[1] Telegram No. 396 of November 16 referred to Anglo-American trade negotiations: see Volume XIX, No. 25, note 3. At an interview on November 16 Mr. Hull handed Sir R. Lindsay a memorandum which stressed the outstanding differences between the American and British proposals, but agreed to accept British proposals as a basis for negotiation. See *F.R.U.S.*, 1937, vol. ii, pp. 83–6.

[2] No. 356.

[3] Mr. F. B. Sayre was Assistant Secretary of State at the State Department.

I have been thinking that something on the lines indicated above may to some degree offer you a way out of the difficulties shown in your telegram No. 510 and I hope that I may be right. If you are willing to proceed with these ideas I suggest the following details of execution.

In my opinion a joint statement by the two Governments would be going too far. Even if on second thoughts they were still willing to join in one I think it would be rather calculated to arouse hostility of strong isolationists in this country and thus defeat its own object. I think too that it would be inadvisable to press Secretary of State for text of statement which he would issue because as you know it is unwise in any way to create the impression that American utterances are influenced by us. I propose therefore that you should prepare immediately the statement which you would wish to issue and should telegraph it urgently to me. I should like to show it to Secretary of State and indicate that if it contains anything likely to embarrass United States Government you would be willing to consider modifications. I should prefer to leave State Department untrammelled by any suggestions from us as to what their statement should contain stipulating that it should not be in contradiction to ours. As to the time-table you could have it as you wish. I imagine you would prefer Monday or Tuesday next and I should be sorry if it were later. A statement made in the House of Commons at 4 p.m. would be matched by a statement here at 11 a.m. which would be quite convenient.[4]

[4] Replying to a question in the House of Commons from Mr. Attlee on November 18 Mr. Chamberlain said that he was very happy to inform the House that informal and exploratory talks about a trade agreement had 'now reached a point at which the Governments of the United Kingdom and the United States feel able to announce that negotiations for such an agreement are contemplated': see 329 *H. C. Deb. 5 s.*, col. 579.

No. 367

Sir R. Lindsay (Washington) to Mr. Eden
(Received November 17, 9.30 a.m.)

No. 398 Telegraphic [F 9665/6799/10]

Immediate   WASHINGTON, *November 16, 1937, 5.33 p.m.*

My immediately preceding telegram.[1]

I have assumed that your telegram No. 510[2] was sent off before you saw my telegram No. 3[3] to Brussels which answers many of your points but I will enquire further at State Department about the actual winding up of conference tomorrow. Meanwhile the President's message did not touch on foreign affairs and I doubt the likelihood of special message while Chicago speech[4] is still fresh in the memory. Mr. Hull said to me today

[1] No. 366.   [2] No. 356.   [3] No. 355.
[4] See No. 291, note 2.

that there is nothing the United States Government can do without legislation and as the Under-Secretary of State said no legislation is contemplated that disposes of all talk of ineffective sanctions. As to suspension of neutrality act see also what the Under-Secretary of State said. State Department's policy on this point is in a state of precarious equilibrium in which they are just able to sit quiet and they only hope this may continue and spare them the necessity of choosing between unpleasant alternatives. Mr. Hull got off on me today some language in the sense of the last words of paragraph 3 of my telegram under reference to Brussels from which I infer the intention to end the conference with some brave words.

No. 368

Mr. Eden to Sir R. Craigie (Tokyo)

No. 483 Telegraphic [F 9704/9/10]

Immediate   FOREIGN OFFICE, *November 17, 1937, 8.5 p.m.*

Japanese Ambassador informs me that he recently telegraphed to his Government urging them to indicate in their reply to Brussels Conference that they none the less desired to see hostilities brought to an end. Japanese Government replied that text of communication to Brussels Conference had already been determined and could not be changed, but that that was their position.

He added that Vice Minister for Foreign Affairs had indicated to you on November 15 that his Government would be disposed to accept offer of good offices[1] and that simultaneously Minister for Foreign Affairs had made similar communication to American Ambassador in Tokyo in even more definite terms[2].

Mr. Yoshida gave it as his opinion that our former offer of good offices had been ignored at the outset, when Japanese authorities anticipated a short campaign, but that now they were thinking differently, especially when faced with decision to open further campaign for capture of Nanking.

If there is any reasonable chance of Japan now accepting Anglo-American good offices, I should be prepared to consider making the offer provided U.S. Government would do the same. It would of course also be necessary to get Chinese Government to accept.

Has Mr. Yoshida correctly represented what Vice Minister for Foreign Affairs said to you? Please ascertain from your U.S. colleague what Minister for Foreign Affairs said to him.

If both sides would accept good offices of His Majesty's Government

[1] See No. 359.
[2] See *F.R.U.S.*, 1937, vol. iv, pp. 189–93: cf. also *ibid., Japan 1931–1941*, vol. i, pp. 413–5.

and U.S. Government, it might be desirable to secure their acceptance before Brussels conference reassembles on November 22. If by then good offices had been accepted, it might be possible for Conference to take note of the fact and suspend action. This might be going behind back of Conference but as prospects of success of latter are practically nil, I do not think that we should be deterred by that consideration.

If you see any objection to procedure outlined above, I hope you will let me know as soon as possible.

You will of course appreciate that you should make no approach to the Japanese in this matter until your U.S. colleague has been instructed to associate himself with you.[3]

Repeated to Washington and Nanking.

[3] Telegram No. 522 to Washington of November 17 instructed Sir R. Lindsay to bring the contents of the above telegram to Mr. Hull's attention, and to ask whether 'if it appears that Japan might accept Anglo-American good offices, U.S. Government would be prepared to join with us in offering them'.

No. 369

Extract from Cabinet Conclusions No. 42(37) of November 17, 1937

[*F 9711/6799/10*]

4. The Secretary of State for Foreign Affairs made a statement as to progress at the Brussels Conference. Any tendencies in the direction that the United Kingdom were frustrating a lead by the United States had been stifled and, as confirmed by telegrams from His Majesty's Ambassador at Washington, co-operation with America at the Conference had been good. He mentioned the following possible future courses for the Conference:

(i) To wind up with a tepid Resolution expressing regret that Japan would not co-operate, if possible accompanied by the appointment of a Sub-Committee to watch the situation, and then to adjourn.

There would be great difficulties in securing the appointment of a Sub-Committee as all the Powers with interests in China wanted to be represented thereon.

The disadvantage of this course was that China would then ask that the Council of the League of Nations should meet to consider what was to be done by the Powers to honour their obligations under the Covenant. The United States did not want the question to go back to Geneva and desired, if possible, to keep the Brussels Conference in existence.

(ii) For the Brussels Conference to pass the tepid Resolution indicated in (i) and then to nominate the United States of America and the

United Kingdom to act as a Sub-Committee for purposes of conciliation.

(iii) To express disapproval of the Japanese action and to refuse to recognise any territorial advantages she might gain or to grant future credits.

The disadvantage of this course would be that it would much annoy the Japanese. Nevertheless he thought that such an announcement subscribed to by the United States would not be by any means futile.

An element in the situation was that the Chinese had hinted that if nothing resulted from the Brussels Conference they might throw themselves on mediation by Germany and Italy. The effect of that upon our own prestige would be very serious. He had received a warning from the Indian Delegate at the Brussels Conference as to the effect of Japanese predominance in China in Burma and India.

The third of the above courses (disapproval of Japanese action and refusal to recognise the consequences or to grant credits) did not commend itself to the Cabinet on a number of grounds. Japan, it was pointed out, had not yet announced any intention of retaining any part of the occupied territory but had rather indicated a contrary intention, and she had not asked for credits either. By putting a proposal into the minds of the Japanese that they might otherwise never have contemplated was calculated to court a rebuff from Japan. The only justification for such a Resolution would be to prevent Japan from acquiring Chinese territory, but it was not likely to have that effect. If it failed as a threat, the Brussels Conference would be more than ever humiliated.

In addition, the Cabinet were reminded that the Japanese were always inclined to associate the United Kingdom with proposals of that kind; that our military position in the Far East was very weak; and that the proposal was calculated to aggravate the present irritation in Japan, with consequences that could not be foreseen. Moreover, the result would be that the Japanese would reject mediation by ourselves or any of the Powers associated with the Brussels Conference, which in any event was unpopular with them. Consequently the view was expressed that, in the unlikely event of the American Delegation pressing this proposal, the United Kingdom Delegates should endeavour to dissuade them by pointing out that threats were inadvisable, particularly if they were not likely to be effective, and that omission to pass a Resolution containing the threat would not prevent the Powers concerned from applying the policy proposed later on if the Japanese should in fact establish a permanent occupation of conquered Chinese territory.

A fourth suggestion was discussed, namely, that if nothing was achieved by the Conference the Governments of the United Kingdom and the United States of America should spontaneously, and independently of the Conference, offer to use their good offices in the direction of conciliation at any time that the parties to the conflict might welcome it. This would forestall a reference to Germany and Italy, and it would be difficult for the contending Powers to accept Germany and Italy as conciliators if they had rejected an Anglo-American offer.

The Secretaries of State for Foreign Affairs and Dominion Affairs, as a result of their experience at Brussels, doubted whether the United States of America would be willing to do this except under authority from the Conference, and it was very doubtful if the Conference could be induced to nominate the United Kingdom and the United States of America as the sole members of a Committee. That depended largely on the French attitude.

The Prime Minister suggested that the United Kingdom Delegates should take soundings as to whether the Conference would be willing to nominate the United Kingdom and the United States of America, and that only if this was impracticable should we propose to substitute a joint effort by the two countries independently of the Conference. An argument that might appeal to the French would be that a reference to Geneva would be avoided by deputing the United Kingdom and the United States to represent the Conference.

The Cabinet realised that resort to German-Italian conciliation after a rejection of an Anglo-American offer would be very serious.

The question was then raised as to whether the co-operation of Germany, with or without Italy, might be sought at the outset. This would be useful not only to avert a rebuff, but to secure a co-operative effort with Germany.

The Secretary of State for Foreign Affairs said that he and the Secretary of State for Dominion Affairs had considered this very carefully at Brussels. The difficulty was that both France and Russia had much greater interests in the Far East than Germany had. For that reason he thought that the suggestion was one that was difficult to work for, though it might be allowed to develop naturally.

The Prime Minister said that he would not ask the Cabinet for a formal decision on the matters discussed, but he had no doubt that the United Kingdom Delegates would take the discussion into consideration in the line they took at the Conference.

The Cabinet then considered the representation at Brussels when the Conference re-assembled on Monday, November 22nd.

The Cabinet agreed

(a) That the Secretary of State for Foreign Affairs could not be spared from London to proceed to Brussels at the reopening of the Conference on Monday next, November 22:

(b) That the Secretary of State for Dominion Affairs should proceed to Brussels on the evening of Friday, November 19th and should endeavour to secure that the Conference should meet on Monday, November 22nd, and if necessary on Tuesday, November 23rd, merely to give formal approval to some arrangement which he would negotiate for bringing it, or at any rate its present stage, to an end:

(c) That in view of the fact that the Secretary of State for Dominion Affairs would, for Parliamentary reasons, probably have to return to London before the formal meetings of the Conference referred to above, the Secretary of State for Foreign Affairs should arrange for one of the Parliamentary Under-Secretaries of the Foreign Office to proceed to Brussels with the Secretary of State for Dominions Affairs to represent him:

(d) That no instructions should be laid down for the United Kingdom Delegates, but that they should take into consideration the various points raised in the Cabinet discussion.[1]

---

[1] Mr. Chamberlain evidently had some instructions of his own for Mr. MacDonald to take back to Brussels. In a letter of November 21 to his sister Hilda, preserved in his private papers, Mr. Chamberlain wrote: 'I have succeeded in curbing our bellicose F.O. which was anxious to finish up the Brussels Conference with more fistshaking at Japan. I have sent Malcolm [MacDonald] back with the strictest injunctions to take part in or to assent to no threats without first referring back to me and as he entirely agrees with my views I can rely on him to carry them out. But I have also made some alternative suggestions of an ingenious character to meet all the difficulties of saving 19 faces. And I am not without hope that before long we may see negotiations for peace opened.'

No. 370

Letter from Foreign Office to Burma Office

[*F 9311/130/10*]

FOREIGN OFFICE, *November 17, 1937*

Sir,

I am directed [by the Secretary of State for Foreign Affairs] to refer to Burma Office letter No. 2887/37 of the 29th October[1] on the subject of the establishment of through road connection between Burma and China and to transmit to you herewith a copy of a telegram[2] which was addressed to His Majesty's Chargé d'Affaires at Nanking in pursuance of that letter. I am also to transmit to you a copy of a telegram from the Acting British

---

[1] This should apparently read 'B 2888/27' (F 8797/130/10). This letter referred to the possibility of the Chinese Government obtaining munitions through Burma: see Nos. 316 and 327. It expressed agreement with the views of the Government of Burma as to respective merits of various routes for prompt delivery, and added that 'Lord Zetland would be content to leave the decision to be taken in accordance with the preference of the Chinese authorities': he would also be glad of information as to whether the prospect of an influx of munitions through Burma to China would justify the Government of Burma in incurring any considerable outlay on road construction.

[2] No. 327.

Consul General at Yunnanfu to H.M. Embassy at Peking[3] in continuation of that of which a copy was enclosed in Burma Office letter No. B 3038/37 of the 5th November[4].

2. The Marquess of Zetland will observe that Mr. Eden has not referred in the enclosed telegram to Mr. Howe to the possibility of bargaining the readiness of the Government of Burma to improve the trans-frontier connection against acceptance by the Chinese Government of the desiderata of the former in regard to the undemarcated frontier. The question of the frontier will, of course, arise if the Chinese Government desire to effect the frontier connection via Kunlong; and in this event they will no doubt recognise the necessity of offering an acceptable settlement. Mr. Eden would, however, deprecate any communication to the Chinese Government which would give the impression that the cooperation of the Government of Burma in facilitating the establishment of road connection between the two countries (which must be of benefit to both countries) was conditional upon acceptance of a settlement of the boundary question upon lines to which they might not in normal circumstances be prepared to agree.[5] Not only does he consider that it would be wrong to take advantage of the present situation in order in effect to impose upon the Chinese Government the solution of this question propounded by the Government of Burma, however intrinsically reasonable that solution may be; but he is also persuaded that, since any solution of the question which could be accepted on the British side must in any event involve concessions by China in relation to what she has claimed in the past (whether with or without justification) any agreement reached now which the Chinese Government could represent as having been forced upon them would be liable to repudiation so soon as the present emergency has disappeared.[6]

[3] Transmitted to the Foreign Office as Peking telegram No. 757 of November 9, not printed (F 9311/130/10).

[4] Not kept in F.O. archives.

[5] In their reply of December 4 (F 10527/130/10) the Burma Office noted that Lord Zetland had observed that 'Mr. Howe has already invited the Chinese Government to expedite a settlement of the frontier question in return for the offer of His Majesty's Government and the Government of Burma to facilitate the transit of munitions of war through Burma'. In these circumstances 'His Lordship does not propose to pursue the matter further at this stage'.

[6] Concluding salutation omitted from the filed copy of this letter, which was apparently signed by Mr. Orde.

No. 371

Mr. Hall-Patch (Shanghai) to Mr. Eden
(Received November 18, 10.30 a.m.)

No. 219 Telegraphic [F 9713/220/10]

SHANGHAI, *November 18, 1937, 3.46 p.m.*

Addressed to Nanking No. 151 of November 17th.
Following from Financial Adviser.
Shanghai telegram No. 147 to Foreign Office[1] and my telegram No. 149 to Nanking.[2]
I had today two hours frank talk with Okazaki. It transpired:

(a) Military want to seize and are being restrained by civil officials.

(b) Tientsin arrangement not satisfactory to military who expect more solid achievement from Matsui who is senior to Tientsin Commander and has a reputation for firmness to uphold.

(c) Civil officials think they will be able to prevent seizure but only if all revenue is deposited direct with Yokohama Specie Bank. Nothing but this will satisfy military that no surplus over cost of collection and service of foreign obligations will reach Chinese Government.

(d) Seizure or not, foreign interest in customs revenue will be respected.

(e) Civil officials deprecate any suggestion of neutral custodian bank or banks for any portion of revenue as quite inacceptable to military.

(f) They also deprecate any foreign Power intervening in any way in negotiations as this would exasperate military.

(g) They hoped British influence would be used to persuade Chinese to accept Yokohama Specie Bank arrangement.

(h) Final decision on Japanese action in Shanghai will be reached in the course of the next few days and negotiations will then be opened between Japanese Consul-General (Okamoto) and Shanghai Commissioner of

---

[1] This telegram of November 16 referred to Shanghai telegram No. 143 of that date in which H.M. Consul General at Shanghai, Mr. Phillips, reported that on November 15 the Japanese naval authorities had completed the seizure of the customs preventative fleet at Shanghai. Telegram No. 147 reported that Mr. Okazaki, Japanese Consul General on special service, told Mr. Phillips that the Japanese 'were determined to stop any revenue reaching Nanking Government' (F 9669/220/10).

[2] In this telegram of November 17 (Shanghai telegram No. 218 to the Foreign Office) Mr. Hall-Patch commented that it seemed useless 'to attempt to obtain acceptance by Japanese of six points proposal for Customs here [cf. Nos. 302 and 329]. But I submit that we should make some proposal satisfactory to us which it will be difficult for Japanese to refuse as otherwise they will state their terms and we may be obliged again to retreat in successive stages as in Tientsin'. Mr. Hall-Patch suggested 'some sort of international supervision of Customs revenue in ports (other than Tientsin and Chingwangtao) where Chinese Government are no longer in control'. This supervision, possibly exercised by an international commission, could ensure that foreign loans could still be serviced.

Customs (Lawford). Hidaka will keep me informed step by step of negotiations.

2. I stressed international character of customs and importance of maintaining it. I pointed out the far-reaching effects of seizure and deplorable impression which would be created by negotiations affecting this important international interest being carried on under threat of military pressure as in Tientsin. The service of foreign obligations would absorb all available revenue for some time to come and Japan had but a small interest in these obligations. It was therefore unreasonable to demand deposit of all revenue in Yokohama Specie Bank. Arrangements could easily be made to hold any surplus when it accrued in a suspense account in Hongkong and Shanghai Bank where revenue was now deposited. Total deposit in Japanese bank would not be accepted by Chinese unless arrangement covered service of domestic loans. Insistence on such deposit would create unfortunate impression in foreign financial circles whose sympathy it seemed inadvisable for Japan to alienate. I thought an arrangement could be reached which would give Japan all she required without necessitating total deposit with Japanese bank and I expressed the hope that he could persuade his military to allow such an arrangement to be negotiated in an orderly manner without threats and intimidation.

3. Okazaki said military 'face' was involved and it would be very difficult to obtain agreement to deposit in neutral custodian bank or banks. He would urge reconsideration of the question as he appreciated advantage of an amicable settlement but frankly he feared his efforts would be fruitless.

4. The issue for Shanghai is now fairly clear and a decision on policy is urgent. There may be some element of bluff in this first Japanese approach and this should perhaps be tested. Should we stand aside and let Japanese divert all Shanghai revenue to Yokohama Specie Bank without making some alternative suggestion? If not, do you consider suggestions made in my telegram No. 149 worth pursuing? If we are to act speed is essential.[3]

Repeated to Peking, Tokyo.

[3] Mr. Eden asked to see minutes on this telegram, and Sir J. Pratt responded on November 19 with a long minute setting out British policy towards the Chinese Customs and the recent history of the service. Mr. Chaplin noted on November 19 that Mr. Young from the Treasury had come to the Foreign Office that morning to discuss the question with Sir J. Pratt, Sir J. Brenan, and himself, and that draft telegrams had been prepared as a result, which Sir F. Leith-Ross wanted to see before despatch: see No. 378 below. Meanwhile an urgent telegram was sent to Sir R. Craigie on November 18: No. 373 below.

No. 372

Sir R. Craigie (Tokyo) to Mr. Eden (Received November 18, 10.45 a.m.)

No. 692 Telegraphic [F 9705/9/10]

Immediate   TOKYO, *November 18, 1937, 4 p.m.*

Your telegram No. 483.[1]

I had certainly not gathered from my interview with Vice Minister for Foreign Affairs on November 15th any definite indication that Japanese Government would be prepared to accept good offices in ordinary sense of this term. There was however . . . [2] suggestion repeatedly put forward in the past and as frequently reported that best way in which Great Britain could assist would be to persuade Chinese Government to enter into direct negotiations with Japanese Government.

At the end of the interview reported in my telegram No. 682[3] I asked Vice Minister for Foreign Affairs for personal expression of opinion as to whether, supposing the moment came for offer of good offices, Japanese Government would prefer Germany to act as intermediary rather than Great Britain or the United States. He said that he thought not.

I then enquired in the same strictly personal manner whether he thought Japanese Government would welcome offer of Anglo-American good offices at appropriate moment. He said he would prefer not to answer this question without consulting Minister for Foreign Affairs.

In order not to arouse any misconception I preferred not to report this part of my conversation until I had learnt Mr. Hirota's view as to which I have still heard nothing. Evidently, however, Vice Minister for Foreign Affairs attached more importance to this conversation than I had myself.

What passed between Minister for Foreign Affairs and my American colleague is reported in my immediately following telegram.[4] He tells me that in his case also there was no more than repetition of suggestion that United States should urge Chinese Government to enter into direct negotiations with Japanese Government.

Mr. Grew and I agree that psychological moment has now arrived when offer of good offices might be acceptable to Japanese Government. We have however no sure indication that Anglo-American good offices would be acceptable.

I suggest as first step that I should be authorised to enquire of Vice Minister for Foreign Affairs *as from myself*.

(A) Whether he is now in a position to answer my question about Anglo-American good offices and

(B) Whether by this term can be understood joint action by the two countries as intermediaries for the initiation of peace negotiations. As regards (B) it would be necessary to make it clear that the Chinese

---

[1] No. 368.
[3] No. 359.

[2] The text was here uncertain.
[4] Not printed: cf. No. 368, note 2.

Government are in no mood yet to engage in direct negotiations with Japan but that my conception of the function of intermediaries would be the passing of armistice and peace terms from one . . .[2] country to the other until a basis had been found for direct negotiations between the parties.

As regards ant[e]-penultimate paragraph question of announcement to Brussels Conference would need careful consideration as Mr. Grew and I feel chance of success of this peace offer would be halved if there is premature publicity.[5]

Repeated to Nanking and Washington.

[5] Mr. Orde noted on November 19 that an answer to this telegram should wait until further information had been received from Washington: see No. 374 below. He commented, however, that the Japanese attitude 'does not seem really to have advanced in the direction of readiness for mediation as distinct from a desire to see pressure put on the Chinese to negotiate direct'.

No. 373

Mr. Eden to Sir R. Craigie (Tokyo)

No. 490 Telegraphic [F 9713/220/10]

Immediate   FOREIGN OFFICE, *November 18, 1937, 9.30 p.m.*

Position disclosed in Embassy Offices Shanghai telegrams to Nanking Nos. 149[1] and 151[2] is under consideration. Meanwhile please make urgent representations to Japanese Government against allowing this question to be decided under military pressure in Shanghai. You should emphasise once again the international character of the Customs and the important British interest not only in the revenues but also in the administration, and ask that urgent instructions be immediately sent to Shanghai to ensure that due regard will be paid to these considerations and to prevent any precipitate action by local military authorities.

You may add that His Majesty's Government are in communication with the other Governments principally concerned[3] and hope shortly to make suggestions for a satisfactory settlement by international agreement.

[1] See No. 371, note 2.   [2] No. 371.
[3] Telegram No. 526 to Washington (No. 240 Saving to Paris) of November 18 instructed H.M. Ambassadors to ask the American and French Governments to instruct their representatives at Tokyo to take parallel action to that in telegram No. 490.

No. 374

Sir R. Lindsay (Washington) to Mr. Eden
(Received November 20, 10.50 p.m.)

No. 414 Telegraphic [*F 9836/9/10*]

Immediate   WASHINGTON, *November 19, 1937, 3.53 p.m.*

My immediately preceding telegram.[1]

Under-Secretary of State commented on aide-mémoire in the following sense[2]:

1. State Department is certain that any leakage will more than imperil success and that secrecy is essential. They are even in doubt whether they will inform Mr. Norman Davis of developments.

2. They would have liked to close or suspend proceedings at Brussels by some kind of announcement of present developments but think considerations of time and secrecy make this impossible.

3. As to four separate steps which they contemplate, first comprises enquiry by Sir R. Craigie of Vice Minister for Foreign Affairs to be followed if response is favourable by separate enquiries by the two Ambassadors of the Minister for Foreign Affairs himself to obtain official confirmation which will be necessary before proceeding further.

4. Second stage would involve agreement between His Majesty's Government and the United States Government that they should not go outside the scope of the Nine Power Treaty and also question of procedure. As regards the latter they are thinking of methods followed at the Conference in 1922 when the Japanese Government stipulated that no pressure should be exercised on them by the two Powers offering their good offices. This was agreed to as a face saving device and in formal meetings which were numerous no pressure was exerted. But there was a great deal of it between the meetings.

5. Approach to Japanese Government must precede that to the Chinese Government otherwise the United States Government and His Majesty's Government might find themselves involved in proposals out of harmony with the Nine Power Treaty.

6. Information received by State Department from the United States Ambassador in Tokyo coincides very precisely with that received here

---

[1] Not printed. Telegram No. 413 transmitted the text of an aide-mémoire handed to Sir R. Lindsay by Mr. Sumner Welles on November 19 in response to Sir R. Lindsay's communication regarding the contents of Foreign Office telegram No. 483 to Tokyo: see No. 368, note 3. The aide-mémoire also referred to the suggestions made by Sir R. Craigie in telegram No. 692 (No. 372), which had been reported to Washington by Mr. Grew: see *F.R.U.S.*, 1937, vol. iii, pp. 687–9. The U.S. Government approved of Sir R. Craigie's first suggestion, to make an enquiry of the Japanese attitude. The aide-mémoire then set out four separate steps to be taken. Further details of this document, as sent to Mr. Grew in Tokyo by the State Department, are given in *F.R.U.S.*, *ibid.*, pp. 699–700.

[2] Mr. Welles's record of this conversation is printed *ibid.*, pp. 697–8.

from Sir R. Craigie up to and including his telegram No. 692.[3]
Repeated to Tokyo No. 2.

[3] No. 372. In telegram No. 703 of November 19, however, received in the Foreign Office at 6 p.m., Sir R. Craigie reported two conversations with the Japanese Vice Minister for Foreign Affairs. He had asked whether the Vice Minister had spoken to Mr. Hirota 'about my earlier enquiry as to whether Anglo-American good offices had been at all in their minds'. Mr. Horinouchi said that Mr. Hirota would welcome such good offices if directed to persuading the Chinese Government to enter into direct negotiations, and had repeated this answer in a further conversation. Sir R. Craigie therefore reported that he and Mr. Grew were agreed that in the circumstances any offer of Anglo-American good offices would be 'premature to say the least. Japanese Government will at the moment accept nothing except an offer to press China to make peace and it would be fatal to make any offer which their people could refuse'.
  Washington telegram No. 416 of November 19 said that Mr. Grew had reported these developments to Washington, and that the State Department agreed that circumstances were at present unfavourable to further steps by the two Governments. Mr. Eden noted: 'I agree.'

No. 375

Mr. Eden to Mr. Howe (Nanking)

No. 663 [F 9799/9/10]

FOREIGN OFFICE, November 19, 1937

Sir,
    The Chinese Ambassador asked to see me this morning when he spoke of the progress of hostilities in the Far East. The Chinese Government had decided to remove their capital to Chungking but it was their intention to continue to defend Nanking. A branch of the Foreign Office would be established at Hankow, but the main portion of that department would remain at Nanking for the time being at least.[1] His Excellency emphasised to me that, when the war had started, the Chinese Government had thought that they would be able to hold out for from six to nine months. Actually the hostilities had been on a wider scale than had been anticipated, with consequently greater demands upon Chinese available stocks of munitions. Under the circumstances, those munitions might well be almsot exhausted by the end of January. The Chinese Government were not contemplating suing for peace but they wished His Majesty's Government to appreciate the true position of their reserves of munitions. Unless they could receive material supplies in this sphere, the position in a

[1] Mr. Howe reported in Nanking telegram No. 679 of November 21 that the Foreign Minister had informed the diplomatic corps that he was leaving Nanking 'at any moment', and had 'officially requested all foreign missions to leave Nanking immediately'. On November 23 Mr. Howe moved most of the Embassy staff on to H.M.S. *Bee*, which proceeded to Hankow. In telegram No. 694 from Hankow of November 29, however, he expressed the opinion that government departments would soon move further inland and that he had arranged to leave for Shanghai on December 3.

few months' time must be truly desperate. If the Nanking Government were unable to maintain their resistance, the result, he feared, would be anarchy all over China.

2. In reply I thanked His Excellency for speaking to me thus frankly about the situation. At the same time, it was not clear what, in the circumstances, he expected His Majesty's Government to do. As he would be aware Hong Kong had been kept open for the transshipment of munitions and some small supplies had come in from this country. The French Government had virtually closed their railway in Indo-China to the supply of munitions, while American Government ships were not carrying any. I, therefore, supposed that the only avenue of supply at present, other than through Hong Kong, was from Russia. His Excellency now asked that we should ensure the arrival of munitions on a large scale. He would appreciate that, in view of the state of our own rearmament, it would not be possible, all other considerations apart, to send such supplies, notably aeroplanes and anti-aircraft guns which His Excellency had mentioned, from this country, so that in effect what we should have to do presumably would be in some way to protect armaments from other countries reaching China through some other port of entry than Hong Kong. Anything of this nature would clearly involve preparations for naval action. His Excellency must be aware that, without arguing the case from other points of view, it would be wholly impossible for this country at the moment to move a fleet to the Far East for such a purpose. The truth was—and we must face it—that action in the Far East depended upon the attitude of the United States and, so far as I had received information recently of the attitude of that Government, there was no indication that they were willing to take any step that would require the approval of Congress.

3. The Ambassador said he fully appreciated the exactness of the summary of the situation which I had given to him. He, of course, understood that His Majesty's Government could take no action in the Far East except in conjunction with the United States. He wondered whether I would agree with his view that the United States Government were some way in advance of United States opinion. I replied that I was confident that this was so. His Excellency continued that Mr. Norman Davis had explained to the Chinese Delegation during the Brussels Conference that he hoped that, as the Conference proceeded, American public opinion would be increasingly interested and more ready to support the President in any action he might desire to take. Unfortunately, His Excellency observed, this hope of Mr. Norman Davis had not been realised. All the same the Ambassador wondered whether it was not possible for us and the United States to encourage Soviet Russia to give more active help to China. It was true that Russia had sent a certain amount of material, but perhaps she could do more than that and even mobilise part of her armies on the Japanese frontier. I replied that I understood the attitude of the Soviet Government to be that they were prepared to take part in any joint

action but only on condition that the risks were shared alike by all having interests in the Far East. The Ambassador then said that he wondered whether it might not be possible for us to take some action in advance of the United States, relying upon United States support in the later stages. I replied that I feared that, more particularly in the present state of Europe, I could hold out no hope that we could pursue such a policy. Indeed, to do so would be to act contrary to the wish which the United States Government had themselves expressed before we went to Brussels. They had asked us to keep in step with them, not rushing ahead or lagging behind. There were two dangers we had continually to be on our guard against when working with the United States Government. The first was that they should believe we were not willing to support them in any action that they might be ready to take. In this respect the United States Government now had no anxieties. The second danger was that the United States Government should not be put in the position in which it could be described by its own public as being dragged at our tail. The Ambassador, who had appeared almost to expect my reply, did not attempt to contest it.

4. His Excellency then said that there were many people who thought that Japan might very likely attack Russia soon in any event. Japan was apprehensive of Russia's power and it was Russia's interests that were more immediately affected by the conquest of China. Moreover the Japanese Government probably thought that Russia was at this moment more vulnerable than usual owing to her internal troubles and the many executions of Generals that had taken place. Japan, indeed, enjoyed the political situation in Europe that suited her best and promoted her conquests in China. A threat of war in Europe suited Japan better than an actual state of war. This was really the situation today.

5. The Ambassador mentioned that there were certain elements in China who desired to use Germany and Italy as mediators with Japan, but that most influential opinion in China was opposed to anything of the kind. Dr. H. H. Kung, he mentioned incidentally, as belonging to this small group which wished to make use of Germany.

6. Finally we spoke of the Conference at Brussels and I explained to the Ambassador that much must depend upon the attitude which Mr. Norman Davis would have been instructed by his Government to adopt. At the same time, it remained, I thought, true that the one hope of achieving any effective result still lay in Anglo-American co-operation. I wondered what His Excellency thought of the possibility of the Conference giving His Majesty's Government and the United States Government some form of mandate in connexion with the present situation. The Ambassador replied that, for their part, the Chinese Government would be very ready to accept that. We then discussed the difficulties which already existed in attempting to set up any form of sub-committee. The Ambassador was at no time critical of the attitude of His Majesty's Government during this dispute but he emphasised that, in the view of his

Government, the Chinese people were fighting to the utmost of their strength and were sacrificing their lives in a cause which was not only Chinese. The triumph of Japanese militarism could not be without its effect on the whole future of the Far East.

I am, etc.,

ANTHONY EDEN

No. 376

Sir R. Craigie (Tokyo) to Mr. Eden (Received November 20, 9.30 a.m.)

No. 704 Telegraphic [F 9854/6799/10]

TOKYO, *November 20, 1937, 2 p.m.*

I fear my telegram No. 703[1] will not be very helpful in solving problem what is to be the next step at Brussels.

A perceptible hardening of opinion and general exaltation are noticeable here. Nothing I am afraid can be relied on to stop these people and bring the Militarists to their senses except the imposition of sanctions (with full American co-operation) and the unhesitating acceptance by all, of the risk of war thereby entailed. Adoption of such a course now might save us infinite difficulties later.

As however this course must for obvious reasons be ruled out I venture to express the earnest hope that Brussels conference may be dissuaded from adopting some halfway measure which while still further provoking Nationalist sentiment here nevertheless stops short at risk of war. There is no room whatever for bluff in the situation which has developed and unreliability of American assurances of armed co-operation are too notorious to need emphasis from me.

The only course which to my mind combines reasonable security with any hope of ultimate success is adjournment of Brussels conference sine die, Great Britain and United States thereafter keeping in closest touch with each other ready to play a part in restoring peace at the first opportune moment. Idea of joint Anglo-American good offices is in principle less unpalatable here than I had thought but Japanese Government have not yet advanced to the point of wishing to act through intermediaries however friendly nor will they do so as long as they feel some hope of being able to force Chinese Government into direct negotiation.

If however Brussels conference decides on action involving further condemnation of, or remonstrance to, Japan or some form of mild assistance to China the chances of useful Anglo-American action to promote peace will in my opinion be fatally diminished. We shall have

[1] See No. 373, note 3.

played into German and Italian hands without having deflected Japanese by one inch from her purpose.

An ineffective application of principles of 'collective security' to a case like the present in which they are unfortunately inappropriate can only hamper the operations of the ordinary processes of diplomacy.

Repeated to Nanking.

No. 377

Sir R. Craigie (Tokyo) to Mr. Eden (Received November 20, 10.30 a.m.)

No. 709 Telegraphic [F 9856/220/10]

TOKYO, *November 20, 1937, 4.50 p.m.*

Your telegram No. 490.[1]

I spoke to Vice Minister for Foreign Affairs yesterday in the sense of your telegram 490. I also reminded him of disagreeable impression created by forcible action of Japanese Military at Tientsin and said that it was most important that early instructions should be sent to Shanghai to prevent similar precipitate action there. Vice Minister for Foreign Affairs did not think there was any danger of precipitate action and instructions had already been sent to discuss this matter in conciliatory spirit with local authorities. He considered, however, that there was no hope at all of Japanese military authorities agreeing to any revenue whatever from Shanghai customs being allowed to reach Chinese Government.

We did not go into any details as this might complicate discussion already proceeding in Shanghai but I concur in Financial Adviser's opinion that speed is essential (see Shanghai telegram No. 151 to Nanking[2]).

As far as is possible to judge from here procedure suggested in paragraph 5 of Financial Adviser's telegram No. 149 to Nanking[3] seems worth trying though I fear in the end we may have to agree to total deposit in Yokohama Specie Bank.

Repeated Nanking and Shanghai.

[1] No. 373.　　　　　　[2] No. 371.　　　　　　[3] See *ibid.*, note 2.

No. 378

Mr. Eden to Mr. Howe (Nanking)

No. 485 Telegraphic [F 9713/220/10]

FOREIGN OFFICE, *November 20, 1937, 7 p.m.*

My telegram No. 490 to Tokyo.[1]

Subject to your views, Mr. Hall-Patch is authorised to negotiate on lines of para. 5 of his telegram No. 149 to Nanking[2], in consultation where possible with his United States and French colleagues, the best arrangement practicable. I will then instruct His Majesty's Ambassador at Tokyo to give all possible support and to endeavour to get the arrangement confirmed by the Japanese Government[3].

2. I am inclined to think that a combination of the two solutions suggested by Mr. Hall-Patch in his telegram to you No. 149 would be the most satisfactory. That is, all revenue should be paid into the Hong Kong and Shanghai Bank (which appears to be already being done) and service of foreign loans effected as contemplated in Agreement of 1912[4] subject to the control of the body of officials referred to in para. 4 of that telegram. From the Chinese point of view, all responsibility for the disbursement of the revenues would then be undertaken by this committee. Vis-à-vis the Japanese, there would, however, be a clear understanding that no payments would be made other than for collection costs and for foreign loans service.

3. In the last resort, it would not be possible to resist in practice a Japanese demand that the revenues should be deposited direct in the Yokohama Specie Bank. It must, however, be secured that their disbursement is controlled in the same way by a board of officials and a clear understanding must be reached with the Japanese that the customs shall be free to draw up to the full amount if required, of revenues

---

[1] No. 373. [2] See No. 371, note 2.

[3] In telegram No. 498 to Tokyo, also despatched at 7 p.m. on November 20, Sir R. Craigie was instructed to inform the Japanese Government that Mr. Hall-Patch was being authorised to negotiate a settlement of the Shanghai customs question, and to say that His Majesty's Government would be grateful if they could 'ensure that Mr. Okazaki collaborates fully with Mr. Hall-Patch and that the military authorities do not interfere in these negotiations'.

[4] Sir J. Pratt explained in his minute of November 19 (see No. 371, note 3) that before the 1911 Revolution the Chinese customs had been administered entirely by Chinese banks and officials. Following the confusion of that year, however, the Chinese agreed in 1912 that foreign Commissioners of Customs at all ports should remit the revenue collections to custodian banks in Shanghai and that the service of all obligations should be handled by an international bankers' commission under the general control of the Diplomatic Body in Peking. Although this agreement was never formally abrogated, after the establishment of the National Government in 1928 the Diplomatic Body had ceased to exercise this function and the Chinese had resumed control of revenues, while continuing to observe the 1912 agreement in respect of the service of foreign obligations.

deposited, first, for costs of collection, and secondly, for service of foreign obligations.

4. I assume that in speaking of 'Shanghai share' of foreign loans Financial Adviser meant appropriate share of liability in event of total collections exceeding that liability, but the possibility that total collections may not leave any surplus must be borne in mind. His Majesty's Government could not agree that foreign obligations had been respected if Shanghai Customs merely paid a percentage (based on the past) towards amounts due.

5. While every effort must be made to secure the acquiescence of the Chinese Government I feel that the integrity of the customs administration is so important that refusal by the Chinese Government of any terms which Mr. Hall-Patch is able to negotiate should not preclude agreement on these terms between the four Governments concerned. The Chinese may upbraid us for abetting the Japanese in controlling the disposal of the revenue, but the practical answer will be that the revenue must in any case be withheld by the Japanese from Chinese control and that our action will assist in preventing a default on foreign loans and a consequent blow to Chinese credit and above all in maintaining the customs machinery on a basis of common interest. The 1912 agreement is of very doubtful value legally as an argument vis-à-vis the Chinese Government.[5]

Repeated to Peking No. 560, to Embassy Offices, Shanghai No. 217, to Tokyo No. 497, to Washington No. 534, to Paris, Saving, No. 247.

[5] This telegram was drafted following discussion with Treasury officials (see No. 371, note 3) and sent to Sir F. Leith-Ross for concurrence before despatch.

No. 379

Sir E. Phipps (Paris) to Mr. Eden (Received November 22)

No. 714 Saving: Telegraphic [F 9859/6799/10]

PARIS, November 20, 1937

The Minister for Foreign Affairs tells me that he received the visit this morning of the Chinese Ambassador, who seemed very depressed, and asked whether Monsieur Delbos advised China to address herself to the League of Nations, in view of the probable failure of the Brussels Conference to obtain any redress for her.

Monsieur Delbos told Mr. Wellington Koo that his advice was to avoid the League, which would be unable to give any practical assistance to China, and to stick to Brussels, where at least the United States was present, however disinclined to help it might be.

In this connexion Monsieur Delbos referred to the conversations that he had at Brussels with you and Mr. Norman Davis regarding the vexed question of the supply of arms and munitions over French Railways in

Indo-China.[1] He repeated his fears about possible acts of sabotage by Japanese agents against those railways and even the bombing of them by Japanese aircraft, the possible occupation of Hainan and the Paracel Islands, and finally the unfriendly feeling of Siam towards France. No arguments of mine could shake him, and I feel strongly that to pursue this matter further will merely irritate the French without serving any useful purpose. He again told me that he had received unofficially Japanese warnings to the above effect, though he admitted that there had been no Japanese 'ultimatum'.

Monsieur Delbos said that the French attitude was perfectly simple and straightforward:

France would do anything under a mutual guarantee by Great Britain and the United States of America, and nothing without it. He complained bitterly, but confidentially, about Mr. Norman Davis' unhelpful attitude at Brussels, and in particular about his unwillingness, despite his pressure upon the French over the Indo-China Railways question, even to consider the possibility of adopting some purely negative action in favour of China by agreeing with other Powers to slow down supplies of oil to Japan.[2]

[1] Cf. *D.D.F.*, Series 2, vol. vii, Nos. 198, 202, 207, 217, 219, 228.
[2] Cf. *D.D.F., ibid.*, No. 253.

No. 380

Sir R. Clive (Brussels) to Mr. Eden (Received November 23)

No. 80 Saving: Telegraphic [F 9949/6799/10]

BRUSSELS, *November 22, 1937*

Following from Mr. MacDonald:

The Conference met in private this afternoon and had before it two drafts which had been put forward by the United States, United Kingdom and French Delegations, the first being a draft report to Governments on the work of the Conference, and the second a draft declaration (see my telegram No. 91).[1]

Dr. Wellington Koo expressed regret that the drafts did no more than re-affirm general principles: nothing was said regarding the 'common attitude' contemplated in the previous declaration of the Conference[2], nor was there any reference to the concrete proposals which he had made at the 7th meeting (see my telegram No. 73 Saving[3]). Referring to the previous declaration, he said that this was a clear case of treaty breaking and of armed force used for the purpose. The issue was of vast importance to the world, and speedy action—moral, material, financial

[1] Of November 22, not printed (F 9834/6799/10): see No. 391 below.
[2] See No. 364.
[3] No. 357.

and economic—was necessary. He again asked that concrete aid should be rendered to China and that supplies should be withheld from Japan. Friendly remonstrances made no impression on the aggressor: that indeed was why China had now been forced to fight and to defend not only her own existence but also the peace and civilisation of the world. China's resources were limited and the results of her efforts could not but be modest. The Powers represented at the Conference with their unlimited resources should surely make some positive, even though indirect, contribution. Failure to act would mean that no distinction was made between the victim and the aggressor, and would represent a new defeat for the forces of peace. He would make no detailed comments on the drafts, but reserve the right to propose amendments after consulting his Government.

M. Michel (Mexico) made a statement to the effect that the conflict was not merely contrary to the principles of international law and prejudicial to the interests of China and other Powers, but also represented a serious menace to all weak countries. No means of bringing about a just solution should be neglected and the Powers should refrain from contributing to the financial and economic resources of the aggressor. The signatories of the Nine Power Treaty were bound to unite their efforts in defence of it and States members of the League of Nations had the duty of calling (through the Far Eastern Advisory Committee) for the application of the relevant positions of the Covenant. He hoped, however, that Japan would alter her attitude.

The Conference proceeded to consider the draft report. After some discussion on the question whether such a report were appropriate at this stage, it was decided to alter the title so as to make it a summary of the essential phases of the Conference's work up to date. This summary would be published and its purpose would be to set forth the situation in an objective manner.

No observations of consequence were made on the greater part of the draft, one paragraph, which dealt with the future of the Conference, being reserved for later consideration.

The Conference finally adjourned until Wednesday afternoon[4] in order that Delegates might consult their Governments regarding the two drafts.

The text of the draft report in its present form is contained in Brussels Conference despatch No. 33.[5]

[4] i.e. November 24.   [5] Of November 22, not printed (F 9962/6799/10).

No. 381

Sir R. Clive (Brussels) to Mr. Eden (Received November 23)

No. 81 Saving: Telegraphic [F 9950/6799/10]

BRUSSELS, *November 22, 1937*

Following from Mr. MacDonald:

The following is a brief appreciation of the discussions at Brussels during the last three days. Contact between the American Delegation and ourselves has been almost continuous. On our return Lord Cranborne, Sir Alexander Cadogan and I endeavoured to get Mr. Norman Davis to agree that the United States and the United Kingdom should make a declaration of their readiness to offer good offices to the two parties in the Far Eastern conflict whenever the situation should seem favourable, keeping other Governments informed of any developments. We urged that if such a declaration were made it would give the Conference a reasonable excuse for adjourning its sittings at least until the new initiative had been given a chance to develop.

But Mr. Davis was from the first strongly opposed to this suggestion. He used all sorts of arguments to combat it, urging especially that such a move was premature. In the same way he resisted the suggestion that the Conference should give our two Governments a mandate to offer conciliation if and when they thought fit. He said that he hoped that such an initiative by the United States and the United Kingdom would become possible a little later, but insisted that it could not be until after the Conference had suspended its sittings. In view of the later telegrams which began to come in from Tokyo and Washington, and which indicated that an offer by our two Governments at the present moment would not be favourably received in Japan[1], we felt it impossible to press this point further.

The American Delegation and ourselves had in the meantime been considering various possible draft declarations by the Conference on its adjournment. It would be wearisome to repeat in any detail the course of arguments which continued hour after hour. It was at the suggestion of the Americans, which they pressed hard, that the two documents were prepared for adoption by the Conference: the first, a summary of the Conference's proceedings up to date, and the second a declaration of the position in which the Conference now finds itself. But the documents which have now emerged and been laid before the Conference are very different from those which the Americans conceived and drafted. The original American draft of the first document referred to above started with a more or less objective account of the Conference's proceedings, but finished with five or six pages of indictment of Japan couched in fiercer language than even Geneva has yet employed. The second document was in the form of resolutions which, amongst other things, called upon the

---

[1] Cf. No. 374, note 3.

two parties in the Far East to cease hostilities immediately. The Americans also desired something in the nature of a hint of possible pressure upon Japan at a later stage, though Mr. Davis kept agreeing that the prospect of American opinion agreeing to any such action had not yet materialised.

Mr. Davis and his principal adviser, Dr. Hornbeck, proved extremely obstinate in maintaining the view that this was the proper way to deal with the situation. Our discussions continued for the best part of two days. Towards the end of them, when Mr. Davis was in his most obstinate frame of mind, I remarked that we might have thought his proposals wise if there had been the slightest chance of following our brave words with effective action. He himself had told Mr. Eden and the rest of us at the beginning of the Conference that if we made two or three reasonable offers to Japan and these were rejected, American public opinion would be gradually worked up to a pitch at which it would support strong action. We had made two reasonable offers to Japan and both of them had been rejected. But the effect on American opinion seemed to have been nil. He and we knew from messages from Washington that his Government did not feel that they could take any action which would require legislation. He himself had suggested that they would be prepared to declare that they would not recognise any alteration of the status quo in China, and that they would not lend money to Japan for the development of any conquest she made. But now we learned that his Government were not even ready to do that.[2] I did not criticise the American Government for their attitude; we in London agreed with them that any such declaration would be, to say the least, premature. But really if those were the facts of the situation, what was the use of our asking the Conference to use the sort of strong language which he had in mind? These remarks were followed by a painful silence. It seemed that for a whole minute Mr. Davis' brain ceased to function. When he recovered his power of speech progress with the drafting became more rapid.

We are not proud of either of the documents which have been produced, but the first is now on the whole, we think, a fair objective report of the Conference's experiences up to date, and the second at least avoids the major foolishnesses which might have gone into it. Despite the many hours of argument and counter-argument between the Americans and ourselves, relations between the two delegations have remained cordial, and co-operation is still complete.

The French delegation were conspicuous by their absence until this (Monday) afternoon. But on being shown the two documents they at once asked that they should be made jointly responsible for them with the Americans and ourselves. The Dominion delegations have all approved both documents in principle, though they are suggesting a few amendments of detail. I am reporting separately on the attitude of the Chinese delegation.[3] It would not appear at present that any insuperable difficulties will be presented by other delegations.

[2] Cf. Nos. 351, 355, and 356.   [3] See No. 382 below.

No. 382

Sir R. Clive (Brussels) to Mr. Eden (Received November 23)

No. 82 Saving: Telegraphic [F 9951/6799/10]

BRUSSELS, *November 22, 1937*

Following from Mr. MacDonald:

Dr. Wellington Koo and Mr. Quo Tai-chi called this morning on the United Kingdom Delegation and the American Delegates were also present at the conversation. They were given copies of the draft of the report and declaration which had been agreed with the United States Delegation, and which were to be circulated to the Conference today.[1]

After reading through these documents, Dr. Koo stated that he could not at the moment make any detailed comments. He would probably have a number of amendments to make. But he wished at once to say that the Chinese Delegation could hardly avoid feeling disappointed: they wanted more encouragement from the Conference than could be found in the documents which he had just read. The Chinese armies had now for some months been putting up a strenuous resistance to the Japanese onset, but the morale of the Chinese people, and indeed of the Government, would suffer considerably if it was felt that they had to continue that resistance without any hope of help from outside. The Chinese army had been provided at the outset of hostilities with certain reserves of ammunition, but the rate of expenditure had been much higher than could ever have been anticipated and the stocks were running very low. It was essential for the maintenance of Chinese morale that some arrangements should be made for assuring the supplies of war material for the Chinese armies.

It was pointed out to Dr. Koo as on the previous occasion, that in point of fact the Chinese Government were free to purchase arms wherever they could find them and to arrange shipment. Mr. Norman Davis added that if an attempt were made to organise the supply of arms to China, that would be certain to give rise to a demand in the United States for the strict application of the Neutrality Act. Mr. MacDonald also pointed out that it would be inevitable that in the event of large quantities of supplies going through Hongkong to China, the Japanese Government would find it convenient to declare a formal state of war and blockade. The result might be that the Chinese Government would receive even less war material than at present.

Dr. Koo insisted that some steps should be taken to facilitate the supply of war material: he did not suggest that the Conference itself could do anything in the matter, but hoped that it might be possible to have discussions 'on the side' in a committee of representatives of countries from which supplies might be expected. It was explained to Mr. Koo that the difficulties, such as they were, in the various countries, were of a

---

[1] See No. 381.

different nature and that any joint meeting would be unlikely to facilitate matters.

Rather fortunately Mr. Norman Davis took the lead in this discussion and was emphatic in his declaration to the Chinese Delegate that it would be impossible for the United States to take any active measures to encourage the shipment of war material to China.

Dr. Koo explained that in addition to the material difficulties of obtaining arms and arranging transport there was also the question of credits. On this point Mr. Norman Davis was even more emphatic that any assistance in the matter of credits would involve legislation which was quite out of the question.

Both Mr. Davis and Mr. MacDonald assured Dr. Koo that they fully sympathised with the Chinese Government in their difficulties and were willing to do anything that might be practicable to assist. They suggested that in the first place Dr. Koo should communicate a statement of China's needs and proposals, and each Government would then examine this statement and see whether any special measures could be devised. It was probably a matter that could be dealt with best through the diplomatic channel in the various capitals where the necessary experts were at hand to consult.

No. 383

Sir R. Clive (Brussels) to Mr. Eden (Received November 23)

No. 83 Saving: Telegraphic [F 9952/6799/10]

BRUSSELS, *November 22, 1937*

Following from Mr. MacDonald:

In the course of a talk with Mr. Norman Davis yesterday, he read me a cable which he had received from Mr. Cordell Hull, in which the Secretary of State complained that articles were appearing in the American press saying that if the Brussels Conference failed, it would be the fault of the Americans.[1] Mr. Hull pointed out that if this charge were freely circulated in the United States, resentful feelings would be aroused and Anglo-American relations would suffer a setback. He hoped that we could do something at Brussels to prevent such stories being written by the press-men here.

I assured Mr. Davis that he could count on our co-operation in combating such statements. As he knew, our policy from the beginning of the Conference had been one of unqualified co-operation with the United States delegation. Mr. Eden at the very beginning had expressed the hope that whatever policy of action or inaction the Conference might adopt should be adopted on the full joint responsibility of both our delegations.

[1] See *F.R.U.S.*, 1937, vol. iv, pp. 217–8: cf. also pp. 221–4.

We were still working in that spirit, and I thought with some success.

Mr. Davis said that he attached the greatest possible importance to Anglo-American co-operation in international affairs. In his view America had only one vital interest beyond her own shores, and that was the security of the British Empire. He then went on to say that the American Government had themselves to blame for the difficulty they were now in. It arose partly from the President's Chicago speech[2]. The expression 'quarantine' used there had been unfortunate. He, Mr. Hull, and the President had discussed the whole situation and the projected speech three weeks before it was delivered, and at that time no expression such as that had been in the speech. The President had inserted it himself without further reference to him.[3] Now American public opinion had forced the President to retreat some way. He (Mr. Davis) had expressed some surprise about the use of the term to the President after his return from Chicago. Mr. Roosevelt explained that he had wished to find some phrase which conveyed a certain impression without implying hostility against Japan. Therefore he did not want to use the word 'sanctions', nor any other words which might seem to indicate that hostile action was a possibility. 'Quarantine' was the best word that he could find. He instanced the case of a community in which there was an outbreak of some fell disease; red flags were put on the houses of the victims, so that everyone might know what places to avoid. Mr. Davis had replied to the President that in those cases of course the red flag was very effective; but supposing a brigand armed with a machine gun entered the street, it was not much good putting a red flag on him.

He said that he was very disappointed at the way that American public opinion had failed to react to Japan's intransigeance. But he still thought that eventually the American Government would be able to take some action such as a declaration of non-recognition of any alteration of the status quo in China, and of an intention to withhold any financial assistance to any Japanese development schemes in China. He thought that American opinion might develop to this pitch in about a month's time.

[2] See No. 291, note 2.
[3] See *The Memoirs of Cordell Hull* (London, 1948), vol. i, pp. 544–5.

No. 384

Sir R. Clive (Brussels) to Mr. Eden (Received November 24)

No. 84 Saving: Telegraphic [F 9959/6799/10]

BRUSSELS, *November 23, 1937*

Following from Mr. MacDonald.

In the course of a conversation with Mr. Norman Davis this morning I asked him whether there was any possibility of his coming over to London for a day or two before he returned to America.[1] We should greatly like the chance of a talk with him about the next steps regarding the Far Eastern situation, and in any case a visit from him to London would be a demonstration to the world that the United States and the United Kingdom were working closely together in this matter.

He replied that he would very much like to come, but that he had to consider the possible effect of such a visit on opinion in the United States. He had talked with Mr. Cordell Hull on the telephone yesterday evening, and whilst the Secretary of State had assured him that he and the President were still anxious to get something done, he had also said that the isolationists were at present very much to the fore. He thought that American opinion would move gradually, but they had to be careful not to give the isolationists a chance to say that the United States Delegation at Brussels were entering into commitments with the United Kingdom.

Mr. Davis told me that before he left Washington both Mr. Hull and himself had pressed the President not to call the special session of Congress. They had warned him that Congress would only embarrass them in regard to the Far Eastern conflict. But the President had taken a different view, and before Mr. Davis sailed it had been clearly understood that the President would send a message to Congress dealing with the Far Eastern situation. He (Mr. Davis) could well understand that it might have been unwise for that message to go to Congress on the first day of its reassembly, but he had expected that it would at least be sent two or three days later. He was disappointed that it had not been sent, but evidently the situation in Washington was rather difficult at the moment. He was afraid that this left us very much in the air, but hoped that we would understand. He also hoped that we would understand his reasons for not coming to London, if he finally decided that such a visit would be inexpedient.

I replied that we would quite understand the position. Our policy was one of co-operation with the United States in this matter, and we were ready to appreciate the Washington Government's difficulties. As he knew, we were prepared to consider any action regarding Japan that the United States Government were ready to consider; but we could not take any action which the United States were not also ready to take. I hoped that his Government understood that position.

Mr. Davis replied that both he and his Government knew that to be the position.

[1] Cf. *F.R.U.S.*, 1937, vol. iv, pp. 228–9.

No. 385

Mr. Eden to Sir R. Lindsay (Washington)

No. 544 Telegraphic [F 9655/26/23]

Most Secret   FOREIGN OFFICE, November 24, 1937, 4 p.m.

Your telegram No. 399.[1]

We are inclined to doubt whether there exists anything quite so definite as an alliance. On the other hand, we have no doubt that machinery has been set up, at any rate as between Germany and Japan, for a very full exchange of information regarding Communist activities, both inside and outside the U.S.S.R., and it is almost certain that representatives of the two General Staffs compare notes regarding the military activities of the Soviet Government itself. Some provision is believed to have been made for consultation between Germany and Japan if either is threatened with aggression by the Soviet Union and for a sort of malevolent neutrality by the other party if one of them is attacked by the Soviet Union.[2] We have no reason to think, however, that any such arrangement extends to Italy.

As regards exchange of information on general matters, no doubt the three parties would like their co-signatories to believe that they keep nothing back, but in point of fact we do not believe that either Germany or Japan keep Italy in their *full* confidence. There has been, however, for some time past the closest collaboration in Europe between Berlin and Rome[3], and no diplomatic document has of late been dealt with by either party without consultation with the other.

We may expect all three to try to use existence of present agreement and alignment as a diplomatic instrument for the promotion of their own interests in the world at large and, if need be, as a means of organising joint pressure against ourselves in particular.[4] But how much more there is to it than this and to what extent the Pact, or such implications of it, would stand up to any strain it is not yet possible to say.

You may so inform Mr. Hull, but as the foregoing is derived from sources which must on no account be compromised, you should emphasise the absolutely secret character of your communication. You may also add that the gunnery practice recently afforded to the German Fleet by the Italian Government in Italian waters and with Italian targets constitutes facilities for which no precedent exists except between allies in war-time.[5]

---

[1] No. 365. Sir R. Vansittart presented the draft of this telegram to Mr. Eden on November 23 with the comment: 'This is about the size of it—fairly and moderately put, and possibly an understatement.' Mr. Eden noted on November 24: 'Yes. A good draft.'
[2] Cf. No. 9, note 3.   [3] Cf. Volume XIX, No. 225.   [4] Cf. *ibid.*, No. 311.
[5] Sir R. Lindsay presented a memorandum in the sense of this telegram to Mr. Hull on November 27: see No. 394 below, and *F.R.U.S.*, 1937, vol. i, pp. 616–7.

No. 386

British Embassy Offices (Shanghai) to Mr. Eden
(Received November 24, 11.10 a.m.)

No. 227 Telegraphic [F 9976/220/10]

SHANGHAI, *November 24, 1937, 5.27 p.m.*

Following from Financial Adviser:

Foreign Office telegram No. 485 to Nanking[1] and telegram No. 498 to Tokyo.[2]

Okazaki informed me today that diplomatic and military representatives here have decided that he cannot be allowed to negotiate with me formally or informally, and that Tokyo had already been so informed. Negotiations must be conducted by Okamoto[3] with Lawford, and Japanese authorities will brook no interference from any quarter whatsoever. The negotiations will be conducted with due consideration to interests of third parties and when concluded these parties can then protest if they consider their interests have been prejudiced. Japanese authorities require control of administration of Shanghai customs and it is for Lawford to produce a satisfactory plan to this end. If the plan is approved, no attempt will be made to disrupt the customs except in so far as necessary to implement this plan.

2. I pointed out that control implied measures which might affect the disposal of revenue or cause changes in the present system of administration, both of which were questions of international interest and should properly form subject of international negotiations. He could not agree. He expressed his personal regret at this attitude, but he could not depart from his instructions.

3. It subsequently emerged that Japanese authorities would not accept any form of international control of customs revenue. The Japanese had to demonstrate to the Chinese people they were the victors in Shanghai. If customs were not clearly under Japanese control, the Chinese would assume that Japan was afraid of the foreign Powers interested in the maintenance of that administration, and any such suggestion could not be tolerated.

4. I summed up by saying that Japanese proposal appeared to be to drive Lawford into a corner, wring concessions from him under the threat of pressure, and then face the Powers concerned with a *fait accompli*. He agreed. I said this was a most unfortunate attitude and again urged the desirability of negotiation. This he could not accept but offered on a personal basis to keep me informed of progress of negotiations with Lawford on condition that I did not communicate this information to American, French or other foreign representatives. This arrangement I did not accept.

[1] No. 378.   [2] See *ibid.*, note 3.   [3] Japanese Consul General at Shanghai.

5. The tone of the discussion was courteous throughout but Okazaki was rather excited. Negotiations on line suggested in your telegrams under reference, however, seem impossible.

6. I have since been in touch with the French Ambassador[4], who concurs, as he has received reports of similar attitude taken by Okamoto with French Consul-General. He thinks it is for the Government concerned now to take up the question again in Tokyo[5]. But for representations there to be in any way effective he holds that they must be collective, identic and rapid. I agree, but if this course is followed my impression from contacts here is that it will cause great resentment which we must be prepared to face.

7. I have also seen American Consul-General but he (?is without) instructions.

8. I will keep you informed of action taken by Lawford but I fear neither he nor Inspector General of Customs will take a strong line. Their anxiety appears to be mainly for their personal position and unless they are assured of the support of the British, French and American Governments in any stand they make, they will accept very rapidly Japanese demands on grounds that no other course is open to them. This impression is shared by French Ambassador and American Consul-General with whom Inspector General of Customs and Lawford have been in touch. Superintendent of Customs, an Administrative Commissioner, and a revenue accountant of Japanese nationality have already in fact been nominated here by the Inspector General of Customs 'as a routine service arrangement'. Moreover, without any demand being made by Japanese authorities, customs inspections are not functioning on wharves in Japanese-controlled areas of the settlement or on the Pootung side. This is described by Lawford as a 'gesture'. Meanwhile the French Ambassador and I have asked Lawford to give us in writing the plan he proposes to submit to the Japanese.

Repeated to Peking, Nanking and Tokyo.

[4] M. P. E. Naggiar.   [5] Cf. *D.D.F.*, *op. cit.*, No. 265.

No. 387

Sir R. Clive (Brussels) to Mr. Eden (Received November 25)

No. 86 Saving: Telegraphic [F 10036/6799/10]

BRUSSELS, *November 24, 1937*

Following from Lord Cranborne:
Brussels telegram No. 80 Saving.[1]
The Conference met in private this afternoon, and further considered

[1] No. 380.

527

the two drafts mentioned in my Saving telegram under reference.

2. Certain amendments put forward to the President by various delegations had already been incorporated in the draft declaration and the Conference, after making a few more amendments of a minor character, decided to combine the two drafts into one and to issue this document as its Report. (This was done at the suggestion of M. de Graeff (Netherlands), who said that while he himself thought the second declaration unnecessary he would not oppose it if the Conference wished it included.)

3. Dr. Wellington Koo said that the Chinese delegation could not regard the result of the Conference's work as satisfactory. He had already shown that concerted action was necessary to restrain the aggressor and restore peace. He noted that the Conference was only suspending its work temporarily in order to afford time for Governments to exchange views and further explore ways of settling the dispute, and he emphasised his conviction that such efforts could only be successful if undertaken promptly and actively: moreover, it was indispensable to consider common action in the form of assistance to China and pressure on Japan.

4. At Dr. Koo's request it was agreed that his statement should be appended to the Report.

5. Count Aldrovandi (Italy) observed that the doubts he had expressed at the opening session with regard to the possible results of the Conference's work had proved well-founded. He was in favour of the Conference adjourning or even dissolving itself permanently. He disagreed entirely with the arguments put forward in the Report. He had no objection, however, to the Report being issued in the name of the Conference provided that the statement he had just made were appended to it.

6. The Report was then adopted, and it was decided that certain documents in which the Chinese and Japanese Governments had stated their case should be annexed to it, Mr. Bruce (Australia) having stressed the need for strict impartiality in selecting these documents.

7. Mr. Norman Davis then made a speech thanking the Belgian Government for their courtesy and M. Spaak for his able Chairmanship, and summing up the results of the Conference's work up to date. The Powers represented would, he said, continue to study the problem with undiminished interest. Indeed the necessity for them to continue their efforts to find a solution was even greater than before. The problem was not a new one, but was simply a new aspect of a situation which had long caused anxiety and involved many varying interests. Much had been gained by the exchange of views which had taken place at Brussels. The problem concerned different Governments in different ways and each would now have a clearer conception of its difficulties. The enunciation of fundamental principles in the Report would contribute to the formation of world opinion.

8. I associated myself on behalf of His Majesty's Government in the

United Kingdom with what Mr. Davis had said. While I understood and fully sympathised with the disappointment of the Chinese delegation, I thought it must be agreed that the conclusions embodied in the Report were those which alone could practically have been reached at this stage of the Conference's work. The Governments represented would keep in the closest touch, and His Majesty's Government would for their part gladly concert with any of them for the purpose of furthering the objects for which the Conference had met.

9. M. de Tessan (France) spoke on similar lines. He hoped that all the Powers would continue to discharge their duties under the Nine Power Treaty. France, faithful to the Conference's terms of reference, would associate herself with all steps taken with a view to ending the conflict by means of a just settlement.

10. Dr. Wellington Koo proposed that the Report should be communicated officially to all Governments for their information. This was agreed to.

11. The Conference listened appreciatively to a short speech by Mr. Jordan (New Zealand) expressing sympathy with China and appreciation of Dr. Koo's advocacy. After a vote of thanks to the Belgian Government and M. Spaak proposed by Senator Dandurand (Canada), the President adjourned the Conference saying that though the Powers participating in it had reason to be disappointed they should not be discouraged by its results.[2]

[2] The Report of the Brussels Conference was transmitted to the Foreign Office in despatch No. 42 of November 25: No. 391 below.

No. 388

Extract from Cabinet Conclusions No. 43(37) of November 24, 1937

[F 10024/9/10]

5. The Secretary of State for Foreign Affairs reported that the situation in the Far East was deteriorating, particularly from the point of view of British interests. He instanced the trouble that had arisen in the Chinese Maritime Customs. Difficulties in this respect had arisen first at Tientsin and, though those had been surmounted, they had now arisen in a more acute form at Shanghai, where the Japanese had seized all the customs vessels.[1] The Governments of the United Kingdom, the United States of America and France had protested but the difficulty had now arisen as to what was to be done with the proceeds of the customs. The amounts were only just sufficient to pay the interest on guaranteed loans. Instructions had been sent to our representatives to try and get the receipts paid into a neutral bank, but the Japanese would probably insist on their being paid

[1] See Nos. 371, 373, and 377–8.

into a Japanese bank. The Chinese would not agree to this, but we should probably have no alternative but to accept. The result was that the Japanese were, in effect, taking our property but we had not the force to resist. He thought the time might come when we should have to approach the United States Government and ask if they would send ships to the Far East if we would do the same.

The Prime Minister said it was clear that we could not put forceful pressure on the Japanese without co-operation of the United States and, while he had no objection to the Foreign Secretary making an approach, he felt sure that the reply would be that American interests were not sufficient to justify the despatch of ships and that American public opinion was not much concerned.[2]

[2] As a result of this discussion a draft telegram to Washington was prepared stating that in view of the Japanese disregard for international interests His Majesty's Government would 'seriously consider increasing their naval forces in the Far East with the object of demonstrating to the Japanese Government that they are prepared in the last resort to support [their] representations by a display of force, provided that the United States Government are willing to take similar action'. The draft instructed Sir R. Lindsay to enquire whether the U.S. Government would despatch 'a suitable number of capital ships' to the region of Manila if British ships were sent to Singapore.

On November 26, however, Sir A. Cadogan discussed the draft with the First Sea Lord, Lord Chatfield, who was concerned that the Cabinet had not realised the implications of such a decision. It would be necesary to send a force which would be almost able to cope single-handed with the Japanese fleet, and there was also a risk that the U.S. Government would not cooperate but 'might allow it to leak out that we had made this proposal, thereby attracting against us to no purpose the fury of the Japanese Government'. He suggested that the draft be reworded 'in such a way as to make it a sounding of the American Government as to their views, rather than as an indication that we were prepared to do something provided that they would follow'. An amended draft was prepared which was initialled by Mr. Eden and despatched on November 27: No. 392 below.

No. 389

Mr. Eden to Sir R. Craigie (Tokyo)

No. 513 Telegraphic [F 9976/220/10]

Immediate   FOREIGN OFFICE, *November 25, 1937, 5.10 p.m.*

Embassy Offices, Shanghai, telegram No. 227[1].

1. His Majesty's Government take the strongest possible exception to the attitude of the Japanese authorities in Shanghai. The Customs administration and revenues are, as has already been recognised by the Japanese Government, an international interest, and His Majesty's Government cannot admit that any arrangement can properly be reached between local Customs officials (influenced by threats of military pressure)

[1] No. 386.

and Japanese authorities in Shanghai without reference to them and to the other Governments concerned. They cannot doubt that the Japanese Government will recognise the right of His Majesty's Government to be fully associated with any negotiations regarding the functioning of the Customs during the present hostilities and they cannot understand how the Japanese diplomatic and military authorities at Shanghai should have had the effrontery to refuse to permit Mr. Okazaki to negotiate with Mr. Hall-Patch and to state that they had 'informed Tokyo' of this decision. Mr. Hall-Patch has, as a matter of convenience, been authorised to carry on negotiations in Shanghai, but any arrangement which he might reach would naturally be subject to acceptance by the Governments concerned conveyed through their representatives in Tokyo.

2. As soon as your U.S. and French colleagues have received instructions, you should make strong representations on the above lines to the Minister for Foreign Affairs personally.

3. Meanwhile you should as a first step present to the Japanese Government in pursuance of the communication which you have made on the lines of para. 2 of my telegram No. 490[2] the arrangement propounded in Embassy Offices, Shanghai, telegram No. 157 to Nanking[3]. You should not disclose that this arrangement has been suggested to Dr. Kung by his own advisers, but you may indicate that you have reason to believe that it might be acceptable to the Chinese Government.

[2] No. 373.
[3] In this telegram of November 23, which was sent to Nanking as a message to Dr. Kung, Mr. Hall-Patch set out a scheme for the administration of the customs which he suggested should be proposed to the Japanese by the British, French, and American Governments. An International Bankers Commission, comprising one representative of each of the American, British, French, and Japanese banks, should act as a trustee for foreign interests. Deposits should be divided equally between the foreign banks, and payments would be made in order of priority out of nett customs revenues. The Inspector General of Chinese Customs would operate this scheme under the supervision of the Commission.

No. 390

Minute by Lord Cranborne

[F 10092/6799/10]

FOREIGN OFFICE, November 25, 1937

As the attitude of the United States Delegation at Brussels is likely to be of considerable importance from the parliamentary point of view in the near future, it may be of use if some attempt is made to assess it, at any rate during the last three days of the Conference. During this period, the United States and British Delegations were in constant, close and cordial contact. Mr. MacDonald, and, after he had left, I, had each day several interviews with Mr. Norman Davis. Moreover, it was agreed between us that should the Chinese Delegation ask for any interviews in connexion with the Draft Resolution of the Conference, we should receive them jointly, as the joint authors of the document. This arrangement had the advantage, from our point of view at any rate, that we could be sure that Mr. Davis was saying the same things to us and the Chinese. In the event, two such meetings were held. At these meetings, Mr. Davis, though not always intelligible, was always frank. He made it abundantly clear to Dr. Koo that the United States could not and would not at the present time co-operate in any measure of material assistance to China. He did not rule out the possibility of a change in the future. But for the moment the situation was unfavourable. There had been a bad setback in business in his country. Isolationist feeling was temporarily dominant. Mr. Davis was indeed at times almost brutal in his frankness. When Dr. Koo explained that French nervousness over the transport of arms through Indo-China might be removed by a joint guarantee by other Powers to make their fleets available in the event of an emergency, he received the blunt reply, 'If the United States Government were willing to send the American Fleet across the Pacific, all these dangers might be removed. But the United States Government are not willing'. Similarly, when Dr. Koo asked for the granting of credits by the United States Government to China for the purchase of arms, Mr. Davis answered, 'That would require legislation. We are not prepared to introduce legislation'.

In private conversation with members of the British Delegation he was more optimistic about the possibility of American action in the future. He did not rule it out. Mr. Hull did not rule it out either. It should, however, be added that Dr. Hornbeck of the United States Delegation, did not share Mr. Davis's optimism. He thought that a very big change would have to come over the United States before there was a chance of any American action other than conciliatory.

In the sphere of conciliation, Mr. Davis remained unalterably opposed to any joint public offer by the United States and Great Britain to mediate in the Conflict.[1] He did not 'want that baby left on our doorstep'. It would lead to nothing but humiliation for both of us. The other signatories of the Nine-Power Treaty would feel themselves entirely absolved from any further responsibility in the matter. Nor, for the same reasons, would he have anything to do with a joint offer of good offices in the future. The position of 'postman' or as he called it, 'errand boy', did not appeal to him. We could not divorce ourselves from responsibility for the terms we transmitted from one party to the other. If they did not accord with the principles of the Nine-Power Treaty, we should be humiliated and disgraced.

While holding this view, he was, curiously enough, attracted by the idea that Great Britain and the United States should take the initiative in jointly putting forward proposals of their own to both sides. It was pointed out to

[1] Cf. F.R.U.S., 1937. vol. iv, pp. 229–30.

him that this too might involve even more direct departure, on the part of Great Britain and the United States of America, from the principles of the Nine-Power Treaty. No terms that conformed to those principles were likely at the present time to be acceptable to Japan. First and foremost, we should come straight up against the question of the territorial integrity of China. He swept this aside, indicating that though obviously we could not agree to any infringement of the territorial integrity of China, we need by no means be so rigid about the administrative integrity. There were, moreover, many other concessions in the economic sphere which China might very properly make. It must, however, be confessed that when he came nearer to concrete proposals, he became vaguer. At one moment, Dr. Hornbeck suggested that China might be asked to recognise the independence of Manchukuo. Mr. Davis at once interrupted, 'Dr. Hornbeck does not mean this as a definite proposal. He is only speaking illustratively'. Similarly, when Mr. Davis made a concrete suggestion, Dr. Hornbeck interrupted with the valuable word 'illustrative'. It was indeed extremely difficult to make out exactly what 'concept', to use a favourite word of his, was moving in Mr. Davis' mind, and it is doubtful both whether he was quite clear himself and whether he was, in any case, speaking on instructions from his Government. We pointed out that recent experience had not convinced us as to the advisability of taking the initiative in recommending solutions in such circumstances as these. Finally, however, I said that I would pass on what he had said to the Secretary of State.

C.

No. 391

Sir R. Clive (Brussels) to Mr. Eden (Received November 26)

No. 42 [F 10044/6799/10]*

BRUSSELS, *November 25, 1937*

The United Kingdom delegation to the Nine-Power Conference presents its compliments to the Under-Secretary of State for Foreign Affairs, and has the honour to transmit herewith a copy of a report of the Brussels Conference dated the 24th November, 1937.[1]

[1] A copy of this Report is also printed in *F.R.U.S., Japan 1931–1941*, vol. i, pp. 417–22. An Extract from Cabinet Conclusions of November 24, when Mr. MacDonald made his report to the Cabinet on the Brussels Conference, has already been printed in Volume XIX of this Series, No. 347.

Report of the Brussels Conference dated November 24, 1937

The conference at Brussels was assembled pursuant to an invitation extended by the Belgian Government at the request of His Majesty's Government in the United Kingdom with the approval of the American Government. It held its opening session on the 3rd November, 1937. The conference has now reached a point at which it appears desirable to record the essential phases of its work.

2. In the winter of 1921–22 there were signed at Washington a group of inter-related treaties and agreements of which the Nine-Power Treaty regarding principles and policies to be followed in matters concerning China constituted one of the most important units. These treaties and agreements were the result of careful deliberation and were entered upon freely. They were designed primarily to bring about conditions of stability and security in the Pacific area.

The Nine-Power Treaty stipulates in article 1 that

'The contracting Powers, other than China, agree

(1) To respect the sovereignty, the independence, and the territorial and administrative integrity of China;

(2) To provide the fullest and most unembarrassed opportunity to China to develop and maintain for herself an effective and stable Government;

(3) To use their influence for the purpose of effectually establishing and maintaining the principle of equal opportunity for the commerce and industry of all nations throughout the territory of China;

(4) To refrain from taking advantage of conditions in China in order to seek special rights or privileges which would abridge the rights of subjects or citizens of friendly States, and from countenancing action inimical to the security of such States.'

Under and in the light of these undertakings and of the provisions contained in the other treaties, the situation in the Pacific area was, for a decade, characterised by a substantial measure of stability, with considerable progress toward the other objectives envisaged in the treaties. In recent years there have come a series of conflicts between Japan and China, and these conflicts have culminated in the hostilities now in progress.

3. The conference at Brussels was called for the purpose, as set forth in the terms of the invitation, "of examining in accordance with article 7 of the Nine-Power Treaty the situation in the Far East and to consider friendly peaceable methods for hastening the end of the regrettable conflict now taking place there.' With the exception of Japan, all of the signatories and adherents to the Nine-Power Treaty of the 6th February,

1922, accepted the invitation and sent representatives to Brussels, for the purpose stated in the invitation.

4. The Chinese Government, attending the conference and participating in its deliberations, has communicated with the other parties to the Nine-Power Treaty in conformity with article 7 of that treaty. It has stated here that its present military operations are purely in resistance to armed invasion of China by Japan. It has declared its willingness to accept a peace based upon the principles of the Nine-Power Treaty and to collaborate wholeheartedly with the other Powers in support of the principle of the sanctity of treaties.

5. The Japanese Government, in replying with regret that it was not able to accept the invitation to the conference, affirmed that 'The action of Japan in China is a measure of self-defence which she has been compelled to take in the face of China's fierce anti-Japanese policy and practice, and especially by her provocative action in resorting to force of arms; and consequently it lies, as has been declared already by the Imperial Government, outside the purview of the Nine-Power Treaty'; and advanced the view that an attempt to seek a solution at a gathering of so many Powers 'would only serve to complicate the situation still further and to put serious obstacles in the path of a just and proper solution.'

6. On the 7th November, 1937, the conference sent, through the Belgian Government, to the Japanese Government, a communication in the course of which the conference enquired whether the Japanese Government would be willing to depute a representative or representatives to exchange views with representatives of a small number of Powers to be chosen for that purpose, the exchange of views to take place within the framework of the Nine-Power Treaty and in conformity with the provisions of that treaty, toward throwing further light on points of difference and facilitating a settlement of the Sino-Japanese conflict. In that communication the representatives of the States met at Brussels expressed their earnest desire that peaceful settlement be achieved.

7. To that communication the Japanese Government replied in a communication of the 12th November, 1937, stating that it could not do otherwise than maintain its previously expressed point of view that the present action of Japan in her relations with China was a measure of self-defence and did not come within the scope of the Nine-Power Treaty; that only an effort between the two parties would constitute a means of securing the most just and the most equitable settlement, and that the intervention of a collective organ such as the conference would merely excite public opinion in the two countries and make it more difficult to reach a solution satisfactory to all.

8. On the 15th November, the conference adopted a declaration in the course of which it affirmed that the representatives of the Union of South Africa, the United States of America, Australia, Belgium, Bolivia, Canada, China, France, the United Kingdom, India, Mexico, Netherlands, New Zealand, Portugal and the Union of Socialist Soviet Republics

'. . . consider that this conflict of concern in law to all countries party to the Nine-Power Treaty of Washington of 1922, and to all countries party to the Pact of Paris of 1928, and of concern, in fact, to all countries members of the family of nations.'

9. In the presence of this difference between the views of the conference and of the Japanese Government there now appears to be no opportunity at this time for the conference to carry out its terms of reference in so far as they relate to entering into discussions with Japan towards bringing about peace by agreement. The conference therefore is concluding this phase of its work and at the moment of going into recess adopts a further declaration of its views.

10. The text of the communication sent to the Japanese Government on the 7th November, 1937, reads as follows:

'1. The representatives of the States met in Brussels on the 3rd November last have taken cognisance of the reply which the Japanese Government sent in on the 27th October to the invitation of the Belgian Government, and the statement which accompanied this reply.

2. In these documents the Imperial Government states that it cherishes no territorial ambitions in respect of China, and that, on the contrary, it sincerely desires "to assist in the material and moral development of the Chinese nation", that it also desires "to promote cultural and economic co-operation" with the foreign Powers in China, and that it intends, furthermore, scrupulously "to respect foreign rights and interests in that country".

3. The points referred to in this declaration are among the fundamental principles of the Treaty of Washington of the 6th February, 1922 (the Nine-Power Treaty). The representatives of the States parties to this treaty have taken note of the declarations of the Imperial Government in this respect.

4. The Imperial Government, moreover, denies that there can be any question of a violation of the Nine-Power Treaty by Japan, and it formulates a number of complaints against the Chinese Government. The Chinese Government for its part contends that there has been violation, denies the charges of the Japanese Government, and, in turn, makes complaint against Japan.

5. The treaty has made provision for just such a situation. It should be borne in mind that the exchange of views taking place in Brussels is based essentially on these provisions, and constitutes "full and frank communication" as envisaged in article 7. This conference is being held with a view to assisting in the resolving by peaceful means of a conflict between parties to the treaty.

One of the parties to the present conflict, China, is represented at the conference and has affirmed its willingness fully to co-operate in its work.

The conference regrets the absence of the other party, Japan, whose co-operation is most desirable.

6. The Imperial Government states that it is "firmly convinced that an attempt to seek a solution at a gathering of so many Powers whose interests in East Asia are of varying degree, or who have practically no interests there at all, will only serve to complicate the situation still further and to put serious obstacles in the path of a just and proper solution".

It should be pointed out that all of these Powers which are parties to the treaty are, under the terms of this instrument, entitled to exercise the rights which the treaty confers upon them; that all Powers which have interests in the Far East are concerned regarding the present hostilities; and that the whole world is solicitous with regard to the effect of these hostilities on the peace and security of the members of the family of nations.

However, the representatives of the States met at Brussels believe that it may be possible to allay Japan's misgivings referred to above; they would be glad to know whether the Imperial Government would be disposed to depute a representative or representatives to exchange views with representatives of a small number of Powers to be chosen for that purpose. Such an exchange of views would take place within the framework of the Nine-Power Treaty and in conformity with the provisions of that treaty. Its aims would be to throw further light on the various points referred to above and to facilitate a settlement of the conflict. Regretting the continuation of hostilities, being firmly convinced that a peaceful settlement is alone capable of ensuring a lasting and constructive solution of the present conflict, and having confidence in the efficacy of methods of conciliation, the representatives of the States met at Brussels earnestly desire that such a settlement may be achieved.

7. The States represented at the conference would be very glad to know as soon as possible the attitude of the Imperial Government towards this proposal.'

11. The text of the declaration adopted by the conference on the 15th November, 1937, reads as follows:

'The representatives of the Union of South Africa, the United States of America, Australia, Belgium, Bolivia, Canada, China, France, the United Kingdom, India, Mexico, Netherlands, New Zealand, Portugal and the Union of Socialist Soviet Republics have drawn up the following declaration:

"1. The representatives of the above-mentioned States met at Brussels, having taken cognisance of the Japanese Government's reply of the 12th November, 1937, to the communication addressed to the latter on the 7th November, 1937, observe with regret that the Japanese Government still contends that the conflict between Japan and China lies outside the scope of the Nine-Power Treaty, and again declines to enter into an exchange of views for the purpose of endeavouring to achieve a peaceful settlement of that conflict.

2. It is clear that the Japanese concept of the issues and interests involved in the conflict under reference is utterly different from the concept of most of the other nations and Governments of the world. The Japanese Government insist that, as the conflict is between Japan and China, it concerns those two countries only. Against this, the representatives of the above-mentioned States now met at Brussels consider this conflict of concern in law to all countries party to the Nine-Power Treaty of Washington in 1922 and to all countries party to the Pact of Paris of 1928, and of concern in fact to all countries members of the family of nations.

3. It cannot be denied that in the Nine-Power Treaty the parties thereto affirmed it to be their desire to adopt a specified policy designed to stabilise conditions in the Far East, and agreed to apply certain specified principles in their relations with China and, in China, with one another; and that in the Pact of Paris the parties agreed "that the settlement or solution of all disputes or conflicts of whatever nature or of whatever origin they may be, which may arise among them, shall never be sought except by pacific means".

4. It cannot be denied that the present hostilities between Japan and China adversely affect not only the rights of all nations but also the material interests of nearly all nations. These hostilities have brought to some nationals of third countries death, to many nationals of third countries great peril, to property of nationals of third countries widespread destruction, to international communications disruption, to international trade disturbance and loss, to the peoples of all nations a sense of horror and indignation, to all the world feelings of uncertainty and apprehension.

5. The representatives of the above-mentioned States met at Brussels therefore regard these hostilities and the situation which they have brought about as matters inevitably of concern to the countries which they represent, and—more—to the whole world. To them the problem appears not in terms simply of relations between two countries in the Far East, but in terms of law, orderly processes, world security and world peace.

6. The Japanese Government has affirmed in its note of the 27th October, to which it refers in its note of the 12th November, that in employing armed force against China it was anxious to 'make China renounce her present policy'. The representatives of the above-mentioned States met at Brussels are moved to point out that there exists no warrant in law for the use of armed force by any country for the purpose of intervening in the internal régime of another country, and that general recognition of such a right would be a permanent cause of conflict.

7. The Japanese Government contends that it should be left to Japan and China to proceed to a settlement by and between themselves alone. But, that a just and lasting settlement could be achieved by such a method cannot be believed. Japanese armed forces are present in enormous numbers on Chinese soil and have occupied large and important areas

538

thereof. Japanese authorities have declared in substance that it is Japan's objective to destroy the will and the ability of China to resist the will and the demands of Japan. The Japanese Government affirms that it is China whose actions and attitude are in contravention of the Nine-Power Treaty; yet, whereas China is engaged in full and frank discussion of the matter with the other parties to that treaty, Japan refuses to discuss it with any of them. Chinese authorities have repeatedly declared that they will not, in fact that they cannot, negotiate with Japan alone for a settlement by agreement. In these circumstances, there is no ground for any belief that, if left to themselves, Japan and China would arrive in the appreciably near future at any solution which would give promise of peace between those two countries, security for the rights and interests of other countries, and political and economic stability in the Far East. On the contrary, there is every reason to believe that if this matter were left entirely to Japan and China, the armed conflict—with attendant destruction of life and property, disorder, uncertainty, instability, suffering, enmity, hatreds and disturbance to the whole world—would continue indefinitely.

8. The Japanese Government, in their latest communication, invite the Powers represented at Brussels to make a contribution to the stability of Eastern Asia in accordance with the realities of the situation.

9. In the view of the representatives of the above-mentioned States met at Brussels, the essential realities of the situation are those to which they draw attention above.

10. The representatives of the above-mentioned States met at Brussels are firmly of the belief that, for the reasons given above, a just and durable settlement is not to be expected of direct negotiations between the parties. That is why, in the communications addressed to the Japanese Government, they invited that Government to confer with them or with representatives of a small number of Powers to be chosen for that purpose, in the hope that such exchange of views might lead to acceptance of their good offices, and thus help towards the negotiation of a satisfactory settlement.

11. They still believe that if the parties to the conflict would agree to a cessation of hostilities in order to give an opportunity for such a procedure to be tried, success might be achieved. The Chinese delegation has intimated its readiness to fall in with this procedure. The representatives of the States met at Brussels find it difficult to understand Japan's persistent refusal to discuss such a method.

12. Though hoping that Japan will not adhere to her refusal, the above-mentioned States represented at Brussels must consider what is to be their common attitude in a situation where one party to an international treaty maintains against the views of all the other parties that the action which it has taken does not come within the scope of that treaty, and sets aside provisions of the treaty which the other parties hold to be operative in the circumstances."

The representative of Sweden made the following statement:

"No one can regret more deeply than does the Swedish Government the fact that the conference's efforts at mediation have so far remained without result. Having to take note of this fact, my Government, which adheres to the principles of the declaration, but which does not possess the same political interests in the Far East as certain other Powers, feels that it is its duty to abstain from voting for this text."

The representative of Norway made the following statement:

"The Norwegian Government accepted the invitation to this conference in the desire thereby to contribute, if possible, to a settlement of the conflict in the Far East by peaceful mediation.
Nobody deplores more than my Government that the efforts of the conference towards such mediation have hitherto been fruitless.
I am quite in accord with the principles underlying the declaration before us and venture to express the hope that it may still prove possible to obtain through mediation a settlement on the basis of those principles.
Referring, however, to my previous declaration made on the 13th instant, I find it proper to abstain from voting."

The representative of Denmark made the following statement:

"I should like to associate myself with the statements just made by my colleagues from Sweden and Norway. Also my country deplores that the efforts for mediation have hitherto not met with success, and I fully share the hope that through means of mediation it may still be possible to obtain some results. For similar reasons as those given by my Scandinavian colleagues, also I think it proper to abstain from voting on the text of this declaration, while fully in accord with the principles laid down therein."

The representative of Italy made the following statement:

"Italy considers the declaration before us as a door open not towards the settlement of the conflict, but rather towards the most serious complications.
Italy does not intend to assume the responsibilities that might devolve therefrom, and she therefore expresses her definitely contrary vote, whilst reserving her attitude as regards all that concerns the subsequent phases of the dispute." '

12. The text of the declaration adopted by the conference on the 24th November, 1937, reads as follows:
'1. The Nine-Power Treaty is a conspicuous example of numerous international instruments by which the nations of the world enunciate certain principles and accept certain self-denying rules in their conduct with each other solemnly undertaking to respect the sovereignty of other

nations, to refrain from seeking political or economic domination of other nations, and to abstain from interference in their internal affairs.

2. These international instruments constitute a framework within which international security and international peace are intended to be safeguarded without resort to arms and within which international relationship should subsist on the basis of mutual trust, goodwill, and beneficial trade and financial relations.

3. It must be recognised that whatever armed force is employed in disregard of these principles, the whole structure of international relations based upon the safeguards provided by treaties is disturbed. Nations are then compelled to seek security in ever-increasing armaments. There is created everywhere a feeling of uncertainty and insecurity. The validity of these principles cannot be destroyed by force, their universal applicability cannot be denied, and their indispensability to civilisation and progress cannot be gainsaid.

4. It was in accordance with these principles that this conference was called in Brussels for the purpose, as set forth in the terms of the invitation issued by the Belgian Government, "of examining, in accordance with article 7 of the Nine-Power Treaty, the situation in the Far East and to consider friendly methods for hastening the end of the regrettable conflict now taking place there".

5. Since its opening session on the 3rd November the conference has continuously striven to promote conciliation and has endeavoured to secure the co-operation of the Japanese Government in the hope of arresting hostilities and bringing about a settlement.

6. The conference is convinced that force by itself can provide no just and lasting solution for disputes between nations. It continues to believe that it would be to the immediate and the ultimate interest of both parties to the present dispute to avail themselves of the assistance of others in an effort to bring hostilities to an early end as a necessary preliminary to the achievement of a general and lasting settlement. It further believes that a satisfactory settlement cannot be achieved by direct negotiation between the parties to the conflict alone, and that only by consultation with other Powers principally concerned can there be achieved an agreement the terms of which will be just, generally acceptable and likely to endure.

7. This conference strongly reaffirms the principles of the Nine-Power Treaty as being among the basic principles which are essential to world peace and orderly progressive development of national and international life.

8. The conference believes that a prompt suspension of hostilities in the Far East would be in the best interests not only of China and Japan, but of all nations. With each day's continuance of the conflict the loss in lives and property increases and the ultimate solution of the conflict becomes more difficult.

9. The conference, therefore, strongly urges that hostilities be suspended and resort be had to peaceful processes.

10. The conference believes that no possible step to bring about, by peaceful processes, a just settlement of the conflict should be overlooked or omitted.

11. In order to allow time for participating Governments to exchange views and further explore all peaceful methods by which a just settlement of the dispute may be attained consistently with the principles of the Nine-Power Treaty and in conformity with the objectives of that treaty the conference deems it advisable temporarily to suspend its sittings. The conflict in the Far East remains, however, a matter of concern to all of the Powers assembled at Brussels—by virtue of commitments in the Nine-Power Treaty or of special interest in the Far East—and especially to those most immediately and directly affected by conditions and events in the Far East. Those of them that are parties to the Nine-Power Treaty have expressly adopted a policy designed to stabilise conditions in the Far East, and, to that end, are bound by the provisions of that treaty, outstanding among which are those of articles 1 and 7.

12. The conference will be called together again whenever its chairman or any two of its members shall have reported that they consider that its deliberations can be advantageously resumed.'

Japanese attacks on British and American shipping: Anglo-American naval conversations

November 27, 1937—January 14, 1938

No. 392

Mr. Eden to Sir R. Lindsay (Washington)

No. 561 Telegraphic [F *10024/9/10*]

Personal & Secret Immediate FOREIGN OFFICE, *November 27, 1937, 12.50 p.m.*

My telegram No. 555.[1]

His Majesty's Government have reached the conclusion that the Japanese Government are unlikely to be effectively deterred by mere representations from damaging seriously the international interests represented by the Chinese customs. Moreover general Japanese attitude shows signs of increasing disregard for rights of third parties or even for the normal courtesies of international life.

In the circumstances His Majesty's Government would be glad to know whether the U.S. Government are beginning to take as serious and anxious a view of the situation as His Majesty's Government do, and whether they feel as His Majesty's Government do that the time has come to take some steps for strengthening our hand in dealing with the Japanese. Such steps would have to be in the nature of demonstrating to the Japanese Government that our two Governments are prepared in the last resort to support representations by an overwhelming display of naval force.

Please therefore inform the United States Government that if they are ready to consider such action, we should be willing to enter into Staff conversations with United States authorities with a view to consider [*sic*] appropriate and adequate combined steps. You will of course realise the necessity for absolute secrecy.[2]

[1] Not kept in F.O. archives.
[2] For the background to this telegram see No. 388, note 2. Sir A. Cadogan had a further conversation with Lord Chatfield, on Mr. Eden's instructions, on November 29, regarding

Repeated to Peking No. 588, to Mr. Howe No. 512, to Embassy Offices, Shanghai, No. 229, to Tokyo No. 520.

the possibility of sending the Fleet to the Far East. Lord Chatfield's view are embodied in No. 402 below.

No. 393

Intelligence (Shanghai) to War Office[1]

No. 3610 Telegraphic [F 10276/35/10]

Secret   SHANGHAI, *November 27, 1937, 2.10 p.m.*

Chinese political situation. Japanese Army is establishing committees to administer occupied territories in Mongolia, Hopei, Shansi and Shanghai area. Nominal heads are Chinese of Anfu party or other individuals prepared to accept Japanese direction but do not as yet include any prominent persons.

Nanking Government organs are being distributed as follows.

Military departments remain Nanking. (?Foreign) and finance Ministries Hankow. Communications and railway ministries Changsha, on last railway open to outside world. Other departments Chungking. Chinese official press report that branches of war and communications Ministries have been established Canton and that Ministries of Finance, Railways and Industries will follow suit.

Chiang Kai-shek is trying to strengthen his position in the Central Provinces by making following recent appointments provincial Governors loyal to him. Chang Chih-chung–Hunan; Ho Cheng-chun–Hupeh; Wu Ting-chang–Kweichow; Chiang Tso-pin–Anhwei. At the same time, former members of the Kuominchun and south western Government, including Chen Chi–Pang and Chiang Kwang-hai, are with following at Hankow.[2]

All (?factor)s point to a realization by Chiang Kai-shek and his former rivals that best course is to hang together as a confederation in interior. They would thus be able to take advantage of any relaxation by Japan and would remain a potential threat to any pro-Japanese administration set up in Central or (?Southern) China. They would also maintain identity as Government of China if any future political bargaining.

It is considered no Chinese General is at present able to advocate cessation of hostilities, since his subordinates realize this would be

---

[1] Received in the Foreign Office on December 1.

[2] Mr. A. Scott, a former Consul in China who was employed in the Foreign Office from November 15, 1937, commented on December 6: 'It is interesting to note that of the appointees named two are of the pro-Jap. party. It may be that C.K.S. in strengthening his own position is keeping in mind the possibility that it may become necessary for him to open neg[otiation]s with Japan.'

followed by disbandment of most of the Chinese army. The peace party thus consist mostly of persons without military affiliations, who dare show their hands only in territory evacuated by Chinese forces.

Unwillingness to surrender is practically confined to the military and intelligentsia, whilst the agricultural and mercantile mass of population are apathetic and would accept peace on almost any terms.

No. 394

Sir R. Lindsay (Washington) to Mr. Eden
(Received November 28, 9.30 a.m.)

No. 433 Telegraphic [F 10138/9/10]

Immediate   Most Secret   WASHINGTON, November 27, 1937, 7.15 p.m.

My telegram No. 432.[1]

I then apprised the Under Secretary of State of your telegram No. 561[2] about Naval Staff conversations of which he took careful notes. He said that he would consult the President but meanwhile he remarked that State Department had the impression that owing to the situation in Europe His Majesty's Government were unable to concentrate very great Naval forces in the Far East. I admitted this impression might exist and suggested elucidation of possibilities could be had through suggested staff conversations.

He then said that arising out of this he would sooner know whether I could now answer Secretary of State's question about precise relations between Governments of Germany, Japan and Italy. I then handed him aide-mémoire of your telegram No. 544.[3] After reading it he said that he would probably wish to speak to me further about this. He thought time had come when our two Governments should exchange very frankly all information on this subject in their possession.

I expect I shall have answer about Staff conversations tonight.[4]

[1] Not kept in F.O. archives: it apparently referred to a conversation between Sir R. Lindsay and Mr. Welles concerning the Shanghai Customs crisis; see *F.R.U.S.*, 1937, vol. iii, pp. 883–4.
[2] No. 392.   [3] No. 385.   [4] See No. 397 below.

No. 395

Sir R. Craigie (Tokyo) to Mr. Eden (Received November 28, 9.40 p.m.)

No. 729 Telegraphic [F 10154/220/10]*

Immediate   TOKYO, November 29, 1937, 2 a.m.

My immediately preceding telegram.[1]

I saw Minister for Foreign Affairs this afternoon[2] one hour after my United States colleague had done so.[3]

After reading my note, His Excellency stated emphatically that he did not want to have trouble with foreign Powers over this question, and that he was determined that due consideration should be given to their views in any settlement reached with Chinese Customs (he remarked in parenthesis that he thought that the military authorities had enough trouble outside the settlement without going to look for more inside). But the Japanese Government felt that as a matter of principle formal agreement on this subject must be not with foreign Powers, but with the Customs Administration as an organ of the Chinese Government. I pointed out that as customs officials were now cut off from contact with the Chinese Government and represented no one but themselves, any arrangement with them (unless approved by the Chinese Government and/or interested Powers) could only be looked upon as a settlement imposed by force. His Excellency held that this would not be the case if the Powers' desiderata were to be given due consideration in preparing the terms of arrangement to be finally reached with customs officials, and that this was his intention.

He said that Okamoto already had instructions to discuss these matters with representative of Powers in Shanghai, but on my insistence he promised to send that [sic] official instructions to get into direct touch with financial adviser and see full consideration was given to our views before any arrangement was come to with the customs. I also urged categorical instructions should be sent to the military authorities on no account to seize the customs pending consideration of the Powers' desiderata, but he declared this to be quite unnecessary, as there was no question of seizure nor of any other action being taken by local authorities without sanction of the Japanese Government.

I was unable to persuade Minister for Foreign Affairs to agree to a round-table conference between representatives of Japan, the other interested Powers and customs. But I think we can, by method of negotiation proposed between the financial adviser (keeping in touch with the proper United States and French officials) and Okamoto, arrive at

---

[1] Not kept in F.O. archives: it apparently reported that Sir R. Craigie and the U.S. Ambassador were to present official notes to the Japanese Government on November 28 regarding the Shanghai Customs; see No. 389.
[2] i.e. November 28.   [3] See *F.R.U.S.*, 1937, vol. iii, pp. 889–90.

much the same result provided Maze and Lawford will hold out against military threats of seizure, which are, in my opinion, purely blackmail. We are far more likely to get satisfactory results by this method than by insisting either that there must be a joint and formal discussion between all interested parties at Shanghai or that any agreement reached between Japanese and customs is to be subject to enquiries of interested parties (latter method raises the question of 'face' with all its dire consequences).

Before leaving Minister for Foreign Affairs, I impressed on him as forcefully as I could the degree of harm which 'the mailed fist' methods of Japanese military would, unless promptly restrained, do to their own country's interest by estranging powerful financial and commercial circles in all countries which counted in the world of finance. What was done now would everywhere be regarded as a test of sincerity of Japan's professions of respect for foreign rights and interests. His Excellency fully concurred and said he had not the slightest intention of alienating the interests I had mentioned.

Repeated to Shanghai.

No. 396

Sir R. Craigie (Tokyo) to Mr. Eden (Received November 28, 8.50 p.m.)

No. 730 Telegraphic [F 10157/220/10]*

TOKYO, *November 29, 1937, 1.40 a.m.*

My immediately preceding telegram.[1]

I feel fairly confident that if financial adviser will at once put forward our desiderata to Okamoto and I back them up here, we should get reasonably satisfactory results. But it is essential that Lawford should agree to nothing meanwhile, and if he yields before these negotiations take effect to what I believe to be a purely imaginary risk in the light of seizure, he would seem to be incurring a serious personal responsibility.

I understand our principal desiderata to be:

1. Deposit of revenue in a neutral bank or banks.
2. Continued payment of sums necessary for service of foreign loans and indemnity and expenses of Customs Administration.
3. Any surplus to remain in the bank.
4. Some form of international control to ensure that above conditions are carried out.

No. 1 would be the chief difficulty, as question of face is involved vis-à-vis Chinese. But I am not clear why we should make big fight over No. 1 if we can secure the other three conditions simultaneously. On the

---

[1] No. 395. Telegram No. 730 was in fact despatched before No. 729, but they have been printed in numerical order.

other hand, I can see that money due principally to third countries should not be deposited in a Japanese bank, but I hope that logic will not be allowed to play too large a part in what should be a practical settlement designed to meet a temporary emergency. We must, of course, resist Japanese effort to settle No. 1 at once and to leave the other matters for subsequent negotiation 'through diplomatic channels' (see Shanghai telegram No. 236[2] to Foreign Office, paragraph 3).

Other suggestions I venture to make are:

1. That we should recognise that Chinese Government are for the moment out of the picture, and that we should make the best arrangement we can without them.

2. That no more publicity should be given than is absolutely necessary to joint representations made here, any public announcement being confined to statement that exchanges of view are proceeding both here and in Shanghai in regard to provisional régime to be set up for administration of Shanghai customs during emergency.

If these recommendations can be approved, I believe matter can be settled not unsatisfactorily. Otherwise, national sentiment here (and presumably also in England) will be further aroused, and a very ugly deadlock may be reached.

Repeated to Shanghai.

[2] Not kept in F.O. archives.

No. 397

Sir R. Lindsay (Washington) to Mr. Eden
(Received November 30, 9.30 a.m.)

No. 437 Telegraphic [F 10254/9/10]

Most Secret   WASHINGTON, *November 30, 1937, 12.48 a.m.*

My telegram No. 433.[1]

1. I was sent for by Mr. Hull this afternoon[2] and I found him more than usually difficult to understand but as result of putting many questions to him the following is an accurate reproduction of what he said.

2. There was first a great exordium on the necessity of most absolute secrecy. If anything transpired about Staff conversations or secret treaties he would get into the worst difficulties with Isolationists in Congress and any possibility of United States Government being able to conduct a far-seeing foreign policy would become more remote. I am sure you will appreciate this and ensure that no leakage can take place anywhere.

3. He also spoke at length on efforts of Administration to educate the

[1] No. 394.   [2] i.e. November 29.

public to a broader view and on the need for patience, from which I inferred that in his opinion you had been travelling too fast in talking about Staff conversations.

4. As to question of relations between the three Powers he said he had lately had information from a secret source which he could not disclose that German-Japanese treaty includes an article the terms of which he gave me textually as follows:

'If either party is attacked or threatened with attack regardless of the circumstances the other must uphold her position and take whatever measures are necessary to uphold her position and both nations will confer on what measures are to be taken for the common good. Opposition to the spirit of the above will be politically resisted by contracting with foreign countries.'[3]

5. The same source had now reported that this article appears also in Italian-Japanese treaty.[4] He regards the source as thoroughly reliable. He had some confirmation of this intelligence from another independent informant. His considered view was that it would be dangerous to act on the supposition that the treaties went less far than this.

6. Text given above is in peculiar language and last sentence hardly makes sense but he insisted that it was right. He gave hint that it was a translation from a foreign language. I will try to get more precise details from Sumner Welles.[5]

[3] See No. 9, note 3. The terms of the article quoted in this telegram correspond broadly to article i of the Agreement printed in *D.G.F.P.*, Series D, vol. i, p. 734, with the important difference that the text in *D.G.F.P.* was limited to the obligation not to do anything to 'ease the situation' of the aggressor should one of the High Contracting States 'become the object of an unprovoked attack or threat of attack by the Union of Soviet Socialist Republics'.

[4] See No. 324, note 2.

[5] On November 30 Sir R. Lindsay sent a letter to Sir R. Vansittart enclosing the text of the 'secret clause' as given to him by Mr. Hull. This letter is filed at F 10616/26/23, together with copies of Washington telegrams Nos. 437 and 438 (see note 7 below). Considerable discussion followed in minutes on this file as to whether to communicate the full text of the secret German-Japanese agreement, as received from British Intelligence sources, to the State Department: cf. No. 9, note 3. Mr. Ronald summed up the situation on December 2: 'It seems to me that we must now choose between three courses, each attended with some danger. (1) We can shut up and decline to say more to the Americans than we have already disclosed to them, in which case we run the risk of irritating them and exciting the suspicion in their mind that we do not trust them. (2) We can answer specific questions put by Mr. Hull and Mr. Welles to Sir R. Lindsay, in which event we run the risks inevitably attendant on transmission of messages by cable, and we cannot tell how far we shall have to go, or (3) we might show Dr. Hornbeck before he returns to America tomorrow the text of the secret agreement and thereby run the risk of the Japanese tumbling to the fact that we can read some of their cyphers.'

Sir R. Vansittart was in favour of showing Dr. Hornbeck a summary of the agreement, rather than the text, and Mr. Ronald did this on December 3, telling Dr. Hornbeck at the same time that 'our information did not bear out story of Italian accession to secret clauses'. Sir R. Lindsay was informed of these developments in telegram No. 579 of December 4, and he was also sent a copy of the summary given to Dr. Hornbeck with a covering letter of December 6 explaining that this method of communication had been chosen as 'not only calculated to provide the Americans with the maximum of information which we feel we

7. As to situation in the Far East United States Ambassador in Tokyo had recently reported from an Italian source that Japanese navy was medi[t]ating a coup, possibly against the Russians, in order to enhance its own prestige. To this he did not attach overmuch importance. As to customs situation at Shanghai United States Ambassador had first represented strong interest of United States Government in integrity etc. of organisation and later had put in formal note insisting on right of United States Government to be consulted.[6] He said that so far Japanese Government had not rebuffed this and there was no indication that Japanese authorities in Shanghai intended to 'run wild'. But their attitude was still ambiguous and he did not pretend to have any confidence in Japanese military authorities.

8. I asked more than once what the answer was to our suggestion of Staff conversations and finally elicited that the answer was to be found in general considerations set forth above and in what would today be said to my Naval Attaché by Navy Department and with this I had to be content.

9. My Naval Attaché who had not seen your telegram dealing with the subject did have conversation with Director of Naval Operations this afternoon but it threw no light whatever on the question at issue.

10. I will make further enquiry tomorrow but meanwhile have no doubt that suggestion of Staff discussions is declined. Secretary of State's tone was entirely friendly throughout.[7]

can safely impart to them but also . . . likely to render unnecessary any further telegraphing on this delicate matter'. Cf. Volume XIX, Nos. 356 and 373.

[6] See No. 395, note 1.

[7] In telegram No. 438, also of November 30, Sir R. Lindsay reported that he had that evening seen Mr. Welles who 'confirmed definitely that [staff conversations] are not now desired mainly because at present State Department do not take quite so pessimistic a view of Japanese intentions as you do'. Mr. Ronald commented on December 1: 'This is a typical American reply, but the situation at Shanghai does appear, temporarily at least, to be a little easier than it was when our telegram in F 10024 [No. 392] was despatched . . .'

No. 398

Mr. Eden to Mr. Howe (Hankow)

No. 526 Telegraphic [F 10157/220/10]*

FOREIGN OFFICE, November 30, 1937, 6.40 p.m.

Tokyo telegrams Nos. 729 and 730 of the 28th November.[1]

1. I agree generally with the views expressed by Sir R. Craigie. Provided that His Majesty's Government are fully consulted before any

[1] Nos. 395 and 396.

arrangement is reached, it appears unnecessary to insist that there should be a formal conference between the interested Powers. On the other hand, there appears to be a real danger that the Inspector-General and Mr. Lawford may capitulate to Japanese threats and agree to something inimical to our legitimate interests. I therefore think that Mr. Hall-Patch should apprise them of the gist of Tokyo telegram No. 729, and advise them to take the attitude in negotiations that they would not agree to anything unless they were satisfied that it was acceptable to the British, United States and French representatives in Shanghai.

2. As regards the position of the Chinese Government, I have already stated in paragraph 5 of my telegram No. 485[2] that the latter cannot be allowed to jeopardise the conclusion of a satisfactory settlement. On the other hand, it would clearly be far better if they could be persuaded at least tacitly to acquiesce in any settlement which is acceptable to His Majesty's Government. Should you see no objection, I shall be glad if you will make every effort to have instructions sent to Sir Frederick Maze giving him a free hand to conclude any temporary arrangement which is approved by the three Powers. This would, I feel, greatly strengthen his position, not only vis-à-vis the Japanese, but also eventually vis-à-vis the Chinese Government; for he must realise that when normal conditions are restored, the latter will be reluctant to accept as an excuse for his present over-timorous attitude the plea of *force majeure*, if that plea cannot be supported by His Majesty's Government.

3. As regards the nature of the agreement to be reached, I consider— though I recognise that there are difficulties which may well preclude it—that the settlement should cover the whole of China, including Tientsin and Chinwangtao. In any event, it must be secured that the North China revenues contribute to foreign loan service, and, on the other hand, that revenues collected in territory still under Chinese control should also do so. I agree with Mr. Hall-Patch that the arrangement outlined in his telegram to you No. 157[3] would be satisfactory as a basis of negotiation. Modifications would no doubt be essential to secure Japanese agreement, but the general principle seems to be sound. I agree with Sir R. Craigie and Mr. Hall-Patch (Embassy Offices, Shanghai, telegram No. 175 to you[4]) that it is hopeless to expect the Japanese to acquiesce in any revenue from the customs reaching the Chinese Government (except, of course, from ports where the former are not yet in control). Although the amount involved can be of little consequence to the Chinese Government, the Japanese might be prepared to accept more of our desiderata in other respects if they were assured that the customs revenues at, e.g., Canton were equally under international control at Shanghai. As regards the custody of the funds, we should, in view of the Tientsin experience, hold out as long as possible for a neutral bank, but as previously stated I am prepared in the last resort to accept the Yokohama Specie Bank; and, in

[2] No. 378.   [3] See No. 389, note 3.   [4] Not kept in F.O. archives.

general, Mr. Hall-Patch should continue to be guided by my telegrams to you Nos. 485 and 493.[5]

Repeated to Peking, No. 605, Embassy Offices, Shanghai, No. 238, and Tokyo, No. 533.

[5] This telegram of November 22 referred to No. 378 and said that an essential part of any arrangements regarding the Shanghai Customs would be 'to obtain definite assurance from Japanese authorities that they would give fullest support to Chinese Maritime Customs in enforcing collection of customs on all commercial imports, including imports from Japan . . .'

No. 399

Mr. Eden to Sir R. Lindsay (Washington)

No. 575 Telegraphic [F 10074/6799/10]

FOREIGN OFFICE, *December 2, 1937, 3 p.m.*

The American press representatives at Brussels in conversation with members of U.K. delegation intimated at least ten days before the conclusion of the conference their intention of attacking the American Delegation for insincerity and laying the blame on their shoulders for conference's lack of success.[1] His Majesty's Government in the United Kingdom would of course deprecate any such criticism as it is their desire that the public should recognise that the two Governments have been and are completely in step. For the sake of future Anglo-American cooperation it is essential that another unseemly wrangle should not develop. At present it appears that American pressmen are disposed to give us credit for what they profess to consider our chivalrous attitude in refraining from blaming the U.S. Delegation and to take up the cudgels on our behalf. This is not a line we should wish to encourage.

I shall be glad if you will keep us informed of such press comment as there is.

[1] This telegram was based on a note addressed to Lord Cranborne on November 23 by Mr. C. Peake, a First Secretary in the News Department, concerning the attitude of U.S. press correspondents at Brussels.

No. 400

Letter from Sir R. Craigie (Tokyo) to Sir A. Cadogan

[*F 71/71/23*]

TOKYO, *December 2, 1937*

My dear Cadogan,

The Ministry for Foreign Affairs have just informed me that, in view of the prevailing anti-British sentiment, the Ministry of the Interior think it advisable that I should have a personal guard whenever I leave the Embassy. Although this is tiresome, I have acquiesced, pointing out that the responsibility for my protection and that of my staff lies of course with the Japanese Gov[ernmen]t. My Soviet colleague is the only one with whom I share this distinction and it is a sad commentary on the deterioration in our relations with Japan. I should not mind so much if other countries came in for their due share of national obloquy, but the Americans and French escape almost entirely and even the Russians are regarded as a sort of traditional bad lot with whom it will be possible to deal later.

The tone of our press, which is far more wounding and contempt[u]ous than anything I see in other nations' papers, has something to do with this. For instance, just when I am getting the J[apanese] G[overnment] in the mood to discuss the Customs Question reasonably with us and to put the brake on their hot-heads in Shanghai, a pompous leading article in the *Times* is telegraphed over full of warnings as to what will happen to Japan if she does not meet our wishes in this matter.[1] If only it could be left to the Ambassador here to deliver warnings in the privacy of the Minister's study, we should get along much faster. And in any case warnings are of little use unless we really mean to take some action if they are neglected—and even so I do beg that the job may be done as much as possible here rather than in the press or in Parliament.

Although conditions have been so unfavourable, I have not been entirely unsuccessful in establishing the beginnings of a position here and, if you would sometimes listen to my suggestions, I believe we could still use it to some effect both as a moderating influence on policy and as a means of preventing a complete *dégringolade* in Anglo-Japanese relations. Putting the matter bluntly, we must try and smother a very natural irritation in order to secure our day-to-day desiderata and build for the future. Above all we must get right out of our heads that these people will be deflected by admonitions or curses: if deeds are not possible, then let us try entirely different tactics: strangely enough, the one thing these people (with some notable exceptions) want is our friendship. Leave the door wide open to this (on the promise of good behaviour) and you will enable us to do a lot here. Close the door (or act so that the Japanese believe the

[1] See *The Times*, November 29, 1937, p. 15.

door to be closed) and this country will go completely to the devil, with the ready assistance of Mussolini and Hitler.

No one knows better than you do how different is the oriental mind to ours and what a different technique is required to that employed in Europe to obtain the same results. But I still feel we can do something by the means I have outlined. This will particularly be the case if something comes of these conversations we appear to be having with Germany.[2] But if, because Japan has committed an aggression, we are now lightheartedly prepared to add her to the number of our sworn enemies, it is best that I should be informed so that I can shape my action accordingly. It would put me in a false position to work for better relations here if there is to be no support from home for this particular policy.

Yours ever,

R. L. CRAIGIE

[2] Cf. Volume XIX, No. 365.

No. 401

Mr. Howe (Hankow) to Mr. Eden (Received December 3, 4.45 p.m.)

No. 706 Telegraphic: by wireless [F 10453/9/10]

Important   HANKOW, *December 3, 1937*

Dr. Kung informed me confidentially this morning that an offer of peace had been received by Chinese Government from the Japanese 'through a third party'. There is little doubt that it is this move which is behind German Ambassador's visit to Nanking where Chiang Kai-shek still is.[1] I was unable to ascertain from Dr. Kung whether above offer was in specific terms or not.

Dr. Kung said that policy of Government was still in favour of resistance. China would not sue for peace. If an offer was received from Japan it was open to China to accept or reject it. Her decision on which of these courses to adopt would depend naturally on the form of the offer but chiefly on whether any or what assistance was given her by the Nine Power Conference or the Powers separately. If it became clear that no material assistance was to be forthcoming then this would influence the attitude to be adopted in considering any offer which came from Japan.[2]

[1] According to *D.G.F.P.*, Series D, vol. i, pp. 787–9, at an interview on December 2 Dr. Trautmann urged General Chiang Kai-shek to agree to negotiate on the basis of the Japanese terms already put to him on November 3: see No. 359, note 2. According to Dr. Trautmann, Chiang Kai-shek agreed to accept the Japanese terms as a basis for negotiation provided that the sovereignty and independence of North China were not violated, that Chinese agreements with third parties were not touched upon, and that the Germans acted as mediators throughout: see *D.G.F.P.*, *ibid.*, pp. 793–6.

[2] On December 3 Mr. Howe and most of the Embassy staff left Hankow for Shanghai: see

Repeated to Peking, British Embassy Offices Shanghai (Shanghai please repeat to Tokyo as my telegram No. 163).

No. 375, note 1. Mr. Gage remained in Hankow with several other members of the Staff to keep in touch with the Chinese Government. In telegram No. 7 to the Foreign Office of December 5 Mr. Gage repeated a telegram from Nanking of December 4 reporting that the Waichiapou had been instructed to inform both the British and Americans of the German approach, which was 'regarded with suspicion as indicating an attempt by Japan to inveigle China into direct discussion'.

No. 402

Mr. Eden to Sir R. Lindsay (Washington)

No. 582 Telegraphic [F 10024/9/10]

Personal & Secret   FOREIGN OFFICE, *December 6, 1937, 6 p.m.*

My telegram No. 561.[1]

It may be useful to Your Excellency to know rather more in detail what is in mind of His Majesty's Government.

In view of Japanese attitude we have to contemplate possibility of reaching a point where they may encroach upon our and other foreign interests to a degree that we find impossible to tolerate.

His Majesty's Government have therefore been considering what means would be at their disposal of making their power felt in Far East.

Capital ship situation in Europe would at present admit of despatch to Far East of a fleet of British capital ships not inferior to Japanese. They would, however, have to be accompanied by a force of cruisers, destroyers, etc. to provide which we should have seriously to denude all our other stations. Even though such a fleet were to be despatched to Singapore, it would have to act there more or less on the defensive and it could not easily engage in any action that would bring direct pressure to bear on Japan. Its despatch would moreover expose us to risk of complications nearer home owing to depletion of our home forces. Decision to send it could therefore only be taken after most serious consideration and in circumstances where our vital interests seemed to require it.

If U.S. Government were disposed to take similar action, problem would be very different. We should still have to send a considerable force, as, if each Government's contribution were markedly inferior to Japanese fleet there would be risk that either or both might suffer defeat or reverse before they were able to join forces and establish superiority.

But if both Governments despatched a considerable force (though less formidable than each would require for dealing single-handed with

---

[1] No. 392.

555

Japan) such a combined superiority might be established as to enable us to bring pressure to bear.

It was with this idea in mind that we suggested Staff conversations that might have elucidated what forces, supposing both Governments were ready to act, each would be able to send, and how cooperation could be effected.

If the U.S. Government were prepared to despatch an adequate fleet, I should be prepared to recommend to His Majesty's Government that they should send a proportionate force to act in conjunction with them, and I have good reason to believe that they would seriously consider it.

You will understand that foregoing is purely for your own guidance and information. I quite realise that it is, for the present at any rate, undesirable to try to press the U.S. Government in the matter.[2]

[2] This telegram was drafted by Sir A. Cadogan on the basis of his conversations with Lord Chatfield: see No. 392, note 2. Sir R. Vansittart wrote on the filed copy: 'I think this is what the S. of S. wanted.'

No. 403

Sir R. Craigie (Tokyo) to Mr. Eden (Received December 6, 5.30 p.m.)

No. 774 Telegraphic [F 10574/6799/10]

TOKYO, *December 6, 1937, 11.30 p.m.*

It is clear that Japan is beginning to feel the need of foreign capital for both present and future requirements at home and in China and Manchuria. Approaches are now being made to the United States financial interests by Japanese industrialists notably by Aikawa of Nippon Sangyo.

Any success obtained by Japan in securing credits in England, France or United States of America would encourage prolongation of hostilities and diminish our chance of exercising moderating influence in final settlement; whereas hope of obtaining economic assistance after the settlement is at present the factor which keeps responsible financial and industrial circles anxious for our good will.

It would therefore be useful if the three Governments concerned could take identical lines with regard to Japanese request for financial assistance in any form. Best answer to any such approach is to say everything must depend on the terms of peace.[1]

[1] In a minute of December 7 Mr. Ronald wrote that Mr. Waley of the Treasury had 'expressed the gravest doubts of the wisdom of advising financial houses to decline to give credit on the political ground suggested by Sir R. Craigie'. A marginal note by Mr. Eden read: 'I am surprised at this. I know of at least one important City House which is in fact taking this action on its own account.' Mr. Orde (December 8) was 'inclined to think that we should encourage the City to use this lever', and Sir R. Vansittart (December 8) stated: 'I wouldn't let *any* of the aggressors have any credits . . . unless they undergo a complete

I have discussed this informally with my United States and French colleagues who agree and are telegraphing to their Governments in the same general sense. My United States colleague states however that State Department are very . . .[2] intervening in such matters though they might be prepared to give advice in the above sense if approached by any United States financial houses.

change of heart.' The Treasury were consulted on the matter in a letter of December 10, and replied on December 16 in favour of a reply on the lines of No. 436 below.
[2] The text was here uncertain.

No. 404

Sir R. Craigie (Tokyo) to Mr. Eden (Received December 7, 1.40 p.m.)

No. 776 Telegraphic [F 10610/9/10]

Confidential   TOKYO, *December 7, 1937, 7.45 p.m.*

Mr. Howe's telegram No. 710.[1]

Events seem likely to move rapidly after fall of Nanking and I should be glad to know for my own information whether any further exchange of views with United States Government has taken place in regard to form and conditions in which Anglo-American good offices would be made available and if so with what result—see my telegram No. 712[2]. In particular it would be useful to know whether His Majesty's Government and/or United States Government would decline to act as intermediary for passing on Japanese terms unless the latter were such as His Majesty's Government could approve.

It is not of course my intention to make use of such information without prior authority but unless I have some general indication of attitude of His Majesty's Government on these points opportunities may be missed for exercising influence in the right direction. Unbending attitude of Japanese Government may not be maintained indefinitely though a decision to withdraw recognition from Chiang Kai-shek would presumably lessen chances of friendly good offices by a third Power.

As regards German and/or Italian good offices I presume position is that while termination of present conflict is more important than means by which this is achieved we should much prefer that ultimate settlement should not be to the credit of these powers.[3]

Repeated to Shanghai Mr. Howe.

[1] In this telegram of December 6 Mr. Howe reported a conversation with T. V. Soong regarding the German Ambassador's approach to Chiang Kai-shek: see No. 401.
[2] In this telegram of November 22 Sir R. Craigie commented on the U.S. aide-mémoire regarding the possibility of Anglo-American mediation: see No. 374.
[3] Mr. Eden wrote 'Yes' in the margin against this paragraph. In a long minute of December 8 on file F 10615/9/10 Sir A. Cadogan argued that 'the time has come to consider

the possibilities of mediation or participation, in some form, in negotiations for a truce or for a general settlement'. He thought it important first 'to clear up with the U.S. Govt. what their attitude would be to any request for their and/or our mediation or intervention' and submitted a draft telegram to Washington on these lines. Sir R. Vansittart (December 9) thought that Mr. Eden would 'wish to mention this projected step to the Prime Minister before actually despatching the telegram', but Mr. Eden wrote on December 10: 'A very good draft. As it does not propose immediate action I think we can send it off without further consultation.' See No. 405 below.

No. 405

Mr. Eden to Mr. Howe (Peking)[1]

No. 710 [F 10665/9/10]

Confidential   FOREIGN OFFICE, December 7, 1937

Sir,

The Chinese Ambassador asked to see me this afternoon when he explained that he had hoped to bring with him the Chinese Ambassador at large[2], but had been prevented from doing so owing to the latter's illness.

2. His Excellency continued that he presumed that I was informed about the recent German attempts to negotiate a settlement in the Far East.[3] I replied that I had received certain conflicting reports and would be grateful if His Excellency could give me his information. The Ambassador then explained that he had received a cable from Nanking from Dr. Kung, the contents of which had been addressed to him personally, and since he was now divulging them he begged me not to repeat them.

3. The German Ambassador had transmitted to Dr. Kung and later to General Chiang Kai-shek certain definite peace proposals which the maintained had the authority of the Japanese Government. His Excellency was quite confident that the German Ambassador had spoken the truth and was quite unimpressed by Japanese denials.[4] These proposals included the creation of a State in Inner Mongolia, similar to that existing at present in Outer Mongolia, this new State to be under Japanese domination; the demilitarisation of almost all the area comprised in the six

---

[1] This despatch was addressed to Mr. Howe at Peking, although he was in fact at Shanghai: see No. 401, note 2.

[2] i.e. Chen Kung-po, Chinese Minister of Propaganda, who was visiting various European capitals on a special mission from the Chinese Government.

[3] See No. 401.

[4] In telegram No. 786 of December 9 Sir R. Craigie reported the Japanese Vice Foreign Minister as saying that the German démarche had been made without the knowledge of the Japanese Government, and that he feared 'it would now be difficult to obtain acceptance by Japan to terms which Minister for Foreign Affairs had outlined to me as being possible in September': cf. D.G.F.P., op. cit., p. 799.

northern provinces of China, these provinces to be administered by a Chinese of whom the Japanese could approve; the creation of a neutral zone round Shanghai which would virtually place that city under Japanese domination; China to join the anti-comintern pact and China to make a trade agreement which would give Japan special privileges in the Chinese market. These conditions, the Ambassador added, had proved quite unacceptable to General Chiang Kai-shek, who had rejected them.[5]

4. At the same time the Ambassador was clearly deeply anxious as to the future. It was the present intention of General Chiang Kai-shek and the Chinese as a whole to continue their resistance to the very last. So long as supplies could reach them resistance would be prolonged. The question was how long supplies would continue to reach them. He feared that the best divisions of the Chinese Army had suffered heavily at Shanghai and time would be needed for the re-organisation of the Chinese Army behind Nanking. The Ambassador fully appreciated our situation and understood that we could take no action which involved sanctions or anything of that character except jointly with the United States, and was also well aware of the present attitude of the United States Government, but he did not conceal his disappointment at Mr. Norman Davis's attitude during the latter part of the meeting at Brussels. His Excellency added that if the Brussels Conference was never to be called together again, the Chinese Government would be compelled to consider whether they should go back to Geneva. At the same time His Excellency clearly felt no enthusiasm for such action and added that the last thing that he wished to do was to embarrass the British and French Governments, who he knew were working in close cooperation and were doing all that they could to help. The Ambassador added in this connexion that supplies were in fact coming through on the French railway in Indo-China, though nothing was being said about it. Certain supplies were also being received from Soviet Russia. His Government had the impression that the Soviet Government were willing to do more than they were doing at present if they could be sure in so doing that they had the general approval of the United States Government and ourselves. I asked the Ambassador what he meant by doing more and he replied that he thought that the Soviet Government might even go so far as to mobilise some troops on the Japanese frontier. I replied that M. Litvinov had never said anything to me at Brussels to imply that such was his Government's view and I had heard nothing of that nature from Moscow. On the contrary M. Litvinov had made it quite clear that his Government was perfectly willing to cooperate in joint action in the conflict in the Far East, provided all the risks were shared alike.

5. Finally the Ambassador said that he had a short time ago left with Lord Cranborne a list of the Chinese Government's suggestions as to the measures of help which they hoped we might be able to give them. I

---

[5] Cf. No. 405, note 1.

replied that I had heard of this list, but had not yet had an opportunity of studying it, and the Ambassador undertook to discuss the matter with Sir Alexander Cadogan.[6]

I am, etc.,
ANTHONY EDEN

[6] On November 29 the Chinese Ambassador had left a memorandum at the Foreign Office setting out Chinese requirements for arms and munitions, with a request that His Majesty's Government would consider what supplies and financial credit could be obtained from Great Britain (F 10659/6799/10). In telegram No. 245 to Shanghai of December 10 Mr. Howe was told that the Ambassador had been given information 'regarding such small quantities of military supplies as might be available for immediate purchase' and that the question of financial assistance was under consideration, although 'question of loan to the Chinese Government for war purposes presents very grave difficulties'. A draft memorandum on this question, concluding that 'in present circumstances there is no prospect of a loan being floated for China in the United Kingdom', was sent to the Treasury and War Office for their comments on December 11.

No. 406

Mr. Eden to Sir R. Lindsay (Washington)

No. 588 Telegraphic [F 10615/9/10]

FOREIGN OFFICE, *December 10, 1937, 6.30 p.m.*

It seems clear that the Japanese Government recently put forward peace proposals to the Chinese Government through the German Ambassador in China. These proposals were rejected by General Chiang Kai-shek.[1] There seems to be considerable doubt whether General Chiang will be able to maintain himself much longer, and his successor might be willing to negotiate on basis of those proposals. If so, negotiations might proceed with assistance of German mediation, and there would presumably be no question of U.S. Government or His Majesty's Government being associated with them.

On the other hand, only yesterday Japanese Ambassador here maintained his conviction that his Government desired Anglo-United States mediation.[2] He confessed that he had received no definite indication from them to that effect but said that he inferred from the 'tone' of their telegrams that they were disappointed that the matter had not been carried further.

[1] Cf. No. 401, note 1. The Chinese Ambassador told Mr. Eden on December 10 that General Chiang Kai-shek had rejected the Japanese terms: No. 406 below. On December 13, however, he admitted that the Generalissimo had 'not rejected these terms out of hand': No. 417 below.
[2] Sir A. Cadogan's record of a conversation with Mr. Yoshida on December 7 is filed at F 10770/9/10.

This seems to me unlikely in present circumstances, but in case events should take such a turn that we were confronted with an invitation from the Japanese Government to participate in some way in negotiations, it seems to me very important that His Majesty's Government and the U.S. Government should agree upon the attitude to be adopted.

In your telegram No. 413[3] you suggested that U.S. Government contemplated 4 separate and distinct steps, the second of which would be consultation between British and U.S. Governments as to nature of good offices and as to procedure involved. It seems to me that it would be desirable to reach agreement on this point in advance, in case we are ever called upon to intervene.

Our idea had been that our role might be to pass proposals from one party to the other. I note State Department consider such procedure would be unwise as it would involve transmission of terms inconsistent with Nine Power Treaty. But I consider this difficulty might be overcome by making it clear that in acting thus we were in no way endorsing proposals or attempting to press them on the other party, but that we were doing so in the hope of eliciting counter-proposals and thus encouraging an exchange of views which might eventually lead to a settlement. State Department in fact add that 'some formula must be found which would make it clear that British and U.S. Governments could not recommend terms of settlement inconsistent with Nine Power Treaty'.

I suggest it would be possible, if invited, to agree to communicate proposals and counter-proposals from one party to the other, without assuming any responsibility for them. It might be objected that that would hardly amount to more than direct negotiation, but it is probable that if Japan were willing to communicate her terms to us she would frame them more moderately than in a direct approach to the Chinese Government. In the light of the conflicting proposals of the 2 parties we could then consult as to the possibility or propriety of attempting to bring the two sides nearer together.

I should be glad if you would put the foregoing to the U.S. Government and request their views, representing to them the importance of our being ready to act together without delay in the event, which I admit is unlikely, of our being called upon to intervene.

Repeated to Tokyo and Embassy Offices Shanghai.

[3] See No. 374, note 1.

C[hief] o[f] S[taff] in [H.M.S.] Bee to R[ear] A[dmiral] Yangtse-Kiang[1]

Unnumbered Telegraphic [F *10816/10816/10*]

Immediate   *December 12, 1937, 10.50 a.m.*

H.M.S. *Ladybird* reports as follows. Begins. British Lumber Company's Tug *Tsingtah* arrived Wuhu from Hsiasanshan[2] at 0730 today with British Consul Nanking, Military Attaché and Flag Captain on board; after these had embarked in *Ladybird* Japanese machine guns opened fire on *Tsingtah* at about 0810. Immediately ordered steam in order to proceed alongside and protest; when I[3] commenced weighing at 0835 a Japanese field gun battery clearly visible on shore opened fire on ships concentrated just above A[siatic] P[etroleum] C[ompany] installation and kept on firing until Ladybird was abreast Wuhu General Hospital and *Tsingtah* was out of range down stream. *Ladybird* [berthed] at 0910. Four direct hits on *Ladybird*, one rating killed, one seriously wounded and several minor injuries including flag captain. Damage to *Tsingtah* unknown. A direct hit was seen on Jardines *Sui[w]o* who was lying astern of *Ladybird*[,] two cables above A.P.C. and one and half cables offshore when action commenced and is still at anchor. Am investigating damage. Ends. *Bee* arrived 0930 and incredible as it may seem was also fired at by shore battery as she turned to come alongside. One shot was fired at a range of four hundred yards and passed over; further firing was stopped by flag captain and Military Attaché who were ashore protesting. I[4] am landing now to endeavour to get in touch with Senior Japanese Military Officer.

[1] Also addressed to the Admiralty, Commander-in-Chief China in H.M.S. *Falmouth*, Senior Naval Officer Shanghai, and British Embassy Hankow, this telegram was communicated to the Foreign Office by the Admiralty.
[2] A minute of December 13 by Mr. Thyne Henderson stated that 'Hsiasanshan, declared a safety zone by the Japanese on Sept. 19, is 13 miles up river from Nanking'.
[3] Presumably the commander of H.M.S. *Ladybird*.   [4] Rear Admiral Holt.

No. 408

C[hief] o[f] S[taff] in [H.M.S.] Bee to Senior Naval Officer Shanghai[1]

Unnumbered Telegraphic [F *10816/10816/10*]

Immediate   *December 12, 1937, 12.25 p.m.*

I have interviewed Colonel Hashimoto temporarily the Senior Japanese Military Officer at Wuhu. I protested strongly against this morning's

[1] Repeated to Commander-in-Chief China, Rear Admiral Yangste-Kiang, and to the Admiralty, who communicated the telegram to the Foreign Office.

extraordinary episode.[2] He made futile excuses but admitted that firing at warships was his mistake and that Japanese had orders to fire at every ship on the river.[3] It is imperative that it be immediately brought home to the Japanese High Command that there are British and foreign merchant vessels and warships at Wuhu and below as the Japanese military at Wuhu appear to be ignorant of this fact. Colonel Hashimoto has been provided with a written statement of the shipping situation at Wuhu and at notified anchorage two miles above Hsia-Sanshan, also of this morning's occurrences. He has agreed that Japanese military shall be suitably represented at the funeral of S.B.A. Lonergan[4] which will take place on shore at 0900 tomorrow Monday.

[2] See No. 407.
[3] The Japanese capture of Nanking was completed on December 13: the order to fire on every ship in the river was presumably aimed at preventing the escape of Chinese troops from the city. Cf. No. 320, note 5.
[4] The rating killed on the *Ladybird*.

No. 409

C[hief] o[f] S[taff] in [H.M.S.] Bee to Senior Naval Officer Shanghai[1]

Unnumbered Telegraphic [F 10816/10816/10]

Important   *December 12, 1937, 6.15 p.m.*

My 1225.[2] I have again interviewed Haschimoto and asked for his advice as to best means of ensuring safety of concentrations above Hsiasanshan.[3] He stated categorically that for the next few days shipping must not move and if it did move would be fired on. He admits he is out of touch with his headquarters. It is useless to argue the point as he has no knowledge of the rights of neutrals or of any undertaking that Japan may have given. He states and I agree that his men are unable to recognise the British flag. *Cricket* who is in charge of concentration has been instructed accordingly. The ships are now proceeding to the notified anchorage and will remain darkened tonight. At Wuhu B[utterfield] and S[wire] tug *Chuting* made passage from A.P.C. installation to alongside *Bee* at B[utterfield] and S[wire] lower pontoon about 1700 without being fired on although all the guns on the bund were trained on her. Haschimoto asked for one hour to get orders to the guns lower down not to fire on her during her return passage. She left here by arrangement with him at 1800 with floodlit white flag and was not seen to be molested. She carried orders

[1] Communicated to the Foreign Office by the Admiralty.   [2] No. 408.
[3] Further bombing attacks on the British shipping above Hsiasanshan took place on the afternoon of December 12. In telegrams despatched from H.M.S. *Bee* at 1.56 p.m. and 4.45 p.m. the Senior Naval Office Nanking reported dive bombing attacks on S.S. *Whangpu* and H.M.S. *Cricket* reported attacks on other British shipping. No ships were hit, and the *Cricket* and *Scarab* had retaliated with machine gun fire.

to ships at and below A.P.C. installation who are out of V/S touch not to move at any cost. Guns on the bund have been firing indiscriminately at anything moving on the river all day. *Bee* and *Ladybird* alongside B. and S. lower pontoon remain covered at point blank range despite my protests. Flag Captain British Consul and Military Attaché are remaining on board *Bee*.

No. 410

C[hief] o[f] S[taff] in [H.M.S.] Bee to Senior Naval Officer, Shanghai[1]

Unnumbered Telegraphic [F 10967/10816/10]

Important   *December 13, 1937, 8.30 a.m.*

Have informed Senior Japanese Military Officer at Wuhu in writing that I intend to proceed (? down river) at noon today Monday to investigate safety of U.S.R.G.B. *Panay* which may have been damaged by air attack. I can get no reply from her by wireless.[2]

[1] Repeated to Rear Admiral Yangtse, Commander in Chief China in H.M.S. *Falmouth*, and to the Admiralty, who communicated it to the Foreign Office.

[2] Further messages from H.M.S. *Bee* received in the course of December 13 revealed that the U.S. gunboat *Panay*, together with the rest of the American convoy, had been destroyed by Japanese bombing on December 12. The crew of the *Panay* abandoned ship: some of the survivors were later picked up by H.M.S. *Bee*. The Standard Oil Company ships *Mei Ping* and *Mei Hsiang* were set on fire, and the *Meian* was beached and abandoned. According to a Reuter's report telephoned to Mr. Peake on December 13, the *Panay*, which was serving as a floating Embassy, was carrying 72 persons, 18 of whom had not been accounted for.

No. 411

Mr. Eden to Sir R. Lindsay (Washington)

No. 591 Telegraphic [F 10961/10816/10]

Most Immediate   FOREIGN OFFICE, *December 13, 1937, 1.5 p.m.*

You will have seen that the Japanese have not only fired on and hit a British warship but have also actually sunk an U.S. warship.[1] They have also made a bombing attack on another British warship. These acts appear to have been deliberate on the part of those firing, and the sustained fire can indeed hardly have been anything else, though those in higher authority will presumably go through all the procedure of diplomatic apology. I mention this to emphasise the aggressive state of mind of those who indulge in these provocative acts. It seems clear that some action will

[1] See Nos. 407–410.

have to be taken by both the United States Government and His Majesty's Government to curb this dangerous spirit before it goes to still more intolerable lengths. There is no doubt that this action should be taken jointly otherwise it will fail to achieve an end which will in any case be difficult to attain. But before considering this action in any detail I would like to have urgently the views of the United States Government.

No doubt United States Government will be contemplating the presentation of a series of stiffly worded demands and if we could have information as to what they are we should be prepared to send similar intimation. More important is the question whether the United States Government will be taking simultaneous action of a more menacing character such as the mobilisation of their fleet or a part of it pending the receipt of the Japanese reply. If anything of the kind were contemplated we should wish to know as soon as possible as in that case we should probably desire to take similar action although of course our ships could not reach Eastern waters as soon as United States ships.[2]

[2] Mr. Herschel Johnson, who called on Sir A. Cadogan on the evening of December 13, said that he had received no official news regarding the sinking of the *Panay*, but had 'only seen a message on his "ticker" to the effect that Mr. Hull at a press conference today had said that the U.S. Govt. cd. not commit themselves to any hypothetical course until they had received all the facts'. Mr. Eden noted: 'This seems wise, so far.'

No. 412

S[enior] N[aval] O[fficer] (Shanghai) to Commander in Chief (China)[1]

Unnumbered Telegraphic [F 11030/10816/10]

Important   *December 13, 1937, 3.25 p.m.*

Japanese Chief of Staff called at 1315 to-day Monday. I was not on board and an apology for incident was made to my executive officer. On my return I went to see Hasegawa he expressed deepest regret for outrages admitting air attack made by naval planes acting against instructions. He stated that Japan must accept full responsibility and has telegraphed Tokyo suggesting reparations. I requested a reply in writing to my protest and this has been promised[2]. I remarked on extraordinary conduct of Colonel Hashimoto[3] which Hasegawa was at first unwilling to believe. He has sent aircraft to drop message on Hashimoto. I have urged

[1] Repeated to Rear Admiral Yangtse, Chief of Staff in H.M.S. *Bee* and the Admiralty, who communicated the telegram to the Foreign Office.

[2] Commander in Chief, China reported in telegram No. 517 to the Admiralty of December 16 that a reply had been received from the Japanese Chief of Staff which was 'satisfactory in tone and contains apology and acceptance of responsibility' but that the Senior Naval Officer's letter had been referred to the Army 'as they were concerned in this case . . . No replies are expected from Army'.

[3] Cf. No. 409.

early down-river release of shipping and H.M.S. *Ladybird* through barrier but was told that this still very dangerous but may be possible in a week. Attitude of Hasegawa is all that could be asked for and his deep concern and distress are manifestly sincere.

No. 413

Mr. Howe (Shanghai) to Mr. Eden (Received December 13, 3.45 p.m.)

No. 716 Telegraphic: by wireless [F 10959/4/10]

SHANGHAI, *December 13, 1937*

Foreign Office telegram No. 527 to Tokyo.[1]

Following from Financial Adviser for Treasury. Begins:

From Japanese officials, bankers, industrialists and military staff officers with whom I am in contact it seems clear that one side of the increasing Anglo-Japanese tension is a misconception that we are giving direct financial support to China. This misconception was evident in Tokyo in May and June owing to Dr. Kung's activities in London[2] and the undesirable and inaccurate publicity surrounding them but since the outbreak of hostilities it has become deep-seated. Even amongst those Japanese civilians well-disposed towards us we are thought to be engaged in financial activities in China which at best are unfavourable to Japan. Amongst the military there are highly placed officers who openly accuse us of lack of neutrality and affirm that if it were not for our direct financial assistance Chinese currency would long since have broken and that its stability is only being maintained by us not out of any wish to help China from a deflation point of view but solely from a desire to frustrate Japan. All efforts to dissipate this misconception locally are received with scepticism and the most irrelevant events are distorted to add fuel to the fire. For instance Rogers' trip to London by air on private affairs is being interpreted as an official visit to mobilise yet greater financial support to enable China's resistance to continue.

2. Some well-considered effort seems to be desirable to make clear to Japan the following points:

A. That His Majesty's Government are giving no direct financial assistance whatever to China.

[1] In Shanghai telegram No. 230 of November 25 Mr. Hall-Patch had reported that the Japanese authorities, anticipating the break up of the Nanking Government, had apparently decided 'to destroy the present financial organisation which they thought was receiving the support from Britain and America'. Foreign Office telegram No. 527 to Tokyo of November 29 asked Sir R. Craigie what he thought was meant by this threat, and instructed him to point out to the Japanese Government that any action which added to the difficulties of the important British financial interests 'would be a matter of grave concern to His Majesty's Government'.

[2] See Nos. 77, note 3, 78 and 92.

B. That British financial institutions here have no relations with Chinese banks or individuals other than the normal relations of banker and client.

C. That our interest in China's financial stability is the general concern of a nation having a large trading and financial stake in this market which will suffer serious prejudice under conditions of currency chaos.

D. That our interest in maintenance of integrity of Customs and Salt Administrations is produced not solely by our concern for legitimate interests of bondholders but also because these organisations are the mainstay of Chinese credit structure and their disruption would adversely affect currency stability.

E. That taking the long view Japan has as great an interest in avoiding a breakdown of China's financial machine as any other nation trading with China.

3. I venture to suggest that these points should be made clear as publicly as possible e.g. by a statement in the House of Commons. Failing this, I suggest diplomatic action in London and/or Tokyo supplemented by a frank talk between the Treasury and Arakawa.[3] Whether these suggestions are acceptable or not I think it most desirable in any case that the Bank of England should make it quite clear to Munakata's successor in London exactly what Rogers is doing here. Japanese bankers and some of the officials have the greatest suspicion of his activities and believe he is a convenient unofficial channel through which is passing the suspected financial assistance of His Majesty's Government to China.

4. Suggestions in two preceding paragraphs are subject to Sir R. Craigie's comments.

5. If any action is taken on these suggestions I should be glad to be advised so that in speaking here to my Japanese contacts I can be conformed.[4]

Repeated to Peking, Tokyo.

[3] Financial Attaché to the Japanese Embassy in London.

[4] Mr. Chaplin, Mr. Ronald, and Mr. Orde favoured the idea of a parliamentary statement on the lines suggested by Mr. Hall-Patch, but on December 18 Sir A. Cadogan stated: 'I am not in favour of advertising non-assistance to China.' Mr. Eden agreed (December 20): '. . . I do not want us to seek to excuse ourselves to the Japanese, or point out to them that we have not done more to assist their victim.' Telegrams 583 and 584 to Tokyo of December 21 informed Sir R. Craigie of this view and set out the lines on which he could reply to any questions from the Japanese Government. Despite further telegrams from both Shanghai and Tokyo requesting permission to give information on this subject to the Japanese, in telegram No. 16 to Tokyo of January 7, 1938 Sir R. Craigie was authorized merely to act on telegrams 583 and 584, and to 'confine yourself to endeavouring to remove misconceptions in conversation with M.F.A. and Vice Minister as occasion offers'.

No. 414

Sir R. Craigie (Tokyo) to Mr. Eden (Received December 13, 2.50 p.m.)

No. 800 Telegraphic [F 10950/10816/10]

Immediate   TOKYO, *December 13, 1937, 8.25 p.m.*

My telegram No. 796.[1]

Minister for Foreign Affairs called on me this afternoon to express on behalf of Japanese Government deep regret at the firing on the *Ladybird* and other vessels involved and at the loss of life and injury caused thereby. Japanese Government had not yet received particulars but had asked for an immediate report and His Excellency promised to communicate with me as soon as this was received. He asked that this message should be conveyed at once to His Majesty's Government.

I thanked His Excellency for his prompt expression of regret and said that I felt sure that continuance of these incidents caused as much dismay to Japanese Government as to His Majesty's Government. With this remark His Excellency cordially and I am sure sincerely agreed.[2]

Repeated to Embassy Shanghai (and for Commander-in-Chief as telegram No. 211).

---

[1] In this telegram of December 13 Sir R. Craigie reported that on receiving news of the attacks on shipping in the Yangtse (see Nos. 407–410) he had called on the Japanese Foreign Minister to protest 'most emphatically' and to urge 'that a suitable apology should be forthcoming at the earliest possible moment'.

[2] Mr. Ronald commented on December 13: 'Expressions of regret are all very well, but what we want and must insist on is the exercise of proper control by the Japanese Govt. over their armies in the field.'

No. 415

Sir R. Lindsay (Washington) to Mr. Eden
(Received December 13, 10.45 p.m.)

No. 464 Telegraphic [F 10976/10816/10]

Most Immediate   WASHINGTON, *December 13, 1937*

I saw Welles this morning and showed him first paragraph of your telegram No. 591.[1] He read it attentively, expressed great appreciation, and said he concurred entirely with views expressed by you.

2. As to action by United States Government, he said that a decision must await arrival of fuller details regarding what had happened, especially as to whether markings of United States gunboat were clear enough to preclude all possibility of error. He himself did not consider

---

[1] No. 411.

even a full apology was sufficient reparation. All he could give me now was his own idea of minimum which United States Government must demand. This should be 1) A full apology, 2) full compensation for all damage done, 3) explicit recognition of treaty right of navigation of river both by warships and by mercantile vessels, 4) full guarantees that modification of this right shall not occur again, 5) punishment of direct offenders, 6) punishment of higher officers responsible for issue of orders which led to bombing.

3. As to this latter point the decision must depend on information to be obtained from Nanking but he mentioned that a telegram from Nanking despatched apparently before bombing took place seemed to indicate that as gunboat and other American vessels left they were being fired upon deliberately by Japanese artillery. He also said that Japanese press officer at Nanking is reported to have stated that foreign ships on Yangtse would be fired on.

4. I assured him that if United States Government were sending a stiff note or notes His Majesty's Government would be anxious to associate themselves with them and equally so if they were to contemplate any naval movement. He welcomed former assurance and promised to let me know immediately any decision that was reached which might be tonight or almost certainly not later than tomorrow morning. If possible he would give me the information before any action was taken. To my latter suggestion he made no direct response but said that he himself believed present incident would arouse liveliest indignation in United States. Later on when we were talking about situation in Europe he said he thought all of us who desire tranquillity had better stop talking and do something.

5. This indicates that he himself and perhaps Secretary of State are impatient at inaction but it does not necessarily indicate much more. Mr. Welles is a highly competent diplomatist but he is not a politician and I do not trust his estimates of public opinion. My immediately following telegram[2] rather confirms my own impression that we cannot yet feel confident of a violent reaction in this country.[3]

[2] No. 416 below.
[3] For Mr. Welles' account of this interview see *F.R.U.S.*, 1937, vol. iii, pp. 798–800.

No. 416

Sir R. Lindsay (Washington) to Mr. Eden
(Received December 13, 11.30 p.m.)

No. 465 Telegraphic [F 10977/10816/10]

Most Immediate   WASHINGTON, December 13, 1937, 4.6 p.m.

My immediately preceding telegram.[1]

On my return to Embassy Under Secretary of State called me to the telephone and said he had just been instructed by President to send following message from him to Emperor of Japan through Japanese Ambassador.[2]

President had been profoundly shocked by indiscriminate firing by Japanese armed forces on American vessels both private and government. United States authorities were assembling all pertinent facts with a view to representations which would shortly be made and he desired that Japanese Government would also prepare necessary material to enable them to respond by making fullest apologies by undertaking to pay (? highest) required compensation, and by giving the most binding assurances that there should be no repetition of such incidents.[3]

---

[1] No. 415.   [2] See F.R.U.S., 1937, vol. iv, pp. 496–7.
[3] In his telegram No. 466· despatched at 4.22 p.m. on December 13, Sir R. Lindsay added that he had told Mr. Welles 'that if he was disposed to have anything like naval conversations mentioned by me on December 1st [see No. 397] I would be able to say something but this elicited no response whatever'.

No. 417

Mr. Eden to Mr. Howe (Peking)[1]

No. 734 [F 11085/6799/10]

FOREIGN OFFICE, December 13, 1937

Sir,

The Chinese Ambassador asked to see me today, when he said that on a previous occasion[2] he had reported to me the terms of settlement which had been brought to General Chiang Kai-shek by the German Ambassador. General Chiang Kai-shek had not rejected these terms out of hand,[3] but had said that he was willing to discuss certain of them. Since then nothing further had been heard from the Japanese and it was indeed evident that the latter had greatly increased their terms.[4] This was but one example of how impossible it was to try to come to any arrangement with

---

[1] Cf. No. 406, note 1.   [2] See No. 406.
[3] Cf. No. 405, note 1.   [4] Cf. No. 406, note 4.

the Japanese. The present position was therefore that all negotiations were at an end and that the fighting must continue. General Chiang Kai-shek and the Chinese Government were now more than ever convinced that they must continue their resistance. To this end they had been for some little time past endeavouring to collect war material and the position in that respect had recently improved. At the same time it was vital for the Chinese Government to receive more supplies. They required direct aid in considerable quantities. It was especially important that this aid should reach them within the next two or three months. The Chinese Government fully appreciated the importance to them of the fact that Hong Kong was being kept open for the supply of munitions. They wished, however, to emphasise the significance of the appeal which they had made to us and to the United States and French Governments for the grant of credit facilities. He greatly hoped that we would consider this question urgently and sympathetically with a view to arranging to give the Chinese Government a real measure of assistance. After all the battle which the Chinese Government were now fighting alone was one in the outcome of which they were not alone interested. The Chinese Government were making great efforts to re-equip themselves. They were now training armies near Hankow and they were receiving certain supplies of aeroplanes from Soviet Russia. These they were concentrating until such time as they had sufficient forces to make effective use of them. But in the end all must depend upon the supplies which they could obtain from overseas. They would not require credits for small supplies, but the big supplies which they sought might have a decisive effect on the war. It was in respect of these that they asked for credit facilities and His Excellency once again earnestly begged that His Majesty's Government would examine his request with a view to some effective assistance being given to China.[5]

I am, etc.,
ANTHONY EDEN

[5] Cf. No. 406, note 6. In a minute of December 20 on file F 11300/4/10 Mr. Orde recorded that on December 10 the U.S. Embassy had telegraphed to Washington to ask what the U.S. Government thought of the Chinese memorandum presumed to have been communicated to them as well as to the British and French Governments. On December 15, however, the answer came back that the Chinese Ambassador at Washington had raised the question but had made no specific request.

No. 418

C[hief] o[f] S[taff] in [H.M.S.] Bee to R[ear] A[dmiral] Yangtse[1]

Unnumbered Telegraphic [F 11103/10816/10]

December 14, 1937, 2.3 p.m.

Okamura of Japanese Embassy and a staff Officer of Admiral Hasegawa's arrived by air. A staff officer of Rear Admiral Konda (who I gather is at Nanking) arrived by destroyer. All three called and have conveyed to me a formal apology for the Wuhu incidents[2] and thanks for assistance given to the Americans[3].

[1] Repeated to Commander in Chief China in H.M.S. *Falmouth*, Senior Naval Officer Shanghai, Hankow, Nanking, and to the Admiralty, who communicated it to the Foreign Office.
[2] See Nos. 407–410.   [3] Cf. No. 410, note 2.

No. 419

Mr. Eden to Sir R. Lindsay (Washington)

No. 594 Telegraphic [F 10976/10816/10]

Most Immediate   FOREIGN OFFICE, December 14, 1937, 3.10 p.m.

Your telegrams Nos. 464[1], 465[2], 466[3] and 467[4].

I think it important that what you said to Mr. Welles should be said to Mr. Hull himself, and I therefore request that you will seek interview with latter at earliest possible moment, and make sure that he is personally aware of attitude of His Majesty's Government.

You should thank Mr. Hull for his courtesy in communicating text of note which United States Government are sending to Japanese Government. You should tell him that His Majesty's Government are drafting a note on similar lines for presentation in Tokyo. British note, in referring to question of specific guarantees of non-recurrence of such incidents, will demand punishment of offenders, which has in fact already been offered to us by Japanese Minister of War. It seems to us that that might be the one effective step that the Japanese authorities could take to deter members of their forces from what they allege to be irresponsible and unauthorised acts. I will telegraph text of note, directly it is ready, for communication to Mr. Hull.

You should however not conceal from him that His Majesty's Govern-

[1] No. 415.   [2] No. 416.   [3] See No. 416, note 3.
[4] This telegram of December 13 forwarded the text of the note which the U.S. Ambassador was instructed to present to Mr. Hirota: see No. 416. See also *F.R.U.S., Japan 1931–1941*, vol. i, pp. 523–4.

ment are somewhat disappointed that note should have been despatched before there had been opportunity of consultation with them. His Majesty's Government feel that in this instance joint action would have been more effective[5].

I wish you moreover to add that His Majesty's Government feel that they cannot contemplate a continuance of this process of successive and increasing outrages followed by simple apology. They fear that Japanese, finding that nothing worse follows, may be encouraged to go to lengths which we shall not be able to tolerate, and that we shall then be faced with the necessity of taking very drastic action. They are inclined to think that it may be better, before it is too late, to take some measures or make some dispositions to show Japan that they are determined to protect their nationals and interests.

We have already sounded United States Government on possibility of naval movements[6], and you should explain to Mr. Hull that what we had in mind was that on such an occasion as this the two Governments might have proceeded, for instance, at least with some measures of mobilisation, to show Japan that we were in earnest and the rest of the world that we were not so unable—as they are beginning to say we are—to defend our legitimate interests.

We feel that we have rather missed a chance of concerting measures with that object. Nevertheless, we feel strongly that the situation has been getting progressively worse, and may be expected to continue to do so. If the United States Government share this feeling, would they be prepared to consider with us some further steps to arrest this deterioration and to uphold the authority of the Western nations in the East.

His Majesty's Government are carefully considering the whole matter and I will telegraph to you shortly, for communication to Mr. Hull, the result of their deliberations.

[5] In his telegram No. 468 of December 14 Sir R. Lindsay had reported that Mr. Welles had told him that 'it had been necessary to send note to Japanese Government immediately in order to anticipate presentation of a note of apology by them. He regretted that this had made previous consultation with His Majesty's Government impossible'. Mr. Orde commented on December 15: 'There is a little in this excuse, but it is not adequate.'

[6] See No. 397.

No. 420

Mr. G. P. Young[1] (Peking) to Mr. Eden
(Received December 14, 4 p.m.)

No. 884 Telegraphic: by wireless [F 11021/9/10]

Immediate   PEKING, *December 14, 1937*

Addressed to Mr. Howe No. 854.

My telegram No. 853.[2]

Meeting of interested parties was held at noon December 14th to settle new administration. According to informant present at meeting composition of new régime which will be announced tomorrow morning is as follows: (For particulars of career see *Who's Who in China*.)

Wang K'e-Min, Minister of Finance, Ch'i Hsieh-yuan, Public Security, Chu Shen Justice, Tang Erh-ho, Cultural Affairs and Secretary General, Chiang Chao-tsung, Kao Ling-wei, Tung Kang, Tsao Ju-lin. President not yet decided but see my telegram No. 847.[3] Name of new Government will be Provisional Government of the Chinese Republic. Propaganda leaflets calling for support of this Government have been freely distributed from aeroplanes this afternoon.

New régime will set up office in old Waichiaopu building. Members include several survivals of Anfu Hankow and Chihli cliques and returned students from Japan but Government is regarded as compromise between demands of Kita and those of Wu Pei-fu.

Repeated to Tientsin and Tokyo.

---

[1] Second Secretary in H.M. Embassy at Peking.

[2] Mr. Young had reported in telegram No. 882 of December 13 that according to a Japanese spokesman Nanking was now considered to be officially occupied and that an announcement concerning a new North China régime would be made on the following day. Mr. Young's telegram No. 853 of December 14 to Shanghai, repeated as No. 883 to the Foreign Office, gave some details of publicity arrangements in connexion with the launching of the new régime.

[3] In this telegram of December 11, repeated as Peking telegram No. 878 to the Foreign Office, Mr. Young reported that according to information given to the Reuters correspondent the President of the new régime would be Ts'ao K'un. Mr. Scott noted on December 13 that Ts'ao K'un 'bought himself the Presidency of China by the most shameless and heavy bribery in 1923 and remained President until Feng Yu-hsiang's coup d'état in Sept. 1924 . . . It is amazing how the Japanese can persuade themselves that they are replacing a bad administration by a good and conforming to the "Kingly way" by putting corrupt ex-Peking Govt. officials into power'.

No. 421

Sir R. Lindsay (Washington) to Mr. Eden
(Received December 15, 9.30 a.m.)

No. 470 Telegraphic [F 11048/10816/10]

Important Very Confidential   WASHINGTON, December 14, 1937, 10.54 p.m.

Your telegram No. 594.[1]

I saw Mr. Hull this afternoon and said to him that you could not hide it from him that you regretted speedy action which had been necessary and that you thought that joint action would have been preferable. An opportunity had thus been missed for taking measures which might have a preventive character. The present situation was exceedingly disagreeable. We were suffering successive and increasing outrages followed by perfunctory apologies which had no meaning and we could not contemplate a continuance of this. The Japanese had come to think that nothing would make us defend our own interests and the situation must grow worse. There were still wider elements of disintegration present, namely that predatory Powers were encouraged while a corresponding discouragement was to be observed amongst all who desire orderly procedure and observance of international law. We might now expect at any moment some action that simply could not be tolerated and action of a very drastic nature might have to follow it. Surely it was advisable to do something to show the Japanese that we are determined to protect our nationals and interests. If we had had more time for consultation in the present instance we would have asked United States Government to contemplate some measure of partial mobilization of the two fleets.

Mr. Hull said that for a long time he had been working day and night to educate the American public on the dangers of isolation and on the necessity of co-operating. A little while ago he had addressed a private meeting of 150 congressmen on the subject and had said things which had opened their eyes. He had had all Under Secretaries of the Government at the State Department to talk to them and he discovered that none of them had ever thought of foreign affairs before. He had had newspaper writers of both east and west up to the State Department in batches. He had inspired the recent leader in *New York Times*, which had made such a sensation; and he had sent for Colonel Knox of the *Chicago Daily News* and had made an impression on him. He was trying to arrange in Congress that pacifist mischiefmakers should have their wings clipped. He wanted the people to know that a fleet was a thing meant to be used and to bring them to the point where it would be possible to move fleet without causing a panic. No-one appreciated more than he did that Great Britain and the United States must cooperate and he was putting around everywhere that the two Governments always sought to consult each other, that they were

[1] No. 419.

575

in close cooperation and were habitually conducting their business along parallel lines and this he regarded as very nearly as good as joint action.

I said that underlying message I had just delivered from you was implication that time factor was of particular importance. It was quite clear that at any moment something might happen in the Far East or elsewhere which might precipitate us into most dangerous position, and United States not being ready we might have to face it singlehanded. He said that he perfectly appreciated this and he had been saying so to the President only today. He did not consider present dangerous tendencies could be stopped by any single Power. I asked him what answer President had made. He merely answered that Great Britain had recently had a great shock in the Mediterranean which had enabled her to face the burden of an enormous rearmament programme, but that nothing of that nature had occurred to the United States yet which was therefore necessarily behind. President quite appreciated dangers of situation and he had it in mind to deliver another address on foreign affairs perhaps during this month, but this could not yet be counted on. Mr. Hull concluded by assuring me that he was always quite willing to listen to anything I might have to say.[2]

[2] For Mr. Hull's account of this conversation see *F.R.U.S.*, 1937, vol. iv, pp. 499–500.

No. 422

Mr. Eden to Sir R. Craigie (Tokyo)
No. 635 [F 11084/10816/10]

FOREIGN OFFICE, *December 14, 1937*

Sir,

The Japanese Ambassador asked to see me this morning, when he said that he had come on a most painful mission. He had been instructed by his Government to offer on their behalf an apology for the incidents which had recently occurred on the Yangtse. His Excellency explained that he had received instructions to do this yesterday, but that he had telegraphed back asking for further information about the incidents. This unfortunately he has as yet been unable to obtain since his Government were not in possession of a report.

2. I replied that I fully appreciated how painful it must be to His Excellency to deliver a message of this character. I could not conceal from him the grave view which His Majesty's Government took of these incidents. It was not as if they were the first. On the contrary there had been unfortunately a sequence of such deplorable events beginning with the wounding of our own Ambassador.[1] His Excellency replied that he

[1] See No. 210.

appreciated the added significance which must be given to this incident, since it was not the first of such happenings. He had also been instructed by his Government to ask me whether there was any message I wished to transmit to them. I replied that we should shortly be addressing a note to the Japanese Government. In the circumstances I must ask His Excellency to urge his Government to meet the terms which would be set out in the note fully and completely with the minimum of delay. Only thus could we hope to repair in part the damage which had inevitably been created to relations between our two countries. There were two further steps which I hoped his Government would be able to take. It was of the first importance that they should issue definite orders to the military commanders to make certain that there was no recurrence of incidents such as these. It was unnecessary for me to emphasise to him how extremely grave any such recurrence must be. Secondly I hoped that it would be possible for the Japanese Government to take steps to improve the tone of their press towards us. There was a tendency to pillory His Majesty's Government as the one Government which was giving help to China and to pretend that our attitude was actuated by some special animus against the Japanese Government. It was even being suggested that only financial aid and the supply of armaments from us made possible the continuance of hostilities by China.[2] The Japanese Government must, however, be aware that statements of this kind gave no true picture of the situation. It was quite true, of course, that opinion in this country was sympathetic to the Chinese, but it was also true that German generals had been organising Chinese resistance. This latter fact was never mentioned. If there was to be a real improvement in the relations between our two countries, it was important that the tone of the Japanese press should be modified. The Ambassador undertook to report what I had said to his Government.

I am, etc.,
ANTHONY EDEN

[2] Cf. No. 413.

No. 423

Sir R. Craigie (Tokyo) to Mr. Eden (Received December 14, 9.45 p.m.)

No. 813 Telegraphic [F 11020/10816/10]

Most Immediate TOKYO, *December 15, 1937, 12.27 a.m.*

I this evening[1] received note from Minister for Foreign Affairs of which text is as follows:

'Your Excellency, the Imperial Japanese Government deeply regret the

[1] i.e. December 14.

occurrence of incidents in which H.M. ships *Ladybird, Bee, Cricket* and *Scarab* were accidentally bombed on December 12th[2] in the neighbourhood of Wuhu and Nanking and I hereby offer a profound apology in their name. I have the honour to inform Your Excellency that the Imperial Government immediately took the necessary measures to prevent recurrence of incidents of this nature and to add that they will deal suitably with those responsible for incidents immediately on completion of their investigations and are also prepared to pay the necessary compensation for damage to your country.

The Imperial Government earnestly hope that the occurrence of these unfortunate incidents will not impair the traditional friendship existing between our two countries.

I await, etc., Minister for Foreign Affairs.[']

I am informed that text is being issued to the press here tonight.

Repeated to Shanghai (and for Commander-in-Chief No. 220).

[2] See Nos. 407–410.

No. 424

Sir R. Lindsay (Washington) to Mr. Eden
(Received December 15, 7 p.m.)

No. 471 Telegraphic [F 11072/10816/10]

Most Secret   Most Immediate   WASHINGTON, *December 15, 1937, 1.20 p.m.*

Under Secretary of State told me today that President wishes to see me most secretly probably Friday afternoon[1]. He will talk about Naval Staff conversations and probably suggest procedure for arranging them.

If you have anything to add to or subtract from your telegram No. 582[2] please telegraph it most urgently not later than Friday morning early.

[1] i.e. December 17.   [2] No. 402.

No. 425

Mr. Young (Peking) to Mr. Eden (Received December 15, 6 p.m.)

No. 891 Telegraphic: by wireless [F 11079/9/10]

PEKING, *December 15, 1937*

Addressed to Mr. Howe, Shanghai, telegram No. 867.

My telegram No. 857.[1]

The composition of the new Government according to further details

[1] In this telegram of December 14, repeated to the Foreign Office as Peking telegram No. 886, Mr. Young referred to No. 420 and reported that the new government, which was to

published today is (A) Political commission with Standing Committee including principal persons concerned under Tang Erh-ho. (B) Administrative Commission under Chairmanship of Wang Ke-min with five sections as follows administrative Wang Ke-min, Peace Preservation Chi Hsieh-yuan, Educational Tang Erh-ho, Legislative Chu Shen, Rehabilitation Wang Ti-tang. (C) Judicial Commission under Tung Kang.

2. Further details to follow by post.

3. Chiang Chao-tsung and Kao Ling-wei remain Mayors of Municipalities of Peking and Tientsin, while last named is reported to have been concurrently named as Governor of Hopei Province.

4. No announcement has yet been published regarding abolition of Peking, Tientsin and other local (Peace) Maintenance Associations etc., but it is generally anticipated that this will follow.

Repeated Saving to Tokyo and Tientsin.

consist of three commissions, claimed 'to enjoy already *de facto* recognition by Japan'. A representative of the new régime had told correspondents that 'it was not a Government of North China but of all China and on that basis would seek the recognition of the foreign powers'.

No. 426

Mr. Eden to Sir R. Craigie (Tokyo)

No. 570 Telegraphic [F 11020/10816/10]

Immediate   FOREIGN OFFICE, December 15, 1937, 6.15 p.m.

Please at once address a note in following terms to Japanese Government. I propose to publish here morning of December 16. Begins.

I have the honour, on instructions from His Majesty's Government in the United Kingdom, to address Your Excellency on the subject of the attacks made by Japanese aircraft and land forces on British warships and merchant shipping at Wuhu and near Nanking on the 12th December[1]. These incidents clearly raise grave issues.

At Wuhu, a British tug which had conveyed from Nanking His Majesty's Consul, the British Military Attaché and the Flag Captain to the British Rear Admiral, Yangtze, was attacked by Japanese machine gun fire after transferring these officers to H.M.S. *Ladybird*. The latter proceeded to join the tug in order to protect her, when she observed a Japanese field-gun battery firing on merchant ships concentrated above the Asiatic Petroleum Company's installation. Firing continued and was directed at H.M.S. *Ladybird* herself. There were four direct hits on this vessel: one naval rating was killed, another was seriously wounded and there were several minor casualties, including the Flag Captain. A direct hit was also seen to be sustained by the British merchant ship *Suiwo*. H.M.S. *Bee* then

[1] See Nos. 407–410.

579

arrived on the scene and was also fired on by the shore battery. The commander of H.M.S. *Bee* landed to protest and was informed by Colonel Hashimoto, the senior Japanese military officer then at Wuhu, that the firing on the warships was due to a mistake, but that he had orders to fire on every ship on the river. At a later interview, the same officer stated categorically that if any ships moved on the river they would be fired on and, despite protests, His Majesty's Ships *Bee* and *Ladybird*, after berthing, remained covered by guns at point-blank range.

Near Hsia-Sanshan, above Nanking, where British merchant ships were concentrated in a part of the river previously designated by the Japanese Commander-in-Chief as a safety zone, three separate bombing attacks were made by Japanese aircraft on them and on His Majesty's Ships *Cricket* and *Scarab*, which were with them.

His Majesty's Government have now been glad to receive Your Excellency's note of December 14th[2] offering the profound apology of the Imperial Japanese Government for the attacks on His Majesty's Ships, stating that measures were immediately taken to prevent the recurrence of such incidents, and adding that they will deal suitably with those responsible and pay the necessary compensation.

His Majesty's Government observe that Your Excellency's note makes no mention of the attacks on British merchant vessels, and I am instructed to request that an assurance may be given that all that is said in that note applies equally to these attacks.

His Majesty's Government take particular note of the statement that those responsible will be suitably dealt with. Adequate punishment of those responsible for the particular attacks under discussion seems indeed to His Majesty's Government to be the only method by which further outrages can be prevented. His Majesty's Government cannot but recall previous incidents in which the Japanese Government have expressed regret for attacks made on British nationals and property and have given assurances that adequate steps had been taken to prevent any repetition. They call to mind the attack made on His Majesty's Ambassador in China while travelling by road from Nanking to Shanghai, the subsequent attack on motor-cars conveying British officials on a similar journey, the attacks on British civilians and military posts on the defence perimeter at Shanghai, as well as other incidents, and the repeated assurances of the Japanese Government of their intention fully to respect the interests of third Powers in the present conflict with China. It is clear that the steps hitherto taken by the Japanese Government to prevent such attacks have so far failed in their purpose and His Majesty's Government must now ask to be informed that measures have actually been taken of a character which will put a definite stop to the incidents of which they complain.[3]

Repeated to Washington No. 605.

[2] See No. 423.   [3] This note was published in *The Times*, December 16, 1937 p. 14.

No. 427

Mr. Eden to Sir R. Lindsay (Washington)

No. 607 Telegraphic [F 10976/10816/10]

Very Confidential   FOREIGN OFFICE, December 15, 1937, 7.30 p.m.

My telegram No. 594.[1]

His Majesty's Government believe[2] that the time has now come when it is necessary to consider whether any dispositions could or should be made to give weight to representations to Japanese Government against successive outrages committed by Japanese forces, and to show that they cannot continue to content themselves with apologies and indemnities.

Such dispositions would necessarily involve some demonstration of naval strength and intention to use it if necessary. But everything would depend on securing co-operation of United States Government.

We have already given hints of this to United States Government who have not responded, and I can quite understand that it might be useless and indeed impolitic to press them again at the moment. Therefore, before instructing you to approach them again in the matter I should be glad to know your opinion as to how far it would be prudent to go.

For your information, we have contemplated the possibility of sending to Far Eastern waters a fleet of eight or nine capital ships with the necessary accompaniment of other units if the United States Government would make at least an equivalent effort. Such a fleet might be ready to sail from here in three or four weeks.

If you think that it is useless to make such a proposal at the present moment to the United States Government, do you think we could usefully suggest some less drastic step by both Governments, such as measures to put the fleet in a state of greater readiness (which in our case would involve calling up naval reservists) and/or naval staff conversations?

We are receiving evidence of loss of prestige in the Far East affecting not only the United Kingdom but also all democracies, and consequently His Majesty's Government think that some action should be taken to restore the situation. We fully realise difficulties which United States Government experience with their public opinion, but hope that they might be willing to consider mobilisation as a first step. That might be sufficient in itself, but if, nevertheless, further outrages should occur, United States Government might then be able to go a step further, and would be more prepared to meet a situation with which we might be suddenly faced.

You will understand that you should make no approach to the United States Government pending receipt of further instructions, but your appreciation of the situation would greatly help me.

---

[1] No. 419.

[2] This telegram was drafted in accordance with conclusion 4. of the Cabinet meeting held on December 15: see No. 429 below.

No. 428

Extract from Cabinet Conclusions No. 47(37) of December 15, 1937

[*F 11160/10816/10*]

3. The Secretary of State for Foreign Affairs said that as soon as he heard of the recent attacks on British and American warships and other ships on the Yangtse,[1] he had asked the American Chargé d'Affaires to visit him. He had pointed out to the Chargé d'Affaires the advantages of concerted action and had asked him to suggest to the American Government that they should postpone sending their note to Japan until they had received a message which he was sending them through his Majesty's Ambassador at Washington. He had then sent telegram No. 591[2] to Sir Ronald Lindsay. Notwithstanding this action, the American Government had sent a note to Japan without consultation with us, though they had sent us an advance copy[3]. The reason they gave for this was that they had learnt that the Japanese Government were themselves sending a note of apology and they wished to anticipate it. On the previous evening, he had sent to His Majesty's Ambassador in Tokyo telegram No. 567[4] containing a note for communication to the Japanese Government. Before that had reached Tokyo, he had received a note of apology from the Japanese Government which was published in that day's Press (Tokyo telegram No. 813)[5]. The first question on which he wanted to consult the Cabinet, therefore, was as to what action he should take on the Japanese note. He had held up action at Tokyo until he had had time to read the Japanese note. After doing so, his inclination was to send our original note subject to some minor modifications. In reply to a question, he said that the action demanded in his note was similar to what the Japanese Government had already promised to accord to the Americans. The principal exception was the demand for the punishment of officers. In that respect, our case differed somewhat from that of the Americans since our ships had been fired on by field guns, whereas theirs had been bombed, and the Japanese War Office had already offered punishment.

The Prime Minister thought that unless some punishment could be secured, we should have no guarantee for any mitigation of these outrages in the future.

The Foreign Secretary drew attention also to the demand he was making for assurances of steps to ensure that British Nationals' ships and property in China will not be subjected to further attacks or illegitimate interference. This went beyond what the Japanese had offered.

---

[1] See Nos. 407–410. [2] No. 411. [3] See No. 416.
[4] This telegram, despatched at 9.15 p.m. on December 14, contained the text of a note of protest to be handed to the Japanese Government: telegram No. 568, despatched at 10.35 p.m. on December 14, instructed Sir R. Craigie to suspend action in view of the receipt of the Japanese note reported in Tokyo telegram No. 813 (No. 423).
[5] No. 423.

The Prime Minister said that the important thing was not to ask for more than the Americans. He thought, however, that the demand for punishment was justified by the difference in the forms of attack.

The Cabinet agreed:

To authorise the Secretary of State for Foreign Affairs

(a) To despatch the note contained in his telegram to Tokyo No. 567 of the 14th December, subject to such minor modifications as he deemed necessary in consequence of the receipt of the Japanese note and the discussion at the Cabinet:[6]

(b) To inform the House of Commons that a note had been received from Japan and that a British note had been despatched to Tokyo.[7]

[6] The modified version of the note was despatched to Tokyo in telegram No. 570 on December 15: No. 426.

[7] Mr. Eden informed the House of Commons accordingly on the afternoon of December 15: see 330 H.C. Deb. 5 s., col. 1168.

No. 429

Extract from Cabinet Conclusions No. 47(37) of December 15, 1937

[F 11155/9/10]

4. The Secretary of State for Foreign Affairs drew the attention of the Cabinet to telegraphic messages between the Governments of the United Kingdom and the United States of America, including the following: . . .[1]

Both he and the Prime Minister, whom he had consulted before sending this telegram[2], were very dubious as to whether the Government of the United States of America would feel able to adopt any suggestions of the kind, but they had felt it was necessary that that Government should be informed as to what we had in mind. He had had further consultations with the Prime Minister and First Lord of the Admiralty on the previous day, as the result of which he had prepared a draft of a fresh telegram[3] to Washington, indicating that His Majesty's Government now thought it necessary to make dispositions enabling them to give weight to representations to the Japanese Government against the successive outrages: that they were considering the possibility of despatching a Battle Fleet to Far Eastern waters; that they earnestly hoped the U.S.A. Government would take similar action; and suggesting in that event that Naval Staff conversations were desirable.

The Prime Minister said that the draft telegram had been prepared as

[1] Fairly lengthy summaries of F.O. telegrams Nos. 591 and 594 to Washington (Nos. 411 and 419), and of Washington telegram No. 464 (No. 415) are here omitted.

[2] i.e. No. 419.

[3] This draft has not been found in F.O. archives, but presumably formed the basis for No. 427: see conclusions (a) to (c) below.

the result of conversations he had held on the previous day with the Secretary of State for Foreign Affairs, the First Lord and First Sea Lord of the Admiralty, and Sir Alexander Cadogan. The telegram, however, was to have been drawn on the basis that we were prepared to send a force to the Far East but that we should not act unless the United States were willing to do so. This point was not clear in the draft telegram before the Cabinet, which, if approved in principle, would have to be amended to bring it out unmistakably.

The First Lord of the Admiralty expressed doubts as to whether it was necessary to send this telegram at all. The first telegram had evoked no satisfactory response. He suggested that the American Government might feel that they were being pressed too hard and be irritated by a further telegram. There was, in addition, the danger of leakage. On the whole he thought that to send a fresh message of the same kind would only exacerbate the situation.

The Prime Minister suggested that if a telegram were to be sent it might contain a proposal somewhat short of sending the Fleet: e.g., a mobilisation, which would be easier for the American Government and yet might in itself be sufficient warning to the Japanese.

The question was raised as to what would be the effect of the despatch of a Fleet to the Far East on the position vis-à-vis Italy in the Mediterranean.

The First Lord of the Admiralty said that it would be necessary to arrange with the French Government to be prepared to look after the Mediterranean in the absence in the Far East of our Fleet. This would involve consultations, as the French might have apprehensions as to the safety of the Atlantic.

At this point the Secretary of State for Foreign Affairs read a fresh telegram[4] from His Majesty's Ambassador in Washington which had only just reached him, the effect of which was that, though the President and the Secretary of State at Washington had been doing their best to bring American public opinion to realise the situation, they were not yet in a position to adopt any measures of the kind now contemplated. The Secretary of State remarked that it appeared that some other event would have to happen before the American Government would be prepared to act in the sense we were contemplating.

The Secretary of State for India was convinced that nothing but a display for [? of] force would have any influence on the Japanese. He would advocate sending the draft telegram, hitching it on to the last sentence of the telegram just read from Washington, where it was stated that the Secretary of State would always be glad to listen to anything we had to suggest.

Another view was that it was clear from the telegram just read to the Cabinet that the American Government, though doing their best to bring home the facts of the situation to public opinion, had given us a strong

[4] See No. 421.

hint that they did not want to be pressed at the moment, and consequently that the only result would be to cause irritation. There was also the danger of leakage.

The Secretary of State for Foreign Affairs said that in any event he would want to consult His Majesty's Ambassador in Washington before sending any further message.

The Prime Minister said that everyone would agree in that, but the question was as to the subject on which we were to consult him. It was clear to him, after listening to the telegram that had just been read, that we could not press the U.S. Government to despatch their Fleet to the Far East. It might be said, however, that we had received evidence of loss of prestige in the Far East affecting not only the United Kingdom but also all democracies. Consequently we thought that some action ought to be taken to restore the situation. We realised the difficulties of the American Government owing to public opinion, but would not that Government perhaps be willing to consider mobilisation as a first step? That might be sufficient in itself; but if, nevertheless, further outrages should occur, the Americans might then be able to do more.

The Secretary of State for Foreign Affairs pointed out that 'mobilisation' was rather a formidable word and it might be better to use some phrase such as 'an improved state of readiness of the Fleet'.

In answer to a question the First Lord of the Admiralty said that if the Fleet in the Mediterranean was to move it would be necessary to call up reservists, and three or four weeks would be necessary before it could start.

The Secretary of State for Dominion Affairs suggested that the Foreign Office should keep in touch with the Dominions Office, who might at the appropriate moment send a message to the Dominions, particularly to Australia and New Zealand, enquiring as to whether they would be willing to co-operate.

The question was raised as to whether, supposing that the American Government decided that there was nothing it could do and the inaction of the two countries was followed by further grave incidents affecting our prestige, any British action could be taken alone to rectify the situation. It was recalled that at the time of the crisis in the Mediterranean the mere movement of ships in that Sea had some effect. Could anything corresponding be done in the Far East?

The Prime Minister pointed out that in the Mediterranean we had already had a strong Fleet at hand. In the Pacific, however, the position was quite different as our Fleet was a long way off. To produce a deterrent effect on the Japanese it was useless to send only a few ships, which might only tempt the hotheads of the Japanese Navy to attack them with a view to their destruction in detail. If we acted alone, therefore, we must send nothing less than adequate forces. But if we were to take action alone that would probably make it harder for the American Government to co-operate afterwards. From that point of view, therefore, it would be wiser not to attempt anything by ourselves. In any event he thought that that question should stand over until a further telegram had been addressed to His Majesty's Ambassador in Washington as to how far it would be wise for us to press the United States Government, and until a reply had been received.

The Secretary of State for the Colonies emphasised the importance of not giving the Japanese an excuse to attack Hong-Kong until adequate forces were available in the Far East.

The Cabinet agreed

(a) That before framing any message to the United States Government containing suggestions for dispositions by the two Governments to give weight to representations to the Japanese Government against the successive outrages committed by the Japanese forces, the Secretary of State for Foreign Affairs should consult His Majesty's Ambassador in Washington as to how far it would be prudent to go:

(b) That the telegram to the Ambassador should take into account the trend of Cabinet opinion. It should convey no impression that His Majesty's Government were at this moment contemplating unilateral action. Assuming that the American Government were not at present able to contemplate the possibility of despatching a Battle Fleet to Far Eastern waters on the understanding that His Majesty's Government did the same, the Ambassador should be consulted as to whether he saw any objection to our suggesting some less drastic step by both Governments, such as measures to put the Fleet in a state of greater readiness (which, in our case, would involve calling up Naval Reservists) and/or Naval Staff conversations: (See also Prime Minister's statement on p. 10 marked 'A'[5]).

(c) That further decisions as to our own action should await a reply from His Majesty's Ambassador in Washington.[6]

[5] i.e. the third sentence of para. 11 of this document.
[6] Telegram No. 607 to Washington (No. 427) was despatched in accordance with their conclusions: cf. note 3 above.

No. 430

Sir R. Lindsay (Washington) to Mr. Eden
(Received December 16, 8.15 a.m.)

No. 472 Telegraphic [F 11116/9/10]

Most Immediate   Very Secret   WASHINGTON, *December 16, 1937, 1.20 a.m.*

My telegram No. 471[1] crossed your telegram No. 607.[2]

[1] No. 424.   [2] No. 427.

Having thought over Under Secretary of State's message I rather expect as a matter of pure surmise:

(1) President will be mainly interested in procedure for secret conversations and that he will decide to send a man from here to conduct them in London.

(2) As I told Under Secretary of State that I should have something to say, I shall have to say something to the President by way of opening the conversation. As to this you can instruct me as you like, if you will do it quickly. If I had to face conversation without further instructions I should be inclined (especially if he is more interested in arranging procedure than in actual conversation) to limit myself in the main to more general terms of your telegram No. 582[3] and I should try to avoid tying you down to definite figure of eight or nine ships, but I would say that three or four weeks would be wanted before the fleet could sail.

I would now not in the least mind in any case urging something in the sense of partial mobilization but I hardly expect he would agree to this yet. I expect he will refuse to take any but the most secret steps until his views are more clear as to the development of opinion in this country.

I await your instructions with interest. Please send them as soon as possible as my appointment with the President is advanced.

[3] No. 402.

No. 431

Mr. Eden to Sir R. Lindsay (Washington)

No. 609 Telegraphic [F 11116/9/10]

Most Immediate   Very Secret   FOREIGN OFFICE, *December 16, 1937, 1 p.m.*

Your telegram No. 472[1].

You are authorised to make such use of my telegram No. 607[2] as you think best. I am sure you can judge better than I can how to approach President in this matter, but I should have thought you could give him at least substance of first 2 paragraphs of my telegram No. 607 in whatever form you think most suitable. I had thought that it would be well also to give him a fairly definite idea of degree of effort we should be prepared to make: I have felt that our attitude hitherto of being ready to do whatever the U.S. Government would do might have become embarrassing to the latter, and that it might be easier for them if we privately told them what our ideas were as to possibilities of action. But this again I leave to you.

I suggest it might be helpful to talk on the line that democracies have to meet rising criticism of inaction and helplessness and that the moment has it seems to us now come to do something to restore our damaged prestige.

[1] No. 430.   [2] No. 427.

Firm action would have its effect not only in the Far East but in Europe, and would give notice to Dictators that democratic Governments are as jealous of their authority as they are, and as willing and as able to maintain it.

Please take an opportunity of expressing to the President and to Mr. Hull the Prime Minister's and my warm appreciation of the helpful and friendly collaboration of the U.S. Government. We understand their difficulties and we wish to do nothing to embarrass them, but[3] they can count upon us to do anything in our power here to facilitate Anglo-U.S. collaboration. More than ever do we believe that only thus can the peace of the world be assured without a shot being fired.[4]

[3] This telegram was drafted by Sir A. Cadogan, but was redrafted from this point by Mr. Eden.

[4] Mr. Chamberlain's keen hopes of profit from the Yangtse situation are shown in a letter from him to his sister Hilda of December 17, preserved in the Chamberlain papers. He wrote: 'The fortunate misfortune on the Yangtse has stirred up the Americans properly and the brilliant account in the *Times* this morning ought to sting them a bit more. It seems to me just a Heaven sent opportunity and you can bet your bottom dollar I am making the most of it. It is always best & safest to count on *nothing* from the Americans except words but at this moment they are nearer to "doing something" than I have ever known them and I can't altogether repress hopes.' He was presumably referring to the report of December 16 from the *Times* correspondent in Washington printed on December 17, p. 16, although there were fuller and more graphic accounts in *The Times* of December 16, p. 14.

No. 432

Minute by Mr. Chaplin on the import of war materials into China via Burma[1]

[F 11293/130/10]

FOREIGN OFFICE, *December 16, 1937*

The present position is that the Government of Burma have intimated their willingness to establish road connexion with China; Mr. Howe has communicated this decision to the Chinese Government.[2] There are already in existence roads within Burma up to the border, one at least of which would serve well for through traffic, if the Chinese Government were to build a road to meet it.

There is no recent news of the construction which is said to have been being [*sic*] undertaken by the Chinese Government. The Government of Burma have emphasised that they must be informed of the Chinese plans as soon as possible, if it is desired that they should undertake improvements to the existing roads, since the work must be done during the dry

[1] Sir A. Cadogan wrote at the top of this minute on December 18: 'I have given most of this orally to the Chinese Ambassador.'

[2] Cf. No. 370.

season, which is already well advanced. A telegram was sent to Mr. Gage at Hankow some ten days ago[3] instructing him to enquire of the Chinese Government how matters stood.

It obviously cannot be expected of the Government of Burma that they should undertake road expenditure until they have information that a road on the Chinese side of the border is under construction.[4]

JNO. CHAPLIN

[3] Foreign Office telegram No. 4 to Hankow of December 8 (F 10527/130/10): cf. No. 439 below.

[4] A further note by Mr. Chaplin read: 'There is no prospect of railway connexion in the near future between Burma and China. Apart from the great physical difficulties of the route and the entirely uneconomic nature of the project the General Staffs of both Burma and India are resolutely opposed to it on strategic grounds.'

No. 433

Sir R. Lindsay (Washington) to Mr. Eden
(Received December [18][1], 9.30 a.m.)

Nos. 481, 482, & 483 Telegraphic [F 11201/9/10]

Important   Very Secret   WASHINGTON, *December 17, 1937, 8.10 p.m.*

My secret interview with the President[2] took place late last night after diplomatic reception at the White House. Secretary of State was present but took no part in the conversation.

The President plunged at once into the question of Staff conversations. He wanted an arrangement such as prevailed from 1915 to 1917 (of which I had never heard before) by which a systematic exchange of secret information had been established between the Admiralty and Navy Department through Gaunt of this Embassy and Captain Pratt (now Admiral on the retired list)[3]. This had been most fruitful. Understanding had then been that the State Department and Foreign Office should know nothing about this and would have denied its existence if anything had transpired. It will be remembered that as Under Secretary of Navy he himself had been personally associated with this arrangement. It became

[1] The date of receipt on the filed copy was given as December 17, presumably in error.

[2] Cf. Nos. 424 and 430.

[3] Captain (later Rear Admiral Sir G. R. A.) Gaunt was H.M. Naval Attaché at Washington, June 1914–February 1918: Captain (later Admiral) W. V. Pratt was at that time Assistant and then Chief of U.S. Naval Operations. In a note of December 20, 1937 on file A 9167/228/45 Mr. Allen recorded a request from the Admiralty for information on this 'naval liaison arrangement which was apparently in force in Washington between 1915 and 1917 . . . The Admiralty had no information themselves about this arrangement but were most anxious to find out what they could as they thought it might be useful to them in their present consideration of the possibility of close cooperation in intelligence matters'. A note on the file stated, however, that no information on this matter was to be found in F.O. archives.

evident that he had not considered the purely practical features of this liaison and he had an open mind as to where conversations should be pursued. In the ensuing discussions he made it clear that officers concerned must be fully familiar with the latest Staff plans and thoughts of their respective Navies and he seemed inclined to think that the secret would be more easily secured in London than here. He thought that he would have no difficulty whatever in finding a suitable person to send over to London at short notice if that were decided upon.

We then had a spell of the President in his worst 'inspirational' mood and I admit that I can give no account of what he said which is both consistent and sensible. First object of Staff conversations, he said, should be to arrange for a blockade of Japan and he used the word 'quarantine' an echo of his Chicago speech[4]. The line should run from Aleutia Island, through Hawaii, mid-way between the Islands to north of Philippines to Hongkong. Japanese mandated Islands would not count and could be starved by military measures. America should look after everything up to Philippines and Great Britain the western section. Battleships should not intervene and should be kept in the rear and it should be a cruiser blockade. In reply to my suggestions he definitely did not want American Fleet based on Singapore. The purpose of blockade should be to cut Japan off from raw materials, and it might take eighteen months to produce results. It would be necessary to bring in at least French and Dutch. The Dutch would lose their exports of oil to Japan and it might be necessary for us to buy it up. There would have to be prohibitions of buying from and of selling to Japan and he admitted that this would necessitate legislation by many States. He denied that blockade like this meant war, as I said it did. In the cases of Abyssinia, Spain and China he had been able to have it as he liked whether what happened was war or not. There was a new doctrine and technique as regards what constituted war. What he was suggesting was within the rights of the Executive under the Constitution and it had happened before in American history that United States had been engaged in hostilities without being at war (this referred to the situation with France in 1798). The occasion of blockade would have to be the next grave outrage by Japanese. They might attack Indo China or Hongkong. In reply to my query about German trade he said that the Germans had no raw material to sell Japan and he said German shipping would not be considerable enough to matter gravely.

All this came out not as one statement but piecemeal in response to my horrified criticisms and questions which I must admit made little impression on him as he seemed wedded to his scheme for preventing a war (but not hostilities). We may hear more of this scheme later as he is always much attracted by his own ideas. It will be mainly for his own advisers to restrain his exuberancy or to bring to practical effort whatever may be useful in his scheme. I myself felt I need not now quench the

---

[4] Cf. No. 291, note 2.

smoking flax especially as general features of lengthy discussions were favourable. I said both as a strategist and as an economist I was completely out of my depth and he agreed that matter must require further and technical study.

I said the best way to prevent war without firing a shot would be for the United States Government to make a demonstration showing clearly that they would not be indifferent to further disregard of normal morality in international affairs. I gave a perfectly frank description of difficulties and dangers of the position of His Majesty's Government; how another outrage might precipitate them into drastic action when possibly United States opinion would still be behindhand; how the loss of prestige in the Far East had an effect on His Majesty's Government of compelling more resentment than the United States Government were feeling disposed to express; and how our apparent impotence may have effect of driving into orbit of the Fascisti States numerous Governments of Europe whose sympathies are normally on our side. I urged that some demonstration by the United States of a decided character would be calculated to stop the rot and give pause to the Japanese aggression and I suggested a naval mobilisation. The President rejected this out of hand and said that mobilisation in America did not count for anything (I understand this is true as naval reserve system here is rudimentary). He also said that a demonstration though it might have effect on a Japanese Government under civil control would have no effect on the military authorities who now govern. However in the course of discussions he did himself bring up a suggestion, which has lately appeared in the press, that naval manoeuvres rendezvous beginning at Hawaii about March 14th might be advanced by a couple of months and I suggested they might so arrange in the course of them that United States Fleet might pay visit to Singapore. At first he reacted against this saying he would not like to venture his battleships so far from their base but later he himself put up the idea of visit to Singapore by squadron of cruisers and this idea appealed to him more and more and he was evidently thinking of it quite seriously. I encouraged this idea as much as I could.

He showed no curiosity to know what force we might be able to put into the Far East, and eventually I had to volunteer the information. I gave in substance all that is mentioned in this connexion in your telegrams Nos. 582[5] and 607[6] mentioned the eight or nine capital ships but putting that as a very maximum measure only to be adopted in vital necessity. He said that he considered this inadvisable and that it was more important that His Majesty's Government should keep their battleships to look after the situation in Europe. He considered that a reinforcement of cruisers, destroyers and long-range submarines in the Far East would be sufficient, though he also mentioned in passing one or two battleships.

I asked how opinion was moving in the United States and he responded

[5] No. 402. [6] No. 427.

very favourably. He had been told that voluntary boycott of Japanese goods in this country had suddenly developed in large proportions. Also that he had had somewhat more than one hundred letters that morning from unknown correspondents of which some 80 per cent were in favour of vigorous action, and of the remainder a large proportion came from secretaries of pacifist societies which he said counted for nothing. In reply to my question he said that the Middle West would go along with the Far West, which is constitutionally anti-Japanese. He admitted however that reports to him were still rather preliminary. I regard all this as satisfactory, but I think it would be inadvisable to build on it yet with any confidence.

We had some passing conversation in which Mr. Hull made his only intervention about the inadvisability of any talk in London about 'joint action' with the United States. This the President endorsed strongly and I am dealing on this subject in a separate telegram.

My last word in conversation was to ask him whether I might report to you that he was definitely considering in detail appointment of an officer to conduct conversations and question of a visit by an American Squadron to Singapore, and he replied definitely in the affirmative. There is of course no reason why you should not send me any observations you may wish me to pass on to the United States authorities on this subject.

From the foregoing you may think that these are the utterances of a hare-brained statesman or of an amateur strategist, but I assure you that the chief impression left on my own mind was that I had been talking to a man who had done his best in the Great War to bring America in speedily on the side of the Allies and who now was equally anxious to be able to bring America in on the same side before it might be too late and if it should be necessary. The utmost friendliness was implicit in everything he said and I myself reciprocated with the utmost frankness.[7]

[7] Mr. Ronald commented on December 19: 'If the Americans are to be induced to take a hand in anything, they have, I think, usually to be led in the first instance to formulate some idea which they can think of and represent to others as spontaneously conceived by themselves without aid or prompting from any one else. The plan sketched out by the President may be a fantastic chimaera as it stands, but it has the supreme merit of being his, the President of the U.S.A.'s, own creation. With care and patience on our part it should not be impossible to preserve the lion's head while yet transforming the goaty body into something more congruous.' Sir A. Cadogan agreed on December 19 that although the President's plan seemed 'rather naive . . . if we wish to secure the President's cooperation (or rather "parallel" action), we should strike while the iron is hot and, while he is in this mood, try to keep him up to the mark'. He submitted a draft reply to Sir R. Lindsay: see No. 441 below.

No. 434

Mr. Gage (Hankow) to Mr. Eden (Received December 17, 8.45 p.m.)

No. 30 Telegraphic: by wireless [F 11210/9/10]

HANKOW, *December 17, 1937*

Addressed to Embassy, Shanghai No. 33, of December 17th.
My telegram No. 31[1].

I saw Donald yesterday[2]. He told me that peace proposals conveyed by German Ambassador[3] were now completely dead owing to subsequent hardening of Japanese Cabinet under pressure from military. Chiang Kai-shek had now no alternative but to carry on and his resignation at present was out of the question. He had made it clear that no peace negotiations were possible unless the Japanese undertook to guarantee Chinese sovereignty. Military situation was far from good and supplies were becoming increasingly difficult to obtain. I gathered that some dissensions are manifesting themselves in Government circles and that Chiang Kai-shek is suspicious in particular of activities of so-called peace party (please see my telegram No. 8[4]) which he has mistrusted ever since Sian incident last year[5]. Chiang Kai-shek's visit to Hankow is probably due to this.

Donald said that Chiang Kai-shek had not expected direct help from Russia. He had made enquiries through the Chinese Ambassador in Moscow and received reply that Russia would not act unless England did. This information was confirmed by Dr. Kung, Sun Fo and Wen Wen-hao who also saw . . .[6] yesterday. Donald thinks Soviet are sedulously propagating story that it is England's fault that China is receiving no direct help from outside. He also believes Soviet do not seriously wish to support Central Government but rather are intriguing for eventual establishment of Communist area in North West provinces. Inactivity of 8th route army pointed to this and idea seemed to be to maintain it intact for use in establishing such a Communist area in the event of collapse of Central Government. Chiang Kai-shek realised this and had already refused an offer by Soviet of ninety aeroplanes for service exclusively with 8th route army. Moreover Soviet pilot . . .[6] Russian aeroplanes already received in China were proving unsatisfactory as they refused to go seriously into

---

[1] This telegram of December 16, repeated to the Foreign Office as Hankow telegram No. 28 of December 17, reported that General Chiang Kai-shek, Madame Chiang Kai-shek and Mr. Donald had arrived in Hankow on December 15 for a short stay and that Mr. Gage was 'endeavouring to make contact with Donald'.

[2] i.e. December 16.   [3] See Nos. 401, 405, and 406.

[4] In this telegram of December 9, transmitted to the Foreign Office as Hankow telegram No. 13, Mr. Gage reported a conversation with the Mayor of Hankow who 'gave an interesting description of alignment of pro- and anti-peace parties with Kwangtung political circles surrounding the Chinese Government'.

[5] See Nos. 22–38, *passim*.   [6] The text was here uncertain.

action. Donald could not say whether this was due to fear or to instructions, but suspicions of the latter. In any case it was hard on Chinese Government who had purchased machines and were paying pilots salaries. According to Donald Chiang Kai-shek has asserted that he has been sold both by the Russians and Communists inside China, to which Madame retorted that they also were being sold by the 'peace' party in China.

From all interviews I have had here including that with General Chang Chun two main lines of thought seem to emerge:

1. That until Japanese people show some sincere desire for peace and can speak with one voice there is no alternative but to continue resistance as strongly as possible. To surrender would be to sell China into slavery whereas although as result of further hostilities she may become a slave there is just a chance that events may combine to undermine her position. It is felt not very sanguinely that such an improvement might come about either through a change in Japanese policy due to economic exhaustion or through some form of eventual foreign intervention brought about by further Japanese outrages on foreign lives and property.

2. Resigned acceptance of unpalatable fact that there is no immediate hope of foreign intervention. In no case have I heard a sharp criticism of England's attitude and our difficulties appear to be fully appreciated. Regret is nevertheless expressed that we should not be in a position to defend our vital political and economic interests in the Far East which Chinese are convinced will be entirely obliterated once Japanese gain control over China. Recent bombing of foreign ships and property on the Yangtse is considered to be a deliberate attempt by Japanese to lower western and in particular British prestige in the eyes of Chinese people. Hope is expressed that a realisation of the stakes at issue will induce England, America, Russia and France or at least a combination of some of the Powers to act together before it is too late.

Repeated to Peking, Commander-in-Chief, General Officer Commanding.

No. 435

Sir R. Lindsay (Washington) to Mr. Eden
(Received December 18, 9.15 p.m.)

Nos. 488 Telegraphic [F 11226/9/10]

Very Secret   WASHINGTON, *December 18, 1937, 1.43 p.m.*

My telegram No. 481.[1]

Today I gave the Under Secretary of State account of my conversation with the President and it coincided well with his understanding of what

[1] No. 433.

had passed. He confirmed that serious consideration is being given to advancing the date of manoeuvres and to the visit by cruisers to Singapore. He also showed some interest which I think was favourable to the idea that facilities of Singapore as a base for some American warships might be made available.

No. 436

Mr. Eden to Sir R. Craigie (Tokyo)

No. 579 Telegraphic [F 11135/6799/10]

FOREIGN OFFICE, December 18, 1937, 11 p.m.

Your telegram No. 774.[1]

You will realise that position of His Majesty's Government is similar to that of United States Government as reported in your telegram. There is no embargo on normal commercial credits, but I understand confidentially that the amount of short term facilities granted by the London Market is already in process of gradual and general reduction. In the event of Japanese interests seeking to obtain credit facilities in London other than those required for normal commercial purposes, the Treasury consider it extremely unlikely that they would succeed but they propose if necessary to ask the market authorities to discourage such discussions. They do not consider it advisable that financial houses should refer to political considerations such as the terms of peace. They have no doubt that Japanese realise that possibility of financial assistance depends not only on reasonable peace but on a number of other conditions. I do not think that at present we can profitably pursue the matter further with the United States and French Governments.

Repeated to Washington and copied to Paris.

[1] No. 403: cf. ibid., note 1.

No. 437

Note from Sir J. Simon[1] to Mr. Chamberlain

T 160/693/F15255/01

TREASURY CHAMBERS, December 18, 1937

I attach:

(1) Note of conversation last night with Mr. Morgenthau[2] on long distance telephone

[1] Chancellor of the Exchequer since May 28, 1937. This note is preserved in the Treasury papers at the Public Record Office.
[2] Secretary to the U.S. Treasury: see Enclosure I to this document.

(2) Memos by Phillips[3] and Warren Fisher[4] in reference to above.

My interim reflections are as follows.

(1) The President was to see Lindsay yesterday afternoon[5] (Washington Time) and I guess that he and Morgenthau have begun to reflect on economic sanctions. To judge from the telephone message (*what* a medium to choose for such a purpose!) they have not got very far.

(2) It is not very easy to be sure what process Morgenthau, or the President, has in mind. One would have supposed that a 'Trading with the Enemy' Act could only be used if Japan was an 'enemy'.[6] Exchange control in such circumstances is a roundabout way of boycotting Japanese goods—by witholding [*sic*] (or at any rate controlling) the provision of *yen* exchange to pay for them. But the U.S.A. has a favourable balance of trade with Japan, and if Japan retorted in kind Japan would not pay her debts to America. Nevertheless, if Japan were prevented from buying war material, this would embarras [*sic*] her—but very slowly, if she has accumulated stocks, as she has—and would operate as a *slow*, and therefore ineffective economic sanction.

(3) As for ourselves, the Elliott [*sic*] Committee has given strong reasons against this sort of economic nagging[7], and we have our Italian experience![8] Moreover, the Dominions would have to be included—and apparently, in the absence of *war* with Japan, this would mean legislation all round the Empire; there is apparently no U.K. statute either.

J.S.

The difficult and very important question will be *how* to reply to Mr. M.[9]

[3] Not printed: Sir F. Phillips was an Under Secretary in the Treasury.

[4] Sir W. Fisher wrote on December 18: 'Over & above the imbecility of economic sanctions, we shd. find ourselves left in the lurch sooner or later by the U.S.A. (who incidentally have no very special stakes in Asia) & Japan wd. scoop Hongkong. Shd. we then add the fatal folly of going to war with Japan & so committing suicide in Europe?'

[5] See No. 433.

[6] This point was explained in a minute of December 20 on the same Treasury file: 'Section 5(b) of the Trading with the Enemy Act, 1917, gave the President power in time of war to "investigate, regulate or prohibit any transactions in foreign exchange", etc. Section 2 of Title I of the Emergency Banking Act of March, 1933 amended the above section to read "during time of war *or during any other period of national emergency declared by the President*, the President may . . . investigate, regulate or prohibit . . . any transactions in foreign exchange . . . and import . . . of currency". I take it that the position now is that the President has power without further consultation with Congress to declare the present a "period of national emergency" and to take such action as he may see fit which could be brought within the words "regulate or prohibit any transactions in foreign exchange" etc.' Sir F. Phillips commented on December 20: 'Power to investigate, regulate or prohibit any transactions in foreign exchange is of course enormously wider than any power we have under the Clearing Offices Act. It is practically equivalent to a complete supervision of trade, import or export.'

[7] See No. 334.   [8] Cf. Volume XVI, *passim*.

[9] Sir J. Simon passed these papers on to Mr. Eden before they were sent to Mr. Chamberlain. Mr. Eden's comments are printed as Enclosure II in this document.

Record by Sir J. Simon of a conversation with Mr. Morgenthau

December 17, 1937

Mr. Morgenthau rang me up on the long distance telephone from Washington at 8 p.m. Greenwich time tonight. He began by saying that he was speaking with the knowledge and approval of the President. He wished to communicate with me by this method because he 'did not wish to use the diplomatic channel'.

The message was for me and the Prime Minister alone. I interposed at this point that I felt sure, if it was a matter affecting foreign affairs, that the Prime Minister would wish the Foreign Secretary to know; and I added that in this country the Prime Minister was accustomed to put even the most confidential matters before the Cabinet.

Mr. Morgenthau said that he must leave that to my discretion.

He then said that they had a law in the United States passed in 1933 called the Trading with the Enemy Act, and that under this law it was possible by executive action to set up an exchange control as against a particular country. He said that they had been considering what they could do if Japan did not give them a satisfactory answer or did not answer at all. He emphasised that they had not decided anything even provisionally. But they wished to let us know, as action of that kind would not be effective if they did it alone.

Mr. Morgenthau's method reminded me so strongly of Mr. Stimson's long distance call to Geneva and the subsequent misunderstanding[10] that I told him that I saw great difficulty in dealing with this sort of matter on the telephone. Sir Ronald Lindsay was in Washington, and I ventured to suggest that it might be a better method to send for him when he (Mr. Morgenthau) could show him (Sir Ronald Lindsay) the Statute and explain his views in detail. Lindsay, of course, was completely to be trusted and would no doubt send a secret message to the Government here.

Mr. Morgenthau then said that he would take this suggestion into consideration.

I said I would of course do my best to deliver this message at once to the Prime Minister. But the message appeared to expect an answer, and I was very unwilling in a matter of such delicacy to use the long distance telephone.

Mr. Morgenthau said he would call up Butterworth and get him to ascertain from me or from my representative at the Treasury what our reactions to his observations might be. He particularly asked that we should not communicate what he had said to Sir Ronald Lindsay.

J.S.

---

[10] Cf. Volume XX, Appendix II.

Note from Mr. Eden to Mr. Chamberlain

17, FITZHARDINGE ST, W.1, *December 19, 1937*

P.M.

Chancellor of the Exchequer has kindly let me see these papers on their way to you. As he says the important question is how to reply to Morgenthau.

In my judgment it is essential that in these critical times we should have one channel, and one channel only, for communication with Roosevelt, and that Lindsay. If once we depart from this we shall get into hopeless confusion and the threads are difficult enough to keep disentagled anyway. Therefore I think that Morgenthau should be thanked, told that Lindsay is handling all matters and projects even the most confidential in connection with Far Eastern situation, and asked to be good enough to get into touch with Lindsay. It might be wiser not to mention that Lindsay has seen the President, for American procedures are so involved that this might be news to Morgenthau!

There remains Lindsay's account of interview with President. I will not weary you with my ideas now, except to say I think it desirable (1) to accept naval officer (2) to try to tie Roosevelt down to present movement of ships rather than future blockade. I have had some conversation with Cadogan on this subject, and he will see Chatfield in the morning. By lunch time I hope to have a draft telegram to Lindsay for you to see.[11]

---

[11] See No. 441 below. Comments on these papers by Mr. Waley, Sir F. Phillips, Sir R. Hopkins, and Sir Warren Fisher are also preserved on this Treasury file. For the draft reply to Mr. Morgenthau see No. 443 below.

No. 438

Memorandum[1] on objects which His Majesty's Government would hope to achieve by sending the Fleet to the Far East

[F 11749/4880/10]

FOREIGN OFFICE, *December 18, 1937*

1. In the event of a decision being taken to send capital ships to the Far East the news will probably become public almost immediately. It seems desirable therefore that the nature of the communications that will then be made (a) to America, (b) to Japan, and (c) to Parliament should be

---

[1] A note by Sir J. Pratt of December 18 stated that this memorandum was the 'result of a discussion between Mr. Peake, Sir J. Brenan and myself and has been drafted in consultation with Sir J. Brenan'.

settled beforehand. These points cannot be decided until the objects it is hoped to achieve by sending the fleet to the East have been formulated with some degree of precision. That question must therefore be examined first.

2. It must be assumed that our naval strength in the Far East will be so great that the Japanese will not care to run the risk of refusing compliance with any demands that His Majesty's Government may make. It does not however follow from this that those demands should be proportionate to the strength of the fleet. If force is used for the protection and maintenance of national interests the only wise and prudent course, however great the preponderance of force, is to combine that policy with extreme moderation and the utmost consideration for the rights and interests of other Powers. His Majesty's Government will in the first instance, of course, insist on due respect for the lives, property and rights, under treaty and international law, of British subjects, but as regards the wider question of protection of British interests generally it seems advisable that these should as far as possible be made to coincide with the legitimate interests of all powers trading with the Far East. The interests protected should be common interests as well as being British interests. This should not be difficult because most of the things that are regarded as British interests, such as the preservation of a stable Chinese Central Government with effective administrative machinery, the maintenance of the Customs administration, the currency system and the credit[2] of the Chinese Government are in fact common interests. To these may be added the principles of the open door and equal opportunity enshrined in the Nine Power Treaty. If the attainment of these general objects is regarded as the main purpose for which the fleet is being sent to the Far East, it will help both to disarm criticism and to secure the support of America. The more particular British interests may safely be left to find their own level later on. If, for example, the Customs administration and the International Settlement are saved from destruction mainly by the efforts of His Majesty's Government too much rather than too little attention is likely to be paid to British claims in the final settlement. It might indeed be advisable to try and secure increased American participation in the Customs and increased German or Scandinavian representation in the Settlement.

3. In carrying out the policy proposed in the preceding paragraph the first question that will arise is how far is it practicable or desirable to insist on a restoration of the status quo? Different sets of circumstances distinguish the cases of North China, the Yangtse Valley, and South China. However great the force at the disposal of His Majesty's Government may be demands should not be put forward of such a character that Japan would prefer to fight even at the risk of almost

---

[2] The words 'currency system' and 'credit' were underlined by Mr. Orde with the marginal comment: 'to support these *now* is tantamount to supporting China in the war.'

certain defeat rather than comply with them. Moreover the inherent incapacity of the Chinese Government, apart altogether from the effect of the recent hostilities, may make a restoration of the status quo unattainable. These considerations apply with special force to the case of N. China. The Japanese now regard their hold on North China as essential for the security of Manchukuo and therefore of Japan itself. The British Navy might be able to force the Japanese armies to withdraw by cutting communications between Japan and the mainland, but this might only cause complete administrative chaos in the regions affected and would certainly cause intense and lasting bitterness against us in Japan. It would be better therefore so far as the North China problem is concerned to stand aside for the time being and confine our efforts to protection of life property and immediate British interests such as the British concession at Tientsin and the Kailan Mining Administration and to such questions as the relation of the Tientsin Customs and Customs revenues to the Customs Administration of the rest of China. It will be important however to avoid giving the appearance of making a bargain, namely, bartering North China to Japan in return for concessions elsewhere.

4. In Shanghai and the Yangtse Valley generally His Majesty's Government would be justified in taking a much stronger line. Had there been a powerful British fleet in Far Eastern waters in July Japan would never have dared to ride rough shod over all our established rights in Shanghai for the purpose of attacking and destroying the Chinese Government; and it was only by the illegitimate use she made of the International Settlement that she has been able to achieve her object. His Majesty's Government cannot undo what has been done but they can insist on a restoration of the status quo at least so far as the International Settlement and extra settlement roads are concerned. The International Settlement is the result of the amalgamation of two areas, one set aside for the residence of British subjects and one for American citizens. Japan was admitted to share in these privileges and His Majesty's Government are entitled therefore to insist that she does not grossly abuse them. The first step therefore should be a demand for the total withdrawal of Japanese forces from the Settlement and roads and an intimation that in future His Majesty's Government will expect to be consulted by any Power that proposes to land forces in the Settlement ostensibly for the defence of the Settlement. If the Japanese do not comply with this demand the fleet must be prepared to enforce compliance by blockade or other forcible measures. Having secured the evacuation of Shanghai the next demand, which should, however, for the present be kept in reserve, should be for the evacuation of the Yangtze Valley with a view to a restoration of the status quo in the whole region. It will be observed that in the case of the International Settlement it should be possible not merely to restore the status quo but to secure considerable improvements in the previous position. This question having been disposed of other questions such as the Customs Administration, currency, etc., should not prove difficult to

deal with.

5. In Shanghai and the Yangtze Valley His Majesty's Government will be dealing with an international situation on an international basis. That is to say the demands they make will be as much on behalf of and in the interests of other Powers such as America as of ourselves. In South China, however, it will be necessary to regard the matter solely from the standpoint of British interests. In South China the greatest of these is Hongkong—a purely British interest—and if Hongkong is to be saved as a British colony immediate action of a drastic character would appear to be necessary.[3] The Japanese are planning landings at various points on the coast south of Shanghai. Among these points are Swatow and Canton. There will probably be hostilities in the immediate future in the region between Canton and Hongkong, violations of British territory and other incidents. The next step will be the establishment of puppet governments in Canton and elsewhere on the North China model, the effect of which would be to render our position in Hongkong first useless and then untenable. It will be much easier to deal with this situation before it has developed than after; for once Japanese forces have consolidated positions on the mainland behind Hongkong the defence of Hongkong will become much more difficult. It is therefore desirable if possible to give Japan prior warning that landings on the coast of China south of Shanghai would be regarded as an unfriendly act and that in particular no landing in the neighbourhood of Hongkong or measures which might lead to hostilities in the hinterland of Hongkong will be tolerated.[4] The preservation of Hongkong is in fact a vital British interest and our

[3] This view was not supported by the Chiefs of Staff in a memorandum of December 21 on the Defence of Hong Kong (C.O.S. 657). Considering the question of the consequences of a Japanese occupation of the mainland behind Hong Kong, the Chiefs of Staff agreed that the long term British occupation of Hong Kong might be affected but could not see that His Majesty's Government could do much about it. They concluded: '. . . we cannot see that any action of a military character which could be taken at the present time would appreciably improve the capacity of Hong Kong to resist capture by Japanese forces which had been able to establish themselves in Kwang Tung [sic] without let or hindrance from us, and were thus in a position, in the worst case, to develop an attack on Hong Kong at very short notice. On the other hand it would be wrong to assume that the mere presence of Japanese forces in the vicinity of Hong Kong would necessarily be a prelude to an attack on the fortress . . . it seems scarcely conceivable to us that [Japan] will deliberately do anything at Hong Kong which is bound to involve her in war with the British Empire.'

[4] Sir R. Craigie in fact on his own initiative on December 27 informed the Japanese Vice Foreign Minister during a discussion of Japanese intentions in Hainan and Canton that 'any operations in this neighbourhood could not fail to impose a further strain on Anglo-Japanese relations'. In a note of December 29 commenting on the present memorandum Mr. Eden said he was 'impressed with the difficulty that will be created for us by any Japanese landing at or near Canton. Should we, can we, in any way reinforce the warning which Sir R. Craigie has already given? Should we not at least tell him that we approve his language and that unless he sees objection he should tell Mr. Hirota that it represents not only his own views but those of H.M.G. The last thing H.M.G. desires, and they believe that Japanese Govt. share their sentiment, is any further deterioration in Anglo-Japanese

position in Hongkong can be completely destroyed, not by any direct attack, but merely by setting up puppet Governments in the adjacent Provinces. Regard for precedent or correct legal procedure should not therefore be allowed to paralyse action while the menace is developing and until it is too late to ward it off.

6. The objects with which the fleet is being sent out may therefore be summed up as follows:

(1) to protect the lives, property and rights generally of British subjects throughout China,

(2) to prevent the development of any threat to Hongkong by the landing of Japanese forces in South China, the occupation of islands or the establishment of Japanese controlled puppet Governments in the neighbourhood of the Colony,

(3) to restore the status quo in the Yangtze Valley and South China generally—namely a régime under the control of the Chinese Government providing for the open door and equal opportunity for all,

(4) to restore the status quo in the International Settlement with, if possible, certain adjustments and secure the immediate withdrawal of the Japanese forces,

(5) to maintain intact the Customs Administration and the Customs revenues,

(6) to protect particular British interests in North China, but otherwise stand aside except in so far as the Tientsin Customs forms part of the general question of the Customs Administration.

7. It is now possible to examine the question of what is to be said to Japan, America and to Parliament when it becomes known that the fleet is about to sail.

As regards Japan apart from the warning about Hongkong, which should be conveyed to her at the earliest possible moment, it would be best to leave her for as long as possible in a state of uncertainty as to our future intentions. Having warned her to cancel the projected landings in South China we should merely inform her that the fleet is being sent out in order to ensure due respect for the legitimate rights of British subjects. We should at the same time explain to America that while the object of sending out the fleet is to protect the legitimate interests of British subjects these interests, with the single exception of Hongkong, are in the main the common interests of all Powers trading to the East. We can point out the international interest in the Settlement at Shanghai, in the Customs Administration and in a régime of the open door and equality of opportunity over as wide an area in China as possible and state that these, plus the purely British interest of Hongkong, are the main objects that we

relations. They cannot but be conscious that such, at the least, must be the effect of any Japanese landing near Hong Kong, & they have thought it wiser and more friendly to let this.be known in advance . . .' A telegram in these terms was despatched to Sir R. Craigie as No. 610 on December 30 (F 11479/9/10).

have in view. It seems unnecessary to discuss details of our proposed attitude towards North China and our proposed demands with regard to the International Settlement until the fleet has actually arrived in the East, but we should of course inform America of the warning given to Japan about Hongkong. The communication to Parliament might be in substance the same as the communication to America.[5]

[5] Sir A. Cadogan (December 21) thought this memorandum 'timely and excellent': 'I think the line to be taken (assuming we are strong enough) is that we intend to take the part which is due to us under the 9 Power Treaty in discussion of a final settlement. That wd. be a warning to Japan, and wd. leave us free to advocate such terms as may seem desirable and practicable when the time comes ... I suggest that we shd. discuss this question of announcing the object of our action, with the U.S. Govt. as soon as possible ... I don't see why the U.S. Govt. shd. find much difficulty in making a corresponding declaration. Their Delegation at Brussels were very keen on reserving all rights under the Treaty and on insisting that the ultimate settlement must be within the 4 corners of that Treaty'. Mr. Eden minuted at this point: 'Yes, this is so.' In a further note of December 29 Mr. Eden expressed agreement with Sir A. Cadogan's proposal, but pointed out that 'it does not seem that United States Govt. are prepared at present to send any force to Far East except four cruisers to Singapore which they will no doubt represent as being on their way home from Sydney': see Nos. 447, 464, 471, and 480 below. On December 28 Sir A. Cadogan had written another long minute on the present memorandum, printed as No. 450 below.

No. 439

Mr. Gage (Hankow) to Mr. Eden (Received December 20, 3 p.m.)

No. 35 Telegraphic: by wireless [F 11346/130/10]

HANKOW, *December 20, 1937*

Your telegram No. 4.[1]

Minister for Foreign Affairs has informed me that Chinese government hope to import large quantities of material via this route in the near future. They have left with me map showing frontier route which they would prefer to use. This map was forwarded to British Embassy Shanghai yesterday by safe opportunity in H.M.S. *Capetown*. Main towns on this route are as follows: Yunnanfu, Hsiangyun, Tali, Hsiakuan, Paoshan, Lungling, Mangshih, Chefang, Shuishi[2], Lashio.[3] I have no copies relevant papers on my file but British Embassy Shanghai will doubtless check and give further details if necessary on receipt of map.

Repeated to Embassy Shanghai and Peking.

[1] See No. 432, note 3.
[2] A note on the filed copy suggested that this should read '(Shui) Jui li'.
[3] A note on the filed copy read: 'This is the route recommended by Burma Govt.'

No. 440

Commander, Shanghai Area (Shanghai) to War Office[1]
(Received December 21, 5 p.m.)

No. 4951 Telegraphic [F 11392/10816/10]

SHANGHAI, December 20, 1937, 5.15 p.m.

Major General Harada Japanese Military Attaché personally presented his apology today to Major General Telfer Smollett on behalf of the Japanese Army for the unfortunate incident of December 12th when British ships were fired at on the river Yangtze[2]. He gave assurances that General Matsui had done everything in his power to prevent the repetition of such an incident. Major General Harada returned from Nanking to Shanghai yesterday.

G.O.C. Hong Kong to pass to C. in C.

Addressed Embassy Tokio and Hong Kong.

[1] Communicated to the Foreign Office by the War Office.   [2] See Nos. 407–410.

No. 441

Mr. Eden to Sir R. Lindsay (Washington)

No. 616[1] Telegraphic [F 11201/9/10]

Most Immediate   Secret   FOREIGN OFFICE, December 20, 1937

Your telegrams Nos. 481, 482 and 483[2].

Your report of interview seems at least to show goodwill of President, though it did not, and perhaps cannot at this stage, formulate any definite plan.

Will you convey to him that Prime Minister and I have learnt with much appreciation of his frank talk with you, and that His Majesty's Government are most gratified to find that his views on the international outlook are very similar to their own. We shall be delighted to receive the officer whom he selects, and will gladly give him all possible facilities. We trust he will come with least possible delay.

The President was doubtless thinking aloud and feeling his way towards

[1] Only a rough draft of this telegram, prepared by Sir A. Cadogan with manuscript amendments by Mr. Eden, has been found in F.O. archives. It is apparently this draft to which Mr. Eden referred at the end of his note to Mr. Chamberlain printed as Enclosure II in No. 437 above. The telegram was despatched on December 20, but there is no record of the time of despatch. Two manuscript additions to the draft, one by Sir A. Cadogan and one by Mr. Eden, are also filed at F 11201/9/10: they are marked 'A' and 'B', but there are no corresponding references in the draft nor any indication as to whether the additions were finally incorporated; see, however, notes 3 and 4 below.

[2] No. 433.

a plan, and for that reason no doubt appears to have been rather self-contradictory. In the earlier part of the conversation he seems to have contemplated a blockade, only to come into operation if the Japanese proceeded to further outrage, and to have rejected the idea of any demonstration now. But later he appears to have contemplated advancing date of manoeuvres and even a visit of American cruisers to Singapore.

His Majesty's Government would prefer that action should not be delayed until further outrages occur. They believe that some preparatory action by the two fleets now, even though such action were parallel and not joint, would be of the greatest advantage. It might indeed in itself suffice to restrain Japan[3] and induce her to have some regard for foreign rights and interests. Even if that were not achieved, and we had to take more drastic action, we should then be more prepared to act quickly as we should be on the spot.

I do not know whether the President can be pressed to this conclusion or whether he is likely to reach it of his own accord, and I leave it to you to judge when and in what manner to approach him again. Of course details will have to await arrival of U.S. naval staff officer, but if the President could be brought to accept in principle the idea of some immediate action, that would be all to the good.

I fully realise danger of speaking of 'joint' action, and we would in all circumstances try to avoid that pitfall. You may assure Mr. Hull that we shall continue to do all we can to meet him in this respect, as indeed we have done hitherto. It would, I suppose, be better to represent any action that we each may be able to take as prompted by determination of each country to protect its own interests.

If any action is to be planned, it will be necessary to take the French Government into our confidence at an early stage, and I understand the President shares that view. But, in view of the danger of leakage by the Quai d'Orsay, I should leave that for as long as possible.[4]

[3] A draft paragraph marked 'A' (see note 1 above) in Sir A. Cadogan's handwriting, which may have been intended as a substitute for the preceding three sentences, ran as follows: 'They believe that some preparatory measures by the 2 fleets now would be of the greatest advantage. They are themselves preparing their fleet for any necessary action, and wd. be glad of some indication whether the U.S. Govt. are doing the same and when they wd. be ready for any action, should that be agreed upon. They believe that public knowledge that such preparatory measures were being taken by the 2 countries, although independently, might in itself restrain Japan . . .'

[4] A draft paragraph in Mr. Eden's handwriting (see note 1 above) which may have been intended for insertion at this point read as follows: 'B. For your own information, I should not exclude possibility of immediate discussion of movements of ships by both govts. to for instance Singapore and Manila respectively, but I imagine that U.S. Govt. are not prepared for any such discussion at present. You have however authority to make our attitude known to President Roosevelt or Mr. Hull if you think it desirable and if you do not consider that it would be regarded by them as an attempt to entangle them.'

No. 442

Sir R. Lindsay (Washington) to Mr. Eden
(Received December 22, 9.30 a.m.)

No. 501 Telegraphic [F 11362/9/10]

Very Secret   WASHINGTON, December 21, 1937, 11.55 p.m.

Your telegram No. 616.[1]

On my return to Washington from Mr. Bingham's funeral[2] I found a message from Secretary of State asking if I had any news for him. I saw him this afternoon and gave him the contents of your telegram under reference.

2. He regarded a blockade as a remoter contingency which must require careful and technical study, and to which recourse could not be had except in the case of some further outrage, if then.

3. I then urged again, in the manner you suggested, advisability of some kind of demonstration of a visible nature and emphasised that it would have preventive effect. In reply he referred to a despatch in yesterday's *New York Times* from Abend, the correspondent at Shanghai.

4. According to this the real culprit in the recent outrage is Colonel Hashimoto. This man has such powerful protection in Japan that he cannot be punished and it is an Admiral who is being made the scape-goat for the bombing. In this way a tense situation is being created between the army and the navy. Moreover the army higher command resents the manner in which Hashimoto is able to defy its authority. Mr. Hull had been told by the editor of *New York Times* that Abend's news came straight from General Matsui. The latter had said to Abend that such news as this if sent from Shanghai to Japan would be stopped by the censor. He wanted it sent to America in the hopes that Japanese correspondents there would contrive to send it back to Japan.

5. Secretary of State pointed out that we thus had not merely the civil Government of Japan at odds with the armed forces but also acute quarrels between the army and the navy and also within the army. Furthermore the Chinese were making the installation of puppet Governments difficult and were destroying Japanese property of immense value. On the whole it seemed to him that Japanese position in China was becoming more difficult. He would not draw any definite conclusion from all this but he would ask you whether the moment might not now be approaching when the civil Government might be able to assert itself and whether anything in the nature of a demonstration just at this moment might not have tendency to check movements that might

---

[1] No. 441.

[2] Robert Worth Bingham had been U.S. Ambassador at London since 1933. He died in Baltimore on December 18. A tribute by Sir Ronald Lindsay was published in the American press on December 19. The funeral took place on December 20 at Louisville, Kentucky.

606

develop in a salutary direction. At the same time he gave me a hint that perhaps some naval preparations are now being made but this part of the conversation was in his most allusive style and I found it impossible to extract definite statements.

6. But a warning that you may at some moment have to inform the French Government provoked a clearly expressed dismay. He said that he had not even informed his own Cabinet colleagues of the conversations. He could understand your own position but begged you to maintain the very strictest secrecy. Could I tell him that you do not propose to reveal anything to the French Government without his previous consent?

No. 443

Minute[1] from Sir J. Simon to Mr. Chamberlain

[F 11748/9/10]

December 21, 1937

Following upon Mr. Morgenthau's telephone message which I reported to you and the Foreign Secretary[2], I saw Mr. Butterworth of the United States Embassy at noon to-day, and in the course of a friendly talk gave him the message in reply which I had shown to you in draft[3]. Mr. Butterworth had a supplementary message from Mr. Morgenthau to deliver which was as follows:

[1] A copy of this minute was sent to the Foreign Office on December 21 with a covering note from Mr. A. J. D. Winnifrith, an Assistant Private Secretary to Sir J. Simon, to Mr. Caccia, linking it with Mr. Morgenthau's telephone message to Sir J. Simon of the previous week (see No. 437) and stating that the Chancellor thought that Mr. Eden would like to see it.

[2] See No. 437.

[3] No trace of Sir J. Simon's message has been found in F.O. archives. An undated and unsigned draft preserved in the Treasury files ran as follows: 'C. of E. has communicated to P.M. message from Mr. M[orgenthau] transmitted by long distance telephone on Friday night, and Mr. Eden, who is Minister specially charged with all aspects of international relations, has also been informed. H.M.G. thank Mr. M. for the information as to powers conferred by *Trading with the Enemy Act* of United States. No similar powers exist in this country save in event of foreign country becoming an enemy and state of war arising, (or in a case covered by Article 16 of the League Covenant) and accordingly special legislation would be necessary both here and in Dominions before such economic action could, in any case, be contemplated. Moreover, experience of H.M.G. and study they have made in earlier instances convince them that every aspect of such problems has to be considered together, and that no separation should be made of economic from political and strategic analysis. P.M. and C. of E. therefore suggest that if this matter is further pursued, this should be through the regular channel of the British Ambassador who is already dealing with very confidential communications on the subject so that all aspects of the present problem may be seen in due relation. Sir John wishes to thank Mr. M. for his courteous communication and sends his kind regards.' According to the Morgenthau Diaries (*op. cit.*, p. 491) the U.S. Treasury concluded from this reply that Sir J. Simon was 'saying "no", indirectly, politely, but emphatically'.

'In pursuance of my telephone conversation with you, it is obvious that the subject is corollary to but an essential part of naval conversations and studies about to be made. The British Ambassador and your Foreign Office have been advised. With full concurrence of Secretary of State Hull, we are asking the American officer who will shortly arrive in London to see you and obtain your views on the economic phase which I discussed with you by telephone Friday evening.'

I understand that the American officer referred to is Captain Ingram[4] of the United States Navy who was over here with Admiral Stanley at the Naval Conference—Mr. Butterworth thought that Captain Ingram[4] had already started.[5] Mr. Butterworth readily took the point that all aspects of the present problem must be considered together and dealt with as a whole, so that 'views on the economic phase' would not be personal to me but would be the concerned view of H.M. Government. If Mr. Butterworth delivers his message with understanding, I do not think we shall have any further trouble over this particularism.

I ought to add (though nothing was said about this in the conversation) that our Debts Clearing Offices and Import Restrictions Act, 1934, authorises a clearing office to be set up if it appears to the Treasury that in the case of any foreign country payments or transfers to persons in the United Kingdom are subjected to restrictions or are prohibited or have been discontinued. There have in fact been a few recent cases in which Japan has made difficulties in providing exchange to pay for imports. But, so far as the Treasury knows, they are comparatively trifling up to the present. In any case the Act was passed to extract payment of debts due to our citizens from defaulting States and not as a means of imposing economic sanctions. I can conceive that, if things develop, an effort might be made to try to apply the Act to her, but it would be a stretch of our powers to attempt it. And I think we are justified in maintaining the view that we, as well as the Dominions, would need further legislative powers. In this connection India and Australia have much greater trade interests at stake than we have (actually in 1936 some 30 per cent. of India's total exports went to Japan) and they will undoubtedly be alarmed by the possibility of Japanese counter measures.

J. S.

[4] A note on the filed copy stated that this should read 'Ingersoll'.

[5] According to Washington telegram No. 510 of December 23 (not kept in F.O. archives) Captain Ingersoll was due to sail in the *Normandie* on December 26.

Mr. R. A. Hall[1] (Yunnanfu) to Mr. Eden (Received January 3, 1938)

No. 34: by Air Mail[2] [F 79/79/10]

YUNNANFU, *December 21, 1937*

His Majesty's Acting Consul-General at Yunnanfu presents his compliments to His Majesty's Principal Secretary of State for Foreign Affairs and has the honour to transmit to him the undermentioned documents.

Reference to previous correspondence:

Foreign Office telegram to Gage at Hankow No. 4 of 8th December 1937[3]

Name and Date	*Subject*
To H.M. Ambassador Peking[4] Despatch No. 108 of 21.12.37	Burma-Tali Road: present position

ENCLOSURE IN No. 444

Mr. Hall (Yunnanfu) to Sir H. Knatchbull-Hugessen (Peking)

No. 108

YUNNANFU, *December 21, 1937*

Sir,

I have the honour to refer to my telegram No. 37[5] to Peking of yesterday's date and to my despatch No. 61[6] of 1st December to His Majesty's Commercial Secretary, Hongkong, concerning the Burma-Tali road. In paragraph 8 of that despatch it was stated that it had been decided to short-circuit Tengyueh and build the road direct from

---

[1] Mr. Hall was Acting Consul General at Yunnanfu and concurrently H.M. Consul at Tengyueh.

[2] A minute by Mr. R. P. Heppel, a Third Secretary in the Far Eastern Department, read: 'This must be almost the first air mail despatch ever received from Yunnanfu. It has outstripped the despatch of 1st December referred to.'

[3] See No. 432, note 3, and No. 439.

[4] Although Mr. Hall addressed his despatch to Sir H. Knatchbull-Hugessen, it was announced in the press on December 21 that in view of the uncertainty as to the date when the Ambassador would be sufficiently recovered to return to duty, it had been decided that His Majesty's Government should be represented in China 'by a diplomat of Ambassadorial rank'. Sir H. Knatchbull-Hugessen was to be succeeded by Sir Archibald Clark Kerr, H.M. Ambassador at Bagdad, who would proceed to China as soon as possible. A copy of the press notice is filed at F 11379/288/10.

[5] Not printed (F 11444/130/10).   [6] Not printed: cf. note 2 above.

Lungling to Yungch'ang [Paoshan] because this carried the great advantage that not only was it more direct, but also that the Shweli River would not require to be crossed and there was already a bridge capable of transporting cars over the Salween so that the only bridges necessary to construct would be a long one over the Mekong and a comparatively short one over the Yangpi.

2. I received a letter from Tengyueh dated 23rd November informing me that the Tengyueh Tupan had received telegraphic instructions to construct the road direct from Lungling to Yungch'ang but that he had replied advocating the Tengyueh route on the ground that this had already been surveyed, whereas on the other route no survey work had been done. On receipt of further instructions he set his surveyors to work on the Lungling-Yungch'ang direct line but no road-builders were called out pending a discussion of the two routes between the Tupan and an engineer of the Yunnan Road Bureau, Mr. Tuan, who was despatched from Yunnanfu for that purpose. A deputation, headed by the Tangpu Representative, was sent from Tengyueh to Yunnanfu to plead that the Tengyueh route be used. The Tengyueh merchants offered to subscribe large sums for the strengthening of the bridges if the road were constructed to pass through Tengyueh.

3. I received another letter from Tengyueh dated 7th December stating that no road construction work had so far begun in the Tengyueh and Lungling districts but preparations for summoning citizen labourers to work on the road had been completed. It was stated that it was likely to be about ten days before road construction would commence. The delay would be due to waiting for Mr. Tuan to decide which route the road would follow.

4. I received a further letter from Tengyueh dated 10th December enclosing an article in the Tengyueh Jih Pao (a new publication since I left) a translation of which forms an enclosure to this despatch.[7] From this it will be seen that the Lungling-Yungch'ang direct route has been definitely decided upon. I am informed that the line will be divided into five sections to be constructed simultaneously, that labourers from Tengyueh District will undertake construction at Lungling and that survey work is just about completed.

I have, etc.,
Ronald Hall

[7] Not printed.

No. 445

Letter from Sir R. Lindsay (Washington) to Sir A. Cadogan

[*F 118/84/10*]

WASHINGTON, *December 22, 1937*

My dear Alec,

Now that I am embarking on secret diplomacy with the United States Government I beg you to remember that it's not always easy for me to see the President. Not that he is unwilling, or that we do not get on well together, but ordinarily an interview with the President takes place at the White House with all the press of Washington watching the Ambassador going into the President's room and cross-examining him as soon as he comes out. Hence vast publicity and dangerous speculation which may be as embarrassing to the President as it is to me. I hardly liked to suggest a secret interview, but this time the President himself suggested it; only the secret arrangements very nearly fell down.

Sumner Welles arranged that my wife and I should take the wife of my junior Secretary, Rumbold,[1] to the White House to be presented to Mrs. Roosevelt, and that while that was going on the President should come across to the private part of the house and he and I should have our talk. All that would have been very simple. However at the Diplomatic Reception on the evening of the 16th, as I was passing before the President he told me that he wanted me to stay behind and have a talk with him after the guests has left. At that very moment Mrs. Roosevelt was whispering to my wife that the interview was to take place the next day as arranged originally by Welles.

I got hold of Welles, who was very angry at having his arrangements put out, but we extemporized what we could to meet the occasion. When the last guest had passed before the President, he and Mrs. Roosevelt withdrew to the private apartments of the White House upstairs, but the State rooms were still completely full with guests trying to go home. A young A.D.C. then seized me, pulled me through the dense crowd, and stuffed me into a lift; and then, coram populo, and glittering with gold braid and stars, I was slowly carried upstairs to the Presence. I felt like a mediaeval saint being translated to Heaven in the presence of ten thousand spectators. Why it wasn't in all the papers next day I can't imagine. As it was the young A.D.C. started blabbing at once and was heavily sat on by the President. And right on the top of that I had a letter from Philip Guedalla[2] who reported to me that the President had been talking freely to him about naval cooperation in the Pacific. So I showed the letter to Sumner Welles and he promised to sit on the President.

In general I am very well pleased with the progress now being made in

---

[1] Mr. H. A. C. Rumbold: Third Secretary in H.M. Embassy, Washington, since October 25, 1937.
[2] 1889–1944: the distinguished biographer and essayist.

public opinion here on the subject of international cooperation, which at the moment means cooperation with us in the Far East. There seems to be almost a conspiracy among the writers of special articles in the press to advocate cooperation, and I myself suspect that the State Department has found it possible to mobilise them. There are so few exceptions that I enclose the worst of them, by Dorothy Thompson, who is very widely read.[3] From Congress there has hardly been a murmur against the cause, except by the negligible Senator Reynolds at the very first moment, and this has not been repeated. The Japanese Ambassador bought some time on the air, uttered a short but emphatic stream of apologies, and was criticised rather sharply for doing so by Senators Copeland and Connally. Landon's declaration of solidarity is I think of considerable importance, not the least because it comes from Topeka, Kansas. The *Panay* incident[4] is slowly producing more and more detail, and all of it of an aggravating character. The United States Naval Court sitting at Shanghai will report at the end of this week and I expect that that will provide more material yet, and the films of the actual events on the *Panay* will come along later.

I hate the idea that bad relations anywhere can be desirable, and outside my own actual negotiations with the State Department I never say anything to anyone about Japan. But it is impossible to ignore the fact that at present the embitterment of American relations with Japan does help to bring us and America closer together and this is of inestimable value. I am always afraid of the reaction in favour of isolation which must surely occur presently, but meanwhile the chief thing for us to do is to avoid mistakes; and the admirable speeches by the Prime Minister and by the Secretary of State in the House last night[5] show that this is fully appreciated by you in England.[6]

Yours ever,

RONALD LINDSAY

[3] Not printed. A copy of the article, entitled *Respects to the London Times*, which appeared in Dorothy Thompson's column 'On the Record' in the *New York Tribune* of December 17, 1937, is filed under F 118/84/10.

[4] See No. 410.   [5] See 330 *H.C. Deb. 5 s.*, cols. 1802–12 and 1878–87.

[6] A minute by Mr. Eden read: 'P[rime] M[inister]. Interesting and on the whole encouraging, for Sir R. Lindsay is ever wisely cautious in his estimates of U.S. action & opinion. A.E.' The copy is marked: 'Seen by P.M.'

No. 446

Mr. Eden to Sir R. Lindsay (Washington)

No. 628 Telegraphic [F 11362/9/10]

Important Very Secret   FOREIGN OFFICE, *December 23, 1937, 9.5 p.m.*

Your telegram No. 501[1].

[1] No. 442.

I hope that we can be sure that message contained in my telegram No. 616[2] has reached President himself.

Would you have any occasion to see him again and to find out how his mind is working and whether he is developing any definite line of action? If any steps are to be taken, we should wish them to be as 'parallel' as possible, and if possible simultaneous. If U.S. Government are developing any action which could only be followed by us at a comparatively long interval, effect would not be so good.

As regards your conversation with Mr. Hull, we believe it is true that there are divided counsels in Japan and we are not without hope that saner elements may be able to reassert themselves to some extent. I am inclined to think this may be due in part at least to press rumours of firm action on the part of U.S. Government and His Majesty's Government, and it may be important to continue quietly with preparations so as to be in a position to keep up pressure if that should prove to be necessary.

But apart from immediate effect in restraining Japanese outrages, we have to consider the future. Unless some pressure is ready to be brought to bear on Japan, it seems likely that she will seek to impose a settlement intolerably unfair to China and designed to destroy foreign rights and interests. I understood from American Delegation in Brussels that U.S. Government took the line that we should not contemplate a settlement that did violence to 9 Power Treaty[3], but it seems unlikely that we shall have much say in the settlement unless we can make a display of considerable force.

Please convey all the foregoing, unless you see any objection, to U.S. Government. You may at the same time assure Mr. Hull that we should not consult French Government until it became necessary to contemplate moving ships ourselves, in which case French Government would have to alter their dispositions. That question is not therefore immediate.

[2] No. 441. [3] Cf. Nos. 344, 351, 356, 360, 381, and 390.

No. 447

Sir R. Lindsay (Washington) to Mr. Eden
(Received December 25, 9.30 a.m.)

No. 512 Telegraphic [F 11473/9/10]

Very Secret   WASHINGTON, *December 24, 1937, 6.30 p.m.*

Your telegram No. 628[1] crossed my telegram No. 509[2] about visit by

[1] No. 446.
[2] Not kept in F.O. archives. This telegram of December 23 referred to the Australian Government's invitation to the United States Government to send one warship to the New South Wales 150th Anniversary celebrations to be held at Sydney on January 26: the U.S. Government replied that they would accept the invitation if a squadron of four cruisers

American cruisers squadron to Sydney and Singapore. It should leave the Pacific coast about January 4th and I hope you will regard this as something which will serve to maintain pressure on Japan.

I saw Under-Secretary of State this morning and repeated to him what I had said to the Secretary of State (my telegram No. 501[3]). I said His Majesty's Government could send naval reinforcements to Singapore and did he think some such action parallel to movement of American cruisers squadron would be appropriate? He said this was the kind of question which could be discussed with United States Staff Officer.[4]

On subject of peace negotiations we had had some inconclusive conversation a few days ago. I now told him that in your view early restoration of peace would be more important than the exact method by which it was achieved but that if German or Italian good offices were invoked His Majesty's Government would not wish to be left out (your telegram to Hankow No. 5).[5] I also repeated considerations mentioned in your telegram under reference. He said emphatically that (? relatively) your view as expressed to Hankow was a . . .[6] under statement of the case. He could easily conceive that peace negotiations might be carried on in conditions which would threaten principle of open door and thus imperil interests vital both to United States Government and to His Majesty's Government.

were invited. In telegram No. 516 of December 28 Sir R. Lindsay reported that the invitation had now been accepted and that the cruisers *Louisville, Milwaukee, Memphis,* and *Trenton* were arriving at Sydney on January 26.

[3] No. 442.

[4] Mr. Eden wrote across the top of this telegram: 'I like the idea of our sending some ships to Singapore to meet Americans there.'

[5] In Hankow telegram No. 10 of December 6 Mr. Gage reported a conversation with the Chinese Vice Minister for Foreign Affairs and asked for guidance as to His Majesty's Government's attitude towards German mediation attempts. Telegram No. 5 to Hankow of December 10 referred to Tokyo telegram No. 776 (No. 404), which Mr. Gage had not seen, and stated that 'Attitude of His Majesty's Government to German or Italian mediation is . . . that, while the termination of the present conflict is more important than the means by which this is achieved we should much prefer that the ultimate settlement should not be to the sole credit of these powers'.

[6] The text was here uncertain.

No. 448

Mr. Gage (Hankow) to Mr. Eden (Received December 27, 11.30 a.m.)

No. 40 Telegraphic: by wireless [F 11524/9/10]

Important   HANKOW, *December 27, 1937*

Addressed to Mr. Howe telegram No. 62.

Donald tells me confidentially further Japanese peace terms reached

German Ambassador last night[1] and have been shown to Chiang Kai-shek. They will be presented to Waichiaopu today.

Donald cannot divulge contents at present but says they are quite unacceptable and appear to have been dictated by the military. He has urged Chiang Kai-shek to (? publish) them and hopes this will be done tomorrow.[2]

Repeated to Commander-in-Chief, General Officer Commanding.

[1] According to *D.G.F.P.*, Series D, vol. i, No. 540, four 'basic conditions' for peace were communicated to Dr. von Dirksen in Tokyo by Mr. Hirota on December 22. See No. 453 below.

[2] Mr. Eden wrote on the filed copy of this telegram: 'The Chinese seem to be standing up well now. We should give what help we discreetly can.'

No. 449

Mr. Eden to Sir R. Craigie (Tokyo)

No. 600 Telegraphic [F 11646/10816/10]

FOREIGN OFFICE, *December 28, 1937, 7.5 p.m.*

Your telegram No. 885[1].

Full text of our note was published here, and consequently text of Japanese reply will have to be published, but I am willing to await decision of Japanese Government as to date of release.

As regards publication in Japan of our note, I do not see any reason why we should insist on that, nor should we, I suppose, be successful in persuading the Japanese Government to publish it if they have reasons, which in their judgment are good, against its publication.

[1] In this telegram of December 28, received in the Foreign Office at 4.30 p.m., Sir R. Craigie said he had received the Japanese Government's reply to the British note concerning the Wuhu incidents (No. 426). His comments were to follow in telegram No. 886 (No. 451 below). He suggested that if 'we propose to accept Japanese reply and so bring public correspondence to an end there is no need to insist on publication of our note here'. The text of the Japanese note was transmitted in Tokyo telegram Nos. 888 and 889 of December 29, not printed: it was published in *The Times*, December 31, 1937, p. 11.

No. 450

Minute by Sir A. Cadogan

[F 11749/4880/10]

FOREIGN OFFICE, *December 28, 1937*

This paper[1] was sent in on Dec[ember] 21st as part of it was of

[1] i.e. No. 438.

immediate topical interest (Hong Kong), but I think it raises a further very important issue which, though not immediate, and though we may never even be confronted with it, should begin to engage our attention now.

The issue arises out of that passage in the memorandum which urges that we should 'combine that policy (of force) with extreme moderation and the utmost consideration for the rights and interests of other Powers'.

If—and it may yet be a very big 'if'—we and the Americans are going to be in a position to dictate to, or at least to influence, Japan, we must know what we are aiming at, and how we propose to use our power.

Assuming for the moment that we *do* make a display of overwhelming Anglo-American naval force in the Far East, what are going to be the immediate repercussions both in that region and in the rest of the world?

In Japan there may be an outburst against us. I do not pretend to know the Japanese, but I cannot help thinking there is a chance that they may react very differently. They have certainly not responded too well to our patience and long-suffering.

In the rest of the world, our friends will doubtless hail with glee firm action on our part. In some of these quarters there may be regrets that we do not dress up our action as action under the League—'collective security'—but probably there will be no very loud-voiced protest at that.

Germany and Italy may be wholesomely impressed or they may secretly rejoice that this adventure may give them the opportunity of putting into effect some of their more nefarious plans. In any case they will howl that America and England, being possessed of naval strength, choose to 'police the world'—naturally for their own selfish ends. They will argue that British naval strength is the great obstacle in the way of their obtaining 'justice', and Germany may dream of denouncing the Anglo-German naval agreement. It might not be hard for the German Govt. to whip up enthusiasm in Germany for embarking once again on a race in naval armaments.[2]

Some of this could be counteracted if, in the event, we were able to show that we were solicitous not only for our own legitimate interests in the Far East, but also for those of other people, and even more if we, with the U.S.A., were ultimately successful in bringing about a reasonably just settlement.

Japan has already more than once been cheated of what she has gained by force of arms, but that has never limited her ambitions nor, seemingly, her power to realise them. And we must recognise that her ambitions arise from her grievances and difficulties. That she has sought to remedy these in the wrong way should not blind us to their existence, and we should be wrong in thinking that a mere return to the status quo (if that were possible) would be a solution of the Far Eastern problem.

The moral of all this is that we should examine whether it is possible for

---

[2] Marginal comment by Mr. Eden: 'Germany can scarcely do this, as well as expand her air force at a great speed and equip her army.'

us to devise the lines of a reasonable settlement. The Americans in Brussels wanted to do this (though they had no concrete suggestions to make), but in those days it seemed to me futile to embark on such a plan when there seemed to be no chance of enforcing its acceptance.

It does seem to me now that the time has come to undertake this work. I cannot myself at this moment make any suggestions as to the form which the plan should take, but I think our experts should start on studies without delay. As soon as the thing begins to take shape, we should have to discuss it with the Americans and keep in close touch with them.

If we and the U.S. could succeed in bringing about a reasonable settlement, we might give the lie to those who say that we are only concerned to maintain the status quo (to our own advantage), and we might show that the 'dissatisfied' nations have a chance of obtaining some reasonable satisfaction of any legitimate claims that they may have without resorting to the dangerous and expensive expedient of war.

It may be said that Japan should be punished for her behaviour, but she will surely suffer enough for her folly: if she has legitimate grievances for which we could find a remedy, let us seek it. If we are strong enough to impose a peace, let us not repeat the errors of Versailles.[3]

[3] In response to Sir A. Cadogan's minute Sir J. Pratt and Sir J. Brenan prepared two long memoranda of January 5 and 6, both entitled 'Sino-Japanese Peace Terms'. These papers, setting out suggestions for 'peace terms to be offered to the belligerents by Britain and America if called upon to mediate' are filed at F 335/16/10 and have not been printed here. As Sir A. Cadogan pointed out in a minute of January 23 'We cannot possibly tell what will be the state either of Japan or of China after a further prolongation of hostilities. Neither can we say with what weight we or the Americans would be able, at any given moment in the future, to intervene. What I wanted was rather an "optimum"—ideal terms that we could impose if we were in a position to dictate'. He thought that the Americans should now be consulted, and suggested that he might send privately to Dr. Hornbeck 'with suitable explanation' a 'suitably edited' paper based on the two memoranda. Mr. Eden expressed agreement on January 28, and on February 14 a 'Memorandum on possible peace terms for communication to the United States Government' was sent to Dr. Hornbeck with a covering letter by Sir A. Cadogan. Both the letter and the memorandum are printed in *F.R.U.S.*, 1938, vol. iii, pp. 89–93. Mr. Hornbeck's reply of April 13, enclosing extensive comments on the British memorandum, is printed *ibid.*, pp. 141–53, and is also filed in F.O. archives at F 4463/16/10. Mr. Howe, who had returned from China to become head of the Far Eastern Department from March 1, 1938, commented on May 16 that the reply was 'largely what was to be expected. It does not offer much prospect of any kind of collaboration or parallel action, [and] assumes that neither side is going to win and will eventually be so exhausted that outside parties will be able to intervene'. Sir A. Cadogan agreed (May 17): 'A lot of this is awful stuff (and in Dr. Hornbeck's recognisable style).' He felt, however, that the exchange of correspondence had been 'useful', and sent a polite reply to Dr. Hornbeck on May 23 (*F.R.U.S.*, *ibid.*, pp. 172–3).

No. 451

Sir R. Craigie (Tokyo) to Mr. Eden
(Received December 28[1], 10.30 p.m.)

No. 886 Telegraphic [F 11673/10816/10]

Important   Confidential   TOKYO, December 29, 1937, 12.5 a.m.

My immediately preceding telegram.[2]

After reading note I said[3] there were two points on which it seemed to me inadequate, namely, (1) No indication of disciplinary measures taken against responsible officers and (2) Insufficient indication of guarantees for the future.

Dealing with point (1) Minister for Foreign Affairs handed me confidentially a list of officers held to have been responsible (see my telegram No. 887[4]) and in reply to my further enquiry stated that they had all been reprimanded. I stated that this punishment seemed to me to be inadequate particularly in the case of Colonel Hashimoto who had not only fired on our two warships and other British vessels but had after the incident kept his guns trained on warships and ordered them not to move. Such action certainly merited more than a mere reprimand. On point (2) His Excellency stated that the whole question of future arrangements for safeguarding shipping on the Yangtse was being carefully considered and he would be glad to discuss this with me shortly.

He then enquired whether he was to take it that I considered reply unsatisfactory on these points. I said that personally I thought that these particular matters would be settled more satisfactorily by a continuance of conversations between us rather than through a further exchange of published notes, but that I did not know what view my Government would take. Minister for Foreign Affairs expressed readiness to discuss both points with me fully.

After American acceptance of Japanese reply in regard to sinking of *Panay*[5] I think it would have unfortunate results if we were to assume a more uncompromising attitude in regard to attacks on our ships. I suggest, however, that our reply should refer to necessity for further conversations to ascertain exact nature of measures to be taken to safeguard in future shipping on Yangtse and British lives and property generally in China. I would not recommend any further *public* reference to nature of punishment as we are more likely to receive satisfaction if I have your authority to press this matter in confidential discussions here.

Repeated to Mr. Howe and Commander-in-Chief.

---

[1] The date of receipt of this telegram was given on the filed copy as December 29, presumably in error.

[2] See No. 449, note 1.   [3] i.e. to Mr. Hirota.   [4] Not printed (F 11676/10816/10).

[5] The Japanese Government's note of apology for the *Panay* sinking was handed to the U.S. Ambassador on December 24: the U.S. Government's note of acceptance was delivered

to Mr. Hirota at noon on December 26. Both notes are printed in *F.R.U.S. Japan 1931–1941*, vol. i, pp. 549–52. Cf. also comments in *From the Morgenthau Diaries, op. cit.*, p. 492.

No. 452

Sir R. Craigie (Tokyo) to Mr. Eden
(Received December 29, 9.30 a.m.)

No. 890 Telegraphic [F 11662/10816/10]

Immediate   TOKYO, *December 29, 1937, 1.5 p.m.*

My telegram No. 885.[1]

Statement was issued last night by the military authorities giving their version of the incidents at Wuhu on December 12th.[2] I was only informed late last night that such a statement was being issued and I was given no previous knowledge of its contents.

I consider publication objectionable not only for this reason but because general tendency of the statement is to put the blame for the incidents on us on the grounds that our ships should not have been where they were. There are also various points on which the statement appears at variance with the facts as known to me. (Assertion in 2nd paragraph of Japanese Government's note that principal points of full report on the incidents had been explained to me by the Japanese military and naval authorities is not true: naval authorities did make communication to the Naval Attaché but no comparable information reached me from the military).

I am taking up this question with Ministry of Foreign Affairs and Ministry of War and will telegraph further comments later.

I have just seen your telegram No. 600.[3] In my opinion situation described above makes it important that our note should be published here.

Repeated to Mr. Howe and Commander-in-Chief.

[1] See No. 449, note 1.   [2] Cf. Nos. 407–410.   [3] No. 449.

No. 453

Mr. Gage (Hankow) to Mr. Eden (Received December 29, 2.50 p.m.)

No. 45 Telegraphic: by wireless [F 11700/9/10]

Important   Confidential   HANKOW, *December 29, 1937*

Addressed to Embassy, Shanghai, No. 79.
My telegram No. 62[1].
Following are the four basic principles of Japanese peace proposals

[1] No. 448.

contained in memorandum handed to Madame Chiang Kai-shek and Dr. Kung (Chiang Kai-shek was in bed with a cold) by German Ambassador as given to me by Donald this morning:

1. China to join Japan and Manchukuo in anti-Communist measures.
2. Demilitarized and special régimes to be established wherever necessary.
3. Economic co-operation with Japan and Manchukuo.
4. Indemnity. Japanese according to Donald also requested Chiang Kai-shek to send a peace envoy to Japan. Upon his arrival Japanese Government would decide when and where they would see him. There would be *no* cessation of hostilities during the peace negotiations.

German Ambassador stated that these terms had been received by his Government from the Japanese Government with the request that they should be passed on to Chinese Government at Chungking and intimated that previous terms presented through him were to be considered cancelled in view of changing military situation. He had accordingly been instructed to leave these terms 'without comment'.[2]

Donald made it clear that the terms were entirely unacceptable as under them, China would virtually cease to exist as an independent nation.

Information contained in this telegram is still confidential but Donald is pressing for early publication.[3]

Repeated to Commander-in-Chief and General Officer Commanding.

[2] The German Government's reactions to the Japanese proposals can be followed in *D.G.F.P.*, Series D, vol. i, Nos. 541–6.

[3] The four basic Japanese conditions were communicated to the Foreign Office in London by the Chinese Ambassador on December 29 (F 11732/9/10). 'The Ambassador added that his Government had indicated that they had rejected these terms, both as a basis of peace and as a basis of discussion.' Mr. Eden minuted to Sir A. Cadogan on December 30: 'We must consider tomorrow whether there is anything further we can do to help China.'

No. 454

Sir R. Craigie (Tokyo) to Mr. Eden (Received December 29, 12.30 p.m.)

No. 892 Telegraphic [F 11701/10816/10]

TOKYO, *December 29, 1937, 6.35 p.m.*

My telegram No. 890[1] penultimate paragraph.

Points in the statement issued by Military which are specially objectionable are:

1. 'Vessels attacked were in dangerous fighting area' where Japanese forces did not dream that foreign vessels could be. This despite warning to foreign shipping given on December 9th.
2. There was dense fog.

[1] No. 452.

3. Vessels gave the impression that they were trying to hide behind a smoke screen.

4. The statement ends 'all these circumstances notwithstanding, we sincerely regret that there should have taken place the present unfortunate affair'.

Counsellor called this morning at my request at the Ministry of Foreign Affairs and pointed out discourtesy of issuing such a statement without previous notification and at a time when . . .[2] was under discussion by the Minister for Foreign Affairs and myself and requesting that the press be informed that I had not seen the statement and could not accept this version of the affair. *Communiqué* on these lines has been issued to the press.

See my immediately following telegram.[3]

Repeated to Embassy Shanghai and Commander-in-Chief.

---

[2] The text was here uncertain.   [3] No. 455 below.

No. 455

Sir R. Craigie (Tokyo) to Mr. Eden
(Received December 29, 12.5 p.m.)

No. 893 Telegraphic [F 11702/10816/10]

TOKYO, *December 29, 1937, 6.50 p.m.*

My immediately preceding telegram.[1]

On the whole I am inclined to recommend that in deciding whether to accept the note from the Minister for Foreign Affairs you should not be influenced by the action of the military in issuing their statement. I think it has been made sufficiently plain here that such methods can only do harm. Moreover enquiries made at the General Staff elicited an expression of regret at the premature publication of the statement which they had intended should be handed to me with the Note. Military Attaché thinks that they would amend the statement in agreement with us if desired. It could perhaps be left with me to make the best arrangements I can for dealing with this Imperial Headquarters' statement after I have received supplementary information for which I have asked Mr. Howe and Commander-in-Chief in a telegram despatched to them to-day.

Repeated to Embassy, Shanghai, and Commander-in-Chief.

---

[1] No. 454.

No. 456

Minute[1] *by Sir J. Brenan on Chinese customs administration*

[*F 11533/220/10*]

FOREIGN OFFICE, *December 29, 1937*

So far as we can gauge the position at the moment (December 28th) it would seem to be as follows. Unless the Japanese can induce the existing Chinese Government to accept their peace terms, which does not appear likely, they will set up a puppet administration under their own control and will claim that it is the government of all China. They are as yet undecided whether this new administration is to be established at Peking or Nanking, and although the Japanese military authorities are supporting the provisional Peking régime the Tokyo authorities have not given it any formal recognition and are waiting on events in the Yangtze valley.

In the meantime the Customs Commissioner at Tientsin, Mr. Myers, has been forced to accept the authority of the provisional Peking government. The North China revenues are being detained in a Japanese bank pending a general settlement and a new customs tariff with reduced duties favouring Japanese trade is about to be introduced in the north. Mr. Myers was informed that the Inspectorate of Customs would be removed to Peking and he was sounded regarding his acceptance of the post of Inspector-General. He replied by pointing out that to set up one Inspector-General against another would ruin the integrity of the Customs service.

In answer to protests by His Majesty's Ambassador at Tokyo the Minister for Foreign Affairs gave soothing but equivocal replies. He ridiculed the idea that the Customs could be seized by force without the sanction of the Japanese Government; he pointed out that the position was regularized in the north by the Commissioner's recognition of the provisional government and said that the whole subject was under interdepartmental discussion. He could give no information about the new tariff. The Japanese Consul-General in Tientsin, however, has admitted that a change is contemplated and the new rates for a number of articles have actually been ascertained confidentially through the Commissioner.

At various times the Japanese authorities have assured us that they desire to preserve a unified Customs service for all China but it is becoming increasingly clear that by this they mean a service for all China

[1] Sir J. Brenan was commenting on Shanghai telegram No. 774 of December 26 in which Mr. Howe referred to the difficulties of Sir F. Maze's position (cf. Nos. 395 and 396, and No. 398) and suggested that 'the time has come when we in conjunction with French and United States Governments must make up our minds whether we should or should not tell the Inspector General of Customs that, when Chinese Government refuse to acquiesce in any action which he proposes to take to safeguard the Customs, he can rely on support of those Powers to see him through vis-à-vis the Chinese Government to the best of their ability'.

under their control. The new tariff will doubtless be applied at all ports occupied by the Japanese forces and that will soon include the whole sea board.

We do not yet know what their next step will be, but it is not unlikely that the Inspector-General and his staff may be offered the alternative of transferring their allegiance and services to a puppet government set up at Peking or Nanking or being supplanted by another administration of more definitely Japanese complexion.

If, in this event, they accept the Japanese offer they may be able to maintain the present international character of the Customs service for some time to come. If not, and if the Powers have to confine their resentment to diplomatic protests, the service will become a Japanese organisation. It is in these circumstances that the Inspector-General now asks for the support of the Powers in coming to terms with the Japanese against the wishes of the Chinese Government. It is suggested that if the Customs personnel disobey the orders of the Chinese Government they are liable to lose their positions and pension rights and the Powers are asked to guarantee that they shall not be financially affected by such action.

It seems to me, however, that the situation is rapidly becoming such that the Customs employees are more likely to lose their positions and pensions if they remain loyal to the Chinese Government than if they transfer their allegiance to the Japanese. A Chinese Government driven into the far interior and deprived of all Customs revenue will have no funds wherewith to pay their Customs staff whereas service under the new masters will at least mean continued salaries, for the salaries are the first charge on the Customs revenue. The general practice is for the Commissioner at each port to deduct from his collection of duty the cost of maintaining his establishment before remitting the balance to Shanghai.

I submit that the question now before the Powers, and His Majesty's Government in particular, is whether the Inspector-General and his staff should be encouraged to remain loyal to the dispossessed Chinese Government, in which case a guarantee of unemployment pay might well be necessary, or whether they should be advised to make terms with the Japanese and continue to run the Customs service on present lines to the best of their ability and for as long as possible. There is no doubt that the latter would be preferable from the point of view of foreign trade, however disappointing such an attitude would be for the Chinese.

I suggest that Mr. Howe might be asked for his observations on the above considerations as I imagine that the idea of the Powers guaranteeing the emoluments of a Customs staff serving a Japanese controlled organization is hardly practical.[2]

---

[2] Mr. Orde did not entirely agree with Sir J. Brenan (December 30): 'Our objective I think must be to preserve the integrity of the Customs administration and not let the Japanese

have an excuse for splitting it up, if we can help it. The question of one or two tariffs, though important, seems secondary, and I am not sure that it is necessary to assume with Mr. Howe (Shanghai tel. 789 [not printed]) that two tariffs are necessarily incompatible with the integrity of the administration though it is only in China that the fiction might be preserved. We must at any rate try to get the Chinese to face facts and as between "face" and the fiction of integrity to prefer the latter, which might turn out to be valuable.' A telegram on these lines to Mr. Howe, instructing him to assure Sir F. Maze that 'we will support him to the best of our ability in any subsequent difficulties i.e. we shall continue to impress on Dr. Kung the need to take a realist view of the situation' was despatched as telegram No. 1 to Shanghai of January 1, 1938 (F 11682/220/10).

No. 457

Sir R. Craigie (Tokyo) to Mr. Eden
(Received December 30, 10.30 a.m.)

No. 898 Telegraphic [F 11697/10816/10]

TOKYO, *December 30, 1937, 3 p.m.*

Vernacular press welcomes settlement of *Panay* incident[1] and general tone has been markedly conciliatory towards United States, great satisfaction being shown that they refused to fall in with Great Britain's alleged proposal for concerted action in Far East.

Asahi expresses conviction that now that United States have settled incident in a friendly spirit Great Britain will follow this 'good example'.[2]

Repeated Embassy Shanghai and Commander-in-Chief.

[1] See No. 451, note 5.
[2] Mr. Thyne Henderson commented on December 30: 'There is doubtless great relief in Japan at having got safely past what looked like an explosive situation. They were clearly more nervous of the U.S. than of the U.K., because the former are in a position to exercise force, while they think we are not. This supplies further evidence, if it were needed, that force is practically the only argument to which the present rulers of Japan are prepared to listen.'

No. 458

Mr. Eden to Sir R. Craigie (Tokyo)

No. 607 Telegraphic [F 11673/10816/10]

FOREIGN OFFICE, *December 30, 1937, 7 p.m.*

Your telegram No. 886[1].

I agree that the Japanese Note is not adequate in the two respects mentioned. I agree, however, that it will be best to deal with these points by means of conversation, as you suggest.

[1] No. 451.

You should address a Note to the Japanese Government in the following terms:

'I have the honour, on instructions from His Majesty's Government in the United Kingdom, to inform Your Excellency that they have noted with appreciation the assurances contained in Your Excellency's Note of the 28th December in connexion with the attacks on British warships and merchant shipping on the 12th December, and have learnt with satisfaction that the statements contained in your Note of December 14th apply to the merchant vessels concerned, as well as to the warships.

His Majesty's Government are bound to observe that their information in regard to the circumstances in which the attacks took place—notably, for instance, on the point of visibility—is at variance with that of the Japanese Government.

His Majesty's Government note, however, with satisfaction that the Japanese Government have taken, or are prepared to take, the necessary measures to deal suitably with the officers responsible for these incidents and to prevent any repetition. As regards the latter, His Majesty's Government consider that the details of these measures and their effective application suitably form the subject of further conversations, in the course of which they do not doubt that they will be informed of the actual steps decided upon.'[2]

We propose to publish above text on Saturday morning.[3]

[2] Discussions on this point continued intermittently until the following May: see Nos. 500 and 579 below.
[3] See No. 449, note 1.

No. 459

Letter from Mr. Eden to Mr. Chamberlain

PREM 1/314

FOREIGN OFFICE, *December 31, 1937*

My dear Neville,

This letter on the last day of 1937 is really to say thank you to you for your unvarying kindness and help to me this year. I really find it hard to express how much I have appreciated your readiness at all times to listen to my problems and help in their solution, despite your many other preoccupations.

1938 is obviously going to be a very difficult year internationally. Our rearmament will still be far from complete and we shall have a very disturbed world to deal with. At the same time there are elements of encouragement: first and foremost co-operation with the United States, though slow and difficult to foster, is now, I hope, making real progress. I shall know more about this after I have seen Ingersoll tomorrow[1], but I am sure that our role in this respect must be to do everything we can privately to encourage the Americans. If they do send some ships to Singapore in a few weeks' time that would be an event of first class importance.[2] Curiously enough that very suggestion was made to me by the Dutch Minister this morning. I, of course, was careful to make no comment which could lead him to think that anything of the kind was likely to happen.

There is one other matter which I should like to mention. I am a little troubled by the fact that according to the account that Chatfield gave us at one of our meetings just before Christmas, we shall it appears be particularly weak at sea from May next year until the autumn of 1939. This unhappily is likely to be a most tricky period internationally, for our Air Force will be only entering on a full stage of development, while our anti-aircraft defence will still be almost non-existent in the modern sense. I have been wondering whether it might not be possible to accelerate some of the naval construction. Quite apart from the usefulness of such an acceleration in strengthening our defences during a critical period, the moral effect upon the world would be excellent. This may be quite impracticable and I did not want to write to you on the subject before Christmas; I only make the suggestion now in the hope that if it appeals to you, you may feel it worth while to have the matter further examined. The fact that commercial orders for new ships have recently fallen off may make it all the more possible to accelerate Admiralty construction.

Cleverly will, I think, have explained to you that we decided to bring Van's appointment out today, in view of guesses which the press were beginning to make on account of his G.C.B.[3] I am sure that it was wise to do this and I consulted Van and he fully approved. Cadogan is settling in here very well and I am confident that the new order of things will work satisfactorily.[4]

Yours ever,
ANTHONY EDEN

[1] See Nos. 460 and 462 below.   [2] Cf. No. 447.

[3] See Volume XIX, No. 408. Sir R. Vansittart's appointment as Diplomatic Adviser to H.M. Government and Sir A. Cadogan's as Permanent Under Secretary for Foreign Affairs took effect on January 1, 1938.

[4] Mr. Chamberlain noted on the top of this letter: 'I have replied to this but I shall want to look at it again when I come to No. 10.' His reply has not been traced in F.O. archives or PREM.

No. 460

Mr. Eden to Sir R. Lindsay (Washington)

No. *1 Telegraphic* [F 95/84/10]

Important   Very Secret   FOREIGN OFFICE, *January 1, 1938, 4 p.m.*

Your telegram No. 512[1].

I was very glad to receive Captain Ingersoll this morning[2] for a preliminary conversation, and he will now get into touch with the Admiralty, who will afford him every possible facility. Record of our conversation is being telegraphed to you.[3]

Meanwhile it seems to me important to clear up, if we can, exactly what is in the mind of the United States Government. So far as I can gather, their idea is to be prepared for action if such is rendered inevitable by further Japanese provocation. What had rather been in our mind was, as you know, that it would be preferable, if possible, to proceed as soon as may be to some demonstration of naval strength, with the double purpose of averting further outrages and of giving us some standing in the discussion of the ultimate settlement.[4]

Can you ascertain whether the United States Government would be likely to adopt our view of the matter? They may see technical difficulties in the way, but they might at least authorise Captain Ingersoll to discuss possibilities on these lines if he has not authority to do so. (For your own information I rather inferred from what he said that he was not expecting to discuss such possibilities but rather dispositions to be taken if war were forced upon United States by Japan).

In any event visit of the United States cruisers to Singapore would certainly be most helpful as evidence of Anglo-United States friendship and I much hope this will materialise.

---

[1] No. 447.
[2] Captain Ingersoll was introduced by Mr. Herschel Johnson of the U.S. Embassy. Sir A. Cadogan was also present.
[3] See No. 462 below. A fuller account of the interview was contained in despatch No. 23 to Washington of January 1, not printed (F 95/84/10).
[4] Sir A. Cadogan noted in his diary on January 1 that Captain Ingersoll seemed 'nice and his instructions seem to be helpful, but even he seems not clear on the *objective*. So after he'd gone, drafted a telegram to Washington to try and draw Americans and urge a naval demonstration *now*'. See *The Diaries of Sir Alexander Cadogan 1938–1945* (ed. David Dilks, London, 1971), p. 31.

No. 461

Mr. Gage (Hankow) to Mr. Eden (Received January 1, 5.45 p.m.)

No. 48 Telegraphic: by wireless [F 105/84/10]

HANKOW, *January 1, 1938*

Addressed to Embassy, Shanghai, No. 86 of January 1st.

In spite of optimism regarding Russian intervention in some quarters here, Donald holds following view.

1. Russia definitely will not fight Japan unless attacked.

2. Russia wants neither China nor Japan to win but both to be impaired ...[1] in order that Communist influences may thrive in both countries.[2]

3. Russian help to China is on the same basis as that of any other country. Aeroplanes supplied have been paid for in cash and pilots salaries are paid at same rate as those of American pilots.[3]

Repeated to General-Officer-Commanding, Commander-in-Chief.

[1] The text was here uncertain.

[2] Commenting on this point in Moscow telegram No. 3 Saving of January 17 Lord Chilston wrote that point 2. 'would certainly be the ideal solution from the point of view of Soviet Government but as a second best they would probably be quite content with the emergence of a stronger and non-communist Chinese Government and a Japan, weakened by the war, whether susceptible to the contagion of communism or not'.

[3] Lord Chilston commented on this point: 'By supplying aeroplanes and services pilots on a regular basis Soviet Government would place themselves on the same footing as other Powers who are assisting China ... though they would no doubt like world communist opinion to believe they were playing a more active and independent part.'

No. 462

Mr. Eden to Sir R. Lindsay (Washington)

No. 2 Telegraphic [F 95/84/10]

Very Secret   FOREIGN OFFICE, *January 1, 1938, 11 p.m.*

My telegram No. 1.[1]

In welcoming Captain Ingersoll this morning I said all we knew of scope and purpose of his mission was that the President had suggested to you desirability of discussing naval plans to meet contingencies in the Far East. I asked if he could tell us a little more of what United States Government had in mind.

2. Captain Ingersoll said Navy Department's plans for naval action in the Pacific assumed that certain dispositions were being made by us. He imagined our plans were drawn up on a similar basis. The President and

[1] No. 460.

Admiral Leahy[2] thought we ought now to exchange information in order to co-ordinate our plans more closely. He could explain American plans and would like to know what ours were. There were also a number of purely technical arrangements which should be made in advance of any co-operation in the Pacific.

3. I asked whether United States Government thought any joint action could be taken now or was action to wait until after next incident. He said Navy Department considered that no movement at all could be made in the Pacific unless full preparation had been made for every eventuality including war. For instance they would not wish to concentrate at Hawaii now only to have to return to coast to make up crews to full strength if war was declared. United States Navy could not take certain steps unless war were declared. He could not therefore say if any action were in contemplation now but after the exchange of technical views during next ten days it might be easier to consider what political decisions might be taken.

4. I told him what we knew of plan to send United States cruisers to Singapore[3] which had been formulated after he left United States of America and suggested that the opening of the new dock at Singapore might afford publishable pretext for visit. We should like to welcome United States ships suitably and would therefore be glad to learn as soon as decision was taken. United States Chargé d'Affaires who was present promised to put this to his Government at once.

5. Captain Ingersoll said that if his visit to this country became known which he hoped it would not it had been arranged that it should be given out that he had come over in connexion with the Washington Treaty with special reference to the question of the limitations on construction of capital ships. Rumour of new ship construction in Japan would make this explanation appear plausible.

[2] U.S. Chief of Naval Operations.   [3] See No. 447.

No. 463

Sir R. Lindsay (Washington) to Foreign Office[1]
(Received January 3, 10.30 a.m.)

No. 5 Telegraphic [F 96/84/10]

Important   WASHINGTON, *January 3, 1938, 1.37 p.m.*

Your telegrams Nos. 1[2] and 2.[3]
I have only uncertain indications of what President has in mind as

[1] Mr. Eden left London on January 3 for a holiday in the South of France: see Volume XIX, No. 411, note 1. Mr. Chamberlain took charge of the Foreign Office in his absence.
[2] No. 460.   [2] No. 462.

regards scope and purpose of staff conversations. Doubtless he is largely influenced by his own personal recollection of what passed between Gaunt and Pratt from 1915 onwards.[4] According to what he said at my interview with him on December 16th[5] these started as merely liaison and developed to such an extent that by the time the war came complete war plans had been elaborated and Admiral Sims'[6] well known mission was really of minor importance. He also told me that while conversations of 1915 had begun with exchange of naval information they had gone on to exchange of 'all sorts of intelligence' (or some such very general expression).

2. I understand you are anxious for a naval demonstration in the Far East but I rather infer that while you will be very glad of visit of United States cruisers to Singapore you may be wishing for something more or for something different. But I note that you are already in communication with United States Embassy about this through United States Chargé d'Affaires. Naval Attaché had oral confirmation from Navy Department that visit to Singapore is intended and I have had indirect confirmation from Welles though nothing has been allowed to transpire as yet. I admit to feeling reluctant to press United States administration too strongly about demonstrations. You may take it that President is willing to make them, but their efficacy greatly depends on effect they have on public opinion here no less than on that which they have on possible aggressor and of that the President is the best judge. He is still educating his public and I expect he is anxious not to frighten them. My impression is that United States Government is at present a horse that will run best when the spur is not used but of course if for any special reason you want him to go any faster I am ready to do my best or you can try through United States Embassy or staff officer as seems best to you.

3. Besides naval demonstrations there can also be diplomatic demonstration and it is possible that President's speech to Congress tomorrow[7] is to be one of the latter. If this comes about it will have been the (? consequence) of pressure from us. In general they greatly prefer to act independently of us and to avoid any appearance of collusion or of joint action.

4. To return to the question of naval staff conversations is it to your interest to define this or to clear up exactly what they have in mind? It seems to me on the contrary far best to leave the scope vague and to make it as vast as possible by trying as occasion arises to widen the field which conversations are to cover perhaps by a process of diplomatic trial and error. So long as strictest secrecy is maintained I do not see how any such danger can be involved by such procedure.

[4] See No. 433, note 3.   [5] See No. 433.
[6] Admiral W. S. Sims was commander of U.S. naval operations in European waters, 1917–18: for details of his somewhat controversial career see Captain S. Roskill, *Naval Policy between the Wars*, Volume I (London, 1968), pp. 51–3.
[7] See *The Times*, January 4, 1938, p. 12: the speech was largely concerned with domestic matters.

No. 464

Foreign Office to Sir R. Craigie (Tokyo)

No. 3[1] *Telegraphic* [F 71/71/23]

Personal and Very Secret   FOREIGN OFFICE, *January 3, 1938, 6.30 p.m.*

Decypher yourself (to both places).

Following from Sir A. Cadogan:

His Majesty's Ambassador in Washington on December 16th had secret interview with President, when latter expatiated at length, though somewhat vaguely, on possibility of a blockade of Japan, to be exercised by United States and British fleets.[2] It seemed that in his idea blockade should be imposed only after next outrage by Japanese naval or military forces. But in course of the conversation he seemed to incline to idea of some immediate action and spoke of advancing date of American naval manoeuvres and sending squadron of cruisers to Singapore. He also decided to send naval staff officer to London to effect liaison and he arrived on December 31st. It seems to be a fact that American manoeuvres have been advanced, and in reply to invitation from Australian Government to send one cruiser to celebrations at Sydney at the end of this month, United States Government asked whether they might send four, which would probably proceed afterwards to Singapore. This has been agreed to.[3]

Possibility of sending fleet to Far East has been under consideration for some weeks by His Majesty's Government, and preparations have been made which would enable it to sail at short notice. His Majesty's Ambassador in Washington informed President, under instructions, that His Majesty's Government were contemplating possibility of sending to Far Eastern waters a fleet of eight or nine capital ships with the necessary accompaniment of other units if the United States Government would make at least an equivalent effort. From this it will be clear to you that His Majesty's Government have no present intention of reinforcing fleet in Far East unless United States Government take parallel action.

It is not yet clear whether United States Government merely contemplate taking necessary dispositions so as to be prepared for action in event of severe further provocation by Japan, or whether, as soon as their preparations could be contemplated, they would consider a naval demonstration in force by both fleets. We are trying to get further light on this.

His Majesty's Government are rather inclined to advocate early demonstration, with the double purpose of averting further incidents and of enabling the two Governments to exert sufficient weight in the discussion of the ultimate settlement. But there may be difficulties in the

---

[1] No. 6 to Shanghai.   [2] See No. 433.   [3] See No. 447, note 2.

way of this. We will keep you informed of further reactions from Washington.

Against this background you may be able to see why we have found difficulty in accepting various suggestions for adopting a conciliatory attitude towards Japanese Government (see, for example your telegrams Nos. 865[4] and 870[5]. Also your private letter to me of December 2nd[6]). Feeling against Japan has been growing here and in America to an extent which you will be able to infer from the fact that we have been having discussions with United States Government such as I have described. For this reason His Majesty's Government have been reluctant to emphasize their desire for friendship with Japan or to advertise the fact that they have not given more help to China, as they are in some sort morally bound to do.

You will, of course, realise that the foregoing is to be treated with the utmost possible secrecy, and the information should, if possible, be kept to yourself alone.

[4] In this telegram of December 24 Sir R. Craigie had complained that he was unable publicly to defend His Majesty's Government against the charge that they were 'through provision of arms and money, the mainstay of China's resistance'. He asked to be given discretion to inform the Japanese Government of the 'true facts', but Mr. Eden minuted 'This is not possible . . .': cf. No. 413, note 4.
[5] Not kept in F.O. archives. [6] No. 400.

No. 465

Foreign Office to Sir R. Lindsay (Washington)

No. 5[1] Telegraphic [F 11777/9/10]

FOREIGN OFFICE, *January 3, 1938, 7.30 p.m.*

Chinese Ambassador on December 31st asked me[2] whether I thought that Far Eastern Advisory Committee[3] should hold a meeting during forthcoming session of the Council. Public opinion in China would expect it. He went on to say that some Chinese thought that if only the League would agree to impose some sanctions United States would cooperate.

I expressed doubt about sanctions notably on oil, proposal of which might give rise to difficulties in Anglo-U.S. relations and would immediately bring up question of joint guarantee of Netherlands East Indies. As to Advisory Committee I said I doubted whether anything useful would come of a meeting but I did not wish to dissuade his Government if they wished to have one called. I suggested that he and Chinese Ambassador at Paris might discuss the matter with M. Delbos, M. Litvinov and myself during Council meeting.

[1] No. 1 Saving to Paris. [2] Mr. Eden.
[3] i.e. the Committee of Twenty-Three of the League of Nations.

His Excellency said his Government naturally would not wish to do anything which might introduce complications into Anglo-U.S. relations and he would invite observations from his colleagues in Washington and Paris.

How do you think Government to which you are accredited feel about meeting of Committee with special reference to the possibility that imposition of sanctions may there be suggested?

Repeated to Shanghai No. 8.

No. 466

Mr. Gage (Hankow) to Foreign Office (Received January 4, 9.30 a.m.)

No. 55 Telegraphic: by wireless [*F 144/16/10*]

Confidential   HANKOW, *January 3, 1938*

Addressed to British Embassy Shanghai No. 97 January 3rd.

My telegram No. 87[1].

I enquired this morning of Vice Minister for Foreign Affairs whether any reply had yet been given to German Ambassador. Vice Minister for Foreign Affairs replied in negative and said that it had not yet been decided whether a blank refusal should be returned or further details of Japanese peace terms called for.

I later had opportunity of speaking to General von Falkenhausen[2] with reference to statements which have appeared in local press regarding peace negotiations and without divulging to him that I was aware of the terms presented by *German Ambassador*. The General believes that responsible Japanese and even young military are anxious to terminate hostilities and would be prepared to negotiate on basis of terms such as those presented by German Ambassador. Reasons he gave were 1. Japan was beginning to feel the severe cost of the war. 2. She felt she was wasting man power dangerously in China and troops were also becoming demoralized. 3. Difficulty of deciding upon the next move and dislike of adventuring further into Chinese territory.

Fundamental Chinese conditions were recognition of Chinese territorial integrity and sovereignty. He thought that there was scope for negotiation of these fundamental conditions within the first, third and fourth basic conditions of the Japanese proposals (he alluded to four conditions himself). As regards second Japanese condition he thought difficulty might be surmounted if normally applied to both sides. Generally speaking he was of opinion that the present occasion was

[1] In this telegram of January 1, transmitted to the Foreign Office as Hankow telegram No. 49, Mr. Gage reported that he had received the four basic conditions of the Japanese peace proposals from the Chinese Vice Minister for Foreign Affairs: see No. 453.

[2] German Military Adviser to the Chinese Government.

favourable for further attempt to find solution to dispute. Asked whether he thought England and America could usefully assist Germany in mediation he replied in the affirmative *provided that they acted together*.

General von Falkenhausen is not in sympathy with National Social Régime in Germany and has always shown considerable independence of official German outlook. The fact that he favours Anglo-American co-operation with Germany in this case whereas . . .[3] even informed us of their *démarche* seems to prove that he is not simply playing German game. I think therefore that it can safely be assumed that his opinion is a perfectly honest one and in view of high esteem in which he is held here I am passing it on for what it is worth.

General von Falkenhausen was formerly German Military Attaché at Tokyo and conviction with which he spoke opinions set out in paragraph 2 gave the impression that he had received information from Tokyo possibly from present German Military Attaché.

It seems possible that an expression of willingness by Chinese to discuss present peace terms may strengthen their case. Discussion should consequently prove validity or otherwise of Japanese claim expressed by Japanese Ambassador in Washington that they are surprisingly mild. Japanese have always complained hitherto of lack of Chinese response to overtures.[4]

I have promised General von Falkenhausen that no mention will be made in Tokyo of source of any information imparted to me by German Adviser.

[3] The text was here uncertain.

[4] In his telegram No. 59 of January 4 (No. 102 to Shanghai) Mr. Gage added that according to Mr. Donald the main difficulty with the Japanese peace terms from Chiang Kai-shek's point of view was 'Japanese insistence on direct conversations. Previous experience of such conversations is bad (Ho Umetsu agreement etc. [see No. 39]) and Chiang Kai-shek has no intention of being caught in the same trap again. It is also considered time will make Japanese more reasonable'.

No. 467

Dominions Office to the U.K. High Commissioner in the Commonwealth of Australia[1]

No. 5 Telegraphic [F 312/84/10]

Secret   DOMINIONS OFFICE, *January 4, 1938, 9.30 p.m.*

Your secret telegram of 28th December[2] Commonwealth Government's telegram of 24th December No. 108.[2] Please deliver following message to Prime Minister[3] begins. In view of the proposal of the United States

[1] Sir G. G. Whiskard. A copy of this telegram was sent to the Foreign Office by the Dominions Office on January 6.

[2] Not traced in F.O. archives.

[3] Rt. Hon. J. A. Lyons.

Government to send squadron which is warmly welcomed here,[4] the question of Royal Navy representation has been most carefully re-examined by the Admiralty but with very great regret they have come to the conclusion that it is impossible to spare ship either from China or East Indies squadron in view of continuing seriousness of the situation in the Far East. Owing to scattered Imperial interests in China and the urgent necessity of holding ships ready to proceed to any one of the many ports where there are British subjects or troops it is out of the question for a ship of the China Fleet to leave the station at the present moment. Moreover if there were a declaration of war between China and Japan followed by a blockade heavy additional duties would fall on His Majesty's ships. It will be appreciated as regards the East Indies squadron that should the situation deteriorate to an extent requiring definite action in the Far East the cruisers of the East Indies squadron must be on their station and it is thought dangerous for any of these cruisers to leave. His Majesty's Government in the United Kingdom feel sure that under existing conditions His Majesty's Government in the Commonwealth will appreciate the force of these over-riding reasons which unfortunately prevent the presence at Sydney of one or more of His Majesty's ships. It is only the gravity of the international situation that prevents their attendance. The *Dorsetshire* has been provisionally detailed for a visit in April as you know and we hope that the international situation will permit of a visit then.

[4] See No. 447.

No. 468

Sir R. Craigie (Tokyo) to Foreign Office
(Received January 5, 9.30 a.m.)

No. 8 Telegraphic [F 291/84/10]

Personal and Very Secret   TOKYO, *January 5, 1938, 10.45 a.m.*

Following for Sir A. Cadogan.
Your telegram[1] which I am keeping to myself is of the utmost value. Following considerations will doubtless be borne in mind:

1. While I feel reasonably sure that resolute Anglo-American action would produce desired effect without war we can never be certain of this in dealing with a nation in which a compound of mysticism and nationalism is apt to distort reason even among responsible leaders. The more Japanese opinion is inflamed against us meanwhile the greater the prospect of hot-heads getting away with it here if and when Anglo-

[1] No. 464.

635

American action becomes feasible. There would always in the Japanese view be a chance of touching off a world explosion.

2. Anti-British sentiment is today less vocal than a month ago (probably owing to Government action) but I am inclined to think it is becoming more deep-seated and therefore dangerous. Advent to power at this juncture of our arch-enemy Suitsugu[2] is not without significance. If we have reason to believe American opinion is hardening against Japan so will Japanese Government also: in such circumstances we cannot altogether exclude possibility of direct attack on us before American opinion has evolved sufficiently to permit of joint resistance to it. Japan would be taking a dangerous chance but so did Germany when she counted upon our neutrality in 1914. Unfortunately Japanese believe that while America might fight on account of another outrage against herself she will not do so merely to help Great Britain. The same calculation applies *a fortiori* to Soviet.

I still feel therefore that the situation demands action along the lines suggested in my telegram No. 865.[3] To demonstrate to these people that they have been fed on falsehoods would strengthen not weaken our position if later we have to defend by forcible action our very existence in China.

I sometimes wonder whether under stress of pro-Chinese sentiment at home His Majesty's Government are sufficiently impressed with real and growing danger inherent in this concentration upon ourselves by these impulsive people of what is fast becoming a bitter hatred.

[2] Admiral Nohumasa Suetsugu, well known for his extreme political views and his opposition to the London Naval Treaty, was appointed Home Minister on December 13 on the resignation of Dr. Eichi Baba on grounds of ill-health. Sir R. Craigie commented in despatch No. 617 of December 17 that the Admiral was 'regarded as one of the strongest characters in Japan today ... a reactionary, though he is not, I believe, essentially anti-British'.

[3] See No. 464, note 4.

No. 469

Sir R. Lindsay (Washington) to Foreign Office
(Received January 6, 9.30 a.m.)

No. 13 Telegraphic [F 184/78/10]

WASHINGTON, *January 5, 1938, 7.40 p.m.*

Your telegram No. 5.[1]

I have spoken to the Under Secretary of State.

Chinese Ambassador had put similar question and had been told that as United States Government was not a member of the League it could express no opinion.

[1] No. 465.

From further conversation I infer attitude of State Department to be that the meeting of the Committee could be of no practical use and might raise serious difficulties and that the Chinese might be wiser to leave the question with Nine Power Conference where it now is. But the Department would not wish to influence decision to be taken.[2]

[2] Cf. *F.R.U.S.*, 1938, vol. iii, pp. 489–90. Sir E. Phipps reported in Paris telegram No. 15 Saving of January 8 that the French Foreign Ministry also felt doubt 'whether anything useful would come of a meeting of the Far Eastern Advisory Committee . . . but agree that it would be unadvisable actually to dissuade the Chinese Government if they wish to have one called'.

No. 470

Sir R. Lindsay (Washington) to Foreign Office
(Received January 8, 9.30 a.m.)

No. 25 Telegraphic [F 314/84/10]

Very Confidential   WASHINGTON, *January 7, 1938, 6.24 p.m.*

Welles asked me on January 4th whether I had any confidential information I could give him about Russia.[1] State Department received absolutely nothing from Moscow, partly no doubt owing to normal difficulties of that post, partly (as he implied only) owing to the well-known incompetence of United States Ambassador there. Points he specially mentioned were

A. What help was Soviet Government giving to China? He received news from Hankow which you also receive but nothing from the Moscow end.

B. Was it perhaps true as he had heard from another European post that the Soviet Government was more interested in spreading its 'cultural propaganda' in the intervening spaces of Mongolia rather than in giving actual help to China.

C. Any reliable news about internal position of the present régime in Russia.

In telegrams and confidential print of the last three months there is little or nothing about all this. Have you any other documents which you could send me for confidential communication to him? Or alternatively and possibly better, could you communicate information to United States Embassy?[2]

[1] See No. 365 and Volume XIX, No. 413, note 2. This State Department request for information is evidence of the exceptional confidence which, in certain directions, existed at this time between the British and U.S. Governments. Similar requests and the general background of consultation in European affairs have been recorded in Volume XIX, Nos. 356, 373, 413, 451–2, 461. President Roosevelt's secret plan in January for a peace initiative, and Mr. Chamberlain's hesitant response, are also documented *ibid.*, Nos. 421–7, etc.

[2] Sir R. Lindsay's immediately following telegram No. 26 is printed *ibid.*. No. 413. Mr.

Ronald minuted on January 10: 'This desire for intimacy is not a new thing, but it has evidently grown recently in intensity; (Mr. Hornbeck had a good deal to say on the subject when he called here on his way from Brussels). Although I fancy we are not likely to receive very valuable information in exchange, I submit that it will be to our advantage to give as much information as we can.' Sir A. Cadogan agreed, and arrangements were made to pass on certain information through the U.S. Embassy in London: see *ibid.*, No. 413, note 4, and cf. *F.R.U.S.*, 1938, vol. iii, p. 7.

No. 471

Foreign Office to Sir R. Lindsay (Washington)

No. 19[1] *Telegraphic* [F 96/84/10]

Immediate   Very Secret   FOREIGN OFFICE, *January 7, 1938, 7.30 p.m.*

Your telegram No. 5[2].

I agree that there are advantages in refraining from trying to define too closely the scope of the conversations, which are developing very satisfactorily. I think it will be possible informally to discuss all possibilities.

I understand American preparations are making good progress, and ours are in their most advanced state short of actual mobilization.

I quite agree that it may be undesirable to press the United States Government unduly, but there are certain points on which it would be very useful if we could be enlightened—points on which I doubt whether Captain Ingersoll could give authoritative opinion.

For instance, I understand that United States Government would not be prepared for naval demonstration except on basis of being prepared for war, which means making up crews to full strength, etc. That could not be done until 'state of emergency' is declared. Can you estimate likelihood of such declaration in absence of further grave provocation?

I hope it might be agreed in any case that, if we find it necessary to order mobilisation or President decides to declare state of emergency, neither side actually proceeds without giving fair warning to the other.

Can you say how far any American action will be dependent on our co-operation?

[1] According to Sir A. Cadogan's diary for January 7 (*op. cit.*, p. 33) this telegram was despatched following a conversation with Mr. Chamberlain on the afternoon of January 7. Sir A. Cadogan had drawn the Prime Minister's attention to reports of Japanese assaults on British officers in Shanghai, the latest of which had been reported that very afternoon (see No. 473 below) and suggested that the 'time had come to tell the Americans we must do *something* (e.g. announce naval preparations) and ask whether they will take "parallel" action'. Mr. Chamberlain agreed, and according to a note to Lord Chatfield from Sir A. Cadogan of January 7 the last two paragraphs of this telegram were added to the draft in accordance with the Prime Minister's wishes. In a letter to his sister Hilda of January 9 Mr. Chamberlain referred to his efforts to 'jolly [the U.S.A.] along': 'I do wish the Japs would beat up an American or two! But of course the little d-v-ls are too cunning for that, and we may eventually have to act alone & hope the Yanks will follow before it's too late.'
[2] No. 463.

Captain Ingersoll has been informed, and has presumably reported, what we should be in a position to do if action were decided upon. It would be interesting to know reaction of United States Government: whether they feel that this goes too far or does not go far enough.

You will of course keep us fully informed of trend of public opinion and of any indication of intentions of United States Government.

On foregoing points your opinion would be valuable: you will judge whether to attempt soundings of United States Government.

I have just seen in the press news of Japanese assault on two British police officers in Shanghai.[3] I have not yet received official report but if press news is confirmed, we may have to consider whether we can still continue to content ourselves with demand for an apology. We may have to consider whether we should not have to go further and, short of ordering mobilisation, announce that we are completing certain naval preparations.

Please inform United States Government at once of foregoing paragraph, in strictest confidence, and ask whether, in the event of our having to proceed to such a step, we could expect any parallel action by them, such, for instance, as sending advance force of cruisers, destroyers and submarines to Hawaii and the rest of the fleet to Pacific Ports. (For your own information Captain Ingersoll has stated that, from a technical point of view, they would be in a position to do this if they wished).

[3] See No. 473 below.

No. 472

Sir R. Lindsay (Washington) to Foreign Office
(Received January 8, 9.30 a.m.)

No. 27 Telegraphic [F 313/84/10]

Immediate   Very Secret   WASHINGTON, *January* 7, *1938, 11.8 p.m.*

Following is a partial reply to first part of your telegram No. 19[1].

I think it most unlikely that United States Government would declare a 'state of emergency' without further grave provocation and moreover that provocation would have to affect American interests or honour.

I think that if United States Government took any action (meaning thereby some definite move of a military nature) they would expect similar action by us. Very likely they would stipulate action by us beforehand.

In general I hope you will not base too sanguine hopes on forward state of naval preparations or on favourable disposition of the administration. Both are in advance of public opinion and it is the latter which decides the pace. I had been hoping to wait till next week when Congress will deal

[1] No. 471.

with Ludlow resolution[2] before reporting on public opinion. I am sure *Panay* affair has made a profound impression which will not be forgotten. It has brought unpleasant possibilities vividly before country and resentment is wide. But at present prevailing feeling is one of relief that it is over. It is talked of no more. People have over-persuaded themselves that termination of the incident has been satisfactory. And though press for most part has kept resentment alive (with various indications that it is being encouraged in this direction by Administration) a vast number of sensible people are thinking of escaping from danger of war and public is not in my opinion likely to get excited over an assault on British policemen in Shanghai. I will try to see Welles tomorrow.

[2] This was a proposal by Mr. L. Ludlow, Representative of Indiana, in favour of an amendment to the U.S. Constitution to transfer the right to declare war from Congress to a national referendum in all cases save that of invasion. The effect of the House of Representatives' vote on the resolution of January 10, 1938, was to reject it by 209–188.

No. 473

Mr. Phillips (Shanghai) to Foreign Office
(Received January 8, 4.20 p.m.)

No. 8 Telegraphic: by wireless [F 334/35/10]

SHANGHAI, *January 8, 1938*

Addressed to His Majesty's Chargé d'Affaires No. 5.
My telegram No. 260.[1]
The following is text of my letter of today's date addressed to Japanese Consul-General protesting against recent assaults on certain British members of Shanghai municipal police. Begins:

I regret that again within a few days I find myself under the necessity of protesting against violence and unlawful actions of members of Japanese armed forces against British subjects.

The facts are as follows: On December 25th Inspector Bennett was proceeding in a police car on wayside road and is alleged to have obstructed a Japanese despatch rider and asked to call at naval landing party headquarters to explain matters. When he called there however a few days later he was assaulted and detained and Superintendent Sinclair who called later to secure his release was similarly ill-treated.

I understand that Chairman of Council sent you full statements of this case in his letter of December 30th and has not yet been accorded the courtesy of an acknowledgement.

[1] This telegram of December 30, 1937, transmitted to the Foreign Office as Shanghai telegram No. 220, referred to a protest made by Mr. Phillips to the Japanese Consul General at the detention for four days of a British subject who had been arrested for theft by the Japanese police.

Another and in some ways more serious case was one in which on January 6th at Brenan road crossing probationary Sergeant Turner was assaulted and so battered that hospital treatment was necessitated, Sub-Inspector Fowler was struck in the face and together with Inspector West manhandled and threatened with loaded rifles and fixed bayonets by a number of Japanese soldiers: in fact it was apparently only due to great restraint shown by Inspector West in his handling of matter and fortuitious [sic] arrival and loyal support given this officer by Sub-Inspector Yamaguchi and other Japanese members of municipal police that consequences were not even more serious. The reason given for this assault was again in its origin a very slight one: probationary Sergeant Turner, who was on duty at the east barrier, considering Japanese sentries were being unnecessarily rough with Chinese peasants passing through requested Japanese P.C. 200 to remonstrance [sic] with them. P.C. 200 refused to do this and Turner left saying that he would report his attitude. Thereupon P.C. 200 alleging Turner had used insulting language in regard to Japanese army instigated Japanese soldiers to assault him and when Fowler and later West arrived on the scene and endeavoured to pacify them continued to assault and threaten all three officers. I would observe that even if it were true Turner had made offensive remarks—of which there is no evidence so that it is merely a case of one man's word against another's while there is always the possibility of a misunderstanding—the Japanese constable had no right to instigate his fellow nationals to make the assault still less had they any right or excuse for committing a breach of the peace of which I complain.

I feel sure that you and the responsible military and naval authorities will agree with me that it is most deplorable that members of the Japanese armed forces should be permitted to act in this lawless manner and I have the honour to request accordingly that you will endeavour to arrange that a strict enquiry be held into these cases and those found guilty suitably disciplined in order to prevent further disorders. Ends.

Repeated to Tokyo, copy to Major-General and Senior Naval Officer.

No. 474

Sir R. Lindsay (Washington) to Foreign Office
(Received January 9, 9.30 a.m.)

No. 30 Telegraphic [F 337/84/10]

Immediate   Very Secret   WASHINGTON, *January 8, 1938, 6.42 p.m.*

My immediately preceding telegram.[1]

Welles then asked me if I had any news of the progress of staff

---

[1] In telegram No. 29 of January 8 Sir R. Lindsay recorded a conversation that day with Mr. Welles, who questioned him about 'the nature of our "naval preparations to be

completed" ': Sir R. Lindsay replied that 'as regards this it was only a question of issuing a statement and that virtually all naval preparations short of actual mobilization had been completed already'. Mr. Welles's record of this conversation is printed in *F.R.U.S.*, 1938, vol. iii, pp. 7–8.

conversations. I said that I only knew that they were developing to your satisfaction and that you would like to know whether the State Department was equally satisfied.[2]

He replied that neither the State Department nor the President had any news of them at all. Instructions to Ingersoll had been that he was to complete his conversations and then return here and report. He thought that possibly Navy Department had received reports and would enquire of them.

I dare say that this may be a disappointment to you. If so I suggest that I be instructed to urge if Ingersoll cannot stay on in London (and very probably his prolonged absence may be highly inconvenient) United States Navy Department should make other arrangement for carrying on an efficient liaison.

[2] In a minute of January 14 Sir A. Cadogan recorded that he had lunched with Captain Ingersoll, who was due to leave England on January 18 and who was 'fully satisfied with his conversations at the Adm[iral]ty . . . I asked him whether he was sure that everything had been carried as far as was possible at this stage, and he assured me that that was so'. Sir A. Cadogan suggested that Sir R. Lindsay might be informed of this, 'telling him, after Capt. Ingersoll's return, to ascertain whether the U.S. Govt. are satisfied . . .' The Admiralty agreed, and a telegram was despatched that evening: No. 487 below.

No. 475

Sir R. Craigie (Tokyo) to Foreign Office
(Received January 10, 9.30 a.m.)

No. 26 Telegraphic [F 340/16/10]

TOKYO, *January 9, 1938, 11.25 a.m.*

Hankow Mission's telegram No. 97 to Shanghai[1].

I feel sure that the Chinese Government would be well advised to continue discussions and endeavour to elucidate Japanese terms. While for many reasons the Japanese would be glad to be quit of this adventure, she is perfectly prepared to push on with it if necessary and as time goes on, influence of military extremists and anti-foreign elements tends to increase. A flat rejection of the terms would simply discourage those elements in this country, represented by the Minister for Foreign Affairs, who wish to negotiate rather than dictate a peace.

I have no doubt that the terms, when elaborated will at first prove quite unacceptable to the Chinese. But from the Chinese point of view the

[1] No. 466.

important thing is surely to keep the ball rolling while they continue their preparations for defence. This would (a) increase difficulty of Japanese military leaders in persuading an apparent reluctant Cabinet to embark on the next phase of operations, such as attack on Canton; (b) tend to bring the Japanese more into the open; (c) permit friendly influences to be exercised here.

If our advice is sought by the Chinese, I earnestly hope that continuance of negotiations may be counselled though it would naturally be preferable if the United States and ourselves be associated in any peace effort.

Repeated to Shanghai.

No. 476

Letter from Mr. Eden to Sir A. Cadogan

[*F 407/84/10*]

PARC PALACE HOTEL, GRASSE, *January 9, 1938*

My dear Alec,

I am afraid that you must be having an anxious time as the outcome of recent Far Eastern developments. It looks from here as though the moment was fast approaching when, if we are to retain our position as a world power, we shall be compelled to move the larger part of the fleet to Singapore. We should not, I think, then overlook the possibility of the following procedure with U.S. Say to them: 'The limit has been reached and we have decided to mobilise our ships and move such and such a proportion to Singapore. We shall announce this (say) today week or in 48 hours.' This would give U.S. time to take parallel action if they so wished, and they probably would. In any event I do not believe that they would sit with folded hands and watch British Empire in jeopardy, if it really came to that.

I believe that our chief difficulty if we did have to move ships would be from the French who would certainly be very jumpy, but Chautemps[1] is sensible and our good relations should help us there. I hear that Flandin[2] is spreading alarm and despondency everywhere on the French Mediterranean shore!

By the bye, in considering Far Eastern problems we must remember to keep the Dutch informed of anything we do. Their help may be important to us one day. They have some good cruisers and a steadily increasing Air Force in the Far East. You will recall my conversation with Dutch Minister just before I left.[3]

[1] Head of the French Government.   [2] Former President of the Council.
[3] A record of Mr. Eden's conversation of December 31 with Count Stirum is filed at F 11776/597/61.

The weather has been lovely since our arrival until today which is still fine, but cloudy. I already feel much better for the change.[4]

Yours ever,

ANTHONY EDEN

P.S. I have, of course, no objection to this letter being shown to the Prime Minister—I am writing to him, but on Italian matters chiefly.[5]

[4] Sir A. Cadogan forwarded this letter to Mr. Chamberlain on January 11 with the following note: 'Prime Minister. The S. of S. has not been seeing telegrams, so does not know that action is being taken more or less on these lines.' See No. 471.
[5] See Volume XIX, No. 418.

No. 477

Sir R. Craigie (Tokyo) to Foreign Office
(*Received January 10, 1.5 p.m.*)

No. 31 Telegraphic [F 383/84/10]

TOKYO, *January 10, 1938, 5.50 p.m.*

My telegram No. 26[1].

Government spent busy day yesterday discussing policy to be followed as regards China. Meeting between representatives of Cabinet and of Imperial Headquarters was followed by emergency Cabinet meeting and meeting of Cabinet Counsellors. Further Cabinet meeting will be held today and it is again reported that combined conference in the presence of the Emperor (see my telegram No. 840[2]) may be held shortly.[3]

According to press there is some divergence of opinion in Cabinet, the new Home Minister favouring declaration of war but other Ministers counselling caution. Indications are however that Cabinet is unanimous in view that Japan must be prepared for a prolonged struggle in order to attain her ends. Question of withdrawal of recognition from Chiang Kai-shek to be preceded by withdrawal of Japanese Ambassador is apparently again under discussion and encouragement is being given to establishment of local autonomous régime.

Activities outlined above made it more important still that Chiang Kai-shek should at this juncture try to keep Japanese in play (see my telegram under reference).

Repeated to Embassy Shanghai.

[1] No. 475.　　　　[2] Not kept in F.O. archives.　　　　[3] See No. 483 below.

No. 478

Sir R. Lindsay (Washington) to Foreign Office
(Received January 11, 9.30 a.m.)

No. 35 Telegraphic [F 407/84/10]

Immediate   Very Secret   WASHINGTON, *January 10, 1938, 6.35 p.m.*

My telegram No. 29[1].

Under Secretary of State for Foreign Affairs tells me by telephone that meeting took place today of President, Secretary of State himself and others after which President decided on following course of procedure in three distinct stages.

(1) He would announce in any case within the next two days that three out of the four cruisers now on their way to Sydney will proceed on a visit to Singapore.[2]

(2) If—but only if—His Majesty's Government decide to issue statement contemplated in last paragraph but one of your telegram No. 19[3] that they are completing certain naval preparations, then within few days announcement would be made here that vessels of United States Fleet in the Pacific are being sent to dry-dock to have their bottoms scraped. This is recognised as a measure of preparatory action.[4] You will see that you must let me know as soon as possible whether you mean to issue statement you contemplated.

(3) Very soon after that announcement would be made here that date for manoeuvres in the Pacific would be advanced by two or three weeks so that they would start about the second week of February.

Finally Under Secretary of State for Foreign Affairs said that he wished to have a confidential conversation with me not at State Department (in order to avoid comment) and he will come to the Embassy for the purpose tomorrow evening.[5]

---

[1] See No. 474, note 1.

[2] In fact the Counsellor of the U.S. Embassy had already telephoned Sir A. Cadogan on January 8 to say that of the four U.S. cruisers visiting Sydney, the flagship *Trenton*, the *Milwaukee* and the *Memphis* would curtail their visit and proceed to Singapore for the opening of the dock there on February 11. Telegram No. 27 to Washington, despatched at 9 p.m. on January 10, instructed Sir R. Lindsay to 'convey to [Mr. Hull] a suitable expression of the thanks of His Majesty's Government'.

[3] No. 471.

[4] Mr. Orde commented on January 11: 'Drydocking will not commit the U.S. Govt. politically as much as a statement by us about naval preparations would commit us . . .'

[5] Mr. Welles' visit to Sir R. Lindsay on January 11 was to deliver President Roosevelt's 'peace plan': see Volume XIX, No. 422.

No. 479

Foreign Office to Mr. Howe (Shanghai)

No. 41 Telegraphic [F 460/78/10]

Secret   FOREIGN OFFICE, January 11, 1938, 11 p.m.

Chinese Ambassador recently stated that he had been informed by his Government that a loan of $150 million had been arranged in United States of America probably with support of United States Government and he hoped that British Government would help to secure similar loan here to be earmarked for currency and service of the Chinese loans. He was informed that such a loan would require a British Government guarantee, that this would necessitate approval of Parliament and that difficulties were very great.[1]

His Majesty's Ambassador at Washington learns on enquiry that no suggestion has been made to the United States Government for a loan.[2] United States Chargé d'Affaires in London states that his Government have no knowledge of any discussions for a private loan.

Chinese request to His Majesty's Government, consideration of which was held up pending information as to United States attitude, is being examined and no final conclusion has been reached, but the chances of our being able to accede to the request appear under present circumstances to be slight.[3]

---

[1] Records of Dr. Quo's conversations with both Sir A. Cadogan and Sir F. Leith-Ross on January 4 are filed at F 199/78/10.

[2] Sir R. Lindsay reported in telegram No. 12 of January 5 that there had been 'absolutely no negotiations here for a loan'. In response to further enquiry he reported in telegram No. 24 of January 7 that no suggestion of a loan had been made to the U.S. Treasury: 'State Department is taking this matter up with Chinese Ambassador here.' Cf. F.R.U.S., 1938, vol. iii, p. 14.

[3] Rumours of an American loan persisted, but in Shanghai telegram No. 109 of January 20 Mr. Howe transmitted a message from Mr. Rogers at Hong Kong that the loan had no foundation: '. . . all houses in New York have turned down proposals which (as in the past) were used by Dr. Kung to bluff Chiang Kai-shek on the occasion of recent political regrouping.' The request for a British loan was, however, renewed: see No. 491 below.

No. 480

Minute[1] *by Mr. Chamberlain on announcement of fleet movements*

[*F 407/84/10*]

January 11, 1938

It is evident that the Americans feel themselves obliged to act with the greatest caution and to take only one step at a time. I am therefore against asking them to commit themselves to any specific action in hypothetical circ[umstance]s and I am sure this would lead to nothing helpful. On our side I feel that this would be a most unfortunate moment to send the fleet away and I would therefore take no immediate action which would involve us in having to do so if the Japanese returned an unsatisfactory reply. At the same time it must be recognised that the provocation on this occasion is worse than ever before since there is no question here of an 'accident' and indeed the action of the military has since been justified and described in the most insulting way by the Japanese spokesman (see this morning's *Times*[2]).

I conclude therefore that we had better not make any announcement yet but I wonder whether the draft telegram to Craigie is sufficiently strongly worded. Should he not be instructed to say at least that His Majesty's Government take a very grave view of the incident which shows a reckless disregard of the most elementary rules of civilised peoples when dealing with foreigners.[3] Coming on the top of so many previous incidents each of which has been followed by assurances from the Japanese Govt. that care would be taken to prevent recurrence His Majesty's Government feel that something more than assurances are now required and that they will regard the response of the Jap. Govt. to their invitation (for suggestions) as a test of their sincerity and ability to control their own subjects. I suggest not necessarily these words but this sort of line.[4]

[1] This minute was in reply to one by Sir A. Cadogan of January 11 reporting a conversation with Lord Chatfield about telegram No. 35 from Washington (No. 478), which he thought 'does not indicate any very great alacrity on the part of the Americans, but . . . is not in the nature of a complete *non possumus*'. After some discussion Lord Chatfield pointed out that if an announcement that the fleet was prepared to sail to the Far East did not have the desired effect 'the only further action that we can take is to send it'. This might have an adverse effect on the Italian negotiations [cf. Volume XIX, Nos. 410–15, 418, 429]. Sir A. Cadogan agreed that 'in whatever way we begin we must recognise that we may be drawn on to the ultimate decision to send the fleet out to the Far East', and asked whether the 'present incidents' were 'of sufficient gravity to justify starting along this road'. He suggested instead a telegram to Tokyo, of which he enclosed a draft (this became No. 482 below). He also mentioned, but did not like, a suggestion by Lord Chatfield that the Americans should be asked 'whether, in case of necessity, they would take *further* action'.

[2] See *The Times*, January 11, 1938, p. 12.　　　　　　　　　　　　[3] Cf. No. 473.

[4] Sir A. Cadogan noted: 'I have redrafted tel. to Tokyo accordingly.' See No. 482 below.

No. 481

Foreign Office to Sir R. Lindsay (Washington)

No. 31 Telegraphic [F 407/84/10]

Immediate   Very Secret   FOREIGN OFFICE, *January 12, 1938, 4.20 p.m.*

Your telegram No. 35[1].

I am instructing His Majesty's Ambassador in Tokyo to make representations to the Japanese Government on the recent attacks on British police officers in Shanghai—see my telegram to Tokyo No. 26[2]—and for the moment propose to wait to see what reply can be obtained from the Japanese Government.

I am very gratified to receive President's message and it is of great value to us to know what the United States Government would be prepared to do in the event of our having to issue some statement. I would of course give you due warning before any such statement was issued, and I would give you the text of it for communication to the United States Government.

Please inform them at once of the above and of the instructions contained in my telegram to Tokyo No. 26.

It would of course be more effective if any announcement made by United States Government could be made *simultaneously* with ours. Is there any possibility of inducing them to do this?

[1] No. 478.   [2] No. 482 below.

No. 482

Foreign Office to Sir R. Craigie (Tokyo)

No. 26 Telegraphic [F 334/35/10]

FOREIGN OFFICE, *January 12, 1938, 5 p.m.*

Telegram No. 5 from Consul General, Shanghai to His Majesty's Chargé d'Affaires.[1]

Please inform Japanese government of the contents and say that His Majesty's Government must protest most strongly against action of Japanese troops and confidently expect that Japanese government will take measures to prevent further incidents of the like nature. If this is not done, it will be impossible to believe that there is not a deliberate intention to undermine morale of Settlement police, which would have disastrous effect on preservation of law and order and safety of Japanese and other nationals, besides arousing the most serious suspicions as to the Japanese intentions towards the existing régime in the Settlement. These considera-

[1] No. 473.

tions are additional to the fact that British subjects have been grossly maltreated, to which His Majesty's Government naturally take the strongest possible exception.

You should make it quite clear to Japanese government that His Majesty's Government take a very grave view of this incident which shows a reckless disregard of the rights of other nationals. Coming on the top of many previous incidents, each of which has been followed by assurances from the Japanese government that care would be taken to prevent recurrence, His Majesty's Government feel that something more than assurances are now required, and they expect the Japanese government to indicate to them the measures that they will take and the instructions they will issue to guard against any repetition. His Majesty's Government will await with interest this information (which I hope may not be long delayed), which will enable them to form a judgment as to the sincerity of the Japanese government and their ability to control their own subjects.

Repeated to Shanghai No. 4, and Washington No. 30.

No. 483

Sir R. Craigie (Tokyo) to Foreign Office
(Received January 12, 9.30 a.m.)

No. 40 Telegraphic [F 485/84/10]

TOKYO, *January 12, 1938, 8 p.m.*

My telegram 31[1].

Combined Conference of Government, Imperial Headquarters and Privy Council representatives was held yesterday in the presence of the Emperor.

What Domei calls 'the supreme China policy of the Empire for the sake of eternal peace in Eastern Asia' previously decided upon by Cabinet was solemnly endorsed.

No statement is being issued for a few days at least and no indication of nature of decision has been allowed to leak out.

The two possibilities most generally canvassed are (1) declaration of war and (2) recognition of provisional Government of Peking and withdrawal of recognition from Chiang Kai-shek. Another report has it that peace negotiations with Chiang Kai-shek having now entered into a crucial stage an important decision on peace terms was called for.

Both amongst my colleagues and Press correspondents I find little belief that it is alternative No. 1 since there are known to have been divergences of opinion in the Government on this issue.

Repeated to Mr. Howe and Hongkong (Governor please repeat to Commander in Chief as my telegram 14).

[1] No. 477.

No. 484

Foreign Office to Sir R. Craigie (Tokyo)

No. 31 Telegraphic [F 340/16/10]

FOREIGN OFFICE, *January 12, 1938, 10 p.m.*

Your telegram No. 26[1].

I do not think that we could take the responsibility of advising continuance of negotiations if Chinese ask our views. If their will to resist is unshaken and if German advisers consider resistance still feasible as they appear to do, Chinese may well 'hope to gain by prolonging the struggle' (your telegram No. 653[2]). Desirable as the termination of hostilities is, the fairness of the settlement which will succeed them must after all be the overriding consideration, and we have always, notably at Brussels, resisted any suggestion that we should urge China to negotiate direct with Japan—a procedure that is unlikely to produce a satisfactory settlement.

Repeated to Shanghai No. 48 and Hankow No. 4[3].

---

[1] No. 475. [2] No. 336.

[3] In Hankow telegram No. 67 of January 14 Mr. D. MacKillop referred to Foreign Office telegram No. 31 and reported: 'Chinese Minister for Foreign Affairs told me today that Japanese terms had not been definitely rejected. Chinese Government had asked for clarification of certain points in them and were now awaiting a reply.' Mr. MacKillop had been appointed Counsellor of H.M. Embassy at Peking on October 9, 1937 in succession to Mr. Howe, but the latter had been asked to stay on until the New Year and overlap with Mr. MacKillop in view of the absence of an Ambassador. Mr. MacKillop took charge of the Mission at Hankow on January 9 to relieve Mr. Gage, who had been recalled to the Foreign Office.

No. 485

Sir R. Lindsay (Washington) to Foreign Office
(Received January 13, 9.20 p.m.)

No. 46 Telegraphic [F 531/84/10]

Important   Very Secret   WASHINGTON, *January 13, 1938, 1.27 p.m.*

Your telegram No. 31.[1]

I have seen Under Secretary of State for Foreign Affairs[2] and informed him of instructions sent to His Majesty's Ambassador Tokyo.[3] It is quite

---

[1] No. 481.

[2] Mr. Welles's account of this interview is printed in *F.R.U.S.*, 1938, vol. iii, p. 19.

[3] See No. 482.

agreeable to State Department that you should await results of these representations before issuing your statement.[4]

Definitely however they will prefer to avoid simultaneous action partly because of their own public opinion (he said we are sick of this nonsense about pulling chestnuts out of fire but must avoid anything that encourages it) and partly because impression on Japan was same whether or not action was simultaneous.

He said announcement about visit to Singapore would come out at any moment now.

[4] Mr. Eden, who had returned to England on January 15 (see Volume XIX, No. 434, note 8) commented on January 17: 'I hope that we shall soon hear further from Sir R. Craigie about this. We cannot allow indefinite delay, & must receive some satisfaction.'

No. 486

Agreed record of conversations between Captain Ingersoll and the Naval Staff at the Admiralty

[F 716/84/10]

Most Secret   *January 13, 1938*

The following memorandum contains the agreed record of the conversations between Captain Ingersoll, U.S.N., and the Naval Staff at the Admiralty.

COMPOSITION, STATE OF READINESS AND INITIAL MOVEMENT OF FLEETS

U.S. Fleet

The U.S. Naval view is that no gesture should be made unless the Fleet now in commission is brought up to 100 per cent. full complement and prepared in all respects for war. The ability to bring the Fleet up to full complement depends on the issue by the President of a Declaration of National Emergency.

The present state of readiness of the U.S. Fleet in commission as regards personnel is as follows:

Submarines and Aircraft on the Pacific Coast 100 per cent.

Advance Force, consisting of 2 Squadrons of heavy Cruisers and 2 Squadrons of Destroyers and 1 Aircraft Carrier is now being completed, as far as practicable, to full complement.

Capital Ships, Cruisers, Destroyers and Auxiliaries on the Pacific Coast, other than Advance Force, 85 per cent. complement.

Atlantic Coast—3 Battleships, WYOMING and 1 Squadron of Destroyers are used as a training Squadron with about 50 per cent. complement.

It is the intention of the U.S. Navy Department to send first to Honolulu the Advance Force, together with about 15 Submarines. These could leave at any time. There are already about 75 patrol planes and about 20 Submarines at Honolulu.

There are 6 Submarines and 36 aircraft in the Panama Canal zone.

It is understood that all available capital ships would probably be sent to Honolulu. Allowing for 2 or 3 ships refitting and 3 on the Atlantic Coast, 9 or 10 capital ships could be ready to sail 10 to 15 days after the Declaration of National Emergency.

Subsequently the Navy Department visualise a gradual advance across the Pacific after air reconnaissance, making use of Japanese Mandated Islands as necessary, and finally establishing themselves at Truk or some other position in the same general area.

They do not at present envisage proceeding immediately to Manila or any other Philippine port.

A Fleet Supply Train with about one month's supplies could sail about 20 days, and transports, tankers and auxiliary vessels about 30 days after the Declaration of a National Emergency.

The U.S. Navy Department intend also to despatch 2 submarines and a small number of aircraft and a seaplane tender to operate from a base at Unalaska.

British Fleet

The Admiralty policy is to send to the Far East a force which is sufficient to engage the Japanese Fleet under normal tactical and strategical conditions. In general, this Fleet would proceed to the Far East as a single tactical unit.

The force which it is at present intended should form the Far Eastern Fleet is as follows: Some of these ships are already in Eastern waters.

Battleships	8	
Battlecruiser	1	
Aircraft Carriers	3	
[1]8″ Cruisers	8	
[1]6″ Cruisers	11	(including 2 attached to Destroyer Flotillas)
Cruiser Minelayer	1	
Destroyer Flotillas	7	
Submarines	25	

together with the necessary Depot and Repair Ships and certain minor war vessels.

[1] *Note in original*: 2–8″ cruisers and 1–6″ cruiser from Australia and 2–6″ cruisers from New Zealand are in addition to the above and all come, probably, under orders of the Admiralty.

The exact composition of the Far Eastern Fleet is subject to modification with the passage of time: for instance, at a later date it may be desirable to send 9 battleships to the Far East and to retain both battlecruisers in Home Waters. The above figures, however, serve as a general guide to British strength in Far Eastern waters.

It is understood that the ships of the Home and Mediterranean Fleets would be ready to sail for the Far East at 10–14 days' notice if mobilisation was ordered after 15th January, 1938.

The British Fleet would proceed initially to Singapore. This base will not be fully completed for 18 months. The dry docks there are ready but Singapore is not prepared at the present time to handle large repairs of ships damaged in action. It can support, mainly by commercial facilities, in other respects the force contemplated to be based there.

General Policy

Both parties agree that, in principle, political movements should keep step with the Naval situation, but it is realised that this may be difficult to accomplish. Both parties also agree that the political and Naval measures of each nation should be kept in step with those of the other nation. To this end it is agreed that it is desirable that the arrival of the British Fleet at Singapore and the U.S. Fleet at Honolulu should, as far as possible, be synchronised. Nevertheless, it is realised that circumstances, and particularly any incidents primarily affecting one nation rather than both, may make it difficult to carry out the above policy.

It is assumed that all waters of the British Commonwealth, including the Dominions, will be available for use of U.S. Naval Forces and that all waters of the United States, including the Philippines, will be available for use of the British Naval Forces.

It is understood that the Government of the United Kingdom cannot definitely commit the Governments of the Dominions of the British Commonwealth to any action in concert with the United Kingdom. The Admiralty feels sure, however, that Canada, Australia and New Zealand would co-operate with the United Kingdom against Japan in the circumstances under consideration.

The Admiralty is not at the present time anticipating any direct aid from the French or Dutch in the Far East, but they consider that it is possible that the latter might adopt a benevolent attitude of neutrality. The Admiralty are not counting on any aid from Russia.

In the event of Germany proving hostile a most serious problem would arise. The Admiralty is not so seriously apprehensive of submarines as they believe that they can successfully deal with them. They are, however, seriously apprehensive of British trade routes in the Atlantic, should the Germans use their 3 Pocket Battleships and the 2 new 27,000 ton ships as commerce raiders.

An even more dangerous situation would arise should hostilities with

Italy also supervene after the greater part of the British Fleet had proceeded to the Far East. It would be necessary for the Admiralty to rely entirely on the alternative route to the East via the Cape of Good Hope. In these circumstances the main problem in the Mediterranean would be to hold the Suez Canal and Egypt. The Admiralty would have to depend on the French Navy to hold the Western Mediterranean and some of her Naval Forces would have to be based on Gibraltar to secure the Western entrance. They would themselves, however, keep anti-submarine forces at Gibraltar. In this connection the Admiralty is of the opinion that the Straits of Gibraltar can be made hazardous for the passage of enemy submarines.

In the event of such a general European war it would almost certainly be necessary to effect a considerable reduction in the British strength in the Far East. With the reduction of British strength in the Far East under these conditions the possible necessity of direct tactical co-operation between the U.S. and British Fleets would require further consideration.

POLICY WITH REGARD TO FORCES NOW IN THE FAR EAST

U.S. Forces

It is understood that the U.S. Navy Department would like the U.S. garrisons now in North China to be withdrawn and that in emergency the U.S. Asiatic Fleet would withdraw from Northern Chinese Waters.

British Forces

The Admiralty is also concerned regarding the British garrisons in North China. Should parallel action in regard to the movements of the two Main Fleets be decided upon, consideration would have to be given to the accurate timing of the withdrawal of the British troops in North China to Hong Kong, and the major units of the British China Fleet would also have to withdraw to that place or to Singapore.

ARRANGEMENTS FOR INTER-COMMUNICATION BETWEEN BRITISH AND U.S. FLEETS

It is agreed that since the two fleets will be widely separated at first and probably for some time there could not be unity of command in a tactical or strategic sense in the near future. It is, however, agreed that strategic co-operation will be necessary and that such co-operation will require common communication facilities.

The following arrangements have been agreed upon to this end:

(a) The Admiralty will distribute to all ships of the British Fleet, and arrange to deposit at the British Embassy in Washington, at Gibraltar and in the Far East for issue to the ships of the U.S. Navy, the necessary copies of the following books:

(1) A suitable Code.

(2) Re-cyphering Tables for use with the Code by the Higher Command.

(3) Re-cyphering Tables for use with the Code by the other Flag Officers.

(4) Re-cyphering Tables for use with the Code by all ships.

(5) A Key Memorandum containing simple recognition signals for use by both Fleets.

(6) A block of War W/T Call Signs for both Fleets.

(b) A copy of the British Naval W/T organisation will be issued by the Admiralty with the books to be distributed to the U.S. Fleet.

(c) The U.S. Navy Department will make available the necessary copies of their Pacific and Asiatic Fleet W/T Organisation for distribution to the British Fleet. These will be deposited as soon as practicable with the U.S. Embassy in London, on board the Flagship of the U.S. Squadron in the Mediterranean, and on board the Flagship of the U.S. Asiatic Fleet.

(d) Commercial W/T procedure will be used for inter-communication.

(e) The Admiralty will propose frequencies for inter-communication if and when the occasion arises.

(f) Direct inter-communication by W/T between individual ships of the two Fleets will not normally be necessary unless tactical co-operation is envisaged.

The inter-communication procedure outlined above will be subject to adjustment between the Commanders-in-Chief of the two Main Fleets.

INTERCHANGE OF COMMUNICATION PERSONNEL

To facilitate inter-communication between the two Fleets it is agreed that the following inter-change of personnel with experience in W/T would be desirable:

(a) 1 Officer and 1 rating from U.S. Asiatic Fleet to be lent temporarily to both Hong Kong and Singapore W/T Stations.

(b) 1 Officer, if and when available, and 1 Chief Petty Officer Telegraphist to be lent temporarily from the British China Fleet to the U.S. Asiatic Fleet Flagship.

(c) 1 Officer and 1 rating to be lent from the British and U.S. Navies to the U.S. and British Main Fleet flagships respectively.

(d) 1 British Officer to be appointed for duty with the U.S. Navy initially at Washington. One officer from U.S. Navy to be attached to the staff of the U.S. Naval Attaché in London and to be available for communication duties.

GENERAL LIAISON

Both parties agree that no further measures for general liaison purposes are necessary at the present time.

Should, however, parallel action be decided upon by the two Governments, it would be necessary to appoint a British Officer with knowledge of war plans to Washington and a U.S. Officer with similar knowledge for duty in London.

STRATEGICAL POLICY

Should the Governments decide that a distant blockade is to be established, the British Naval Forces will be responsible for the stoppage of Japanese trade on a line running, roughly, from Singapore through the Dutch East Indies past New Guinea and New Hebrides, and thence round to the Eastward of Australia and New Zealand.

The U.S. Navy will be responsible for operations against Japanese trade throughout the West Coast of North and South America, including the Panama Canal and the passage round Cape Horn.

The U.S. Navy will also assume responsibility for the general Naval defence of the West Coast of Canada.

In these circumstances it is agreed that no hard and fast line of demarcation between the areas in which the two fleets will operate need be laid down at this stage.

R. E. INGERSOLL,
Captain, United States Navy.

T. S. V. PHILLIPS,
Captain, Royal Navy.

No. 487

Foreign Office to Sir R. Lindsay (Washington)

No. 40 Telegraphic [*F 337/84/10*]

Very Secret   FOREIGN OFFICE, *January 14, 1938, 8.20 p.m.*

Your telegram No. 30[1].

Records are, I understand, being sent to Navy Department by United States Embassy bag.[2]

Captain Ingersoll states that he is fully satisfied with his conversations, in which United States Naval Attaché has been associated. He is sure that everything has been carried as far as is possible at this stage. The Naval Attaché could carry on if this is necessary and an official in the Navy Department had already been deputed to be ready to come over if that were desirable.

When Captain Ingersoll gets back, you might ascertain whether the United States Government are satisfied and inform them that we should gladly welcome any further collaboration or liaison that they may think desirable and convenient.

[1] No. 474.   [2] See No. 486.

CHAPTER VI

Discussions on financial assistance to China and possibilities for mediation: Anglo-Japanese agreement on Chinese Customs administration

January 17—July 27, 1938

No. 488

Sir R. Craigie (Tokyo) to Mr. Eden (Received February 28)

No. 14 [F 2293/84/10]

TOKYO, *January 17, 1938*

His Majesty's Representative at Tokyo presents his compliments to the Secretary of State for Foreign Affairs and has the honour to transmit to him the undermentioned documents.

Name and Date	*Subject*
From Japanese Government, 16th January	Statement on China policy of the Imperial Government[1]

ENCLOSURE IN No. 488

Even after the capture of Nanking, the Japanese Government have till now continued to be patient with a view to affording a final opportunity to the Chinese National Government for a reconsideration of their attitude. However, the Chinese Government, without appreciating the true intentions of Japan, blindly persist in their opposition against Japan, with no consideration either internally for the people in their miserable plight or externally for the peace and tranquillity of all East Asia. Accordingly, the Japanese Government will cease from henceforward to deal with that Government, and they look forward to the establishment and growth of a

---

[1] A summary of this statement was transmitted to the Foreign Office in Tokyo telegram No. 57 of January 16 (F 623/84/10).

new Chinese régime, harmonious co-ordination with which can really be counted upon. With such a régime they will fully co-operate for the adjustment of Sino-Japanese relations, and for the building up of a rejuvenated China. Needless to state, this involved no change in the policy adopted by the Japanese Government of respecting the territorial integrity and sovereignty of China as well as the rights and interests of other Powers in China.

Japan's responsibilities for the peace of East Asia are now even heavier than ever before.

It is the fervent hope of the Government that the people will put forth still greater efforts towards the accomplishment of this important task incumbent on the nation.

No. 489

Sir R. Craigie (Tokyo) to Mr. Eden (Received January 18, 6.15 p.m.)

No. 68 Telegraphic [F 744/84/10]

TOKYO, *January 18, 1938, 11.20 p.m.*

In the course of my conversation today with the Minister for Foreign Affairs I asked whether there was anything he could tell me in regard to the recent declaration[1] whether [sic] it would be issued by the Japanese Government. He said that Chiang Kai-shek's reply to Japanese peace terms had been a curt request for further elucidation.[2] As the terms had been stated clearly and fully there was no need for further elucidation and Japanese Government considering Chiang Kai-shek had no serious intention of discussing peace terms decided to have no further relations with him. German Government had similarly informed Chiang Kai-shek that they were not prepared to act further as intermediary.[3] Intention of Japanese Government was to accord their recognition to a Government of China which would win the confidence not only of Chinese but also of the Japanese people.[4]

In reply to further enquiries Mr. Hirota admitted that no such Government was at the moment in sight. He added that hope of Japanese Government was to see emergence of a single strong government and that

[1] See No. 488.   [2] Cf. No. 484, note 3.
[3] Sir N. Henderson confirmed in Berlin telegram No. 27 Saving of January 29 that 'Germany has definitely abandoned rôle of postman for Japanese peace conditions and, inasmuch as Japanese Government has now refused to treat with Chiang Kai-shek, has no intention of resuming it'.
[4] Mr. Thyne Henderson minuted on January 19: 'A. There seemed, to everybody except the Japanese, considerable need for elucidation. Even the Germans seemed to think so, as they asked the Japanese to give the Chinese plenty of time. B. The Germans are gradually dissociating themselves from the Japanese. C. It will take great skill to avoid disputes with Third Powers if the Japanese keep up their present arrogant tone.'

they had no desire to encourage creation of a number of 'autonomous' governments.

I found the Minister for Foreign Affairs more than ever impressed with the necessity for preventing incidents and disputes with third Powers now that considerable prolongation of conflict was to be anticipated.

Repeated to Mr. Howe.

No. 490

Mr. MacKillop (Hankow) to Mr. Eden (Received January 19, 8 p.m.)

No. 72 Telegraphic: by wireless [F 786/16/10]

HANKOW, *January 19, 1938*

Addressed to Embassy Shanghai No. 60.

My telegram No. 47.[1]

President of Executive Yuan has informed me that Japanese reply was received yesterday through German Ambassador. It was to the effect that the Chinese Government had had Japanese proposals before them for a considerable time . . .[2] could therefore only regard request for elucidation of proposals as indication of lack of sincerity and desire to elude negotiations on the part of Chinese Government. Japanese Government had therefore decided to bring negotiations with Chinese Government to an end.[3]

---

[1] No. 67 to the Foreign Office: see No. 484, note 3.   [2] The text was here uncertain.
[3] In Tokyo telegram No. 72 of January 19 Sir R. Craigie reported that the Chinese Ambassador was leaving Tokyo on the following day, though some of his staff would remain. The Japanese Ambassador in China had also been recalled, although the Counsellor would remain.

No. 491

Mr. MacKillop (Hankow) to Mr. Eden (Received January 19, 6 p.m.)

No. 74 Telegraphic: by wireless [F 787/78/10]

HANKOW, *January 19, 1938*

Addressed to Embassy Shanghai No. 63 of January 19th.

President of Executive Yuan asked me to call this morning and delivered long oral message which he asked me to transmit to Sir F. Leith-Ross with a view to ensuring sympathetic reception by Sir F. Leith-Ross of a request for assistance which had or would be made to him

---

[1] Telegram No. 74 was actually received in the Foreign Office before No. 72 (No. 490), but they have been kept in numerical order.

by Chinese Ambassador in London.[2] Dr. Kung felt entitled to make this request not merely because he knew Sir F. Leith-Ross to be a sincere friend of China but because he considered British political and economic interests to be deeply involved.

British Empire had important possessions in the Far East and South Seas. It was the Japanese navy's desire to constitute a chain of those possessions for the benefit of Japan to obtain control of natural resources and man-power of China and if she succeeded she would dominate this part of the world within ten years at the most.

Imports from Great Britain had always been an important factor in China's trade and the Chinese Government believed they would increase with China's prosperity. Great Britain had large investments in Chinese railways and real estate and a privileged position in administration of China customs service while final currency reform carried out with British help ensured stability of Chinese exchange and protected British economic interests which would suffer if currency were endangered.

Arrangements had been made with private financial interests in United States with approval (as Dr. Kung understood) of United States Government for grant of a loan to China for general purchasing purposes and a contract had been signed.[3] His Excellency understood that Sir F. Leith-Ross had made enquiries in Washington and was aware of this. The amount borrowed in Washington was not secured on customs revenue of China and he felt that Great Britain was morally and legally bound as participant in League resolution to render assistance to China and grant of assistance would be in her own interest. During His Excellency's visit to England[4] agreement in principle had been reached for loan of £20,000,000 to China through the agency of Hongkong and Shanghai Bank to be secured on customs revenues. Japanese aggression had supervened and it would probably now be impossible to float loan on the open market. But security was good. Whatever the amount raised in London the money would not be touched but would act as an additional currency constituent and an assurance would be given that it would not be withdrawn. In short credit sought would be purely a book transaction. Knowing Sir F. Leith-Ross' influence in the counsels of His Majesty's Government His Excellency had instructed Chinese Ambassador to represent to him the true state of affairs and trusted that Sir F. Leith-Ross would recognise necessity and wisdom for facilitating an arrangement which would strengthen China's resistance and consolidate currency reform and stability of foreign exchange thereby safeguarding British

[2] Cf. No. 479.

[3] Cf. No. 479, notes 2 and 3. In a letter of January 21 to Sir A. Cadogan commenting on this telegram Sir F. Leith-Ross said that he had still received no confirmation of this supposed loan, and 'information obtained from Washington seems to indicate that Dr. Kung's statement on this point is not accurate'.

[4] See Nos. 75, note 3, 77 and 92.

investments in China which would suffer from any weakening of Chinese currency.[5]

[5] In his letter to Sir A. Cadogan (see note 3) Sir F. Leith-Ross suggested that one way to help China might be for the Treasury or Bank of England to buy a block of silver from the Chinese Government and realise it gradually on the market. He had not, however, put this idea to the Treasury yet and meanwhile submitted a draft reply to Dr. Kung: see No. 495 below.

No. 492

Mr. Affleck (Tientsin) to Mr. Eden (Received January 19, 6 p.m.)

No. 5[1] *Telegraphic: by wireless* [F 806/15/10]*

TIENTSIN, *January 19, 1938*

Following addressed to Embassy, Shanghai, No. 14 of 18th January.

Following is my information of present customs situation in North China in so far as affected by political considerations:

Relations between Wang Ke-min, the chairman of Peking Provisional Government, and Japanese appear to be somewhat strained. Wang is reported to be showing much personal independence in his dealings with Japanese military, and there are persistent rumours that, in spite of fact that his régime is disavowed by Central Government, he is in touch with Dr. Kung and T. V. Soong. It is worth noting in this connexion that Wang has not yet given his approval to proposed reduction of certain items in tariff which were put forward by Japanese and were to come into force originally on 1st January, then on 15th January, and are still not promulgated.[2]

The new Superintendent of Customs, Wen, seems also at variance with Wang. It is practically a certainty that recent telegram received by commissioner purporting to come from Wang and instructing that customs revenues should be quartered in the Bank of Chosen and that the Bank of Hopei and Chitung Bank were to act as customs collecting banks

[1] This telegram, and all others of file 15/10 of 1938 relating to the problems of the Chinese Customs and Salt administrations, have not been kept in F.O. archives, although about 100 relevant documents have survived in the Confidential Print volumes for this period. Documents printed in this Volume taken from the Confidential Print are indicated, following the usual practice of the Collection, with an asterisk.

[2] Cf. No. 456. The Peking Provisional Government announced on January 21 that the revised customs tariff would be put into effect in North China the following day. In telegram No. 68 to Tokyo of January 27 Sir R. Craigie was instructed to enter a strong protest with the Japanese Government, and Sir R. Craigie reported in telegram No. 132 of February 1 that he had addressed a note to Mr. Hirota 'conveying your strong disapproval of action of Provisional Government' and expressing 'confident expectation that the Japanese Government would secure immediate withdrawal of new tariff'. The U.S. and French Ambassadors made similar protests, on the grounds that the Provisional Government's action was calculated to disrupt the Chinese customs administration.

originated from Wen himself, who is interested in at least the Bank of Hopei. This is borne out by meekness with which Wen accepted commissioner's refusal to act on instructions.

As regards remittances, Japanese appear to be now realising that embargo is reacting against themselves just as much as it was intended to react against Central Government. Japanese consulate is giving close attention to this question, and there appears to be a reasonable hope that remittances for foreign loans may be resumed in the near future, probably in February.

Reverting to tariff, it might be advisable at this juncture for Central Government to take the initiative by a reversion to say (? 1931) tariff, with very generous terms for exports, a gesture which would undoubtedly stimulate trade under present conditions, bring in ample revenue for loans, and incidentally take the wind out of Japanese sails. The introduction of a considerably reduced tariff, no matter by whom it is introduced, would immediately relieve a great deal of distress and be popularly acclaimed, particularly if attention is paid to exports.

The customs continue to function normally in Tientsin and Chinwang-tao. A notice appeared in Japanese press to-day that illicit trade in Chitung would cease on 20th instant. Cargoes on the way or already landed would pay Chitung customs tax up to 30th January, after which regular customs duties would have to be paid.

Repeated to Tokyo and Saving to Peking.

No. 493

Mr. Phillips (Shanghai) to Mr. Eden (Received January 20, 7 p.m.)

No. 23 Telegraphic: by wireless [F 832/35/10]

SHANGHAI, *January 20, 1938*

Addressed to His Majesty's Chargé d'Affaires Shanghai telegram No. 18 of January 20th.

My telegram No. 12 and my telegram No. 15.[1]

Japanese Consul General has addressed to me a reply regarding Mr. Bennett's case of December 29th in which he encloses copy of his reply to Chairman of Council dated January 18th. In latter letter he gives the reply of Rear Admiral commanding special landing party which seeks to place responsibility for the incident upon Inspector Bennett on account of obstructing . . .[2] motor-cycle. Rear Admiral accuses Bennett of being under the influence of liquor on December 25th and of being insolent at interview on December 26th at branch headquarters. He states that as

---

[1] Of January 14 and 16, not printed: see, however, No. 473.
[2] The text was here uncertain.

662

Sinclair supported Bennett he was asked to leave and Bennett was restrained by a gesture. The assaults are denied and no fault on the part of Japanese naval landing party is admitted. The Rear Admiral expressed the hope that municipal authorities will issue strict instructions for avoiding similar traffic incidents and he states that on their side they will do everything possible to promote desired co-operation and a better understanding.

Japanese Consul General in his letter to me communicates the hope expressed by naval landing party headquarters that more caution should be exercised by Japanese and British alike in order to prevent future incidents and invite[s] my particular attention to remarks of Rear Admiral on necessity for co-operation and better understanding. While . . .[2] are not . . .[2] anxious to press matter too far they will take no further step without our approval and Commissioner of Police will report further. It is hardly likely to . . .[3] any ground for charge made against Mr. Bennett. I am sending copies of replies to Tokyo.[4]

Repeated to Tokyo, Commander-in-Chief for information. Copy to Major General and Senior Naval Officer.

[3] The text was here uncertain: 'substantiate' was suggested on the filed copy.

[4] Sir J. Brenan commented on January 24 that the Japanese 'never admit that their man can be in the wrong. It is hinted that to suggest such a thing is an insult to the Imperial Japanese Navy and the Emperor. All sorts of aspersions are cast on the victim of the assault and downright lies are told about his conduct to justify his treatment. . . When finally it is clear to everybody that the Japanese are hopelessly in the wrong they try to settle the matter, as they are doing now, by saying that all the Japanese desire is cooperation. . . It is to be hoped therefore that this sort of reply . . . will not be allowed to close the case, and that if satisfaction is finally unobtainable H.M.G. will leave the Japanese Govt. in no doubt as to their extreme dissatisfaction'. Mr. Orde wrote (January 25): 'Obstinate lying and slander are the usual Japanese tactics in these cases. I agree with Sir J. Brenan.' See No. 498 below.

No. 494

Sir E. Phipps (Paris) to Mr. Eden (Received January 21)

No. 44 Saving: Telegraphic [F 811/84/10]

PARIS, *January 20, 1938*

M. Delbos[1] remarked to me again last night that he was more and more convinced that, so long as the United States did not come out into the open against Japan, Great Britain and France must decline to be drawn into the Far Eastern conflict. If, on the other hand, the United States did decide to fight Japan, we could do anything we liked, for in that case the

[1] M. Chautemps announced the resignation of his government on January 14, but formed a new government on January 18 in which M. Delbos retained his position as Minister for Foreign Affairs: see Volume XIX, No. 435, note 3.

United States would be with us, not only in the Far East, but in Europe as well.

I observed that that happy day seemed as far distant as ever, and M. Delbos regretfully agreed.

No. 495

Mr. Eden to Mr. MacKillop (Hankow)

No. 9 Telegraphic [*F 912/78/10*]

FOREIGN OFFICE, *January 22, 1938, 11 p.m.*

Your telegram No. 74.[1]

Please convey following reply for [from] Sir F. Leith-Ross to Doctor Kung.[2]

I duly received your message of the 19th instant. I have been kept in touch with the situation by the Chinese Ambassador and, as I have told him, I am anxious to do anything possible to help support the financial position of China[3]; but, as Doctor Kung recognises, it is not possible in present circumstances to raise a market loan, while question of a guaranteed loan would obviously raise serious political difficulties. I have not been able to obtain any details of contract arranged with American financial interests and it might help if I could be informed how similar difficulties have been overcome as regards the United States of America.

Repeated to Shanghai No. 83 for repetition to Rogers Hongkong. Copy to British Embassy Shanghai for Financial Adviser.

[1] No. 491.   [2] See *ibid.*, note 5.

[3] A draft memorandum on the possibilities of financial and material assistance to China is filed at F 1098/78/10. In a letter of January 26 to Sir F. Leith-Ross Mr. Orde said that Mr. Eden had been considering this memorandum and that while 'it seems impossible to do anything involving submission to Parliament he would very much like to help', and would like Sir F. Leith-Ross's views. None of the possibilities considered in the Foreign Office found favour with the Treasury, however, and Sir F. Leith-Ross concluded in his reply to Mr. Orde of February 1 that 'it seems to me that the only way in which the London market could help the Chinese Government would be by arranging a credit secured on silver which would enable the Chinese to sell their stocks of silver gradually to repay the credit'.

No. 496

Mr. MacKillop (Hankow) to Mr. Eden (Received January 26, 6.15 p.m.)

No. 80 Telegraphic: by wireless [*F 1201/84/10*]

HANKOW, *January 24, 1938*

Addressed to Embassy, Shanghai telegram No. 76, January 24th.

Recent telegrams from here have covered a wide variety of subjects and

I should like to attempt a personal synthesis.

After pondering the Japanese terms Chinese Government . . .[1] to keep peace discussions alive by a request for details.[2] Reply[3] came as a shock but it is still hoped in some quarters that a further chance will be given. Dr. Kung's attitude is that after necessary political and military reorganisation the fight must go on: but it is doubtful whether dispositions (or disposition) can be said to exist for a regular and determined defensive battle still less for attack. As regards currency stability Minister of Finance has hoisted a private flag of distress. Doubt is permissible whether economic structure of territory as yet unoccupied by Japanese is adequate to contemplate support of administration of modern type with foreign obligations and also to bear cost of waging modern war and vast additional purchases abroad which will be required if ambitious projects of Minister of Economics are brought into operation. If they are not, the economic structure of this territory will continue to be in the main a primitive one. This territory has inadequate communications with the outside world while the area beyond the front where there is a large concentration of foreign interests has become a coast without adequate hinterland and its economic life seems also to be suffering. Such revenue as it may produce over and above service of foreign obligations is lost to National Government.

Very considerable doubt must be felt whether task of rationally organising remaining territory and at the same time keeping up supplies to military forces is within the capacity of National Government. Barring an act of God in the form of foreign intervention it will be miraculous if this administration does not crack long before financial anaemia obliges Japanese to relax grip. This is not of course to say that Japanese will be able soon enough for their needs to develop such relations with the civilian populations as will permit of the invaded territory to be administered and exploited at not undue heavy cost. As regards military and political standpoints the Chinese position is infinitely weaker than Japanese; the financial and economic strain on Japan would therefore have to be of immediate and decisive effect if it was to be of countervailing benefit to National Government since the latter's own losses in this field have been so severe.[4]

As regards act of God Chinese Government hope that Great Britain, United States and Soviet Union or one or some combination of two of those Powers will decide to intervene actively; failing this that one or more of the three will be embroiled in war as results of grave incident or of failure on the part of Japan to respect important foreign . . .[1]

---

[1] The text was here uncertain.   [2] See No. 484, note 3.   [3] See No. 490.
[4] Mr. Scott remarked on January 31: 'I fancy that her [China's] funds must be nearing exhaustion and in default of fresh credits it is I agree probable that financially she will "crack" before Japan.'

No. 497

Memorandum by Sir J. Pratt on British Policy in the Far East

[F 1023/78/10]

FOREIGN OFFICE, *January 24, 1938*

What is the policy of His Majesty's Government in the present crisis in the Far East? Policy is the means adopted to attain a given object. In the present case the objects of His Majesty's Government are (a) to defend threatened British interests while the conflict lasts and (b) to endeavour to secure that the terms of the settlement shall be such as to afford the maximum opportunity to British trade, industry and finance in the new régime inaugurated in China. In this memorandum an attempt is made to deal with (b).

If a powerful British fleet is sent to the Far East policy will become a comparatively simple problem. His Majesty's Government will be in a position to insist on a settlement that shall carry into effect the principles of Article I of the Nine-Power Treaty. Such a settlement would provide ample opportunity for Japan, equally with other nations, to develop her interests in China. It is no part of the policy of His Majesty's Government that Japan should be either ruined or destroyed.

If the British fleet is not sent out to the Far East the struggle may end in the complete victory of Japan; it is unlikely to end in the complete defeat of Japan but it may end in something like a stalemate. Which of these alternatives would be more favourable to British interests? By a complete Japanese victory is meant the cessation of organized Chinese resistance to Japanese domination. Such a victory would be followed by the progressive and fairly rapid elimination of all British interests in China beginning with North China, then Shanghai, the International Settlement, the Yangtse Valley generally and the Customs Administrtion and finally South China and Hong Kong. While the issue is yet in doubt the responsible leaders of Japan will do their utmost to avoid complications with foreign Powers. They will refrain from exercising belligerent rights at sea, they will make every effort to prevent the young officers committing further outrages and they will give every possible assurance calculated to keep foreign governments quiet. From September 1931 to February 1933 Japan's representatives at Geneva never ceased reiterating that Japan was respecting and would continue fully to respect the Covenant, the Kellogg Pact and the Nine-Power Treaty, that she had no territorial ambitions, and that she was the champion of the open door in Manchuria. The same simple tactics are being repeated now. Mr. Hirota has just announced that Japan 'would not only respect to the fullest extent the rights and the interests of other Powers in occupied areas of China but was prepared also to leave the door wide open to all Powers and to welcome their cultural and economic co-operationin China.' These tactics should not deceive a

666

child and it is disturbing therefore to find that the Diplomatic Correspondent of *The Times* in today's issue (January 24) states that appreciation of these assurances is expressed in British official circles.[1] For there is no doubt that the sole object of Mr. Hirota's speech was to keep official circles quiet until Japan was ready to expel British interests from China as she has expelled them from Manchuria.

If China continues to put up a vigorous resistance to Japanese aggression that is the only hope British interests have of saving something from the wreck. There is just a chance that the conflict may be so prolonged in time and enlarged in space that Japan may be forced to relinquish her more extreme designs upon Chinese sovereignty and treat for peace with a Chinese Government on more or less equal terms. That would give us an opportunity to maintain our footing because the Chinese Government will look to us and to other friendly nations to act as a counter-weight to Japan.

If this diagnosis of the situation is correct the proper policy for His Majesty's Government to follow is to give China every possible encouragement and support in the hope that she will thereby be enabled to carry on the struggle so long that in the end Japan will be forced to agree to reasonable terms of peace. It is not sufficient that this policy should be accepted by the Foreign Office as being the proper policy for His Majesty's Government. It must also be accepted by the Treasury and other Departments of His Majesty's Government. It must also be accepted by the Bank of England and that section of the City that is specially interested in Far Eastern finance. It is also desirable that responsible business houses should receive some guidance in the matter. In 1932 the Shanghai British community—to their shame—openly applauded Japanese aggression hoping that foreign privilege would be fortified by Chinese defeat. Even today they are not much wiser for they believe that Japan would show greater regard for foreign interests than China and that, in any case, as China is certain to be defeated, it is to their interest to seek good relations with Japan the most powerful country in the Far East. In fact there is only one way to get fair play from Japan and that is not to seek for favours, but to insist upon just consideration. Nevertheless the Bank of England and the City share the view of the merchants with the result that while His Majesty's diplomatic representatives are encouraging Chiang Kai-shek to continue resisting until a fair peace is possible the British Consortium banking group—which enjoys the complete support of His Majesty's Government—considers that financial pressure should be put upon the Nanking Government in order to force them to compromise with Japan and make an early peace. It seems unnecessary to point out the disastrous consequences that may flow from our thus seeming to speak with two voices. If the Consortium base their financial policy upon political

[1] A report of Mr. Hirota's speech to the Imperial Diet on January 22, and comments by the 'Diplomatic Correspondent', are printed in *The Times*, January 24, 1938, p. 12.

considerations they should at least be the same as those upon which the policy of His Majesty's Government is based.[2]

There are many who still regret the passing of the Japanese alliance: there are many more who, realising that it cannot be restored, yet desire that His Majesty's Government should cultivate close relations with Japan because she is the strongest power in the East. There is however only one ground on which alliances, ententes or a common policy can be based and that is community of interest. There was community of interest with Japan in 1902—the desire to check Russia—and therefore an alliance was possible. Russia practically disappeared from the East when the Great War broke out and from that moment the Foreign Office has been aware that the interests of Japan and Great Britain in the Far East are diametrically opposed. Great Britain desires to see a prosperous and United China. To Japan this is as great a nightmare as a Europe united under one sovereignty would be to British statesmen. Japan has therefore promoted separatist movements and has blocked the political and economic development of China. In 1935 British policy in the Far East fell into confusion. It was believed that we could hunt with the hare—develop China—and ride with the hounds—co-operate with Japan. Sir F. Leith-Ross was accordingly sent out on an impossible mission,[3] but it was soon discovered that the success of the currency reform and the rapid progress China was making towards unity and prosperity had aroused the bitter hostility of the Japanese.[4] To some extent it is we who have brought down this Japanese attack upon the Chinese and inevitably we have roused hopes that having brought them thus far along the road we would not leave them in the lurch when the crisis came. There is not much that we can do to help the Chinese but national honour no less than a regard for our own interests demands that we should at least give them all the encouragement we can and not advise them to surrender. It seems important that steps should be taken to ensure that this is recognized by all the Departments and the interests concerned as being the policy of His Majesty's Government.

---

[2] Mr. Orde commented on February 3: 'I certainly think that we should try to get the Consortium Banks to change their attitude.' In a long letter to Sir F. Leith-Ross of February 9 Sir A. Cadogan summarized the arguments in Sir J. Pratt's memorandum and suggested that financial and commercial houses in the Far East, especially those comprised in the Consortium, should 'receive some guidance', possibly through the Treasury and the Bank of England, as to the considerations upon which the policy of His Majesty's Government is based'. He asked Sir F. Leith-Ross's views as to how to go about this, and concluded: 'The Banks may feel that in view of Japan's need for money they do not run the same risk of being deprived of their position in China if Japan gets control as commercial firms would do, but such an attitude seems short-sighted in their own interest as well as contrary to the general interest.'

[3] See Volume XX, Chapters V and VI.   [4] See *ibid.*, Chapter VII, *passim.*

No. 498

Foreign Office[1] to Sir R. Craigie (Tokyo)

No. 66 Telegraphic [F 832/35/10]

FOREIGN OFFICE, *January 26, 1938, 5.45 p.m.*

Mr. Phillips' telegram No. 18[2] to His Majesty's Chargé d'Affaires.

You should make it clear to the Minister for Foreign Affairs that His Majesty's Government cannot accept the explanation offered by the Rear Admiral commanding the landing party and will not be satisfied with vague expressions of a desire for co-operation and a better understanding by the municipal council.

In this and in the other cases under consideration police officers of British nationality have been maltreated by Japanese troops without any adequate excuse.

As stated in my telegram No. 26[3] His Majesty's Government take a very grave view of these incidents and unless they are to be left with the conviction that the Japanese Government are utterly careless of the rights and feelings of British subjects they expect to receive some expression of regret and to be informed what steps have been taken to prevent a repetition of such conduct towards their nationals.

Repeated to Embassy, Shanghai, No. 92.

[1] Mr. Eden left London on January 25 to attend the League of Nations Council meeting in Geneva.

[2] No. 493.

[3] No. 482.

No. 499

Sir R. Craigie (Tokyo) to Foreign Office
(Received January 27, 1 p.m.)

No. 106 Telegraphic [F 1107/510/61]

Confidential　　　　　　　　　　　　　　　TOKYO, *January 27, 1938, 8.25 p.m.*

In the course of interview today Vice Minister for Foreign Affairs speaking unofficially confidentially referred to announcement made by United States Navy Department on January 13th to the effect that three American cruisers were to be sent at the invitation of the British Government to participate in celebrations connected with opening of Singapore dock (? base)[1]. A further report reached Japanese Government quot[ing] an alleged denial by British Admiralty that ships were attending as result of an official invitation. Vice Minister for Foreign Affairs wondered whether I could give him any information on the subject particularly as to whether an invitation had been despatched. On my

[1] See No. 478.

replying that I had no official information, His Excellency went on to say that it seemed to him personally a little unfortunate for such an invitation to be sent (if it had been sent) to United States and not to Japan as the other great naval power in the Pacific, adding that he had even seen it alleged that meeting at Singapore was intended as a demonstration of Anglo-American solidarity against Japan.

I replied that as Japan was actively engaged in hostilities in China I thought an invitation to send a Japanese ship to attend official celebrations at Singapore might be considered hardly consistent with neutral attitude we had consistently adopted. This seemed to me more likely explanation than the idea of a naval demonstration. But I would not conceal from His Excellency that generally expansionist trend in China and hostile attitude towards foreign interests adopted by some Japanese authorities on the spot must inevitably have the effect of bringing Great Britain and United States closer and closer together. His Excellency made no comment on this but as he seemed to attach some importance to the matter I promised to pass on to you his unofficial enquiry.

I feel sure that sending of these American ships has already had a salutary effect on Japanese opinion. But it would be clumsy to over-emphasise the moral and I hope I may be authorised to return a friendly answer particularly as there are distinct signs of a desire in high quarters to bring about a *détente* in Anglo-Japanese relations.[2]

Repeated to Embassy Shanghai.

[2] According to a note on this file Mr. Chamberlain was 'very interested' in this telegram, and 'anxious that Craigie should make it clear to the Japs. that the Americans invited themselves & that we had not asked them': cf. Nos. 447, 462, 464, and see No. 501 below.

No. 500

Sir R. Craigie (Tokyo) to Foreign Office
(Received January 29, 10.20 a.m.)

No. 117 Telegraphic [F 1195/5/10]

TOKYO, *January 29, 1938, 5.35 p.m.*

Foreign Office spokesman informed Reuters correspondent in reply to enquiry that Japanese Government considered *Ladybird* incident closed.[1]

As you are aware (see my telegram No. 39)[2] I am endeavouring to secure assurance that Colonel Hashimoto has been punished. May I indicate to Japanese Government that until we have some further

[1] See No. 458.
[2] In this telegram of January 11 Sir R. Craigie gave an account of a meeting with the Vice Minister for Foreign Affairs that day when he again complained about Colonel Hashimoto's 'gross negligence and lack of judgment' and said that he did not see how his government 'could be expected to regard the incident as satisfactorily settled so long as Colonel Hashimoto remained in command of his unit'.

guarantee for the future such as his punishment would afford we cannot consider the matter definitely closed?[3] It is important that no public reference should be made to fact that I am pressing for punishment of Hashimoto who, incidentally, appears to have strong political protection.

Repeated to Commander-in-Chief.

[3] The Foreign Office concurred. Mr. Orde commented on February 7: 'We may not get him punished but clearly we cannot regard the incident as properly closed if he is not.'

No. 501

Foreign Office to Sir R. Craigie (Tokyo)

No. 78 Telegraphic [F 1107/510/61]

FOREIGN OFFICE, *January 29, 1938, 10 p.m.*

Your telegram No. 106.[1]

I approve your language.

The facts are, however, that there was never any question of issuing a formal invitation to foreign Governments to attend a comparatively small function like the opening of the new dock at Singapore. The United States Government having proposed to bring some of their cruisers back from the celebrations at Sydney by way of Singapore, it was suggested to them that the visit might be timed to coincide with the opening of the dock.

It was agreed with the United States Chargé d'Affaires that any inquiry here from the representatives of foreign Governments should be answered on the above lines, and an informal enquiry by a Secretary of the Japanese Embassy was dealt with accordingly.[2]

You should speak to the Vice Minister in the sense indicated.

[1] No. 499.
[2] According to a letter from the Admiralty of January 21 the U.S. Naval Attaché in London had also been approached by a German journalist and by the French Assistant Naval Attaché as to the nature of the 'invitation' issued to the U.S. Navy to visit Singapore.

No. 502

United Kingdom Delegation (Geneva) to Foreign Office (Received January 31)

No. 19 [F 1215/78/10]

GENEVA, *January 29, 1938*

The United Kingdom Delegate to the League of Nations presents his compliments, and has the honour to transmit copies of the undermentioned paper, of which a copy has been sent to Paris.

ENCLOSURE IN NO. 502

GENEVA, *January 28, 1938*

Far East

A meeting took place to-day (January 28th) at the Secretariat at which were present the Secretary of State, Lord Cranborne, M. Delbos, Mr. Litvinoff, Mr. Wellington Koo and Mr. Quo Tai-Chi.

THE SECRETARY OF STATE said that the purpose of the meeting was to take stock of the present situation and decide what could be done.

MR. WELLINGTON KOO said that he had received instructions from his Government to bring the Far Eastern situation before the Council and to request that the procedure contemplated in Article 17 of the Covenant should be carried out. The Brussels Conference had disappointed China.[1] The Chinese Government thought that the League of Nations should consider the taking of steps which might lead to the cessation of hostilities or, if they were not prepared to do that, should at any rate react in some way to the Japanese aggression.

THE SECRETARY OF STATE then asked what it was exactly that the Chinese Government desired.

MR. WELLINGTON KOO said that the Chinese Government urged that the Council should proceed under Article 17 and invite Japan to take part in the discussions. The Chinese Government did not expect the application of the whole gamut of sanctions as a result of this procedure but thought that some concrete measures might be devised. The Covenant of the League was designed to deal with just such a situation as had arisen, and the Chinese Government thought that the League had now a chance of showing its vitality by taking some positive action.

MR. LITVINOFF asked whether it was desired that the League should establish aggression by Japan.

M. DELBOS said that the United States and Holland were both vitally concerned. As regards the application of sanctions by the United States the Brussels Conference had shown that there was really no hope.[2]

THE SECRETARY OF STATE said that it was necessary to take into account the realities of the situation. He thought that the fact that hostilities had not spread further south in China was due to an appreciation in Tokyo of the importance of growing co-operation between the United States and the United Kingdom. Would the application of sanctions really help China? Sanctions would entail a blockade by [?of] Japan and would result in the application of the neutrality legislation by the United States. China

---

[1] Cf. No. 387.

[2] See No. 355.

would thus be in a worse situation than at present. It was not sanctions that would improve her situation, but she might benefit from what help interested Powers could give her individually.

Mr. Wellington Koo said that the League might give an example to the United States. At the present the U.S. Government said that if the League were to take some decision they would give it their sympathetic consideration, while the League said that they could take no decision without being assured of the co-operation of the United States. It would seem to be a vicious circle.

The Secretary of State reminded Mr. Wellington Koo that at Brussels Mr. Norman Davis had ruled out the possibility of the application of sanctions.

Lord Cranborne said that Mr. Norman Davis had in fact made it clear that the United States could not consider anything which involved legislation such as sanctions inevitably would.

M. Delbos alluded to the European preoccupations of France. She could not undertake any definite action in the Far East unless full co-operation were forthcoming from the United States. He feared that if the European Powers were to take a decision to apply sanctions they would find that the United States could not cooperate.

The Secretary of State said that there had been a certain development and education of public opinion in the United States since the Brussels Conference. He would not wish to do anything to hinder that.

Mr. Wellington Koo said that in the view of the Chinese Government opinion in the United States had so far evolved that if the League were to take action the United States could follow. He asked whether France and Great Britain had recently enquired in Washington in regard to the possibility of the application of sanctions to Japan.

The Secretary of State said that they had not put this question recently to Washington but they had been led to understand that the U.S. Government would much prefer that the Far Eastern question should continue to be treated by the Brussels Conference rather than at Geneva.[3]

Mr. Wellington Koo suggested that an approach might be made to Mr. Leland Harrison.

Lord Cranborne said that it was quite clear that the United States wished to avoid any connexion between the Brussels Conference and the League of Nations.

Mr. Wellington Koo said that hostilities had been raging in China for six months. China would continue to resist Japan's aggression, but she felt that the cause of law and order throughout the world was at stake and that if she failed not only would she suffer but all other nations as well. The Chinese Government very much hoped that they would be able to obtain

[3] In Geneva telegram No. 4 of January 30 Lord Cranborne reported that the U.S. Consul had told him that the Chinese Ambassador at Washington went to see Mr. Hull on January 29 to enquire 'what was attitude of United States Government towards a possible convocation of Brussels Conference': see *F.R.U.S.*, 1938, vol. iii, pp. 578.

help from Members of the League.

M. DELBOS suggested that the U.S. representative here should be asked whether his Government were ready to reopen the Brussels Conference.

MR. LITVINOFF suggested that the U.S. Government might be told that there was a group of States in the League who were ready to help China and might be asked whether, in those circumstances, the United States would co-operate with such a group. If the United States were not ready to assist then there was no hope of doing anything.

MR. WELLINGTON KOO said that his Delegation at the Brussels Conference had submitted a memorandum to the other Powers represented there. It might be possible to take up some of the suggestions contained in that memorandum while avoiding the use of the word 'sanctions'.

THE SECRETARY OF STATE doubted the possibility of putting forward any concrete measures to the United States Government. He said that His Majesty's Government had given some study to the question of sanctions as had probably other Governments. Their point of view was that sanctions would be either effective or ineffective. If they were effective the nations applying them must be ready to carry them through to the end, which meant possibly military action. If they were ineffective they were not worth applying.

M. DELBOS said that as far as France was concerned she was ready to go to all lengths provided there was solidarity.

MR. LITVINOFF asked whether it was sure that sanctions would provoke hostile action by Japan.

THE SECRETARY OF STATE said that if sanctions were effective this was likely.

MR. WELLINGTON KOO suggested that negative sanctions should be applied, such as a refusal to sell certain goods to Japan.

M. DELBOS said that such action was possible if everybody participated in it.

THE SECRETARY OF STATE said that he was ready to examine any proposals in conjunction with the United States. His Majesty's Government were not prepared to act without full co-operation from the latter.

MR. WELLINGTON KOO said that Japan existed on differences of opinion between the Powers anxious to promote peace. If some common action, however mild, were taken by these Powers it would create a tremendous impression on Japan.

THE SECRETARY OF STATE agreed that it might be possible to approach the United States Government and ask them what they were prepared to do. This however, would not be much comfort at the moment to Mr. Wellington Koo, the difficulty of whose position he fully appreciated. What could the Council do in the circumstances?

MR. WELLINGTON KOO suggested that the Council might start procedure under Article 17.

This suggestion was not enthusiastically received.

Mr. Wellington Koo then pointed out that the Chinese Government found it most difficult to understand the League's failure to take action under Article 17.

The Secretary of State said that the Chinese Government surely saw that the League could not act without the co-operation of the United States.

Mr. Litvinoff said that it was quite out of the question that the Council and Assembly should vote in favour of sanctions. In any event it was only the interested Powers who would take action.

The Secretary of State said that it was quite clear that nothing that was done at Geneva alone would impress Japan. A resolution of the Council, however, might give some satisfaction to China.

Mr. Wellington Koo said that the report of the Advisory Committee was in fact an acknowledgement of Japanese aggression and ought really to have been followed by some action by the League.

Lord Cranborne said that Japanese aggression could, of course, be formally established, but that there appeared to be no advantage in doing this unless it were to lead to action against Japan by the League. It was clear that the latter could not act without the United States.

Mr. Wellington Koo then suggested action by the Council under Articles 10 or 11.

M. Delbos said that there would certainly be strong opposition in the Council to any such suggestion and thought that the only course was for those countries particularly interested in the Far East to ask the United States whether they were prepared to co-operate.

The Secretary of State said that a resolution by the Council might recall the passage in the Assembly's resolution of last October concerning the extension of individual aid to China.[4]

Mr. Wellington Koo urged that the Council should advance a step further and should recommend that nations particularly interested should concert together to give aid to China. He pointed out that at present all the Members of the League were well-disposed towards China but were unwilling to act singly. He thought that it might be possible to set up an unofficial committee of interested Powers with the object of laying down a concerted plan.

The Secretary of State asked how China would benefit by that. If more war material reached China as a result would not Japan declare a blockade?

After some further discussion the Secretary of State suggested that the Council might authorise certain of its Members to get into touch with non-Member States.

Mr. Wellington Koo thought it would be necessary to tell the United States what interested Powers were ready to do.

Mr. Litvinoff said he thought that the Netherlands, for instance,

[4] See No. 288.

would be ready to co-operate but would require full military protection.

After further discussion it was decided that a draft resolution should be prepared for a later meeting. The resolution should recall part of the Assembly's resolution of last October and should authorise interested Members of the Council to concert among themselves and with non-Member States in the study of possibilities. It was further decided that there should be no speeches at the Council meeting apart from that of the Chinese representative, who undertook to speak in harmony with the resolution. The Secretary of State, however, advised Mr. Wellington Koo that it would be better to make no speech at all.[5]

[5] In a minute of January 28 Sir A. Cadogan recorded that Mr. Eden had telephoned from Geneva to say that 'after a rather difficult day's discussion, he and two of his colleagues have been able to agree on a draft resolution relating to the Far East'. The draft was amended during further discussion on January 29 and 31, and the agreed text was then circulated to the Council delegations: see No. 504 below.

No. 503

Mr. MacKillop (Hankow) to Mr. Eden[1]
(Received January 31, 7.50 p.m.)

No. 88 Telegraphic: by wireless [F 1502/84/10]

HANKOW, *January 31, 1938*

Addressed to Embassy Shanghai telegram No. 89 January 31st.
My telegram No. 76.[2]

You have no doubt seen agency messages minimising importance of Sun Fo's visit to Moscow[3]. They suggest either that he has received a rebuff or that he has been persuaded that it is impolitic for Chinese Government to single out Soviet Government as their special (?saviour).

My telegram under reference was not wholly a statement of my own views but was meant to be in the main an objective summary based on known facts and statements of Chinese spokesman. My personal view goes further. The strongest impression which one forms here is of the supineness, incapacity, disunion, irresponsibility and ill-founded optimism of the Chinese Government—optimism based almost wholly on hope that other countries including prominently our own will be willingly or (? unwillingly) involved in war and that a great catastrophe will save something out of the wreck for Chinese Government.

It can be stated fairly in their defence that their machinery of government and even their centre of gravity has been forcibly displaced,

[1] Mr. Eden returned to the Foreign Office on January 31. [2] No. 496.
[3] Dr. Sun Fo, son of Sun Yat-sen and President of the Legislative Yuan, had returned recently from a visit to Moscow on a secret mission which, the Chinese Ambassador told Mr. Eden on January 18, was connected with Soviet help to China. Dr. Quo said that Russia was now giving 'a very considerable measure of help to China in war material and in personnel'.

that they have never before been called upon to discharge full normal obligations of centralised sovereignty over this territory, that it is a difficult country to administer on modern lines, and that they are deprived of foreign advice and of the wealth of Shanghai to which they formerly had access. But real question for us is surely not respective deserts of blame or sympathy but whether they are capable of existing given all possible sympathy and assistance including a measure of armed intervention amounting to a high proportion of the total effort which any one of the countries on which they are relying is capable of bringing to bear *here*. In my opinion answer is that they will disintegrate as soon as they are forced to leave Hankow, perhaps sooner than that if renewal of Japanese offensive is delayed for an appreciable time, whether or not they receive such material and imponderable aid.

I have spoken of Chinese Government and not of China. Latter unlike the former is probably indestructible. I do not know whether Japanese will on balance derive anything but loss from her adventure. That is in any case a question of long term.[4]

[4] For the views of Mr. Howe and the British Military Attaché on this telegram see Nos. 506 and 508 below.

No. 504

Mr. Edmond (Geneva) to Mr. Eden (Received January 31, 11 p.m.)

No. 5 Telegraphic: by telephone [F 1266/78/10]

GENEVA, *January 31, 1938*

Following from Lord Cranborne:

The following is the text of a draft resolution on the Far East which was agreed by me with the French, Chinese and Soviet representatives this evening.[1] It will be circulated confidentially by the President of the Council tonight to the other Council Delegations. The President is calling a secret meeting of the Council for 12.30 p.m. tomorrow to consider it.

'The Council,

Having taken into consideration the situation in the Far East,

Notes with regret that hostilities in China continue and have been intensified since the last meeting of the Council,

Deplores this deterioration in the situation the more in view of the efforts and achievements of the National Government of China in her political and economic reconstruction,

Recalls that the Assembly by its Resolution of October 6th 1937 has expressed its moral support for China and has recommended that Members of the League should refrain from taking any action which

[1] See No. 502, note 5.

might have the effect of weakening China's power of resistance and thus of increasing her difficulties in the present conflict and should also consider how far they can·individually extend aid to China, <u>calls the most serious attention of the States members of the League to the terms of the above-mentioned resolution,</u>

Is confident that those States represented on the Council for whom the situation is of special interest will lose no opportunity of examining in consultation with similarly interested powers the <u>feasibility</u> of any further steps which may contribute to a just settlement of the conflict in the Far East'.

The modifications introduced into the text of the draft Resolution as the result of today's negotiations are indicated by underlining. They do not materially affect the sense of the Resolution.[2]

[2] At the Secret Session of the Council held on February 1 Mr. Jordan, the New Zealand representative, summed up the views of a number of the delegates when he said that 'there was nothing whatever in the resolution. It merely reaffirmed the something, or rather the nothing, which had been done at the Assembly' (see No. 288). The French representative accepted the draft without comment: M. Litvinov expressed disappointment. Lord Cranborne explained that the resolution had necessarily to be in vague terms because so much depended on the attitude of non-member states. Dr. Wellington Koo, while expressing some disappointment, said that he understood this point. After some further discussion the resolution was sent forward to be considered by the Council on February 2: see No. 507 below. Mr. Eden told the Cabinet on February 2 of the difficulties encountered in drafting the resolution, adding that 'he himself was not particularly satisfied with the draft... The matter, however, was one of great difficulty, on which he might have to approach his colleagues before long'.

No. 505

Sir R. Craigie (Tokyo) to Mr. Eden (Received February 2, 9.30 a.m.)

No. 135 Telegraphic [F 1348/35/10]

TOKYO, *February 2, 1938, 11.35 a.m.*

Your telegram No. 86.[1]

I have handed to Vice Minister for Foreign Affairs today letter enclosing Japanese Consul General's letter to His Majesty's Consul General with enclosures summarised in his telegram No. 18 to Mr. Howe.[2]

In my letter I have stated above communications had left a very bad impression on me. There was no doubt in both cases violence was offered and yet there was no word of regret and no sign that it was gross breach of

[1] This telegram of January 31 referred to No. 498 and asked how matters stood: 'Delay in Japanese reply is regrettable from every point of view. You should avoid if possible being involved in detailed discussion of provocation (which seems in any case to have been very slight if any) and concentrate on the main issue of brutal assaults which nothing could justify.'

[2] No. 493.

discipline and international courtesy that Japanese armed forces should strike members of Settlement police. If this spirit were to be allowed to prevail heavy responsibility would rest on commanding officers of Japanese forces for any further incidents.

In regard to Mr. Bennett I emphasised that he bore excellent record; had attended naval landing party headquarters voluntarily and without obligation to do so; both he and Sinclair had nevertheless been subjected to violence and former had been forced against his will to remain when latter was compelled to leave room.

I expressed hope that Japanese Government would shortly declare willingness to give full satisfaction in these cases which would otherwise remain further cause for Anglo-Japanese irritation. They only went to confirm impression in my mind that Japanese naval and military authorities in Shanghai were determined to act towards nationals of third Powers in an arbitrary and high handed manner. Vice Minister for Foreign Affairs after reading letter said he thought Mr. Okamoto's letter must have been despatched before he had received instructions sent to him after my last conversation with His Excellency on this subject. He would do his best to hasten reply of Japanese Government.[3]

Repeated to Consul General Shanghai.

[3] Mr. Thyne Henderson wrote on February 3: 'This is all to the good, but it doesn't get us much further. The Japanese Govt. will not dare to censure their military in Shanghai and we shall only receive a prevaricating answer.'

No. 506

Mr. Howe (Shanghai) to Mr. Eden (Received February 2, 4 p.m.)

No. 223 Telegraphic: by wireless [F 1551/84/10]

Secret   SHANGHAI, *February 2, 1938*

Following is a summary of the Military Attaché's[1] appreciation of the situation.

It should be read in conjunction with Mr. MacKillop's telegrams Nos. 76[2] and 89.[3]

Chinese army has been organised and equipped by foreign countries whose representatives have for the most part given entirely misleading advice as to China's ability to Japan. Soviet military Attaché has encouraged the Chinese to believe that the Japanese were bluffing and that some form of active assistance would be forthcoming from Soviet Government: General von Falkenhausen has continually asserted that the Chinese are strong enough to resist and even to drive the Japanese from North China. French authorities in the past have practically promised

[1] Major W. A. Lovat-Fraser.   [2] No. 496.   [3] No. 503.

facilities (not implemented) for free importation of munitions via Indo-China, Donald and Malley have supported vigorously the bellicose and ill-founded attitude of Madame Chiang Kai-shek though they do not speak Chinese and are [? not] in a position to realise the facts.

Territorial situation is that Japanese have overrun five important provinces and part of two more, have captured Nanking, driven the Government to Hankow are in occupation of Tientsin, Tsingtao, Shanghai, Hangchow and are in a position to take Canton and advance on Hankow.

Chinese army is irreparably smashed and air force is eliminated. The only hope of the new . . .[4] lies in provision of facilities for importation of war material. The Soviet Government are most unlikely to afford serious assistance in this difficulty and it would be most unwise for His Majesty's Government to bolster up dying cause.

The only hope of the Central Government most of whom are men with unsavoury records is to prolong resistance in the hope of embroiling a third party preferably Great Britain.

The Chinese are not fighting our war and have done nothing but harm to our interests having brought about serious international situation in Shanghai and gravely jeopardised our commercial interests in Central China.

Central Government should therefore receive no encouragement to continue . . .[4] support whatever in attempt to import war material via British territory. End of summary.

Air Attaché[5] considers that we should not encourage any shipment of aircraft and supplies on grounds

(a) that they encourage the Chinese to no purpose and

(b) antagonise Japanese.

While I feel that you should be in possession of these views I do not agree with them.

My own observations will follow.[6]

Repeated to Mission Saving and Peking.

[4] The text was here uncertain.   [5] Wing Commander H. S. Kerby.   [6] See No. 508 below.

No. 507

Mr. Edmond (Geneva) to Mr. Eden (Received February 3)

No. 17 Saving: Telegraphic [F 1397/78/10]

GENEVA, *February 2, 1938*

Following from Lord Cranborne:

Council met at midday today, first in private and then in public, to deal with the appeal of the Chinese Government, which figured as No. 24 on the Council agenda.

The Council had before it a draft resolution which had been prepared after consultation between the United Kingdom, French, Soviet and Chinese delegations and had been submitted to the other Members of the Council by the President on the previous day.[1]

In the private meeting it became clear that the Polish and Peruvian representatives intended to abstain from voting for the resolution and to base their abstention on their dissatisfaction with the procedure followed in drawing it up. An attempt was made to dissuade them from ventilating this question in public and a somewhat confused discussion took place which continued for three-quarters of an hour. Neither the Polish nor the Peruvian representatives were to be moved from the attitude they had assumed, and the Council proceeded to meet in public session.

After the President had presented the resolution to the Council, Mr. Wellington Koo (China) made a speech. He said that since the last meeting of the Council Japanese aggression in China had been intensified. He referred to the cruel and barbarous conduct of the Japanese military forces at various places in China. He said that the establishment of puppet governments by the Japanese proved that they intended to destroy Chinese independence and sovereignty. He asserted that this was not Japan's only aim but that she also wished to undermine and destroy all foreign interests in China. The Chinese Government would continue to defend the country's sovereign rights and territorial integrity. No settlement which did not guarantee this would be acceptable to China. He reminded the Council that China had appealed to Articles 10, 11 and 17 of the Covenant. He could not conceal the disappointment of his country at the result, or rather at the lack of result of the Assembly's resolution and of the Brussels Conference. He maintained that were the League to take decisive action in the present instance it would regain its lost prestige. Public opinion throughout the world demanded the application of the covenant. He terminated what was, on the whole, a moderate speech in the circumstances, with the assertion that China was not fighting for her own hand alone but for the peace of the world.

Senor Quevedo (Ecuador) said that in signifying his agreement with the resolution he desired to make it clear that the Ecuadorean Government accepted it on the understanding that if the resolution involved action with a view to putting an end to the conflict which engaged the responsibility of League Members, the matter should be brought before the Council before any decision on it could be taken. The responsibility of League Members could not be engaged without the approval of the constitutional organs of the League. This was without prejudice of course to any action which League Members thought fit to take individually. His Government could not have accepted the resolution if they thought that its last paragraph had involved a delegation of powers to a few States.

M. Komarnicki (Poland) made the usual Polish complaint against the

[1] See No. 504.

procedure adopted in preparing the resolution. He said that his Government could not accept a resolution giving the support of the League to action by some Members outside the League. He would accordingly abstain.

Señor Calderon (Peru) complained that too short a time had been given for the Members of the Council to consider this resolution. He had not been kept *au courant* with the negotiations day by day. He was therefore unable to appreciate all the implications of the resolution. He would abstain from voting on these grounds.

I then supported the resolution and in a short speech made clear the position in regard to the method of work which had been adopted on this occasion. As there was no rapporteur for this question the Chinese representative had consulted certain delegations. Informal discussions had ensued and as soon as they had reached a point at which communication could be made to the other Members of the Council this was done and a draft resolution was submitted to them. This procedure was justified by the unusual position. Its sole object was to facilitate the Council's work. There had never been any intention of pressing the Council to agree in haste to a ready-made resolution and the United Kingdom delegation for its part had been ready to prolong the present session of the Council for so long as might be necessary for other delegations to arrive at a considered decision on the resolution.

M. de Tessan (France) and M. Stein (U.S.S.R.) associated themselves with my remarks as also did Mr. Wellington Koo (China) who said that his Government was ready to accept the resolution though they were disappointed at what they regarded as an insufficient response to their appeal for assistance. They hoped for more concrete results and maintained their reservation to bring the matter up under Articles 10, 11 and 17.

The resolution was then adopted with two abstentions and the 100th Session of the Council was declared closed by the President.[2]

[2] The full record of this Sixth (Private, then Public) meeting of the League of Nations Council is printed in *L./N.O.J.*, January–June 1938, pp. 117–25.

No. 508

Mr. Howe (Shanghai) to Mr. Eden
(Received February 3, 9.30 a.m.)

No. 226 Telegraphic: by wireless [F 1452/84/10]

Secret   SHANGHAI, February 3, 1938

My telegram No. 223[1] and Mr. MacKillop's telegrams Nos. 76[2] and 89.[3] Military Attaché believes central government to be finished. Mr.

[1] No. 506.   [2] No. 496.   [3] No. 503.

MacKillop, who does not go so far, thinks they will crack when forced to leave Hankow if not earlier but does not foresee subjection of China as a necessary concomitant.

My own views are these.

If Powers stand aside completely central government may well crack before economic and financial pressure compels Japan to relax her grip. Moreover it is possible *but by no means certain* that if we were to encourage China to make peace with Japan on any terms they might lose heart and seek to negotiate. But this would not necessarily bring about peace.

Whatever may happen in North, Southern leaders will not easily accept Japanese domination nor will they agree to any terms recognising economic or political domination of the North by Japan. I think that if Chiang Kai-shek were to endeavour to make peace on such terms Kuangsi generals would assume control and would have behind them not only sympathy of vast majority of Chinese but some of the best organised forces in the country i.e. their own . . .[4] men and Communist troops.

Even if Japanese claimed[5] what are believed to be their nearer objectives their approximate territory would still be bounded by a line running from Paotou to Changsha and thence to position[6] covering only about one-fifth of the country (excluding Tibet and Sinkiang) (? and) enormous forces would be necessary and enormous risks have to be taken if they were to proceed further. Let us assume every vestige of central government control gone in occupied area even including the port of Canton: Japanese in full control of customs, salt etc: a crash of the entire financial structure based on revenues reserves and credit of central government. Even then I do not rule out possibility of a central government under leadership of Kuangsi group continuing to function effectively (by Chinese standards) in the rest of China. I think they might well succeed in 'rational organisation' of this remaining territory maintaining a fighting force which while . . .[7] effective attack would make establishment of peaceful government by Japanese puppets in neighbouring provinces exceedingly difficult. So long as there is an effective Chinese Government in any part of the country claiming to be the government of China it must attract better elements and prevent drift towards any bogus organisation.

If I am right in this view then whether or no we supply Chiang Kai-shek with arms and financial assistance and whether or no we discourage its will to fight there will still remain a central government in lineal succession to government which we have recognised and in more or less effective control of four-fifths of the country. If arms and financial assistance were available government would be by so much stronger. I do not suggest we should provide this government with any special facilities but I do not

---

[4] The text was here uncertain.

[5] It was suggested on the filed copy that this word should read 'gain'.

[6] It was suggested on the filed copy that this word should read 'coast'.

[7] The text was here uncertain: the words 'unable to undertake' were suggested on the filed copy.

agree that we should restrict those supplies which this government is able to obtain by reason of our . . .[4] neutrality.

Our League obligations permit us to sympathise with incessant difficulties of Chinese Government and this attitude seems to have full support of current popular opinion in Great Britain. Though we should not go out of our way to provoke Japan nothing is to be gained by attempting to placate her. British interests in Japanese dominated territory would receive no more consideration simply because we had thrown over central government. Japanese find us in their way all along the line. Our only fault is that we got there first. We are feeling their pressure at a hundred points and a policy of weak conciliation will not get us anywhere.

I hold further that it is to our definite advantage to break Japanese stranglehold on Chinese coastline by encouraging building up line of communication—road rail and air—across Chinese Western frontier. Internal communication system in West China is expanding rapidly under impulse of government war needs and I believe it important to our future trade to link up this system with Burma at as many points as possible.[8]

Repeated to Mission and Saving to Peking.

[8] Mr. Orde commented on February 8: 'I myself much prefer Mr. Howe's judgement to Mr. MacKillop's or the Military Attaché's. The latter takes too narrow a professional view and the former makes too little allowance for what the Chinese can do with a Govt. which is below Western standards of efficiency.' Sir A. Cadogan agreed (February 8): 'In these matters I should certainly give preference to Mr. Howe's judgment. I expect—and hope—that he is right in maintaining that Japanese aggression has produced a national feeling that never existed in China before. . . When it comes to looking round for ways of assisting them, we find difficulties everywhere. Other papers show that there is not much prospect of financial assistance. . . Burma communications are the most hopeful field.'

Mr. Eden wrote across the top of the filed copy of this telegram: 'I agree emphatically with this telegram. We must review means of helping China. I have spoken to Sir F. Leith-Ross. I presume that India are dealing with my views on Burma road problem?' After a talk with Mr. Eden on February 9 Sir A. Cadogan wrote: 'I understand from the S. of S. that a C[ommit]tee is to be formed, under Ld. Cranborne's chairmanship, to consider help to China': see No. 517 below.

No. 509

Mr. MacKillop (Hankow) to Mr. Eden (Received February 3, 7 p.m.)

No. 102 Telegraphic: by wireless [F 1548/84/10]

Secret   HANKOW, *February 3, 1938*

Addressed to British Embassy Shanghai No. 115.
Your telegram No. 223 to Foreign Office.[1]
While I have felt it my duty to report on the situation here as I see it I have not felt it so to advise on policy as the latter is necessarily governed by

[1] No. 506.

considerations which are not fully known to me and which I could not in any case see in proper perspective.

Still less have I felt it my duty to discourage Chinese Government or to advise them on their proper course. What I have said has been that His Majesty's Government have consistently expressed sympathy with China and have consistently done everything open to them to bring the present conflict to an end by peaceful methods stipulated in resolution of the Brussels Conference by which His Majesty's Government are bound: and that support given by Great Britain individually before hostilities began, notably regarding currency reform and stabilisation, has been of great and admitted service to China since hostilities began.[2]

[2] The Foreign Office evidently viewed the argument between Mr. MacKillop and Mr. Howe with some unease. Sir J. Brenan minuted on February 9: 'So long as Mr. MacKillop clearly understands that it is not his duty to discourage the Chinese Govt. from continuing their resistance he will at least do no great harm.'

No. 510

Mr. MacKillop (Hankow) to Mr. Eden (Received February 4, 5 p.m.)

Nos. 103 & 104 Telegraphic: by wireless [F 1549/84/10]

HANKOW, *February 4, 1938*

Addressed to British Embassy Shanghai No. 116 of February 4th.
My telegram No. 115[1].

If I am permitted to say a word on general policy I should like it to be this. I have always taken it to be the case that in these Sino-Japanese conflicts as in comparable matters since they put their signature to the Covenant of the League of Nations His Majesty's Government have been and are anxious as far as lies in their power to ensure that it shall be considered collectively with other nations interested in preservation or restoration of peace. As an individual government their main concern has been to take the lead therefore, which is their right and duty in such collective consideration but not to dominate it since that would be to defeat the principle of collective responsibility.

As an individual government it would ill become them to stand out publicly as first to advocate and practice a policy *parcere superbis et debellare subjectos*.[2]

The vice of our post-war China policy has been its duality. We have been fellow members with China of League of Nations and at the same

[1] No. 509.
[2] To make this point Mr. MacKillop here inverted the nouns in a familiar Virgilian quotation. The original (*Aeneid VI*, line 853) reads: 'Parcere subjectis et debellare superbos', which may be adequately translated by 'to spare those subjected (to Rome) and to tame by war the proud'.

time we have exercised within her territory 'simalacrum' [*sic*] of sovereignty which has been incompatible with such fellowship and yet has never been (it could not be at such a . . .[3] without an obvious disproportionate strain) based on a force sufficient to make it in fact what it purported to be. The present hostilities therefore brought a real Japanese force into the presence of . . .[3] real British one and existence of the latter has been a heavy political liability which is due to a China policy illogical and unjustifiable in itself a . . .[3] shadow of Central Government and in complete contradiction with our general policy.

[3] The text was here uncertain.

No. 511

Mr. Eden to Sir R. Craigie (Tokyo)

No. 60 [F 1472/84/10]

FOREIGN OFFICE, *February 4, 1938*

Sir,

The Japanese Ambassador asked to see me this afternoon when he said that he had been instructed by M. Hirota to leave with me the two attached documents, the first being a report of a speech by M. Hirota[1] and the second an aide-mémoire in explanation of it[2]. His Excellency continued that he would like to make certain additional observations on his own account. I would perhaps recollect that shortly before my departure for Brussels His Excellency had been to see me and suggested that His Majesty's Government, possibly jointly with the United States Government, should offer their good offices to bring hostilities in the Far East to a close.[3] At that time, however, the Japanese Government were relying upon German mediation and had advised him not to proceed further with this suggestion. It had always been the Ambassador's conviction that the German mediation would come to nothing. Germany was too busy sending arms to China and trying to keep in with both sides in furtherance of her own interests. Events had proved him right and the German attempt had failed. He now wished to suggest to me that the moment had perhaps come when His Majesty's Government might reconsider his suggestion. The war was putting a severe strain on Japan, both financially and economically. Moreover her actual military commitments in the field in China were heavy. The Japanese Government did not, he felt sure, wish this state of affairs to continue indefinitely. Of course, it might be that it was our view that it was best for us that the conflict should continue and both sides exhaust themselves but, if we did not take that view—and I

[1] Not printed: see No. 497, note 1.   [2] See Enclosure in this document.
[3] It is not clear to which interview Mr. Yoshida was here referring.

interjected that, of course, we did not—then His Excellency once again begged me to consider whether we could not informally approach both sides.[4] We should shortly have a new Ambassador in China[5] and he, in conjunction with you, might be able to facilitate progress.

2. I replied that I presumed that the Ambassador contemplated the good offices of ourselves and the United States Government jointly. I felt sure that we should not be willing to act in the Far East except in conjunction with the United States Government. His Excellency assented, though without any enthusiasm. I then asked him whether his Government was aware of the suggestion which His Excellency was making. The Ambassador replied that he was speaking entirely for himself, but that he felt sure that the Japanese Government would be found to be interested if we were willing to undertake this task. I replied that I would, of course, give very careful consideration both to the memorandum which His Excellency had left with me and to the observations which he had himself made. I appreciated M. Hirota's action in thus explaining his view to us. In the meanwhile I would only make one or two preliminary observations.

3. There had, of course, been a considerable deterioration in the relations between our two countries in recent months. That was inevitable in the light of the view we took of Japanese action in China. In addition we had certain special obligations towards China, as had recently been made clear by the declaration of the Council of the League.[6] There were also many difficult Anglo-Japanese questions, notably the position at Shanghai. His Excellency at once agreed with the last-named observation but contended that the longer hostilities lasted, the more acute these difficulties would become. I then showed His Excellency a copy of the evening paper from which it appeared that Japan was now beginning a campaign for the conquest of Southern China. I pointed out that if these facts were accurate then I feared that the prospects of improving Anglo-Japanese relations for which he had pleaded would inevitably be affected. As you had already explained to M. Hirota, an extension of hostilities to the neighbourhood of Hong Kong would inevitably increase the risk of grave complications between our two countries.[7] The Ambassador replied that he was surprised to read this report and himself doubted its accuracy. His own information was that, while an attack in

[4] At a meeting of the Cabinet on February 9 Mr. Chamberlain drew attention to the preceding ten words of this despatch and asked Mr. Eden 'if it was the intention of the Foreign Secretary to follow up this suggestion?' Mr. Eden 'replied in the affirmative', but pointed out that the task 'was one of great difficulty and delicacy, as the Germans had found, and he felt that it could only be carried out hand in hand with the United States of America. On that basis he was prepared to consider making the attempt'. At the Cabinet meeting on February 23, after Mr. Eden's resignation, Mr. Chamberlain brought the subject up again, reminding Lord Halifax of Mr. Eden's undertaking and asking him to take up the matter himself.

[5] See No. 444, note 4. Sir A. Clark Kerr left Bagdad on January 31 and arrived in Shanghai on February 24.

[6] See Nos. 504 and 507.

[7] See No. 438, note 4.

South China had been contemplated some little time ago, the idea had been definitely abandoned on account of the large increase in military commitments which it would entail.

4. Before leaving, the Ambassador said that Viscount Ishii was shortly returning to this country. On the occasion of his last visit, which His Excellency admitted had not been conspicuously successful, Viscount Ishii had spent much time in explaining Japan's past attitude and aims. On this occasion he hoped to make some proposals for the future and His Excellency, therefore, greatly hoped that I would be able to see Viscount Ishii again.

I am, etc.,

ANTHONY EDEN

ENCLOSURE IN NO. 511

Aide-Mémoire on Anglo-Japanese relations

Strictly Confidential

It has always been the earnest desire of the Japanese Government to promote and perpetuate the most amicable relations between Japan and Great Britain. Of late, however, incidental to the present hostilities in China, unfortunate misunderstandings seem to prevail to the detriment of cordial relations between our two countries. The Japanese Government feel deeply perturbed by the development of an unhappy atmosphere through these misunderstandings and are anxious to dispel it in order that Anglo-Japanese co-operation may be restored for the benefit of peace in the Far East. It was this desire which prompted Mr. Hirota the other day to declare before the Imperial Diet that the Japanese Government would firmly adhere to the settled policy of cultivating traditional friendship with Great Britain, and that it was their hope—fully reciprocated, it is believed, by the British Government—that the peoples of our two countries will realise the importance of Anglo-Japanese relations and unite in earnest efforts to improve them.

2. The ultimate aim of the Japanese Government in prosecuting the present hostilities is the attainment of an enduring peace in the Far East by the inauguration of an established and solid understanding between Japan and China. With this aim in view, the Japanese Government, both prior to and during the present hostilities, have exerted unremitting efforts to obtain reconsideration of the anti-Japanese policy of the National Government. This having failed, the Japanese Government have, as set forth in the statement of January 16th,[8] reluctantly come to the decision that they will cease to deal with the National Government.

The policy of the Japanese Government is not directed towards any

[8] See No. 488.

territorial aggrandisement whatsoever nor towards the separation of North China from the rest of China. The Japanese Government will respect to the fullest extent the rights and interests of the other Powers. The policy of the Open Door will be maintained for the purpose of promoting the welfare of the Chinese people, and the Japanese Government will welcome the cultural and economic co-operation of the other interested Powers, especially of Great Britain, in the rehabilitation of China. Such being the immutable policy of the Japanese Government, it is earnestly to be desired that the Government and people of Great Britain should understand the realities of the situation in the Far East and, believing in the assurances of the Japanese Government, should enter without misgivings into full and friendly co-operation with Japan in the major task of reconstructing China and rehabilitating the Chinese market.

3. The Japanese Government regret deeply that since the outbreak of hostilities, unfortunate incidents have occurred in which British interests have unwittingly been involved. It is more than gratifying that these incidents have been settled amicably on the basis of a genuine goodwill, and the Japanese Government are confident that our cordial relations have not been fundamentally affected. The Japanese Government are taking all possible precautions to prevent the recurrence of any such incidents and ask for the full co-operation of the British Government in this respect.[9]

[9] Mr. Yoshida's communication was received with some scepticism in the Foreign Office. Mr. Orde remarked on February 9 that 'what the Japanese mean by co-operation is money, the use of which they would control'. Sir A. Cadogan wrote on February 10: 'I flatter myself that I don't "misunderstand" Japanese policy. I take no credit for that, for it's plain as daylight. All this stuff about no territorial ambitions and respect for foreign interests is exactly what was given off by the Japanese Govt. while Japan was getting a good stranglehold on Manchuria. Look what they have done to foreign interests there since. . . Mr. Yoshida is a nice little man and possibly himself well-intentioned, and his comm[unica-tio]n deserves a polite reply of some sort. But we really can't be fooled beyond a certain point. He admits himself that he is "speaking entirely for himself" which is extremely obliging, but utterly useless.' He suggested that the best thing to do 'would be for the S. of S. to see him again and to say that H.M.G. would be willing for their part—as they have always stated—to offer their good offices in conjunction with the U.S.A.' Mr. Eden agreed: see No. 521 below.

No. 512

Mr. Howe (Shanghai) to Mr. Eden (Received February 7)

No. 257 Telegraphic: by wireless [F 1602/84/10]

SHANGHAI, *February 7, 1938, 4 p.m.*

Mission telegram No. 116[1].
Mr. MacKillop refers to duality of our post war policy, but duality is

[1] No. 510.

more apparent than real, and so far as it is real it is the outcome of historical circumstances.

Extra-territorial system (Mr. MacKillop's 'simulacrum of Sovereignty') was imposed on China when she was not in a position to resist it. That is in fact the only condition under which extra-territoriality can endure. We have, since the war, not only been adopting a more liberal attitude on moral grounds, but have been uncomfortably aware that China was growing up and that her continuous subjection would need the use of force which we did not want to use. We have been gradually relaxing our grip as a result of policy deliberately adopted in 1926, and the reason why more progress has not been made is only that China's inability to set her own house in order has made it impossible for us to let her have unhampered control of large British interests, which have grown up under the shelter of extra-territoriality, and jurisdiction over lives and properties of individuals. Our China policy is perfectly consistent and coherent and I do not agree that it is in complete contradiction with our general policy. Of course if the Japanese are prepared to send a million men to China to impose an *illiberal* policy, which is in direct conflict with ours, it is unfortunate for us, but it does not follow that our policy is either illogical or unjustifiable.[2]

Not repeated to Hankow.

[2] Mr. Thyne Henderson commented on February 9: 'And that answers Mr. MacKillop.' Mr. Orde wrote (February 10): 'Bird's eye views are good, but Mr. MacKillop's is taken from a height which flattens out the mountains. We should let Mr. Howe know that we agree with him. He can do as he likes about informing Mr. McK., but the latter will eventually see this tel. & the reply in sections—after Mr. Howe leaves China.' Mr. Howe was transferred to the Foreign Office on March 1, where he succeeded Mr. Orde as head of the Far Eastern Department. Mr. Orde was appointed H.M. Minister at Riga, Tallinn, and Kovno from April 23, 1938.

No. 513

Mr. Eden to Sir R. Craigie (Tokyo)

No. 109 Telegraphic [F 1054/287/10]

Secret   FOREIGN OFFICE, February 7, 1938, 11 p.m.

The Japanese forces have occupied certain islands off the South China coast. A number of them could all be used, in varying degrees, as naval and air bases in an attack on Hongkong. The retention by Japan of any of these islands is therefore strategically undesirable.[1]

[1] On January 7 the Admiralty communicated to the Foreign Office a secret telegram of January 2 from the Captain on the Staff, H.M.S. *Tamar*, listing the islands off the South China coast occupied by Japan. In a letter to the Admiralty of January 10 Mr. Orde said that Mr. Chamberlain would be grateful 'if he may be informed whether in the opinion of the Lords Commissioners of the Admiralty any special significance, strategic or political,

Unless you see grave objection I think we might endeavour to extract from the Japanese Government some more specific assurances than those of a general character hitherto given.[2] You might refer to the Japanese assurances in regard to Hainan and other islands, to their disclaimer of any territorial designs and to their professed desire to cultivate friendly relations with us. You should go on to say that circumstantial reports have reached us that Japanese have occupied certain islands not far distant from the South China coast. You should avoid being drawn into discussion as to exactly which islands are in question seeing that most of our reports have reached us from confidential sources. In conclusion you should say that you have been instructed to remind the Japanese Government in the friendliest possible way that any permanent occupation of islands in the vicinity of Hongkong could not fail to have detrimental effects on relations with His Majesty's Government and say that His Majesty's Government would welcome renewed assurances that no such occupation is in contemplation.

Repeated to Shanghai No. 134 and Commander-in-Chief.

attaches to the occupation of any of these islands or groups of islands'. The Admiralty replied on January 25 that while islands north of Formosa were of no strategical significance, those between Formosa and Hong Kong 'could all three be used, in varying degree, as naval and air bases in an attack on Hong Kong', and another six islands, south and west of Hong Kong, could also be used as naval and air bases. The Admiralty suggested that Sir R. Craigie should be authorized to tell the Japanese Government that 'any permanent occupation of islands in the vicinity of Hong Kong would have seriously detrimental effects on our relations'. Mr. Orde agreed, and approved the draft of the present telegram. Cf. No. 438, note 3.

[2] Cf. No. 438, note 4.

No. 514

Mr. Eden to Sir R. Lindsay (Washington)

No. 105[1] *Telegraphic [F 1345/15/10]**

FOREIGN OFFICE, *February 8, 1938*

(To Washington only.) Your telegrams Nos. 431 and 432.[2]

(To both) Chinese Customs.

Representations were made to Japanese Government on 28th November by United States, French and British Ambassadors insisting on the right of their Governments to be consulted in regard to any arrangement

[1] No. 19 Saving to Paris.

[2] These telegrams of November 27, 1937, not printed, referred to instructions sent to Mr. Grew to make representations to Mr. Hirota regarding the Shanghai customs: see No. 395, note 3.

contemplated.[3] These representations have been ignored, and on 23rd January His Majesty's Chargé d'Affaires at Shanghai reported[4] that new proposals had been communicated to Shanghai Commissioner of Customs to effect that Shanghai Customs revenue accounts were to be opened with Yokohama Specie Bank in the name of the commissioner; the commissioner to draw on these for administrative expenditure and foreign loan quotas; amount of quotas to be determined by the Japanese Government in consultation with customs authorities; and any accrued surplus to remain in the account.

Japanese consul-general has told inspector-general that he expects him to take orders from his Government, since Japanese are in military occupation. This attempt to short-circuit the interested foreign Powers was fortunately resisted by the inspector-general, and the representatives of these Powers are now being asked to agree to deposit in the Yokohama Specie Bank. United States consul-general has replied that he cannot discuss this until assurances requested in Tokyo by United States Ambassador (see Tokyo telegram No. 869[5] to Foreign Office of the 24th December) have been received.

His Majesty's Government are gravely perturbed by the recent indications of the Japanese intention to use the revenues for their own purposes to the detriment of the loan services as soon as they have obtained control of them. The assurances hitherto given are at best equivocal; General Matsui has stated in a press interview[6] that ample financial resources drawn upon the customs revenues are to be placed at disposal of a new Chinese régime, and that the foreign loan services will have to suffer; the Japanese Minister for Foreign Affairs has told a committee of the Lower House that Japanese Government will 'supervise Shanghai Customs and take over a fixed part of the revenue'; and His Majesty's Ambassador at Tokyo has been given to understand that revenue is to be made to bear expenses of 'other administrations' as well as Customs Administration before loans are served.

Unless deposit in the Yokohama Specie Bank is prevented, there will be little or no hope of safeguarding the position. This point is therefore essential, and I shall be glad if you will urge it informally upon Government to which you are accredited.

If deposit in the Yokohama Specie Bank can be prevented, it will be necessary next to consider on what lines negotiations should proceed. His

[3] See Nos. 395 and 396.

[4] In Shanghai telegram No. 135 January 23, not printed (F 923/15/10).

[5] Not kept in F.O. archives: see, however, *F.R.U.S., Japan 1931–1941*, vol. i, pp. 733–4 for the text of a note presented by Mr. Grew to Mr. Hirota on December 23 asking for assurances that the integrity of the Chinese customs would be preserved.

[6] In telegram No. 198 of January 29 Mr. Howe reported the chief points of an interview between Mr. H. G. Woodhead, Editor of *Oriental Affairs*, and General Matsui, chief of the Japanese General Staff, who made a number of controversial comments on Japanese policy in China and was critical of British policy in the Far East. Sir R. Craigie had been instructed in telegram No. 94 of February 1 to protest to Mr. Hirota about the General's remarks.

Majesty's Government are for their part prepared to suggest to Chinese and Japanese Governments that customs funds in areas controlled by the Japanese should be deposited in the Hong Kong and Shanghai Bank, and that control over them should be vested in a body of officials nominated by Powers interested in customs loans (compare my telegram No. 485[7] to Shanghai). Please ask Government to which you are accredited whether they are prepared to support this proposal. I think it will greatly strengthen our position if we can agree on a positive alternative to Japanese terms.

Please see my immediately following telegram.[8]

Repeated to Embassy Offices, Shanghai, No. 136.

[7] No. 378.

[8] In telegram No. 106 to Washington (No. 20 to Paris) Mr. Eden said he had received further information that the French and U.S. Governments might consider the deposit of part of the revenue in the Yokohama Specie Bank if the Japanese Government gave the required assurances to the U.S. Government. Mr. Eden felt, however, that 'Legitimate Japanese interest in revenues is not great enough to justify custody by Yokohama Specie Bank of any part of the revenues and I think it is most desirable that a further stand should be made against it'.

No. 515

Sir R. Craigie (Tokyo) to Mr. Eden (Received February 9, 1.45 p.m.)

No. 178 Telegraphic [F 1648/287/10]

Secret   TOKYO, *February 9, 1938, 6 p.m.*

Your telegram No. 109[1].

I saw Minister for Foreign Affairs this morning and carried out your instructions.

He at first showed considerable irritation asking why we thought it necessary to make these constant demands for assurances when the Japanese Government had already given to His Majesty's Government all assurances that could reasonably be expected of them in present difficult circumstances. Referring specifically to Hainan His Excellency said they could not possibly give a permanent pledge not to occupy: Japan was engaged in a serious struggle and, if it was not to be prolonged, she might be forced to occupy more Chinese territory whether insular or on the mainland. I pointed out that assurance asked for was against 'permanent occupation' but his somewhat irascible reply was that if war was to be permanent, so would occupation be.

I warmly rejoined that your anxiety in this matter was entirely reasonable: Hongkong could not in any sense be regarded as a threat to Japan but occupation by Japan of islands in the vicinity of Hongkong

[1] No. 513.

could legitimately be regarded as a threat to that colony. His Excellency saw the force of this and agreed that Japanese Government desired to do nothing which might prove seriously prejudicial to Anglo-Japanese relations but he was unable to make any commitment detrimental to the conduct of the present naval and military operations. The most I could get him to say was that Japanese Government's declaration that they had no territorial designs in China applied equally to islands and mainland.[2]

While interview ended on a friendly note it cannot of course be regarded as satisfactory. My impression is that Minister for Foreign Affairs is under constant pressure from Ministry of Marine to agree that occupation of certain islands should not necessarily be strictly limited to the period of hostilities; while the declaration in regard to 'no territorial designs' still holds good, Minister for Foreign Affairs must realise that an undue prolongation of the struggle may upset all previous calculations and ultimately necessitate a change in policy in this matter of occupation of territory.

I am sure it has been a good thing to give the Minister for Foreign Affairs a warning as to ill-effects on Anglo-Japanese relations of a permanent occupation of islands in the vicinity of Hongkong but I feel reiteration of request for assurances as regards further . . .[3] merely provoke irritation without producing any guarantees on which reliance can be placed for more than a few weeks ahead.[4]

Repeated to Mr. Howe and Commander-in-Chief.

[2] Marginal comment by Mr. Eden: 'not much use.'
[3] The text was here uncertain.
[4] Mr. Eden wrote across the filed copy of this telegram: 'This is a disturbing telegram, both for French and ourselves.' A copy of the telegram, together with copies of the correspondence with the Admiralty, was sent to Sir E. Phipps for the information of the French Government.

No. 516

Mr. Eden to Mr. Howe (Shanghai)

No. 151 Telegraphic [F 1551/84/10]

FOREIGN OFFICE, *February 10, 1938, 11 p.m.*

Your telegram No. 226[1].

I entirely agree with you. Moreover I regard it as imperative that nothing should be done or said to discourage the Chinese.

Neither Service Department is disposed to agree with pessimistic views reported in your telegram No. 223[2].

It is of course perfectly right and proper that Service Attachés should

[1] No. 508.   [2] No. 506.

express their views to *you* in this way, but I hope all concerned will bear in mind warning contained in my telegram No. 207[3].

Repeated to Hankow No. 16, Peking No. 35.

[3] Of November 15, 1937, not kept in F.O. archives: it apparently warned against indiscreet remarks to outsiders.

No. 517

Minutes of the First Meeting of the Interdepartmental Committee on the possibility of rendering assistance to China, held at the Foreign Office on February 11, 1938, at 11.30 a.m.[1]

[*F 1788/78/10*]

Secret

PRESENT: Viscount Cranborne (*in the Chair*); Mr. Orde, Sir J. Pratt, Sir J. Brenan (Foreign Office); Sir F. Leith-Ross, Chief Economic Adviser; Vice-Admiral Sir W. James, Deputy Chief of the Naval Staff, Captain G. E. Creasy (Admiralty); Sir V. Warrender, Lt.-Colonel A. F. Harding, Colonel W. P. J. Akerman (War Office); Wing Commander D. L. Blackford (Air Ministry); Mr. N. E. Young (Treasury); Mr. E. P. Donaldson (Burma Office); Mr. Heppel (Foreign Office) Secretary.

Lord Cranborne referred to the Resolution passed by the Council of the League of Nations on the 2nd February,[2] in which, after referring to the Assembly's Resolution of the 6th October[3] recommending that the members of the League should consider how far they could individually extend aid to China, the Council expressed its confidence that 'those States represented on the Council for whom the situation is of special interest will lose no opportunity of examining, in consultation with other similarly interested Powers, the feasibility of any further steps which may contribute to a just settlement of the conflict in the Far East.' Dr. Wellington Koo had seen the Secretary of State in connexion with this Resolution and had made various demands, many of which were out of the question, but it was necessary that His Majesty's Government, having subscribed to the Resolution, should review the means at their disposal of rendering assistance to China. Dr. Koo had asked, *inter alia*, for (1) munitions, (2) lorries, (3) loans and credits and (4) the prevention of the

[1] See No. 508, note 8. Following a discussion between Mr. Chamberlain and Mr. Eden on February 9 concerning the League Council Resolution of February 2 (see Nos. 504 and 507), letters of invitation were sent out on February 10 to the Burma Office, Admiralty, Treasury, War Office and Air Ministry, asking them to send representatives to a meeting the following day. Lord Cranborne was to be Chairman, and Sir F. Leith-Ross was invited personally to attend.

[2] See Nos. 504 and 507.

[3] See No. 288.

export of war material to, and the withholding of credits from, Japan. The present meeting had been convened for the purpose of preliminary discussion and it was proposed to hold a second meeting at which the considered opinions of the Departments concerned would be reviewed.

2. Lord Cranborne observed that it was the policy of His Majesty's Government to delay applications for the export of arms to Japan, but that as the action taken by the Council was a recommendation, and not a decision, it did not override our treaty obligations towards Japan. At present, there were two contracts in process of fulfilment.

3. As regards lorries, Sir F. Leith-Ross said that the Export Credits Guarantee Department would not be precluded from operating, but that they would not regard exports to China as an attractive proposition.

4. Lord Cranborne asked that the Admiralty, War Office and Air Ministry should consider again whether there were any stocks of munitions of any kind which could possibly be made available. The representatives of those Departments agreed that this should be done. Sir V. Warrender referred to the Cabinet decision that exports of munitions from surplus Government stocks should not be permitted either to China or to Japan. It was agreed that the Service Departments should take into consideration the possibility of this decision being modified. If it were modified, Sir V. Warrender thought that a certain number of Hotchkiss guns and a certain amount of war-time ammunition might be available, but, if it were not, the War Office knew of no sources from which the Chinese might obtain supplies, apart from Messrs. Alvis-Straussler Limited and the Soley Armament Company, whose representative, it was understood, was already in touch with the Chinese Embassy. In answer to a question by Wing Commander Blackford, Lord Cranborne said that the purpose of the Committee would be to examine only the technical possibilities and that the political issue would no doubt be considered by the Cabinet, if such possibilities were found to exist. He anticipated that, if any assistance were given, publicity would be avoided as far as possible. It was observed that the volume of war material imported through Hongkong was already increasing considerably, but most of it appeared to originate in Italy and Germany.

5. *Financial Assistance*

Mr. Young said that it was quite clear that no loan could be floated in London by the Chinese Government without a guarantee by His Majesty's Government, which would of course require the prior approval of Parliament. He said that consideration had been given to the possibility of purchasing silver from China, but that neither the Treasury nor the Bank of England was in a position to do so.[4] In any case, silver had been bought from China by the United States in such large amounts that the further quantities available might not be very great. Japanese credits in London had been reduced, he believed, to less than half of their normal volume,

---

[4] See No. 495, note 3.

(purely on business grounds), and probably any attempt by the Japanese to get special credits (apart from ordinary commercial transactions) would fail of itself. It would, however, be possible to discourage anyone proposing to give such credits.

6. Mr. Orde mentioned the possibility of diverting the Boxer Indemnity monies which were paid to the Chinese Government Purchasing Commission in London, but pointed out that this would necessitate a new Act of Parliament. It would also increase the temptation to the Japanese to seize the customs revenues, out of which the indemnity is paid.

7. Sir F. Leith-Ross said there were two other possibilities. First, the Hongkong and Shanghai Banking Corporation might be moved to do something to help the Chinese currency at all events, but their feeling was at present very negative. The best method of approaching the Bank would be for Sir A. Clark Kerr to speak to Sir V. Grayburn at Hongkong. Secondly, there was the question of the Burma-Yunnan road: motor transport might be provided in order to help to make this undertaking a commercial success.

8. Mr. Donaldson said that the Government of Burma had been asked for their views on the construction of an all weather road. There were at present two fair-weather roads on the Burma side, the first from Lashio (rail-head) to Muse, a distance of under 120 miles, which could be used by motor traffic until the end of May; the second from Bhamo to Muse via Namkham with a recently completed bridge over the Shweli, usable by motors in dry weather, though not in good condition. It would take a considerable time to construct an all-weather metalled road by either of these routes, and the Government of Burma could not contemplate incurring the cost of constructing it without arrangements being made for its recovery. Sir J. Brenan said that he understood that some kind of a road existed as far as Muse on the Chinese side, but that there was no bridge across the Salween.

9. *Conclusion*

Lord Cranborne said that the meeting seemed to show that action might be taken under the following five headings:

(1) An approach to the Hongkong Bank.
(2) Construction of the Burma road.
(3) Release of surplus Government stocks of war material.
(4) Discouragement of Japanese applications for credits.
(5) A general review of possibilities by the Service Departments.[5]

[5] The Committee never met as a whole again. It was agreed that questions of finance and the Burma Road could be dealt with by the Treasury and the Burma Office, and when consulted by Mr. Orde, Mr. R. A. Butler, who succeeded Lord Cranborne as Parliamentary Under Secretary of State for Foreign Affairs on February 26, ruled that the question of reversing the prohibition of government sales of surplus arms stocks should not be pursued (April 8).

No. 518

Minute by Sir J. Pratt on the Burma-Yunnan road[1]

[*F 1850/79/10*]

FOREIGN OFFICE, *February 12, 1938*

One of the proposals for rendering assistance to China now under consideration is that a safe road for the supply of munitions should be provided by the construction of a good all-weather road from Lashio to Yunnan. As it is unlikely that there would be any great volume of commercial traffic along such a road for many years to come the revenue raised by levying tolls would not provide an adequate return on the capital sum expended. The Government of Burma cannot therefore be expected to provide the necessary funds, nor would H. M. Government be justified in doing so merely for the purpose of providing the present Chinese Government with a means of procuring munitions. Taking the long view, however, there are strong reasons why H. M. Government should not hesitate to provide or guarantee whatever sum may be necessary (it will not be very large) for the building of this road.

It seems probable that in the course of a few months the Japanese will gain possession of the whole coast of China and of the Yangtse as far as Hankow and that the Chinese Government will then retreat and maintain an organised existence in the interior provinces. The more secure the Japanese are in their conquests and the freer they are from anxieties the more certain and the more rapid will be the extinction of British interests in territory under their control. It is important therefore that the Chinese Government in the interior should be as strong as possible and capable of maintaining indefinitely an active and vigorous resistance to Japan. A glance at the map will show that such a Government would be in touch with France (Indo-China) Great Britain (Burma and Tibet) and Russia (Outer Mongolia and Sinkiang). France will be afraid to cultivate close relations with this Government because Indo-China, which is completely blanketed by Hainan, is at the mercy of Japan. Both Great Britain and Russia are strategically in a much stronger position and it is in the interest of both to help China against Japan. There is no great objection to China receiving help from Russia. Nevertheless, it would not be desirable that, say, Szechwan should fall as completely under Russian influence and control as Sinkiang. Great Britain, through Burma, should cultivate the

---

[1] A covering note of February 13 by Sir J. Pratt read: 'Mr. Orde. After the meeting on Friday [No. 517] Lord Cranborne asked for a memo. on the political implications of the Burma-Yunnan road. Tokyo telegram No. 191 is also relevant in this connection.' In Tokyo telegram No. 191 of February 12 Sir R. Craigie said that the establishment of road communication through Burma at an early date 'constituting as it would route for transition of arms independent of any blockade Japan may impose, would provide valuable means of pressure on Japan in certain eventualities. We need some more cards in our hands. Might I be kept informed of any developments in this matter?'

closest possible relations with the interior provinces of China. The first step in such a policy would be the immediate construction of a good road from Lashio to Yunnan.

The first thought of a Chinese Government established in the interior, with the coast and the Yangtse in Japanese hands, would be to divert the trade of the interior away from the Yangtse and out through some other channel. Hongkong *ex hypothesi* would be blocked. Indo-China for the political reasons indicated above would also be to some extent blocked. The way out through Sinkiang is too long and too hazardous. There remains only the trade route to Burma. It is possible therefore that the Lashio-Yunnan road, though primarily a political proposition, would justify itself on commercial grounds much sooner than present indications would appear to warrant.

J. T. Pratt

No. 519

Sir R. Lindsay (Washington) to Mr. Eden
(Received February 14, 9.30 a.m.)

No. 119 Telegraphic [F 1818/15/10]*

WASHINGTON, February 13, 1938, 6.38 p.m.

Your telegram No. 105[1] and your telegram No. 106.[2]
Following is reply of United States Government:
'The receipt acknowledged of British Embassy aide-mémoire of 9th February, on the subject of Chinese Maritime Administration at Shanghai. In that aide-mémoire question is asked whether United States Government would be prepared to support a proposal of the Chinese and Japanese Governments that customs funds in areas controlled by Japanese should be deposited in Hong Kong and Shanghai Banking Corporation, and that control of such funds should be vested in a body of officials nominated by foreign Powers interested in customs loans.

United States Government has given careful consideration to statements of fact and comment contained in British Embassy's aide-mémoire, but feel constrained frankly to state that plainly expressed attitude of Japanese authorities towards Chinese Maritime Customs situation at Shanghai indicates to this Government that Japanese authorities would reject any proposal which contemplated international control of customs revenue at Shanghai or any proposal which contemplated the initial deposit of customs revenues in other than a Japanese bank. It would further appear that insistence upon proposal outlined in aide-mémoire of British Embassy might result in unilateral action by Japanese authorities and failure to obtain from them assurances of a general nature in regard

<hr>

[1] No. 514.

[2] See *ibid.*, note 8.

to preservation of administrative machinery of Chinese Maritime Customs and in regard to serviceing [*sic*] of foreign loans and indemnity quotas.

For these reasons the United States Government does not feel that it can take action which His Majesty's Government suggests in regard to representations which His Majesty's Government contemplates making.

United States Government realises, however, that His Majesty's Government may wish to continue with action outlined in British Embassy's aide-mémoire and desires to avoid any procedure which would tend to prejudice or weaken British position. United States Government is accordingly instructing United States Ambassador to Japan and United States consul-general at Shanghai to consult with their British colleagues, and, if the latter so desire, to hold in abeyance further approaches to Japanese authorities for the present. They are being further instructed that if their British colleagues do not express a desire for postponement of further American approaches to Japanese authorities, they are authorised either alone or accompanied by similar action on the part of the British and French diplomatic and consular officials to acquaint Japanese Government with fact that they have information in regard to character of Japanese proposal made at Shanghai to Commissioner of Customs for a settlement of customs problem; to refer assurances which the United States Government has already requested of Japanese Government to re-express an earnest and emphatic desire to receive from Japanese Government positive assurances that no action will be taken or countenanced that will disrupt the Chinese Customs service or jeopardise the serviceing [*sic*] of foreign loan and indemnity quotas from customs revenue, and that serviceing [*sic*] of such loan and indemnity quotas will be considered and treated as first charge on customs revenue after deduction of costs of Chinese Maritime Customs Administration.'[3]

[3] Cf. *F.R.U.S.*, 1938, vol. iii, pp. 655–6.

No. 520

Sir R. Craigie (Tokyo) to Mr. Eden (Received February 15, 11 a.m.)

No. 203 Telegraphic [F 1867/15/10]*

TOKYO, *February 15, 1938, 5.10 p.m.*

Your telegrams Nos. 105[1] and 106[2] to Washington.

United States Ambassador has informed me of reply returned to representations made by His Majesty's Ambassador at Washington, namely, that while our proposal could not be accepted, United States Government did not desire to prejudice action taken by us. I have also seen draft communication which my United States colleague was

[1] No. 514.　　　　　　　　　　　　　　　　　　[2] See *ibid.*, note 8.

authorised to make to the Japanese Government if my French colleague and I concurred.

Essentials of this draft were (1) United States Ambassador is aware of recent Japanese proposals to Shanghai commissioner: (2) before examining any plan for customs United States Government expect to receive assurances that customs will not be disrupted, and foreign loan and indemnity obligations will be treated as prior charge after Customs Adminstration costs: (3) such assurances should be accompanied by clear statement that, in any arrangement made, administration machinery and procedure will be maintained and foreign loan and indemnity quotas provided for 'on an equitable and unconditional basis.'

I have indicated my view that this communication would convey the impression that given assurances United States Government might raise no particular objection to recent proposals, although we know the latter to be incompatible with the former. I therefore asked that if any communication were made either it should be simple reminder of earlier request for assurances or at the least (1) should be omitted from draft. I also suggested *full* service loans should be insisted upon and that reference to 'equitable basis' should be omitted, since it implied that quotas were susceptible of reduction in some manner.[3]

I consider it most important that United States should join us in rejecting recent Japanese proposals, otherwise Japanese will be encouraged in their present attitude, and I have so informed my United States colleague.[4]

Repeated to Mr. Howe.

[3] Mr. Hull agreed on February 15 that Mr. Grew could omit this phrase from his projected aide-mémoire to the Japanese Government: see *F.R.U.S.*, 1938, vol. iii, pp. 657–8. Mr. Grew presented his note on February 17: see *F.R.U.S.*, *Japan 1931–1941*, vol. i, p. 740.

[4] Sir R. Craigie did not, however, think that a common front with the United States should necessarily be maintained at all costs. Commenting in his telegram No. 234 of February 19 on Shanghai telegram No. 328 of February 17, in which Mr. Howe had expressed the opinion that 'United States Government are not prepared to move from the line they originally took up, or to do more in regard to customs than seek general assurances in Tokyo', Sir R. Craigie said he felt it 'essential that, *pari passu* with demand for assurances, we should endeavour to reach practical agreement with Japanese Government. . . Having somewhat laboriously brought the Japanese Government to the point of realising that they cannot legitimately settle this question without at least an official consultation with us, I think it would be a pity now to abandon this position and leave responsibility to customs officials . . . unless we are prepared to assume this responsibility . . . all that will remain of rights in customs will be a bundle of worthless assurances'.

No. 521

Mr. Eden to Sir R. Craigie (Tokyo)

No. 94 [F 1883/84/10]

FOREIGN OFFICE, *February 15, 1938*

Sir,

The Japanese Ambassador came to see me this afternoon when I told him that the memorandum by Mr. Hirota, [1] which His Excellency had been so good as to leave with me, had now been carefully examined by us and that there were one or two points in connexion with it which I would like to put to His Excellency. It had been suggested by the Ambassador himself at our last meeting that possibly there might be an opening shortly for the good offices of His Majesty's Government in the Far Eastern conflict. As I had then explained to him, however, it would not, I thought, be possible for us to offer our good offices except in conjunction with the United States. His Excellency would appreciate that, in the light of the similarity of our positions in the Far East and the parallel action which we had been taking, it would be only natural that we would wish to approach the United States if any such step were contemplated. At the same time, before doing so, I would be grateful if the Ambassador could tell me whether his suggestion had been repeated to his Government and, if so, what was their present view.

2. In reply the Ambassador explained that Mr. Hirota and the Japanese Government had been much troubled in the concluding months of last year by the rapid deterioration of Anglo-Japanese relations and by the anti-British propaganda which was being indulged in in Japan. I would remember that I had several times spoken to His Excellency on this subject, pointing out that some of the charges made against us were without justification. He had faithfully repeated these conversations, with the result that Mr. Hirota, impressed by the dangerous situation which was developing and by our complaints, had made a public speech about Anglo-Japanese relations[2] and submitted to us the memorandum to which I had referred. This speech and the action which the Japanese Government had taken had had a good effect in damping down anti-British propaganda, and the position in this respect had greatly improved. As regards good offices, the Japanese Government felt that it would be better to observe how matters now developed between our two Governments and also whether the situation in the Far East were auspicious for their use. In the view of the Japanese Government that moment had not yet come. If they in any way modified their view, His Excellency would, of course, tell me, but he fully understood that we should then wish to communicate with the United States Government.

3. Finally I reminded the Ambassador that Mr. Hirota's memorandum

---

[1] See Enclosure in No. 511.

[2] See No. 497, note 1.

had made certain references to Anglo-Japanese relations. I thought it best to speak frankly about that. The Ambassador would know as well as I what was the state of British public opinion with reference to the hostilities now raging in the Far East. To that subject I had nothing further to add today. There was, however, another issue which also affected Anglo-Japanese relations, viz., British interests in the Far East, as to which His Majesty's Government were naturally sensitive. I thought it must be clear to both of us that the attitude which the Japanese Government and, above all, the Japanese authorities on the spot adopted to important British interests in the Far East must have an inevitable reaction on Anglo-Japanese relations. Unfortunately we frequently had to contend with difficult local situations. In this respect I had only to mention Shanghai. His Excellency replied that he fully appreciated our position in this matter and that he would once again emphasise this aspect of Anglo-Japanese relations to his Government.[3]

> I am, etc.,
> ANTHONY EDEN

[3] Mr. Eden reported this conversation to the Cabinet on February 16.

No. 522

Sir R. Craigie (Tokyo) to Mr. Eden (Received February 16, 9.30 a.m.)

No. 212 Telegraphic [F 1897/35/10]

TOKYO, *February 16, 1938, 4.45 p.m.*

My telegram No. 135.[1]

Military Attaché has been informed confidentially by Director of Military Intelligence of General Staff that Corporal Toya was 'severely reprimanded' for his action in striking a British policeman. General Homma stated that if provocation had not been so great he would have been still more severely punished.

This information should be treated as confidential.[2]

Repeated to Mr. Howe.

[1] No. 505.
[2] Sir J. Brenan remarked on February 17: 'This is a very inadequate reply to our formal protests.' Mr. Orde agreed (February 18): 'What we want is something from the Jap[ane]se Gov[ernmen]t and something which we can publish. See tel. No. 135 to Tokyo.' This telegram, despatched at 10.15 p.m. on February 16, read: 'It is now more than a month since the incident took place and His Majesty's Government are still without satisfactory reply. You should impress on Japanese Government harm that such delay is bound to have on [*sic*] Anglo-Japanese relations and press for a very early answer.'

No. 523

Sir R. Craigie (Tokyo) to Mr. Eden (Received February 18, 12.30 p.m.)

No. 226 Telegraphic [F 1991/84/10]

TOKYO, *February 18, 1938, 6.40 p.m.*

I learn from German Military Attaché who is usually well informed that Japanese Army were not in favour of recent decision to break off dealings with Chiang Kai-shek and that policy was pushed through by industrialists working through Prime Minister and Minister for Foreign Affairs. On the other hand I learn from one or two sources (including my United States colleague) that in recent weeks the most intransigeant member of the Cabinet in all that appertains to China has been Mr. Hirota. This may not be unconnected with plan reported in my telegram No. 225.[1]

Repeated to Mr. Howe.

[1] This telegram of February 18 (F 2026/68/23) said that according to press reports the Japanese Government were considering the establishment of an East Asiatic Affairs Bureau to control political, economic, financial, and cultural activities in China. The bureau would be attached to the Cabinet, and presided over by the prime minister, with Mr. Shiratori as Assistant Director-General. Sir R. Craigie thought that in fact the bureau would tend to remove the conduct of Chinese affairs from the hands of M. Hirota.

No. 524

Sir R. Craigie (Tokyo) to Mr. Eden (Received February 18, 10.10 p.m.)

No. 235 Telegraphic [F 2065/15/10]*

TOKYO, *February 19, 1938, 1.40 a.m.*

My immediately preceding telegram.[1]

From the point of view of our future influence with the Japanese Government, I attach great importance not only to the substance but also to the method of settlement of the customs question. Here is a sphere in which our rights and interests are particularly well defined, and if Japanese authorities find that they can virtually dictate a settlement, with the interested Powers reduced to lodging a vain protest, whether on the basis of fresh assurances or not, they will be encouraged to treat our rights and interests with even scantier respect in other spheres. This is, therefore, the line on which we should make our firmest stand.

From this point of view I think it is important to maintain principle that in matters affecting our interests there must be direct consultation with us (not via some third party, such as customs officials). Vis-à-vis the Japanese Government, our future position in China would be better safeguarded by

[1] See No. 520, note 4.

negotiating a settlement, providing, if necessary, for some temporary spur in the service of foreign debt during the present emergency than by simply lodging a protest when in due course the Japanese take full charge and arbitrarily decide what amounts of foreign loan quotas . . .[2]. Similarly, I have ventured to urge that we should not be too uncompromising about deposit in Yokohama Specie Bank of revenue from territory under Japanese control, provided that we receive assurances as to amounts to be allocated to foreign loans service and can secure reasonable rights of supervision. If conditions of agreement were not fulfilled by the Japanese, our assent to deposit in Yokohama Specie Bank would be withdrawn.

It is certainly unfortunate that United States support on practical issue should not be forthcoming at the critical moment, but in long experience I have found this usually to happen, and I trust that we shall not thereby be diverted from continuing our own efforts to settle matter in a most . . .[2] like way. So long as the Customs hold firm and 'young officer' element can be restrained, we still have a good chance of success along the lines outlined above.

As soon as we have received Japanese proposals (see your [?my] telegram No. 205)[3] I will submit my detailed estimate of maximum we are likely to be able to secure from Japanese Government by process of negotiation.

Repeated to Shanghai.

[2] The text was here uncertain.　　　　　　　　[3] Not kept in F.O. archives.

No. 525

Sir R. Craigie (Tokyo) to Viscount Halifax[1]
(Received February 21, 12.25 p.m.)

No. 250 Telegraphic [F 2073/35/10]

TOKYO, *February 21, 1938, 7.30 p.m.*

Your telegram No. 135.[2]

Vice-Minister for Foreign Affairs informed me today that according to a message he had received from Shanghai, Japanese Consul-General had addressed letters both to British Consul-General and Mr. Franklin in regard to Mr. Bennett and Mr. Turner cases and not having received a reply to either letter had concluded that matter was regarded as settled. On my repeating that this was by no means the case the Vice-Minister for Foreign Affairs suggested that settlement of these two questions could best be discussed informally between Mr. Phillips and Mr. Okomoto and

[1] Viscount Halifax was acting Foreign Secretary following Mr. Eden's resignation on February 20: see Volume XIX, No. 568, note 2, No. 570, note 1, and Appendix I. Lord Halifax's appointment as Foreign Secretary was announced on February 25 and effective from March 1.
[2] See No. 522, note 2.

at my request promised to request Mr. Ok[a]moto to adopt conciliatory attitude. I pointed out that it was in Japanese interest as well as ours that those guilty of such assaults should be adequately punished.

I should be grateful if Mr. Phillips could now try this method leaving me to intervene again later if satisfactory results are not achieved.

Repeated to Mr. Howe.

No. 526

Viscount Halifax to Sir R. Craigie (Tokyo)

No. 154 Telegraphic [F 2065/15/10]*

FOREIGN OFFICE, *February 24, 1938, 6.40 p.m.*

Your telegram No. 235[1] and Mr. Howe's telegram No. 343.[2]

In view of the American attitude[3] the time seems to have arrived for a concession regarding the deposit of funds in return for adequate safeguards. This concession should, if possible, be restricted to the deposit in the Yokohama Specie Bank of the Japanese share in the loan services and of surplus after meeting the foreign loan obligations in full.

If it is impossible to secure this, we would be prepared to consider alternative under which full revenues in the Japanese-occupied areas are deposited in the Yokohama Specie Bank, but quotas accruing in respect of the foreign obligations are transferred regularly to the foreign banks interested. We could, however, only contemplate this second alternative if the Japanese Government gave you formal assurances in writing on the following lines:

1. That the full services of the foreign obligations will be maintained without interruption on due dates, provided the revenue collections are sufficient; but otherwise unconditionally.

2. That the foreign obligations will be treated as a first charge on the revenue after the cost of maintaining the Customs Administration.

3. That the foreign loan quotas will be settled by agreement with all the Powers concerned at weekly or monthly intervals as may be agreed and the amounts so settled shall be transferred forthwith by the Yokohama Specie Bank to the banks nominated by the Powers concerned or responsible for the service of the loan, i.e., in our case there would be paid

---

[1] No. 524.

[2] In this telegram of February 19 Mr. Howe reported a conversation between Mr. Hall-Patch and Mr. Okamoto, who said that if the total customs revenues were deposited in the Yokohama Specie Bank he would be prepared to give assurances that the full service of foreign obligations would be maintained provided revenue collections were sufficient.

[3] The phrase 'In view of the American attitude' was omitted from the otherwise very full paraphrase of this telegram given by Sir R. Craigie to Mr. Grew on February 25: cf. *F.R.U.S.*, 1938, vol. iii, pp. 661–3.

to the Hong Kong and Shanghai Bank the quota in respect of the British Boxer indemnity and in respect of the loans serviced by the bank.

4. That any preventive launches, &c., still detained will be returned to the Customs.

5. That Customs authority shall be exercised in regard to all Japanese non-military imports.

6. In addition to the above, it is highly desirable to have a uniform tariff for all China. An assurance that the Japanese authorities will arrange for this with the Inspector-General on the 1931 basis, or otherwise, would help to relieve our anxiety regarding the integrity of the Customs Administration.

If the Japanese Government will give you written assurances regarding points 1 to 5 and, if possible, 6, we would then authorise the financial adviser in Shanghai, subject to discussion of details locally, to waive further objections so far as His Majesty's Government are concerned. This would, of course, not imply any responsibility for attitude of Chinese Government or other parties concerned.

It should be understood quite clearly that any arrangement on either of above bases would be temporary and for the period of hostilities only.

You should keep in touch with your American and French colleagues on the lines indicated in your telegram No. 234[4] with which I concur. I am instructing His Majesty's Ambassador at Paris to inform the French Government that these instructions have been sent to you, and that you will be communicating their purport to the French Ambassador.

Repeated to Shanghai, No. 196, and Paris, No. 45, Saving (by post).

[4] See No. 520, note 4.

No. 527

Sir R. Craigie (Tokyo) to Viscount Halifax
(Received February 26, 4.30 p.m.)

No. 271 Telegraphic [F 2318/15/10]*

TOKYO, *February 26, 1938, 8.45 p.m.*

Your telegram No. 154.[1]

Vice-Minister for Foreign Affairs asked me to call this morning and said he desired to reply to representations I had made at our last interview (see my telegram No. 232).[2]

[1] No. 526.

[2] In this telegram of February 18 Sir R. Craigie transmitted the text of a note addressed by him to Mr. Hirota on December 27, 1937, drawing his attention to the importance attached by His Majesty's Government to the maintenance of the integrity of the Chinese Customs service and asking for assurances that it would be preserved.

707

Taking the first question of general assurances, his Excellency said that while Japanese Government had every intention of maintaining (to full extent which present abnormal situation permitted) integrity of Customs and service of foreign loans, they were opposed to giving assurances of the scope desired by the United States Government because of the danger of subsequent misunderstanding and misinterpretation. Thus to give assurance that Japanese Government would not countenance action which would 'disrupt' customs service might invite the argument that the mere fact of Japanese occupation of certain Chinese ports constituted in itself a breach of such an assurance. Japanese Government, therefore, greatly preferred method of settling the matter by detailed negotiations and specific assurances, which would leave less scope for future misunderstanding.

He understood that, in our view, the most important point was the maintenance of service of foreign debt. I said that this was *an important point*, but that integrity of Customs and unimpaired authority of Inspector-General of Customs were, in our view, an equally if not more important consideration.

Vice-Minister for Foreign Affairs then observed that Japanese Government were unable to understand the ground of our objection to deposit of revenue with Yokohama Specie Bank. Prior to the present incident, revenues had been deposited with Central Bank of China and deposit with Hong Kong and Shanghai Bank had been a purely emergency measure. Japanese Government felt strongly that on the analogy of arrangements existing before the outbreak of hostilities revenues in the areas controlled by Japan should be deposited with a Japanese bank. They felt this all the more keenly because they would eventually be responsible to any new Chinese Government which emerged for custody of revenues in the occupied zones. I replied that our view had always been that since Central Bank of China was no longer functioning, revenues should be deposited with a neutral bank or banks. Furthermore, it seemed to us illogical that revenues, the major part of which would return to neutral banks for service of foreign loans, should first be deposited in a Japanese bank. Finally, it seemed to us inadmissible that Japanese Government should seek to settle the question of deposit of revenues in advance of other questions involved, such as service of foreign debt.

Vice-Minister for Foreign Affairs then referred to the method of fixing loan quotas, maintaining that these should be based on figures for recent months, seeing that revenue receipts at different ports were now quite abnormal. Principle to which the Japanese Government attached importance was that revenues in occupied territory should not be expected to make up for any defaults and deficiencies in territory still under the control of National Government. He added that any arrangement reached in regard to Shanghai would be made applicable to all other ports in occupied territory.

I then enquired whether the Japanese Government would not agree to

708

deposit in Yokohama Specie Bank Japanese share of loan service and of any surplus (after meeting foreign loan obligations in full), leaving British and other shares to be deposited in neutral banks. His Excellency regretted that it would be impossible for the Japanese Government to agree to this in the circumstances at present obtaining.

I then put before His Excellency points 1 to 5 in your telegram under reference, saying that if I could receive definite assurances on these points, I would suggest to my Government deposit in Yokohama Specie Bank of full revenues in occupied areas. His Excellency was, at first sight, prepared to accept points 1 and 2. As regards point 3, he felt settlement of loan quotas weekly or monthly would be difficult, and that Japanese Government had in mind a quota settlement to last one year. On my demurring to this, he said point was a technical one which he would wish first to discuss with his experts. As regards points 4 and 5, he was prepared to agree in principle, but here again consultation would be necessary before he could give me a definite reply.

Before leaving, I observed that, as he knew, His Majesty's Government considered it highly desirable to have a uniform tariff for all China and that I hoped that he would be able to give me parallel assurances in the sense of point 6 on your telegram. He replied that Japanese Government had this matter under consideration and hoped to send an early answer. In reply to his enquiry, I said that I could not guarantee Chinese Government's acceptance of 1931 tariff, but that if the Japanese Government accepted, I knew that you were prepared to do what you could to secure acquiescence of the Chinese Government and that personally I thought that this might be forthcoming.

As Vice-Minister for Foreign Affairs desired to consult with experts before giving any final answer, it was agreed that we should meet again this evening at 8.30.[3]

I am keeping my French colleague and my United States colleague informed.

Repeated to Sir A. Clark Kerr.

[3] See No. 528 below.

No. 528

Sir R. Craigie (Tokyo) to Viscount Halifax
(Received February 27, 1.15 p.m.)

No. 274 Telegraphic [F 2267/15/10][1]

TOKYO, February 27, 1938, 5.15 p.m.

My telegram No. 271.[2]

On resumption of our conversation yesterday evening, Vice-Minister for Foreign Affairs submitted counter-proposal which, after some discussion, was worded as follows:

'1. Total revenue collected by Maritime Customs within areas under Japanese occupation to be deposited with a Japanese bank (Yokohama Specie Bank).

2. From revenues thus deposited payments to be made by bank on due dates for service of foreign obligations, the quota for each port being decided upon in accordance with principle of full service of such foreign obligations.

3. A temporary quota for each port calculated on basis of actual gross revenue for a given recent period, to be decided after discussion at Shanghai between Japanese authorities and representatives of interested Powers.

4. Payment of foreign obligations to be treated as a first charge on revenue after deducting maintenance expenses of Customs Administration.

5. Provision to be made for payment of Japanese portion of Boxer indemnity and of arrears on that indemnity.'

Discussion on above proposal may be summarised as follows:

Point 2. Japanese Government consider only sums representing share of a particular port in foreign loan and indemnity service should be remitted from local branch of Yokohama Specie Bank to neutral bank responsible for service of foreign obligations, balance remaining in Yokohama Specie Bank at disposal of Japanese and local Chinese authorities. Vice-Minister for Foreign Affairs recognised, however, that this might not be practicable arrangement, and is prepared to consider suggestion that sums for service of foreign obligations should be remitted regularly to special account to be opened by Inspector-General of Customs in Shanghai. He insisted, however, that once service of foreign loans had been adequately provided for, foreign Powers could not claim *locus standi* for regulating disposal of surplus (if any) in occupied area. I

---

[1] This telegram has not been kept in the F.O. 371 files nor in the Confidential Print. A copy has, however, been preserved in a separate collection of telegrams in the Foreign Office.

[2] No. 527.

raised question of service of domestic loans and drew attention to serious effect in position of Chinese bank and currency if service were now to be suspended. His Excellency said that Japanese Government desired to avoid undermining of bank and currency and would be prepared to take into account any unofficial representations or suggestions we might make on this score, but he considered that this question should be treated separately from that of service of foreign obligations and integral Customs Administration. Just as Central Government had normally received for their own purpose surplus of customs revenue after discharge of obligations, so it was only equitable that any such surplus in occupied area should now be available for Chinese Provisional Government for such local services as education, police, &c. He added that the whole arrangement must be subject to consent of Provisional Government of Peking, but agreed that this was a matter between Japanese Government and Provisional Government, with which we could have no concern.

Point 3. Basis of calculation of quotas tentatively suggested by Vice-Minister for Foreign Affairs was average of last four months of 1937. He was strongly opposed to monthly revision of quotas, saying Japanese Government wished to fix them for one year ahead, but he would, I think, be open to suggestion for revision at some shorter interval.

Point 5. I pointed out that Boxer indemnity was included in general term 'service of foreign obligations' in paragraph 2, but Vice-Minister for Foreign Affairs observed that that paragraph only related to revenues coming from occupied territory, whereas Japanese Government wished to make it clear that Japanese share of Boxer indemnity should no longer be withheld from revenue originating in Chinese territory. He understood since, incidentally, arrears of Japanese share of indemnity had been accumulating in a special account in name of Inspector-General of Customs.

We then dealt with points 4 and 5 in your telegram No. 154.[3] Vice-Minister for Foreign Affairs asked that these points should not be made an integral part of proposed arrangement, though he recognised their relevancy to question of customs revenue. Customs launch question was being taken up with Ministry of Marine, but was rendered difficult by allegations that launches in areas controlled by Chinese had been used for running the blockade. I suggested that Inspector General of Customs might possibly be in a position to give guarantee that launches would be used exclusively for preventive purposes, and Vice-Minister for Foreign Affairs appeared to think this might help. As regards payment of duties on Japanese non-military imports, his Excellency entirely accepted principle, but stated that owing to abnormal conditions it might take a little more time to secure necessary distinction between military and non-military imports in Shanghai area. I urged that this should be treated as a matter of urgency, to which his Excellency agreed, adding that

[3] No. 526.

reduction of tariff had already led to improvement in northern area. Turning then to point 6 in your telegram, Vice-Minister for Foreign Affairs stated that suggestion of introduction of 1931 tariff was receiving careful consideration as a matter of urgency, but it was not yet possible to say what would be final decision of Japanese Government. First reaction to proposal was not unfavourable. As regards denial of responsibility on the part of His Majesty's Government for attitude of Chinese Government or other parties concerned, Vice-Minister for Foreign Affairs fully agreed, but expressed hope that we would do our best to obtain consent of Chinese Government to any arrangement acceptable to other parties concerned. I said that this would certainly be done, adding that I was keeping my United States colleague and my French colleague fully informed. His Excellency also agreed that proposed arrangement should be regarded as being for period of hostilities only.

My comments follow.[4]

Repeated to Sir A. Clark Kerr, No. 185.

[4] See No. 529 below.

No. 529

Sir R. Craigie (Tokyo) to Viscount Halifax
(Received February 27, 2 p.m.)

No. 275 Telegraphic [F 2319/15/10][1]

TOKYO, *February 27, 1938, 7.13 p.m.*

My immediately preceding telegram.[2]

Points mentioned in your telegram No. 154[3] are for the most part covered by Japanese counter-proposal, though phraseology is somewhat different. As regards points 4, 5 and 6 of your telegram, I feel we should get better results by treating them as matters of urgency, to be settled in parallel negotiations, rather than as conditions to be attached to our acceptance of deposit of revenues in the Yokohama Specie Bank. I am hopeful that amicable settlement of the latter question will lead to early arrangement on all three points.

The least satisfactory aspect of Japanese counter-proposal is that any surplus, instead of being transferred to Inspector-General of Customs' account, would remain in local branch of Yokohama Specie Bank for use of authorities in occupied areas. This conflicts with method suggested in Shanghai telegram to Foreign Office, No. 361,[4] but I feel we are on delicate ground in claiming to have a say in the use of surplus after

[1] Not kept in F.O. 371 or Confidential Print: copy taken from telegram collection; see No. 528, note 1.
[2] No. 528.   [3] No. 526.   [4] Of February 24, not printed.

satisfaction of foreign obligations, and I hope that we may be able to meet Japanese on this point.[5] I am also convinced that the best chance for securing continued service of Domestic Loans is to utilise argument about safeguarding position of banks and currency instead of attempting to include this question in our proposed arrangement.

The other unsatisfactory point is the Japanese method of calculating quotas (which I see differs from that proposed in Shanghai telegram No. 361), but on this compromise should not be impossible, and there is something to be said for avoiding a monthly wrangle in regard to size of individual quotas.

I should be grateful for early instructions, as the moment is opportune for settlement. It is, at all events, satisfactory that Japanese Government should thus recognise their responsibility for helping to meet service of foreign obligations in full and should display readiness to discuss all these matters frankly with representative of His Majesty's Government. If we can secure agreement here on general rules which should govern determination of quotas and method of transmission of funds, their detailed application could then be worked out in Shanghai.[6]

Repeated to Sir A. Clark Kerr.

[5] In Shanghai telegram No. 381 of March 2 commenting on this telegram, Sir A. Clark Kerr stated: 'I think that we should hold out for a surplus at all ports under Japanese control to remain in suspense account of the Inspector General of Customs. . . If we cannot obtain this concession, Central Government will have no inducement whatever to abstain from action which will disrupt customs service. . . I agree that we are on delicate ground if we insist that surplus goes to service of domestic loans, but originally the avowed goal of Japanese in demanding deposit in Yokohama Bank was simply to insure [sic] that no surplus reached Central Government. This goal is reached by the surplus going to a suspense account of the Inspector General of Customs at that bank, and a strong stand before making concessions beyond that point seems necessary'. Sir A. Clark Kerr's view was supported in F.O. telegram No. 185 to Tokyo, instructing Sir R. Craigie to make a stand on this point: see note 6 below.

[6] Foreign Office telegram No. 176 to Tokyo of March 3 referred to Nos. 527, 528, and 529 and stated that the Japanese counter proposals went 'some way to meet our requirements', and went on to list those points which remained unsatisfactory, including surplus disposals (see note 5 above). The negotiations on these points now began in earnest, but the general lines of eventual agreement had in fact been drawn. Sir R. Craigie had discussions with the Vice-Minister for Foreign Affairs on March 9, 14, 16, and 19, commenting in telegram No. 324 of March 15 that 'Japanese Government are genuinely anxious to set up machinery which will, in fact, guarantee full service of foreign obligations, and discussion really resolves itself into examination of the best method of bringing this about'. The only point on which deadlock had been reached was that of surplus disposals. On March 23 the Japanese Vice Minister for Foreign Affairs submitted a new draft agreement: which Sir R. Craigie described in telegram No. 363 of March 24 as 'the best I can hope to get here': he communicated this draft to the U.S. Ambassador, and it is printed in F.R.U.S., 1938, vol. iii, pp. 671–4. There followed some final negotiations on points of detail, and in Tokyo telegram No. 381 of March 26 Sir R. Craigie reported that the Vice-Minister for Foreign Affairs had again 'pressed very strongly for early establishment of customs agreement': see No. 550 below.

No. 530

Viscount Halifax to Sir R. Craigie (Tokyo)

No. 165 Telegraphic [F 2073/35/10]

FOREIGN OFFICE, *February 28, 1938, 6 p.m.*

Your telegram No. 250.[1]

The suggestion that these cases should be left for discussion between the two Consuls-General at Shanghai when the Minister for Foreign Affairs will 'request' his own subordinate to be conciliatory is entirely unsatisfactory, and cannot be accepted as a reply to the serious communications which you were instructed by my telegram No. 26[2] and subsequent telegrams to convey to the Japanese Government.[3]

As previously stated British subjects in the performance of their official duties have been subjected to brutal assaults by members of the Japanese forces; assaults which even the amount of provocation alleged but not proved by the Japanese authorities is quite inadequate to justify. Experience has shown that no satisfaction is to be expected from the Japanese civil officials in Shanghai in questions involving the conduct of the Japanese troops, and we are not prepared to accept the sort of reply reported in Shanghai telegram No. 18 to His Majesty's Chargé d'Affaires[4].

Even though we may not be in a position to exact reparation for insults and injuries of this nature nothing will be gained by the quiet acceptance of rebuffs for fear of irritating the Japanese. It is better to be insistent in demanding redress and if that cannot be obtained to leave the Japanese Government in no doubt of our resentment. You should therefore address a note to the Minister for Foreign Affairs recapitulating the facts and stating that His Majesty's Government cannot accept the excuses hitherto offered by the local authorities as any justification for the assaults. They expect to receive from the Japanese Government themselves and not from any local official an expression of regret and an assurance that

---

[1] No. 525. [2] No. 482.

[3] In a long minute of February 24 Sir J. Brenan reviewed the history of the Shanghai assault cases (see Nos. 473, 482, 493, 498, 505, and 522) and pointed out that 'it was proposed at one time to make this a test case to be followed, if necessary, by action of some sort. The intention . . . was to impress on the Japanese Government that the issue was really grave and, failing a satisfactory solution, would lead to serious impairment of our relations'. He expressed some doubt whether Sir R. Craigie had 'understood the real purport of the instructions or effectively conveyed their intended warning to the Japanese Government', and suggested that 'we should first convince our own Ambassador and then instruct him to renew his representations in writing, making it clear that unless we receive an expression of regret we shall not regard the incident as closed'. Mr. Ronald and Mr. Orde expressed entire agreement with Sir J. Brenan, but Sir A. Cadogan remarked on February 27 with regard to the draft of telegram No. 165: 'I have toned down the telegram a little (we must remember that circumstances have changed).'

[4] No. 493.

measures have actually been taken to prevent a repetition before the cases can be considered as closed.

Repeated to British Embassy Shanghai No. 210.

No. 531

Sir R. Craigie (Tokyo) to Viscount Halifax
(Received March 1, 2.30 p.m.)

No. 280 Telegraphic [F 2426/35/10]

TOKYO, *March 1, 1938, 8.30 p.m.*

Your telegram No. 165.[1]

I regret that you should have gained the impression that I favour 'quiet acceptance of rebuffs for fear of irritating Japanese'. The very strong representations that I have on several occasions made in this case (for example see my telegram No. 135[2]) hardly seem to justify such a conclusion. There was also no suggestion in my telegram No. 250[3] that the case should be 'left for discussion' at Shanghai since I specifically proposed further intervention here if no results were achieved locally. But Vice Minister for Foreign Affairs having declared his conviction that settlement could best be discussed locally I considered this procedure advisable *as a stage in negotiation.* If Mr. Phillips reports shortly that Vice Minister for Foreign Affairs' recommendation has been carried out without result I shall be in a better position for securing satisfaction this end. Whatever the outcome of discussion at Shanghai I had not of course contemplated that expression of regret should come from any source other than Japanese Government.

That a note will be necessary before long if Japanese attitude remains unchanged I entirely agree but this will only leave one further unsettled case as a source of irritation between the two countries whereas the securing of satisfaction by reasoned argument is surely preferable where it is practicable. I venture therefore to express strong hope that I may be authorised to postpone despatch of note until completion of course of action which I had mapped out on the understanding that delay will not in any case exceed a fortnight.[4]

Repeated to Embassy Shanghai.

---

[1] No. 530.   [2] No. 505.   [3] No. 525.

[4] Sir R. Craigie's defence of his position produced further minuting in the Foreign Office. Mr. Thyne Henderson noted on March 2 that Sir R. Craigie had not yet sent in a note: his contacts had been unofficial, and a great deal had been done via the Military Attaché. 'Doubtless this is the best way of settling the question. At the moment when it arose, we thought we were going to adopt a "forward policy" vis-à-vis Japan and were really looking for an excuse to show firmness... Now, as Sir A. Cadogan says, circumstances have changed, and we must presumably concentrate on settling the incident.' Sir J. Brenan

(March 2) thought that a 'fortnight's delay will make no difference to the position, but we do not want to be rude to the Ambassador who is having a difficult time, so better agree.' Mr. Ronald, however, thought that 'Sir R. Craigie is being unnecessarily umbrageous', and that sufficient time had elapsed since his last interview with the Vice Foreign Minister (see No. 525). He submitted a draft telegram, which was despatched on March 3 (No. 532 below).

No. 532

Viscount Halifax to Sir R. Craigie (Tokyo)

No. 174 Telegraphic [F 2426/35/10]

FOREIGN OFFICE, *March 3, 1938, 7.30 p.m.*

Your telegram No. 280.[1]

My telegram No. 165[2] was designed to strengthen your hands in dealing with the Japanese Government as providing you with evidence which you could show them of the serious light in which His Majesty's Government continue to regard this matter and I am sorry that you should have read into it a reflexion on your conduct of the case. Let me assure you that none was intended.

Mr. Phillips' telegram to His Majesty's Ambassador Shanghai No. 45[3] however confirms me in my opinion that local discussions are unlikely to contribute to a settlement and, unless Mr. Phillips has by then informed you that he has strong reason to expect the early receipt of any constructive suggestions from his Japanese colleague, I think you should on Monday next March 7th present a note to the Vice Minister and inform him that His Majesty's Government are waiting with some impatience to learn what measures the Japanese Government are taking and what instructions they are issuing to guard against any repetition of these assaults.

Repeated to Shanghai No. 220.

[1] No. 531. [2] No. 530.
[3] In this telegram of February 25 (No. 62 to the Foreign Office) Mr. Phillips reported a conversation with the Japanese Consul General who 'continued to stand up for local Japanese attitude towards these cases and I am not very hopeful of achieving any satisfactory progress towards a settlement'.

No. 533

Sir R. Craigie (Tokyo) to Viscount Halifax
(Received March 11, 10.30 a.m.)

No. 316 Telegraphic [F 2739/35/10]

TOKYO, *March 11, 1938, 4.45 p.m.*

Your telegram No. 31 to the Consul-General Shanghai[1].

I carried out March 7th instructions in your telegram No. 174[2] addressing note to Minister for Foreign Affairs briefly recapitulating facts of the cases and drawing His Excellency's attention to five written but unofficial communications already addressed to Japanese Government on one or other of the cases.

I referred to statement of Japanese Consul-General Shanghai that local naval and military authorities saw no reason to change their view (Consul-General's telegram No. 55 to His Majesty's Ambassador[3]) and observed the matter was in any case viewed by His Majesty's Government as too serious for settlement locally without reference to governments concerned. Not the slightest expression of regret had yet been received from Japanese authorities who allege provocation, which I did not admit, and who appeared to consider it consonant with the dignity and discipline of armed forces to use violent methods in such circumstances. His Majesty's Government were awaiting with some impatience to learn what steps Japanese Government were taking to prevent repetition of such incidents and felt entitled to an expression of regret from Japanese Government.[4]

Repeated to Sir A. Clark Kerr (and for Consul-General Shanghai telegram No. 10).

[1] Of March 9, not printed (F 2562/35/10). [2] No. 532.
[3] Of March 6, not printed (F 2614/35/10): cf. No. 532, note 3.
[4] In Tokyo telegram No. 438 of April 9 Sir R. Craigie reported that as he had received no reply to his note of Mach 7 he had sent another note on April 8 pressing the Japanese for an early answer. In a minute on file F 3836/35/10 of April 21 Sir J. Brenan suggested that 'in view of the Japanese attitude we had better put the cases in cold storage until we are in a position to press them more effectively. The Ambassador might end the correspondence temporarily by expressing dignified resentment and by leaving it on record that the cases remain open for eventual settlement'. In a further minute he concluded that 'it would be better to let the Ambassador deal with [these cases] as he is doing with all the other unsettled questions and bring them up periodically in interviews with the Ministry for F[oreign] A[ffairs]. . .' Mr. Howe and Sir A. Cadogan expressed agreement on June 20.

No. 534

Viscount Halifax to Sir A. Clark Kerr (Shanghai)

No. 251 Telegraphic [F 2921/25/10[1]]*

FOREIGN OFFICE, *March 16, 1938, 11 p.m.*

Your telegram No. 429[2].

Proposal communicated to me by Chinese Ambassador on 15th March is as follows:

Loan of 20 million sterling to be raised for Chinese Government through private banks, with encouragement (not guarantee) of His Majesty's Government, to run for fifteen years and to be secured on wolfram and antimony monopolies, with customs surplus as collateral.

I said that, while I could not, of course, express any opinion about his proposals, I would see that they were at once referred to the proper quarter and would let him have a reply as soon as possible.

Before he left His Excellency said that Chinese were waging by no means unsuccessful guerrilla warfare against Japanese troops, who were very much strung out. There was no prospect of negotiation, which would be premature and in any case could hardly be initiated by Japanese, who had ceased to deal with Central Chinese Government. If, and when, time did come for negotiation, [he] did not think that any satisfactory result could be achieved without the association of His Majesty's Government and United States Government in the conversations.[3]

Repeated to Hankow, No. 26.

[1] None of the papers on file 25/10 have been preserved in F.O. archives. Some papers have been preserved in the Confidential Print volumes, and some in a separate collection of telegrams: cf. No. 528, note 1.

[2] In this telegram of March 13 Sir A. Clark Kerr stated: 'China's efforts so far to maintain her currency and credit have been beyond all praise but we must face facts. . . Any large scale financial assistance to China now can only be an act of high policy unrelated to any ordinary financial considerations.'

[3] A slightly fuller account of Dr. Quo's interview with Lord Halifax on March 15 was sent to Shanghai in despatch No. 165 of March 15.

No. 535

Viscount Halifax to Sir A. Clark Kerr (Shanghai)

No. 272 Telegraphic [F 3075/25/10]*

Secret   FOREIGN OFFICE, *March 25, 1938*

Your telegram No. 384[1] and my telegram [*sic*] No. 165[2].

The proposal for a loan has been fully and sympathetically considered, but the conclusion reached is that no loan or credit, such as suggested by Chinese Ambassador to me or by Soong to you, is possible.

I note from your telegram No. 430[3] that Hong Kong and Shanghai Bank arrange to advance £2 million on silver.

Question whether any further such advance would be possible could best be discussed with Sir V. Grayburn at Hong Kong, as Treasury believe it most unlikely that any substantial credit secured on silver could be arranged in London and undesirable that it should.

The above is for your own information. I do not consider that it would be desirable to give too blunt a reply to the Chinese Government, since I fear this would, however unjustifiably, be taken as implying an unwillingness on the part of His Majesty's Government to help and might afford a pretext for a discontinuance of the service of foreign loans and might weaken the resistance of Dr. Kung and Mr. T. V. Soong to wholly unsound financial policy. I would, therefore, propose to say that the question whether proposal for a loan is a feasible one would have to be studied by the banking authorities and that this should be done by discussion between the Chinese Government and the Hong Kong and Shanghai Bank in Hong Kong. The question is clearly one which will require somewhat prolonged examination.

Subject to your views, I propose to reply on the lines of the above to the Chinese Ambassador.

---

[1] In this telegram of March 3 Sir A. Clark Kerr recorded a conversation with T. V. Soong who asked if a loan for China in London might be possible: the Ambassador replied that he did not think either a loan or credit would be possible in present circumstances.

[2] See No. 534, note 3.   [3] Of March 13, not printed.

[4] Telegram No. 273 to Shanghai of March 25 added that 'we are, on the other hand, greatly interested in any arrangement which would enable us to obtain control of Chinese wolfram and antimony', though further information on the possibilities was required. Cf. No. 541 below.

No. 536

Letter from Burma Office to Foreign Office

[*F 3290/79/10*]

BURMA OFFICE, *March 25, 1938*

Sir,

With reference to the correspondence ending with your letter of the 28th February 1938, No. F 2214/79/10[1], regarding the proposed highway from China to Burma, I am directed by the Marquess of Zetland to transmit herewith, for the information of Viscount Halifax, a copy of a telegram[2] received from the Governor of Burma[3] in reply to the telegram sent to His Excellency on the 9th March[4], of which a copy was enclosed in this Office printed letter No. B.1206/38 dated 11th March[2].

It will be observed that the Governor has authorised the commencement of work to make the road from Lashio to the Burma-China frontier up to an all-weather motorable standard at a cost of Rs.2½ lakhs which will be borne by the funds of the Federated Shan States. The improvement of the standard of the bridges on this road will also be undertaken at the expense of the Federal Fund and every effort will be made to complete the work by the end of May.[5]

Lord Zetland is confident that Lord Halifax will share his satisfaction at this report and he would accordingly propose, if there is no objection, to inform Sir Archibald Cochrane that His Majesty's Government greatly appreciate the steps which have been taken in the matter.

It will be seen that it is doubtful whether the Bhamo-Muse road via Namkham can be in efficient operation as an all-weather motorable road before the rainy season of 1940 and that, until then, it will only be usable

[1] Cf. No. 518. In telegram No. 48C of February 17 the Governor of Burma expressed doubt as to whether the Chinese would have completed their part of the road construction before the rains started, and stated that he did not want to saddle Burma with the extra expenditure involved in bringing their part of the road up to standard prematurely. A copy of this telegram was sent to the Foreign Office, and in a letter of February 28 to the Burma Office Lord Halifax said that he hoped that 'in view of the strong political and ultimately commercial considerations which appear to him to favour the development of adequate communication between Burma and China the cautious programme contemplated will not be allowed to prejudice adoption of a higher standard of road should it appear that the Chinese road is likely to attain a higher standard'.

[2] Not printed.   [3] Sir Archibald Cochrane.

[4] This telegram referred to Burma telegram No. 48C (see note 1 above) and asked the Governor of Burma to expedite the preparation of detailed estimates for the completion of the Burmese side of the road.

[5] In telegram No. 329 of March 16 Sir R. Craigie referred to his telegram No. 191 (see No. 518, note 1) and asked to be kept 'informed of the position as regards the proposal for road communication'. In telegram No. 232 to Tokyo of April 4 Sir R. Craigie was informed that the road from Tali to Lashio was expected to be completed to all weather motorable standard by the end of May, although he was not to make use of this information without permission.

during dry weather from mid-December to mid-May. In these circumstances, Lord Zetland does not propose to press the Governor to proceed further with this section of road but will await a further expression of His Excellency's views after consideration of the estimates for its improvement which have been called for.

The Governor's telegram has been repeated to His Majesty's Ambassador at Shanghai and copies of this letter and of its enclosure are being sent to the departments represented on the Inter-departmental Committee on the possibility of rendering assistance to China, in case it should be desired that that body should take cognisance of the new developments.

I am, etc.,
G. Graham Dixon[6]

[6] Acting Assistant Secretary in the Burma Office.

No. 537

Letter from Sir R. Craigie (Tokyo) to Mr. Ronald

[F 1883/84/10]

TOKYO, March 25, 1938

My dear Nigel,

I presume that Orde will by now have left for Riga and that you are in charge.[1] I hope for your sake you are not having too heavy a time, although I am afraid that the bombardment of telegrams from here and Shanghai on the Customs question may have proved a little overwhelming! Here the pressure keeps up pretty steadily but I find the work interesting and we both contrive to enjoy life in our new post.

I was very interested in your despatches Nos. 60[2] and 94[3] of February 4th and 15th (F 1472 and F 1883) in regard to the conversations with Yoshida and the Japanese desire for improvement in Anglo-Japanese relations. I am afraid that the Japanese will consider that our reception of the very friendly advance made in the Aide-Mémoire left on February 4th was somewhat chilly and they are only too easily choked off in such matters. However perhaps this was inevitable in present circumstances. I should be very grateful if in the case of important interviews of this kind, I could have a short telegraphic summary as despatches take from a month to six weeks to arrive. I have been once or twice placed in a somewhat embarrassing position when either Hirota or Horinouchi referred to some interview which Yoshida has had at the Foreign Office and I have had to plead ignorance. Even a mere catalogue of the subjects discussed would be better than nothing.

I am greatly looking forward to my first experience of the cherry

[1] Cf. No. 512, note 2.   [2] No. 511.   [3] No. 521.

blossom season which should now be shortly upon us. While gardening here is not quite so interesting as with us owing to the absence of flowers, nevertheless the Japanese gardens with their marvellous arrangement of trees and shrubs are a great joy and we are just arriving at the time when they will be at their best.

Yours ever,
R. L. CRAIGIE

No. 538

Viscount Halifax to Sir R. Craigie (Tokyo)

No. 177 [F 2832/84/10]

FOREIGN OFFICE, *March 26, 1938*

Sir,

I have read with some interest the pronouncement made by the Japanese Foreign Minister on the subject of the hostilities in China which you communicated to me in your Excellency's despatch No. 57 of the 4th February[1].

2. Mr. Hirota's argument has prompted me to certain reflections. It seems to me that international law will prove tougher than its critics imagine, if for no other reason than that in the long run it is easier to have rules than to have a state of complete chaos. Although there may be periods when the rules of international law are extensively violated, yet in general they persist, because international relations between countries cannot conveniently be carried on on any other basis.

3. Mr. Hirota's pronouncement does, however, raise a point of general interest to which I should like to call attention. It is specifically directed to trying to make out that what is occurring in the Far East, although it bears all the ordinary marks of a war, is not in fact a war. It has as a matter of fact been in the interests of both parties, for reasons I need not enter into here, to take this view of what is happening. It would be open to the Chinese at any time to convert what is going on into a war by declaring that they considered themselves to be at war with Japan. In the same way any third country which chose to do so could say that for its part it regarded what was happening as being a war, and that it would conduct

---

[1] Not printed. The despatch forwarded the text of a statement by the Japanese Minister of Foreign Affairs in the House of Peers on January 25, 1938. The gist of the statement was that the China 'incident' did not constitute a state of war because the situation differed from that in Europe 'which has been regulated in accordance with the conceptions of International Law'. It went on to assert that Japan was fighting only 'the Chiang regime', as 'a faction which stands for anti-Japanese resistance'. In the Foreign Office this statement was commented upon at length by Mr. G. G. Fitzmaurice, the Third Legal Adviser, and it was thought that the substance of his minute would be of interest to the missions in Tokyo and Shanghai. It accordingly makes up the bulk of the present despatch.

itself accordingly and would apply the strict rules of neutrality. In brief, the question whether there is or is not a war does not in the last resort depend exclusively on the views of the parties themselves.

4. This plea that hostilities do not constitute war, or, alternatively, that the situation is one to which the rules of international law do not apply, has been put forward on several occasions recently. It will be recollected that the Italians persistently denied that the hostilities between themselves and Ethiopia constituted a war. They said it was a colonial expedition or a police operation. They also refused to admit that the ordinary rules of international law were applicable as between themselves and Ethiopia. Germany has similarly advanced a plea that the ordinary rules do not obtain as between herself and Austria, and both Germany and Italy have put forward somewhat analogous pleas in justification of their action in prematurely recognising Franco as the true Government of Spain and denying that status to the Barcelona Government. Now we have the Japanese denying that the Chinese Government is the true Government of China or that they are at war with China itself or that the hostilities amount to war.

5. Behind all these instances there will be found reasons of a similar character. These are partly psychological and partly practical. So far as psychology goes, the Italians were never prepared to admit that Ethiopia was a State having equal rights with other States. In spite of Ethiopia's membership of the League, they constantly reiterated that the allegedly barbarous character of her Government placed her outside the pale. Ideological reasons similarly account for the attitude of Germany and Italy towards the Barcelona Government. Racial reasons account for the attitude of Germany where Austria was concerned. Again in China, the Japanese are concerned to deny the status of China as a normal State. They wish to regard it as a congerie of separate elements over which the Nanking Government holds no true sway.

6. But there is clearly more than ideology in it. The alleged inferior status of Ethiopia was an essential part of the Italian case of trying to persuade the world that the Covenant was not applicable. The allegation that what was going on was not a war was clearly directed in part to getting round the charge that Italy had 'resorted to war' within the meaning of article 16 of the Covenant, or had employed war as an instrument of national policy within the meaning of the Kellogg Pact. A somewhat similar idea was in the minds of the Japanese in 1931–32, and it is probably also in their minds now. Again, in the German-Austrian case the insistence that Austria was not really a separate country from Germany was clearly useful in order to enable Germany to deny that what occurred constituted aggression in the true sense of the term. It was also a useful ground on which to deny the right of other countries to interest themselves in the matter. Again, by denying the right of the Spanish Government to be called a Government, on the plea of its allegedly Bolshevik leanings, Germany and Italy were able to make out some sort of

plausible case for the premature recognition of Franco as the legitimate Government of Spain, and thereafter to seek to justify a series of actions vis-à-vis him which could not otherwise have been justified. Similarly, it suits Japan's book to make out that they are not waging war on China, but merely carrying on a private quarrel with the Nanking Government, which they purport to regard as a mere faction not representative of China as a whole.

7. I am sending a copy of this despatch to His Majesty's Ambassador at Shanghai.

I am, &c.,
HALIFAX

No. 539

Sir R. Craigie (Tokyo) to Viscount Halifax
(Received March 30, 10.5 a.m.)

No. 389 Telegraphic [F 3468/71/23]

Confidential   TOKYO, March 30, 1938, 4.38 p.m.

During the past fortnight the General Staff have approached the Military Attaché[1] on three separate occasions to ascertain whether it is possible for them to make some concrete gesture to indicate their desire to improve relations. Military authorities state that they have been active in gradually damping down anti-British activities in the press and elsewhere, are prepared to allow a language officer to be stationed in Formosa and are anxious to do more if possible. They therefore ask for some definite suggestions, for example specific British railway interests in China which they might guarantee to protect. Could these be furnished for study. On their side they state categorically that Chiang Kai-shek régime will disappear and though it is fully realised that proportion of British munitions being supplied to him is less than that from other sources, the fact remains that all these foreign munitions are passing through a British port. Could not Hongkong be closed to all foreign munitions. If this is considered un-neutral then munitions to Japan and China might be simultaneously stopped. France had closed Indo-China frontier and Germany had stopped sales to China; could not Great Britain close Hongkong? Military authorities further urged that such a gesture would be very well received in Japan and would have a far better effect on Anglo-Japanese relations than a tardy recognition of Japan's victory after all was over. Possibility of Anglo-Japanese co-operation in China might have less chance of success if such matters were to be left in abeyance until the end of hostilities.

[1] Major General Piggott.

724

In view of your telegram No. 503[2] of 1937, Military Attaché was careful not to encourage any belief that transit of munitions via Hongkong could be stopped.[3]

[2] Of November 23, 1937, not printed (F 9884/31/10).

[3] Foreign Office officials were not impressed by this telegram. Mr. Ronald wrote on March 31 that he regarded the Japanese approaches through Major General Piggott as 'merely a try-on and not necessarily indicative either of more friendly feelings towards us or of war strain manifesting itself in Japan'. Sir J. Brenan agreed (April 1): 'A bargain is in fact proposed in which we are to put forward our terms for stopping the flow of supplies to China and helping Japan to end the war and get out of the mess she is in.' Sir A. Cadogan (April 2) drew attention to the League Resolution (see Nos. 504 and 507) 'under which we pledged ourselves to assist China so far as might be possible. Our policy must continue to be to keep Hong Kong (and eventually the Burmese route) open. . . Our attitude shd. be explained to Sir R. Craigie'. See No. 542 below.

No. 540

Sir R. Craigie (Tokyo) to Viscount Halifax
(Received March 31, 11.55 a.m.)

No. 396 Telegraphic [F 3544/16/10]

TOKYO, *March 31, 1938, 5.15 p.m.*

I note from your despatch No. 94[1] that on February 15th Japanese Ambassador was informed that it would not be possible for us to offer our good offices except in conjunction with the United States. There is no doubt that if time ever arrives to offer good offices, combined Anglo-American action would be the best course from every point of view. I have however recently received indications from one or two well-informed quarters that public opinion here is unlikely to welcome or even accept joint action owing to implication of pressure in so powerful a combination. On the other hand I am told that influential opinion is coming more and more to the view that when the right time comes good offices by either United States or Great Britain (and preferably Great Britain) would be best and surest method of settling dispute.

I do not at present moment see any prospect of useful intermediary action except in improbable event of Chiang Kai-shek being willing to retire in order to bring peace to his country. But situation might change at any moment and I should be grateful if I might be informed for my confidential guidance whether His Majesty's Government would not altogether exclude possibility of using their good offices should they receive indications that independent action would be welcome in both Tokyo and Hankow. It might for instance be possible to envisage a situation in which either Great Britain or United States might act as intermediary with the concurrence and . . .[2] of other powers though not

[1] No. 521.

[2] The text was here uncertain.

ostensibly in combination with it. I realize of course that a decision on such a matter must necessarily depend on circumstances of the moment but a general indication that we do not definitely exclude possibility of independent action would be of value to me.

Opinion even in moderate circles seems to me to be increasing in favour of an early advance on Hankow as being best means of hastening end of National Government. The successful conclusion of this military operation could only have the effect of further stiffening of Japanese terms and rendering yet more difficult future protection of our own interests in China.[3]

Repeated to Embassy Shanghai and Hongkong (for His Majesty's Ambassador).

[3] Mr. Ronald expressed the opinion on April 1 that 'we should not definitely exclude the possibility of mediation by one Govt.' and suggested that this telegram should be repeated to Washington and the opinion of the U.S. Government sought. Sir A. Cadogan agreed: 'If the best chance of hastening the conclusion of hostilities were to lie in mediation by ourselves alone I should not like to see it turned down. I do feel however that we shd. be in a very difficult position. Mediation between 2 parties is hard enough, but it would be much harder if it were accompanied (as it doubtless would be) by a fusillade of irresponsible American criticism' (April 6). See No. 543 below.

No. 541

Viscount Halifax to Mr. J. D. Greenway[1] *(Shanghai)*

No. 305 Telegraphic [F 3704/25/10]*

Secret   FOREIGN OFFICE, *April 5, 1938*

Reference Foreign Office telegrams Nos. 272 and 273[2].

Chancellor of Exchequer saw Dr. Sun Fo and Chinese Ambassador on the 31st March, and explained that market loan could not be arranged on any reasonable terms and Government guarantee was not practicable. Apart from possibility of further credits on silver such as had already been arranged with Hong Kong Bank[3], best possibility seemed to be commercial arrangement for purchase of Chinese production of wolfram and antimony referred to in Foreign Office telegram No. 273.[4] He promised to consider how best British commercial interests could be got to take up negotiations for this purpose. Chinese said that Mr. T. V. Soong would be the best representative on Chinese side. They hinted that Dr. Kung might not be aware of proposal.

Treasury would be glad of Rogers's comments.

Repeated to Hankow No. 3 Tour, and Hong Kong.

[1] Appointed First Secretary in H.M. Embassy in China on November 21, 1937.
[2] See No. 535, and *ibid.*, note 4.   [3] See *ibid.*
[4] In a letter to Mr. Chamberlain of April 5 (PREM 1/303) Sir J. Simon expressed the view

that 'the Chinese production of these metals, and particularly of wolfram, is of the first order of importance to us on defence grounds', and mentioned that if reports that the Germans were trying to obtain the Chinese metals were correct the British position, with her small reserves, would be very difficult. He suggested that Britain should purchase a large part of Chinese antimony and wolfram production for the next three years, and in return grant the Chinese Government a credit which they could repay out of the proceeds of the exports: 'Insofar as the financial arrangements help to strengthen the Chinese currency ... we should be killing two birds with one stone ... here we have a good opportunity of using our financial power effectively in the national interest, and it is a matter of some urgency to see if it can be arranged.' Mr. Chamberlain agreed to Sir J. Simon's suggestions in a letter of April 6; cf., however, No. 584 below.

No. 542

Viscount Halifax to Sir R. Craigie (Tokyo)

No. 235 Telegraphic [F 3468/71/23]

FOREIGN OFFICE, *April 6, 1938, 4 p.m.*

Your telegram No. 389[1].

I regard these advances with considerable suspicion and attribute them in large measure to recognition by the Japanese of the fact that deterioration of relations with the Union of Soviet Socialist Republics, coupled with Japan's growing unpopularity in United States of America calls for a special effort to improve relations with Great Britain (compare concluding paragraphs of your despatch No. 72[2]).

I am asking War Office how valuable they regard presence of language officer in Formosa.

If the suggestion about British railway interests relates to their protection during hostilities, this should be superfluous if the general assurances already given have any value. If it relates to position after the war it amounts to proposal for division of China into spheres of economic influence and as such is not suitable for discussion now, though in some form it might perhaps be considered as part of the general settlement to be negotiated with Japan when the conversations broken off last summer are taken up again. Real intention of the general staff is obviously to give us vague promises—and we know from experience how worthless such promises are—in return for which we are to close Hongkong, and help Japan to end the war and extricate herself from her difficulties.

Policy of His Majesty's Government remains as stated in my predecessor's telegram No. 503 of 1937[3] and we have no intention of disregarding our obligations under the League Resolutions.[4] We shall do our best to keep Hongkong open and to help China in her desire to provide herself with alternative channel of supply through Burma.

[1] No. 539.
[2] Of February 12, not printed (F 2844/152/23).
[3] See No. 539, note 2.
[4] See Nos. 504 and 507.

I have no confirmation of the statement that Germany has stopped sales to China and I am asking His Majesty's Ambassador at Berlin and Governor of Hongkong whether they have any knowledge of this. I am also asking His Majesty's Consul General at Saigon what is present position in regard to transit of arms through Indo-China.

No. 543

Viscount Halifax to Sir R. Lindsay (Washington)

No. 253 Telegraphic [F 3544/16/10]

FOREIGN OFFICE, April 7, 1938, 11.45 p.m.

Tokyo telegram to Foreign Office No. 396.[1]

As at present advised my own feeling is that, though we should much prefer joint mediation, we should not definitely exclude the possibility of mediation by one Government and that it is not of any great importance whether that Government be His Majesty's Government or the United States Government if the Japanese set any store by one doing it rather than the other. I do however think that whoever mediates ought to keep the other neutral Governments, including the German Government, reasonably well informed of the progress of negotiations.

Please so inform the United States Government and invite their views explaining that we shall not try to form any final opinion on the point until we hear what they think. You might take the opportunity to enquire whether the State Department have yet formulated any views on the matters dealt with in Sir A. Cadogan's letter to Mr. Hornbeck of February 14th.[2]

[1] No. 540.   [2] See No. 450, note 3.

No. 544

Sir R. Craigie (Tokyo) to Viscount Halifax (Received April 9, 11 a.m.)

No. 442 Telegraphic [F 3942/84/10]

TOKYO, April 9, 1938, 5.25 p.m.

My telegram No. 392[1].

The new German Ambassador[2] called today. In the course of a general discussion I gained the impression that he was genuinely anxious for such

[1] Not kept in F.O. archives.
[2] General Ott, German Military Attaché at Tokyo, had received a personal telegram from Herr Hitler on March 24 offering him appointment as German Ambassador to Japan in succession to Dr. von Dirksen, who had been recalled: cf. Volume XIX, No. 492, note 1.

collaboration between the two Embassies as was possible in the present circumstances. As regards China he thinks it most unlikely that Japanese Army will embark on any further large scale offensive after the present Lunghai operations have been brought to an end. He believes that the Japanese already have a heavier task on their hands in consolidating the position in Central China than they had anticipated and that from a purely military point of view any further extension of their military responsibilities and commitments would be unwise. (To my Belgian colleague he had previously remarked that after Nanking the Japanese General Staff had hoped to be able to reduce number of divisions in this area to three but had been obliged instead to increase their number.) On the political situation he said that the German Government had done their best to bring about peace and had failed but they hoped that some other Power might prove more successful. For the moment he saw no way out of present imbroglio though he had a vague feeling that some typically oriental means of escape would be discovered from a situation which was rapidly becoming unbearable for both sides.

I hear from several sides that Germans are disappointed at military performance of their own associates and are still taking such opportunities as offer to counsel moderation.

Repeated to Embassy Shanghai.

No. 545

Sir R. Craigie (Tokyo) to Viscount Halifax
(Received April 12, 2.35 p.m.)

No. 458 Telegraphic [F 4000/12/10]

TOKYO, *April 12, 1938, 3.45 p.m.*

My immediately preceding telegram.[1]

After finishing discussion in regard to North China I handed to Minister for Foreign Affairs a memorandum setting forth the thoroughly unsatisfactory position in regard to navigation on the Yangtse, observing that this continued discrimination against British vessels and British trade on pretexts which had been discarded one after the other constituted a clear breach of the Japanese Government's assurances. I also communicated to His Excellency a memorandum outlining a series of cases on which I had been vainly addressing representations to the Japanese

[1] In this telegram of April 11 Sir R. Craigie reported that he had spoken to the Japanese Foreign Minister that day in accordance with his instructions in telegram No. 230 of April 4 to the effect that foreign interests should have some say in the rationing of foreign exchange by the new Chinese Federated Reserve bank. The Foreign Minister promised to discuss the matter with Sir R. Craigie after studying the question.

Government during the past few months, drawing attention in support to the Mr. Bennett and the Mr. Turner cases and question of access to property in Shanghai. I said that whatever might be arguments advanced by the Japanese local authorities in support of the attitude in each individual case, the cumulative effect of all these cases was to demonstrate the existence of an underlying determination on the part of certain Japanese authorities to undermine, discredit and discriminate against British interests in China by every means in their power.

His Excellency listened to this diatribe with some surprise, declaring that most of the Japanese[2] were under the impression that Anglo-Japanese relations were improving. As regards Central China he had understood that the change in High Command[3] had been beneficial to Anglo-Japanese relations.

I replied that I was the first the recognise the improvement in the situation so far as this country was concerned and I knew that my Government had appreciated His Excellency's efforts to remove mis-understanding and repress newspaper recriminations. Nevertheless atti-tude of Japanese local authorities in occupied territory in China appeared to be as bad as, if not worse than, it had been a few months ago and evidences of an intention to discriminate against foreign interests more palpable than ever. I suggested that the best way to deal with this somewhat menacing situation was for the Japanese Government to make it clear once and for all to their authorities on the spot (whether civil, military or naval) that it was the definite policy of the Japanese Government to endeavour to work with, rather than against, Great Britain in these matters and that the policy of exploiting the military situation in order to benefit Japanese economic interests must cease. I had consistently recommended to my Government a policy of seeking cooperation with the Japanese Government whenever possible in safeguarding of British interests during present emergency, but I could hardly be expected to continue to offer such advice unless the Japanese Government were ready to take energetic steps to bring about a change in the policy of their local authorities. Settlement of these various cases which were causing so much friction would be far more valuable to future Anglo-Japanese relations than any amount of 'gestures' or propaganda, such as were recommended in certain quarters in Japan.

The Minister for Foreign Affairs repeated his desire to see all questions relating to protection of British interests in China settled satisfactorily and he particularly agreed with the last sentence of my observations. He promised to go into all these matters carefully and see whether some

[2] This statement was underlined and queried on the filed copy.

[3] On February 23 it had been announced that General Matsui, Japanese Commander in Chief, and his two principal divisional commanders had been recalled. General Matsui was succeeded in the Chief Command by the Inspector General of Military Training, General Shunroku Hata.

action could not be taken to bring about a better state of affairs between our respective authorities in China.[4]

Repeated to Shanghai.

[4] In telegram No. 267 to Tokyo of April 15 Sir R. Craigie was congratulated by Lord Halifax on 'the excellent manner in which you presented our case' and said that he would be glad if the Ambassador on the next suitable opportunity would 'inform Minister for Foreign Affairs how unreservedly I approved the terms of the communication which you made to him'.

No. 546

Sir R. Lindsay (Washington) to Viscount Halifax
(Received April 16, 9.30 a.m.)

No. 201 Telegraphic [F 4129/16/10]

WASHINGTON, April 15, 1938, 11.4 p.m.

Your telegram No. 253[1].

Following is substance of State Department's reply of April 14th of which text by bag[2].

United States Government are impressed with Sir R. Craigie's view that there is no prospect at present of useful mediatory action and so far as their own information goes neither Chinese nor Japanese Governments would be prepared at this stage to agree with terms of peace acceptable to the other; they appreciate cogency of views that Japanese public opinion would be unlikely to welcome or even to accept collaborative mediation by United Kingdom and United States owing to implication of pressure and that in such circumstances mediation by one rather than by more than one government stands better chance of success and they agree that situation may change. They think it advisable before assuming a definite attitude to the question of mediation by one as distinct from more than one government to await a time when development of conflict is such as to render opportune the offer by a third country or countries of good offices. They consider that any government or governments undertaking mediation should keep other principally interested governments reasonably well informed of progress of negotiations and they will wish to communicate with His Majesty's Government in case of any significant development and trust we will keep them informed of our attitude and thought.[3]

I am sending by bag leaving April 20th a reply from Mr. Hornbeck to Sir A. Cadogan's letter (? of February 14th) of which I have been given a copy[4].

[1] No. 543.
[2] Not printed: see F.R.U.S., Japan 1931–1941, vol. i, pp. 463–4.
[3] Sir R. Craigie was informed of the substance of the American reply in telegram No. 271 to Tokyo of April 19.
[4] See No. 450, note 3.

No. 547

Sir R. Craigie (Tokyo) to Viscount Halifax
(Received April 16, 1.30 p.m.)

No. 483 Telegraphic [F 4130/16/10]

Confidential   TOKYO, April 16, 1938, 5 p.m.

While Japanese Government are most anxious for a settlement there are as yet no signs at all that they are prepared to offer terms which have any chance of acceptance or to accept foreign mediation in promoting settlement. For . . .[1] Japan apparently militarily successful and capable financially to meet the strain . . .[1] her terms are likely to stiffen in proportion to her sacrifices and she will tend increasingly to endeavour to recoup herself economically in occupied areas for her failure to bring Chiang Kai-shek to his knees (see my telegram No. 425[2]). The only event likely to reverse this tendency would be elimination of Chiang Kai-shek as the embodiment in the public mind of Japanese of leadership in China.

As regards Japan's staying powers our view is that economically and financially she can, barring unforeseen circumstances carry on campaign for another year on present scale. The economic difficulties will steadily grow and after a . . .[1] must be increasingly serious but there is no indication at present that she is likely to be deflected from her course by these considerations.[3]

I fear therefore that when Japanese Ambassador expresses contrary opinion the wish is father to the thought. Nevertheless I feel we should constantly . . .[1] watch and take advantage of any new development such as a possible change of Government, to reconsider position. In this connexion I should be grateful for any guidance you can give me in answer to my telegram No. 396.[4]

Repeated to Embassy, Shanghai (for Sir A. Clark Kerr).

---

[1] The text was here uncertain.   [2] Not kept in F.O. archives.

[3] Sir J. Brenan commented on April 20: 'Sir R. Craigie estimates that the Japanese can carry on the war on the present scale for another year. . . We are also told that the Chinese can continue their resistance for at least a year so that by next spring the chances of useful mediation should be much brighter. In the meantime our interests will pass through a pretty grim time.'

[4] No. 540: cf. No. 546, note 3.

No. 548

Sir R. Craigie (Tokyo) to Viscount Halifax
(Received April 19[1], 11 a.m.)

No. 494 Telegraphic [F 4154/71/23]

TOKYO, *April 19, 1938, 4.13 p.m.*

My telegrams Nos. 389[2] and 449[3] and your telegram No. 258[4].

In preparation for formal conversation in the near future Military Attaché has twice discussed Anglo-Japanese relations with General Homma, Director of Military Intelligence, General Staff, and on the second of these occasions Military Attaché put the following points to him:

(a) I agreed with General Homma's view that Anglo-Japanese relations could more easily be improved now than after the war;

(b) Friendly gestures which General Staff advocate were insufficient while underlying causes of friction remained. (General Homma agreed but emphasized psychological effect on Japan of exchange of gestures.)

(c) Offer of General Staff to guarantee protection of . . .[5] British interests in exchange for closure of Hongkong indicates that General Staff did not at present intend to implement Japanese Government's assurances of respect for all our interests. (He was impressed by this.)

(d) Both British public opinion and dictates of neutrality ruled out any likelihood of the closure of Hongkong. Some recent figures of munitions imports from Germany were given to him orally.

(e) Military Attaché urged General Homma to consider earnestly what Japan could do to eliminate discrimination against British interests, obstruction and incidents, and suggested that vague instruction to higher commanders to avoid 'injuring rights of foreign Powers' might be made more definite, e.g. that specific orders be issued to subordinate commanders including captains and subalterns to ensure that their units understood Japanese Government's policy of friendship and co-operation with Great Britain as laid down by Minister for Foreign Affairs in the Diet on 22nd January (see your despatch No. 60[6]). In other words all ranks must be warned to work with and not against British representatives in China. (General Homma regarded this suggestion as of considerable practical value.)

---

[1] The date of receipt was given on the filed copy as April 18, apparently in error.
[2] No. 539.
[3] In this telegram of April 11 Sir R. Craigie referred briefly to some of the points raised in No. 542.
[4] Of April 13, not printed (F 3711/717/10).   [5] The text was here uncertain.   [6] No. 511.

No. 549

Memorandum by Mr. Gage[1] on the new China-Burma Highway from Yunnanfu (China) to Lashio/Bhamo (Burma)

[*F 4304/79/10*]

FOREIGN OFFICE, [*April 21, 1938*]

1. General Data

Distance from Yunnanfu to Lashio	738 miles
Distance from Yunnanfu to Bhamo	724 miles
Distance from Yunnanfu to Burma frontier	618 miles
Distance from Burma frontier to Lashio	120 miles
Distance from Burma frontier to Bhamo	106 miles

The frontier road to Burma forks near Muse, eleven miles from the Chinese frontier, one branch passing through Kutkai to Lashio and the other through Muse and Namkham to Bhamo. From Lashio Rangoon can be reached by rail and road, and from Bhamo by river.

Specifications etc. of Chinese highway from Yunnanfu to Burma frontier

Length	618 miles
Maximum width	27 feet
Minimum width	21 feet
Maximum gradient	8%
Highest point (at Hsiakuan)	6,200 feet
Maximum capacity of bridges	15 tons
Number of suspension bridges	2
Number of workmen employed on new Hsiakuan-Burma frontier section	170,000
Proposed date of completion:	end of June, 1938.

Progress on Chinese highway up to February 18, 1938

Yunnanfu-Hsiakuan (275 miles) Complete, except for re-surfacing, re-bridging and widening.

[1] Mr. Gage, who had been relieved at Hankow by Mr. MacKillop (see No. 484, note 3) elected to return to England by way of the proposed new highway from Yunnanfu to Lashio, a journey which he completed between January 27 and February 18. Afterwards he wrote a detailed report with maps and 43 photographs, filed at F 2657/79/10. Mr. Orde commented on March 30 that it showed the Chinese to be improving the road 'with immense energy (170,000 men at work). On the Burma side prospects are good also . . . the next question is lorries to operate on it. Sir F. Leith-Ross and I spoke to the Chinese Amb[assado]r today and gathered that the Purchasing Commission (Boxer Indemnity) had funds which cd. be used for that and that Export Credits might supplement. Mr. Gage is emphatic about the high morale in Hankow.' Later Mr. Gage prepared a resumé of his report which is printed here as being briefer and with some more recent information than the original report.

Hsiakuan-Nangshih (287 miles) This is an entirely new section commenced in December 1937. Cutting three quarters complete. Three large bridges over Rivers Yangpi (stone), Mekong (suspension) and Salveen (suspension) yet to be completed. New bridge required across Mekong, present bridge over Salveen can be strengthened and enlarged up to specification. Laying of all-weather surface not commenced. Width and gradient on completed cuttings up to specification.

Nangshih-Burma frontier (56 miles) Motorable in dry weather. Under partial reconstruction to meet required specification for width, gradient and bridging. Laying of all-weather surface not commenced.

Specification for improved Burma frontier road to Lashio

Length	120 miles
Maximum width	16 feet
Minimum bridge capacity	
all-weather surface	7½ tons
Date of completion of work:	end of May, 1938.

State of Burma frontier-Lashio road on February 18, 1938

By the above date no decision had been taken to improve the road up to specification set out above and scarcely any work was therefore in progress. The surface was earth and motorable in fine weather. Average width as far as Kutkai about 10 feet. Gradients and curves exceed Chinese maximum.

State of Burma frontier-Bhamo road (106 miles) It is understood that this road is unsuitable for heavy traffic, from Muse onwards. Decision has been taken not to improve it at present. The road, however, appears to be more important for ordinary trade than that to Lashio, in view of the comparatively low cost of river transport from Bhamo to Rangoon, as opposed to rail from Lashio.

2. General remarks

From Yunnanfu the China-Burma highway connects with an existing highway to Kweiyang, whence other highways radiate to the important centres of Changsha, Nanchang, Chungking and Kweilin. From Changsha and Chungking Hankow can be reached by river and from the former also by rail. Thus the new highway forms an artery to the heart of China. It is anticipated that on completion of the China-Burma highway most of the above-mentioned centres will be reached from Rangoon in from 12 to 14 days.

3. *Possible results of construction of new highway*

(1) By ensuring an additional and secure line of communications for the importation of supplies it will encourage the Chinese Government to continue resistance. The highway itself is invulnerable to Japanese attack and the outlet port of Rangoon is well-placed strategically, as it lies behind Singapore.

(2) It affords a desirable outlet for trade from China through British territory. Under present conditions with the blockade of the Yangtze and the consequent elimination of Shanghai, the only alternative outlets are Canton which is very vulnerable and Haiphong in French-Indo China whence Yunnanfu is reached by the French railway from Hanoi. Rangoon has the advantage over Haiphong of being 2,500 sea-miles nearer to Europe. Moreover the capacity of the French railway from Hanoi is limited and the cost of transport on it is high. The use of river transport in Burma in conjunction with Diesel-engined lorries should assist to make transport along the China-Burma highway a commercial proposition.

(3) In addition to extraordinary trade which may be forced along the Burma-China route by the present abnormal conditions, the highway should form the shortest and probably the cheapest route for new trade with the hitherto little developed provinces of Yunnan, Kweichow and possibly also southern Szechuan. Yunnan is rich in minerals, particularly in tin and it is probable that wolfram can also be mined there. It also has a promising climate for fruticulture and a health resort for the Far East. Moreover signs are not lacking of an intention to make Yunnanfu an industrial and cultural centre of China.

(4) The city of Rangoon, river and rail transport in Burma and British commercial interests in general should benefit, the latter not only from the trade mentioned under (2) and (3) above but also from orders placed by the Chinese Government for transportation material. An order is already about to be placed for 200 British-made lorries.

(5) By granting to the Chinese the necessary facilities in Burma in connexion with the new highway we have an opportunity of rendering positive assistance to China and at the same time protecting and advancing our own political and commercial interests at little cost and no danger to ourselves.

(6) The province of Yunnan marching as it does with Burma for 600 miles can in a sense be considered a bulwark of our Indian Empire. On this assumption, in the increasingly unlikely event of the collapse of the Central Government in China the preservation of the independence of this province might become an important British interest, which would be threatened either by the establishment in it of Japanese influence or of a state of anarchy. The new highway should assist us to extend a stabilising influence into the province and at the same time leave Japan in no doubt as to our interest in it. French political interests from Indo-China probably run parallel to ours.

736

4. *Suggestions for encouraging British trade in this area*

(1) Encourage purchase of Diesel-engined lorries to reduce cost of transport.

(2) Ensure good service along highway for British vehicles sold.

(3) Ensure through official or semi-official organisations that Chinese receive advice regarding most suitable type of transport available. Foreign competition, particularly in Diesel-engined transport, is very keen.

(4) Endeavour to secure remission of duty on Burma Oil Company's products sold for use of Chinese highway authorities, otherwise it may be found cheaper to import from Indo-China.

(5) Encourage establishment of aircraft assembly plants in Burma and consider possibility of British or Sino-British Aviation Company operating from Burma into China. This would assist the defence of Burma as well as trade.

No. 550

Sir R. Craigie (Tokyo) to Viscount Halifax (Received April 22, 6.40 p.m.)

No. 506 Telegraphic [F 4350/15/10][1]

Important TOKYO, *April 22, 1938, 10.35 p.m.*

Subject to your approval, I have now reached agreement with Vice-Minister for Foreign Affairs.[2] Points outstanding have been dealt with as follows:

(a) *Basis of Calculation*. Japanese Government agree to accept basis of calculation as actual gross collections of import, export and inter-port duties for previous month.

(b) *Tientsin–Pukow Loans*. Japanese Government agree to accept contingent charge in respect of Tientsin-Pukow and Hukuang Railway loans, on condition that we raise no objection to inclusion of similar contingent charges in respect of Japanese loans. Text (to be included in an agreed record[3]) is still under discussion.

(c) *North China Currency Question*. Japanese Government undertake that quotas of northern ports will be paid in Chinese national currency (see exchange of letters in my telegram No. 508[4]). In return, I give assurance proposed in agreed record.

Japanese intend that the whole of arrears now immobilised in Hong

---

[1] Not kept in F.O. 371 or Confidential Print: copy taken from telegram collection (see No. 528, note 1).

[2] Cf. No. 529, note 6.

[3] The agreed record of Sir R. Craigie's conversation with Mr. Horinouchi was transmitted in Tokyo telegram No. 513 of April 23, not printed.

[4] Not printed: for the final text of these letters see No. 565 below.

Kong and Shanghai Bank at Shanghai, Tientsin and Chinwangtao (after deduction of foreign loan collections for March) shall be used exclusively for payment of northern quotas, thus contributing to solution of transfer difficulty (see agreed record). For this purpose we abandoned paragraph 5 C of former draft agreement (repayment of overdraft).

(d) Japanese Government propose safeguarding clause contained in paragraph 4 B of present draft arrangement should be transferred to their covering note and somewhat amplified, in view of the decision to accept monthly basis of calculation. They point out that any radical change in economic situation in China (such as serious collapse of Chinese currency) might render present arrangement unworkable and necessitate its reconsideration. They therefore propose to add to their draft covering note (of which text was transmitted in my telegram No. 414[5] and amended in my telegram No. 473[5]) following words at the end of paragraph 1 after 'described therein': 'It is understood that measures are of a temporary nature for duration of the present hostilities, and will be subject to reconsideration in the event of radical change in economic conditions under which above measures are prepared.'

Text of draft arrangement (revised so as to take account of above amendments) is contained in my telegram No. 507[6].

My comments follow.[7]

Repeated to Sir A. Clark Kerr.

[5] Not printed.
[6] Not printed: for the final text of the agreement see No. 565 below.
[7] See No. 551 below.

No. 551

Sir R. Craigie (Tokyo) to Viscount Halifax (Received April 23)

No. 512 Telegraphic [F 4384/15/10]*

TOKYO, *April 23, 1938*

My telegram No. 506[1].

I think that under proposed arrangement we secure our main desiderata.

It is true that we have to abandon clause 5 (c) of former draft, but as it now appears that amount of overdraft which can be shown to relate specifically to Shanghai share of service of foreign obligations is under 1 million yuan (balance having been paid out of revenues from Chinese-controlled ports), concession is not very considerable and has the merit of helping to ease the transfer difficulty in respect of northern quotas.

Question of provision for exchange for transfer to northern quotas has

[1] No. 550.

proved difficult of solution. It will be seen that Japanese Government gives a definite and unconditional undertaking to pay these sums (estimated at about 2 million dollars per mensem) in Chinese national currency. But I was only able to obtain assurance in these terms by promising, subject to (? Chinese authorities') approval, that British authorities in China would do what they properly could to lend assistance in this matter. Vice-Minister for Foreign Affairs was most insistent that we should endeavour to persuade Bank of China and the Bank of Communications in Tientsin to sell remittance Bills against their credit balances in Shanghai. I pointed out repeatedly that I could see little chance of Chinese banks agreeing to do anything of the sort, but on Vice-Minister for Foreign Affairs urging that without this method being at least tried he could not obtain required assurance in regard to payment of quotas in yuan, I promised to ask for your authority to say 'this proposal would be placed before Chinese banks concerned.' A more practical method of obtaining necessary exchange is that importers in North China should pay certain proportion of their customs duties in foreign currency, and in this perhaps His Majesty's Consul in Tientsin may be able to give some indirect assistance. It is, of course, understood that assistance is limited to provision of exchange necessary to remit northern quotas and we remain judges as to extent of assistance which can 'properly be given.'

As regards paragraph 2 of draft arrangement and point 3 of draft record, it will be seen that words 'duly . . .^{2}' have been omitted because they lead to quite unnecessary dispute as to which loans have been recognised by National Government and which have not. It will be seen, however, that Vice-Minister for Foreign Affairs in draft record agrees that Tientsin-Pukow Railway loans fall within the scope of agreement, and we thus secure our point. As regards Japanese loans mentioned, Vice-Minister for Foreign Affairs states that there is no present intention of putting forward claim that they should be serviced from customs, but Japanese Government feel bound to make a reservation on this point to counterbalance their concession in regard to railway loans in which we are interested. It is fully understood that our assent to include Japanese loans binds no one but ourselves (i.e., Chinese Government would retain right to . . .^{2} British bondholders were Japanese Government to put forward any claim that their loans should be serviced from customs).

Japanese Government ask that exchange of letters (see my telegram No. 508^3) should not be published, as it is difficult for them to acknowledge publicity [sic] that northern quotas cannot be paid in new currency. They would also prefer substance of exchange of notes rather than that texts should be published, and will submit proposals to this end. As regards draft record of conversation, it is proposed that this should be kept strictly confidential, though I am informing my United States colleague and my

---

^{2} The text was here uncertain. ^{3} See No. 550, note 4.

French colleague that the points mentioned were provisionally agreed to and, as in my discussion with Vice-Minister for Foreign Affairs, texts of all other draft documents have been handed over to my two colleagues.

It is obviously desirable that the proposed arrangement should, if possible, apply to March collections of revenue, and for this and other reasons speed is necessary. If, therefore, proposals have your general approval, I suggest substance of proposed exchange of notes and of text to be enclosed in Japanese note should be communicated confidentially to Chinese Government forthwith, leaving time meanwhile for your more detailed examination of various texts.

In estimating value to us of an arrangement on these lines I hope general considerations mentioned in paragraphs 1 and 2 of my telegram No. 235[4] will be taken into account.

Repeated to Embassy, Shanghai.

[4] No. 524.

No. 552

Sir A. Clark Kerr (Hankow)[1] *to Viscount Halifax*
(*Received April 26, 9.30 a.m.*)

No. 14 Tour Telegraphic: by wireless [F 4581/16/10]

HANKOW, *April 26, 1938*

In the course of a conversation yesterday Minister for Foreign Affairs reviewed circumstances which had led to the present armed conflict between China and Japan and all the phases through which it had passed and said that things seemed now to have come to a deadlock.

There were reasons to believe that Japan wanted peace but she was . . .[2] by her own action which amounted to withdrawal of recognition of Chinese Government from any move in that direction. In her turn China wanted peace also provided it were honourable and lasting but she too could make no move for if she did it would give the impression that she was suing for peace. That she would never do for so long as Japan persisted in her aggression China would continue to resist and as time passed she was becoming more and more convinced of her power to make her resistance effective.

His Excellency went on to say that if it seemed to His Majesty's Government that the time was opportune some friendly Power or group

[1] After taking charge of the Embassy at Shanghai on February 24 Sir A. Clark Kerr decided to make a tour including visits to Hankow and Chungking. He left Shanghai for Hong Kong on March 29, arriving at Hankow on April 5. After flying to Chungking he returned to Hankow until April 25 (telegram No. 14 Tour was drafted on April 24) and then returned via Hong Kong to Shanghai, arriving on May 1.

[2] The text was here uncertain.

of Powers (say Great Britain, United States and France) might singly or severally make some *démarche* which might prepare the way for negotiations. He thought that in the first instance this *démarche* (which should be made simultaneously to each side) should be of an unofficial nature.

There could be no question of China accepting the four points put to them some months ago through the German Ambassador[3] or anything like them but they would be ready to agree to any reasonable terms that would preserve the sovereignty, independence and administrative integrity of China. They would also be ready to agree to economic co-operation with Japan on the basis of equality and reciprocity but not to any form of co-operation which was domination in disguise.[4]

Repeated to Embassy Shanghai.

[3] See No. 453.
[4] In telegram No. 19 Tour of April 26 referring to this conversation Sir A. Clark Kerr said that according to Dr Kung the Chinese Government had recently received unofficial overtures about peace terms from 'a Japanese known to be in close touch with his Government'. These terms included a withdrawal of Japanese troops, an indemnity for damage done in Shanghai and elsewhere, and a 'settlement' of the Manchukuo question.

No. 553

Sir R. Craigie (Tokyo) to Viscount Halifax (Received April 27, 9.30 a.m.)

No. 526 Telegraphic [F 4462/71/23]

TOKYO, *April 27, 1938, 1.30 a.m.*

Your telegram No. 274[1] dealing with two points:

1. Whether equitable relations can be more easily improved now than after the war.

2. Whether chances of rescuing our interests in North China from shipwreck are likely to diminish the longer the war lasts.

View I have expressed on point 2 is largely based on trend which has become steadily more noticeable in the last few months towards establishment of an exclusive Japanese . . .[2] in North China—a trend which during my first few months here was confined to extremist military circles. If present economic . . .[2] due to prolongation of an anomalous situation could be relieved at an early date I consider it might still be possible to save something from the wreck. But I admit that any view on this point must necessarily be speculative and in present circumstances largely academic.

[1] This telegram of April 21 referred to paragraph (a) of No. 548 and asked Sir R. Craigie to 'amplify your view, with which I find it difficult to agree'. It also referred to a statement in Tokyo telegram No. 449 (see *ibid.*, note 3) that the chances of saving British interests in North China would decrease the longer the war lasted.
[2] The text was here uncertain.

As regards point 1 the view in (A) of my telegram No. 494[3] may perhaps have suffered from over-compression in drafting. It would be better expressed as follows: Unless we succeed during period of hostilities in arriving at some working arrangement with Japanese for safeguarding of intrests in China, thus reducing present causes of friction, agreement for their adequate protection after the war is likely to prove more difficult. This proposition I believe to be correct irrespective of view that may be held on point 2.

In support of this proposition I submit the following arguments.

1. There are still important elements here which believe that the only hope of promoting an early economic recovery in China lies in co-operation of Japanese with Great Britain and United States.[4] These elements are not vocal but they exercise a certain influence behind the scenes. As the war proceeds however the extremists (and particularly the advocates of totalitarian methods) gain steadily in influence while the tendency of military authorities in China to resort to independent action is likely to grow. This process has been in operation before my eyes for eight months and I see no prospect of its reversal in the near future. As the strains and stresses grow so does the tendency to resort to unorthodox methods.

2. If the struggle is to be indefinitely prolonged I apprehend that when it ends these extremist elements will have gained so predominating an influence[5] in the counsels of this country that without some good spadework meanwhile the difficulty of concluding satisfactory arrangements at termination of hostilities will be greatly enhanced. It would not be right to exclude altogether the possibility that economic situation of this country might in time become so grave and the response so poor to the makeshifts of a policy of self sufficiency that even a purely militaristic or authoritarian government might be forced to see reason; on the other hand this is not a contingency in any case we should be justified in relying on.

3. The prolongation of period of armed occupation, the resultant creation of vested interests and probable disappointment in the military and political results of present adventure may be expected to combine to strengthen the trend in favour of exclusive economic exploitation by Japan of all parts of China which can be brought effectively under Japanese control.

4. The present moment is obviously inopportune for conclusion of any agreement with Japanese relating to post-war period but working arrangements for protection of our interests during the emergency would appear to be the logical sequel to our numerous protests and warnings and the only thing lacking to their attainment so far has been Japanese goodwill. If powerful aid of Minister of Defence can be enlisted in support

[3] No. 548.   [4] Marginal comment by Mr. Howe: 'Because they want our money!'
[5] Marginal comment by Mr. Howe: 'That depends on the ending.'

of Minister for Foreign Affairs' somewhat feeble efforts in this direction it would be easy ultimately to capitalise such goodwill as now exists. This is the purpose of conversations which Military Attaché has heen having with Director of Military Intelligence.

5. The type of working arrangement I have in mind is that which it is hoped to conclude in relating to customs i.e. an arrangement of limited scope and having no direct bearing on major political problems. Another possible subject for a modus vivendi would be protection of our railway interests in China. Such arrangements may be unattainable but if attainable they are surely desirable. Even an oral understanding as regards methods by which respect for British interests can most effectively be secured would be better than nothing.

I venture to express the hope that as defined above objective towards which we are working will meet with your approval.

It may be asked what inducement the Japanese have at the moment for reaching an understanding for better protection of our interests in China.[6] Here lies the difficulty. As stated under 1 all saner Japanese realise that China cannot be put on her feet again in any foreseeable future without British and American assistance and that a prolonged economic struggle with us in China will not be the best method of restoring the shaken financial fabric of Japan herself. I do not suggest that we should here and now promise co-operation for the future (which must be dependent on Japan's own behaviour) but merely that we should not shut the door upon it. Manchukuo seems to me the classic example of operation of American-inspired policy of non-recognition and non-co-operation *à outrance*—a policy which has had disappointing results even from China's point of view. While nothing can of course be guaranteed I believe a different technique (applied now rather than at the termination of hostilities) may secure better results for ourselves and China.[7]

[6] Marginal comment by Mr. Howe: 'Exactly.'

[7] Marginal comment by Mr. Howe: 'This assumes that China will be another Manchukuo.' In a minute of May 4 Mr. Howe commented: 'The Ambassador's whole case rests on the assumption that the Japanese are going to win the war, an assumption which I do not myself believe in, and I think that there is at least an equal possibility, if not of a Chinese victory, then certainly a stalemate.' Sir A. Cadogan agreed (May 7): 'It may be that the Chinese will lose all the battles except the last one.' Sir J. Brenan also submitted two long minutes criticizing Sir R. Craigie's reasoning, which were combined by Mr. Ronald into a despatch sent to Sir R. Craigie on May 17: No. 575 below. Meanwhile telegram No. 335 to Tokyo of May 16 thanked Sir R. Craigie for his 'efforts to formulate some constructive practical suggestions for saving our position in the Far East . . . but I am afraid that in spite of your arguments I adhere to the view expressed in my telegram 274' (see note 1 above).

No. 554

Sir A. Clark Kerr (Hong Kong) to Viscount Halifax
(Received April 29, 9.30 a.m.)

No. 1 Special Telegraphic: by wireless [F 4639/15/10]*

HONG KONG, April 28, 1938

My telegram No. 18, Tour Series.[1]

I found Chiang Kai-shek very suspicious about customs negotiations and he pressed me hard for full explanation. He claimed that any agreement concluded between ourselves and Japan at the present stage would be damaging to China, in that it would be represented by Japanese as moral support for them and possibly their puppet Government, under whose control certain of the ports would fall, into some form of recognition. If we were unable to give China active support we might at least give her passive support by refraining from concluding an agreement with her enemy.

2. I told him on very broad lines what we were trying to do and claimed that it might be regarded as active support of China, basing my remarks upon the last paragraph of your telegram No. 8, Tour Series,[2] but he was not persuaded, and in the end I said that I would let him have from Shanghai explanation that would convince him.[3]

Repeated to Shanghai for Tokyo and Saving to diplomatic mission.

[1] Not printed.
[2] This telegram of April 13 left it to Sir A. Clark Kerr's discretion as to whether he informed the Chinese Government of the customs negotiations. The last paragraph stated that if he did so he should 'explain that our policy has been to seek every means of maintaining authority of customs service and avoiding seizure of customs throughout the occupied area, and that the arrangements contemplated must be regarded as a whole in the light of this alternative'.
[3] See No. 561 below.

No. 555

Sir A. Clark Kerr (Hong Kong) to Viscount Halifax
(Received April 29, 9.30 a.m.)

No. 2 Telegraphic: by wireless [F 4551/84/10]

HONG KONG, April 29, 1938

Tokyo telegram No. 483[1].

It is most unfortunate that Japanese are still thinking in terms of beating Chiang Kai-shek to his knees and are unwilling to treat with him

[1] No. 547.

on grounds that he is the embodiment of anti-Japanese feeling in China. In many ways it is true that he is, at any rate at present, because, as I see it, he has now become the symbol of Chinese unity, which he himself had so far failed to achieve, but which the Japanese are well on the way to achieving for him. And, in the minds of the Chinese people he and those about him stand for the independence and integrity of China and for leadership in her struggle against Japan which has now become a national affair.

2. At the same time although Chiang Kai-shek is now this symbol, national feeling is so exacerbated that if he were to disappear, others just as anti-Japanese would take his place.

3. The days when Chinese people did not care who governed them seem to have gone and I much doubt whether provinces over which war has passed or those behind the line (with the exception of Sinkiang) would now accept the rule of any group willing to treat Japanese on lines they seem to contemplate.

4. It would be foolish to try to forecast the outcome of the war, but I am bound to say that my visit to Central China from out of the gloom and depression of Shanghai has left me stimulated and more than disposed to believe that provided the financial end can be kept up Chinese resistance may be so prolonged and effective that in the end the Japanese effort may be frustrated.

5. The Chinese themselves are persuaded of this. Their spirit is high and their determination strong and their recent military successes in Shantung have taught them that Japanese troops, hitherto considered invincible, can be beaten.

6. As has been said they feel they have got their second wind and that their strength lies in their realisation that they are fighting for their existence, in their consequent desperation, their immense endurance and capacity to suffer, their new and high morale, weight, bulk and 5 to 1 preponderance in man power. They are relying on all this but they are also relying on financial help from outside[2] and mainly I am sorry to say upon such help from us.

7. Finance is their main weakness but to it must be added their inexperience (though they seem to have learned the lessons of Shanghai and Nanking) inferior equipment, loss of most of their ports and some absence of harmony on home front.

8. Here Chiang Kai-shek is obstinate and difficult to work with. Dr. Kung is no good as Minister of Finance. Friction between the two brothers-in-law prevents Soong from pulling his weight which at this stage would be of utmost value.

[2] In telegram No. 5 (Special) of April 30 from Hong Kong Sir A. Clark Kerr added that he had asked Chiang Kai-shek what help he was getting from abroad: 'He said very considerable material support was coming from Russia on a barter basis . . . and that an agreement had just been reached with France for a fifteen years credit for sixteen million dollars for railway material'.

9. Nevertheless apart from Dr. Kung and his follies they are making in their muddling way a good job of things in extremely difficult circumstances.

Repeated to Shanghai for Tokyo and saving to Diplomatic Mission.

No. 556

Sir R. Craigie (Tokyo) to Viscount Halifax (Received April 29, 8 p.m.)

*No. 533 Telegraphic [F 4570/15/10]**

TOKYO, *April 29, 1938, 11.20 p.m.*

Your telegram No. 290[1].

Result of further long discussion with Vice-Minister for Foreign Affairs is given in my immediately following telegram[2], but before you consider this I should like to submit my view of more general aspects of this question.

We have now been negotiating here uninterruptedly since the middle of February. At that time I expressed the view that threat in regard to 'forcible taking over the Customs' need not be taken too seriously, but subsequently delay has undoubtedly led to a revival of earlier impatience of the Japanese military authorities in Shanghai. The recent formation of renovation Government[3], which is determined to get its hands on revenues at an early date, has increased the tension still further. It is under these circumstances that I had hoped that a certain discretion would be given me in dealing with less important matters, and this has been my only excuse for begging for the very prompt consideration of proposals put forward in my telegram No. 512.[4]

Vice-Minister for Foreign Affairs now informs me, confidentially, that if we fail to put new arrangements into force as from Sunday, 1st May,

[1] This telegram of April 27 contained Foreign Office comments on points of detail in the draft customs agreement: see No. 550. The main remaining point of difficulty concerned the new North China currency which had been instituted by the Japanese: Sir R. Craigie was instructed to try and secure Japanese acceptance of responsibility for transferring the North China quotas even if collected in foreign currency.

[2] Not printed: telegram No. 534 of April 29 transmitted the Vice Minister for Foreign Affairs' response to the points raised in Foreign Office telegram No. 290 (see note 1 above).

[3] In telegram No. 523 of March 28 Sir A. Clark Kerr had reported the inauguration of a new Japanese-sponsored régime in Nanking called the 'Reformed' Government. The manifesto of the new régime, summarized in Shanghai telegram No. 535 of March 29, stated that its objects were 'to restore sovereignty as before the war, save the people from war, reconstruct peace in Far East and strengthen relations with Europe and America'. It would not conflict with the Provisional Government, which would continue to handle Central Government matters, and the two would be amalgamated 'when communication on Tientsin-Pukow and Lunghai railways is restored . . . since it is not intended that there shall be two Governments in China'.

[4] No. 551.

there is a danger that renovation Government (and by this, of course, he means the Japanese military on the spot) may take independent action. They are determined to put their finances on a more satisfactory footing from May onwards. I have satisfied myself that the risk is a real one, and that this is not merely an attempt to exercise undue pressure. It is easy to reproach the Japanese Government for their lack of authority over their subordinates in China, but this will not get us any further.

It is a little difficult for me to judge from your telegrams whether you consider this agreement really worth having or not. If it is I feel sure that we should conclude at once without making further difficulties on point of detail. Further, it would be easy to find some pretext, such as the transfer difficulty, for allowing negotiations to lapse, whereupon Japanese authorities in China would take their own measures. I realise the political difficulty of concluding any arrangement at all with Japan in the present circumstances. But we presumably decided to face that difficulty when we started on these negotiations, and the result is a good deal better than I had personally anticipated at the outset. We have at least advanced beyond the stage at which the Japanese Government even refused discussion of these matters at all with representatives of foreign Powers.

It will be seen that I have secured most, though not all, points mentioned in your instructions. In addition I have obtained reference insertion of paragraph 5 (c) in the old draft, whereby nearly 4 million dollars will be refunded to Central Bank. This will go some way to make the agreement more palatable to the Chinese Government, and is a concession which I have only obtained with the greatest difficulty. I hope that in view of this you will not think it necessary to insist on those points . . .[5] to which I have been unable to obtain Japanese assent.

If agreement so amended is considered to be generally in British interests, I earnestly hope that I may receive instructions to enable me to exchange notes by morning of 1st May.

Repeated to Shanghai for the Ambassador.

[5] The text was here uncertain.

No. 557

Sir A. Clark Kerr (Hong Kong) to Viscount Halifax
(Received April 30, 9.30 a.m.)

No. 3 Telegraphic: by wireless [F 4582/84/10]

HONG KONG, *April 29, 1938*

I spent some hours with Chiang Kai-shek on April 24th. He had much to say about the military situation which he claimed to be good and to promise well for the future.

2. He explained that general Chinese plan had provided for withdraw-

al from Hankow into the west and it had been decided on as part of a policy to lure the Japanese armies into the interior and away from their bases. Recent Chinese successes had been due to length and weakness of Japanese lines of communication and for this reason they could be repeated again and again.

3. He said that a retreat from Hankow now seemed remote and asked what view His Majesty's Government in the United Kingdom would take if nevertheless it came about. Would they withdraw recognition from Central Government? I said I thought I could assure him that so long as Central Government held together as the legitimate government of China our policy would remain unchanged.

4. He then asked what in my opinion was the best course for Chinese to take. Should they continue to resist? I said my purely personal opinion was to the effect that they should.

5. He replied that given certain circumstances he had no doubt they could and would. The country was with the Central Government and elements formerly opposed to them (Communists and Kuangsi Generals) were now fighting on their side. He was sure that he could deal with Japanese armies. It would take time but Chinese were contemplating and preparing for long campaign. Their ability to carry it on and bring it to a successful end depended however upon their getting financial help from outside.

6. I asked how long China could hold out (a) without help, and (b) with it. To (a) he replied, still some months, and to (b), a year or so . . .[1] years if flow of supplies from abroad continued. When I mentioned Canton he said he thought Japanese were so deeply engaged elsewhere that any threat to that port was now remote.

7. He then asked with a mixture of sadness and bitterness why we were not giving China more support. It was true that she was fighting for her own existence but it was not unfair to claim that she was fighting for us too and that the whole position in China depends on her success. Further, had we contemplated the significance to ourselves of the defeat of China and her subjugation by Japan? It would mean that the Japanese with the man-power of China could and would make the Yellow Peril a real thing.

8. He asked whether lack of support from us was due to unwillingness, fear of Japanese, or party dissensions at home. I dismissed the last two and explained in regard to the first the difficulties of raising money in London without adequate security. But this obviously left him unconvinced for he replied that if we did not think it worth while to help China she would lose the war. It did not seem to him that in all the circumstances in seeking help from us he was asking over-much and that if we gave it he could . . .[1] it from America and France also. This, followed in due course by a few sharp words to Japan, would be all that was wanted to give Japan the jolt she needed to bring her to her senses. He appreciated that the situation in Europe had . . .[1] impossible for His Majesty's Government to give Japan

[1] The text was here uncertain.

748

this jolt but the situation was clear . . .[1] hoped that the time was coming when His Majesty's Government would be able to make some show of strength. I did not encourage this hope but he persisted in it.

9. He ended a very strong appeal that help should not be withheld and begged that I should pass it on to you.[2]

Repeated to Shanghai for Tokyo and saving to Diplomatic Mission.

[2] Minutes on this file show that the question of financial help for China was still under consideration by the Chancellor of the Exchequer, to whom Lord Halifax had written on April 25 regarding the scheme for credits for China based on the security of her wolfram and antimony supplies (cf. No. 541, note 4). Sir R. Vansittart noted on April 30 with reference to telegram No. 3: 'I hope we can avail ourselves of this to give the antimony deal another good push.' Sir A. Cadogan (May 4) also expressed the hope that an arrangement on these lines could be made, although he feared that 'most of the money may be wasted by the Chinese' on the 'purchase of unsuitable material such as heavy guns. . . But it is perhaps true that there will be a more lively sense of gratitude toward us if we help them in the moment of their greatest difficulty'. He and Mr. Howe suggested that Lord Halifax should draw the Chancellor's attention to telegram No. 3. In a letter to Sir J. Simon of May 9 urging that a means be found to accede to China's request for financial assistance, either through the wolfram scheme or through some other means, Lord Halifax pointed out that 'China is fighting the battle of all the law-abiding States and she is incidentally fighting our own battle in the Far East, for if Japan wins, our interests there are certainly doomed to extinction. . . Every consideration, therefore, of honour and self-interest impels us towards doing what we can to keep China alive'.

No. 558

Sir A. Clark Kerr (Hong Kong) to Viscount Halifax
(Received April 30, 9.30 a.m.)

No. 6 Telegraphic: by wireless [F 4697/16/10]

HONG KONG, *April 30, 1938*

My telegram No. 2 from Hongkong[1].

Chiang Kai-shek gave me some indication of peace terms which the Chinese would be willing to accept.

2. To conditions stated in last paragraph of my telegram No. 14 tour series[2] he added that Japanese troops must be withdrawn from all provinces of North China other than those originally composing Manchuria. He said that China would not feel safe unless some third Party was party to the negotiations concerning these provinces and would wish that Power to act as guarantor of any agreement reached. I said I foresaw difficulties about that.[3]

[1] No. 555.　　　　　　　　　　　　　　　　　　　　　　　[2] No. 552.
[3] Mr. Howe commented on May 6: 'General Chiang Kai-shek has always maintained that he will not make peace until the Japanese take their armies out of China and I believe that he is sincere in this. As long as he remains in power I do not believe that Japan can recoup herself in North China for the cost of the war. Subject to what Sir R. Craigie has to say we can only tell the Chinese M.F.A. that we shall gladly do what we can in the way of mediation

749

3. His Excellency confirmd Dr. Kung's statement that China would be willing to see Manchurian question settled on basis of Irish Free State[4].

Repeated to Shanghai for Tokyo and Saving to Diplomatic Mission.

as soon as we know that both sides are ready to accept mediation but that we see no sign of this yet—in Japan.' Sir A. Cadogan agreed (May 6), and telegram No. 315 was despatched to Tokyo on May 7 asking for Sir R. Craigie's observations on No. 552 and the present telegram.

[4] Dr. Kung had made this observation in the course of the discussion with Sir A. Clark Kerr reported in telegram No. 19 Tour: see No. 552, note 4.

No. 559

Viscount Halifax to Sir R. Craigie (Tokyo)

No. 300 Telegraphic [F 4571/15/10]*

FOREIGN OFFICE, May 1, 1938, 6 p.m.

Your telegrams Nos. 533[1] and 534.[2]

1. Treasury agree that latest amendments represent substantial improvement, and if you are convinced that military danger is serious, you are authorised to sign texts as amended rather than risk breakdown. But we have not yet received Sir A. Clark Kerr's views[3] nor been able to consult Ministers here, still less to obtain Chinese Government's reactions. In view of political and financial importance of securing effective agreement, it [sic] much prefer to wait a day or two, and we hope that if you indicate to Vice-Minister our position, he will agree to defer completion till Wednesday.

2. In notifying decision to Vice-Minister, you should, if you see no objection, say that our acceptance is based largely on oral assurances given by him. We are glad to note his desire to work with us in the whole matter, and we trust that he will do his best to secure satisfactory settlement of difficulties which remain to be dealt with, especially smuggling, North China currency and method of utilisation of balances.

3. We assume from your telegram No. 534, point 3, that Japanese Government only ask us to put before Chinese banks proposal that they should remit to Shanghai payments made to them in Tientsin in *Chinese national currency*. You should, if possible, obtain confirmation on this point, which is of great importance. It seems from your telegram that our comments on North China currency have reached you in corrupt form.

4. We should also like to see beforehand precise terms of statement to be issued to the press. It is most important that this should not be drafted in such a form as to antagonise Chinese susceptibilities. Delay would enable us to arrange for simultaneous publication here.

Repeated to Embassy, Shanghai, No. 379.

[1] No. 556.   [2] See *ibid.*, note 2.   [3] See No. 560 below.

No. 560

Sir A. Clark Kerr (Shanghai) to Viscount Halifax
(Received May 1, 6.10 p.m.)

No. 688 Telegraphic [F 4646/15/10]*

SHANGHAI, *May 1, 1938, 10.47 p.m.*

I am satisfied that final concessions by Japanese, referred to in Tokyo telegram No. 534,[1] gave us as much as we can well hope for and, indeed, more than I had expected. I hope, therefore, that you will permit Sir R. Craigie to conclude agreement.

2. Notwithstanding Chinese objections (which are inevitable in the circumstances), I think an agreement most desirable. I have been counting on it as spearhead of future negotiations on many other issues, such as railways, conservancy, river navigation discrimination against British trade, &c. If Customs Agreement is not brought to fruition, our prospects in these other negotiations will be jeopardised. Failure to reach an agreement will, moreover, not really help Chinese, and, apart from the fact that I think proposed agreement is of advantage to China, this formal recognition by Japan that she cannot ride roughshod over foreign interests in China may indirectly benefit Chinese Government.

3. My own information is that, if agreement is not concluded soon, there is a real risk of combined action by semi-independent Japanese authorities here.

4. I agree with Sir R. Craigie's suggested solution of 'relevant overdraft' question and with suggestion to frame his note vaguely rather than positively, so that we waive objections to arrangement prepared instead of positively approving only one feature of it. This enables us to explain to Chinese that we are tacitly acquiescing in arrangements which we are unable to prevent.

5. It seems futile to expect Japanese to put up their quotas in foreign currency, and I think we should concentrate on getting them in Chinese legal tender without promising any assistance in the way of pressure on Chinese banks to facilitate remitting.

6. As regards assurances referred to in Tokyo telegram No. 536,[2] I have never expected to get a satisfactory assurance about Chinese domestic loans, but it is important that they should be mentioned in order to please the Chinese. If an agreement is reached it will be in Japanese interest to stop smuggling, and this involves returning customs vessels, so that I think we can count on both. I therefore consider the exact wording of these assurances is not raised.

[1] See No. 556, note 2.

[2] In this telegram of April 29 Sir R. Craigie stated: 'I agree that assurances are in a form not particularly satisfactory but with the exception of that relating to domestic loans I am confident that they will in practice be sufficient to secure early improvement both as regards smuggling and customs launches.'

7. Your telegram unnumbered of 27th April to Hong Kong[3] reached me only to-day. There is no doubt that reactions of Chinese Government will be unfavourable, though I do not think that they will go to the length of destruction of customs service to prevent its execution.

8. Both Chinese Government and Rogers express concern over the possible effects of agreement on Chinese currency. It is, however, a question of Japanese policy. If they wish to damage currency they will be able to do so in any case; in fact this would be easier if there were no agreement.

9. I regard it as of the first importance that Chinese Government should be notified (not consulted) of the terms of arrangement before it is concluded. I am accordingly intimating to Mr. MacKillop text of arrangement and a full summary of all accompanying documents, and instructing him to inform Minister of Finance in confidence of arrangement with . . .[4] of contents of accompanying documents.

10. I am also sending to Chiang Kai-shek through Mr. MacKillop promised arguments in favour of agreement (see my telegram No. 1 from Hong Kong of 28th April[5]).

Repeated to mission, Hankow, Tientsin and Tokyo.

---

[3] This telegram asked Sir A. Clark Kerr to 'forecast attitude of Chinese Government on the whole agreement and, in particular, on the questions of currency in North China and deposits in Hong Kong Bank'.
[4] The text was here uncertain.
[5] No. 554.

No. 561

Sir A. Clark Kerr (Shanghai) to Viscount Halifax
(Received May 1, 6.15 p.m.)

No. 689[1] Telegraphic [F 4611/15/10]*

SHANGHAI, *May 1, 1938, 10.40 p.m.*

Following addressed to mission, Hankow, No. 371:
'My telegram No. 368[2].
Following is message for Chiang Kai-shek:
"When I saw your Excellency in Hankow I promised to write from Shanghai and explain reasons why we found it necessary to discuss customs questions with Japanese. On my return here I find that matter had suddenly become one of extreme urgency, since Japanese have indicated that unless understanding is reached by 3rd May, they propose to take over all Customs Administration in occupied territory unconditionally.[3]

---

[1] This telegram was despatched, but not received, before No. 560: they have been kept in numerical order.
[2] Presumably a repeat to Hankow of No. 554.
[3] Cf. No. 556.

It is probable, therefore, that arrangement will be concluded on 3rd May.

It was clearly impossible for Chinese and Japanese to come to terms with regard to customs, and we were faced with a position in which unless we took some initiative ourselves, the Japanese would take over Customs Administration in occupied territory unconditionally, turning it into a Japanese Administration run primarily for Japanese benefit, and destroy organisation which has been foundation of China's credit in the past and will undoubtedly be so again in the future.

We deliberately refrained from consulting the Chinese Government during the negotiations, since it was evident from the first that the Japanese would not agree to terms (e.g., bank of deposit and internal loans) which would satisfy China's minimum demands, and it accordingly seemed to us better to make no communication to the Chinese Government until an agreement had been reached, and then to face them with a *fait accompli* for which they could disavow responsibility, but I do most earnestly hope that the Chinese Government, even while refusing to accept the arrangement as binding upon themselves, will not take any measures which will make it unworkable.

If the arrangement does not go through, there will be complete disruption of customs service, which Japanese will take over and run for their own benefit.

The advantages which Chinese obtain from the agreement are: (1) that Japanese are definitely committed to payment of appropriate share of foreign obligations secured on customs (thus maintaining China's credit on international market); (2) payment in Chinese national currency and not in any new puppet currency (thus supporting national currency vis-à-vis puppet currency); (3) formal integrity of Customs Administration is preserved with its international personnel, which Chinese Government must realise has proved to be one of the most valuable safeguards of Chinese interests.

His Majesty's Government have secured these assurances from the Japanese Government only after months of negotiation, and I am convinced they are the best we can obtain. Though I fully appreciate their shortcomings from point of view of Chinese Government, I am confident that if your Excellency carefully considers results of failure to make such an agreement, you will agree with me that in the interests of Chinese Government an agreement is greatly preferable to unconditional seizure of customs by Japanese."'

Repeated, Saving, to Tokyo.

No. 562

Sir R. Craigie (Tokyo) to Viscount Halifax (Received May 2, 1.30 p.m.)

No. 549 Telegraphic [F 4612/15/10]*

TOKYO, *May 2, 1938, 6.5 p.m.*

Your telegram No. 300.[1]

I am grateful for authority conveyed in first paragraph.

I at once called on Vice-Minister for Foreign Affairs and spoke as authorised.

He fully appreciated difficulty and would have liked to meet your wishes. But he found himself already obliged, as result of strong representations from Ministry of Finance and from Japanese authorities in Shanghai, to withdraw concession he had made in regard to reinsertion of paragraph 5 (*c*). He reminded me that this concession had only been made as the price of an immediate agreement, his idea being that he would be able to face dissentient authorities with *fait accompli* of signature, but that pressure was now so strong that he felt obliged to withdraw it. I pointed out that concession had been made with a view to signature on 1st May, and that I should consider I had been ill-used if, when I came on 2nd May to announce agreement, I found concession withdrawn. Vice-Minister for Foreign Affairs pointed out that I was now asking him to defer signature until 4th May, and that it was quite impossible for him in the circumstances to hold concession open any longer. Furthermore, although no untoward event had yet occurred in Shanghai, he was momentarily expecting trouble.

As I understand that you attach importance to this concession, and particularly as you have already mentioned it to Chinese Government (see your telegram No. 301[2]), I argued very strongly for its retention, and Vice-Minister for Foreign Affairs finally agreed to ascertain whether, if notes were to be exchanged to-day, this could still be on the basis of my telegram No. 533.[3]

He has since replied in the affirmative, and I have therefore been reluctantly obliged to avail myself of authority conveyed in paragraph 1 of your telegram to exchange notes this afternoon. I am quite satisfied that this is necessary to avoid loss of paragraph 5 (*c*), and probably also a complete breakdown.

Vice-Minister for Foreign Affairs has agreed to defer the issue of *communiqué* to Japanese evening papers of 3rd May in order to give time for your observations on *communiqué* to reach me to-morrow morning.[4]

Repeated to Sir A. Clark Kerr.

[1] No. 559.　　　　　[2] Not kept in F.O. archives.　　　　　[3] No. 556.
[4] The *communiqué*, was, however, sent to the press by the Foreign Office in London, and printed in *The Times* of May 3, 1938, p. 15. The last sentence of paragraph 1 read: 'It is further understood that the Governments of the United States and France do not propose

to raise any objection to the temporary application of these arrangements.' Cf. No. 563 below.

No. 563

Sir R. Craigie (Tokyo) to Viscount Halifax (Received May 4, 11.40 a.m.)

No. 559 Telegraphic [F 4730/15/10]*

TOKYO, *May 4, 1938, 4.35 p.m.*

My telegram No. 556.[1]

My United States colleague read to me this morning telegram he had received from his Government, substance of which was that they were only prepared to concur in agreement if it could be shown (*a*) that it was approved by the Chinese Government, and (*b*) that it would work. Meantime, they desired to reserve their position. As regards (*b*), they understood that it was my view that the whole agreement must break down if Chinese Government (as was their right) refused to provide foreign exchange for payment of northern quota.

I observed in reply that United States Government tended to make the worst of arrangement instead of trying, in the interest of Anglo-American co-operation in the Far East, to make the best of it. They should at least recognise that, had not some temporary arrangement been made, a default on service of foreign debt and forcible action against customs in the Japanese-controlled areas would have been highly probable—an event which would have seriously affected American interests as well as ours. We had kept the United States Government informed of every step in the negotiations, they had raised no objection at any time, and all we now asked was that they should give it a fair trial and not raise eleventh-hour objections.

As regards (*a*) above, it seemed that Chinese Government would, if only for political reasons, be unable to express approval of arrangements, but this did not mean that they would not privately regard it as the better of the two evils or that they would necessarily wish to impede its operation. But attitude of United States Government, which I felt might be based on insufficient information, would certainly encourage Chinese Government

---

[1] In this telegram of May 3 Sir R. Craigie reported that Mr. Grew had told him that the U.S. Government were unlikely to agree to express any opinion on the customs agreement and that they would consequently be opposed to the reference to their attitude in the last sentence of the *communiqué*: see No. 562, note 4. Sir R. Craigie explained that it was too late to make any change in London, but that the sentence would be omitted from the version of the *communiqué* issued in Tokyo. He expressed regret at the misunderstanding, explaining that at the last moment matters had to move more quickly than anticipated. In telegram No. 557 of May 3 Sir R. Craigie admitted that he had not made it sufficiently clear that the last sentence of paragraph 1 was still subject to United States concurrence, but he commented that the U.S. attitude throughout the negotiations 'has been very unhelpful and in marked contrast to that of the French Government'.

to take a short-sighted view of their ultimate interest in the whole matter. I added confidentially that it had also been the view of His Majesty's Ambassador in China that it put Chinese Government in a position of having to express a definite opinion on arrangement. Point (b) above was, I said, based on a misunderstanding, because my view was that if Chinese Government refused to assist in supplying foreign currency to pay northern quotas, it should be possible to secure the necessary foreign exchange from payment of a proportion of customs duty in Shanghai from foreign currency.

The Ambassador promised to put these arguments forcefully before his Government.[2]

Repeated to Sir A. Clark Kerr.

[2] According to *F.R.U.S.*, 1938, vol. iii, the U.S. Government were meanwhile considering a *démarche* of their own to the Japanese Government regarding the customs: see pp. 698–99.

No. 564

Sir A. Clark Kerr (Shanghai) to Viscount Halifax
(Received May 4, 8.20 p.m.)

No. 700 Telegraphic: by wireless [F 4757/15/10]*

SHANGHAI, *May 4, 1938*

Following is repetition of mission, Hankow, telegram No. 353 of 3rd May:

'Your telegrams Nos. 368 to 371[1].

I saw President of Executive Yuan yesterday afternoon and communicated your personal message, text of agreement and summary of correspondence. Vice-Minister for Foreign Affairs was also present.

Dr. Kung did not take communication too badly, although he was evidently much depressed, and said that it was most regrettable that a Power friendly to China should make an arrangement which would reinforce Japanese militarism and Japanese military capacity without participation of China and without consulting Chinese Government. He asked to what extent United States and French Government had been consulted on final texts. I was unable to inform him.

Vice-Minister for Foreign Affairs, who was inclined to criticise agreement somewhat severely, requested that Chinese Government should be supplied with text of correspondence summarised in your telegram No. 370[2] as soon as this should be available.

Dr. Kung handed me a copy of an instruction to Chinese Ambassador in London, dated 1st May, containing text of *note verbale* to be handed to Foreign Office, which I am repeating to you in my immediately following telegram[3]. He also gave me a copy of a further telegram to Chinese

[1] See No. 561, and *ibid.*, note 2. [2] Not kept in F.O. archives. [3] Not printed.

Ambassador, dated 2nd May, setting out his personal unofficial observations on proposed agreement, for the information of Sir F. Leith-Ross. This is very long, and if, as I assume, agreement will be signed on 3rd May, it seems unnecessary to telegraph [t]ext. Tone is critical.'

No. 565

Sir R. Craigie (Tokyo) to Viscount Halifax (Received June 7)

No. 276 [F 6072/15/10]*

TOKYO, *May 4, 1938*

My Lord,
With reference to my telegram No. 549[1] of the 2nd May regarding the conclusion of an agreement relating to the China customs revenues, I have the honour to transmit to your Lordship herewith copies of the following documents exchanged between the Minister for Foreign Affairs and the Vice-Minister for Foreign Affairs on the one hand, and myself on the other, at the Ministry for Foreign Affairs on the evening of the 2nd May:

(1) Translation of note from the Japanese Government with enclosure regarding the disposal of the China customs revenues.
(2) Copy of my note in reply.
(3) Copy of letter addressed by me to the Vice-Minister for Foreign Affairs requesting assurances regarding the currency in which foreign loan quotas will be paid.
(4) Copy of Vice-Minister's letter in reply giving these assurances.
(5) Record of meeting between the Vice-Minister for Foreign Affairs and myself elucidating certain points in connexion with the arrangements.[2]

2. I also have the honour to enclose a copy of the *communiqué* relative to the above which was issued to the press by the Ministry for Foreign Affairs on the 3rd May.[3]

I have, &c.,
R. L. CRAIGIE

ENCLOSURE 1 IN No. 565

Japanese Minister for Foreign Affairs to Sir R. Craigie

Translation   TOKYO, *May 2, 1938*

Your Excellency,
As a result of the conversations which have recently taken place between

---

[1] No. 562.   [2] Not printed: see No. 550, note 3.   [3] Not printed: see No. 562, note 4.

your Excellency and Mr. Horinouchi respecting the service of the foreign obligations secured on the Chinese Maritime Customs revenue and other relevant matters, I have the honour to inform your Excellency that the Japanese Government, after obtaining the concurrence of the Chinese authorities in the occupied areas, are now desirous of dealing with these matters on the lines set forth in the accompanying document and are prepared to effect the measures described therein. It is understood that the measures are of a temporary nature for the duration of the present hostilities, and will be subject to reconsideration in the event of a radical change in the economic conditions under which the above measures are proposed.

I trust these arrangements will prove acceptable to His Majesty's Government in the United Kingdom.

I avail, &c.,
Minister for Foreign Affairs

SUB-ENCLOSURE

All duties, surtaxes, dues and other revenues collected by the Chinese Maritime Customs at each port within the areas under Japanese occupation shall be deposited in the name of the Commissioner of Customs with the Yokohama Specie Bank or, where the bank has no branch, with any other bank or banks to be agreed upon.

2. From the import, export and inter-port duties and the flood relief surtax thus deposited, foreign loan quotas shall be remitted, at intervals which should not exceed ten days, to the Inspector-General's account at the Yokohama Specie Bank in Shanghai in order to meet in full on due dates the service of the foreign loans and indemnities which were secured on the customs revenue in July 1937.

3. The service of foreign loans and indemnities secured on the customs revenue shall be treated at all ports in China as a first charge on the revenue after deducting the maintenance expenses of the Customs Administration (including the share of the expenses of the inspectorate-general) as certified by the Inspector-General of Customs, and such customary payments and grants (hitherto deducted from gross revenue before payment of foreign obligations) as are similarly certified.

4. (*a*) Foreign loan quotas for each port shall be determined monthly in proportion to the share of that port in the total gross collections for all ports during the preceding month.

(*b*) Calculations in respect of foreign loan quotas shall be based on the gross import, export and inter-port duty collections of the Chinese Maritime Customs and these quotas shall be determined as set out in (*a*) above by the Inspectorate-General of Customs, with the agreement of Japan and the other Powers concerned.

(*c*) Any insufficiency of customs revenue to meet the quota of any port

758

within the areas under Japanese occupation in North China and in Central China shall be made good from the customs revenue of other ports in the respective areas.

5. (*a*) The arrears on the Japanese portion of the Boxer Indemnity held in a suspense account at the Hong Kong and Shanghai Bank since September 1937 shall be paid to the Japanese Government.

(*b*) Future payments of the Japanese portion of the Boxer Indemnity, as well as the Japanese share of the Reorganisation Loan of 1913, shall be made in the same manner as in the servicing of all foreign loans and indemnities secured on the customs revenue.

(*c*) The arrears on the foreign loan and indemnity service for January and February 1938, at present deposited in the Hong Kong and Shanghai Bank at Shanghai (amounting to 3,966,576.32 dollars), shall be released to meet the relevant overdraft for which they act as security.

(*d*) The balance of the customs accounts with the Hong Kong and Shanghai Bank in each port under Japanese occupation shall be transferred to the account of the Commissioner of Customs at the branch of the Yokohama Specie Bank in each port at which such a balance exists and utilised for future foreign loan quota payments.

6. The above arrangements shall come into effect on the 3rd May, 1938, and shall apply to the customs collections beginning with March 1938.

ENCLOSURE 2 IN No. 565

Sir R. Craigie to the Japanese Minister for Foreign Affairs

TOKYO, *May 2, 1938*

Your Excellency,

I have the honour to acknowledge the receipt of the note which your Excellency was good enough to address to me on the 2nd May respecting the service of the foreign obligations secured on the Chinese Maritime Customs revenue and other relevant matters.

His Majesty's Government in the United Kingdom recognise that the present position creates great difficulties for which it is urgently necessary, in the interest of all countries concerned, to find a solution, and I have accordingly been authorised to state that His Majesty's Government will, for their part, raise no objection to the application of the temporary measures set forth in your Excellency's note and its enclosure.

I am further instructed to take this opportunity to emphasise once more to your Excellency the interest which my Government take in the maintenance in every respect of the authority and integrity of the maritime customs service.

I avail, &c.,
R. L. CRAIGIE

Sir R. Craigie to the Japanese Vice-Minister for Foreign Affairs

Confidential TOKYO, *May 2, 1938*

My dear Vice-Minister,

With reference to the notes which are being exchanged to-day in regard to the Chinese Maritime Customs, I should be glad if, in order to avoid future misunderstanding, your Excellency would be so good as to give me an assurance that the quotas for foreign obligations payable by the northern ports in Japanese occupation will be remitted in a currency which will enable the Inspector-General to effect the necessary transfer into the currencies in which the foreign obligations are serviced. This question arises particularly in connexion with the recent decision to create a new currency in Northern China.

Believe me, &c.,
R. L. CRAIGIE

ENCLOSURE 4 IN NO. 565

Japanese Vice-Minister for Foreign Affairs to Sir R. Craigie

Confidential TOKYO, *May 2, 1938*

My dear Ambassador,

With reference to your letter of to-day, I am glad to be able to give you the assurance that the quotas for foreign obligations payable by the northern ports in Japanese occupation will be paid in Chinese national currency ('Fa-Pi'), on the understanding that the Inspector-General of Customs will arrange for the supply of the necessary amount of foreign exchange for the conversion of these sums from Chinese national currency ('Fa-Pi') into currencies in which the foreign obligations are serviced.

Believe me, &c.,
KENSUKE HORINOUCHI

No. 566

Sir R. Craigie (Tokyo) to Foreign Office (Received May 7, 9.30 a.m.)

No. 571 Telegraphic [F 4865/84/10]

TOKYO, *May 7, 1938, 11.46 a.m.*

Sir A. Clark Kerr's telegrams Nos. 2[2] and 3 Tour[3].

[1] Lord Halifax left London on May 7 for Geneva to attend the 101st session of the League of Nations Council. The session ended on May 15.
[2] No. 555. [3] No. 557.

It may be useful if I indicate my estimate of present Japanese attitude:

Hopes of a progressive weakening of Chiang Kai-shek's position as a result of setting up of Peking and Nanking Governments having disappeared there can be little doubt that a more active conduct of the campaign is now in prospect. First objective will be to administer a striking defeat in Lunghai area. This would clear the way for an advance on Hankow and there are growing indications that this advance will be undertaken should the expected victorious termination of Lunghai campaign fail to shake Chiang Kai-shek's determination to resist. Japanese of course realise that this means a further extension of their military commitments and lines of communication but they believe political results of the fall of Hankow would justify these risks (particularly through anticipated accretion of strength to provisional régimes in Peking and Nanking). Once Hankow had fallen I should expect to see a formal Japanese recognition of these régimes. That prosecution of the campaign on this scale would necessitate great sacrifice both parties fully recognise but there is no doubt that determination to 'see the thing through' is increasing even in circles in Japan which would normally be regarded as moderate.

As regards justification of a loan to Chinese Government this would necessarily increase China's powers of resistance and correspondingly embarrass Japanese but I doubt myself whether it would make much difference to the ultimate outcome of military campaign. On the other hand were such a loan to be sanctioned and encouraged by His Majesty's Government it would mean revival of anti-British feeling here in its most intense form and the end of all hopes of protecting our interests in China by process of friendly co-operation to that end. I am not in a position to estimate whether the gains to be anticipated from such a policy would outweigh its dangers but it would be unwise to under-estimate the risks of serious complications ensuing with this country were a 'political' loan of this character to be granted to China.[4]

Repeated to Sir A. Clark Kerr.

[4] Sir J. Brenan commented on May 11: 'It is as well to see both sides of the case. If we were to give substantial financial assistance to China the immediate result might and probably would be intensified Japanese antagonism and interference with our commercial interests on a scale hitherto avoided. Although we believe that a Japanese victory will mean the gradual elimination, in the long run, of many important British interests in North and Central China, the long run may bring with it political changes in the world situation causing the Japanese to modify their programme. If the Japanese, with nothing more to fear from us, except war, were to harrass our coastal shipping, seize the Customs, alter the tariffs to our detriment, tighten the blockade so as to exclude British exports, occupy British premises and so on, all on the plea of military necessity, we should have to submit or go to war, and His Majesty's Government do not want to go to war with anyone, and certainly not in the Far East. I believe that wholehearted assistance to China in spite of the risk of immediate damage to our local interests would be good policy from a wider Imperial point of view, but I gather that the chances of a political loan are nil [cf. No. 535], so it is hardly worth arguing about.' Mr. Howe agreed (May 13) that there were 'no chances of a political loan but there is no reason (at least in my opinion) why we should not give China financial

help in other ways viz. credits for antimony or purchase of silver'. He noted on May 19, however, that according to the Treasury 'the Chancellor has got all the papers on this question and is now considering it. I suppose we must just wait for his reply to the S. of S.'s letters (see last one of May 13 [see No. 557, note 2])'. Sir A. Cadogan agreed (May 19), and Sir R. Vansittart added (May 20): 'I hope we shan't wait very long.' See No. 584 below.

No. 567

Sir A. Clark Kerr (Shanghai) to Foreign Office (Received May 7, 8 p.m.)

No. 726 Telegraphic: by wireless [F 4969/84/10]

SHANGHAI, *May 7, 1938*

My telegram No. 7 from Hong Kong[1].

As I understand it His Majesty's Government consider Japanese peace terms as we know them at present are disastrous to our Far Eastern position in general and that the best hope of maintaining this position is that Japan should be forced to moderate her demands and agree to peace on terms compatible with integrity of Chinese sovereignty. Further that His Majesty's Government see in continued Chinese resistance a hope that something may happen to bring this about but that although they are pledged to do everything possible to support China against aggression they find it difficult at present to offer appreciable material help.

It seems to me that we cannot escape the fact that there is force in Chiang Kai-shek's claim that to some extent Chinese are fighting our battle as well as their own for it is only a Japanese failure which can save us from this disaster to our position in the Far East.

As I have said in my earlier telegrams my visit to Central China has brought me to the belief that if we can play our part in the sense he suggests and so enable the Chinese to gain time it is by no means impossible that they themselves may well be able to bring about a situation in which the Japanese would be obliged to assent to a decent peace. Chinese are convinced that under certain conditions they can do even more than this.

For what it is worth it should be noted that limit they now set upon their efforts is two years while Military Attaché's telegram No. 483[2] puts the staying power of Japan on present scale at one year.

In view of what Chiang Kai-shek has said to me about his need for financial help and his hope that he may get it from us it seems to me that the time has come to take stock of things and to make up our minds whether we consider our position in the Far East important enough to justify a determined effort to save it or whether we are going to leave it to be destroyed. If it is worth saving we shall have to contribute to the cost; if it is not, in fairness to Chiang Kai-shek we ought to tell him once and for

[1] Not printed.

[2] No. 547.

all that he cannot count on us and let him shape his plans accordingly.

My own view which I hold strongly is that the effort would [? should] be made. I recognise that it may be something of a gamble but it is a gamble that offers good hope of success whereas the alternative is a promise of nothing but disaster. By showing this country some tangible mark of support *now* which would contribute to save it from Japanese domination we would put the Chinese under an obligation to us which would stand us in good stead when the time comes for reconstruction in which we ought I think to play a prominent part. It would also I submit do something to show that we are paying something more than lip service to the League principles.

Although it would be in my opinion a moderate premium to pay for the insurance of our position in the Far East I appreciate that for obvious reasons His Majesty's Government cannot let China have anything in the nature of political loan but I gather from Grayburn that London would be likely to take up Wolfram-Antimony scheme if assured privately of same backing by His Majesty's Government[3]. Inasmuch as the security seems to be a good one I would urge strongly that this backing should not be withheld.

If anything is to be done I think it should be done soon before financial situation deteriorates beyond redemption.

I recognise that what I have said conflicts to some extent with views expressed in my telegram No. 412[4] but strength of Central Government's resistance was not at that time apparent and in any case my views have been considerably modified by my visit to Hankow.

I would add in order that there may not be misunderstanding that I have no illusions about effects upon our position here of a successful emergence by China from the present war. It would bring with it abolition of extra-territoriality and entire recasting of our relations with this country. But I feel that these are in any case overdue and that most helpful prospect for the future of the Far East is offered by a strong and independent China which is no longer subject to exploitation by any predatory Power.[5]

Repeated to Mission and Tokyo and Saving to Hongkong.

[3] Cf. No. 557, note 2.   [4] Of March 11, not printed.
[5] Sir A. Cadogan sent a copy of this telegram to Lord Halifax at Geneva on May 11, saying that in view of the urgency Sir J. Simon's attention might be drawn to it. Meanwhile telegram No. 418 to Shanghai of May 11 read: 'I agree with your views. For your information only, the question of financial assistance to China either in connexion with the antimony scheme or by any other means which may be possible is being earnestly considered.' For Sir R. Craigie's views on telegram No. 726 see No. 570 below.

No. 568

Sir R. Craigie (Tokyo) to Foreign Office (Received May 10, 12.30 p.m.)

No. 581 Telegraphic [F 4981/16/10]

TOKYO, *May 10, 1938, 5.45 p.m.*

Your telegram No. 315[1].

I find it difficult to believe that the present moment would be opportune for a *démarche* such as the Chinese Minister for Foreign Affairs has suggested and I fear that a premature and abortive move might further exacerbate the feeling between the two countries. While I have not mentioned the proposal of the Chinese Minister for Foreign Affairs to any of my colleagues I have not found one who considers that at the present moment no [? any] mediatory action by third parties stands any chance of success.

The Chinese Minister for Foreign Affairs informed Sir A. Clark Kerr that China was not prepared to accept the four points[2] 'or anything like them'. On the other hand I have no reason to believe that Japanese Government are at the moment prepared to consider anything less than the four points. Recent pronouncements by public men in this country (see my immediately preceding telegram[3]) are as uncompromising as ever.

Only on one point do the Japanese and Chinese desiderata appear to coincide, namely, that peace must be a lasting one. This conception of a 'war to end wars' (Sino-Japanese) makes a great appeal to all sections of the population but unfortunately it is a repudiation of an equally stubborn conviction that only when China has been convinced once and for all of Japan's military might can there be any hope of a lasting peace. So far I have been unable to discover any argument capable of persuading responsible Japanese that a peace based on a mutual assumption that a colossal blunder has been made for which neither side is entirely guiltless might afford an equally promising basis for a lasting peace.

I have not discussed these matters for some time with the Minister for Foreign Affairs and I propose to take an early opportunity to introduce the subject in general terms in order to ascertain whether His Excellency has changed his ground since our last talk in regard to peace terms. I expect to meet with the usual response that Japan is determined to press until the last vestige of power of Chiang Kai-shek's régime has been destroyed. If however the Minister for Foreign Affairs' approach to the question were to be less uncompromising the opportuneness of Chinese Minister for Foreign Affairs' proposal might perhaps be reconsidered.[4]

Repeated to Sir A. Clark Kerr.

[1] This telegram of May 7 referred to Nos. 552 and 558 and asked for Sir R. Craigie's observations on the Chinese suggestion that the moment might be opportune for mediation.

[2] See No. 453.   [3] Of May 10, not printed (F 4977/84/10)

[4] Sir J. Brenan minuted on May 12: 'I submit that the time has not arrived to offer

764

mediation, however tentatively. We should find ourselves, as in 1932, acting as Japan's mouthpiece in imposing harsh terms on China.' Foreign Office telegram No. 427 to Shanghai of May 12 referred to Tokyo telegram No. 581 and instructed Sir A. Clark Kerr to tell Dr. Kung that although His Majesty's Government 'should always be ready to do what we could in the way of mediation', it seemed that 'the Chinese and Japanese are still far apart in their ideas regarding a possible settlement and that attempted mediation by third parties could lead to no useful result at the present time'.

No. 569

Mr. Edmond (Geneva) to Foreign Office (Received May 10, 6.40 p.m.)

No. 15 L.N. Telegraphic: by telephone [F 4984/78/10]

Important   GENEVA, *May 10, 1938*

Following from Secretary of State.

At a meeting of Council this morning Mr. Wellington Koo (China) stated that resolution adopted by the Assembly and the Council had not been carried out[1]. The members of the League had undertaken to consider what assistance they could individually render to China, but the latter is still having serious difficulties in obtaining supplies. Though the tide of war had recently turned in favour of Chinese Japanese atrocities were getting worse; the Japanese army are preparing to use gas and Mr. Koo asked that steps should be taken to prevent this.

Japan was a deliberate aggressor. The procedure for dealing with exactly this case was laid down in Article 17 of the Covenant. There was no risk that the application of the provisions of the Covenant in this case would entail endless complications with other States. China could fight her own battles but she expected material aid and co-operation from other Member States. He asked the Council to take concrete measures in execution of the provisions of the Covenant and of the resolutions of the Assembly.

The President of the Council said that his colleagues would no doubt wish for time to reflect on the Chinese representative's declaration and suggested the adjournment of this question to a later meeting.

It will be necessary for me to take part in the discussion of this declaration and I should be grateful for your views as soon as possible on the substance of my observations.

[1] See Nos. 288, 504, and 507.

No. 570

Sir R. Craigie (Tokyo) to Foreign Office (Received May 10, 4.50 p.m.)

No. 582 Telegraphic [F 5039/15/10]*

Confidential   TOKYO, *May 10, 1938, 8.30 p.m.*

Sir A. Clark Kerr's telegram No. 726[1] raises a question of great difficulty. He himself rules out the possibility of a political loan, but urges that His Majesty's Government should give their backing to scheme which would secure credits for China on a commercial basis.

If granting of such credits would really have effect on insuring our future position in Far East, the question deserves most careful consideration, for none can guarantee our future if Japan's victory were to be complete and overwhelming. Moreover, Japanese respect strength, and so far our protests against maltreatment of our interests in China have lacked any forceful backing. On the other hand, the granting of such credits (especially if responsibility were not to be shared with United States and France) would lead to an overwhelming outburst of fury against Great Britain, the ultimate consequences of which it is difficult to predict. If gamble came off, we should earn undying hatred of these people; if it failed, the fact that we should have made attempt will never be forgotten, and we should, moreover, have set the seal upon our losses in China.

Sir A. Clark Kerr considers the alternative of [*sic*] assisting China is a promise of nothing but disaster. While I agree that outlook is grim, I do not regard it as quite so hopeless as this. Even without financial aid, China's resistance may prove sufficiently prolonged so to undermine Japan's capacity for political and economic domination that conditions wrung from a dismembered China may in course of time prove to be as worthless to the victor as those wrung from Germany after the war.

When Chiang Kai-shek speaks of being able to hold out only for a few more months without financial assistance, he may purposely be underestimating his staying power. Doubtless, the currency cannot be maintained for much longer and Hankow may be lost, but his reserves should be sufficient to prevent 'puppet' Governments from maintaining themselves without Japanese assistance, and until those Governments can be so maintained, economic strain on this country must continue.

A consideration which it seems to me must always be present to our mind is that, whereas in a world war or threat of a world war the attitude of China would not be a determining factor, the reverse is true of Japan. Any breach of our relationship with Japan which is of such a character as to bring her irrevocably a German (? dependence) is bound sooner or later to react upon our defensive position in Europe—a risk which we can presumably ill afford to take at the moment.

If United States (and possibly French) banks could be associated in

[1] No. 567.

granting of such credits, risks of such a movement would obviously be *pro tanto* diminished, and I presume nothing would in any case be done without first ascertaining whether such support would be forthcoming. If it were forthcoming, and if United States Government were prepared to share in hazards of undertaking, the proposal would take on another complexion.[2]

Repeated to Sir A. Clark Kerr.

[2] The question of financial assistance to China was considered by the Cabinet Committee on Foreign Policy on June 1: see No. 584 below.

No. 571

Foreign Office to Mr. Edmond (Geneva)

No. 23 Telegraphic [F 4984/78/10]

Immediate   FOREIGN OFFICE, *May 11, 1938, 2.15 p.m.*

Your telegram No. 15[1].

Following for Secretary of State:

I fear it is very difficult, for reasons which are present to your mind, to say much at the Council about assistance to China.

You will not have overlooked the fact that the League resolution bound Members to consider what assistance they could *individually* render to China. This therefore is a matter to be arranged direct between the Chinese Government and other Governments, and it is not clear that the latter are answerable to the Council itself. (Nor, I should have thought, was it in China's interest that any arrangement made should be publicly announced to the Council).

If Chinese Delegate has now 'asked the Council to take concrete measures in execution of the provisions of the Covenant and of the resolutions of the Assembly', i.e. to act in its corporate capacity, he seems to be going beyond existing resolution.

If we must try to show that we have done what is possible to meet our obligations under League resolution I suggest we can only draw attention to the fact that His Majesty's Government have already taken practically all steps which are open to them *as a government* to implement their undertakings to give assistance to China, such as, for example, keeping Hongkong open. The needs of our own armament programme preclude us from permitting export of munitions on a large scale to foreign countries. We are always prepared to consider any further suggestions that may be put to us by the Chinese Government, who are aware of the difficulties with which we are confronted in various respects.

We might go on to suggest that there may be possibilities of China obtaining help from non-governmental sources. Should Chinese Govern-

[1] No. 569.

ment consider that this method of approach presents possibilities, China may rest assured that His Majesty's Government will regard such efforts from the standpoint of her undertakings under the League's resolutions.

As regards gas, reply might be to the effect that we have no information that Japanese army are in fact intending to use gas.

No. 572

Mr. Edmond (Geneva) to Foreign Office (Received May 11, 8.35 p.m.)

No. 19 L.N. Telegraphic: by telephone [F 5038/78/10]

Important   GENEVA, *May 11, 1938*

My telegram No. 15[1].

Following from Secretary of State.

Mr. Wellington Koo asked to see me this evening in order to give me his ideas of possible action by the Council in connexion with the Sino-Japanese conflict. He first of all mentioned possible measures against Japan such as embargo on arms and oil, refusal of financial assistance and boycott of Japanese goods. He did not appear to put these forward with any conviction that they would prove acceptable. He then detailed measures of assistance to China which he thought might be taken:

1. An acknowledgement by the Council of China's effort in defending her territory.

2. Encouragement of League members to restore the trade and transit facilities enjoyed by China before the outbreak of hostilities (this is aimed at France).

3. That the Council might encourage members of League to help China with arms and money.

4. That the Council pay serious attention to the allegation made by the Chinese representative regarding the possible use of gas by Japan, might denounce it as an infringement of international law of the gas protocol and might consider inviting those of its members who have Military Attachés in China to collect information on the subject in collaboration with Chinese Government.

I reminded Mr. Wellington Koo that China enjoyed reasonable transit facilities at Hongkong and as far as His Majesty's Government were concerned they were considering what help they could give China individually. I said that I would consider the other points raised by him and thought that perhaps Council might find it possible to say something on the subject of poison gas. I suggested Mr. Wellington Koo should take an early opportunity of laying his idea before the Council and should arrange with the President for a meeting for that purpose.

[1] No. 569.

Of Chinese proposals 1. seems to me irritating to the Japanese without having any practical value for the Chinese; 2. scarcely concerns us and we presumably maintain Hongkong position but if a resolution is possible though this is unlikely, do you see any objection to our concurring? 3. is dealt with by your telegram No. 23[2]. 4. I should have thought that we might concur in a properly worded anti-gas resolution. I should suppose that idea of Military Attachés collecting information is undesirable but I should be glad of arguments against it.[3]

[2] No. 571.
[3] A note on the file stated that Sir A. Cadogan and Mr. Howe discussed the terms of a reply to this telegram: see No. 573 below.

No. 573

Foreign Office to Mr. Edmond (Geneva)

No. 29 L.N. Telegraphic [F 5038/78/10]

Important   FOREIGN OFFICE, *May 12, 1938, 5 p.m.*

Your telegram No. 19[1].

Chinese Government have never been permitted by us to entertain any hopes of imposition of sanctions against Japan. As regards the detailed measures put forward by Dr. Koo our views are as follows:

(1) We agree that this may irritate Japan without having any practical value but it is no doubt put forward to give China 'face' and we see no great harm in it.

(2) I see no objection to our concurring. You will no doubt remember that we took up with M. Léger during recent visit of French Ministers[2] question of transit of arms through Indo-China. M. Léger said that transit of war material through Indo-China was absolutely prohibited and made it clear that there was no chance of French Government reversing their policy. French Government apparently take no account of League resolutions nor Chinese complaints.

(3) I agree that we might concur in a properly worded anti-gas resolution. I see no objection to our saying that we are prepared to authorise our Military Attaché in China to receive and examine any information or reports regarding the use of gas.

[1] No. 572.   [2] See Third Series, Volume I, Chapter III.

No. 574

Mr. Edmond (Geneva) to Foreign Office (Received May 16)

No. 25 Saving: Telegraphic [F 5234/78/10]

GENEVA, *May 14, 1938*

Following from Secretary of State.

Resolution on China, the text of which is being transmitted separately[1], was adopted by the Council this evening, Poland abstaining.

Mr. Wellington Koo thought that the resolution left much to be desired, but he accepted it on condition that the question remained on the agenda on the same terms as heretofore. He said China should enjoy at least the same import and transit facilities as she had had in peace time.

M. Bonnet[2] said that France had done her best to help China. He expressed the hope that neither China nor Japan would use poison gas.

I said His Majesty's Government had done their utmost, within the limits imposed upon them by their own situation, to implement previous League resolutions in China, and would continue to do so. I hoped that the information about the anticipated use of gas would prove in the end to be unfounded but I thought it a wise precausion that governments in a position to do so should obtain information on the subject.

M. Souritz (U.S.S.R.) accepted the resolution, though he would have liked it to be more concrete.

M. Komavinchi [?Komarnicki] (Poland) while abstaining from voting on the resolution as a whole expressed his government's concurrence in that portion of it which dealt with the use of poison gas.

[1] Not printed (F 5235/78/10). Reporting to the Cabinet on May 18 Lord Halifax described the outcome of the proceedings at Geneva as 'the adoption of a Resolution of sympathy with China, the endorsement of previous Resolutions, and a Resolution condemning the use of poison gas if it should be resorted to'.
[2] French Minister for Foreign Affairs since April 10, 1938.

No. 575

Viscount Halifax to Sir R. Craigie (Tokyo)

No. 305 [F 4462/71/23]

FOREIGN OFFICE, *May 17, 1938*

Sir,

In my telegram No. 335[1] I undertook to set out in some detail the reasons why I find myself unable to agree with your Excellency in thinking that it would be both easier and more advantageous to improve our

[1] See No. 553, note 7.

relations with the Japanese now rather than after the cessation of the present hostilities.

2. It seems to me that our primary aim and object must be—and I have good reason to believe that this view is shared by the United States Government—to do all that may be possible to induce the Japanese to recognise that principles, interests, law, treaty provisions and the public opinion of many countries too powerful to be disregarded in the long run are opposed to Japan's present policies and methods, and that it may pay Japan to abandon those policies and methods once and for all in her dealings not only with China but with all other foreign countries. Our secondary, though possibly more immediate, object must be to safeguard British rights, property and interests in China. Although it will obviously be unwise to adopt too rigid an attitude, I am satisfied that it will not pay us in the long run to derogate too far from the first of these objectives in the hope of attaining something of immediate benefit under the second.

3. If, for instance, we were to pursue the line advocated in your telegram No. 526[2] and were to try to arrive at some 'working arrangement with the Japanese,' I have no doubt that a point would rapidly be reached at which we should be asked to give something concrete in return for the safeguarding of our interests. That something could only be the abandonment of China's cause as exemplified by the stoppage of supplies through Hong Kong, work on the Burma-Yunnan road and the recognition in some form of the legality of Japan's aggression—in fact, a complete *volte-face* and the repudiation of our League obligations.

4. You suggested (paragraph 5) that an attempt might be made to negotiate some arrangement of limited scope analogous to the Customs Agreement and having as its object the protection of our railway interests in China. This idea appears also to commend itself to His Majesty's Ambassador in China (see paragraph 2 of Shanghai telegram No. 688 of the 1st May[3]). I am not at present convinced that it will be to our interest in the long run to act quite in this way. The Customs Agreement,[4] though in many ways a considerable achievement, in effect amounted to a withdrawal by His Majesty's Government of their opposition to the seizure of the customs revenues in the occupied territories, provided that the foreign obligations secured thereon continued to be paid. The Chinese, not entirely without justification, are liable to regard the agreement as a selfish deal, and I understand that His Majesty's Government are already being accused in the United States press of saving their interests at China's expense. Any agreement designed to secure analogous treatment for our railway interests would, I fear, involve an admission that the Japanese might appropriate the railways, which, of course, are Chinese property, provided that they paid off British loans and debts secured thereon. That may conceivably prove to be a solution for those areas in which we abandon hope of retaining any political influence, but to my mind it is

---

[2] No. 553. [3] No. 560. [4] See No. 565.

much too early to abandon hope for Central China. In any case, I am not sure that this is what the Japanese had in mind when they asked the military attaché for suggestions as to how they might protect specific British railway interests.

5. I remain then in principle averse from any idea of entering into any such formal arrangement as the Customs Agreement on any other subject, though naturally I should favour the negotiation of informal *ad hoc* arrangements to cover such subjects as those mentioned by Sir Archibald Clark Kerr, railways, Whangpoo conservancy, river navigation and discrimination against British trade, wherever this may be done solely to avoid unnecessary friction and without obvious benefit to the aggressor or detriment to the victim and I shall be glad if you will continue to explore the possibilities in this direction.

6. To turn to your Excellency's contention that, unless we succeed during the period of hostilities in arriving at some working arrangement with the Japanese for the safeguarding of our interests in China, an agreement for their adequate protection after the war is likely to prove more difficult. It seems to me that this proposition might be examined with advantage in the light of what the Japanese might be expected to do if hostilities ended to-morrow. It will be clear from the texts of the Bills recently passed by the Diet, the substance of which appeared in the *North China Herald* of the 30th March, that the principal object of the Japanese in forming the North China Development Company and the Central China Promotion Company is to ensure the immediate control and the ultimate elimination of foreign enterprise in these two areas. At first they set out merely to make provision for the orderly development of the areas in question on well-considered lines and to prevent reckless competition between Japanese interests. In the initial stages foreign capital is to be invited to invest in these companies, but it is made abundantly clear that the foreign shareholder is to have no participation in their direction or control. The two monopolistic 'national policy' companies are to control all public utilities, the supply of electricity, gas and water, transport and communications on land and water, mining and salt manufacture. As you are aware, we have considerable interests in the port of Shanghai itself, including such public utilities as the waterworks, gas company, tramways and omnibus services. The electric light and power company and the telephone company are American. The activities of these companies are not confined within the boundaries of the foreign settlement; they extend outside and are to a large extent dependent on the goodwill of the Chinese authorities in the surrounding district. The water-works company, for instance, draws water from the river and supplies it to extra-Settlement areas under a Chinese municipal franchise; the Settlement telephone system is connected with that of other districts, and so on. Once they have displaced the present Chinese authorities and are firmly installed in their special city completely encircling the foreign Settlement, the Japanese, without overt or active interference, would in a short time

be able to make things so difficult for the British and United States companies inside the Settlement that they would have to admit Japanese participation and control or sell out at a loss. If other methods proved too slow, the Japanese could always instigate labour troubles, as they have done with the Kailan Mining Administration in North China. This process of squeezing out foreign interests and enterprise would be easy and expeditious in the Shanghai area: in the north there would be even fewer obstacles in the way.

7. It would seem then that if the war were to end to-morrow, the Japanese would be likely to give effect to these grandiose and ambitious plans to the early detriment, if not extinction, of all foreign competition. Such an extensive programme, however, would require a considerable capital. Our hope must be that neither capital, nor Chinese, nor foreign co-operation will be forthcoming in sufficient quantity to make the schemes a success. I am inclined to think that that hope is more likely to be realised the longer hostilities continue. Military operations while they last constitute a considerable strain on Japanese finance; economic development, or exploitation of the expected gains will inevitably constitute another strain. Surely, our position will be at its strongest when on top of the first strain the second strain is making itself most apparent? The need for foreign help at that stage will be at its maximum and at its most obvious, even to the totalitarians, and I find it difficult not to believe that the terms most advantageous to ourselves, and incidentally to the Chinese, will then be obtainable.

8. The arguments used in your telegram No. 526 appear to me to be based on the expectation that the Japanese will in the end achieve a complete victory. I was much impressed by the views expressed in Sir Archibald Clark Kerr's telegram No. 2 from Hong Kong of the 28th April[5], and I for my part am not yet convinced that the Japanese will necessarily win the war. They can perhaps go on winning battles for some time to come, but it is not easy to see how they will succeed in subduing the whole of China, or even bringing the greater part of it under effective control for the purpose of economic exploitation. I anticipate that the unsubdued portion may well in the end frustrate their efforts to pacify and develop the occupied territory. They cannot make an economic or political success of their adventure by force of arms alone, and this is already recognised by the saner elements in Japan, as is evidenced by the peace feelers and tentative invitations to mediation which they constantly put forward. I continue to think that the outcome of the war may yet be something approaching a stalemate, and it seems to me that in playing for such a stalemate His Majesty's Government may repose the best hope for the survival of British influence in the Far East. An immediate peace on Japanese terms would face us with the prospect outlined in paragraph 6 above, and I cannot see that it could be much worse. A Japan exhausted by

[5] No. 555.

a lengthy war may well be compelled to abandon a good part of her ambitious plans and may have to listen with more respect to our views regarding the proper treatment of the interests of other nations.

9. Finally it seems to me that the earlier the war ends the more likely Japan is to be able to finance and prosecute her schemes outside China proper, the extrusion of the Russians from the Maritime Province and the southward expansion. The earlier they attain success in China therefore the more immediate the danger to the British, Netherlands and United States dependencies in the South Seas. It seems to me then that it will not be to our interest to do anything now which may be of direct or indirect assistance to Japan, for, if we do, we should increase the probability of the early extinction of our interests in China itself and the danger to our possessions in the Far East generally.[6]

I am, &c.,
HALIFAX

[6] For Sir R. Craigie's reply to this despatch see No. 600 below.

No. 576

Sir R. Craigie (Tokyo) to Viscount Halifax
(Received May 19, 12.15 p.m.)

No. 604[1] Telegraphic [F 5386/12/10]

TOKYO, May 19, 1938, 3.50 p.m.

My telegram No. 458[2].

I reminded Minister for Foreign Affairs this morning that I had as yet noticed no tangible results from the serious representations I had addressed to him on April 11th in regard to treatment by Japanese authorities of British interests and subjects in China, a communication which had subsequently received your full approval. On the contrary further instances of discrimination or ill-treatment had occurred and I drew special attention to Wil(? kinson) case[3] in regard to which I spoke very strongly. As an instance of high-handed action affecting Customs and International Settlement I mentioned the arrests made by the Japanese gendarmerie (see Shanghai telegram No. 759[4]). I spoke again in the sense reported in my telegram No. 458, but even more pointedly and enquired whether there was no way of bringing home to Japanese military and naval authorities in China the great disservice they were doing to their

[1] Telegrams Nos. 603 (No. 577 below) and 604 were despatched in reverse order.
[2] No. 545.
[3] Mr. E. S. Wilkinson, head of Thomson & Co., Chartered Accountants, had been arrested and wounded by Japanese military authorities in Shanghai on May 13 while out birdwatching.
[4] Of May 12, not printed.

country's interests by their present proceedings. His Excellency would be as well aware as I of constant pressure that was being brought to bear on His Majesty's Government to depend, for protection of British interests, on the provision of economic assistance to Chinese National Government rather than on Japanese Government's assurances which were not implemented locally. Finally I handed to Minister for Foreign Affairs a list of various cases in regard to which my representations had either been left without reply or met with no satisfaction.

Minister for Foreign Affairs said he believed one of the main causes of the difficulty continued to be the bad personal relations existing between Japanese and British authorities in China for which Japanese could certainly not be held entirely to blame. Settlement of outstanding difficulties and the prevention of fresh incidents would be facilitated by an improvement in these relations. For this reason both Japanese Government and Japanese authorities had welcomed the decision that Major General Piggott should visit Shanghai (see my telegram No. 603[5]) and it was greatly to be hoped that this would have good results.

I agreed with Minister for Foreign Affairs as to the great importance of improving personal relationships, but said that, even if one made allowances for emotional stress under which Japanese officers in China were working, it nevertheless was entirely inadmissible that they should permit personal antagonisms to jeopardise their country's interests and obstruct the execution of declared policy of their Government. I hoped that impending visit of the Military Attaché would be used not only to improve personal relationship but as an opportunity for a renewed effort to settle outstanding cases of discrimination and ill-treatment.

His Excellency agreed that the visit should be made signal for such an effort and promised to do what he could in this direction. He will study carefully the various documents I left with him and appreciated my point that present moment was not suitable for the making of any striking 'gesture' (as had been advocated by some) but should rather be used for an unostentatious removal of existing grounds of dispute between our two Governments with a view to a better understanding when war was over.

Repeated to Sir A. Clark Kerr.

[5] No. 577 below.

No. 577

Sir R. Craigie (Tokyo) to Viscount Halifax (Received May 19, 1 p.m.)

No. 603 Telegraphic [F 5412/12/10]

TOKYO, *May 19, 1938, 5.25 p.m.*

After consultation with Sir A. Clark Kerr it has been decided that the

Military Attaché should pay a short visit to Shanghai in the course of which it might be possible for him to assist in discovering and removing some of the causes of personal friction between certain of the British and Japanese authorities in Shanghai.[1] Military Attaché has of course no illusions as to the difficulties involved but I feel his visit can do no harm and may be productive of much good. He is due to arrive on May 30th.

It is possible that some of our authorities in Shanghai do not quite appreciate the importance of personal element in our efforts to secure better treatment for British interests in China. To the Japanese mind this matter of personal contact plays a part which to our mind appears exaggerated in approach to all such questions and it is difficult for our countrymen who have not lived in Japan fully to appreciate this. It is furthermore obvious that apparent inadequate control exercised by Japanese Government over their naval and military authorities in China and by those authorities over their subordinates makes it particularly . . .[2] for officers smarting under a mistaken sense of grievance to thwart policies of their Government. I would go so far as to say that a pre-requisite for adequate protection of our interests in China consists in an improvement in their personal relations particularly in Shanghai. If this can once be achieved our task in Tokyo will be greatly facilitated.

I do not for a moment suggest that there should be any truckling—quite to the contrary. But it is possible to combine firmness in protection of our interests with utmost politeness and patience, of which qualities I fear a large stock is necessary. Japanese affirm that there has been far less personal friction in the case of other nationalities, the relations maintained with Japanese by Americans being comparatively good.

I have ventured to submit the above considerations because I believe that if Military Attaché's visit cannot be turned to good account there is a danger that situation may go from bad to worse. Minister for Foreign Affairs assures me that Japanese naval and military authorities are prepared to made a special effort to use the opportunity so presented for eliminating personal difficulties and misunderstandings and I earnestly hope their opposite numbers among British authorities will be prepared to reciprocate.[3]

Repeated to Sir A. Clark Kerr.

[1] Major General Piggott had exceptionally long and affectionate links with Japan: see Volume XX, No. 486, note 5. He had spent three years in Tokyo as a child, and had already served three terms in Japan during his career, including his appointment as Military Attaché 1921–6. With his knowledge of Japanese and friendships extending over many years with some of the senior Japanese officers he was a strong believer in the importance of personal contact at the higher official levels as a means of removing some at least of the causes of Anglo-Japanese friction. His autobiography, *Broken Thread, op. cit.*, gives a good account of his visit to Shanghai in May 1938 (pp. 302–8).

[2] The text was here uncertain: the word 'easy' was suggested on the filed copy.

[3] In private and personal telegram No. 458 of May 24 to Shanghai Mr. Howe told Sir A. Clark Kerr that he was 'not optimistic that [General Piggott's visit] will achieve any lasting improvement in the relations between ourselves and the Japanese military at Shanghai. . .

There seems to be no doubt that there is a definite anti-British sentiment in the Japanese Army in China which manifests itself down not only to the junior officers but also to the rank and file. . .' He criticized General Piggott for tending to the view that 'the bad relations between ourselves and the Japanese at Shanghai are the fault of our officials there', but then went on to make more personal criticisms of the attitude of Major General Telfer-Smollett, Commander of British troops in Shanghai (F 5412/12/10).

No. 578

Sir R. Craigie (Tokyo) to Viscount Halifax (Received May 19, 2.45 p.m.)

No. 605 Telegraphic [F 5389/84/10]

TOKYO, *May 19, 1938, 7.40 p.m.*

In course of my talk today[1] with Minister for Foreign Affairs I brought conversation round to the question of Japanese aims in China. The upshot of the fairly long conversation which followed may be summarised as follows: Japanese Government believe victory at Hsuchow which now appears a foregone conclusion[2] will apart from its general effect on military situation have a serious effect on Chiang Kai-shek's personal position. It will be necessary for the General to decide at *Hankow* what his future course is to be—he will be unable to retire progressively into the interior because of reluctance of the provinces hitherto unscathed by war to offer their territory as scene of future operations. For this reason Japanese Government do not believe Chiang Kai-shek can in any case hold out indefinitely. With reference to Japanese Government's declaration of January 16th[3] Minister for Foreign Affairs pointed out that even from Chiang Kai-shek's own point of view it would be impossible for him to negotiate for peace in the rôle of a defeated General—he would be obliged in any case to give way to others before negotiations started. Should he decide to do so without undue delay it should be possible for reconstituted régime at Hankow to enter into discussion with Provisional Government in Peking and Nanking for constitution of a government representing the whole of China with which it would be possible for Japan to negotiate for a lasting peace. To a government so constituted it would be possible for Japan to offer more generous terms than those offered and rejected by Chiang Kai-shek.

I said that my information as to the personal position of Chiang Kai-shek did not at all coincide with Minister for Foreign Affairs and that so far as unoccupied China was concerned he appeared to be the accepted ruler and the national hero. But I thanked His Excellency for his

[1] See No. 576.
[2] A general offensive against the important town of Hsuchow, which stood at the junction of the Tsinpu and Lunghai railways, was launched at the beginning of May by Japanese troops who had been advancing along the railways since the end of March. Hsuchow fell on May 20.
[3] See No. 488.

explanation of the method by which Japanese Government hoped that peace would eventually be restored and I felt sure that it would be useful to you to know what was in his mind.[4]

Repeated to Sir A. Clark Kerr.

[4] Commenting generally on this telegram Sir J. Brenan remarked that the Japanese Government presumably realized 'that they cannot negotiate a real peace with a puppet Chinese government of their own creation. . . They must negotiate sooner or later with the authorities who are conducting the resistance on the other side. They have rather foolishly declared that they will have no further dealings with Chiang Kai-shek and have tied their hands so far as he is concerned, so they are now working for a split in the Chinese camp and are suggesting that more favourable terms will be given if Chiang retires . . . J. F. Brenan. 23/5.'

No. 579

Sir R. Craigie (Tokyo) to Viscount Halifax (Received May 21, 11 a.m.)

No. 611 Telegraphic [F 5456/5/10]

TOKYO, *May 21, 1938, 5.25 p.m.*

Since my telegram No. 39[1] I have on two occasions reminded the Japanese Government that in connexion with Wuhu incident we expected punishment of Colonel Hashimoto.

The Director of Military Intelligence had now informed the Military Attaché confidentially that Colonel Hashimoto has been placed on the retired list. His exact words are interesting: 'We have had the greatest difficulty in bringing this about owing to his political influence but we have at last succeeded'.

I think this is a clear case of removing a source of friction and there is no doubt that it has been done in face of many obstacles largely as a result of our representations.[2]

Repeated to Sir A. Clark Kerr.

[1] See No. 500, note 2.
[2] Mr. Howe commented on May 24: 'It takes a great deal of effort to remove one dug-out colonel.'

No. 580

Viscount Halifax to Sir R. Lindsay (Washington)

No. 445 [F 5558/15/10]*

FOREIGN OFFICE, *May 25, 1938*

Sir,

You will no doubt have observed in the printed sections Sir Robert

Craigie's telegrams to me Nos. 556[1], 559[2] and 570[3], in which he expressed some disappointment at receiving no support from his United States colleague in connexion with the arrangement recently negotiated with the Japanese Government in regard to the China Customs.

2. As your Excellency is aware, I consider it very desirable that there should be close and friendly co-operation between ourselves and the United States Government whenever this is possible. There are many difficulties in the way of achieving this, and disappointments are inevitable from time to time. I do feel, however, that it would be foolish to allow ourselves to be unduly discouraged whenever the United States Government do not give us all the support for which we might have wished. And I think that it is necessary to make a serious effort to understand the United States point of view whenever they fail to collaborate. As I feel that Sir Robert Craigie's telegrams, as they stand and without full knowledge of their context, may give rise to the impression that in the matter of the China Customs the United States Government have behaved in such a manner as seriously to prejudice the hope that we may some day achieve a real co-operation in the Far East, I have endeavoured in the following paragraphs to set out the sequence of events as they have been reported to me, and so remove any false impression as to the extent to which the United States may be regarded as having failed us in this particular matter.

3. In the earlier stages of the discussion of the customs problem, a certain measure of parallel action was achieved on several occasions by the British, French and United States representatives at Tokyo, and this had the effect of restraining the Japanese from drastic action, for instance the seizure of the Customs Office at Shanghai, and of bringing them to a frame of mind in which they were prepared to negotiate a settlement with the interested Powers. (The United States and French Governments also supported the representations made by His Majesty's Ambassador against the introduction of new tariff rates by the local authorities in North China.) When, however, in February last, it became plain that the Japanese Government were prepared to negotiate a detailed settlement, it was found that there was a fundamental difference of method between His Majesty's Government and the United States Government. The earlier parallel action had taken the form of a request for certain general assurances, for example, that the administrative integrity of the Customs would be maintained, and that the service of the foreign loans should not be prejudiced. The United States Government took the line that these assurances must be forthcoming before any detailed plan could usefully be examined, while the view of His Majesty's Government was that with the demand for assurances a detailed arrangement ought to be negotiated

---

[1] See No. 563, note 1.   [2] No. 563.
[3] This telegram of May 6 referred to the U.S. proposal for a *démarche* regarding the customs agreement; see *ibid.*, note 2.

under which Japan would be expressly bound to provide for third parties' interests in a certain way. Our objections to the method advocated by the United States Government were that the Japanese Government would refuse to give satisfactory general assurances, because this would limit their freedom of action too much; secondly, if any assurances were obtained, the Japanese would manage to evade them; and, thirdly, Sir Robert Craigie feared that the United States Government, having obtained their assurances, would rest content and not support a later demand for specific guarantees, while the Japanese Government, for their part, would receive the impression that they were at liberty to make, within the framework of these inevitably vague assurances, whatever specific arrangements they pleased.

4. The United States Government's objection to our method was, I presume, that any detailed negotiations would lead to a compromise, which might be interpreted as a bargain with the aggressor at China's expense. Sir Robert Craigie was of opinion that the United States Government held this view so strongly that they would persist in their refusal to join in asking for specific guarantees, even after the general assurances had been obtained, and even if these assurances were obviously unsatisfactory. How far this was justified is, perhaps, a matter for some doubt, seeing that in a note addressed to the Japanese Government on the 12th February, the United States Ambassador had used the words: 'Before examining any plan for a settlement of the Customs problem, the United States Government expect to receive from the Japanese Government broad and positive assurances . . .'[4] However that may be, Sir Robert Craigie summed up the situation on the same date by saying: 'Actually, the divergence goes deeper than the method, for while we are prepared to fight for our rights in China, step by step, the Americans are not, and prefer to take refuge in generalities, for fear of becoming too deeply involved in protecting "vested interests."'

5. Early in January, the Japanese communicated to the customs authorities at Shanghai a plan under which they would obtain complete control of the revenues. His Majesty's Government thereupon endeavoured to persuade the United States and French Governments to support them in pressing upon the Japanese an alternative plan under which the revenue would be placed out of Japanese reach, and its control would be vested in some kind of international body. The French Government, though sceptical of success, agreed to associate themselves with the proposal, but the United States Government declined, on the ground that the Japanese Government would be so exasperated that they would not even give the general assurances which the three Powers had already demanded. They proposed instead that all three Governments should join in a further demand for these general assurances. With this proposal His Majesty's Government were, at first, disposed to concur. But,

[4] Cf. No. 520.

for the reasons given above, Sir Robert Craigie deemed it essential to negotiate a detailed plan simultaneously. As the United States Government did not agree with this method, he suggested that Great Britain, as the Power chiefly concerned, should take the lead in the negotiations, and that he should keep his French and United States colleagues informed of developments. Joint action by Great Britain and France was ruled out, seeing that this could not but emphasise the divergence of their views from those of the United States Government. This divergence, of course, resulted, among other things, in its being impossible to ask as much of the Japanese Government as had been hoped.

6. The Foreign Office, at the instance of the Treasury, now took the line that, in view of the United States attitude, little more could be hoped for than a satisfactory settlement as regards foreign loan quotas, and this the Treasury were more than anxious to obtain. Sir Robert Craigie was accordingly authorised to negotiate with the Japanese Government on this basis in the manner suggested by him.

7. This isolated action was, therefore, to a large extent of our own choosing. We could have adopted the United States method, but chose not to do so because we feared that it would produce no results. And, in fact, the Japanese Vice-Minister for Foreign Affairs very soon confirmed that his Government were not prepared to give any general assurances. Having chosen this line, His Majesty's Government could no longer expect much assistance from the United States or French Governments. In fact, however, the United States Ambassador not only offered no comments on Sir Robert Craigie's periodical reports of developments, but actually received instructions at the last moment, after the arrangement had been all but concluded, to inform his British colleague that the United States Government saw certain objections to the arrangement and must reserve their position in regard to it.

8. Having just brought to a successful conclusion a long, arduous and delicate negotiation which appeared likely to benefit United States as well as British bondholders, Sir Robert Craigie was naturally somewhat disappointed, and in his telegram No. 557 of the 3rd May[1] he gave vent to his exasperation, saying that the United States 'attitude throughout the negotiations has been very unhelpful, and in marked contrast to that of the French Government.' On the whole, however, I am inclined to the view that the failure of the United States Government to co-operate in this particular matter must be attributed to the fundamental divergence of opinion as to method referred to in paragraph 3 above, and to the different character and scope of the United States interests involved as compared with those British interests to safeguard which His Majesty's Government were working. It is too early to judge whether the line to which His Majesty's Government finally committed themselves was the right one; only time can show this, and it is possible that in the end the United States view will be proved to have been the wiser. On balance, I feel that we should certainly not allow ourselves to be discouraged by this

apparent setback to Anglo-American co-operation, and still less allow the impression to persist in our minds that the United States Government have been guilty of a serious deviation from the principles of Anglo-American co-operation, to which they profess to attach so much importance.

9. I am sending copies of this despatch to His Majesty's Ambassadors at Tokyo and Shanghai.[5]

I am, &c.,

HALIFAX

[5] The Customs agreement was never implemented: the Chinese Government refused to allow funds to be transferred from the Hongkong and Shanghai Bank or to release the Boxer Indemnity funds, although current revenues began to be deposited in the Yokohama Specie Bank. The further course of negotiations on this issue has not been documented in this volume, but can be followed in the Confidential Print.

No. 581

Viscount Halifax to Sir R. Craigie (Tokyo)

No. 379 Telegraphic [F 5775/16/10]

FOREIGN OFFICE, May 31, 1938, 10 p.m.

The Japanese Ambassador informed me on the 31st May that in his opinion the recent cabinet changes[1] resulted from the recognition of the growing unpopularity of the war and that new Foreign Minister was anxious for better relations with this country.

He then reverted, though without specific instructions, to the request that His Majesty's Government should mediate at the appropriate moment, to which I replied that we had never been able to feel any great assurance that any basis of mediation in fact existed. His Excellency said that except for the cessation of the anti-Japanese movement in China and, in his opinion, 'some special provision' with regard to the provinces bordering on Manchuria, the Japanese Government would make no preliminary conditions for mediation. Chinese territorial integrity would be preserved and foreign interests respected.

When His Excellency asked that you should be sent the requisite instructions, I replied that you were already sufficiently aware of my views and that you would be able to advise whether there is any opening for useful action by His Majesty's Government at any time.[2]

Repeated to Shanghai No. 481.

[1] It was announced in Tokyo on May 26 that General Kazushige Ugaki was to replace Mr. Hirota as Foreign Minister: Mr. Ikeda became Minister of Finance, and General Araki Minister of Education.

[2] Sir R. Craigie replied in telegram No. 668 of June 2 that he did not feel that 'formation of new Government offers any immediate prospect for successful mediation' and that Mr. Hirota had been removed because of his well-known opposition to an intensification of the

China campaign: if an advance on Hankow had been decided upon 'no good opportunity for mediation seems likely to occur until that objective has been achieved'. He would, however, 'watch carefully for the slightest sign that any step on the part of His Majesty's Government would be welcome'.

No. 582

Sir R. Craigie (Tokyo) to Viscount Halifax (Received May 31, 4.10 p.m.)

No. 660 Telegraphic [F 5849/71/23]

TOKYO, May 31, 1938, 11.10 p.m.

Minister for Foreign Affairs[1] received heads of Missions this afternoon. In the course of my necessarily brief interview Minister for Foreign Affairs referred to traditional relations of friendship between Japan and Great Britain, expressed his regret that these should recently have become clouded and declared his firm intention of doing everything in his power to eliminate all causes of discord. It was His Excellency's intention to examine personally all questions at issue and he wished to emphasize that he would always be at my complete disposal for discussion of such matters. He had had little experience as a diplomat but he believed in absolute frank treatment of such questions and hoped he could rely on me to approach matters in the same spirit.

After I had warmly responded to this overture I enquired whether I might inform you that assurances given by the former Government in regard to protection of foreign rights and interests in China held good in every way. General Ugaki replied with emphasis that I could not only inform you that policy of the Government in this respect was the same as that of its predecessor but that as far as British rights and interests were concerned, you could rely on an even more strenuous effort being made in the future to ensure this protection. Often the authorities on the spot were inclined to be influenced by false reports and rumours but His Excellency repeated that he desired to treat all such questions from wider standpoint of ultimate interests of our two countries and to liquidate them as quickly as possible.

In taking my leave I said that I felt sure that you would be glad to learn of assurances I had received and that he could rely on the co-operation of His Majesty's Government and British authorities in China in settling outstanding difficulties and preventing new ones from arising.

Repeated to Sir A. Clark Kerr.

[1] i.e. General Ugaki.

No. 583

Sir R. Craigie (Tokyo) to Viscount Halifax (Received May 31, 7.40 p.m.)

No. 661 Telegraphic [F 5850/71/23]

TOKYO, *June 1, 1938, 12.5 a.m.*

My immediately preceding telegram[1].

I was much impressed with friendliness and sincerity of new Minister for Foreign Affairs. Although I had met him previously I had not had an opportunity to discuss Anglo-Japanese relations and there is no doubt in my mind that he intends to make a very real effort to put our relations on a better footing and to settle outstanding problems. The General is a man of energy and strength of character and I feel no doubt that if he really intends to implement the assurances he gave me today useful results will follow. I was particularly impressed by his obvious desire to discuss with me individual cases of difficulty in our relations—a readiness which had never been displayed to the same degree by his predecessor who was prone to depute such tiresome matters to his subordinates.

Possibly diplomatic office may diminish the General's first enthusiasm in this respect but I am of opinion that he will stand up to the army and navy in a way his predecessor has not dared to do and that prospects for a more rapid settlement of outstanding questions have definitely improved.

In this first interview I was careful to avoid any controversial questions. If you feel disposed to authorise me to express gratification at the assurances which I have transmitted to you I feel sure that it would be all to the good.[2]

I venture also to express the earnest hope that until this new prospect of improving our situation in China has been explored no irrevocable step will be taken such as the granting of credits to China. Taking a somewhat longer view than Chinese Government can be expected to take in present circumstances I am as convinced today, as when I first arrived, that there are other and more efficacious methods of assisting China to her feet than granting direct assistance to her in present struggle and driving of Japan irretrievably into the camp of landgrabbers and totalitarians.

Repeated to Sir A. Clark Kerr.

---

[1] No. 582.
[2] Sir R. Craigie was so authorized in Foreign Office telegram No. 387 of June 3.

No. 584

Extract from Conclusions of the Thirtieth Meeting of the Cabinet Committee on Foreign Policy held in the Prime Minister's Room, House of Commons on Wednesday, June 1, 1938, at 5.30 p.m.

Cab. 27/623

Secret

PRESENT: Mr. Chamberlain, Prime Minister (*in the Chair*); Sir J. Simon, Chancellor of the Exchequer; Lord Halifax, Secretary of State for Foreign Affairs; Mr. M. MacDonald, Secretary of State for the Colonies; Lord Hailsham, Lord President of the Council; Lord Stanley, Secretary of State for Dominion Affairs; Sir T. Inskip, Minister for Co-ordination of Defence; Mr. O. Stanley, President of the Board of Trade; Mr. R. S. Hudson, Parliamentary Secretary, Department of Overseas Trade; Sir R. B. Howorth (*Assistant Secretary*).

2. THE SECRETARY OF STATE FOR FOREIGN AFFAIRS raised as a matter of urgency the question of the Chinese request for financial assistance, and copies of a Memorandum were handed round at the Meeting by the Secretary of State for Foreign Affairs. (For convenience of reference a copy of this Memorandum is attacked to these Conclusions, see Appendix I[1]).

The Secretary of State for Foreign Affairs observed that his Memorandum had been prepared in consultation with the Treasury.

THE CHANCELLOR OF THE EXCHEQUER said that while the Treasury had had an opportunity of seeing an advance copy of the Memorandum, they had not participated in its preparation, and it must not be regarded as in any way representing the Treasury point of view.

THE SECRETARY OF STATE FOR FOREIGN AFFAIRS said that the short point was that some little time ago the Government of China made a proposal that we should in some way assist them to raise money on certain metals which are essential for armament production and of which the Chinese supplies are the largest in the world, the metals in question being wolfram and antimony.[2]

The Chancellor of the Exchequer would no doubt inform the Committee as to the economic aspects of the proposal, but there was a very large political aspect as well, and as the Committee would observe there were powerful arguments set out in paragraphs 8 to 15 inclusive of the Memorandum in favour of helping China and strong reasons to the contrary set out in paragraph 16. In the face of these conflicting opinions it would now be necessary for the Committee to reach some decision.

---

[1] See Appendix to this document: neither drafts nor the final copy of this memorandum have been kept in F.O. archives.
[2] See Nos. 535 and 541.

Lord Halifax added that his own instincts were all strongly in favour of assisting China in some such manner as was now proposed. From the point of view of morality, China's case strongly appealed to him, and there was also the powerful argument that provided adequate financial assistance could now be given to China she might in the end succeed in defeating Japan owing to the exhaustion of the latter. The arguments from the point of view of our own defensive arrangements were not perhaps so strong, but they could be used to supplement the other arguments. In any event, it was imperative that the Government should make up their minds as to the action to be taken with as little delay as practicable.

THE LORD PRESIDENT OF THE COUNCIL recalled a recent telegram in which it was suggested that China might approach the United States of America on somewhat similar lines. Might it not be as well to interest the U.S.A. in the proposal so that if the United States agreed to share our responsibilities in the matter we should not be left alone to face a Japanese outburst of fury?

THE SECRETARY OF STATE FOR FOREIGN AFFAIRS thought that in this matter the U.S.A. would certainly refuse to join in any common action with us.

THE CHANCELLOR OF THE EXCHEQUER said that broadly speaking the views of the Treasury were summarised in paragraph 16 of the Memorandum. His advisers had provided him with very formidable support for the views expressed by Sir R. Craigie in his telegram of the 10th May 1938 (No. 582), a copy of which is annexed as Appendix II to these Conclusions[3]. He (the Chancellor of the Exchequer) felt that it was exceedingly difficult to decide whether the proposal should be accepted in principle, and if so what precise form it should take. The matter needed the most careful and exhaustive examination. He then read to the Committee extracts from Sir R. Craigie's telegram, and pointed out that no language could have conveyed a plainer or more serious warning, and that it was the language of the man on the spot who was in the best possible position to judge of how Japan was likely to react to our acceptance of any scheme for giving assistance to China.

THE MINISTER FOR CO-ORDINATION OF DEFENCE pointed out that Sir R. Craigie's telegram did not appear to take account of the arguments set out in paragraph 10 of the Memorandum that in the event of a Japanese victory our interests in the Far East were certainly doomed to extinction, and that in particular we should be excluded from China and our immense vested interests there would be destroyed. It appeared to him that the answer to the question raised in the Memorandum very largely depended on whether the opinions expressed by Sir R. Craigie or by Sir A. Clark Kerr were the right ones.

THE LORD PRESIDENT OF THE COUNCIL enquired whether Sir R. Craigie

[3] See No. 570.

accepted the view that in the event of a Japanese victory our interests in China were doomed to extinction.

The Chancellor of the Exchequer said that as he read the telegram Sir R. Craigie was prepared to admit that our future prospects in China would be by no means bright if Japan proved successful.

The Prime Minister pointed out that almost every other important country was sending supplies of all sorts to China, and that while apparently other countries could lend money and show favour in other ways to China with impunity we alone would be subject to intense Japanese hostility and to threats that Japan would be drawn definitely into Germany's orbit if we ventured to comply with China's request for financial help. All this was a somewhat hard measure and difficult to understand.

The Chancellor of the Exchequer observed that none of the other countries in question had given hostages to fortune such as we had given in the case of Hong Kong. So far as the practical side of the problem was concerned it was clear and agreed by everyone that there could be no question of a British Government loan to China or of British Government credit being made available in any form. There remained therefore a Chinese loan raised in the usual way in the City of London. Regarded as an ordinary commercial proposition, the difficulties in the way of the suggestion in the opening paragraphs of the Memorandum appeared well-nigh insuperable. The metals in question which were to form the security for the loan were still under the ground, and it was by no means certain that China would remain in control of the surface during the period of three years when the undertakers were to recoup themselves by extracting the metals. We ourselves did not require these particular supplies for our own defence purposes. As explained in the Memorandum, if we were engaged in war we should rely on supplies from Burma.

The Governor of the Bank of England had ascertained from the Hong Kong and Shanghai Bank that Sir Vandeleur Grayburn, the Chairman of that Bank, was arriving in London on June 2nd. In any case nothing could obviously be done until the whole question had been discussed with Sir Vandeleur. The alternative suggestion that a book credit might be opened which would enable the Chinese Government to draw on London as the supplies of metal came forward did not seem very attractive.

The Chinese apparently hoped to obtain about £20,000,000. Sir Frederick Leith-Ross thought that in favourable circumstances the City might conceivably produce about £1,000,000.[4] Would a sum of this order make any real difference and enable China to continue her resistance? It must be obvious that any value to China lay not in the financial aspect of the proposal but in the psychological aspect that she was at least receiving some direct help from Britain, and that this might encourage other countries to follow our example. The fact that we were not going to, and

[4] *Note in original*: It afterwards appeared that Sir Frederick Leith-Ross had taken the view that in favourable circumstances the City might conceivably produce about £5,000,000.

could not in fact, give China any substantial help might be of some small assistance from the point of view of Chinese propaganda, and might for a brief period help to sustain the Chinese currency, but it would certainly infuriate the Japanese and might involve us in the most serious consequences, vis à vis Japan. In short, we would run very substantial risks of doing China little, if any, good while creating the maximum amount of trouble and danger with Japan.

THE PRIME MINISTER pointed out that in paragraph 3 of the Memorandum it was stated that it would not be possible to interest British firms in any proposal on the lines of the wolfram scheme, unless it was actively supported by His Majesty's Government.

THE CHANCELLOR OF THE EXCHEQUER observed that it was quite possible that on his arrival Sir Vandeleur Grayburn would say that the proposal was one which he could not for a moment recommend his Bank to entertain.

THE PRESIDENT OF THE BOARD OF TRADE said that the proposal seemed to him to be an attempt by the Chinese Government to obtain a British Government loan disguised in the form of a commercial transaction. The disguise was extremely thin and regarded as a purely commercial proposition the proposal seemed extremely unattractive.

THE MINISTER FOR CO-ORDINATION OF DEFENCE agreed that the security offered appeared to be very miserable and inadequate.

THE PRIME MINISTER asked whether, even if China obtained the money from us, what guarantee was there that she would not immediately hand it over to Soviet Russia? She had obtained large supplies of arms and ammunition from that country, and she no doubt was being pressed for payment.

THE SECRETARY OF STATE FOR FOREIGN AFFAIRS said that he had no information to show how China proposed to use the money if she obtained it. He realised that it would be most difficult, if not impossible, for the Committee to reach any decision on the present occasion. In the view of the Foreign Office China might well fight the Japanese to a stalemate and the opinions expressed by Sir R. Craigie should be largely discounted. He himself agreed that the proposal was a very bad commercial proposition, very thinly veneered. At the same time we must all sympathise very greatly with China in her difficulties. It was very disturbing to him that whenever any chance arose of helping China in some concrete form we were at once faced with these objections based on fear of the possibility of Japan's hostile reactions.

THE PRESIDENT OF THE BOARD OF TRADE enquired whether the Secretary of State for Foreign Affairs would be prepared to recommend the Cabinet to authorise a Government loan of £20,000,000 to China.

THE SECRETARY OF STATE FOR FOREIGN AFFAIRS replied in the negative. The Foreign Office attached very considerable importance to the first argument in paragraph 17 of page 7 of his Memorandum that some small help by us might encourage others to follow our example.

THE PRIME MINISTER said that all his sympathies were with the point of view which had been expressed by the Secretary of State for Foreign Affairs. He very strongly resented our being singled out by Japan for differential treatment to our great detriment as compared with other countries in all matters connected with China. At the same time he was satisfied that this particular proposition was an inherently bad one. We must remember that our position in the Far East was a very vulnerable one, and that if we were attacked by Japan in strength, we were not in a position, at all events at the outset, to defend ourselves. If in consequence of adopting this proposal we provoked Japan to take some action of a violent and outrageous character he was convinced that no useful purpose would have been served by entertaining the proposal.

THE SECRETARY OF STATE FOR FOREIGN AFFAIRS expressed the view that Japan was unlikely to indulge in any violent reactions against us. The last thing that the Japanese authorities desired was to get into serious trouble with Great Britain at a time when they had more than they could successfully manage in conducting the war in China.

THE PRIME MINISTER thought that before any financial decision was taken it would be necessary to hear what Sir Vandeleur Grayburn had to say, and also to ascertain whether there was any possibility of securing the co-operation of the United States.

THE SECRETARY OF STATE FOR FOREIGN AFFAIRS enquired why we were satisfied with the small stocks of wolfram which had already been acquired, namely 1,000 tons, while the German Government apparently required 20,000 tons to complete their war requirements.

THE MINISTER FOR CO-ORDINATION OF DEFENCE pointed out that in the event of hostilities, Germany, unlike ourselves, would be unable to make use of supplies from Burma.

In reply to an enquiry whether it might not be possible to rig the wolfram market and so make certain of recovering our money, THE CHANCELLOR OF THE EXCHEQUER said that he had no information on the point, but mentioned that the world price of wolfram had dropped very substantially in recent months. He had spoken to Lord Riverdale in regard to the matter, but the latter had regarded the proposition as a hopelessly impracticable one.

THE LORD PRESIDENT OF THE COUNCIL said that all the members of the Committee were agreed that there could be no question of a British Government loan or of a Government guarantee. The best course would be to wait and see what Sir Vandeleur Grayburn had to say. Personally he (Lord Hailsham) would greatly deprecate any steps being taken to discourage persons from lending money to China in present circumstances.

THE CHANCELLOR OF THE EXCHEQUER pointed out that the Chinese Government greatly needed large numbers of lorries for transport purposes and wondered whether we might not be able to arrange supplies on export credit terms.

THE PRIME MINISTER thought that assistance of this character would not be enough to make any difference.

THE SECRETARY OF STATE FOR THE COLONIES said that he also sympathised with the point of view expressed by the Secretary of State for Foreign Affairs, but he felt that on the information given to the Committee by the Chancellor of the Exchequer the amount of money which it would be possible to raise in the City for China would not be sufficient to make any difference to China's powers of resistance.

THE SECRETARY OF STATE FOR FOREIGN AFFAIRS recognised that the Committee had reached no decisions on the matter that day. He would ascertain what Sir Vandeleur Grayburn had to say about the proposition, and would also make soundings as to the attitude of the United States towards possible co-operation. In the event of his further examination producing any gleam of hope he would invite the Committee to give the question further examination after Whitsuntide.

The Committee agreed with the action proposed to be taken by the Secretary of State for Foreign Affairs in regard to the matter.[5]

APPENDIX TO NO. 584

Memorandum on the Chinese request for financial assistance

May 31, 1938

Two or three months ago, the Chinese Government enquired in Hong Kong and also in London as to the possibility of obtaining credits in London—£20 million was the amount mentioned—on the security of the wolfram and antimony which are produced in the Central and Southern Provinces of China under a Government monopoly system, the British creditors to have the whole of the output for three years. Sir F. Leith-Ross, who has been in constant touch with the Chinese Ambassador and other Chinese representatives on the matter, and the Treasury have endeavoured to ascertain whether it would be possible to interest British firms in such a proposal as a commercial proposition. It has also been considered whether the purchase of these supplies from China is essential for our own defence requirements.

2. As regards the defence aspect, there might have seemed to be obvious advantages in obtaining supplies of raw metals which are essential for armament production and of which the Chinese supplies are the largest in the world, and of depriving Germany of the access which she has

[5] According to a note from Mr. Waley to Sir F. Phillips of June 2 (PREM 1/303) the question of a loan to China was discussed that day by Foreign Office, Treasury, and Bank of England officials, and Sir Vandeleur Grayburn. The latter said that it was impossible to grant any credits to China unless they were guaranteed by His Majesty's Government, and this would require special legislation. Mr. Waley concluded: 'It is thus really an academic question whether H.M. Government is, or is not, in favour of financial assistance to China unless and until the Foreign Secretary puts forward a proposal for a guaranteed credit.'

hitherto had to these supplies. But the view held by our own defence experts is that the small stocks which have been already acquired, viz. 1,000 tons, are regarded as adequate on the ground that satisfactory alternative sources of supply (Burma) would be available to us even in time of emergency. In contrast to our own defence requirements as stated above, the German Government have offered to buy up to 20,000 tons to form their war resources, while they actually purchased 8,000 tons of wolfram and 2,000 tons of antimony from China in 1937.

3. As regards the commercial aspect, enquiries have been addressed to the Hong Kong and Shanghai Bank in Hong Kong, to which no reply has yet been received, and discussion will probably be necessary with Sir Vandeleur Grayburn, the Chairman of the Hong Kong Bank, when he reaches England at the end of this month. But it may be taken as certain that it will not be possible to interest British firms in any proposal on these lines unless it is actively supported by H. M. Government. The commercial difficulties are that uncertainty may be felt whether these supplies will remain under the control of the Hankow Government and whether it will continue to be possible to export them from China, and also market conditions are unsatisfactory. The price has been falling heavily in recent months; and British buyers who already have adequate commercial stocks will not buy more at present prices without Government guarantee against loss.

4. One suggestion which has been made is that a book credit should be opened which would only actually be drawn upon as and when exports actually leave China. This would not be of much real help to the Chinese Government, though it might be welcomed for psychological reasons. It would certainly be far more satisfactory if a real credit could be arranged, even though for a much smaller sum than that mentioned by the Chinese.

5. Another proposal which has been put forward is that the British and Chinese Corporation, acting together with the China Development Corporation, should construct a railway from Yunnanfu to connect with the Burmese railways. The British and Chinese Corporation wrote on the 14th April to the Burma Office to say that they understood that the Chinese Government might be willing to grant a concession for such a railway, but that in the first instance they wished to ascertain the views of the Burma Office. The British and Chinese Corporation have not received details of this proposal from the Chinese Ministry of Communications, and have not yet explored the commercial prospects of the line. If the Burma Office are sympathetic, and if the scheme appears attractive on further examination, it is possible that the British and Chinese Corporation would grant some small immediate credit to the Chinese Government in return for obtaining the concession. The Burmese Government would have to build about fifty miles of railway on the Burmese side of the frontier.

6. In the meantime, the Chinese have completed a road suitable for motor traffic right through to the Burma frontier. The Burmese

Government have built a road on their side, which is not as wide as the Chinese road. The whole question of Burma-China communications may in the future be one of great importance from the point of view of British relations with China and active assistance in the development of Burma-China communications would constitute a concrete sign of our goodwill and should constitute both an economic and political asset. The Soviet Government are being far more active than we are in improving their overland communications with China.

7. Both as regards the wolfram scheme and as regards Burma-Yunnan communications, the time has now come when it is urgently necessary to decide whether His Majesty's Government desire to use all the influence they have to encourage British interests to give financial assistance to China. On this important question, two opposite views have been expressed.

8. The argument in favour of helping China may be stated as follows:

Few people expected the Chinese Army to recover from its staggering defeat at Shanghai at the end of last year, and it did not seem then to be practical politics to consider material assistance to China on any extensive scale. The Chinese have, however, made a remarkable recovery and all our information goes to show that provided their financial situation and supplies of war material can be maintained, they are undoubtedly capable of a prolonged and effective resistance against the Japanese.

9. The attached telegram from our Ambassador in China (Hong Kong No. 3 of April 28th[6]) giving an account of a recent conversation with General Chiang Kai-shek is typical of many reports we have had lately. The French have recently granted a credit of approximately £1 million for railway material to the Chinese Government, and the Russian Government is also granting considerable supplies on credit, while even Germany is supplying China with large quantities of munitions on credit. It is their financial situation which causes the Chinese great anxiety, particularly as this affects the maintenance of the currency.

10. China is fighting the battle of all the law-abiding States, and she is incidentally fighting our own battle in the Far East, for, if Japan wins, our interests there are certainly doomed to extinction. The Japanese Army and other high authorities have left us in no doubt about that. Our immense vested interests in North China and Shanghai will be the first to go and the Japanese Army and Navy set no limits to their appetites on the Continent and in the south Seas. If China can only fight Japan to a stalemate, we and the Americans will then be able to intervene with effective results and safeguard our position for another generation.

11. Moreover, we are committed by two Resolutions of the League of Nations to give every assistance we can to China and, on the 14th May, the League Council adopted a further Resolution urging that the Members of the League should do their utmost to give effect to previous Resolutions

[6] No. 557.

and should take into serious and sympathetic consideration any request the Chinese Government might make in conformity with them.[7]

12. Sir R. Craigie assumes that Japan is bound to emerge victorious from her war. Even supposing that this is correct, if the war goes on much longer the victory will be but Pyrrhic. In point of fact, the longer it continues the greater the strain on Japan's resources and the less likely she is at the end of it to be in a position to give effect to those grandiose schemes for exploiting the territory of her victim, details of which have already been embodied in Bills passed by the Diet. These schemes, there can be no doubt, will spell ruin and extinction for many British and other non-Japanese interests not only in North but also in Central China. The less help from outside which China gets now, the more quickly the war is likely to be over and the more likely it will be that Japan will be able to put her plans into effect and the nearer the time when British interests in China may be expected to be sent packing. To refrain from assisting a valuable potential customer in her hour of need because it would irritate an unscrupulous competitor, whose one idea is to secure that customer for his sole exploitation, seems an argument of questionable validity.

13. It should not be impossible to meet any Japanese complaint that the loan was dictated by political motives: it could be represented as an ordinary commercial transaction in which His Majesty's Government were interested solely on account of their natural and legitimate desire to acquire control of the Chinese antimony output for their own rearmament purposes.

14. Every consideration, therefore, of honour and self-interest impels us towards doing what we can to help China. For a comparatively small sum of money, we may in this way be able to preserve our vital interests in the Far East.

15. This view is strongly supported in the attached telegram from our Ambassador in China (No. 726 of 7th May[8]).

16. On the other hand, the opposite view is strongly advanced by our Ambassador in Tokyo in the attached telegram (No. 582 of 10th May[3]). He points out that the granting of British credits (especially if responsibility were not to be shared with the United States and France) would lead to an overwhelming outburst of fury against Great Britain, the ultimate consequences of which it is difficult to predict. Whatever the issue of the war, we should have earned the undying resentment of Japan, and it is unsafe to exaggerate the weakening effect that the war will have upon her. And the danger of permanently incurring Japanese resentment is very great. Whereas in a World War the attitude of China would not be a determining factor, the reverse is true of Japan. Any breach in our relationship with Japan which is of such a character as to bring her irrevocably under German domination is bound sooner or later to act upon our defensive position in Europe. Sir R. Craigie adds that if the

[7] See No. 574. [8] No. 567.

United States Government were prepared to share in the hazards of the undertaking, the proposal would take on another complexion. By their purchases of Chinese silver the United States Government have already extended considerable financial assistance to China, but it is extremely unlikely that they would be prepared to take part in any joint scheme of financial assistance.

17. To sum up:

A. It is not suggested that to lend China the little money which is all that is likely to be forthcoming will enable her to win the war in a strategical sense. But to lend her what we can

(1) may encourage others to do the same (although there is no indication that the United States Government are at present encouraging American financial interests to help China, they have themselves given such assistance since the outbreak of the hostilities by the purchase of Chinese Silver Stocks at favourable rates, and it is not inconceivable that they might be moved to further efforts by our example. It should also be borne in mind that United States arms manufacturers have supplied China with an enormously greater quantity of material than we and, for all we know, may be ready to grant China the same sort of long-term credit facilities which have been extended to her in Germany, Russia, France and Italy);

(2) will enable us to fulfil our obligations under the League Resolutions; and

(3) even if it does not help China to secure final victory will render Japan the less likely to be able to give effect to her plans for the elimination of foreign interests and competition in China.

B. On the other hand,

(1) the United States and other Governments may not be prepared to share in the hazards of the undertaking;

(2) we run the risk of incurring the resentment of the Japanese, a very vindictive people, and this may result in bringing them more within the German orbit; and

(3) the amount of assistance which we may find ourselves able to give is likely to be on a very limited scale and would not be calculated to postpone for more than a very short while the financial collapse of China, if that financial collapse is otherwise inevitable.

18. It is between these two opposite views that the Foreign Policy Committee are called upon to decide.

No. 585

Viscount Halifax to Sir R. Craigie (Tokyo)

No. 386 Telegraphic [F 5850/71/23]

FOREIGN OFFICE, *June 3, 1938, 10.30 p.m.*

Your telegram No. 661[1].

In your telegram abovementioned you state that you are convinced that there are more efficacious methods of assisting China to her feet than granting direct assistance to her in the present struggle and driving Japan into totalitarian camp. This seems to imply that we should stand aside until China has been knocked down by Japan.

I very much doubt whether a victorious Japan astride a prostrate China would allow us to co-operate in the latter's rehabilitation on any terms which we could accept. We are moreover bound in honour by three resolutions of the League of Nations[2] to give what help we can to China in her present struggle with Japan.

Furthermore is not Japan committed already to the totalitarian triangle?

The above are my first and perhaps rather hasty reactions to the last paragraph of your telegram under reply and I should welcome any further views on the above points as soon as possible. We shall naturally take into account as far as we can the new situation which has arisen in Japan by the advent of the reorganised government.

[1] No. 583.
[2] See Nos. 288, 507, and 574.

No. 586

Sir A. Clark Kerr (Shanghai) to Viscount Halifax
(Received June 5, 9.30 a.m.)

No. 879 Telegraphic: by wireless [F 6006/1155/10]

SHANGHAI, *June 4, 1938*

Addressed to Tokyo telegram No. 511 of June 3rd.
Following from Major-General Piggott.[1]

I have visited several Japanese posts on perimeter and talked with many non-commissioned officers and men and a few officers. All branches of the Service are represented even in small guards of a dozen men; their general attitude is grossly slovenly and occasionally discourteous; discipline is obviously and patently lax and there is no sign of esprit de corps. Much of Japan's loss of prestige and popularity in the eyes of the foreign observer is due to appearance and actions of these indifferent representa-

[1] See No. 577.

tives of their country's army. It would have been much better policy if say Imperial Guard had been detailed for these unspectacular and tedious duties; incidents would have been far fewer and Japanese prestige would be far higher. I propose making friendly and sincere representations in this sense to General Staff on my return to Tokyo.

No. 587

Sir A. Clark Kerr (Shanghai) to Viscount Halifax
(Received June 5, 8 p.m.)

No. 889 Telegraphic: by wireless [F 6145/1155/10]

SHANGHAI, June 5, 1938

Addressed to Tokyo 518 June 5th.
Following from General Piggott.
His Majesty's Ambassador dined with me June 3rd to meet General Hata. The Commander-in-Chief in the presence of twelve other Japanese naval and military officers and civilian officials re-emphasised equal determination to restore Anglo-Japanese cordiality and settle local incidents promptly. The ...[1] of admiration and unconcealed liking for Major-General Smollet[t] on the part of all Japanese present was sincere and these new happy relations are good augury for the future.[2]

Major-General and staff called with me June 4th on Lieutenant-General Ito, commanding all troops in Shanghai area, at his Headquarters half a mile from Major-General Smollet[t]'s house and established friendly contact hitherto non-existent.

[1] The text was here uncertain. [2] Cf. No. 577, note 3.

No. 588

Sir R. Craigie (Tokyo) to Viscount Halifax (Received June 7, 9.30 a.m.)

No. 689 Telegraphic [F 6135/25/10]*

TOKYO, June 7, 1938, 12.10 a.m.

I have carefully considered, in consultation with principal members of my staff, your telegram No. 386[1], and my observations are as follows:

2. When referring in my telegram No. 661[2] to 'direct assistance' I had in mind such financial assistance as might (with governmental encouragement and support) conceivably be forthcoming in present circumstances, and, in particular, a loan or credit in the neighbourhood of £4 million to

[1] No. 585. [2] No. 583.

£10 million, such as press reports allege to be under consideration.[3] Assistance on a really large scale (e.g., loan of £100 million) would clearly be most efficacious method of all in assisting China. But if, as I presume, so large a loan is out of the question, I consider alternative of offering inadequate assistance (i.e., a sum which might be expected to prolong the struggle a few months only) would leave us with the worst of both worlds; it would not save China, but it would finally alienate Japan and render nugatory such help as we might be able to afford to China by other methods.

3. This does not imply that we should stand aside until China has been knocked down by Japan. But intervening in all matters where we have the right to intervene (e.g., for protection of British rights and interests in China), we are indirectly benefiting China by making it difficult for Japan to obtain complete economic strangle-hold in occupied areas; by leaving the door open to possible future co-operation with Japan we render it less likely that advocates of more violent methods will obtain immediate control over Japan's China policy; by preserving some degree of impartiality we are making it easier for Japan ultimately to accept British or Anglo-American mediation, with the advantage that that would connote for China. Consistent adoption of these methods, while it guarantees nothing, does, in my opinion, hold out some prospect of success. On the other hand, adoption of policy of ineffectual or insufficient assistance to China, coupled with bleak hostility to Japan, offers no such prospect.

4. As regards other Powers' co-operation with Japan for China's rehabilitation, I agree that this may prove to be impracticable whatever policy we pursue, but I believe that persistence along the lines outlined in preceding paragraph is more likely to achieve the desired result than any other course at present open to us.

5. League of Nations resolutions do not presumably imply that risks inherent in offering assistance to China should be incurred by ourselves alone. Moreover, I suggest that we alone must be judges as to how best we can assist China. If His Majesty's Government were to decide that partial and inadequate assistance to China would only make matters worse, they would not appear to be acting contrary to League of Nations resolutions by adhering to policy outlined in paragraph 3 above.

6. As regards totalitarian argument, it would be wrong to regard Japan as irretrievably committed to more than the immediate purpose of Anti-Comintern Pact. In so far as this pact is respected here as an alignment with totalitarians for purposes wider than suppression of communism, this is due indubitably to national conviction that Japan urgently needs friends in present emergency. My forecast on this point is that, provided Japan is not so weakened by present struggle as to stand urgently in need of military assistance against Russia, and provided

[3] Cf. No. 584.

pressure of events meanwhile does not necessitate even closer association with totalitarians (there are rumours respecting Tsingtao), Japan's tendency after the war will be to gravitate towards those Powers (such as Great Britain and United States of America) from which she can hope to draw economic sustenance, of which both Japan and China will stand so badly in need.

7. I trust you will consider the case presented above as sufficiently strong to defer any decision to give financial assistance to China at least until there has been time to test assurances and intentions of new Japanese Government.[4] It is worth considering in this connexion whether announcement of a credit to China coming so soon after General Ugaki's assumption of office might not either seriously undermine position of a statesman on whom it is permissible at present to pin some hope, or, alternatively, deflect him along a completely new and undesirable path.

8. I have in recent weeks spared no pains to bring it home to responsible Japanese that if Japan goes back on her assurances, we have a rod in pickle for her. It appears that hints, which have, of course, to be used with discretion, have reached their mark if only because the Japanese can never be quite sure how far we might go if severely provoked. But unless the dimensions of the rod can be greatly increased, it is best left where it is.

Repeated to Sir A. Clark Kerr, No. 510.

[4] Cf. No. 582.

No. 589

Letter from Sir A. Clark Kerr (Shanghai) to Mr. Howe

[F 7673/12/10]

Private and Personal   SHANGHAI, *June 7, 1938*

My dear Bob,

There was good deal in Tokyo telegram No. 603[1] of the 18th May about our relations with the local Japanese, that we here did not much like. I do not propose to hit back because that would be silly and in any case you know all about the situation and the sort of thing that we have had to put up with.

But the Consul General[2] has been fussed lest it should be thought that he and his staff have been lacking in patience. There can be no question that, in exceptionally exasperating circumstances, he and all those about him have, to their great credit, managed to maintain good personal relations with their Japanese colleagues. I have told the Consul General that I would put this on record.

[1] No. 577.   [2] Mr. Phillips.

Meanwhile Piggott has come and gone and I think that his visit has been worth while. Wisely, I believe, Telfer-Smollett took advantage, before Piggott's arrival, of an unexpectedly handsome apology from Hata about a nasty incident on the perimeter, to call and to end the feud, and so the bridge was built and to it Piggott added the garlands and the streamers.[3] And now everything in the military garden is beautiful.

In my private telegram to you of the 27th May[4] I said that I hoped that a visit here might pacify Piggott. I think that this hope has been fully justified, for he was shocked by a good deal of what he saw. 'My God! how the Japanese Army have let me down.'

Yours ever
A. C. K.

[3] Cf. Nos. 586 and 587.   [4] Not traced in F.O. archives.

No. 590

Sir R. Craigie (Tokyo) to Viscount Halifax (Received June 13, 9.30 a.m.)

No. 719 Telegraphic [F 6347/1155/10]

TOKYO, *June 13, 1938, 3.15 p.m.*

My telegrams Nos. 603 and 604 of March [May] 18th.[1]

Military Attaché has now returned from Shanghai and has given me a detailed account of his visit. Report follows by bag.[2]

It is clear from what I have heard from His Majesty's Ambassador in China and from Japanese sources that visit has produced and will produce valuable results locally and these in turn are likely to react favourably on all our dealings with Japanese Government and Japanese authorities.

Military Attaché had interview at the general staff yesterday and emphasised points in Shanghai telegram No. 511 of June 3rd[3] as regards indifferent Japanese troops on perimeter; his representations were well received and he is not unhopeful that a change may be made.

Repeated to Sir A. Clark Kerr.

[1] Nos. 576 and 577.
[2] Not printed. The report, which was forwarded to the Foreign Office in Tokyo despatch No. 410 of June 18, ran to 18 pages of typescript and is filed at F 7419/1155/10.
[3] No. 586.

No. 591

Sir R. Craigie (Tokyo) to Viscount Halifax (Received June 14, 2.10 p.m.)

No. 730 Telegraphic [F 6449/25/10]*

TOKYO, *June 14, 1938, 7.50 p.m.*

Your telegram No. 407.[1]

I agree credit which would be devoted, under guarantee, exclusively for the maintenance of currency would not be open to the same objections as one for general purposes, including purchase of munitions. But to avoid too unfavourable a reaction here it would be desirable to show that Chinese Government would not be enabled, on receipt of new credits, to release for other purposes a portion of reserves now kept as backing for currency. Also it would be important in advance publication that I should be enabled unofficially to warn the Japanese Government and to explain the reasons for the step. The main thing is to be able to show here that we are acting on behalf of British, not merely on Chinese, interest. Also 'credit' would be easier to defend than a 'loan'.

I cannot pretend that currency credit to China would help the situation here. While more moderate elements appreciate that the maintenance of China currency stability is in Japan's ultimate interest, there are other influential elements who urge that Japan's first business being to win the war, undermining of China currency and credit is a means to this end, and, nevertheless, if credit is not too extensive and above conditions could be fulfilled, I think that we could prevent irreparable harm being done to our relations with this country.[2]

[1] This telegram of June 13 referred to Nos. 583 and 588 and asked Sir R. Craigie whether his objections still applied to a loan for currency purposes. 'If Chinese currency collapses, position of British banks to China will be very difficult, and they may have to be helped out by the City if not by the British Government. The Japanese cannot really object to a loan given to help the Chinese currency, since they have constantly assured us that they are anxious to avoid any breakdown of the Chinese currency.'

[2] In a memorandum of June 17 (PREM 1/303) Sir F. Phillips noted that he had spoken to the Deputy Governor of the Bank of England, Mr. Catterns, in the light of Tokyo telegram No. 730. Between them they disposed of all the arguments put forward by the Foreign Office in favour of a loan to China, and concluded that it would amount to 'assisting China with cash with little prospect of ever seeing our cash back'. Sir Warren Fisher expressed agreement with this view in a minute of June 18: 'As I see it that issue is a perfectly clear one—are we prepared to support China financially in her resistance to Japanese aggression (& to be of any use the assistance wd. have to be on an effective scale)? If so we must face the consequences & recognise that we shall earn the undying hostility of Japan who sooner or later—perhaps at a time when we are at death grips with Germany—will take her revenge. Thus to risk our country's security, indeed survival, would be nothing short of a crime, equalled only by the folly of it as nothing that has been suggested in the way of financial assistance can be effective. The trumpery odds & ends of help that have been mentioned simply cannot be a determining factor & cd. only result in the worst of every world, infuriation of the Japanese against ourselves & no real benefit to China. To be effective scores of millions wd. have to be contributed; indeed, except in form we shd. have to range

ourselves & our resources on the side of China. Do the protagonists of China favour this? So far all that they have advocated is backstairs provision of a pittance, useless to China & provocative to Japan. I sincerely trust that the Govt. will have nothing to do with this dangerous—& in the long run possibly suicidal—nonsense.' In a minute to Mr. Chamberlain on June 21 Sir J. Simon also expressed agreement with Sir F. Phillips' memorandum and suggested that the Foreign Office should be informed of this view: see No. 595 below.

No. 592

Sir A. Clark Kerr (Shanghai) to Viscount Halifax
(Received June 27, 9.30 a.m.)

No. 1022 Telegraphic: by wireless [F 7001/62/10]

SHANGHAI, *June 27, 1938*

Japanese pressure affecting our long established interests here continues undiminished. The projected setting up of development companies in north and central China under Japanese control heralds yet greater difficulties.

2. Our representations so far have met with little or no response and our interests here, if present tendencies continue, are faced not only with heavy realized losses but with a bleak prospect of slow extinction in future. Should they complete the military strangle-hold which Japanese already exercise over the Yangtze and main railways there is every evidence that revival of trade and industry in occupied provinces in so far as any revival is possible while military occupation lasts, will only be allowed on terms which mean a virtual monopoly for the Japanese. In these circumstances, continued vigour and initiative of our trading interests in this important market can hardly be permanent even if hostilities cease.

3. Repugnant as any idea of reprisals is to me, the time has now come to consider what indirect pressure could be applied in the last resort to Japan which might supplement the so far fruitless diplomatic action and bring home to her the necessity of respecting our rights and interests in China and of maintaining the principle of equal opportunity.

4. The pressure I have in mind would be questions [*sic*] for example, legislation restricting Japanese banking activities in Great Britain and Crown colonies on the lines of legislation in force in the United States and Dutch East Indies restricting foreign banking activities. Or again possibly some form of unofficial pressure tending to handicap Japan in London discount and re-insurance market.

5. I realize that any pressure of this nature has grave and far-reaching implications, nevertheless I submit that the question of what measures (short of war) can be applied by us alone (or in conjunction with France and America) which might bring Japan to her senses, merits serious consideration in virtue of almost negligible results produced by nearly a year of activity and continuous diplomatic pressure.

6. I shall be glad to learn if you think this suggestion worth pursuing.[1]
Repeated to Tokyo.

[1] The possibility of economic retaliation against Japan had already been considered in a memorandum of May 23 by Sir J. Brenan dealing with injuries and losses suffered by British subjects and interests in China (F 5554/62/10). Sir J. Brenan pointed out that although economic sanctions on an international scale had been ruled out by the A.T.B. Committee (see No. 334, note 15) the possibility of 'economic retaliation of limited scope directed against particular Japanese measures in China injurious to British interests' had not been examined. He also referred to Dr. Hornbeck's letter of April 13 to Sir A. Cadogan (see No. 450, note 3) in which Dr. Hornbeck stated that the U.S. Government were examining the possibility of commercial reprisals against both Japan and China for damage to American interests in the Far East, and asked whether a similar study was being undertaken in Britain.

Copies of Sir J. Brenan's memorandum had been sent to Sir F. Leith-Ross, the Treasury, and other interested Departments with covering letters suggesting that the subject should be examined by an interdepartmental committee. Sir H. Knatchbull-Hugessen, who had now joined the Economic Relations Section of the League of Nations and Western Department, was asked if he would run the committee if formed, and minuted on May 30 that he would 'willingly undertake it'. By the time Shanghai telegram No. 1022 arrived, the Colonial Office and Dominions Office had indicated their willingness to participate in a committee, but the comments of the Treasury, Board of Trade, Department of Overseas Trade and India Office were still awaited. Foreign Office telegram No. 60 to Hankow of July 5 informed Sir A. Clark Kerr that 'Establishment of Interdepartmental Committee to study this question is being considered but difficulties are of course great. Our most obvious weapons are double edged and I can give no indication as to whether any action will be possible'. Meanwhile Sir R. Craigie had expressed his agreement with Sir A. Clark Kerr: see No. 594 below.

No. 593

Sir R. Craigie (Tokyo) to Viscount Halifax (Received June 28, 4 p.m.)

No. 791 Telegraphic [F 6976/84/10]

TOKYO, *June 28, 1938, 8.10 p.m.*

Minister for Foreign Affairs observed to me today that he had been informed by Minister of Finance gist of conversation recorded in my telegram No. 758[1] and desired to thank me for this frank expression of my views. In the course of that interview I had referred to position of His Majesty's Government in regard to question of mediation (I had in fact repeated statement made by Prime Minister in Parliament on May 11th[2]).

[1] In this telegram of June 20 Sir R. Craigie reported a conversation with 'a personality holding influential position in the Japanese Government' regarding the implications for Anglo-Japanese relations of recent Cabinet changes in Japan.
[2] In answer to a question on May 11 Mr. Chamberlain stated: 'His Majesty's Government would be glad to offer their services either alone or in conjunction with other Powers to bring about an equitable peace between China and Japan. They do not, however, consider that any useful purpose would be served by offering mediation until both sides have indicated their willingness to accept it.' See 335 *H.C. Deb. 5 s.*, col. 1558.

Minister for Foreign Affairs was of opinion that it would be difficult for Japan to accept any form of foreign mediation so long as China was receiving assistance in men and material from foreign Powers. China was incapable of resisting Japan unaided and so long as this foreign assistance continued war must be prosecuted. As one instance of what His Excellency had in mind he mentioned that it had been announced in House of Commons that British Government were considering granting of a long term credit to Chiang Kai-shek's régime.[3] This could only have effect of prolonging the war and it would be extremely difficult to adjust many difficulties that confronted us so long as such aid continued. A further point to be remembered was this: Hankow would undoubtedly be taken before very long; when that happened the present Chinese Government would become a regional régime exercising little control over any area in China other than relatively small region actually occupied by Chiang Kai-shek's personal forces. At the same time there would be large areas where Japanese forces would not be able to exercise full control. In these un-controlled areas communists would function and their doctrines flourish. He hoped that this aspect of the question would not be lost upon His Majesty's Government. In reply I stated that so far as my memory served me only statement made on this subject in House of Commons was to the effect that if British financial houses desired to offer a credit to Chinese Government no difficulties would be placed in their way by His Majesty's Government. I did not see how any other would be compatible with neutrality. I then reminded His Excellency how little concrete assistance had up to now been furnished to Chinese Government by Great Britain, observing that as Japan was a highly industrialised state and China was not it was natural that latter should draw more heavily on foreign resources than did Japan. His Excellency remarked he had not wished to suggest anything had occurred which was contrary to international law but that a useless prolongation of the war by furnishing of outside aid was contrary to dictates of humanity. On my observing that Chinese believed (and many people with them) that if they could prolong the war sufficiently they could also win it and that argument of humanity was therefore unlikely to carry conviction abroad His Excellency said that in that case it would be necessary 'to fight it out to the end.'[4]

[3] Cf. 336 *H.C. Deb. 5 s.*, cols. 1179–80.

[4] Sir A. Cadogan remarked on June 30: 'The Japanese create chaos in China, and then warn us against the dangers of the resulting communism (if it results). They continue to wage war against Chiang Kai-shek who devoted his energies to the stamping out of communism. The M.F.A. "had not wished to suggest anything had occurred which was contrary to international law". I should hope not. Japan, quite lawlessly, and without declaration of war, is laying waste a country with which we are on friendly terms, and where we have considerable interests. We should have a perfect right, in international law, to furnish assistance, financial and other, to China. Lectures from Japanese on international law, at this moment, I find rather trying.' Lord Halifax wrote: 'Yes, H. 1/7.' There is a reference to this telegram in Third Series, Volume VIII, No. 12, note 3.

No. 594

Sir R. Craigie (Tokyo) to Viscount Halifax (Received June 29, 2.30 p.m.)

No. 794 Telegraphic [F 7031/62/10]

TOKYO, *June 29, 1938, 8 p.m.*

Shanghai telegram No. 1022[1].

I agree with Sir A. Clark Kerr that it would be well to consider what form of indirect pressure could be applied to Japan in support of our representations and how it could progressively be applied. It would be particularly useful to know whether any such action is practicable if ultimately considered to be desirable.

I have already hinted to Minister for Foreign Affairs that certain perfectly neutral action is open to us which might benefit China and have left it to be understood that we may be ready to take it if our rights and interests were further trampled upon (see my telegram No. 790[2]). As the Minister for Foreign Affairs has more than once indicated his intention of doing everything possible to improve Anglo-Japanese relations and as I believe results may be expected before very long it would now clearly be wise policy to give him a little time in which to effect improvement. If in the course of say next month or six weeks there is no substantial change for the better we might then start to put the screw on.[3]

Repeated to Shanghai.

---

[1] No. 592. [2] Of June 28, not printed (F 6975/12/10).

[3] Sir J. Brenan commented on July 2: 'In spite of Sir R. Craigie's desire to give the Minister for Foreign Affairs time to improve Anglo-Japanese relations, I submit that no results worth having will materialise until we do something to frighten the Japanese. It is not reasonable to expect otherwise. General Ugaki may succeed in giving us a sop here or there; the release of a captured launch, permission for a few people to return to Nanking, satisfaction for some minor incident. But the fundamental Japanese policy to exploit China at our expense and to expel British influence from the Far East will only be modified by the fear of British intervention on an appreciable scale in some form or another. Failing forcible action, or serious economic reprisals [cf. No. 592, note 1], the only thing we can do to frighten the Japanese is to let them think that we might give financial assistance to China to prolong the war. . . It is to be hoped therefore that this telegram will not be regarded as a reason for postponing consideration of the loan to a later date.' Sir H. Knatchbull-Hugessen agreed (July 4): 'The moment seems to have come when we should take stock of all the weapons which we can use if required.' Sir A. Cadogan and Lord Halifax added their initials on July 4. Cf. Nos. 595–6 below.

No. 595

Memorandum[1] by Lord Halifax on assistance to China

Cab. 24/277

Secret   FOREIGN OFFICE, *July 1, 1938*

A very important, urgent and difficult question arises for decision, viz., whether His Majesty's Government should provide support for the Chinese currency, which is in a critical condition. Unless a substantial loan or credit can be made available, the Chinese Government will almost certainly be forced to suspend the service of their foreign debts and to restrict still further the convertibility of their currency. This must inevitably lead to a further fall in the Shanghai exchange (which cannot be controlled by the Chinese Government) and may precipitate a flight from the currency and a run on the Chinese Banks which could only be stopped by declaring a bank moratorium. The adverse effects of such measures would be felt not only by all trading and financial interests in China, but would extend to the political sphere; once the confidence of the Chinese people in the currency is undermined, the Central Government may itself be disrupted and China broken up into a number of separate régimes which would not be able to sustain the burden of resistance to Japan except in the remote interior. On the other hand, Mr. Rogers, who is the Adviser of the Chinese Central Bank, and who is in this country until the end of this week, takes the view that (apart from unforeseen developments) a loan or credit of twenty millions should enable the position to be held for a substantial period—probably a year—before which time the Chinese hope that Japan may be sufficiently exhausted to make peace on reasonable terms.

2. Other proposals have been made on previous occasions for affording help to the Chinese Government, but for one reason or another no action was found possible in regard to them, and it appears clear that no loan of substantial amount can be raised without a British Government guarantee. Meanwhile, the Chinese Government continue to ask what we can do to implement the League Resolution,[2] and on the 21st June I

---

[1] Circulated to the Cabinet on July 6 as C.P. 152(38). This memorandum was based on a paper dictated in the Treasury by Sir J. Simon on June 24, a copy of which was sent to Lord Halifax as a basis for discussion. According to a note of June 28 by Sir H. Wilson, the question of a currency loan to China was discussed that morning by Mr. Chamberlain, Sir J. Simon, Lord Halifax, Sir A. Cadogan, Sir J. Brenan, Sir R. Hopkins, Sir H. Wilson, and Sir F. Leith-Ross. Lord Halifax said that on balance he favoured a loan: Sir J. Simon pointed out that as legislation would be necessary a loan could not be camouflaged. Mr. Chamberlain said that as the issues involved were so important he wished to see a Foreign Office memorandum, with either comments or a separate paper from Sir J. Simon: see No. 596 below.

[2] Cf. No. 574.

informed the Chinese Ambassador[3] 'that we would be ready to consider any practicable proposals and would be glad to find some way of affording financial assistance to China in accordance with the League Resolutions that would not be open to the objections which we had felt in regard to the proposals hitherto made,' and I promised to draw the attention of the Chancellor of the Exchequer to these representations. It is evident, therefore, that a decision on this question in the name of the Government as a whole is urgently required.

3. Very large issues are involved. The position in the Far East is that Japan aims to dominate and exploit China for the furtherance of the Japanese programme of imperialist expansion. Her more immediate objective is to reduce the Chinese to submission and to recoup the unexpectedly heavy cost of the war by exploiting to the utmost the occupied areas in north and central China. This is to be done by monopolising the foreign trade of the country to the detriment of the influence and commerce of other nations, especially British trade and influence, which has predominated in China for the last century. The process is already far advanced and the methods have been frankly disclosed. These include puppet governments applying Japanese regulations, a customs administering a discriminatory tariff, a non-convertible currency, the seizure of the railways (belonging to British and other foreign bondholders), the control of all communications and harbours and the establishment of corporations monopolising all important industries and public utilities. If Japan wins the war there can be little doubt that British influence will be excluded, British financial interests largely lost, and British trade with China will within a short period be reduced to negligible proportions.

4. The only serious resistance now being offered to the accomplishment of this programme is that of the Chinese people. They are fighting gallantly for their independence and incidentally they are fighting the battles of the British and the Russians, who may be regarded as the next obstacles to the fulfilment of the Japanese imperial destiny. The Russians have recognised the obligation by supplying China with aeroplanes and other war material. The Chinese, however, are desperately in need of financial assistance and are asking Great Britain for help in this respect. Their immediate danger is a collapse of the currency on account of the depletion of the foreign exchange reserves on which the note issue is secured. Apart from the direct and harmful effects on local British interests, such as banks and industrial enterprises, a collapse of the currency would probably entail a default in the service of China's foreign obligations and possibly the disintegration of the Chinese Government itself and the end of organised military resistance to Japan.

5. The best hope for the preservation of British influence and interests

[3] This interview actually took place on June 16, but was reported to Sir A. Clark Kerr in telegram No. 544 to Shanghai of June 21.

in China lies in a prolongation of the hostilities until Japan is exhausted, or at least until she is brought through war-weariness to a state of mind when she will be ready to invoke the mediation of third Powers and accept terms of peace that would allow a fair share of the China market to other nations. Apart, therefore, from the obligations assumed at Geneva there are cogent reasons of self-interest why His Majesty's Government should grant financial assistance to China.

6. As stated above, it is estimated that the sum of £20 million would enable China to maintain the currency and prolong the war for another year while continuing the service of her existing foreign debts. It is understood that the Chinese Government would be prepared to offer the best security available (whether a charge on Customs or exports of wolfram or both). These securities should be valuable if China survives the war, but they are in present circumstances admittedly precarious. Repayment would be looked for in the distant future and possibly in benefits other than cash. There is also the danger of Japanese resentment, of which Sir R. Craigie has spoken very gravely, and the likelihood of an intensified obstruction to British interests in the occupied areas. It is not probable, however, that Japan, who is already in serious difficulties over the China campaign and has to be prepared for a Russian war, would go to the length of provoking a conflict with Great Britain. There is, of course, the possibility that another year of warfare may leave the combatants in the same relative position and that a further loan to China may then be required for the same purpose. On the other hand, if China is not able to maintain an organised resistance, we may soon find ourselves face to face with a Japan flushed with success, allied with the 'Have-not' Powers in Europe and with her hands free to pursue her expansionist ambitions in the South Seas and throughout Asia. It is undeniably a gamble, but we have to choose between two very disagreeable alternatives: (1) Either we can make a loan now, at the price of possible or perhaps probable loss of a large part of it, and if Sir R. Craigie is right, of incurring just Japanese resentment, in the hope of saving something in the future, or (2) we must resign ourselves to accepting the probable extinction of British interests in China, with all that that means to us economically and politically, consoling ourselves with the almost certainly illusory hope of Japanese gratitude for our self-restraint.

7. It is difficult to assess with any accuracy the monetary value of the British interests referred to, but it is probably in the neighbourhood of some £200 million. That loss in itself would obviously be considerable, but there is more to it than that. China at the beginning of last year offered probably the most promising field in the world at that time for economic expansion. Not only did it appear likely that she could absorb in the course of the next ten years an increasing quantity of British exports, but also she could, by taking the exports of other people, have added considerably to that world prosperity on which we must at all times so largely depend. The Japanese invasion has already largely extinguished

any hopes we may have entertained regarding the contribution to the expansion of world trade afforded by the development of the China market. Japanese plans for the future exploitation of China will effectually rule out the extension of non-Japanese enterprise in China and cause the early extinction of existing foreign enterprise on the model of what has been done in Manchuria. In fine, if the Japanese are allowed to give effect to their known plans, British interests in China will be strangled, the retention of Hong Kong rendered problematic, and a severe blow struck at British prestige in the Pacific, with possibly grave consequences to the unity of the Empire.

8. There is no doubt at all that we are under the strongest moral obligation to help China so far as we prudently can, both because she is the victim of outrageous aggression and because of the League Resolutions to which we are a party. It may well be that the maintenance of Chinese currency is an important British interest, in view of the financial consequences which would ensue if it collapsed, though the view of the Bank of England is that it is not essential that we should give a loan to China to protect the position of British banks, and that we ought not to use the position of these banks publicly as a defence for making a loan to China, since this would cast discredit on their position which is, in fact, undeserved. But the question which transcends all others in the matter is not a merely financial question, but one of high general policy, viz., whether assistance of this sort given to China is going to bring about such resentment in Japan as that of which Sir R. Craigie has warned us, with grave consequences which might not be limited to the Far East. The Japanese Government have constantly assured Sir R. Craigie that they are anxious to avert any breakdown of the Chinese currency, and this was repeated as recently as the 14th May, when the Vice-Minister for Foreign Affairs said that 'it was to the interest of the Japanese to maintain the Chinese currency, as, if it deteriorated, it would adversely affect the new currency in the north'—not to mention the Japanese yen. On the other hand, Sir R. Craigie, in his telegram of the same date, warns us that, 'while more moderate elements appreciate that the maintenance of China's currency stability is in Japan's ultimate interest, there are other influential elements who urge that, Japan's first business being to win the war, undermining of China's currency and credit is a means to this end.'[4]

9. More recently, however, the Ambassador would appear somewhat to have modified his views regarding the dangers of incurring Japanese resentment on this subject. In his telegram No. 772 of the 24th June,[5] referring to Anglo-Japanese conversations in Shanghai on measures to deal with a possible currency crisis, he expresses the opinion that the Japanese are nervous about the financial situation in the occupied areas, and that our bargaining position is now stronger. He thinks, therefore,

[4] Sir R. Craigie's warning was contained in telegram No. 730 of June 14 (No. 591).
[5] Not kept in F.O. archives.

that we can safely hint to the Japanese that, 'unless they can put forward proposals which secure our rights and interests and tend to increase rather than restrict trade, we shall be forced to consider measures for our own protection, such as credits in support of the Chinese currency.' But it is right to make it clear that the course suggested as alternative (1) in paragraph 6 above is at once more definite and immediate, as it is also based on wider considerations, than anything suggested by Sir R. Craigie, and it may be taken that he would regard it with misgiving.

10. If, however, His Majesty's Government do decide in principle to give financial assistance to the Chinese, its most suitable form would be a loan to maintain the currency, since this could be represented, in answer to Japanese protests, as a measure for the protection not only of British interests, but also of Japanese interests. Such a loan would require legislation, which would presumably take the form of a short Bill authorising the conclusion of a Loan Agreement, the text of which would have to be negotiated with the Chinese Government and be appended. Doubtless the pretext that the support of the Chinese currency served Japanese as well as British interests would not remove Japanese objections, for the real motive for the loan would not be hidden from them; but in such a matter it is important for reasons of publicity, and not least from the point of view of the Japanese Government in dealing with their own people, that a plausible explanation should be provided for the transaction.

11. It has been suggested that the United States should be sounded as to whether they would join in some scheme of assistance to support the Chinese currency. The draft of a telegram prepared for this purpose is annexed,[6] but before the telegram is sent it is desirable to decide what the intentions and policy of His Majesty's Government in the matter are. The United States Government might be unwilling to join in such a scheme and could reply that they had already provided assistance to China by buying silver from her. It would be unfortunate if Japan were to learn that America had declined to join in a plan put forward by His Majesty's Government, and it follows that the major point of policy should be decided first.

CONCLUSION

12. Apart from the financial considerations that arise, my view is that the necessity and the possibility of doing something to protect British interests and prestige in China and in Asia should on balance outweigh the risk and consequences of Japanese resentment.

H.

6 Not printed.

No. 596

Note[1] *by Sir J. Simon on assistance to China*

Cab. 24/277

Secret   TREASURY CHAMBERS, *July 1, 1938*

The Foreign Office memorandum on assistance to China[2] contains paragraphs which put very forcibly the considerations which may be urged in favour of affording such assistance, but in my view it does not bring out with corresponding emphasis the considerations in the other direction which must be fully weighed before so grave a decision is taken. I must therefore ask leave to supplement the memorandum by calling specific attention to the following points.

1. Sir A. Clark Kerr originally urged that His Majesty's Government should give their backing to a scheme which would secure credits for China on a commercial basis and he himself ruled out the possibility of a political loan, doubtless on the ground that this would be regarded as throwing our weight on the Chinese side in the war against Japan. Sir R. Craigie commented (telegram No. 582 of 10th May[3]) that if the granting of such credits would really have the effect of insuring our future position in the Far East, the proposal for commercial credits would deserve the most careful consideration 'for no one can guarantee our future if Japan's victory were to be complete and overwhelming'. But Sir R. Craigie went on to warn us that in his view, if we intervened to this extent, this 'would lead to an overwhelming outburst of fury against Great Britain, the ultimate consequences of which it is difficult to predict. If the gamble came off we should earn undying hatred of these people; if it failed, the fact that we should have made the attempt will never be forgotten and we should moreover have set the seal upon our losses in China'.

2. The Foreign Office memorandum refers in paragraph 9 to a modification of the view held by Sir R. Craigie as I have quoted it in paragraph 1 above. But I must remind my colleagues that his acquiescence in a credit for currency purposes (see telegram No. 730 of 14th June[4]) is qualified by two main conditions.

He says:

(a) That it would be desirable to show that the Chinese Government would not be enabled on the receipt of the new credit to release for other purposes a portion of reserves now kept as backing for currency.

(b) That the credit should not be 'too extensive'.

I am advised as regards the first condition that it is impossible to devise an arrangement which would effectively satisfy it. The Foreign Office memorandum itself admits that the purpose and the effect of financial

---

[1] Circulated to the Cabinet on July 6 as C.P. 157(38): cf. No. 595, note 1.
[2] No. 595.   [3] No. 570.   [4] No. 591.

assistance to China, however described, would be to sustain the Chinese resistance. Must it not also be conceded that the Japanese would so regard it?

As regards the second condition, we cannot pretend that a loan of £20 millions is not 'extensive' in amount, however insufficient for the major political purposes. If, however, Sir R. Craigie's condition that the credit should not be 'too extensive' means that we ought not to do enough to affect Japan's chance of winning, why give a credit at all?

I share to the full the view that right in this matter is on the side of China and that Japanese resentment would be ethically unjustified. But I think it is necessary to draw my colleagues' special attention to the serious nature of the warning addressed to us as to the possible consequences to ourselves of intervening in the conflict.

3. The proposal to secure assistance for China through the City of London on a commercial basis was fully investigated, both in connection with proposals for acquiring wolfram and in connection with other forms of security, and the conclusion was reached that, as a commercial proposition, it was so unattractive as to be impracticable. It is only because the hope of getting assistance for China through non-Governmental channels has been dashed that the suggestion now comes forward (which was at first treated on all hands as impossible) that Government credit should be provided. This requires an Act of Parliament, and the Bill would be necessarily the subject of public debate. No doubt it would be warmly supported in indiscreet speeches by Members of the Opposition, and I find it difficult to believe that, if Japan would have resented British assistance provided through the City of London, she would not regard a Government guaranteed loan, authorised by a special Act of Parliament, with even greater resentment. Whether it is right or wrong to do these things, it would certainly be wrong to decide to do them without maturely measuring this risk.

4. We have just decided to find £16 millions as an exceptional measure to cement our attachments to Turkey. It is a serious matter, on the financial side, to follow this up by deciding to give £20 millions away in the Far East, unless we are confident that we shall gain political advantages of at least equal value. I fully realise that even this wholly exceptional process would stand us in good stead if thereby we saved the whole Far Eastern situation and restore British interests there on a secure basis, and I do not minimise the serious consequences to British trade and prestige in the Far East which are likely to follow from a Japanese triumph. But we must ask ourselves whether we can rely on the calculation that £20 millions given away now can really be expected to secure that China will win the war within twelve months, and we must consider what we are going to do if at the end of twelve months these hopes are not realised.

5. The financial and commercial considerations, serious as they are, do not constitute the crux of the matter. The main anxiety seems to me to be whether the action now proposed is one to which we can commit our

country having regard to the dangerous state of Europe. If, in spite of the 'hint' which Sir R. Craigie thinks we could safely give to the Japanese (paragraph 9 of the Foreign Office memorandum), we take the proposed step and it does not secure China's victory within twelve months but incurs the continuing hostility of the Japanese have we not greatly increased the danger of being engaged at some time in the future in simultaneous hostilities in Europe and the Far East? Our military advisers have consistently urged that it should be a prime object of our foreign policy to avoid that possibility.

6. There are thus considerations of the utmost gravity and importance on the other side in this matter, and I am circulating this note to make sure that my colleagues have the above considerations fully before them at the same time as the powerful and persuasive arguments which lead the Foreign Office to urge that we should take the risk and act as proposed.

J.S.

No. 597

Extract from Cabinet Conclusions No. 31(38) of July 6, 1938

Cab. 23/94

6. The Cabinet had before them the following Most Secret documents on the subject of Assistance to China:

A Memorandum by the Secretary of State for Foreign Affairs (C.P. 152(38))[1] posing the question whether His Majesty's Government should provide financial support to China to the extent of £20,000,000, and adducing arguments which led him to the conclusion that the necessity and the possibility of doing something to protect British interests and prestige in China and Asia should, on balance, outweigh the risk and consequences of Japanese resentment:

A Memorandum by the Chancellor of the Exchequer (C.P. 157(38))[2] putting forward considerations of the utmost gravity on the other side, and drawing his colleagues' special attention to the possible consequences to ourselves of intervening in the Sino-Japanese conflict, having regard to the dangerous state of Europe.

The discussion showed that the arguments for and against the provision of financial support to China were very nicely balanced. The Chinese, with their backs to the wall against a peculiarly brutal aggression by Japan, were fighting the battle of Western Nations in the Far East. If Japan obtained control of a large part of China, British trade would gradually be frozen out, as had already happened in Manchukuo. A Deputation which the Foreign Office had received on the previous day from the China

[1] No. 595. [2] No. 596.

Association had been unanimous on this subject, though some members of it had not been favourable to the proposed financial support owing to the hostility that it would provoke in Japan. The proposal was consistent with the Resolutions adopted at Geneva, which so far it had been found impossible to implement. Most of the experts on China were reported to agree that great danger to that country arose from the collapse of the currency. While the proposal could be represented and supported as a British interest, the loan could not be tied up by conditions which would prevent the Chinese Government from applying it to war purposes. It was admitted, therefore, that the loan would amount to intervention on behalf of China. Attention was drawn, however, to the following telegram that had been received from His Majesty's Ambassador in Japan:

'I have received hints from fairly responsible quarters that Anglo-Japanese action (to be taken with the assent and co-operation of Chinese Government) for preventing collapse of Chinese national currency would, if obtainable, be agreeable to Japanese Government. . .' (Tokyo telegram No. 815, of 5th July.)[3]

The Foreign Secretary had already sent a telegram[4] asking for the precise meaning of this passage.

The Cabinet were informed that India was watching the struggle between China and Japan with the utmost interest, with a strong bias in favour of China. Something was being done in Burma to improve communications with China. If nothing was done by this country it would give the impression that we were afraid to act or were unable to do anything.

The admission that the proposal amounted to intervention in China was used as a powerful argument against its adoption. In this connection attention was drawn to the earlier warnings of His Majesty's Ambassador in Tokyo as to the effect it would have in the alienation of Japanese opinion from this country. It was suggested that the real ground for the proposal was to secure China from defeat. £20 millions, however, was not likely to prove sufficient for this. What was to happen at the end of the year if this proved to be the case? Were we to find another £20 millions? As to the views of the China Association, they would naturally want a backing for China, and it was particularly significant that some members of it did not want it. The passage quoted above from Sir Leslie Craigie's telegram showed that what the Japanese had in mind was Anglo-Japanese action, and did not detract from the gravity of the Ambassador's warning against purely British action. It was stated that some of the experts did not consider that the collapse of the currency would have such critically serious consequences as had been suggested. China had great powers of resilience. The first effect of a collapse would probably be the suspension of payment of interest on Bonds which had hitherto been paid. The effect

[3] Not printed.   [4] No. 454 of July 5, not printed.

on British banks would, of course, be serious, but, in the view of some experts, not catastrophic. Whatever financial resources were left after collapse of the currency would be used for financing the war instead of for paying the interest on debts. One suggestion was that if the £20 millions were forthcoming it would involve us in doing everything we could to help China to win the war. We could not stop at that point.

It was stated that a somewhat similar proposal had been made at Geneva a year ago by Dr. Kung, who had openly admitted that his object was political in order to bring out the fact that the United Kingdom was on the side of China.[5] While the latest proposal was in line with the Resolution taken at the League of Nations, it was stated that it went beyond what had then been visualised.

Another reason given against the proposed financial support to China was that, as constantly urged by the Chiefs of Staff Sub-Committee, it was very important to avoid simultaneous war with Germany, Italy and Japan. At the present moment, when our relations with Italy threatened to deteriorate, it would be a great mistake to antagonise Japan. Failure to support China might involve loss of prestige in the Far East, but this would be inconsiderable compared with the consequences of an unsuccessful war.

Two suggestions were made for easing our position in relation to Japan if the loan was made to China, viz:

(1) That we should ask other Powers interested, including especially the United States of America, to co-operate in the loan:
(2) That we should follow up the idea of Anglo-Japanese co-operation contained in the Tokyo telegram referred to above.

Another suggestion was that Australia and New Zealand ought to be consulted before a decision was taken.

The Cabinet were reminded of a proposal that had been made two months ago for a commercial loan to China on the security of the deposits of antimony and wolfram in that country.[6] That proposal had been rejected by the City of London on commercial grounds. It was suggested, however, that in the event of His Majesty's Government providing financial support to China they might secure part of it at any rate on these deposits. This would also have the advantage of preventing Germany from acquiring these important metals. A variant of this proposal was that we should purchase the whole of these deposits. The objection to this proposal, however, was that the deposits were still in the ground. To pay for them as and when they were received would not help China; but to pay for them in advance would be as irritating to Japan as a mere loan.

Another suggestion was that in return for a loan we should obtain an extension of the leased territory at Kowloon. In this connection the Cabinet were informed that an extension of the leased territory was being

[5] Cf. No. 92.

[6] See Nos. 535 and 541.

examined, but this was not considered a favourable moment for opening the question.

The Prime Minister, summing up the discussion, said that the arguments were very nicely balanced. The Foreign Secretary had put both sides fairly in his memorandum, and when he found his colleague, after considering both sides of the question, still urging action, he himself found it difficult to oppose. Nevertheless he could only agree to the proposal with grave misgiving. It was not disputed that the object of the proposal went beyond mere support to the Chinese currency in the interests of British banks. Serious as the failure of the currency would be, the attempt was made to justify the proposal on the ground that we must support China in the war. In fact, the proposal amounted to intervention. The more effective that intervention was, the more disagreeable it would be to the Japanese. We had no guarantee that after a year Japan would be reduced to such a state of exhaustion as to agree to terms which would be fair to China and leave us a proper share of the trade of that country. We should then be told that another £20 millions was necessary. He felt that this was rather a long vista and that we were being committed to a policy based on the supposition that our interests were against a Japanese victory and that we must do all we could to prevent it. He himself was not prepared to dispute that a Japanese triumph might result in a situation in Northern China resembling that in Manchukuo. He was not certain, however, that China would collapse. China had always shown great powers of recuperation. The Japanese operations might be less successful in the future than in the past. The Chinese had received a good deal of munitions from Soviet Russia, which had not yet, he believed, been paid for, except to some extent by barter. It was by no means unlikely that the Soviet might continue to furnish support. Our money might well go to Russia instead of to the Bondholders. The result, therefore, of a loan might be bad. The situation would be different if we only had to consider Japan and ourselves, when the present proposal might be faced. But we could not limit the question to these two nations. In Spain we had adopted a policy of non-intervention so as to avoid spreading the conflict. Were we certain that to adopt an opposite policy in China would not have that very effect? In this connection it was interesting to note that the Germans had just withdrawn all their Generals, although they had very large interests in China. He did not see how any device, such as purchases of wolfram, could hide the real object of a loan. Was it not probable that Signor Mussolini, who was in a captious mood, might not stigmatise our action as directed against the Dictator Countries in general? The Prime Minister then recalled the repeated warnings of the Chiefs of Staff Sub-Committee as to the necessity of avoiding a war with three nations at once. If we were to become embroiled in the Far East, Germany might seize the opportunity to do something in Czechoslovakia, or Italy in Libya. He agreed that the situation would be much improved if the United States of America could join us, as suggested in paragraph 11 of C.P. 152(38) and in the draft telegram attached thereto.[3] He had, however, been opposed to sending the telegram until the Cabinet had made up its mind. There was always a danger that Washington might announce that they had refused a British suggestion of the kind. On the previous day, however, he had seen the American Ambassador, who had just returned from Washington, and who had given a very favourable account, from our point of view, of President Roosevelt's attitude towards, and desire to co-operate with, His Majesty's Government. The Ambassador had also been reassuring as to the President's intentions over the application of the Neutrality Law if we became engaged in war. The Ambassador had also shown himself very desirous to help. This led him to suggest that the American Ambassador might be a better, as well as a slightly less formal, channel for taking soundings as to the possibility of American co-operation in the proposal before the Cabinet than His Majesty's Ambassador in Washington. He suggested, therefore, that the decision should be left over while a little fresh light on certain aspects of the problem was obtained from Washington and Tokyo.

The Foreign Secretary agreed that a delay in making so grave a decision was reasonable. He did not underrate the objections to his proposal. He agreed that it would be easier to apply it if other nations would join. He had to see the American Ambassador the same day, and he would sound him on the question and ascertain if he was willing to sound the American Government. He agreed also that it was desirable to await Sir Leslie Craigie's reply to his latest telegram to clear up the point quoted earlier in this summary. He raised the question as to whether the Governments of Australia and New Zealand should be consulted.

The Prime Minister thought it would be premature to consult the Dominions and that it would be better to wait until the Cabinet had had a further discussion.

The Cabinet agreed

(a) To postpone the question of whether financial support should be provided to China until the next regular weekly Meeting of the Cabinet:[7]
(b) That in the meanwhile the Secretary of State for Foreign Affairs should
    (i) obtain from Sir Leslie Craigie the further information he had already asked for as to the meaning of the proposal contained in Tokyo telegram No. 815 of the 5th July, quoted in the above summary;[8] and

---

[7] See No. 599 below.

[8] In telegram No. 818 of July 6 Sir R. Craigie, while admitting that there was a growing conviction in well-informed Japanese circles that something must be done to support Chinese currency, still felt that 'proposed action by His Majesty's Government alone would (for psychological and political as also for technical reasons) have a shattering effect here, though the consequences would be greatly mitigated if conditions suggested in my telegram No. 730 [No. 591] could be fulfilled'.

(ii) take discreet soundings with the American Ambassador as to whether he thought it would be advisable to ascertain whether the Government of the United States of America would be willing to co-operate in financial support to China, and whether His Excellency would himself be prepared to take soundings in Washington:[9]

(c) That consultation with the Governments of the Dominions should be postponed until the Cabinet had had a further discussion on the subject.

[9] Lord Halifax spoke to Mr. Kennedy in this sense on July 11: See *F.R.U.S.*, 1938, vol. iii, pp. 535–6.

No. 598

Minutes of a meeting of the Interdepartmental Committee on the possibility of retaliation against action by Japan in the Far East detrimental to British interests, held at the Foreign Office on July 12, 1938[1]

[F 7991/62/10]

A Committee of representatives of the Treasury, Board of Trade, Department of Overseas Trade, and the Colonial, Dominions, India and Foreign Offices met at the Foreign Office under the chairmanship of Sir H. Knatchbull-Hugessen on 12th July 'to consider what action could be taken in the economic sphere by His Majesty's Government in the United Kingdom or could be suggested as possible to the Governments of the Dominions, India and Burma, as a means of deterring Japan from further attacks on British interests in the Far East'.

The following is a brief summary of the conclusions provisionally reached: (it should be noted that no opinion is intended to be expressed as to the desirability of taking any of the action considered to be possible).

[1] See No. 592, note 1. The Board of Trade, Department of Overseas Trade, and Treasury had not been uncritical of the proposal to set up an interdepartmental committee. A letter from the Board of Trade of July 8 expressed the opinion that the A.T.B. Committee had already adequately examined the question, and in any case measures of economic retaliation would infringe the Anglo-Japanese Treaty of 1911. In a letter from the Treasury of July 8 Mr. Waley told Mr. Ronald that the Treasury view was that any reprisals 'would have to be of the nature of those specified in A.T.B. 155' (see No. 334). Mr. Waley also enclosed a copy of a minute of July 8 by Sir J. Simon, who shared the Treasury's doubts about the proposed committee: 'I should have thought it would in any case be better to refer any enquiry as to possible reprisals to the [A.T.B. Committee] which has already gone elaborately over the ground from another angle and is fully seized of the essential proposition that people should only go in for reprisals who are prepared to go in for war.' It was agreed, however, that the meeting which had already been arranged for July 12 should go ahead, and all Departments agreed to send representatives.

There are few lines of action which would not infringe the Anglo-Japanese Commercial Treaty of 1911, but the following are possible:

(1) *In the Colonies*: a. The duty of exports of iron ore might be increased. This would increase revenue and would adversely affect Japan, who takes 1½ million tons annually. The Van Zeeland Report[2] while condemning measures of this kind insists that there should be reciprocity and Japanese obstructiveness to British trade seems to afford sufficient justification.

b. Restrictions might be placed on the issue of licences to fish in Malayan waters; this industry is largely in Japanese hands. Similarly administrative difficulties and delays might be opposed to Japanese applications to enter and reside in Malaya and to ply certain trades, though as regards residence and trading such covert administrative discrimination would be contrary to the spirit of the Anglo-Japanese Treaty.

c. Restrictions similar to those mentioned under (b) above might be imposed in certain other colonies.

(2) *In the United Kingdom*: it is just possible that certain classes of goods might be found which are imported almost wholly from either Empire or Japanese sources (e.g. canned salmon). The import duty on these might be raised (The Board of Trade are enquiring further into the position regarding canned salmon).

(3) *In India*: as regards cotton exports to Japan the Japanese market is so important to India as to put the question of restriction practically out of the question.

It is *not* considered that any restrictions of Japanese financial operations in London would be effective: Japan has already lost her credit as a result of the war.

It was found that more effective measures would only be possible if individual Colonial Territories were withdrawn from the operation of the Treaty or if the Treaty were terminated. 12 months would have to elapse before such withdrawal or termination became effective. We should then be free, in the territories concerned, to place discriminatory duties on Japanese imports, restrict Japanese undertakings and obstruct Japanese shipping. As far as the Colonies are concerned, none of them stand to lose by being out of the Treaty. On the other hand to go further and terminate the Treaty entirely might have serious consequences for the United Kingdom, although Japan would presumably stand to lose more because of her very favourable balance of trade with the United Kingdom (imports 3 millions sterling, exports 12 millions).

The Committee think also that complete denunciation of the Treaty would have an unfavourable psychological effect in Japan, where it would be likely to provoke retaliation with the possibility of wider political consequences. The Committee accordingly decided not to examine in further detail the action which could be taken after termination of the

[2] See Volume XIX, No. 440.

Treaty, either as regards any one or more colonies or *in toto*, until they knew whether it was considered desirable to run the consequent political or economic risks of retaliation by Japan. It was, however, observed that a more effective and perhaps less risky procedure would be for His Majesty's Government to warn the Japanese Government that continued action by them against British interests in the Far East would make it necessary for His Majesty's Government seriously to consider the withdrawal of certain colonies from the operation of the Treaty or possibly its complete termination. It would be represented to the Japanese Government that we could not continue to give them most favoured nation treatment if we were in effect though not in theory denied the same treatment in territories controlled by them, and were actually prevented from carrying on our business there.

Attitude of the Dominions. The Committee noted that some of the Dominions had favourable trade balances with Japan and were therefore in a vulnerable position. Neither Australia nor Canada were likely to favour action resembling sanctions against Japan, though New Zealand probably would. In any case, the Dominions would expect to be consulted before His Majesty's Government in the United Kingdom took the step of denouncing the Treaty.[3]

[3] In a long minute of August 10 commenting on the conclusions of the meeting Mr. Heppel summarized the course of action to be taken as follows: '(1) application of such reprisals as are possible without infringing the letter of the [Anglo-Japanese] Treaty . . . (2) application of such further reprisals as are possible when the Treaty has ceased to apply to certain colonies (3) denunciation of the Treaty *in toto* – i.e. an unrestricted trade war.' He considered that 'we should begin (1) at once, with a view to proceeding to (2) if (1) is ineffective, and in the meantime consult the United States in particular as regards (3).' Copies of the minutes were sent to the Departments on August 23 with a covering letter discussing possible courses of action, and referring to Tokyo telegram No. 980 of August 18, in which Sir R. Craigie expressed the view that the 'moment is approaching when we must conclude that method of friendly negotiations here has failed'. Telegram No. 980 is printed in Third Series, Volume VIII, No. 32.

No. 599

Extract from Cabinet Conclusions No. 32(38) of July 13, 1938

Cab. 23/94

8. In accordance with the Conclusion mentioned in the margin,[1] the Cabinet resumed their discussion of the question whether financial support should be provided to China, and again had before them the following documents:

[1] See No. 597.

A memorandum by the Secretary of State for Foreign Affairs (C.P. 152(38)):[2]

A memorandum by the Chancellor of the Exchequer (C.P. 157(38)).[3]

The Secretary of State for Foreign Affairs reported that, as requested at the meeting of the Cabinet referred to in the margin, he had seen the American Ambassador who had not adopted an encouraging attitude on the prospects of collaboration by his Government in giving financial assistance to China, although he had been generous in his expressions of sympathy with our attitude.[4] Both he and the Secretary of State for Dominion Affairs, he thought, had sounded the Australian High Commissioner (Mr. Bruce) who had expressed the clear opinion that Australian public opinion would be in favour of a loan to China if this were practicable, but not if it would involve risk of trouble with Japan. He himself had replied that this was exactly our own attitude. He had had examined the suggestion for an advance based on a purchase of wolfram. He thought this project could be dressed up to a certain extent, but he could not escape the conclusion that if anything effective was to be done, it must be by means of a direct loan. The real difficulty was the uncertainty firstly, as to whether the proposed loan would prove sufficient; secondly, as to how far we should be committing ourselves by a loan; thirdly, whether a collapse in China would of certainty take place if we did not make a loan, and fourthly, as to what would be the Japanese reactions. In all this uncertainty, he could quite understand that opinion was likely to be divided on this matter. He himself was not much impressed by Sir Robert Craigie's recent telegrams as to the improved attitude of the Japanese Government towards this country, which was not likely to affect the long-range policy of Japan.[5] He did recognise, however, the danger that would arise if the Japanese Government reacted badly to a loan to China, more particularly if they took some action, for example, against Hong Kong, to which we could make no effective reply. He was given to understand that some time ago when a question had arisen of sending a fleet to China, ten or twelve capital ships had been deemed necessary. That would be a grave risk to take in the present European situation with Signor Mussolini in a curious and somewhat inexplicable frame of mind and with a somewhat critical situation in Central Europe. In these circumstances, he was rather impressed by the American Ambassador's comment 'that the British Empire had enough trouble on its hands at the moment without gratuitously taking on more'. If he had to give his own opinion, which he did with great reluctance, he would have to say that his mind was very much influenced by the Italian situation and he would advise against taking the risk of an adverse reaction in Japan. He had considered the possibility of a tentative approach to the Japanese Government in order to ascertain what their reaction was likely to be. He

[2] No. 595.   [3] No. 596.   [4] See No. 597, note 9.   [5] Cf. *ibid.*, note 8.

820

thought, however, that no result was likely to ensue except discredit. If the Japanese reacted badly, we should be in a worse position than before.

If the Cabinet decided not to make the loan, the Foreign Secretary suggested that he should not make any approach to the Japanese Government, but that he should inform the Chinese Ambassador that he had examined the question of a possible advance; that he had ascertained that the Chinese had no satisfactory commercial security to offer and that any plan that might be dressed up to meet the difficulty would be seen through. He thought that was a better course than to adopt a stiff line with the Japanese. He was informed that if he were to convey a decision of this kind to the Chinese, they would probably default on their foreign loans, but he did not know how much free money this would put at their disposal: he believed that the amount would not be large. If China defaulted, it was anticipated that the Japanese would denounce the customs agreement. If the Cabinet decided not to assist the Chinese and they were to default, he hoped that we should not be too harsh with them on that account.

The President of the Board of Trade said that on the previous evening he had been visited by a Member of Parliament, who was the Director of a British firm concerned in Chinese business. The Member had reported to him that Mr. Wellington Koo had asked if his firm would co-ordinate all their purchases in different parts of the world. In doing so, Mr. Koo had impressed him with the strength of the Chinese financial position and their ability to pay for purchases in all parts of the world.

The Chancellor of the Exchequer supported the view of the Foreign Secretary. The great difficulty in reaching a decision was the number of unpredictable factors in the situation. But for that very reason, he thought the Cabinet ought not to be too despondent of the prospects. It was by no means certain that Japan, even if successful in the war, could thereafter deal with so vast an area of territory as was involved, to our exclusion. Neither was it certain that China could be forced to collapse. In addition, all his information was to the effect that a loan of £20 millions would not prove sufficient. He supported his remarks by summarising memoranda he had received both from Sir Charles Addis, who had very long experience of China, and from the Bank of England. He shared the disappointment and distress of the Foreign Secretary in this matter and agreed in the course he proposed.

The Secretary of State for India recalled that, at the meeting of the Cabinet referred to in the margin, he had given some reasons in favour of the proposal. While he did not feel it possible to dissent from the Foreign Secretary's deductions, he felt bound to point out that continued inaction was not increasing our prestige in the world at large. In support of this, he quoted an opinion he had received as to the danger that Siam, though still friendly to this country, would in the event of a war between Japan and ourselves 'sit on the fence' and only come down on the side of the winner: also from Pandit Nehru who had told him that he had found people on the continent of Europe expressing doubt as to whether we were in a position to take a strong line, though he had noticed that on two occasions when we had done so, the results had been satisfactory, namely, in the case of the Nyon Agreement and the recent threat to Czecho-Slovakia.

The Prime Minister recalled that, at the previous discussion on this question, he had expressed doubts rather similar to those of Sir Charles Addis. He was even more strongly impressed by the considerations arising out of the state of Europe. It was his conviction that this was not the moment to embark on a policy calculated to produce reactions in Germany and Italy which would force us to face the dilemma of choosing between the risks of conflict and inaction. Consequently, he welcomed the advice of the Foreign Secretary. Referring to the remarks of the Secretary of State for India, he agreed that Siam was likely, in the event of an Anglo-Japanese conflict, to 'sit on the fence' and only to come down on the side of the winner. That, however, only showed the danger of a challenge to Japan, which might not produce the desired effect. He agreed also with what Pandit Nehru had said. It was, however, wrong to draw the conclusion that, because on certain carefully selected occasions we had adopted a firm attitude, we should necessarily repeat it on occasions that were less suitable. It was necessary to bear in mind in these matters that our defensive arrangements were still far from complete.

The Secretary of State for the Colonies supported the views of the Foreign Secretary and the Prime Minister and the grounds on which they were advocated. He thought that our prestige in the world, though not high, was rising and in support of this he instanced the confidence of the Government of the United States of America in our foreign policy.

The Cabinet agreed:

(a) That, in view of the serious international situation and the reactions that might be caused first on Japan and subsequently in Europe by the adoption of the proposals in C.P. 152(38) for giving financial support to China, those proposals should not be adopted:

(b) That the Secretary of State for Foreign Affairs should make an appropriate communication to the Chinese Ambassador on the lines suggested by him in the discussion summarised above.[6]

[6] The Chinese Ambassador was informed of this decision in a letter of July 26 from Lord Halifax, which concluded with an expression of the 'extreme reluctance with which His Majesty's Government have been forced to this conclusion'.

Sir R. Craigie (Tokyo) to Viscount Halifax (Received August 8)

No. 509 [F 8491/12/10]

TOKYO, *July 14, 1938*

My Lord,

I have read with great interest the despatch No. 305[1] of the 17th May last in which Your Lordship was good enough to set forth the objections to the thesis that it would be more advantageous for us to seek to improve our relations with the Japanese now rather than after the cessation of hostilities. It has been of great value to me to be furnished with your views in such detail—all the more so in that Your Lordship's despatch discloses the existence of certain misapprehensions as to the nature of the views which I have attempted to put forward from time to time by telegram. In particular I have never at any time recommended that an attempt should be made in present circumstances to conclude arrangements with the Japanese Government applicable to the post-war period. My recommendations have related purely to the conclusion of such *ad hoc* arrangements as might prove practicable for protecting our foreign rights and interests in China during the current crisis, without prejudice either to the peace settlement or to the conditions which may obtain in the Far East after the war. Furthermore, from the use of the expression 'working arrangement' which appears in paragraph 3 and elsewhere in your despatch I gather you may have considered (possibly through faulty telegraphic transmission) that I was envisaging some formal arrangement covering in a single document all or most of our interests in China. In all my telegrams, however, I have used the word 'arrangements' in the plural and the type of *ad hoc* arrangements which I had in mind are precisely those the conclusion of which Your Lordship specifically approves in paragraph 5 of your despatch. If in my telegrams I have quoted the recent Customs Agreement[2] as an example, this was not because I saw any particular virtue in the fact that it took the shape of a *formal* agreement but because this *ad hoc* method of protecting our interests seemed to me one which could with advantage have a wider application. The more informal and provisional such arrangements are in appearance, the better for all concerned. Your Lordship lays it down in paragraph 5 that any *ad hoc* arrangements must be 'without obvious benefit to the aggressor or detriment to the victim.' It seems to me that the Customs arrangement would pass this test before any unprejudiced court and I entirely agree that no provisional arrangement for the protection of our interests should be made in future which does not conform to this formula.

2. Turning to paragraph 6 of your despatch, I note that here again the argument seems to rest on the assumption that I am proposing some form

[1] No. 575.   [2] See No. 565.

of settlement with the Japanese which would be applicable to the post-war period. This, as stated above, is not the case, nor have I ever contemplated that we should 'give something concrete in return for the safeguarding of our interests' (see paragraph 3 of your despatch). My proposal has been, and still is, that we should hold the Japanese Government to their promises of respect for our rights and interests in China by laying down in a detailed and concrete form the actual procedure by which this can best be achieved in relation to our various groups of interests (shipping, railways, factories, etc.)

3. In paragraph 7 of your despatch it is stated that our hope must be that neither capital nor Chinese nor foreign cooperation will be forthcoming in sufficient quantity to make Japanese schemes for the development of China a success; that hope, you consider, is more likely to be realised the longer hostilities continue. Subject to one or two reservations which I examine in paragraphs 5 and 6 below, these propositions appear entirely sound. It is in fact reasonable to expect that the Japanese Government will become more and more amenable to foreign influences as it is borne in upon them that, far from being able to develop China in the grandiose and somewhat exclusionist manner of their dreams, they may eventually become dependent on foreign assistance to save the very financial structure of Japan herself.

4. It will be seen from the preceding paragraphs that no such divergence of view in fact exists on the above points as would appear to be the case from a first perusal of Your Lordship's despatch.

5. The first point on which I feel a reservation should be entered is the following: if driven too hard, Japan may definitely abandon any further attempt to fulfil her, at present, genuinely assumed undertaking to protect foreign rights and interests in North China and may decide instead to set up a State which, completely independent of the rest of China, would be developed, like Manchukuo, in Japan's exclusive interest. Such a decision might mean a prolonged postponement of adequate schemes for the development of this area, a temporary pauperisation of its inhabitants and an added strain on Japan's financial resources. But the rulers of Japan have the habit of thinking in decades rather than for single years ahead and they would be prepared to face what they would regard as temporary difficulties and embarrassments rather than run the risk of seeing their armies return to Japan virtually empty-handed. This is a solution of the problem which would leave China definitely dismembered and Japan, at grips with all but the totalitarian States, engaged on a sterile economic contest with ourselves in Central China from which nothing but ill could be expected. Japan may not be rich enough to develop China on her own resources but she is sufficiently powerful to prevent anyone else from doing so with that sense of confidence and security which would be so necessary for the success of the enterprise. This opens up so grim a prospect that however slight may appear today the chances of an early re-establishment of China's complete independence and integrity, I feel

that it would be unnecessarily *défaitist* to abandon such hope at the present time or to base our policy on the assumption that North China is already as good as lost.

6. Another point on which I feel a reservation should be made is that there exists a limit to the extent to which Japan can suffer exhaustion without upsetting the whole equilibrium in the Far East and without grave risk to our own future interests. If, for example, Japan's financial and economic exhaustion were to become really serious, the danger of an attack by Soviet Russia could not be disregarded and he would be a brave man who would predict that our interests in China or our prestige in the Far East would benefit from a Russian victory over Japan. Even if matters did not proceed to the length of war, there is little doubt that Japan, under the menace of a Russian attack, would feel obliged to depend for her safety more and more on German aid and Germany, while not in the habit of sponsoring the weak, would nevertheless feel reluctant to lose altogether such advantage as she would still derive from association with Japan as a makeweight to Soviet Russia. It seems to me therefore that there are possible dangers in an undue prolongation of this conflict and, while Japan is still some way from the degree of exhaustion which would bring these new factors into play, this aspect of the question is one which should not be lost from view.

7. In the preceding paragraphs and in Your Lordship's despatch this question of the duration of the present hostilities has been dealt with primarily from the point of view of the effects on British interests. There is however the all-important humanitarian aspect of this question and, even without the public declarations which have been made on this subject, I am aware that it is the desire of His Majesty's Government that no favourable occasion should be lost of bringing the conflict to an end, on terms acceptable to China, quite independently of the opportuneness of the moment from the more narrow aspect of British interests.

8. In conclusion I may perhaps be permitted to offer a few general observations on the reaction of Anglo-Japanese relations on our position in Europe. It is no idle speculation to suggest that one of the underlying causes of our anxieties in the field of foreign affairs during the last few years has been the inevitable estrangement of two old friends—Italy and Japan. With Germany growing to unprecedented strength under the present dictatorship, we can afford to give no hostages to fortune. Even if in pre-war days we placed no undue reliance on active assistance from either Italy or Japan, we could not even then have contemplated with equanimity an increasingly intimate relationship between these Powers and Germany. Today this process is one which we have an even greater interest in arresting. The effort to re-establish more friendly relations with Italy is already in progress, but the path to reconciliation must necessarily be a difficult one in view of the intense bitterness engendered on both sides during the period of crisis. As regards Japan, the problem seems to me to be whether, without abating our just condemnation of the

recent aggression in China, there are not things which can be done and measures which can be taken to prevent the bitterness on either side assuming such proportions as to add to the dangers which already surround our own country. In face of acts of armed aggression, the expression of measured resentment in Great Britain is natural, spontaneous and valuable, but the very spontaneousness of such expression seems to impose on all concerned an added responsibility for establishing a nicely calculated relationship between the country's powers of defence and its capacity to make and confront new enemies. So far as Japan is concerned, we are in any case likely to do more constructive work by considering plans for the cure of the disease from which these advocates of expansion suffer rather than by chafing at its unpleasant symptoms. Edmund Burke once said that the criticisms of friends are different from the invectives of enemies. This is a truism which is particularly applicable to the case of Great Britain and Japan. Just as the inception of a new phase of Japanese imperialism synchronised with the termination of the Anglo-Japanese Alliance, so the prospect of a re-established friendship between the two countries would afford the best hope visible today of weaning Japan from her foolish policy of armed imperialism. Of the cynic who denies that any such hope exists, I would enquire whether the alternative of constant bickering and impotent condemnation is not likely to leave China for years in a state of unrest and economic distress. I maintain that such a hope in fact exists; that a test of its strength involves no risks; and that, given encouragement from our side, Japan's recent experiences in China may tend to hasten rather than to retard its fruition.

I have etc.,

R. L. CRAIGIE

No. 601

Letter from Mr. Howe to Sir A. Clark Kerr (Shanghai)

[F 7673/12/10]

FOREIGN OFFICE, July 19, 1938

My dear Archie,

I quite understand your feelings on the receipt of Tokyo telegram No. 603,[1] about which you wrote in your letter of the 7th June.[2] I seriously considered at the time taking up with Craigie some of the points in that telegram which were particularly irritating, but came to the conclusion that no very useful purpose would be achieved by doing so.

I have just read Piggott's account of his visit to Shanghai[3]. It is exactly what I expected. He seems to think that it is only necessary to throw a few saki or cocktail parties and all our difficulties with the Japanese are solved

[1] No. 577.   [2] No. 589.   [3] See No. 590, note 2.

by the soothing assurances of goodwill which they elicit from the Japanese. This is not to say that I consider that his visit did not achieve some usefulness, but the real test will be to what extent the Japanese in Shanghai meet our many grievances there.

Please tell Phillips that he need not be anxious lest it should be thought that he and his staff have been lacking in patience. On the contrary, I think we might accomplish more if we lost our tempers occasionally. For example, I have always thought that our military people might take a much stronger line on the spot whenever incidents arise which involve them with the Japanese. In the Kaoru case, when the Colonel of the Durham Light Infantry was threatened with a revolver by Kaoru, it was a heaven-sent opportunity for our people to beat him up and throw him back over the barbed wire, for we had the perfectly good excuse that as he was dressed in Chinese clothes, we thought he was a Chinese.[4] However, all that is dead and gone.

We did our best for the Chinese over the question of a loan, but, as you have probably gathered, the Powers-that-Be felt that in the existing critical situation in Europe they would not be justified in taking any risk, however slight, of provoking the Japanese to take further, and possibly more direct, action against us in the Far East. There was also the added feeling that if we did give them a loan of £20,000,000 there was no guarantee that this amount would have had any decisive effect on the outcome of the struggle and that we should not afterwards be asked for more. The above is, of course, only for your own information.

I hope that you and Lady Clark Kerr are not finding Shanghai unbearable, but it is not a very pleasant place even in normal times in the summer.

With best wishes,
Yours ever,
R. G. HOWE

[4] Details of this incident of March 28 can be followed on file 1155/10.

No. 602

Letter from Burma Office to Foreign Office

[*F 7754/79/10*]

BURMA OFFICE, *July 20, 1938*

Sir,

In continuation of this Office letter No. B.2496/38,[1] dated 18th May 1938, I am directed by the Secretary of State for Burma to forward herewith 6 copies of a memorandum on road communications between

[1] Not printed.

Burma and China which has been compiled in this Office from information received from the Government of Burma. The Marquess of Zetland would suggest that if Viscount Halifax desires to communicate to the Chinese Ambassador such of the information contained in the memorandum as may be useful to His Excellency, it should be suitably edited before transmission.[2]

Copies of the memorandum have been sent to the Treasury, Admiralty, India Office, War Office, Air Ministry, Board of Trade, the Department of Overseas Trade, Export Credits Guarantee Department, and Sir Frederick Leith-Ross.

I am, etc.,

E. P. DONALDSON[3]

ENCLOSURE IN NO. 602

Memorandum on the existing position and forecast of developments concerning the Burma–Yunnan road compiled from information received from Burma up to 17th June 1938

Confidential   BURMA OFFICE, *July, 1938*

I. *Road from Lashio to Muse* (*Kingyaung*)

1. This section of the road will be completed up to an all-weather standard from the 1st December 1938; surfacing even to a width of 10 ft. may not be completed by that date, but the amount of rainfall normally expected from then until the break of the following rains will not make the road unusable at any time; surfacing to a width of 16 ft. will be completed before the break of the rains in 1939.

The delay in making the road fit for motor traffic has been caused partly by lack of labour, (as the Chinese who come to the Shan States for work in the non-cultivating season naturally return home on the approach of the cultivating season) and partly by exceptionally early heavy rain which began on the 8th May and has been virtually continuous ever since.

2. The question of strengthening the two suspension bridges on the road over the Nam Makhka and Nam Hkai rivers so as to carry a load equivalent to a line of lorries each weighing 5 tons when loaded, or an 8-ton road roller, is being examined in consultation with the consulting engineers in England. It is anticipated that all the bridges on this road will be up to a gross lorry weight standard of 7½ tons before the break of the rains in 1939.

3. It has been suggested that the road, when improved, might not be able to be kept in effective repair if more than 800 tons a day (this being only two-thirds of the traffic which the railway could deliver daily at

---

[2] A note on the filed copy of July 27 stated that an abbreviated version of the memorandum (with omissions from paragraphs 1, 4, 5, 6, 7, and 9) had been prepared for the Chinese Ambassador.

[3] A Principal in the Burma Office.

Lashio) had to pass over it. This figure is, however, not likely to be reached owing to the insufficiency of transport. The distance from Lashio to Yunnanfu is about 618 miles; under the most favourable conditions 12 days would be the least time occupied by a journey to Yunnanfu and back by lorry; the average load per lorry would be 4 tons; thus 2,400 lorries would be needed to carry 800 tons a day. Even taking the figure of 300 tons a day, the minimum requirement of lorries would be 900. The transport consideration by itself seems likely to impose a practical limit on the utilisation of the road, so that the Public Works Department will be able to maintain the road in an effective motorable condition.

4. As regards the maximum load for bridges, the best information available in Burma is to the effect that the bridges on the Chinese road will limit the gross lorry capacity to $7\frac{1}{2}$ tons. (The Chief Public Works officer of the Federated Shan States reported that he was told in March 1938, when he inspected a considerable portion of the Chinese road, that $7\frac{1}{2}$ tons would be the figure for the two large suspension bridges over the Salween and the Mekong. When one of the Chinese engineers was in Rangoon he stated that their intention was to build to a 10–ton standard, but admitted that he had not been able to obtain his requirements for a suspension bridge over the Mekong to carry 10 tons and had been compelled to design a bridge of 5-ton carrying capacity, but he added that, the normal engineering margin of risk being large, he hoped to be able to get 10-ton lorries over his 5-ton bridge!) It has been understood that the Chinese Government Purchasing Commission in this country has strongly recommended 6-wheel lorries, which will weigh 3 tons and carry a load of $4\frac{1}{2}$ tons, for use on the road and is therefore suggesting that a lighter lorry altogether should be used. The authorities in Burma entirely concur in this view, based on experience of local conditions.

II. *Road in Chinese territory from Kingyaung (near Muse) to Talifu*

5. Experience with newly made roads in Burma suggests strongly that even the Chinese will not be able to keep the road fit for through traffic before next cold weather. It is impossible to believe that the new road will be better than that carrying a well-established bus route between Hsiakuan and Yunnanfu which was described in Mr. Peter Fleming's article in the *Times* of 18th May 1938[4] as very bad. Actually the exceptionally early and heavy break of the rains at the beginning of May made this road impassable for motors for the time being and several lorries from Burma were stranded in May at various points on the Chinese road. Mr. C. M. Chen, the official from the Chinese Central Government's Ministry of Communications now in Rangoon, has abandoned any idea of establishing through traffic on this section until next cold weather.

[4] This was the second of three articles by Mr. Fleming entitled 'The Burma Road to China' which appeared in *The Times* on May 17, 18, and 19, 1938 each on pp. 17 and 18 with photographs on p. 20.

III. *Road from Bhamo to Muse*

6. This can be dealt with in three sections, as follows:

(1) *Bhamo to Shweli Bridge section.* The estimate for making this road up to all-weather standard 10 ft. wide is Rs.12,70,000 and up to 16 ft. wide Rs.22,38,000. These are advance estimated figures, which have not yet reached Government officially. It is doubtful whether, apart from considerations of cost, labour would be available in sufficient quantity to enable the road to be finished, even up to a 10 ft. width, by the rains of 1939. The same considerations in an accentuated form make it quite certain that the road could not be brought up to all-weather standard 16 ft. wide before the rains of 1940. For reasonably heavy traffic a width of 16 ft. would be necessary as, with the present 10ft. width, one-way traffic on long sections of the road has to be enforced. The cost of making a road in this hill section (through the whole length of which the alignment is perforce that of a 'mountain road' climbing from about 350 feet at Bhamo to about 5,000 feet at the watershed and dropping to the Shweli at about 2,000 ft.) is much higher than in the Northern Shan States, both because the rainfall is heavier and because the hills are much closer, whereas much of the country through which the Lashio-Muse section passes is comparatively open in character.

(2) *Shweli Bridge to Namkham Section.* No difficulty is anticipated in bringing this section up to all-weather motorable standard by the break of the rains in 1939. The work can be put in hand at the end of the present rains.

(3) *Namkham-Muse Section.* Nothing can be done with this section which lies in low ground in the Shweli Valley flooded in the river's high season, until after the present rains, when the construction of the necessary embankment will be put in hand. Difficulty is, however, anticipated as regards labour, and it is consequently not anticipated that this section will be brought up to an all-weather motorable standard for reasonably heavy traffic before completion of the Shweli Bridge–Namkham section.

IV. *Preference for the Lashio–Muse road over the Bhamo–Muse road*

7. The main practical reason for concentrating on work on the road from Lashio to Muse is that it is both quicker and cheaper, to establish through communication *via* Lashio than *via* Bhamo; a secondary consideration has been that the Shan States Federation is able and willing to bear the cost involved by the former road which lies wholly within the Federation area, whereas expenditure on the Bhamo–Muse road falls almost wholly to be found from the revenues of Burma. Moreover, the Lashio road can be prepared for through all-weather traffic by the next cold weather whereas a similar state of things cannot be hoped for by the Namkham route within an extra year.

8. Goods could be forwarded from Rangoon to Railhead at Lashio in

1 ½ to 2 days in case of urgency and need only be handled at Rangoon and Lashio, whereas goods would not reach Bhamo from Rangoon by river in less than 10 days. Freight can be carried through from Rangoon to Bhamo on 'flats' without breaking bulk, though a shallower draught steamer has to be used above Mandalay than below. It is only very occasionally that the river above Mandalay is too low for the passage of loaded 'flats' towed by the steamers. But when this does occur it is in the cold season when the roads are in their best condition. The handling of heavy goods at Bhamo would however present difficulties because, owing to the varying depth of water in the river at that place, the steamers have to tie up at various points on the bank which would sometimes be as much as a mile below the town and permanent wharfage arrangements are thus impracticable. It is doubtful whether this difficulty can be solved by dredging.

9. The Bhamo–Muse road was mainly designed as a strategic road to facilitate lateral communication between Lashio and Bhamo along the Chinese frontier and its utility for traffic between Burma and China is a later development.

V. *General Conclusion*

10. The general conclusion to be drawn from these reports is that it may be possible for goods in lorries of 7 ½ tons gross weight to be carried continuously between Lashio and Yunnanfu after about the 1st December 1938, but that the route *via* Bhamo cannot be available for heavy traffic until about May 1940, and is bound always to be very much the slower route from Rangoon.

No. 603

Sir R. Craigie (Tokyo) to Viscount Halifax (Received July 27, 6.25 p.m.)

No. 900 Telegraphic [F 8129/16/10]

Confidential   TOKYO, *July 27, 1938, 9.3 p.m.*

My telegram No. 791[1].

In the course of interview today Minister for Foreign Affairs reverted to the question of British mediation. He and his colleagues had given careful consideration to what I had said in the course of an interview on June 27th and they were appreciative of friendly disposition of His Majesty's Government. They were, however, very doubtful of possibility of concluding peace with Chiang Kai-shek and His Excellency mentioned, as an instance of the latter's unreliability, that he was engaged at this moment in endeavouring to ascertain by indirect means the attitude which Japanese would adopt in peace negotiations. The Japanese Government

[1] No. 593.

831

did not, however, believe in the sincerity of Chiang Kai-shek's intentions so that peace negotiations would be difficult at present moment. It would therefore be a problematical matter for His Majesty's Government to take any initiative at the moment. If, however, later information should show that General Chiang Kai-shek was sincerely and honestly trying to make peace with Japan, Japanese Government would be quite prepared to reconsider question. If Japan's object were accomplished Japanese Government would be willing to do their best to restore peace.

After thanking His Excellency for this interpretation of Government's position I observed that so far as I knew, there was no question of His Majesty's Government taking any initiative at this time. Their position remained exactly as stated by the Prime Minister in House of Commons.[2] As regards opening of peace negotiations on their part it seemed to me that the difficulty did not lie so much in the lack of sincerity on part of Chiang Kai-shek but in the nature of Japanese Government's peace terms. If Japan were really ready, as her leaders had often declared, to offer terms which would constitute territorial and administrative integrity of China and lay solid foundation for future of Sino-Japanese friendship, I thought peace could be made tomorrow without loss of another life.

His Excellency then enquired why I thought lasting peace could only be concluded with Chiang Kai-shek and his régime. I said the General was the one great patriot who had emerged from the welter of Chinese affairs during the last generation; that he had never been either violently anti-Japanese or pro-Communist; that the Japanese declaration of January 16th[3] had, if anything, increased his prestige; that no peace concluded with régimes at Peking and Nanking which left Chiang Kai-shek régime in permanent opposition could be a . . .[4] one; and that if, after a patched-up peace, the threat of a further war were to remain suspended over China, the finance necessary for the recovery of the Far East would obviously not be forthcoming.

Minister for Foreign Affairs agreed that Chiang Kai-shek had been less anti-Japanese than many of his officers but nothing could alter the fact that during the last ten years the education offered in the schools had been rabidly anti-Japanese. Nevertheless Chiang Kai-shek had at one time been prepared to adopt policy of friendly co-operation with Japan and Japanese Government were watching until he displayed a readiness to return to his former position. That moment had not yet arrived and it might be necessary to wait for some time to come.

While above conversation was inconclusive it is interesting as confirming my suspicions that General Ugaki is not a supporter of the January 16th declaration. The conversation (coupled with that reported in my telegram under reference), also discloses the interest which Japanese Government are taking in the idea of British mediation or good offices. What His Excellency doubtless hoped was that I might indicate readiness on our

[2] See No. 593, note 2.   [3] See No. 488.   [4] The text was here uncertain.

part to leave Chiang Kai-shek to his fate; but I am also left with the impression that if Chiang Kai-shek were prepared to move from his position of no negotiations pending withdrawal of Japanese army, the moment might soon become propitious for negotiations. So long, however, as Chiang Kai-shek's position remains as stated, it is useless for me to attempt to probe Japan's present terms, but I should say they do not differ widely from those reported in Shanghai telegram No. 1129[5] on the basis of Tani's statements. This would not necessarily represent Japan's last word.[6]

Repeated to Shanghai.

[5] Of July 26, not printed (F 8140/84/10).
[6] Mr. Ronald commented on July 29: 'I have an uncomfortable suspicion that these hints about the possibility of British mediation are intended to flatter and soothe and are by no means indicative of the true attitude of the Japanese Govt. towards this possible means of terminating the dispute.' Sir G. Mounsey agreed: 'I find it difficult to conceive any possible ground for successful mediation at present.' Sir L. Oliphant added on August 2: 'I agree with Sir G. Mounsey.'